Bevis Hillier

Bevis Hillier, formerly editor of *The Connoisseur* and *The Times* Saturday Review, has written twenty-five books (mainly on art) in addition to the three volumes of his authorized biography of John Betjeman. He is a Fellow of the Royal Society of Literature.

Praise for *Betjeman: The Bonus of Laughter*

'One of the most difficult parts of the biographer's art is bringing to life the inter-connecting groups of people who move around the subject, to give an idea of their world. Hillier achieves this superbly well . . . Whatever happens to John Betjeman's reputation, he has had the best and most sympathetic biographer he could have wished for' Artemis Cooper, *Evening Standard*

'Magnificent . . . Buy this volume, and its two predecessors . . . as a cultural monument, as well as a thoroughly pleasurable read' Jackie Wullschlager, *Financial Times*

'An admirable, venerable achievement – devoted and compassionate but sharply perceptive about the man's foibles and his petty vices . . . A biography this good abolishes time in its own way, and triumphantly ensures Betjeman's survival' Peter Conrad, *Observer*

'Bevis Hillier brings his monumental life of John Betjeman to a triumphant conclusion . . . a true work of scholarship, intelligent, generous, sympathetic, and often entertaining' Allan Massie, *Literary Review*

'I enjoyed it enormously' John Gross, *Sunday Telegraph*

'Hillier's labours on behalf of Betjeman are a mighty enterprise, equal in stature to Leon Edel's biography of Henry James' Roger Lewis, *Independent*

BETJEMAN
The Bonus of Laughter

BEVIS HILLIER

JOHN MURRAY

First published in Great Britain in 2004 by John Murray (Publishers)
A division of Hodder Headline

Paperback edition 2005

1

A CIP catalogue record for this title is available from the British Library

ISBN 0 7195 6557 X

Typeset in Monotype Sabon by Servis Filmsetting Ltd, Manchester

Printed and bound by
Clays Ltd, St Ives plc

John Murray (Publishers)
338 Euston Road
London NW1 3BH

I made hay while the sun shone.
   My work sold.
Now, if the harvest is over
   And the world cold,
Give me the bonus of laughter
   As I lose hold.

John Betjeman, 'The Last Laugh',
A Nip in the Air, London 1974

Max Miller, the great priapic God of Flashness, dies. 'There'll never be another.' As old John Betjeman says, an English genius as pure gold as Dickens or Shakespeare – or Betjeman, come to that.

John Osborne, diary, 8 May 1963; *Almost a Gentleman:
An Autobiography*, London 1991

It is the sort of book, were one a famous man, one would wish written about himself. It is sympathetic, but not a whitewash.

John Betjeman, reviewing Hilton Brown's *Rudyard Kipling*
in the *Daily Herald*, 19 September 1945

I often met Jerrard Tickell [whose novel about a cow, the 'Venus de Milko', she was involved in filming], in the Connaught Hotel, where, he said, he met colleagues during his days in Intelligence. He introduced me to his friend, John Betjeman; he and Tickell struck me as two very loveable eccentrics as we sat with our drinks, talking about *Appointment with Venus*. Betjeman said, 'History must not be written with bias – both sides must be given, even if there is only one side' . . .

Betty E. Box, *Lifting the Lid: The Autobiography of
Film Producer Betty Box*, OBE, Lewes, Sussex, 2000

TONICH
OLASIA
INORME
MYFRIE
NDOFFO
RTYFIV
EYEARS
HISWIF
ERONAA
NDTHEI
RDAUGH
also TERMYG
ODDAUG
HTERVE
RITYWI
THLOVE

CONTENTS

List of Illustrations   ix
Preface   xi
The Story So Far   xvi

 1 Wantage   1
 2 'Vic. Soc.' and 'The Dok'   27
 3 The *Daily Telegraph*   52
 4 *Summoned by Bells*   79
 5 Back to Cloth Fair   117
 6 The Euston Arch   126
 7 Australia 1961   146
 8 The Coal Exchange   163
 9 A Natural Showman: Television in the Sixties   183
10 Barry Humphries   204
11 The Battle of Bedford Park   219
12 *High and Low*   236
13 John Nankivell   249
14 Pylons on the March: Preservation in the Sixties   259
15 Mary Wilson and a Journey to Diss   275
16 Back to Australia   289
17 The Church of England Ramblers   306
18 *Metro-land*   330
19 With the Andersons, the Pagets and Joyce Grenfell   354
20 'A Heavy Crown'   363
21 *A Passion for Churches*   398
22 Radnor Walk   421
23 Heaven and Hell on Television: The Seventies   446
24 The 'Green Giant' and Other Campaigns:
    Preservation in the Seventies   454
25 *Banana Blush*   471
26 Simon Jenkins and a Trip to Southend   485
27 '. . . As I Lose Hold'   499
28 *Time with Betjeman*   529
29 His Last Bow   549
30 '. . . Whose Death Has Eclipsed the Gaiety of Nations'   575

CONTENTS

Epilogue   592

Appendix 1: 'A Walk with Mr Betjeman' by Tom Driberg   619
Appendix 2: The Last of Penelope   624

Acknowledgements   627
Notes   630
Bibliography   717
Index   721
Copyright Acknowledgements   746

ILLUSTRATIONS

Black-and-White plates

1. Count Gleichen's statue of Alfred the Great at Wantage
2. Anne Baring
3. Candida Betjeman, 1960
4. John with Penelope after receiving the CBE, 1960
5. Campaigning to save Lewisham town hall, 23 August 1961
6. John with Veronica Sharley
7. Penelope at Wantage
8. The wedding of Candida Betjeman and Rupert Lycett Green
9. Invitation to the opening of the Coal Exchange, London
10. Philip Larkin and John during filming in Hull
11. John with Paul Betjeman and the Baring family
12. In Cecil Beaton's house
13. John and Mervyn Stockwood, Christ Church, North Brixton
14. John as a temporary train driver
15. John with John Nankivell at Exeter University, 1967
16. Bust of the Prince of Wales, modelled by David Wynne
17. *The Animals of Farthing Wood*: John's controversial choice for an Arts Council Prize
18. John in Spain, 1971
19. John, Mervyn Stockwood and Lady Elizabeth Cavendish on holiday
20. Liverpool Street station, 1904
21. Plans for Liverpool Street's modernization, 1971
22. The Clifton Suspension Bridge and the Avon Gorge
23. Clifton hotel plans
24. John and Simon Jenkins on Southend Pier, 1976
25. With Valerie Jenkins, 1974
26. At home
27. Dr Gregory Scott
28. John with the Rev. Harry Williams in *Time with Betjeman*, 1981
29. With Osbert Lancaster
30. With Bevis Hillier at Radnor Walk, 1982
31. 'Sir Les Patterson' visits John at Radnor Walk
32. John and Lady Elizabeth Cavendish at Chatsworth
33. Mary Wilson greets John at Scilly, 1981
34. Lady Elizabeth Cavendish

35. The naming of British Rail's the 'Sir John Betjeman', 24 June 1983
36. John's grave, St Enodoc, Cornwall

                              Colour plates

 1. John trying on Mervyn Stockwood's mitre
 2. 'The Battle of Bedford Park': Christmas card, 1963
 3. At the wedding of Verily Anderson and Paul Paget, 1971
 4. John on the grand staircase of the City Hall, Belfast
 5. John between blue and gold trains
 6. John in a recording session with Jim Parker, *Time with Betjeman*,
      1981
 7. With John Sparrow
 8. On the cliffs at Trebetherick in *Summoned by Bells*, 1976
 9. John in front of Blisland Church, Cornwall
10. John and Lady Elizabeth Cavendish at Trebetherick
11. With Jonathan Stedall
12. John holding Archie and Jumbo during filming of *Summoned by
      Bells*
13. John with his grandson, David Lycett Green
14. Presentation of a model of the Euston Arch, 24 June 1983

The author and publishers would like to thank the following for permission to reproduce illustrations: *black-and-white plates* 1, Christopher Loyd; 2 and 11, the late Mollie Baring; 3, Candida Lycett Green; 4, 7 and 8, the late Hon. Lady Betjeman; 5, William Norton; 6, Veronica Sharley; 10, Sotheby's; 12, by courtesy of Cecil Beaton Studio Archive, Sotheby's; 13, Jane Bown; 14, Gordon Whiting; 15, John Nankivell; 16, The Worshipful Company of Goldsmiths; 18 and 19, William Westenra and the late Bishop Mervyn Stockwood; 20 and 35, British Rail; 21, Bernard Kaukas; 22 and 23, Paul Chadd, QC; 24, Sir Simon Jenkins; 25, Valerie Grove; 26, the late Sir John Betjeman; 27, the late Dr Gregory Scott; 28, 29, 31 and 32, Jonathan Stedall; 30, Tara Heinemann; 33, Lady Wilson of Rievaulx; 34, Advertising Standards Authority; 36, Bernard Mattimore; *colour plates*: 1, the late Bishop Mervyn Stockwood; 2, the late Tom Greeves; 3, Janie Hampton; 4, Kenneth Savidge; 5, Photograph by Snowdon; 6, 7, 8, 9, 10, 11, 12 and 13, Jonathan Stedall; 14, Bernard Kaukas; *integrated illustrations*: p. 11, Toby Rushton; p. 76, *Daily Telegraph*; pp. 101 and 102, *Sunday Times*; p. 114, Express Newspapers; p. 127 Hulton Archive; p. 220, Victorian Society; p. 245, © Punch Ltd; pp. 272–3, Wally Fawkes ('Trog'); p. 285, *Private Eye*; pp. 373 and 376, by kind permission of Lady Lancaster; pp. 461 and 470, Dr Gavin Stamp; p. 473, Cicely Herbert; p. 483, Julia Whatley; p. 515, Humphrey Stone; p. 564, Sir William McAlpine; pp. 589 and 591, Dr Donald Buttress.

PREFACE

This volume has one attribute which cannot be equalled for almost a thousand years: it was begun in one millennium and finished in another. There is no merit in that fact – but it does provoke thoughts about the nature of time, such as John Betjeman expressed in 1957 on returning to England after a stint as a professor of poetry in Cincinnati: '1860 over there seemed as old to me as Perpendicular does here, and Red Indians seemed as long ago as Anglo-Saxons, and what is time anyway.'

The present year (2004) marks the twentieth anniversary of Betjeman's death; and in two years we shall be celebrating the centenary of his birth. As a Christian, he was expected to view history *sub specie aeternitatis*, and to an extent he did so. When, in 1947, his wife Penelope was converted to Roman Catholicism, he wrote in his poem 'The Empty Pew':

> In the perspective of Eternity
> The pain is nothing – but, ah God, in Time!

But history impinged on him. His life was enclosed by the twentieth century like a ship in a bottle. He lived through both world wars and each of them affected him: the first, by threatening families who had German-sounding names; the second, by precipitating him into a succession of uncongenial jobs. The status of his country changed dramatically in his lifetime. In the year of his birth, 1906, the British government issued a Blue Book recording that the British Empire occupied one-fifth of the land surface of the globe and had a population of four hundred million. In 1956, when he was fifty, Britain's imperial pretensions suffered a blow from which they never recovered, when the United States forced Anthony Eden's government to halt its invasion of Suez.

Betjeman had an almost Proustian fascination with the way humans parcel up time. He wrote morosely about reaching fifty, both in a *Spectator* article and in a poem – lamenting that he was 'half a century nearer Hell'. He was seventy when he authorized me to write his biography, in a characteristically joshing letter: 'By all means write my life. You writing, Jock [Murray] publishing, should assure a modest sale in the circulating libraries among the older folk . . .'

That letter was written in 1976 – when Harold Wilson sprang a surprise and resigned as Prime Minister; Jimmy Carter was elected President of the United States; Chairman Mao died; Isabel Perón was thrown out in a bloodless coup in Argentina; the Israelis freed Idi Amin's hostages in a raid on Entebbe, Uganda; Patty Hearst was found guilty of armed robbery; Princess Margaret and Lord Snowdon split up; the long, hot summer broke all records; the Sex Pistols ran riot on a television chat show; Carl André's notorious bricks went into the Tate Gallery; and Lester Piggott won the Derby for the seventh time.

It is a chastening thought that some people who are now Members of Parliament or Fellows of All Souls were in their prams then. For them – and also because I cannot assume that all the readers of this volume have read the other two – I am inclined to recapitulate some of the things I wrote in the earlier prefaces. First, those who would prefer a short, compact biography of Betjeman – 'A shilling life will give you all the facts' – should be advised that two such books exist: Derek Stanford's *John Betjeman* (1961) and Patrick Taylor-Martin's *John Betjeman: His Life and Work* (1983). In my preface to the first volume, I stated that 'Neither book weighs more than an avocado pear.' (Mr Taylor-Martin wrote to me: 'I hope I am not a *dud* avocado.') And for those who find the written word itself too taxing, my own *John Betjeman: A Life in Pictures* (1984) tells the story in photographs and drawings, with the minimum of verbiage.

Taylor-Martin modestly begins his book: 'This is not the last word on John Betjeman.' My book will not be the last word either, but I have set out to create a more fully fleshed portrait. At the same time, I am not an admirer of the vacuum-cleaner school of biography. It has also been called the Nennian method, after the medieval Welsh historian Nennius. 'Coacervavi', he coolly admitted, 'omne quod inveni' – 'I have made a heap of all that I have found.' Yet in one sense I feel kinship with Nennius, and with his predecessor Bede: we are not only biographers; we are, willy-nilly, 'sources' too, chroniclers with direct access to some of the people in our chronicles. I have had advantages which no future biographer of Betjeman can have: friendship and long talks with him and his wife, and interviews with many of his friends and associates.

Why do people read biographies? To live, vicariously, somebody else's life? To escape into someone's life? To learn from others' mistakes? For the pleasure of saying to oneself, smugly if ungrammatically, 'Thank God I wasn't him!'? To enjoy a novel whose plot is – as far as the biographer can make it – true? Those answers could apply to the life of just anyone. But in the case of someone famous, like John Betjeman, the responses change. Philip Larkin, writing about

Betjeman's verse autobiography, *Summoned by Bells*, concluded: 'Although the book ends in ostensible failure ("Failed in Divinity!") it is really a triumph. Betjeman has made it. He has become Betjeman.' *That* is what interests us about the famous: how the chrysalis becomes a butterfly, the ugly duckling a swan. By what alchemy does John Betjemann lose an 'n' and gain a 'K'?* How does the school dunce, the university joker, the BA (failed) Oxon develop into the best-loved poet of his generation, an arbiter of taste and a prince of the media?

The life of almost anyone would be worth reading, provided it were based on adequate materials – letters, diaries, recollections. How much more is that true of somebody who was a considerable poet and of whom Maurice Bowra remarked as early as the Twenties, 'Betjeman has a mind of extraordinary originality; there is no one else remotely like him.' His own letters have been admirably edited by his daughter, Candida Lycett Green. Naturally I have drawn on her two volumes – as she drew on my first volume in her first – and I acknowledge the debt with much gratitude. But also Betjeman saved, from about the age of twenty, virtually all the letters he received. (Most of them are now lodged at the University of Victoria, British Columbia.) His reputation was of someone bumbling, who needed to be chivvied by officials like the Town Clerk of Oxford because he was in such a muddle. Yet he kept all this correspondence. What does that tell us about him? It tells us that he was pretty sure he was going to be famous and that people would be interested in him; tells us, too, that he *wanted* them to take that interest, was up for it. When a man has left us such prodigal resources to help us understand him, it would be churlish – a snub by posterity – to burke the challenge.

---

* As recorded in my first volume, the poet was born John Betjemann, but later dropped the second 'n'. In the volume of Proust's *A La Recherche du Temps Perdu* entitled *A l'ombre des jeunes filles en fleur*, the narrator recalls:

> I was barely conscious of who Albertine Simonet was . . . Even the name, Simonet, which I had already heard spoken on the beach, I should have spelt with a double 'n' had I been asked to write it down, never dreaming of the importance which this family attached to there being only one. The further we descend the social scale the more we find that snobbery fastens on to mere trifles which are perhaps no more null than the distinctions observed by the aristocracy, but, being more obscure, more peculiar to each individual, surprise us more. Possibly there had been Simonnets who had done badly in business, or worse still. The fact remains that the Simonets never failed, it appeared, to be annoyed if anyone doubled their 'n'. They were as proud, perhaps, of being the only Simonets in the world with one 'n' instead of two as the Montmorencys of being the premier barons of France. (Translated by C. K. Scott Moncrieff and Terence Kilmartin; revised by D. J. Enright, London 2000.)

By a weird coincidence, the firm which took over G. Betjemann & Sons when that company came to an end in 1945, was called Symmonet, Bowers & Co.

Betjeman not only spreads out for us the map of his life; he points us along the route. He was a man of exceptional honesty. It might be enjoyable to research and write the life of somebody dishonest – exposing the truth beneath the fabrication. The late Philippa Pullar had that experience when she wrote about Frank Harris; A. J. A. Symons and Donald Weeks had it in questing after Baron Corvo. A publisher recently said to me, 'When you have finished your Betjeman trilogy, you ought to write a new life of Compton Mackenzie: somebody who wrote so much about himself must have had a lot to hide!' The idea has some appeal; but what has been so rewarding in writing about Betjeman is the feeling that he is somehow on one's side, anxious that one should get through to the real him. He is even honest about having been *dishonest* – as when, in *Summoned by Bells*, he confesses how he fibbed that his 'mater' was ill to get out of fighting another boy. And the honesty was not only retrospective. In 1933, when his bisexual friend Alan Pryce-Jones became engaged to Joan Eyres-Monsell (it did not last, and Pryce-Jones married another woman), Betjeman – who wed Penelope later that year – wrote to him:

Darling Bog,
    I am so sorry I have not written before. Of course I am delighted. You've scored all along the line. But there is one thing you must do before you marry – you must explain that you were once inverted. She won't mind at all. In fact she obviously knows as she is quite aware that old Graham [Eyres-Monsell] and I and all our friends are inverted. I think it is mad not to be honest and clear up the embarrassment of a prickly conscience. Actually inversion is an additional charm. It worked very well with Philth [Penelope] although I have now decided that I daren't marry her – money and emotion and fear getting in the way.

There are two ways of writing a biography. One is the strictly chronological, in which one simply sets down the events in a person's life in the exact order in which they happened. The other is the 'tectonic' method – a series of overlapping plates. The chronological system has its advantages: as in a train going through stations, you always know just where you are. But a biographer is only as good as his sources; we do not have a detailed 'time-map' of most people's lives. And even if I knew what John Betjeman was doing on every day of his life, I would still prefer the tectonic method. For example, it seems to me better to cover his work – and tribulations – as Poet Laureate in a single chapter than to present them as fitful outcroppings in a seamless narrative. Again, his happy collaboration with the musician and composer Jim Parker, which continued for several years, is best appreciated as a symphony rather than as a series of divertimenti: that way, it is possible to show development; success; a dying fall.

The broad time-frame of this final volume is 1960 to 1984, but sometimes I have trespassed beyond it. In a chapter on Betjeman's contributions to the *Daily Telegraph*, I have reached back to the early Fifties; in that on his rôle in the Victorian Society, to its founding in 1957. And, because Penelope Betjeman has been so vivid a presence in all three volumes – her own biography has been a sub-plot of my book – I have also stretched forward, in an appendix, to record the manner of her death in India in 1986.

Introducing the first volume, I wrote: 'This book is not a "critical biography". That seems to me a bastard art-form, one which yokes two disciplines that do not belong together – historical narrative and literary criticism.' While I have not wholly rescinded this self-denying ordinance, I have so far relaxed it, in an Epilogue to this volume, as to indicate why I thought John Betjeman worthy of a grand canvas, not a miniature. In reviewing Alan Sheridan's masterly life of André Gide in 2001, I suggested that with a biographer of such empathy, his subject's blood almost begins to course through his own veins. I do not claim that that Metaphysical conceit applies to me; but, having immersed myself in Betjeman's life for twenty-eight years, I feel equipped to attempt a summing up of the poet and the man. My essay is the heat of a sport that will be much practised when his centenary dawns.

John Betjeman authorized this biography, both in his jokey letter of 1976 to me and in a more formal agreement with the publisher. 'Authorized' does not mean 'bowdlerized' or 'censored'. He created his own myth through his writings and his television stardom. The myth was nearer reality than most myths are: in general, he was as likeable as he seemed. There may be some for whom the revealing of any flaw in him will seem the desecration of a national monument; but I have no training as a hagiographer. I have tried only to discover the truth and to tell it. For myself, I can say of my subject what his contemporary A. J. P. Taylor wrote in the preface to a life of Betjeman's sometime employer Lord Beaverbrook: 'I loved the man.'

THE STORY SO FAR

John Betjeman is born in north London on 28 August 1906, the only child of Ernest Betjemann (thus spelt) and his wife Bess. The Betjeman(n) family is probably of German origin but in the anti-German frenzy of the First World War it claims to be Dutch. Ernest is the third generation to run a London cabinet-making firm. Its products include smart dressing-tables, games boxes and tantaluses sold at Asprey's, sometimes to maharajahs. Ernest fervently hopes John will follow him into the firm as 'the fourth generation', but as a child John shows himself hopelessly unhandy with a chisel. At an early age he is convinced that he will be a poet. A lonely child, he treats his teddy-bear, Archibald Ormsby-Gore ('Archie'), as an intimate – a make-believe sustained all his life and borrowed by his friend Evelyn Waugh for the character of Lord Sebastian in *Brideshead Revisited*.

John first attends Byron House, a Highgate nursery school, where he falls in love with a girl called Peggy Purey-Cust. Then he moves to Highgate Junior School where the young T. S. Eliot is a master. John presents him with *The Best Poems of Betjeman* but Eliot tactfully makes no comment. John goes on to the Dragon School, Oxford, where Hugh Gaitskell, the future Labour leader, is a fellow pupil and friend. John shines in acting and has poems published in the school magazine. Already he is exploring and learning about architecture. While he is at the Dragon School the Betjeman family moves to Church Street, Chelsea. Holidays are in north Cornwall, where Ernest builds a house. Later, Cornwall becomes John's second home.

From 1922 to 1925 he is at Marlborough College – then more like a concentration camp than a school – with the poets Louis MacNeice and Bernard Spencer, the art historians Anthony Blunt and Ellis Waterhouse, the future film stars James Mason and James Robertson Justice, the historian John Bowle, and Graham Shepard, son of the illustrator of the Pooh Bear books. John is regarded as a clown and a bit of a dunce (he loathes the sarcastic classics master A. R. Gidney) but wins a poetry prize, is acclaimed as an actor and co-founds *The Heretick*, a rival to the school magazine. He falls in love with another boy, Donovan Chance.

John scrapes into Magdalen College, Oxford, in 1925 and reads English. Here he blooms and makes such friends for life as Maurice Bowra, Osbert Lancaster, John Sparrow and Kenneth Clark. He is something of a tuft-hunter, seeking the friendship of Irish aristocrats in whose country houses he stays – the Marquess of Dufferin and Ava, Edward, Earl of Longford, Lord Clonmore and Pierce Synnott – and of the millionaire Edward James. Patrick Balfour (later Lord Kinross) is also a close friend. John acts in the Oxford University Dramatic Society and edits *The Cherwell*, the University magazine. But again he does not excel academically; he hates his tutor, C. S. Lewis. He fails a divinity examination ('Divvers'), in spite of his lifelong interest in, and devotion to, religion and the Church of England, and leaves without a degree.

He takes two prep-school teaching jobs, an unorthodox but inspiring master; becomes private secretary to the Irish statesman Sir Horace Plunkett; and joins the staff of *The Architectural Review*, where he is expected to champion the Modern Movement. Following the example of his friend the architectural writer P. Morton Shand, he claims as pioneers of the Modern Movement architects and designers he really admires – Voysey, Ashbee and Lutyens. His first book of poems, *Mount Zion*, is published by Edward James in 1931; his book on architecture and style, *Ghastly Good Taste*, in 1933.

From the late 1920s on, he pursues aristocratic 'gels' – Camilla Russell, Lady Mary St Clair Erskine, Pamela Mitford and Penelope Chetwode, daughter of Sir Philip (later Lord) Chetwode, Commander-in-Chief of the Army in India. The Chetwodes regard him as a scruffy and penniless journalist and would prefer Penelope to find 'somebody with a pheasant shoot'. Penelope herself is torn between love for John and a desire to become an Indologist. The courtship is stormy. Penelope, in her torturing indecision, takes refuge with an aunt in the south of France. At the urging of Nancy Mitford, John follows her there and they agree to marry. There is a backsliding by John when, during Penelope's absence in India, he becomes engaged to one of her best friends, Wilhelmine (Billa) Cresswell (later Lady Harrod), but Penelope wins him back and the three remain great friends. John and Penelope marry clandestinely at Edmonton in 1933. In the autumn of that year, Penelope breaks the news to her dismayed parents. The couple live first in a little flat near the British Museum, next in St John's Wood, then in a street off the Strand.

*   *   *

The year 1934 brings three great changes in John's life: he becomes film critic of the *Evening Standard*; he and Penelope move to Uffington, Berkshire; and, in June, his father dies. John finds that he has not, after all, been cut out of the will. At the funeral, his father's 'other family' by a mistress appears. John bows out of the film-critic job after a year and a half.

With more free time on his hands, he begins a short-lived diary in which he records meeting G. Bernard Shaw and Dean Inge; a visit to the 'Uranian' poet Dr E. E. Bradford; the revival of his Oxford friendship with W. H. Auden; and his misery at the thought of the coming war, in which – at this stage – he intends not to fight.

He begins editing the Shell Guides to English counties for Jack Beddington, the petrol company's publicity manager, himself writing the first guide on Cornwall (1934) and that on Devon (1936). Beddington takes him on to the staff at Shell-Mex House as an advertising copywriter.

The Betjemans make more friends in the Uffington area. Maurice Bowra often comes over from Oxford. Osbert Lancaster is also a frequent visitor, and there are hilarious amateur concerts. John and Penelope organize the Uffington Coronation celebrations in 1937. In the same year their son Paul is born. The painter John Piper becomes one of John's best friends; his wife, Myfanwy ('Goldylegs'), one of the poet's muses.

John Murray publish John Betjeman's 1937 verse collection *Continual Dew*, favourably reviewed by Evelyn Waugh and others. In 1938 John Miles issues John's *An Oxford University Chest*. To improve his income, John needs constantly to find freelance work; this includes 'home hints' for the *Daily Express* (with some help from the Uffington blacksmith). He eventually takes a staff job as editor of the magazine *Decoration*. In breaks from the office he stays with the Longfords in Ireland and, at T. S. Eliot's request, attends a Student Christian Movement summer camp. He obtains freelance work on BBC radio, some of it through the spy Guy Burgess.

As war looms, he joins the (Royal) Observer Corps at Uffington, watching for enemy aircraft. He tries to get into the armed forces (having changed his views on fighting) but is rejected by all of them. His Oxford friend Sir Kenneth Clark finds him a job in the films division of the Ministry of Information, where his main rôle is to commission film scripts. In the canteen he meets Joan Hunter Dunn, a catering assistant, and he writes a poem about her.

In January 1941 John is posted to Ireland, bringing his family with him, as press attaché to the British Representative in Dublin. He gives help to Laurence Olivier in the filming of *Henry V*. He appears to have a subsidiary rôle as an intelligence agent for Britain. Perhaps as a result, he gets on to an IRA hit-list, but is spared when the IRA read his poems and conclude he cannot possibly be a spy. While in Ireland he is greatly attracted by Emily, Lady Hemphill, who figures in his poem 'Ireland with Emily'. The Betjemans' daughter, Candida, is born in Dublin in 1942.

Between 1943 and 1951, John is a regular freelance book-reviewer for the *Daily Herald*, the '*Daily Express* of the Left'. He has a talent for recognizing the books that will later be regarded as classics. He gets his mother, 'Colonel' Kolkhorst and other friends to précis books for him, but increasingly finds the work an intolerable chore. In 1944, after a brief spell back at the Ministry of Information, he joins 'P' Branch (Priority and Production) of the Admiralty in Bath, with the novelist Richard Hughes as his senior and the future Lord Weinstock as one of his juniors. He is not happy in the job, but renews contact with his old friend P. Morton Shand who is living in Bath, and develops a strong crush on Shand's young daughter Mary, about whom he writes poems.

In 1945 the Betjeman family move to The Old Rectory in Farnborough, Berkshire, bought for them by Penelope's father. In March John learns of the death, in action in Burma, of his great Oxford friend Basil, Marquess of Dufferin and Ava, and writes a threnody. In June he enters a nursing home to have a sebaceous cyst removed from his stomach and is nursed by Mary Renault, the future novelist. In Farnborough, Paul and Candida temporarily acquire Berkshire accents, though Paul is soon sent off to the Dragon School. Penelope is the disciplinarian of the household; never at ease with young children, John often escapes to stay with Kolkhorst and his camp circle at Yarnton Manor. In December 1945 his verse collection *New Bats in Old Belfries* is published, again to mainly favourable reviews.

From January 1945 to the spring of 1946, John is head of the British Council's books division. Most of his colleagues regard him as a hopeless administrator. Between 1946 and 1948 he is secretary of the Oxford Preservation Trust, founded to protect the city's and University's buildings and environment. Again he is not very effective. In 1947 the Betjemans' marriage suffers a crisis when Penelope becomes a Roman Catholic convert. In bullying letters, Evelyn Waugh tries to convince John that he, too, should 'go over to Rome'; but the poet feels his place is in the ill-attended Anglican parish church in Farnborough. He becomes ill; recovering, he falls in love with Margaret Wintringham, a young socialist married to the publisher and wine expert Edmund Penning-Rowsell, but the two hold back from a full affair. In 1950 another love-interest comes into John's life: his new secretary Jill Menzies, whom he calls 'Freckly Jill'. For her he develops 'a grand, long-lasting, platonic passion'.

The Betjemans keep up with all their old friends: the Pipers, the Lancasters, John Sparrow, Maurice Bowra and – more controversially – Sir Oswald and Lady Mosley. Lecturing at Charterhouse

School, John meets Patrick Cullinan (now a well-known South African poet). He invites him to Farnborough and later gives him a sort of master-class in writing verse.

John's freelancing as a radio broadcaster – largely interrupted by the war – takes off again. In the 1940s he becomes better known as a broadcaster than as a poet. In 1947 W. H. Auden edits a selection of Betjeman poems for an American readership, under the snide title *Slick but not Streamlined* (which John hates). In 1949 John becomes 'literary adviser' – in effect, literary editor – of *Time and Tide*, the magazine founded and edited by the redoubtable Lady Rhondda. It is a sad time for him because his mother, Bess, is very ill. (She dies in 1952.) Towards the end of 1953 Lady Rhondda invites him to the Caprice restaurant in London and sacks him. He takes revenge in a satirical poem, 'Caprice'.

In 1951, dispirited by changes in Farnborough made by a local farmer, the Betjeman family move to a Victorian house in Wantage, Berkshire. They make friends with the Barings at near-by Ardington, and for years the two families are 'inseparable'. At Ardington John enjoys some of the home comforts that Penelope, often preoccupied with her horses' welfare, fails to offer.

On 29 May 1951, at a London dinner-party held by Lady Pamela Berry, John meets Lady Elizabeth Cavendish, a lady-in-waiting to Princess Margaret. Guy Burgess, also invited, does not turn up; Anthony Blunt, who does, leaves early, ill with anxiety as he knows that Burgess and Donald Maclean, like himself Soviet spies, have fled the country. John and Elizabeth exchange no words, but fall in love.

In 1952 Murray publish a selection of Betjeman's prose writings. The final choice is made by Myfanwy Piper, who also suggests the book's felicitous title, *First and Last Loves*. John adds a jeremiad of an introduction, 'Love is Dead', attacking contemporary mores and indicating a depressed state of mind. In 1953 he unsuccessfully opposes a scheme by Magdalen College, Oxford, to create what he considers a 'suburban' rose garden on the other side of the High Street. On the eve of the garden's formal opening, he and Patrick Cullinan (by now a Magdalen undergraduate) creep out at dead of night and plant a garden gnome among the rose bushes. Murray publish another slim volume of Betjeman poetry in 1954, *A Few Late Chrysanthemums*. John Sparrow writes to Murray that he thinks the new poems '$\alpha + + + \ldots$ perhaps the best of the collections you have yet published of him'. The book wins the £250 Foyle's Poetry Prize. In the same year John rents a flat in Cloth Fair, near Smithfield Market in the City of London. He usually spends the weekdays there, the weekends with his family at Wantage.

The Betjemans live beyond their means. They attempt to bring in more money with King Alfred's Kitchen, a café-cum-bookshop in Wantage, and with a duck farm run by Penelope. Neither enterprise yields adequate profits. The children are growing up. Paul is sent to Eton, does his National Service and reads geography at Oxford. Candida attends St Mary's, Wantage. In 1957 John spends a month as a visiting poetry professor in Cincinnati, accompanied by Penelope. He is a great success but the Betjemans do not entirely enjoy the experience. John misses Elizabeth and Penelope finds the cocktail parties and the suffocating central heating 'ghastly'.

In 1958 the Cloth Fair flat is severely damaged by a fire. While it is repaired, John moves into a riverside flat in Rotherhithe rented by his friend Antony Armstrong-Jones from William Glenton, a London shipping reporter. Later in the year John scores his greatest critical and commercial success with Murray's publication of his *Collected Poems*. It is the publishing phenomenon of the year, and its royalties help to restore the family finances. In December 1958 Princess Margaret presents the poet with the Duff Cooper Prize. On Christmas Day John writes to Jock Murray: 'Of course next year there will be the reaction and I shall suffer contempt, neglect & frustration, but I can now always look back to a really thrilling moment of triumph . . .' In 1960, with some of the profits from *Collected Poems*, John buys a house called Treen in Trebetherick, Cornwall, as an extra home.

1

WANTAGE

I'm jolly glad Arne [Anne Baring] was the instigator of painting King Alf. Though he was a very great king, it is a very poor piece of sculpture of him ...

John Betjeman, letter to Mollie Baring, 25 July 1960

I felt increasingly that the play was about *me* ... Oh, my dear boy, I can't exactly thank you for such an agonizing self-analysis.

John Betjeman, letter to John Osborne, 10 September 1964

Candida never quite forgave her parents for moving, in 1951, from the Georgian Old Rectory in Farnborough, downhill to their almost parodically Victorian new house, The Mead, in red-brick Wantage. But there was one compensation for the move: it brought the family much nearer to Desmond and Mollie Baring and their children at Ardington House.[1] The Barings became the Betjemans' best friends in the district. An early encounter between the two families, just before the Betjemans left Farnborough, presaged and symbolized their future relationship. Penelope was bossing about a group of children, including her own and the Barings', in rehearsals for a nativity play. Mollie Baring was ordered to shine a torch on the Virgin Mary's face. John Betjeman, arriving home, was horrified to find that Mollie had not been offered a drink, and asked her to join him in 'that little room on the left'.[2]

Always, Mollie and John conspired together to enjoy the comforts and minor luxuries that Penelope frowned on. Again, when the Barings' sons, Peter and Nigel, helped Paul dig up potatoes on the Betjemans' land – an exercise which Penelope saw as their 'helping to earn their keep' – John gave the boys a pound note each, 'an *enormous* tip then', Penelope grumbled.[3] Ardington House – early Georgian, with wide lawns sweeping down to a landscaped lake – became for John not so much a bolthole as a different world into which he could escape. He compared it to the paradise into which the Pied Piper led the children of Hamelin.[4] The two husbands differed from each other in a positive–negative way: John the effervescent showman, 'Dezzie', though quietly humorous, self-effacing. The wives were opposites, too. Penelope was born to the purple but almost oblivious of class distinctions; while Mollie, a bookmaker's daughter, was acutely aware of the social niceties she had had to pick up. But these were opposites who attracted each other: the differences spiced the friendship.

Desmond and Mollie did everything they could to help the Betjemans. 'Candida was virtually brought up at Ardington,' Mollie said. In 1960 John was able to make some return for the Barings' kindness in what seemed, at the time, an episode of high drama. On 20 April 1960, the *Wantage Herald* reported that an outrage had been perpetrated in the Berkshire town. Under the headline 'KING ALFRED IN THE RED', the newspaper stated: 'Workmen were busy on the statue of King Alfred the Great in Wantage Market Place today removing paint from it. Dark red paint was found today daubed on the face and on the battle-axe. Police are making enquiries.'[5] The granite effigy of Alfred had been sculpted by Queen Victoria's nephew, Count Gleichen, in 1886, and the craggy face was said to have been modelled on that of Lord Wantage, a kinsman of the Betjemans' friends the Loyds.[6] (Christopher Loyd's father overheard one old lady saying to another, as she pointed at the axe-wielding Alfred: 'It's so like dear Lord Wantage, and of course he was always so keen on forestry, wasn't he?')[7]

'Everyone knew the painting hadn't been done by oiks', Mollie Baring recalled, 'because little sonnets were stuck on the paint, and Latin tags coming out of his mouth – it was done most beautifully, marvellously thought out.'[8] The police investigation exposed the culprits – fifteen girls at St Mary's School, among them Anne Baring. Mollie, on her way to Goodwood, was summoned back to be interviewed by the police. 'I was a magistrate at the time and so were most of my friends. Someone said to Anne, "You'll probably end up in court." And she said, "Well, what will that matter? It will only be in front of Mummy, Mrs Lonsdale and Mrs Knight!" '[9]

Of the fifteen graffiti artists, twelve had just left St Mary's; but three were staying on, including Anne. Sister Brigitta, the school's formidable headmistress, decided that they must be expelled. Though Candida (who was not involved in the incident) had left the school some time back, John was still a governor. The Conservative MP for Abingdon, Airey Neave, and his wife Diana, were also governors. Their daughter was one of the vandals, but she had left the school.

One must not be too rude about Airey Neave, who was known as 'Hairy Knees' [Mollie Baring said]. He had been a hero in the war, escaping from Colditz Castle; and he died a hero's death, blown up by the IRA. But I must say he was frightfully pompous. He went round saying, 'This is going to affect the [Conservative] Party. These girls must be expelled.' It was so preposterous. I mean, who the hell was going to vote Labour because some girls at St Mary's, Wantage had painted a statue? He and his wife said to Sister Brigitta: 'You must take a very strong line on this.' So I was really fighting terrific odds. I suppose one must be fair to Airey Neave and see his point of view. He didn't want people to say, 'It's only because he's an MP and his daughter was in it that they've all got off.'

Anne didn't mind very much if she was expelled. But I thought it would be a pity. She was very brainy. I thought it wasn't going to do her much good. So I rang Penelope to find out where John was. 'Oh, he's up *there*,' she said. 'I don't care where he is,' I said. 'I must speak to him.' Time was running out.[10]

Penelope meant that John and Elizabeth were staying with the Dowager Duchess of Devonshire at Edensor, Derbyshire. Mollie telephoned the Duchess, who told her that John and Elizabeth were out walking. Mollie replied: 'The moment John comes in, will you ask him to telephone me. It is important.' John later told Mollie that when he got the message his first thought was that Penelope or Candida had been killed. He rang Mollie and, on hearing the problem, gave immediate advice: she should write at once to Lady Cynthia Colville, who was the Queen's governor of St Mary's. 'So I sat up all night writing Lady Cynthia an impassioned letter,' Mollie said.[11]

Meanwhile, John went to work on Sister Brigitta. He had already had one brush with her, in 1958. Candida was in trouble then. She had copied out some lines from Andrew Marvell's 'To His Coy Mistress' which she had found in the school library –

> My vegetable love should grow
> Vaster than empires, and more slow.

She had substituted the words 'D-cup bras' for 'empires' and passed the lines to a friend. 'Her explosion of laughter caused the piece of paper they were written on to be confiscated and shown to Sister B. who, not knowing her Marvell, took the lines to be an invitation to lesbian frolics. She was at the time cross-questioning the whole school on the question of masturbation.'[12] John and Penelope were called in to see the headmistress, after which meeting John wrote to Sister Brigitta with some asperity:

One thing on reflection greatly disturbed me in that shattering interview I had with you (and may I say that Mrs Betjeman was even more shattered than me), and that was that you told me the chaplain had said to you he was greatly disturbed by the sex in the school, because of what he had heard in the girls' confessions. I do not think that even in the most general terms a priest should make such a breach of confidence. Once at Lancing a boy was expelled shortly after he had been to confession and it took years before they could get anyone to go to confession again. It would be really terrible for the faith of the school if what you said to me became known outside the community.[13]

John had not been content just to raise this matter with Sister Brigitta; he had gone over her head and written to Father Raymond Raynes, the Warden of the Order of St Mary's Convent, to express dismay at the chaplain's betrayal of the girls.[14] This had hardly smoothed the way for him to raise another delicate matter with the headmistress and ask a favour of her. But, when necessary, John could be very tough. He told Sister Brigitta that if the statue-painters were expelled, he would resign as a governor.[15] Given his fame, this would ensure that the vandal-scandal reached national newspapers, not just local ones. Lady Cynthia Colville also appealed for mercy toward the miscreants. 'And I grovelled,' Mollie Baring said. 'The girls were going to be in the sixth form, which carried tremendous privileges. I said, "Why don't you let them stay but take away all their privileges?" – Anne was very upset about that. And Sister Brigitta accepted that compromise and let them stay on.'[16]

On 25 July 1960 – at that stage it was not yet known whether the headmistress would relent – John wrote Mollie a long 'note of consolation and advice'. Though the letter was for Mollie, its contents were chiefly designed to cheer up Anne. 'I'm jolly glad Arne was the instigator of painting King Alf,' he wrote. 'Though he was a very great king, it is a very poor piece of sculpture of him . . .' He added: 'Schoolmasters and mistresses lose all sense of proportion. If they allow the newspapers into their schools with all the accounts of ridiculous undergraduate and student rags that they contain, they must expect emulation from the more high-spirited of the girls.'[17] He suggested that it was no disgrace to be sent down from a girls' school – rather the reverse. 'Arne will look at the statue of King Alf with pride in future years, if she is sent down.'[18] He thought she should leave anyway to go abroad or to a tutor 'as she is clever and sensitive and now too old probably for school'.[19] He advised Mollie not to confuse boys' schools with girls' schools. 'Expulsion from the latter is an honour and is fast becoming one from the former.' He reminded her that he had been sent down from Oxford, 'and I don't regret it'. His final advice was: 'Have a drink and give one to Dezzie.'[20] Mollie remembered how the affair of the statue ended. 'All the girls involved had to pay £30 – which seemed fantastic in those days – to have the statue cleaned. Within one month the boys of Wantage had repainted it!'[21]

In the middle of the crisis over King Alfred, his descendant Princess Margaret married Antony Armstrong-Jones (Lord Snowdon), on 5 May 1960, in Westminster Abbey. John and Penelope were invited. So was William Glenton, Armstrong-Jones's landlord in Rotherhithe.[22] He and the Betjemans agreed that 'for moral support' they would go to the Abbey together.

> As part of the arrangement [Glenton recalled] I was to collect them in my car – but when I arrived at the Kensington house where they were spending the night there was, at first, no reply to my knocking. Only after I had hammered hard for several minutes did the door open, and the plump figure of John, still in pyjamas, appeared. Both he and his wife had overslept, and when I announced that we had only half an hour to get to the Abbey, there was pandemonium. As I helped John to find his clothes, half of which he had mislaid, I kept catching glimpses of a half-dressed female figure dashing up and down stairs – his wife was hunting for her belongings. It was more like a quick change at the Windmill, and how John managed to get ready in time without putting his ancient morning suit on over his pyjamas I do not know.
>
> But we were, I suppose, as respectably dressed as anyone as we took our places among that strange mixture of famous and unknown faces in the Abbey. I was surrounded by such contrasting groups as the Chelsea Set and a party of estate workers, from Tony's father's North Wales estate, and the well-known characters I could identify ranged from Noël Coward and Margaret Leighton to Jean Cocteau.[23]

Three days after the wedding, Noël Coward wrote in his diary: 'I forgot to mention that during the week I met, at long last, John Betjeman and, of course, loved him immediately.'[24] (The friendship developed.[25] John read the address at Coward's memorial service in 1973 and the playwright left him one of his own oil-paintings in his will.)[26]

After the first two public events that affected John in 1960 – Alfred red, Margaret wed – came a third: the arrival in Wantage of a new vicar. John had always found the previous vicar, the Rev. Arthur Chetwynd-Talbot, a 'dull old stick', and disliked his wife, who had annoyed him by uprooting all the box hedges in the vicarage garden.[27] So he was delighted when a new priest, John Schaufelberger, came to the town. In September 1960 John wrote to Harry Jarvis: 'He is full of jokes, calls everyone "my dear", likes embroidering and I think cats or maybe dogs, lives with his old mother, is dark-haired and forty-four and thank God is *very High*. I hope that Our Lady will come back into prominence and life and a little vulgarity.'[28] A ribald nickname for the new incumbent was soon in circulation: 'Shufflebugger'.[29] The curate, the Rev. Harry Bloomfield, was his boyfriend. 'Soon they became an accepted couple in the town,' Candida records. 'They were known as "Hinge and Bracket"[30] and were very happy and certainly filled the church.'[31]

John enjoyed their company. In 1976 Schaufelberger recalled:

John would totter down here on a Saturday morning and say, 'Boys! I've brought a bottle of sherry. Just to have a little drink before lunch.' He sometimes came on to lunch at our cottage, where he once said, 'There's only one thing missing here. That's the sound of the sea.' And then he heard the sound of a train rushing by, because the cottage is quite near the main railway track that goes through from Paddington. So he said, 'Oh well, the sound of the train makes up for the lack of the sound of the sea.'[32]

'John came to church very faithfully,' said Schaufelberger.[33] It was at church that John met Bart and Jessie Sharley, who lived in a small terraced house in the road called Portway, in Wantage. John invited the Sharleys back to The Mead for a drink with Penelope, and the two couples became friends. The Berkshire society in which John and Penelope normally moved was of people whose sons were sent to public schools and whose daughters became debutantes – even people who had seats in Westminster Abbey at the Coronation in 1953. Some of these friends could not understand why the Betjemans spent so much time with the Sharleys.[34] Bart and Jessie were not at all grand. He was a primary-school teacher at King Alfred's School in Wantage; she had been secretary to a director of the Rootes company in London. They had two daughters, slightly younger than Candida – Veronica (Ron) and Diana. 'Penelope called us The Bug Family,' Ron recalled. 'She always said that John should have married Mummy and she should have married Daddy – and all the children would have been prime ministers.'[35]

Although John often appeared on television, the Betjemans had no television set. Like many middle-class families in the 1950s, they regarded it as *infra dig* to own a set. They had their books, their piano and their gramophone: what need of this ugly machine pumping out its generally banal entertainment? Not to have a 'telly' was as much the done thing as to drive a Land Rover. Still, when John appeared on the 'idiot box', he could not resist asking the Sharleys – who did have a set – if he might come round to Portway and watch himself.[36] The Sharleys were useful to Penelope, too. Jessie and the two girls all helped in King Alfred's Kitchen from time to time. 'I can see John now, washing up at the caff,' Ron said. 'We used to leave him the big soup saucepan with about two inches of sediment at the bottom which no one had stirred. The sink leaked so you had to stand on boards balanced on bricks. He had this enormous apron on. I used to say, "You hold it here and I'll run round you to tie it." '[37]

The Sharleys were quite unawed by John's fame. Bart had a countryman's wisdom and horse sense. Neither he nor Jessie was afraid to tell the Betjemans when they thought they were making a mistake.

Penelope came round one morning [Jessie recalled] and she said, 'Darling, I'm so depressed,' and she put her arms round me. I said: 'What's the matter with you?' She said, 'I'm not making use of the gifts God's given me.' I said: 'Of course you're not.' She straightened up and said, 'What do you mean?' I said, 'The trouble is, Penelope, you want to write a book but you're fiddling about down at the café. I said, 'You're doing nothing. Why don't you stick to one thing?' She said, 'You're right, darling.' And do you know, it's funny, because I'm not an intellectual like she was, but she always used to come to me if she was down.

Anyway, the next morning she came over about nine o'clock. She said: 'I'm going to Oxford.' I said, 'Oh, are you?' 'Yes, I'm going to do some writing. You don't believe me, do you?' She comes back about four o'clock, roaring with laughter. She said, 'You won't believe this.' I said, 'Oh yes, I do believe it.' So she said, 'What do you mean, believe it?' I said, 'You haven't done *any* writing, have you?' 'No,' she said, 'I found a book and I just sat and read it, then came home.'[38]

Jessie often accompanied Penelope when she gave lectures.

They used to think I was her secretary. One day she was due to give a lecture on Indian temples, in Reading. She said, 'I don't quite know where it is, but you go past the hospital – the Royal Berkshire I think it's called.' We get to Tilehurst and Penelope sees an ambulance. 'Follow that!' she says. 'It's bound to be going to the hospital.' 'Don't be so silly,' I said, 'it may be going to pick someone up.' But we followed it. She said, 'We'll ask those boys.' I said, 'They don't look as if they've got much brain.' They gave some skew-whiff directions. We came to a large house, lit up. She said, 'Let's ask there – will you go?' I said, 'No, *you* go.' She came back, puffing. 'They haven't got a clue.' We came to a road with a hall at the end of it. She said, 'I expect this is it.' I said, 'There's no light.' We got all her slides out of the car. A priest came out and said, 'Can I help you?' 'Yes,' she said, 'I've come to lecture to the Townswomen's Guild.' He said, 'It's tomorrow night.'[39]

The greatest bond between the Betjemans and the Sharleys was a sense of humour, on both sides. They teased each other without taking umbrage. John particularly liked Ron Sharley, an attractive, sparky teenager.

I did silly things that made him laugh [she recalled]. A lot of malapropisms – I suppose I do have slight dyslexia. He used to sit and read to me a lot. He had a wonderful book of limericks and he adored that, because I used to sit and giggle, and he'd giggle too. They weren't all Edward Lear. Some of them were naughty modern limericks. And he'd say, 'Ooh, I'd better not tell you this one, you're not old enough.' But then he did, of course. There was one – I can't remember all of it, but it begins 'There was a young lady of Wantage Of whom the town clerk took advantage . . .' and it ends with her saying, 'You've completely altered my frontage!'[40]

When John was away from Wantage, he wrote her letters giving advice on her love-life and career. (At one stage she became matron at Wellington College.) 'I am so glad you are in love,' he wrote.

It's the only tonic for nerves.

> "God is love" the Bishops yell,
> Yes I know, but Love is hell

as my secretary quoted to me last week about her own state of mind.[41]

A year later, he wrote: 'Love is a searing experience, more often painful than a pleasure, but it makes people wiser, kinder and more full of humour than those who never know it.'[42] Ten years on he was still writing to her: 'I very much enjoy your dotting your "i"s with "o"s. It makes your letter look nice and Swedish. If you draw a line at an acute angle through all your "o"s it would complete the Scandinavian effect.'[43] In 1963, when Ron was sixteen, John gave her lunch at the Royal Automobile Club in London.

We sat in this huge dining-room and I was the only female there, other than the waitress, who was a bottle-blonde cockney and obviously knew him very well. I think her name was Flo or Betty or something. John and I sat opposite each other and Archie and Jumbo sat opposite each other. We had a super time. The Great Train Robbery had just taken place and the waitress said, 'Oh, you're very rich today. Have you pinched some from the Great Train Robbery?' At the other tables were all these elderly men. I felt rather conspicuous, sitting there with a teddy-bear and an elephant.[44]

John was also fond of the Sharleys' other daughter, Diana. Jessie Sharley remembered:

When Diana was working in London, John rang her up one day and said, 'Are you coming down [to Wantage] at the weekend, Diana?' She said, 'Yes.' He said, 'Will you do something for me? I've written a poem and I want to read it to somebody.' He said, 'It's no good reading it to Penelope because she goes to sleep halfway through.' So when she came home, she said, 'What do you think? Poor old John, he was sweeping up the hall. He'd just given a lecture at the VC [the Victoria Cross Gallery which the first Lord Wantage, a holder of the medal, had created to house paintings of valorous exploits]. He said, "Penelope doesn't *see* dust and dirt."' So Diana said, 'Oh, John, let me finish it for you.' But he said, 'Well, I've just about finished now'; and he read her the poem.[45]

John found Diana a job. 'John was at our house one day,' Jessie recalled, 'and he asked, "What is Diana going to do when she leaves the secretarial college in Oxford?" I said, "Well, she's talking about trying to become a secretary to one of the almoners at the Middlesex [Hospital]." "What does she want to go there for? Why doesn't she come to Bart's, where she'd be near me?" That very week he wrote to Mr Carus-Wilson, the Governor of the hospital; and the next week there was a letter to say that when she left the college she'd got the job.'[46]

The Betjemans' and Sharleys' children were less close to each other than their parents were. 'Paul I adored,' Ron said. 'I had a wonderful schoolgirl crush on him. He was always very kind, just like his father, but I don't think he specially noticed me. At that time he had this terrific thing with serpents, he loved snakes. He kept a snake in a glass tank in the library at The Mead, with a volume of the *Encyclopaedia Britannica* balanced on top to stop it escaping.'[47] Ron saw little of Candida. 'Candida was very much with the yuppies – my sister and I didn't fit into that group. We were sort of glorified village kids, I suppose. She mixed with the Old Etonians and so on – people like Herki [Hercules] Bellville.[48] He was quite sweet – just like a streak of lightning, very tall, very slim.'[49]

Many of Candida's friends were the children of her parents' friends – the Barings, Clives, Harrods, Lancasters, Pipers and Powells.[50] But in Oxford she met a new group of friends, the pioneers of the 1960s

satire movement, including Richard Ingrams, William Rushton, John
Wells and Paul Foot. She fell in love with Ingrams, who had film-star
looks to match her own. 'I first saw him in the Town and Gown in
Oxford,' she later said. 'It was an awful little egg and chip place. With
neon lights. It became my home from home. I went there every single
day for six months because I knew Ingrams would be there. Foot, Peter
Jay[51] and Rushton would be there as well.'[52] Ingrams and Rushton
were both involved in producing the undergraduate satire magazine
Mesopotamia (*Mespot* for short – it was named after a spit of land
in the River Cherwell). Rushton drew the cover design and several
cartoons for a 'sackcloth and ashes' issue – the cover was of sackcloth,
the pages were to be burnt for ashes, and pasted on the back were
mustard and cress seeds from which to grow a frugal meal for the
penitent.[53] Candida – then taking a sculpture course at the Oxford
'Tech' – went round college rooms selling the magazine.[54] *Mespot* was
a prototype for *Private Eye,* which she helped to launch in 1961. By
then she had a job sub-editing copy about fur coats for Jocelyn Stevens
on *Queen* magazine. In the evenings she went to the Pavilion Road,
London house of Mary Morgan, Richard Ingrams's future wife, and
stapled together the copies which Mary had collated. She posted some
to her friends. John Piper was the first person to take out a subscription.[55] Jocelyn Stevens found out she was moonlighting for *Private
Eye*, and sacked her.[56] As a result, he was evermore lampooned in the
magazine as 'Piranha Teeth'. Like her father, Candida knew how to
keep a feud on the boil.[57]

She later wrote of her friends of that time: 'If they seemed like eager
university students, they often alarmed my father. He felt vulnerable
among them.'[58] At first, he took against the lymphatic and noisy
Rushton, and wrote a rude rhyme about him.[59] Rushton retaliated
with amusing caricatures of John. But in time John came round to
Rushton. Ingrams, too, became a friend and in 1971 John began
contributing a 'Nooks and Corners' column to *Private Eye,* pillorying
bad architecture and the assaults on good buildings. He always called
Ingrams 'old Pressdram' – the latter word was the magazine's tele-
graphic address.[60]

Candida writes of her father: 'When he got to know young people
of whom he was frightened, the rewards were often great.'[61] One of her
friends was David Dimbleby, son of the television broadcaster Richard
Dimbleby. He remembered a picnic on the downs with the Betjemans.
John asked him what he intended to do when he left Oxford. On learning that the young man was undecided, he advised him to go into a
monastery for a week to think things over. Dimbleby did not; but the
idea of finding calm in a crisis stayed with him, as did the memory of

From left to right: John Betjeman, Evelyn Waugh, John Sparrow (seated), C. P. Snow and Cyril Connolly. The cartoon by Rushton originally appeared in The A to Z of National Culture

John's kindly curiosity.[62] The picnics on the downs usually took place at Knighton Bushes, where John would perform his set-piece of chanting Vachel Lindsay's 'Congo', beating time on a cake-tin lid.[63] 'Boom, Boom, BOOM' – the sound that had so annoyed Mr Summers at Heddon Court prep school[64] – echoed round the Berkshire hills.

John's attitude to Candida's romances was relaxed and *laissez-faire*: 'It will probably blow over,' was his reassuring refrain in letters to Penelope, who looked on more anxiously. While she did not have her own mother's snobbish attitude to her daughter's suitors, she naturally hoped that she would marry somebody pleasant and of good character. Candida became a debutante. Penelope recalled in 1976:

> John greatly disapproved. He just thought Candida should have a job. He thought coming out was an absolute waste of money. He was becoming like his father. It was exactly what his father would have said if he'd had a daughter.
>
> Anyway, Candida came out, it was tremendous fun. [Lady] Mary Clive's daughter came out the same year and they were great friends.

Mary had a flat in London, near Peter Jones. And we used to entertain. Our way of entertaining was much more fun than giving dances. We used to have big cinema parties for films like *Ben-Hur*. I would do most of the food and Mary provided the crockery and help. We used to give them a large dinner first and then all go to the cinema.[65]

The Betjemans gave a party for Candida.

It was quite memorable, a barn dance. Paul came out from Oxford with his band and played the music. The place was owned by some nice people with a pony cart, over near Longworth, somewhere right down the Thames – I think they bathed in the Thames at night. We all drove over; we had, I think, eleven pony carts. Simon Hornby drove the trolley cart and I drove my four-wheel cart with a famous gossip lady from the *Tatler*. We had a lovely dance, it was so different from the London dances. Everybody seemed to enjoy it.[66]

After Candida was fired from *Queen* magazine, and before she became secretary to John's former Admiralty boss Richard Hughes, she was invited to a house party in Venice, in a palace that belonged to Countess Munster, a sister of Penelope's old schoolfriend, Nicolette Hornby.

Peggy Munster lent her palace to her nephew, Simon Hornby – later chairman of W.H. Smith. And Simon at that time rather fancied Candida, I think would have liked to marry her. He invited her as his girlfriend, rather. And John said, 'On no account must Candida go.' He was not going to pay for her to go. 'It's time she got a job,' he said, 'and she could perfectly well get a job at W.H. Smith in Oxford, selling pencils.' And I said, I suppose from a motherly instinct, 'She might meet some eldest sons.' I told him, 'This is ridiculous. It's only for a week, she can get a job afterwards.' We had an awful row about it. He was so self-contradictory: I mean, he loves grand people himself. Finally, I paid her return fare; and there she met Rupert Lycett Green – one of the most successful marriages of all time! After Venice she got the job with Richard Hughes and Rupert used to go and see her. He'd lorst his licence for dangerous driving, so he had to go by train and get a taxi.[67]

John and Penelope were delighted and relieved when Candida and Rupert became engaged.

She could have married absolutely the wrong person [Penelope said]. She was a terrible flirt. At one time she was in the beginnings of a sort of hippie movement led by [Sir] Mark Palmer. He was the king hippie. He was up at Oxford then, he got sent down for drugs. But she used to come out with him and his various friends and they used to cut out the knees and elbows of their jeans and jerseys to look as dishevelled as possible. Mark was always charming to me. He was a very good horseman. But the friends he brought out with him never spoke to me at all, they were frightfully rude. Candida said he wanted to marry her but she didn't want to marry somebody who never did anything. Quite right!

So he then started this gypsy thing of getting caravans and horses and getting lots of girls and boys together who wanted to lead that sort of dropout life. They went all over England. They went down to Cornwall and he was beaten up in Padstow because he rather stole the thunder from the Padstow 'Obby 'Oss dance, with all his pretty debs and caravans. And then he had a liaison with Peggy Cuthbertson (who now lives with Desmond Guinness) and they lived together in Montgomeryshire. I went to stay with them. They had an old gypsy doing fencing on their small-holding. I can't describe the squalor, I CANNOT describe the squalor. The next morning I realized there was a huge hole in the wall of my bedroom which was covered up by a piece of old carpet on the outside. And their great theory at the time was that you must never never spend one moment doing any housework, it was an absolute waste of time. The *gypsy* took me aside and complained of the dirt and the mess! So I was very relieved that Candida didn't end up with Mark.[68]

Sir Mark Palmer did not come to nothing, as Penelope implied, but became a successful horse dealer. He and Candida remained good friends; in 2000, when she was suffering from cancer, he was her companion on the long cross-country ride she described in *Over the Hills and Far Away* (2002). Rupert Lycett Green was much more Penelope's idea of a desirable son-in-law. 'He has beautiful manners,' she wrote to John.[69] He was a grandson of a baronet, Sir Edward Lycett Green, a Yorkshire master of hounds. The family had gained some notoriety in the Baccarat Scandal of 1891. A gentleman was caught cheating at cards at Tranby Croft, near Doncaster, the home of Arthur Wilson, a Hull shipowner. The Prince of Wales (later Edward VII), who was present, had to testify at the unsavoury court case which followed. The scandal only came to light because Arthur Wilson's young son blabbed to his sister – Rupert's grandmother.[70]

Twenty-five in 1963, Rupert Lycett Green was Byronically handsome. In that year he founded Blades, the tailors, in Mayfair, London, naming it after the elegant fictional club where James Bond had his greatest gambling triumph in *Moonraker*. It made for young-men-about-town the new suits with long jackets and hip-hugging, tapered trousers. In 1967 Jonathan Aitken – a grandson of John's old boss in Dublin, Lord Rugby – included Lycett Green in his book *The Young Meteors*. Aitken thought Blades was the male fashion-house equivalent to Annacat, the 'glossy Brompton Road boutique' owned and run by the ex-debutantes Maggie Keswick and Janet Lyle.[71]

A Blades suit [Aitken wrote] costs between £70 and £90 and since [Lycett Green] has seven hundred regular customers after four years in business, the formula is evidently a successful one. The atmosphere of Blades is very like that of a grand club. Customers can sink into comfortable leather sofas and read glossy magazines while awaiting a fitting, or chat with their friends while buying a shirt, belt or tie.[72]

'I started the place because I couldn't buy a decent suit anywhere in London,' Lycett Green told Aitken, adding:

When I first joined the army, if I wore anything outrageous . . . the reaction seemed to be, 'Christ, what the hell is that young bounder doing?', but by the time I left two years later if you wore something that looked smart they'd be prepared to say, 'Christ, that's a smart suit' or 'What a great shirt' or something like that. Previously, to remark on that sort of thing would, anyway in the army, make one vaguely suspicious of odd tendencies in the person paying the compliment, but the shortage of birds made everyone completely re-think about dressing properly. It was just luck we happened to start Blades at the time of the boom.[73]

Just as John had replicated his father's sternness in prescribing army service to make a man of Paul, Penelope insisted on a marriage settlement between Rupert and Candida, in almost the same words that her father had used thirty years earlier when very grudgingly outlining a possible settlement for John and Penelope; though Penelope began her cross letter to Rupert (4 April 1963) with a half-humorous touch of melodrama – '*I AM IN A PURPLE PASSION* . . .'[74] The wedding took place on 25 May 1963. Candida wore a gown of white organdie trimmed with frills and with a long train.[75]

John wore with his morning dress Henry James's waistcoat, given to him by the novelist's former secretary, Theodora Bosanquet.[76] Penelope's arrival was remembered by a Wantage neighbour, Stella Hollister:

It was a very big wedding with toppers and tails. Mrs Betjeman was mucking out her horses or something and she arrived at the church about a quarter of an hour before the bride was due. They were all changing at Dr Squires's house, next to the church. And she dashed in there – all the crowds of people waiting outside to see them go in – dashed in, covered in dirt and with bits of straw sticking out from everywhere. She washed her face, put on what passed, with her, for finery, and came out – the mother of the bride![77]

There had been difficulties over the guest-list for the 'family lunch-eon'. Penelope had invited the Sharleys to it.

The closest friends went to the lunch [Jessie Sharley said], the others to the ball. Angela Wakeford[78] was very upset. 'Do you know, Jessie,' she said, 'we haven't been invited to the luncheon. I can't understand it. We've been friends with John and Penelope for so long.' So I didn't say anything to Angela, but I said to Penelope, 'Angela's very unhappy. Why not let her and her husband have our tickets? We don't mind.' 'Don't you dare say that!' she said. 'You're coming.' I thought it was a bit unkind, really.[79]

At the lunch, which was at Faringdon, Robert Heber Percy released a flight of Lord Berners's coloured doves. John Schaufelberger, who might have been expected to enjoy such campery, felt that 'it was a falsity'.[80] All the *Private Eye* crowd were at the ball that evening. Candida recalls: 'Nicole [Hornby], who was very tall and quite alarm-ing, waltzed JB, who was smaller, around the dance floor at great speed. My mother . . . bravely intercepted and put an end to it, insist-ing that JB would be sick.'[81]

On their honeymoon, Rupert and Candida drove round the world in a customized Land Rover. 'We made no preparations,' Candida wrote, 'but for my buying a pair of white leather thigh boots because I was so frightened of snakes.'[82] They drove through Belgium, Germany, Austria, Yugoslavia, Bulgaria, Turkey, Persia, Pakistan and India. They saw the temples of Angkor Wat in Cambodia – the treat that Penelope had denied herself by her marriage to John thirty years earlier. They were held at gunpoint in Kabul, turned the Land Rover over in Jaisalmer, saw 'a spider with a body the size of a Big Mac' in Cambodia and a man strung from a lamppost in Baghdad.[83] When they got back to England they found nobody was interested in their photographs; but Penelope was thrilled that Candida was four months pregnant and sent her imperious notes about relaxation exercises and the importance of breast-feeding.[84]

With Rupert installed at Blades, he and Candida were at the centre of Swinging London of the Sixties.[85] Their friends included the dress designer Ossie Clark, who designed frocks for Candida (David Hockney, also a friend, painted her portrait in one of them); the pop artist Derek Boshier; the poet Christopher Logue and the interior decorator David Mlinaric – another of Jonathan Aitken's 'young meteors'. Lady Henrietta Rous, who edited Ossie Clark's diaries in 1998, noted that Rupert and Candida 'were known as "Tailor and Cutter" – she the "Cutter" for her notoriously sharp wit'.[86]

Candida's parents were much less at home in the Swinging Sixties. Penelope did not even know (or affected not to know) who the Beatles were. In September 1963 Diana Sharley made a tape-recording of an evening that John and Penelope spent with the Sharleys at their home in Portway. The Betjemans knew the recorder was on, and there was some playing to the gallery; but gradually they forgot about it. This unique 'oral document' takes us, as closely as it is possible to get, into the Betjemans' company when John and Penelope were in their fifties. Bart and Jessie Sharley, Diana and 'Ron' were all present. So was Ron's boyfriend, Tony de Sousa. At that time Ron was the cook at All Hallows, Shepton Mallet, a Roman Catholic preparatory school which sent pupils on mainly to Ampleforth and Downside. De Sousa, himself an Old Amplefordian, was an assistant master there.

On 27 September, Penelope was due to appear on *Woman's Hour* on the radio, to talk about her new book, *Two Middle-Aged Ladies in Andalusia*. (One of the ladies was Penelope; the other was a mare which the Duke of Wellington had lent her in 1961 to ride across Andalusia – an adventure partly inspired by George Borrow's *The Bible in Spain*.) As the 1963 recording opens, John is about to take Penelope through a dummy run for the radio interview, assuming a mock, slightly patronizing inquisitor's tone.

JB: I'm going to give you an interview about your book.

PB (*squawks*): No, no, I'm not going to!

Sharleys: Oh go on, Penelope, *do!*

JB: Miss Chetwode, I understand that you have for some time been married to a journalist in Wantage. What made you first want to go to Spain?

PB: It comes on the first page of my book. Shows you haven't read it.

JB: Oh, I wonder if you'd mind . . . I've read your book with great pleasure, but I opened at the *second* page; and I was very interested to know that you found Spain so interesting a country. Could you tell me why it interested you so much – such an interesting place?

    (*Long silence*)

JB: Miss Chetwode?

    (*Sharleys giggle*)

A voice: Sssssssh!

PB: It was interesting because it was so unlike England. You see, England is nothing but internal combustion engines, and in Spain you simply saw people going about on mules and horses and donkeys, which

I much prefer to motors. I think Wantage would be a very much happier place if everybody went about on mules and horses. I think, for instance, Mrs Sharley would look charming on a mule.

JB: And so you're not in favour of progress?

PB: No – *damn* progress is what I say.

JB: Heh, heh; heh, heh . . . Could we stop now?[87]

On the tape, John next reads 'Upper Lambourne' (*sic*) and 'Diary of a Church Mouse'. Then he reads 'Devonshire Street, W1', introducing it with these words:

This refers to Dr Stephen Ward who was extremely good as an osteopath and cured some rheumatism I had in my knees; and I remember that when I was in the waiting-room of his surgery I saw across the way, in Devonshire Street, two old people coming out from the opposite house and the man had one of those large brown envelopes with your X-ray photographs in it and his wife was with him and it made me think of this.[88]

Everyone in the room would have known who Dr Stephen Ward was. A figure notorious in the Profumo scandal of that year, he had committed suicide two months earlier, by a drugs overdose. It was at Ward's country cottage on Lord Astor's Cliveden estate that John Profumo, Secretary of State for War, had first seen the beautiful call-girl Christine Keeler as she frolicked naked in the swimming pool. The minister and the prostitute had begun an affair. It was Ward again who had tipped off MI5 that Keeler was also having a liaison with the Soviet naval attaché Eugene Ivanov. In June he had been put on trial for allegedly living off immoral earnings. Claiming that the Establishment was taking revenge for his exposé of a Government minister, Ward, while admitting that he was 'a connoisseur of love-making' and 'a thoroughly immoral man', denied that he had ever taken money for prostitution or procuring girls. However, he was convicted while still in a coma from the overdose. He never recovered to be sentenced. In November 1963 John wrote to his old friend John Sutro, 'I would dearly like to see penned those immortal lines you recited on the Ward case. They must not be hidden only in your memory . . . We will guard the secret if there's libel.'[89] Sutro's clever squib began:

HIC JACET VIR FAMOSUS STEPHEN WARD*
By our Society ruined and abhorred . . .

---

* Here lies a famous man, Stephen Ward.

FIAT JUSTITIA RUAT LEX[†]
With WARD we bury the delights of sex . . .
This hypocritical and false campaign
Ended one Saturday in heavy rain
When saying farewell to all the lies and cant
'BARBITURI VOS SALUTANT' . . .[‡90]

As the September evening at No. 6 Portway continued, Jessie Sharley put more logs on the fire and John recited two more of his poems, 'Beside the Seaside' and 'Wantage Bells', which had been written in celebration of Candida and Rupert's wedding –

> Where are the words to express
> Such a reckless bestowing?

When he finished reciting, with a few stumbles caused perhaps by tiredness or drink, John said: 'It's easier to read to oneself and you get the full hang of it; and Tennyson, who wrote every word that he wrote to be read out loud and *said* it about fifty times before he committed it to print, is *marvellous* out loud.'

Diana Sharley: When you write yours, you don't just sit down and say, 'I'm going to, today'? Do you wake up in the middle of the night and write, ever?

JB: Oh, Lord, no. In the early morning I remember stuff and never have a pencil by my bed. I generally write on a bit of . . . whatever's in my pocket, if a line comes to me, and then compose the rest of the stuff round it – weeks later, it might be. It's all crossed. You know, you get a mood, you want to put something down and a line occurs to you that suggests the mood. Then you build round the line. It's a very slow process and then I'm never satisfied with it.

Diana Sharley: Do you read it to yourself, do you read it out loud?

JB: I recite it out to myself, out loud, best of all when driving a motor-car alone. Because you're entirely alone then – no one can get you on the telephone – perfectly at ease. And then you say the stuff out loud until it comes out in the right order, as you think.

[†] Let justice be done, to hell with the law.
[‡] In this line Sutro has punningly adapted the gladiators' salute on entering the arena, '*Ave Caesar, morituri te salutant*' (Hail, Caesar, those about to die salute you'; Suetonius gives '*Ave Imperator, morituri te salutant*' – hail Emperor . . . – in *Claudius*, 21) to refer to Ward's overdose of barbiturates.

I'm sure that poetry is meant to be read out loud and I think [...] out loud, on their own, without music. I think it's probably a later de[...] opment than music. I think that obviously what first started must have been the bards saying things to these airs, and then the airs departed and the words were left. Well, now they're trying to get back to music and words together with this jazz, which is really a very good idea; but a poet who's any good at all must be able to stand on his own, like Tennyson did.

Ron Sharley: You ought to write pop songs.

JB: I couldn't, because my sentiments are so un-pop.

Ron Sharley: I'm sure if you got someone like the Beatles to sing it, you'd roar to the top.

PB: Who are the Beatles?

    (*laughter*)

Ron Sharley: They're a pop group . . . And you'd get about half of what they make out of it.

JB: Well, it's a nice idea, yes.

Ron Sharley: Wouldn't you like that?

JB: Yes, I think so. But I'm old, you know – my emotions have all died.

Ron Sharley: Well, *I'd* buy it, if no one else did.

JB: Oh, you are good and loyal and kind to me. You'll remember me when I'm fifty-seven! [He was fifty-seven then.]

    (*giggles*)

JB (*to Penelope*): Plymouth, ought we to go?

PB: Yes.

Diana Sharley (*to Penelope*): You're looking very tired.

PB: Terribly tired. I awoke at four o'clock.

JB: It's very good that she should look tired. Because she's been over-excited and wrought up for so long, it's very much better she should go to bed tired.

PB: (*indignantly*): Not over-excited! My God, I haven't been excited. I'm absolutely bored stiff with that house and our possessions.

Ron Sharley: Where are you going for Christmas, Mr Betjeman?

JB: I don't know, haven't thought about . . .

PB (*interrupting*): Cornwall, you always go to Cornwall.

JB: Generally. I expect I shall go and stay with Joc Lynam and Peggy Lynam Thomas down at Trebetherick. Or I shall be with Mr Piper.

Ron Sharley: Have you been to Cornwall this year?

JB: No. Oh, well, earlier this year, yes. I'm going down in October, I hope.

Ron Sharley: You're not coming through Shepton, are you? If it's on a Monday, I'll be able to come and see you.

JB: Monday's your day orf, is it?

Ron Sharley: Yes: Monday afternoon.

JB: What's on the menu that day? Is it fruit tart?

u a fruit tart, John?

a definite thing every [day of the] week? I can tell you [at St Margaret's, Bushey, Herts]. There was plum duff on uesday was jam tart; Wednesday it was stewed fruit and hursday it was rice pudding; Friday it was spotted dog; and Sa y it was bread and jam.

Ron Sharley: What about Sunday?

PB: Sunday we used to have something like plum tart and custard, or apple tart.

Ron Sharley: Well, the boys usually have either dead man's leg or mangled baby once a week.

$\left.\begin{array}{l} JB \\ PB \end{array}\right\}$: What's mangled baby?

Ron Sharley: Jam roly-poly pudding!

PB: Oh.

Ron Sharley: And then they have hair-oil and toenails.

JB: What's that?

Ron Sharley: It's treacle pudding with cornflakes.

JB: *Toenails!* Isn't it marvellous, that sort of graphic description that only schoolboys know?

Ron Sharley: And then there's baby's bottom.

JB: What's that?

Ron Sharley: Pink blancmange.

PB: How disgusting!

JB: Tell me some more names.[91]

There the recording of the Wantage evening ends; but immediately after it, on the same tape, Diana recorded the *Woman's Hour* interview of Penelope by Teresa MacGonagall on 27 September. One reference to John was made.

PB: The roads [in Andalusia], thank God, are nice and bad, which keeps the tourists away. The whole country was a complete revelation to me; it was a sort of idyll, which I don't suppose I shall ever repeat again.

Teresa MacGonagall: Off the beaten track like that, didn't you ever come across bandits?

PB: No. The last bandits are said to have been driven out into France in 1955. They were mostly, as is well known, remnants of the Civil War of the Thirties. My husband was very nervous and he wrote out to me and said would I insure my life with a bank, because he didn't think he'd be able to pay the ransom if I was captured by bandits, but in point of fact I didn't meet any real ones.[92]

Inconsequential as it is, the 1963 tape gives a fly-on-the-wall view of the Betjemans' strained relationship at that time. There is still affectionate fun between them: the mock radio interview, the shared enjoyment of the schoolboys' names for puddings. John can feel concern about Penelope's tiredness. But she flares up at his suggestion that she is 'over-excited': on the contrary, she is fed up with having to take responsibility for The Mead and their chattels. Her snappish interruption to insist that John will be spending Christmas in Cornwall illustrates her displeasure over his separate life with Elizabeth Cavendish. (John is dissimulating when he suggests that he may stay with Joc Lynam and Peggy Lynam Thomas in Trebetherick, or that he will 'be with Mr Piper' – when in fact he will be at Treen, his own house in Trebetherick, with Elizabeth.) The tape also tells us what John wished to be known about his way of writing poems, and reveals that a visit to the lurid figure of Stephen Ward was the genesis of one of his most tender poems. It may have been Elizabeth Cavendish who introduced him to Ward, whose patients included members of the royal family.

In 1964, Osbert Lancaster's wife Karen died of cancer. She had been sick for some time – too ill to attend Candida's wedding in May 1963. John had always called her 'Kareen', because he knew it irritated her; but now he wrote Lancaster a heartfelt letter of commiseration. He also dedicated to Karen's memory his poem 'Autumn 1964'. Before the funeral baked meats were cold, Ann Fleming's rumour mill was grinding away. On 15 November 1964 she wrote to Evelyn Waugh: 'The widower Lancaster is deeply involved with a tall beautiful lady-journalist called Anne Scott-James; post-obsequies he wished to take her to Cornwall to join J Betjeman and E Cavendish, but E Cavendish did not feel up to it . . .'[93] (Lancaster married Anne Scott-James in 1967.)

Though John's relationship with Elizabeth was now generally accepted in and some way beyond his circle it was still causing awkwardnesses. Ron Sharley remembered that 'Penelope used to have to say to his London secretary, "Can I make an appointment to see John?" '[94] For a while, Ron had a job in a golf club in Cornwall. 'I used to visit him in Trebetherick,' she said. 'He would say to Elizabeth, "You go and do the shopping, then Ron and I will go for a walk." We used to walk for miles along the beach. Everyone down there called Lady Elizabeth "Mrs Betjeman", but I'm afraid I blurted out: "*That's* not Mrs Betjeman." '[95] Some people who had been friends with John and Penelope for years still kept their distance from Elizabeth.

It was always slightly embarrassing [Mollie Baring said] because I didn't ever ask Lady Elizabeth to stay at Ardington. I was Penelope's friend.

He would have stayed with us more often if I had said, 'Will you and Elizabeth come?' Also, there was a celebrated party held by the d'Avigdor-Goldsmids,[96] at Somerhill. My daughter Anne was Chloë d'Avigdor-Goldsmid's best friend, and Chloë asked Anne to the party. But she also asked John and Elizabeth. Anne rang me and said, 'But I can't go, Mum, can I?' And I said, 'No, I don't think you can.' She said: 'They don't understand. Loving Penelope as I do, I just don't feel I can go.'[97]

Candida, on the other hand, accepted Elizabeth; naturally, she did not want to be alienated from her father. 'I certainly never thought twice about the situation,' she writes. 'Like JB, Elizabeth was a listener and easy to get on with.'[98] In 1964 John and Elizabeth had supper with the Lycett Greens at their new house in Chepstow Villas, Notting Hill Gate, London – 'and from then onwards [Elizabeth] was part of the Lycett Green family'.[99]

In that year, John Osborne exposed to public view John's guilt over his double life, in his play *Inadmissible Evidence*. Improbably, he and John had become friends and, possibly as early as 1958, John had stayed with him at his mill house in Sussex.[100] It is hard to think of anyone less likely to get on with John than the bileful playwright, angriest of the Angry Young Men. The pioneer of 'kitchen sink' drama might have been expected to lump John with Noël Coward as a reactionary fribble, and the title of one of Osborne's later books, *Damn You, England*, could stand as the exact antithesis of John's outlook. But Osborne's sharp, often scatological humour amused John. Still more winningly, it was clear that Osborne was a genuine fan of his. In May 1963 the dramatist wrote in his diary: 'Max Miller, the great priapic God of Flashness, dies. "There'll never be another." As old John Betjeman says, an English genius as pure gold as Dickens or Shakespeare – or Betjeman, come to that.'[101] And again, on receiving a 'spiffing note' from John on his birthday in December 1965: 'What did Trollope say – muddle-headed Johnny? It's deep honesty that distinguishes a gentleman. *He's* got it. He knows how to *revel* in life and have no expectations – and fear death at all times.'[102] A wit and a fan of John's Osborne might be; but, as his wives and most of his friends found out sooner or later, he could suddenly turn on them and spit venom. He might have echoed one of the speeches in *Inadmissible Evidence*: 'I myself am more packed with spite and twitching with revenge than anyone I know of.'[103]

John attended the first performance of the play at the Royal Court Theatre in Chelsea on 9 September 1964. He wrote next day to congratulate Osborne on 'a tremendous play', adding: 'It is the most heart-rending and tender study of every man who is not atrophied.

We want to avoid giving pain and we want to be left in peace. Love makes us restless and we resist it. I felt increasingly that the play was about *me* . . . Oh, my dear boy, I can't exactly thank you for such an agonizing self-analysis. I can only reverence the power and generosity in you which makes you write such a shattering and releasing piece.'[104] John was almost certainly dismayed by the play, but realized there was no point in protesting about a *fait accompli*. Osborne was in any case a dangerous man to offend.

Though the play's central figure, Bill Maitland, is a solicitor, John identified with him so closely that he signed his letter to Osborne 'Bill Maitland-Betjeman'; Osborne himself later referred to John by that name in his diary. And indeed, the resemblance between the poet and the stage character was so obvious that friends of John, such as Tristram Powell, the film director son of Anthony and Lady Violet Powell, recognized him in Maitland.[105] One of the clearest signs that Osborne had John in mind is his giving Maitland the line, 'I have always been afraid of being found out.'[106] This was a recurrent theme in John's breast-beating – almost a signature tune.[107] Then there are Maitland's Betjeman-like views on modern architecture. He says of a developer: 'I'm always seeing his name on building sites. Spends his time pulling down Regency squares – you know – and putting up slabs of concrete technological nougat. Like old, pumped-up air-raid shelters. Or municipal lavatories.'[108] On top of these indications, Maitland, who is married with two children, has a mistress called Liz and is tormented by the pain he causes by his love for the two women. It is unlikely that Osborne consciously had Elizabeth Cavendish in mind when he named Maitland's girlfriend: that would have been too malicious even for him. What may well have put the name in his mind was the previous year's runaway bestseller *The Spy Who Came In from the Cold* by John Le Carré, whose hero (or anti-hero) also has a girlfriend called Liz. This passage of dialogue between Maitland and his clerk must have seemed painfully near the knuckle to John:

HUDSON: I don't know.
BILL: What? How she puts up with me?
(HUDSON *nods*.)
BILL: Which? Anna or Liz?
HUDSON: Either of them.
BILL: But especially Anna.
HUDSON: There must be some compensations. You've got two nice kids.
BILL: They're all right. I don't think they think we're as nice as we assume
    they are.[109]

Of John's two children, Candida was now 'off his hands', but Paul continued to give some concern. In 1963 Penelope had come to see John Schaufelberger, 'dressed as usual in a pair of old jodhpurs'. She burst out: 'The Powlie has embraced the Mormon faith. At his age, of course, anything like that is permissible. I, in my youth, embraced Zen Buddhism. But at least that has some authenticity – but he has wedded himself to *a bloody fairy story*!'[110] Paul had come back for the wedding from America, where he had enrolled at the Berklee School of Music.[111] Dick Squires, the Betjemans' next-door neighbour in Wantage, saw him on that visit. 'We had tea in our garden,' Squires recalled. 'Paul said, "This is a very nice cake, delicious," and I said, "Oh yes, it's coffee cake" – and he immediately, without thinking, spat it out on the lawn, because coffee's a stimulant forbidden to Mormons.'[112] Osbert Lancaster commented, 'If the Field-Marshal knows that his grandson is playing the jazz saxophone and has become a Mormon, he must be rolling about in his grave.'[113] Paul's conversion was less of a joke to John. He wrote to his friend Father Harry Williams, at that time Dean of Chapel at Trinity College, Cambridge, for his advice and was much consoled by it. Williams wrote:

> You must inevitably be very worried about your son Paul. But what occurs to me is that if he wanted, as most sons do, to be different from his parents and didn't want to be an agnostic, you and his mother haven't left him a great deal to choose from. He could have become a Methodist or Baptist, but that would have been frightfully dull. Mormonism is different, calculated to surprise and shock, and a positive religion. I don't at all believe that God pours His reality and love only into certain specified doctrinal bottles. From a certain point of view, every form of religion is slightly dotty. If humour is the perception of incongruities, one of the funniest things is the contrast between God Himself and the largely absurd religions we all profess. The fact that to us Mormonism seems funnier than Anglicanism does not mean a great deal. God gets through to us not so much in spite of but by means of our ridiculous notions . . . But of course I realise how easy it seems when one is not oneself personally concerned about someone.[114]

Sending this on to Penelope, in the hope it would help her as it had helped him, John said that when he wrote to Paul he would merely say, 'Love to the Mormons', or 'God moves in a mysterious way His wonders to perform', and make no fuss about it. But he asked her not to tell people about it too much. 'It will probably pass off & if it doesn't it's better than Marxism I suppose or nothing at all & may be full of charity & make the P[owlie] less selfish.'[115] One perennial

difficulty for Paul was that, with his distinctive surname, wherever he
went in Britain people said to him, 'Oh, are you related to that marvellous . . .?' In America, hardly anyone had heard of John Betjeman.
There, Paul could be – as his Eton housemaster had discerned he
wanted to be – himself. Eventually he became an American citizen and
taught music in New York.

With Paul in America, with Candida married and John, for the most
part, in London, The Mead was even less a centre of family life. In
November 1963 the Betjemans let it, for eight months, to an interior
decorator called Tom Parr.[116] From the early 1960s onwards, Penelope
did a lot of travelling. King Alfred's Kitchen was at last sold in 1961,
as 'more trouble than it was worth'.[117] That year, Penelope made the
trip to Andalusia, keeping a diary of the journey which John declared
'a work of genius'.[118] In 1965 she decided to write a book about the
Kulu Valley in northern India. Published in 1972, it showed how
impressive an Indologist she could have been if, instead of marrying
John, she had dedicated herself to scholarship. In the later Sixties and
the Seventies she spent several months at a time in India, sending John
regular letters about her adventures. Her attitude to Elizabeth
Cavendish softened a little. When she heard that Mollie Baring was
going to Cornwall and would be seeing John and Elizabeth, she asked
her to tell Elizabeth how much she appreciated the devoted way she
was caring for John. 'How else could I go gallivanting off to India?'
she asked. Mollie recalled: 'I told Elizabeth, who said, "How very kind
of you." She invited me to visit her when I was in London. But I never
went.'[119]

In June 1964 John wrote to Penelope, who was in India:

> I was ever so pleased to have your two letters, one a continuation about
> the horrible thunderstorm you experienced in Simla and the other about
> your trek on horseback among the jeep-infested Himalayas. I had not
> realised that [the] whole world, even India, was in the devil's grip of the
> internal combustion engine.[120]

In the same letter he reported that The Mead had been well cared for
by Tom Parr and, according to Candida, had become 'a fashionable
rendezvous'.[121] He was relieved to find that he did not feel chained to
his library there; and he suggested they look for a smaller place. This
might have been a moment for the Betjemans, while remaining on
affectionate terms, to go their separate ways, to sell The Mead and
make good use of the proceeds. Neither John nor Penelope seems to
have contemplated this course. Why not? John's letter implied that his
whole concern was for Penelope: 'Like you, I have shed much of the

need for possessions but know you will want your pony and field for it to graze – and a smaller house.'[122] In other words, he was not going to shrug off his share of financial responsibility for her. This probably was in the forefront of his thinking; but a sub-motive may have been that it suited him, as the very public figure he now was, to continue to seem conventionally and happily married. For her part, Penelope still loved him, had found no other partner and hoped he might one day come back to her; also, her religion was particularly hostile to any backsliding from the marriage vows. And John, in his way, still cared greatly for her, telling friends, 'I love nobody in the world more; but we just can't live together.'[123]

A half-hearted quest for a smaller house began; but the Mead property itself had been reduced over the years. In the late 1950s Penelope had sold three fields, Colonel Robinson's old dairy and O'Brien's cottage, The Gogs, to Robert Reedman, an architect who lived nearby with his friend Maitland Bradshaw.[124] Reedman, in turn, gave one of the fields to Georgie Sale – the boy whom Candida had threatened to hang[125] – for his twenty-first birthday.[126] Penelope also sold one and a half acres to a Mr Avenall. 'That must have caused conflict,' Dick Squires said, 'because Avenall was a self-made man who had set up a squalid little factory in the middle of Wantage making spare parts for car factories. A lot of the products needed bits punched out of sheet metal – a fiendish banging noise. There were great complaints to stop this, led, of course, by John. So Penelope, in her enjoyment of a good bargain, was selling the land to the person John had been campaigning against.'[127] More land, Squires recalls, was sold to 'a stock-market whizz-kid with a Mercedes and an Audi' who amused the neighbourhood by his flamboyant name-dropping – 'So sorry we don't have the best silver coffee-pot tonight: I've never forgiven my grandmother for giving it to the Czar.'[128]

In 1965 the Betjemans divided the house in half, letting the front part to a middle-aged lady with a terrier,[129] and occasionally spending time together in the other part. Candida noted sadly that The Mead was now 'altogether different from how we had found it when we first came in 1951':[130] new houses had been built on the fields which had been sold on either side of the drive, and the houses were soon surrounded by 'municipal shrubs'.[131]

'VIC. SOC.' AND 'THE DOK'

Oh fearful was our task, for evil was the mask
  of Benevolent Authority on Vandalism's face
when the Betjeman Brigade vowed to start a new Crusade
  to preserve Victorian relics from Oblivion and Disgrace.

Peter Clarke, 'November 5th, 1957'

The idea of a pressure group to protect Victorian art and architecture
was hatched between John and the Countess of Rosse in 1957.
Michael Rosse, the sixth Earl, was exactly a month younger than
John and had known him at Oxford. In 1935 he had married Anne
Armstrong-Jones, sister of the designer Oliver Messel and mother of
the future Lord Snowdon. She had been one of the Bright Young
People. To James Lees-Milne, who attended the first 'get-together'
of the Victorian Society, she was 'so affected, but a real worker'.
In the war he had seen her in a hospital ward, scrubbing the floor in
'one of those ghastly turbans that charwomen wore at that time –
she really *led* these women with cigarettes drooping out of their
mouths'.[1]

The first informal meeting was held in the Rosses' London house,
18 Stafford Terrace, an appropriate venue since the Victorian interior
had remained – as it still remains – almost undisturbed from the days
when it had been owned by the Countess's grandfather, the *Punch* cartoonist Linley Sambourne.[2] Two of the people Anne Rosse wanted to
attend this first meeting on 5 November 1957 were brave enough to
decline. Nikolaus Pevsner, showing the sense of humour that John
always denied existed, wrote to her on 30 October, 'I deeply regret
that a long-standing engagement with Guy Fawkes makes it impossible for me to be present at the meeting next Tuesday.'[3] However, he
wanted her to know how much in sympathy he was with the forming

of such a group. He suggested that the society should set itself four main tasks:

1) To draw up a list of Victorian buildings which must be preserved.
2) To try to get this accepted by the Ministry of Housing and Local Government and incorporated in their lists of Buildings of Architectural or Historic Interest, and to be scheduled there as Grade II and not Grade III.
3) To make the list known to county, city and rural district authorities.
4) To watch over the fate of buildings listed by the Victorian group, just as the Georgian Group watched over Georgian buildings.[4]

Reasons for preserving buildings, he suggested, might be:

1) Pure architectural value.
2) Historical value.
3) A special and exceptional importance in the history of Western architecture.[5]

He felt most strongly about the third reason. 'Britain in the Victorian age was leading in many fields of Western architecture. Things happened here specially early and specially characteristically. The quality of being specially characteristic does not make a building always specially beautiful, but in spite of that, such buildings ought in my opinion to be included in the list.'[6]

Pevsner confined his comments to architecture; but Sir Kenneth Clark, who also had to decline Lady Rosse's invitation, mentioned the decorative arts as well, and gave shrewd advice on the politics of such a group.

As to buildings, your list will have to be severely critical, otherwise you will find yourself called in to try to save two-thirds of the town halls in the Midlands, practically all the Insurance Offices in the country, and many other buildings, which, although they have something to commend them, must take their chance in the general course of architectural development.

With regard to decorative objects, the problem is almost of the opposite kind because so many of these have been destroyed already . . .[7]

Both these responses correspond with their authors' comic stereotypes – Pevsner's for categorization and 'admin', Clark's for love of 'agreeable' objects.

Most of the other art-world grandees Lady Rosse had invited were present among the aspidistras and antimacassars in the first-floor drawing-room of Stafford Terrace on Guy Fawkes' Night, 1957. Besides Lord and Lady Rosse, John, and James Lees-Milne, they included Lord Esher, Oliver Messel, John Pope-Hennessy of the Victoria and Albert Museum and his brother James, the architect H. S. Goodhart-Rendel, John Piper, Osbert Lancaster, Sir Hugh and Lady Casson, Belinda Norman-Butler (a great-granddaughter of Thackeray), J. M. Richards of *The Architectural Review*, the art critic Nigel Gosling, Christopher Hussey of *Country Life* and the novelist Rosamond Lehmann.[8] Among the younger people present were Peter Clarke and his friend from Cambridge days, Thomas Greeves, who had both met John in 1938 when he gave a lecture at Cambridge on 'Antiquarian Prejudice'.[9] By 1957, Clarke was Assistant Secretary of *The Times*. On that newspaper, he was renowned as a mimic; I remember how, ten years later, the saloon bar of the Baynard Castle pub would be thronged with his colleagues at lunch-time, helpless with laughter at his lisping rendition of a William Rees-Mogg editorial conference. In the generation just junior to John's, he was perhaps the person most like him. He was a keen explorer of Victorian architecture and a very accomplished versifier. Tom Greeves had gone to Cambridge in 1936 to read architecture and music; the only person to have done so before was Goodhart-Rendel. He became a designer of Piranesi-like architectural fantasias, on which John was to write an admiring article in *Country Life*.

Peter Clarke had become friends with Pevsner by parodying him. In 1954 Clarke had written a piece for *Punch* called 'Non-Stopography', taking off various kinds of guidebook. One of the skits was obviously aimed at Pevsner, the '*Bricks of Britain* Series (a Bauhaus-to-house search) for Art-historians who like to do the thing thoroughly'. It contained such entries as:

> *Smogge Hall*. C.18. Offices of Northmet and British Restaurant. 1 – 2 – 3 hop 1 – 2 – 3 window arrangement. Characteristic double-hollow-chamfered waterspout. Not specially nice.
>
> *Slaughterhouse* (Waterhouse?). Beefy, hamfisted. . .

Not for the last time, Clarke contrasted John's demonstrative manner with Pevsner's dogged, meticulous notes, in 'the poetic-nostalgic approach', an unmistakable take-off of a Betjeman guide.

> From '*The Last Rows of Somers Town*' (with 100 drawings in pen and wash of Nonconformist Chapels in stormy weather).
>
> 'Ah, Smoggy Fields! Victim of Progress and the Welfare State! Yet your ragged elms and stuccoed railway-station (Sancton Wood, 1848, but ruined by British Railways of course) recall to me a bright morning on

which I set out with my great-uncle to see the opening of the White City. What art-nouveau panes may not still lurk in your Ladies' Waiting Room? What sets of tennis may not be played out in the dusk on your Municipal Courts? What etc.? Ah! etc., etc.'[10]

Pevsner read the article and was so amused by its on-target barbs that he wrote to congratulate Clarke. The correspondence led to an enduring friendship. Clarke was invited to the inaugural meeting to consider the formation of the Victorian Society. He suggested to Lady Rosse that Tom Greeves, who by now lived in Victorian Bedford Park, should also be asked along.

After mulled claret had been doled out with a silver ladle, Lady Rosse welcomed her guests and hoped they would find the surroundings in tune with the subject which was to be discussed. She and Mr Betjeman, she said, had called this meeting of people whose opinion was authoritative to consider whether the time had not come to form some organization to preserve not only the architecture but some of the furnishings and other things made and designed from the 1830s onwards. She added that Victorian furnishings were often either deplored or admired merely as a pose, and she hoped the attitude of any new group which might be formed would be one of sincerity.[11]

John then spoke. He said he thought the formation of a group was the only way of tackling the problem of preservation, and read out the letters that Pevsner and Clark had sent Lady Rosse. He suggested that the meeting should consider whether the new group ought to extend its activities to cover the Edwardian period.[12] Two other ticklish questions to be discussed were: should the Victorian group be founded as an independent organization, or as a branch of the already existing Society for the Protection of Ancient Buildings (SPAB)? and what should be its relationship to the William Morris Society? Lord Esher said that the SPAB was 'supposed to stop at 1715'.[13] R. H. C. Briggs from the William Morris Society feared 'some overlapping . . . and the splintering of effort' though he also pointed out that Morris had rebelled against much that he found in Victorian England.[14] Casson was sure the time to form a group was before the period became fashionable.[15] Osbert Lancaster agreed: 'Victorian' was not yet a desirable adjective in estate agents' vocabulary.[16] To discuss and resolve the difficulties, an 'organization committee', with John as one of its members, was set up.

Peter Clarke wrote a poem about the inaugural meeting, based on Macaulay's 'Battle of Naseby'.

November 5th, 1957
Macaulay helps to found the Victorian Group

Oh wherefore come ye late from deserted W.8
    when rockets are bursting and bonfires burn red?
And why these quiet 'Hear-Hears!', poets, architects and peers?
    and what was your plot, all ye authors well-bred?

Oh fearful was our task, for evil was the mask
    of Benevolent Authority on Vandalism's face
when the Betjeman Brigade vowed to start a new Crusade
    to preserve Victorian relics from Oblivion and Disgrace.

On that bleak November night how mellow was the light
    of candles as they flickered on the Sambournes in the hall!
And the Earl of Rosse was there to receive us on the stair,
    and Hussey and Lord Esher and the 'Father of Us All'.*

Supported (though by proxy) by Sir Kenneth and 'The Dok'† – See
    our Lion-Heart‡ arouses us: 'The Foe is at the Gate!'
Will you let the Pass be sold? Fight as Morris fought of old
    to save our priceless heritage before it's all too late!
. . .

Then hark! Angry notes swell those pure aesthetic throats!
    Now Georgians, Victorians and Morris-men unite!
'For mahogany chiffoniers! For jet! For gasoliers!
    For Burges and for Butterfield! For Teulon and for Tite!'

While outside a steady drizzle made the children's rockets fizzle
    (and a dog a-whirl in Outer Space left adult minds aghast)¶
What the Present could involve never dampened our Resolve:
    Though we might not have a Future, we would fight to save the Past![17]

Until the Victorian Society could attract enough members and subscriptions to afford its own premises, it was allowed to hold its

---

* This was how Kenneth Clark described Goodhart-Rendel, in relation to the appreciation of Victorian architecture in the preface to the London 1950 edition of his *The Gothic Revival*.
† Nikolaus Pevsner.
‡ John Betjeman.
¶ The date of the meeting coincided not only with Guy Fawkes' Day but also with the launching of the Russian rocket *Sputnik II* with a dog on board. This launch showed how far in advance of America the Russians were in rocket technology; hence Clarke's gloom about 'The Future' two lines later.

meetings in the SPAB's rooms at No. 55 Great Ormond Street, London. On 16 December 1957 the organization committee met representatives of the SPAB there. J. M. Richards chaired the meeting. John was among the Victorians' delegates, with the Rosses and Lord Esher. It was decided that the Victorian Society should be a sub-committee of the SPAB but with its own chairman and secretary. That was just how the Georgian Group had started in 1936.

Ian Grant, an architect, who was thirty-two in 1957, was the first young blood to come into the society, though by 1958 Mark Girouard, the architectural historian, and his friend Thomas Pakenham, the journalist and historian - both eight years younger than Grant – had joined the committee.[18] Grant had studied at the Architectural Association in the late 1940s, qualifying in 1949.

> When I qualified [he recalled in 1994] I went to work for people who built glass-walled office blocks. And then, as used to happen in those days, people approached me to build bathroom extensions, things like that; and I came to the conclusion that I wasn't terribly interested in 'modern' architecture and that really I was interested in traditional architecture, especially of the nineteenth century.[19]

Grant attended the first full meeting of the society; again at Stafford Terrace, on 25 February 1958 – the meeting at which the body formally constituted itself as the Victorian Society. (It was usually referred to as 'the Vic. Soc.'.) John sent apologies for his absence. Lord Rosse took the chair on this occasion. 'He was marvellous,' Grant said. 'I liked Michael Rosse immensely, and I have never seen anybody who was able to manage an annual general meeting with the skill that he did – I mean at the Georgian Group. He gave Anne Rosse a great deal of encouragement about the Victorians but he felt that one chairmanship was quite enough. The first chairman of the Victorian Society was old Lord Esher. Anne Rosse was a typical ex-deb, immensely snobbish and extremely conscious of her position in life. I remember her saying to me, long after, "Oh, Ian, you used to come to Stafford Terrace in the early days. I think you were a bit frightened of us, weren't you?" And I thought to myself, "No, I wasn't. I was just absolutely fascinated to see how the other half lived."'[20]

At the meeting Lady Rosse attempted a definition of the society's objects: 'Both she and Mr Betjeman wanted to ensure the continuity and saving of things, not only architecture, but furniture, glass, carpets, jewellery, silver etc. to make the public aware of the beautiful design and craftsmanship of this period; to encourage museums to display such things, particularly in the provinces, in order to create

a general consciousness of Victorian art and to discover and save
beautiful rooms which were likely to be destroyed.'[21] Christopher
Hussey successfully proposed a formula in which these aims could be
summarized: 'the study and appreciation of Victorian architecture
and decorative arts with a view to preserving outstanding examples'.[22]

Lord Esher, as chairman, 'was the archetype of an elderly
Edwardian nobleman', Grant recalled. 'He used to sit slumped in his
chair at the Victorian Society committee meetings. "What do you
mean by that?" "Can you explain that statement?" When somebody
suggested that the society ought to have a constitution, he said: "For
God's sake, we don't need a constitution! This country hasn't got one
and we don't need one for the Victorian Society." '[23] Another regular
at committee meetings was Canon Mortlock, the Vicar of St Vedast,
Foster Lane. 'I think Anne Rosse had roped him in,' Grant said. 'He
used to appear in black, with a clerical collar. And he'd no sooner sat
down than he fell asleep. He never took any part in the proceedings at
all. Just slept right through.'[24]

William Gaunt had agreed to be the society's first secretary, but
resigned after a few weeks 'because of pressure of work'. A Mrs Jenks
took over, but was felt to be less than satisfactory.

In October 1958 [Grant recalled] John Betjeman asked me to lunch at the
Athenaeum. There was to have been a third person who didn't turn up; I
never knew who it was. But what John was actually doing was softening
me up to try to persuade me to become secretary. I remember the lunch.
He had ordered, specially, an extremely good bottle of claret. And there
was a very elderly wine waiter with a hooked nose fast approaching his
hooked chin – a real Mr Punch figure. He tottered up with this bottle
cradled. He offered John Betjeman a glass and John said, 'Ooooh! Ooooh!
It smells like *old books*!' And the old waiter said, 'Oh, Mr Betjeman! I 'ope
it doesn't *taste* like them!'[25]

At the end of lunch, Grant 'virtually said, "Yes, all right, I'll be secretary" '. Then 'John donned a straw boater and unchained his bicycle
from the railings and wobbled off up Waterloo Place.'[26]

In the society's early years, John attended meetings fairly regularly.

He used to appear [Grant remembered], usually after the meeting had
begun, and creep around the back and sit somewhere rather inconspicu-
ous – perhaps next to the snoring Canon Mortlock. And the chairman
would say, 'Oh John, how nice to see you!' What I remember of his contributions to meetings was his absolutely phenomenal memory. In those
days there wasn't a case-works sub-committee, we discussed all that in the

33

ittee. And the most obscure church in Devonshire would be
and he'd say, 'Oh yes! Now, don't tell me . . . Bodley, isn't it?
wonderful stencilled decoration in the apse.'[27]

As well as his memory, one could rely on his sense of the absurd. After inspecting a house one day, John and Grant travelled back by train.

There were these grab-handles wobbling about. I said, 'Don't you think those look rather suggestive?' He said, 'Oh yes!' And he always carried a fish-bass with bits of correspondence in it. 'Oh, yes,' he said. 'John Osborne sent me a postcard. I think I've got it here.' He bent down and pulled it out. It was one of those Donald McGill sort of cards showing the interior of a library and a very nubile young lady is sitting with downcast eyes at one table; opposite her is a young man, blushing furiously, and there's a big notice in the background saying SILENCE. And a uniformed attendant is tapping the young man on the shoulder and saying, 'Did you titter?' and he says 'No! I never touched her!'[28]

At a meeting on 16 December 1958, the committee decided, with an irony that would only later become apparent, that 'the Boardroom at Euston station would be a suitable place to hold the Annual General Meeting', but British Railways cannily refused permission. At the same meeting, a proposal for a Victorian fashion show was discussed. It was eventually held in 1960. Ian Grant described what happened:

It was the first really important activity the Victorian Society ever had. A woman called Charmian Lacey undertook to arrange [it]. She managed to borrow an enormous collection of genuine Victorian clothes and found a collection of girls to model them. At first we were terrified there weren't going to be enough people, so the other amenity societies were circularized, the Georgian Group and the SPAB. We did actually turn people away in the end.

It was a marvellous occasion . . . brilliantly organized by this girl. I was upstairs, faffing around trying to make myself useful. And one of the uniformed porters came up to me and said, 'Mr Grant, there's a man downstairs making an awful fuss. He's trying to get in without a ticket. He's called Mr Bet-something-or-other.'

I said, 'Oh my God, he's our deputy chairman; and I'm sure he hasn't got a ticket.'

I went downstairs and John, wearing his grotesque old hat, all out of drawing, and carrying his fish-bass, had managed to make his way from the entrance right to the bottom of the staircase, but they wouldn't let him in. He was absolutely furious. He said, 'Oh, I see that you've got to be properly dressed to get into places like this.' And fortunately I just burst into fits of laughter, in which, in a moment, he joined. It must just have been instinct. But it was a difficult moment. I mean, he was meant to be on the receiving line – receiving guests with Anne Rosse.[29]

At the meeting of 19 January 1960 (by now the society had 289 members) John was congratulated on his CBE, announced in the New Year's honours list. At this meeting, too, the threat to Euston station appeared for the first time, a faint storm-cloud on the horizon.*[31]

Ian Grant's architectural practice was growing. In February he had announced that he would like to resign, and the committee agreed to employ a new secretary at a salary of £500 a year. The post went to John's old friend Peter Fleetwood-Hesketh, who had illustrated *Ghastly Good Taste* with many a Victorian fane.[31] In 1976, in his ornate flat below the SPAB'S committee-room in Great Ormond Street, Fleetwood-Hesketh recalled how he had been 'pressganged' into taking the job.

I was coerced by John Betjeman and Mark Girouard into being secretary of the Victorian Society. I'd never been secretary of anything before. Various excellent people, William Gaunt, Ian Grant and others, had done secretarial work without any premises at all in their spare time because they all had jobs. And the only place they had to work was on the corner of a table in the SPAB, mostly after hours.

And then these devoted people couldn't carry on any longer, because they all had their own work, and John and Mark Girouard swung round on to me and said, 'Look here, we can't get anybody to be secretary of the Victorian Society' – which I was a founder-member of anyway – 'Will you take the job?' And they said, 'If you don't, we can't get anybody else and the Victorian Society will expire.' So to that appeal I thought I must respond sympathetically; but it was slightly awkward because at that moment I was High Sheriff of Lancashire, which meant being rather occupied, you know, with local affairs. So I said, 'Of course! The moment I can get free from this, I will try.'

So in due course I came to a committee meeting of the Victorian Society when they were thrashing out their troubles. It was in the SPAB committee room, upstairs here. And they said, if only we could have that vacant flat downstairs for an office; but we aren't allowed to, because the planning authority say it has got to be residential. So I said, 'Well, look here'. . . I had only just recently given up Freda's [his wife's] flat we had in

* See Chapter 6, 'The Euston Arch'.

London . . . I said, 'Why don't we take it as a flat and live in it, so it will be "residential", but the Victorian Society's work will be done there.' John thought that was an excellent plan, so it was all arranged – this became my flat in theory, but the offices of the Victorian Society in fact. So in this very room were fought the battles of Euston and the Coal Exchange.[32]

Fleetwood-Hesketh was a talented artist and a willing and hard worker. Most people found him very likeable; but some thought him a snob and a bore – among them the diarist Frances Partridge, who was 'sickened' by the man her best friend, Julia Strachey, had once hoped to marry.[33] Hesketh's stage-aristocrat drawl was so mannered that even John – usually indulgent to what others considered affectation – tried to imitate it phonetically (without success) in a letter to Rupert and Candida.[34] The Hesketh drawl was added to Peter Clarke's repertoire of impressions. Clarke and Greeves together made a tape-recorded skit of a typical Victorian Society meeting, with Lord Esher barking 'What the devil?', Hesketh drawling 'Now, look *he-ah*!', Lady Rosse saying, 'I must ask my solicitor about that,' and the high, excited voice of Thomas Pakenham breaking in at times.[35]

The Annual General Meeting of May 1960 was held in the Criterion Restaurant, Piccadilly – the 'Cri' of John's early poem 'The 'Varsity Students' Rag'. In 1961 John himself unexpectedly became responsible for an important Victorian property – Tower House, Melbury Road, London. The remainder of the lease was left to him in the will of E. R. B. Graham. The house was a whimsical masterpiece by William Burges, the architect of Cardiff Castle and Castell Coch. Above the chimneypiece in the drawing-room were carved personified adjectives and other 'parts of speech', with a cockney 'dropped aitch' falling down the wall.[36] In 1963 John reported that the house had been bought by Richard Harris, the film actor, who was 'very keen to keep it as it was'. John thought that 'the Society need not worry about it further'.[37] This may have seemed over-sanguine considering that Harris was usually characterized in the popular press as a 'hellraiser'. And in fact Tower House continued to cause concern. In 1965 Lady Turnbull, wife of Sir Richard Turnbull, a former Governor-General of Tanganyika, bought a lease of about fifty years and initiated a restoration of the structure and décor. The Royal Institute of British Architects lent drawings. The Historic Buildings Council made a grant of £4,000 towards the structure. The Greater London Council granted nearly £3,000 towards the decorations. On 30 November 1967 *The Times* devoted a whole page to the results of nearly two years' work. On 10 December the same paper, to the outrage of John and others in the Victorian Society, announced Lady Turnbull's decision to sell the remainder of her lease. But at least the house had been preserved, like its distinguished neighbour Leighton House, where the artist Sir Frederic Leighton had created an Arabic court with fountains, Moorish tiles and other lustre tiles by William De Morgan. Sir Lawrence Alma-Tadema's old house in St John's Wood, once the home of John's parents-in-law, fared less well; in *Apollo* magazine in December 1962 the art critic Mario Amaya deplored the way it had been allowed to fall into decay.[38]

The National Provincial Bank building at Bishopsgate was another structure in which John took the keenest interest. It was 'a marvellous Victorian, slightly curved building in Bishopsgate, ostensibly a single-storey building of the 1860s by Parnell.'[39] Its case was raised at the meeting of 6 March 1962. Fleetwood-Hesketh reported that he had consulted a friend who was a director of the Bank and who thought 'that rebuilding might eventually be necessary but not for several years'.[40] John was not going to be fobbed off with that kind of evasiveness. 'Mr Betjeman suggested that the Secretary try to have a preservation order made on this building, which the City Architect is said to be fond of. It was decided to press for up-grading and that a letter be sent to the chairman of the bank and the City Architect asking what proposals were envisaged, and saying that this Society would object to demolition; also referring to Professor Pevsner's published opinion in *Buildings of England*.'[41] A public inquiry later found in favour of its preservation. 'And this really set the City developers absolutely on their elbow,' Ian Grant recalled, 'because they suddenly realized that just because it was "Victoriana", it didn't necessarily mean that they were going to be allowed to pull it down. It was a real turning-point.'[42]

Next Balliol College, Oxford, wanted to demolish its Waterhouse block. However, on 5 February 1963, John reported that 'so much money would be required for rebuilding that the dons were beginning to lose heart'. It was agreed a letter of protest should nonetheless be sent to *The Times*. This duly appeared in March and drew an angry reply from the notoriously ill-tempered Master of Balliol, Sir David Lindsay Keir. The society pressed for the Balliol buildings to be 'regraded, not degraded'.[43]

Balliol was worth fighting for; but, mindful of Kenneth Clark's sage advice to Lady Rosse before the society was founded, the society did not press for every Victorian relic to be preserved. At the meeting of 5 June 1962 photographs of the Pimlico Road fountain were passed round. 'The Committee . . . decided that it would be a pity for the fountain to disappear altogether, but it was not of high enough quality for the Society to take strong action.'[44] On the other hand, the committee in general and John in particular were alarmed at the way the fine terracotta houses of Norman Shaw were being picked off by developers in Fitzjohn's Avenue, the broad rise that joins Hampstead and Swiss Cottage. On 2 April 1963 it was reported that several had been demolished already and more were threatened.[45] The fuss over Fitzjohn's Avenue served as a rehearsal for the much bigger and more successful battle to save Bedford Park which began in the same year when the Bedford Park Society was founded with John as its president.*

John's attendance at the Victorian Society's meetings had become gradually more intermittent. Monica Dance, secretary of the Society for the Protection of Ancient Buildings, warned Ian Grant: 'John is a great one for lost causes and new societies, but when they begin to gather momentum he loses interest.'[46] John was far too easily bored to be a good committee man. Canon Eric James gave an example of his fragile attention-span.

I first met John Betjeman when the future of St Peter's Vauxhall was under discussion in the Sixties. We were both appointed to a Commission which the Bishop of Southwark, Mervyn Stockwood, had set up. John Betjeman represented the Victorian Society. I was then Canon Precentor of Southwark Cathedral.

The meetings ... began at 5.0 p.m. and the members of the Commission sat round a large rectangular table which virtually filled the room and allowed little or no space for movement in the room once people were sat at the table.

At the first meeting ... we were just about to begin when John Betjeman arrived, looking very flustered and embarrassed. There was only one vacant seat, next to me, and I tried to look welcoming. He came and sat down and huffed and puffed and unfolded his papers which seemed to be in complete disarray.

The meeting had not been in session for more than half an hour when I noticed he was scribbling furiously. Suddenly, he pushed what he had written in front of me. It said: 'Do you know the Two Chairmen?'

I thought he must be going gaga, and simply wrote below what he had written: 'It is not two chairmen but the chairman and his male secretary,' and pushed the note back to JB.

Immediately he started scribbling furiously again, and then back came the piece of paper on which he had now written capitals:

'WRONG! 1 out of 10. "The Two Chairmen" is a pub near here. If you had the courage to say to *the* Chairman soon that you had a train to catch you would give me the courage to join you, and we could repair to "The Two Chairmen."'

* See Chapter 11, 'The Battle of Bedford Park'.

It was just after opening time when we arrived and just before closing time when we left, having laughed our way through most of the evening.[47]

When in 1963 Lord Esher died and Nikolaus Pevsner succeeded him as chairman, John virtually ceased to attend meetings. He detested Pevsner, who became a hate-figure in his later years to rival those demons of his youth, A. R. Gidney, C. S. Lewis and Farmer Wheeler. Immediately Pevsner was elected chairman, John suggested that a new post of deputy chairman should be created, and proposed for it his old friend John Brandon-Jones, who was elected.[48] It is possible that this was John's way of ensuring that there would be a counterbalance to Pevsner at the top, somebody he himself could 'nobble' if Pevsner tried to push through unpalatable measures.

Nikolaus Pevsner was four years older than John. He had seen the way things were going in Germany and had come to England in 1930 in the German intellectual diaspora. At first he taught Italian to History of Art students at the Courtauld Institute. His *Pioneers of the Modern Movement from William Morris to Walter Gropius* was published in 1936. In 1939 he was interned for two months as an enemy alien, then released. Offered a choice of several jobs, he said yes to a staff post under J. M. Richards at *The Architectural Review*; to editing King Penguin books (when the original editor was killed in an air raid in 1941); and to teaching art history at Birkbeck College, London. He was Slade Professor of Fine Art at Cambridge from 1949 to 1955. His great series the Penguin *Buildings of England* began in 1951, the year in which his *High Victorian Design* was also published.

Ian Grant had little love for Pevsner, but he thought that in the relations between John and Pevsner the animosity came solely from John's side. 'Certainly John disliked Pevsner intensely,' he said, 'but I don't think Pevsner even noticed. He wasn't *human* enough to notice.'[49] The evidence does not support this view. Pevsner's aggression was more subtle and oblique than John's; but, once he realized he was in a fight, he fought.

Dr Timothy Mowl, who has written a book on the rivalry between the two men,[50] thinks that, initially, John's writings may even have influenced Pevsner. He postulates that an article John contributed to *The Architectural Review* in 1930 – the year Pevsner first came to England – may have given the German scholar the idea that William Morris and the British arts-and-crafts men pioneered modern design and were forefathers of Le Corbusier and Gropius.[51] That idea was the basis of his own *Pioneers of the Modern Movement*. John had himself derived the theory from his friend and mentor P. Morton Shand, who expanded it in articles in *The Architectural Review* between 1934 and

1935. In what Mowl considers 'an apparently innocent but actually rather provocative disclaimer' in the foreword to his book of 1936, Pevsner wrote that he had not known of Shand's articles 'until I had almost finished my research. The fact that his conclusions coincide in so many ways with mine is a gratifying confirmation of the views put forward in the book.'[52] Mowl comments: 'Given Pevsner's interests and the *Archie Rev's* prestige it is difficult to believe that he had missed a single issue of the magazine since he first settled in Britain. That Foreword must have acted like a red rag to a bull as far as Morton Shand was concerned . . .'[53] Shand wrote a sour review of the book;[54] and, as John was such a close friend of his,[55] it is likely that this episode predisposed him against Pevsner.

Even if it did not, what happened in the 1940s must have done. In 1941, when the architect and designer C. F. A. Voysey died, John sent an obituary appreciation of his old friend to *The Architectural Review*. It was not used; instead, a tribute by Pevsner appeared.[56] Because of his *Pioneers* book, *he* was now seen as the expert on Voysey and all that school. Mowl thinks that 'There is no need to look any further for the source of Betjeman's subsequent dislike of his rival . . .'[57] But the antipathy had other causes, too.

Richard Ingrams and others have suggested that there was 'nothing personal' in John's low view of Pevsner.[58] It was (they contend) simply a matter of colliding tastes: John, whose response to buildings was largely instinctual and related to the people who lived or had lived in them, deplored the 'Teutonic thoroughness' with which Pevsner categorized architecture, with hardly any mention of human associations, his 'graceless' prose and lack of humour.[59] John did indeed hold those opinions; but the bitterness of his animus against Pevsner suggests a more personal vendetta. Others took the view that John was piqued at Pevsner's 'muscling in' on his territory; at his superior scholarship; and at his acceptance by the art-history establishment to whom John was a self-publicizing 'funny-man', a journalist, poet and 'television personality'. Again, there was some truth in this assessment. As a genuine foreigner, not just an Englishman with a funny foreign name, Pevsner had been able to write with more objectivity than John on 'The Englishness of English Art', a natural Betjeman subject.[60] Pevsner pulled academic rank on John. The only book of his which he ever deigned to notice publicly was *Ghastly Good Taste* (1933). This he described as 'memorable', but only for the eccentric typography of its title-page. He understood that Betjeman had been 'an undergraduate at Oxford' – a dry way of sneering at the poet's degreelessness.[61] In 1966, appealing to John Summerson to help save St Pancras station, John wrote: '. . . I have been so denigrated by Karl Marx

[J. M. Richards] and the Professor-Doktor [Pevsner] as a light-weight wax fruit merchant,[62] I will not carry the necessary guns.'[63]

John can hardly have failed to take as a slighting reference to himself a passage in Pevsner's *Pioneers* book of 1936: 'What attention is paid to Victorian buildings and design is still, with a very few exceptions, of the whimsical variety.'[64] In 1944 Pevsner delivered an editorial rebuke to John. Five years earlier, he had taken exception to a Betjeman article in *The Architectural Review* which had the sub-title 'How to Like Everything'.[65] Pevsner now called this 'a genial over-statement'.[66] Mowl plausibly suggests that another Pevsner article, on Norman Shaw, 'was contrived pointedly to re-evaluate and admire a Victorian architect whom Betjeman had casually dismissed'.[67] (John later came right round to Norman Shaw, particularly in the campaign of 1963 to save Bedford Park, with its houses by Shaw and his disciples.)[68]

In November 1946 John's friend Alan Pryce-Jones was appointed to the staff of the *Times Literary Supplement*.[69] He became assistant editor and the recognized heir to the editorship in July 1947.[70] (After he was made editor in 1948, his absenteeism, as a social gadabout, prompted a Betjeman joke: 'Captain Bog [his nickname for Pryce-Jones] had to ask a policeman the way to Printing House Square.')[71] John was now able to snipe at Pevsner from under the cover of the *Lit. Supp.*'s anonymity. In September 1947 he contributed a leader, 'The New Pedantry'. He suggested that 'The introduction of professionalism into such subjects as literature, architecture and art too often turns enjoyment to ashes' and regretted that 'the vanity of prefixing "Doctor" or "Professor" to a surname and some letters after it' had crept from Germany and America into Britain.[72]

In that post-war period, there was competition between the county guides John edited for Shell and for John Murray, and Pevsner's Penguin series of *The Buildings of England*,* with their very different approaches. The Murray guides got off to the quicker start, with *Buckinghamshire* and *Berkshire* in 1948 and *Lancashire* in 1950. The first *Buildings of England* volume was published in 1951. Mowl judges that by then 'the race was running level'.[73]

Open warfare between the two men broke out in 1952. In January, reviewing L. T. C. Rolt's *The Thames from Mouth to Source* in *Time and Tide*, John delivered a sideswipe at Pevsner.

> [Rolt] writes with an eye for landscape unimpaired by antiquarianism. He sees a building and he knows its history, but he does not isolate it from its

---

* Now published by Yale University Press.

setting and function and classify it as though for a museum, as do our Herr-Professor-Doktors of today.[74]

In March, John complained in a letter to James Lees-Milne: 'I travel third and am cut by people who count and looked down upon by the new refugee "scholars" who have killed all we like by their "research" – i.e. Nikolaus Pevsner that dull pedant from Prussia.'[75]

Pevsner was buffeted again in John's *Time and Tide* review (10 May 1952) of Bruce Allsopp's *Decoration and Furniture: The English Tradition*. The author's generalizations, such as 'the famous Gothic Revival architects like Scott and Waterhouse were not the true heirs of Pugin', might sometimes miss the mark, but they were 'infinitely preferable to . . . windy Germanic pontificating and bogus accuracy'. And writing to Morton Shand on 31 October, John described Thomas Howarth's new book on Charles Rennie Mackintosh as 'a singularly ugly book, and a typical "thesis". I think Granny [Pevsner] appears on every page.'[76] John's almost manic hatred for Pevsner in that year is illustrated in the foreword to *First and Last Loves* by a stab of venomous xenophobia: 'The Herr-Professor-Doktors are writing everything down for us, sometimes throwing in a little hurried pontificating too, so we need never bother to feel or think or see again.'[77] What caused this outpouring of bile against Pevsner in 1952? One answer may lie in an internal office memo of 1951 in the BBC archives: 'Please note that Mr Betjeman wishes never again to appear in a discussion programme with Professor Pevsner.' John was clever; but Pevsner was more learned. Had he been condescending to John, or scored points against him, humiliating him on a radio programme?

Whatever the reason for John's attack on him, Pevsner did not take it lying down. He fired back what Mowl considers 'a raking, provocative and deliberately hurtful broadside'.[78] In his *London: Volume 2* of 1952, he disparaged John's favourite living architect, Sir Ninian Comper – and his admirers. Of Comper's St Cyprian, Marylebone, he wrote:

> If there must be medieval imitations in the C20 it is here unquestionably done with joy and care. Beyond that appreciation can hardly go. There is no reason for the excesses of praise lavished on Comper's church furnishings by those who confound aesthetic with religious emotions.[79]

The architect Alan Rome and the historian A. L. Rowse, who both knew John and Comper, suggested that John disliked Pevsner for scorning Comper's architecture.[80] In 1991 Father Anthony Symondson SJ contributed to the *Thirties Society Journal* an article on 'John Betjeman and the Cult of J. N. Comper'. Comper (1864–1960) was

Bodley's most distinguished pupil. Symondson thought that 'Nobody did more to keep Comper's work alive than Betjeman,' though he could not 'altogether forgive him for comparing Comper's appearance to Col. Sanders, the proprietor of Kentucky Fried Chicken, in his 1974 television film *A Passion for Churches*,* a comparison which has sunk indelibly into people's memories'.[81]

The Betjeman–Pevsner feud continued in 1953. In June, sending on to Osbert Lancaster a note from Lord Chetwode in which the field-marshal expressed admiration for one of Lancaster's cartoons, John added: 'See me on Pevs in next TLS . . . INTEGRITY & TRUTH must be safeguarded against official closed shop of ART HISTORIANS.'[82] The anonymous review appeared in the *Times Literary Supplement* of 3 July. In it, John tore to pieces the latest Pevsner on County Durham, pointing out many inaccuracies.[83] Pevsner's letter to the *TLS*, replying to the criticisms, is described as 'an incoherent, apologetic disaster' by Mowl, who adds: 'He had deliberately hurt Betjeman in that vulnerable area where religious enthusiasms and aesthetic judgments interact. Now he himself had been ridiculed as an outsider whose scholarship was inadequate in an English context.'[84]

A friend of Pevsner's, the architectural historian Alec Clifton-Taylor (who had known John since they were at Oxford together)[85] was so incensed by the *TLS* review that he asked John – not realizing he was its author – if he would let him defend Pevsner in *Time and Tide*. John brusquely refused. 'We cannot continue to praise Pevsner,' he replied. 'The guides . . . are neither complete as a catalogue nor distinctive as a personal approach.'[86] In his Reith Lectures of 1955, Pevsner hit back: 'Making England responsible for the fancy-dress ball of architecture in the Victorian Age is not complimentary to the aesthetic genius of the nation.'[87]

By now, the Betjeman–Pevsner row was attracting notice beyond the art-world coterie. As early as November 1955 – two years before the Victorian Society was founded – Peter Clarke contributed to *Punch* a wickedly pointed poem originally entitled 'Poet and Pedant'.

> POET: A POET-part-Victorian
> part-Topographer – that's me!
> (Who was it tipped you Norman Shaw
> in Nineteen Thirty-three?)
> Of gas-lit Halls and Old Canals
> I reverently sing,
> But when Big-Chief-I-Spy comes round

---

* See Chapter 21, ' "A Passion for Churches" '.

I *curse* like anything.
Oo-oh!

PEDANT: *A crafty Art Historian*
of Continental fame,
I'll creep up on this Amateur
and stop his little game!
With transatlantic thoroughness
I'll note down all he's missed.
Each British Brick from Norm. to Vic.
you'll find upon my list!
(Aside: Ah-h-h!)

POET: I tawt I taw a Gothic arch
a-peepin' out at me.
I *did*, I *taw* a Gothic arch,
and breathed a soft: 'O-gee!'

PEDANT: *(I analyzed it long ago upon the B.B.C.)*

POET: I thought I saw a Folly tall
of stucco built and thin wood
It played on my emotions
as a visit to 'East Lynne' would.

PEDANT: *(Ho-Ho, that was no Folly tall*
but a Mortuary by Inwood.)

POET: I thought I saw a Packing Case
a-looming over the City.
So large and square and out of place
it filled my soul with pity.

PEDANT: *(No doubt Advanced Headquarters*
of the Barbican Committee.)

POET: I thought I saw a Tennis Girl
admiring a Piscina in
a Pugin Church near Holloway –
the first I'd ever seen her in.

PEDANT: *(He did not know she was my stooge –*
a highly-cultured Wienerin!)

Contre Danse ('Summerson's icumen in')
In abidingly lyrical   *Full of Danish empirical*
Mildly satirical   *Quite unhysterical*
                              – neo-Ruskinian

(Rah for Sir Ninian!)
                              Tecton-and-Gropius –
Strict on Subtopias –

Fine Arts Commissioners   *Bauhaus Practitioner's*
Poetry Versed.   *Knowledge I burst!*

Lost in a world that is all Norman Shavian
Wright, Le Corbusier, Nash and Basévi-an
Peristyle, Metope, Squinch, Architravian.
    ('*I* was the one who discovered it
    FIRST')

Epilogue
All things bright and Butterfield
    With Features Great and Small,
All things weird and Waterhouse
    Work wonders for us all![88]

Clarke devoted another spoof to Pevsner's Germanic steamrollering, 'Fröhliches Weihnachten von der Pevsnerreise' ('Merry Christmas from Pevsner Tour'), designed to be sung to the tune of Schubert's song 'Die Forelle' ('The Trout'). It was considered too scabrous to publish but was gleefully circulated among Victorian Society members and others, some of whom assumed that John was its author. It began:

    1
From heart of Mittel-Europ
    I make der little trip
To show these Englisch Dummkopfs
    some echt-Deutsch scholarship.
Viele Sehenswürdigkeiten*
    By others have been missed,
But now comes to enlighten
    Der Great Categorist.

    2
Der Georgian und Viktorian
    Ist so-wie-so 'getan'
By Herr Professor Richardtson
    Und Dichter Betjemann:
Wile oders gifs you Stevenage,
    Stonehenge und Gilbert Scott,

---

* 'Many places of interest'.

From Pleiocene to C. 19
I gifs der blooming lot.[89]

In the 1960s, Pevsner admired Sir William Holford's buildings for
the new precincts of St Paul's Cathedral;[90] John complained that they
were characterless and blocked the view of Wren's masterpiece. The
rivalry of the guidebooks continued. In 1963 John wrote to Lady Juliet
Smith, who was writing the Shell Guide to *Northamptonshire*:

> It is no good trying to write a comprehensive impersonal catalogue. That
> is being done already in Pevsner's *Buildings of England*, and does not tell
> you what the place is really like, i.e. whether it is strung with poles and
> wires, overshadowed by factories or ruined army huts, whether it is sub-
> urban or a real village, nor whether it is a place of weekend hide-outs and
> carriage-lamp folk with wrought-iron front gates by the local smith.[91]

'We have got Pevsner on the run,' John crowed in a letter of 1966 to
John Piper.[92] He was wrong: the Pevsner guides were becoming a
national institution, and John himself found them useful, as a sheep-
ish approach to Pevsner's secretary, for a free copy, showed.

Even Pevsner's friends conceded that he was not an easy man, nor
the soul of diplomacy. When he died in 1983, Ian Sutton wrote in the
Victorian Society Annual that he was 'the benevolent despot of the
Victorian Society . . . Under his chairmanship the Committee was an
energetic and devoted body, though it was not a democracy . . . On the
whole he was impatient of procedural niceties . . . Nor did he have any
time for facetiousness, one of the few English qualities that he neither
acquired nor wanted to acquire.' Pevsner's admiration for the
International Style, Sutton thought, 'went with his lack of sentimentality . . . about architecture, about other people, above all about
himself. As a historian he was immune to nostalgia; literary and historical associations weighed little with him . . .'[93] It sounds like a blue-
print for somebody unlikely to get on well with John.

As the Professor's letter to Lady Rosse showed, it was not quite fair
to say that Pevsner had no time at all for facetiousness. Several examples of his dry wit are on record. Before going into hospital for an operation he said to the committee, 'As you know, I am a scheduled ancient
monument. No major internal alterations are permitted. I look to you
to ensure my preservation.'[94] He recalled going on a Victorian Society
lecture tour of America with the Duke of Gloucester. 'I had somehow
flattered myself,' he said, 'that I was an acceptable travelling companion, even for royalty. So I was rather disconcerted to find my trunk
labelled in large letters PROFESSOR PEVSNER. NOT WANTED

ON VOYAGE.'[95] Tom Greeves remembered Pevsner's reply to a man who wanted to alter his important Victorian house virtually to the point of demolition. 'Tell him', Pevsner said, 'he can pull down the first storey. Tell him he can pull down the second storey. But he must leave the third storey *exactly as it is.*'[96]

Ian Grant disliked Pevsner almost as much as John did. 'John Newman telephoned me after Pevsner died,' he recalled, 'and said, "I wonder if you can possibly give me something for the auction we're holding to raise something for a Pevsner Memorial Prize. You must have known him well and realized what a charming man he was." And I said, "I didn't think he was charming at all. I thought he was a charmless Kraut." There was an appreciable pause during which I could hear a gobbling noise at the end of the line.'[97] What had most turned Grant against Pevsner was a brush he had had with him over the *Victorian Society Annual*. Jane Fawcett, who had become the society's secretary just after Pevsner became chairman, had asked Grant if he would edit the *Annual*, and he had agreed. Some of the contributors were very slack in handing in their articles. Pevsner, reasonably enough, held Grant responsible.[98]

Bruising as such encounters could be, Pevsner's ruthless insistence on efficiency was what the Victorian Society needed at that stage of its development. Under the Esher–Rosse–Betjeman régime, it had shambled, in a gentlemanly, shabby-genteel way, from crisis to crisis. On 16 October 1963, Thomas Pakenham presented a report, as clear-eyed and unsentimental as even Pevsner could wish, on the working and future expansion of the society. 'For virtually all its life,' he said, 'the society has been living beyond its means and now the reckoning approaches. Four fifths of our accumulated funds have been dissipated ... We have continued to spend nearly double our income.' He added: 'Dr Beeching would find plenty of scope for his talents in our society.'[99]

It was largely thanks to the efficiency of the Pevsner–Fawcett partnership that the society achieved so much in the years that followed the destruction of the Euston Arch and the Coal Exchange. St Pancras station and the Foreign Office were saved. The appointment of Lord Kennet as the minister responsible for preservation and his introduction of the 1967 Town and Country Planning Act and the 1968 Civic Amenities Act gave the society essential powers; official recognition and compulsory notification of threatened listed buildings came with the first, while the 1968 Act, by establishing 'conservation areas', helped stop the systematic destruction of Victorian cities. With the arrival of 'spot listings' in 1974 the society was able to short-circuit the inadequacies of the post-1830s lists by ensuring that full statutory protection was given to threatened buildings, under emergency regulations, within twenty-four hours. St Pancras and Liverpool's Albert Dock were spot-listed as Grade I. In important campaigns, such as that to save St Pancras, John continued to play his flamboyant rôle in public; but after 1963 he was seldom seen at the committee meetings, where Pevsner hustled the members through the agenda.

John did continue to take part in the architectural rambles organized by Peter Clarke. These expeditions were to be among the most popular and pleasurable of the society's activities. They included 'Mayfair, or Marching through Neo-Georgia', 'Kensington Gore and other Battle Scars', 'The City of Holmes, Soames, Pickwick and Pooter', 'Swinging through Chelsea from Savage to Sedding' and (with an ecumenical indulgence towards the 1930s) 'Semi-detached Edgware'. Tom Greeves was nearly always of the party; together, he and Clarke drew a parody of an H. M. Bateman cartoon: 'The Man who tried to look at a Mediaeval Building on a Victorian Society Outing'. (All the other members are looking on aghast, one is dropping his spectacles and umbrella in goggling astonishment.)[100]

Even John had things to learn from Clarke's encyclopaedic familiarity with nineteenth-century buildings. Sometimes John, Clarke and Greeves went off on more exclusive jaunts of their own. 'One time we visited Wormtree Hill in south London,' Greeves recalled. 'Peter got Betjeman and we all went over to see it. I remember it was a boiling hot day. Peter was dressed up in a sort of Palm Beach suit – it was a *very* hot day – and Betjeman made a pointed remark. He said he didn't think one should make concessions to the weather. He didn't approve of people who dressed specially in very light clothes – thought it would be better if they just carried on, ignoring the weather.'[101] Clarke got his own back on John. First, he told him he had invented a heavy-duty garment called a 'PevJak', a jacket with deep poacher's pockets capable of holding sixteen volumes of Pevsner's *Buildings of England*. Then he wrote a limerick about John, one of a series with architectural themes, later published under the Betjeman-derived title 'New Brickbats and Bouquets' –

> What was *that* looming up through the murk
> which made Betjeman stop with a jerk?
> 　'A gas-works by BUNNING!'
> 　he cried 'Come a-running !'
> (Alas, just a castle by SMIRKE.)[102]

John recognized that Clarke was – to use an anachronism – a sort of clone of himself. He was conscious of a certain amount of hero-worship from the younger man, and enjoyed it. The two became friends beyond the Victorian Society. Clarke wrote some of the best parodies of John's verse, rivalled only by Patrick Leigh Fermor's[103] and Alan Bennett's.[104] Some of these appeared in the *New Statesman* before the Victorian Society was founded, including 'Fulham by Gaslight' which evoked the London suburb in 1854, 1944 and 1954. The first two stanzas run:

1854
Radiant gas in Craven Cottage, flares on Eel Brook Common glowed;
Hissed the jets from Bishop's Palace to St Thomas, Rylston Road.*
Oh! The cabbage-laden wagons rumbling up to London town.
Oh! The shapely green gas-holder, wobbling gently up and down!

1944
Gone, the fields and *Cottages Ornés* 'neath the surge of Walham Green.
Gone, the great Imperial Gas Works, built when Adelaide was Queen.
Lone, the Baths of Deighton Pearson! Lost amid the red-brick swell
Churches by Sir Arthur Blomfield *Kunstgeschichters* know so well.[105]

Though Clarke was friendly with both men, it amused him, in his slightly feline way, to play on John's dislike for Pevsner. The term 'art-historians', in Clarke's parody 'Bungalowood, or A Stately Home "Adapted to Modern Residential Requirements"', is also intended as a sideswipe at the Pevsner camp. The mock-Betjeman poem, about the auction of a country house, begins:

With a sandwich-lunch and a Thermos, we sat,
    Myfida and I,
on a mounting-block in the stable-yard, as we watched the 'Big House' die
in the closing stage of a Golden Age 'neath a leaden Wiltshire sky.

Oh, the dealers and art-historians were having a *splendid* day,
(and the National Buildings Record man kept quoting the P.R.A.)†
while the clock on the Barry Chapel was ticking our lives away . . .[106]

Clarke's 'Hymn', a take-off of one of John's earliest and best-known poems, suggests the new attitudes to Victorian architecture that the Victorian Society was trying to foster.

---

* A church by Pugin.
† At a Royal Academy banquet, Sir Alfred Munnings, the president, had said that modern art was 'money for jam!', adding for good measure a question which in 1950s England was thrillingly *risqué*, 'Wouldn't you like to give Picasso a kick up the arse?'

The Church's restoration
in Eighteen Sixty Three,
is *not* the aberration
we thought it used to be.
That pulpit so hamfisted,
those pews we used to damn;
that roof so dark and twisted,
were *all* by Buckton Lamb!

That aisle we once were cool on,
that crimson glass as well
we've learnt are works by Teulon
by Clayton and by Bell.
Forgive the youthful blunder
we knew not where to look.
But could you really wonder?
We had no Penguinbook . . .[107]

In 'MCMLXXXIV' he gives a Betjemanesque version of the year to which Orwell's novel had given the most sinister undertones of the century.

Autumn, and we are skimming down MI,
Pam at the wheel and Pevsner in the boot
His 'Londbirm, Volume X' is *very* large.
Past the old Rugby cooling towers we purr
(The Morris-Comper touches ninety-five)
Ashby St Ledgers – Ah, no time to look
Now life is lectures, lectures all the way
To acolytes from Solihull to Slough
On Pugin, Middle Stumpers, Baillie Scott.
  On, then. Past Bugbrooke, Yardley Gobion,
Ah, Luton . . . (Fifty lines omitted here) . . .
  Summon us home, oh Bells of Clement Danes,
In time for tea at Television House
(Kupcakes, perhaps, and Shippam's potted paste),
– What's that, a *Pearson* church? 'All Saints', by Jove!
We've overshot the mark. This must be *Hove*.[108]

Peter Clarke did not live to see the year 1984 (as it happened, the year of John Betjeman's death); he and his wife were killed in a car crash in 1975. Yet the central prophecy of his poem was fulfilled. The Victorian age had been rehabilitated; and, while Pevsner had not produced a

'Londbirm, Volume X', Victorian architecture was indeed studied seriously, with university lectures on such as Pugin and Baillie Scott – whose house John had chosen as a *poste restante* to fool the Chetwodes when honeymooning with Penelope.[109] Pevsner's disciples gave their master nearly all the credit for the Victorian reprieve; 'he saved a century', it was said, a tag which adhered to him.

To John, too, however, must go much of the credit for de-stigmatizing Victorianism – as co-founder of the society with Lady Rosse, as affectionate champion of Victorian architecture in poetry and prose, and above all in his television broadcasts, which won over the public to Victoriana more effectively than a hundred well-researched works by Pevsner could have done. Only with the public on its side could the society persuade MPs and other powerful figures that they would not become laughing-stocks by supporting its campaigns. Neither man's achievement is diminished or eclipsed by that of the other. One might see them as the 'tough cop' and the 'gentle cop' going to work on an obstinate customer – the firm smack of *Kunstgeschichte* followed by the soothing caress of poetic nostalgia. But even this contrast is unfair: Pevsner had his moments of geniality, and John was not all smiles.

Pevsner won the battle of the guidebooks. In the long run the tortoise beat the hare – Pevsner's dogged application outdistancing John's inspired dilettantism. But it was John who triumphed in the battle of the styles. After the war, Pevsner's views seemed temporarily to prevail. With a Labour Government, a shortage of materials, and an urgent need to rehouse bombed-out people, his pro-Bauhaus theories and taste for austere buildings had more appeal than John's and Piper's arguments in favour of individuality and decoration and against doctrinaire aesthetics.[110] But history eventually settled for John's more catholic taste, comprehending Victoriana, suburbia and decorative eclecticism, not for Pevsner's fealty to the International Style. Mowl attributes John's win to his 'sheer omnipresence' in the 1970s,[111] but some credit, too, must be given to human nature, which rebelled against 'a machine to live in' and craved some 'chintzy, chintzy cheeriness'.[112] It has been claimed that John came to 'like and recognize' Pevsner;[113] but the hatchet was never quite buried. In 1982 John said to me: 'Why is it that when you've read what Pevsner has to say about a building, *you never want to look at that building, ever again?*'

THE *DAILY TELEGRAPH*

Sir, – It is much to be regretted that Mr Bernard Levin, in your issue for December 27, was compelled through lack of space to cut short his catalogue of words suitable for book reviews. To assist his further researches, I append herewith an extract from my forthcoming work *The Reviewer's Lexicon* (O.U.P., 50s.):

Accomplished, agreeable, *Angst*, Angus Wilson, archetype, astringent, A. J. Ayer, Betjeman, bitchy, born writer, by and large, catalyst, Charlus, *chichi*, *cliché*, clinical, compassion, *conte*, contemporary, creative, crystallisation (see Stendhal), delicious, deliriously (funny), disquieting, dotty, Empson, excruciating, father (mother)-figure, Freudian, Geiger counter, gimmick, Grigson, historicity, *Howards End*, integration, intellectual integrity, jejune, Leavis, mellifluous, Nancy Mitford, nostalgic, *panache*, *pastiche*, penetrating, polarisation, predicament (esp. artist's), private myth, Proustian, round the bend, saddening, scholarly, semantics, sensibility (exquisite), significant, Stendhal (see crystallisation), subtopian, Swiftian misanthropy, twentyish, unequivocal, *voulu*, *Weltanschauung*, whimsy, *Zeitgeist*.

Yours faithfully,

JOCELYN BROOKE

Letter to the editor of *The Spectator*, 3 January 1958.

Though John had found reviewing for the *Daily Herald* an intolerable chore, he still needed the extra income that this kind of part-time job brought him. As a result he began writing for the *Daily Telegraph*, and his association with that paper lasted from 1951 until 1969. John had two links with the Berry family which owned the *Daily Telegraph*. His brother-in-law, Roger Chetwode, who committed suicide in 1940,[1] had married Patricia Berry, Lord Camrose's daughter. And Michael Berry, Patricia's brother, had married Lady Pamela Smith, sister of John's friend Freddy Birkenhead. Through these connections, John became a book reviewer for the paper a few months after giving up his *Daily Herald* column. He was hired as a fiction critic, though occasionally he was also sent poetry, 'funny' books or works on architecture and the railways.

Leaving the *Herald* and joining the *Telegraph* (again as a freelance) was in theory a big leap. He was moving from the most left-wing of the popular newspapers to the most right-wing – in terms of male readers, from cloth caps to bowler hats. It might also be assumed that his new readers had received more formal education than his old ones. There was, however, no discernible 'change of gear', between John's reviews for the *Herald* and those for the *Telegraph*. As he seldom wished to express strong views on politics, the polarized political stances of the two papers did not signify. Neither did he feel the need to adopt a different style to address a different class. People who watched his television programmes saw that he got on just as well with railwaymen as with the owners of country houses. In his reviewing, he similarly made no distinction between his blue-collar and white-collar readers. He offered each of them 'essence of Betjeman' which, like Bovril, could be enjoyed (or not enjoyed) by any class. As on the television, he did what he was paid to do: be himself.

Contributing critiques of novels for almost the whole of the 1950s, he worked for two literary editors. The first was Edmund Clerihew Bentley, who was in his seventies when John began working for him. Bentley had written the classic detective story *Trent's Last Case* and invented the clerihew. His son Nicolas, the cartoonist, was a friend of John's; after *Mount Zion* was published in 1931 John had a fan letter from Nicolas and replied, 'You must illustrate my next effort if I don't kill myself . . .'[2] – but the idea came to nothing. Everyone liked E. C. Bentley. Enthusiasm was less widespread for H. D. Ziman, who became literary editor when Bentley died in 1956. He was known to everyone, including his family, as 'Z'* – though John, when exasperated by him, sometimes called him 'Zimple Ziman'.[3]

In 1988 Anthony Powell, recalling John's character in his Journal, wrote: 'He had extraordinary powers to charm . . . On the other hand he would take unreasoning dislikes: for instance, Ziman, Literary Editor of the *Daily Telegraph*, whom Betjeman could not hear mentioned without a stream of objurgation. Admittedly Z could be maddening . . . but *au fond* he was sound, good-natured, tried to do his best about books and reviewers.'[4] Others have portrayed Ziman less charitably. Duff Hart-Davis, in *The House the Berrys Built* (1990), described him as 'one of the greatest bores ever to send people fleeing down the corridors of No. 135 [Fleet Street]'[5] and claimed that Colin

---

* Pronounced 'Zed' in the British way.

Coote, the *Telegraph*'s editor, had made him literary editor because he
was 'unable to stand [his] contributions to leader-writers' conferences
any longer'.[6] In an obituary of Ziman published in the *Telegraph* in
1983, however, David Holloway (his deputy and successor as literary
editor) wrote: 'His attention to detail was famous and his contributors would tell of long arguments over the telephone of the use of a
single word or a comma. Z was almost always right.'[7] But such petti-
fogging discussions were not much to John's taste.

There were compensations. The Fifties were a good decade in which
to be a fiction critic. They saw the rise of the so-called Angry Young
Men, led by John Wain, John Osborne, Kingsley Amis and John
Braine, and the Beats, led by Jack Kerouac. Iris Murdoch's early novels
appeared. Such classics as L. P. Hartley's *The Go-Between*, William
Golding's *Lord of the Flies* and Salinger's *The Catcher in the Rye* were
published; also Waugh's war trilogy and *The Ordeal of Gilbert
Pinfold*. It was *the* decade for science fiction. Of the older generation,
Compton Mackenzie and John Cowper Powys were still going strong.
P. B. Abercrombie, Ivy Compton-Burnett, William Cooper, Isak
Dinesen, Lawrence Durrell, Francis King, Robin Maugham, Brian
Moore, Alberto Moravia, Anthony Powell, Barbara Pym, William
Sansom, Elizabeth Taylor and T. H. White were all reviewed by John.

Those were the high spots. As early as March 1952, after little more
than a year of reviewing, John wrote, in a notice of William Sansom's
A Touch of the Sun:

> Week after week I notice what I think is the best of the competent middle-
> brow output from which I select. Week after week I am inclined to lower
> my standards by thinking 'this one is better than last week's best, so it
> must be first-class', until I come up against a book like this of Sansom,
> which is so much better than the average 'excellent' of my reviews that I
> begin to remember what 'good' means.[8]

Three months earlier, he had ventured an opinion of what *was* good
in contemporary fiction, when reviewing L. P. Hartley's *My Fellow
Devils*, 'a leisurely and haunting love story with no sex in it':

> Most novels worth reading today are either cerebral or religious. To the
> cerebral belong the books of Ivy Compton-Burnett and Henry Green and
> Elizabeth Jenkins. They are a specialized taste, full of intellect and
> subtlety, as it were unfutile crosswords. Religious novelists like Dorothy
> Sayers, Evelyn Waugh and Graham Greene are mostly Catholic, Anglican
> or Roman. But romantic fiction has lately deviated either into cynical sex
> stories or silly slop with a little history thrown in.[9]

In England we look back on the Fifties as the decade which emerged from the greyness of post-war austerity, first with the vivid splashes of the Festival of Britain (1951) and the Coronation (1953); then with the rise of a new teenage culture, with rock 'n' roll, Teddy boys, coffee bars, skiffle groups, quiffs and ponytails. In a book of poems which John reviewed favourably for the *Telegraph*, Thom Gunn wrote of Elvis Presley –

> He turns revolt into a style, prolongs
> The impulse to a habit of the time.[10]

So to find religion identified as one of the major ingredients of Fifties fiction might strike one as Betjemanesque quirkishness, of a piece with his interest in Sandemanian meeting houses and the Strict Baptists. But the Roman Catholics Greene and Waugh were two of the precellent novelists of the time. Iris Murdoch, too, was exercised by religion, noble and perverted; Barbara Pym mirrors in prose much the same middle-class Anglican world depicted in Betjeman poems; and the works of John Cowper Powys are also instinct with religion in their craggy, pagan way.

In the more than fifty years since John began reviewing for the *Telegraph*, posterity has had time to make up its mind about the fiction of that time. Reading his notices now, you realize – as with his *Daily Herald* reviews – how seldom he failed to seize on quality. In February 1954 he hailed Kingsley Amis's *Lucky Jim* as a comic masterpiece – 'I do not remember to have laughed so much at a new funny book . . . since when I first read Evelyn Waugh's "Decline and Fall" – and that was in 1928.'[11] William Faulkner's *Requiem for a Nun* 'walks like somebody in a thick tweed suit into the slick and formally dressed company of other modern novels. The warp and the woof show.'[12] He enjoyed Elizabeth Taylor's wit in *The Sleeping Beauty*, especially the fragment of dialogue about a businessman's domineering mother –

'And very forthright. You know where you are with her.'
'Yes, but you don't want to be there.'[13]

John ranked Taylor with Elizabeth Bowen, Christine Longford and Elizabeth Jenkins. He always had high praise for William Sansom and William Cooper. He defended Barbara Pym from the charge of creating *petit-point* characters whose concerns were rarely more momentous than whether to serve Darjeeling or Lapsang Soochong.[14]

Though he did not know it at the time, Barbara Pym was just as taken by his writing as he by hers. As early as 1938 she had written a boyfriend what she called 'a Betjeman poem' (lamentable in scansion); described herself as 'chirping' John's 'Hymn'; and told the novelist Robert Liddell of her attempts to convert a foreign friend to John's verse. ('Friebert is being educated to enjoy the poems of John Betjeman, but naturally it is rather difficult, particularly when I have to explain such lines as "The incumbent enjoying a supine incumbency", but I make him read them aloud, which is really a treat.')[15] In 1943 she 'listened to a John Betjeman programme in the *How* series – *How to Look at a Town* – simply delightful of course – ending up with a Non-conformist chapel!'[16] Ten years later, John was not the only reviewer who admired her *Excellent Women*. Marghanita Laski praised it in *The Observer* and the *Church Times* reviewer thought it revealed 'flashes of insight into female characters worthy of Jane Austen'.[17] But, Pym's biographer writes, 'Perhaps the review that pleased her most was the one in the *Daily Telegraph* from John Betjeman – one of her favourite poets as a writer who, in some ways, influenced her more than any novelist . . .'[18]

Another Church of England spinster whose novels John praised, was Rose Macaulay. In 1956 he released, in a review of *The Towers of Trebizond*, some of the anger which Penelope's becoming a Roman Catholic, and Evelyn Waugh's ham-fisted attempts to convert him too, had provoked. He thought it:

> the best book she has written, and that is saying a lot. Roman Catholics may not enjoy it, nor will extreme Protestants, for Miss Macaulay is unashamedly, honestly, learnedly, charitably 'high Anglican', and this is her testament.
>
> At a time when people are wanting to tie the love of God down to hard and fast definitions, when Liberalism is at a discount, when to long for complete faith and not to have it is regarded as an illness which can only be cured by submission to the Pope or revivalist 'conversion', the views of Miss Macaulay expressed here will seem shocking indeed, especially to the self-assured. Her church does not fall into
>
> > such things as sentimentalism and exaggeration and puritanism and pietism and the Reformation and the Counter-Reformation and revivalism and Lourdes and Lisieux and reliquaries and pictures of the Sacred Heart in convent parlours and Salvationism and evangelical hymns, and many more such barriers to religion, which daunt those not brought up to them and keep them out, like fundamentalism and hell fire.[19]

John rarely savaged a book. Knowing the pains of authorship, if he could find merit, he did. Many writers, besides Rose Macaulay, took encouragement from his reviews. In 1956 he wrote: 'Catherine Cookson's "The Lord and Mary Ann" ... is a completely successful sequel to her novel "A Grand Man" ... What makes this book so good is its frank realization of the terrors as well as the joys of childhood – the terrors of going home from school and being taunted by a bigger girl, the repulsive Sarah Flanagan and her gang ...'[20] Forty years later, Dame Catherine Cookson, who was born two months before John in 1906, wrote:

> I was delighted by Mr Betjeman's opinion of my work. I did not have the nerve to write to him: to me he was a great man, a great poet.
>
> After my first novel, *Kate Hannigan*, was banned in Ireland, and then some of my friends (so-called) suggested that my second, *The Fifteen Streets*, and my third, *Colour Blind*, should go the same way, Mr Betjeman's words were as balm to my bruised soul – and I confess that I name-dropped him on every possible occasion.[21]

John's praise for Catherine Cookson – who was dismissed by some critics as merely a popular romantic novelist – illustrates his independence of judgement. As a reviewer, he was hardly affected by 'received opinion', the consensus of other critics. In the *Telegraph*, as in the *Herald*, he did not for instance join in the chorus of admiration for Ivy Compton-Burnett's novels. He approached her gingerly, making his feelings clear when he wrote of her *Darkness and Day* (1951), 'There are those who live only till her next novel appears. And here it is.' He described the book as pointillist – 'all done with little blobs'.[22]

Recognizing the great talent of Iris Murdoch, which was to flower in such novels as *The Black Prince* (1973) and *The Sea, The Sea* (1978), he was severe on what he saw as the failings of her earlier books. Of *The Bell* (1958) he wrote:

> Here is someone who really knows how to write, who can tell a story, who can delineate character, and who can catch at atmosphere with deadly accuracy and who even dares to invade the private thoughts of a man and put them down so that your reviewer can believe them ...
>
> Unfortunately, however, [the book] shows no understanding of the purpose of the religious life. Iris Murdoch describes superbly the terrifying silence of that part of the chapel where the nuns unseen are still with adoration, but she does not seem to know whom they adore, nor is she very accurate on the niceties of liturgical worship.
>
> It is unlikely for instance that the priest who lives with the lay community should play so small a part in its worship. The bishop who comes in at the end of the story is a mere caricature. But it is the plot which is the chief weakness of the book. This deviates into a mere adventure story, in

which Dora and Toby haul up a medieval bell, by means of a crane, out of the lake and try to substitute it, without anyone finding out, for the new bell which is to be blessed by the bishop the next day.

It is possible that this story of the bell has some symbolic significance which has escaped me. But it seems to me as though suddenly, about three-quarters of the way through, Miss Murdoch had handed her manuscript to Angela Brazil and said, 'You finish it.'[23]

By contrast, Monica Dickens, generally regarded as just a popular novelist who wrote about things she knew about, such as nursing, received the highest commendations from John. Reviewing her *The Winds of Heaven* (1955), he wrote: 'I do not know why Monica Dickens does not have articles written about her work by literary pundits. She seems to me one of the acutest and wittiest exposers of humbug and power mania, one of the most affectionate and humorous observers of the English scene, particularly of the pretensions of genteel suburban life, that we have.'[24] In another review he credited her with having inherited 'some of the genius of her famous ancestor'.[25] (She was the great-granddaughter of Charles Dickens.) John used the word 'genius' only twice more in his *Telegraph* reviews. One novelist singled out for this accolade was Mark Bence-Jones – later better known for his non-fiction books on Irish country houses. The philosophy implicit in Bence-Jones's *Paradise Escaped* (1958) could hardly have been further from John's own. John paraphrased it: 'God has made human beings like a lot of curious beetles crawling around the face of the earth and then He has made a lot of ridiculous rules which they cannot possibly keep just in order to mock at them.' But John found the book an 'amusing and devastating . . . picture of post-Edwardian country house life'. It was the best description he had read of 'the irresponsible monied, drinking and hunting set in Eire'. Another quality in the book appealed to him still more.

> Christopher's mother is a Roman Catholic of a rather lapsed kind and the girl Christopher loves is even more lapsed. But how well this writer understands love:
>
>> Long did we kiss: much we had to tell each other. Yet when we sat with my aunt and her friends, we did not, I think, long to be alone. The thought of tomorrow was pleasure enough, as, with a great thirst, one hesitates to quench it, but pauses blissfully, drink in hand.[26]

The other novelist who won John's highest praise was Evelyn Waugh, for *The Ordeal of Gilbert Pinfold* (1957). The review appeared under the headline 'About a Novelist Going Mad'.

I ask myself: 'Is this novel autobiography?' It is certainly a picture of hell on earth. It is not a picture of madness but of the stages leading to it. I have an idea that most of us are haunted by voices such as these.

I know that in times of depression I hear arguments such as Mr Waugh describes going on in my head, indeed in moments of searing self-examination I discover what I am really like underneath through the medium of these arguments which expose one's secret shames. The picture is most unpleasant. I would say that the ordeal of Gilbert Pinfold is self-examination written as a novel but unlike other such works, which are generally dreary and self-pitying, this, because it is by Mr Waugh, is readable, thrilling and detached.

What is it that makes Waugh so good a writer? Is it just his careful use of grammar and punctuation, narrative power, conciseness and Firbankian gift for the unexpected? I think it is more than these. It is something which comes in from outside – that is genius.[27]

In his own case, John often spoke of the help he received 'from the Management' – looking heavenwards.

Reviewing Bertrand Russell's collection of short stories *Satan in the Suburbs* (1953), John wrote of the title piece, 'One might say that there is not meant to be any heart in the story . . . One must answer that, in fiction, ideas are rarely enough.'[28] Two months later, he wrote of Rosamond Lehmann's *The Echoing Grove*, 'Miss Lehmann's characters, though civilized and humane, are rather too purposeless for me. Though one cannot blame them for not knowing why they exist, I feel rather depressed to find none of them faintly interested in anything but their relationships with friends and lovers.'[29] He expected a literary work, like a piece of music, to move towards a destination. Too much Fifties fiction, he wrote, was 'sexy twitterings'.[30] Others of his distastes become evident in the nine years of *Telegraph* reviews. He found Carson McCullers's *The Ballad of the Sad Café* (1952) 'too well written'.[31] A frequent criticism is that a writer has 'tried to do too much'[32] – a mistake he rarely made in his own work.

Himself the master of a fine prose style, he was repelled by slovenly or overdone writing, though he made an indulgent exception for Ursula Bloom's *The Abiding City* in 1958: 'Why this book, which is idiotic in style ("She finished the cigarette and took a last look at the Alps etched against the sequinned gown of the sky") and improbable in plot, held me, I do not know. Perhaps there is a streak in me which likes sentimental nonsense in reaction from the realism and sophistication of better novels.'[33]

Though he had been a friend of Flann O'Brien in Ireland, John was caustic about what he saw as pretentiously experimental writing.[34] In

1953 he reviewed together Ernest Frost's *A Short Lease* and Peter Vansittart's *A Little Madness*.

> Both Ernest Frost and Peter Vansittart are interesting stylists who delight in words. Both have written novels about art students in England, so there is a reason for noticing their books together. Both are inclined to overwrite and to strive after stylish effects, perhaps in unconscious apology for the dreariness of their drifting characters. Thus Mr Frost:
>
>> 'The Art School funny boy,' Betty said, rough as soda. One saw, now, the alcohol twisting her eyes and the painful way words flew around inside her mouth before coming out.
>
> And thus Mr Vansittart:
>
>> After she had gone I stood drenched with perspiration that poured over me from the torpid air, scalding my armpits, dripping down my body, then slowly icing. The sunlight was starved and biting, and I went home tired out, unable to assess the afternoon.
>
> I should think so after an experience like that.
>
> If these were first novels, I would not single out such extravagances. But they are both third novels. By all means let us have the language kept alive by experiment. Let us also be sure of what we mean.[35]

Embedded in the *Telegraph* reviews are fragments of autobiography; reading certain novels, especially about childhood, John experienced 'the shock of recognition'. Jocelyn Brooke's *The Passing of a Hero* (1953) stirred memories of the boys who had outshone him at school, but whom he had eclipsed in later life, such as J. P. W. Mallalieu at the Dragon School, whom John unaffectionately recalled in *Summoned by Bells* as 'Percival Mandeville, the perfect boy . . . Upright and honourable, good at games . . .'[36] John wrote of Brooke's novel:

> Many of us have known Pryce-Foulger, Mr Brooke's hero. He was so successful at his private school, so good-looking and so good at games and a favourite everywhere, with a true sense of 'playing the game'; at the same time he was slightly ridiculous. Then he let himself down by making a rude noise just at the most serious moment of the headmaster's speech.
>
> At Oxford his ample money made him try to move in social circles which did not really want him. Then he became 'literary', but one knew that nothing he wrote would be any good. He stood for Parliament and was elected: the war came, and he was killed . . .
>
> Poor Pryce-Foulger never knew about himself. He remained a successful schoolboy looking about for prizes for which he no longer qualified . . .[37]

In 1952 John reviewed G. F. Green's *In the Making*. 'G. F. Green, with a terrifying intensity and power of recollection, has put himself right into the mind of his hero Randal Fane, so that when I read it my own childhood came back to me with its delights and terrors – the summer term and being ashamed of not having passed the swimming test, the first discovery of poetry, the changing friendships.'[38]

In a notice of Aldous Huxley's *The Genius and the Goddess* (1955), John recalled the impact Huxley's early fiction had made on him at school.

Never shall I forget the thrill with which these startled eyes, those of a schoolboy in 1923, first ran over the pages of Aldous Huxley's 'Antic Hay' – the daring thoughts disguised in scientific language, the blasphemous unconvention of the conversations, the bold mention of the unmentionable. 'How difficult it is in these days,' says Aldous Huxley in his latest novel . . . 'to remember the strength of the old taboos'.

Yet I find my old shockability coming back as I read this new short novel, an alternative title to which could have been 'Youthful Reminiscence of Sex by an Adult in Later Middle Age'.

Aldous Huxley seems to have regained the quality which I thought he had lost in those longer later books, starting with 'Point Counter Point', of delighting in the use of words. Though he has never been sufficiently recognized as such, he is a very good poet. 'Leda', his book of poems, made an unacknowledged impact on poetry in the 'twenties.[39]

Let off the leash of fiction criticism to review Edmund Blunden's *Poems of Many Years* in 1957, John paid tribute to another poet who had influenced him at school.

I find all the pleasure coming back to me that I first had in the poems as a schoolboy . . . They wear well. They are not in the least 'folky' or 'stooky' as one suspected, after so long an absence from them, they might seem to the more sophisticated taste of one's middle years.

I cannot go back to Austin Dobson, whose 'Ballade of Beau Brocade' seemed to me when I was fourteen to be the very essence of the eighteenth century, with anything but a nostalgic recollection of early experience. But I can go back to Blunden because he has nothing spurious about him.[40]

Assessing the slender volumes of new poets in 1960 – 'paper boats set on the stream of fame' – John remembered his own elation at being published. 'It is a great help to a poet to see himself in print. The first poems he has printed, even if it only be in the school magazine, he reads again and again. To come out with a whole book, even if it be very thin and only bound in paper and even if he has had to pay the printer's bill, is the most fulfilling moment of his life.'[41]

John's days as an assistant master at Thorpe House and Heddon Court were brought back to him by a novel of 1956.

> Those who have had the hilarious experience, as I have had, of being a preparatory schoolmaster, will know that 'Young Seeley-Bohn', by Donald Gilchrist . . . is the real thing. Seeley-Bohn is a boy of about ten, that age when boys are unfeeling barbarians to one another, but extremely sensitive inside themselves, and this Mr Gilchrist understands. He must be a very good schoolmaster.[42]

The sour memory of his battles at the Ministry of Information gave an extra sharpness to John's review of a novel of 1952. 'Mr William Mole has surely been in the Civil Service. His first novel, "Trample an Empire", is a defence of individualism. Robin Portock is a Civil Servant who finds himself up against the repulsive kind of ambition which will do anything for power. His "Ministry of Coordination" is all too probable. It is a relief to find in this exciting tale that Robin and his girl friend outwit the power-maniacs.'[43] In 1954 he wrote another heartfelt notice which it is impossible not to relate to his own situation:

> Let 'A Villa in Summer', by Penelope Mortimer, be a warning to anyone who thinks he can lead a happily married life half in London and half in the country . . . The discomforts of "roughing it", running out of oil and coal, rushing to catch the country bus in the cold rain at seven in the morning, steamily drying in the draughty train to London and going through the same process the other way round in the evening, have seldom been better described. It is this, the expensive discomfort of such semi-rurality, its exhausting demands on the body and inadequate compensation to the spirit, that impresses me most in this really excellent novel.[44]

Roughing it in deep country might not be to John's liking; but a novelist who evoked the suburbs was usually rewarded with an appreciative mention. 'Nothing I have read this week', he wrote in April 1953, 'is so good as the opening of Alexander Baron's "The Human Kind", which describes an expedition on a racing bike, with a crowd of youths, out of the East End to Epping and home in the evening rain, skidding on the tramlines.'[45] The descriptions of Epping Forest reminded him of the 'beanfeasts with my father's firm' which he recalled in his poem 'Essex'; as that poem appeared in *A Few Late Chrysanthemums* (1954), it may even have been inspired by Baron's book. In Tom Clarkson's *The Pavement and the Sky* (1951) he admired the author's 'prose poems' about the Borough of St Pancras – 'the poor streets and the hollow pleasures of pin-tables; the sight of girls in summer frocks in public parks; of wide boys with flashy ties and crimped hair-styles. It is far more London than those Festival books of photographs which are still, belatedly, pouring into the bookshops.'[46] In the same year he again praised William Sansom: 'He has turned middle-class suburban life into poetry and made a rhapsody of half-spoken love affairs in tea-shops; he has written affectionately of the majority of us who are dog-lovers with an expensive wireless set in our house, but very few books.'[47]

In American novels John found no such reassuring points of reference; and that was only one of the reasons why American fiction, in general, left him cold. Anti-American feeling was rife in England of the 1950s. There was rankling resentment that the United States had 'come into the war late'; bad blood among British servicemen whose wives had been unfaithful with wartime GIs, 'overdressed, overpaid, oversexed and over here'; outraged virtue by some British wives who had been propositioned in vain; even hard feelings in parents whose daughters had been carried off as GI brides. New York had not been bombed, like London. Throughout the 1940s Americans had seemed so indecently rich while England suffered from shortages and rationing. And now in the Fifties, as England at last struggled out of austerity, her cultural mandarins deplored the import from America of Elvis the Pelvis, horror comics, bubble gum, and films which either exploited sex or showed America winning the war single-handed. (John was in any case jaundiced against the Hollywood establishment which had tried to get him sacked as film critic of the *Evening Standard* in the Thirties.) Many British people were shocked by the McCarthy purges of alleged and genuine Communists and by America's Cold War belligerence with, looming in the background, the atom bomb which America had dropped and which threatened civilization itself. At the end of the Fifties the brazen palace of the new American embassy, rising amid the old brick houses of Grosvenor Square, seemed to symbolize the 'brashness' and 'vulgarity' with which the Americans were so often credited. Much of the anti-American feeling was unjustified – irrational prejudice. But for a time it was fashionable for people who thought themselves cultured to do down things American.

As early as February 1951 John wrote: 'Seldom have I read a less inviting beginning than Frederick Buechner's first chapter of "A Long Day's Dying". I learn that he is a very young American writer and that Mr Isherwood thinks highly of him. Reverence for youth and

Mr Isherwood helped me plough through pages of Henry Jamesian description of a man having a face massage.'[48] A week later, reviewing some ghost stories by H. P. Lovecraft, he asserted:

> Ghost stories are an English speciality . . . But the Americans cannot do it, except for Henry James and Edith Wharton, and they became so Europeanized as to count as English writers. When I started 'The Haunter of the Dark and Other Tales of Terror' by H. P. Lovecraft, I hoped that here might be someone of the James and Wharton school. But no. This is an unsubtle American book with cobwebs, winding passages, terrible rites and vast pseudo-scientific and pseudo-archaeological imaginings.[49]

He found the stories unfrightening – 'They remind me too much of Boris Karloff and not enough of the devil.'

John could write approvingly of Mary McCarthy's novel *Cast a Cold Eye* (1952), because 'Mary McCarthy is one of those American story-tellers who are so much at home to English readers that only the place-names and an occasional phrase remind us that we are not reading about some cultivated circle of comfortable compatriots';[50] but when he reviewed her *Memories of a Catholic Girlhood* five years later, and realized how American she was – and an atheist at that – he described her as 'a dry, dispassionate creature'. Only by translating her experiences into English terms could he understand them. 'The chapter describing a visit to the State of Montana, where Mary first learned how to drink raw spirits and what men are like, is – in terms of English social life – like a description of a nice girl from South Kensington sent to stay with a vice gang in Stepney.' And he ended the review with another thump at Roman Catholicism: 'When these memoirs were published serially in the United States Miss McCarthy received abusive and menacing letters about her criticisms of certain aspects of her Roman Catholic upbringing. Lay Roman Catholics threatened to cancel their subscriptions to the magazine and attempted to constitute themselves a pressure group.'[51]

In 1959 John reviewed a book by America's leading architectural historian, Henry-Russell Hitchcock, the Penguin volume *Architecture: Nineteenth and Twentieth Centuries*. Hitchcock was uncongenial to John not only as an American writer, but also as an adherent of the school of Pevsner. John wrote in the *Telegraph*:

> On the ramparts of that impregnable, ugly nineteenth-century castle Art History, the bearded American figure of Henry-Russell Hitchcock stands alone.

Though he inhabits this forbidding castle, one feels he is unconcerned with the scramble for comfortably endowed chairs and official honours that is going on inside its walls.

Unlike his predecessor in this field, H.S. Goodhart-Rendel, who has done more for the appreciation of nineteenth- and early twentieth-century architecture and earned less thanks than any living man, Mr Hitchcock cannot write interesting or good prose . . .[52]

American poetry got even shorter shrift from John than American prose. Reviewing an anthology in 1956 – *The Faber Book of Modern American Verse* with an 'adroit preface' by his friend W.H. Auden – John complained that 'America is so large that there is no intimacy and people are always on the move.' He added:

> American muse, whose strong and diverse heart
> So many men have tried to understand
> But only made it smaller with their art,
> Because you are as various as your land . . .

writes Stephen Vincent Benét, and goes on for too many stanzas saying the same thing in different ways.

This is the weakness of these poets, though not of the best of them. Their poetry is very individual, and since they have not the innuendoes, subtleties, literary conventions and nostalgic topography that we have on our academic island, they substitute for them shock tactics and bright ideas, and tend to become caricatures of themselves.[53]

It becomes clear that the word 'American' was itself a pejorative term for John. But his prejudice did not prevent him from recognizing the quality of J.D. Salinger's *The Catcher in the Rye* (1951) – 'The manner of telling is conversational and full of American slang. But the boy himself, through all his strangeness and his chronic indolence, is somehow sane and charming. The book carries its reader along through the force of the narrator's personality and outlook.'[54] In 1952 Edmund Wilson was complimented on his prose style and for depicting Americans who had at least had recognizable counterparts in Europe of the 1920s.

'I Thought of Daisy' is a novel by a critic. Its author, Edmund Wilson, writes direct, easily understood literary criticism which stimulates or may anger but which never confuses or bores its readers. He is the enemy of jargon and of that involved Germanic pretension which passes for criticism in so many of the arts today.

He is a very pro-American American. In this novel he is constantly differentiating types of Americans, as a regional writer in England emphasizes atmosphere and accents, varying from county to county. Yet the people he describes, artists, poets and musicians of New York living in Greenwich Village in the nineteen-twenties, are, beneath their accents and origins, like artists, poets and musicians anywhere in Western Europe of the twenties. They are mostly a frustrated, hard-drinking lot, constantly seeking soul-mates and then moving on to new ones.[55]

Two years later, John and Edmund Wilson met in London, and liked each other. Wilson wrote in his diary: 'Since Dylan Thomas's death, he is, I suppose, the best poet in England – a minor poet, perhaps, but a very, very good one.'[56]

John made a point of reviewing novels about homosexuality – not only because of the 'percentage' of homosexuality that he acknowledged in himself, but also because this was a subject increasingly in the news. In the Forties homosexuality could barely be mentioned in the press. In the Fifties it was brought to the fore by police tactics (much condemned in *The Spectator*) in the arrest of Lord Montagu and the actor John Gielgud; the book *Against the Law* by Montagu's co-defendant Peter Wildeblood; the defection to Russia of the homosexual spy Guy Burgess and his accomplice Donald Maclean; the plays of Tennessee Williams; the Kinsey Report which suggested that as many as 20 per cent of men had had some homosexual experience; and the Wolfenden Report which in 1957 recommended that the law should be changed to permit homosexual relations between 'consenting adults in private'. It was significant that the often reactionary *Telegraph* could publish, on the same page as one of John's fiction reviews in 1955, a fair-minded review of Wildeblood's book by Sir Basil Henriques, under the headline 'The Homosexual and the Law'.[57]

Even in his first year as a *Telegraph* critic, John reviewed novels about homosexuals, though sometimes he warned his readers that 'Some may regard this book as "unhealthy".' ('Unhealthy' was then the favoured euphemism for any book whose sexual content might shock. The novels of Ivy Compton-Burnett were denounced as 'unhealthy' in *Country Life*, even though her close friend Margaret Jourdain was the magazine's leading contributor on antiques. In reviewing Edgar Mittelholzer's *The Weather in Middenshot*, about black magic in the then British Guiana, John devised a more extravagant euphemism – 'This writer . . . does not specialize in what is savoury.')[58] In February 1951 John was sent Fritz Peters's *Finistère*, a novel about homosexuality issued by the left-wing publisher Victor Gollancz. On 25 February John wrote to Alan Pryce-Jones: 'Have you read FINISTERRE [*sic*]? My dear! Never read anything so outspoken in my life. It will be banned (Gollancz) for certain.'[59] The book was not banned, but certainly it was strong meat for the early 1950s; later homosexual novels tended to be described as 'in the tradition of *Finistère*'.[60] John wrote: ' "FINISTERE" is a very good and a very depressing novel. The subject of which it treats is delicate and tricky. It can easily be made sentimental or obscene. Mr Peters steers clear of both dangers. His pity for all the characters purges the book.'[61] The book ends with the suicide of the main ones. This might be seen as an expiation of homosexuality demanded by society at the time, comparable with the insistence – in that era – that film villains must always come to grief by the end of the film, never profit from their crimes.

In November 1953 John wrote:

I review belatedly 'The Heart in Exile', by Rodney Garland, because it is the sort of novel which twenty years ago might have been hounded into the law courts by some morality publicist. It is a completely honest story, written by a psychiatrist about homosexual life in London. There is no self-pity in it, no sentimentality, no attempt to defend or condemn homosexuality.

A young man on the eve of his marriage to a girl kills himself and the story is of a psychiatrist's search among the young man's friends for the reason of his suicide. Now that there seems to be another drive against male homosexuals, this book will tell those who want information about this 'underground' movement more than they can gather from police court reports or the remarks of magistrates and judges.[62]

In 1954 John reviewed Garland's next novel, clearly based on the Burgess–Maclean affair.

'The Troubled Midnight' by Rodney Garland starts, as did 'The Heart in Exile', with a knowledgeable account of post-war homosexual life in London. It then changes into a good spy story about two missing diplomats. Mr Garland . . . is best at quick and perceptive character studies of young and middle-aged men.

I wish, instead of cashing in on topical themes, he would turn his gifts to a novel showing up the Gestapo method of certain sections of the police in this country. It would be a crusading novel worth writing, and it need not confine itself to police methods with those suspected of sexual offences.[63]

John Betjeman is seldom thought of as an agitator for social reform – rather as the tradition-bound celebrant of a cosy status quo. But it took some courage to lay into the police on behalf of homosexuals in the early Fifties. His anger was partly provoked by the jailing, in 1953, of Rupert Croft-Cooke, who had 'got himself into "a spot of bother" with a sailor'.[64] John, who had met Croft-Cooke through Lord Kinross, wrote to Kinross in October 1953: 'What happened about poor old Rupert C-C? I thought of him all yesterday and the day before. Oh, now I see today's *D Telegraph*. To hell with these dreadful laws. He won't win his appeal. No appeal ever does get through. I wish I could somehow help him. Prayer I suppose is the only thing.'[65] John wrote favourable reviews of two Croft-Cooke novels, *Fall of Man* (1955)[66] and *Seven Thunders* (1956).[67] Croft-Cooke went on to write *Bosie* (1965), *Feasting with Panthers* (1967) and *The Unrecorded Life of Oscar Wilde* (1972).

When John reviewed *Finistère* in 1951, he avoided the word 'homosexuality', hinting only that 'The subject of which it treats is delicate and tricky.' But in 1958, when he reviewed the anonymous novel *A Room in Chelsea Square*, the notice appeared under the headline 'Bitter Attack on Homosexuals' – so far had openness progressed. Instead of defending a novel on the side of homosexuals, John found himself in the unusual position of chiding a novelist who attacked them.

Rarely have I read so talented, amusing and unlikable a novel as 'A Room in Chelsea Square'. Its author is anonymous, and those who read his book will see why. That he is a 'he', there can be no doubt, for the only woman in it is the only character without a personality . . .

Whether he intended it as such I do not know, but the novel succeeds in being one of the most bitter attacks on homosexuals I have read. There is a malice in the chief character, Patrick, of which no woman is quite capable: it is so calculated, ingenious, heartless and underhand.

Patrick, who was left one of the richest men in England when Mummy died, and who had a good eye for pictures and young men, liked to encourage talents and good looks, particularly the latter. Despite the fact that age had worn out his own beauty, he still could obtain pleasure with his money and had no illusions about himself.

The story concerns a young man whom Patrick, because his desires are not gratified quickly enough, gradually reduces to utter dependence.

The world into which the young man is introduced is as horrible as the brain can devise. There is Stewart Andrewes, the newspaper editor ('He knew what the British public wanted. It wanted what he made it want. Two things only. Sex and scapegoats.') And Ronnie Gras, the fat dress-designer with his passion for food and wine and his girl-slave of a secretary: 'I hate being kissed where my hair is receding. I'm reminded of my age.' . . .

If this world did not exist, there would be no need for the author to be anonymous.[68]

John's remark, in reviewing Fritz Peters's *Finistère*, that 'His pity for all the characters purges the book,' enunciates the theme that recurs most often and most insistently in his reviewing: that a novel must be written with heart, with sympathy, even pity. The quality he most deplored was what he called 'uncharity'. This was the defect which, for him, ruined *Festival at Fairbridge*, J. B. Priestley's topical novel designed to 'cash in on' the Festival of Britain in 1951.

I dislike much of the book [John wrote], because so much of it is bad-tempered. The slapstick comedy too often deviates into theatrical 'business'. None of the chief characters is alive. Mr Priestley shares at any rate this with Dickens – he cannot draw good women. Nor can he draw good men. The only people he can describe accurately and sometimes brilliantly are those he dislikes or despises, and they are many.

His chief indication that he approves of a man is that he smokes a pipe. There are at least five pipe-smokers in the novel, all approved of by the author. A pipe and a stiff whisky and a leather armchair, socialism combined with plenty of brass and taciturn silence broken by rudeness, seem to be the qualifications for a hero. Qualifications for villainy are interest in the Third Programme and documentary films, a critical faculty, liking modern literature or art or verse-drama, or being Conservative, or Communist . . .

The great comic novelists wrote out of love for their fellow-creatures and hatred of oppression. Mr Priestley's book sounds peevish and disappointed beside them.[69]

Nancy Mitford was a friend to whom John had once light-heartedly proposed marriage, but he could not take the heartlessness of her novel *The Blessing*. He found the plot 'a little too heart-rending to be in keeping with the funny characters . . .'.[70] The best he could say for the novel was that it was 'unforgivably entertaining' and that there were, he was pretty sure, no hidden allegories in it. He rated it much below her *The Pursuit of Love* – unlike Evelyn Waugh, who assured her that *The Blessing* was 'by far the best of your writings'.[71]

In some of John's *Telegraph* reviews one sees the germ of a Betjeman poem, a phrase or idea which later recurs more tellingly in verse. His scorn at the pipe-smokers in J.B. Priestley's Festival novel anticipates a stanza in his later poem 'Monody on the Death of a Platonist Bank Clerk' –

These are his pipes. Ah! how he loved them,
   Puffed and petted them after walks,
After tea and a frowst with crumpets,
   Puffed the smoke into serious talks.[72]

Again, in *Summoned by Bells* (1960), John wrote of his Marlborough
schooldays:

Doom! Shivering doom! Clutching a leather grip
Containing things for the first night of term . . .
   Those few who read Dean Farrar's *Eric* now
Read merely for a laugh; yet still for me
That mawkish and oh-so-melodious book
Holds one great truth – through every page there runs
The schoolboy sense of an impending doom . . .[73]

Eight years earlier, reviewing *In the Making*, G.F. Green's novel of
'terrifying intensity' about a boys' school, John wrote:

Above all this book has in it that great feature of school life we all forget,
the sense of impending doom. People laugh at 'Eric' and Dean Farrar's
other school novel, 'St Winifred's', yet I think that for all their mawkish-
ness those stories are more like school than many more recent realistic
school stories, because they are full of that sense of disaster ahead, and
the sudden unreasoning fury of those in authority, whether parents, older
boys or masters. Here is G.F. Green on his hero's impending fateful visit
to his headmaster:

Randal went to Mr Western's study after breakfast, which had been
brought to him in the Sick Room. The fire was splintering in the grate
and a white morning mist shone in the window.

Oh, dreaded tidy sanctum! Expulsion? A beating? Public disgrace? In how
many minutes will Mr Western arrive?[74]

In January 1954 John wrote: 'The way that women love the most
loathsome men, and love them the more the more horrible they are,
is the theme of "A Bed of Roses" by William Sansom. I would find it
hard to discover a nastier good-looking, self-confident bully than
Guy Harrowby. The description in the opening chapter of this book
of how he locks up his girl-friend Louise in a clothes cupboard, and
her emotions as he smashes her glass toys, relics of childhood, so
that she can hear him doing it from her dark prison, is probably the
most powerful thing in the book.'[75] In his poem 'Huxley Hall', which

appeared in *A Few Late Chrysanthemums* later that year, John wrote:

> Barry smashes Shirley's dolly, Shirley's eyes are crossed with hate,
> Comrades plot a Comrade's downfall 'in the interests of the State'.[76]

In June 1951 John reviewed Peter Fleming's adventure story *The Sixth Column*, about a Russian plot to turn Britain into 'a sort of garden suburb of Europe'.

Here is an example of Peter Fleming on the British desire to excel in some field other than that in which they are by nature and training qualified for success:

> ... the senior Civil Servant would exchange his prospects of a knighthood for one really good photograph of a Great Northern Diver feeding her young, the don dreams of Everest. The trait has in general a civilizing effect and helps to keep us a nation of amateurs, but its consequences can occasionally be dangerous.

> It is such engaging comment which reminds us that here is someone who is more than a thriller writer.[77]

John's poem 'Mortality', published in *High and Low* (1966), contains the lines:

> The first-class brains of a senior civil servant
>   Shiver and shatter and fall
> As the steering column of his comfortable Humber
>   Batters in the bony wall . . .
> That very near miss for an All Souls' Fellowship
>   The recent compensation of a 'K' –
> The first-class brains of a senior civil servant
>   Are sweetbread on the road today.[78]

In May 1959, reviewing a collection by the young poet Christopher Logue, John wrote:

Christopher Logue's 'Songs' are angry young stuff by a poet who speaks vigorously for himself.

> 'Logue grinds his axe again. He's red,
>   Or cashing in.' And you are right.

> I have an axe to grind. Compared to you
> I'm red and short of cash. So what?
> I think, am weak, need help, have lived,
> And will, with your permission, live.

The format of his book and the way the poems are printed in various types, sometimes heavy, sometimes italic, sometimes small and often sans serif, remind me of early Vorticist publications, as do the poems. Logue is obviously a poet. He writes poetry because he must . . .[79]

Logue's being upbraided by name for 'cashing in' with his poetry may possibly have suggested a line in a poem of John's (again published in *High and Low*), ironically entitled 'Reproof Deserved *or* After the Lecture' – 'Betjeman, I bet your racket brings you in a pretty packet . . .'[80]

Even works which did not influence John could appeal to him because images or themes in them chimed with those of his own verse. In *Patrick Campbell*'s *Omnibus* (1954), a collection of newspaper 'funny pieces', John enjoyed the story 'Saved by the Bell'.

> I like his description of the Australian sports-girl:

>> . . . as strong as a kangaroo. She looked indeed quite like a kangaroo, bleached and sun-burned, with her longish nose, short, compact arms and powerful springy legs.

> And I like the large foreign lady who has been roped in to play 'Murder' at a country house party and who says 'Pleace, boyss! Strankle jaintly. Else veel foll down my draiss.'[81]

There tower the powerful women of John's 'Invasion Exercise on the Poultry Farm', 'The Licorice Fields at Pontefract' and 'The Olympic Girl'. In May 1955 he praised a similar character in Dennis Parry's novel *Sea of Glass*: 'Varvara, this grand, athletic, vigorous girl, comes striding through the pages, bursting with life and teeming with hockey-girl attraction and sweet Russian *naïveté*.'[82] Perhaps when he reviewed Michael Swan's first novel, *The Paradise Garden*, in 1956 its central character, 'Anna Falconer, who lives on the banks of the Beaulieu river, and is the only child of a crushed mother and a bullying retired major of a father', reminded him of Clemency, General Buckland's daughter, whom he had put into his poem 'Youth and Age on Beaulieu River, Hants'.[83] And he may have been tickled by the echo of his own poem 'Eunice' in Lewis Gibbs's novel of 1958, *Gowns and Satyr's Legs*. ('Its author has a witty style of which this is a specimen:

"Miss Gray's Christian name was Eunice, which had the effect of giving her surname the life and colour it so badly needed." ')[84]

When Bentley and Ziman sent him poems to review, John was usually generous in his response, even with poets whose style was quite foreign to his. He admired Dylan Thomas, and the compliment was returned: Thomas recalled, in a recording, how he had read Betjeman poems to an audience of bemused 'bobby-soxers' on an American campus. However, John preferred Thomas's incantatory prose to his poems. In August 1955 he wrote of the Welshman's *A Prospect by the Sea*:

> Dylan Thomas's imagination and sense of words is [*sic*] wholly Celtic, and he owes something to T. F. Powys and James Joyce. But he makes an interesting contrast with Thomas Hardy, whose poetry he so much admired. Hardy's novels seem to me to be a preparation for his poetry, Dylan Thomas's poems and early prose writings seem to me the preparation for his later clear prose, much of it autobiographical, which may be found in 'Portrait of the Artist as a Young Dog', 'Under Milk Wood' and the four pieces at the end of this book. Finally, I would commend to all literary aspirants his piece in this book called 'How to be a Poet'.[85]

In 1960 John applied his 'odious comparisons' technique in reviewing the Scottish poet Alastair Reid (who is also credited with composing the most celebrated modern palindrome, about T. S. Eliot).

> Alastair Reid is a young poet between boards and he certainly deserves to be. 'Oddments, Inklings, Omens, Moments' well describes the clear moments of vision he has been vouchsafed and which he puts down so freshly and sharply. I take one stanza (if such it can be called) from his poem 'Pigeons'.
>
> > Arriving in rainbows of oil-and-water feathers
> > they fountain down from buttresses and outcrops
> > from Fontainbleau and London,
> > and squat on the margins of roofs with a gargoyle look,
> > they note, from an edge of air, with hooded eyes,
> > the city slowly lessening the sky.
>
> This seems to me exact, interesting and original. I cannot help comparing it with the first stanza of a poem called 'The Sparrows' from 'Begging the Dialect' by Robin Skelton:
>
> > From a sour garden wrinkled with trees,
> > in the well of yellow houses, tall
> > as yesterday's syllables, the birds,
> > plucking at crumbs, step into mind,

> random and delicate, with all
> the desperate aplomb of their kind.

Here the description is so literary and cerebral that I forget about the words in puzzling out the simile about syllables.[86]

Ironically, it was to be Robin Skelton, a lecturer in English at the University of Victoria, British Columbia, in the 1970s, who was largely responsible for persuading the University to purchase the bulk of John's papers.

John recommended the Cornish poet Charles Causley[87], the veteran Ralph Hodgson ('I recaptured the exaltation the poems gave me years ago')[88] and 'that beautiful, too little appreciated poet, Bernard Spencer' – who had been at Marlborough with John.[89] In 1959 he reviewed *Jiving to Gyp*, a book of poems by Royston Ellis, an eighteen-year-old boy from Rickmansworth. 'It ashamedly and vigorously sets down in a series of rhythmic sketches what it is like to leave Rickmansworth and mother and go "Jiving to Gyp" in Soho "in cuddly sweater / and trousers typically tapered".'[90] John added that the poems reminded him of *Wild Party*, the book he had daringly bought for a Heddon Court pupil in the 1920s.

In 1957 he had reviewed another poet of contemporary life, Thom Gunn – 'the poet of, among other things, motorcyclists, though I rather doubt whether those who attend scrambles and rallies will learn his poems by heart'.[91] In the same review John praised *The Descent into the Cave and Other Poems* by James Kirkup, the homosexual poet whose poems he had published in *Time and Tide*. 'Mr Kirkup writes free rhythmical verse – that is to say he writes lines which clearly are not prose but which rarely conform to a known metrical form. He writes with complete clarity of expression. Quite how remarkable a poet he is you will realise when I tell you that he manages . . . to make a moving and even beautiful poem, neither facetious nor filthy, out of a Public Convenience.' Readers of the *Daily Telegraph* who bought the book on John's say-so would have found themselves reading these lines:

> With what passionate relief
> Men entered here, and made their scrolls
> Of joyous water; with what voluptuous ferocity restrained
> Themselves no longer, confessing dreams beyond belief!

In his memoir *A Poet Could Not But Be Gay* (1991), Kirkup remembered John with gratitude.

When he was reviewing for the *Daily Telegraph*, Betjeman made a very perceptive remark, that modern poems were becoming more and more like short stories. With the decline of the short story (and the short-story market) in Britain, the poets were taking over the usual domestic–provincial–academic themes of that form, and translating or rather transposing them into verse of the Larkin school, for the most part (unlike some of Larkin's work) extremely dreary, banal and anti-poetic, giving contemporary poetry the bad name from which it has still not recovered . . . Betjeman sent me a cutting of the review he did of my book of poems, *The Descent into the Cave*, with a note saying, 'to an obviously un-Telegraph man'. It was a very good review, one of the few the book received. He also invited me to lunch at Kettner's and to what he called the 'Bertie Woosterish' Wheeler's in Charlotte Street, mainly I think to fish for information about the 'Barone' Seymour Kirkup, the eccentric mediumistic painter and member of the Pisan Circle who discovered Giotto's portrait of Dante. His oddity and his friendship in later life with Swinburne must have attracted Betjeman's passion for unusual Victoriana.[92]

In 1960 John gave up reviewing books for the *Daily Telegraph*, contributing instead a column about architecture, 'Men and Buildings'. The heading made clear his view that buildings should never be considered just as aesthetic *objets*; the shellfish mattered as much as the shells. The series brought him a new friend (though she was mainly a pen-friend), the artist Leonora Ison, whom the *Telegraph* asked to illustrate his articles. She had already proved her ability as a newspaper artist by making drawings for three pieces on historic houses by J. H. Plumb.[93] She and her husband Walter had written books on two of John's favourite cities – Bath (in 1948) and Bristol (1952).[94] She was a friend of John Summerson, who thought her 'one of the very best architectural draughtsmen of her generation'.[95] John respected her too, and the 'Dear Mrs Ison' of his many letters to her never changed to a 'Leonora' overture. Her ancestors interested him, especially one of her great-grandfathers, James Wilkinson, who translated Swedenborg's works and was a friend of Henry James.[96] In the Thirties Leonora and Walter Ison shared a house in Doughty Street, London, with Robert Harling – the writer–designer with whom John had several spats in that decade when editing the magazine *Decoration*.[97] In 1952 Walter became architectural editor of *The Survey of London*. It was either Robert Harling or Leonard Russell, Walter thought, who recommended Leonora to the features editor of the *Telegraph* to be John's illustrator.[98]

The partnership worked very well. Leonora knew her rôle was that of an accompanist, not a soloist. She could draw stylized vignettes

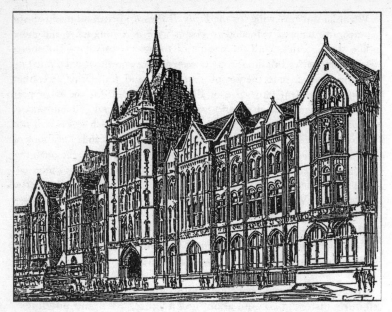

Drawing by Leonora Ison of the Prudential Assurance Building, High Holborn

comparable with the wood-engravings of her friend Reynolds Stone; but in the *Telegraph* her line, though still fastidious, was freer, more flexible.

John would write to tell Leonora what London buildings or country town he was about to cover, often making suggestions for drawings in rough sketches of his own. She did not always accept his ideas. In March 1961 he wrote to her: 'I quite agree. Your sketch of the Jewellery quarter gives a much better impression than mine.'[99] Seven months later he asked her to think of a beautiful village and also one that had been ruined by road-widening, then to draw them. When she did so, he wrote: 'You could not have chosen a better contrasting view. It says just what I want.'[100] A typical note from him ran: 'I must congratulate you on that really brilliant pair of drawings – subtle, unexaggerated, funny and moving.'[101] He could be more critical, as in September 1962: 'Yes, v[ery] nice. BUT some buildings in each drawing must be clearly identifiable and you might need to show a little more of the left hand one in (2) so as to establish visually (as no one ever reads my articles or the captions) that they are both drawings of the same street.'[102]

Often John used the *Telegraph* column for an eleventh-hour attempt to save a building. He wrote an article in 1963 when the riverside buildings at Rotherhithe, where his and Elizabeth's friend Lord Snowdon had lived, and John had taken refuge after the Cloth Fair fire, were threatened by the London County Council.[103] As too often happened, the buildings were demolished all the same. In John's letters to Leonora, his anger at what was happening to the City of London frequently broke through. In February 1964 he wrote:

> If you go to Route 11 on the Barbican site, you will see . . . the tatty masonry of the demolished church of St Alfege [*sic*], London Wall, carefully preserved like a weedless and pointless rockery amid the new glass blocks. Above it is one of these pointless podia passes along which Londoners are meant to stroll in warm weather, if there ever is any, looking at the shops and looking down at the traffic on Route 11. If you can show this lip service to the old in its inhuman setting and all its ridiculousness, I should like to title it 'Antiquarianism Run Mad' . . .[104]

The Betjeman–Ison collaboration came to an end that year. On 27 July he wrote to her:

> I have become the subject of a take-over bid and fear that this is to be our last article together in the Daily Telegraph. I have been transferred to one of these new colour supplements, which will mean, I expect, the use of photography and I do not know who will be taking my place. It is sad to think our long association on the coarse newsprint of the Daily Telegraph is to end. I expect Brian Harvey [the *Telegraph*'s features editor] will be getting in touch with you. How odd it is to think that the only time we met on the job personally was when I talked to you on a bitterly cold day in Queen's College, Oxford, when you were drawing the new lodgings for the Provost. I am sad to think of no more letters to Whitstable to you and the O.C. [Old Cartographer],[105] for your drawings have been a more essential part of Men and Buildings than my prose.[106]

As his swansong, John had decided to write about some of the older architects he had known, including Lutyens. With his usual thoughtfulness,[107] he wrote to Leonora: 'As coming to London in summer is even nastier than coming at other times, I have thought of two Kentish houses which might not be too inconvenient for you from Whitstable . . .' [108]

Peter Fleetwood-Hesketh took over the column from John. Leonora found him 'rather tiresome' and, Walter recalled, 'his successor, John Chisholm, chose such uninteresting subjects that she decided it was time for her to make a change and concentrate on flower painting. Her retirement brought the "Men and Buildings" articles to a close.'[109] John and Leonora continued to correspond intermittently, and in 1983, as her last commission, she made several drawings to supplement those which had appeared in the *Telegraph*, for Frank Delaney to use in his book *Betjeman Country*. In his introduction, Delaney wrote: 'Mrs Ison captured Betjeman country in its heyday, at a time when he was most prolific . . . and Mrs Ison echoed the world as he saw it, a sort of visualizing amanuensis.'[110]

By moving to the *Telegraph*'s colour magazine, John received higher fees for his articles; but he also fell into the clutches of one of the most notorious editors in Fleet Street. John Anstey was a man of some surface charm. In his large office, with its well-stocked cocktail cabinet, he would talk expansively and wittily. Like a caliph in his harem, he surrounded himself with no fewer than four secretaries – more than the editor of *The Times* boasted. He was a renowned bottom-pincher who thought it a joke to dowse one of his secretaries with a fire-extinguisher. He was also known as a great sacker. His successive features editors took the same sort of gamble on survival as Henry VIII's wives. None of this need have bothered John; but what did affect him was Anstey's bizarre method of editing. When an article came in – from John or anybody else – Anstey would send it round to various members of his staff for their comments and criticisms. It was then the task of the hapless features editor of the moment to write the contributor a letter summarizing all the criticisms and suggesting the many ways in which, it was felt, the article could be 're-jigged' and 'improved'.[111] The pay was good and other authors were prepared to put up with this humiliating treatment; but to John it became insufferable. In June 1969 he wrote to Mary Wilson: 'I *may* be landing a job editing a sort of gazeteer of the UK which may free [me] from the hateful *Daily Telegraph Magazine*. I am to do what will, pray God, be my last article for it, today or tomorrow.'[112] In fact he stayed the course another four months. On 16 October he wrote to Patrick Leigh Fermor: 'I've chucked the *D[aily] Telegraph* and dropped two and a half thousand pounds per annum plus five hundred expenses. And has it been worth it? My God, yes. It's freedom. News-paper men are shits.'[113]

4

SUMMONED BY BELLS

Tell me exactly what you think of the new Betjeman poem. The brief verdict at Cambridge was 'It stinks', which is surely a little exaggerated. Dick Routh[1] *per contra* puts it at the very top of all the poems he had read, which again seems to lack balance.

Rupert Hart-Davis[2] to George Lyttelton[3], 12 January 1961. *The Lyttelton Hart-Davis Letters 1955–1962: A Selection*, ed. Roger Hudson, London 2001 edn.

John's generation was given to premature autobiography. In 1926 Beverley Nichols brazenly published *Twenty-Five* – the age he then was. Christopher Isherwood was thirty-four when his *Lions and Shadows* appeared in 1938; Cyril Connolly thirty-five when *Enemies of Promise* was published in the same year; John's Magdalen friend Henry Green (Henry Yorke) also thirty-five when *Pack My Bag* was issued in 1940; Stephen Spender forty-two when *World within World* came out in 1951. Tom Driberg published a discreet memoir, *The Best of Both Worlds*, at forty-eight in 1953 (his full flagrancies only appeared in *Ruling Passions*, issued after his death). John was fifty-four when John Murray published his verse autobiography *Summoned by Bells* in 1960.

The impulse toward early self-portraiture was so marked in the males of John's generation that it is tempting to seek an underlying psychological cause. They grew up in the shadow of the First World War. Another war was threatened, and soon it was upon them. The menace of nuclear weapons supervened.[4] Did they feel a need to put themselves on record in case they were snuffed out? Alternatively, all these autobiographers were sent away to prep schools and public schools. Perhaps the shocks and traumas of those experiences fixed their interest on their schooldays, as an earthquake stops the clocks. Reviewing a book on Cyril Connolly, Peter Ackroyd has written: 'It is hard to think of another generation of English writers who have come so exclusively from the upper middle class and who have been so obsessed with their education. The result was, of course, that many of them remained perpetually immured in their adolescence.' Again, with the rampant exception of Henry Green, all these men were homosexual or bisexual. The hankering after 'lost youth' is a recurrent theme of 'Uranian' poets' love. The autobiographies deal primarily with infancy, school and university; at the end of the television adaptation of *Summoned by Bells* (1976), John confessed that no other part of his life was of interest to him.[5]

Early in 1960 John did his friend Cecil Roberts[6] the service of correcting the proofs of his *Selected Poems 1910–60*, which included 'The Old Brown Hat (John Betjeman's)' about a burst of inspiration John had enjoyed in 1952. John wrote to Roberts from a house near Killarney about the phenomenal sale of his own *Collected Poems* and the ensuing publicity. 'He was now apprehensive,' Roberts wrote. 'I had recommended him to go into a sort of Wordsworthian "retreat" and to get on with a blank verse poem, à la "Prelude".'[7] John wrote to Roberts:

> I would have written before had I not spent two weeks of Irish peace, walking and driving and loitering and in the mornings going on with my blank verse autobiography, which few will read and fewer praise, but which is what I want to do. I hope you will not be disappointed with it. I am going to stop when I am twenty-three, as after that I got into the old literary groove we all know. It covers early childhood, Cornwall, Dragon School (as far as I've got), London in the twenties, Marlborough, Oxford, ending with being a private schoolmaster after being sent down. So the Wordsworthian seclusion you prescribed is being indulged in so far as it is financially possible.[8]

Roberts's memoirs, deliberately ambiguous, might give the impression that John had shut himself away to write a 'Prelude' on his suggestion, and that that was the genesis of *Summoned by Bells*. It was not so. As long ago as 1941 John had sent John and Myfanwy Piper the typescript of a long autobiographical poem in blank verse to which he referred in letters as 'The Epic'. At that stage, most of the poem was about the Betjemanns' Cornish holidays. Large parts of it were siphoned off and published, with some emendations and changes of names, as 'North Coast Recollections' (first in the *West Country Magazine*, Spring 1947, then in *Selected Poems*, 1948). Other extensive passages were used, again with some changes, in *Summoned by Bells*. A few passages in the early version of the 'Epic' were never published – less because John thought them of inferior quality than because he felt they were too harsh about his parents and might give offence to surviving relatives. One passage never used was this:

> Last year on picnics it was just the same
> 'John, don't go down the cliff path! John, come back!'

'Why don't you get into the open air?'
'Why don't you go and play like other boys?'
'John, run and get my bag. It's in my room.
And don't disturb your father, he's asleep.'
'John, do as mother tells you. Get her bag.'
'O! Father, but I thought you were asleep.'
'Don't argue. Run and do it. Cut along.'
John do, John don't, John run, John cut, blast damn.
'O! John, the pain I suffer when I walk.'

Also never published were Mrs Betjemann's comments on her teeth –

'Wilfred [Ernest] would never pay to have them done,
Though, goodness knows, he never stints himself.
Last week I found his tailor's bill – he'd paid
Seventeen guineas for a shooting suit.'

Part of Ernest's complaint to John was cut out –

'My boy, when I was your age I was made
To scrub my father's shop at half past six;
At seven I made the head assistant's tea,
And, sharp at eight, was rolling calico.
Yes, real work! and now I look at you . . .

The cruellest passage John excised was this:

These hideous people, were they really his?
That sagging woman with her 'Craven A'?
This beefy business man with steely eyes –
'Sir James was telling me the other day' –
The studied ease with which he said 'Sir James',
The half-pay colonels whom he called his friends,
Their jolly voices and class-conscious air,
The war-time captains who were more his sort:
'How well he thought of men who made their way' . . .
And in some gas-lit bedroom did they mate?
And say was I the undesired result?

The bulk of *Summoned by Bells* was written between the early
months of 1958 and the early months of 1960. When the poem
was broadly completed, a typescript was sent first to Tom Driberg,
then to John Sparrow, for them to make comments and to suggest

possible changes. Preserved in Murray's archives, the typescript bears copious marginalia by Driberg, Sparrow and John, with the odd addition by Jock Murray. Driberg and Sparrow expressed themselves with great freedom and often with a jocose *de haut en bas* tone, as when the word 'proffering', in John's line 'My father, proffering me half a crown, said . . .', draws from Sparrow the comment, 'How many times must I tell you that you must not drag out such words into three syllables. TD is right.' (Driberg had written: 'Awkward scansion – As he proffered half a crown?'[9] In the published version, John opted for 'My father, handing to me half-a-crown'.) Driberg is severe on mixed tenses. Sparrow is for ever replacing 'which' with 'that' – 'John Sparrow is a great which-hunter,' Jock Murray quipped.[10]

John did not accept all Driberg's and Sparrow's suggestions meekly. The poem begins:

> Here on the southern slope of Highgate Hill
> Red squirrels leap the hornbeams . . .

Sparrow wrote in the margin: 'You are *sure* these were hornbeams? and *red* squirrels?' John wrote: 'Yes.' A little further on came the lines:

> Then Millfield Lane looked like a Constable
> And all the grassy hillocks spoke of Keats.

'Not to you,' wrote Sparrow, 'who had not heard of them then. Omit.' John left the lines in, retorting, 'But there is a lot I wouldn't have noticed at that time . . .'[11] Where John wrote of his surname:

> That tee-jay-ee, that fatal tee-jay-ee
> Which I have watched the hesitating pens
> Of Government clerks and cloakroom porters funk . . .

Driberg suggested the more metrically correct 'bureaucrats' instead of 'Government clerks'. John wrote under the suggestion, 'I don't mind' but eventually chose to vary the steady metre with an irregular heart-beat, and left the line as it was.[12]

Many other suggestions John accepted. Where he wrote of his mother's bridge-playing friends in Chelsea:

> Did they in anger sometimes leave the house
> After those hot post-mortems?

Driberg commented ' "In anger" is misplaced. Perhaps: "Did they, I wonder, leave us in a huff . . ." ' John made the change suggested.

And where John wrote, of Colonel Kolkhorst's 'Sunday mornings' at Oxford,

> If that's what heaven's like it won't be bad . . .

Driberg wrote, 'A *wee* bit sentimental in the Godfrey Winn manner?' John responded 'I agree' and deleted the line.[13]

    John agonized most about the lines that described the love he had felt for Donovan Chance at Marlborough.[14] Partly at Sparrow's urging, partly on his own initiative, he deleted large passages from this section of the poem – which, however, survive in the typescript at Murray's.

> O dreadful sin against the Holy Ghost!
>   Sin for which ~~Blanksome~~ Major was expelled   Branksome
> The only sin which could not be forgiven
>   Even by God in chapel.
> 'Break temptation's fatal power,
>   Shielding all with guardian care;
> Safe in every careless hour
>   Safe from sloth and sensual snare
>   Thou our Saviour
> Still our failing strength repair.'
>
> This nameless evil sapped one's strength for games,
> It made the mind too weak to pass exams,
> Rotted the will, for ever stained the soul
> And drove its victims on to suicide.
> There were unmentionable forms of sin
> For which one went to prison. Oscar Wilde
> Had practised them. Thus life was only safe
> Exchanging scandal with contemporaries:
> And love, of course, was poles apart from sex.

In the original, these lines were followed immediately by the lines which introduce Donovan Chance in the published poem, beginning, ' "Coming down town?" I had not thought of him . . .'

    Other early drafts of the Marlborough poem which, in the published version, begins 'The smell of trodden leaves beside the Kennet . . .' contain these stanzas:

> ~~I could not analyse the new emotion~~ Intense and inexplicable emotion
>   Here by the fives-courts, by myself at last

~~I revelled in the warm enclosing ocean~~ I longed to meet the
                                      warm enclosing ocean
  Of love to come and persecution past
Here 'twixt the church tower and the chapel spire
Rang sad and deep the bells of my desire.

Sad, deep and vast, bells through the branches pealing
  Under the clouds which raced from Granham Hill
Gave me that guilty, dread religious feeling
  Those lovers know whom only dreams fulfil.
Lit windows rose impersonal and grim
But lights in one house class-room shone on him.

Though Mr Gidney's hours were now no brighter,
  Nor could I concentrate on verbs ~~in Greek~~   in μί
Yet dark school passages were made the lighter
  By the mere whirlwind of his rushing by.
The labs might show him meddling with retorts
Or goalposts frame him in his muddy shorts.

'Vainly we offer each ample oblation.'
  The hymns in chapel had a meaning new
'Richer by far is the heart's adoration'
  Lucky, by Jove, were his hymn book and pew
He read the one and rested on the other
'Oh brother man, fold to thy heart a brother.'

(Then followed the stanza beginning 'The smell of trodden leaves . .
.', later transferred to the beginning of the poem.)[15]

How could I have withstood those five years flowing
  From boredom on to boredom; how endure
Without romantic love to keep them going –
  Romantic love so rarefied and pure
That the sole reason why it never died
Was just because it was unsatisfied.

Hot summers of discovering liberation
  Moving from Oscar Wilde to *Antic Hay*
Commanding Officers' exasperation
  On Corps parades: The tedious Molière play:
Escaping cricket by the skilful ruse
Of biking off to sketch with Mr Hughes.

'Castle and Ball' when stopping in my motor
  To drink within your warming-pann'd recess

I still recall my mother's fearful floater
~~By coming down in far two young a dress~~ When she came
                    down in far too young a dress
For Prize Day and I recollect my dread
As the lounge listened to the things she said.

(Sparrow wrote of this: 'Irrelevant stanza. It's not good. It doesn't reproduce the anguish or the [romantic?] ecstasy.')[16]

Fresh and refreshed I motor past the College
    Whose prison walls look still the same and close
Round those grim classrooms of pedantic knowledge
    Where the years showed me who were friends and foes
Two things your stern conventions taught me well:
What joy it was to love and to rebel.

(Sparrow wrote: 'This lyric is not up to standard. Try to remember what being in love at school was *really* like.')[17]

In the original version of the Marlborough poem, John wrote:

Was God what I was waiting for, or love?

Sparrow commented: ' "Was God what I was waiting for?" is a false note. God was not what you were waiting for, nor did you think it was Him. Don't mention Him.'[18] For the published version, John changed the line to

Perhaps what I was waiting for was love!

In the early draft, John's description of his love as 'a delightful illness That put me off my food and off my stroke' is followed by the couplet:

Electric currents racing through my frame –
Was this the love that dare not speak its name?

These lines were cut from the printed version and replaced by a less explicit couplet; however, John recycled the 'electric current' notion in the next chapter, in recounting his love for Biddy Walsham in Cornwall –

                      If my hand
By accident should touch her hand, perhaps
The love in me would race along to her
On the electron principle, perhaps . . . ?

In the typescript, the Marlborough poem, in its six-line stanzas, was followed by the continuation of the main narrative of *Summoned by Bells*, beginning:

> Desire for what? I think I can explain
> The boys I worshipped did not worship me
> The boys who worshipped me I did not like . . .
> And life was easier in terms of jokes
> And gossip, chattered with contemporaries –
> Till one there was – yes one there was whose light
> Irradiated all the summer term
> Neither through what he did nor what he thought –
> His interests were chiefly motor-cars,
> His friends not my friends – did we come together
> The usual greetings in the gravel court,
> The shouted joke, flying along with books
> He to the Science, I to the History Sixth,
> The wink across the parted chapel pews.
> Occasional visits after lunch down town.
> To Stratton, Sons & Mead for groceries,
> Agreement upon masters we disliked
> And priggish boys and prefects in the house –
> These were of each of us the outward sum
> And sex, the sin against the Holy Ghost,
> Was quite unthinkable. It would pollute
> The freckled innocence of one who seemed
> So perfect that I now believed in God
> So handsome his existence was enough . . .

Very little of this passage survived in the published poem, perhaps as a result of Sparrow's remonstrance in the typescript's margin:

> 'The boys I worshipped . . .' These lines just won't do. Who are these 'boys' (plural)? *What is this 'worship'*? You introduce this whole poignant theme with two flat lines and it turns out to be only *one*, after all. And you don't give the feel of it. He might be anybody. Try to *remember* Donovan C! Give personal details of *him*! Recreate your feelings for him – if you ever had any, and I am beginning to suspect you of not having done so. Don't insist too much on the innocence of the passion (which I readily accept), but convey its intensity (as you do so well for 'John Lambourn' in 'North Coast Recollections'). In short this is NOT up to snuff. You must try again. Sorry, but so it is.[19]

Sparrow, supremely uninterested in girls, also wanted John to cut the lines about his childhood feeling for Biddy Walsham, in the 'Cornwall in Adolescence' chapter. Opposite the last line of the penultimate 'paragraph' of that section, ('She would explain that I was still a boy') Sparrow wrote: 'PLEASE end this canto here. It is such a good end and leads on so well to the next, "The Opening World". And the lines about Biddy Walsham are not in keeping or in context and are NOT good in themselves – second-grade Betjeman. What goes before is first-grade. Don't spoil it.'[20] John took Sparrow's criticism seriously, and right up to a late proof stage was undecided whether to cut the Biddy Walsham passage. Eventually he followed Elizabeth Cavendish's and Jock Murray's advice and left it in.

One passage John did decide to omit was about Hugh Gaitskell and about alleged black magic at Exeter College, Oxford.

> New College waits us with her Wykehamists!
>   Already half a don,
>   Sparrovian John
> Among his spreading rows of leather spines
> Knows not of that bare room whose bright bulb shines
> On essays, scholar's gown and lecture-lists,
> And hard and new
> On your Left Book Club books in orange row,
> Gaitskellian Hugh
> G.D.H. Cole,
> Infuse my soul,
> But ere you quite convert us let us go
> Past the Bodleian with its rows of bikes
> To Gothic Exeter so full of spikes
>   And was black magic practised there? Did we
>   After a High Church dinner party see
> In those dim colleges that front the Turl
>   Satan's forked tail uncurl
> In deadly battle with the exorcists?

Another passage John cut, perhaps for fear of a libel action by C. S. Lewis, was about the references supplied to him when he sought a job as a prep-school master.

> Sir Cyril Norwood kindly praised my gifts;
> The Reverend J.M. Thompson praised my work;
> Roy Harrod and ~~Maurice Bowra~~ wrote a line   John Bryson
> But that coarse Ulster puritan and prig,
> My tutor, wrote a damning reference
> Which only said that I was amiable.

          I wisely left it from the envelope
          To J.H. Hope, Esquire, Heddon Court,
          Cockfosters, Barnet, Herts.

John's poem about being a cricket master at Heddon Court did not
appear in the hardback edition of *Summoned by Bells*, but was
published separately and was later tacked on to the paperback
edition. But, even in its published form, the poem differed signifi-
cantly from the typescript version. With most of John's cuts and
alterations, one feels he was wise to make them; but in the case of
the 'Cricket Master' poem, some of the amusing original lines –
presumably based on John's own experiences – are a regrettable
loss.

          'The MCC sends down an A team here.'
          'Oh thank you very much, I'll like the work;
          I'm keen on cricket, very keen indeed.'
          A last year's number of *The Cricketer*
          Was in the common room when I arrived
          And there I read a letter giving tips
          Called, 'teaching bowling to the young idea'.
          'Encourage boys to learn the art of breaks
          By painting a white patch before the crease'.
          So with a pail of whiting and a brush
          I hurried out to mark one in the nets.
          Though J.H. Hope had given me my post
          His elder partner Summers was away
          Upon the morning of my interview.
          I met him now in company with one,
          A thick Devonian called Huxtable,
          A new assistant too. The piercing eye
          Of Mr Summers registered dislike
          On sight of an aesthetic type like me.
          'Well, let us have a knock-up in the nets.'
          We strolled towards them. 'What on earth is this?'
          'Oh that's a patch I always like to paint
          To show the boys where they can pitch their breaks.'
          'Then go and get a pail and wash it out.'
          I did as I was told, while Huxtable
          And Summers looked sardonically on.
          'Now let's see how you bat. With but one pad
          No gloves, and knees that knocked in utter fright,
          Vainly I tried to fend the hail of balls

> Hurled at my head by Huxtable
> And at my shins by Summers. Evening light
> Threw its long shadows on the playing- field;
> Crossing to supper in the afterglow
> Huxtable took my arm: 'Well Betjeman,
> D'you want to know what Summers said to me?
> *He didn't think you'd ever held a bat.*'

As those lines show, John for the most part left people's real names in the typescript. 'Summers' and 'Huxtable' were altered to 'Winters' and 'Barnstaple' in the published version. The typescript reveals the true identities of others given pseudonymns when the poem was printed. 'Mr Purdick', the deaf invigilator at Marlborough, was in reality Mr Patrick –

> '*Do you tickle your arse with a feather, Mr Purdick?*'
> '*What?*'
> '*Particularly nasty weather, Mr Purdick!*'
> '*Oh.*'

And the boy who was covered with ink and treacle and hoisted in the giant waste-paper basket was Ingle – L.D.C Ingle, who had entered the school with John in 1920 and, according to the *Marlborough College Register*, did indeed leave early, as recorded in the poem ('Never to wear an old Marlburian tie'), and became a horticulturalist. In the poem, John called him 'Angus'. Though this retained the 'ng' sound and had the right number of syllables, it caused difficulties with the original line –

> Though Ingle's body called 'Unclean! Unclean!'

'Though Angus's body . . .' disrupted the scansion; so John had to change the line to –

> Though the boy's body called 'Unclean! Unclean!'

As early as 29 April 1959 Jock Murray could write to Leonard Russell, the literary editor of the *Sunday Times,* 'The vicissitudes of the present work have already been considerable.'[21] The poem's fitful progress can be traced in Murray's archives. On 13 February 1958 Jock Murray wrote a memorandum for the rest of the senior staff. 'John Betjeman called. He has actually started his Memoirs in blank verse. At the beginning he read three or four pages which are first rate.'[22] It was planned that the blank verse would be broken by poems on a given incident or person and also by line illustrations. For the earlier parts of the poem, the pictures would be extracted from books contemporary with the time about which John was writing. The later parts – Oxford days onwards – might have vignettes by Osbert Lancaster, 'excluding people'.[23]

Murray wrote to John on 19 March: 'The first chapter is marvellous. Forge on as fast as you can. Don't show it to too many people before it is in proof. Send more as soon as you can but let us only plan the style of the book when the typescript is finished. Nothing must divert you from putting it all down.' He added: 'Congratulations.'[24] Before John received Murray's warning about showing the poem to others, he had already sent the early pages to Stephen Spender for his opinion. Spender at once asked whether he might be allowed to publish them in *Encounter*. John had to write back, disappointingly, that 'Jock Murray says it cannot be published until it is complete. It is only part of a grand plan with which I am continuing.'[25] At that time, he was writing the lines about the Dragon School, which were to be followed by 'a chapter on Marlborough followed by a chapter on Oxford followed by being a schoolmaster with the great world of literature waiting to open its bronze doors as a finale'.[26] There was another good reason why John could not release the poem for publication in *Encounter*: he had signed a contract to allow the *New Yorker* first choice of his poems. 'I don't think it likely that they will want this epic,' John wrote to Spender, 'as it will be incomprehensible to the Americans . . . but they will have to be offered it . . .'[27]

On 2 September 1959, in another memo to the staff, Jock Murray recorded that he had just had lunch with John to celebrate the sale of 56,000 copies of the *Collected Poems*. While staying with Elizabeth Cavendish in Derbyshire John had completed another chapter of his verse memoirs and had nearly finished the Marlborough section.

> We went out on to the bombed site by St Paul's [Murray wrote] and he read the new twenty pages or so which are very good indeed . . .
>
> As to production: this is going to be a bit fancy. The area to be slightly larger than *Continual Dew*. It will have line illustrations in text at the breaks for pauses in the verse. Michael Tree is obviously in the running as being one of the illustrators. Piper might do Marlborough. Lancaster would probably do Oxford though there would be no human beings in any of the drawings. There is at present a plan to have a section at the end of the book devoted to advertisements to include commodities, railways, hotels, books – all items which were in evidence about the 1920s. Original blocks to be used where possible.[28]

Murray's 'at present' was probably a hint that, if he had his way in the matter, the plan to use old advertisements would be dropped at a later stage – and indeed it was. Michael Tree, Elizabeth Cavendish's brother-in-law, was not an artist in the same league as Piper and Lancaster; but it became clear to Murray that John was quite determined to have the book illustrated by Tree and he gave way on this point. (Lancaster wickedly echoed the song, 'I think that I shall never see A poem lovely as a Tree.')[29] John may have wished to please Elizabeth or cultivate Tree; or perhaps he genuinely thought that his scratchy, amateurish, 1910-guidebook style was right for the book. Tree made his drawings of Marlborough, St Enodoc Church and other locales, on the spot.

On the day after his lunch with John, Jock Murray wrote to the poet's then secretary, the Rev. Gordon Owen, 'Much looking forward to a typed copy of the continuation of the Great Work . . . Just for the record, I turned down on JB's behalf a request for a Christmas feature, a story or poem, from *Woman & Beauty*.'[30] On 11 September Owen sent Murray pages 27 to 54 of the poem. In a memo of 15 September Murray noted, 'Betjeman's thought for the title of his new book – the memoirs – is "Summoned by Bells".'[31] Although John later proposed a series of other possible titles, *Summoned by Bells* was eventually used.

In November, after staying with Elizabeth Cavendish, John wrote to Candida: 'I have written a lot of my verse autobiography but it is not yet finished . . . I have been working in the Derbyshire Dales – great folding limestone rocks, little black cottages, ivy and tinkling water falls. It is lovely beyond words. I shall not finish my autobiography this side of Christmas which is annoying.'[32] In February 1960 he did another stint of hard work in Cornwall. On the 10th he wrote to Penelope: 'I've *finished* the Epic. Now I will have to spend several weeks revising it and cutting the dead wood of which there is a lot and rendering some of the blank verse in lyric form, as there might be too much blank verse. I have no confidence in the thing. I doubt if it will even be a *succès d'estime*.'[33] On the same day he sent Jock Murray a postcard: 'The Epic is finished today but not yet revised and cut down. Some additional suggested titles to ~~summoned~~ Called by Bells – A Brillant Career; Not Cricket.'[34] On 22 February, Murray's editorial assistant Jane Boulanger wrote to John (the publisher was away with a bad cold) to thank him 'for the safe return of the corrected draft sent from the low level refreshment room at Crystal Palace'.[35] On 26 February, Murray, back at work, wrote to Katharine White, the deputy editor of the *New Yorker* and wife of E. B. White who wrote *Charlotte's Web*, 'Dear Mrs White, Rejoice. John Betjeman has finished his verse memoirs. The revise is being typed now but I send with this letter up to p. 47 which includes four sections. To me it is exciting and of course vividly recognizable. I wonder if it will ring any bells among an American audience. I hope so much that you will like it – all of it, or at least some of it.'[36] It was planned as an autumn book, he told her. He hoped she would permit part of the poem to be used in the *Cornhill Magazine* which was celebrating its centenary that year.[37] On 29 February he sent her the second and final instalment of the poem, adding, 'John Betjeman thinks that he may be omitting the lyric to Edward James but I am trying to persuade him to leave it in. This poem you saw separately and rejected it and it was subsequently published in *Punch*.'[38]

On 12 March John wrote to Murray suggesting types that he thought might be used for the book: 'The effect should be spacious.'[39] Two weeks later B. A. Young of *Punch* wrote to Murray saying that John had agreed in principle to *Punch*'s serializing his verse autobiography but had raised various points. Young added: 'According to John the poem "shows him up for the weak, bad, vain and selfish man that he is". I refuse to believe this – and in any case it need not involve the poem's being bad itself.'[40] Murray hastened to tell Young about the *New Yorker* arrangement. John's comment about the work was typical, he wrote. 'I expect he will wish us to advertise it as the work of an old hack writer.'[41] Tom Driberg had made his first set of corrections to the typescript by 29 March. The next day, John wrote to Murray asking that a copy of his epic should be sent 'post-haste' to Derek Stanford in Hounslow 'to help the poor fellow write his book about yours ever . . .'.[42] Jock Murray advised strongly against this, and suggested that Stanford should be told he could see a proof.

The *New Yorker* wrote on 1 April to give its decision: it wished to use a heavily cut version of the poem as a 'profile', at a flat fee of $2,500. Rachel MacKenzie, Mrs White's assistant, wrote that if John insisted he be paid at the 'line rate' the magazine would want to reconsider, because that would be 'out of line for a profile'.[43] John was with Elizabeth Cavendish in Derbyshire. Murray wrote to tell him of the *New Yorker*'s proposal. 'I want to talk to you about this but meanwhile I am doing a little haggling about terms with them.'[44] He suggested to Rachel MacKenzie ('I do not want to seem to be too grasping on John Betjeman's behalf . . .') a compromise payment, halfway between the line rate and the $2,500 fee suggested.[45] This proposal was accepted. The *New Yorker* promised to publish its extract before September. 'Timing is important,' Murray told Rachel MacKenzie. '. . . John is making some final corrections.'[46] This was to prove an over-optimistic assessment. Only on 14 April did the typescript go off to John Sparrow at All Souls for his comments. John wrote to him:

Darling Spansbury,

This is dictated in Jock's office because I have to go away. Jock is signing it. Here is the MS of my childhood epic. The provisional title is Summoned by Bells but you may think of another one. I thought of Lachrimae Rarum [*sic*]. [Here, Jock Murray wrote a large 'NO' in the margin.]

... It is very kind of you indeed to look at this work. You knew my parents, and you will be able to judge one of the chief things that bothers me about it, and that is: am I too hard on them, since they are dead and cannot answer back? I do not think my mother comes out of it very well. Yet I rather like what I have written about her. O Lord, what a cad one feels . . . [47]

The *New Yorker* sent an advance cheque for John, an initial payment of £1,000. However, Jock Murray was shocked by the copyright terms printed on the back of the cheque and told Mrs White that before it was cashed he must be assured that John would retain copyright in the poem and that he would be able to serialize it after its appearance in the *New Yorker*. [48] While that difficulty was being sorted out, another embarrassment had to be dealt with. John confessed to Murray that he had written a short poem on Princess Margaret's wedding for *Harper's Bazaar* in London. [49] Murray made him confess also to the *New Yorker*; Mrs White was very understanding and even agreed that the epithalamium ('not at all in JB's best form', Murray considered) might be printed in American *Harper's* too.

John Sparrow sent back the first part of the typescript on 27 April, expressing his admiration for Driberg's criticisms. He added: 'I think that John should put in a lot more work on the poem. It contains so much that is really his best work, and it will be his most important work. It is a pity that it should be spoilt by flat passages and careless blemishes. There are a great number of these and it should take him a great deal of time and trouble to remove them all, but I am sure it is worth doing.' [50]

Thanking Sparrow for the return of the first forty pages, Murray wrote, 'It is such a good work that nothing necessary should be spared.' He asked for the rest of the typescript back 'so JB can take it on 6 May to Derbyshire where he has promised that he and his typescript will be incommunicado'. [51] On 6 May Murray sent John, in Derbyshire, the full typescript with 'all the Driberg–Sparrow–Betjeman marginal conversation' and a clean duplicate on which John was to mark his final corrections for the printer. 'Please consider with the greatest caution', Murray urged, 'any of the deletion suggestions made by Sparrow. In one or two cases I think he is wrong because a book of this kind needs a stretch of breath-regaining narrative between the gems (mixed metaphor!).' [52] On 4 May Mrs White of the *New Yorker* wrote reassuring Jock about the copyright rubric on the back of John's cheque. Murray replied: 'I wish I could send you a finally revised typescript now but the process of revision has been incredibly complicated and a kind of running conversation has been carried on by John Betjeman's helpful (?) literary friends in the margins of the typescript. However, I spend next weekend with him when I hope we will settle on the final version . . .'[53]

On 17 May Murray wrote to her again, after spending the weekend with John at Elizabeth Cavendish's house; luckily, the poet had made only a few changes to add to those already sent to New York.[54] Five days earlier, the publisher had written for his staff a further memo about *Summoned by Bells*. At a meeting attended by Murray, John, Elizabeth Cavendish and Michael Tree, it had been decided to use Antique Old Style type. Initial capitals were to be used at the start of each section. 'At first it was thought that Michael Tree might design these, but it was decided to see what types the printer [Clowes] had and if it would be possible to get Morris Kelmscott caps.' Tree's drawings were to be finished by the end of May. ('Nothing was said about payment,' Murray noted.)[55]

Serial rights in Britain were complicated because everybody seemed to want them. The following, Murray recorded, had applied: the *Sunday Times*; *Punch* (rejected as it was agreed that '*Punch* was not the right place'); the *Daily Express* via George Malcolm Thomson;[56] who said that the features editor was very keen and would outbid anybody; Marcus Morris[57] of *Harper's Bazaar* and other glossy magazines (the request came through John); the BBC (Douglas Cleverdon,[58] also via John); Stephen Spender of *Encounter* and Kingsley Martin of the *New Statesman*. 'JB at the moment prefers the *Sunday Times*,' Murray wrote. 'However he has agreed definitely that an extract should be allowed to be printed in the centenary *Cornhill*.'[59]

Like a war leader making plans for the peace to come, Murray had been discussing with John what he might do once the brouhaha over the launch of *Summoned by Bells* had died down.

JB'S great wish [Murray wrote] is to be able to do no writing, except occasional poems, for eighteen months. I explained that this was the time during which this was possible as he was earning large royalties and it was agreed that he would refuse all offers of literary work except occasional reviewing of books he wanted to review. There are many plans for books for us, including STREET, NORMAN SHAW, a volume of topography articles, an Approach to Victorian Architecture, the next volume of memoirs etc., so that he had no excuse for accepting any proposals from other publishers. However, in order to tie up with his wishes for a relaxed life for eighteen months, he agreed that a book of topographical verse would be an excellent idea and that this would fit nicely into his idea of writing occasional poetry. This would make a book on the lines of A Poet's View of Landscape and Buildings and he definitely approved of this plan. It would lend itself to excellent and varied illustrations.[60]

Murray had also asked John what he was in fact committed to in the way of future work for other publishers. John sheepishly revealed that he was meant to be collaborating with Robert Furneaux Jordan on a picture book about churches which Edmund Penning-Rowsell would publish at Vista Books. Murray suggested that this might be in competition with the Collins volume, 'but [John] said he did not mind doing Collins down and never wanted to do another book for them!'.[61] Second, he had signed a contract for a photographs book in collaboration with Edwin Smith. 'However, he says that this is so long overdue that it can be written off.'[62] Paul Elek had asked him to work with the photographer Eric de Maré in choosing photographs and supplying text about National Trust properties. Murray offered to get him off this hook, and wrote to Elek saying that John could not undertake the book for at least a year, 'and possibly not then if the text needed was as much as or more than 10,000 words'.[63] The message was clear: if more golden eggs were going to be laid, they were going to be laid for Murray.

Early in June, to Jock Murray's hair-tearing frustration, John decided to rewrite the end of the Marlborough section of *Summoned by Bells*. Murray sent the revised pages out to Katharine White for incorporation in the *New Yorker* version, with a wry note of apology (' I think I mentioned when we met that John Betjeman . . . was not a stranger to the unexpected . . .').[64] But a week later John changed his mind again and reverted to the original lines about the school. By 15 June he had made his corrections to the *New Yorker* text. Sending them to Mrs White, Murray wrote, 'He is honestly very grateful for what you have done and sincerely likes the result . . .' He assured her that she need not fear libel actions as 'the names of his school friends are all false' and promised to find out from John what the mysterious phrase 'blob work' meant in the lines about Byron House school –

> what happy, happy steps
> Under the limes I took to Byron House,
> And blob-work, weaving, carpentry and art . . .[65]

On 17 June Jock Murray wrote to Mark Clowes, of the printers William Clowes & Sons of Little New Street, London EC4 : 'My dear

Mark, Rejoice with me! and mark carefully that the finally revised, titivated, polished manuscript of John Betjeman's SUMMONED BY BELLS is completed and should be with Clowes by Monday. Keep an eye on it, for it is a gem, and we shall need a lot of friendly collaboration to get it through for the Autumn . . .'[66] Meanwhile the American rights had been sold to Houghton Mifflin. Lovell Thompson of that firm wrote to Jock Murray that he wanted to make the American edition 'somewhat like yours – harmonious but not identical'. On 20 June Murray sent Thompson plans for the jacket, which were very different from the version finally adopted:

> There is still much debate as to the general plan for the jacket. There is no proof; there are only ideas floating in three heads. The most likely plan will be a very large suitable type for the title on a sky blue background; under it, possibly McKnight Kauffer's three little white clouds which was used on his earlier book of poems, *Continual Dew*; below that a line drawing of a bell; and below that the author's name. The alternative was a William Morris typographical design; and another idea was a *trompe l'oeil* picture of a school notice-board with a notice stuck on to green baize with a dirty drawing pin and the title and author on the notice – putting the author's name above the title for obvious reasons.[67]

John had strong views about the jacket. He cared about the physical appearance of all his books, and particularly of this book which, as autobiography, was to represent him more than any other. On 8 July he sent Murray a wood-engraving of a bell from Messrs Mears & Stainbank of the Whitechapel Bell Foundry.[68] On 20 June he wrote him two letters. In the first, he asked: 'What do you say to leaving out the basket incident in the Marlborough chapter. . .?'[69] Murray persuaded him to leave the episode in; but it says much for John's tenderheartedness that he was prepared to sacrifice one of the most dramatic set-pieces in the poem to spare Ingle's feelings. The second letter contained John's suggestion for the jacket.

> I telephoned today to say to Miss Boulanger, who will tell Miss Debenham (ask her if she is Molly Higgins's daughter), that the right kind of dust wrapper is BROWN PAPER of the light, rather straw-coloured variety printed on with black ink and, if need be, red to diversify the black. This will go superbly well with the olive green of the binding and is the same colour right through and the right sort of wrapping paper for style of the book.[70]

Virginia Debenham of John Murray was indeed the daughter of John's former lover Molly Higgins, who had married Gilbert (later

Sir Gilbert) Debenham, a contemporary of his. (Debenham's father, Sir Ernest Debenham of department-store fame, interested John because he had commissioned the architect Halsey Ricardo to build a – still surviving – blue-and-green-tiled palace in Addison Road, Kensington, with William De Morgan fireplace tiles inside.)[71] Adapting the Mears & Stainbank wood-engraving, she made a drawing of bells which John approved as a motif for the jacket.

Jock Murray was not enthusiastic about the brown-paper idea. 'Part of the charm of that colour', he replied to John, 'is in the actual material of the brown paper and there is a danger that when it is matched in an ink it will look rather like French mustard. However we will get a colour sample of it. We may yet find that our first choice is the better.'[72]

By now the book was in galley proofs. John wrote to Murray from Derbyshire on 22 July:

My dear Jock,

1 I have corrected the proofs and now await Spansbury's and Tom Driberg's comments.

2 A copy of the proofs should go to my only surviving aunt, my mother's sister, whose name is Mrs F. Howard. I have not her address up here. If you ring up Noel Gosse (see London telephone book) his wife who is my cousin would give it to you. I am rather nervous of her reaction to the portrait of my mother in the 'Cornwall in Adolescence' chapter.

3 I am inclined to agree with Spansbury that the Biddy Walsham bit which ends that chapter is a bit out of key but it strikes, Elizabeth says, a more cheerful note. It is also a bit *normal*, after the Marlborough chapter!

4 I still can't make up my mind about the basket bit. Like the picture of my mum's hypochondria, it is interesting – but ought one to be interesting at the expense of other people's feelings? Anyhow, you have, I know, told the Sunday Times to omit it . . .

5 The caps are awful. What about a Caslon Display initial or Baskerville?

6 The italics are awful and will not do. You must get italics from another fount even if they are not the write [*sic*] size.

7 If you have a couple of pages over, we might have a very funny index of proper names, eg Sanatogen, C. S. Lewis, Euthymol, Attlee, Rt Hon Earl, John Dugdale, Michael Dugdale, J. D. K. Lloyd, London and South Eastern Railway.[73]

Against the last suggestion, Murray wrote another large 'NO' in the margin.

On 23 July, after receiving Murray's letter about the jacket, John wrote, 'Oh! I did not mean try to reproduce brown paper but use brown paper itself. I send an example of colour and printing on it. If carrier bags of brown paper can take the names of firms in printing on them, then so can dust jackets . . .'[74] On 29 July Murray sent a sample of paper, which he thought gave the impression of being brown paper but was better than 'the horrible synthetic substance that you sent'.[75] John gave his blessing to this compromise.

In the middle of August, both Jock Murray and John were on holiday – Murray in Audierne, Brittany, John on the Isle of Jura, Argyllshire, where he was staying with Michael Astor. The harassed Jane Boulanger acted as go-between. She wrote to Murray on 17 August, enclosing the page proofs.

> I hate to intrude on your holiday with this, but you did ask for it! Mr Betjeman has been sent his for correction and a set is going off to Mr Driberg. Mr Betjeman rang up to approve the blurb for the jacket and he also wanted us to have 'Gilbert Debenham's daughter's bells' put on the fly-leaves. I think his idea is to have a small bell block on the endpapers. Can we have your views on this latest idea? Or if you are against it, perhaps you could let Mr Betjeman know direct. It isn't easy for us to turn down his ideas, as you know . . .[76]

On 19 August she wrote: 'Summoned again by Betjeman. I am sorry! Here is the proof of the wrapper, which I am sure you should see before it goes off finally. With great trepidation I have sent one to the author and pray that he will not surface with several new suggestions. Anyhow, we shall just have to say "Too late" and this I will endeavour to make clear when I write with it.'[77]

John was full of suggestions. He wrote to Miss Debenham about the dust-jacket. 'I agree with you wholly about the placing of the pears but I am not sure that pears are the right things here. Is there something in the type specimen book which is a bit more vertical? Something Art Nouveau-ey . . . and not suggesting too much Faber & Gwyer or one of the university presses, but looking like early EVERYMAN editions with a strong hint of J. M. DENT & SONS and Letchworth Garden Suburb.'[78] Concerning the endpapers, he wrote:

> As you see from the enclosed postcard Major John Grey Murray MBE seems to think I wanted them in colour. Not at all. I wanted them in black and the left hand one in the front could have a panel let into it thus [drawing of 'This book belongs to . . .'] which was a popular device of about MCMX when this poem was written. Contrary to the Major, I think printed endpapers with the Debenham bell design and the suggested panel will blend very well with the Antique type and the title page, but . . . I don't insist. I only *know* I am right.[79]

On 25 August, writing from Derbyshire, John sent yet more elaborate suggestions for the endpapers.

> If it is decided to have the Debenham bells on the endpapers, I have a very good idea about them. As you know, English bells are rung right round [drawing] and so on till they are up again. If you are to cut out your bells and paste them like this [drawing] the endpapers would give a wonderful effect of ringing bells but perhaps this is asking too much. They should read from left to right starting down, going by quarters round till they are up and down again the same way.[80]

Returning to Albemarle Street from his wet holiday in France, Jock Murray was horrified to learn of all John's new proposals, only three months away from publication. However, the 'bell changes' endpapers were agreed to. (Philip Larkin, in his review of the book, described them as 'awful'.)[81]

A set of page proofs was sent to Cecil Roberts, who usually lived in Italy but was staying at the Milton Court Hotel in South Kensington. He came over to Albemarle Street to discuss his suggestions with John, just before John went off on 31 August for a two days' retreat at Nashdom Abbey in Buckinghamshire, where Adrian Bishop had once been a monk. Page proofs also went to the poet Richard Church and to Stephen Spender, who wrote to Jock Murray, 'It is his best work and certainly a classic of our times because it is so beautifully founded on experiences intensely lived and accurately remembered.'[82] Murray asked permission to use this comment in pre-publication publicity. Spender wrote back: 'Yes. I meant it!' The *New Yorker* extract had appeared on 27 August. Philip Larkin wrote to Murray on 14 September, 'I am greatly looking forward to *Summoned by Bells*, something of which I have already seen in the *New Yorker*. I wish there were more of it, but there it is. One cannot be lengthy without being tedious (see Coleridge) and Betjeman is incapable of that.'[83]

Houghton Mifflin told Murray they would like to use on the jacket of their edition Osbert Lancaster's 1948 caricature of 'Mr John Betjeman awaiting inspiration and the 4.47 from Didcot'.[84] Murray moved quickly to scuttle this idea. 'I cannot help feeling personally that the caricature is rather a "family joke" and not a suitable kind of portrayal for those who do not know him. I rather feel that it might tend to make him a joke, which would be a pity in connection with this marvellous and moving autobiography . . .'[85]

Good news came from the Book Society: *Summoned by Bells* was to be its 'alternative choice' for December. The preliminary order would

be for not fewer than six hundred copies. In early October Sir Isaiah
Berlin, the Oxford philosopher, returned the page proofs he had been
sent. Like the *New Yorker*, he was worried about libel possibilities.
Jock Murray reassured him: 'The line which refers to the Highgate
Junior School reads "A hell-hole in the side of Highgate Hill". This
would hardly have encouraged parents to send their children there and
this would have been particularly damaging when one thinks how
many parents will be reading the book. To make it really obscure for
any jury it has been changed to "Avernus in the side of Highgate
Hill"!'[86] Douglas Cleverdon of the BBC wrote to tell Murray how
enjoyable it had been to record the poem, which was to be broadcast
in three separate programmes.[87] (John received 400 guineas for the
entire recording.)

Not since the Festival of Britain nine years earlier had there been a
publicity campaign so clamorously and successfully orchestrated as
that for the launch of *Summoned by Bells*. It began as early as 24 July
with a note by Leonard Russell, literary editor of the *Sunday Times*,
in his 'Mainly about Books' column. 'John Betjeman has just completed his finest work, a long autobiographical poem in blank verse
called *Summoned by Bells* (Murray, November). Fresh from reading it
in manuscript, I abandon all the usual literary equivocations, and call
it a masterpiece.'[88] By this stage the *Sunday Times* had secured the
serial rights. As the publicity machine cranked into high gear, Jock
Murray asked John's secretary what his commitments were in the
coming months. The answer was:

> Friday 21 October, Bristol Grammar School prizegiving
> Tuesday, 25 October, Raynes Girls' School prizegiving
> Wednesday, 26 October, read poetry at the American Embassy to a group
> of American service wives. (Would it be in order for him to read the *New
> Yorker* version of Summoned by Bells?)
> Wednesday, 7 December, sale of work at Repton School
> Friday, 9 December, Oxford Society dinner at Manchester.

John turned down the idea of a book-signing session at Bowes &
Bowes in Cambridge, but was tempted by the idea of a signing and
poetry recital at Bentall's of Kingston. He also agreed to a signing
session in February 1961 at Lear's Bookshop in Cardiff, in spite of
Murray's opinion that 'it seems to me a waste of your time'. The
clincher, for John, was that the Bishop of Llandaff would be in the
chair.

Leonard Russell wrote to Murray in some distress: he had read
that John was to make an Associated Television programme with

Sir Kenneth Clark in early November, in which he would recite a large chunk of *Summoned by Bells*. This, Russell claimed, would infringe the *Sunday Times*'s first serial rights. 'We are spending an enormous amount of money on advertising the serial and by extension the book and I for one shall have an eternal grievance if John is going to recite passages from the book on television. I know you will do what you can to get this serious matter cleared up.'[89] Murray replied that printed serial rights did not include television rights; but in fact he had already written to Clark telling him that publication date was 28 November and that Murray would not be able to give leave to quote five minutes of *Summoned by Bells* until publication or thereafter.[90]

A less remediable disaster befell the limited edition of the poem, for which Michael Tree had drawn a portrait of John. When Edmund Penning-Rowsell wrote to ask Jock Murray for one of the limited-edition copies, Murray replied, 'Oh dear, I wish I had thought of this sooner. John's limited edition has been oversubscribed over four times . . . In any case, the tea trolley at the printer's works in Beccles crashed over the whole edition and has ruined them all. I hope to retrieve a few tannic copies which will doubtless be of high bibliographical value in a few years' time.'[91] Penning-Rowsell replied: 'What a calamity about the tea trolley! This story was recounted to me also by the author, to whom I suggested that he should sign the copies in tea.'[92]

On 4 November the *Daily Telegraph* trumpeted: 'more than a literary sensation – an experience all must share. The life poem of John Betjeman . . . John Betjeman recites a passage from his autobiography to Leonard Russell, literary editor of the *Sunday Times*.' Two days later, the *Sunday Times* published the first of three serial extracts under a Gothic canopy ornamented with gargoyles of mischievous schoolboy heads. The artist Charles Mozley also drew an impression

Drawing by Charles Mozley, Sunday Times, *6 November 1960: the first publication of an extract from* Summoned by Bells

of the schoolboy John, based on early photographs. The newspaper
drawings were far more evocative than Michael Tree's in the book. On
15 November, thanking Lovell Thompson of Houghton Mifflin for a
copy of the American edition, Murray wrote: 'It makes a very elegant
volume. I rather envy you not having had to design the book with illustrations!' He added: 'After a first printing of nearly 80,000 we are furiously reprinting. It looks like scoring a publicity jackpot.'[93]

On the same day John, who was in Cornwall, wrote asking Murray
to send him a dozen copies. 'I must send one to George Seferis, and
have I sent one to Noël Coward?'[94] An all-male celebration dinner was
planned for publication day. Murray had asked John to compose a
light poem to go on the menu. John sent these lines:

How sweet the bells of Clerkenwell
Are ringing loud and wild
Across the gaslit warehouse where
The Murray stocks are piled.
The nobs may come from Albemarle
The Major and Sir John;
It is Fleet Ditch which makes them rich
And the warehouse thereupon.

IN THE MAGAZINE SECTION

Summoned by Bells—I	Art 34	Gardening ...30
by John Betjeman 21	Autolycus 35	Gramophone
The Autobiography of	Ballet 35	Records ...34
Peter Scott—V 23	Books	Mainly for
Life in Russia, 1960—III	31, 32 & 33	Children ...36
by Ronald Hingley 24	Mainly About	Mainly for
The Great Oil	Books 31	Women
Battle—III	Bridge 36	27, 28 & 29
by Robert Henriques ...25	Chess 36	Music 34
	Crossword ...39	Theatre 35
	Family Clinic 28	Travel 37
	Films 35	TV & Radio 40

Jock Murray wrote back diplomatically: 'Thank you for . . . the poem, which is highly enjoyable, but for this particular purpose I think it is rather a dig at Albemarle Street and for some it might widen the gap between Number Fifty and Clerkenwell Road, which we try to bridge. I shall use it for private circulation.'

Two days before publication, *Smith's Trade News* published an interview with John by Ruth Martin. She visited him at Cloth Fair. He told her the latest news from Murray's: that 'two requests had been received for *Summoned by Bells*. One was for *Summoned by Bills*; the other, for *Some of my* Belles'.[95] John's Oxford friend Michael Dugdale – mentioned in the poem – wrote up the publication-day party on 28 November in his diary.

Back to finish the Betjeman poem so as to be able to say, this evening, that I had done so. It is successful, I think, but not his masterpiece. Would I have read it had I known neither the author nor some of the events and people it describes? I doubt if I should have got to the end.

Then to the party, and a very good evening it proved to be. We met at Jock Murray's beautiful office in Albemarle Street. We were the following: Jock, Betjeman, John Bryson, Ben Bonas, John Dugdale, Tom Driberg, Philip Harding and myself. In fact the entire available cast of 'Summoned by Bells'. Some talk and drink and laughter – for none of us have been in the habit of meeting a great deal of late. We then moved off to a near-by restaurant, and dined off oysters and sole bonne femme, and a bottle of white wine which Tom ruthlessly sent back as being corked. I sat between Betj. and Bryson with Driberg opposite, and got, therefore, the pick of the conversation. The bores (Dugdale and Harding)[96] contrived to get banished to the far end, whether by accident or design. I was able to expound my theory of the reliability, or not, of the BVM [Blessed Virgin Mary] as the only witness from whom we get the nativity story. And this to Tom and Betj., both of whom are exceedingly High Church.

Then back again to Albemarle Street, and brandy, and much reminiscing of such forgotten figures as Sandy Baird,[97] Alec Macindoe,[98] Denzil Branch.[99] And of course g'Ug (and I had the pleasure of pointing out to Betj. that he had misspelt this name G'ug.['Colonel' Kolkhorst]).[100]

'Will John Wain spoil my sales?' asked JB in the voice of one who did not think that anyone could do that.

A very perfect evening.[101]

John wrote to Jock Murray the next day: 'What a jolly evening. One of the happiest in my life. No strain and all affection. The only blot was that I too much assumed the rôle of host. I do thank you warmly.'[102]

John was in need of some affection and comforting at the party. The day before, *The Observer* – whose cantankerous literary editor, Terence Kilmartin, thought he had been promised the rights and was furious at being scooped by the *Sunday Times* – published the brutal John Wain review mentioned by Dugdale. Deriding 'timid reviewers', with their 'squeals of adulation' for John's work, Wain scorned his 'complete lack of the skills of the true poet, his wooden technique, his watercolours slapped at the canvas, his incuriosity about literary art', and added:

> Most of his poems are written either in hymn-metres or in metres usually associated with 'light' and comic verse. These forms, themselves loaded with the kind of suggestion he means to convey, are the literary counter-part of Betjemanian *bric-à-brac* in the world of objects – yellow-brick steeples and the rest. To manipulate them needs no more skill than is shown by the men who write the jingles on Christmas cards. And that so many people find Mr Betjeman the most (or only) attractive contemporary poet is merely one more sign that the mass middle-brow public distrusts and fears poetry.[103]

The Bookman quoted these dismissive lines under the crosshead 'Summoned by Jingle Bells'.

Punch, which had also been eager to secure the serial rights, now published a similarly disobliging review, by Julian Symons, under the heading 'Private Giggles'. A whiff of sour grapeshot?

> The Betjeman, like the South Sea Bubble, grows and grows . . . here indeed is a poet for the Plain Man. But Mr Betjeman's critical reputation at least must surely be badly damaged by this long stretch of autobiography, written for the most part in singularly blank verse which contains so many object-lessons in the art of sinking. ' "Haven't you heard," said D. C. Wilkinson, "Angus is to be basketed tonight." ' 'Ah-hah,' say the Betjemanites.' 'but Betjeman himself knows that such lines are funny. Yes, and a little bit sad, too. He anticipates all your criticisms.' Perhaps he does: but still the product of this tear-in-the-eye whimsicality is not poetry.[104]

In the *Sunday Times* on the same day as Wain's *Observer* diatribe, Raymond Mortimer, a friend of John's, could muster only a qualified enthusiasm for the book.

> We are gripped by the story: we chuckle at phrasing; we are deeply touched by the candour and the strength of feeling: the book is triumphantly read-able. Yet I must finally confess to disappointment. If this brilliant versifier

had not chosen, except in a few passages, to go so near to prose, might he not have given us the truth, and poetry as well?[105]

While Wain and Mortimer criticized the poetic technique, Robert Pitman, the *Sunday Express* columnist, attacked what he took to be the 'kinkiness' of its subject-matter, in a parody of John's more familiar style.

> Have you read the latest Betjeman?
> But, my dear, you simply must!
> He's adored by Princess Margaret;
> Yes, he's madly upper crust.
> What? You say it's all in poetry?
> Ah, I promise you won't mind;
> He's not baffling like old Eliot,
> His is quite a different kind.
> If it wasn't for the printing
> And the lines all set in rows
> And some rather *weird* descriptions
> You would almost say it's prose.
>
> What's the story? Well I grant you
> That there isn't very much
> It just tells how little Betjeman
> Was descended from the Dutch;
> How his father was a bully
> And his mother rather vague . . .
>
> But before the bit on Oxford
> There is something rather *odd*
> In the way he notes each belting,
> Each debagging, every rod,
> Every nurse's spanking fingers,
> Every bully's boot unkind
> Which made imprint almost daily
> On the Betjeman behind.
> He gives each humiliation
> In such detail that you'd say
> There'd be not much book left over
> If you took the pain away . . .[106]

Walter Allen wrote a friendlier review in the *New York Times* that Sunday, but it took some days for the cutting to reach England. On publication day, the American magazine *Newsweek* reported that

'John Betjeman, 54, is an ingratiating English eccentric who is his country's probable next Poet Laureate . . . In syntax and emotion he is as easy to understand as a singing commercial. This rare quirk in a poet of quality has enthroned him as a popular performer on British television and boomed him into one of the world's best-selling bards'. Under this assessment, the magazine published an interview with John.

'I don't call it poetry,' John Betjeman objected the other day, as he chalked a cue stick in London's Athenaeum Club. 'What I write is what I mean. I'm not striking an attitude. Nostalgia is a word critics always use about my writing. I describe what people have been through. I can't write about the future because I don't know the future. What else is there to write about but the past and the present?' An amiable, modest man, with a pink face topped by sparse wisps of hair and a mouth full of slightly scrambled teeth, Betjeman is awed by his success as 'Britain's No. 1 pop poet'. 'True pop poets,' he says, 'are the ones who write the lyrics of songs. Cole Porter is the greatest. I happen to write lines that rhyme and scan and that people who read novels understand . . .'

Betjeman often writes his poetry on the backs of envelopes and the margins of books while riding on the train between his Berkshire country home and a London flat which is usually a jumble of books and drying laundry. He goes about in a fearsomely battered felt hat, a shapeless Tattersall coat and owns some clothes which used to belong to Henry James. He cruises the streets of London on a bicycle, cultivating unlikely acquaintances. Princess Margaret calls him 'a friend . . . and my favourite poet'.[107]

Two reviews of the kind that Jock Murray described as 'not very *helpful*' appeared on 29 November. The *Birmingham Post* reviewer, who confessed himself a great admirer of John's work, found the 'uneasy blank verse' no more than 'fair'.

Perhaps those critics who over the years have suggested that blank verse was his true medium have done him a disservice . . . 111 pages of nostalgia is perhaps a bit much . . .

Indeed this mist of nostalgia seems to have muffled that personal voice we know from his shorter poems: the giggling voice, the sad, responsible voice in those lovely elegies for dead friends, the waspish, satirical voice and the fearful voice. This may be a triumph of objectivity, but it tends to diminish the poem to one more Edwardian memoir with Nanny for muse . . .

I prefer Mr Betjeman brief, intense, angry and passionate in his anger. Here that wretched teddy-bear gets between me and his poetry.

The *Daily Express* made a similar point more viciously.

> The reader must trudge through pages of 'Do you remember, Joan, the awkward time When we were non-co-operative at sports, Refusing to be organized in heats?' Whether Joan remembers that awful afternoon when John laughed and furious Miss Tunstall sent him home to bed, seems doubtful indeed; but it is likely that as she reads Betjeman's account of the affair Joan will groan. She will not groan alone. *Summoned by Bells* is one of the flatter poems in the English language.

The *Financial Times*'s notice by David Pryce-Jones (Alan's son) was more encouraging. '*Summoned by Bells* is the complete Betjeman keyboard, the final resolution of this mandarin–philistine . . . He is writing as a kind of intuitive sociologist of the middle classes, achingly aware of the minute particles of daily life that go towards making a tautly class-ridden childhood.'[108]

Also on 29 November, Philip Larkin wrote to Jock Murray from Hull to thank him for a copy of the book. 'It has been much in my thoughts during the last few days as the *Spectator* were good enough to send me a copy for review, which I hope should be appearing in their next issue or so. I enjoyed the poem very much indeed, and though my notice is not a rave, I hope it should do something to counteract Mr Wain in the *Observer*. I did not spot a single misprint this time! But why did you use Goudy italic with Old Style Antique?'[109]

Murray replied:

> I am so glad you feel able to do something to counteract those critics . . . who appear to take pleasure in attacking the book on the wrong premises. The kindest interpretation is that some of the critics were expecting too much and something different and are not flexible enough to consider with understanding what had been offered.
>
> You are very expert to have spotted the Goudy italic. The type selected was Antique Old Style (series 161) of which there was only one set of matrices in a shed at the printers in Somerset. Unfortunately it had no italics in the smaller size and Goudy italics seemed the only fount to match without excessive heaviness.[110]

More than one critic commented on the prose-like quality of the verse. On 1 December the *Daily Express* – returning to the charge – dealt with this aspect sarcastically. 'Perhaps through some technical difficulty to do with a jammed typewriter Mr Betjeman's manuscript appears to have been delivered to the publisher in lines that do not extend fully across the page . . .' To illustrate his ponderous jest, the

Express writer amalgamated several lines of the poem into prose passages, without changing any of the words.

On 30 November the *Southern Evening Echo*, Southampton, put in its jab: 'In all the comments . . . which have been made about John Betjeman's verse autobiography in the last week or so, the most alarming was the suggestion that he might be the next Poet Laureate. Mr Betjeman, I suspect, is incapable of state poetry. I don't think he is capable of great poetry, either. *Summoned by Bells* is an enormous middle-class success because it offers a great number of people a kind of lucky-dip from which they can extract little parcels of the familiar past tied up in neat and easily recognizable metres.' The reviewer thought that what really irritated many intelligent and well-read people was 'neither the poet nor his work, but what is claimed for both by his more fanatical devotees'.

Stephen Spender hailed the book as 'a landmark in English letters' in *The Bookman*. He thought it 'a break-through' in that it represented 'a fusion of the poet's particular talents with the opportunity to write such a poem which the time somehow offers'. Spender added: 'Of course it might be said that Betjeman does not give us any answer to the problem of the world of Bomb. An answer to that objection might be that no poet can give an answer; but it may be admitted that his world is a bit too cosy, too guarded from attack by mockery and heaped-on self-mockery, though there are signs in this book of his moving towards what might be called the larger apprehensiveness.'[111]

December brought a kinder press. On the 1st, the *Times* reviewer had some patronizing things to say, but conceded:

> The more one reads through it all; the more plain does it become that what Mr Betjeman has brought off is not the *Prelude* of today but a lightweight version of *Sinister Street*. The young John and Michael Fane in Sir Compton Mackenzie's once bestselling novel have much in common. Mr Betjeman has caught the moods of a sensitive boy preoccupied with High Churchmanship as appealingly for this generation as Sir Compton Mackenzie did for the young men who are said to have bought his more or less autobiographical double-decker before the First World War.

P.N. Furbank's *Listener* critique, on the same day, was more barbed and ironic, but he credited John with some technical virtuosity.

Oh Mappin, Webb, Asprey and Finnigan!

Can one think of another writer who, like Betjeman, has made a whole artistic career out of parody? It is a strange and certainly a fruitful achievement: the late chrysanthemums have been not few but many. Everything works in Betjeman's verse when he is filling out someone else's pattern with his own delicious overtones.

> What time magnolias bursting into bloom
> By Balliol's brain-grey wall . . .

goes the splendid mock-Spenserian lyric in his new autobiographical poem. The body of the work is a pedestrian blank verse metre, sometimes Tennysonian, sometimes debased Augustan, and endless shades of brilliant bathos play round it: 'The foursome puffing past the sunlit hedge With rattling golf bags.' But of course there are times when he is not sending his form up, and then the writing sags into a mild and flabby Georgianism. The truth is that, fascinating and dazzling performer though he is, Betjeman is not really a poet. There is no new poetical shape he wants to make for himself. This sounds grudging but I think makes a necessary distinction.

Furbank tried to fathom why John's poetry was so popular.

Betjeman's present vogue is part of contemporary English chauvinism. The English cannot hear too much about themselves at present. In the decline of their imperial greatness they are studying and inventorying themselves with passion and the richness of their preposterous socio-architectural inheritance dazzles them. An eye trained simultaneously upon class and architecture, and a tone which parodies both, have thus made Betjeman peculiarly topical . . .

On 2 December William Plomer, perhaps the poet of that time who had most affinity with John, gave him a straight 'rave' in the *Daily Telegraph*. ('In this poem his humanity, his precision in detail, his powers of enjoyment, and the playful wit that never quite hides his seriousness are all to be found in plenty. It will increase the admiration and affection he has won by being himself . . . But it may annoy literary prigs who find popularity unforgivable.') John wrote to him: 'The last sentence of your kind review . . . has saved me from a nervous breakdown brought on by persecution mania. I really thought the verse not bad and complete in itself and it was much worked on. Fuck Wain and the prig in *The Times* who was probably Griggers [Geoffrey Grigson]. I've gone away to escape further blows.'[112] Jock Murray also wrote Plomer a grateful letter. 'How refreshing and how welcome to read you in the *Daily Telegraph*. You are the first in the press to approach John's *Summoned by Bells* as a human being and not as shark. (One of the BBC Critics even went so far as to refer to the

author and the book as waspish!) Up to now the attacks have been
relentless but you seem to have marked the turning of the tide. From
the material point of view, the book seems to have benefited from
attack, for sales are phenomenal – but their dimensions must be kept
from those who are likely to review his next book.'[113]

Larkin's review appeared in *The Spectator*, and was all that poet
and publisher could have hoped for. 'He is an accepter, not a rejecter,
of our time, registering "dear old, bloody old England" with robust-
ness, precision and a vivacious affection that shimmers continually
between laughter and rage . . . Although it remains a mystery how Mr
Betjeman can avoid the traps of self-importance, exhibitionism, silli-
ness, sentimentality and boredom, he continues to do so. Why should
we accept his teddy-bear when we want to stuff Sebastian Flyte's down
his throat?. . . No doubt sincerity is the answer, a sincerity as unselfconscious as it is absolute . . .'[114]

Like Furbank, the *Times Literary Supplement*'s reviewer (2 December) tried to analyse why John's poetry was so popular. Few living poets,
he wrote, were memorable, even fewer commanded large sales.

To these gloomy and all too just generalizations Mr Betjeman is a
notable – by far the most notable – exception. Where his fellow poets sell
in the two figures, he sells well into the five. Where they are known only in
a small coterie of the elect, he is a national figure. What is the reason for
this? Mr Betjeman's personality is certainly far better known than that of
any other living English poet. Of most of the poets the public has no sort
of picture. Even of such public personalities as Mr Eliot or Dame Edith
Sitwell they do not feel that they know them intimately. Mr Betjeman they
know as if he was a private friend. 'Such a modest man,' said of him
recently a bank clerk in the Midlands. Why is this?

Television, of course, has greatly helped; but television is not the whole
explanation. Readers would still surely have felt that they knew Mr
Betjeman had they nothing but his verse through which to know him, and
the reason is that his verse is always, essentially, autobiographical. He has
created characters as clear and as well known as those of any novelist, and
he has left the public in no possible doubt about his tastes and prejudices.
He has expressed them with simplicity. Mr Betjeman is, like so many of
the wisest and most likable of men, one who has never fully grown up. 'A
clever fifteen' was once the verdict on him of a psychologist after examination . . . He also preserves unashamedly the faith of the child.

'For myself,' John wrote in *Summoned by Bells*, 'I knew as soon as
I could read and write, That I must be a poet.' He added, no doubt
with F. R. Leavis in mind:

>   Even today,
>   When all the way from Cambridge comes a wind
>   To blow the lamps out every time they're lit,
>   I know that I must light mine up again.

Dr John Broadbent, Fellow of King's College, Cambridge, took these lines as his text when reviewing the book in *Time and Tide* (3 December). Like Robert Pitman of the *Express*, but with more finesse, he wrote his review in verse.

>   Arise, smooth Waller, from the hoary Cam
>   Descend from out your crusty wine-room frame,
>   King's only poet (so far) help me choose
>   A Christmas quip, *bon mot* or epigram
>   Wherewith we may relume the lamp of Betjeman.
>
>   His poetry has the virtues of bad prose?
>
>   Like slackened conversation it invites
>   Vague sympathies; makes no demands, nor bites.
>   Churchwarden murmur leads us to the pew
>   And lets pretend he, we (and I) are you,
>   Ensouled all in one tea-cosy memory
>   Of lovely spankings, bicycles and sherry . . .
>
>   'Those far sun-gilded days' of early childhood
>   Shine with inherent glamour; but the verse
>   Does not create the thing that it refers to.
>   For, 'the more hilarious moments', lyrics
>   Trickle through all complexities of metrics
>   With fun-poking, shy nostalgia; but their feet
>   Are at Moorgate, and their heart under their feet . . .
>
>   So have a happy Xmas with this book;
>   Stuff it in stockings, pore i' the inglenook,
>   Smack Pam's so darling bottom with its spine
>   And toast the poet in your British port-type wine
>   For his gentle sly self-laughter, no self-pity
>   And his simply using verse to tell a ditty.
>
>   Funless and stark by chilly Cam we glisten
>   Our sterile quivers stacked with bitter ice;
>   But Queen and people touched at heart will listen
>   For the tale *is* touching, and the poet nice.

In compensation for this and so many other reviews which failed to take John seriously, V. S. Pritchett's *New Statesman* review, also on 3 December, observed that 'Mr Betjeman's real subject is not nostalgia, but the sense of insecurity, the terror of time and pain. The laughs come at the point of agony. If it sounds like the chuckle of *The Diary of a Nobody*, it has far more of the delighted scream of the fiend.' Pritchett thought that John's genre was very English: 'it is perpetuated only by very clever, frightened, defensive people who are given sedulously to ritual . . .'. At a second or third reading, the verse disclosed its essence: 'he is a true excavator of drama'.

In the evocation of suburban youth and family troubles; the visit to father's works; the conflict between father and son, the miseries of prep school and public school, the romantic holidays in Cornwall, we recognize the fidelity of observation, the painful anxiety for truth in the determination to amuse and touch. But these would be fatally lulling but for the short thrilled power of dramatizing a scene in a line or two. Nervous of prolonging these scenes, Mr Betjeman makes often too quick a getaway; but they whizz back like a cane and are sharp enough to raise a weal.

Alan Pryce-Jones reviewed the book in the *New York Times* (4 December). Either from modesty or from embarrassment, he did not reveal that he figured in the poem ('Alan Pryce-Jones came in a bathing-dress And, seated at your low harmonium, Struck up the Kolkhorst Sunday-morning hymn . . .'). Almost thirty years before, he had written a bitter-sweet review of John's first book, *Mount Zion*. Now he did the same for *Summoned by Bells*. In the book's favour he wrote:

The following things are clear about Mr Betjeman: he is a martyr to guilt, to insecurity, Anglo-Catholic high jinks, to Victorian architecture, to a class-consciousness rare even among the British, to the private joke, to suburbia. He is also – we have Mr Edmund Wilson's word for it – one of the two 'most considerable English poets writing today'. The evidence for both these statements is contained in this blank verse autobiography, written almost on the scale of *The Prelude* . . . Mr Betjeman is a miniaturist. His special skill is to pack some element of everyday experience in the gift wrapping of a very personal sensibility. In a sense therefore all his work is autobiographical. He is the least objective of poets even when the matter of his verse is of a kind which seldom provokes a poet to strong feeling. Electric trains, acetylene lighting, a brawny girl on a bicycle, an old gym shoe are to him what the figures on the Grecian urn were to Keats;

and now for the first time he has woven all his preoccupations into a single unified design.

Against the book, Pryce-Jones had this to say:

John Betjeman . . . is likely to make the rash assumption that he and his readers are all part of some whimsical fancy which has suddenly come into his head. This is unfair on the reader. Unless he happens to have been on the spot at the time, it forces him into the snobbish attitude of smiling at jokes he cannot possibly understand. The Oxford section of the poem, for instance, is full of intricate references which nobody outside the inner circle of Mr Betjeman's friends can hope to unravel. This is where Mr Betjeman's charm has to come to the rescue of his talent. By nudging and whispering and smiling up at his audience, he manages to convey that the party to which he has taken them, uninvited, has been a marvellous success. The morning after brings its doubts, however. Who were all those people? And what on earth were they up to?

On 9 December, sending John a favourable but uninspired review by Peter Quennell in the *Weekly Post*, Jock Murray wrote:

A survey of all reviews makes most fascinating reading. Though the envious sharks got the lead at the start, they have been well and truly routed now, so you have no excuse for indulging in symptoms of persecution mania.

News of progress: the approximate figure of sales before publication was 35,000. Sales today are passing the 50,000 mark.

I have just seen – for approval – the first copy of the limited edition which in modern parlance looks smashing. The edition should be ready for signing just before Christmas. I am afraid you will have to keep the major portion of an afternoon for this.[115]

By the end of 1960 John was to many Britons not just one of the most famous Englishmen, but one of the best-known people in the world. In a 'round-up of the year' cartoon for New Year's Eve, Cummings of the *Daily Express* showed him with (among others) Prince Philip, President Kennedy and Chancellor Adenauer.

The full 75,000 first printing of the book was sold, and Murray reprinted. In January 1961 Rupert Hart-Davis wrote to his friend George Lyttelton:

Tell me exactly what you think of the new Betjeman poem. The brief verdict at Cambridge was 'It stinks', which is surely a little exaggerated. Dick Routh *per contra* puts it at the very top of all the poems he had read,

CUMMINGS' NEW YEAR'S EVE FANCY DRESS PARTY

Sir Brian Robertson as 'The Triumph of Steam' — Mr Macleod as 'The White Man's Burden' — Dr Adenauer as a gold brick — John Betjeman as 'St George and the Dragon' — Mr Kennedy as Father Christmas in reverse — Prince Philip as 'The Spirit of Anglo-German Friendship'

which again seems to lack balance. It appears to me to have every merit except the poetic. Amusing, vivid, moving, full of stuff, obviously the work of a delightful, wise and excellent man. And I suppose it *does* gain by being in blank verse rather than prose? If I say that it doesn't do to me what poetry does – or did – you will answer: 'You must remember you are old and grey and full of sleep'. Leavis[116] has not yet pronounced; he probably thinks it beneath his notice. His disciples at Girton, it is said, send to Coventry any girl who likes it.[117]

In February John received a warmly appreciative letter about the work from his old Magdalen friend Martyn Skinner, writing as one poet to another. The two men had kept in touch. John had admired Skinner's *Letters to Malaya*, a wartime poem in heroic couplets which had won the Hawthornden Prize; and from time to time he gave his opinion on the majestic epic 'The Return of Arthur' that Skinner was writing, for which John would eventually write a foreword. He replied to Skinner on 23 February 1961:

What pleases me most is that you (& John Sparrow) alone know – or at any rate have expressed – the laborious technique that went to make it seem effortless & readable & concise at the same time. I knew that I had done that, but until you wrote I did not realise anyone had consciously seen that I had made that particular effort. It involved cutting out a lot of dead stuff. Now that you have written I feel immensely cheered up for this awful publicity (much of it well-meaning) has been getting me down.[118]

The same year, John wrote his poem 'Lines written to Martyn Skinner before his Departure from Oxfordshire in Search of Quiet – 1961', which begins sardonically –

> Return, return to Ealing,
>   Worn poet of the farm!
> Regain your boyhood feeling
>   Of uninvaded calm . . .[119]

Another spirit of the Oxford past summoned up by the book was Edward James, who wrote several rambling letters to say how much he had enjoyed the poem, especially the parts about himself. A friend had sent him John's *Punch* poem 'Edward James' of 1958, which was incorporated in *Summoned by Bells* ('They tell me he's in Mexico, They will not give me his address . . .'). James had given strict orders to his agent at West Dean, Sussex, that he was not to divulge his Mexican address to anybody; but on the illogical whim of the petulant, spoilt rich man he was, he fired him for not having given John his address.[120] In return for a complimentary copy of *Summoned by Bells*, James prepared a magnificently bound copy of his own recent poems written under the pseudonym 'Edward Silence', and hand-painted an elaborate dedicatory title-page for John; but when he had finished the decoration, he was so pleased with his artistry that he kept the book and never sent it – at least living up to his pseudonym.

In March 1961 Derek Stanford's book about John was published.[121] Philip Toynbee, who roasted it in *The Observer*, took the chance to summarize what he took to be John's achievement.

It had to happen soon, but it does seem a pity that it had to happen through the dull and obfuscating medium of Mr Stanford. (He was first on the ball with Dylan Thomas too; and this ordeal is not the least of the dubious fates which seem to attend the achievement of popularity in verse. Think of Mr Stanford, all you young poets, when you set foot on the primrose path!) This is a bad book indeed and my only excuse for reviewing it is that I find the subject of it deeply interesting.

Mr Betjeman has three more or less distinct claims on our attention. There is the simple claim of his verse itself – its uniqueness of tone and method. There is the fact that the 'Collected Poems' have sold over 80,000 copies and 'Summoned by Bells' 60,000 copies. There is finally the fact that Mr Betjeman has changed our vision to the extent that certain English scenes or buildings immediately evoke his name.

It is fashionable – which does not mean that it is wrong – to decry the verse; but my own view is that the point is usually missed in the more savage attacks. Betjeman is a pasticheur – which means that the claims made by the verse (they are not the same as the claims made for them by its more ardent admirers) are obstinately modest . . . I must add, with a real regret, that I cannot apply this approbation to Mr Betjeman's last poem. 'Summoned by Bells' seems to me to be an almost unmitigated disaster – a gross case of a writer miscalculating not only his capabilities but the whole nature of his talent . . .[122]

'An almost unmitigated disaster' was the most crushing of the verdicts on John's most ambitious poem. But in his otherwise ambivalent *Sunday Times* review, Raymond Mortimer put the case for it: 'We say to ourselves, not "This is poetry" but "This is the truth." '[123]

BACK TO CLOTH FAIR

On his return from Rotherhithe to a refurbished 43 Cloth Fair, JB's shambling figure once more became a familiar sight around Smithfield meat market and Aldersgate. His suits were hopelessly out of shape through heavy books being constantly shoved in their pockets; he always carried a fish basket into which he stuffed more books. He wore a brown felt hat and occasionally the most revolting semi-transparent grey plastic mac which used to embarrass me as a style-conscious teenager.

Candida Lycett Green (ed.), *John Betjeman: Letters*, vol. ii: *1951 to 1984*, London 1995

In 1959 John came back to a Cloth Fair restored and titivated by 'the Partners', Lord Mottistone and Paul Paget. Tory Dennistoun had left to marry John Oaksey – then a successful point-to-point rider and later a popular racing commentator. John now decided to employ male instead of female secretaries. Through his friend Canon Freddy Hood, who tried to find jobs for clergymen who were in 'a spot of trouble', he employed several in the early Sixties. 'Perhaps he thought they would not be constantly leaving to get married,' Candida speculates;[1] but there was another reason, too, for his taking on Hood's protégés. 'There, but for the grace of God . . .' he would say.[2] Asked by Osbert Lancaster what an ex-priest had been 'done' for, he replied, 'Bare ruined choirs, where late the sweet birds sang'.[3] In 1970 John contributed to a fund for Bishop Gordon Savage, whose affair with a Bunny Girl had been exposed in the press and who, as Bishop of Buckingham, was inevitably the subject of ribald limericks. The fund enabled Savage to emigrate to Tenerife.[4]

Harry Jarvis, who had been chaplain at Summer Fields prep school, Oxford, was one of the priest–secretaries.[5] His rôle was not only secretarial. It also resembled that of a batman to an officer ('Make the bed, make the tea, open the champagne at midday')[6] and private chaplain to a lord. Sometimes he took John's confession formally, in church; more often John used him as 'a confessor out of the confessional, so to speak'.[7] The two men became great friends.

You never had to say anything twice to John [Jarvis told Candida in 1994]. He was with you straight away. His friendship meant an enormous amount to me; he was never shocked and never, at that particular time, judgmental. He made me laugh the whole time: he was so spontaneous.[8]

John took Jarvis on City walks. Once he led him up to a poky room at the top of the Victorian red-brick building of the Prudential Assurance Company in Holborn and they climbed on to a window ledge to get a view of St Paul's, which from ground level was becoming obscured by brutalist office blocks. 'You could still see St Martin's spire framed against St Paul's dome,' Jarvis remembered.[9] He had no idea how John knew about the Prudential eyrie; but John had probably been introduced to it by Osbert Lancaster, whose considerable wealth came from his paternal grandfather, formerly secretary of the 'Pru'.

Jarvis was a sympathetic confidant on John's private life. In August 1960 John wrote to him from Wantage:

As the calm mentor of my life and the only person who knows its twisted strands, please remember in your prayers Phoeble [Elizabeth Cavendish] and me and Penelope and Paul and Candida. I must not make Phoeble unhappy as I do with my ties here. How can I hurt least? It is all very fraught, I know that.[10]

John's relationship with Lady Elizabeth, so settled in later years, was still in the balance. Elizabeth did not want to break up the Betjemans' marriage and had tried to give him up.[11] In 1954 John had written to Jack Beddington: 'I am ill from a broken heart at present and the pleasures of life seem very far away.'[12] Elizabeth's distancing herself from him at that time provoked a poem for and about her,[13] 'The Cockney Amorist', which, because of its sensitive personal context, John witheld from publication for twelve years –

> Oh when my love, my darling,
>   You've left me here alone,
> I'll walk the streets of London
>   Which once seemed all our own.
>
> The vast suburban churches
>   Together we have found:
> The ones which smelt of gaslight
>   The ones in incense drown'd;

> I'll use them now for praying in
>   And not for looking round . . .
>
>   . . .
>
> I love you, oh my darling,
>   And what I can't make out
> Is why since you have left me
>   I'm somehow still about.[14]

Was there a veiled threat of suicide in that last stanza? Or just the romantic implication, 'I shall die of a broken heart'?

That the relationship was still on/off in 1955 John had made explicit in a poem of that year. In August, he and Elizabeth, with her sister and brother-in-law Anne and Michael Tree, made a tour of Germany, Austria and the Alps, ending in Venice.[15] He wrote to Penelope from a Garmisch hotel on 19 August: 'We went yesterday from here on a tour of mad queer King Ludwig II of Bavaria's castles and palaces. Linderhof, of which I enclose a postcard, seemed to me rich beyond dreaming. The atmosphere was exactly like being in Gerald [Berners]'s . . .'[16] During the trip John wrote 'In the Public Gardens' about Elizabeth –

> In the Public Gardens,
>   To the airs of Strauss,
> *Eingang* we're in love again
>   When *ausgang* we are *aus*.
>
>   . . .
>
> Among the loud Americans
>   *Zwei Engländer* were we,
> You so white and frail and pale
>   And me so deeply me;
>
>   . . .
>
> In the Public Gardens,
>   Ended things begin;
> *Ausgang* we were out of love
>   *Und eingang* we are in.[17]

In March 1960 John wrote to Father Harry Williams:

Feeble is getting v[ery] pale and washed out again. Partly it is insecurity about me. I love her. But I also love – and very deeply – Penelope and the kiddiz. If Feeble falls in love elsewhere, I will be able just to get along. Of course, without her, I would probably write nothing more except the dreariest hackwork and would get still more into debt. But I don't really mind about that. I do mind about not hurting Feeble. I'm so glad we are in your prayers.[18]

Harry Jarvis told Candida:

I do not think that at any stage he wanted to leave Elizabeth; he never wanted to leave either of them in fact. Sometimes I think that he thoroughly enjoyed dealing with guilt, to some extent anyway. He was happy some of the time but he went through long periods of being very, very unhappy and consumed with guilt. It was definitely a case of loving two women, I know he loved them both. I did not advise him what to do, he had a very deep love for Penelope but he just could not live with her which made for an impossible situation. They were incompatible in a way.[19]

At his most tormented, John put his feelings about the situation into his poem 'Guilt' –

> I haven't hope. I haven't faith.
>   I live two lives and sometimes three.
> The lives I live make life a death
>   For those who have to live with me . . .[20]

In contrast with the tribulations of his private life, John basked in public fame after the publication of *Summoned by Bells*. Journalists beat a path to his door. One of the best writers among them was Kenneth Allsop, who wrote a profile of John for the *Daily Mail* in December 1960.[21] Allsop's face was even more familiar to the television-viewing public than John's, as he was a co-presenter of the popular *Tonight* show, with Cliff Michelmore, Fyfe Robertson and Derek Hart. John knew Allsop slightly as a fringe figure of Princess Margaret's circle: Derek Hart was a great friend of the Snowdons and had introduced Allsop to them. Allsop, who had lost a leg in a road accident, limped up the narrow staircase of No. 43.

The Poet of 1960 [he wrote], the only English mass-circulation bard since Kipling . . . is flat out in his flat spin through his London morning.

John Betjeman, the minstrel of middle-class suburbia as well as Top People's unofficial laureate, is floundering bemusedly about his tiny house in Cloth Fair, behind Smithfield meat market, looking like a flood victim in search of somewhere to be cast up.

His ash-powdered suit apparently clove to him some time ago down-stream. He has two cigarettes going at once. He has just been gulping a cup of tea and is now sloshing out some whisky.

His secretary is vainly trying to get his pen to connect with the bottom of some typed letters. Christopher Hollis drops in, so does a young woman wanting the Betjeman autograph on her copy of his new smash best-seller . . . *Summoned by Bells*. The telephone bell shrills continually, relentlessly summoning him.

In a brief interlude between calls from an importuning TV producer and an editor Mr Betjeman relates a conversation a friend has just had with Earl Attlee: 'Attlee's a dear old thing. He said "Betjeman's such a relief." "A relief from what?" my friend asked. "From other poets," Attlee said.'

Mr Betjeman screeches with laughter, revolving once or twice inside his motionless suit, and, forgetting the whisky, snatches at the teacup.

Then the laughter dies as if a fuse has blown and his face crumples back into its more customary sag of apprehensive dolour.

Swivelling upon his secretary, he says tensely: 'I have to be at the Oxford and Cambridge Club at one o'clock, you know, and my front tyre's flat again. You must get a new tyre – this so undermines one's faith in bicycling.'

He turns to his awaiting interviewer and says: 'My dear chap, I'm fright-fully sorry. Let's escape into the bedroom out of all this *hell*.

'Will you lie on the bed, or shall I? I will. Rather jolly – like being psycho-analysed.'

In the fall of quiet there is opportunity to consider the autumnal, but blazing, flowering of fame and fortune for John Betjeman.

Now 54, and a working poet all his life, it is only in the past few years that he has been adopted by the British as a national emblem, a sort of Uncle Unicorn.[22]

Here we see John moving into position the stage-props of his public persona – the rumpled suit; the cigarettes and whisky to establish his blokishness. He even manages to let Allsop know that he rides about London on a bicycle. The Lord Attlee quotation is there to defend John from any taint of the highbrow. In the interview he attacks his usual targets – chromium fish-and-chip shops, stork-necked concrete fluorescent lamp standards, Civic Centre adult education courses and television lounges in road-houses. 'Betjeman expresses tribal nostal-gia for a vanished security,' Allsop writes. John's new worry, he tells Allsop, is of not being able to pay his taxes. His old apprehension about death is always there. 'I dread the idea of extinction, and I think about death every day.' As the whisky takes effect, John lets some of his resentment at the criticism for *Summoned by Bells* glint through.

Mr Betjeman gives a bellow of laughter, and remarks with appreciable pleasure that in its first three days 'Summoned by Bells' sold 4,500 copies, and that the printing presses are whirling off more by the hour – despite the disparagement of some critics.

'Well,' Mr Betjeman reflects kindly, 'I could hardly expect the approval of these poor accentless, rootless, joyless brain-boxes.

'It is understandable that, not being very good poets themselves, they are envious if one is lucky enough to be more widely read. However, to keep this in proportion I keep reminding myself that Ella Wheeler Wilcox sold like this.'[23]

An interviewer from *Everywoman* visited John a few days later and was treated to a variation on the Betjeman act, tailored to the magazine's readership. The article was headed 'The Gentle Rebel of Rhyme'.

Forty-three Cloth Fair stands, like a little old doll's house, in a tiny court, down a narrow lane off Smithfield Market . . .

Inside the doll's house, up a flight of Tom Thumb stairs, in a wonderfully unbusinesslike office, surrounded by Morris wallpaper, a bowl of pebbles, curtains of altar-cloth, empty tea-cups, an ancient typewriter, a Rossetti drawing, a patchwork of letters and other papers and two or three unbanked cheques, sits Britain's top-pop poet, John Betjeman, propped like a large grey teddy bear in an easy chair.

In one hand, he holds a cylindrical tin of fifty cigarettes, one of which burns remotely in the other hand until a shower of ash cascades upon his lap.

He says: 'Oh, my poor fellow! Fancy having to come here and write about me . . .'

His eyes are sad and his cherubic mouth droops from a melancholia that is far from the chortling Betjeman we have seen on TV.

At the thought of writing, the furrows on his brow stretch from temple to temple; almost joining up with the wispy, fly-away hair that umbrellas his ears.

'I find writing is a fearfully laborious business,' he complains. 'I don't like doing it, do you? I suppose you're like me, you've got no pension to look forward to. It's awfully worrying. I'm no good at business, at all.

'Of course, one can go on writing after people in other professions would have to retire, but I loathe the idea of *having* to sit down and write something. When I compose, I recite aloud – in the street, in trains, wherever I happen to be. People are inclined to regard it as a slightly eccentric habit.

'You know, it took me years to write *Summoned by Bells*. I suppose I said each line over ten or twenty times, constantly changing it, until it

seemed right. Then I showed it to some friends. They suggested *more*
alterations. I'm amazed that so many people like it, aren't you? . . .

'By the way, have you seen my millipede? Maxwell Knight, that natur-
alist chap on television, gave me one. It died, but before it died it laid an
egg, and my present millipede was the result.'[24]

Suddenly, Mr Betjeman has cheered up immensely.

'Fascinating creature,' he says. 'I keep it warm with an electric bulb
covered by a flowerpot and feed it on carrots, and veg that isn't quite fresh.
It sleeps a lot. But when it moves it's marvellous – all those legs like ripples
in the sea undulating over a long shore. I keep it here, at the flat.'[25]

As the article was to appear in a women's magazine, John turned
the conversation to Penelope and the children.

'My daughter is studying typing and shorthand now,' says Betjeman,
'probably spending a good deal of time looking at undergraduates – or the
other way round. She's very pretty.'

He dreams a moment. 'Smashing! A raving beauty!

'Paul is reading geography at Oxford, but his great interest is jazz –
advanced jazz. I think he'll be a musician. He's done his National Service,
you know. He got along very happily as a private, then some silly fool in a
club advised me to persuade him to become an officer. He became one. He
was never happy again.'[26]

Rather than give a formal interview, John let the *Everywoman*
reporter, like Kenneth Allsop, join in his life for a while – a sort of
'audience participation'.

Three visitors from the BBC squeeze into the office. A bottle of liqueur
whisky is plopped beside the teapot and we stand in a solemn circle,
glasses in hand, at eleven thirty in the morning, while the leader of the new
arrivals, an Australian, responds somewhat tonelessly to Mr Betjeman's
earnest plea that he should sing *Waltzing Matilda*.

'Charming fellows,' recalls the poet absently, some time after they have
departed.

John Betjeman swoops upon a shelf and hands down an ancient photograph depicting some twenty or so men in Edwardian costume, a few in
bowlers, a few in toppers, posed statuesquely in a clearing in Epping
Forest.

'What do you make of it? A Midsummer Night's Dream perhaps?
Actually it was taken on a staff outing of my father's firm,' he says. 'I think
this one, here, must be my father.'[27]

John talked to the interviewer about his friends, 'old Tom' (Driberg), 'old Osbert' (Lancaster) and 'old John' (Piper).

'I try to do a bit of painting myself at times,' says Betjeman, squinting in recollection of the effort. 'I spend hours, concentrating like mad, then old John comes along and does a hundred times better in a few strokes. It's rather disheartening.

'My father used to paint a little, you know. He did that one, up there.'

The poet points to a landscape in watercolour among the miscellany of pictures on the wall. Then he snatches another, smaller painting from its hook, places a large hand over part of it to conceal the signature, and demands excitedly, 'Guess who did this . . .'

He removes his fist. 'An early Gerald Kelly![28] I was lucky to get that. Isn't it spiffing!'

And, his triumph complete, the prize is swished back, without ceremony, on to the wall where it hangs, quivering, a little lopsided.

One feels, in this small, immensely personal den of Betjeman's, that one has dodged for a moment the bulldozers of conformity; stepped outside the topsy-turvy world where it is too often clever to be tough and despised to be tender, smart to be smart and absurd to be simple.

'If I hadn't married,' says John Betjeman, the gentle rebel, 'I think I should still be a schoolmaster – extremely quaint and cranky by now, but very happy, I'm sure.[29] There's nothing more exciting than arousing enthusiasm for the things that you enjoy among young children.

'Children respond to poetry with three times the gusto of adults. They are quite fresh and ready for it. What's more, they write poetry better than adults, too. How about: "The square dark squeeze of a dead man's tomb"? *Brrr!*'[30]

From the early 1960s to the mid-1970s, John enjoyed a giddy social life, with a constant succession of lunch-parties and dinner-parties. In 1960 Ben Bonas, his friend from Marlborough days, organized an Old Boys' reunion, a black-tie dinner. Louis MacNeice and John Edward Bowle attended, but Anthony Blunt had to decline because, Bonas told John, 'he is busy with Poussins in Paris'.[31] John saw a lot of Tom Driberg. In 1961 he took him on a memorable tour of the City which Driberg wrote up in the *New Statesman*.* The article shows John at the pitch of his powers, describing old buildings and their history with a connoisseur's delight and abominating the New Brutalism.

John's nearest neighbour in the City, except for the Partners, was Andrew Graham, the wine correspondent of *The Times*, who lived in

* See Appendix 1, 'A Walk with Mr Betjeman'.

the Charterhouse and needed help to empty the many cases of wine he received. He had written amusing novels illustrated by Osbert Lancaster. Having been comptroller (catering manager) of the British Embassy in Paris under both Duff Cooper and Gladwyn Jebb, and secretary of a St James's club, he knew everybody. There were boozy lunches at Graham's flat and later with the *bon vivant* Oliver Van Oss, who had been at Magdalen with John and became Master of the Charterhouse when he retired as headmaster of Charterhouse school. In November 1963 the American versifier Ogden Nash wrote to John: 'I cannot leave without sending you my warmest thanks for the truly glorious two hours you so generously devoted to me, from the opening whisky on through the Charterhouse visit . . . I am still tottery.'[32]

The Garrick Club was another temptation. Fleet Street, today no more than a metaphor, was then still a thrumming reality. (It can be seen as it was then, in the 1963 comedy film *Brothers in Law*, based on Henry Cecil's novel.) John's freelance journalism took him to Fleet Street; and the Garrick was a convenient haven near the City and the newspaper offices. Too often for the health of his bank balance, he entertained there. His publisher, Jock Murray, recalled:

> He was a marvellous host. And unfortunately he was fond of oysters, smoked salmon and champagne. And I remember his accountant, a Mr Masterson, who was also a poet (which is perhaps why he stayed with that accountant) coming into the office and saying, 'Oh, Mr Murray, is there any royalty? Because John is rather in the red.' And he said, 'You know, there are times when I find myself going down on my knees and praying, "O Lord God, prevent John Betjeman from going to the Garrick Club."'[33]

Among the friends John most enjoyed seeing were Ian and Ann Fleming. Ian Fleming was becoming famous through the James Bond books and films. John had first known Ann through her brother Hugo Charteris, novelist and playwright.[34] Her celebrated bitchiness was entertaining so long as it was not turned on oneself; John, who had taken against Evelyn Waugh when the novelist tried to bully him into becoming a Roman Catholic, especially enjoyed the story of how, when Waugh affectedly proffered her his Victorian ear-trumpet, she had banged it smartly with a spoon. In December 1963, a few months before Ian Fleming died, John wrote him a fan letter to cheer him up.[35] Fleming replied: 'A thousand thanks, my dear John, for, I think, the most unexpected and charming letter I have ever had. But as Annie said when she delightedly read me the letter, "Tell him that *he's* the person that created a world."'[36]

THE EUSTON ARCH

At times the urge to preserve the past, with which the Sixties were obsessed, took on the proportions of mania . . . Often the name of John Betjeman was attached to appeals, and eventually Mr Eric Lyons, himself an architect, coined the phrase 'Betjemanic depressives' to stigmatize collectively those who would preserve at all costs everything from the past, be it a wrought-iron lamp-post due for replacement in Chelsea, a Victorian church in Essex complete with its 'blue-jowled and bloody' stained glass, or the celebrated Doric portico at Euston Station.

Bernard Levin, *The Pendulum Years: Britain in the Sixties*,
London 1970

Accepting the Foyle's Poetry Prize in 1955, John said: 'Poets are prophets.'[1] There would seem to be a mysterious link between poesie and prophecy; William Blake is only the most obvious example.[2] John, too, had this gift. In 1933, still in his twenties, he wrote in *The Architectural Review*: 'Hardwick's Doric Arch at Euston is the supreme justification of the Greek Revival in England . . . If vandals ever pulled down this lovely piece of architecture, it would seem as though the British Constitution had collapsed . . .'[3] He lived to see the arch demolished. Its destruction became a *cause célèbre*, an oriflamme for every future conservation battle. As Dr Dan Cruikshank has said, 'The arch had symbolized the might of the railways. Now it was to symbolize institutionalized vandalism and the triumph of stupidity and greed over beauty.'[4]

Euston station was built by the London and Birmingham Railway, a company formed in 1830. The company wished to site its London terminus somewhere in the King's Cross area, but farmers and landowners resisted plans to run lines over their property. Only in 1838 was Parliamentary permission received to extend the line 'to a certain place called Euston Grove; on the north side of Drummond Street near Euston Square'. The directors of the company wanted the new station

to express the importance of the first trunk railway to link the capital and the provinces. It was planned by their engineer, Robert Stephenson, son of George Stephenson of *Rocket* fame. The design was entrusted to Philip Hardwick. The Doric arch was the central feature, a gateway linked to flanking lodges by ornamental gates.

The Euston Arch stood seventy feet high and was supported on four fluted columns each eight feet six inches in diameter. The total length of the façade was 300 feet and it cost the company £35,000. It was built by W. and L. Cubitt using some 80,000 cubic feet of stone from the Bramley Hall quarries in Yorkshire. Behind this entrance were the arrival and departure platforms, offices and waiting-rooms. Although at the time the line to Birmingham was far from complete, Euston station was opened on 20 July 1837, with a service between London and Boxmoor in Hertfordshire. As Victoria had become queen exactly a month before on the death of her uncle William IV, the station just came within the purview of the Victorian Society.

The first reference in the press to the possibility that the arch might be threatened was on 22 January 1960. In a paragraph headed 'PROPOSALS FOR EUSTON STATION ARCH', *The Times* reported that the London County Council town planning committee would have no objection to the removal of the Doric arch at Euston Station – so that the site might be used in the London–Manchester electrification scheme – provided it were re-erected in another 'appropriately dignified and open setting'. The LCC were deferring a decision on the station's Great Hall, which the British Transport Commission (the body charged with overseeing the nationalized British Railways)[5] wanted to remove for the same purpose, to obtain professional advice.

The British Transport Commission had long wanted to see the station redeveloped. Since the building was put up in the 1830s the needs of passenger, freight and parcels traffic had, like the population, vastly increased. The main-line and Underground stations were unequal to the demands made on them. These demands would become greater still when the Commission electrified the main line from London to Birmingham, Manchester and Liverpool. Euston station occupied a large area of land, set back from the Euston Road. The Commission wanted to bring it forward, with longer platforms – which would also be more suitable for trains which were longer and faster than those of the nineteenth century. In addition, London Transport wanted to resite the entrance to Euston Underground station. Beyond these practical issues was the question of 'image', to use a term that became popular in the 1960s. Bernard Kaukas, then deputy to the chief architect of the London Midland Region of British Railways, and – perhaps surprisingly – later a good friend of John's – recalls that the attitude of the Region's general manager was: 'We are coming to the end of the electrification. What an embarrassment if at Euston there is what everyone but the conservationists considers a wretched mish-mash of buildings and platforms, in which it is hellish to try to get a train.' Kaukas concluded: 'No way were they going to have this archaism at the end of the electrified line.'[6]

For a time no decisive action was taken, because British Railways were waiting to hear from the LCC whether the Council would give planning permission for extra storeys to be added to the new station, containing thousands of square feet of lettable office space. Eventually the British Railways Property Board was refused permission to add two extra storeys to each of its ten-, twelve- and sixteen-storey blocks. But this decision, Kaukas recalls, was so slow in coming that the London Midland general manager told his chief architect, Roy Moorcroft, 'I'm no longer prepared to wait any longer for planning permission for a development. You will design and we will build just a railway station.'[7] (British Railways needed no permission for that.)

The British Transport Commission's architects, led by Frederick Curtis, decided that the Doric arch could not be retained in its then position on Drummond Street, facing the present Platform 9. The Commission therefore notified the LCC, as planning authority for the area, of their intention to demolish it. They had to give such notification because the arch was listed by the Ministry of Housing and Local Government as a building of special historic or architectural interest. In the list prepared in 1951 the arch had been registered as Grade II★ – meaning that it was outstanding in the second class. Although copies of the list had been issued to the Society for the Protection of Ancient Buildings and the Georgian Group in 1951, no suggestion that the building was incorrectly listed was made until 1960.[8]

On 27 January 1960, five days after its first paragraph on the Euston Arch, *The Times* reported that the LCC had been told it would cost British Railways £180,000 to take down the Doric arch and re-erect it. The same issue recorded that the LCC was resisting a threat to the Aldwych Theatre. At last, it seemed, Victoriana were news. The first public figure to campaign against the proposed demolitions at Euston was not John, but Woodrow Wyatt, a maverick politician who was then in the Labour Party but who, twenty-five years later, would be among Margaret Thatcher's and Rupert Murdoch's closest friends. (Mrs Thatcher had him ennobled in 1987 as Lord Wyatt of Weeford.) John had first met him soon after the war. They had made jaunts together to such places as Stourhead, and often met later when staying at Chatsworth.[9] With his cigars and gourmandizing and boisterous humour, Wyatt could be fun; but he was not widely respected. When he asked Clement Attlee why he had not made him a minister, Attlee allegedly replied, in his laconic way, 'No good!'[10] Wyatt was an opinionated journalist and a bombastic television interviewer; but as a defender of Britain's heritage he had at least two credentials: he was a kinsman of the Regency architect Benjamin Wyatt; and in 1957 he had helped John save the Regent's Park Terraces.[11] In 1996 he recalled how he and John had decided to challenge British Railways in 1960 and 'confound their knavish tricks'.[12]

John wrote to Wyatt on 28 January 1960:

Dear Woodrow,

How right you were in raising the matter of Euston Great Arch when you did. The bloody British Transport Commission has now come into the open. I am doing a little piece in the *Telegraph* on Monday week. But that immediately gives a political slant, because it appears in that paper, to something that is far more important than politics. I think that there should be a survey made at the instigation of Parliament of all railway architecture and preservation orders put on those stations, viaducts, bridges and tunnel entrances which are worth preserving. In architectural and historical significance they are obviously equal to ruined castles.[13]

John's *Telegraph* article duly appeared on 8 February. It began in conciliatory style. 'The LCC has given permission to British Railways to demolish the Great Arch at Euston, and the attendant lodges. It has made the wise condition "provided that they are re-erected on another site in an appropriate, dignified and open setting".' However, John could not maintain this politeness for long. Later in the article, his anger broke through.

There is very little written about railway buildings. The names of the architects of some of our grandest stations such as Temple Meads are forgotten.

Partly because of this and partly because of an incredible insensitivity to architecture on the part of the British Transport Commission in the past, a great many splendid buildings have been mutilated or allowed to decay.

Unfortunately, he noted, railway enthusiasts were mostly interested in engines, train speeds and the history of railway development, rather than in buildings. But Euston had been built 'with all the courage and swagger of a time which was convinced of a glorious future'. He ended with a suggestion. 'I can think of no worthier memorial to the fact that Britain built the first railways than to reconstruct this Arch, its lodges and railings on the Euston Road itself.'

Meanwhile, Woodrow Wyatt was getting his campaign under way. The *Times* Parliamentary report of 10 February 1960 included the headline 'CHANGES AT EUSTON: "VANDALISM" TO DESTROY GREAT HALL'. Sir Keith Joseph, then Parliamentary Secretary at the Ministry of Housing and Local Government (but twenty-five years later the 'Mad Monk of Monetarism' and 'a Thatcherite before Mrs Thatcher'), reported to the House of Commons that the British Transport Commission had given notice that it intended to remove both the Great Hall and the Doric arch at Euston. The Ministry was 'considering the matter'. Wyatt intervened: 'It would be an act of vandalism to destroy the Great Hall and Shareholders' Room at Euston, which was the first railway station to be built in any capital city in the world, and has been designated as an historic monument.'

A speech by Julian Snow, Labour Member for Lichfield and Tamworth, showed that the conservationists were not going to have things all their own way. 'There are mixed views about the Doric arch,' he said. 'While it has an historic quality, not everybody is convinced that it has artistic merit.' The next day, Wyatt tabled a motion calling for the preservation of the Great Hall and the Shareholders' Room, and asking that the Doric arch should be resited. On 18 March the LCC appointed three advisers to report on the architectural and engineering aspects of Euston. On 16 April Wyatt wrote to *The Times*: only the Ministry of Housing and Local Government could now stop the destroyers.

On 19 April *The Times* published a strong letter from Nikolaus Pevsner. 'If the Euston Arch were destroyed,' he wrote, 'that would be the worst loss to the Georgian style in London architecture since most of Soane's Bank of England fell shortly before the war.' No doubt

Pevsner calculated that there would be more sympathy for 'Georgian' than for 'Victorian'. He thought it was a challenge to the railways' architect. 'The Romans, in building the most beautiful railway station there is, could make a feature of a fragment of Roman wall inside it. Could not an English architect enhance the symbolic character of the old architecture by making it a monument inside his new building?' Pevsner missed the point: it was, in part, precisely *because* of its symbolism that British Railways wanted to get rid of the arch. Ian Grant has commented: 'It was for imagistic reasons and no other that British Railways wanted to demolish the arch. It symbolized to them the old steam age which was an image they wanted to put behind them.' Support for Pevsner came in a letter to *The Times* from J.J. Hodgson: '[The arch] is completely appropriate as the gateway to the great industrial towns and cities of the north. Massive, grimy, Ozymandias-like, it symbolizes the industrial revolution. Nobody could travel to Cheltenham or Tunbridge Wells through such an arch. But for Wigan and Stockport it is so right.'[14]

John was temporarily quiescent. With Elizabeth Cavendish, he was taken up with preparations for the wedding of Princess Margaret and Antony Armstrong-Jones (Lord Snowdon), which he and Penelope attended on 6 May.[15] But Wyatt was still on the warpath. In a reply to him in Parliament on 18 May, Sir Keith Joseph said he regretted it, but the Great Hall had to go. On 11 June John's friend Sir John Summerson contributed a long signed article to *The Times*, 'A GREAT MUSEUM PIECE DOOMED'. That headline was written by a sub-editor, not by Summerson. As justification for his heading, the 'sub' could have pointed to the last paragraph of Summerson's piece: 'It is the station itself which is the great museum-piece commemorating as no other structure in the world the moment of supreme optimism in the marriage of steam and progress.' But between the headline and the peroration were 1,600 words of damning faint praise.

John always called Summerson 'Coolmore', not just because it was his mother's maiden name, but because it seemed to fit him: there was something of frigid neo-classicism in his character. His article on Euston was severe to the point of disparagement. Its first sentence was defeatist and deprecating. 'Euston station as it stands at this moment (but will not stand for very much longer) is, perhaps, the greatest railway curiosity in the world.' A *curiosity*: something that had no place in the brave post-austerity Britain of the 1960s. He wrote:

It was . . . in 1835 that the station was begun and almost from the first the idea of the station comprehended the fantastic idea of the portico.

Fantastic it was, this structure costing £35,000 and useful only by virtue of the iron gates and lodges on either side of it. As an approach to the modest little station building which stood behind and a little to the right of it, it was manifestly absurd. But that was not the point. It was the gateway to a much greater structure than that, to the line itself and all the railway works as far as Birmingham, where the passenger was received in the shadow of another huge and equally useless classical propylaeum.[16]

Fantastic . . . manifestly absurd . . . useless: with friends like Summerson, Euston hardly needed enemies. More withering observations followed.

Today the Euston portico or 'arch' (as it is wrongly but perhaps irrevocably called) stands in grossly embarrassed relationship to everything around it. It must be imagined in its first setting, seen across the square from Euston Road with the sky behind it, framed between stucco terraces. It is a Greek portico – Greek Doric, based, no doubt, on the Agora gateway at Athens recorded by Stuart and Revett; Greek Doric partly perhaps as an act of stylistic vanity but also because that order seemed to have the toughness, the precision and power of the railway age. In 1835 to be Grecian was to be modern.

Grossly embarrassed . . . stylistic vanity: Summerson was pulling the pins from grenades which the enemies of Euston were to hurl. The Great Hall was 'today little more than an overblown waiting-room'.

It is very much a young man's design. Philip Hardwick has forsaken the Greek and embraced the Italian Renaissance; he has noted the splendid frieze in the saloon of the Palazzo Massimi [Rome]; and he has been impressed by illustrations of the vestibule of Schinkel's Berlin Opera House. He has tried to combine every sort of grandeur (not forgetting the French stair) in a creation of over-powering monumentality. The success of his efforts must be a matter of opinion.

In the weeks that followed, Summerson's words gave the cue to less temperate critics. A letter to *The Times* from the Conservative MP Sir Frank Markham (28 June) deplored the idea that the arch might be moved to another site.

I wonder if those advocating re-erection realize the size of the arch and the attendant lodges, and that its reconstruction on another site would require nearly a quarter of an acre of valuable land? Have they considered who should pay for the added cost of removal and re-erection? I suggest that if lovers of monstrous railway eccentricities wish to retain the arch, they only, and not British Railways, should pay for it.[17]

The question of who might pay for the moving of the arch was aired in Parliament early in July 1960. *The Times* reported the debate under the headline 'HOME FOR EUSTON'S DORIC ARCH: NO MONEY FOR REMOVAL'. Sir Frank Markham had asked the Minister of Housing and Local Government what progress had been made in negotiations between the LCC and the British Transport Commission, about the removal of the arch. Sir Keith Joseph replied: 'The LCC has been informed by the BTC that the commission would raise no objection to the re-erection of the arch if a suitable site can be agreed, but they are not willing to pay for it.' Joseph added that there was no possibility of a contribution from the Government.[18]

In the meantime, John had been stirring things up behind the scenes. Although in 1953 he had lost a battle to prevent Magdalen College, Oxford, from creating a rose-garden in the High Street, it had taught him the value of a decision by the Royal Fine Art Commission.[19] No public body could wholly ignore such a recommendation, even if the intention was to defy it eventually; so the Commission could at least defer catastrophe. John used his influence with the RFAC, and his vote; the Commission recommended that the Euston Arch should be preserved. In the Commons on 21 July 1960, Woodrow Wyatt asked the Prime Minister, Harold Macmillan, whether he would appoint a minister with the responsibility of implementing the RFAC's recommendation. 'No,' Macmillan replied. 'Such action would be entirely inconsistent with the Commission's status as an advisory body.' Wyatt was not to be put down.

> Will the Prime Minister look into this, and check the careless vandalism that is going on under his Government? The RFAC have recommended to the Ministry of Housing and Local Government that Euston Station should not be pulled down and the Doric arch not destroyed. It has been totally ignored. These are wonderful monuments to the railway age which should not disappear entirely. (*Some Ministerial laughter*.)[20]

That was the trouble with having Wyatt on one's side: no one took him very seriously. Macmillan replied that the Commission's letter on the subject was being studied. The next speaker was a politician who was far more respected, John's old schoolfriend and flatmate Hugh Gaitskell, the Leader of the Opposition: 'There is considerable doubt if the Commission has the resources to enable it to fulfil its extremely important functions adequately.' But he was fobbed off too.

Macmillan agreed the Commission needed extra staff and said he would 'look into it'.[21]

So far, the tabloid press had taken no interest in the fate of the Euston Arch. It was more interested in the fate of a man who, on 18 April 1960, was seen spreadeagled on the roof of the first coach of a Euston-to-Glasgow express. The train's stoker spotted him as it neared Boxmoor station. As the train was approaching a bridge, the stoker, Mr Bannister, 'sprayed the man with a hose to prevent him from standing up'.[22] It was in 1961 that the public furore over the arch broke out. The year began quietly enough, with the announcement in January that the London-to-Midlands electrification would be complete by 1966. In April, in the Royal Fine Art Commission's 17th annual report, Lord Bridges drew attention to the need to rebuild 'the Great Arch at Euston' on an adjoining site.[23] It must have seemed ironic to John that while one of his greatest friends, John Summerson, was damaging the Euston cause, two of his hate-figures were supporting it – Pevsner and Bridges.[24]

The Minister of Transport entered the dispute: Ernest Marples, an on-the-make politician whose character was well hit off in a *Private Eye* cover which showed him peering into an aluminium dustbin, with the voice-balloon 'What's in it for me?' In a Parliamentary written reply of 13 July 1961, he announced that 'it will not be possible to save the historic buildings at Euston, including the Doric arch'. Expert advisers to the Ministry of Works, he said, had estimated that the cost of dismantling and re-erecting the arch alone, without its flanking lodges, would be about £190,000, compared with £12,000 for simple demolition. The arch weighed about 4,700 tons, and to brace it and move it on rollers would cost even more. The Government's decision 'had not been reached without regret at the passing of a major monument of the Victorian railway age, but there was no practicable alternative'. The British Transport Commission had been told they could 'proceed on this basis'. In other words, the green light had been given for demolition. Two days later *The Times* printed a furious letter from John Gloag. The arch, he wrote, was 'an example of the genius of early nineteenth-century architects working in the classical idiom, which was then a living and inspiring tradition'. He demanded: 'Would any European country allow such a landmark of architectural history to be removed, on economic or any other grounds, without some attempt to raise the money for its preservation or re-erection?'

The last word on the arch had not been spoken, though things looked black from the *Times* headline of 27 September, 'EUSTON MUST LOSE ITS DORIC ARCH'. A last-minute plea by the Royal Fine Art Commission had been unsuccessful, the paper reported.

'Contractors are due to begin pulling [the arch] down this week.' The Commission thought that the least that could be done was to preserve it in a way that would not interfere with railway operations, even if that involved substantial extra cost. *The Times* added: 'The Victorian Society, whose chairman is Mr John Betjeman, is making an effort to save the arch by starting a public fund. It aims to raise £90,000, which it believes will be necessary to move the arch nearer Euston Road. In the meantime the Minister [Marples] has been asked to delay demolition.' Aside from his own article in the *Telegraph*, this was the first time that John's name had been publicly mentioned in connection with the save-the-arch campaign. The next day, *The Times* reported that demolition of the arch would now begin in about two weeks' time. A representative of the contractors, Leonard Fairclough Ltd of Adlington, Lancashire, had told the paper that the job would take several weeks. It would be done by hand so as to cause as little inconvenience as possible to station and road traffic. A spokesman for the London Midland Region said it would be impossible to blow up the Portland-stone arch because of the adjacent buildings. 'But', he said, 'the demolition will be complete.'[25]

On 29 September it was reported that in a reply to a letter of protest from Ivor Bulmer-Thomas of the Ancient Monuments Society, Marples's assistant private secretary had said: 'Although the arch was not ornamental it was a formidable structure.' The columns, nine feet in diameter (actually eight feet six), were hollow, with a void, four feet five inches square, for their entire heights. The flank walls were also hollow and the ends of the walls consisted of stone blocks of fifteen to twenty tons apiece. The whole edifice was carried on a system of relieving arches in the foundations, and because the jointing throughout was very fine, meticulous care would have had to be taken to avoid damage if the arch were to have been removed with the view of recreating it. In spite of this bleak answer, Bulmer-Thomas told *The Times* that 'the efforts of the society to save the arch were continuing'.

The Victorian Society was still trying to raise money. On the night of 1 October it sent a telegram to the Prime Minister:

> Sincerely hope demolition of the Euston portico may be postponed to give us a chance of raising funds for its removal to an appropriate site. If immediate demolition is unavoidable we earnestly and with great respect entreat you to ensure that the stones are numbered and stored to make further reerection possible, as was done for Marble Arch and Temple Bar.

The Times reported on 2 October, 'EUSTON ARCH: NO CHANGE OF PLAN'. A Ministry of Transport official commented: 'People have been in touch with the Prime Minister about it, and he has been in touch with us, but there has been no change of plan.'

Representing the Victorian Society, John made a television appeal. By now the arch was covered in scaffolding, bearing the signboards of the general contractors, Fairclough, and of the demolition firm, Valori. Standing in front of the arch, John's bespectacled interviewer said:

> The Victorians built to last. They built this gateway to Birmingham in granite. Now, 125 years later, it is to come down. But who is this, pushing his way to the foot of the gallows with a last message of hope? Who but Mr John Betjeman of the Victorian Society?

Turning to John, he asked, 'Why should we bother with this arch?' John replied:

> It was the first bit of railway architecture in the world of any size – it's very grand-scale. Fine stone – granite. And if it were moved forward in front of the new Euston Station, it would be the most magnificent public monument in London.[26]

On 16 October some of the protesters staged a dramatic public demonstration. A group of young architects led by G.H. Slater met in the Great Hall at Euston at lunch-time and marched to the portico where Slater and a colleague named Mustoe climbed on to the scaffolding to attach a fifty-foot banner with the inscription 'SAVE THE ARCH' on it. A member of the demolition team removed it. *The Times* reported: 'Apart from a few cries of "Ban the bomb", lunch-hour travellers were unperturbed by the demonstration. The idea of the protest had been thought of only on Saturday and there had been no time for publicity; this partly explained the attendance of fewer than half of the expected 150 demonstrators. Mr Colin Boyne, editor of the *Architects' Journal*, and Sir John Summerson were also present . . . Mr Slater emphasized that this might be the last opportunity to avert what he regarded as an act of vandalism by the Government, and his warning was strengthened by the ominous scaffolding covering the portico and the noise of pneumatic drills that have already demolished an adjoining lodge.' The report added that the possibility of moving the arch had been put forward by a Canadian firm, Nicholas Brothers, which had offered to move it on rollers at an estimated cost of £90,000. The Victorian Society had raised a forlorn £1,000 towards this. The society had received a letter from the Prime Minister stating that the possibility of numbering and storing the stones would be examined.[27]

By appearing at the demonstration, Summerson was doing his best to atone for his barbed words of the year before; but the gesture came too late. On the day after the demonstration, *The Times* published an editorial headed 'NOT WORTH SAVING'.[28] It was the arch's death-warrant. John's old colleague from 'Archie Rev' days, J. M. ('Karl Marx') Richards, had been *The Times*'s architectural correspondent since 1947. He had got on well with the editors Robin Barrington-Ward and William Casey, but found their successor, Sir William Haley, far less easy to work with. Haley had been a telephonist on *The Times*, had left when his suggestion for improving the telephone service was rejected, had risen to be director-general of the BBC, and had returned to the newspaper in triumph as editor in 1952. (The man who had rejected his telephone suggestion committed suicide.) Though a forceful leader and a man of obvious integrity, Haley was shy and aloof; J. B. Priestley said he was the only man he had ever known with two glass eyes. Among the 'Black Friars', as Lord Northcliffe had called them, the Oxbridge mandarins of Printing House Square, Haley felt insecure about his cultural credentials. Parading the learning of an auto-didact, he contributed each week a somewhat pedantic article about books, under the pseudonym Oliver Edwards. (An article headed 'MARY MacCARTHY' turned out to be about the nineteenth-century novelist, with not a hint that a famous contemporary novelist of the same name existed.) He had respect for the paper's experts – the wine correspondent, the museums correspondent and so on – but if any of them seemed to challenge his authority as editor, Haley would smack them down. Unfortunately, Richards's rather prickly personality was of exactly the kind to cause friction with Haley. Richards recalled:

[Haley] was genuinely high-minded, but had a fondness for making dogmatic pronouncements, at least about architecture, based on nothing but prejudice and a total absence of visual judgement . . . I had several conflicts with him, culminating in the case of the Euston arch . . . When I thought the time had come for *The Times* to add its weight to the campaign, which I was already supporting, of course, in *The Architectural Review* [of which Richards was now editor], I spoke to Haley. He turned down my request with some scornful generalization about Victorian architecture, and I had to resign myself to *The Times* not intervening. Next morning to my indignation – and my embarrassment, because my connection with *The Times* was well known in the architectural world – *The Times* had a leader, written I afterwards discovered by Haley himself, under the heading 'Not Worth Saving', declaring that the public campaign should be ignored and the Euston arch demolished as a useless and outdated object.[29]

One suspects that Haley was out to teach Richards a lesson: you don't argue with the editor, whose decision is final. But Haley was not without subtlety. He wrapped his criticism of the arch in a more general attack on conservationists who were indiscriminate in their crusades and thus weakened their case when something worth saving was threatened. Many would have seen these remarks as aimed directly at John, the most persistent campaigner, and the best known.

> Vandalism is always threatening the faces of city and countryside [Haley wrote] and perpetual vigilance in resisting it is a mark of good citizenship. But those who launch defensive campaigns need a sense of proportion no less than do architects. If they lack this guide when profitably to fly to arms and when to accept some change as harmless or even desirable they run the risk of wearying other people by their lamentations . . . The clamour against removing the Euston portico is a cautionary case in point.[30]

Haley noted that one critic of the arch, at the time of the Great Exhibition, had called it 'gigantic and very absurd'. Clearly Haley had ordered up the Euston Arch cuttings from the *Times* 'ID' (Intelligence Department or library). He seized on Summerson's too cool appraisal of 1960, which was now flung back in his face – 'stands in embarrassed relationship to everything around'. Haley concluded: 'Whether we dismiss [the arch] as some of our ancestors did as "Glyn's Folly" (in reference to SIR STEPHEN GLYN, the first chairman of the London and Birmingham Railway) or hail it as a Hardwick masterpiece, we should think twice before devoting to its preservation funds that could be so much better spent elsewhere.' [31]

When he read the leader, Richards considered resigning, but decided that that would be a purposeless gesture. 'I have never believed in resigning. It is something you can do only once, and I would be denying myself further opportunities of exerting influence through the columns of *The Times*, even though such opportunities were proving to be disappointingly fewer than I had hoped. I am fairly sure that Haley's pronouncement influenced Harold Macmillan, the Prime Minister.'[32]

As a desperate last measure, the Victorian Society and other groups had approached Macmillan again and he had agreed to receive a deputation. The meeting took place on 24 October. The deputation, led by Sir Charles Wheeler, president of the Royal Academy, included John, Richards, Summerson, Pevsner, the then Earl of Euston, Hugh Casson and Peter Fleetwood-Hesketh.

Richards later wrote: 'Macmillan listened – or I suppose he listened; he sat without moving with his eyes apparently closed.

He asked no questions; in fact he said nothing except that he would consider the matter . . .'[33] Fleetwood-Hesketh recalled the Prime Minister as slightly less taciturn:

> The whole thing was organized by an old friend of mine, Sir Hamilton Kerr.[34] He was absolutely splendid. He organized this delegation. I think it was held at the Admiralty, because Downing Street was being rebuilt. We'd provided Macmillan's people for months with all the information. We all sat down at this table. Macmillan was there; on his right was Ernest Marples; on Marples's right was myself and then the rest of the deputation. And within a minute or two of the beginning of the meeting it transpired that in spite of our having supplied them with all the relevant information, Macmillan knew absolutely nothing about it. You would have thought he'd never heard of the Euston Arch. He said: 'I understand you want to pull it down stone by stone and build it up again.' Well, *months* before we had said that was out of the question. What we proposed to do was to move it on rollers, which had been done in every other country for years – Canada, America, France, Germany. But whatever information we had fed into that Prime Ministerial office, evidently hadn't percolated. And that beautiful thing could have been left where it was, or moved forward on rollers for £90,000. Why didn't they agree to that? It was sheer pique on the part of British Railways and the Government. They were so outraged that anybody should dare to criticize them. They were savages![35]

Hugh Casson's memory of the meeting was that 'We were courteously received but it was quite clear that we had got absolutely not a single inch. I don't think that Macmillan, really – like many aristocratic people – had ever taken much notice of Victorian architecture. Most of them had inherited great Georgian houses. The idea of something attached to a railway station – this wasn't of much interest.'[36] (In later years Casson was fond of pointing out that 'the three architectural mistakes made in London since the war' – in his opinion, the removal of the Euston Arch, the siting of the Hilton Hotel and the selling-off of County Hall – had all happened under Conservative governments.)[37] Macmillan himself may have come to regret the destruction of the arch. His biographer, Sir Alistair Horne, writes: 'Macmillan . . . probably drew more personal invective over a misguided decision determining the fate of the Doric Arch at Euston Station than over all the rest of the Beeching Cuts.'[38]

Ten days after Macmillan saw the deputation, Sir Charles Wheeler, as its leader, received his reply. *The Times* gave the gist of it in a main home-news story headed 'EUSTON PORTICO FATE INEVITABLE,

SAYS MR MACMILLAN: LITTLE OR NO PROSPECT OF
FINDING AN ALTERNATIVE SITE'. The Doric arch could not be
saved, Macmillan wrote. There was the question of time: 'It is urgently
necessary to get ahead with this work [of rebuilding the station].'[39]

Bernard Kaukas thinks that this argument would have been particularly telling in the minds of the Government and the Railways.

> I am sure that by that time Macmillan's advisers, who had been talking to
> the permanent secretaries in the Department of Transport, were being
> told, 'We cannot wait any longer. We've got to have this station completed
> in time for the Queen to open it.' When you think the Queen had to be
> booked a year ahead anyway – a minimum of a year – somebody was
> saying, 'If we go on like this we're never going to get anything done' and
> the London Midland manager, a powerful, good manager, said, 'Finish!
> Enough!'. . . A sorry story – but the truth usually is a sorry story, isn't it?[40]

A movement needs a martyr. A religion needs a human sacrifice; a
conservation movement needs an architectural sacrifice. Though the
loss of the arch was grievous – 'Eustonasia', it was called at the time –
the conservationists learned new cunning. They realized they had left
everything too late, they had not mobilized their forces in time, they
had failed to raise enough money, their generals were too far from the
front line. Developers learned something too. The row brought odium
on the Railways and the Government. In future, developers perhaps
thought twice before planning the casual demolition of a listed building. 'Remember the Euston Arch' was the word in boardrooms.

The immediate result of the Euston demolition was a conservation
backlash, moving from the particular to the general: were *any*
national monuments safe in this philistine Government's keeping? The
different 'amenity societies', often rather sniffy about each other,
closed ranks for an onslaught on official vandalism. In a joint statement on 6 November, the SPAB, the Victorian Society and the
Georgian Group said: 'We are seriously concerned about the threat to
other great architectural monuments in the custody of the Ministry of
Transport. We intend to press the Government to make clear their
future intentions in regard to such buildings at the earliest possible
moment.' The portico, they pointed out, was being destroyed against
the advice of the three officially appointed bodies concerned. 'The
English people are losing their finest triumphal gateway to make room
for a building which they must pay for, but the plans and elevations of
which they have never been allowed to see.'[41]

Frank Valori, managing director of the company responsible for
demolishing the arch,[42] was so upset at having to do it ('he cried all the

way to the bank', as a cynical later commentator said) that he presented the Victorian Society with a silver model of the arch, 'to perpetuate the building's memory'. On 6 March 1962 Lord Esher, as the society's president, accepted the gift. *The Times* reported:

> Lord Esher frankly admitted that this generous gesture made him feel as if some man had murdered his wife and then presented him with her bust by Epstein. But, he added, Mr Valori was a benevolent executioner who, as a man of taste with a respect for the architecture, had undertaken the demolition without pleasure . . . The guilt lay in the low mental capacity of what were called top people. [This was a snarling reference to the then familiar advertisement, 'Top People Read *The Times*' and hence to Haley's editorial.]
>
> It was to the retarded mentality of those who set out to govern us that this artistic outrage was to be attributed. It would happen again and he foresaw dozens of silver replicas passing into the society's headquarters in Great Ormond Street.[43]

After this speech of graciousness, ungraciousness, good taste, bad taste, wit and bile, drinks were served. John was at the party. In this less formal setting, and not for the notebook of the man from *The Times*, Esher was heard to remark, in his booming, bassoon-like voice: 'I am often accused of preferring buildings to people. Well, the Euston Arch is *irreplaceable*. People? They can be replaced quite easily. And with a certain amount of pleasure.'[44] Later, as if in mimicry of the granite original, the miniature silver arch 'went missing'. It has never been recovered.

Apart from his *Telegraph* article, his television appearance, his words to the Royal Fine Art Commission and his joining the deputation to Macmillan, John kept in the background during the Euston Arch campaign. He did not write letters to *The Times*, clamber about on scaffolding or (with the exception of Wyatt) lobby MPs. Yet when people looked back on the scandal of the Euston Arch and execrated Macmillan, Marples, British Railways and Haley, it was always John who was mentioned as the leader of the campaign to save it. Bernard Kaukas firmly believed that John had led the deputation to Macmillan.[45] Bernard Levin also helped perpetuate this myth of John's central rôle, in his book about the 1960s, *The Pendulum Years* (1970). In, for him, a rare and perverse aberration of taste, Levin reviled, or affected to revile, the arch.

> At times [he wrote] the urge to preserve the past, with which the Sixties were obsessed, took on the proportions of mania. There was nothing

so ugly, so dirty, so useless, so lacking in any kind of aesthetic, historical
or stylistic attraction that it was impossible to find a group of people
willing to solicit funds for its removal to a permanent home. Often the
name of John Betjeman was attached to appeals, and eventually Mr Eric
Lyons, himself an architect, coined the phrase 'Betjemanic depressives' to
stigmatize collectively those who would preserve at all costs everything
from the past, be it a wrought-iron lamp-post due for replacement in
Chelsea, a Victorian church in Essex complete with its 'blue-jowled and
bloody' stained glass, or the celebrated Doric portico at Euston Station.
This last created the greatest preservationist furore of the decade . . .[46]

Levin said he found it difficult to believe that most of the protesters
about the arch had ever set eyes on it.

In 1978 John Pinches, a firm of medallists, conscripted John for a
somewhat kitsch exercise, a series of silver medals, mounted in a blue
and gold leatherette case, to be sold as 'Betjeman's Bygone Britain'.
On the front of each medal would be depicted a British building that
had been destroyed; on the back, a text written by John would be
engraved. Of course there was a Euston Arch medal. On the back
John's text read: 'Euston Propylaeum London 1836–39. Doric gateway
to the first trunk railway in the world. Arc. Philip Hardwick.
Destroyed by British Rail [sic] 1961.' The London bookseller Ben
Weinreb, a friend of John's, called this set of medals 'The Revenge of
Betjeman'.

More scathing still were the words John wrote about the new
Euston in his and John Gay's book, *London's Historic Railway
Stations*.

What masterpiece arose on the site of the old station? No masterpiece.
Instead there is a place where nobody can sit; an underground taxi-
entrance so full of fumes that drivers, passengers and porters alike hate it.
A great hall of glass looks like a mini-version of London Airport, which
it seems to be trying to imitate. On its expanse of floor and against its
walls passengers lie and await trains, which they are not allowed to enter
from the platforms below without the permission of uniformed gen-
darmes at the barriers, who imprison the travellers in the hall until the last
possible moment. A constant stream of lengthy official verbiage pours
over the waiting queues: 'buffet car and refreshment facilities will be available on this service', 'will Mr MacAlpine awaiting a passenger from Crewe
kindly contact the Information desk'; hygienic and slippery buffets may be
glimpsed on upper floors, and less hygienic and more slippery bars are
entered from the hall itself. The telephone boxes are open to the full blast
of the Tannoy system and the Irish drunks who have always haunted

Euston . . . The smell of sweat and used clothes, even in winter, is strong in this hall, for there is something funny about the air-conditioning. In hot weather it is cooler to go to the empty space in front of the station, where the portico could easily have been rebuilt . . .[47]

In 1960, when Summerson had insisted in his *Times* article that the arch should be called a portico, John had teased him with a skit on *Prufrock* –

> In the room the women come and go,
> Talking of Euston portico.[48]

On the Pinches medal he gave it the still fancier name of 'propylaeum'. But in folk memory it remained 'the Euston Arch'. Its destruction could be considered the greatest failure of John's career as a conservationist; but in time he wore the defeat with pride, like a duelling scar. Though he did not win all his future fights, he entered them as a battle-hardened veteran – or at least with the *reputation* of a battle-hardened veteran. He learned lessons from the Euston fiasco and became genuinely more formidable. But he was haunted by a feeling that he had not done enough.

The new Euston station was opened in 1968. In that year, the architects Alison and Peter Smithson published their book, *The Euston Arch and the Growth of the London, Midland and Scottish Railway*. The Smithsons had been unlikely allies of John in the campaign to save the arch. As designers of the Hunstanton secondary modern school, Norfolk (1949–54), they had been celebrated pioneers of the New Brutalism – the architectural style that John specially abominated.[49] But they felt passionately about the arch. In her section of the 1968 book, Alison Smithson (a novelist as well as an architect) wrote:

> What stuff for a novel lies in the rubble – or buried in the rockeries made from the broken stone – or smoulders in the ash-trays ground out of the Doric guttae rumoured to be gracing the desks of railway top brass . . .
>
> Who were the men who really could have countermanded the destruction order?
>
> Somewhere you would think were two or three who would know the power of meaning in the object involved.
>
> Why were these men not found by the writers of the Royal Fine Art Commission letters, by the architects who picketed the place with such genteel sobriety, by the men who went to the Prime Minister and limply left without a promise – or a scene?[50]

Several of the journalists who wrote about Euston in 1968 also went in for blame-laying and scapegoat-hunting. The *Sunday Times* published a swingeing article by John Fielding on 22 September. He viewed the whole Euston saga as 'an acid reminder of how to throw away money'.

By failing to exploit a site in an area where office accommodation brings in almost £5 a square foot and freehold land sells for almost any price you like to pull out of a hat, the railways – and ultimately the taxpayers – have abandoned an asset potentially worth a good £40 million.

On 14 October 1968 – the day the new station was opened by the Queen – Michael Baily, the respected transport correspondent of *The Times*, contributed an article headed 'Lost opportunity'. He wrote: 'As a piece of urban planning in the capital of a country with severe traffic and transport problems it stands as a monument to ignorance and bureaucratic bungling.' The fault with BR's plans, Baily thought, was not that they were too ambitious but that they were not ambitious enough. 'If there is anywhere in London that deserves mile-high sky-scrapers it is at the centre of the main railway terminals.' Workers could be brought right into their offices by trains 'originating in darkest Surrey', relieving buses and roads of congestion. Baily thought British Rail should be stripped of the property-developing function in which they had proved themselves so incompetent.[51]

Both Fielding and Baily compared British Rail's performance with the rival Euston Centre rising near-by (opened 1969). Fielding wrote:

Four hundred yards to the west of Euston [station] stands Joe Levy's 400 ft office tower at Euston Centre, an embarrassing indication that dealing with many of the same authorities over the same period of time as the rail-waymen, private enterprise pulled off one of the biggest development coups of the century.

Why, he wondered, had there been planning permission for the Centre, but no planning permission for the station? A book that would have given him the answer (he and Baily had evidently not read it) was *The Property Boom* (1967) by Oliver Marriott, financial editor of *The Times* – a penetrating exposé of the commercial-property business since 1945. Marriott devoted a chapter to 'The Euston Centre: Joe Levy and Robert Clark'. He laid bare the way in which, at every turn, the LCC valuers had favoured the private property developers D.E. and J. Levy and Robert Clark. Because, in the early 1950s, Joe Levy had obtained outline planning permission from the LCC for

a 120,000 square foot office block, he had the Council 'over a barrel';
also, the LCC 'needed a private developer who would fit in with its
own plans'.[52] A cosy relationship was established. The LCC made
closing orders on houses and flats. Marriott concludes: 'Throughout
the LCC was . . . exceedingly cooperative with Joe Levy. It was almost
like having a fourth estate agent in the consortium.'[53] And great
secrecy was preserved. Only in 1960 did insiders wake up to the
possibility that Stock Conversion (the Levy–Clark company) 'might
be a vast iceberg'.[54] Not until 1964 was something like the full story
uncovered – by Judy Hillman of the *Evening Standard*.[55] After George
Brown put a ban on new offices, in November of that year, Joe Levy
gleefully referred to his Euston Tower as 'Monopoly House'.[56]

Oliver Marriott does not so much as mention the Euston Arch. But
it is clear from his book that John, in his efforts to save the arch, was
pitted not just against British Railways, but against the LCC with its
bias in favour of Levy and Clark. 'If British Railways had been allowed
to build its offices,' Bernard Kaukas said, 'that would have paid for the
Doric arch to be moved anywhere you like.'[57]

AUSTRALIA 1961

I cannot say his book makes me want to go to Australia, even if I could afford the passage.

John Betjeman, reviewing Donald McLean's novel *No Man Is an Island*, 'Life in a Silver Mining Town of Australia', *Daily Telegraph*, 21 January 1956

Oi'm *loovin* Aussieland.

John Betjeman, letter to Penelope Betjeman, 7 November 1961

In 1961 John's former employers, the British Council, flew him to Australia for a five-week cultural tour. He was to sing for his supper by giving lectures. Before he left, though, there were some problems to sort out. The Euston Arch controversy was not quite played out.[1] He was dissatisfied with his current secretary, the Rev. Mr Jourdain, the latest in the long sequence of 'non-secular secs'. On 21 October John wrote to Penelope that he had had to get rid of him. 'He is very conscientious & pathetic but really too incapable to be able to deal with things in my absence & know what was important from what was not. He has got a better paid, if duller job with the Metal Box Company.'[2] In his place John was taking on another part-time clergyman, the Rev. R. N. Timms of Brockham, Surrey, who would look after his affairs in his absence.

John was worried about his son Paul, who was jobless and staying with Gerard Irvine at 'St Philbert's' (St Cuthbert's Clergy House, Philbeach Gardens, London). Paul had applied for a job as a trainee interior decorator with the leading designer David Hicks. He had desperately swotted up in homes-and-gardens magazines but had been turned down ('thank goodness', John wrote to Penelope,[3] who was on her riding holiday in Spain*). On 25 October he wrote to her, under a sketch of herself and her riding companions: 'Oi keep himagining yew as mooch the toiniest person on the expedition accompanied boi

---

* On this holiday, see Chapter 1 of the present volume, 'Wantage'.

Spanish villains & always wearin that round at yew wore at the airport when oi saw yew off.'[4] In another letter: 'BEWARE OF BRIGANDS!'[5]

John left London on a BOAC airliner on Sunday 29 October. In an article about the trip which he later wrote for *Vogue* he recalled: 'An official of the British Council in London asked me to lunch before I went, to warn me not to patronize the Australians. Such had not been my intention, but I can see what he meant. It is a mistake to expect a welcome simply because one comes from England.'[6] He added:

Why did I, in the first instance, accept an invitation to go? The air journey was even more formidable than I had been told and I strongly advise visitors to break the journey with two nights' rest on land on the way. One reason for going was the natural desire we all have to escape from Mr Marples' traffic problems and the depredations of 'developers'. Besides that, I was invited for November, which is springtime down under. Another reason was that I would have none of those language difficulties which make the continent of Europe so difficult for one who has had the advantages of a public school education. The overriding reason was to see what it was like. Sir Kenneth Clark and the late Neville [*sic*] Shute[7] had long urged me to go there, telling me I would enjoy it. I had a suspicion it might be like America and I had spent a month of March [in Cincinnati] in the Middle West when the land was brown and dry and robins as big as pheasants hopped about on the porch swings and the sun sank early behind Lutheran steeples in the land of Uncle Tom's Cabin. Australia was quite unknown to me and to most of my friends. I read the *Penguin Book of Australian Verse* on my way out, which was a better guide to the people and scenery than any official brochure.[8]

Re-reading the Penguin anthology, he reminded himself how Australian poetry had formally begun with Erasmus Darwin's vision of Sydney Cove in 1788 and continued with the odes of Michael Massey Robinson, whose aspiration to the title of poet laureate was recognized by a government grant of two cows. In 1819 the unfortunately named Barron Field, a correspondent of Charles Lamb, had published *First Fruits of Australian Poetry*. In *Thoughts* (1845) Charles Harpur had used Australian local words and avoided English associations. His disciple Henry Kendall, author of *Poems and Songs* (1862), had styled himself 'Native Australian Poet' and had spoken of 'the Muse of Australia'. His poem 'Bell Birds' made John eager to hear these chiming birds when he got to Australia –

> The silver-voiced bell-birds, the darlings of daytime!
> They sing in September their songs of the May-time;

When shadows wax strong, and the thunder-bolts hurtle,
They hide with their fear in the leaves of the myrtle.[9]

John also enjoyed the *Bush Ballads and Galloping Rhymes* (1870) of
Kendall's contemporary Adam Lindsay Gordon, a 'southern Byron',
and the poems of A.B. ('Banjo') Paterson. He was amused to find that
there had been a precious *fin de siècle* aestheticism in Australian
poetry as well as in English. Victor Daley, author of *At Dawn and
Dusk* (1898) and *Wine and Roses* (1905), had written:

> I have been dreaming all a summer day
> Of rare and dainty poems I would write;
> Love-lyrics delicate as lilac-scent,
> Soft idylls woven of wind, and flower, and stream,
> And songs and sonnets carven in fine gold . . .[10]

In the best aesthetic tradition, Daley had died of tuberculosis. John
also noted from the potted biographies that Rosemary Dobson, born
in Sydney in 1920, was a granddaughter of the English 1890s poet and
essayist Austin Dobson.

Of the living poets represented in the Penguin book, there were two
John decided he would try to meet while in Australia: Douglas Stewart
and Judith Wright. In Stewart's poem 'Two Englishmen' was a characteristic Australian blend of prickliness about the English and grudging
admiration for their arrogance. The poem describes A.W. Kinglake's
meeting an English military man in the desert, both bound by the code
that 'One did not speak without an introduction'.

> And while their Arab servants rushed together
> With leaps and yells to suit the glad occasion
> Each Englishman gazed coolly at the other
> And briefly touched his hat in salutation
> And so passed by, erect, superb, absurd
> Across the desert sands without a word.
>
> But when they'd passed, one gesture yet endures;
> Each turned and waved his hand as if to say,
> 'Well, help yourself to Egypt' – 'India's yours',
> And so continued grandly on his way;
> And as they went, one feels that, truth to tell,
> They understood each other pretty well.[11]

Stewart was also capable of a Betjemanesque satire of suburban
mores:

Seven pairs of leopardskin underpants
Flying on the rotary clothes-line. Oh, look, look . . .[12]

But John was going to Australia in quest of the Australian, and he
found it in the exhilaration of Stewart's lines –

> Schute, Bell, Badgery, Lumby,
> How's your dad and how'd your mum be?
> What's the news, oh, far from here
> Under the blue sky burning clear
> Where your beautiful business runs
> Wild as a dingo, fresh as a brumby?[13]

Judith Wright was even more ur-Australian than Stewart (who was
born in New Zealand). She was born in 1915 at Thalgarrah Station
near Armidale, New South Wales, into a pastoral family who had been
pioneer settlers of the New England district. In 1960 she had published a prose history of her family, *The Generations of Men*. She was
close to the land, a passionate conservationist. Sometimes the tone of
her poetry is too elevated and self-consciously 'poetic' for most
readers, the echo hollow. But in her best poems, her candour carries
its own austere nobility, as in 'The Blind Man' –

> Oh, I,
> red centre of a dark and burning sky,
> fit my words to music, my crippled words to music,
> and sing to the fire with the voice of the fire.
> Go sleep with your grief, go sleep with your desire,
> go deep into the core of night and silence.
> But I hold all of it, your hate and sorrow,
> your passion and your fear; I am the breath
> that holds you from your death.
> I am the voice of music and the ended dance.[14]

John's journey was broken by a night in Singapore. He had told
Penelope that he would be staying at the Raffles Hotel, but in fact
wrote to her on 31 October from the Hotel de l'Europe, 'I spent last
night here and I CAN ABSOLUTELY UNDERSTAND your passion
for the gorgeous East.'[15] He had been round the city with a man who
had 'gone native'. John could see it would take a lifetime to understand
it. He knew the differences between their Berkshire neighbours –
in class, wealth and religion. But in Singapore, where Christian, Indian
and Malayan were mixed, 'with Communism on the doorstep, with

an increasing population and a decreasing number of jobs available because of it', he saw that he would never be able to disentangle the social strata. 'So I lie back and enjoy the wonderful smells, the little figures of men and women and the extraordinary vegetation and horrifying squalor of the Chinese, Injun and Arab quarters.'[16] He had seen a Buddhist temple – 'v ugly and lots like RC art of the '80s' – and a Mogul temple even uglier. He had admired the Roman Catholic and Church of England cathedrals, 1820 neo-classical, the Anglican one 'vast and *high*'. 'But all I long for is us again back at Wantage and in peace and though I've never been to Aussieland, my longing for home is so great I would gladly forgo the trip.'[17] He added a drawing of himself and Penelope in bed at Wantage with Archie the teddy-bear.

'The aeroplane here from London', he complained, 'is three hours late and I will go and enjoy some Chinese food in the airport caff. Singapore is like Torquay set down in a tropic swamp. It will go Commie quite soon, but that is probably better than the Chinese Secret Society by which it is run at present.'[18]

The next day he wrote to Penelope on BOAC stationery: 'I'd better write to you now while I'm on the plane between Darwin and Sydney while I have some time as my Aussie programme looks pretty full and you may only get postcards from me.'[19] The landscape below him looked 'toasted brown' with just a few dead sheep and cattle scattered over the earth. John was sitting next to a nice Australian engineer, who told him that when he was asleep in New Guinea one night, 'he was woken by a sharp stab like a surgeon's knife between his shoulder blades and then another on his buttocks and a third at the back of his leg. He flashed a torch and it was a straw-coloured centipede about a foot long. He said it was not a poison bite, only a bleeding incision. He rides on huge turtles on the coast of Malaya . . .'[20] John had been sorry to leave Singapore. 'Although I realise it was very secondhand and modern East compared with elsewhere in Injer and China, I had a spell (and a smell) I shall never forget.'[21] In the wet heat he had thought of the cold Penelope must be suffering in the Granadian mountains.

John was welcomed to Sydney by Norman Williams, the British Council's chief representative in Australia, and his wife Margery, a leading 'literary hostess', who was the same age as John. John reported to Penelope that Williams was 'v kind and protective and looks v like the Commander [George Barnes, formerly head of the BBC Third Programme]'.[22] In the same letter, of 4 November, he wrote:

I write this at six in the morning in bed as there is really no other time of peace. Even so I found Sydney very invigorating and unbelievably beautiful. The Aussies are very kind and *clever*. Although there are things about the life here that remind me of the miseries of Cincinnati, the place is really much more English and therefore familiar. Sydney is a series of bays mostly tree bordered and really very vast and grand like Plymouth Sound going on for miles and with Trebetherick bungalows in gardens full of palms, jacaranda trees, and tamarisks and HUGE CEN-TIPEDES and very loud mouthed birds. The older houses, of which there are hundreds, are charming with rich cast iron work . . . [*He draws two*.] You expect Cobbers in slouch hats and rifles to come out on to the verandahs & fire guns at kangaroos. The colours of the flowers are amazing. The sea is a series of lakes all over the town. The C of E is very low, the RC is very Irish indeed & both dominate the city with their respective cathedrals. The Aussies are not materialistic, it seems to me, though a lot of big business is causing hideous slabs to arise in some charming suburbs. I am never left alone, as I suspected would be the case, but by just treating myself as a parcel, I get along all right . . .[23]

Three days later he wrote to her again:

Oi'm *loovin* Aussieland. This is a glorious time to be here, late spring with the most violent coloured trees & flowers & always, here in Sydney, glimpses of the sea & ships. The Jacaranda trees are out, bright purple flowers, no leaves, & as big as sycamores. Then there are weird palm like plants with flowers like exotic birds – cockatoos. Yesterday I went to a small inland town called Orange in NSW which was, of course, like Polzeath laid out on a grid system but here & there surviving these charm-ing old Colonial houses with ironwork verandahs on two floors & thence to where they first found gold where there were some derelict mines . . . & a varied farm or two, all in the style of old Cornwall – this is because the Cornish were pioneers to the goldfields in about 1840 which here is as old as Stonehenge . . . The gravestones of old prospectors, just like Georgian headstones in English churchyards, are just put anywhere beside the road on the old properties, & have the awesomeness of Avebury. The country

I went to was like the downs & full of horses & the people were all
Plymmi [Penelope] type people & I have an idea you would be very happy
here . . . I only hope Spain is being as good for you as Aussieland is for
me . . .[24]

On 11 November he wrote from Newcastle, New South Wales:

From your letter I can see Archie would be v shocked by Spain. I don't think
he would dislike Sydney which is so low that it is the only Anglican diocese
to recognize that heretical church in South Africa which broke away from
the C of E because the C of E wasn't low enough. All the rest of Aussieland
is high – & v well attended too. The Cathedral here in Newcastle is magnificent, strong, huge & simple brick building of the eighties.

   Oh I *do* love the Aussies. The accent is not one by which you can tell
birth, class or region or education. Apparently it is purely fortuitous
whether an Aussie has an accent or not. Last night I was given a huge

iguana yellow & black & about 6 feet
long which had been shot that afternoon. But we thought it would go bad
in this intense heat & so we dumped it
in the back of a 'yewt' (which is what
the Aussies call a utility van – a 'bewt
yewt' would be a beautiful utility van)
which was parked outside the club
where I am staying. I was also given two big centipedes, but alas, they have
died in the night. Do take care of your sweet ijjus little self all alone in
those Sierras. I pray for you every day. Yesterday I crossed the Mooney
Mooney Creek & thought of nooni nooni [the Betjemans' private expression of endearment]. [25]

The Williamses introduced John to Douglas Stewart, one of the two
poets he most wanted to meet. Stewart had become the grand pan-
jandrum of Australian letters. Seven years younger than John, he had
been literary editor of *The Bulletin* (the famous 'Red Pages') for the
twenty-one years up to 1961, but had just resigned the post to become
literary adviser to Australia's leading poetry publisher, Angus &
Robertson. Twenty years later, Rodney Hall wrote in an introduction
to *The Collins Book of Australian Poetry*: 'Almost every poet in this
anthology between [Kenneth] Slessor and [Geoffrey] Lehmann had
to submit their poems to him, in one or other of his rôles, to achieve
publication.'[26] Stewart put out the flags for John. In the *Vogue* article,
John wrote: 'I went to a party given by Douglas Stewart, the poet, in

a suburb of Sydney and recall a spider's web as big as a sheet between the eaves of the verandah of his bungalow and the ground. In the middle of it was a beautiful green spider as big as one's hand which everyone took for granted as a common sight.'[27]

The Sydney sight which made most impression on John was the Technical College, whose premises were once a prison for the penal colony which was the origin of the city. 'The Principal', John wrote, 'showed me a yard outside his room where prisoners were once flogged. Forty-five lashes was the average sentence. There were rings in the walls to which the men were tied and channels in the stone floor leading to a hole where the blood drained away.' He added: 'A very small percentage now of Australians is descended from convicts, but the memory remains – particularly, of course, in Celts. Many people, especially those from South Australia which was founded by free settlers, may, as you get to know them, talk about their ancestry, which is nearly always from people who immigrated of their own free will.'[28]

John's tour was to take in the capitals of the five states and Tasmania. His trip to Brisbane was made while he was still based in Sydney. On 17 November he wrote to Penelope:

I did a long 600 miles through bush & scrub & terrific heat to Brisbane by car & came back, thank God, by air. Brisbane is all banana trees & parrots & bright flowers & koala bears & little white wooden bungalows built on stilts. It is a warm, welcoming & tropic city. J.L. Pearson's Cathedral is his finest work I've seen all in the lovely pale yellow & pink local stone. I met a gecko – a lizard with a frill round its neck – on the road & we picked it up – put it on a fence where it lay stock still disguised as a piece of bark.

Brisbane is very high & the RC Archbishop & ours are both very old & great friends & Catholics of both denominations get on well together there – unlike Sydney which is low & Irish.[29]

From Brisbane John made a detour to the wild country near Mount Tamborine, where Judith Wright, the other poet he wanted to meet, lived with her husband J. P. McKinney (author of a natural history of European thought, *The Structure of Modern Thought*) and their daughter Meredith. 'Nor shall I forget standing in the rain forests below Mt Tamborine near Brisbane with Judith Wright, the poet,' John wrote in *Vogue*. 'We heard cicadas loud as jet engines outside London Airport. They stopped suddenly and in the hush one could almost hear the jungle growing in the steamy depths below us where parasite climbed on parasite and strange and huge flowers burst from the greenness and the crack of the stock-whip bird increased the strangeness.'[30] In 1995, at eighty, Judith Wright recalled John's visit.

> Douglas Stewart referred him to me but the visit was a very brief one . . .
> Tamborine Mountain is an hour and a half's drive from Brisbane, where
> I think he was staying, and we (my husband was alive then) asked him to
> lunch, but Jack wasn't well enough (heart trouble) to ask him overnight,
> so I cooked him a hasty lunch and we walked down the National Park
> tracks into the rainforest. This impressed him deeply but I think he was
> for some reason in search of a bird-eating spider – which doesn't exist in
> the rainforest there but only near Cairns (and for all I know may be extinct
> even there at this stage) . . .[31]

Judith Wright also remembered that, during John's visit, she and he 'discussed the plight of the Aborigines, which has always been a pre-occupation of mine'.[32] Legislation affecting the aborigines was a leading topic in the press during John's stay in Sydney. Judith Wright's views may have influenced him, for he wrote in *Vogue*: '[The aborigines] are a comparatively tall and distinguished nomadic people with great skill in hunting and trekking, and they live an entirely communal life. Their way of life is so different from that of the later settlers that I am sure they will come to harm if they are westernized and exploited as tourist attractions.'[33]

By mid-November John was back in Sydney, where he was *the* social catch of the season. His daughter writes: 'One well-known Sydney lady, having failed to get him to dinner, dared not admit her failure in the eyes of the city and printed in the paper an account of a dinner she never gave.'[34] On 18 November John wrote to Penelope, who was still in Spain:

> I had the most wonderful letter I have ever had from you today from
> INFERNO. It was so graphic and thrilling, I felt I was there with you . . .
> I read out the non-nooni [non-endearment] parts of your letter to the Brit
> Council people in Sydney and they said you must be a marvellous writer.
> I said you were. I do hope you do a book. Your letter gives a picture of con-
> ditions I should scarcely have believed possible . . . It's odd that I should
> travel thousands of miles to find Golders Green by the sea and you should
> go only a few hundred and find yourself back centuries. The oddest thing
> about Aussieland is the way the moon's 1/4 is the wrong way round and the
> bath water whirls away from the bath in the opposite direction to that which
> it does in England.
>   The birds are amazingly noisy & one sounds like a whip being cracked
> which old Patrick [Kinross] would like very much. Another sounds like
> church bells. Parrots fly about & finches with vivid red backs & triangular

blue butterflies. There are a lot of queers in Sydney. I have only just dis-covered them – interior decorators of course. Their favourite adjectives are 'interesting' & 'fabulous'.[35]

The next day, John met more of Sydney's homosexuals at a grand party the Williamses held to say farewell to him as he left for Canberra and Melbourne. The Australian novelist Patrick White, a future Nobel laureate, was there with his Greek lover Manoly Lascaris.[36] White was still at that time a great friend of Margery Williams, whom White's biographer describes as 'foremost of the women Lascaris called "Patrick's lady disciples"'.[37] On 20 November White wrote to his friend Frederick Glover, a Sydney bank manager and playwright: 'Last night we went to a party given by the British Council for John Betjeman (whom we liked immensely), and there we found all the heads of the Establishment.'[38]

The often cantankerous novelist was no doubt well predisposed because of the favourable review John had given his novel *The Aunt's Story* in the *Daily Herald* in 1948. ('Patrick White must be one of the best living writers of English prose. But this does not necessarily mean he will be popular. He demands effort and he has his mannerisms. He is a dead loss to the libraries, a great asset to English literature.')[39] White was familiar enough with John's verse to quote from his poem 'Banana Blush' in his autobiography, *Flaws in the Glass* (a book so gratuitously unpleasant about almost everyone that it was nicknamed *Claws in the Arse*): White's friend Cynthia Nolan, wife of the Australian painter Sidney Nolan, had committed suicide in the Regent Palace Hotel, London, the scene of Lilian's tribulations in the poem.[40] Born in London in 1912 of Australian parents, White had been sent to Cheltenham College, the subject of another Betjeman poem.[41] Although he said he wrote about Australia because it was 'the only country I really know in my bones',[42] and had some glum memories of his years in England ('the walks in cold rainy afternoons, and the dismal tea-room at the end'),[43] he could write that 'apart from the accident of blood, I feel I am temperamentally a cosmopol-itan Londoner,[44] and 'I am at heart a Londoner, only by fate an Australian.'[45] There was much in his character and preoccupations that corresponded with John's. A letter that he wrote to a London pen-friend, the stage-struck young writer Jean Scott Rogers, has exactly the tone of John's badinage, the same teasing curiosity: 'But what kind of a person are you really? Are you a sport in a plaid skirt; or a Bohemian in spectacles and a Spanish hat; or a seductive siren with a willowy waist and magnetic eyes; or the taffeta ingenue; or the leafy nymph . . .?'[46]

John chose the right moment to leave Sydney for Canberra. The lead story in the *Sydney Morning Herald* of 20 November was of the torrential rain which had caused the biggest Sydney floods in five years. On the 19th the swollen George's River had burst its banks at Moorebank, with loss of life and homes. The other big story was that Governor Nelson Rockefeller's explorer son was being sought in New Guinea. (He was never found.) In Canberra John stayed with the Governor-General of Australia, Lord De L'Isle and Dudley VC and his wife Jacqueline, who, like Penelope, was the daughter of a field-marshal (in her case Lord Gort VC). Three years younger than John, De L'Isle was a descendant of the poet Sir Philip Sidney and the owner of one of John's favourite houses in England, Penshurst Place in Kent. On 23 November John moved on to Melbourne, from which city he wrote to Penelope:

> The time of my whirlwind Aussie tour is now nearing its close. I stayed yesterday and the day before with the Governor General himself at Canberra (Ld de Lisle [*sic*] and Dudley VC). I got some idea of the sort of luxury you must have been brought up in Injer which is I [?know] why you can stand troglodyte caves now.
>
> Canberra, as I told you, is like Welwyn set down in a basin of the hills round Urbino. Melbourne where I am now is, in its old parks, like Paris if none of the houses were more than two or three storeys high. It spreads out into bungalows, the older types very pretty with ironwork verandahs

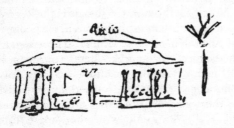

> and charming wooden fences to the gardens, all of different patterns. There are iris everywhere in the broad streets of Melbourne, but alas a tremendous amount of the most hideous and out of scale contemp I've ever seen, so that most of the city is ruined by half-baked skyscrapers. I am staying in Trinity College, Melbourne University . . . I have a nice room. I remember you every day at Mass and hope you are not falling off your horse. Gerry [Wellesley, Duke of Wellington] is now on the high seas bound for Canberra with Rupert Gunnis [the authority and author on British sculpture]. They are going to stay with the de Lisles.[47]

The 'joy and wonder of Aussieland' were not palling in spite of rain and cold in the last few days. He had found that Loelia, Duchess of

Westminster was making a similar tour, 'but we've not been able to meet though we've talked on the telephone'.[48] The actress Vivien Leigh and Moura Lympany the pianist were also on the Australian circuit.[49] John sent an enthusiastic letter to Candida from Geelong Grammar School on 26 November. 'Painting is very good and so is the poetry. In fact it is like what England must have been in the reign of the first Elizabeth.'[50] In a postscript he added: 'They talk here about giving one a "tingle" on the telephone.'[51] He used this expression for the rest of his life.

Three days later he wrote to Penelope again, thanking her for 'another WONDERFUL letter': 'I *did* laugh at the idea of the plastic cruet set being on the chimney piece amid all those lovely earthenwares.'[52] He was still enjoying the tour. He had spent the previous two nights in Hobart, staying with Lord Rowallan, the Governor of Tasmania (formerly the Chief Scout) and his wife Gwyn, a sister of Jo Grimond, the Liberal leader. The Rowallans' son and heir, Arthur Corbett, was shortly to be at the centre of a *News of the World* scandal when the courts disallowed his marriage to the sex-change model April Ashley (later a neighbour and friend of Penelope Betjeman's in Hay-on-Wye, Hereford).[53] Corbett's sister Fiona was a schoolfriend of Candida Betjeman.[54] Lady Rowallan hired a small aircraft and took John and Fiona on a jaunt. John recalled in the *Vogue* article:

> Never shall I forget flying in a small chartered aeroplane low over the sinister 'horizontal bush' in an unexplored part of Tasmania. Here men walk over the tops of the trees, but if they fall down into the wood below there is said to be no way out, and there are stories of skeletons being found with manacles on them – skeletons of convicts who tried to escape from the cruel penal establishment of Port Arthur. We were flying to the forgotten city of Zeehan, once the third largest in Tasmania and now with only a few hundred people, a hospital, an opera house and scattered wooden houses and shops in a sea of sweet-scented white iris, with pink mineral mountains all round.[55]

The opera house was now used only as a cinema, on Saturdays, John noted in another article.[56] In his letter to Penelope he described the second part of the air trip in 'Tazzie': 'Then we flew over tremendous mountains with rock formations like the Giant's Causeway on their peaks & over steamy rain forests with glimpses of ferns & palms struggling up & flowering till we came to an inland lake with a white sandy shore & brown water containing the most primitive form of fish – indeed of animal life in the world. It was called Lake Pedder & the silence was so terrific you could touch it.'[57]

John gave a lecture at the University of Tasmania. Among those who attended were the Hobart engineer Charles Parks and his wife Dorothy, a writer and broadcaster who admired John's poetry.[58] After the lecture they spoke to him and Dorothy Parks revealed that she was a granddaughter of the English Victorian architect E. Bassett Keeling, who had designed some London churches and the Holborn Restaurant, dying in the 1880s. John wrote a fulsome inscription in her copy of his *English Parish Churches*. Later she sent to him in England, via her son, the lecturer and translator Philip Parks, some booklets about contemporary Australian architecture. In his letter of thanks to Philip Parks, John referred to Tasmania as 'that heart-shaped island of allure'.[59] He said he had enjoyed Australian architecture, 'but I could have done without the Colonial Mutual Life Building in Melbourne'.[60] Parks had reminded him of his ancestry and John wrote: 'How wonderful to be a great-grandson of E. Bassett Keeling! My old friend Goodhart-Rendel used to say the Bassett Keeling church in Penge was the most extraordinary building in England.'[61]

From Hobart John moved on to Adelaide. With ecumenical goodwill on both sides, he was staying at Aquinas College of the University of Adelaide, 'whose Rector, Father Richard Scott SJ,' he wrote to Penelope, 'is mad on church art'. By 2 December he was on two days' retreat with the Kelham Fathers in Adelaide. 'Here it is only "Bridle-high",' he wrote, 'but then the Revd Bridle[62] was one of the first two Kelhamites[63] so it is fitting to have come here for a break. I must say I need one after all this feting & lecturing. The enclosed cutting will make you laugh. It's nice being put on a par with old Loelia . . .'[64]

The city of Adelaide made a big impression on him.

> Australian architecture's most remarkable manifestation [he later wrote] . . . is in town planning. Nowhere in the world is there so splendid a town plan as that of Adelaide. Colonel Light, an English artist and surveyor, looking across a flat stretch of bush on the shores of a gulf off the Indian Ocean, visualized a city on the grid system with five public squares and a green belt and a suburb, and wide streets with the country and mountains visible from any street.
>
> He had this vision in 1836 and even today it dominates the city of nearly 400,000 with streets still wide enough to cope with an age of too many motor-cars.[65]

On 4 December John flew to his last destination in Australia, Perth – a four-hour flight, first over sea, then over desert. He wrote Penelope a letter on the aeroplane. 'The one lesson Aussie [h]as taught me is that the C of E & RC live in amity there in a marvellous way.'[66] Perhaps Penelope was intended to interpret that as a parable for their married life. John reported that he would be returning to England via Singapore and arriving at London airport on the morning of 9 December. He asked Penelope to send an overcoat to the airport for him. 'I did not want to be burdened with one in the heat of Aussieland & it was still quite warm when oi set out & scorching here now boot will be cold in England.'[67] In an earlier letter he had warned her that he was 'bound to be *very toired*' when he arrived.[68]

What John needed most when he came home to Wantage was a good rest – almost a period of convalescence. But he still found time to write an article on Australian architecture, which appeared in the *Daily Telegraph* on 18 December, barely more than a week after his return. The article showed that, while he had concentrated on the cities, he had also pressed the organizers of his tour to let him see small towns in the country.

The average country town is at a crossroads, with a bank on one corner built in a solid-looking classic style, broad-eaved and with decorative details which, even if incorrect, are elegant and strangely Australian. There may be a town hall and post office in variants of this style and always on one or more corners an hotel, two storeys high, with verandahs of richly patterned cast iron.

The High Street will also have cast-iron verandahs over the shops giving an appearance of the Rows at Chester, if they were executed in cast-iron with wooden walls behind. The private houses are . . . bungalows, oblong in shape, with a large verandah in front, again with patterned cast-iron shedding intricate shadows on to the weather-boarded house wall.

This style of house – derived partly from India and mainly from the Regency houses of a town like Cheltenham – continued in Australia until the 1920s. Corrugated iron may not sound an attractive roofing, but in Australia, especially when painted black or grey or allowed to rust, and elegantly bent over the verandah roof, it looks well.[69]

John admired the houses' gardens, where hibiscus of every colour and lantana grew and mesembreanthemums cascaded 'in sheets of crimson'.[70] But the *Telegraph* article was also a chance to release some of the bile that had built up during the long, taxing journey – 'Thus if it were not for the hoardings, the sky signs, the cats' cradles of wires, the plethora of poles, the brash shop fronts, and the over-abundance of hideous petrol stations which disfigure the more prosperous towns, Australia would have, as it does in many parts, the pleasantest architecture in the world.'[71]

Since the early pioneering days, John observed, Australia had developed an architecture of her own. 'It first appears in the great brick cathedrals by Horbury Hunt at Newcastle, Armidale and Grafton and in the grand churches of St John's and Holy Trinity, Launceston, Tasmania, by Alexander North, and in the houses by R.S. Dods in Brisbane. All these are late Victorian and Edwardian.'[72] Canberra was 'a dream not yet wholly fulfilled, for it is unfinished – an enormous Welwyn Garden City for diplomats and civil servants . . .'.[73] He thought the best recent architecture was domestic, variations on the verandahed bungalow in concrete, wood and glass.[74] He had also seen 'exciting new buildings like the Music Shell and the Olympic Swimming Pool in Melbourne'.[75] But there was one more outburst of fretfulness against modern Australia. 'Nowhere did I see an office building in a capital city of any distinction at all. Here, alas, the fatal influence of the "developers" and the architectural magazines from Europe and America has produced glass boxes with unconsidered skylines. These are not suited to the hot sunlight of a wonderful and variegated continent.'[76]

John particularly enjoyed three aspects of the Australian tour. First, he liked being lionized, without the saturation hospitality that he and Penelope had endured in Cincinnati. With Penelope and Lady Elizabeth Cavendish safely in England, he was even free to flirt a little at parties. Second, there was his surprise at finding so much unspoilt Georgian and Victorian architecture: '*No one had told me . . .*' he wrote.[76] But John could be fêted or could look at Victorian buildings in England. What entranced him in Australia was the prodigality of Nature. 'First there was the light, with its dazzling clearness everywhere. Next there was the brilliant colour of flowers, trees, rocks, birds, reptiles and insects.'[77] In Australia John recaptured some of the exaltation he had felt as a youth, swooping down the Cornish hills on his bicycle in the search for wild flowers.[78]

The gum-trees of Australia are of every shape and colour. Some look like British elms, others like oak or ash. There are hundreds of varieties of mimosa, or wattle, whose flowers vary from pale gold to deepest orange. The scarlet of the flame-tree flares on the mountain sides. The millions of flowers which appear everywhere after the rain give an impression of luxuriance, like the tropics one reads about in *The Swiss Family Robinson*. There are trees of vast height, and some of the palms and pines look like the fossilized plants in coal . . .[79] In Canberra, how odd it was to see pink parrots flying about the trim suburban avenues and find snakes slithering over the municipally mown grass between the footwalk and the road, which is seductively called 'the nature strip' in Australia. How pleasantly embarrassing, too, to be sitting in a drawing-room making polite conversation and suddenly to burst into giggles caught from the maniac laughter of the kookaburra birds on the lawn outside.[80]

John's liking for Australia was reciprocated. The official British Council report on his visit was eulogistic.

Because of his unique qualities Mr Betjeman was an ideal visitor for Australia. He aroused in his audiences and acquaintances that pleasant sensation of nostalgia for 'Home' which is a feature of the old Australian character ... The professorial and academic architects he met were amazed by his knowledge of Australian architectural history, and by the clarity of the canons of taste he applied to Australian buildings ... His poetry was a major factor in his popularity in Australia ... The agents for Mr Betjeman's publications sold out their stocks of his books during his tour . . . In Melbourne Mr Betjeman's programme was crowded and rushed ... A very successful tour. Press and public alike were convinced of the sincerity of Mr Betjeman's liking for Australia. The visit will remain a yardstick by which Australians will measure the success of other Council visitors.[81]

John 'recycled' his impressions of Australia in a number of articles during the 1960s. By 1963, when he wrote the piece for *Vogue*, he had imposed some kind of pattern on his memories.

I am hard put to it to say which state capital I preferred – Sydney with its oysters and delicate white wines, its old streets of verandahed terraces and its sudden glances of sea; Melbourne with its palatial public buildings in a classic style like the London clubs and its superbly laid out botanic garden and its great art gallery: Adelaide, which must be the best planned city in the world ... Brisbane, where the houses are on stilts and toast-rack trams waft you in a warm breeze past banana trees and shops: Perth, where black swans glide on lapis-blue water and immense parks of trees and flowers slope down to the river: or Hobart below its many-coloured mountains on the edge of the most beautifully landscaped harbour I have ever seen.

The further north you travel in Australia the hotter grows the weather and the slower comes the speech. All the states have distinct character. South Australia is the most English, New South Wales the most vigorous, Victoria the most official, Queensland the most countrified, Northern Territory the most primitive, while western Australia and Tasmania seem to be separate leisurely countries.[82]

In 1964 he was roped in to contribute an article ('Beneath the Wattle Tree') to a three-page section of the *Daily Express* designed to encourage emigration to Australia and supported by a large advertisement for

Consolidated Gold Fields Ltd of London EC2.[82] On the strength of his single trip, John was billed as one of the 'important writers who know Australia well'. Among his fellow contributors was Neville Cardus, the writer on cricket and music, who assured prospective immigrants that 'Nearly every Australian girl can play the piano reasonably well – no, not "pop" music, but Beethoven. The Australian girls are unique. Good-lookers as a rule...'[83] John offered the more rarefied temptations of 'diamond light', the bell-bird's chimes and 'vast Gothic cathedrals in honey-coloured local stone or variegated brick'.[84] In 1968 he returned to these topics in an article for the *Daily Telegraph Magazine*, headed 'John Betjeman's Kangaroo Island: Old-Fashioned Betjemanesque Pleasures'.[85]

Besides spawning the somewhat repetitive articles (in every one of them, Canberra was compared to Welwyn), the Australian tour of 1961 served as a thorough reconnaissance for John's four Australian television films ten years later – rather as his excursions to suburban London cinemas as a film critic in the 1930s gave him a framework for his celebrated *Metro-land* film of 1972. In 1961, with his verse autobiography published, John was already beginning to transform himself from Bright Young Thing and *enfant terrible* into Grand Old Man. The arduous legwork he put in then, at fifty-five, might have proved too punishing at sixty-five, when the onset of Parkinson's Disease, which would reduce him to an invalid in his last years, first became apparent.

THE COAL EXCHANGE

For God's sake come & speak. We must save this building. What is really behind its destruction is a speculator who has his eye on the rest of the island site on which it stands.

John Betjeman, letter to Woodrow Wyatt MP, 18 February 1961

The fate of the Coal Exchange is being decided this week. The Common Council should vote against this wickedness.

J. O. Grindlay, letter in *City Press*, 9 March 1962

Despite the lessons of the Euston Arch débâcle, it turned out that in conservation forewarned is not always adequately forearmed. The case of the Coal Exchange was one of the first taken up by the Victorian Society, which was aware of the Corporation of London's designs on the Exchange two years before British Railways' threat to the Euston Arch came to its notice. The forewarning enabled the society to make trouble for the developers in Parliament, at the Guildhall and in the press. Even so, it only won a reprieve for the building. The Exchange was demolished a year after the Euston Arch, in 1962. The aesthetic and historical arguments were urged as eloquently as John and his allies knew how; the developers opposed them with the unanswerable argument of big money.

If anything, the scandal of the Exchange was greater than that of the arch, though its fate never roused such a public outcry. The building in Lower Thames Street, London, near the Billingsgate fish market (soon itself to disappear) was begun in 1847. The architect was James Bunning – the man with whom Peter Clarke associated John's name in his limerick.* It was opened by the Prince Consort in 1849. The exterior was not unlike that of a Regency church, its rounded portico crowned with a two-storey turret. This gave no indication of the interior. Walking through the portico, the visitor found himself in a large

---

* See Chapter 2, ' "Vic. Soc." and "The Dok" '.

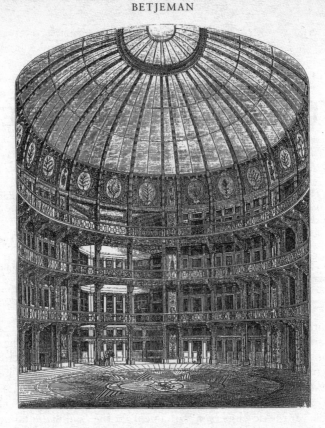

Interior of the Coal Exchange

domed court, fifty feet in diameter and almost wholly constructed of
cast iron. The circular court was surrounded by tiers of small offices
reached by galleries. The principal iron supports were moulded with
a cable motif derived from the ropes used in the coal mines and by the
colliers that carried the coal by sea to London. The three galleries and
the dome were decorated with arabesques and paintings by Frederick
Sang of colliers, collieries, tree ferns, coal miners and towns associated with the industry. Curved iron ribs formed the dome. Originally
the spaces between the ribs had been filled with ground glass and the
eye of the dome with amber glass, but that had been shattered by
bomb blasts in the war.[1]

The rotunda was the earliest example in England of a public building constructed with extensive use of cast iron. In that, it anticipated
the Crystal Palace, built two years later. There was no equivalent

surviving cast-iron monument of such an early date in the country. The American design historian Henry-Russell Hitchcock, in his book on early-Victorian architecture, described the Coal Exchange as the London rival of Labrouste's Bibliothèque Nationale in Paris, another iron structure.[2] He added that the Exchange was 'more typically Victorian than more famous edifices in cast-iron like the Crystal Palace or King's Cross Station'.[3]

John was already concerned about the future of the building before the Victorian Society was founded in 1957. He learned that the Corporation of the City of London had plans to demolish it, ostensibly as part of a road-widening scheme. John thought that the real reason was to clear the site so that part of it could be sold or redeveloped. In March 1956, writing to the secretary of the Council for the Care of Churches, he raised – lightly enough – the question of the threatened Exchange. 'Darling Miss Scott, Indeed we must keep up the fight but I am told that [Anthony] Eden wants to show himself as a strong man here at any rate, even if he can't in Cyprus. If we do save it, you and I might go away to the south of France together.'[4] In September of the same year he contrived to deliver the annual speech of the Society for the Protection of Ancient Buildings in the Coal Exchange.

As you are all converted, there is no need for me to say to you why you like the building. Goodness knows why one likes one building and not another! ... I see so many distinguished people here who, I know, can answer these questions. I see that great man, John Summerson; I won't mention names any more, but I can see Mortimer Wheeler, Marshall Sisson[5] and people who really do know, so I am nervous of speaking ... I do not know about proportion ... It is one of those subtle things that you do not notice until you see it wrongly done ... The relation of one building to another in a street and in a village has something to do with proportion. The relation of this building to its street is considerably better that the relation of, let us say, some of those white cliffs that have arisen in this city next to St Paul's Cathedral ... I wonder what Morris would have said if he had known the SPAB was ever going to meet in a building put up in 1847 [sic, for 1849]! I think he would have said, 'It's all right if it's a good building.' We know how Morris tests one ... This surprisingly light, airy, fantastic, imaginative interior is what he would have liked. It seems to me rather like the City itself, this building: a bold front and a good brain inside ... Let us not write the Victorians off as no good.[6]

The peril the Exchange was in was first noted at the Victorian Society in June 1958. With John in the chair, the Committee decided to send a letter of inquiry to the Corporation and also inform J. M. Richards and *The Architectural Review* in the hope of publicity.[7] It was three months, though, before Richards, as architectural correspondent of *The Times*, wrote in the paper about the building. And although his article appeared under the headline 'London's Cast Iron Victorian Masterpiece', it was sparing in its commendation.

> The Coal Exchange in Billingsgate . . . is one of London's semi-public buildings that are less well known than they should be. It is significant that more anxiety has been expressed over the Roman hypocaust that survives beneath it (and which care is being taken to preserve even should the Coal Exchange itself have to go) than over the fate of the building. The hypocaust has but little beauty, but objects of antiquarian interest always seem to be more highly valued than objects of visual interest.
>
> Not that the Coal Exchange is so important a work of architecture as to require preservation without question, however inconvenient to the City's road improvement schemes, especially since its usefulness for the purpose for which it was built seems to have come to an end . . .[8]

Richards went on to speak of 'the architectural riches within', and their uniqueness, but the article was not the ringing call for rescue that might have given the Victorian Society heart and the developers pause. The 'on the one hand . . . on the other hand' preamble gave the nod to the Corporation that the architectural establishment might accept they had a reasonable case.

Almost a full month passed before Lord Esher, the Victorian Society's president, commented on Richards's article, in a letter to *The Times*. He chose to take it as read that Richards was in favour of preservation. 'I should like to add my name to his recommendation to your many readers who work in the City and explore its streets, that they should visit [the Coal Exchange] before it is too late . . . I have no doubt they will regret that they will be among the last to see it standing.'[9] That sounded like a defeatist acceptance of a *fait accompli*; but Esher continued:

> Many are yet to be convinced that there is any necessity to destroy the building. During the war there was widespread regret at the loss of buildings of architectural distinction and historic interest. We felt that their going was a loss to our lives. We have to remember that the wartime losses in the City were very great. There is little left, and the prestige of the City is such that any action the authorities take to preserve their remaining treasures cannot but influence other local authorities. Soon enough we shall have a City of enormous office blocks, flanked to the west by St Paul's

and to the east by the Tower, through which the Lord Mayor will annually
proceed as a reminder of better days.[10]

After these only too prophetic words, Esher asked the Corporation's
committees to reconsider the Exchange's fate.

On 21 October 1958 the Victorian Society decided to write a further
letter to the City Clerk, with copies to a number of MPs.[11] On 23
October, W. E. Sykes, chairman of the Coal and Corn and Finance
Committee of the Corporation of London, wrote to *The Times* in
reply to Esher. He said that the Corporation had taken fully into
account the historical interest of the building, but that Lower Thames
Street must be widened to seventy-six feet as part of the County of
London Development Plan, 'designed to enable traffic to by-pass the
congested Bank intersection'. The only alternative to demolishing the
Exchange, that he could see, was to demolish 'a very considerable
part' of the Custom House, on the south side of Lower Thames Street;
but the Custom House was a listed building, and the Coal Exchange
was not.[12] John replied to this, from Cloth Fair, on 25 October.

It is good to learn from Mr Sykes's courteous letter yesterday that the
Coal, Corn and Finance Committee of the Corporation of London had
'great reluctance' in concluding that the demolition of the Coal Exchange
is inevitable. Before it is too late perhaps the committee will increase its
reluctance and so save this distinguished building.

  Since Lord Esher wrote on October 15 protesting against the proposed
vandalism, I think the Corporation may well find the Coal Exchange has
been given equal status with the Custom House on the statutory lists of
buildings of historic and architectural interest. If it is really necessary to
make a wider road between the traffic blocks at Blackfriars Bridge and the
Tower, then perhaps the authorities concerned will consider the compara-
tive merits of the Coal Exchange and the Custom House architecturally
since either the whole of the former or a slice from the back of the latter
must be sacrificed to traffic.

  The Custom House, largely rebuilt by Sir Robert Smirke in 1825,
depends for its distinction on the charming façade it presents to the river
and on the famous Long Room. Neither of these would be affected by
alterations to the uninteresting façade the Custom House presents to
Lower Thames Street. The Coal Exchange, only 20 years younger than
Smirke's Custom House, is a unity, not a piece of façadism. Its round
porch and tower are a fine feature as street architecture, its side elevations
are original and thoughtfully designed, its domed entrance hall leads one
naturally to the really splendid glass and cast-iron round the galleried hall
of the Exchange itself. Indeed to the look of Lower Thames Street the Coal

Exchange is infinitely more important than the back of the Custom House. It is moreover a pioneer building in cast iron . . .[13]

John went on to suggest that the Coal Exchange was 'by no means useless'. When it had been threatened, its tenants had sent a signed petition to the Corporation deploring its impending destruction. And when it had been used for the SPAB meeting it had 'served its purpose as a public hall admirably without disturbing the office tenants'. As the Guildhall Art Gallery had not been rebuilt, would not the Coal Exchange make an excellent gallery or museum? 'I repeat', he concluded, 'that it is still not too late to reconsider this decision. Particularly is it important to keep the building standing till the last possible moment. We do not want to see its site as one more gap among the new cliffs of the City while the rest of the proposed new route remains uncompleted, or is abandoned altogether.'[14]

Four days later, John's old friend the photographer Eric de Maré wrote to *The Times* to support him. 'Mr Betjeman's arguments in his letter . . . are sensible. Of course we must keep the Coal Exchange – just as we must keep the Shot Tower and the Albert Bridge.'[15] (The shot tower was soon to be pulled down, and the Albert Bridge was only saved by forceful campaigning by John and others.)[16] What was important, de Maré thought, was to preserve 'some historical and cultural continuity in a city'. If necessary, the whole of the Coal Exchange could be moved back on rollers – 'a perfectly feasible thing to do as I know, for some years ago I edited a special issue of a technical magazine on the moving of large old buildings in this way'.[17]

Somebody who did not agree with John was David Young of Sloane Avenue, Chelsea, who wrote on 30 October:

I recently had the opportunity of working for a short time in the Coal Exchange and would like to put forward some practical points in defence of the Corporation of London's decision to demolish it. The City of London is the centre of the commercial world of Britain, the Commonwealth, and the sterling area. It is important that we should keep it in the most efficient and presentable form possible. The Coal Exchange may be 'a pioneer building in cast iron', to quote Mr Betjeman's letter on October 25, but it is in bad repair, cold, dirty, and no longer of any use to the coal industry.

We must not be sentimental about buildings of this type: it seems incredible that Mr Betjeman deems it more important to keep the Coal Exchange standing until 'the last possible moment' than to solve the City's vital problem of traffic congestion.[18]

In November Victorian Society members were invited to visit the City Planning Office and see the plans for widening Lower Thames Street. Ian Grant, Mark Girouard and the architectural historian Peter Ferriday were dispatched to visit the Coal Exchange and asked to come up with a proposal for diverting the road.[19] On 16 December, at a Victorian Society meeting chaired by Lord Esher, John reported that he and Ferriday had discussed with the Corporation's planning officials 'a slightly different roadway' which would enable the Exchange to be saved. But the meeting 'produced no results, and it was pointed out that Lord Esher's letter to the Ministry of Housing and Local Government, which followed it, and which asked for a round table conference of all interested parties, was still unanswered and was obviously being "sat on" '.[20] Ferriday had drafted a letter for Esher and John to sign and send to *The Times* or *Sunday Times*, preferably with a picture. 'This they agreed to do after they had rewritten it.'[21] By 13 January 1959 the letter had not been published in *The Times*; J. M. Richards was asked to try and find out the position.[22]

By 17 February, the society evidently thought it had won the day with its alternative plan: the moment seemed to have arrived for congratulatory articles to be submitted to the press.[23] By March two tenants had been found. No further action seemed to be needed.[24] On 12 May Fleetwood-Hesketh said he had been unofficially told that the City planning department was examining a scheme to arcade the pavement under the Coal Exchange along Lower Thames Street.[25] The society now became preoccupied with preparations for its fashion show,* but found time to write to Mr Bayley Reynolds at the Ministry of Works to find out the Ministry's reaction to the society's suggestion that part of the Custom House should be removed, as an alternative to demolishing the Exchange, 'as this had never been officially broached'.[26] By 21 July the society had received a brusque reply: the Ministry was 'unwilling to have the Custom House reduced in any way'. But the Ministry had requested the City Corporation to examine the possibility of moving the Coal Exchange bodily backwards.[27]

No further mention of the Coal Exchange was made in the society's minutes for six months;[28] in the meantime, the case of the Euston Arch had suddenly supervened, requiring an urgent campaign. Bernard Miles of the near-by Mermaid Theatre was, reassuringly, allowed to use the Coal Exchange for rehearsals; also, theatrical and photographic museums expressed interest in taking over the building.[29] The society's *Annual Report* for 1961–62 stated that 'Action taken by our

* See Chapter 2, ' "Vic. Soc." and "The Dok" '.

Society resulted in demolition being postponed until the end of 1960.'[30] But then the building was again threatened.

At the meeting of 29 November that year, Christopher Hussey, the architectural historian and former editor of *Country Life*, reported that following a meeting he and Mark Girouard had attended earlier that day at County Hall, there now appeared to be 'no hope of retaining it on its present site', though the London County Council might keep the dismantled iron frame for re-erection elsewhere.[31] John was absent from that meeting; but he was present on 3 January 1961 and possibly galvanized the committee into action, as the minutes noted: '*Coal Exchange*. Agreed that further efforts should be made to save the building.'[32] On 2 February, as a result of these representations, the Court of Common Council gave the Exchange a temporary reprieve.[33]

On 8 February the defenders of the Coal Exchange held a press conference. John, speaking for the Victorian Society, appeared with Sir Mortimer Wheeler, the archaeologist and 'television personality', and Nikolaus Pevsner to appeal for the building's preservation. Wheeler described it as 'a national monument in the fullest sense of the phrase' and added that its destruction would be unforgivable.[34] John said that while his society realized the importance of widening Lower Thames Street it felt – and here the Georgian Group was in agreement – that if any building must go the authorities should level their first attack at 'the much less attractive rear façade of the Custom House opposite'.[35] He urged the Corporation of London to seek an alternative use for the Coal Exchange – 'this airy and top-lit galleried building' – suggesting that it might house the Corporation's own collection of paintings and sculpture which had been removed from Guildhall art gallery before the war.[36] Pevsner, *The Times* reported next day, 'agreed with Mr Betjeman that the "featureless back" of the Custom House could be demolished to let the road through'.[37]

The day after the press conference, John's old friend Tom Driberg raised the matter in Parliament. In some ways Driberg was, just as Woodrow Wyatt had been in the case of the Euston Arch, an unfortunate choice. Conservatives, who might by definition have favoured conservation, regarded him as an extreme left-winger verging on Communism. Others, in that less enlightened age, were put off by his open homosexuality: it was Winston Churchill who, seeing Driberg with his rather plain wife, allegedly commented, 'Well, buggers can't be choosers, I suppose.'[38] On the other hand, Driberg was a clever and articulate aesthete: and there might be some Labour support for saving a building that commemorated the coal industry.

Driberg spoke at 11.25 p.m. He began cautiously, trying to dispel the prejudices that MPs might feel against an early-Victorian building.

Count Gleichen's statue of Alfred the Great at Wantage. In 1960, John saved Candida's friend Anne Baring from being expelled from St Mary's, Wantage, for painting the figure red

Candida Betjeman (later Lycett Green) in 1960

John with Penelope in 1960 after he was appointed CBE

Campaigning to save Lewisham town hall, 23 August 1961: John with thirteen-year-old William Norton

John with Veronica ('Ron') Sharley
at the wedding of her sister Diana to
Eric Kendrick on 7 September 1968

The wedding of Candida Betjeman
and Rupert Lycett Green at
Wantage Church on 25 May 1963

Penelope in the garden at Wantage

John with his son Paul (*left*) and the Baring family in the grounds of Ardington House, *c.* 1962

In Cecil Beaton's house: (*left*) John and Cathleen Nesbitt, the actress who had been Rupert Brooke's girlfriend and had nearly married him; *(right)* Lady Elizabeth Cavendish with Beaton's secretary Eileen Hose

An embossed invitation to the opening of the Coal Exchange, London, by Queen Victoria in 1849. John tried to save the building, but it was demolished in 1962

Philip Larkin and John making a BBC *Monitor* television film in Hull in 1964

THE CORPORATION OF LONDON
request the honor of

Company at the opening of the

NEW COAL EXCHANGE
HER MAJESTY QUEEN VICTORIA
on Tuesday 30th October 1849

Realizing a schoolboy dream: John as a
temporary train driver

John with Mervyn Stockwood in the open-air
pulpit of Christ Church, North Brixton

In 1967 John arranged for his friend, the artist John Nankivell, to have an exhibition at Exeter University

In 1980 John's choice of Colin Dann's book *The Animals of Farthing Wood* to receive a £7,500 Arts Council prize for a children's book was widely condemned. Later the book was adapted into a hugely successful television series

'You knelt a boy, you rose a man. And thus your lonelier life began' ('A Ballad of the Investiture, 1969'). The maquette of this bust of the Prince of Wales was modelled by David Wynne and made by David Thomas. It was cast in eighteen-carat gold, the eyes and crown set with lapis lazuli

We are only just beginning to realise that Victorian architecture at
can be very fine indeed. There are always these cycles of taste. No only
the architects, but the poets, painters, novelists of the period immediately
preceding our own are out of fashion; then we begin to be interested in
them again, and can see them in perspective, without the excessive adulation to which they are, perhaps, subjected in their lifetime, or the excessive disparagement which follows their death.

It is only quite recently that the Victorian Society has been formed and
has begun to educate public opinion on this matter, and indeed has warned
us, perhaps only just in time, that we must act quickly if we are to preserve
at least specimens of the best building of that once much ridiculed age.[39]

He quoted Sir Mortimer Wheeler's praise for the building, adding,
'Those who have seen Sir Mortimer on television will be able to
imagine the rolling eye, the superb mustachios, and the orotund enunciation.'[40] A quotation from Sir Mortimer had appeared in *The Times*
that morning: the Coal Exchange expressed 'an era of urban revolution as no other surviving building is capable of doing. Even the careful
preservation of a tattered Roman hypocaust in its basement is a happy
symbol of that decade [the 1840s] which, more than any other, saw a
new flowering of scientific and humanistic understanding throughout
the country.'[41] Driberg thought that some people were 'seduced by the
fallacy of earliness': 'Just because the building opposite, the Custom
House, is earlier than the Coal Exchange, it is automatically assumed
that it must be better.'[42] Here Sir Keith Joseph, Parliamentary Secretary
to the Ministry of Housing and Local Government, interrupted to say
that the Minister was not 'seduced by the fallacy of earliness', he was
simply following the advice of his advisory committee, which had
graded the Custom House Grade I and the Coal Exchange Grade II.[43]

'I suggest, then,' Driberg riposted, 'that the advisory committee is
seduced by the fallacy of earliness.' He further pointed out that even
the Georgian Group, which was primarily interested in preserving
buildings of the period of the Custom House, agreed with the
Victorian Society that the Coal Exchange ought to be saved perhaps at
the cost of shaving off some small part of the Custom House. He
added:

If there were a proposal to pull down St Paul's or St Stephen's, Walbrook,
for road development, obviously the Minister would never allow it – but
just because, and only because, the Coal Exchange was built in the nineteenth century, instead of the eighteenth or the seventeenth century, the
threat is real. Yet, of its kind and period, it is a building of quite exceptional character and merit.[44]

Driberg hoped that the Parliamentary Secretary was going to tell the House, that night, either that a decision had been taken to reprieve the building or that there was to be a public inquiry.

> I feel that he can hardly refuse a public inquiry. I am assured that it would be technically possible to divert the projected road by the few yards needed, and the public inquiry would also examine various possible future uses for this building, some of which have been suggested by Mr John Betjeman, who told us on the BBC this morning that when the last tenants were given notice – they had been working in offices there – they had found it so agreeable and convenient a place to work in that they sent an appeal of protest against having to leave.[45]

Driberg hoped that 'that noble galleried rotunda' could be preserved where it was, and as it was. 'If the Minister can bring that about, I am sure that Londoners of the future will bless his name.'[46] As Driberg sat down, an unexpected champion of the Coal Exchange stood up to speak, Colonel C.G. Lancaster, the Conservative Member for South Fylde. He wished to support the preservation of the Exchange 'on the ground that I expect I am the only person in the House who made use of that building for the purpose for which it was built. Like everybody else who did so use it, I know that one could not but be impressed by the noble features of a very distinguished building which has played a very significant part in the City of London and in the commerce of this country.'[47] William Deedes, the former journalist on whose adventures Evelyn Waugh had partly based his novel *Scoop*, also supported Driberg, hoping that 'the movable object will resist the irresistible force'[48] – a phrase which must have taxed to the utmost Deedes's Churchillian diction.

Sir Keith Joseph rose to reply. 'It would be a pleasure', Joseph said, 'to reply to such a constructively and moderately put debate if only one could be as forthcoming as hon. Members wish.' He wanted to be constructive and helpful, but he was sorry to say he could not go as far as hon. Members were hoping. Evading Driberg's arguments about the growing regard for Victorian architecture, he clung to the letter of the listings. He reminded the House that there were 140,000 listed buildings. It was not possible to preserve them all. The Coal Exchange, he repeated, was graded Grade II, the Custom House Grade I. Further, the Exchange had been neglected. It had suffered war damage and (here was an adroit jab at the Labour Party) 'the use to which my hon. and gallant friend the Member for South Fylde [Colonel Lancaster] referred was brought to an end by nationalization'.[49]

'In 1958,' Joseph continued, 'when the plans for demolition were first made public, the Royal Fine Art Commission and the Ministry's advisory committee both urged that every effort should be made to find ways of keeping the building; but neither of them said, as they have both said about some buildings, that the building must be kept at all costs . . .'[50] All the alternatives to demolishing the Exchange which Joseph had before him involved pulling down part of the Custom House. There had been a Custom House on the site for five hundred years. 'There would be the maximum resistance from the users – the Customs authorities – the owners – the Ministry of Works – and a public outcry, which would be equally justified, if that building, let alone Billingsgate Market, were touched.'[51]

Joseph offered a sop to the conservationists. He still hoped that somebody might pay to move and re-erect the building. With this end in view, he would see 'whether it is possible to keep this building up until the very last moment, at least to maximize the opportunity for sympathizers to preserve it'.[52] (This would seem to be a direct echo of John's letter to *The Times*.) Meanwhile, records could be taken and models made. The Minister would not hold an inquiry, as the cost of such an inquiry would fall, not on him, but on the local authority. However, Joseph was prepared to ask the Minister to appeal to the City for a stay of execution. (Apparently he was unaware that one had already been granted on 2 February.) 'One thing which would be intolerable', Joseph said, 'would be if the building were demolished and, in the interval between its demolition and the start of the construction of the road on the site, a proposal came to light which might have saved the building by having it re-erected elsewhere.'[53]

As John wrote to Woodrow Wyatt on 18 February, the temporary reprieve which the Court of Common Council had granted the building gave an opportunity for 'a full and constructive discussion'.[54] He invited him to a meeting in the Society of Antiquaries' rooms at Burlington House on 3 March. This, at last, was to be the 'round-table conference' for which Lord Esher had pressed in 1958. To it were invited members of the Corporation of London, the London County Council, the Government departments concerned, and representatives of societies who might find an immediate use for the building or who were interested in it because of its architectural quality. Sending Wyatt the formal letter of invitation which went out to everybody, John added an urgent scribble in the margin – 'For God's sake come & speak. We must save this building. What is really behind its destruction is a speculator who has his eye on the rest of the island site on which it stands.'[55]

At the Burlington House meeting, which was chaired by Mortimer Wheeler, a committee was appointed to organize the Coal Exchange campaign: the MPs Brian Batsford and Tom Driberg, C.S. Chettoe, P. Chamberlin, Sir Albert Richardson, Lord Mottistone and Mark Girouard.[56] On 9 March 1961, John chaired a meeting of this committee at the House of Commons. Driberg opened the meeting by reading a letter from Sir Keith Joseph. There was general indignation at Joseph's bland assertion that 'While the historic significance of the construction of the Coal Exchange is recognized, there are reservations as to the artistic quality of the building.'[57] It was agreed that this slight should be countered by reference to the observations made by Henry-Russell Hitchcock and the reassessment by Pevsner. In his letter Joseph said he had looked thoroughly into the matter and had found himself compelled to the conclusion that the only hope for the Exchange was for a practical scheme for its re-erection on another site – perhaps of the rotunda only.[58]

The committee was not prepared to accept this view. John asked Richardson, Mottistone and Chettoe to outline their respective schemes for saving the Exchange. Richardson pointed to the number of 'poor buildings and vacant sites' near the Exchange. His suggestion was that a new one-way road should run to the north of the Exchange and that an open piazza should be created. The committee liked this plan but urged that the Watermen's Company Hall in St Mary-at-Hill should also be preserved. Mottistone's idea was to push back the Exchange by ten feet and have a footway through part of the Custom House. Chettoe's scheme envisaged an elevated roadway right through, an express route from Blackfriars to the Tower with four lanes of traffic on the ground and two on top. Chamberlin was asked to investigate what it would cost to re-erect the Exchange on another site, say in Kew Gardens. After a long discussion of the alternative routes, it was agreed to proceed with Richardson's proposal; a deputation would wait on the Minister of Housing with sketches by Richardson and plans drawn up by Chettoe.[59]

Keith Joseph received the deputation, on 17 April 1961, and Richardson's, Mottistone's and Chettoe's different schemes were all put to him. Joseph seemed to prefer Mottistone's plan, though he described Richardson's as 'highly dramatic and the most poetical scheme'. He confessed himself 'considerably shaken' by what the deputation had told him.[60] On 29 May Joseph's private secretary wrote to the Victorian Society to say that the City was now examining the three suggested schemes.[61] For the next six months the society again allowed the Coal Exchange issue to go cold while battle proceeded over the Euston Arch.[62] At the meeting of 7 November 1961, at which it was concluded that 'The Battle of Euston is lost', it was decided that Ashley Barker of the London County Council should be consulted about the

Coal Exchange.[63] Barker met several members of the committee on 14 November and presented a suggested modification of Mottistone's plan, which would cost £125,000. The LCC considered the other plans unworkable.[64]

On 24 November the Town Planning Committee of the LCC reported Barker's findings to the Minister of Housing.[65] At a Victorian Society meeting on 5 December, the committee stated plainly and pointedly its belief that there was no need to widen Thames Street for the sake of the traffic, which was not heavy, 'but that what seems urgent to the City Corporation is the demolition of the Coal Exchange so that they can make a highly profitable development of the site as soon as possible'.[66] The case for retention would be enormously strengthened if a practical use could be found for the building: could it be an extension to the London Museum? Or a Light Engineering or Electronic Building Centre? The London Museum and Sir Vincent de Ferranti, chairman of Ferranti Ltd, were to be approached. While these behind-the-scenes moves were made, it was decided to delay a renewal of the press campaign.[67]

'Keith Joseph knew how to be courteous and knew how to charm,' Peter Fleetwood-Hesketh said. 'He also knew how to deliver a rabbit-punch.'[68] On 24 January 1962 the Ministry of Housing wrote to the City Corporation to say that the three schemes for saving the Exchange had been considered; that the first two had been found impracticable, while the third, Mottistone's, though workable, would cost £125,000.[69] The Ministry's letter contained this sentence: 'Lord Mottistone's scheme appears to him [the Minister] to be not impracticable, but it would involve drastic alteration to the exterior of the building and would substantially reduce the accommodation it provides, thus making the problem of finding a suitable use for it even more difficult.'[70] The Minister therefore thought it right to release the Corporation from its undertaking to defer the demolition of the building. In fact Mottistone's plan involved 'arcading' the pavements on both sides of Lower Thames Street; so, as the Victorian Society's annual report stated, 'The accommodation would thus be somewhat reduced but the external appearance, far from being "drastically altered", would scarcely be changed at all.'[71] Neither Mottistone nor the Victorian Society was informed of the letter's contents, or that it had been sent. It was by mere chance that they heard of it later.

The Society at once approached several MPs and peers, asking them to raise the matter in Parliament. At the same time the Society sent an illustrated brochure. *The Case for Preservation*, to every member of the City Court of Common Council. The brochure quoted some views on the Exchange: '*Professor Nikolaus Pevsner*: "Among the twelve irreplaceable buildings of nineteenth-century England"; *Ian Nairn, in the* "Daily Telegraph": "How Robert Adam might have built if he had lived in the mid-nineteenth century"; *Professor R. Furneaux Jordan*: "Posterity will revile us if we do not do something about it." '[72] At a special 'Coal Exchange' meeting held on 21 February, the Victorian Society decided 'to withold press or other publicity for the time being, so as not to prejudice the Society's relations with the City'.[73] In spite of this, *The Guardian*'s architectural correspondent contributed an article the next day, headed 'END OF THE EXCHANGE: Preservation pleas fail'.[74]

In early March 1962, a Mr J. O. Grindlay wrote to *City Press* from Queen Victoria Street, which runs parallel to Lower Thames Street: 'The fate of the Coal Exchange is being decided this week. The Common Council should vote against this wickedness. Everything in these days is being done to facilitate the movement of traffic. The motor dominates the life of the nation. It makes for enormous unnecessary expenditure and it overrides everything else. It is time to stop. Cannot the City set an example?'[75] Tom Driberg again raised the matter in the Commons on 6 March. The ministerial reply was that nothing could be done 'as the decision to demolish had already been taken'.[76] This was not strictly true, as the Court of Common Council was due to discuss precisely that question on 8 March.

A debate was held in the Lords on 7 March. Lord Conesford – the former Henry Strauss QC – asked Her Majesty's Government what steps they were taking to prevent the destruction of the Coal Exchange.[77] In reply, Earl Jellicoe, as Joint Parliamentary Secretary, Ministry of Housing and Local Government, rehearsed the Government's reasons for releasing the Corporation from its undertaking to defer demolition.[78] Conesford rose again: 'My Lords, does my noble friend recognize that . . . its destruction would not be allowed in any other civilized country? Does he know that the noble Lord, Lord Mottistone, has devised a perfectly practicable scheme for saving everything essential at an estimated cost of £125,000?'[79] Jellicoe replied that he was indeed aware of Lord Mottistone's plan; but the fate of the Coal Exchange was now a matter for the City Corporation.[80] Several peers spoke in favour of saving the Exchange. They included Lord Molson, a figure of fun to the Evelyn Waugh generation, known as 'Hot Lunch Molson' from his assertion in their Oxford days that 'Only a hot lunch will do.'[81]

My Lords [Molson said], may I ask the Parliamentary Secretary whether Her Majesty's Government realize the greatly increased interest in Victorian architecture and the growing view that many fine buildings were erected at that time, some of them masterpieces? Do Her Majesty's Government realize how great is the concern that, first of all, the Euston Arch should be demolished, in spite of the protests from all those most qualified to express a view about its architectural importance, that now the Coal Exchange is going, and that, in the evening papers yesterday, we now hear that the Shot Tower, which has come to be regarded as an important and, I may say, a much beloved landmark in London, is also to be demolished? Are Her Majesty's Government prepared to do something to preserve the great monuments erected in the nineteenth century, which are coming to be regarded with every year that passes as of greater importance?[82]

Jellicoe replied: 'My Lords, I am afraid I have not "mugged up" the Shot Tower as yet, but I would assure my noble friend that we are well aware of the growing interest in Victoriana.'[83] Only one peer made a speech hostile to the Coal Exchange: the Earl of Albemarle, a man of eighty who that morning had put himself to the trouble of contacting the Corporation's surveyor and visiting the site.

Is it not a fact [he asked] that the access is quite out of date? The only entrance to the building is on a corner. The only entrance to the offices on the ground floor and on the first floor is by a circular stone staircase; and for getting up to the second, third and fourth storeys the only access is from the first floor by angular iron staircases. Is he not further aware that the office accommodation is entirely a question of dark cubby-holes with little stairways, thoroughly out of date with anything any of us have seen in the way of modern offices? . . . If the cultural uses which are being suggested here were found for this building, would not the smell of fish from Billingsgate Market immediately opposite be . . . objectionable?[84]

Albemarle's aspersions on the Exchange were mild compared with those made by D. G. Mills, chairman of the City Corporation's Streets Committee, when the question of the Coal Exchange was debated at length, the next day, by the Court of Common Council at Guildhall. He spoke of it as 'this dingy, brown-painted, miserable place'.[85] Of the iron railings, he said he had seen better examples in public houses. He added that the Exchange would not be agreeable to the Streets Committee for a public lavatory.[86] The case for the Exchange was made by Alderman Sir Edmund Stockdale, who said he was rising for the first time in sixteen years other than as Lord Mayor.[87] And there was a pointed question as to whether it was intended to demolish Tower Bridge. Replying, Sir William Rowland, chairman of the Bridge House Estates Committee, denied that the committee was considering demolishing the bridge, even though it was 'well known' that the bridge had been 'coping for some time with a density of traffic which was never envisaged when it was constructed'.[88] On a vote, Rodway Stevens, chairman of the Coal and Corn and Finance Committee, obtained a majority decision to demolish the Coal Exchange and to invite tenders for this work.[89]

What was the Victorian Society to do now? The alternatives seemed to be, in order of merit:

1. A buyer who could use the building as adapted under the Mottistone plan.
2. To dismantle the iron rotunda (fifty feet in diameter and seventy-five feet high) and move it to a new site, for example as part of the Barbican scheme.
3. A museum, perhaps the Victoria & Albert, to preserve a section of the rotunda.[90]

The annual report of the Victorian Society, 1962–63, recorded: 'To make the building more widely known Mr Betjeman persuaded the City to open it to the Public for a time before demolition, during the City Festival, arranging a photographic exhibition of Victorian architecture in the Coal Exchange itself, and showing the building on television.'[91] The Exchange was opened to the public from 2 to 27 July 1962.

At the Victorian Society meeting on 3 July, the secretary read out a letter from Frank Valori, the contractor who had demolished the Euston Arch and who had now been commissioned to take down the Exchange. Valori was suggesting that 'the Victorian Society should handle the work of dismantling the rotunda themselves, and pay him compensation for that part of his Contract with the Corporation of London which he would be deprived of carrying out. The Society would not be able to adopt this suggestion.'[92] On 25 July the City informed the society that demolition could no longer be postponed and would begin as soon as practicable after the building was closed to the public on 27 July.[93] They added that the Roman hypocaust under the Exchange – 'a very ordinary bath,' the society's annual report sourly noted – would be preserved.[94] The society inquired into the possibility of obtaining plastic moulds of the different parts of the rotunda for reproduction in any suitable material, and re-erection; but the cost was prohibitive.[95]

Its inquiries went further afield. On 26 July, at the eleventh hour, it received an enthusiastic approach from Eric Westbrook, director of the National Gallery of Victoria, Melbourne, and Roy Grounds, architect of the new Cultural Centre being built in Melbourne. The two men expressed their wish to acquire the rotunda for re-erection as the nucleus of the new centre. They asked for rough estimates for dismantling it and shipping it to Melbourne. The society accordingly asked the Corporation for a deferment of demolition to allow a chance to obtain the necessary information.[96] Meanwhile, on 2 August in the House of Commons, Dr Barnett Stross asked the Minister of Housing why the Coal Exchange had never been placed on the Ministry's statutory list of protected buildings.[97] Frederick Corfield, replying for the Minister, said he could add nothing to the Parliamentary Secretary's reply to Mr Driberg on 6 March, which (the society considered) was irrelevant and, at the time, untrue.[98]

By 3 August the society had obtained a very rough estimate, of some £40,000, for dismantling the rotunda, all contingent expenses and transport to Melbourne, where the National Gallery of Victoria would accept it as a gift; the further £40,000 necessary for re-erection would be underwritten in Australia.[99] The Agent General for Victoria and the Victorian Society asked the Corporation to stop demolition to enable this plan to be carried out. At the same time attention was drawn to the City's Coal Market Fund, untouched since the closure of the Exchange and showing an accumulated balance of over £40,000. The society suggested that the City might use this to dismantle and transport the rotunda to Melbourne as a gift to the Government of Victoria.[100] On 12 August there was a comic piece of tastelessness in the *Sunday Times*, in which John's old friend from Ministry of Information days, Ernestine Carter, who was by now the paper's fashion editor, used photographs of models lolling against the ironwork of the Exchange. 'LAST LOOK AT THE COAL EXCHANGE in San Clair's low-belted, double-breasted, dark mixed tweed, sleeved in rib-knit, 10½ guineas at Woollands, London.'[101]

On 20 September the Court of Common Council announced that the Coal Market Fund could not be used, but that, 'because it appears to be the first serious indication that anyone . . . considers the Coal Exchange Rotunda sufficiently important to spend money on it', they had ordered a postponement.[102] The next day, the society's secretary, Peter Fleetwood-Hesketh, was told by the Town Clerk that if he could get promises of £20,000 in a nominal four weeks (in fact three weeks and three days) the City would provide the other £20,000 needed. In the event of failure, demolition would proceed.[103] The unexpected offer sounded not ungenerous; but did the Corporation cynically calculate that the money would not be raised in so short a time?

In the weeks before the deadline, Fleetwood-Hesketh wrote individual letters to chairmen and directors of over ninety companies.[104] Frank Valori volunteered to dismantle the rotunda and forgo payment for two years, and the Port Line offered to undertake shipment to

Australia at low cost.[105] By 18 October only £1,000 had been raised.[106] On 16 October Fleetwood-Hesketh pointed out to the City that the society's initial object, which was shared by the Australians, was *preservation*. He explained that dismantlement and delivery to some suitable place for storage, with a view to eventual re-erection in Britain, would, on the estimates they had, amount to just over £24,000. If the City would contribute the £20,000 already offered, only £4,100 would be needed to achieve the society's objective. Given a little more time, there seemed every chance of raising that sum.[107] But on 18 October Rodway Stevens told the Court of Common Council that, since the Victorian Society had failed to raise £20,000 in three and a half weeks, the City Architect had been instructed to resume demolition. 'The announcement was greeted with applause,' *The Times* reported, 'and there was no discussion.'[108]

However, on 7 November it was found that the rotunda was still intact, and Lord Esher wrote to the Town Clerk, repeating the points made in Fleetwood-Hesketh's letter of 16 October.[109] The Town Clerk acknowledged Esher's letter and said that a special meeting of the Corn and Coal and Finance Committee would be called to consider it, though he did not say when the meeting would be held.[110] It took place on 12 November, when it was decided not to delay demolition.[111] Fleetwood-Hesketh was incensed to learn that on 9 November, after Esher's letter must have been received at the Guildhall, Valori had received 'a very urgent telephone call' from Mr Fiske, of the City Architect's department, insisting that he begin demolition without fail on 12 November, the very day the special meeting was to take place.[112]

On 14 November, Fleetwood-Hesketh received a telegram, soon confirmed by letter, from the museums director of Durham County Council, requesting information about the rotunda with a view to its re-erection in that county.[113] After ascertaining that, apart from the removal of a few sections of the balustrading, the rotunda remained intact, the inquiry was reported to the Town Clerk.[114] Fleetwood-Hesketh asked whether demolition could again be deferred, whether the City would uphold its offer of £20,000, and if a reasonable length of time could be granted in which to raise the necessary funds. But the Corporation had had enough.[115] The Town Clerk replied (untruthfully, Fleetwood-Hesketh thought) that demolition had advanced so far as to preclude the possibility of dismantling for re-erection. The City's offer of financial help was withdrawn and there was to be no extension of time. Demolition would continue.[116] The magazine *Steel and Coal* had pithily and accurately summarized the situation on 19 October under the heading 'Adieu – The Coal Exchange has had it'.[117] It only remained to tell the Victoria & Albert Museum that there now seemed no chance of preserving the Exchange whole, so they could make sure of getting the bits that they wanted and that had been promised to them in the event of demolition.[118] At a meeting on 3 December the Victorian Society decided that the cause was lost.[119] Demolition followed. Two cast-iron griffins from the Exchange were erected on Victoria Embankment in 1963 to mark the City boundary[120] – in its way, as ironic a gesture as Valori's presentation of the Euston Arch model to the Victorian Society.

For years afterwards there were bitter post-mortems. In 1973 the *City Press* ran a story under the headline 'Why did the Corporation pull the Coal Exchange down?'

> Over ten years ago the Coal Exchange in Lower Thames Street was demolished. Jane Fawcett, secretary of the Victorian Society, is still asking the question why, since nothing has been done to the site – a windswept plot of vacant land . . . It now appears that far from using the site for the road-widening scheme there may well be a mammoth office block built there instead. The City Corporation say that there has been a road actually over a third of the site for the past five years, and that the City's Planning Committee have approved an office development application from Fitzroy Robinson and Partners for the other two thirds of the site . . . Mrs Fawcett told City Press she disagreed with this first claim: 'As far as I know the pavement has been narrowed but the site has not been eaten into.' . . .
>
> *The big question still remains, ten years later – should the City have gone ahead with demolition? Why couldn't Common Council wait until the building had been resited, since it has not exactly sprung into action now that the building has gone? And why is the City considering using the site for a purpose different from that given as the reason for demolition? After ten years of red tape, these questions will probably never be answered.*[121]

John's suspicions about the Corporation's ulterior plans had proved well founded. In 1977 Jennifer Freeman wrote in *Built Environment*:

> Remember the Coal Exchange in Lower Thames Street? Fifteen years ago J. B. Bunning's cast-iron masterpiece was demolished by its owner, the City Corporation, the greatest architectural loss of that authority's post-war rampage . . . Recently completed in its stead stands the (pseudonymously) named St Mary's House, 85,000 sq ft of offices designed by Fitzroy, Robinson and Partners for the Legal and General Assurance Society. It is an irregular, eight-storey block with tinted glass windows, finished in grey polished granite and arranged round a central car park. After so long a hiatus the City Corporation must eagerly anticipate the reinstatement of a substantial ratepayer.

Conservationists may bitterly reflect that the rates foregone while the site lay vacant must far exceed the £125,000 refused to restore the building in 1962. Lower Thames Street is now transformed into a major east–west artery which pedestrians cross at their peril, for there are no crossings and few subways. The Coal Exchange could easily have been retained. At the narrowest place the Exchange stood 43 ft across the street from Billingsgate Market. Further west on the Southern Route, for example at Blackfriars Underpass, the highway is only some 40 ft wide. Pedestrians could have been accommodated by insetting the pavement into the entrance vestibule and providing a subway to link with the proposed riverside walk. An ideal tenant for the Coal Exchange might have been the London Metal Exchange which has needed new headquarters for several years.[122]

Why did John and his friends fail to save the Coal Exchange? The tragedy of its loss cannot be attributed entirely to the City's greed, duplicity and philistinism. To use legal language, there was perhaps 'contributory negligence' by John and the Victorian Society. He was a great catalyst in any controversy or campaign; but he lacked 'follow-through' and staying power. He wrote striking letters to the newspapers. His appearances on television fascinated. He was astute at smelling out his opponents' motives. But he was no organizer. He could get the public's attention but could not keep it. As his friend Philip Harding (whose office in the brand-new *Times* building overlooked Upper Thames Street in 1962)[123] was fond of saying, 'Brag is a good dog; *but Holdfast is a better*.'[124] Months went by with no discussion of the case at Victorian Society meetings, and with no public campaigning. The Corporation was not kept wincing in the pillory. Part of the trouble was that the society had too few officers and not enough troops. Then again, the crisis over the Euston Arch distracted it from the Coal Exchange: the small force was fighting on two fronts at once, and one was neglected. Peter Fleetwood-Hesketh's rearguard action was tenacious, but it came too late. The real villain of the piece was Keith Joseph, whose silky politeness lulled the preservationists into false confidence, and who then struck with no warning or quarter given. The architect of Thatcherism was in training for his profession.

The loss of the Coal Exchange was a blow to John's vanity as well as to the English architectural heritage. In both the Euston Arch and the Coal Exchange campaigns he was the front man; both ended in failure. John was now on his mettle to achieve a success. All that he had learned from the defeats of 1961 and 1962 was brought into play in the campaign of 1963 – the Battle of Bedford Park.

A NATURAL SHOWMAN: TELEVISION IN THE SIXTIES

And now prepare for the unexpected.

John Betjeman, television film on *Devizes*, 1962

Throughout the 1960s, John worked on a television *ABC of Churches* with the BBC producer Kenneth Savidge, who was based at Bristol.[1] The two had first got to know each other in radio work when Savidge was a Religious Broadcasting assistant. He recalled:

There used to be a magazine programme devised by the organizer of religion, a saintly man called the Rev. Martin Willson, whom Frank Gillard, the war correspondent, had met in North Africa when Martin was a chaplain. Gillard thought Martin would be the man to run religion in the newly formed 'Western Region' of the BBC, as John always called it – the West Region. I was his assistant. And that radio magazine, *The Faith in the West*, was the origin of John's *Poems in the Porch*.* I remember once – one of the *Poems in the Porch* begins

> Septuagesima – seventy days
> To Easter's primrose tide of praise . . .

---

* John's pamphlet *Poems in the Porch* was published by the Society for Promoting Christian Knowledge (SPCK) in 1954. In an 'Author's Note', he wrote:

These verses do not pretend to be poetry. They were written for speaking on the wireless, and went out over the Western Region at the request of the Rev. Martin Willson, Director of Religious Broadcasting in the West. Owing to the numerous requests for copies of them, the SPCK have kindly consented to publish them in printed form, and in order to compensate for the shortcomings of the verse, I have prevailed on my friend, Mr John Piper, to provide the illustrations.

and half jokingly we suggested, 'How about

> The Gesimas – Septua, Sex and Quinq
> Mean Lent is near, which makes you think.

And for the broadcast version only he adopted that, but the version printed in *Poems in the Porch* is not quite as skittish – the line reads

> The Gesimas – Septua, Sexa, Quinq . . .[2]

Savidge graduated from radio to television. By then, the Rev. Martin Willson had already filmed the first of the *ABC of Churches* (Aldbourne, Wiltshire). Savidge was given the job of making the rest. In 1959 he went to see John at Cloth Fair.

We had not actually met at that time [Savidge recalls]. All our radio work had been done 'down the line'. I wasn't awed; but it was slightly daunting as he came in with Elizabeth Cavendish nursing a lap-dog. Elizabeth gave the impression that she thought broadcasting wasn't quite respectable – I later knew this was far from true. I thought: 'I'm not quite sure whether I shall want to work with this man very much.' But after the second or third meeting I think he realized I was moderately competent and not a total fool. There were drinks and jokes and it all fell into place.[3]

John and Savidge made three films a year for the *ABC*. They reconnoitred in the spring and filmed in the summer. 'B' was inevitably Blisland, Cornwall, one of John's favourite churches. At Dummer, Hampshire, John surveyed a cupboard in the gallery crammed with oil lamps, jam jars and discarded harvest festival decorations, and commented: 'Some corner of a country church that is forever Church of England.'[4] In a piece of scene-setting in Hove, he said, 'The terraces here are far too grand ever to have bathing dresses hanging out of their windows.'[5] Savidge told John's daughter:

He delighted in the different clerics we met all round the country . . . At Inglesham on the upper reaches of the Thames above Lechlade, JB arrived down the infant Thames in a punt propelled by the willowy son of the incumbent, who was called Father Thomas. Father Thomas was very modern and said immediately, 'Call me Padre,' and then he said, 'I bet you don't do this for nothing.' John and I doubled up laughing afterwards and 'Call me Padre' then became a stock description of a certain sort of cleric.'[6]

At Kingston, on the Isle of Purbeck, Dorset, a church by G.E. Street, they approached the incumbent, Father Lloyd, who said, '*Television?*

I can't think why on earth anyone would want to put my church on television. Are you sure you have come to the right place?' But he was very co-operative.[7] At Minstead, Hampshire, whose church had a family pew like an opera box, lived Patrick Garland's father, who had been deputed, years before, to introduce John to 'Sex with ladies' in Paris.[8] He served the crew venison sandwiches.[9] At Ottery St Mary, Devon, whose exterior is modelled on Exeter Cathedral, John talked about Coleridge's association with the place. Parkstone, Dorset, was 'a Roman basilica beside suburban Bournemouth tennis courts'. In the Unitarian Church at Taunton, Somerset, Coleridge was mentioned again: he used to walk over from Nether Stowey to worship there. 'U' was predictably Uffington: the film began with John bowing three times into the eye of the White Horse. Savidge wanted him to recite G.K. Chesterton's lines –

> Before the gods that made the gods
>   Had seen their sunrise pass
> The White Horse of the White Horse Vale
>   Was cut out of the grass.

Usually John did whatever the producer asked him to do; but he refused to recite Chesterton's verse – whether from jealousy (*he* was the poet of Uffington) or from distaste for Chesterton's Roman Catholicism, Savidge was not sure.[10] However, in an ecumenical spirit, John did allow 'W' to be the chapel of Wardour Castle, Wiltshire – the only Roman Catholic place of worship in the series. 'Y' would be Yaverland on the Isle of Wight; 'Z' had to be Zennor – 'a strange Celtic kingdom at the end of England'. But for some time both John and Savidge were puzzled what to do about 'X' – until John hit on the idea of going to the church of the Hospital of St Cross, Winchester, the almshouse founded by Henry de Blois in the 1130s. At the entrance John asked for the Wayfarer's Dole – the horn beaker of beer and piece of white bread given free to any traveller who requests it. One of the brothers of the Hospital at that time was Dick Young, the disreputable former schoolmaster who was the original of 'Captain Grimes' in Evelyn Waugh's *Decline and Fall*.[11] Ken Savidge remembers that he gave the men 'copious draughts of refrigerated Amontillado'.[12] (A few years later, Brother Young's death caused yet another scandal: it was found that he had left – and not to the Hospital – a fortune which should have disqualified him as a poor brother; also a fine collection of porcelain which went to the Ashmolean Museum, Oxford.)[13]

The *ABC* series was made with the BBC's Outside Broadcast Unit (OBU).

Although it was somewhat more cumbersome than film [Ken Savidge said] (with film you had a crew of six people, while OBU could be up to twenty-five), you did have the advantage of four or five cameras all working at once and you could do long 'takes'. You could do a take in which John walked down an aisle and talked about details of bench-ends, and actually slot them in, which you can't do with a single camera.[14]

Savidge thought that John was a television 'natural'.

I don't know what it means, except that I recognize it when I see it. It's nothing to do with technique. An invidious comparison: if you think of someone like Lord Clark of Civilization[15] – the scholarship! the erudition! You sat and wondered at them. But – I wouldn't use the phrase 'showing off', but he was *displaying*. It was a good lecture and you sat passive and absorbed. But the great thing about John was that he wanted you to *share* his love and enthusiasm. He wasn't without vanity, but it didn't show on screen. Another good comparison is Patrick Moore.[16] I'm not the slightest bit interested in astronomy; but if I happen to see *The Sky at Night*, I think, 'Well, it obviously matters a great deal to *him* – I wonder perhaps whether I ought to be taking an interest.'[17]

'Crews loved working with John,' Savidge said. 'They virtually queued up to do so.'[18] John was friendly and remembered their names. Often he joined them in a pub for the lunch break, paying for the drinks. 'He was always sneaking off to the pub with them,' Savidge told Candida. 'I remember losing him completely in the village of Edington – eventually I found him an hour later in the pub with the drivers.'[19] After the *ABC* filming of Hove, John, Savidge and the crew went to a pub in Brighton. 'An executive and his "bird" came in and John said, "I bet they'll order ten Seniors[20] and a Babycham." And they did.'[21] On a free morning, John would play golf with crew members. His golfing shoes came in useful in filming. 'If we were working at a site where there was a lot of walking along gravel drives, he would bring them so that the recordist got really crisp sound from footsteps.'[22] There were jokes and there was laughter. 'John was the very antithesis of the performer who regards the crew as a collection of anonymous technicians, with whom he need not concern himself. He kept everybody happy, and for a producer this was a real godsend.'[23]

He did much of your work for you [Savidge added]. If there was a hold-up, he'd ask the floor manager, 'Is Ken talking? Do stop him, we want to get on.' This of course did nothing but get the crew on his side – and indirectly on my side. He knew the business. He knew what would work and what wouldn't. He was always very keen to think of the audience, 'our readers', as he called them. He'd say: 'Do you think our readers will understand this?' And he had a very just estimation of the place of television – he realized it was like journalism.[24]

John enjoyed the technical jargon used by the crew, such as 'inky dink' (one of the smallest lamps), 'dolly' (moving platform for a camera), 'apple and biscuit' (a type of microphone), 'basher' (a powerful light, giving overall illumination), 'pups' (much smaller lamps, for bringing out detail in, say, a stone carving) and 'to barn door off 2k' (a two kilowatt lamp fitted with a shuttering device called a 'barn door', enabling one to vary the amount of light the lamp produced).[25] If some of the equipment became outdated and had to be replaced, he affected acute nostalgia for the redundant machinery. When the old '405 line scanner' went, he composed a valedictory ode –

> Farewell, articulated scanner,
> Sad victim of some heartless planner.
> What happy days were spent with thee
> By Eric, Jack and Ken and me,
> A-churning out the ABC.[26]

There was a second stanza, which Savidge has forgotten, except the opening lines, 'And now behold a newer van, Equipped with 625 to scan . . .'[27] From a remark of John's, the mobile VT recording van became known as 'Ray's cinema'. 'We had lost track of JB,' Savidge recalled, 'though we could hear him as he was wearing a radio mike. "I'm in the cinema with Ray" (watching a playback of the sequence we had just recorded), he finally announced. Ray Burgess was the recordist and for long afterwards the mobile recording van was known as "Ray's cinema".'[28]

The one person in the BBC who never quite understood John was Frank Sheratt. His title was West Region Programme Executive, though John always called him 'The Accountant'. 'Fancy a grown man like that going around with a teddy-bear!' Sheratt said to Savidge.

He was a quiet, kindly Lancastrian [Savidge recalls]. JB liked to imagine him sitting at a high desk, with pince-nez, writing with a quill pen. Once, particularly dissatisfied with a contract, John threatened to ditch the BBC and go and work for 'those commercial people down next to the crematorium' (a reference to Television West and Wales, now Harlech Television). That little difficulty was surmounted – though John did some

W – but poor Mr Sheratt was completely nonplussed when
d one set of expenses, which went something like this:

n Cloth Fair to Heathrow £17s 6d
Morning papers 1s 10d
Coffee in Forte's 4d
Tip to waitress £5[29]

John made a number of films with Savidge that were outside the
ABC sequence, including one on Truro Cathedral and another on *One
Thousand Years at Milton – from Milton Abbey*. Savidge has preserved the script of the Milton Abbey film, which contains this characteristic piece of Betjeman patter:

A cunning Cornish lawyer called Sir John Tregonwell (that's his brass in
the Abbey – you can see he was Cornish, incidentally, by the choughs on
his arms), fixed up Henry VIII's divorce from Catherine of Aragon and the
Abbey and its lands were his reward.

That's a little kiddy of his, who fell from the roof of the Abbey, but
wasn't killed because his skirts acted as a parachute.[30]

In May 1962 Maria Aitken, a granddaughter of John's wartime boss
Lord Rugby and later a well-known actress, wrote to John from
Sherborne School for Girls, asking him to talk to the school's literary
society. He agreed to do so, telling her that he expected to be in
Sherborne some time between 25 and 29 May. 'With a very nice Old
Harrovian called Jonathan Stedall and his Secretary, Miss Diana Gray,
I am making a reconnaissance of the town for a series of films on towns
in the West Country which I am making for the commercial television.
We thought of Sherborne as a school and abbey town with good streets
and what looks good on television is plenty of detail, carved stone and
wood and why not some young feet running down the polished floors
of school passages?'[31] The films were made for the short-lived TWW.
When the company closed down, John took part in a filmed tribute to
it, entitled *Come to an End,* in which he said, 'TWW – or Tellywelly as
I call it – was a good firm to work for . . . They found for me a young
producer, Jonathan Stedall, who had just started with them. We liked
the same jokes and we had the same point of view and we worked out
our programmes unhampered by accountants and officialdom.'[32]
Stedall, who was twenty-three in 1962, later wrote of John: 'For me he
was, in a way, like the father I never had – but without the complications.' Stedall too, after public school, had been expected to go into the
family business, the steel engineering firm Stedall's of High Holborn
and Clerkenwell; but his parents divorced, 'so I hardly saw my father

as a child and did not build up guilt as John did'.[33] Jonathan was a second cousin of Marcus Stedall, who had not only been at Marlborough with John, but owned a cliff-top house at Trebetherick.[34] For Jonathan's benefit, John wrote a satirical poem about Marcus –

> Safe in Somerset or Surrey,
> Marcus Stedall counts his chips,
> While down here the breakers hurry,
> Smoothing slate and smashing ships . . .[35]

John gave the talk at Sherborne School for Girls. He dined first with (Dame) Diana Reader Harris,[36] whom Maria Aitken had temptingly described as 'the most beautiful headmistress in England'.[37] Stedall thought her name was 'Rita Harris', and John ever afterwards referred to her as that.[38] (Stedall quickly noticed John's fondness for giving people nicknames. 'He even gave God a nickname – "The Management".'[39] During the filming at Sherborne, John and Stedall stayed at the Coker Motel. 'And there was a very beautiful receptionist I took up with, with blue eyes, so she became "Blue-eyes". John knew that I saw her subsequently, she was my girlfriend for a while. That was just an affectionate label – but perhaps, too, he couldn't be bothered to remember her name.')[40]

At the dinner with Dame Diana, John felt cold. He borrowed her fur coat and delivered his lecture in it. 'He was, of course, an enormous success and totally disarmed everyone,' Maria wrote to her mother. 'Not only the girls, who were all enchanted by him, but even the most astringent of the spinsters on the staff.'[41] From Maria he gained some inside information for use in the Sherborne film, in which he comments: 'You see these girls, well they shouldn't be wearing their school uniforms in the town. They should be wearing summer dresses.'[42] In the film he also visited the famous public school for boys, reciting an absurd school song beginning, 'When King Alfred was at Sherborne . . . ' At Lord Digby's School for girls (today an arts centre) he pointed out the Baroque staircase paintings by Sir James Thornhill 'who painted the inside of the dome of St Paul's Cathedral'.[43]

Stedall also filmed John in Marlborough, Bath, Clevedon, Devizes, Northlew, Chippenham, Crewkerne and Sidmouth. Over thirty years later, and ten years after John's death, when the 1962 films were found in the archives of HTV and were rescreened with much panoply as *The Lost Betjemans*, Stedall told the *Daily Express* that in filming Marlborough College 'It was a major struggle to get him through the gates. I had to practically push him.'[44] John had written a poem to go with the film –

Shades of my prison-house, they come to view,
Just as they were in 1922;
The stone flag passages, the iron bars,
The dressing gowns, the faggings, hats and scarves . . .

The dining Hall we're looking at is new.
I wonder if it smells of Irish stew,
In the same way the old one used to do? . . .[45]

By 1962 John had twenty-five years' experience of television work. He ranked as one of the leading pioneers of the medium, with Compton Mackenzie, Mortimer Wheeler, Gilbert Harding, Malcolm Muggeridge, David Attenborough and A. J. P. Taylor. He had perfected his television technique. In front of the camera he seemed to be able to cast off all self-consciousness. He talked, not in carefully honed passages of prose, but as one might chat to a friend, with jerky inconsequence, asides and second thoughts. In Devizes, he said:

I think a church is a very good place from which to start on a tour of this too little regarded Wiltshire assize town of Devizes. And, by the way, always look down alleys if you want to find the real history of a town. I mean, look at those half-timbered houses. Built before brick was used and when stone was so rare it was only used for castles and churches. I should think that's fifteenth century. Late fifteenth. And then notice that splendid altar tomb surrounded by railings in the churchyard there. Mid-Georgian, from the look of it. Now I wonder where he lived, who lies under there. Across the road, in that house? Probably not. He was dead before that: this house, I should think, is about 1790. It's a Devizes version of the Adam style, with Ionic capitals to the porch . . .[46]

As a natural showman, John knew the value of suspense and surprise. 'I never thought of looking at Crewkerne until this visit. I'm glad I stopped. You never know . . .'[47] When he spies the illicitly dressed Mädchen in Uniform in Sherborne, he asks, 'Will they be caught?' (They are not caught.) In another of the West Country films he asks: 'Where are all these old lanes leading? Each comes a cart's distance from some farm or hamlet to one secret, hidden village. They're all leading to Northlew, which was once marked quite big on the old maps of Devon.'[48] In that film he made a telling comparison between Northlew, which had been ruined by the coming of the railway ('Steam power displaced horses and drained the trade away') and Swindon, which was *made* by the railways. 'In Swindon it has always been an honour to be employed in the [locomotive] works – "inside", as they call it in the town.'[49] In 1994, when the film was reshown as one of *The Lost Betjemans*, it was realized what a historic record John had created. In one and the same film were seen old Northlew villagers who had been alive in the 1890s when the London and South Western Railway brought its ruin; and the great sheds of the old Swindon railway works, still in clanging, hammering use in 1962. But if one industrial glory had gone, by compensation another, which John had found moribund in '62, had been restored by 1997 when the actor Nigel Hawthorne presented a further series of *The Lost Betjemans*. 'And now prepare for the unexpected,' John had said in the Devizes film. 'Devizes hides one of the great engineering triumphs of the world – the Kennet and Avon Canal, built 1794 to 1810 – twenty-nine locks descend here from the chalk downs . . . Look at it today. England's most wonderful waterway, forgotten and neglected.'[50] Hawthorne was able to report that the canal had been brought back to use.

In 1951 John had agreed with the pioneer television producer Mary Adams that there was 'not enough silence in television'. He practised what he preached. Reaching the covered market in the film on Devizes, he says, 'There's no need for me to talk here. Just have a look round.'[51]After the camera has had time to forage round the market, John interrupts the silence with an afterthought:

> Oh, and I forgot this. The Bear 'otel in the marketplace, a relic of coaching days. Look at that ironwork. About 1800, I should think. And then follow along to the older part. Sir Thomas Lawrence,[52] the portrait painter, was born here; his father was the innkeeper. I like that great fat lettering across the front . . .[53]

For just one of the West Country films, John wrote a commentary in verse – because he thought verse suited the 'verandahed world' of Sidmouth –

> Farewell, seductive Sidmouth by the sea! –
> Older and more exclusive than Torquay.[54]

In the films on Bath and Clevedon, he deployed another of his talents, mimicry of voices. In Bath he conducted an imaginary conversation with a heartless developer. 'Today's building', he said in the developer's estuary twang, 'must express itself honestly and sincerely, as in this feature, which might be termed the *vital buttock* of the construction . . .'[55] In a small Clevedon hotel, in winter, he imagined what the permanent residents were thinking or saying. A television critic noted that 'One is writing . . . a brave letter . . . to say how she has made a home in this blank, bland room.'[56] Alan Bennett later adopted a similar technique for a programme filmed in a Harrogate hotel, and in his *Talking Heads* series of the 1980s.[57]

In 1963 John took part in a television 'profile' of his old friend Hugh Gaitskell, the Labour leader.[58] In 1964 he made a programme about branch-line railways, after Dr Beeching had done his 'devilish' work.[59] In June that year he was paid 200 guineas to take part in a Monitor programme about Philip Larkin, produced by Patrick Garland. In the crew was John Boorman, the future director of such feature films as *Deliverance*, *The Emerald Forest* and *Hope and Glory*. He had previously worked with John on a film about Swindon, and remembers John's telling him his somewhat well-worn anecdote about Field-Marshal Sir Philip Chetwode's views on how his son-in-law should address him.[60]

John interviewed Larkin in Hull, and rather took command. In a Hull graveyard, he harangued him about the social classes of those buried there, where they might have lived, and what he himself felt about death. Larkin submitted with a good grace: John was older, more famous and much more used to the television camera – though Alan Bennett, reviewing Andrew Motion's biography of Larkin in 1993, wrote: 'He was interviewed, or at any rate was talked at, by Betjeman, and typically, of course, it's Larkin who comes out of it as the better performer.'[61] Larkin was flattered by John's ability to reel off Larkin poems from memory. But after the filming Larkin wrote to Garland with wry good humour, suggesting that he retitle the film *To Hull with John Betjeman*.[62] 'The only question was what kind of a film could be made out of the inexplicable scraps you found you had brought back with you ... I can see it taking shape: Betjeman ("Uncle Abel") shows me my father's grave: "Ay, 'e wor a reet skipper, was your dad – a great seaman – a great gentleman ..." '[63] When the film was transmitted, Larkin wrote to Garland: 'I was sorry that our remarks about death had been excised. The whole programme had a rather funereal tone ... '[64] and reported that he had received an abusive letter from 'a dotty old lady from Edinburgh objecting to the "grey sludge of my mind" '.[65]

In 1965 John wrote a television play with Stewart Farrer, *Pity about the Abbey*. The plot was that Westminster Abbey was sold to Texas to make way for traffic improvements and offices; Farrer added some 'love interest'.

> *Architect*: Something had to be sacrificed. The new Treasury building replaces ... the Abbey!
> *Developer*: Good. Pity about the Abbey, though.

Architect: Mr Page, no one regrets having to make this
　decision more than I do, but . . .

The developer's daughter (half the love interest, with a blonde beehive
hairdo) comes in and looks at the architect's model.

Daughter: But what have you done with the Abbey?
Developer: I've got rid of it. Why?
Daughter: But you *can't*!

There were no great repercussions when the play was first transmitted in July 1965; but unfortunately, when it was repeated in 1966,
Godfrey Samuel of the Royal Fine Art Commission sent a script of it to
the architect Lord Esher, another member of the Commission. The
script was passed around and John heard that it had reached Lord
Bridges[66], whom he detested. 'Now, why I am annoyed about this,' John
wrote to Esher, 'is that the film was a very serious argument disguised as
a comedy, against developers of an unscrupulous sort . . . Though I don't
expect many of the Commissioners have television sets (I haven't one
myself), had they seen the play, I should have expected to have had letters
of congratulations and thanks. As it is, I gather from others, but not
from Godfrey, that there is a general impression in the Commission I
have behaved in an ungentlemanly fashion. I am so thunder-struck by
this that I must ask you to let me have your reactions.'[67] Esher replied
mildly: '. . . I'd say that I am all for the Commission, like any other official body, being made fun of, but not by one of its members, even though
of course I know and sympathize with what you wanted to put over.'[68]

John appeared solo in the programme *A Man with a View* (April
1966). The *Times* reviewer identified some of the qualities that made
him so effective on television.

In last night's film Mr John Betjeman visited Poole; and both, one could
say, were seen to good advantage. Mr Betjeman sketched the history of the
place, took us on a conducted tour of the old part of the town, and then
explored its suburban surrounds. Characteristically, his deepest affection
was reserved for the old umber-coloured brick, and the narrow streets,
'built for shelter and for friends'.

　What makes Mr Betjeman such a delightful guide is not merely the
strength of his feelings but also his eye for the out-of-the-way detail. He
pointed out, for instance, two codfish, made of marble, decorating one
Georgian fireplace. His informality is also a great asset: he is the first man
one has seen on television standing on a suburban bench and peering over
a hedge to get a better view of the house beyond.[69]

In November 1966 John went to the Holy Land to make the BBC
Television film *Journey to Bethlehem*, to be screened at Christmas. On
11 November he wrote to Candida from the American Colony Hotel,
Jerusalem:

> I cannot recommend Jerusalem too highly. But this hotel is *the* place – old-
> fashioned, huge bedrooms, flowers and endless servants and quiet and run
> by Anglicized Americans.
>
>   Now this is the very *odd* thing about Jerusalem which makes me so glad
> I came. It really does make you aware that Christ (whether he was God is
> for the moment irrelevant) lived and walked here. There the devotion of
> centuries, despite raids by Persians, Romans, Moslems and modern com-
> puters, make one see that Christ was God i.e. Man and God in one. And
> that is brought about by the churches here (Eastern Orthodox, Coptic,
> Syrian, Latin and the dear old C of E) all sucking honey from the rose of
> Jerusalem like bees. I am most surprised at how I love this city. But come
> at this time of year, not in pilgrim time . . .[70]

John went to Bethlehem, the Garden of Gethsemane and an Arab
refugee camp. On 29 November, back at Cloth Fair, he wrote to
Duncan Fallowell, a teenager who had become a friend after writing
him a fan-letter from St Paul's School in 1965, 'I was laid low with 'flu
for six days after the excitement of Jordan. Nobody had told me how
beautiful the place was and how hot it was going to be. The colours
of the desert were just like they are in Holman Hunt's *Scapegoat* . . .'[71]
The trip had made financial, as well as physical, demands on him. In
December he wrote to his then agents, David Higham Associates:

> I spent £110, exclusive of hotel bills, out of the £120 which the BBC
> allowed me in travellers' cheques for my stay in Jordan. The rest went in
> taxi fares, baksheesh, booklets and donations to churches which we filmed
> and some of it was spent in returning hospitality. It is worth noting that
> the American Colony Hotel liked us so much they took 50% off the bill,
> though I pointed out that the BBC would be the only beneficiary of their
> generosity.[72]

Since he had come back, he had sent off many copies of his books to
people who had helped ('Oddly enough the postage is more expensive
than the books').[73] Higham Associates wrote to Margot Robbins of
the BBC on 14 December: 'John Betjeman had to use a fantastic
amount of personal charm to get what was necessary for making the
film at all, since he and the producer appear to have been given very
little help by the BBC . . .'[74] In the circumstances Higham felt the

Corporation should reimburse John for the books he had sent out and for a Garrick Club dinner he had given the Jordanian Ambassador in London. The BBC paid up.[75]

John was still in demand for panel games. He took part in several sessions of *Call My Bluff*, in which he guessed the meanings of recherché words with such old friends as the giggling Arthur Marshall and the stuttering Patrick Campbell. Anthony Burgess wrote that the game 'was based on the complacent acceptance of ignorance by the ignorant, so long as it was the higher ignorance'.[76] Robert Robinson chaired *Call My Bluff*. He also presented the literary quiz *Take It or Leave It*, which was often produced by the young Melvyn Bragg.[77] Extracts from famous authors were read out without attribution and the panellists had to say who the writer was. 'Betjeman was a regular participant,' Robinson recalled, 'and always referred to the programme as *Money for Jam*: he didn't feel it necessary to say more than, "I say, it's awfully good," or if the passage in question featured names like Serge or Alexandrovna he might opine that it was "certainly Russian".'[78]

Anthony Burgess, who sometimes appeared on *Take It or Leave It*, remembered John's hopelessly off-target guesses:

> Two actors would read out in turn from works of literature and the writers were asked to identify them. The game was not competitive. The right answer was flashed on the viewer's screen, though not the participants' monitor, and the viewer had the superior pleasure of knowing who wrote what while his literary betters stumbled. John Betjeman regularly said, 'Surely that's Thackeray' while the viewer's screen said Edgar Wallace or John Dryden.[79]

Other panellists were Lord David Cecil, Angus Wilson, Kingsley Amis, V. S. Pritchett, Elizabeth Jane Howard, Bernard Levin and John Gross. The occasional publisher was let in; but when Anthony Blond, correctly identifying a passage as from *Scouting for Boys* by Lord Baden-Powell, added that in West Germany a statue had been erected to the hero of Mafeking inscribed *Der Grosse Britische Homosexuell*, the contribution had to be cut.[80] It was Blond who, in 1970, reissued John's 1930s book *Ghastly Good Taste*.

On 2 January 1967 John wrote to David Attenborough (then Controller of BBC2 Television): 'I have been having a very jolly time filming the Edgware Road with Julian Jebb. In its way it was as thrilling and dangerous and mysterious as those jungles you used to explore and where centipedes rushed out to bite your ankles.'[81] Jebb, who was a grandson of Hilaire Belloc, was a sensitive, amusing, slightly fey character who had joined BBC TV in 1967, researching and producing features for the Arts Features department. The film was still being made in October. On 1 November John wrote to his friend Terence de Vere White:[82]

> It was mighty kind of you to give me so good a luncheon as you did at dear distinguished Boodle's yesterday. St Margaret smiled down at us. It was very wet and alarming at the top of Marble Arch to which we climbed and there were little rooms inside the arch lit by gas *and* electric so that if one went out, the other was there to come to the rescue. I don't think Television is anything but a minor art – except now and then when immediacy, as at Churchill's funeral,[83] gives it an extra dimension – but I think it is delightful team work.[84]

The film was transmitted on 31 January 1968 as *Contrast: Marble Arch to Edgware – A Lament by John Betjeman*. Stephen Hearst, the Viennese-born Head of Arts Features, wrote to John: 'May I tell you how delighted I was with the results of your collaboration with Julian Jebb? *Marble Arch to Edgware* had originality, heart and wit and I am most grateful. It would be good to be able to interest you in other arts features programmes over the coming year.'[85] John replied: 'I am pleased beyond measure by your kind letter to me . . . It was a joy working with Julian J. and his crew. We share outlook, jokes and eye . . .'[86]

In the same year John made *Pride of Place*, a series of films in stately homes, walking round the rooms with Arthur Negus, star of the antiques show *Going for a Song*. One of the houses they browsed in was Mereworth Castle, owned by Elizabeth Cavendish's brother-in-law, Michael Tree, the illustrator of *Summoned by Bells*. John on his own and Negus on his own were masters of their particular genres; but, together, they outdid each other in theatrical old-codgerliness and gasps of 'Just look at this!' The double-act was satirized on one of *Private Eye*'s thin plastic records, issued with the magazine:

> *John Betjeman*: Oh, gosh, look at this, I think we've come to the smallest room in the house. Shall we go in?
> (*Sound of door creaking open. Sudden screech of female occupant.*)
> *Arthur Negus*: Oh, this is very interesting, John. Just look at these old legs. They're varicosey, I think. Yes, they're by Carlo Varicosi, who was active in these parts – who was *very* active in these parts – about 1780. I wonder if there's a mark. Let's have a look at the bottom.
> (*A further squawk from occupant*)

In 1968 the BBC had a sudden windfall from colour television licence fees. It spent some of it on a series called *Bird's-Eye View*, a three-year project in which England was filmed from a helicopter. The production was entrusted to Edward Mirzoeff, a young film-maker with an ironic but sympathetic approach to his subjects.

> One of the first things that came to mind [Mirzoeff recalls] was that we had to bring in writers; it was quite important that, given the nature of the view from above, the remote view from the helicopter, you had to personalize, and John was suggested as one of the possible writers. I had never met him; I knew of him, of course. He came to Kensington House [BBC offices in west London] and we met in the bar and talked about it. He was charming and thought it a lot of fun as an idea. He actually found it quite hard to say no to almost any proposal we made eventually – not that he would *do* things, he would just say yes and afterwards you found that saying yes didn't necessarily mean that he was going to do it at all. That's how we first met and we made thirteen films in the helicopter series of which John wrote three and I directed two of those three.[87]

John had all kinds of visions of what it meant to film from the air. Mirzoeff decided to show him what it did mean. At that stage, he was planning to take the writers along with the crew every trip, so that they could see what was being filmed. 'It was an idea we very quickly disabused ourselves of.' He and the crew met John at Kidlington Aerodrome near Oxford, where the helicopter was kept. Mirzoeff said, 'Let's just have a flip round and show you what it's like.'

> Unfortunately, the internal communication system that day had a gremlin in it which meant that we couldn't talk to each other by radio in this noisy machine; but we could gesture – not something that John much liked. We took off, there was a Polish pilot, Captain Novak – he changed his name from Shuvalski to Novak, I could never quite understand why – who was a daredevil. We had said, let's go and find a number of landmarks that John might know and see what they looked like from above, country houses and churches and so on. It was a misty day, grey and gloomy. And we were wandering over Northamptonshire in a rather desultory way, a manifestly odd way; and eventually the pilot turned round and shouted at the top of his voice over the engine: 'I'm not sure where we are. Sir John knows England very well. Perhaps he could recognize a church spire.' And you could see the look of terror on poor John's face. It wasn't an experience he was enjoying. He pulled his cheque book out of his inner pocket and he wrote on it and handed it to me. It said: 'PLEASE CAN WE GO HOME NOW?' which we did as quickly as possible. We drove him back to Oxford station where we went into the buffet and he asked for a double brandy. That was the first moment he began to unfreeze, and we began to

think it might be possible, because we started joking about the horrible experience that he'd had, and we began to hit it off.[88]

Later, Mirzoeff and the crew went back into the air and shot film for the first *Bird's-Eye View* programme, 'The Englishman's Home'. The footage ranged from archaeological sites to Norman castles to Elizabethan mansions to 1960s shops and houses. The film editor, Edward Roberts, reduced the mass of material to about two-and-a-half hours. John was invited to Roberts's screening-room in Soho, London. 'Two-and-a-half hours later,' Roberts remembers, 'we said, "What do you think of that, Sir John?" "Very boring." '[89] 'There was a lot of early stuff in that film,' Mirzoeff explained. 'John found archaeology unbelievably dreary – ruins said nothing to him. We eventually realized that. But we also appreciated that his ability to write verse, and to personalize through his verse to the picture, was absolutely unique.'[90]

'The Englishman's Home' was savaged by Sean Day-Lewis in the *Daily Telegraph*:

> Mr Betjeman was invited to air his prejudices and he did so predictably, and with more illogicality than usual, in a poetic manner that at best sounded like tongue-in-cheek parody of his own verse. He rhymed with reverence about everything up to the 1920s, even the post-1918 Sussex bungalow suburbs, and was acid about all building since 1945. His apparent view was that an eighteenth-century masterpiece like Castle Howard and a high rise twentieth-century block of flats are genuine alternatives.[91]

John may not have seen these words, as he had written to Mirzoeff asking him not to send him reviews. 'I only notice the bad ones, and they give me terrible persecution mania.'

John agreed to go up in the helicopter for another programme, 'Beside the Seaside'. Novak flew high above Trebetherick, then did a dive on an island. John gave his highest-pitched laugh and gasped, 'It's just like getting drunk.' Mirzoeff said: 'I don't think John enjoyed that either, really, but he decided to pretend that he had.' The film traced the history of the seaside and 'going on holiday'. 'The Cornwall parts in particular were quite close to him,' Mirzoeff said, 'and by then he had got the notion of what you had to do to write to this impersonal sort of film, the way you personalize it, creating characters, creating mythical people that you talk about – it was the same kind of thing that he did, rather embarrassingly, in restaurants when he said in a stage whisper, "Do you think it's an office romance?" He was actually filmed in that film, from the helicopter, with his walking along the coastline, going over a stile, coming to the edge of a cliff, taking off his hat and waving it.'[92]

In telling the history of the seaside, the film started in Weymouth and moved up to Clevedon, where John's old school friend Sir Arthur Elton lived. 'So we had "Can we get old Arthur into the film?" "It's not that sort of film, John" – and then all the way round the coast of Somerset, Cornwall and Devon. We didn't go as far as Brighton because we'd done Brighton in the previous film; but we brought it right up to date with power-boat races, in which John was convinced that executives and chairmen were involved. He hated that, of course, and was very scathing about it – though it was visually very exciting.'[93]

In one scene, the helicopter hovered above a Butlin's holiday camp. John excelled himself in the verse commentary for this section. Two schoolgirls are together in an aerial chair-lift.

> Shirl and Sheila just are friends;
> For boys they do not care.
> They tell each other secrets
> In the safety of the air,
> Regardless of what's going on
> In chalets over there.

An old man and two children are seen on the roller-coaster.

> The twins inveigle grandpa
> On the switchback by a trick
> But grandpa has the laugh of them –
> For both the twins are sick.

John was paid £750 for the *Bird's-Eye View* series.

In 1968 and 1969 he made another film with Julian Jebb, *Tennyson: A Beginning and an End*. In the preliminary stages of research, an incident occurred in which John was inclined to discern a supernatural intervention. Sir Edward Pickering, the newspaper editor and vice-chairman of Times Newspapers, later recalled in the *Tennyson Research Bulletin*:

One night in 1968 I was catching the 6.50 Waterloo/Portsmouth train which took me to my home in Haslemere. I entered a carriage, sat down and found John Betjeman in the opposite seat. Immediately he launched into a sad story of how he was doing a television series on the life of Tennyson; how he was on his way to Farringford (Tennyson's Isle of Wight home) to record part of the series; but how he lacked material for the second part dealing with Aldworth (Tennyson's Haslemere home for the last twenty-five years of his life). By an astonishing coincidence, I had that week received from Sir Charles Tennyson (Tennyson's grandson and biographer) an essay recalling memories of life at Aldworth with his grandfather . . .[94]

Pickering handed John a copy of the essay and thought no more of it until September 1968, when John wrote to him:

What I wanted to ask you was whether you knew I was going down to Portsmouth by the 6.50 that evening, when you got out at Haslemere, and I was bound for the Isle of Wight? If you did not know then the coincidence is most extraordinary because of what happened the next day. You will remember that you gave me a very useful essay on Aldworth by Sir Charles, which I was able to make use of, when we filmed the following Friday at Aldworth. But on the next day to that on which I met you, our last shots on the island after doing Farringford were of Emily Tennyson's tomb in Freshwater Churchyard. The sun shone and the camera was to pan up to the Downs beyond Farringford, after which there was to be a mix into the view from Aldworth. While this was happening I was to read 'June Bracken and Heather' which as you will remember was Tennyson's dedication to Emily of his last book of poems. Twice we couldn't take the shot because of noise, once from hovercraft or some such thing, and the other time from aeroplanes. At the third take there was silence enough, and when I came to the bit about the June blue heaven, all the birds around burst into song, as though it were spring, and the cameraman noticed the startled look on my face.

I ask you the question at the top of the previous paragraph because if our meeting was a true coincidence, it looks as though the Tennysons are watching you and me.[95]

Julian Jebb described filming on the Isle of Wight in his diary for 1969.

Monday August 14th

John is very cheerful and immediately takes out maps and guides from the large broken-down raffia shopping bag which he always carries with him. After he has rested at our hotel we start on our walk to Farringford, which is now a hotel and where we have arranged to dine. We are in the country at once, going through tree-lined lanes; the sun is setting. We are already looking for suitable location set-ups for shooting.

'This is much the best view,' I said as we came into a muddy lane covered by a nave of thickly-leaved elms. 'We don't need to go any further.'

John paid no attention but started to walk up the path, murmuring 'I say, it's beautiful.' And so it was. Soon we came to a crumbling farmhouse with an entrance topped by two stone balls. The path became narrower, a muddy track with chickens darting about in disarray and very thick leaves overhead. This opens on to a cliff path which is bordered by honeysuckle, willow herbs and 'old man's nuisance'. I point the latter out to him and he says he invented this name himself in one of his poems. I had completely forgotten this, indeed I believed I'd invented it myself!

John talked about Tennyson's extreme short sight and how he used to leap into ditches when he was on one of his six-mile walks to examine flowers and lichen at a quarter-of-an-inch distance.

August 22nd

John and I meet at King's Cross for the journey to Lincoln. We and the weather are both very sunny. When we get to Lincoln we collect the hired car and take the road to Louth, where we are going to stay the night. We drive beyond the town to the sea and come upon an enormous Caravan Ground in the early evening light. It is called Golden Sands. Holiday-makers, with their skin burnt more by the wind than the sun I suspect, are beginning to return from the beach with grizzling children. John is delighted with the place, a mile or so away from Mablethorpe where Tennyson had a cottage. He takes off his shoes and socks and we walk over the enormous sands to the sea.

Returning to London we have a fantasy about a new series of guide books John will edit called 'Betjeman's Dim Counties'. Clackmann, Renfrew and Bedford will launch the series.

September 9th, Freshwater

I have bought a denim cap and an oil-cloth coat, which I consider suitable clothes for a film director. John wears a grey suit, carries a rolled umbrella and the collected works of Tennyson, and wears his famous brown hat. We take the first shot – John walking up the lane towards the camera, and at once one feels relief. We shoot a good deal more in the verdant gloom, all mute. Occasionally large middle-aged women in trousers stop and stare at us until they are politely asked to move on. John and I dine together at the Farringford hotel. I sketch again what I want the film to be like.

'What we've got to show is how funny Tennyson was. And how nice. We'd have liked him more than Byron,' John says.

'And how famous he was,' I interrupt. 'Never before or since has the most famous man in England been a poet.'

September 10th

After lunch we go to Tennyson Cross on the top of the cliffs. It is a very steep path and this time the whole thing is a bit like the crucifixion. Chris, the assistant cameraman, is Christ carrying the great weight of the camera on his shoulders. When we reach the summit, everyone disappears for a few minutes in awe at the stunning view – the wrinkled sea, the gulls submerged in air, the huge picture. Were it not for the ugly cross it would be a perfect setting for some huge work of art – for King Lear or Walkyrie.

When we are in the middle of walking through a fairly elaborate approach shot of John bobbing into view I realise that there is no one at the camera, which is placed by the cross about fifty yards away. I start signalling and shouting, to no avail. I hurry irritably to find what has happened. Libby has dropped one of her contact lenses out of her eye. For what seems like innumerable precious minutes the crew of nine souls get down on their knees and search the close-cropped turf for a quarter-inch disc of transparent plastic. Eventually we are helped with a battery torch. The scene is rather Tennysonian but the lens is never found.

September 16th

Travel to Lincoln with John and Sir Charles Tennyson. Sir Charles is an angelic man, though not in the sense that his great uncle, Horatio, described the breed as being like a species of clumsy poultry. His face is vivid with humour, warmth and sense. We film Sir Charles reminiscing to John about his grandfather surrounded by the relics in the Usher Museum, Lincoln, then make for Tetford, a village near Somersby.

September 17th

Tetford. In the afternoon I make John rest as the rest of us tear off to find a suitable location for the opening and closing shot of the film. I want a bosky knoll or dell where I will strew pictures, books and other relics of Tennyson. To my slight consternation Sir Charles decides to accompany us. I feel he will be disapproving of this 'imaginative' flight, or anyway not see its point, which is to try and integrate in one shot the two aspects of the film: the inspiration from nature and the accumulation of objects and mementoes which a long public life endows. At last I find an ideal spot: a clearing surrounded by tall trees sloping steeply down to Tennyson's Brook and to the left a leaf-framed view of stubbled wold. Terry and I get to work feverishly. We festoon every rock and leaf with manuscripts, photographs, files – until the glade begins to look like the drawing room of some eccentric Tennysonian at Christmas-tide. We quickly, almost guiltily, take two or three long running shots, then, when it is rumoured that John is on the way, we rearrange all the objects down the hill in a cascade. He arrives in very good spirits, rested and very funny. 'Oh, I say, a psychedelic dell!'

The light is fading (oh how many times during the last fortnight does the light begin to fade, the electric saw to drone, the tourists to arrive just

as we are reaching the crux of the day's work!) and I begin to feel
first time that megalomania which is said to beset film directors. The frustration of waiting for the lighting to be finished, for the combine harvester
to be located, bribed and silenced becomes intolerable. 'Let's shoot!' I
screamed. 'It doesn't matter about the noise or the light.' The crew went
on imperturbably: if you're going to throw a temperament, clearly it has
to be more dramatic than this. I bit off my fingernails, chain-smoked and
glared impotently. At last, in twilight we took the shots. I really mind
about them more than any in the film. Sir Charles, of course, did not dis-
approve in the least.

We have been an exceptionally happy and united crew. The atmosphere
has been extraordinarily gay and we have a whole bag of private jokes and
references which have grown up during the film. This is partly John's
genius for getting on with people, which really consists in paying careful
attention to everyone and having a very good memory.

On John's last night we have a celebration dinner. John and I do a
parody of *Woman's Hour*. Box cameras flash and the best from the White
Hart cellars is produced. We talk about the excitements of filming and all
the crew agree that it is among the five chief pleasures in life . . . [96]

When Tristram and Georgia Powell published Jebb's diary in 1993,
the sound-recordist Andrew Barr contributed to the book a memory
of John during the making of the Tennyson film.

Whose film was it, Julian's or John Betjeman's? Certainly Julian was passionate about some moments that had to be included, and to us he was a
serious film-maker. Yet a fledgling sound-recordist had to fear if the extraordinary scenes were to be realized. John Betjeman was frequently to be
positioned a long way from the camera, requiring the use of the then unreliable radio microphone; the first evening, he stood in a gale on top of
Tennyson Down reciting 'Sunset and Evening Star'. It was only a whiff of
what was to come. Then a long scene was played with the [future] Poet
Laureate up to his knees in the North Sea. It looked idyllic, but loud and
quite unrecognizable explosions declared that a bombing range had been
chosen for this idyll. Even the radio microphone would not do. Julian was
unrepentant. Briefly belligerent, he would walk off demanding a miracle
without delay on all such occasions. [97]

For now, there was harmony between John and Jebb. Two years later,
it was to be irretrievably disrupted.*

* See Chapter 15, 'Back to Australia'.

BARRY HUMPHRIES

Not a word is wasted. Not a point is missed. He hits the nail on the head every time and his phrases linger in the mind for months after one has heard them.

John Betjeman, programme note to Barry Humphries's revue,
A Nice Night's Entertainment, Melbourne 1962[1]

John was a friend of Barry Humphries long before the Australian comic became famous in Britain in the late 1970s as Dame Edna Everage, 'housewife superstar' – a *monstre sacré* with 'natural wistaria' hair, diamanté-studded butterfly spectacles, basilisk eyes, twitching scarlet lips, a rich falsetto voice and sublimely over-the-top costumes. He first heard his name in the British Council office at Sydney on his 1961 trip to Australia.[2] Somebody there had two 45rpm records Humphries had made, *Wild Life in Suburbia* (1958) and *Wild Life in Suburbia: Volume Two* (1959). John played them over to himself dozens of times.

Even more than the monologues by Edna Everage, the aggressively genteel Melbourne housewife, he enjoyed the Pooter-like musings of Humphries's other creation, Sandy Stone, an elderly, decent, childless man of the suburbs with a battleaxe wife called Beryl. Sandy's account of his banal week, on the 1958 record, began, in a quavery drawl: 'I went to the RSL [Returned Servicemen's League] the other night and had a very nice night's entertainment.' John enjoyed Sandy's turn of phrase: 'I had a bit of strife parking the vehicle'; 'I don't say no to the occasional odd glass'; 'Beryl makes a lovely sponge finger'.[3] Like John in his poems about suburbia, Humphries brought out the pathos of his characters as well as the comedy.

John made a flattering reference to Humphries in one of his Australian press conferences of 1961. A friend sent Humphries a newspaper cutting of the compliment. Humphries discovered John's Cloth Fair address and wrote to him in ink, making several drafts of the letter before he sent it.[4] At the time the Australian was living in Grove Terrace, Highgate Road[5]– the very row of Georgian houses in

which John once said he would have liked to live as a sm
rather than in the ugly Parliament Hill Mansions near-by.[6] Humphries
received a prompt reply, in an envelope bearing a Manx stamp.

The letter within [Humphries wrote], inscribed with a fountain pen in
Arts and Crafts calligraphy, contained an invitation to lunch the following week. Although I had been an avid explorer of old London since my
arrival in June 1959, I had never visited Smithfield. Following my enthusiasms, as a Melbourne schoolboy, for the works of G.K. Chesterton,
Arthur Machen and Thomas Burke, I had rambled around Notting Hill,
Clerkenwell, Canonbury and Limehouse, but as I rang John Betjeman's
doorbell in a tiny passage off Cloth Fair I saw the twelfth-century soot-
stained fabric of St Bartholomew the Great for the first time.

The poet greeted me effusively and we went up two flights of narrow
stairs to his small flat with its William Morris wallpapers, beetling book-
shelves and, over the fireplace, a faded Arcadian improvisation in watercolour by Conder, an almost forgotten artist of the 1890s who had always
interested me.

John dispensed bubbly in pewter tankards with boyish exclamations
such as 'I am as rich as Croesus' and 'You are a great genius', at which the
other luncheon guests – two members of the high Anglican clergy –
exchanged glances that were appropriately reverential and sceptical.[7]

After several drinks the four men – Gerard Irvine was one of the
priests – set off down the street to John's favourite restaurant in
Aldersgate. The street where John's great-grandfather had lived, and
which he had celebrated in a poem, 'seemed miraculously to have survived the Blitz', Humphries wrote, though it was soon to be demolished and replaced by 'brutalist' buildings. They lunched at Coltman's
Chophouse with more champagne, roast beef, Brussels sprouts and
Players cigarettes, 'which John dispensed from a round tin in his
already book-ballasted poacher's pocket'. Afterwards they 'floated
back to Cloth Fair', stopping for a browse at the bookshop of Frank
Hollings, then run by John's friend 'Dusty' Miller.[8]

John was still talking excitedly [Humphries wrote] about the Victorian
architecture he had seen in Australia: St Patrick's Cathedral by William
Wilkinson Wardell and St Paul's Cathedral by William Butterfield, both in
Melbourne and St John the Evangelist in 'Brizzie' [Brisbane] – John
Loughborough Pearson's unfinished masterpiece. He loved the Victorian
shopping arcades of my home town and described one of his most
thrilling moments in Australia: when his taxi from the airport into

Melbourne took him through the euphonically named suburb of Moonee Ponds, Mrs Edna Everage's girlhood haunt.[9]

John took Humphries to see the Coal Exchange on the eve of its destruction.

Together [Humphries wrote] we climbed its spiral stairs and wandered through its forsaken offices which could so easily have been converted to another purpose (recycling had not yet been invented). John pointed out that it was a favourite trick of the developer to allow a building to fall into a state of advanced desuetude so that by the time the conservationists had got their act together, he could point to the crumbling wreck, now a derelict latrine, and say, hammer at the ready: 'You want to save that! You must be joking!'[10]

Barry Humphries was born in 1934 in a prosperous district of Melbourne, the son of a builder of smart Art Deco houses.[11] His first and favourite nanny was called Edna.[12] He was educated at Melbourne Grammar School and Melbourne University. He early discovered the pleasures of shocking. One repeated practical joke was to leave a spattered deposit of Heinz Russian Salad – a diced potato and mayonnaise concoction closely resembling human vomit – on a pavement. When enough disgusted pedestrians were giving it a wide berth, holding their noses, Humphries, dressed as a tramp, would kneel beside the mess, take a spoon from his top pocket and devour several mouthfuls.[13] For a time he was banned from Qantas air flights for the similar trick of pretending to use his sick-bag, then slowly eating the contents to the distress of other passengers. At university he staged two 'Dada' exhibitions and a revue, *Call Me Madman!* Later, with the help of 'a beautiful undergraduate' called Germaine Greer, he mounted a show at the Victorian Artists' Society which included a display of 'Platytox' boxes, a new 'product' designed to eradicate the much loved platypus. The boxes were filled with sawdust, but the public were gratifyingly outraged.[14]

In 1954 he took a job with EMI, smashing old 78rpm records with a hammer to make way for the new 45s.[15] At nights he acted with the newly formed Union Repertory Theatre Company at Melbourne University. Brenda Wright, who acted with him in *Love's Labour's Lost*, became his first wife in 1955. Edna Everage was born in the same year. John Sumner of the Union Rep had asked Humphries to play Orsino in a country tour of *Twelfth Night* in Victoria. At each place the company visited, the lady mayoress would thank them for their performance. On the way to every destination Humphries, at the back of the bus, amused the rest of the cast by predicting, in a piercing falsetto, what the next speech of thanks would be like.[16] In December 1956 he presented Edna Everage on stage for the first time in a Christmas revue. He again performed the Edna sketch in two revues at the new Phillips Street Theatre in Sydney in 1956 and 1957, acting alongside the ageing Max Oldaker, 'last of the matinée idols', who, he noted, rouged his ears, a rejuvenating trick.[17] In 1957 he was invited to make a weekly television programme as the Bunyip, a legendary Aboriginal swamp creature, but was sacked from children's television for his racy slang.[18] A stage production of the Bunyip had also starred Rosalind Tong, a New Zealand dancer who looked to Humphries 'just like Botticelli's *Primavera*'. He married her early in 1959, as soon as a divorce from Brenda was settled.

In May 1959 Humphries and Rosalind set sail for Europe from Port Melbourne. A photographer friend persuaded him to put on Edna's conical hat and peer through the porthole waving a handkerchief. The photograph was used on the record sleeve of *Wild Life in Suburbia: Volume Two*.[19] Among several letters of introduction Humphries brought to London was one from Max Oldaker to Charles Osborne, the young Australian editor, critic, poet and actor.[20] With his very long, lank hair and shabby clothes, Humphries presented himself at the English-Speaking Union in Charles Street, Mayfair, but was escorted out by a commissionaire.[21] He found a job in an ice-cream factory and went to theatre auditions.[22] Rosalind worked in a greengrocer's.

In November 1959 Humphries won the part of Jonas Fogg, a madhouse-keeper, in a musical version of *Sweeney Todd, the Demon Barber of Fleet Street* at the Lyric, Hammersmith.[23] The reviews were poor and the show closed a few days before Christmas.[24] 'So, as the Sixties dawned, I was out of work again'; but in June 1960 Humphries made his West End debut as the undertaker Mr Sowerberry in Lionel Bart's musical *Oliver!* at £15 a week.[25] (He also understudied Fagin.) It was the musical success of the decade. The Humphrieses moved from a Notting Hill basement to the Grove Terrace, Highgate, flat owned by two Australian friends.[26] It was soon after this change of address that Humphries met John for the first time.

The two men had an uncanny – as Dame Edna would say, 'spooky' – amount in common; Humphries was almost an Australian *Doppelgänger* of John. Both were born in city suburbs and into the upper-middle class, with nannies. Both their fathers supplied the luxury Art Deco market – Humphries senior with houses, Betjemann *père* with furnishings. Both would have been the fourth generation to enter the family business had they not disappointed their fathers by refusing to do so. Each early decided what he wanted of life. John told a small girl: 'I'm going to have long hair when I grow up and be a poet.'[27] Humphries, asked by his mother when he was five what he wanted to be eventually, said, 'I want to be a genius' – and long hair was part of his recipe for fame, too. ('Why don't you get your fucking hair cut?' demanded the Australian poet Kenneth Slessor[28] when the young Humphries interrupted him in a snooker game to mumble something about his long-term admiration for his work.)

Both John and Humphries hated their schools, especially sports and prefects with canes, and both took their revenge in verse. Humphries wrote:

> Where are they now – the prefects? Stripped of their awesome powers.
> Do they miss their footy comrades in the Lifebuoy-scented showers?
> Do they long to cane a slacker or humiliate a shirk
> As they Volvo down to Portsea leaving Judy in the Merc?
> They don't miss English literature or algebra or sums,
> But as middle age envelops them, a poignant feeling comes
> When, with thumping heart, they recollect those tight blue
>   schoolboy bums.[29]

Both found they could appease the bullies by making them laugh. Both liked to shock with elaborate practical jokes: Humphries's exploits with the potato salad are reminiscent of John's falling down in the street with a mouthful of Eno's Fruit Salts and frothing at the mouth. Both left university without degrees, leaving legends behind them.

Each was fascinated by 'decadence', particularly by Oscar Wilde. John's interest in Wilde had led him to correspond with Lord Alfred Douglas. Clive James headed the chapter about Humphries in his memoirs, 'The Green Gladiolus', in reference to Wilde's green carnation and Edna Everage's custom of hurling gladioli into the audience.[30] John and Humphries read and collected neglected writers of the 1890s. John wrote about Wratislaw and Dowson and Theo Marzials. Humphries liked Matthew Phipps Shiel, the writer of fantasy, Havelock Ellis, Anna Wickham and *fin de siècle* romances by Marmaduke Pickthall, Haldane MacFall and Count Stenbock. The two could happily spend a lunchtime discussing these writers, enthusiasm parried by enthusiasm. 'Count Stenbock!' John would breathe. 'Matthew Phipps Shiel!'[31]

In a Melbourne bookshop, Humphries had acquired a broken set of *The Yellow Book* – 'more muddy brown than yellow'. The volumes had made him an enthusiast for the illustrations of Aubrey Beardsley.

In 1998, when the Victoria & Albert Museum held a large Beardsley exhibition, Humphries wrote in *Harpers & Queen:*

> When I visited London for the first time . . . there were still a few people alive who had actually known Beardsley. John Betjeman, whom I met about this time and who shared my love of the Nineties, characteristically decided, after a long lunch, to ring them up, while I eavesdropped on several strange conversations with bewildered old gentlemen. One recipient of such a call was so confused he thought Beardsley was still alive, and another, the evocatively named architectural painter Maresco Pearce, recalled that the artist always pronounced his Christian name 'Ahr-bry'. That was about as close as we got to Beardsley, but the experience was eerily like telephoning the nineteenth century.

(Elsewhere, Humphries recalled that Augustus John was another of the Nineties figures John telephoned.)[32]

John and Humphries were also much taken by neglected artists – John by Tuke and Julius Olssen, Humphries by little-known Australian Impressionists. Both men owned works by Charles Conder, an effete English–Australian artist who often painted his nebulous blue idylls on silk in the shape of a Japanese fan.[33] A friend of Wilde and Lautrec, Conder had died of syphilis in 1909. John thought Conder should have a daughter named Anna – Anaconda. (For similar reasons, he maintained that a City restaurateur named Bubb should have called his daughter Cilla.)

Another trait John and Humphries shared was a love of the music-hall, also pre-eminently an art of the 1890s. During his early years in England, Humphries went to the Metropolitan Music Hall ('the Met') in the Edgware Road, where he saw the last of English music-hall – Hetty King, the male impersonator, G.H. Elliot, the 'Chocolate-Coloured Coon'[34] and Randolph Sutton, who brought the house down with 'On Mother Kelly's Doorstep'.[35] 'To stand with a pint of Guinness at the back of the circle and watch the show', Humphries wrote, 'was exactly like being in a painting by Sickert.' Humphries went to see Randolph Sutton so many times that he was able to sing 'On Mother Kelly's Doorstep' for John. 'And John went to see Randolph Sutton at his home, somewhere on the south coast,' Humphries recalled. 'He became his friend and got him to perform, alongside Tommy Steele, at the City of London Festival in 1962.'*[36]

John and Humphries both enjoyed dated slang, such as the 'Devil if I understand!' of John's poem about an old poet at the Café Royal.[37]

---

* See Chapter 20, 'A Heavy Crown'.

In one of his monologues, Sandy Stone referred to a car jaunt as a 'spin' – the same expression used by John's 'Retired Postal Clerk'.[38] The love of *désuète* slang was counterpointed by a hatred of modern jargon – 'viable', 'basically', 'image', 'infrastructure', 'book storage unit', 'disadvantaged' (for a slum-dweller) and 'community' (as in 'the gay community'). Dame Edna sweetened her most venomous sallies with the language of bogus liberalism – 'compassionate', 'sharing', 'caring'. Both were incensed by the idea that their work should be 'relevant'.

Although John and Humphries loathed parroted jargon, both rev-elled in brand names. Craven 'A', the brand of cigarettes mentioned by John in two poems, was also part of Humphries's nostalgia. Describing the hairdressers of his childhood, he wrote: 'Behind the small lino-topped counter was a positive reredos of cigarette packets and smoking slogans: We too smoke Turf! Three Threes Always Please, Country Life, City Club, Temple Bar, Ardath,[39] Craven "A", Capstan and the less popular filtered lines designed to appeal to women and pansies, like Garrick and Du Maurier; names that aroused a distant resonance of sophistication even if you didn't know they were named after dead actors.' Edna Everage evoked the Melbourne of her childhood in a poetry of brand names –

> The Melbourne of my girlhood was a fine Rexona Town.
> Her smile was bright with Kolynos and Persil white her gown,
> Her Bedgood shoes with Nugget shone, she scorned inferior brands,
> And in her Lux-white gloves there slept her soft Palmolive hands . . .[40]

John wrote of Elaine in 'Middlesex':

> Well cut Windsmoor flapping lightly,
>   Jacqmar scarf of mauve and green
> Hiding hair which, Friday nightly,
>   Delicately drowns in Drene;
> Fair Elaine the bobby-soxer,
> Fresh-complexioned with Innoxa . . .[41]

Humphries could have had a career as a poet, just as John could have done as an actor. The school magazine at Humphries's first school rejected one of his poems on the ground that it was so good it would only discourage the other children. Dame Edna often launches into verse at moments of high emotion – 'I feel a poem coming on.' John's influence on Humphries's verse is obvious, and is meant to be. Peter

Coleman fairly describes as 'Betjemanesque' Humphries's 'Wattle Park Blues'[42] and there is a clear debt to John's 'In Westminster Abbey'[43] in Edna's Christmas Prayer ('for an up-market audience'):

> Hear my prayer O heavenly Lord
> Make me visible across the board.
> May my bottom line be Virtue
> Lest I ever bug or hurt you.
> And help me to unite the Nations
> In on-going worship situations.
> Up-tight and hassled though I be
> Teach me to be up-front with Thee
> And though my in-put be minute
> When Thou my shortfall dost compute –
> Pray let my daily print-out say:
> Thy servant was relevant *per se*.[44]

Both men recognized the virtues of suburbia as well as such cosy absurdities as Sandy's Cries of London table-mats and Edna's mulga-wood serviette rings. Humphries sees himself as 'sinking artesian wells into the suburban desert . . . I'm in the boredom-alleviation business, aren't I?' Both rejected the label of 'satirist' – partly, perhaps, because they did not want to seem merely part of the trendy sixties 'satire movement' – but accepted there was an element of caricature in their work, characterized by Humphries as 'lying to get at the truth'. Both were obsessively interested in taste, particularly in notions of 'bad taste'. John wrote *Ghastly Good Taste* when he was twenty-seven; Humphries, besides staging the Dada shows and publishing an anthology of bad Australian verse, wrote a book on Australian kitsch;[45] and his entire career could be seen as a sustained assault on good taste. But both wanted to save the good as well as revile the bad. Humphries was as passionate a conservationist as John.

Again, both John and Humphries keenly relished what the Australian called 'the voluptuous satisfaction of vengeance'.[46] (One of Dame Edna's theatre shows was billed as *Back with a Vengeance*.)[47] John waged his vendettas against Gidney, C. S. Lewis, Farmer Wheeler and Pevsner in verse and prose. A friend of Humphries told one of the star's biographers: 'If Barry feels wronged or betrayed, he will not forget. He will continue to keep them on a kind of hit list. He goes after them with humour and contempt, putting them down with little asides.'[48] Sometimes, Humphries favoured more physical means of retribution. At university, coming up behind somebody who had bullied him at school he emptied a large sack of white paint powder over his

head.[49] (When the victim turned round, clown-faced, Humphries realized he had attacked the wrong man.)[50]

Striking as it is, however, the comparison between John and
Humphries cannot be carried too far. They differed in significant
ways. As the paint-powder incident illustrates, Humphries was more
extreme than John, more shocking. They were drinking companions
in the 1960s; but, while John liked his drink, Humphries became for a
time an alcoholic. A more central difference from John was
Humphries's imperviousness to religion. For a time he was a Sunday-
school teacher in Melbourne. 'I felt I was a terrible hypocrite,' he
recalls, 'mouthing the teachings of the Church of England to these
indifferent brats, and at the same time writing agnostic and frankly
anti-clerical verses for the school magazine. The rapture of an authen-
tic spiritual experience has always eluded me.'[51] John was assailed by
doubts, but he lived and died in the Church of England.

In 1961 Cliff Hocking of Melbourne, who was beginning his career
as a theatrical impresario, came to Humphries with the idea of a one-
man show featuring Edna Everage and Sandy Stone.[52] Humphries
liked the idea but was tied by his contract in *Oliver!* The management
would not release him.[53] Eventually a doctor got him out temporarily
on the grounds that he was 'having a sort of breakdown';[54] then
Humphries made sure of his release by an accident on a holiday in
Cornwall. He was staying, not with John and Elizabeth, but with a
friend at Zennor, near the farm where D. H. Lawrence and Frieda had
lived.[55] He fell down a precipice, dislocated his shoulder and fractured
an arm. (Joan Littlewood sent a telegram: 'GET WELL SOON,
BIRDMAN.')[56] After recovering from his injuries, he and Rosalind set
sail for Australia. Elizabeth Cavendish and John came to see them
off.[57] On 30 July 1962 in a church hall in central Melbourne, Edna,
dressed in a Jackie Kennedy pillbox hat with veil, a red coat and pearls,
opened *A Nice Night's Entertainment*. John had written a blurb for
the programme. 'Barry Humphries', he predicted, 'is one who, I have
no hesitation in saying, will become internationally famous, because
he is an artist with words, imagination and mimicry who belongs to
the great tradition of music hall and theatre.'[58]

The show was a success and was taken on to Newcastle and
Adelaide. Then came a summons from Broadway: would Humphries
resume his rôles as Sowerberry and as Fagin's understudy in *Oliver!*?
The money was good and the engagement was only for three months.
He accepted.[59] In New York he met Peter Cook, who was starring in
the American run of *Beyond the Fringe*.[60] Back in London, Humphries
made the first of his two unsuccessful attempts in the 1960s to present
his Australian characters on stage. In May 1963 Peter Cook, who was

running the Establishment Club in Soho, London, asked him to fill in for the American Lenny Bruce, at £100 a week, when the British authorities refused to allow that 'obscene drug addict' to make a tour of Britain.

Before the day of his debut, Humphries went along to the club to spy out the land. It was a long room in Greek Street which had been redecorated by Sean Kenny, the designer of *Oliver!*, 'in a kind of heavily timbered, Tudor-Constructivist style'. In a bar at the front, 'young satire groupies loitered; pale-faced girls with fringes, pearlized lips and eyes like black darns. They said "Yah" and "Soopah" a great deal and they all seemed to know Dudley Moore quite well.'[61] As he watched the show, Humphries began to wonder whether this audience would crack a smile at Edna and Sandy. Eleanor Bron and John Fortune did a funny sketch about middle-class (British) pretentiousness. John Bird impersonated Harold Macmillan 'to a convulsed audience'. One 'unprepossessing fellow' got a lot of laughs with a monologue about the royal barge sinking in the Thames. 'He looks like a Methodist minister's son,' Humphries thought, as the girls around him 'hooted and soopahed'. Later he learned that David Frost *was* a Methodist minister's son.[62] The show gave Humphries some laughs but left him anxious. In the Fifties, Melbourne friends had said, 'I hope you won't be doing Edna in Sydney. *She's far too Melbourne*. They'll never get the point.' The success in Sydney had proved them wrong, but Soho in the Sixties might be a different matter. Writing as Edna, Humphries later recalled: 'The cold hand of fear entered my breast and gave my heart a little squeeze.'[63]

John turned up at the Establishment Club to support his protégé on his opening night. In her autobiography *My Gorgeous Life* (1989), Dame Edna described the scene.

That evening the little tables in the club were packed with celebrities, and kind, supportive Peter [Cook] pointed some of them out to me as we nibbled our steaks in the corner. That jolly little balding man with the wavy upper lip was John Betjeman, the famous poet, who apparently adored me. Over there in a grubby pink suit was a droopy man whose arms were too long for his body, chain smoking cigarettes with the wrong fingers. His name was Tynan, a critic apparently, and I blushed to think he had the same Christian name as my own manly little son. Jean Shrimpton, the famous glamour-puss, was looking bewildered. Holding forth at her table was a carrot-headed, camel-faced man in a crumpled corduroy suit called Dr [Jonathan] Miller, who seemed to be trying to knot his arms together with some degree of success. I even noticed a few journalists with notebooks at the ready.[64]

There was some poetic licence in this account: Peter Cook was in fact still in America, and Humphries was glad he was not in the club to witness his humiliation. On the pocket-handkerchief stage, he launched into Edna's opening song, a hymn to 'The Old Country'. The pianist was an Australian girl. No one had warned Humphries that 'acute anxiety sometimes caused her to strike so many wrong notes that a tune could become unrecognizable'. Through clouds of cigarette smoke, he could see the critics scribbling glumly in their notebooks. His punchlines fell flat – 'As for those who say the English don't bath enough – I always say it would be a funny old world if we all smelt the same, now wouldn't it?'[65] Humphries later told John Lahr: 'I was so nervous I don't think I did justice to whatever material I had, anyway. I didn't *feel* funny. When you don't trust the audience, it doesn't trust you . . . I mystified people. Not many turned up. A few barracking Australians, a kind of claque; who did me more harm than good. It was the wrong time and the wrong place.' Peter Cook (who no doubt heard the full story from staff or punters) told Lahr that in the annals of the Establishment, no turn went down worse. 'The stoniest of stony silences,' Cook said. '*Nobody* found Barry remotely amusing. It was dreadful. Must have been dreadful for him. There were about three or four people who thought this is very very funny. Mainly John Betjeman, John Osborne, and (later) me. I felt ashamed of my fellow-Londoners for not appreciating him.'[66] Backstage, after his performance had finished to 'the most perfunctory smattering of applause', Humphries bitterly cursed himself 'for ever having agreed to trot out these whimsical provincial marionettes, who never made so much as a single reference to the Rt. Hon. Harold Macmillan'. In the person of Dame Edna, he recalled:

> I had a bit of a weep afterwards. Barry had gone home in a huff, the worse for a few sherries I'm afraid, but Peter was very sweet and told me on the quiet that the audience had all been drifting out to the bar throughout the Humphries section and he thought my material would catch on eventually with discerning people. Talking of which, gorgeous John Betjeman popped in to say he'd watched it all from a shadowy corner of the room and he had thought it was all 'marvellous' and 'sheer genius'. Were they just being nice, I wondered? Or should I get on the next plane back to Australia?[67]

The reviews were bad. Bamber Gascoigne in *The Spectator* called Humphries's turn 'distinctly soporific'.[68] The *Daily Mail*, repelled by the 'lank, dirt-coloured lady-length hair flapping across his face', described him as 'like an emu in moult'.[69] After three painful weeks, Nick Luard, the club's business manager, told him they would have to cut his season short. The ignominy of failure was alleviated by the birth of the Humphrieses' first child, Tessa, on 14 May 1963.[70] On the same day Spike Milligan invited Humphries to take the lead in his new play (written with John Antrobus) *The Bed-Sitting Room*.[71] In 1964 Humphries played the balladeer in Lionel Bart's *Maggie May* and took several rôles – one as a nun – in Joan Littlewood's production of *A Kayf up West* by Frank Norman, a scar-faced old lag described by Humphries as 'a home-grown Genet'.[72]

One of the few people who had been impressed by Humphries's act at the Establishment was the cartoonist Nicholas Garland.[73] In 1964 Peter Cook brought Garland and Humphries together to draw and write a comic strip for *Private Eye* about an Australian innocent abroad, 'a colonial Candide in an Akubra hat'.[74] The character was christened Barry McKenzie. (With an extra dash of narcissism, the astrology column that Humphries also wrote for the magazine was headed 'Madame Barry'.) The first strip appeared in the magazine on 10 July 1964. McKenzie and his oafish mates blundered and chundered[75] through England of the Swinging Sixties, directing their ribald mockery at the flower people, avant-garde film-makers, television producers and organic-food addicts. As Peter Coleman observes, ' "Bazza" McKenzie was the first Humphries character to catch on in England, at a time when Edna and Sandy still left British audiences unmoved.'[76] McKenzie became a cult figure and several of his scatological euphemisms passed into the language – 'chunder'[77] and 'Technicolor yawn' for vomit; 'strain the potatoes', 'point percy at the porcelain' and 'shake hands with the unemployed' for urinate; 'pork sword' and 'one-eyed trouser snake' for penis, and so on.[78] The strip lasted, with some interruptions, until March 1974 when the then editor, Richard Ingrams, axed it.[79] Humphries's association with *Private Eye* brought him further within John's ambit, because of Ingrams's friendship with Candida.

John and Humphries met often, sometimes giving each other rare books or pictures as presents. They would go to art exhibitions together, or to Abbott and Holder's shop in Barnes to look at watercolours and drawings.

> On a summer afternoon [Humphries remembered] we would sit under the enormous weeping beech in the garden, and Eric Holder would bring out bundles of paintings and drawings and spread them on the grass for our amusement.
>
> 'Art never lets you down,' said John, as if most other things did.
>
> One day we chose about six pictures between us, all very fairly priced . . . John bought a big seascape by Laura Knight,[80] a breezy

watercolour by Robert Anning Bell[81] (given to me after John's death) and a nude boy on a rock in Cornwall by Henry Scott Tuke,[82] who specialized in such subjects and was patronized by Edwardian schoolmasters and clergymen with Greek inclinations and more recently collected by Sir Elton John.[83]

When the pictures were spread out on the lawn, John and Humphries would walk along them, up and down, 'as if inspecting troops'.[84] 'My purchases were quite modest at that time,' Humphries says. 'I might come away with a Phil May sketch.'[85] (Though the Victorian cartoonist – 'Film A' as he was once mistranscribed by a secretary, to John's amusement – was British, he worked in Australia for a while.)[86] 'But John would buy much more expensive things. I had to be very careful not to admire anything too much as I would at once be given it.'[87]

In 1964 the Humphrieses moved into a flat in a Georgian house at No. 25 Maida Avenue.[88] It was near the Grand Union Canal in the heart of the Little Venice district, where lived John's friends Lord Kinross, Lady Diana Cooper, the composer Lennox Berkeley and his wife Freda – 'the Paddington set', as John called them. When the reporter R. J. Scholfield visited Humphries in Maida Avenue in January 1965, he noticed one of John's gifts on view.

There [Humphries] benevolently rules a household consisting of fair-haired New Zealand wife Rosalind, daughters Tessa, twenty months, and Emily, six weeks, and a French *au pair,* Dominique. The drawing-room, with its air of decadent Edwardian luxury, might have been designed as a fortress against Mrs Everage. The walls are crowded with designs by Charles Conder depicting the lesbian boudoirs of Balzac's novels, bulgy creatures lolling and intertwined, like hurdles of worms . . .

Squeezed between the lesbians are other paintings by Tom Roberts, Holman Hunt, Arthur Boyd and Abraham Louis Buvelot. On the lavatory wall hangs a sketch of Humphries's old school, Melbourne Grammar. The donor of this work was John Betjeman, who picked it up in a junk shop.[89]

John did everything he could to champion and promote Barry Humphries. He constantly played the Sandy and Edna records to his friends, not all of whom were captivated. When Humphries first met Osbert Lancaster, the cartoonist said that he did not know any Australian comedians, 'but there's one that John Betjeman insists on playing who is a terrible bore'.[90] Humphries did not dare to admit it was he. During the early Sixties John was invited by the BBC to make a programme about his special loves. He suggested Humphries as one of his enthusiasms and the Corporation tentatively approached the

Australian to recite one of his monologues. The BBC soon backed out, thinking that Humphries's act would not be to the taste of their viewers. 'And John Betjeman was so embarrassed about this,' Humphries recalled. 'He felt so responsible – though of course I didn't hold him responsible. So he sent me this beautiful vellum-bound 1890s book which must have cost him at least double his fee. It was the visitors' book of Amaryllis Hacon, the wife of Llewellyn Hacon, the lawyer who funded the Vale Press.[91] And it had all these signatures in it – Beardsley, Wilde, Conder, Shannon, Ricketts . . . It arrived by special delivery. He sent it just because he was disappointed that the BBC had erased me from the programme.'[92]

In the later Sixties, Humphries had a success in Australia with the revue *Just a Show*; but when that was transferred to London in 1969 – again John attended – it flopped as dismally as the Establishment act. However, somebody at the BBC enjoyed the revue and Humphries was offered his own television series, *The Barry Humphries Scandals*. It was to be produced by Dennis Main Wilson, who had produced *The Goon Show* in the late Fifties and, it was thought, 'could do no wrong'. The series was pulled off the air to prevent Humphries singing a song he had composed, 'The Spunk Song'. It began:

> The English have a quality
> I'd like to sing about
> It's not the sort of quality bestowed on wog or Kraut
> When things are on the sticky side
> You never throw a tizz
> A special something sees you through
> I'll tell you what it is –
> Spunk, spunk, spunk
> You're so full of British spunk
> You're never in a panic
> You're never in a funk
> So in a time of crisis
> There's nothing quite so nice as
> Singing spunkspunkspunkspunkspunkspunkspunk . . .[93]

A later verse started

> The dissolution of the monasteries
> Was a very sad affair,
> It was so iconoclastic
> There was stained glass *everywhere*,
> The poor old abbots in their habits

Said, 'My God, what's hit us?'
So each of them slipped
Down into his crypt
And sang this *spunk dimittis* . . .[94]

When nervous BBC men explained to Humphries that there was a
double entendre to the word 'spunk' of which, as an Australian, he
was probably unaware, he pretended not to understand them; but privately he was considering a companion-piece on British phlegm.
Humphries sang 'The Spunk Song' to John, who cried with laughter.[95]

For Barry Humphries, 1970 was the worst year of his life. His television series was cancelled. His marriage to Rosalind Tong was dissolved. He broke with his Australian impresario, Cliff Hocking. The
Australian authorities served writs on him for unpaid taxes. He
returned to Australia, 'ill and mad'. Mixing anti-depressant drugs and
several glasses of schnapps, he was arrested in Melbourne as drunk
and disorderly. His lawyer got him off most of the charges by emphasizing his 'depression'; but two days later – his medication doubled –
Humphries was mugged and left in a Melbourne gutter. A passing car
dumped him off at St Vincent's Hospital.[96] 'I must have spent many
months in the Dymphna Ward of St Vincent's Hospital,' Humphries
wrote. 'John Betjeman wrote me a long and comforting letter containing much information about the life and good works of St
Dymphna herself.'[97]*

---

* In the 1970s, Barry Humphries found sobriety and success. See Chapter 27, ' " . . .
As I Lose Hold" '.

THE BATTLE OF BEDFORD PARK

Yes, it was Bedford Park the vision came from,
De Morgan lustre glowing round the hearth,
And that sweet flower which self-love takes its name from
Nodding among the lilies in the garth.
And Arnold Dolmetsch touching the spinet,
And mother, Chiswick's earliest suffragette.

John Betjeman, 'Narcissus', *London Magazine*, October 1965

The dogs do bark in Bedford Park,
The Festival to praise,
There's not a flaw in Norman Shaw;
The sunflower gardens blaze.

John Betjeman, 'A message from our patron', programme of the
second Bedford Park Festival, 1968

In May 1952 Peter Clarke and Tom Greeves, with Greeves's wife Eleanor, visited their friend Derick Behrens, who was a neighbour of John's in Wantage. Behrens, an atomic scientist at Harwell, had been at King's College, Cambridge, with Clarke and Greeves. He had heard how his two friends had met John in Cambridge before the war and about their trip to the gasworks.* He took his guests to The Mead for tea. 'We sat around John Betjeman, on the lawn, in an adoring circle,' Eleanor Greeves recalls. 'His long-suffering wife went off to feed the ducks.'

In 1951 Tom and Eleanor had moved to Bedford Park. It is an estate of arty villas, many of them designed by Norman Shaw, near Turnham Green Underground Station in London.[2] Bedford Park interested John because it was the first 'garden suburb' and the prototype of all the decorative suburbia he both celebrated and satirized.

---

* See Chapter 2, '"Vic. Soc." and "The Dok"'.

'Why did you come to Bedford Park?' John asked Greeves. 'Was it because of Norman Shaw?'

'Not a bit of it. We came because it was the cheapest house of its kind we could find in London. We very nearly went to Putney.'[3]

Turnham Green station, thirty minutes from the City, was opened in 1869. In 1875 Jonathan T. Carr, a cloth merchant with artistic connections (he was a brother of the art critic Comyns Carr), bought forty-five acres near-by for speculative development. His first choice of architect was E. W. Godwin, the Japanese-inspired artist who later designed the white drawing-room of Oscar Wilde's house in Tite Street, Chelsea. Some simple brick-and-tile houses were built to Godwin's designs, but they were harshly criticized in the trade press for impractical planning.[4]

The next architect Carr picked was R. Norman Shaw, who was at the height of his career. In 1872 Shaw's City office block, New Zealand Chambers, had drawn public attention to the new 'Queen Anne' manner, which began as a rebellion against the 'churchy' neo-Gothic. The style owed less to Queen Anne's reign than to English vernacular tradition – with some Renaissance flourishes and Dutch gabling. Shaw's first design for semi-detached villas in Bedford Park was published in the *Building News* in November 1877 and was followed in the next year by five more designs, drawn by the magazine's editor, Maurice B. Adams.

❋Bedford·Park·Estate· TURNHAM·GREEN ❋ Perspective·View·of·VILLAS ·R·Norman·Shaw·ARO·

The 'Queen Anne' front elevation of each house was embellished with a brick panel containing a sunflower motif – one of the emblems of the Aesthetic Movement led by J. M. Whistler and Oscar Wilde. For Carr's own occupation Shaw designed the imposing Tower House in Bedford Road. The foundation stone of a church was laid in 1879 and in 1880 the Tabard Inn was opened, with tiled friezes by William Morris's pupil William De Morgan[5] and other tiles by Walter Crane. The inn sign was painted by T.M. Rooke, a pupil of Edward Burne-Jones and friend of John Ruskin. Rooke lived in Bedford Park from 1879 to 1942. Among other early residents were the young W.B. Yeats; York Powell, Oxford's first professor of history; George Haité, who designed the Victorian cover of the *Strand Magazine*; Sidney Paget, who illustrated the Sherlock Holmes stories in the *Strand* in the 1890s; and Cecil Aldin, well known for his paintings of dogs.

'For years,' Yeats later wrote, 'Bedford Park was a romantic excitement.'[6] He remembered T.M. Rooke's house, where he and his sisters took dancing lessons. 'The dining-room table, where Sinbad the Sailor might have sat, was painted peacock-blue, and the woodwork was all peacock-blue and upstairs a window niche was so big and high up that there was a flight of stairs to go up and down by and a table in the niche.'[7] G. K. Chesterton met his future wife in Bedford Park, at a meeting of the community's debating club, of which she was secretary. Frances Blogg was the daughter of a Bedford Park stockbroker; her parents disapproved of Chesterton because his income was only £1 5s a year. The objections were overcome and the couple were married in 1901 by John's future friend Conrad Noël;[8] but the feeling of being looked down on may have given extra bite to the satirical portrait of Bedford Park which opens Chesterton's novel *The Man Who Was Thursday* (1908). He called it 'Saffron Park' and described it as 'the outburst of a speculative builder faintly tinged with art'.[9] In his *Autobiography* of 1937, Chesterton was still mildly disparaging of the 'red-brick catacombs' and their 'manufactured quaintness', but he had to concede that Bedford Park had 'conquered the world'. What had once seemed so fanciful was now familiar. 'To-day, model cottages, council houses and arty-crafty shops – to-morrow, for all I know, prisons and workhouses and madhouses may present (outside) the . . . picturesqueness which was then considered the preposterous pose of those addicted to painting pictures.'[10] There is still a gulf between this grudging concession and John's joyous '*Et in Suburbia Ego*', his idea that the suburb is admirable and likable, 'the fulfilment of every man's dream – a house of his own in the country'.[11]

The visit of Peter Clarke and the Greeveses to Wantage in 1952 reminded John of the charms of Bedford Park. Six months later he wrote to Clarke, 'I am now thinking of little else than Bedford Park. I am going to try to get "Patmac's", who now own the Tabard Inn, to allow me to redecorate it in the Norman Shaw style.'[12] In 1955 Patmac's indeed commissioned an architect to renovate the Tabard's interior, but not at all as John would have wished. Greeves, as one of the pub's regulars, heard of the plan and telephoned the Society for the Protection of Ancient Buildings. He was told: 'You should get hold of John Betjeman.' He did so. Horrified by the news, John telephoned the architect, then rang Greeves to give him a lifelike imitation of the architect's reply, which was not conciliatory. The next day, Greeves was at the Tabard.

> Somebody said, 'Look, there's the architect. Why don't you go and talk to him?' So I did. He was just responsible for that particular pub. I said, 'Can you explain to me what you're doing?' He looked at me rather narrowly and said, 'Now look 'ere: for thirty years we've been doing up pubs. There's nothing you can tell us about it.'
>
> I said, 'Oh. Well perhaps you could answer one or two questions: for example, what are you going to do with that fireplace?' It was the one with the Walter Crane tiles.
>
> 'Oh, we're 'aving that out.'
>
> 'Oh,' I said, 'what are you going to put in its place?'
>
> 'Well, I thought a nice piece of Tudor brickwork.'
>
> I said, 'Do you know who designed that fireplace?'
>
> 'No.'
>
> I said, 'He was a better architect than you or I will ever be.'
>
> 'Oh, oo's that?'
>
> 'Norman Shaw.' Then he looked at me and he said, 'You're not Mr *Betjeman*, are you?' Of course, they'd been having a very persistent Mr Betjeman on the telephone.[13]

John's protests had their effect. Although the Tabard was redecorated, the more drastic plans were abandoned and the De Morgan and Crane tiles left in place. During the decoration, however, a painting of the Tabard, which had hung in the interior, disappeared. Tom Greeves asked John if he would mention this fact in his 'City and Suburban' column in *The Spectator*. John obliged in the issue of 7 October 1955:

> I wish I were a director, or at any rate an influential employee, of the firm of Patmac's, who own, among other attractive premises, the Tabard Inn, Bedford Park, Chiswick. There it stands among the delightful houses of that earliest experiment in suburban planning for 'artistic people with moderate incomes'. Many an old art worker of the William Morris

tradition lived here, beating opals into pewter or painting sunflowers on panelling or weaving homespuns. Here the youthful Yeats lived when he first came to London and in the noble room above the Tabard, panelled in cedarwood from a City church, no doubt artistic people from the suburb listened to William Morris lecturing or to ladies playing the clavichord. The Tabard Inn was designed by the great Norman Shaw and the walls of its public bar are lined with tiles by William De Morgan, but since the recent redecoration of this historic place, a beautiful painting of the Tabard as first conceived has disappeared. I could have wished, too, that the redecoration had been in the Morris style for which Norman Shaw designed the building.

The painting was recovered, but not as a result of John's paragraph. It was found years later at the back of an upstairs cupboard at the Tabard, into which it had been tidied away before the redecoration.[14]

John again mentioned the Tabard in an article headed 'Suburbs Common or Garden' in the *Daily Telegraph* of 11 August 1960. This time the inn was described as having been a place 'where men could play the clavichord to ladies in tussore dresses, and where supporters of William Morris could learn of early Socialism'. (When John set his 1965 poem 'Narcissus' in Bedford Park, the clavichord became a spinet – 'clavichord' does not rhyme with 'suffragette'.)[15] In the *Telegraph* article John called Bedford Park 'the most significant suburb built in the last century, probably the most significant in the Western world'. This ringing claim was to be a battle-cry in the 1960s campaign to save Bedford Park from destruction. And in the article John fired the first fusillade of the battle: 'It is sad that the winding roads of this leafy garden suburb are now cut through by heavy traffic and that the fences so carefully designed as part of the whole composition are dilapidated or altered. But the spirit of Bedford Park is still there and it is probably one of our most charming and important monuments; nor is its usefulness past.'

By the date of John's article, only a few of Bedford Park's buildings had come to grief. In the 1930s Jonathan Carr's Tower House, by then a convent school, was demolished and was replaced by flats. There was some bomb damage during the Second World War and the Chiswick School of Art (1881) was destroyed. Later the clubhouse which had been a centre of community life was bought by an industrial firm which remodelled the interior.[16] For years after the war, little development took place because there was not much money around and severe building regulations were in force. But in 1962 Tom Greeves was outraged when Acton Council demolished The Bramptons, a large house in Bedford Road and built an old-people's home on the site, in yellow brick. He wondered whether a group could be formed to protect Bedford Park. 'So I sounded out people in the pub, but I didn't get much response. Even Peter Clarke wasn't very encouraging. He said, "Oh, you won't get much support in Bedford Park because people won't like there to be any control over what they do with their houses; they don't want to be interfered with." '[17] Greeves did not feel like founding a society on his own, so he wrote to Mrs Christine Shaw of the Old Chiswick Protection Society to alert her to what was happening. Mrs Shaw put the matter before her committee, but no action was taken.

In February 1963 a Tabard drinking companion of Greeves, Norman Bond, suggested he should write to Frank Adams, a local stained-glass artist, to see if he would be interested in co-founding a society. 'I have come to the conclusion', Greeves wrote to Adams, 'that we ought to do something before it is too late – before we find that a lot of interesting houses have been pulled down.' He added that he had been doing some research and had made a plan defining the limits of Bedford Park. On it he had marked all the buildings of architectural interest. By consulting early architectural journals in the Royal Institute of British Architects' library, he had so far identifed seven types of house by Norman Shaw and two types by Godwin. 'Apart from the historical interest, the point of all this is to try to get a sub-stantial number of houses listed under Town Planning. Only a few are at present listed'[18] – and those few were only listed as Grade III build-ings, which meant they could be demolished without too gruelling an inquiry if permission were obtained from the Ministry of Housing and Local Government.

Greeves had no reply from Adams, but about a week later Norman Bond showed Greeves an article in the *Acton Gazette*. The piece was headed 'A BETJEMAN BROADSIDE: It's sounded in defence of Bedford Park'. It told how a leading Acton Conservative, Harry Taylor, aged eighty-two, had 'declared war on Town Hall progress planners'. They were, he complained, 'destroying the unique nature of Bedford Park with their barrack-like building and ugly "develop-ments" '.

Unless a 'keeping in keeping' movement starts soon, the character of the old place could crumble away. Unless Mr Taylor can form a protection society, 90-year-old mansions could make way for more and more flats.

Forward the 'John Betjeman Brigade'! A pitched battle for preservation is about to begin!

The new three-storey old people's flats going up in Bedford-road are the latest, biggest and blackest blots on the residential landscape, says Mr Taylor . . .

'The whole trouble started when Bedford Park was split between Chiswick and Acton. It should never have happened. It divided one of London's finest suburbs and has led, indirectly, to these eye-sores being erected. Because the South Ward includes Acton Green a Socialist councillor is almost certain to be elected to the Council. Therefore there won't be a protest over any new plans for this area.

'It is about time the Bedford Park people started a protection society, like the one at Strand-on-the-Green. According to John Betjeman we have got the finest Garden City in England. We should stop it being spoiled with flats, nurseries and other unsuitable buildings.'[19]

The page-seven story was 'flagged' on the paper's front page with a photograph of the white-haired, mustachioed Taylor and a paragraph in which John's praise of Bedford Park in the *Daily Telegraph* of three years before was more accurately quoted.

Greeves was slightly put out by Taylor's headline-grabbing initiative on his own pet subject, and was concerned that Taylor seemed intent on making political capital out of the campaign; but he wrote to him that he agreed with him and would like to meet him. As soon as Taylor received the letter, he came round to see Greeves. He had already collected several signatures of people who would like to found a society.

He was a remarkable fellow [Greeves recalled]. He was really just a builder who had done a bit of delving into the history of Bedford Park because it was virtually his home town – he was born near here, retired, and came back to live here. He wasn't by any means an educated man; but he was a go-getter. He was a rabid Conservative, he couldn't stand the Labour-controlled Acton council or anything to do with the Labour Party. I think he thought the Bedford Park Society was going to be a sort of branch of the Conservative Party.[20]

At Easter 1963 Tom and Eleanor Greeves went on holiday. When they returned, Greeves found an agitated note from Taylor enclosing a letter from Mr Spurrier, the town planning officer of Middlesex County Council. Spurrier said that he had seen the *Acton Gazette*, understood that a Bedford Park Society was being formed, and thought they might like to know that there was an application to demolish No. 3 Newton Grove (the house opposite the Greeves's) and build flats. 'What on earth should we do?' Taylor asked. Greeves said: 'The thing to do is to get stationery printed: we haven't formally founded the society, but we'll pretend it exists.' Greeves had the headed paper printed. 'I wrote letters all round, and in the end we saved that house. That was a great triumph.'[21]

In May a committee was formed. Greeves and Taylor persuaded Arnold Walker to be chairman. He was just finishing his term as the last Mayor of the borough of Brentford and Chiswick, which in 1964 was amalgamated with Hounslow. It was Walker's idea to ask John Betjeman to be the society's patron. Not all the committee thought this a good idea.

To some of them [Greeves remembered] Betjeman was a figure of fun. 'We don't want to get associated with him,' they said. 'He's a crank.' He did have a reputation for preserving trivia. The Stretchworth Dairies, for instance. He had said, 'Cambridge is much more interesting than Oxford because it has got that wonderful dairy.' Of course, I knew it was irony and that really Betjeman felt deeply. Anyway, Harry Taylor suggested we should get Sir Albert Richardson as a patron, as well as Betjeman. And in fact Richardson was asked, but he died soon afterwards,[22] which solved the problem.[23]

In his letter of May 1963, inviting John to be patron, Arnold Walker reminded him of what he had written about Bedford Park in the *Telegraph* article of 1960. The Bedford Park Society, he told him, already boasted around 350 members awaiting a constitution. 'It would be a very gracious act on your part if you would give them merely the encouragement of your name . . .'[24]

John replied from Cloth Fair on 15 May:

Dear Mr Mayor,
   Full willingly and with a sense of honour, will I be a patron of the Bedford Park Society. As you know, the best way to protect it against Clore and Cotton's[25] agents is to get the paper of the society printed at once and write on it a letter of protest to the Middlesex County Council planning officer with a copy to the Secretary of the Royal Fine Art Commission.
   With best wishes,
                    John Betjeman
God bless you for encouraging so excellent and vital a society. Afraid I am away such a lot I cannot do more than give advice.[26]

Later in 1963 John telephoned Tom Greeves to ask if he would help him make a television film about Bedford Park. Greeves heard nothing more for several weeks.

I thought, 'Well, that's that: he's getting information from somewhere else.' However, one morning about nine o'clock the telephone rang and it was John Betjeman. He said something like this: 'Oh, my dear chap,

I'm so sorry; but you know those dreadful television people, they've gone to Bedford Park and I don't know what they're doing. I'm afraid I can't come today. Please go and find them and tell them what to do.' All I had to do was to show them the right streets. We went on a tour with a camera mounted on a lorry, a sort of slow progress. You could see the buildings on either side, and I'd say: 'That's worth taking; that's worth taking' and so on. And also we did some interiors in the Tabard Inn – which I took part in, I appeared as a local drinker of beer. The producer said, 'Could you possibly impersonate a customer?' I said: 'I *am* a customer.' When the film was made, John Betjeman dubbed a commentary on to it.[27]

Almost eighty people attended the first public meeting of the Bedford Park Society in May 1963. They agreed that the main aim was to get buildings listed. Through the Victorian Society, Greeves got an introduction to Anthony Dale, chief investigating officer on the listing committee of the then Ministry of Housing and Local Government. Greeves showed Dale his map of Bedford Park and the many photographs he had taken. Dale asked Greeves which buildings he thought should be listed. He replied: 'Well, if you're going to list Bedford Park you cannot pick and choose – it must all be saved.' Dale was astonished. 'You can't expect me to list *all* these houses,' he said. 'They're not worth it! Architecturally, they're just not good enough. And look at the lay-out. I mean, there isn't one. Compare it with Hampstead Garden Suburb [which had recently been listed].'[28] Greeves had not expected this kind of rebuff. He consulted Nikolaus Pevsner, who was also on the listing committee. 'This is awful,' said Greeves. 'Yes, it *is* awful,' Pevsner agreed. 'I will see what I can do.' But in committee Pevsner's proposal that a large number of the Bedford Park houses should be listed was vehemently opposed, and scuttled, by that philistine in aesthete's clothing Sir John Summerson, who had already virtually drafted the death warrant of the Euston Arch in his *Times* article of 1960.[29] On 16 October 1963 Pevsner wrote to Greeves:

Dear Tom,
    This is, alas, to let you know that I lost the battle over Bedford Park. The treatment was fair. Everybody had a chance of speaking, and in the end it was put to the vote. I am, of course, very distressed.
    Yours sincerely,
                Nikolaus Pevsner[30]

Greeves showed this letter to Peter Clarke. The word 'battle' suggested to Clarke a subject for a Christmas card. Clarke and Greeves occasionally combined their artistic talents to design a topical

Christmas card to be sent to a few Victorian Society friends. The 1963 card represented 'The Battle of Bedford Park' (after the Battle of Turnham Green fought near-by during the Civil War). The card shows John Summerson 'attacking' Bedford Park, which is 'defended' by John Betjeman and other members of the Victorian Society brandishing umbrellas and sticks – a 'Betjeman brigade' indeed. John and Pevsner were shown together, rallying the pro-Bedford Park troops.[31]

The great setback of 1963 was followed by another in 1964: the death of Harry Taylor. Admittedly some of the members had thought him more of a liability than an asset. To him, the best way of gaining influence for the society was to lobby Members of Parliament. He wrote them what seemed to Greeves 'ridiculous' letters. Greeves remembered: 'One of his celebrated lines was: "Bedford Square is listed. Why not Bedford Park?" '[32] Arnold Walker said to Greeves, 'We must try and curb Brother Taylor!'[33] Greeves himself always felt some ambivalence towards Taylor, who got all the public credit as the 'founder' of the Bedford Park Society, though Greeves had had the idea first. But it was Taylor's belligerent initiative that had started the society; and his bombast kept it in the news. His last success, before he became ill, was to drum up support for a public lecture by Ian Fletcher, a Reading University lecturer in English who later edited a book about utopias, *Romantic Mythologies*, himself contributing the section on Bedford Park.[34] 'Taylor did a very good publicity job,' Greeves said. 'The hall of the Chiswick Polytechnic was packed out. People had to be turned away.'[35] The first annual general meeting was postponed because of Taylor's illness. Greeves visited the old man in hospital and was able to tell him that Ealing Council had promised they would consult the society on every building that came under threat.[36] Taylor died in November 1964.

New blood was coming into the society to replace the old. During the 1960s a number of young people moved into Bedford Park – among them the barrister Marcus Edwards, the literary agent Andrew Best (who represented John at Curtis Brown); the painter Alexander Hollweg, a grandson of Bismarck's chancellor, Bethmann Hollweg;[37] John Scofield Allen, a special adviser to the Prime Minister, Harold Wilson,[38] and his wife Philippa, at one time a well-known television presenter; and Mark Glazebrook, an Arts Council officer, with his then wife Elizabeth. Tom Greeves, with not entirely mock crustiness, called these new arrivals 'the trendies'. Bedford Park was suddenly 'in'. There was an *art nouveau* revival: the sinuous, 'whiplash' line of the 1890s was given new currency by London exhibitions of the artists Alphonse Mucha and Aubrey Beardsley and books by Mario Amaya, Maurice Rheims and Robert Schmutzler.[39] Bedford Park was not itself *art nouveau*; but in Schmutzler's book, particularly, Walter Crane was hailed as *the* precursor, if not pioneer, of the style.[40] And the original dream-vision of Bedford Park, which Yeats had glimpsed as a child – a walled-off community of artists with daily newspapers kept out – was also compatible with the 1960s revolt against materialism, the concepts of the 'dropout' and the 'commune'.

In 1965 Father Jack Jenner arrived in Bedford Park as the new vicar of St Michael and All Angels Church. Tom Greeves disapproved of Anglican priests calling themselves 'Father'; but Jenner soon won him over by his zeal for conservation. Naturally enough, Jenner's first concern was for the church – later a main location for the 1990 film *Nuns on the Run*. He asked Andrew Best if he knew any potential donors of money to help repair the church roof. Best and his then wife Gemma had recently come to live in Woodstock Road. Best suggested that a festival should be held, partly to raise money, partly to raise consciousness of Bedford Park's history and quality.[41] Jenner thought that an excellent idea. A committee was formed. John Betjeman, approached by Jenner, agreed to be patron of the festival as well as of the society.

To launch the campaign to restore the church roof, a party was held on the vicarage lawn on 19 July 1966. John was the guest of honour. The Bishop of Kensington and the Mayors of Ealing and Hounslow were also present. John made a speech. 'We are standing right in the centre of the world's first garden suburb,' he said. He praised Norman Shaw's church:

> The church is not too large, because Bedford Park was a manifestation of early Socialism, and the designers did not expect everyone in the community to want to go to church. For the 'non-worshipping aesthetes', tennis courts were provided on a recreation ground around the church. The high church tradition maintained at St Michael's comes directly from Shaw, a Scot, though partly Irish, with high church predilections . . . The chapel is a miracle of how to get atmosphere in a small place.[42]

Those in John's audience who had read his *First and Last Loves* (1952) might have noticed that the speech marked a volte-face: in the book he had said the church lacked mystery.[43]

After the speech, Mark Glazebrook's wife Elizabeth, in the costume of a Victorian maid, served tea and tea-cakes. 'The dress wasn't of a very saucy nature,' she recalls. 'It was quite decorous – a long black dress with a small white apron and a white mob cap.'[44] John sat down next to Glazebrook on a bench. 'You must be a happy man,' John said. 'Not only do you have a beautiful wife dressed up as a Victorian maid.

(How did you manage to get her to do it?) You also have a Bedford Park house by Norman Shaw, with a shell porch.'[45] Glazebrook later commented: 'Little did he know that we were just in the throes of getting divorced. In fact, I think it was the Victorian costume that put the lid on it for me. She's a very good *ex*-wife. My life was in ruins – I was out of a job, too. But it was a lovely idyll.' Glazebrook further points out that his house, which could be seen over the vicarage garden wall, was by E. J. May, not Norman Shaw.[46]

Mark Glazebrook had recently contributed an article on Bedford Park to the *London Magazine*. 'And John Betjeman had read my article, being a friend of the editor, Alan Ross, and a reader of and contributor to the magazine, and he was a little bit tickled by it, I think. I'd mentioned in it, without having ever met him, that I imagined he'd been amused by the slightly eccentric types in the early community of Bedford Park, which I had described as "thinly peppered with major-generals of modest means".' John asked the young art critic, 'Are you a relation of the Glazebrook who did the portrait of Anthony Hope which hangs in the Garrick Club?' Glazebrook knew there was a portrait of Lord Milner at the National Portrait Gallery, which Roy Strong[47] had banished from the staircase; and that the family had had a few examples of the artist's work which they had sold as theatrical props.

> I said, 'It must be my great-uncle, my grandfather's brother, Richard de Pitville Glazebrook' – a semi-fashionable Edwardian portrait painter, not at all bad.[48] And John Betjeman said, 'Look, I'm going to take you to the Garrick, and we'll toast the Glazebrook in champagne.' So the day dawned and I went along to the Garrick Club. The silver tankards were produced. We drank a good half-pint of champagne each before lunch, and we went down to lunch in that nice big room at the Garrick. He ordered a bottle of claret and said, 'I believe in getting drunk in the lunch hour.' Pause, and a lot of giggles. And then, after the perfect interval, he said, 'And then again, in the evening.'[49]

Mark Glazebrook was thirty in 1966 and John was twice that age, but there was no generation gap. Glazebrook had much of John's charm, wit, artistic interests and helpless susceptibility to jokes. A week after the Garrick lunch he visited John in Cloth Fair. As usually happened when John made a new friend, he both volunteered and invited confidences. He told Glazebrook that he felt he should never have married Penelope Chetwode. 'The reason he had done – and of course I know that things change in old men's memories from reality and I know nothing about it – but what he *said* was that he got married because he thought that if one had carnal knowledge of someone, one had to marry them. It was only later that he discovered that you didn't have to – it wasn't the law or a religious obligation. That was his excuse, it seemed to me – he'd made this marriage that didn't work out entirely right. What marriage does?'[50]

In turn, John soon found out what was bothering Glazebrook: the unease which the over-privileged were being made to feel in the 'class-less society' of the 1960s. The probing began innocently. 'I was at school with a Glazebrook,' John said. 'Short chap, rather good at squash. Wiry.' Mark Glazebrook told John that that was his uncle Rimington, who had become High Sheriff of Denbighshire. ('Rimington tried to import Friesian cattle into Wales, but it all went slightly wrong.')[51] Under questioning which from anybody else might have seemed intrusive, Glazebrook spilled out his feelings of insecurity.

The reason why you felt a sort of love for Betjeman [he recalled] was that he understood what people who had had a privileged background sensed in the age of the common man. He had a very soft spot for slightly hope-less but charming aristocrats and middle-class people like my family, with good values. You got the feeling that it was important to *him* that your grandfather[52] had founded the Royal Cornish Yachting Club and your uncle had played squash at Marlborough and your father was director of the Midland Bank in its heyday.[53] He made you feel less of an endangered species.

I remember feeling this awful thing that I don't feel now at all – a sort of guilt that I'd had this privileged childhood, being sent to Eton, where my father knew the housemaster. There were many middle-class people like me – we weren't out of any particular top drawer, we weren't grandees in any way. I mean my grandmother was rather critical when I was sent to Eton – 'Marlborough was good enough for your father.' (My father was there slightly before Betjeman's time.)

Somebody like myself who in theory had an impeccable background – Eton, Welsh Guards, Cambridge – could feel great insecurity. And John Betjeman understood that.[54]

The two men also talked about art. Glazebrook, who in the late 1960s was to become art critic of the *London Magazine* and director of the Whitechapel Art Gallery, was compiling a catalogue of David Hockney's works. He remembered:

John Betjeman said he'd discovered a similarity between Hockney's work and Henry Scott Tuke, whom my mother's family knew in Falmouth, Cornwall.[55] And one of the things he said was, 'Tuke was a high-minded old Quaker; and David Hockney likes to put the world to rights, too, doesn't he?' And they both liked painting boys in the nude – Tuke by the sea, in Hockney's case in showers. 'Both exactly the same,' he said. And I told him that my mother had said that Tuke was allowed to come to dinner not wearing a dinner jacket, because he was an artist. And Betjeman was very amused by this and said, 'Oh yes, Tuke would have come in an old fisherman's pullover.' I discovered from my mother that, actually, he came in an extremely smart suit.

And I told John Betjeman my mother was very innocent in her understanding of homosexuality – this 'nice young man' Mr Tuke lived with, and so on. But when she was in her nineties, she said to me: 'I suppose that Mr Tuke must have been one of "those men" – you know.'[56]

For the first Bedford Park Festival of 1967, under John's patronage, Glazebrook organized an exhibition of works by Bedford Park artists of the 1880s. A catalogue was published with a reprint of his *London Magazine* article. In tandem with this show, Alex Hollweg hung an exhibition of works by living Bedford Park artists. One of the works caused a public scandal – an etching of a penis on a cart, bearing the label 'PENIS WAGON'. 'An outraged letter was sent to the *Chiswick Times*,' Alex Hollweg recalls. 'I had reporters in brown mackintoshes at my front door and the Vicar shouting down the telephone, "Don't say anything! Don't say anything!" It turned out it was all a put-up job. The man who wrote the outraged letter was a friend of the artist. He did it partly to send the whole thing up and partly to get it publicity. The Vicar removed the etching and hid it in his downstairs loo.'[57]

Tom Greeves, as secretary of the Bedford Park Society, had been co-opted on to the festival committee. At first he was dubious about the trendies' plan. Their object was to raise money; to him, getting the houses listed was the all-important objective. But then he realized that the festival could be a context for the campaign for listing. He agreed to mount an exhibition of his photographs of Bedford Park. For about a year before the festival, the society had been trying to save No. 1 Marlborough Crescent, one of the finest houses, but it was demolished because it was not listed. In the exhibition Greeves showed the empty site; other photographs illustrated unsuitable alterations that had been made to several houses.[58]

During the campaign to save No. 1 Marlborough Crescent, Arthur Grogan of the Greater London Council Historic Buildings Division had come to investigate. Greeves showed him round the district, and although Grogan was unable to save the Marlborough Crescent building, he became interested in Bedford Park. By luck he was transferred to the listing committee of the Ministry of Housing and Local

Government just before the first festival. Greeves telephone[
said, 'You must come and see the exhibition, I've got the
graphs.' Grogan came to the show (John was also there – he
Lady Elizabeth Cavendish), and said, 'It's scandalous that this place
has not been listed.' By that time Port Sunlight, Lord Lever's 'ideal
village' for the workers at his soap factory, had been listed as well as
Hampstead Garden Suburb. 'I've only just arrived in the job, and there's
a lot of hostility towards Bedford Park,' Grogan said. 'But I'll do my
best.'[59] The next day he was seen in Bedford Park with a notebook.[60]

In July 1967 a 'summit' meeting was held in the Greeves' house in
Newton Grove: two representatives of the GLC, two from Ealing
Council, two from Hounslow Council and Arthur Grogan from the
Ministry. 'Grogan was the last to arrive,' Greeves recalled. 'We sat
round a table and waited for him to appear. We were all discussing
what could be done.' When he arrived, Grogan kept them in suspense.
He went out to the kitchen with Eleanor Greeves to help her bring in
coffee on trays. As he came into the room, carrying a tray, he said:
'We're going to list 356 houses. Is that what you wanted?'[61]

Grogan had brought a plan with him. He indicated the houses
which the Ministry had decided to list, provisionally, as Grade II.
Greeves said of Grogan: 'He looks a mild sort of person, but he's not.
I've since asked him how he got round the committee, but he's rather
reticent and doesn't like to give away any secrets.' In the same year the
Civic Amenities Act was passed. Both the local authorities announced
that they were going to make their sectors of Bedford Park 'conservation areas'. Those areas were not established officially until 1969 for
Ealing and 1970 for Hounslow: but there were no further demolitions
in Bedford Park. The second festival, in 1968, was a celebration. John
wrote one of his less sophisticated poems for the programme.
Beginning 'The dogs do bark in Bedford Park' (a pastiche of an old
nursery rhyme),[62] it was printed as 'A message from our patron'.

In 1975 Bedford Park celebrated the centenary of its founding and
John made a second television programme about the suburb. Again he
asked Tom Greeves for help. On the day of the filming, Greeves was to
pick him up at Cloth Fair and was also to collect some books that John
said he wanted to give him. When Greeves arrived at Cloth Fair he
found that John had already left. John had told the cleaning woman
that he wanted to go by Underground. He had left sandwiches and
wine for Greeves, and the books – nine large volumes of offprints of
Maurice B. Adams's illustrations to the *Building News*. 'It was an
incredibly generous present,' Greeves said.[63]

When Greeves got back to Bedford Park he found the television
crew in the garden and John in the house talking to Eleanor. Greeves

brought in the Maurice Adams books and the two men looked through them. John was particularly amused by a drawing of the Georgian church at Ealing that had been 'improved' by S.S. Teulon.[64]

The BBC television producer, Margaret McCall,* came in and said, 'We're all ready, John.'

'Oh dear, what shall I say?' John asked Greeves.

'Well,' Greeves suggested, 'why not start by describing the sort of people that Bedford Park was built for? At that time, I gather, people had begun to take an interest in how their houses were furnished. Before that, it would be considered rather effeminate for a man to do that – it was left to his wife or the builder.'

'Ooh yes, that's good,' John said.[65]

Filming began outside. John sat in a chair in the garden. In his lap was a group of De Morgan tiles which Tom Greeves had salvaged when No. 1 Marlborough Crescent was demolished. An Underground train came past and Margaret McCall stopped the filming.

'I'm afraid we're going to get the noise of these trains,' she said.

'Oh, I *love* the Underground,' John said. 'Could we please have the train noise *in*?'

Heavy rain began falling, an April shower. Margaret McCall said: 'We'll have to come back and film a bit more and make sure we've got the sound of the trains in.' (This was later done, without John, and his voice was dubbed on.)[66]

'Let's go to the Tabard and have a look at the De Morgan tiles,' John suggested when the crew had left. He and Greeves, with Margaret McCall and her secretary, went into the private bar where the tiles could be seen, a wide frieze below the ceiling.

'Aren't these *marvellous*!' John exclaimed.

And suddenly [Greeves recalled] he noticed there was another occupant of the bar, an Irish character who'd obviously been refreshing himself considerably. This man said:

'And h'what is you all looking at those tiles for?'

John Betjeman said: 'Because we're lovers of art, that's why.'

'Oh, you're lovers . . . shure, and wasn't I an art student meself?'

'Oh, were you? In that case, you'll know all about William De Morgan.'

And then the Irishman noticed Margaret McCall and her secretary. 'And who are those *females* you've got wid yer?'

So I was about to say, 'Look, I think we'd better go into the other bar,' but John Betjeman wasn't going to give up. He said, 'I think you'd better have a drink and then perhaps you won't be so rude.'

* On Margaret McCall, see Chapter 16, 'Back to Australia'.

The Irishman said: 'Oh, thank you, sir. I'll have a large Irish whiskey.' So he went and bought him a drink and he calmed down.[67]

Tom Greeves did not see John again. But in 1983 – a year before John's death and twenty years after the victory in Bedford Park – he sent him a copy of a small book he had written on the history of the place. John replied, above a shaky signature, that the booklet had brought him 'fresh memories of Bedford Park as it was but I am delighted to hear that now it is even better . . .'.[68]

Most of the credit for winning the Battle of Bedford Park must go to Harry Taylor, Tom Greeves and Arthur Grogan. Without these three men Bedford Park today might be as devastated as Fitzjohn's Avenue, Hampstead, of which the red-brick houses by Norman Shaw and E. J. May, which were a largely unspoilt sequence in the mid-1960s, have been shockingly gouged into by later developments. But John's contribution to the victory was not peripheral. He was already fighting to save the suburb in the 1950s, before anyone else. His *Daily Telegraph* article of 1960 gave the Bedford Park Society its battle-cry. His poem 'Narcissus' (1965), though affectionately satirical, was the best evocation of the suburb's early days and 'atmosphere' since Yeats and Chesterton had described it.

By agreeing to be patron of the society, John threw the weight of his public fame (never higher than after the publication of *Summoned by Bells* in 1960) behind the campaign, even at the cost of opposing his old friend John Summerson and linking arms with his old enemy Nikolaus Pevsner. He attended the festivals and wrote a poem for one of the programmes. And in two television appearances he kept Bedford Park in the public eye. The almost total victory that he helped to win could not compensate for the ruin of the Euston Arch and the Coal Exchange; but it re-nerved John's confidence as a gladiator of conservation. From now on, no letter of complaint to the press, about historic buildings, seemed valid without his signature.

HIGH AND LOW

When I think how few of our friends have fulfilled their first promise or how little one has oneself done from first hopes your achievement in poetry stands up solid and splendid and encouraging and defiant. The old boy [Ernest Betjemann] must be pleased – he was after all an artist, and the worms won't have taken that from him.

Sir Maurice Bowra, letter to John Betjeman, 29 October 1966
(after receiving his copy of *High and Low*)

In 1965 Jock Murray decided it was time to persuade John to publish a further 'slim volume' of his poems – a chaser to the runaway success of *Collected Poems* in 1958. The usual process began, by which secretaries rummaged through desk drawers and magazine editors were plagued for lists of the Betjeman poems they had published in the last few years. In January 1966, with John's agreement, Murray sent Lord Birkenhead the poems he had so far managed to marshal.

Birkenhead – son of the great lawyer and Lord Chancellor F. E. Smith – had been at Oxford with John, who respected his judgement. He had written an introduction to the *Collected Poems*. On 10 January he wrote back to Murray that he would read the new poems with great interest, adding, 'The next step is to overcome [John's] reluctance about their publication. I will try to get hold of Elizabeth Cavendish some time soon and have a talk with her as to how this could best be done, as I know she is very keen on their coming out.'[1]

The letter is revealing. In John's lifetime, most of the public would have been surprised to learn that he was reluctant to go into print. Their impression of him was of a man constantly invading their homes on television or sounding off in newspapers and magazines – hardly a shrinking violet. What few of them can have guessed was how acutely sensitive he was to unfavourable reviews of his work. His poetry meant so much to him – he told Candida, 'I know nothing in the world, not even love, quite as fulfilling as completing a poem to one's satisfaction'[2] – that an attack on it had almost the force of a physical wound. Birkenhead's letter also makes clear the recognition by John's friends that the best way of getting him to do something was to have a quiet word with Lady Elizabeth – rather as a courtier wanting a favour from Louis XIV would approach Madame de Maintenon.

Birkenhead thought a few of the poems were sub-standard. Murray wrote to him on 22 March 1966:

[John] accepts your suggested omissions with the exception of Narcissus and 'possibly Archibald'.[3] 'Both,' he says, 'are really psycho-analytical poems.' Would you think it wise to give way to him on this? I would find it hard to vote on it, but in view of his feelings I would be inclined to accept Narcissus but omit Archibald . . .[4]

The poem 'Narcissus', very probably about John's childhood feelings for Billy Bouman, the boy next door in Highgate, had appeared in the *London Magazine* in 1965.[5] Birkenhead agreed with Murray: 'Narcissus' should stay in, but 'Archibald' should be left out. 'Although I do not mind it myself,' he wrote, 'I am sure it will be regarded by the critics as "whimsical" and will draw a great deal of fire.'[6] Murray wanted Birkenhead to write a preface to the new book, as he had done for *Collected Poems* in 1958; but the peer replied that he had already said what he wanted to say, in the 1958 essay, and suggested Osbert Lancaster be asked instead.[7] On 29 March Murray wrote to Birkenhead:

NARCISSUS is provisionally going into the proof but I still have qualms about it . . . ARCHIBALD is out.

I did mention the suggestion [about the preface] to Osbert, who looked at me very quizzically and said that he would like to talk to you. If you are really determined not to preface, please bring all your powers of persuasion on to him.[8]

Another difficulty still to be resolved was the order in which the poems should appear. John wrote to Murray: '. . . I think you should group them under Cornwall, the Irish melodies, sex, wrath and the world to come, and in the wrath section of course come any funny ones.'[9] Murray did not find that too helpful. The eventual section-headings used were 'Landscapes', 'Portraits', 'Light and Dark' and 'Personal'; but to the extent that the poems about Cornwall and those about Ireland were grouped together in two distinct clusters (within 'Landscapes'), John's hint was acted on.

All through the first half of 1966, new poems were being added to the corpus, and old ones disinterred. Some of them caused Murray further disquiet. In a postscript to his letter of 29 March to

Birkenhead, he wrote: 'I think we are all agreed that the later poem about the car accident should not be included.'[10] This was an angry poem about an angry man – a bad-tempered driver overtaking another on the A30 and being killed. Into its viciousness could be read John's hatred for the new motorways that were slicing through the old England. The A30 linked places he loved, such as Shaftesbury, Sherborne, Crewkerne and Stockbridge, where the canopied entrance to the George Hotel juts over the pavement to the kerb. Consulted again by Murray, Birkenhead replied:

> I do not think the poem about the car accident should be included. It seems to me extremely bad and quite unworthy of him. But I have written to John saying that I do feel that the poem which begins 'When father went out on his basic'[11] should be put in. If he cannot remember it or has not got a copy, I have it in my head and could write it out for you.[12]

By 13 April, however, Birkenhead was having second thoughts about 'When father . . .'. 'It belongs, after all, to a bygone age of rationing and shortages and might seem out of place now. It is a pity because I think it is one of the funniest he ever wrote . . . A whole generation has arisen which would not know what "basic"[13] meant.'[14] John suggested the title 'A Memory of 1940' for the poem,[15] but in fact it was not included and was never received into editions of the *Collected Poems*. But he continued to press that the 'car accident' poem should go in. Murray reported this to Birkenhead on 22 June, adding that the poem had now been given the title 'Meditation on the A30'.[16] The publisher was distinctly peeved that, when he told John that both he and Birkenhead were against its inclusion, John was able to produce a letter Birkenhead had written him on 21 March in which he wrote, 'I should certainly put in A30.'[17] One argument Murray advanced against the poem was that the volume was already to include a poem about a car accident – 'Mortality', with its reference to 'The first-class brains of a senior civil servant'. But John was so adamant about the A30 poem that in the end it was included as well.

Two big questions remained to be decided: who should write the preface? and what should the book be called? Osbert Lancaster had finally declined to introduce the poems. John resolved this difficulty by writing a verse preface addressed to Jock Murray – pastiching the 'Epistle' which Lord Byron had addressed to Murray's ancestor, John Murray II, in 1817.[18] Becomingly modest, John's preface ended:

> MURRAY, your venerable door
> Opened to BYRON, CRABBE and MOORE

And TOMMY CAMPBELL. How can I,
A buzzing insubstantial fly,
Compare with them? I do not try,
Pleased simply to be one who shares
An imprint that was also theirs,
And grateful to the people who
Have bought my verses hitherto.

The title gave more trouble. John's first suggestion was *Evensong*,[19] which seemed unsatisfactory to Murray on two counts: first, that it bore no relation to many of the poems in the book; and second, that John seemed to be implying that this was a farewell or near-farewell performance and that not many more golden eggs were to be expected from this goose. By 15 June, two other titles were also in the running: *Consoling Seas* (an adaptation of the last line of John's poem 'Winter Seascape') and *Seventh Wave*.[20] By 27 June the field had narrowed to two: *Evensong* and *A Few Cut Flowers* – though the latter seemed too much an echo of *A Few Late Chrysanthemums* of 1954.[21] It is not clear from the surviving correspondence whether the title finally adopted, *High and Low*, was suggested by John, by Murray or by somebody else. While, like *Evensong*, it had obvious religious connotations, it was less specific, more comprehensive. It could refer to the contours of landscape or to John's mercurial spirits as well as to Church of England rites. John was still having afterthoughts in September, when Murray wrote to him firmly: 'Yes, indeed, too late for a change of title. Besides, your later thought[22] would provide irresistible temptations to your imaginary enemies amongst the critics.'[23]

As usual, Tom Driberg was asked to suggest amendments to poems. Murray wanted to pay him a £25 'advisory fee', but John said, 'Double it' – because (Murray told his staff in a memo) 'JB said that Tom Driberg was hard up and he valued his advice.'[24] Birkenhead was also full of suggestions, mainly about John's unseasonal references to flowers. In the poem 'Cornish Cliffs' John referred to primroses and gorse flowering at the same time. 'This could certainly not happen where I live,' Birkenhead wrote from Oxfordshire. 'It is possible that they might briefly coincide in the Cornish climate, but I am doubtful about this.'[25] In 'Inexpensive Progress', John wrote of poinsettias in the rockery on an English roundabout. 'Of course the poinsettia is a tropical flower,' Birkenhead added, 'and the only way this could happen would be if it was grown in a greenhouse and then planted out. I cannot see local authorities doing this, somehow . . . In the same poem I suggest that "yellow" vomit might be more effective than "coloured" vomit.'[26] On 15 June Murray thanked him: 'It was quite a labour finding a more realistic alternative to poinsettias.'[27] Originally, the stanza Birkenhead complained of had read:

> Destroy the ancient inn-signs
> But strew the road with tin signs
>   'Keep Left,' 'M4,' 'Keep Out!'
> Command, instruction, warning,
> Poinsettias adorning
>   The rockeried roundabout.

In the published version, John simply altered 'Poinsettias' to 'Repetitive'. He also adopted the helpful suggestion about the chromatics of sick –

> When all our roads are lighted
> By concrete monsters sited
>   Like gallows overhead,
> Bathed in the yellow vomit
> Each monster belches from it,
>   We'll know that we are dead.

In August, when page proofs were ready, Jock Murray was dismayed to learn that John was on the point of going abroad to stay at Simon Stuart's villa in Italy with Harry Williams and others of the Church of England Ramblers.*[28] Murray sent the proofs urgently to Cloth Fair and invited John to lunch with him and Tom Driberg – the meal to be followed by an afternoon session at Albemarle Street to agree on corrections for the printer.[29]

In October, as publication day loomed, Murray was again perturbed to hear that John, whose dislike of 'abroad' was well known, was about to go on his travels again, this time to make a BBC television film about the Holy Land.† Murray did his best to get him to promote the book before he left. On 12 October he wrote to let him know that Miss Jocelyn Ferguson of the BBC's *World of Books* programme was very keen to interview him about *High and Low*. 'You would not be talking to a critic,' he soothingly continued, 'and might be asked to read one of the poems. This would be really worth doing . . . if you had a spare half hour between coming to London and going to Jordan.'[30]

John did take part. He also found time to grant an interview to William Foster of *The Scotsman*. He gave Foster the full eccentric-old-

---

* See Chapter 17, 'The Church of England Ramblers'.
† See Chapter 9, 'A Natural Showman: Television in the Sixties'.

codger treatment, so that the resulting article had much to say about the poet and his way of life, but little about the new book.

> In his bedroom [Foster wrote], the windows are shuttered and double-glazed and its occupant sleeps with ear-plugs 'to keep out the diesel-breathing, gear-changing lorries, the most devilish noise on earth'. As we talked the phone rang insistently ('damn, it's going to do this all morning') and the poet hopped about the room like a gnat on a summer evening. Then he poured me a whisky which he was sure had been improved by being drained through charcoal.
>
> He said that he had always wanted to be a practising architect . . . 'But, oh dear, I should have tried to be so with-it that I'd have been very out-of-date by now.'
>
> Betjeman is married to Penelope Chetwode [who is] working on a book about a remote valley in the Himalayas.[31] 'Even when she leaves a note in the kitchen about the whereabouts of the butter, her writing has distinction,' says the poet loyally.[32]

John told the reporter about his early life and the many times he had been sacked. ('The round, crab-apple face crumples like a paper bag at the thought of how near he came to failure.') He also talked about death and 'an Anglican nun, dying in hospital, who told him it was no more frightening than packing up your books at the end of term'.[33] Foster asked John about his architectural conservation campaigns. (He thought John had 'given the nation a sense of outrage'.) John told him, 'with a defensive grin', that nearly all the people on his side were under forty. ' "You won't find the Victorian Society composed of a lot of greybeards and the people who oppose that rent-collecting slab over there are the young." He wags an angry flipper at a block of flats just beyond his own windows that seems to mock him in its square, uncompromising twentieth-century way.'[34] Foster ended his article:

> The familiar bedlam seemed to be breaking out again as I left. Betjeman was saying to someone on the telephone: 'I fell in love with Judi Dench[35] on television. I would like to see her every day of my life.'
>
> A BBC producer, who was about to feature the poet on a television hook-up from the Holy Land, called in to discuss camera angles on the manger. The poet began performing again. 'But what's Bethlehem really like? Is it as nice as Didcot or as big as Wantage?'
>
> There was the unmistakable gurgle that whisky only makes when it has been drained through charcoal.[36]

As John prepared to leave for the east, there was good news from the west. The American publishing house of Houghton Mifflin, though they regarded *High and Low* as rather too slim a volume for their market, nonetheless ordered 2,000 sets of sheets of it.[37] Murray asked Craig Wylie of that firm whether he might be interested in taking the wrapper that Murray's were using, 'printed in a most eye-catching, dazzling red-puce'.[38] Wylie tactfully replied that Houghton Mifflin would prefer to design their own jacket, 'though we think your jacket very attractive'.[39]

By the end of October, John's friends had received their complimentary copies. Maurice Bowra wrote to him on the 29th:

When I think how few of our friends have fulfilled their first promise or how little one has oneself done from first hopes your achievement in poetry stands up solid and splendid and encouraging and defiant. The old boy [Ernest Betjemann] must be pleased – he was after all an artist, and the worms won't have taken that from him. Your poetry is of course entirely your own (though you owe a bit to old Tom Hardy), but it is also the poetry of our times. It is these small corners of towns and villages, of the countryside and the suburbs that we have left to us out of the vast nature that was once there. Silly for us to go Wordsworthing about and you are the guide to secrets around the corner, which we should all have missed if you had not spotted them and given them just the right shape that keeps them real . . .[40]

Of the thirty-four poems in the new book, nearly half had not appeared in print before,[41] though a few were of some vintage. ('In Willesden Churchyard' was first printed in *Vogue* in 1957.)[42] There was a more strongly autobiographical element than in any previous Betjeman collection. In 'Tregardock' he made bitter reference to 'journalism full of hate'. 'Old Friends' was about the people he had known in Cornwall since childhood – 'Where is Anne Channel who loved this place the best, With her tense blue eyes and her shopping bag falling apart . . .?' 'A Bay in Anglesey' was written while staying with his friend the Marquess of Anglesey at Plas Newydd. Two poems, one easily decodable, the other less so, alluded to Lady Elizabeth: 'A Lament for Moira McCavendish' and 'The Cockney Amorist'. Two others expressed, obliquely, his hatred of Lord Bridges: 'Good-bye' and 'Mortality'. In 'Lines written to Martyn Skinner . . .' he addressed his old friend of Magdalen days.[43]

The death of George Barnes was commemorated in 'The Commander'; that of Ned Burden, secretary of the St Enodoc Golf Club, in 'The Hon. Sec.'. 'A Russell Flint' was about his affection for 'Freckly Jill' Menzies. 'Agricultural Caress', about a girl who had attracted him in Farnborough, was now thought safe to print, with some changes to names. The three poems grouped as 'Personal' were about giving a lecture, being sacked from *Time and Tide* by Lady Rhondda and driving across the cricket pitch at Heddon Court. John's *saeva indignatio* gave passion to 'Matlock Bath', 'Inexpensive Progress' ('O age without a soul') and 'Harvest Hymn', the poem which infuriated Britain's farmers when it was published as a letter in the *Farmers' Weekly*. Based on a favourite hymn, the poem begins:

> We spray the fields and scatter
>   The poison on the ground
> So that no wicked wild flowers
>   Upon our farm be found.
> We like whatever helps us
>   To line our purse with pence;
> The twenty-four-hour broiler-house
>   And neat electric fence.

On 18 November 1966 Jock Murray wrote to John: 'Greetings on your return. *High and Low* was published most successfully in your absence and, with hardly any exceptions, has been splendidly received.'[44] Contrary to John's fears, most of the reviews had indeed been excellent. Several of the critics noticed an improvement and a greater adventurousness in his technique – among them, Cyril Connolly ('he is more than ever expert in the traditional metres which he affects')[45] and Gerard Meath, O.P. in *The Tablet* ('There is . . . a new swaying counterpoint that swings through "Caprice" echoing the harmonic discord of the poet's feelings').[46] Two leading critics repudiated the view that John was merely nostalgic and cosy. John Gross wrote in *The Observer*:

It is easy, while trying to define in a few words what one means by Betjemanesque, to give a false impression, to make the poet sound like a mere collector of Victoriana, whose interest in the past can be summed up in that dread word 'jokey'. In fact he is a serious, not to say an impassioned writer, who uses objects and landmarks to conjure up the eternal moment, the sudden stab of terror, intimate feelings and buried memories . . . It often escapes notice that most of his poems, and not just the satirical ones, are set firmly in the present – not the swinging pseudo-present, but the real world up the road.[47]

John Carey wrote in the *New Statesman*:

Mr Auden once claimed that the spirit of his Aunt Daisy inhabited Mr Betjeman.[48] It was kindly meant, but reflects the popular suspicion that Mr Betjeman, for all his tasteful delicacy, lacks power. In fact, what his poetry constantly implies is raw passion . . . He fronts the world's bullies with quivering rage.[49]

Even Geoffrey Grigson, reviewing the book in *Country Life*, sweetened his usual disdain for John's poetry with an amused anecdote about him.

O tempora et amores, O, if holidays in North Cornwall were the same, and O Anglo-Ireland before Dev and disaster; and back in Betjemanshire, O, thumpetty-thump, for that lost – if ridiculous – confidence in pitch-pine and Minton tiles and St Aubyn mudscrapers, oil lamps and Tortoise stoves, and *Now the day is over* –

> *Or were they both too much restored*
> *In 1883?*

Talking of *Now the day is over*, I once went with Mr Betjeman to Lew Trenchard, in search of recollections of its authoritarian–antiquarian, piano-fingering rector, Baring-Gould (he wrote that children's hymn). On the way we had lunch, I think in Tavistock.

There were salt cellars of a slightly peculiar shape on the table. 'O,' said the inventor of Betjemanshire, 'dew-spoons.' I knew my inventor better than the third of us, who was younger and on guard, but was taken in, up to the last sentence and the last delighted total giggle or breakdown, by the disquisition on dew-spoons. Again, in the usual small neat volume, dew-spoons and other such – 'now the day is over' – are on view, half fantasy and all feeling, the delighted giggle sometimes changing to an undelighted snarl or shudder about death – 'night is drawing nigh' – and other rude intruders into the province of Lost Delight.[50]

Only one of the many articles about the book really got under John's skin. This was a skit in *Punch* by Basil Boothroyd, a veteran contributor to that magazine. Under a cartoon by Leslie Illingworth, he pictured John with the controversial journalist and television star Malcolm Muggeridge, engaged in a dialogue in Willesden cemetery. John's half of the conversation consisted entirely of quotations from *High and Low*.

The scene is Willesden cemetery. JOHN BETJEMAN and MALCOLM MUGGERIDGE saunter among the graves.

Mugg: We should come here more often. One of life's few remaining pleasures is contemplating the inestimable blessing of release.

(*He stops to read a headstone.*)

Who's this fortunate guy?

Betj: 'Where is Anne Channel who loved this place the best, With her tense blue eyes and her shopping-bag falling apart . . . ?'

Mugg: Not here, my dear John. I'm not unaware that you had another book of poems out last week, but this enviable plot has nothing to do with the deceased ladies in your life. It appears to be occupied by a gentleman called William Trundle. Nineteen-twenty-two. He should be about ready to move over. (*Laughs uncontrollably.*)

Betj: 'The heart in me's dead, like your sweetest of daughters, And I would that my spirit were lost on the air.'

Mugg: I recognise the quotation, old boy. That's your girl-friend Moira McCavendish. I see her as the Joan Hunter Dunn of Erin, distasteful though the concept may be. On the whole I prefer your moving obituary of the golf-club secretary. My only feeling—

Betj: 'The flag that hung half-mast today
Seemed animate with being,
As if—'

Mugg: My personal feeling—

Betj: 'As if it knew for whom it flew
        And will no more be seeing.'
Mugg: Yes. Did these weary old eyes deceive me, by the way, or did I read
        in your foreword that the ineffable Tom Driberg had kindly corrected
        your grammar, and punctuation? I only ask because any politician is
        naturally a figure of farce, and I couldn't help thinking it an odd choice.
        However, putting that aside, I fancy I detect a distressing streak of anti-
        death sentiment here, and I regard it as a great mistake. (*Laughs with
        sudden gusto*) . . .[51]

Perhaps the reason John detested this article was that he saw it as
cattily 'outing' his close friendship with Elizabeth; he may also have
resented the snipe against Driberg. The article earned Boothroyd his
lasting enmity. Anthony Powell, who, as a former literary editor of
Punch when Muggeridge was in the chair, knew Boothroyd, noted
John's loathing of him. Unaware of its origin, he considered it one of
John's 'unreasoning dislikes'.

Again Basil Boothroyd on *Punch*, another object of Betjeman hatred,
[was a] Three-Men-in-Boat/Pooter-type figure, with quite a good idea of
a joke, who ought to have represented all Betjeman supposedly stood up
for in the Suburban world, even if he happened not to like Boothroyd's
pieces in *Punch*.[52]

High and Low sold well. On 8 December Murray sent John a copy
of the second printing. 'Already it is going at a tremendous speed,' he
wrote, 'and the third printing is in train . . .'[53] By then the book was
fifth in the *Evening News*'s list of non-fiction bestsellers – behind *The
Guinness Book of Records*, Nancy Mitford's *The Sun King*, Harold
Nicolson's *Diaries and Letters* and Randolph Churchill's second
volume in the great biography of his father which was to be completed
by (Sir) Martin Gilbert.[54] Kingsley Amis chose *High and Low* as one
of his Books of the Year;[55] and Philip Larkin, after receiving a copy,
wrote to Jock Murray: 'Nearly all the poems are new to me, but from
a quick first reading I feel confident that they will become part of my
verbal memory as all the others have.'[56]

John agreed to one more interview, with Graham Lord of the
Sunday Express, a clever journalist who in a number of newspaper
profiles became a sort of vaudeville commentator on the poet's later
years. Lord began his piece by suggesting that the little book, with its
'repulsive pink jacket', was 'just not the sort of book a bestseller is
likely to be'. He asked John to account for its success.

'Perhaps it's appearing on TV that's done it,' he suggests.

'They say: *"I've seen that old man. Isn't he the one that's always going on about old houses? OK, Mavis, buy his book. He's all right, it'll be clean."* And, of course, dear boy, they're wrong.'

Balancing his vaguely diamond-shaped body precariously on his bed, legs crossed, outstretched arm waving a glass of vodka, he laughs.

A bleat of a laugh. A shy leer that stretches slack lips against long, pro-truding teeth, and chases grooves along his nose and brow towards a white, fuzzy-tonsured scalp.

At first, a guarded man – 'I hate being interviewed. You don't want to write something nasty, do you?'

Then hospitable – 'Have a stale cigarette, dear boy. I used to smoke 60 a day. I've given it up now. But I'm longing for you to smoke. Please blow it in my direction.'

Above all, a sensitive man – 'I hate arrogance' . . .[57]

He talked to Lord about the poems. 'My themes are that you're all alone, that you fall in love, that you've got to die.'[58] He confessed to feeling insecure about the future: would he still be able to afford vodka in ten years' time?

It was insecurity that made me fall in and out of love so often. I think by nature I'm masochistic. So far as the body is concerned I prefer taking orders to giving them. I've never seen Joan Hunter Dunn since I wrote that fantasy for her. As you get older what you want is quiet and kindness. Loyalty, gentleness. It doesn't matter about looks.[59]

At lunch in a pub near Cloth Fair, Lord saw another side of John's character.

Over steak-and-kidney pie . . . young men nod and murmur 'That's John Betjeman' as he walks out to a neighbouring bank with quick short steps to cash a cheque.

He returns affronted, almost sulky. He had to wait in a long queue of market porters paying in great piles of money. Indignant, he sets off after lunch to change to another bank.[60]

In that moment of petulance, Lord saw John's 'for public consump-tion' persona lifted; his evident vulnerability endeared John to him still more.

In 1978 Jock Murray wrote to John to ask if he would give permis-sion for a small reprint of *High and Low*. He replied:

Ta for yorz of April 16th re re-printing my verse. Do anything you like for I know you are an honourable and a true friend. Bring it out in stained glass or in newsprint, it doesn't matter.[61]

In 1970 the contents of *High and Low* had been added to the new edition of *Collected Poems*.

13

JOHN NANKIVELL

Penelope said to me when we were motoring in Leamington last Sunday, about
a sunlit house we passed, 'It looks just like a John Nankivell' & so it did. That
is what being an artist is.

John Betjeman, letter to John Nankivell, 22 December 1967[1]

On a fine July day in 1967, John was returning to The Mead after
morning service in Wantage Church, his summer suit creased, his
boater rakishly askew. As he neared the house, he saw a lean, dark-
haired young man standing at the front door, holding a large parcel.
'I thought,' John later told his visitor, '"What's that Cornishman
doing, knocking at my front door? And what's that parcel under his
arm?"'[2]

Though he was born in Cheltenham and grew up in Ilfracombe in
Devon, the stranger, John Nankivell, *was* Cornish by ancestry. The
surname means 'Valley of the wild horses' in the old Cornish language.[3] He turned to face John. 'I was wondering, Mr Betjeman . . .
I've got some of my drawings here and I was wondering if you'd look
at them and tell me what you think of them.'[4]

'We-e-ll . . . we-e-ll . . .' John looked uncertain, but after some hesitation invited Nankivell in. The artist recalls:

The Mead was cool and white-walled, much smaller than I had imagined.
A homely kitchen, with a large dresser, crowded with colourful plates. The
passage walls were hung with luminous Pre-Raphaelite paintings. We
passed the sitting-room, full of flowery patterned sofas and dominated by
a high, black lacquer Chinese cabinet, surmounted by two bronze Thai
dragons.

I was led upstairs to a large, long, low room, converted from several bed-
rooms into a library, not without strain to the rolling floor, I felt. Dark pink-
red walls and deep, tall shelving held thousands of inviting books: art,
architecture, poetry and other literature. We sat in two comfortable old
armchairs. He looked intently at my drawings, which were of Ilfracombe.

I knew that he was enthusiastic about the place, from his book *First and Last Loves*;[5] he admired the high Victorian resort as much as I did.[6]

John was impressed by the drawings. Though they depicted Ilfracombe's buildings with careful detail, there was something about the perspective – a hardly perceptible distortion – that saved them from being drily academic; it was as if the buildings were reflected in a lake with a slight shiver across its surface. 'We got on as well as I had always hoped and imagined,' Nankivell writes, 'sharing, it seemed, the same love of wayward and hybrid architecture – "rogue", he called it – with such architects as Teulon,[7] White[8] and Burges[9] and their polychromatic brickwork, turrets, towers and grotesque carving. We talked and talked.'[10]

The conversation was not all about architecture. With gentle questioning, John learned about Nankivell's background, his life and his present difficulties. There was artistic talent in the family. Nankivell's paternal grandfather George had been trained as a sculptor in Harry Hems's West of England company,[11] working on church interiors and house interiors in England and Ireland, but in old age, when John Nankivell knew him, had run a large quarry in Devon with sixty workers, supplying the raw material for foundation stones and church monuments all over Devon.[12] Rather as John Betjeman's father had wanted his son to take over the family cabinet-making business, George had wanted John Nankivell's father Leslie to run the quarry; but instead Leslie became a teacher at St Luke's College, Exeter. 'I would have quite liked to take on the quarry,' Nankivell told John, 'but I was too young when it was flourishing and it was all disposed of by the time I was fourteen or fifteen.'[13]

Nankivell, born in 1941, attended Ilfracombe Grammar School, where he was 'bottom of virtually every subject except art'.[14] He went on to Reading University's School of Art.

It was very traditional [he later recalled] – in the sunset of the High Renaissance, if you like. It had a lovely old professor called J. Anthony Betts. He drew wonderfully. He had the most fantastic visual memory. It was said that he could look at a Rembrandt drawing, work out how he had begun it and then, by memory, do the whole thing, stage by stage. The department was small and intimate and the professor had collected beautiful works of art. There was an original Cézanne watercolour in the secretary's office. The other tutors were also traditional. They could all draw and paint well. The year behind me was the first of the revolution – the students who told the staff they were wasting their time. They all promised to be really big in modern art – but I've never heard of them since. I enjoyed my time at Reading, studying fine art and then specializing in typography and illustration. I learned a lot and they let me be fairly individual and eccentric.[15]

In 1962, while at Reading, Nankivell contributed to the University magazine, the *Kennet Review*, a passionate attack on most of contemporary British architecture.[16] Though John Betjeman was nowhere mentioned in the article, the editor – rather to Nankivell's embarrassment – headed it 'Betjemania'.[16] And indeed much in the piece could have been written by John Betjeman, including the prophetic 'Our buildings of today will turn into new slums' and 'The Gothic revival produced its bastards, but even the most unpalatable results have definite convictions, and in this age of compromise this is welcome . . .' Nankivell's warm praise for Edwin Lutyens also chimed with John's views. Nankivell showed that he was not a reactionary by his enthusiasm for Oscar Niemeyer's Brasilia and Basil Spence's new University of Sussex, which was then being built at Brighton. John Betjeman might not have gone as far as Nankivell when the young man suggested how the 'tasteless' new architecture that generally prevailed might be curbed: 'some sort of despotic governing body, based purely on aesthetic grounds, and containing the greatest of our architects . . .'. Apart from that, the two were completely in step.

In 1965, Nankivell was appointed art master of Segsbury, a new, mixed-sex comprehensive school at Wantage. He took lodgings opposite the school with a local doctor called George Greenhalgh and his wife Mary. Their red-brick Edwardian house, Challow Park, had formerly been part of Lord Berners's estate. Some of the parents of Nankivell's pupils disapproved of him, because he dressed in Swinging Sixties style; drove around in a fast sports car, a finned Sunbeam Alpine; and seemed to have a succession of girlfriends. An incident in 1967 led to his leaving the school.

The head was rather limited in some ways, a bit repressive. He was most insistent on the wearing of the school uniform, which was dull and dire. It was designed by his wife; unfortunately, I didn't know that when I told him it was dull and dire – it was dark, dirty red. He was more interested in that than in anything else (or so it seemed to me), which was sad. And the school tended to operate on two levels. When the head was around, people conformed; when he wasn't, they didn't. So parties would go off to London. They would leave looking very school-uniformy and when the bus got round the corner they would relax and bloom into beautiful clothes. I took a party of students to London to see the Picasso exhibition. They said to me, 'Do we have to wear school uniform, sir?' – and, being only twenty-six and wanting to be liked by the kids, I said they needn't.[17]

The children enjoyed the Picasso show. So, rather to his surprise, did Nankivell. 'It made me laugh, because it was his sculptures.'[18] Towards the end of the day, the students were given some time by themselves.

Unfortunately, one of the lads, who was not allowed to smoke at home, smoked himself silly. I didn't see it. No one saw it. They all came back in one piece but unknown to me this boy had spent all his money on fags and when he got home he told his parents that he'd been out of school uniform and that he'd been allowed to smoke.[19]

The head demanded that Nankivell write him a letter of apology about the episode. Nankivell said: 'I'm sorry, I don't think I have anything to apologize for. We had a wonderful day in London. The kids had a magic time. And I didn't give permission for anyone to smoke.' On that, the head sent him home for the day. Nankivell consulted his head of the year, a likable man called Lewis Hosegood, who published books of poetry.[20] 'What should I do about this?' Nankivell asked him. 'The head wants me to apologize.' Hosegood said, 'If I were you, I'd rather cut off my nose than apologize.'[21]

In Wantage, Nankivell had a good friend – though not girlfriend – called Miriam Fletcher.

I went to see her and she said, 'You have these options' – this, this and this. '*Choose*. Choose what you want to do.' And I thought, 'Sod it, I'm not going to apologize.' So instead I sent the head a letter of resignation – which was an awful shock to him, I'm told. It was only about two weeks before the end of the summer term. The deputy head said: 'I'm sorry about this, but you've made a mistake. The head is not a big enough man to just rip it up and say, "Let bygones be bygones: you've learnt your lesson."' Sure enough, my resignation was accepted. Everyone said: 'Great! You've escaped!' But now I was out of a job.[22]

Nankivell soon found work, as a painter, decorator and sign-writer with a local firm, Campbell's of Wantage. He was sent to Grove Research Establishment, an offshoot of near-by Harwell. He painted 'NO ENTRY' and 'DANGER KEEP OUT' signs, complex flow charts and flaking water towers. At lunch-time, he sketched the workmen as they played cards and gossiped. One person who did not congratulate him on his change of career was his landlady, Mrs Greenhalgh. 'She said to me one day – and I didn't understand what she was getting at – "I really wanted a *professional* person in my house." Of course she meant a doctor, lawyer or teacher – not a painter and decorator. But I didn't catch her drift – I was green, socially – and I didn't move out.'[23]

After a while, Nankivell himself began thinking, 'What the hell do I do with my life? Do I go back to teaching?' He did not want to work as a painter–decorator for ever. 'My parents were a little disappointed that their darling son had ended up out of education. They were very supportive, but they were not terribly happy.' In his anxious, undecided frame of mind, Nankivell went to see Miriam Fletcher.

She was a very considerable psychologist. She knew some quite eminent psychologists and psychiatrists, like the Lake brothers;[24] she was very much into R. D. Laing,[25] all that sort of area. She was a 'mother' to a lot of people who needed advice. A gypsy who met her one day said, 'You're an "old soul",' and she did have that sort of aura about her. She was definitely the wisest person I'd met – my mentor and confidante.

There were times when she got really irritated with me; and this was one of them. I was telling her how much I admired John Betjeman. I had chosen his poems as the art prize at school; I shared his views on architecture and had written this article which they headed 'Betjemania'; I was glued to the screen whenever he was on television; and here he was in Wantage, but I had never met him.

Miriam said: 'Well, you don't really want to meet him in case he doesn't like your work, in case he thinks it rubbish.'

I said, 'No, no, I just don't like to impose on him. I know he doesn't like meeting new people. I can't inflict myself on him.'

She said, 'Yes you can, you *can* – all he can say is, "Go away, I don't want to see you." Or he might actually say, "Yes, hello."' She said: 'Get out of my sight. I'm sick and tired of you. You've got no backbone. You'll never do anything in your life if you go on like this. You need an extra push – so I am barring you from this house until you have made up your mind what you are going to do.'[26]

Nankivell brooded about his future for a week or two, and did not call on Miriam. One of the girls he had taught at Segsbury was Margaret O'Brien, the daughter of the Betjemans' groom;[27] she helped Penelope with her ponies. She would often tell Nankivell, 'They're down this weekend,' talking about the Betjemans 'as if they were the royal family'.[28]

One day – during this miserable time when I'd been expelled from Miriam's house and was full of uncertainty – Margaret said, 'He's down this

And she told me that Candida would be out riding on Sunday
…elope Betjeman would be at Mass in East Hendred. So I thought,
… this is the weekend. This is the moment of truth.' I rolled up a load of
…y drawings and wrapped them in brown paper, and I went ambling down
the drive of The Mead, past the back of the house and round to the porch
at the front. I'm knocking on the front door. Unknown to me, the lady who
lived there – because the Betjemans had leased out the front part of the
house – was away; and I was on the point of giving up when, out of the
corner of my eye, I saw John Betjeman returning from church.[29]

On that July day in 1967, Nankivell was twenty-six, John Betjeman
was sixty. The encounter was not unlike one of Max Beerbohm's cartoons of the Old Self confronting the Young Self. Both Johns had
strange, trisyllabic surnames which needed explaining to people
(inevitably, Nankivell was nicknamed 'Nanki-Poo' by student wags).
In each case, there was a strong link with Cornwall. Both were brilliant creators with a touch of eccentricity; and John Betjeman, the
writer, was as capable an amateur artist as John Nankivell, the artist,
was a skilful amateur writer. Both loved Victorian architecture. Both
rebelled against authority and, when young, suffered social slights
which rankled in later years. And both were susceptible to women.

John Betjeman was so taken with Nankivell that he invited him to
breakfast at The Mead the next day, the Monday.

It was then that I met for the first time the formidable and terrifying
Honourable Mrs Betjeman and an even frostier daughter, Candida. They,
fully knowing John Betjeman's weakness when faced with his 'fans', were
understandably suspicious of me, this interloper into their family life.
'I spend my life protecting John from people like you,' Penelope told me
years later, 'and somehow you slipped through the net – thank God!' Yet for
a while it was a delicate situation, somewhat softened by Penelope's quick
appreciation of my drawings, and by the growing warmth and support of
John, who seemed genuinely interested in my then vague future.[30]

John Betjeman had come to hate driving, particularly after his car
suddenly broke down in Trafalgar Square. Nankivell became his unofficial chauffeur.

Sometimes, when he was invited out to dinner, our departure would be
delayed when he discovered buttons missing on his jacket or, more often, his
waistcoats. I would have to sit beside him on the sofa or bed, frantically
sewing before we could set off and somewhat worried lest I stick a large
needle into his stomach.

One morning, arriving at The Mead early to collect him and Penelope to set off south to the opening of the restored Crofton Beam Engine down on the Kennet and Avon Canal, I found a great scene in progress. John, always nervous and highly strung before such events, especially when he had to speak, was desperate to set off, being terrified of a last-minute rush. But Penelope would not start, because she was expecting a long overdue visit from 'the Bendix man': her huge washing-machine stood silent and malevolent amid mounds of linen in the laundry room.

John got more and more agitated, eventually becoming beside himself and yelling 'Plymouth!', one of his nicknames for her. When eventually the unfortunate man arrived, he was quickly abandoned to his task – but not before he'd suffered from the frustrations of both of them.[31]

By the time the three of them reached the Crofton opening, John had become more his usual ebullient self. They were greeted by Penelope's cousin Lord Methuen, the artist and owner of Corsham Court.[32]

'He's the most psychic man in Britain,' Penelope said to me, in one of her shattering whispers. 'He's spent most of his life on the Astral plain.' Impressed, I asked, 'Where's that?'[33]

It was a splendid occasion. After the speeches, John, chuckling and a bit unsteady, climbed to the top of one of the huge boilers and turned a shining brass wheel, releasing the steam. The glittering engines, slowly at first, began to lift hundreds of gallons of river water into the canal. The tall red building shook and the guests applauded. Even on our way back, John was tireless and we stopped at Froxfield to visit a tiny jewel of a Gothic revival chapel, hidden away in a Restoration courtyard of almshouses.[34] As a youth, I had watched on television what he called his perambulations; now I had one to myself .[35]

Another day, Nankivell drove John and Penelope to tea with the Rev. Hugh Pickles, Vicar of Blewbury.[36]

He was a gentle, eccentric man, utterly dotty on cricket. His rambling vicarage, deep in the centre of the downland village, was beside the cricket field, and we spent a hilarious evening, after a leisurely walk, and a typical vicarage tea, watching the Reverend's countless out-of-focus and often upside-down slides of the local cricket tournaments, while John at his wittiest made continual, delicate and priceless asides.[37]

John introduced Nankivell to his friends. He took him to lunch with Christopher Loyd at Lockinge. Loyd praised Nankivell's drawings ('Don't you think they're like the young Augustus John's?' John

Betjeman asked) and gave him a tour of his Canalettos and Corots. Nankivell was also taken to meet the Barings at Ardington. In the evenings he returned to his lodgings in Challow Park and told his land-lady, Mrs Greenhalgh, of his adventures. 'Imagine her confusion! I had been driving around with John Betjeman, whom she longed to know but had never met. And her painter–decorator had been hobnobbing with the owners of the grand houses she most aspired to visit. She never again mentioned her preference for a "professional" lodger.'[38]

Nankivell repaid John's kindness by giving him several of his archi-tectural drawings: John particularly liked one of Cranmore Tower, an Italianate folly above Shepton Mallet.[39] But John also found a way of boosting Nankivell's income by commissioning and paying for draw-ings as wedding presents or as gifts for his godchildren;[40] and in 1967 he arranged for an exhibition of the drawings of Ilfracombe to be staged at Exeter University. He knew Christopher Corcoran and Adam Hylton, young architects in the County Planning Department of Devon in Exeter; they had contacts at the University who were able to offer gallery space. Nankivell borrowed a mass of 'in retrospect rather awful' frames from the young, hippie Lord Weymouth (later Marquess of Bath), whom he had met independently of John.[41] Nankivell was half delighted and half embarrassed when John volun-teered to come down and open the show.

> He came all the way down from London on the train, by himself. I met him at Exeter St Davids station and took him up to the University in the Sunbeam Alpine. There was a reception. He made a lovely speech. I wanted to take him out for a meal afterwards, but he said, 'No, I want to get back to London,' so I took him back to the station and put him on the train. I was so touched by that. It made a nice splash for me; it sparked off a lot of local news.[42]

In 1968 John and Nankivell made a short television film about the Ilfracombe drawings, with the BBC producer Michael Croucher. It lasted about eight minutes. The camera panned over the drawings and John gave an extempore commentary.[43] In 1970 he recommended Nankivell to the publishers Mitchell Beazley as '*the* man' to illustrate a new series of guidebooks to English towns based on Tallis's *London*, with its elevations of Regency streets.[44] 'I visualize it', John wrote to Nankivell, 'as a sketchbook and as something you can put in your pocket when walking about in the town.'[45] Unfortunately, the man at Mitchell Beazley who was most keen on the idea died young, soon afterwards, and the project was dropped.

In 1970 Penelope left for India for a year and let The Mead to an American psychologist and his family for fifteen guineas a week.

'She is going with three people called Elizabeth, whose surnames are Simpson [sic],[46] Cuthbert[47] and Chatwyn [sic],' John wrote to Harry Jarvis, 'and she is taking John Nankivell[48] to do some drawings. It is costing the earth, but let us hope it will repay at any rate part of itself.'[49] Elizabeth Chatwin was the wife of Bruce Chatwin, the future travel writer and novelist. Penelope knew him, too. She described him to Stuart Piggott, on a pony-trap ride in 1968, as 'certainly a "flaming homo"'.[50] Chatwin had been a star pupil of Piggott at Edinburgh University, and one Edinburgh research fellow thought that both men 'were much fonder of each other than they were of any women'.[51] Bruce Chatwin was originally to have been part of the group going to India but he reneged, telling his wife in 1970, 'Penelope seems to be very demanding and I'm afraid that eccentricity has an uncommon tendency to develop into egomania. This is perfectly all right as long as you don't have to travel with it.'[52]

John Nankivell remembers the preparations for the epic journey. Not all the portents were good.

Penelope had made a fatal mistake. She'd gone to Oxford and bought two vans. She had fallen for a handsome young salesman who had persuaded her to buy these two Morris J4 vans. They had engines between the front passengers high up, which made them abominably hot when we travelled overland to India and were a disaster in lots of ways; though, to do them credit, they did go overland to India and back twice in the end.

Dick Squires was going to do up the vans as caravans for the group. My mother gave me some money to go to India; Jock Murray gave me £200 to go to India (which I later returned because I didn't illustrate a book). I had this money, but it wasn't quite enough to finance my trip. So then – because I was still in Wantage – I stayed with the Squires and helped Dick do up the vans. We spent the summer making them up really grandly; I was earning my keep.

Before we left for India, I was intending to put my sports car up on blocks at the back of The Mead; but the last day or two were total disasters, because Dick Squires had forgotten to give me all the injections I needed and I had the most dire time getting them done on the last day. But we packed the vans. We were all loaded up: Elizabeth Simson with masses and masses of shoes; me with beautiful boxes with things like silver hair brushes which the others thought very freaky; and Penelope with her saddles and tack and God knows what. And one lovely night in September with the Wantage bells ringing madly – they were ringing specially for us – we set off. Virtually all Penelope's friends turned out around The Mead to wave us goodbye.[53]

That month, Bruce Chatwin was in Istanbul, his biographer records, 'when he heard a familiar voice: "Oh my dear, we've been raped." It was [Penelope] Betjeman – and Bruce was more or less the first person to whom she related an experience that thrilled her so much that her husband . . . John Betjeman, sent her account of it out as a Christmas card.'[54] No one had in fact been raped; but when a lustful Turkish soldier had tried to drag Elizabeth Simson out of their van and Simson held on to the steering wheel, Penelope had dropped the copy of Robert Byron's *The Road to Oxiana* that she was reading and shouted, 'Elizabeth, Elizabeth, I will go. I'm too old to have a baby.' She jumped out of the van and interposed herself, stroking the man's wrist and caressing his head. Elizabeth Simson roared off in the van to seek rescuers. She flagged down a carload of Americans and they returned to find Penelope sitting in a cornfield, laughing hysterically. She had raced off into the field and hidden in the corn. The Turk had fled. Bruce Chatwin went back to England but it was planned that he would join his wife in India before Christmas. However, he wrote to her that 'Penelope is the last person I want to show me round Delhi and would put me off for ever.'[55] When Chatwin went on his travels, there could be only one star. In the end, he did not join the party in India, though he flew to Teheran in March 1971 to bring his wife home.[56] Chatwin's feelings about Penelope were to change completely during the next two decades. When she died suddenly in India in 1986 (he attended the funeral there), he wrote to a friend, 'The loss is hardly bearable.'[*57]

John Nankivell made a masterly series of drawings on the tour of India in 1970–71. John Betjeman and Penelope both attended the private view of an exhibition of them at Hartnoll & Eyre's gallery in London.[58] Nankivell was valued by John as a creative artist, a friend, a driver and one of the young men – others were Mark Girouard, Simon Jenkins, Gavin Stamp, Glynn Boyd Harte, David Watkin and myself – who shared his appetite for 'rogue' architecture and his distaste for the New Brutalism.[59] But, like Chatwin, Nankivell also became a great friend of Penelope. In the years of John's and Penelope's widening separation, he was able to act as an ambassador between their courts, an Ariel traversing continents, materializing with Penelope in Chelsea, Simla, or with John in Chelsea, London, and welcomed by each of them.

---

* On Chatwin's friendship with Penelope, see also Chapter 21, 'Radnor Walk', and on the funeral see Appendix 2.

PYLONS ON THE MARCH: PRESERVATION IN THE SIXTIES

Do not be too discouraged by this defeat. We lose far more battles than we win
but the tide is bound to turn, at any rate in your time if not in mine, in our favour.

John Betjeman, letter to thirteen-year-old William Norton,
16 May 1962

Between 1958 and 1963, as we have seen, John took part in three great
campaigns to save nineteenth-century buildings: the Euston Arch, the
Coal Exchange and Bedford Park – two defeats and a victory. He still
found time to protest at the axing of railway lines; at the taking over
of Ince Blundell Pantheon, near Liverpool, by an order of nuns which
refused public access to the sculpture collections housed there since
1811; and at the deterioration of the Great Barn at Avebury, Wiltshire.

John was drawn into the Avebury controversy by his Oxford friend
Lord Moyne (Bryan Guinness). In December 1959 the historian
(Dame) Joan Evans visited her godson, the biologist Sir Francis
Knowles, at Avebury Manor. On a walk round the village with
Knowles, she was appalled by the dilapidated state of the Great Barn,
a thatched seventeenth-century building in the care of the National
Trust.[1] Used as a store by a local farmer, it was near collapse. The
Trust's sole interest in Avebury was the neolithic stone circle there,
which Alexander Keiller, the marmalade king, had sold them in 1942.
(Stuart Piggott, who had worked for Keiller on the site, wryly
described his style of archaeology as 'megalithic landscape gardening'.)[2] The barn had no connection with the stone circle; as a local historian put it, it was 'not Avebury-relevant'.[3]

On 6 December 1959, Sir Francis Knowles wrote to Lord Moyne to
tell him of Joan Evans's concern about the barn;[4] and at Moyne's

urging, John drafted a letter to *The Times* which went the rounds in 1960 and was signed by such *eminenti* as Lord Methuen, Lady Violet Bonham Carter and Sir Mortimer Wheeler, as well as by Joan Evans, Moyne and John. The letter might never have been sent off if the National Trust had been prepared to abandon its policy of concentrating on the prehistoric stones in Avebury at the expense of old buildings.[5] John put pressure on his friends in the Trust, Robin Fedden[6] and James Lees-Milne (Fedden paid the barn a visit)[7] but the Trust was unyielding. The letter appeared in *The Times* on 12 January 1961. The *Daily Herald* took up the story in the best tabloid style on 13 January:

> Farmer Farthing's old barn is a massive place that stands on sixteen piles, each of them an oak tree, so they say. And the Wiltshire village of Avebury is having a sly rural chuckle at all the bother it is causing 'they outsiders' . . .

The National Trust, the *Herald* alleged, wanted to pull the barn down: 'There are holes in the thatch.'

The difference between this conservation campaign and most of the others that John fought was that for once the campaigners had money (Moyne's Guinness millions) while the owner, the National Trust, had little to spare. Letters supporting the campaigners flooded in to *The Times*, including a passionate one from John's friend Lord Rosse. Questions were asked in the Commons and, by Moyne himself, in the Lords. The Trust, embarrassed, caved in. Moyne gave first £6,000, then a further £8,000, to restore the barn, which was turned into a rural-life museum with a successful vegetarian restaurant called Stones.[8]

Brian Edwards, who worked in the museum as a volunteer and has written about the Avebury campaign,[9] thinks it was the beginning of the popular preservation movement which was celebrated in the Kinks' pop song of 1967, 'The Village Green Preservation Society' –

> We are the Office Block Persecution Affinity –
> God save little shops,
> China cups and virginity.

> *

> We are the Skyscraper Condemnation Affiliate –
> God save Tudor houses,
> Antique tables and billiards.

> *

> *Preserving the old ways from being abused,*
> *Protecting the new ways for me and for you –*

What more can we do?
God save the village green . . .[10]

The interest was no longer just in stately homes built and owned by aristocrats. 'It was "Save the schoolhouse"; "Save the park"; "Save the buses",' Edwards says.[11] It went with the fashion for rural communes, organic food and real ale. The Wiltshire Folk Life Society was founded in 1975. In 1996 the barn was rethatched at a cost of £30,000. Eventually the National Trust took it back and extended the Alexander Keiller Museum in it.[12]

In May 1961 John appealed with Lord Euston, Benjamin Britten, Hugh Casson, Peter Hall, Bernard Miles, George Rylands and Donald Wolfit for £35,000 to preserve the St Edmundsbury Theatre Royal, built in 1819 by William Wilkins, architect of the National Gallery, London. Since 1926 it had been used as a barrel store by a brewer who had now offered it on a long lease. It was, the *Times* signatories claimed, 'the only surviving Regency theatre in the country'.

John's main preservation battles can be traced in the columns of *The Times*; but he was in many skirmishes besides. Anyone who wrote to him for help to save a building or a stretch of country received an answer, and usually active help. In May 1961 a thirteen-year-old schoolboy, William Norton (who in maturer years was styled Metropolitan of the Catholic Apostolic Church), wrote to John about a threat to Lewisham town hall, a building of 1874 by George Elkington.[13] John referred the case to the Victorian Society, and suggested that Norton should collect signatures on a petition. On 19 August, John sent a handwritten letter from Cloth Fair:

Dear William,

I hope I may address you by your Christian name as our Secretary of the Victorian Society does. You have done a splendid job of getting those signatures. Publicity and signed protests are the only way to move councils. I cannot believe it is beyond the ingenuity of an architect with imagination to incorporate the old building by Elkington with the proposed new additions. This has been done up to now, why should it suddenly stop? No building with such stone work and picturesque outline as Elkington's T. H. [town hall] could be built today. They are going to destroy something which is irreplaceable.

I am suggesting to the Secretary of the Victorian Society that he brings the subject up at our next meeting, & I hope the C'ttee will ask him to refer the matter to the Royal Fine Art Commission. I hope that that hard-headed body (on which I sit) will take notice and refer the matter to the Minister. Let me know if I can do more to help – but I won't be about much

this Autumn. I go to Cornwall in Sept[ember], the Faroe Islands probably
in October & Australia in November.

Do you know a rather fine late Victorian Church in Catford by
E.R. Robson? I remember being much impressed by it . . . I have not my
books with reference to it here or I could give you its name and date. God
bless you and good luck. Fight on and don't be put off by officials &
bigwigs.

Yours sincerely,

John Betjeman[14]

This letter gives the impression that John was 'signing off'; but he
had second thoughts and on 23 August met Norton outside Lewisham
town hall, with Peter Fleetwood-Hesketh and a *Daily Herald* reporter
and photographer in attendance. Next day, the paper published a photograph of John and Norton (see plate) and reported:

That knight of the great steam age, *John Betjeman*, best-selling poet,
preservationist, vice-chairman of the Victorian Society, does not spare
himself in the fight against the Philistines who want supermarkets,
bowling alleys and bingo halls everywhere.

Yesterday, accompanied by his faithful squire, *Roger* [*sic* for *Peter*]
Fleetwood-Hesketh, secretary of the Victorian Society, he journeyed into
south London to give moral support to a remarkable 13-year-old schoolboy who is trying to stop Lewisham Council from pulling down its
Victorian Gothic town hall.

The boy, *William Norton*, wrote to him about it.

They went, of course, by train 'Ex-Holborn Viaduct, arriving Catford
at nine minutes past three,' said Betjeman.

The poet, with the inevitable shapeless hat and well-chewed cigarette,
boarded the train clutching a large brown-paper parcel tied with green
string.

'A picture – a little memento for the boy,' he explained. [Another,
unidentified, newspaper cutting kept by Norton reveals that John
inscribed the back of the picture, 'This memorial to Sir Walter Scott was
never put up. Let's hope that a memorial as great and impressive will one
day be put up to William Norton in gratitude for his effort to save
Elkington's work, the Lewisham town hall.'] . . .

William Norton, flushed with excitement, was waiting on the platform
at Catford to take the poet round the town hall.

William, whose widowed mother works for the Post Office (his father
was a police sergeant), has collected 1,300 signatures against the demolition, which is to make way for a new building with an underground
car park.

Betjeman's verdict: 'The chaps who built the town hall had a medieval dream. Now the Council wants to replace it with a plan run up by chaps with beards and duffel coats in an expresso bar.'

John wrote to Norton that evening, 'It was most enjoyable visiting Elkington's municipal shrine today,' and sent him a list of Victorian buildings in Lewisham to look out for, including the Mission Church, Algernon Road ('It is not in Pevsner'). He added: 'Have a nice holiday. I hope we'll meet again & I'll meet your parents [*sic*] & brother'.[15]

Lewisham town hall was demolished. John wrote to Norton on 16 May 1962:

I am sad about our defeat over Elkington's Town Hall, particularly sad as what will replace it will almost certainly be a building of no distinction at all if it is anything like the latest additions to the site. Do not be too discouraged by this defeat. We lose far more battles than we win but the tide is bound to turn, at any rate in your time if not in mine, in our favour. I think the thing to do in your borough is to note groups of buildings which are spaciously laid out among trees and wide roads and which are worth keeping as whole streets or roads. Also look for views of a restful nature from frequented streets which could be spoiled by slabs on the skyline in the distance. There are of course individual buildings to be watched too. Keep in touch. You have fought a good fight and alas there will be many more before we all go up in an explosion.[16]

As the Lewisham case illustrates, part of John's rôle as a preservationist was to mount desperate last-minute campaigns to try to save threatened buildings. But also, in a more leisurely way, he kept an eye on the buildings he admired – visited them, made recommendations about them, publicized them in television programmes and gave money to them. He did all of these things for St Michael's College, Tenbury, Worcestershire. The college had been founded as a model choir school in 1856 by the Rev. Sir Frederick Ouseley (1825–89), known to his pupils as 'The Bart'. It was built in a massive Gothic style by the young architect Henry Woodyer, a pupil of William Butterfield. (Woodyer was also to design Dorking Church, buildings at Eton College, and parts of Tyntesfield, Somerset.) In 1961 John visited St Michael's with the poet Christopher Hassall – the beloved and biographer of Edward Marsh. An old boy of the college, Hassall had written a poem about it for the centenary celebrations in 1956.[17] The school's official history records:

One very memorable event for many of the boys was the visit of John Betjeman to the College. He took the boys on a tour of the College, and brought the buildings to life as only he can, as well as telling the boys a great deal about the architect, Henry Woodyer. He noted particularly the patterns of his hinges and ironwork, the patterns of tiles on the floor of the church, the span and symmetry of arch upon arch of windows and woodwork, and boys tramped all over the College, looking at the usual from unusual angles. Mr Betjeman very generously awarded a prize for the boy who did the best drawing of some feature typical of Woodyer's detail work.[18]

The school magazine reported (July 1961): 'These two eminent literary figures did us a great honour by spending the night with us ... To have poets of such standing reading their own works to thirty-five boys in the Dormitory at night is an experience few preparatory schools can have enjoyed ...'[19] Hassall and John managed to keep a straight face when the headmaster, Warden Desmond Stride, told them it had always been his aim to instil into boys the three 'C's – Christianity, Classics and Cricket.[20] In 1963 John introduced a BBC television programme about the school.[21] In 1971, when it was discovered the church needed rewiring, some recommendations about lighting which he had made ten years earlier were followed.[22] In 1981 John returned to the college to film with Jonathan Stedall. 'Sir John [as he had by then become] recalled his first visit ... when he listened to Christopher Hassall reading his splendid "Poem for Christmas Day" [sic] to the boys in bed in the Big Dormitory, which brought back so many happy memories.'[23] After the visit with Stedall, he sent a generous cheque to the warden and wrote: 'You have humanized Anglican church music for me. Henry Woodyer is very pleased up in heaven and soars with the arches and calls for more spikes against the sky as some of them have fallen off.'[24] The buildings survive; but St Michael's ceased to be a choir school in 1985 and is now an international independent boarding school, run by a group with headquarters in Madrid.[25]

In April 1962 John had protested, with a group of artists and writers, when one of the routes under consideration for the South Wales Motorway (M4) was to run 'through the heart of the Berkshire Downs ... one of the few remaining tracts of land in southern England still almost free from "development" '.[26] In June he even managed to secure Maxwell Fry as a co-signatory (with Maurice Bowra, Kenneth Clark, John Piper and others) to support the LCC preservation order on Robert Street, one of the three surviving sections of the Adelphi, London, built by the Adam brothers. 'If Robert Street is destroyed,' they wrote, 'for no other reason but that some individuals would find its destruction profitable, then why should not the same argument apply to Albany, for example, or any of London's historic squares?'[27]

On 26 September a news story appeared in *The Times* headed 'HAMPSTEAD GARDEN SUBURB CLASH: Move fails to oust directors'. Shareholders of the Trust wanted to end the appointment of J. F. Eccles as a director. The board had sought to sell a third of the suburb controlled by the Trust to a Cotton–Clore company (Suburb Leaseholds Ltd) which controlled the rest. The Hampstead Garden Suburb Protection Society thought there was 'a danger of a suburb of much higher density being developed, in which case it would no longer be a garden suburb'.[28] In October a fund was opened to promote in Parliament a private Bill safeguarding the future of the suburb. The sale to the Clore–Cotton group went ahead nonetheless, and on 30 October John joined forces with Pevsner, commenting that 'Many onlookers must have felt that, no matter how excellent the interests of the new landlords, commercial development could no longer be ruled out . . .'[29] The two men applauded the Bill to preserve the *whole* suburb; already £3,000 of the £8,000 needed had been subscribed.

In June 1963 John signed a letter with, among others, A.L. Rowse and the satirist John Wells, begging the Admiralty to think again over its application to use 355 acres of moorland at Zennor in Cornwall for training troops to use helicopters. According to the co-signatories, 'three rocky hills of exquisite grandeur' were threatened.[30] On 21 June a *Times* news story recorded an Admiralty assurance that 'nothing would be done which might tend to disfigure the countryside';[31] the Zennor site had been chosen because within easy reach of RN Air Station Culdrose.

John was in the news again in December: 'SUPERMARKETS RUIN OUR TOWNS: MR BETJEMAN'S ATTACK'. On 2 December about 350 leaders of Lincolnshire opinion met in Lincoln for a conference on Lincolnshire past, present and future. The conference 'began with an assault by Mr John Betjeman against supermarkets, which were "wrecking the West Country"'.

Two habits of thought were helping to spoil our towns. One was the idea that nothing mattered except money. The other was the modern point of view that there was always another side to the argument.

Mr Betjeman said: 'You know that on the wireless you are never allowed to express an opinion unless someone else disagrees with you. It comes of allowing ourselves to be dominated by the Civil Service, which likes to gather power to itself on its way up from prefect to knight to nobleman. It does not mind what decision is made so long as it makes the decision.'

If amenities would be destroyed by the widening of a road, the civil servant would say, 'I would be the first to tell you that we should not broaden the street at all, but there are other considerations.' Mr Betjeman pounded the table. 'Well, there aren't,' he said. Supermarkets could be sited on the outskirts of towns.[32]

On 31 August 1964 John mounted another of his favourite hobby-horses in a letter headed 'PYLONS ON THE MARCH'. He would never allow his name to be taken in vain without retaliating; and three days earlier, a Joseph Wilby of Chiswick had mentioned him slightingly in a *Times* letter. If one engaged in research, Wilby was sure, one would find men of the seventeenth and eighteenth centuries 'campaigning against the building of those monstrosities, the windmills, which mar the Sussex landscape'. And he was 'more than sure that the John Betjemans of the twenty-first and twenty-second centuries will still be campaigning for the preservation of the pylons which carried that ancient form of power to the homes of their forebears'. John snapped back:

> One of your correspondents advocating the case of the Minister of Power for putting up pylons regardless of public opinion brings my name into a letter likening pylons to windmills.
>
> May I point out the falsity of this analogy? Windmills could never be put underground. Windmills never marched in straight lines from a central generating station. Windmills were hand made and not all of a pattern . . .
>
> It is sentimental to glorify pylons. We all really know why pylons are to be allowed to industrialize and change the character of downs and modest agricultural landscape . . . The reason is money.

Just as John was not too proud to court his 'enemies', such as Maxwell Fry and Pevsner, to persuade them to join his campaigns, so he was not afraid to pillory his friends if their actions threatened the landmarks he cared for. Sir William Holford had signed several of John's gang-bang letters, but no quarter was shown him when, in November 1964, John thought his plans for the precincts of St Paul's would block the Cathedral and destroy the famous skyline. 'What is to happen to the churches, livery halls and historic buildings which give the City character and are at present at ground level?' John asked. 'Are they to disappear along with the old alleys with their little shops where we used to walk in our lunch hours? It looks to me as though the City will become a second-rate New York.'[33]

In July 1965 John took revenge on the 'developers' and the hated Civil Service in the television play he wrote with Stewart Farrer, *Pity about the Abbey* – about the proposed replacement of the abbey by an office block.* Three months later, life almost imitated art, when the Civic Trust supported a plan to redevelop Whitehall, proposed by Sir Leslie Martin and Professor Colin Buchanan. 'Mr John Betjeman said that he could not agree to the pulling down of the old Foreign Office. Westminster was a city, a park, and the centre of government, not just a place where we stood back respectfully and looked at different government offices.'[34] Tom Driberg, perhaps to tease John, said the Houses of Parliament should be left as a 'museum of democracy' and that a new House of Commons, about thirty storeys high, should rise on the south bank of the Thames.[35]

In 1966, John fought to save two major Victorian works, the iron choir screen in Hereford Cathedral (1862), designed by Sir Gilbert Scott and made by Skidmore and Sons of Coventry; and St Pancras station (1869–74), designed by Scott's son Sir George Gilbert Scott. Hereford Cathedral Chapter wanted to remove the screen to a museum, though urged by the Royal Fine Art Commission to keep it. After *The Times* published a photograph of the ornate screen, Canon Dawson of Salisbury wrote:

> I doubt whether the plea for retaining the Scott–Skidmore screen in Hereford Cathedral will be greatly enhanced by the publication today of your photograph of it in all its depressing enormity . . .
>
> The eye can hardly avoid it. Its spiky, blatant vulgarity is such that it effectively destroys any enjoyment in the architectural qualities of the Cathedral itself . . . It was a debased fashion which put in these metal screens 100 years ago irrespective of their surroundings.[36]

John countered this affront to the Victorians with a display of erudition.

> Your correspondents who decry the screen at Hereford forget the practical purpose of screens in cathedrals. They enable the cathedral clergy and choir to say and sing the daily offices undisturbed by visitors and pilgrims on their way to shrines at the east end . . .
>
> The original stone screen at Hereford was on the west side of the tower crossing with, as was usual, the organ above it. It was all but destroyed by Cottingham, the first Victorian restorer of Hereford, who also removed a good renaissance altarpiece behind the high altar to reveal a Norman arch and the rather awkward-looking spandrel of a column supporting the retrochoir. This was part of the Victorian craze for 'open vistas', which Canon Dawson seems to share.

* See Chapter 9, 'A Natural Showman: Television in the Sixties'.

It was then felt that the newly revealed east end was an anticlimax and that the cathedral had a tunnel-like effect. Consequently Scott, the next Victorian called on, and whose sense of scale no one will question, made the present iron screen which is light enough for the choir and high altar to be seen through it . . .

Hereford was not built, as were the modern cathedrals of Guildford, Liverpool and Coventry, for huge congregations, and its proportions will be destroyed if the present screen is removed . . .[37]

The next day, Jane Fawcett of the Victorian Society wrote to say that the Herbert Museum, Coventry, where the screen was supposed to be going, had not enough room for it, neither could it afford the £2,000 being asked for it.[38] Nevertheless, the screen was removed. In 1984 it was acquired by the Victoria & Albert Museum.

John admired all the Scott family of architects and in 1944 had again written to Sir Giles Gilbert Scott (designer of the red telephone kiosks), asking this time if he would let him write a chronicle of the family over the past century and a half.[39] (Scott replied, 'I am much interested in your proposal', but the book never materialized.)[40] So John was prepared to do battle when, in September 1966, British Rail announced their intention to redevelop both the King's Cross and St Pancras termini. J.M. Richards, as *The Times*'s architectural correspondent, assessed both buildings on 3 September. They were, he thought, of first-rate quality. With Lewis Cubitt's King's Cross (1851), character was derived from function; the station was 'one of the forerunners of modern architecture', a work of 'heroic engineering'. St Pancras was different: its designer was 'a highly conscious artist'. It was a contribution to the London street scene and in particular to the skyline. Though the earlier station would be 'a very great loss', St Pancras would be the greater. 'It is unique, and it would mean a loss of visual richness and excitement.'

After this, John might have felt that he did not need to reiterate the case for the defence; but over St Pancras he encountered, for the first and last time in his campaigning career, an adversary able to turn on him his own weapons of irony, ridicule and provocative flippancy. Sir Edward Playfair, a suave alumnus of Eton and King's, Cambridge, had served with the Inland Revenue and the Treasury. He had become Permanent Under-Secretary of State for War and Permanent Secretary at the Ministry of Defence. Then he had moved from the Civil Service into industry, as chairman of International Computers and Tabulators. Like John Maynard Keynes, he was a finance man with an arts bent: he had served with John on the Royal Fine Art Commission and was a future chairman of the National Gallery. The usual philistine or mercenary opponents of conservation, who spoke of buildings outliving their usefulness or standing in the way of commercial progress, John could swat easily enough. But when Playfair's letter appeared at the top of the *Times* correspondence page on 6 September 1966, John recognized a superior foe who would need to be tackled with greater finesse.

No one could make the case for St Pancras better than your Architectural Correspondent [Playfair wrote] . . . Could you find space for one who positively loathes the building? My reason for asking it is that (morally at least) the conservationists have it all their own way.

They are the experts and the men of feeling; those who do not share their views (as your Correspondent implies) are ignorant followers of an obsolete fashion.

In fact, of course, his reaction and mine are both subjective, though his is much better informed. St Pancras gives a lift to his spirit: mine droops at its sight and I have never passed it without hoping . . . that it would soon be demolished. As a critic, I do not count against your Correspondent; as voters, ratepayers, passers-by, and railway-travellers we are equal. Haters of St Pancras should register their feelings as emphatically as its lovers do.

Not enough is said about the virtues of demolition. [The present taste is for] the national junk-yard, the museum with far too many walls, plans distorted to accommodate the fashionable, the obsolete and the unusable, and restrictions placed on today's achievements in favour of the dead.

Anyway, what fun it would be. Think of our delenda list, starting with Elizabethan vulgarities . . . and rising to a climax in modern times, with St Pancras at its head, advancing through Waterhouse (*opera omnia*) towards that arch-delendum the Ministry of Defence. It is a pity that we destructionists are so passive: we need an anti-Betjeman to lead us.

John could not let this pass; but instead of rehearsing all the pro-St Pancras arguments, as he would have done with a stolider opponent, he brushed Playfair aside with disdainful brevity.

Sir Edward Playfair wrote amusingly to you in your issue of September 6 and in his last line refers not very flatteringly to me.

I have heard of him as a senior civil servant who resigned to take up more constructive work in the computer industry. But now he seems to have taken on a new job on behalf of the demolitionists and to have developed into an unashamed developer. Surely in human reason they have devoured enough already?[41]

James Lees-Milne reacted to the Playfair letter with less equanimity. To him, an assault on a building was as heinous as an attack on a person. 'Sir Edward Playfair', he wrote, 'may, for all I know, be a very funny man. But there are certain subjects, like cancer, cruelty and Philistinism, which are not amusing. That Sir Edward can see neither architectural merit nor beauty in St Pancras Station is of little interest to anyone. That he is the first person to have been a member of the Royal Fine Art Commission who publicly takes sides with the vandals is, however, enlightening. Preservationists will take note of his admission.'[42] Another friend of John's, the photographer Eric de Maré, wrote, 'The facetious tone of [Playfair's] letter devalues a very serious subject . . . The future of St Pancras is . . . a test case which will decide whether or not this country is to retain any architectural appreciation at all or any pride in itself and its past – whether or not it is going to live . . . by unreal, sterilizing and restrictive money values only, or by those true values which make life worth living for all of us.'[43] St Pancras was saved. In 1996, at eighty-five, Sir Edward Playfair blandly recalled: 'I knew John, but only as a fellow-member of the Royal Fine Art Commission, where he displayed . . . his usual common sense: he was a useful member, as well as being a delightful man . . . I have no letters from him, and only remember receiving one: he had had a letter from someone asking him to intervene to save the kitsch decoration of a bank branch which NatWest [the National Westminster Bank] proposed to destroy. As I was then a director of NatWest, John sent it on to me, saying that he did not think it worth preserving.'[44]

A month after the St Pancras row, John composed verses to be sung by the London Welsh Male Choir at a Guildhall banquet in aid of the Barnado centenary. The four-stanza poem was to be sung to the tune of Handel's March from *Scipio*. John made it a condition that the pointed second stanza should not be omitted –

> The many-steepled sky
> Which made our City fair
> Buried in buildings high
> Is now no longer there.[45]

In March 1967 he supported an objection by the Warwick Society to the demolition of the Bear and Baculus public house in Warwick.[46] In April he wrote, with Quintin Hogg and John Summerson, to appeal for £25,000 to save St Mary's, Bryanston Square, a Smirke church of 1825, from dry rot.[47] He figured in a front-page news story in *The Times* of 2 June, next to an account of the gambling underworld shooting of John James Buggy, 'last seen at a card table in a Mayfair club'. The regional committee of the National Trust in Cornwall had rejected John's poem in support of Enterprise Neptune, a campaign to save nine hundred miles of British coastline. One Trust member claimed the poem was 'poetic licence run amok'. The poem ('Delectable Duchy') described Cornwall as 'a pathetic sight'. *The Times* reported: 'He paints a grim picture of a county overrun by the litter of tourists, and where beauty spots have been spoiled by caravan sites and holiday development.'

Mr N.J. Savage, a member of the regional committee, said the poem had been rejected because it was felt to be against the best interests of the Neptune campaign. 'We feel it gives the impression that Cornwall is already spoiled beyond redemption,' Savage said, adding that he would like Mr Betjeman to write another poem painting Cornwall as a county of 'beautiful, unspoilt coves which could be in danger of being ruined'. Lord Antrim, a friend of John's and chairman of the National Trust, said he would investigate the rejection. The offending poem was published in *A Nip in the Air* (1974). The unnamed person apostrophized in it was John's childhood friend, Joan Kunzer (*née* Larkworthy).

> Where yonder villa hogs the sea
> Was open cliff to you and me.
> The many-coloured cara's fill
> The salty marsh to Shilla Mill.
> And, foreground to the hanging wood,
> Are toilets where the cattle stood.
> The mint and meadowsweet would scent
> The brambly lane by which we went;
> Now, as we near the ocean roar,
> A smell of deep-fry haunts the shore.
> In pools beyond the reach of tides
> The Senior Service carton glides,
> And on the sand the surf-line lisps
> With wrappings of potato crisps . . .

In August 1967, two months after the row about the Cornwall poem, John again wrote to *The Times* about the buildings obscuring St Paul's Cathedral. The protruding Juxton House had fulfilled the fears he had expressed earlier in the decade. Now, agreeing with Professor Sir Keith Hancock, who proposed that a subscription should be opened to demolish what John called 'the building which seems to project into the west front of St Paul's', he demanded that the owners should 'let us know what price they set on this building which has earned no rent for them since it was built some years ago and is still empty'.[48] In July 1968 he launched a £7,000 appeal to restore the

Cartoon by 'Trog', 6 October 1969

7 October 1969

8 October 1969

John Moore cottage, one of sixteen medieval cottages in Church Street, Tewkesbury, as a museum in memory of John Moore, the Gloucestershire novelist, playwright and broadcaster who had died the year before.[49] On 10 August, J.M. Richards, whom John had called 'Karl Marx' since their days together on *The Architectural Review*, reviewed his *Pocket Guide to English Churches*: 'This essay is one of the most brilliant things Mr Betjeman has written.' Two days later, John was writing to *The Times* in connection with the real Karl Marx – appealing for funds for Marx House on Clerkenwell Green, London, built in 1738 for the Welsh Charity School but by now owned by the Marx Memorial Library. In November the Government

9 October 1969

20 October 1969

21 October 1969

promised that plans for the London motorway box and ring road would be 'thoroughly ventilated and tested in public', after John declared that the Greater London Council could not be allowed to make a 'line of death' round inner London, 'cutting off parts of it and producing terrible stench and noise'.

In 1969 Betjeman the preservationist was affectionately satirized by the cartoonist Trog (Wally Fawkes) in his 'Flook' comic strip in the *Daily Mail*. The artist caught brilliantly both John's appearance and his way of talking – which by then, the height of the Swinging Sixties, was as much a period piece as some of the buildings he was trying to save.

The big campaign of 1969, however, was not an attempt to save a building, but a protest against the proposal for a new airport at Wing, Buckinghamshire. The name might be apt, but, John told the Roskill Commission at Aylesbury on 16 July, 'only Stansted would be a worse choice than Wing . . . for London's third airport. The scenery here in north Bucks is the sort that Henry James described as "unmitigated England".'[50] (The main front-page news was the lift-off of Apollo II, the day before, on its way to the moon.)[51] John would probably have protested about the proposed airport of his own volition; but he was goaded on by his friend Lady Pamela Berry, whose house at Oving, Buckinghamshire, was near the proposed site. She wrote to him: 'I can't begin to tell you how thrilled we are that you have agreed to come and address us on the subject of the airport menace . . . Everyone is wildly excited about your appearance . . .'[52] John wrote a poem for the Wing Airport Resistance Association (Wara), conjuring up a picture of a bulldozed Vale of Aylesbury. It was a variation on William Cowper's 'The Poplar Field' (1784), which begins:

> The poplars are fell'd, farewell to the shade
> And the whispering sound of the cool colonnade . . .

Early in 1970 Candida accompanied John to a large meeting of protesters at Oving, and he recited his poem.

> . . .
> The birds are all killed and the flowers are all dead
> And the businessman's aeroplane booms overhead;
> With chemical sprays we have poisoned the soil,
> And the scent in our nostrils is diesel and oil.
> The roads are all widened, the lanes are all straight
> So that rising executives won't have to wait.
> For who'd use a footpath to Quainton or Brill
> When a jet can convey him as far as Brazil?[53]

The Wing Airport scheme never took off. Stansted, with no Lady Pamela Berry and no Betjeman poem to defend it, was not so lucky.

MARY WILSON AND A JOURNEY TO DISS

The third thing I want to thank you for is existing . . . Thank you, dear Mary,
and go on being kind to the bald old journalist who signs himself
　　Yours with love
　　　　　John

　　　　　　　John Betjeman, letter to Mary Wilson, 11 January 1968

In 1969 John went on a train journey to Diss, in Norfolk, with Mary
Wilson, wife of the Prime Minister, Harold Wilson. The two had first
met, two years earlier, through the Earl of Drogheda, chairman of the
Royal Opera House and later of the *Financial Times*.[1]

> Lord Drogheda used to invite me to join his party at Covent Garden [Lady
> Wilson recalls]. I had admired John Betjeman for a very long time and had
> seen him on the television, and I thought, 'That's the man I would like to
> meet!' I saw the guest list of the party when I got to Covent Garden and
> I said to Garrett Drogheda, 'Is John Betjeman *really* coming?' And he said,
> 'Yes.' I said, 'Oh how marvellous, I've always wanted to meet him.' So he
> said, with his characteristic rather cool manner, 'Oh well, I must change
> the table plan, then,' which he did. I sat next to John and we had a lot of
> conversation. We wrote to each other soon afterwards; and so began a
> friendship.[2]

Mary Wilson wrote to John on 10 November 1967: 'I did so enjoy
meeting you and it would be delightful if you could come to tea and a
proper talk.'[3] She enclosed two of her own poems, a carol and 'After
the Bomb'. John replied that he liked both the poems, but thought the
carol the better of the two. 'It is so *good* like you are, really good.'[4] By
20 November the two had met again. On that day John wrote, 'I *did*
enjoy our talk. It was noble of you to see me at a time of stress like

that must have been.'[5] (It was the month sterling took a fall, when Harold Wilson was derided for assuring the public that the pound in their pockets had not been devalued.)[6] In her reply, Mary Wilson wrote: 'Could I, without appearing rude about your handwriting, ask if you could possibly address your letters to me in a fair, round hand, because the messengers mistook Mrs for Mr. Consequently your letter went downstairs and was opened by Philistine hands.'[7] In December she dined with him at the Garrick Club. 'Oh dear. Never again the Garrick,' he wrote to her. 'What a gauntlet of eyes. I never thought it would be like that as I very rarely go there in the evenings.'[8]

In a regular feature headed 'Mrs Wilson's Diary' (based on the long-running radio serial *Mrs Dale's Diary*), *Private Eye* portrayed Mary Wilson – 'Gladys' – as a cosy *Hausfrau* with strictly domestic horizons. This travesty related to Harold Wilson's reputation as a tough little nugget from oop north who was partial to HP Sauce – a condiment mocked by John himself in his poem 'Lake District'.* Mrs Wilson was not *grande dame*, but she was an attractive, kind and sensible woman, the sort that had always appealed to John. Cynics thought that he was sucking up to her in the hope of ingratiating himself with the Prime Minister;[9] and it was through Wilson, in 1969, that he received his knighthood. Perhaps John was a little over-gushing in his praise of her poems; but it is clear that he felt genuine affection for Mary Wilson and that he was able to ask her advice or confide in her when he was depressed.

She would go to tea with him, or he with her. He 'found the lift at Number 10 Downing Street very erotic', Lady Wilson told Candida Lycett Green. 'It was lined with red suede and always took a very long time to reach its destinations.' He told her 'how he imagined all the things that had happened in it'.[10] Apart from dinners at the Garrick Club (John relented on the 'never again'),[11] they kept their friendship private; there was no knowing what a malicious gossip columnist might insinuate if their innocent companionship was observed. As a result, some of their meetings had almost the air of lovers' trysts. 'I'll meet you on the bridge in the middle of park at three p.m.' Mary Wilson wrote to him in January 1968.[12] He replied with a jokey verse:

---

* I pass the cruet and I see the lake
  Running with light, beyond the garden pine . . .
  I pledge her in non-alcoholic wine
  And give the HP Sauce another shake.

(The 'HP' stands for 'Houses of Parliament'.)

> I will be on the bridge at St James's
> When the clocks are striking three
> And if the rain is falling
> I will telephone up to thee
> Till then accept all love from
> Henry Wadsworth B.[13]

When they met in each other's homes, they would often spend the whole afternoon reciting and talking about poetry. 'Now how many people', Lady Wilson asked in 1982, 'would know enough poetry to talk about it as he did and know every poem that you mentioned? We had lovely quoting sessions, back and forth, and then we'd rush to the reference book to make quite sure whether we were right or not. And he liked me to read to him, which I always found rather embarrassing, because he reads things so much better than I do. I used to read to him – and then he'd go to sleep. Very soothing.'[14] The poets they read were mostly John's old favourites.

> Tennyson, *Maud*. Newbolt, 'There's a breathless hush in the close tonight.' Noyes's 'Highwayman' [Lady Wilson recalled]. Anything with a sort of beat to it. One afternoon I read the whole of *Maud* to him – no mean feat! I'm very fond of certain poets whom he's not very fond of. I like Longfellow. He doesn't like Longfellow – hates *Hiawatha*! He did a spoof of *Hiawatha* for me – 'Anyone can do it, darling.' But after I had visited Longfellow's house in Cambridge, Mass., I brought back a tray for John and he gave me his copy of Longfellow, inscribed to me.
>
> Another poet I like is Edgar Allan Poe. I love *The Raven* – very spooky. Anything really dramatic and juicy like that. My favourite poem of all is 'My soul there is a country, far beyond the stars' – Henry Vaughan. But there are often moods in which one likes to quote Dowson or Flecker.[15]

As the two bandied poems back and forth – 'poetical ping-pong', as John described it – they sometimes made discoveries.

> It is thrilling if you suddenly find something, and say, 'I've just read this poem by Hardy which I've never understood or liked before' [Lady Wilson added]. He's very fond of Hardy, because Hardy's poems are so strange. And one day John and I discussed a poem by Longfellow called 'The Children's Hour'. It describes that hour –
>
> > Between the dark and the daylight,
> >   When the night is beginning to lower,
> > Comes a pause in the day's occupations
> >   That is known as the Children's Hour.

Then the children creep down to the study to take the writer by sur-prise – 'Grave Alice and laughing Allegra And Edith with golden hair'.

> Do you think, O blue-eyed banditti
>   Because you have scaled the wall,
> Such an old moustache as I am
>   Is not a match for you all!
>
> I have you fast in my fortress,
>   And will not let you depart,
> But put you down into the dungeon
>   In the round-tower of my heart . . .[16]

'Such an old moustache as I am' – we thought it was such a funny phrase. But then I realized, when I read it in a book, that it was what Napoleon used to call his soldiers, 'Old Moustaches'.

Another poem about which John felt I'd made a discovery was John McCrae's 'In Flanders Fields' –

> In Flanders fields the poppies blow
> Between the crosses, row on row
>   That mark our place . . .
>
> We are the Dead – Short days ago
> We lived, felt dawn, saw sunset glow,
>   Loved and were loved, and now we lie
>   In Flanders fields.
>
> Take up our quarrel with the foe:
> To you from failing hands we throw
>   The torch; be yours to hold it high.
>   If ye break faith with us who die
> We shall not sleep, though poppies grow
>   In Flanders fields.[17]

Do you know, it wasn't until I'd known that poem by heart for years and read it over and over again, that I suddenly realized the significance of the last lines: which is, that poppies make people sleep. I told John. 'Isn't that exciting,' he said. We used to get so excited; it was almost like being drunk.[18]

The sense of intoxication in each other's company was disapprov-ingly noticed on one of their rare sorties in public. 'He had such an *infectious* laugh,' Lady Wilson said in an interview with Candida Lycett Green. 'We were once walking from the House of Lords along the Embankment past the Henry Moore statue and I said, "John, come and look at this building." It was covered in turrets and balconies and towers. Of course John knew all about it and how it was designed by two brothers and he described an imaginary conversation between them – "Well, that bit looks a bit plain, let's put another balcony on it," and we were craning our necks upwards and laughing. The policeman who walked by took us to be drunk and disorderly.'[19]

Such merriment was only one aspect of the friendship. What Mary Wilson found especially sympathetic in John was his admission that he was afraid of things. 'Most people wouldn't say, "That's very frightening" – but he does, which is very endearing. He suffers terrific guilt, too. I'm a great guilt-feeler as well; and what John really dislikes are the guilt-*givers*. We've talked a lot about that.'[20] Because Mary understood John's melancholy side, she became, as Candida writes, 'a gentle support which he knew he could always turn to'.[21] 'I . . . knew when he was worried about something,' she told Candida. 'He had this habit of putting his hand to his mouth and biting his knuckles.'[22] The friendship existed almost in isolation. In spite of their deepening rapport, neither found the other's friends very congenial. John once took Mary to dinner with John Osborne and Jill Bennett, 'but it didn't work'.[23] And John was not interested in politics. When Mary talked about somebody who had been to dinner at No. 10, he would say, 'Is he Left, darling?'[24] The only time he sent her a 'political' letter was in August 1969, after Harold Wilson sent British troops into Ulster following a week of sectarian violence. On 16 August John wrote to her:

I am sorry indeed that the Irish are so keen on drawing attention to themselves and are furious at not having been in the limelight for so long they have tempted the PM away from the Scillies [where the Wilsons spent their holidays].[25] If there's one thing nastier than a Belfast Presbyterian, it's a Belfast Catholic. When I was the UK press attaché in Dublin for a year in the war the true Nazis (other than the Nazi Embassy in Dublin and my opposite number there) were the Northern Irish Catholics, not de Valera's lot. It was up there the Nazis carried on their propaganda and used Catholic [?provocateurs] in Harland and Wolff's shipyard. 'Sure there's nothing to choose between them. It's a struggle of two imperialists. Let the best man win. Oi'm for Hitler meself. England's difficulty is Oireland's opportunity.' That was the sort of thing I used to hear, and it made me furious.

  Ulster is three equally divided groups: Church of Ireland landowners and old-fashioned Presbyterians and pro-England nice business people and anti-British, as well as the 26 counties and Irish Catholics, anti-everything and with all the worst jobs. Nothing will solve the Ulster problem short of mass transportation or a change of heart. Neither is likely. They love quarrelling.[26]

John encouraged Mary to read him her poems. In January 1968 he wrote to her: 'I am as certain as I am of stars in the sky that there is a lot of good poetry already written by you and more to be written. Somehow, you must be given self-confidence about it. Good poets are always shy of criticism or even of showing their poetry, for if it is good it is part of themselves, a newborn vulnerable baby when first written and a worn old bore years later but still part of one.'[27] He gave her tips on poetical tradecraft. In October 1969: 'A piece of advice when stuck with a poem you are writing. Read someone else's poem, preferably poems you like, even old favourites. When I'm up the spout in writing an article, I always turn to Hans Andersen to [*illegible*] my prose.'[28] Two months later: 'I don't think it matters having a lot of 1/2 finished poems to turn to when in the mood. Tennyson worked that way.'[29]

His encouragement was constant; but one of her poems he singled out for special praise. This was 'Mamzelle' which, he wrote, 'should be in all anthologies'. It was about a schoolgirl crush on a French mistress – the kind of feeling John had written about in his 'Myfanwy' poems. Mary told him who Mamzelle was: Geneviève Gérard Marchant, who had been her French teacher at Milton Mount College, Crawley, a school for Nonconformist ministers' daughters.[30] Two of the six stanzas run:

> My mouth is dry as she goes by –
> One curving line from foot to thigh –
> And, with unEnglish liberty
> Her bosom bounces, full and free;
> Pale skin, pink lips, a wide blue stare,
> Her page-boy fall of silky hair
> Swings on her shoulders like a bell;
>   O how I love Mamzelle!
>
> She cannot get her idioms right,
> She weeps for Paris in the night
> Or, in the tension of the Match
> She laughs when someone drops a catch!
> The other staff are not unkind
> But distant; she tries not to mind,
> And I would gladly go through Hell
>   Just to protect Mamzelle.[31]

John sent Mary early drafts of some of his poems, too. The Wilsons owned a painting of stormy seas by Julius Olsson RA. John bought an Olsson of a sunlit scene and wrote a poem about it. He sent the poem to Mary, with a note: 'What about this? I've just made it up. I got the picture from a dealer in Falmouth, Peter Jackson. It's not as big as yours

and it's bright sunlight and in a very 1920s frame with "dull gold".'[32]
He also sent her an early version of his poem 'The Last Laugh' –

> I made hay while the sun shone;
>   My work sold.
> Now if the harvest be over
>   And the world cold,
> Give me the strength to be grateful
>   As I lose hold.[33]

In a later flash of inspiration – the sort he claimed came 'from the
Management' (God) – John changed the penultimate line to 'Give me
the bonus of laughter'.[34]

In February 1968, Mary read John a poem she had written about
Fulbourn in Cambridgeshire, where she had lived from the age of five to
ten. She had total recall of that time, she told him, but did not remember
much of Diss, where she had been born. Her father was a Congregational
minister and they lived in the Manse. She wondered whether the house
was still standing, and whether the Mere, a large ornamental lake in the
middle of the town, was as she remembered it.[35] For his part, John
wanted to revisit Diss Church where the Tudor poet John Skelton had
been vicar for twenty-five years. Long before Ben Jonson became the first
official Laureate, Skelton had been created 'poet Laureate' by the universities of Oxford and Cambridge, an academic distinction. He wrote
Garlande of Laurell, a self-glorifying poem describing the crowning of
the author among the great poets of the world.

'Oh, Diss is a wonderful place,' John said. 'Why don't we go
there?'[36] They planned the train journey they would make, and that
evening John wrote the poem later published as 'A Mind's Journey to
Diss' – 'a mind's journey' because they had not yet made it.

> Dear Mary,
>   Yes, it will be bliss
> To go with you by train to Diss,
> Your walking shoes upon your feet;
> We'll meet, my sweet, at Liverpool Street.
> That levellers we may be reckoned
> Perhaps we'd better travel second;
> Or, lest reporters on us burst,
> Perhaps we'd better travel first.
> Above the chimney-pots we'll go
> Through Stepney, Stratford-atte-Bow
> And out to where the Essex marsh
> Is filled with houses new and harsh

> Till, Witham pass'd, the landscape yields
> On left and right to widening fields,
> Flint church-towers sparkling in the light,
> Black beams and weather-boarding white,
> Cricket-bat willows silvery-green
> And elmy hills with brooks between,
> Maltings and saltings, stack and quay
> And, somewhere near, the grey North Sea;
> Then further gentle undulations
> With lonelier and less frequent stations,
> Till in the dimmest place of all
> The train slows down into a crawl
> And stops in silence . . . Where is this?
> Dear Mary Wilson, this is Diss.[37]

When the poem was printed in *A Nip in the Air* (1974), one critic unkindly wondered where else Mrs Wilson might have worn her walking shoes, if not on her feet. Others teased John about the intimate tone of the lines. Robert Nye – never a Betjeman fan – wrote in *The Times*: 'Can our Poet Laureate really be asking the wife of our Prime Minister to accompany him on a railway trip to Diss, Norfolk, for an unspecified purpose? Diss is the Latin for hell, of course,[38] but that is no excuse. The poem . . . ends with a line to make the stuffed owl hoot: *Dear Mary Wilson, this is Diss*. It is all rather splendid and I await the denial from Downing Street.'[39]

The visit had in fact been made eighteen months after John's poem was written. In Diss, it took Mary a little while to get her bearings. Much had changed.

> But once we went up Frenze Road, where we had lived, I immediately rec-
> ognized the house. So we looked at that and then I said, 'It's going to be
> rather funny, because people are going to recognize you.' We went down
> into the town and some people in the offices of the newspaper saw John
> and rushed down and said, 'Sir John, are you visiting the town for any
> reason?' and he said, 'Oh, no.' And he engaged them in conversation while
> I slunk away. And then we had tea in a tea shop. There was a paragraph in
> the local paper – but nothing about me![40]

Mary mentioned the tea-shop interlude in the poem she wrote in reply to John's 'Mind's Journey', on their return.

> Dear John,
>   Yes it is perfect bliss
> To go with you by train to Diss!

Beneath a soft East Anglian rain
We chug across the ripening plain;
Moon-daisies and the standing hay –
We come to Diss on Market Day,
Where cloth-capped farmers sit around,
Their booted feet firm on the ground;
They talk of sheep, the price of corn;
We find the house where I was born;
How small it seems! for memory
Has played its usual trick on me.
The chapel where my father preached
May now, alas! only be reached
By plunging through the traffic's roar;
We go in by the Gothic door,
To find, within the vestry dim,
An old man who remembers him.
Now, as we stroll beside the Mere,
Reporters suddenly appear;
You draw a crowd of passers-by
Whilst *I* gaze blandly at the sky.
An oak-beamed refuge now we find –
The scones are good, the waitress kind –
Old ladies, drinking cups of tea,
Discuss their ailments cheerfully.
Across the window-ledge we lean
To look down on the busy scene,
And there among the booths below
Fat, jolly babies kick and crow
As, wheeled by mothers young and fair,
They jolt around the Market Square.
The church clock rings a warning chime
Just to remind us of the time;
We climb the hill as daylight fails,
The train comes panting up the rails,
And as the summer dusk comes down,
We travel slowly back to town.
What day could be more sweet than this,
Dear John – the day we came to Diss?[41]

The two poems were printed on facing pages in the *Sunday Times* colour magazine.[42] The next issue of the *Sunday Times* carried a letter from Mrs Barbara Laming of Eynsford, Kent: 'I thought Mary

Wilson's poem about Diss was much better than John Betjeman's. Perhaps she should be our next Poet Laureate.'[43]

In 1970, Sir Robert Lusty of Hutchinson brought out a collection of Mary Wilson's poems. Just before publication, he held a celebratory dinner-party at the Garrick Club, inviting, besides Mary Wilson, John; Lena Wickman, the glamorous London representative of the Swedish publishing house Bonnier; John Guest of Longman who later edited *The Best of Betjeman*; and Ogden Nash and his wife Frances who happened to be in London. 'It was a hilarious evening,' Lusty recalled, 'and in charge of the proceedings was Joan, then the Garrick's leading character-waitress and herself a poet of some enthusiasm, who had contributed a talk to the BBC on What Poetry Means to Me.'[44] Joan was renowned for having a Shakespearean tag to suit every occasion. (When a soufflé collapsed: 'O, what a fall was there!')[45] Lusty wrote in 1975:

> Now scattered far and wide are the verses composed that evening. Ogden fell heavily for Mary Wilson and wrote delightfully for her. Mary Wilson wrote a poem for him and John Betjeman distributed his favours. Joan the waitress went into a corner to compose a response to the tributes accorded her. Around midnight Mrs Wilson was delivered back to 10 Downing Street by Messrs Guest and Betjeman, and Ogden Nash expressed his conviction that there was not much wrong with this country.[46]

John read the proofs of Mary's poems. He warned her what to expect from the critics: 'People will be envious and humiliating, of course – but not *real* people.'[47] Some of the reviewers recognized the quality of the poems. Others wrote of 'doggerel' and 'naivety'. One comment that piqued her was, 'Of course, she has been inspired by the work of Sir John Betjeman.' She retorted: 'I have been writing poems since I was six!'[48] Hutchinsons sold 85,000 copies of the book.

The satirist John Wells, in his fortnightly 'Mrs Wilson's Diary' in *Private Eye*, persisted in ascribing to her absurdly jejune and schmaltzy verses. In the issue of 30 May 1975 he imagined her visiting the Chelsea Flower Show with John: the spoof diary entry was accompanied by a cartoon by Candida's old friend Willie Rushton.

> Oh Chelsea, famed for bud and bloom
>   For pensioners and buns
> Where now the fragrant roses loom
>   Athwart the rusting guns.
>
> Mecca of all green-fingered folk
>   In this last week of May

Where sweet old ladies pry and poke
  Beneath the blossoms gay.

O could we but for ever rove
  Within thy fragrant tents
And savour Nature's treasure trove
  Regardless of expense!

I have always loved the Chelsea Flower Show, so imagine my pleasure when
Harold accepted a delightful gold-embossed invitation to join Sir Monty
and Lady Fison[49] in the CBI Dig for Victory Tent on the opening day. I was
particularly delighted when Sir John Betjeman immediately agreed to
escort me, as I knew that Harold would be tied up talking shop with Sir
Monty and his colleagues. So we set off, on a lovely May morning, with
Mr Haines[50] at the wheel of his Mini, and myself, Harold and Lady

Forkbender[51] in the back. There was Sir John, waiting for us on the doorstep of his bijou artisan's cottage in Chelsea, a delightful lady passer-by brushing the collar of his coat and adjusting his floppy hat.

'Gosh, isn't this fun?' he panted as he clambered in to join us in the back of the vehicle, coming to rest, somewhat cautiously, on Harold's lap. Luckily we had not far to go, as I could see Harold was not wholly at ease trying to smoke his pipe with Britain's Premier Poet perched incongruously on top of him. Once through the wrought-iron gates, with the glorious scent of the flowers and the music of a military band drifting through the trees, we were in another world . . .

It is hard for me, even now, when I have rubbed shoulders with potentates and astronauts, to realise my good fortune in walking side by side with Sir John through massed banks of carnations. With his dignified gait and silver-topped walking-stick, doffing his panama right and left to the many people who recognized him from his performances on TV, he cut a distinguished figure, and I was delighted with his observations about the teeming life on every side. 'Gosh, Gladys,' he whispered, 'do look at the old lady in gloves. I bet she's come up for the day on the 8.40 stopping train from Stroud. Mrs Sniggs the Vicar's wife, glad to get away from the old boy for a bit. Lunch at Barker's, and then back on the 4.15.'

What a privilege to be vouchsafed this glimpse into the workings of the creative mind! . . .[52]

In real life, the friendship between Mary Wilson and John continued. When the Wilsons moved to Lord North Street, their next-door neighbour was Ava, Lady Waverley, a friend of John's. (He usually referred to her as 'Ava, Lady Quaverley'.) John unsuccessfully tried to persuade her to give up part of her garden to the Wilsons. Later, Lady Waverley said to Mary: 'Does your husband smoke his pipe in bed?' 'Sometimes, yes.' '*I can smell it through the wall*.'[53] Another day, John came to see Mary and knocked on the Wilsons' front door. Lady Waverley promptly appeared at *her* front door and hijacked him, insisting he should come in for a drink.[54]

The friendship between John and Mary lasted until his death; but their correspondence petered out, because in his last years of illness she very often visited him at Radnor Walk, so there was no need to write. In all, he wrote her seventy-five letters. Some were from Cloth Fair and Radnor Walk. He always sent her letters and postcards when on his travels – in Australia, Romania, Spain, Italy, Biarritz and Iceland. ('I loved Iceland,' he wrote, 'its scenery and people, its clear light, low shot at this time of year, its many mad-looking mountains, all shapes and colours, wide green meadows and golden-haired beautiful people who speak softly and gaze wonderingly or grimly at distant horizons we can't see in our myopia.')[55] Frequently he wrote from Cornwall: the correspondence shows just how often he was there with Elizabeth from the late 1960s onwards. Sometimes the tone was rapturous.

The hot smell of Nivea Cream on Brummy [Birmingham] limbs tanning in glorious June weather here, is more potent than thyme. The sea pinks are just over . . . The elders are creamy green, the sea is emerald with purple shadows . . . The blackbirds are in full song and the thrushes. A goshawk has been seen here . . .[56]

At other times a shadow falls across paradise:

When I first get down here, as now, I am stunned by the beauty of light and blossom, a pink Montana clematis in the porch, a wattle (mimosa) bigger than ever, the orchard going into bloom, high seas and high winds and I think, 'Oh, I'll write later. This is just absorbing.' But I don't write. I seem to be drying up except in the early morn after an early bed and not too much drink, and even then I get self-conscious and welcome any distraction. I know it's the same with you . . .[57]

And then there are days when depression engulfs him:

I did like getting your telephone call. Sometimes in Cornwall I feel trapped. I do now . . . I think we live in a Press state, run by gloom-casters – those school bullies who give the ITN TV news.[58]

In Cornwall, John and Elizabeth were near the Isles of Scilly, which the Wilsons regarded as their real home. (When Harold Wilson resigned as Prime Minister in 1976, John relayed to Mary a remark a taxi driver had made to him: 'He's all right. He can go to the Sicilies.')[59] In March 1970 John and Elizabeth took a helicopter trip to Tresco to visit the gardens there. (The Wilsons were in London.) John wrote to Mary:

We walked up the granite quay and through the gate after we had crossed that mysterious football pitch and there was that high shorn avenue up to Neptune and the peacocks in full splendour two thirds of the way up. The camellias are out, the scented heathers and the bushes that smell of curry and Eliz who knows all about shrubs and flowers was in heaven at all this sunlit beauty and so was I . . . It was for me a marvellous day and everywhere I thought of you and almost saw your ghost on the shore and down by the quay and in the little lanes back to the airport. I couldn't imagine you in Tresco Gardens. But I saw you going across to Bryher. God!

it was wonderful. It must keep you all sane and brave as you seem to have it as a hide-out. But I wouldn't like to live there for ever – certainly not on Tresco. Personalities are too strong. Like the Irish, the Cornish say what they think you want to hear, not what they mean . . .[60]

In spite of these reservations, John was to return to the Isles of Scilly, ten years later. This time, Mary Wilson would be there to greet him.*

* See Chapter 27, ' "... As I Lose Hold" '.

BACK TO AUSTRALIA

Off to Aussie this morn (DV).

Sir John Betjeman to the author, 14 September 1971

Penelope was in India when John wrote to her on 18 June 1971; the monsoon, he imagined, had started. John speculated that the cholera and riots in Bengal had delayed the mails, but he had received thirteen pages of her 'fascinatin doiary', photocopied for him by Jock Murray. Unfortunately John would miss Penelope's homecoming. On 14 September he was to fly to Australia again, this time with a BBC film unit. 'I am v. excited about Australia,' he wrote, '& have 3 films worked out. Tasmania, Sydney & Melbourne Cathedral, Brisbane & district.' He would be returning in early December via Chicago, 'where I am picking up a dollar or two reading moi verse'.[1]

On 7 July he wrote again to commiserate with her on hearing from 'Kneecoal' (Nicole Hornby) that Penelope had been bitten on the 'broadwoods' (legs) by poisonous insects. 'Ow orrible. What sort?' But the letter that began so lightly brought melancholy news: Maurice Bowra had died of a heart attack the Sunday before. 'Very sad for me. Not for him. He had a strong belief in the next life & in personal survival & often talked to me about it. He said we would meet our friends . . . He was looking forward to meeting [Adrian] Bishop . . . Oh God! you and I will miss him!'[2] The next day Ann Fleming drove John to Oxford to attend the private funeral with John Sparrow.

Sparrow wrote a lapidary epitaph on Bowra, later published in the *Times Literary Supplement*. It read almost as if it were translated from a Latin original. Sparrow thanked John for the help he had given in refining the verse by supplying alternative words ('eg "justly" in l.4'). John thought the valediction a brilliant exercise, at once the wittiest and the most moving of his friend's occasional poetry.

C. M. B.

Which of the two, when God and Maurice meet,
Will occupy – you ask – the judgment seat?
Sure, our old friend – each one of us replies –
Will justly dominate the Grand Assize,
Assume the sceptre and ascend the throne,
Trump the Last Trump, the loud Last Post postpone,
And claim the Almighty's thunder for his own.
Then, if his stern prerogative extends
To passing sentence on his sinful friends,
Thus shall we plead our cause at Heaven's high bar:
'Be merciful! you made us what we are;
Our jokes, our joys, our hopes, our hatreds too,
The outrageous things we do, or want to do –
How much of all of them we owe to you!
Send us to Hell or Heaven or where you will,
Provided only you'll be with us still;
Heaven, lacking you, too dull would be to bear,
And Hell will not be Hell if you are there.'[3]

On 14 July John wrote to Penelope, 'Maurice's death will leave Oxford empty & sad for hundreds of us.'[4] The words were similar to those he had used to describe the desolation he had felt when his childhood friends the Boumans had left Highgate to live abroad.[5] Bowra's death reminded John of his own mortality: more than anyone, he had been the moulder of his youthful self. John's sixty-fifth birthday was near. Five days before it, on 23 August, he wrote to Penelope again. 'Oi am off to a party at No. 50 [Albemarle Street] to meet Austry lyon booksellers, v useful for my forthcoming films in Aussieland.' He was doleful that he would not be seeing her until the end of the year – 'it is sooch a long time away what with Austry lya.' He added 'If the Powlie [Paul Betjeman] is willing to see me I will tell it when I go back by USA but as it doesn't write, it is hard to get in touch with it.'[6] He sent love from Archie the teddy bear and Jumbo. As the date for embarkation came closer, John was markedly less enthusiastic about the Australian trip. Optimism gave way to a chilling of the feet. 'Oi am ter leave Sept 14,' he wrote on 12 August, 'oonless oi can put it off.'[7]

On the morning of his departure he found time to send me a letter of thanks for a book. The letter was in his most extravagant *art nouveau* lettering and ended:

MY ELDEST GRAND DAUGHTER [Lucy Lycett Green] FELL OUT OF
A TREE ON SUN MORN & IS BADLY INJURED IN PADDINGTON

HOSPITAL HENCE CHANGE OF MOOD & PEN ♡ OFF TO AUSSIE
THIS MORN (DV) c/o FISHER, ABC 145 ELIZABETH ST GPO BOX
487 SYDNEY NSW 2001 AUSTRALIA LOVE FROM
JOHN B
ART LETTERER &
LOITERER & LOVER[8]

The 1971 tour of Australia was to be altogether a more organized visit than the one of ten years before. This time John had the benefit of briefings and introductions from two Australian friends living in London: Barry Humphries, whose stage impersonations of 'Edna Everage' were soon to be a West End hit, and Frank Tait, Lady Elizabeth Cavendish's next-door neighbour in Chelsea. Tait introduced John to Guilford Bell of South Yarra, one of the few modern architects John admired.[9] The British Embassy and consulates and the British Council were sent his itinerary. The airlines gave him the red-carpet treatment all the way. For John, at sixty-five, a little cosseting and ceremony were welcome. In 1961 he had still been a young man pretending to be old. Now he was an old man trying to recapture his youth. There was a touch of senescent wistfulness in the commentary he made in Brisbane: 'How well I remember ten years ago what fun it used to be careering down the hill by tram past the Custom House with its crisp carved Corinthian capitals of local stone . . .'[10]

Not that the 1971 trip was devoid of fun. John was delighted that the producer in charge was Margaret McCall, who had already worked with him on the *Four with Betjeman* series that had included the film on Bedford Park.* She was the kind of dominant, vivacious woman he responded best to. The film crew called her 'Big Marge' (she was five foot eight inches tall) and recorded a version of the Shirelles' 1961 pop song 'Big John', dubbing in the word 'Marge' throughout.[11] As it happened, her father was Australian, though the family had emigrated from Australia to California where he became a well-known Congregational minister, 'McCall of Berkeley'. She trained as an actress at Northwestern University, then came to RADA in London where she met her future husband Philip Broadley, later a television scriptwriter. McCall decided she wanted to get into directing and producing. 'I pulled a few rather delicate strings. But mostly I was very clever. Because I could always get the person that nobody else could get, you know? I knew that if I could say, "I've got Robert Graves," I would be given the programme to make. I spent a lot of money of

---

* See Chapter 11, 'The Battle of Bedford Park'.

Philip's to go to them, went to Majorca and found that Graves loved having his own poetry recited to him. About the programme, Graves kept on saying no no no no; but I kept quietly at it and eventually he said yes. He was coming back here for an operation and he agreed.'[12] She made programmes on Graves, Lawrence Durrell and Graham Sutherland. Durrell's biographer writes that the novelist 'was power-fully attracted to her'. She accompanied him on his travels, but refused to be booked into the Shelbourne Hotel in Dublin as 'Mrs Durrell' and the two split up because 'she would not have him on his terms'.[13]

McCall had had little formal training. 'But before I even went in I was watching the television screen like mad; and one does get timing from the theatre. I just kept my ears flapping because I was fascinated. And when I went in first I kept asking questions, like "What is CSO?" – colour separation. As a director I was never content to leave shots to the cameramen. I was always looking through the viewfinder. They used to be furious. With the energy of youth I thought I knew better than they did – and I did.'[14] Eventually the BBC put her on a training course; David Attenborough gave her a staff job and she was entrusted with *Four with Betjeman*.

In some ways, she thought, John and Robert Graves were similar. 'They both had this very fey quality which went well beyond intellect. Graves used to show me where the fairies lived underneath the trees – and mean it. John *almost* did that.'[15] But in other ways John was quite different from the arts celebrities she had filmed before.

> John was a natural. The camera liked him. A natural is not easy to find; and that's why I got into the habit, with the others, of trying to question them about something they did not know I was going to question them about, to make them *think* – they were not natural otherwise. But it was a very bad thing to do with John. He liked to be forewarned of the ques-tions. Where we were going to; what we were going to see; what he was going to say.[16]

Julian Jebb was also directing part of the series, though his friend Tristram Powell thought that 'Working in television did not nurture his abilities, which were literary and critical rather than what is loosely called creative.'[17] Jebb had got on well with John when making the film about the Edgware Road in 1967[18] and the one about Tennyson on the Isle of Wight and in Lincolnshire.[19] He had also made a television film about Dieppe with Barry Humphries, with whom Margaret McCall thought he was 'madly in love'.[20]

The film-makers had Lady Elizabeth Cavendish to contend with as well as John. He had insisted that it be written into his contract that the BBC should pay for her to accompany him on the tour. Margaret McCall remembered:

> The first time I was introduced to this enormous and very healthy-looking lady, John said, 'Oh, look at poor Feeble! Look at those little wrists! You know, she can't carry anything' – all this caper. I liked her very much: and without her John, being a little boy, couldn't have gone through with it. She took care of him, completely. She told him what to do and what not to do. She cooked terrible dinners – pieces of dried toast. And, after we came back, when John wanted to give Philip a book about Greece, she didn't want him to give it away. She ruled John's life.[21]

To make the long outward journey less gruelling for John, 'stopovers' were arranged at Teheran and Bangkok. In Teheran McCall noticed for the first time his 'chameleon' nature. 'His fear I always remember and – the other side of the coin – he would be very much braver than we were.'

> When we got to Teheran, John was terrified, with all these native people around, coming out of a crowded station. He was quivering and didn't know what to do. Got him into a taxi, drove through the very busy streets and got him into a crash where people were out drawing their guns rapidly – and he loved it! Loved it and it was very dangerous.
> We stayed at a very nice hotel there. That was my first introduction to really good caviar. John and I sat outside on the lawns having caviar and Feeble went around, as she would – very adventurous lady – seeing what Teheran was like. Came back and swept John and me up and said, 'We've got to go into all the bazaars.' And the only way to get there . . . there weren't any taxis, the way you do it in Teheran is to jump on the back of an empty cart and go as far as you want and jump off. And to see John – little fat John – doing that! He *did* it – and again there was no fear – and enjoyed it, loved it. And this has always been incredible to me, that he had this double nature: this fear that went right through his life, maybe cowardice, maybe not cowardice, it doesn't matter, but sensitivity; and, then, suddenly pushing forward where nobody else would dare to tread.[22]

In Bangkok there was another splendid hotel. Because she was Princess Margaret's lady-in-waiting, Lady Elizabeth was given the royal suite, with large gilt lions outside it. 'But John immediately took it over and kicked her out,' Margaret McCall remembered.[23] McCall herself got 'Bangkok tummy' by drinking a glass of water with ice in it. Her illness caused an embarrassing incident at the beginning of the Australian tour.

When you get Bangkok tummy it isn't very funny. I was wretched with it and apparently I forgot that when John and Feeble got to Australia they were supposed to have a full reception from the Governor-General, a grand reception – white gloves, the lot. And somehow the information had been given to *me*. It should never have been given to me because I was producing – something quite different. Anyway, I forgot. And they all turned out in Sydney – pipe bands, champagne – and John wasn't there. Both of them were very nice about it.[24]

Margaret McCall had decided to begin filming in the north of the country and then to move southwards, ending in Tasmania, where Julian Jebb would be allowed to make the last film. John and the team drove to a desert place in Queensland called Charters Towers, almost in the outback.

I hadn't worked with John that much [Margaret McCall said] and I still, at this stage, thought that the best way of doing it was not to tell him exactly what was going to happen, so that you would get, not the set answer, but the look of trying to find his own answer. Spontaneity, more expression. Of course he was such a professional, I didn't need to do that.

On this first opening, out he came with Feeble to this goldrush town of Charters Towers – it was right off the tourist beat – and met me at what were the ruins of something or other. And he wouldn't come out of the car, he was so terrified. He was jittery – 'I don't know what all this is about; I can't do it.' And Julian Jebb – later John gave him hell but they were still friends at that point – told him, 'Now John, just remember how you've started so many programmes. "Now, where am I?" are your opening words, and after that you are going to be quite calm.' It was like a hypnotist. The crew were waiting around, the lighting people and so on. And finally he emerged from the car and started, 'Now, where am I?' and off he went.[25]

The ruin was the iron skeleton of the old Charters Towers gold exchange, which had once had a roof of stained glass. 'Where on earth is this?' John asked, standing in the centre of the former building in a white hat, blue flowered shirt and grey slacks. 'This is the stock exchange, the gold stock exchange, of Charters Towers. And in the boom years of the 1880s and '90s, this place was crowded.'[26]

There was another anxious moment in Charters Towers. 'It was a sort of shanty town,' said McCall, 'and there was one pub, a rickety pub. And I said, "I want to film you, John, going into that pub, and inside that pub." He shuddered. However, he played the game – he went in, terrified because here were all these pretty rough Australians in the outback drinking their beer. Very shortly, he had them in his hand. They were laughing and joking, and I think we all drank quite a bit.'[27]

The film went on to show the straw-hatted boys of the public school Thornburgh College. 'These great schools', John said, 'were once the mansions of millionaires of the gold-rush days.'[28] And then came the sequence that everyone remembers from John's Australian films. He is waddling along the passages of a suburban house.

Australian houses inside, you see, are very like many English houses: flowered carpet in the hall; china ducks on the wall; a hatstand and flowers on it; and then round the corner here's a room we all sometimes have to use: beautifully decorated – pale mauve, an embroidered seat and lace curtains. All very like an English house; EXCEPT, you see, up there . . . a tarantula spider.[29]

'Some people think we hired the tarantula from a zoo,' Margaret McCall said. 'But we didn't. It was just there. Quite harmless. It had been sitting there for several years. The cameraman gave it a tiny prod but it didn't do anything except raise its ugly head.'[30] The 'tarantula in the loo' image entered the visual repertoire of advertising agents. Twenty years after John's film was shown, an advertisement for Carling lager showed roistering Australians in a bar telling an Englishman the way to the outside lavatory and guffawing at the thought of the tarantula which awaits him. The pommie calmly puts the spider in a box, comes back into the bar with it, frightens them all away, and drinks a leisurely lager.

In John's film, the *coup de théâtre* with the tarantula was followed by another in the deserted Venus Crushing Mill at Charters Towers. To this mill, built in 1872, prospectors had brought their quartz to be pounded by enormous hammers into dust from which they hoped to extract gold. The wind flapping a piece of tin brought into John's mind 'what it would be like if all the hammers were pounding' – and the BBC sound-effects department supplied the missing din, giving John the air of Prospero conjuring up a storm.

From Charters Towers, he moved on to Camden Park, New South Wales, the first of Australia's 'stately homes' to appear in the programmes. 'Before it was gold, it was wool . . . White man's wealth in New South Wales is symbolized by Camden Park.'[31] The serious history of the house was covered, but first there was a music-hall double-take on the verandah. John pointed with horror to a centipede on the ground; then picked it up and revealed it was 'of rubber, from Hong Kong'.[32] The house had been built in the 1830s by John

MacArthur, a soldier who retired as a settler and introduced Merino sheep to the region. 'He was a man of taste as well as a farmer,' John judged from the well-filled library and the well-designed dining-room. 'And if you're Yours Truly and you're in a dining-room, what is the first thing you think of? Wine.'[33] John led the way down to the cellars. 'The family had their own vineyard. One thing I can assure you about Australian wine. Since I've been down under I've drunk a lot of it, and some of it, drunk here in Australia, is really *magnificent*.'[34] John's flushed face and his slightly muffing his lines in this passage suggest that he had been liberally sampling the Camden Park vintages.

In 1971 John was for the first time showing signs of infirmity. In fact these were the first symptoms of the Parkinson's Disease which blighted his last years and enforced the old-mannishness he had some-times adopted as a pose. 'It was a lot of work for one man,' said Margaret McCall, 'and, what I've never forgiven myself for, I never knew he had Parkinson's Disease. Sometimes I used to see him walking like an old man and I'd think, "Why does he do this to me?"'[35] It was now clear that walking any distance really did tax him. In the rest of the first film he travelled by train and by tram – his favourite means of transport. The train ran from Melbourne to Bendigo, fol-lowing the pioneer trail to gold. 'You see the real country from [the train],' John commented as he rode through 'Australian Impressionist' scenery, 'not those awful petrol advertisements which ruin the roads.'[36] The former copywriter of Shell petrol posters might have felt a twinge of guilt as he delivered that line.

Arrived in Bendigo, John said, 'Now let's see the city that gold built – by tram.' He waved in the direction of 'splendiferous and prominent public buildings'.

It was staying in one of those verandah'd hotels that Dame Nellie Melba was kept awake all night by the Windsor chimes in the post office tower. In deference to her they were silenced at 11 pm and the custom has con-tinued ever since.[37]

John was not only nostalgic about the past; he was also nostalgic about the present, by anticipation. As the tram trundled to its ter-minus he intoned: 'By the time this film comes out the trams will all too probably have been scrapped from the streets of Bendigo.'[38]

On 29 September, John wrote to Candida from Sydney:

Darling Wibz,

I am gradually thawing and growing less dotty. We are all four very happy because Australian wine is so good. So is Australian architecture right through to Moderne and real contemp[orary]. I am ravished by it and you will be. The hotels are awful. The one at Bendigo smelt of cats and my pillow smelt of pipe smoke. The motels, though they are all 'do it yourself', are good. Rupert's white hat and suits are v[ery] good. So far it has been v[ery] cold in Melbourne and Tazzie [Tasmania] and this suits me. Brizzie will be sweltering. I've bought a lovely rubber centipede. I often think of poor fallen Lucy and hope she is okay . . . [Lucy recovered.] Julian is our life and soul, Eliz[abeth] organises us all and supports me when I lose my balance (physically) and Margaret McCall is highly efficient and kind and calm. We all get on v[ery] well and drink a lot . . . Have seen a lot of Barry H[umphries] and his two wives. Start filming in N[orth] Queensland among snakes and scorpions next week . . .[39]

Though John found the work tiring, he was still ready for a bibulous dinner and dancing in the evening, after a rest in his hotel room.

The assistant cameraman knew all about wine [Margaret McCall remembered] – you know how John loved wine. That and oysters. He couldn't get enough oysters. So every night he and the crew and I had a trestle table of different wines to taste. Well, we got to some restaurant, and brought along this very nice wine to our table to taste. And the proprietor said, 'We don't allow people to bring wine in here. We have our own wine and we will not have people bringing wine in here.' John was furious. He didn't say much, he just stood up and led us all away. He would not have it, you see: this nice boy, being insulted, who'd given us so much joy. John was livid.

Also, dancing with John was an emotional experience. He danced very well. Most fat men do, I find – they're very light on their toes. And of course he enjoyed it, and one more or less bounced off his stomach. And Julian Jebb would take off on his own and do his own pirouettes and improvisations.[40]

The second film, entitled 'Pomp and Circumstance', blended Melbourne and Sydney. It began staidly with John walking through the entrance colonnade of the Parliament House of the State of Victoria in Melbourne. To him this building, finished in the 1890s, symbolized Melbourne – 'calm, self-assured, dignified; good clubs, stables full of good horses; shops and fashion; imperial prosperity'.[41] Through the columns he pointed out the Princess Theatre 'where many a time no doubt Dame Nellie Melba sang'. So far the film was the kind of architectural tour that any competent guide could have presented. But then John launched into one of the histrionic interludes in which he made the dry stones live.

Peter Kerr or Carr as he probably called himself in Scotland, which he came from, Peter Kerr did the style and the decoration. Now there's an interesting thing about him. He started work articled to an architect called Archibald Simpson in Aberdeen, and then he went and worked at Dunrobin Castle in Scotland. And there he met Sir Charles Barry, the great architect of the Houses of Parliament in Westminster; and Sir Charles Barry was at heart a classical man – he liked the Greek and Roman styles. And I can imagine that dear old thing saying in his London voice to young Peter, 'Now look 'ere my boy, if you're going out to Australia and you get the chance to build some houses of parliament, don't you use that Gothic style. *You use the classic.* And by Jove, he did – full-blooded Roman Corinthian, look at it.'[42]

'My boy' is how John's father habitually addressed him, and, according to Penelope, Ernest Betjeman had a cockney accent.[43] It is possible that John was imitating him in his Barry impersonation, as he had imitated him long before in his *Artsenkrafts* play at Oxford.[44]

Later in the film, John visited Rouse Hill House, a verandahed mansion eight miles south-east of Windsor, New South Wales, on the road to Parramatta. 'From about the 1820s until today the Rouse family and its descendants have lived in this house. All the Victorian bric-à-brac has been left undisturbed since it was first collected by Hannah Rouse on her trips abroad in the '60s and and '70s.' John led the way into Hannah's bedroom. 'Her picture remains on the mantelpiece: which is it? The lower one? No, the top one.'[45] The teasing question was one of John's techniques for holding the viewer's interest.

In Melbourne he wandered through the Botanical Gardens, laid out by William Gilfoyle, a landscape gardener of Queen Victoria's reign. 'His motto is said to have been, "There's always something pleasant round the corner." Come and look.'[46] The Block Arcade in Melbourne inspired him to a piece of vaudeville verse –

> Below this dome fate and fashion meet
> In marvellous Melbourne, safe from rain and heat.[47]

The date of the Arcade is 1891, but John pointed out that a similar structure in England would more probably date from about 1871. All over Australia he noticed this 'time-lag' in architecture. Showing a barracks near Sydney, he commented: 'If it were in England you'd say it was about 1820; but as a matter of fact it's about 1848. The architect, a Royal Engineer, Colonel Barney, used the local Sydney sandstone.'[48] And here John homed in on one of the piquant details that enlivened all his television work: 'The soldiers used the sandstone for sharpening their sabres and bayonets' – he indicated the scars in the stone.[49]

From the barracks, the team plunged into what John called the heart of Sydney. 'The Anzac Memorial dominates the vista. Perhaps a bit too strong for today – a bit too reminiscent of Lalique and of Raemakers cartoons[50] and of the paintings of Frank Brangwyn.'[51] Here is another trait of John's television persona: he makes no concession to popular taste. The average viewer might well be familiar with the Art Deco shapes of Lalique glass, but would be unlikely to have encountered a Raemakers cartoon of the First World War or a Brangwyn painting. It was part of John's appeal that he did not talk down to his audience; rather as Irving Berlin and Jerome Kern introduced into their popular songs the most subtle note-transitions and modulations, he relied on the viewers to catch the sense of his recherché comparisons.

The film ended inside the Memorial, with the sculptures of the Manxman Reyner Hoff. 'Inside, emotion: the idea here was to give an impression of the horror of war. A naked Anzac soldier lies stretched on a shield and sword . . . Incised in the pavement are these words: "DON'T SPEAK: CONTEMPLATE." '[52] John told Julian Jebb that he thought that would be a good motto for a television film-maker: as far as possible, architecture, landscape and works of art should be allowed to speak for themselves, not cluttered with gratuitous commentary.[53]

There was so much to see and show in Australia that the unit decided there would have to be four films, not three as John had originally envisaged. The third film was based in Brisbane and Sydney. 'Nobody told me that Brisbane is so beautiful a city,' John said in his commentary.[54] He pointed out the 'exuberant Frenchified' Parliament House; the *art nouveau* Presbyterian church of St Andrew ('how dashing for its date!') and St John's Cathedral, designed by John Loughborough Pearson, the architect of Truro Cathedral in Cornwall, and completed by his son, Frank Loughborough Pearson. 'The cathedral in what he called "Brizzie", he was agog to do that,' Margaret McCall remembered. 'You can imagine what a job it was, lighting that interior. It took hours and poor little John was sitting there. I couldn't say, "Go off", because we needed him. He was so impatient, and once that got into his blood you couldn't do a thing with him. He still gave a very good performance in the cathedral. At least he couldn't drink while he was waiting in there – always a danger in other breaks in filming.'[55]

On 9 October John wrote to Candida, 'We are now in a sort of Montego Bay of N[orth] Queensland . . . The sea is grey and polluted-looking and huge things called sting wasps with tentacles as long as cricket pitches kill the surf bathers.'[56] On 14 October he wrote to her again, from Brisbane. 'I have huge mosquito bites. We've been doing a lot of filming in tropic islands of Cairns and Townsville. I saw a cassowary. Horned head. Black beak. Huge eyes. Black and blue feathers. Ten foot high. Terrifying. Julian talks to the Aussie crew in Aussie. They don't seem to mind and think he's married.'[57] (Jebb was homosexual.)[58]

From Brisbane there was another train ride to enjoy, on the narrow-gauge railway from Cairns to Kuranda, nine hundred miles north. 'He sat with the driver on this little choo-choo train and chattered away,' Margaret McCall remembered. 'Oh, he loved it; he took over the driving part of the way.'[59] The railway – originally steam but by 1971 diesel – was built in the 1880s to bring down minerals and timber from the mountains to the port of Cairns. 'Built by Italians and Irish, buried beside the track,' John said as the train rattled on. 'And now it's a tourist attraction. And let's be attracted tourists.'[60]

From the railway he looked down on the Barren Falls, from which McCall cut deftly to the EI Alamein Fountain in Sydney, with linking words from John: 'How Australians love the water! What tricks they like to play with it!'[61] And thence to the Sydney Opera House, poetically described by John as 'a regatta in full flight arrested at the water's edge'.[62]

On 17 October he wrote to Mary Wilson.

We have moved into a flat overlooking Sydney harbour. Very beautiful but very hot and noisy kiddiz on the same floor. Queensland was TERRIFIC. How very good Alan Moorehead is on Captain Cook in the Pacific with *Fatal Impact*. The Whites should never have come here. There's not such a thing as progress. Better a trodden path from hut to hut and the rattle-snake bites cured by a witch-doctor.

If I were young, I *think* I would settle out here. People are all so nice to each other. I can't get over it. I'm not of any consequence here and they're nice to me too even though I'm a 'Pom'.[63]

On the same day he also wrote to Candida: 'After the trials and mosquitoes of Q[ueens]land, I am feeling better and less full of self-pity.'[64] He had seen Eileen Ross-Williamson, widow of the man who had succeeded him as press attaché in Dublin in 1943.[65] Her flat was hung with John Piper paintings of Northamptonshire and of Welsh mountains.[66]

Today [John added] I've got to film an ultra-modern house with glass walls in a jungle suburb. All the pictures are mobiles and so are the kiddiz' toys. You can't tell one from t'other. I *think* I can make myself like it. On Sunday next we film the State Cinema here in full colour – it is

Mexican–Jacobean with a picture gallery and a monkish parlour and melodious organ – tiptop 1927.[67]

In the resulting film, John said of the Cinema (actually built in 1929 to the designs of Henry Eli White), 'I think it must be the most luxurious, lavish and splendid super-cinema left in the world.'[68] Barry Humphries had tipped him off about the surprise of the cinema's art gallery – 'the last thing you'd expect to find in a super-cinema', John said. It was full of Australian Impressionist paintings.

The film ended on a sour note, with John's abhorring the city's modern tower blocks. 'As we sail past Government House in Sydney Harbour, that little 1840 castle in its landscaped park, its towers and turrets seem sadly to say, "We're sorry, we didn't know all that was going to happen." '[69]

John dreaded making the Tasmanian sequences because Julian Jebb was to direct them, and Jebb had 'got across' him. Margaret McCall remembered:

Julian Jebb – 'JJ' we called him – was putting on an act and John said he didn't do his job properly – didn't get the reference books John wanted, and so on. And with Feeble's backing John got up a great hatred against poor Julian, who was a very sensitive little creature.[70] I had told Julian before we left London that he could have the last film to direct, which was Hobart, Tasmania. But, to make matters worse, the crew were very fond of me and not at all fond of Julian, because Julian threw his weight around. He'd say to an experienced cameraman, 'We can't use you unless I see what work you've done' – can you imagine what the reaction to that was? And he danced a jig when we came off the 'plane; and John of all people didn't want to be obvious. Julian was pretending to be something he wasn't. He wasn't all that sincere, he was playing a game.

So when the time came for Hobart . . . What I had been used to doing with John was knocking on his door and sometimes he was running round *tout nudité*, giggling away; and Feeble was pretending that she was horror-struck when she wasn't. So come Hobart, little Julian goes and knocks on his door, the door opens and John shouts 'GO AWAY! GO AWAY! GET OUT OF IT!' and bangs the door. So I found Julian walking by the river, ready to commit suicide. John's door was still closed so I went and saw Feeble. '*What*', I said, 'is going on? I promised JJ that he could do this, and I see no reason why he shouldn't. He's been okay as far as I'm concerned.' And she, being a magistrate, which made her very fair, went over to my side: 'Right, then he must do it.' And I went up in her estimation because I stood up against her, and against John too, of course. And John immediately gave in. He did what madam said he would do. I think the whole episode was caused not just by his dislike of Julian; it was also that he had got used to working with me.[71]

Barry Humphries encountered the group and later gave his assessment of the fraught situation.

I happened to be in Melbourne and John came to see me at the Windsor Hotel, where I was discussing the script of *Barry Mackenzie* with Bruce Beresford.[72] Well, when John arrived, we both realized that he was falling-over drunk. I was thinking, 'There isn't going to be a film.' John was merry, but it was so disturbing. And Jebb was not much better. Like John, he was drinking a lot and mixing it with pills. So you'd got a producer and a presenter who were both unfit for work. John wasn't well enough. And, when he got to Tasmania, he was terribly depressed by the atmosphere of the place. Oh, and there they took on board another depressive, a Tasmanian producer who later committed suicide – so that made three of them. And eventually a film had just to be cobbled together. And there was more. There was an inevitable loss of privacy in making a film with a small group of people travelling together. John was homesick. There was a 'territory' thing between Big Marge and Jebb. Elizabeth didn't like Jebb's assumption of intimacy with John; his extreme preciousness got on her nerves, too. And she was, frankly, getting worried about John, and wondering how much more he could take. So she took it out on Jebb.[73]

Jebb was allowed to make the Tasmanian film. John, exhausted by the months of filming, was not at his most tractable, but McCall, as producer of the series, was present all the time and was able to cushion him against Jebb's occasional bumptiousness. '*And* I had to edit Julian's footage severely,' she said. 'But Julian did get some unusual shots.'[74]

I think Hobart has a horrifying atmosphere. It was where all those convicts were tortured. And of course it had the same effect on John as it had on me. We went into the cells. John was again a-quiver and of course Julian Jebb insisted that we went into every last cell. So that worked on his fear. Hobart has what's called vibrations. Not nice. Julian shot down into where they tried to get away, these poor souls. But the best shot Julian ever took of John, which started the Tasmanian film, was John in the rain forest with an English umbrella over him. It was such a lovely contrast. Julian had little brilliances like that.[75]

John visited more stately homes in Tasmania than in the whole of the rest of Australia; but he did not play down the horrors of Hobart. Ironically quoting the old advertisements for 'the heart-shaped island of allure', he said, 'It was a dump for undesirables, this beautiful island.' At Point Pure 'boys from Fagin's kitchen were reformed. And this is the Island of the Dead. Only prison officers had headstones.' In the deaf and dumb cell, prisoners were kept away from all light and sound by four doors. 'Despite the beauty of Port Arthur[76] . . . I still seem to hear above the waves and the whisper of the leaves groans of chain-gangs and the cries of the flogged.'[77]

With relief, John turned from convicts to architecture. 'Crowning all, St John's Church of England, 1825. Charming Colonial Gothic *outside*; but *inside* . . . !'[78] He pursed his mouth like a parrot's beak and nodded mysteriously. Inside was flamboyant restoration work by a Kendal man, Alec North. 'He invented his own kind of Gothic in the 1890s, with a strong hint of *art nouveau* about it. I mean, look at that capital: gum leaves and gum nuts and those are ring-tailed possums.'[79] As a further example of North's style John showed Holy Trinity, Launceston, Tasmania. 'Now you can't call that a slavish copy of the Middle Ages, can you? Good on yer, North.'[80]

From the grotesqueries of North's churches, John and Jebb moved on to three classical Tasmanian mansions: Quamby, a long, low white bungalow built by the political prisoner Richard Dry whose son became Governor of Tasmania; Panshanger ('I wonder why I like it so much . . . Is it the colour of the stone, which is like pale toast? I think it's one of the most beautiful houses anywhere');[81] and Woolmers, still in the hands of the Archer family who had built the house in 1817. Inside Woolmers, John commented how dark the Victorian dining-room must have been in the days of candles. A candelabrum of oil lights had been installed in the 1890s; gasoliers in the 1920s. John added in his archest manner: 'Any other light here comes from two newly created Dames: Dame Electricity and Dame Television.'[82] In the sombre room he staged his last grand *coup de théâtre* of the series.

> Let's see what this room would look like in the original glimmer of the lights of Woolmers.
> *Turn down the gas.*
> *Lower the lamps.*
> *Snuff out the candles.*[83]

As the last lights were extinguished the house was left in darkness. If in the Venus Crushing Mill John was Prospero, here he was Othello – 'Put out the light, and then put out the light.'

The Tasmanian film ended with a passionate tirade against commercialization.

This is Frederick McCubbins's painting *Lost in the Bush*. There is a new bush. The trees are pylons. The leaves are direction-signs. The creepers are wires. The hills are office blocks and flats. The wild beasts are motor cars, with their feeding places. The mist is oil fumes. The scent is diesel. The new bush has reached to the ends of the earth. It has reached Tasmania.[84]

During the last three weeks of filming, according to Margaret McCall, John could not wait to get back to England. On the interminable journey home he amused himself by writing a poem, which was published in *A Nip in the Air* (1974).

Back from Australia

Cocooned in Time, at this inhuman height,
   The packaged food tastes neutrally of clay.
   We never seem to catch the running day
But travel on in everlasting night
With all the chic accoutrements of flight:
   Lotions and essences in neat array
   And yet another plastic cup and tray.
'Thank you so much. Oh no, I'm quite all right.'

At home in Cornwall hurrying autumn skies
   Leave Bray Hill barren, Stepper jutting bare,
     And hold the moon above the sea-wet sand.
The very last of late September dies
   In frosty silence and the hills declare
     How vast the sky is, looked at from the land.[85]

It was, in fact, December, not September, when Lady Elizabeth and John arrived back in England. Julian Jebb was home by 6 December, on which day he telephoned his great friend Frances Partridge, the Bloomsbury survivor, writer and diarist.[86] A week later, he was meant to join her at a party at the Reform Club, 'but after one or two telephone calls [Partridge wrote] I realised he was in dire distress, and drove round to see him'.

I think he was suffering from sheer understandable exhaustion after his Australian tour. But he had the desperate person's desire to press to extremes, to tell me he was 'ill', feeling suicidal. His use of 'ill' I've long ago noticed is an emergency exit whether for himself or others; but I was saddened by his haunted expression, and large tragic eyes, and tried to give sensible advice while dreading being too much of a hospital nurse or schoolmistress.[87]

That year, Frances Partridge spent Christmas with the David Cecils at Cranborne, Dorset.[88] On Christmas Eve they all went to dinner with 'the Trees, Andrew Devonshire's handsome sister and her flashy husband (who appeared in a bright cherry-coloured velvet evening suit, bulky and genial)'.[89] Partridge added: 'Elizabeth Cavendish, Betjeman's "Feeble", was also there. David [Cecil] has twigged that there were difficulties in Australia. I was interested that the forceful Feeble said she had been knocked out for three weeks by the thirty-four-hour flight home.'[90] If Elizabeth and Jebb, respectively twenty and twenty-eight years younger than John, and fitter than he, were exhausted, how much more so must he have been.

The Australia films were shown on British television ten months later, in an order different from that in which they had been shot. 'Oi'm glad you liked the Aussieland films,' John wrote to Penelope on 9 October 1973. 'Oi loiked the last oone best, about the State Cinema [*sic*, for Theatre], Sydney and Brisbane.'[91] Before the public screening, a private one was organized for the Prince of Wales, who loved Australia, and for Princess Margaret, who was about to go there for the first time. After the film show there was a dinner. Among those invited was (Sir) John Drummond, who had persuaded the Australian Broadcasting Corporation to put up some money to help the BBC make the films. He wrote:

The other guests were Lord Snowdon, Elizabeth's mother, the Dowager Duchess of Devonshire, the writer and diarist James Lees-Milne and his formidable wife Alvilde, Patrick Garland, who like me had Australian connections, and his then girlfriend, Jenny Agutter. We dined in a top-floor room at Rules in Maiden Lane, chosen by John – perhaps not entirely tactfully, because Edward VII used to entertain his girlfriends there. At one moment four of us trooped in procession through the crowded restaurant to the gents. I could sense people saying to each other, 'The Prince of Wales, Lord Snowdon, John Betjeman, and who's that with them?' 'He must be the private detective,' I heard a woman say. The evening culminated in a spectacular row between Princess Margaret and Lord Snowdon, after which he refused to leave and she had to be driven back to Kensington Palace in Patrick Garland's Mini. In fact we all trooped back and were there until two in the morning, since the Princess never seemed to tire. James Lees-Milne wrote of the occasion in his diary,[92] but better than that was the letter he wrote to John Betjeman, in which he said he found Princess Margaret 'very very very frightening but beautiful and succulent like Belgian buns'.[93]

THE CHURCH OF ENGLAND RAMBLERS

In one of the restaurants [John Betjeman] discovered in a town in Calabria the padrone was so pleased at our obvious appreciation of the food that he brought John a book to sign. John wrote not his name but that we were members of the Church of England Ramblers Association. The padrone took the book to the local lawyer, who was lunching at a table near to ours, hoping he would be able to decipher it. There was much mystification and shaking of heads and arguments, and we left before the riddle had been solved. Presumably it never was.

The Rev. H.A. Williams CR, *Some Day I'll Find You*, London 1982[1]

In November 1958 Edward Heath, as Chief Whip of the Conservative Government, arrived at No. 10 Downing Street for his morning meeting with Harold Macmillan.

'You look annoyed,' said the Prime Minister to the future Prime Minister.

'I *am* annoyed. You've made a Commie a bishop.'

Maintaining his reputation for unflappability, Macmillan looked only mildly surprised. Heath explained that Mervyn Stockwood, who had just been appointed to the Southwark see, was a red-hot radical and an outspoken critic of the Government. Macmillan thought for a moment. Then he said, 'Who is the diocesan in your constituency [Bexley]?'

'Chavasse of Rochester.'

Macmillan grinned. 'Oh, that's all right then. He's old. He'll die or retire soon and then I'll give you somebody you like.'[2] (Heath had only four years to wait. Chavasse died in 1962 and was replaced by the 'safe' David Say, who had been domestic chaplain to the Marquess of Salisbury and was later High Almoner to the Queen.)

Even a Labour prime minister might have thought twice before advancing Stockwood to the important see of Southwark. (And indeed, in 1974 a quarrel between Stockwood and Harold Wilson denied Stockwood the Archbishopric of York.) His capacity to provoke had not lessened since John had first met him at Cyril Tomkinson's table in Bristol in 1939.[3] Yet his beautiful resonant voice, his urbanity, wit, hard work and flair for making himself agreeable to people in high places, had all helped to propel him upwards in the church hierarchy, first as Vicar of St Matthew Moorfields, Bristol, next as an honorary canon of Bristol Cathedral and then, from 1955 to 1959, as Vicar of the University Church, Cambridge.

John and Stockwood had never lost touch, but Stockwood's Cambridge appointment, in particular, brought them together. Bishop Stockwood recalled:

> Simon Phipps [much later Bishop of Lincoln] was chaplain of Trinity then. He had grown up with the royal family – his father was a Gentleman Usher to the Queen. He was a close friend of Princess Margaret and was one of her advisers in the 'Townsend affair'.[4] And Lady Elizabeth Cavendish was the Princess's lady-in-waiting . . . John was Elizabeth's friend . . . you can see the whole set-up. Simon was a very dearly beloved friend of mine. Trinity had nominated me to be Vicar of the University Church, so I could go and eat at Trinity whenever I liked, and I saw a lot of Simon. And through him I saw a lot of Elizabeth and John.[5]

Simon Phipps was a cousin of John's friend, the mimic Joyce Grenfell, who was born a Phipps. His *Times* obituary in 2001 credited him with 'the same kind of wit and gentle humour as hers'.[6] In one of her wartime journals she described him as 'a nice creature, very civilized and rather sensitive'.[7] He had the unusual credential, for a future bishop, of having been president of the Cambridge Footlights. 'Gorgeously arrayed in female attire, he sang some very popular numbers, including "Botticelli Angel" and – curiously prophetic – "I wish I were a line in Crockford's".'[8] 'He was marvellously talented at organizing that sort of thing,' Stockwood said. 'And when I was Vicar of the University Church, it was a fun show – John Cleese and David Frost were with the Footlights, all those people.'[9]

> I can *see* John there, at my house in Cambridge, with Simon. It was quite a modest house. They hadn't had a vicar before at the University Church. It had always been a don at Trinity; that was one of the problems. All dons were in holy orders until about the 1870s. So they just looked after Great St Mary's from Trinity. Then, when the law changed and dons were allowed to marry, they depended on Trinity men of means, and that continued. They tried to get Charles Raven, who married a millionairess who died on her honeymoon. And so, for the first time in their lives they had

to find an ordinary clergyman, and they had to find a house for him. They found me, and put me in a nice house in Madingley Road – nothing pretentious.

And that is where the friendship with John developed. It had been, in my Bristol days, just a nice acquaintanceship . . . But it became a close companionship in the Cambridge days. And at that time I got John to lecture too. I used to get people of all sorts of persuasions to come and give lectures on a hundred and one things – the American and Russian ambassadors, for example, and scientists, people like Nevill Mott [then Cavendish Professor of Experimental Physics at Cambridge], the people who split the atom.[10]

The friends Stockwood helped to bring together were mainly bachelors. Two who became lasting friends of John and Elizabeth were Raymond Leppard, then a fellow of Trinity and lecturer in music, and the Rev. Harry Williams, Dean of Chapel at Trinity. In his earlier years, Williams had been regarded as a conservative theologian;[11] but now he was making a name as a revolutionary preacher, in sermons later gathered in his book *The True Wilderness*.[12] Penelope thought it disgraceful that he, a priest, abetted John – as she saw it – in his unfaithfulness to her.[13] Williams was outwardly a plump, worldly cleric with a sly wit much appreciated at high table and by John. But in a much later autobiography, *Some Day I'll Find You*, he described a searing mental breakdown and wrote with brave candour about his homosexuality and affairs with men.[14] He and Simon Phipps did not find their dog-collars too restricting: neither was the cartoonist's stereotype of a strait-laced vicar. When they spent a week together on Mykonos, Phipps wrote a verse on the back of a handbill –

> I saw Apollo's torso
> And a portion of his *morceaux*
> Which they'd hidden most discreetly in the grass.
> But the rest was rather bitty
> As his legs are in the Pitti
> While Lord Elgin had carried off his arse.[15]

Back in Cambridge, knowing the rhyme would amuse the then Master of Trinity, Lord Adrian, Williams recited it to him in the ante-chapel before Sunday Evensong. When the undergraduate organist suddenly stopped playing, the Dean of Chapel was heard bellowing '*arse!*', followed by Adrian's guffaw.[16]

The Stockwood–Williams circle in Cambridge also included Simon Stuart, the younger brother of Lord Castle Stewart;[17] Lord

Rossmore, a Trinity undergraduate with whom Stockwood stayed on fishing holidays in Ireland;[18] Julian Grenfell (later Lord Grenfell) of King's, president of the Cambridge Union in 1959; Graham Storey of Trinity Hall, the editor of Dickens's letters; and David Cobbold (now Lord Cobbold) of Knebworth, the Victorian Gothic house where Dickens had taken part in amateur theatricals. There were also three future suffragans of Stockwood's: John Robinson, a Trinity lecturer in divinity who was to shock the theological world in 1963 with his bestseller *Honest to God*; David Sheppard, an undergraduate at Trinity Hall, a future England cricket captain and Bishop of Liverpool; and Hugh Montefiore, Dean of Gonville and Caius College, who later provoked headlines and a rebuke from the Archbishop of Canterbury by suggesting that Christ might have been homosexual.[19] Though an Oxford man, Ned Sherrin, the television director and impresario, became one of the group after meeting Stockwood in a television debate on censorship.[20] John and Elizabeth fitted into this coterie, with its Church of England beliefs, its jokes, *bon vivant* tastes, spattering of titles and mixture of muscular Christianity and campness.

When Stockwood was appointed Bishop of Southwark – straight from the University Church at Cambridge – in November 1958, no bishop's house was available for him. 'The original bishop's house', he recalled, 'had been taken over during the war as a home for backward children, and it would have created a scandal if they had been turned out.'[21] So, as soon as Stockwood was appointed, John said he would help him, with the architect Paul Paget, his neighbour and landlord in Cloth Fair, to find a suitable house. John said: 'Come round and see us tomorrow afternoon. We'll do what we can; we'll ring around, and so on.' When Stockwood arrived at John's house in Cloth Fair the next day, he found both men bubbling with excitement.

'We think we've found the *exact* place,' John said. 'We don't really know who lives there at the moment, or whether it's up for sale, but we think it may be possible. It's right on the river, very near the cathedral. We've been given a telephone number.'

John rang the number and a deep voice answered:

'Hello? The Provost of Southwark speaking.' (Southwark Cathedral has a provost instead of a dean.)

'I'm speaking on behalf of the Bishop Designate of the diocese,' John said. 'We understand your house may be for sale.'

'Oh,' said the Provost, 'I'm expecting to see him tomorrow; and I'm afraid my house is *not* for sale.' The Provost was George Reindorp, later Bishop of Guildford and Bishop of Salisbury. When Stockwood went to see him the next day, he said, 'Have you come to get my house?'[22] The house the new Bishop eventually moved into had the Betjemanesque address No. 38 Tooting Bec Gardens.

Once Stockwood was installed as bishop, John accompanied him on journeys which were part episcopal progress, part 'church-crawl'.

I had two marvellous church-crawls with Elizabeth and John [Stockwood recalled]. We did about ten churches each time, starting early in the morning, about seven o'clock, and ending late in the evening. Preferably, churches with clergy who were quite the most dotty in the diocese. John would say, 'Take me to a church, the odder and madder the better.' He loved laughing at the Church of England.

It's a huge diocese. We'd go to Deptford or Woolwich and then we'd go right down south to Gatwick Airport; and there was one at Tatsfield, I remember, which is the most remote church in the Surrey hills. It was very old but it had never been given a name, and one of the first things I had to do as bishop was to give it a name. We named it St Mary. John was very interested in this lovely, isolated church; and the vicar, who was a very understanding man, knowing that we had a very busy day and that a little refreshment would be welcome . . . there was no real vestry there but he put out on a little table gins and tonic. And in came some American visitors who hadn't the remotest idea that this was not normal practice. They thought this was absolutely splendid, doling out gins and tonic.[23]

One of the churches John visited with Stockwood was Christ Church, North Brixton, which has an open-air pulpit engraved, 'REPENT YE AND BELIEVE THE GOSPEL'.

In that particular church [Stockwood said], they still preached in the black gown. In the old days, right up to the end of the last century, it was customary for the parson, with a three decker pulpit . . . having worn the surplice, when he reached the third Collect, he went into the vestry, removed his surplice and put on the black gown. John loved Christ Church, North Brixton. He went into the vestry – I rather think there was an interregnum in the vicars – and he put on the black gown and went up into the open-air pulpit. He said, 'Do I look like a Low Church Father?' Later, when Jane Bown of The Observer wanted somewhere suitable to photograph John and myself, we posed together in that open-air pulpit (see plate).[24]

Beverley Nichols sometimes joined John and Stockwood on their expeditions. He lived in the diocese, at Ham Common, just on the border of Richmond Park. 'He had the most lovely, lovely garden,'

Stockwood remembered. 'His faith was not as pronounced as John's, although his father was a clergyman.[25] But I met him early in my episcopate, in 1959, and we became close friends.'[26] Nichols introduced Stockwood to his friend Princess Alexandra, who lived near-by at Thatched House Lodge, Richmond.

I saw a great deal of him [Stockwood added]. When my job took me to the Richmond Park area I'd feel quite free to call at his house and say, 'Is he in?' He might say, 'No, I've got guests' – it was very relaxed, just as it was with John. And you know, it's very difficult – it isn't that one wants to sound grand – but your calendar, your programme, when you're a bishop, is so packed with dates and your intimate friends are very few. There are not many people you can ring at the last moment and say, 'Look, could I drop in for supper tonight?' or even, 'I've got an hour off before the next engagement; could I just come in and rest and shut my eyes?' I hadn't more than a dozen friends like that, and John and Beverley were among them. They got on very well with each other, too. Both Old Marlburians, of course; they'd spend hours discussing how much they hated their Latin master.[27]

In 1966, the Port of London Authority took John, Stockwood and Nichols from Westminster Bridge up the Thames. 'Incredibly beautiful; you'd never realize how lovely it is,' Stockwood said in 1990. 'When you go up to Richmond, you go through whole areas where you don't see anything except trees and fields. We had a picnic. I can see myself, twenty-four years ago, with John and Beverley, eating strawberries. That was an immensely happy day.'[28]

Stockwood was an enthusiastic ecumenist. Before accepting the parish of St Matthew Moorfields, Bristol, in 1941, he had made one condition: 'I must have a free hand to cooperate with the Free churches and to run the parish on an ecumenical basis.'[29] In the 1950s he allowed the American evangelist Billy Graham to preach at the University Church in Cambridge; John was interested in that experiment, and wrote about it in *The Spectator*.[30] As a short break between leaving Cambridge and taking up his duties in Southwark, Stockwood went to Capri. On his return journey Julian Grenfell joined him in Rome. Pope John XXIII granted them a private audience and told the bishop-to-be, through an interpreter, that he knew of his deep concern for Christian unity, which he shared. He said he hoped that he and the Archbishop of Canterbury might meet.[31]

A few days later, when Stockwood stayed with Archbishop Fisher at Lambeth Palace the night before his consecration ('May 1st was chosen by the Archbishop, though he had forgotten it was Labour Day'), he told Fisher about his visit to the Vatican. 'He was not pleased. "When you are older, Stockwood, you will be careful before allowing these Roman Catholics to pull the wool over your eyes." '[32] (Fisher did, however, go to the Vatican eventually.) Within a few weeks of his consecration, Stockwood was in trouble with the Apostolic Delegate, Archbishop O'Hara, for speaking on the wireless in aid of the week's good cause, birth-control clinics. 'The Delegate was furious,' Stockwood later wrote. '. . . He maintained that had Pope John known of my views on contraceptives he would never have received me at the Vatican. I doubt it.'[33] It was entirely characteristic of Stockwood that he had managed to offend both the Church of England and the Roman Catholics while striving for ecumenism.

Intellectually, John saw the point of ecumenism; emotionally, he was less committed, since he felt resentful about what he felt was Penelope's apostasy. But both John and Beverley Nichols were, as Stockwood put it, 'fixtures' at an annual party which John called 'the Ecumenical'.

> When I went to Southwark first [Stockwood said] it was in the hard days of no dealings between the Roman Catholic Archbishop of Southwark and us Anglicans. But then, as the thaw gradually came under John XXIII, the Archbishop [Cyril Cowderoy] and I became very close friends. I always had lunch with him on St George's Day and he always came to me the last week of December, near St Thomas's Day, because it was the day he was made a bishop and I was made a priest. We used to have this wonderful party, always with John and Beverley – and many others besides. And I suppose this went on for twenty years. The first time the Archbishop was very nervous about the whole thing; I remember [Lord] Hailsham and [Lord] Longford were there. But then it became so much less formal, we used to have glorious parties.[34]

The guests were waited on by Stockwood's cook–chauffeur, a Christian Arab called Munir (known as El Fhatah), a former barman at the Panorama Hotel, Jerusalem, whom the Bishop had brought to England.[35] Besides John, Elizabeth and Nichols, they often included John Robinson, Hugh Montefiore, David Sheppard, Tom Driberg, Norman Hartnell, the Queen's dressmaker; Barbara Cartland, the romantic novelist; Frankie Howerd, the comedian; Eric Crabtree, a leading London hairdresser of John's generation; Ned Sherrin and his friend Caryl Brahms;[36] and leading clergy of the Roman Catholic Church, the Orthodox Church and the Church of England. 'Mervyn's Palestinian cook cooked as badly as he drove the bishop's car,' Sherrin wrote, 'but the friendly nature of the feast made up for burnt chicken and sausages.'[37]

John's collinses to Stockwood show his enjoyment of these junketings. On 17 December 1968 he wrote:

> My dear Mervyn,
>   Every moment of that dinner was a pleasure. The old Archbishop [Michael Ramsey][38] grew more and more cheerful; I dare say he would rather not have been inflicted with Tennyson under whom you all bore up bravely, but it made it all the nicer for him when it was over. He is a very warm old thing and very lovable. Nothing will change his opinions. I expect he thinks of us all – clerical and lay alike – as larky heretics, and I know he enjoyed himself, as I did . . .[39]

On 27 October 1969:

> The ecumenical banquet was as heavenly as ever. The new bishop of Woolwich [David Sheppard] quite makes me wish that I were Low. It's so splendid that he doesn't mind jokes about High and Low and he is obviously calm and good. I thought Beverley in splendid form, and so are we all . . . I hope Fathers Miles and Wallis [sic][40] have a blessed Christmas together, with all the other Fundamentalists in your glorious diocese. Down with pleasure-loving worldliness![41]

David Sheppard (now Lord Sheppard of Liverpool), who had been consecrated Bishop of Woolwich only nine days before that meal, remembers the ecumenical lunches.

> Usually they took place in the week before Christmas. I found myself each time sitting next to Cyril Cowderoy, the very traditionalist Archbishop of Southwark. He talked to me of his devotion to the memory of Napoleon. He said: 'I'm sure I love our blessed Lord very much more, but Napoleon means so much to me.' One evening John arrived with colourful silk ties as gifts for us. I still have this flamboyant fuchsia tie – but I can never think of the right occasion to give it an airing![42]

Ned Sherrin recalls that the ecumenical lunches came to an end 'when three very nice Americans (two black), who founded an *a cappella* singing group, joyously told the old *Sunday Express* (in its broadsheet form – must have been the Seventies) of the wonderful hospitality. They went well over the top in terms of the luxury of the hospitality and an impression was given of the Bishop pushing the boat out while the poor in his parish starved.'[43]

John and Elizabeth went on holidays with Mervyn Stockwood, Harry Williams and others of their set. Osbert Lancaster, who twice

met a group of them – once on a Greek island and again among the
royal tombs of the Escorial – christened them 'the Church of England
Ramblers Association'.[44] The name stuck, and Williams mystified some
readers when, in 1972, he dedicated his book *True Resurrection* to
members and honorary members of the association: it was thought
that a celestial metaphor was intended.[45] There were fourteen Ramblers
in all, but they were never all present. Because of John's antipathy to
'abroad', Elizabeth sometimes left him in England when off with the
Ramblers. In 1962 she went to the Middle East with Stockwood and
Williams. According to Stockwood's biographer, 'the management of
the King David Hotel in Jerusalem . . . assumed that Lady Elizabeth was
Mervyn's mistress and could not comprehend why they did not share a
bedroom. As the hotel filled up, with a consequent lack of spare accommodation, ever more pressing hints were made that it would be greatly
appreciated if Lady Elizabeth would kindly vacate her room and move
in with the bishop.'[46] While still in the Holy Land, the party heard it
announced on their car radio that 'The Bishop of Southwark is now
touring Israel with Lady Elizabeth Cavendish, his lady-in-waiting.'
(The newscasters had muddled up some information about Elizabeth's
rôle in Princess Margaret's retinue.)[47] In Salamanca one summer,
Elizabeth, Simon Phipps, Graham Storey and Harry Williams followed
the directions of a youth advertising what called itself the Hospederia
Oxford. It soon became clear that it was a brothel, but they stayed there
nonetheless, as all hotel rooms were booked for the town's annual
fiesta. 'At least,' said Phipps, 'it wasn't the Hospederia Cambridge.'[48]

On a later holiday, Simon Stuart and Harry Williams arrived at the
Spanish frontier, from France, with the other Ramblers' luggage in the
car as well as their own. Two customs officials ordered them to open
one of the suitcases. 'It turned out to belong to Elizabeth Cavendish,
and contained, naturally enough, brassières, panties, dresses and an
outfit of cosmetics,' Williams wrote. 'The two customs officials gave
us both severely old-fashioned looks and called over two policemen to
examine the haberdashery . . . At last they allowed us to continue our
journey, but not before they had put on a show half of resignation and
half of disgust.'[49]

In April 1966 John was induced to accompany Elizabeth and
Williams to Apulia and Sicily. On 1 May he wrote to William Plomer:

I came back from Sicily – wild irises, Greek temples, shepherds and sheep
bells and at Syracuse Cathedral the first Mass of Easter when the gong-like
bells rang out and the lights suddenly filled that Greek Doric temple of
Athens with Christian walls between the columns and all in honey-
coloured stone like the wine – I suddenly realised what I saw with my eyes

and heard – that BC and AD become one with the Resurrection and it didn't matter whether one was R[oman] C[atholic] or C[hurch] of E[ngland].[50]

Mollie Baring received a less rhapsodical postcard from Palermo, dated 31 March. 'Too much sun, tho' exquisite octopus to eat . . . and ruined palaces of the great.'

Simon Stuart was rich. His mother was a daughter of the financier Solomon Guggenheim, who had himself married a Rothschild. Stuart had a villa at Ancona, Italy, at which Elizabeth, John and Harry Williams stayed in August 1966. He was host both to them and to an undergraduate reading-party. 'I am very surprised I like abroad so much,' John wrote to Penelope on 22 August. 'This place is a paradise of olive trees, little hills . . . among the farms and little walled towns and shrines of our lady and smells of sage.'[51] Stuart's house (which John drew for her) was of pale eighteenth-century brick and looked towards Urbino. Senigallia was the local market town – 'very beautiful with a sixteenth-century chapel full of Barroccios'.[52]

Simon S has a car [he added] and so have the undergraduates. Servants look after the house which is well supplied with baths and *toilets* and, thank God, no telephone. We lunch in and go out to dinner and have mussels and local wine and pellegrino. I at last feel rested and uncoiled after that spate of telly[53] and thankful no one knows me or sees me. Harry W has written a long treatise on Evil while here and Simon is writing a book on education[54] but all I am up to is reading Agatha Christie. I can't even read Pater.[55]

Stuart was a master at Haberdashers' Aske's School. As he did for most of his friends, John soon devised a nickname for him.

John called me 'bad Simon' [Stuart wrote] to distinguish me from 'good Simon' – Simon Phipps . . . mostly I think because I had affairs with boys (though not in his company).[56] Thence I became 'Wicked' or 'The Wicked' – which I always suspected carried more affection than was offered to 'The Good'. I always enjoyed his euphemism for 'queer' – 'I say, he was a bit unmarried, don't you think?' . . . A.L. Rowse told me years before I met him that JB was utterly tormented by boys – but I never saw anything to substantiate that, unless I adduce his declining to give a lecture at Haberdashers' – which he could have regarded as a torment with no possible reward.[57]

Stuart regarded himself as only an honorary Rambler. ('"The Ramblers" reached me at a late stage, fully formed by others. It felt

like a standing joke which I'd never really understood.')[58] But he was
with John, Elizabeth and others of the Association on three holidays
abroad: Umbria in 1966, Biarritz in 1970 and the French Pyrenees, followed by Barcelona, in 1971.

> John was terrified of having to talk to foreigners [he wrote]. Once in a
> church in the Pyrenees a Frenchman approached him: he peremptorily
> summoned 'Feeble, Feeeeble, FEEBULL!' to come and defend him from
> the unbearable. And when I told him a young German would be a co-guest
> at dinner, he said, deeply anxious: 'Will I have to speak a foreign lan-
> guage?' Yet it wasn't ordinary xenophobia – in Umbria he was very happy
> chatting to the not-much-educated couple who looked after us, in pidgin
> Italian, and gave them a charming water-colour he did of the house. In the
> Pyrenees we stayed in a small hotel where Monsieur was a top chef, and
> when he walked through the dining-room, JB and Harry warmly
> exclaimed '*Artiste!*' and ordered the top vintage on the wine-list. On that
> occasion, Elizabeth and I went into a titled huddle and discovered we both
> thought it wicked to spend so much on a bottle of drink – a puritanism
> from which the bourgeoisie was delightedly free.[59]

Harry Williams also remembered the rapport John established with
some of the 'natives'. In Italy John had an infallible way of dealing
with such mishaps as punctures.

> Seeing our distress a car would stop and its occupants get out and come
> over to us. John would then say in the charmingly persuasive and ingrati-
> ating voice which none of the rest of us could imitate: 'Siamo Inglese,
> molto stupidi. Tutti Italiani intelligenti.' This was invariably greeted with
> loud protests of 'No, no, *Inglese* intelligenti,' and before we knew where
> we were they had changed the wheel for us.[60]

Graham Storey was with the Ramblers on the visit to Italy in 1966. He
remembers 'how mercilessly we all teased John about his goggling
admiration for the Italian boys we saw'.[61]

In April 1967 John and Elizabeth went to Spain with the Ramblers.
Mervyn Stockwood took a holiday there every year for the sake of his
health. He had always had trouble with his chest. When he was offered
Southwark in 1958, Kenneth Carey, the principal of Stockwood's old
theological college, Westcott House, advised him not to accept the see.
Years later Stockwood asked him the reason for his advice and was told
that in his Westcott House file there was a note to the effect that he
suffered from such bad health it was unlikely he would reach the age
of thirty. Knowing that, Carey thought Southwark would kill him.[62]

Philip and Susan Richardson, who were friends of Stockwood's (Susan, a dedicated Anglican, helped him out in the diocese), owned a house in Moraira, a cape on the eastern coast of Spain, south of Valencia and north of Alicante.

It's just north of Benidorm [Stockwood said in 1990]. John did a painting of Benidorm, which I still have. He thought Hell would be rather like Benidorm.

The first year I went, I took John Robinson with me. Later on, I usually took four or five people. On three occasions John and Elizabeth came over and we had a marvellous time. We got on so well; mind you, at the same time we knew how to go our own ways, which is very important. Elizabeth was never all that keen on John joining us younger ones – I was several years younger than John, and there'd be others, like my chaplain, who'd be much younger than myself. So we would go off on long expeditions and John would potter around near the house with Elizabeth.[63]

In London, shortly before the 1967 holiday, Stockwood had married the actor Hywel Bennett and Cathy McGowan, presenter of the television pop show *Ready Steady Go*. He had met them through Ned Sherrin, who acted as master of ceremonies at the wedding reception in the San Lorenzo restaurant. Sherrin sat Stockwood next to Roger Moore, who at that time was playing Leslie Charteris's sleuth 'the Saint' in a television series. (Newspaper photographs the next morning were captioned 'The Bishop and the Saint'.)[64]

At the reception, which was on a Saturday night [Stockwood recalled] I asked Hywel where he and Cathy were going for their honeymoon.

'Near a place called Moraira in Spain,' he said.

'Are you?' I said. 'What day are you going?'

He said: 'We're going tomorrow.'

I said, 'Really? I'm going out there on Monday with John Betjeman and Elizabeth Cavendish.'

So we had the most wonderful fortnight. Hywel and Cathy loved John. We met every day of the fortnight. We once drank Spanish brandy, and how any of us got home, I've no idea.[65]

John reported to the television director Jonathan Stedall, on 24 April:

The C of E Ramblers had a lovely time in Spain – green grass, wisteria, arum lilies in flower, oysters, prawns, good local wine and wall-flower-stuffed cliffs of Baroque in Santiago and those same Atlantic rollers on the shore above near Corunna. We saw twenty-seven things that *thrilled* us all – not bad in fourteen days . . . Feeble's got a job as location advisor for *The Charge of the Light Brigade* and is v excited.[66]

On 8 February 1968, John wrote to his Oxford friend Lionel Perry, who now lived in Co. Donegal, to tell him that he, Elizabeth, Harry Williams and Simon Stuart were going to Lerwick for a fortnight before Easter on 30 March – 'Shetland is very bracing and beauteous.'[67] In the event, Stuart did not join the other three on that trip.[68] Harry Williams remembered the holiday with special clarity, because on it he received what he considered a 'divine imperative'.[69] He had left for the Shetlands in a state of tension, hoping for a respite from a question that was troubling him. He was nearly fifty and was wondering whether to leave Cambridge and become a monk in the Community of the Resurrection at Mirfield, Yorkshire. He travelled to Lerwick with John and Elizabeth. The morning after their arrival they woke up to find thick snow on the ground, which immobilized them for two days. They stayed in the hotel, reading and watching television. One of the programmes they saw was Lord Snowdon's film *Don't Count the Candles*, about growing old. 'The film reminded me savagely . . . of the choice I had to make,' Williams wrote. 'In what context was I to live the rest of my life? I thought it a filthy trick of fate to confront me almost immediately on my arrival in Shetland with the problem from which I had gone there to escape for a week or two.'[70] He cursed the snow and tried to find some relief by repeating several times to John and Elizabeth that Snowdon had made an appallingly bad film. 'They were surprised at my vehemence and clearly wondered what lay behind it.'[71]

Tension eased when the fishing fleet arrived back in Lerwick. The fishermen, with weeks of pay to spend, packed the pubs and were very hospitable to the strangers. Williams thought he only remained sober because of his excellent training as a drinker at Trinity College. The fishermen carried a half-bottle of whisky in their hip pockets. 'One of them – he must have been round about twenty-five – slipped in the snow, cut himself slightly and bled a little. Feeling the moisture, he put his fingers to the wound and then sucked them. "Thank fuck," he said, "it's only blood." '[72]

The next day, with the snow almost gone and the sun shining, the party hired a car and explored the rugged country. They had a launch at their disposal and, with the weather holding, went to Yell and Unst, where they spent two nights, and to several of the smaller islands. At Fetlar they saw a snowy owl which was nesting there and were given lunch at the house of a kirk elder.[73] One expedition, Williams regretted.

On Vaila we visited a largish house whose furnishings and decoration, all in spotless condition, hadn't been changed since 1880. It was a bit eerie as the old lady who owned the house was bedridden upstairs and her fairly constant geriatric cries and moans made the house feel as if it were haunted. I think we were wrong to visit it. She didn't know we were there and we were intruders. I had agreed to accept her housekeeper's invitation to see the place, and it was certainly a curiosity finding ourselves in a house which looked exactly as it had almost ninety years before. But I felt now that we had been discourteous, to say the least. It was a relief when we left.[74]

On the mainland they were invited to lunch by Sir Basil Neven-Spence, who had been MP for Orkney and Shetland and was now Lord Lieutenant. As a widower, he did his own cooking and served an excellent meal. The interior of his house 'looked as if it had left Harrods only the day before': he had had it refurbished for a recent visit of the Queen. After lunch they followed in their car as he led them, in his, along cliff roads with the sea hundreds of feet below. He had already told them that his brakes were deficient, and Williams expected to see him disappear at any moment. On leaving, they 'absolutely refused' his offer to lead them back to their garage.[75]

The evenings were spent in the bar of the Lerwick hotel, talking about what they had seen in the day and what they planned for the next day. All three of them made friends with the barmaid, Dolly, a woman of about fifty, who knew a lot about Shetland lore. Williams later wrote: 'We were (somewhat provincially, I suppose) amused by the way the islanders spoke of Aberdeen as if it were a foreign city in the far south, much as we might speak of Milan. John was particularly intrigued by the fact that the nearest railway station was at Bergen. It would be fun, he said, to have it stamped upon one's writing paper.'[76]

On Easter Sunday Williams thought he had better go to church, 'partly out of a sense of duty and partly not to upset John, for whom at that time . . . attendance at the Holy Communion on Sunday was a bit of a neurotic compulsion; all the more so, therefore, on Easter Sunday'.[77] The three of them went to the small episcopal church in Lerwick for the eight o'clock morning service. The priest was 'a youngish man attended by the usual adolescent server in his middle teens'.[78] It was here that Williams, as he later put it, met his doom. The priest read the usual Prayer Book epistle for Easter Sunday 'and a sentence of it burnt itself into me like fire: "Ye died, and your life is hid with Christ in God." The words overpowered me. It was like being struck fiercely in the face.' From that moment, Williams knew that he was being invited 'to die somehow to an old life in order to find a truer identity in the encompassing mystery of which I had been so long aware'.[79] In practical terms this meant leaving Cambridge and asking if Mirfield would give him a try.

> At the time [he wrote] I said nothing to Elizabeth and John about what had happened to me in church. I knew them both intimately, but the experience was at the moment incommunicable. In any case, if I had tried to speak of it I was sure I would break down, and I remembered that it was their holiday as well as mine. As there would be no change in my attitudes and behaviour, the easiest thing seemed to say nothing. But unperceptive is the last thing Elizabeth ever is. She saw something was up, but with her usual sensitivity she asked no questions. All she did that morning was unaccustomedly early to say: 'Let's go and see Dolly and have a drink,' to which I agreed with alacrity. The bar was closed. But Dolly was about and brought us large glasses of Glen Morangie.[80]

Back in Cloth Fair after the fortnight in Shetland, John wrote to Lord Wemyss about the holiday, praising the Queen's Hotel at Lerwick and Voe House at Voe, but also asking his advice 'as how best to stop the Lerwick Town Council destroying the remaining old parts of the town'. He thought the most serious threat was to Annesbrae, a charming laird's house of 1791, which was empty.[81] Probably as a result of John's concern and Wemyss's representations, the house was saved.[82] John had enjoyed the Shetland holiday so much that he returned there in 1973, when his poem beginning 'Fetlar is waiting . . .' was written.

A few days after returning to Cambridge, Harry Williams wrote to the Superior of Mirfield asking to become an aspirant. He told a few intimate friends, and was taken aback to find that 'Elizabeth Cavendish was totally opposed to what I had done.'[83] In the spring of 1969 he stayed with her and John in Cornwall. After the first calming week there, he felt at dinner that something was in the air. 'I was right. Elizabeth told me straight out that she thought I was making the most catastrophic mistake in going to Mirfield and said she was going to spend the evening telling me why.'[84] Williams remembered how her mother, the Dowager Duchess, had told him one evening in Derbyshire that Elizabeth had a rough tongue but a kind heart. He had witnessed 'the most passionate quarrels' between mother and daughter, by the end of which the two would be shouting at each other things like 'If that's what you mean, then for God's sake say so!' But the quarrels left no trace. 'Sitting that evening at Trebetherick I remembered those occasions, fastened my seat belt, and prepared for the worst.

John's face, meanwhile, was a mixture of concern, anxiety, amusement and reassurance. He remained silent most of the time, but every now and then he interjected a sort of miniature scherzo which sounded irresistibly funny.'[85] Williams proceeds to write what is in effect a delicious one-act play, a double act by John and Elizabeth in which the characters of both, and their interplay, are revealed.

'First of all,' said Elizabeth, 'you enjoy conviviality. You get a great deal of pleasure out of parties and dinners. There's nothing wrong in that, and it's just silly to cut yourself away from it. It's a much more important side of your life than you imagine, and you'll feel the loss of it desperately.'

At this point John interjected the first of his scherzos. Sounding like the Walrus in Alice in Wonderland he said gravely: 'I suppose you reach a state where a *petit beurre* tastes delicious.'

'And then,' Elizabeth went on, 'what about your holiday travels? You've often said they're the best part of your life. Certainly they liven you up. Won't you be more than half-dead without them?'

'Oh, those ceramic tiles at Caltagirone. I shall never forget them,' said John.

I had no secrets from Elizabeth. She knew all about me, and she continued: 'And young people, the undergraduates and those you've been able to make permanent friends of like Simon and James and William and that young man – what's he called? – who works at Rota's,[86] and those amusing young Fellows, what's the name of the one who's such a good mimic, you know, the one who's a scientist? And that lovely old man who kissed me when I came to the Ladies' Night, the Russian, Susie, no, Bessy, something – won't you be cutting yourself off from your life-blood if you can't see them?'

'I thought that young man in front of us in church on Sunday was very handsome. Do you think he noticed us?' said John.

'What I'm getting at is this,' said Elizabeth. 'What you say and write is of enormous help to hundreds of people. I know because I've met a lot of them. It's not conventional parson's stuff. You get to the heart of things. But this depends upon your imagination. And imagination needs to be fed. It's parties and travel and young men, however much it sometimes hurts, and interesting people, which feed your imagination. It'll dry up without that sort of stimulus. And we shall all be the losers. And for what? I'm going to have my say. For a fit, for what is probably no more than a passing fit, a fit of – yes, I'm going to say it – a fit of conceit. Yes, I don't care what you think, of conceit, spiritual conceit. I don't know the technical name for it, but I'm sure it exists. Is it 'accident' or something like that? And it won't work because you're simply not like that. You're not the stuff from which stained-glass windows are made.'

'Kempe's windows in Wakefield Cathedral are rather good,' said John.

'I'm sorry,' said Elizabeth, 'but I've got to say what I think. I think you're being madly silly, utterly insane, criminally stupid.'

She paused and I said, 'But I've done it now. I've resigned from Trinity.'

'Yes, I know,' she said. 'But there are dozens of other things you could do which would keep you in circulation. One thing you must promise me – if when you go to Mirfield it doesn't work, you must be humble enough to admit it frankly and leave. I mean this with all my heart – you mustn't be wasted. People need terribly what you have to give them.'

'I would like a glass of port,' said John.[87]

The dialogue shows how unfeeble 'Feeble' could be when she chose. It also shows how John usually wanted to avoid confrontations and dissipate tension. Williams went to Mirfield and stayed there, though with many revivifying sorties to London.

In Williams's last years at Trinity College, Prince Charles was an undergraduate there. Williams was the first person Charles met in January 1966 when visiting the college for the first time with his father;[88] and the Prince's biographer, Jonathan Dimbleby, writes that Williams was 'to exert much influence over his undergraduate life'[89] and that, after Charles came up in the autumn of 1967, he was 'a frequent guest at the Dean's table'.[90] John was sometimes there, too.[91] At the end of the Lent term each year, the undergraduates got up a revue, with many satirical references to the dons. In 1969 Charles, who was an addict of *The Goon Show*, was in the cast. To the tune of 'Lily the Pink', the actors sang:

> Let's get drunk, get drunk, get drunk
> For Harry the monk, the monk, the monk.[92]

Charles's presence meant that the song was published the next morning in the *Daily Telegraph* and other national newspapers. A letter John sent Mary Wilson suggests that he may have had a hand in the squib's composition.[93]

In May John and Elizabeth attended Williams's fiftieth birthday party at the Savoy (Williams was by no means ascetic). On 1 July John and Williams were both present at Charles's investiture as Prince of Wales, an event stage-managed by Lord Snowdon at Caernarvon Castle. At Charles's request, John wrote a ballad to commemorate the occasion. He began it by describing the evening on which Charles asked him to write the poem – an evening spent with the Prince, Harry Williams, Elizabeth and two of Charles's Trinity friends, William Hastings Bass (later Earl of Huntingdon) and Edward Woods, younger son of the then Dean of Windsor.

> The moon was in the Cambridge sky
>   And bathed Great Court in silver light
> When Hastings-Bass and Woods and I
>   And quiet Elizabeth, tall and white,
> With that sure clarity of mind
> Which comes to those who've truly dined,
>   Reluctant rose to say good-night;
> And all of us were bathed the while
> In the large moon of Harry's smile . . .[94]

The ballad, which John described as 'a sort of rhyming letter',[95] tells of the poet's train journey to Wales (he travelled with the Earl of Euston, later Duke of Grafton)[96] and of the ceremony itself, in which the Queen crowned Charles as Prince of Wales and the Prince swore to be her 'liege man of life and limb and to live and die against all manner of folks'.[97]

In 1969, after a trip to Iceland, following in the footsteps of William Morris, John again went to Spain with the Ramblers. ('Out of the ice box into the fire,' he commented.)[98] In a letter dated '1 Advent 1969', he wrote to Mervyn Stockwood:

Dear Mervyn,
  Father Miles[99] has indeed excelled himself in this issue. The story of the Nun and the RC Father is very encouraging reading. Could you not ask Father & Mrs Miles to join you and Beverley and poor, white, quiet, washed-out Elizabeth and me in Spain? They would do so much to correct the Spanish to the doctrine of Free and Socialist Grace through the Triune Covenant . . . Poor WQWOE immensely enjoyed her WQWO evening with you and the new Bishop of Woolwich [David Sheppard] and the inland China missionaries. She has . . . come back into the world quite *Low Church*. It is very kind of you to ask her to Spain and I look forward to coming for a week on my return from *Iceland* . . .[100]

The next year, Simon Stuart took a house in Biarritz and invited out John, Elizabeth, Harry Williams and Joe Bain, who had been a colleague of Stuart's when he taught at Stowe. Queen Victoria had spent her winters in the Belle Epoque town; the Ramblers were there in high summer. John wrote to Stuart from Cloth Fair on 20 August 1970:

My dear Simon,
  That was the best holiday I could imagine. Sitting here in my city room pitying myself (9.30 a.m.) I think if I were at Biarritz now I would be just about waking up & shuffling over the floor to the hall & out on to the

terrace & I would hear Harry's laugh & you would get up & fetch me a boiled egg & coffee & the others would have finished except for poor Elizabeth who, white & quiet & inarticulate, would not yet have appeared. I laugh a lot too at the thought of Joe struggling through the Channings.[101] I wonder if he even got through it. When I go over in my mind those glorious all too few days I can't sort out an order for a series of marvellous experiences – that first dinner under the trees in the village, the interior of St Per [? St Peire], bathing in all those many self-conscious crowds, the evening walk by the sea at St Jean-de-Luz, the thronged church there, that restaurant, Biarritz itself & the Palais Hotel, the cathedral at Bayonne & its cloister – perhaps best of all, exceeding these, the harmony of our company. You are a generous host & a welcoming. The C of E Ramblers will live for ever.[102]

John's next holiday with the Ramblers was not such a success. In September 1971 he wrote to Mary Wilson: 'I've been with the C of E Ramblers to France and Barcelona and *hideous* Andorra.'[103]

I behaved very badly about Andorra [Simon Stuart admitted]. JB wanted to go because, like Everest, it was there. *My* car, and I was the only driver. The mountain bends up, and then down, were wearing. I'd've loved to stop for some *tapas* and eaten it on the mountain, but it was not to be. The big-paunched cabal voted for four full courses in a baking road-side restaurant of filthy food. I sulked. But I'd prepared a more effective revenge – you couldn't cross frontiers without a car insurance document – 'gree' ca''. We got into Andorra, but at the far end I discovered I'd left it at the hotel in France. The car was hugely expensive, but so unreliable that I had filled the boot with £100 of spare parts. The authorities were convinced we were running a scam in contraband goods. It was one? two? three? hours before they let us go. There were some harsh words, but JB's forbearance was total.[104]

In Barcelona, John 'nosed out all the lesser-known Gaudí buildings'.[105] (Forty years earlier, when John was on *The Architectural Review*, Evelyn Waugh had written an article on the *art nouveau* architect for the magazine.)[106] In the funfair the Ramblers met David Hockney, 'and JB was delighted with *his* delight at having acquired enough wealth to send his aged parents on a cruise – "and they're goin' first class"'.[107]

In spite of the contretemps in Andorra, the witty, 'Wicked' Simon Stuart remained a favourite of John's. Sometimes, John stayed with him at his Sussex house, which had the Betjemanesque name Windyridge.

Harry [Williams] told him he wasn't allowed to want to go to church because it upset me [Stuart wrote]. I'm pretty sure he did so, though, but I knew of nowhere that used incense etc. I found I was out of red wine and went into the pub to remedy that if possible. The landlord asked, had a bomb gone off, I behaved so timidly. Actually it had. My brother's house in Tyrone had been blown up by the IRA. John's comment was, 'They can't bear Georgian.' He always referred to his poems as 'my verses' in a self-disparaging way, but perhaps that was because an aura of Leavis still hung about me. It was only after he'd been here more than once that I discovered he'd pilloried 'Windyridge' as a cosy, suburban nomenclature.[108] It still worries me, like my fish-knives.

Perhaps it was when my marriage was approaching [in 1973, at forty-three, Stuart married Deborah Jane Mounsey and they had three children] that he volunteered that he didn't think he could face the whole ordeal of husband and fatherhood all over again. I recognized a world of anguish there, but didn't take warning. Actually that ended our association – meeting my fiancée he embarked on making a fuss of her; but Feeble put paid to that, by cutting her then and subsequently. Harry glossed, 'She can't bear women,' but I think it carried some snobbery too.[109]

John's last trip to the Continent with the Ramblers was in Lent 1972. Mervyn Stockwood had again been loaned the Richardsons' house at Moraira. He thought it would be a good idea if both his suffragans, Hugh Montefiore and David Sheppard, joined him with their wives. The Sheppards did not come, as one could not fly and the other could not travel by sea;[110] but Montefiore and his wife Elisabeth joined Stockwood, John, Lady Elizabeth and Lord Rossmore (Montefiore supervised him in the New Testament in Cambridge), who was recovering from his broken engagement to a pop star.[111] (Ulick O'Connor, the writer, actor, champion boxer, pole-vaulter and rugby player described 'Paddy' Rossmore in his diary for 1970 as having 'the look of a fine-boned medieval monk'.)[112] Rossmore was a keen photographer and his black-and-white photographs (see plates) evoke the sunlit days in Moraira: the wrought-iron and marble table on the verandah, loaded with bottles of gin, martini and wine, with local wines in wicker-cased bottles under the table; Mervyn Stockwood pouring champagne (wearing a three-piece suit – he found it difficult to 'go casual'); Elizabeth Cavendish in pullover and slacks; John carrying a pottery wine flask back from the local shop; the company lolling on the verandah, drinking and laughing. 'I have memories of a very happy house party,' Bishop Montefiore writes, 'and the countryside was looking idyllic with all the almond blossom out. I remember John Betjeman laughing uproariously when seated on a model steam railway when we took a journey; and also his delight in the delicious *gambas* served with an apéritif before meals. It was here that Betjeman wrote his moving poem "The Costa Blanca".[113] The poem, consisting of two sonnets, is about an English couple who have a house built in Spain. In the first sonnet the wife describes what tempts them to Spain ('Skies without a stain. Eric and I at almond-blossom time Came here and fell in love with it . . . Good-bye democracy and smoke and grime . . .'); in the second sonnet, the husband, five years on, pours out their regrets about the move, and their yearning for their 'Esher lawn'.

> That Dago caught the wife and me all right!
> Here on this tideless, tourist-littered sea
> We're stuck. You'd hate it too if you were me:
> There's no piped water on the bloody site.
> Our savings gone, we climb the stony path
> Back to the house, with scorpions in the bath.[114]

The two sonnets might be taken to represent the two sides of John's ambivalent feelings about 'abroad'.

The holidays with the Ramblers ended; but John's friendship with Stockwood continued. A strong link between them was their mutual friendship with Gerard Irvine. Stockwood and Irvine had been priests together in the Bristol diocese in the 1940s. 'I and others', Stockwood said, 'felt Gerard could have been on a wider scene.'[115] One difficulty was Irvine's voice, which was breathy and gabbling, not unlike Lord David Cecil's. 'Gerard was inclined to be excessively High Church,' Stockwood said, 'and when he celebrated the Holy Communion people would say, "He says the Roman Mass." It wasn't so at all. He was saying it in English but in such a way that no one could hear what he said.'[116]

Irvine became priest of St Matthew, Westminster, near the Houses of Parliament, where he was able to be of use to Mervyn Stockwood. In 1974 Stockwood founded a group called 'The Caps and Mitres', consisting of twelve academics and twelve bishops. They began by meeting at All Saints, Margaret Street, where Michael Marshall was Vicar. But in 1975 Stockwood appointed Marshall Bishop of Woolwich and Gerard Irvine offered the group the hospitality of St Matthew, Westminster. 'There couldn't have been a better place,' Stockwood said, '– the whole setting of the tumbledown vicarage, and so central; though some of the bishops did raise an eyebrow when they saw Tom Driberg in the corridor.'[117] Driberg had come to live at the vicarage in 1969; Gerard Irvine allowed him two upstairs rooms rent-free on condition that he redecorated them.

My lovely Arab cook Munir used to come and cook for the Caps and Mitres at Gerard's [Stockwood recalled]. We used to meet at six o'clock and have drinks; then about half-past six we got down to work and some-body read a paper. At half-past eight we had a stand-up supper and then at nine we would resume until ten. It was a marvellous mix of people. This is the great thing about getting people to meet around a table. I always said to my chaplain, 'You've got to have one High, one Low; one inner city, one outer city in the "gin and Jag" belt, and so on.' You mix them up and the personal relationships transform everything. You see, most bishops never meet socially. They only meet at official functions. With the Caps and Mitres, there were two golden rules: first, no minutes, no record of any-thing that anybody said; number two, everybody, no matter who he was, was addressed by his Christian name, whether he was an archbishop or ... whatsisname at Cambridge, doesn't believe in anything, he's frequently on the box.[118]

As the host, Gerard Irvine used to have a drink with the Caps and Mitres before and sometimes after the meeting. The presence in the Westminster vicarage of two of John's best friends, Irvine and Driberg, often brought him to the house. When the Caps and Mitres were there, he too would be invited for drinks with them; even Driberg joined the group on occasion. In the catering, Munir was joined by Irvine's housekeeper, a German woman who, John was fascinated to learn, had appeared in *Mädchen in Uniform*, the 'unsuitable' film to which he had taken his Heddon Court pupil Vincent Hollom in 1931. Tom Driberg, according to his biographer, 'conceived a fierce dislike' of this woman. 'She brought out the most pathological side of his misogyny; he refused to drink out of any cup or eat off any plate that she might have used, no matter how many times it had been washed.'[119]Only in Sartre's *Huis Clos*, perhaps, has a more piquantly disparate, not to say discordant, set of characters been brought together in one room: the twelve dons with John, a BA (failed) Oxon; the twelve church prelates with Driberg, a representative of most of the deadly sins and a Communist who had lauded Stalin's Russia; the housekeeper from Hitler's Germany; the Christianized Arab cook; the frothy-voiced Irvine; over all, the booming bonhomie of Stockwood.

A further bond between John and Stockwood was that John encouraged the Bishop to write humorous occasional verse. He liked the poem that Stockwood had written in the 1940s when the Bishop of Bristol, F. A. Cockin, got into trouble with the Anglo-Catholics ('Spikes') for not wearing his mitre at appropriate times.[120] Some thirty years later, in 1977, Stockwood sent John a new poem, 'The Diocese'. The lines were mildly Rabelaisian, for a bishop.

The Diocese is quite my scene.
With Tooting Bec and Canon Dene
In scarf and hood at table's end
The north of course – no modern trend
Like wafer bread or Series Two,
We stick to 1662.
Not far away is Father Smith,
A very different kind of fish;
He bows and bobs and shows his arse
When genuflecting at the Mass.
To Rome he has a private line –
HH Pope Paul, VAT 69.
To Wimbledon we now must jump –
The parish church is middle stump . . .
Within a mile is Somers Town
With Father Francis in black gown.
He thinks the Mass a Roman fable
And keeps away from Holy Table . . .
To cheer the radicals let me tell
Of our port of call in Camberwell.
In *Gay News* you've read a hundred times
The permissive letters of Canon Rhymes;
He seeks to make St Giles effectual
By reserving his seats for the homosexual;
His brisk confrontations, his counselling, his breadth,
His sermons, his pamphlets, his dialogue in depth
Are greatly admired by many a sod
Who thinks Havelock Ellis wrote *Honest to God*;
But if to be 'with it' you really aspire
Then pull down the church – the mitre – the spire.
St Peter St Helier and Deaconess Kroll
Will not be content till she's usurped the rôle
Of a priest at the altar in unisex cope
– Her first step to Rome and becoming the Pope.
She condemns His Holiness for telling a fib
When he says Holy Scripture is against Women's Lib.[121]

John wrote to Stockwood on 10 January 1977:

That poem . . . that beautiful summary of the Diocese, must not perish in
a filing cabinet. May I suggest you have it typed out with plenty of space
between each line on the saintly ground floor of Bishop's House and then
have a copy sent to me. The more I think about it, the more it warms my

heart to the Diocese and the Bishop and the Suffragans ... It certainly is a wonderful thing that has grown up since your appointment, and that thing is THE Diocese. Before you came it had very little character. Now Southwark has more character than any diocese always excepting Sodor and Man.[122]

METRO-LAND

[Sir John] takes you to Chorleywood and leaves you feeling you have voyaged up the Orinoco.

Richard Last, reviewing *Metro-land*, *Daily Telegraph*, 27 February 1973

In *The Secret Glory* – the novel which profoundly influenced John in his teens[1] – Arthur Machen indicated the rich material awaiting the writer who would choose the suburbs as his subject, 'who has the insight to see behind those Venetian blinds and white curtains, who has the word that can give him entrance through the polished door by the encaustic porch!'.[2] What was needed, Machen considered, was a writer 'able to tell the London suburbs the truth about themselves in their own tongue'.[3] In his later years, Machen moved into the suburbs, to Amersham, Buckinghamshire, where John visited him and heard stories of Oscar Wilde, whom Machen had known.[4] Amersham was in that region of suburbs known, from its penetration by the Metropolitan Line of the London Underground railway, as 'Metro-land' – a name made popular in the Twenties and Thirties by property developers promoting their villas in Neasden, Wembley, Chorleywood and other dormitory towns along the Line. (Evelyn Waugh borrowed the name for Lady Metroland in *Decline and Fall*, 1928.)

In one of his film criticisms of 1934, John deplored the lack of good films about London. 'The possibilities of London have never yet been explored,' he wrote. 'There are the corrugated lanes of Finsbury Park, the clatter round the Peckham High Road, the quiet squares of Clerkenwell and Islington, the rutty roads of some half-finished bit of Metroland, all waiting to be photographed and immortalized as René Clair has immortalized Paris.'[5]

In 1972 John got the chance to practise what he and Machen had preached. In that year he made the television film *Metro-land*, directed by Edward Mirzoeff – by common consent the best of all John's television appearances, a classic of television art. The BBC film was first screened on the night of 26 February 1973.

Mirzoeff had seen John's potential in making the helicopter *Bird's Eye View* films in the late Sixties. He thought the seaside programme was more successful than the previous one; but both he and John felt that it still bore little relation to the way ordinary people lived. John was sure that most people liked living in cities, especially in suburbia. He and Mirzoeff began to plan a third film, with the working title 'Joys of Urban Living'. Mirzoeff recalled: 'It was a time when suburbia was absolutely a pejorative term. It's very hard to go back to that now; but the only thing that had been written, that anyone knew of, in favour of suburbia, was a book by John's old *Architectural Review* colleague J.M. Richards called *Castles on the Ground*, which had the same sort of theme. Nobody else had done this.'[6] Even John himself had written, in a *Daily Herald* review of 1945, 'Country and town lives do not marry. Their illegitimate child is suburbia.'[7]

Before any filming could begin, the idea had to be sold to the BBC. Mirzoeff got John to write a letter to Robin Scott, the Controller of BBC2.

It is a rich theme [John wrote] and could be full of praise and stimulation. Most people are suburban and won't admit it. What trim gardens we could show, what shopping arcades, front halls, churches, schools and human-scale paths and bicycle tracks and open spaces. I see it as a thanksgiving for traffic-free privacy throughout Britain – but not Southern Ireland, which isn't suburban, as is yours gratefully and ever,

John Betjeman[8]

Scott gave the project his blessing.

What parts of London should be filmed for the programme? To debate this question, Mirzoeff and the film editor Ted Roberts took John to lunch at one of his favourite restaurants, Wheeler's in Old Compton Street, Soho. It was Roberts who came up with the idea of making the Metropolitan Line the 'spine' of the programme. He pointed out that St John's Wood, near the beginning of the Line, could be regarded as the historical beginning of suburbia. Mirzoeff was enthusiastic. As for John, Roberts was preaching to the converted: no fewer than three of the poems in John's collection of poems *A Few Late Chrysanthemums* (1954) were about the Metropolitan Line.[9]

John suggested that the film should be called *Metro-land*. He said the film should be like the variety shows he remembered from the music-hall of his youth: the act should be changed every four minutes. 'If you don't like what's on now, you know it will soon change.' Several months of research began. The team needed to know when the Pinner Fair and the Croxley Green Revels would be held. Eddie Mirzoeff remembers sitting for two hours with the local historian of Chorleywood, who was a dentist. 'It was rather boring and we glazed over. And finally, just as we were leaving, quite sure there was nothing in Chorleywood, he said, "And of course there is a man who has built his house round a Wurlitzer organ removed from the Empire, Leicester Square." ' At Wheeler's, John and Mirzoeff had high-mindedly agreed that they were not out to show 'interesting people' but only 'how ordinary people lived in suburbia' – but Len Rawle and his mighty Wurlitzer were irresistible.

The film begins with a careering, speeded-up ride along the Metropolitan Line, past hedgerows, under bridges and through stations, to the music of 'Tiger Rag', played by the Temperance Seven when they were still (in 1956) the Royal College of Art Jazz Band. The record was in Ted Roberts's collection, and he played it at a breakneck 45rpm instead of 33⅓rpm.

Then watercolour covers and pages are shown from the developers' brochures mentioned in John's spoken introduction:

> Child of the First War, forgotten by the Second,
> We called you Metro-land. We laid our schemes
> Lured by the lush brochure, down byways beckoned,
> To build at last the cottage of our dreams,
> A city clerk turned countryman again,
> And linked to the Metropolis by train.

After a still of Quainton Road station, John is discovered in the bar of Horsted Keynes station, drinking beer. He walks from the bar on to a platform littered with old chocolate machines, enamel notices and antique leather baggage and steps into a third-class carriage with the slogan 'Live in Metro-land' engraved on the metal door-plate. ('It was real stuff,' Mirzoeff recalls, '– but all installed by our designers through the night.') This sequence was in fact filmed on the Bluebell Line – which, unlike the Metropolitan Line, still had steam trains – at about six o'clock in the morning before commercial business started. 'We were all feeling very dopey,' Mirzoeff says. 'You'll notice that the pint glass of beer John is meant to be drinking in the bar (it was actually ginger beer) is in fact finished, he's sucking at an empty glass. The sense was that he was meant to be in a *Brief Encounter*ish little buffet having a glass; but it took such an endless time for this steam train to turn up that he'd drunk it all and didn't know what to do with the glass. He knew he was meant to drink it and he'd already drunk it. There was a terrible embarrassment about knocking back this empty glass.'

In the carriage, as fields flash past, John is reading a 1910 copy of the *News of the World*. Then he looks out of the carriage window and sees, in black and white, the view from the Metropolitan Line in 1910, rushing past. John was a friend of Michael Robbins, then managing director of the London Underground. At an early stage of the research for *Metro-land*, John wrote to him to tell him what was planned and to ask for his approval and co-operation. Robbins wrote back that he thought it 'a lovely idea' and that he would be delighted to help. 'Extraordinarily enough,' he added, 'by some strange coincidence we discovered some film in the cupboard this week that might possibly have some relevance.' This was the film made from the Metropolitan Line in 1910. Mirzoeff thought it a 'stroke of genius' on Ted Roberts's part 'to use the moment where John gazes out of the window in the train and to see outside the window the old black-and-white footage'.

The stroke of genius was almost nullified by a most unexpected obstacle. On receiving the 1910 film from Michael Robbins, Mirzoeff had offered it to the BBC but was told that 'the BBC doesn't hold any film that it has not shot itself'. He was advised to give it instead to the National Film Archive, who knew how to preserve old film. So Mirzoeff went to the NFA and said, 'Look, we've discovered this. It's extremely rare. Could you please look after it?' The NFA representative said, 'It's magnificent! We've never seen anything like it!' and it was accepted for the collection immediately. Mirzoeff recalls what followed.

> The attitude of the then archivist was that the best way to preserve film was for no one ever to see it. When, some weeks later, we said to the NFA that we wanted to make use of the film, we were told by a crabby official, 'You can't possibly touch it. It's far too rare and delicate.' I said, 'This is utterly ridiculous! You wouldn't *have* the film but for us. We *must* borrow it, because we want to give the impression of Sir John Betjeman looking out of a train window into the past.' We asked if we could make a copy, and they said, 'Under no circumstances. It's extremely valuable archive film.' There was a terrific row – quite a long drama. And eventually they very grudgingly released it – at full archive price, to our dismay, making quite a dent in our budget.

After the early-morning session on the Bluebell Line, John took all the team back to the country home of his other favourite film-director, Jonathan Stedall, where he had spent the night. Drinks were dispensed and John held a 'school prizegiving', inscribing copies of his books to members of the team. Mirzoeff's was inscribed 'To the head prefect'. In the copy of Simon Wilson, the sound recordist, John wrote: 'To Simon, who recorded the flowers growing'. This was a standing joke: in recording a background track at Quainton Road station, Wilson had pointed a microphone at a flowerbed, and John had pretended to think that he was recording the flowers growing.

The film moves on to the exterior of the Baker Street station buffet, about which John had written in his poem 'The Metropolitan Railway'. Now he asks: 'Is this Buckingham Palace?' and then, as the camera moves inside,

> Are we at the Ritz? No. This is the Chiltern Court Restaurant, built above Baker Street station, the gateway between Metro-land out *there* and London down *there*. The creation of the Metropolitan Railway.

In 1972, when the film was made, the restaurant where H. G. Wells and Arnold Bennett had eaten when they lived in Chiltern Court (the flats above the station) was still open; John was able to sit at a crisply laid table and to evoke the ladies from Pinner and Ruislip who, after a day's shopping at Liberty's or Whiteley's, would sit waiting for their husbands to come up from Cheapside or Mincing Lane. 'While they waited they could listen to the strains of the band playing for the *thé dansant* before they took the train for home.' Only eleven years later, when Frank Delaney wrote his *Betjeman Country*, the place had been closed down, the restaurant gutted.[10]

John resists the strong temptation to recite his ready-made poem about the buffet, though he allows himself an echo of its opening two words as the 1910 archive film shows a train leaving Baker Street station –

> Early Electric – punctual and prompt.
> Off to those cuttings in the Hampstead Hills,
> Of St John's Wood, Marlborough Road . . .

Standing amid the remains of the defunct Marlborough Road station, John points out the house where Thomas Hood died. 'Thomas Hood the poet. He wrote: "I remember, I remember, the house where I was born", and the railway cut through his garden.' This gives John the cue to add: '*I* remember Marlborough Road station because it was the nearest station to the house where lived my future parents-in-law.' He did a piece about the house's having once belonged to the artist Alma-Tadema, but this ended up on the cutting-room floor, with many miles of other reluctantly rejected footage. In the film John emerges from the old Marlborough Road booking hall – which by 1972 had become an Angus Steak House.

> Farewell old booking hall, once grimy brick,
> But leafy St John's Wood, which you served, remains . . .

There are several shots of St John's Wood villas, where artists and kept women lived in the Victorian age;[11] and John shows No. 12 Langford Place, the sinister 'helmeted house' where lived the Rev. John Hugh Smyth-Piggot whose disciples believed him to be Christ and indulged in free love. John knew all about the Rev. Mr Smyth-Piggot, his country house The Agapemone and his Clapton chapel with 'wonderful stained glass by Walter Crane', from reviewing for the *Daily Herald*, in 1945, Joseph Shearing's *The Abode of Love*, the story of the Agapemonites. But another cutting-room casualty was the St John's Wood house of the television announcer Mary Malcolm. 'The crew loved filming at Mary Malcolm's,' Eddie Mirzoeff remembered, 'because she produced an extremely fine bottle of chilled white wine. It was the first day of real filming, and like all crews they thought, "*This* is going to be all right!" and they shot a lot of film in Mary Malcolm's garden. She was very charming; but in fact it was never used.'

From the lowering casements of Langford Place, the train hurries on to Neasden, a town which Candida's friends at *Private Eye* magazine had turned into a byword for suburban gaucheness, investing it with a hopeless football team, Neasden United, for which the player 'Baldy' Pevsner scored own goals and whose manager Ron Knee was usually 'ashen-faced' in defeat. *Private Eye* had issued a record of 'The Neasden Song', sung by the cartoonist and actor William Rushton. It began, 'Neasden: you won't be sorry that you breezed in!' Eddie Mirzoeff decided to use it in the film soundtrack to accompany shots of a Neasden milk float and of rows of shops in Neasden Parade. There was a snag, however.

The record [Mirzoeff recalled] was one of those floppy things that used to come inside the front cover of *Private Eye*. But if you happened to get that particular one, 'The Neasden Song', you couldn't hear the words, because they had mixed it so badly. So we had to go back to them and say, could they find the original tracks, which, by some sheer miracle, they could. We remixed it completely, so that the words were now much clearer and the backing far less strong.

In his commentary, John falls in with the unflattering image of Neasden:

Out of the chimney-pots into the openness,
Till we come to the suburb that's thought to be commonplace,
Home of the gnome and the average citizen,
Sketchley and Unigate, Dolcis and Walpamur.[12]

But then he goes on to show another side to Neasden, as he introduces the eminent ornithologist Eric Simms in Gladstone Park – 'the start of the well-known Neasden Nature Trail'. Of course there is an element of send-up in this too. In his precise, deadpan voice, Mr Simms describes the commonest birds as if he were David Attenborough pointing out jungle exotica. 'There are something like nine hundred pairs of house-sparrows within half a mile of my house and many of them can be found in the park. One of the very common birds round here is the London or feral pigeon. That's a cock blackbird looking for worms. That's a hen blackbird which has just come out from the shrubberies. The second most interesting part of my Nature Trail at Neasden are the allotments in Brook Road, and there's such a good view from the top here that I can pick birds up at a great distance.' Eddie Mirzoeff remembers:

> Much more than now, the word 'bird' was slang for 'girl', so there were all kinds of *doubles entendres* – 'It's a marvellous place for coming to watch young birds at this time of the year' and so on. John wondered if he was being cruel to Mr Simms. He was a very uncruel person and he was sensitive to that. There was quite a lot of heart-searching as to whether we were sending him up slightly too much. But in fact we got Mr Simms in and showed it to him, and he loved it, didn't think we were sending him up at all. He wrote an autobiography after that and there was a whole chapter about being filmed for *Metro-land*.

After Neasden, Wembley – 'an unimportant hamlet Where for years the Metropolitan didn't bother to stop'. On the way, the sad story of 'Sir Edward Watkin's dream', an Eiffel Tower for London. Watkin, chairman of the Metropolitan Line, thought thousands would pay to climb the tower, and announced a five hundred guinea prize for the best design. But when the first stage was opened, with its Turkish baths, shops and Winter Gardens, no crowds arrived. The tower rusted and was dismembered in 1907. As John relates the tale of the Wembley Tower, Mirzoeff throws across the screen, in quick succession, the preposterous competition designs. And then follows a grand *coup de amphithéâtre*: John says 'This is where London's failed Eiffel Tower stood, Watkin's Folly as it was called' – and the camera pulls back to show that he is standing in the middle of the football pitch in Wembley Stadium.

Wembley also gives John the chance of an autobiographical flashback. In 1924, at eighteen, he had visited the British Empire Exhibition with his father. He had preferred the Imperial pavilions of India, Sierra Leone and Fiji 'With their sun-tanned sentinels of Empire outside', to the Palaces of Industry and Engineering 'Which were too much like my father's factory'. He had had to wait in the Palace of Arts 'While my father saw the living models in Pears' Palace of Beauty'. (One might have thought that, at eighteen, John was old enough to accompany his father into the Palace of Beauty – but he seems to want to convey the idea that he was still a large-eyed child at the Wembley Exhibition; perhaps, too, he wants to present his father as coarse, a dirty old man, and himself as a refined young one.) To the music of Walford Davies's 'Solemn Melody', a 1924 shot of the Basilica in the Palace of Arts is shown, replete with murals by A.K. Lawrence and Eric Gill. Then, the murals stripped, we see John in the Basilica, beside a Humpty Dumpty pantomime prop. The music switches to 'Masculine Women and Feminine Men' by the Savoy Havana Band, and King George V and Queen Mary are seen riding on the miniature railway in the Wembley Pleasure Park.

> Oh bygone Wembley, where's the pleasure now?
> The temples stare, the Empire passes by . . .
>
> But still people kept on coming to Wembley.
> The show-houses of the newly built estates.
> A younger, brighter, homelier Metro-land:
> 'Rusholme', 'Rustles', 'Rustlings', 'Rusty Tiles',
> 'Rose Hatch', 'Rose Hill', 'Rose Lea', 'Rose Mount', 'Rose Roof',
> Each one is slightly different from the next,
> A bastion of individual taste . . .

This suburban idyll is followed by one of the best lines in the film, 'Roses are blooming in Metro-land' (after the haunting First World War song 'Roses are blooming in Picardy'). Frank Delaney noted in his *Betjeman Country* (1982) that the rose house-names had gone. 'On Oakington Avenue [Wembley] no more "Rusholme", "Rustles" or "Rustlings" – only numbers, the new egalitarian snobbery . . .'[13] But in fact, Mirzoeff reveals, 'Those houses never had those names – we made them up from a book of house names John brought into the cutting-room.'

On to Kingsbury station, near which John appears on the battlements of Highfort Court, where 'a speculative builder . . . let himself go, in the Twenties'. And then to Harrow, with the public schoolboys raising their shallow-crowned straw hats at 'Bill', the register-taking, to the sound of one of the rousing Harrow songs that used to make Sir Winston Churchill weep on his return visits to the school. John had something of a fixation on Harrow.[14] In north Harrow, away from the school, the camera zooms in to front-door stained-glass panels by the

Whitefriars Glass Company of Harrow – sunset, bulrush and bluebird motifs – to the music of 'Sunny Side of the Street' by Jack Hylton's band. John was not present at the filming of the Sunday-morning sequence that followed – gardening, lawn-mowing and washing cars to the sound of *Family Favourites* on the wireless (from the actual broadcast on the day of filming, Sunday 25 June 1972) – 'Down by the Lazy River' sung by the Osmonds, the young American brothers with gleaming teeth who were then the heartthrobs of English teenage girls. The car-washing sequence makes great play with sudsy water dribbling down car windows. Four magazines of film – at ten minutes a magazine – were used up on the car-washing alone. 'It's a banal occupation,' Mirzoeff said, 'but we found a way of making it interesting, with the water running down like lava.'

From Harrow, on to Harrow Weald and Grims Dyke, the half-timbered mansion which Norman Shaw built for W.S. Gilbert, the lyricist of the Savoy Operas. John regarded it as 'a prototype of all suburban homes in southern England'. The BBC research team had learned that a meeting of the Byron Luncheon Club was to be held there and addressed by the historian Elizabeth Cooper. Eddie Mirzoeff 'did a recce' at an earlier meeting and realized he would be able to make striking picturesque capital out of the Tory ladies' hats.

Elizabeth Cooper was the local historian [he said]. She was blonde and rather chubby and pretty and John strongly took to her; she very much took to him, too. The idea was originally to use her speech to give us facts about whatever was being shown; but it became clear that the fun was not so much in that as in the faces and the hats. I knew they were going to look like that because of my preliminary recce.

We could not film John at the lecture – he would have been talking while Elizabeth Cooper was talking; and he'd have been looking down at the ladies and they'd have been craning upwards to look at him. So we filmed him separately, arriving at the top of the stairs and looking as if he saw them, when in fact they weren't there. That was one of the more ludicrous events – my standing there and saying, 'Pretend I'm a woman wearing a strange hat, John. Try and smile! Go on, think of a curious sort of hat on my head.' Poor man.

The stratagem worked. There is an almost Hitchcockian suspense as John climbs the oak staircase, beckoning us on. 'If I go up there I'll see – goodness knows what. Let's go and look.' Then he appears to burst into the hall of hatted ladies and his face breaks into a smile of bemused delight. Elizabeth Cooper is describing Grims Dyke as 'the most beautiful house in Harrow, one of the most interesting both

architecturally and historically'. John comments, 'Dear things, ind
it is', and, to the accompaniment of 'Tit Willow', goes on to describe
how Gilbert was drowned in the garden pond in 1911. 'After a good
luncheon he went bathing with two girls, Ruby Preece and Winifred
Emery. Ruby found she was out of her depth, and, in rescuing her,
Gilbert died, of a heart attack, here – in this pond.'

It was the pond, as much as the house, that made Eddie Mirzoeff
want to film at Grims Dyke.

Grims Dyke was one of the places that John cared about [he said]. It was,
to be frank, a bit off the beaten track of the Metropolitan Line, but it was
by Norman Shaw, whom he was passionate about. I was not sure it would
make a good sequence; but once we got the sense that not only was there
the building but also the pond and the story of W.S. Gilbert drowning
which you could write suggestively, with Ruby and Winifred having the
bathe after lunch – these two young nymphs – we knew it would work.
The sense of risqué frolics, which are slightly implied in what you see.
John named the girls, too: it was so typical of him, to get the names of the
little people. It's always *particular* things, it's naming anything; all names
have resonances to them, and Ruby and Winifred are such period names.

John's commentary continues 'Funereal from Harrow draws the
train' but with a swift music-hall change of scene and mood we are
suddenly among the roundabouts and ferris-wheels of the Pinner Fair,
held once a year on St John the Baptist's Day. Festival gaiety and a
tradition from the Middle Ages elicit from John a couplet in the
manner of Keats's *The Eve of St Agnes* –

> It is the Feast Day of the Parish Saint,
> A medieval Fair in Metro-land.

The next part of the film was meant to be a tour of the architectural
glories of Moor Park Golf Club, a great house of the early eighteenth
century. To Baroque music, John would talk amusingly about the
Venetian *trompe l'oeil* allegories of gods and cupids; he might also try
his hand at a stroke or two on the course. That was what eventually
happened; but not before a storm in a tea caddy had been played out.

The plan was [Eddie Mirzoeff recalled], we would film inside the clubhouse first of all – do all the architectural stuff, get that out of the way. It
was a massive lighting job. John was due to come to Moor Park station.
He liked to come to the locations by Underground, not by car; he thought
it was in the spirit of the film to come on the Metropolitan Line – sort of

'method acting'. So we arranged to meet him at the station. The team were at the golf club much earlier to sort out the lighting and other problems.

He was late. We were sitting there waiting. There was no sign of him. We didn't know what had happened. Christine Whittaker, one of our young researchers, had been sent to collect him. Time went by and eventually we saw a Mini appear with John in it. It drew up and we all lined up outside Moor Park Golf Club waiting to greet him good morning. He came out of the door looking like a thundercloud, saying, 'I know I'm only the *artiste* and therefore the least important person in this team . . .'

I thought, 'Oh God, something's gone wrong'; turned round and noticed that everybody had disappeared, edging away and leaving me to face this . . . this major difficulty. What had happened, Christine quickly explained, was that Moor Park station – we hadn't realized – had two exits. She was at the main exit, he went to the other exit. He stood there and waited and waited and waited and thought we'd forgotten all about him; and finally, when Christine went exploring and found him, he was in this terrible temper. What could we do? Clearly he was in no state to start talking about architecture. I think somebody went and got some gin and tonic. I had to make a quick decision, and I decided we'd do the easy bit first. I knew that John played golf quite well. He played it down in Cornwall and enjoyed it. So I said 'Let's do the golf bit first – change everything around.'

If you look quite carefully at the piece he does just before he hits the golf ball – he says the nearness of golf to London is the attraction of Moor Park Golf Club – he's very, very serious. It's an absolutely dead straight face, there isn't the flicker of a smile. He's still fuming at the fact that he hasn't been picked up on time. There's this turbulence. And we say, well, can we do the drive off? (It was going to be quite a big sequence, his playing golf.) And he does this grandiose swing and completely misses, this first take. And you had this marvellous moment when he suddenly broke up laughing and the cameraman went on filming, and all the tension disappeared, just like that. It was the most magic moment in the film, I think.

After the golf-club sequence, George Glanville, the officious, jobsworth Moor Park gate-keeper (who had formerly been in the military police) is shown, first chatting ingratiatingly to a lady member, then implacably turning away a non-member at the entrance barrier. Mirzoeff had earlier toyed with the idea of letting John arrive at the barrier as a non-member. 'We'd worked it out, what was going to happen,' Mirzoeff said. 'I said to John, "Can you plan what you're going to say if George stops you?" He said, "If George says, 'You can't go through here,' I'm going to say, 'Oh, I thought this was an *urban clearway*.'" Of course, once we saw the state John was in, we couldn't let him loose on George. In any case, we had the feeling that John wasn't terribly good with people. He was a one-man show, not effective as an interviewer. He would have got very angry. He didn't care for George, and he was happier not to encounter him. Everybody else took hours in arguing with George, who clearly enormously enjoyed having an argument. Eventually we sent Christine Whittaker along to be stopped by him, and filmed her. He didn't realize it was set up. We said to Christine, "For God's sake don't argue with him; just turn round and go away." '

The next section of the film, heralded by a pipe band, was of the Croxley Green Revels, with the crowning of a local sort of 'Queen of the May'. The commentary for this part of the film included a joke of Mirzoeff's that John thought was the funniest joke of the entire programme –

> The Croxley Green Revels –
> A tradition that stretches back to 1952.

'He thought it was hilarious,' Eddie Mirzoeff said in 1991. 'And in 1972 it *was* quite funny to speak of a tradition stretching back to 1952; but when the film is re-run today, people scratch their heads and think, well, yes, that is going back some.'

The Croxley Green sequence also contains one of the memorably comic images of the film: a small boy eating an ice-cream cone and getting vanilla all over his face. 'Actually, we cheated,' Mirzoeff admitted. 'The small boy was in fact filmed at the Rickmansworth Donkey Derby, another Metro-land carnival. We eventually decided we hadn't room for both the Croxley Green sequence and the Rickmansworth sequence, so we cut out Rickmansworth. But we couldn't bear to lose the ice-cream boy, so he was shown as if on the sidelines at Croxley Green.'

As Chorleywood comes into view ('Where in '89 the railway came') John says: 'This is, I think, essential Metro-land.' The 'country quality' survived there – 'Oak, hazel, hawthorn, gorse and sandy tracks . . .' A child hurtles round the Chorleywood cricket pitch in a game of rounders, and a boy utters a line which, in both sense and rhythm, could come straight from a Betjeman poem: 'Mrs Hill, we've got eight rounders now.' John knew what he wanted to show in Chorleywood: 'The Orchard', the family home which C.F.A. Voysey had built for himself and his wife in 1900. 'I think it was the parent of thousands of simple English houses,' John says, perhaps forgetting that he has already brought a similar paternity suit against Norman Shaw's Grims Dyke. As if in counterpoint to the tradition stretching back to 1952, he makes full play of the fact that he, speaking in 1972, had known the architect and his wife who had lived in that house built in Victoria's reign.[15] In his affectionate tour of the house, John shows his genius for television commentary. It is neither literary prose nor verse, but a series of effortless impromptus which yet manage not to be inconsequential:

> Voysey liked to design every detail in his house. For instance, that knocker, Voysey. A typical curious-shaped handle, Voysey. And this handle or iron hinge with what seems to be his signature tune, the heart. It's there at the end of the hinge, it's here round the letterbox, it's also round the keyhole and it seems to be on the key. That's a Voysey key, and in the house he did everything down to the knives and forks.

There was genuine improvisation in this intimate patter; John veered right away from the scenario that had been agreed with Mirzoeff. Throughout the sequence filmed in The Orchard, John is holding a small book. Why, never becomes clear. The book was Beatrix Potter's *The Tale of Mrs Tittlemouse* (1910). John had read the book in childhood, and the Voyseys' house reminded him of one of its picture-captions: 'Such a funny house! There were yards and yards of sandy passages, leading to storerooms and nut-cellars and seed-cellars, all amongst the roots of the hedge.' Mirzoeff agreed that at some point in the filming of The Orchard John should open the book and read those words. The idea came to nothing. 'The best-laid plans of mice and men . . .' Mirzoeff quoted ruefully.

> Because of continuity John was holding the book in all the bits of looking at the door and the key and the Voysey heart shapes, and he had it in the main piece that he was going to do, which he was quite nervous about doing, in fact, as he always was with the main pieces. But it was an absolutely characteristic Betjeman thing that while he was trying to remember what he was meant to say . . . I think it was the most extraordinary occasion of all the films I did with him, in which you actually see the mind working, quite clearly, and suddenly thinking of this other point, of how he was not very tall and the lintels of the doors are very low and that you could see this if he walked to them . . . and then he just did it, in midstream, without any warning. I mean, the focus could have gone completely; as it happens it was all right. We were open-mouthed that he was going to improvise in that way.

The spontaneity of the unexpected move, Mirzoeff thought, more than compensated for losing the twee charm of the *Tittlemouse* extract. The patter is all Betjeman:

The plan of the house radiates out from this hall. Extreme simplicity is the keynote. No unnecessary decoration. The balusters here for the stairs, straight verticals, giving an impression of great height to this simple hall. But as a matter of fact, it isn't a particularly high house; in fact, it's rather small. I knew Mr Voysey and I saw Mrs Voysey; they were small people and in case you think it's a large house, I'll just walk – I'm fat I know, but I'm not particularly tall – and I'll stand by the door here and you can compare my height with the ledge and the door.

Mirzoeff now had to build the rest of the sequence round the new move.

Once he's got there, *now* what are we going to do? We've got to get him somewhere else. So we had him walk through to the far little round window and talk about 'This pane which opens to let in the air from Beechy Bucks . . .' And because this hadn't been planned either, and had to be improvised as well to make up for this wonderful thing he had thought up, we'd forgotten all about *Mrs Tittlemouse* by this stage. There was no way you could get it back, because the new thing was something so good. And you can see in the film when he does that piece about Beechy Bucks, he looks . . . there's a very characteristic shifty look of the eye. Every time I see the film I look for that moment; because that was Take 6 or 7 or 8 and I'd been saying, 'No, it's going wrong again, John,' and he gives this 'Oh God', you know, nervous glance, 'Have I got away with it this time?' And of course he *had*. He had this very rare gift, an ability to talk to a piece of glass, a lens, as if it were a human being, and to say things like, 'Come with me, and I'll show you wonders.' How you say this to a piece of machinery is extraordinary. He was not arch or ingratiating. There is an *engaging* quality in the eye.

Also in Chorleywood, and a contrast to the arty-crafty restraint of The Orchard, was the Art Deco glare and blare of Len Rawle's cinema organ. John, who had first heard the instrument in the Empire, Leicester Square, as a film critic in the 1930s, and had visited the revolving house of the Wurlitzer family in Cincinnati in 1957, would surely feel at home in this sequence. In fact, however, Len Rawle's house was the scene of one of the film's worst crises.

We had planned to film at Len Rawle's house the whole day [Mirzoeff said]. It was a difficult thing to film. Mr Rawle has this extraordinary Wurlitzer which he plays in the living room and which you have to crawl behind to get inside. John arrived at ten o'clock, again by the Metropolitan Line at Chorleywood; and he announced to a totally astonished film unit that he was going to leave by 10.45 – the first mention of this. Some time later we found that he had double-booked himself with another film crew for another film the same morning. He was making a pair of films with Jonathan Stedall – *London on Sunday* and *London in the Country*, two half-hour films that Ted Roberts actually cut as well. With his usual inability to say no to anybody or anything, John had arranged to be at Cloth Fair with Jonathan Stedall and a film crew at half-past eleven, and he'd sort of thought that would be all right – in spite of the fact that we had made it absolutely clear that this would be a full day. He literally walked in at ten saying 'Well, I've got exactly three-quarters of an hour. I must be away at 10.45.' The extremely equable and placid cameraman, John McGlashan – 'The Bishop' as John called him, he really was a bishop in some obscure church – threw a fit at that point. He said to me, as if it were my fault, 'I just cannot be expected to work in this way. How do you think I can do this in three-quarters of an hour? There's no possibility whatsoever of being able to film the sequence with Sir John not here.' I said to John, 'You can't do this. It's absolutely not on.' And he got into a tizz, as he quite often did. You could see he was getting upset – because he was guilt-ridden, as usual. And tempers got extremely frayed.

In the end what Mirzoeff managed to do was to film John walking in from outside and standing by in one shot while Len Rawle played the organ. 'A wide shot and a close-up: that was it. 10.45 came and off he went.' For the rest of the day Len Rawle played the organ and smiled happily at the open space where John should have been. By sleight-of-hand editing it was made to seem as if John were there, enjoying and responding to the playing.

> O happy indoor life in Chorleywood
> Where strangest dreams of all are realised,
> Mellifluating out from modern brick
> The pipe-dream of a local man, Len Rawle,
> For pipe by pipe and stop by stop he moved
> Out of the Empire Cinema, Leicester Square,
> The Mighty Wurlitzer
> Till the huge instrument filled half his house
> With all its multitude of sound effects.

Len Rawle bears John no ill-will for his perfunctory visit. To him, it was the event of a lifetime.

The house is much changed since that time [he said in 1990]. We've extended it front, back and sides – not to accommodate a larger instrument;

the 'Mighty Fertilizer' is still there. That wonderful film has taken my wife
and me around the world; we became quite famous as a result of it. We
made about twelve records and I'm one of the few people who plays these
machines now.

I remember Sir John coming in, with a plastic carrier bag. I was fearing
the moment of his arrival, but he came out of the taxi and he just shuffled – his Parkinson's Disease, sadly, was quite evident at that time and it
certainly isn't evident on the film; he must have made a massive effort, I
think, to have accommodated some of the movements which were wanted.
And as he came in our front door, his face lit up.[16]

As Len Rawle plays 'Crimond' and 'Varsity Drag' (an ironic link with
John's poem 'The 'Varsity Students' Rag'), his wife and two daughters
are seen in the background on a sofa. After the screening of the film
in February 1973, John's and Elizabeth's friend Peter Shaffer wrote to
John: 'What an adorable programme on Metro-land, enchanting,
lyrical . . . O o o that Wurlitzer man and the mum and child [sic]
reading unconcerned on the sofa . . .'[17]
When the Rawle performance had been filmed, Mirzoeff realized
that he had forgotten to record John's laugh at the end.

What were we to do? We had to record the Sir John Betjeman laugh. It was
a high-pitched laugh, not an easy thing to imitate. So we edited the film,
showed it to him and said, 'Look, you do a giggle.' He said: 'Well, I can't
do a giggle.' So Ted said, 'We'll put you in a recording booth and we'll tell
you funny stories, and then you'll laugh.' Ted had a string of what he
thought were funny stories. But there were no laughs. It was desperate. For
story after story, John's face just got longer and longer. He tried, but it was
impossible. But he had brought along a couple of friends. They started
telling him stories. At the end there was a sort of half-laugh, and we had
to make do with that.

To the strains of the Wurlitzer pumping out 'Chattanooga Choo
Choo', John rides on to the end of the line at Amersham, where he
delivers a dummy valediction, the kind of sign-off couplet with which
Shakespeare signals the ends of acts –

> In those wet fields the railway didn't pay,
> The Metro stops at Amersham today.

He does not pause in Amersham to reminisce about his visits to
Arthur Machen; but he cannot leave the area without showing the fate

of a Modern Movement house familiar to him from his days on *The Architectural Review*.

In 1931 all Buckinghamshire was scandalized[18] by the appearance high above Amersham of a concrete house in the shape of a letter Y. It was built for a young professor by a young architect, Amyas Connell. They called it 'High and Over'.

'I am the home of a twentieth-century family,' it proclaimed, 'that loves air and sunlight and open country.'

It started a style called moderne – perhaps rather old-fashioned today.

And one day, poor thing, it woke up and found developers in its back garden.

Goodbye, *High* hopes and *Over* confidence – In fact, it's probably goodbye England.

Like The Orchard, High and Over came to the film through John's direct knowledge, not through the team's research. 'We wouldn't have found either of them without him,' Mirzoeff admitted. It was almost certainly John who wrote the caption about High and Over when it was given a page in *The Architectural Review* of November 1932:

STRAIGHT LINES AND STRAIGHT THINKING

HIGH AND OVER, AMERSHAM, BUCKINGHAMSHIRE, Amyas Connell, *architect*. Although this house may not fit in with the local use of brick and tile in Buckinghamshire, the straight lines of the cantilever-reinforced concrete construction in the house, and the long terraced garden walls, have been designed to merge in with the lines of the chalk hills behind and around it. Since it is a twentieth-century building it is designed with the object of getting as much sunlight and as many fine views as possible. For this reason it is more logical than the 'Elizabethan' bijou residences that are being built elsewhere in the district. The Elizabethans did not require views from hills, nor sunlight. We do . . . The plan shows how every room has three outside walls each pierced with windows. The whole house is of cantilever construction in reinforced concrete so that the horizontal lines are not a 'jazz modern' affectation, but a logical outcome.

So in 1932 John (if it was he who wrote the caption) was careful to deny that the house was 'jazz modern', while forty years later he concedes that it is 'moderne' – much the same thing. Freed from de Cronin Hastings's leash, he has come round to Art Deco,[19] as the style is also known; but he still seems more gleeful than dismayed at the nemesis by encroachment that has overtaken the house that began with such health-and-efficiency pretensions. 'Clean lines' were never John's thing.

And now the film moves towards its perfect pastoral coda. In a straw hat – perhaps to indicate the mood of nostalgic retrospect – John peers down from the battleship-grey iron bridge at the disused Quainton Road station. 'Where are the advertisements? Where the shopping arcade, the coal merchant and the parked cars?' Quainton Road was to have been 'the Clapham Junction of the rural part of the Metropolitan'.

But, alas, all that has happened is that there a line curves away to the last of the Metropolitan stations in the country in far Buckinghamshire, which was at Verney Junction.

And I can remember sitting here [on Quainton Road station] on a warm autumn evening in 1929 and seeing the Brill tram from the platform on the other side with steam up ready to take two or three passengers through oil-lit halts and over level crossings, a rather bumpy journey to a station not far from the remote hill-top village of Brill.

In the film's last scene, John is leaning on a fence at Verney Junction. The ghost station was named after the Buckinghamshire family whose near-by seat, Claydon House, had been a country refuge for Florence Nightingale. John turns to camera: 'The houses of Metro-land never got as far as Verney Junction. Grass triumphs. And I must say I'm rather glad.'

Most of John's work on the film was done, not on location, but in the cutting-room.

It was one of those films that fell totally into place in the cutting-room [Eddie Mirzoeff said]. The shooting was not, as it happens, particularly enjoyable. It was quite difficult and edgy, it wasn't one long laugh on the road. John was always pushing towards certain things – he was saying,

why don't we do this and why don't we do that, which didn't seem relevant to what we were actually doing. It was a strained time, in fact, on the
road. The laughs were all in the cutting-room. Some films are an endless
struggle to get the structure right and the pace right; and that one, for
some reason, wasn't – in the cutting-room.

To some extent John enjoyed the process and the craftsmanship of
editing. He liked coming in to Document Films, Ted Roberts's editing
studio in Soho.

A mythology grew around it [Eddie Mirzoeff said], as it grew around a lot
of the things John was interested in. On his way up Wardour Street he
would always pass a music publisher – gone now – called Peters Editions
(with the two words on the shop sign very close together); and he'd say,
'Look, there's Peter Sedition, the well-known anarchist.' And there was a
man called Ben Henry OBE, whose name he got obsessed by. Henry lived
on the floor below Document. Nobody ever met him, but John would see
the sign on the door and ask, 'And how is Ben Henry OBE and his kiddiz
and his little wife?' The fantasies grew. It was a nice friendly small film-
editing place, and he felt at home there. He wrote all his films – everything,
not only mine but everybody else's too – in the cutting-room.

Mirzoeff asked John to write 'treatments', and he did; 'but the
treatments bore absolutely no relation to the films themselves. They
were wild and bizarre, strange ideas – nothing ever that you were
really talking about or wanting to do'. So John's commentary was
always written to the cut footage in the end. He would sit at a
Steenbeck editing machine, which he had learned how to work, and
would go backwards and forwards on it with reams of paper. Mirzoeff
recalled: 'He'd write in his tiny spidery hand, which he couldn't read
and nobody else could read, many many pages of iambic verse and of
prose – just throwing papers on the floor one after another.'

If John was up against a 'writer's block', as often happened, he
would go off to another room at Document. His favourite, because it
was the only one where he could be certain of being on his own, was
a tea cupboard, which he called 'the composition cell'. He would sit
there trying to get the verse right. Then he would come back and say,
'What about this?' Ted Roberts, who had a talent for pastiche, would
be sitting trying to write the same kind of verse. He would hand it to
John and say, 'What about this?' And John would usually say, 'That's
much better than mine, let's throw away mine.' Then Mirzoeff would
tactfully chip in, 'No, John, but perhaps it's edging you towards what
you want to say.'

There was an extraordinary rapport between John Betjeman and Ted Roberts [Mirzoeff said]. John would write a line of verse and Ted would cap it with another rhyming line, which was usually pretty obscene. And they would shriek with laughter. And then: 'What about putting that in the film?' 'No, we can't really put that in the film.' Then John would remember limericks, he would talk about Gerald Berners who had composed wonderfully funny and obscene limericks, none of which I can now remember. And then he'd get on to the poems of the Rev. Bradford, which were all about boys. He had this gift of remembering large chunks of extremely funny poetry which he'd reel off. It was absolutely magical. Those were great days. At other times, I must say, it wasn't like that at all. John's idea was that anything was better than writing – *anything*. Always, coming in to look at the assembled film, he would say, 'Oh, it doesn't need words at all; let's go and have a drink.' And we'd say, 'No, it really does need words, John.' 'Oh *dear*.'

It usually took John three to four weeks to write the commentary for a fifty-minute film. He came in most days, sometimes staying the whole day, sometimes going after an hour – 'It's no good, I'm not in the mood.' He arrived mid-morning or after lunch.

Quite often he brought friends [Mirzoeff recalled] – people he was fond of or just people he was seeing that day. 'Let's go to the cutting-room and see the film' – which meant that no work was done. My face would fall when I saw him walk in with people. There were exceptions, such as his friend Margie Geddes.[20] He was particularly close to her and trusted her judgement. He was always convinced that the film was no good, frightful, a disaster. We would show sequences to Margie Geddes and she would say, 'But this is wonderful, John,' and he would be temporarily lifted by that. So we were quite pleased to see her. She helped to shore up this lack of confidence that John always had. It wasn't just about working; I was struck in the early days by the genuine sense he had, that this was a temporary phenomenon, that he was in vogue and therefore able to scratch a living, but that it wouldn't last and that he would unquestionably end in the workhouse. He used to say that regularly as a joke – but it was one of those things that you knew *wasn't* a joke. He had a terror that suddenly one day it would all go away. Coupled with the fear of death, which was very manifest, was the fear of poverty. He lived by his wits, he felt; one day, quite soon, people were going to see through it. And as a result he was always susceptible to adverse criticism. He hated the faintest whiff of anybody disliking anything. He was terrified by what the critics would say about his television programmes. Hours were spent in the cutting-room writing the scathing reviews that he was sure were going to be written about

Metro-land. Instead of writing the commentary, he was writing these stinking reviews. They were put in sealed envelopes to be opened after the actual reviews had been published. The reviewer he feared most was the son of one of his friends – Sean Day-Lewis, son of Cecil Day Lewis, John's predecessor as Poet Laureate. Sean would invariably pull apart a Betjeman programme, saying it was bitty, had no structure, had nothing going for it. John was paranoid about what Sean was going to say. And Sean's reviews were quite vitriolic, actually. John had this constant sense of uncertainty. The impression of the man on television and the man himself were two different things. He was by no means the person that the world thought it saw.

Often John tried to dispel his depression with drink. 'He hated the blank piece of paper,' Mirzoeff said 'And when he sat in front of the Steenbeck machine he'd say gloomily, "There's so much film on the *left*-hand side; and so little on the *right*-hand side [that is, completed]." It was a burden to him; and the thought of just having a laugh, which was John's great thing in life, and not having to sit and work, was extremely tempting. "Let's go and have a drink," he'd say; or "Why don't we have another drink and then we can go to my club and have lunch there." '

To be honest [Mirzoeff added] I was the puritan of the three of us, saying 'We haven't got the time, we haven't got the money.' John and Ted both thought I was a killjoy – 'Go away and let us enjoy ourselves.' And Ted was saying, 'The more we actually make him enjoy it, the more likely he is to come back and perhaps write something.' But in fact he never came back and wrote anything. Once you went and had a few glasses, nobody was in a state to write anything.

Mirzoeff did ban drinking in the cutting-room. In the early sessions John would arrive holding a bottle of burgundy and a bottle of whisky in his string bag. He was usually holding his teddy-bear Archie, too, and Archie's companion Jumbo came occasionally. One day John arrived and said, 'Jumbo is very depressed indeed,' meaning that he himself was depressed. 'How can we cheer him up?' Ted said. 'Let's give him a ride.' He put Jumbo on the flat plate rewind machine that went round and round – and Jumbo went round as if on a merry-go-round. After a while John said, 'Jumbo *is* enjoying himself,' and Mirzoeff knew that everything was going to be all right. 'It was ludicrous, really; but it was rather touching.' As a result of the drinking ban in the cutting-room, John gained a taste for tangerines. Document was near the fruit market in Berwick Street. The assistant constantly had to be sent out for 'another bag of those lovely tanjers' – 'Can we have some more tanjers?'

When the commentary had been finally worked out, and Gina Hobson had managed to type John's near-illegible notes, a day was set for recording the commentary right through. Eddie Mirzoeff arrived at Document at about nine o'clock in the morning. Ted Roberts was already there, with a very serious expression on his face. 'I think you'd better have a word with John immediately,' he said.

Mirzoeff thought: 'Oh, God, what's happened now?' He walked over and said, 'Hello, John, how are you?'

He said: 'A-a-a-a-a-ll r-i-i-i-i-i-ght.'

Mirzoeff thought. 'Why is he sounding so slow?'

He sounded terribly slow and slurred and sleepy. We clearly had a major problem. We thought that something awful had happened, and we asked him could he remember the name of his doctor. Eventually we found the name of his doctor [Jill Parker][21] in his address book and we rang her and said, 'Sir John sounds terribly funny; can you possibly have a word with him?' He spoke on the phone to his doctor. Finally, we spoke again, we got handed the telephone, and we said to the doctor, 'What's the matter?' And she said, 'He's perfectly all right; no problem at all. The only thing is that he was clearly feeling very nervous about recording the commentary, had some difficulty in sleeping, and took a sleeping pill at about a quarter to six this morning. So actually he's fast asleep.' Great! What do we do? The doctor said, 'Well, there's only one thing to do, and that's to put him to bed immediately.'

I said, 'We're in a Soho commentary-recording theatre.'

She said: 'I don't care where you are, put him to bed *now*.' She said, 'He'll be all right in a few hours.'

We turned to the dubbing mixer and said, 'What are we going do? Is there a bed?' and the man said, 'Yes. Curiously enough we often work quite late here and there is a camp bed.' We suggested to John that he might like to lie down on this bed, and he thought, yes, that was quite a good idea; and somehow or other a blanket was produced, and we tucked him into this bed, said Good-night, switched the light off and tiptoed out. I stood outside in absolute despair. I asked the people who ran the place whether they had a rate for sleeping as opposed to a rate for commentary recording, because we didn't want to pay the full rate. Anyway, we went away, came back about lunch-time – and he'd gone.

He'd left a message: 'JUST GONE FOR A DOZEN OYSTERS AND HALF A BOTTLE OF BUBBLY. BE BACK BY TWO.' He'd gone to Wheeler's. He came back full of beans, perfectly all right. We started recording that afternoon – and it was brilliant.

On 23 February 1973 a private showing of the film was held for John
and his friends at Colour Film Services, off Portman Square, London.
Among those present were Lady Diana Cooper, her son Lord
Norwich, Barry Humphries and John's old aunt Queenie Avril.[22] 'We
all went and had champagne in the Portman Hotel opposite,' Mirzoeff
said, 'not a piece of architecture that John approved of, but the champagne was all right and Barry Humphries paid for it.'

Less happy was the private viewing at Kensington House arranged
for Aubrey Singer, Head of Features Group at the BBC.

We were going to run the film for the first time as a complete film [Mirzoeff
recalled], and we asked Aubrey to it, as he was our boss. But he said he
couldn't come because he was going to America; and we said, 'Oh what a
shame, we thought you might have enjoyed it.' I thought; in that case, let's
get the film manager and my wife Judith, and a few other people. Then at
the last moment Aubrey changed his plans, said he was taking a later flight
to America and would turn up at the preview. We said, fine, feel free. He
came along, walked in, took one look at this group of people, glowered
throughout the film and walked out at the end without a word; and I
thought, what's the matter with him? Later he sent me a note saying 'If
you invite me to previews you will never, under any circumstances, invite
anybody else; I think this is outrageous.' I thought, for God's sake! And
therefore he took against *Metro-land*. He was just not in the mood to like
it, come what may.

Aubrey was known to John as 'Brigstocke' – because 'Brigstocke' was
the kind of executive name that he made up. And, apart from writing
adverse criticisms of his own film, John would say, 'What is Brigstocke
going to say about this? He'll find it frightfully boring, won't he?
Brigstocke won't let this be shown, will he?' I don't think Aubrey ever
knew that he was called Brigstocke.

Luckily the critics took a more favourable view of the film than
Singer, after it was screened on 26 February 1973. It was recognized
not only as a high point in television history, but as a benediction on
suburbia. John and Mirzoeff liked best an *Evening Standard* review by
Simon Jenkins which took flight in Betjemanesque verse:

GIRTHING SUBURBIA

> Panorama's breath is bated,
> World in Action holds its hand.
> For at 10.10 on the TV
> Betjeman's gone to Metro-land.

'Dad, it's Pinner on the Telly,'
Chintz mock-Tudor lounges cry.
'Do you think we ought to watch it
Or Come Dancing? Mum would die.'
Turn the knob and draw the curtains,
Hatch End, Ruislip, Rickmansworth.
Pork-pie hat and suit from Harrod's
On figure of suburban girth
Will touchingly reveal your secrets,
Architectural Peyton Place.
Unsteady gait, a pause, a gesture,
Betjeman smile on Betjeman face,
Popping up along the platform,
Prep-school boy on exeat,
Epitome of people's poet
Environmental laureate.
Metro-land was built for those who
Rode to work by Metroline,
Turn-of-century exotic
Homes to reach by high-tea time.
The camera traversed the dreamland,
Baker Street to Croxley Green,
Where golf and pool and Jag and rounders
Paid homage to the Beauty Queen.
It encapsulates affection
Deeply planted, not absurd,
By a man who knows that pictures
Are as mighty as the word.
For an hour he held enraptured
Pinner, Moor Park, Chorley Wood.
'Well I'm blowed,' they said, 'He likes us.
'Knew one day that someone should.'[23]

WITH THE ANDERSONS, THE PAGETS AND JOYCE GRENFELL

I now had [my tonsils] ripped out and John Betjeman came to see me. All the nurses were a-twitter that the Poet Laureate was coming to see me. And when he did arrive, he made up a poem about me . . .

Edward Anderson, interview, 1999

Lord Mottistone, John's co-landlord at Cloth Fair, died in 1963.[1] He had become Surveyor to the Fabric of St Paul's Cathedral, a post in which Paul Paget – his partner in business and in life* – immediately succeeded him. For a time, Paget was desolated; but in 1971, to everyone's amazement, he married. Winifred Hector, John's friend at Bart's Hospital, remembered: 'When we heard the news at Bart's, we said: "*MARRIED?!*" '[2] The architect's bride was the author Verily Anderson, widow of Captain Donald Anderson, a man much older than herself who had served in the Indian Army under Penelope's father and had been chief press officer for the 1951 Festival of Britain. By an almost Dickensian coincidence, John already knew Verily. Her maiden name was Bruce and she was of that Bruce family which had looked after John's Heddon Court pupil Kenric Rice when Rice's parents went to China and 'advertised' him in *The Times*.[3] Kenric had been 'like a brother' to her; and, through him, John had met the Bruces in the late 1920s, including Verily and her father, the Rev. Rosslyn Bruce, whose life she wrote as *The Last of the Eccentrics* (1972). 'John came to see us in 1929,' Verily Anderson Paget recalled. 'I would have been about fourteen. Any

---

* See *John Betjeman: New Fame, New Love*, pp. 502–3 and 506–7.

young man coming to the rectory, of course, was a source of excitement; but we weren't terribly hit by John, we didn't think him very attractive. He adored clergymen, so he doted on my father. They had the same sort of jokes.'[4] Rosslyn Bruce had been narrowly beaten by Hilaire Belloc in 1899 for the presidency of the Oxford Union. He became a well-known breeder of Skye terriers and sold Queen Victoria the puppy, Rona II, which appears in William Nicholson's woodcut of the Queen. Rosslyn Bruce's sister Kathleen married, first, Scott of the Antarctic,[5] then the first Lord Kennet, whose son, Wayland Young (second Lord Kennet), was John's ally in conservation battles.*

Verily Anderson's accomplishments were as varied as her father's. She studied at the Royal College of Music with Benjamin Britten, but did not take her Finals. She published over thirty books. Elizabeth Bowen wrote in a review of her autobiographical book *Spam Tomorrow* (1956):

> I feel I can best conjure up Mrs Anderson by saying she has one practically unknown gift: she can write what might seem a sustained tall story and at the same time make it convincing: at times, grimly so. She became a debutante, applied for a job as a companion, was almost annexed by a white slave trafficker and had a success designing toffee papers. She and Donald, a man of the most fascinating age, fell in love irrevocably though calmly upon the outbreak of World War II (which is, at least from the point of view of one young girl, brilliantly described). She became a FANY [First Aid Nursing Yeomanry]. She was court-martialled for driving into a gate-post and later deserted in order to marry Donald young. Married life in a top-floor West End flat took place during the Blitz. Previous to the excruciating birth of her first child, she spent a month in a pre-maternity institution known as The Barrens. This is a genuinely bizarre book. Those who agree with it will become incurable addicts of *Spam Tomorrow*.[6]

Something that recommended Verily to John was that she was a close friend of his friend, the entertainer Joyce Grenfell. He and Grenfell had been in touch since the 1940s, when he suggested for her monologues about 'a lady who speaks in a rosy soft voice and loves all "lovely" things and no sudden noises or vulgarity. She will probably wear homespun and a necklace of painted cotton reels.'[7] Verily

* See Chapter 2, ' "Vic. Soc." and "The Dok" '.

remembered Grenfell's saying, 'I had to do a television programme with John Betjeman the other day; I always think he's rather unsavoury – well, really, *savoury*, more.'[8] (She disapproved of his drinking and smoking.) But gradually the two had become friends, their sense of humour overcoming all differences. Verily had first met Joyce Grenfell on a *Woman's Hour* radio programme.

And then [Verily recalls] I was put on to edit for four years the *Girls' Friendly Society Magazine* – and having babies and writing books and helping out with the Festival of Britain. And I interviewed her for the magazine. Well, really, she interviewed me. I mean, I went to her dressing-room, all ready with questions to ask, and she asked me questions instead. She was terribly interested in the family, because she had no children of her own. And gradually she sort of crept into our lives, especially after my husband died in 1957. In 1963 I was very ill and in hospital and she just took over. She'd come and see me in hospital – they had strict visiting hours in those days, but she paid no attention to that. And then she'd go back to our flat and cook a stew. She was wonderful. I had no idea she was a Christian Scientist; it didn't seem to match up. I mean, she was asking what drugs I was on and so on. And when she did eventually let on, I was very interested. I didn't quite *become* one, but I wrote for the *Christian Science Monitor* and she became a great friend, as did her sweet husband Reggie, who outlived her by many years.[9]

Verily's mother, who had married Rosslyn Bruce in 1908, was Rachel Gurney of Northrepps Hall, near Cromer in Norfolk.[10] Verily knew Northrepps well as a child. Paul Paget also knew it through his uncle, Samuel Hoare, and was a distant cousin of Verily's, as his mother was 'half Gurney Hoare, half Hart-Davis'.[11] In the mid-1960s, Joyce Grenfell bought a cottage at Northrepps for Verily and her family. 'She said, "You find a nice cottage and we'll buy it and then you can be our tenants." So I said, "What about the rent?" – and that was 1s. And after a bit she said, "Oh, it's such a bother – *you* have it" – and gave it to us.'[12] And in Northrepps Verily met Paul Paget.

We must have paddled at fashionable Overstrand as children [Verily recalls] as we both had grandparents in the area. But he said that we met at Northrepps Church – it is curious that *he* remembered, it's usually the women who remember these things – he said it was a Remembrance Day service and out in the graveyard he saw this woman 'with masses of hair and even more children'. We both retired from London, a year or two before the Grenfells gave us this cottage, whence Paul came as a change from the formality of his inherited household at the other end of the village. We fell in love.[13]

On 7 June 1971 Joyce Grenfell wrote to her friend Virginia Graham: 'Verily Anderson and her cousin companion Paul Paget joined us for dinner on Saturday. He is an architect. Not the marrying kind. A *dear* man. They are enjoying each other's company so much. It really is a most lovely thing for both.'[14] One month later, one of Verily's daughters, Janie (later Joyce Grenfell's biographer), was about to marry Charles Hampton in Northrepps Church. And one of Verily's other daughters, Rachel Anderson, 'got Paul on the mat and said, "What's all this? You're going to have the reception of my sister's wedding in your house and put up a marquee for two hundred or so people. But where does my mother come into all this? *What are your intentions towards her?*" And Paul, telling the story, said he replied, "Would it be all right if I married her?" And Rachel said, "Oh yes, that would be all right as long as it's not on the same day." '[15]

On a hot summer's day, when John dropped in as he so often did, Paul asked him to be best man. 'I had on a light summer dress,' Verily recalls. 'We thought John would find it a great joke, our getting married at a total age of 127, and we expected some awful crack. But instead he came slowly towards me with his arms outstretched, wearing his most sacred *Sesame and Lilies* expression, whispering reverently as he bestowed a holy kiss: "All in white!" '[16] Verily and Paul were married in August, twenty days after Janie – not, like her, in Northrepps but in St Bartholomew the Great, with John as best man and Joyce Grenfell as 'a rather mature bridesmaid'.[17] The bride wore a white spotted dress from Grenfell's wardrobe. Grenfell was taller and thinner than Verily but, as she said, 'Your width takes up the length.'[18] A colour photograph of the wedding party was taken (see plate), a very Seventies tableau. As a wedding present John gave the couple John Sell Cotman's *Specimens of the Architectural Antiquities of Norfolk* (1818), a set of sixty etchings. 'He inscribed it in pencil, "In case you want to give it away to someone else" – as if we ever would,' Verily remembers.[19] The inscription ended: 'from . . . John Betjeman and his fellow bachelor Elizabeth Cavendish'.

After the wedding, Paul and Verily moved into the splendour of Templewood, the shooting box the Partners had designed for Sam Hoare. On the façade were sphinxes from the demolished Nuthall temple and Ionic columns from the old Bank of England.[20] John and Elizabeth were already familiar with the house, as they had stayed there with Paget in 1969. After that visit, John had written to Paget:

Dear Paul,

What a glorious crowded visit. Here is a
picture of poor white washed-out quiet
Elizabeth looking at a Norfolk water lily
midst the reeds and the rest of us. The
journey back was quiet and comfortable. We
dined at the Great Eastern and had some
Beaujolais. I had a bath when I got home,
cut my finger- and toe-nails and slept like a
log . . .[21]

John had given Paget advice on an allegorical painting the architect
had planned for the ceiling of the grand hall, painted by Brian
Thomas, the artist who later created *The Sailor's Return* on the
blocked-up window at Cloth Fair. John suggested a scene of Heaven
and Hell. 'You should have all the people you like at one end and all
the people you hate at the other,' he said.[22] In Thomas's original
design, based on John's suggestions, was a menacing full-frontally
nude Devil. Under his feet were the damned, among whom, John
urged, Nikolaus Pevsner should be portrayed. But this plan was later
abandoned in favour of the Four Seasons. 'Spring' showed Paget as a
Cambridge athlete – 'something he certainly *wasn't*', as his stepson
Eddie Anderson commented.[23] 'Summer' was a scene of Norfolk
where his grandparents had lived and to which he had always intended
to return. A swallow-tailed butterfly peculiar to Norfolk hovered in
the air. Northrepps Church was depicted, with a do-gooding aunt
leading people in and an unctuous parson stooping in the porch.
Cloth Fair and Mottistone Manor were also painted. (Lord
Mottistone had left Paget the mansion on the Isle of Wight and most
of his other property.) After Paget married Verily, Thomas returned
and painted two *grisaille* amendments, *Babies and Books* and *Babies
and Music*. Eddie felt there should have been a third depicting a
decanter and two glasses on a silver salver.[24]

Eddie's main career was to be in television; but in 1972, having
been expelled from school, he was working as Lord Leicester's game-
keeper on the estate at Holkham Hall. There he fell seriously ill with
a quinsy – acute inflammation of the tonsils. He was brought to
Templewood to recover.

I was lying in Paul's dressing-room in some distress [he recalls] – agonizing pain. And I was just beginning to get better when John Betjeman came to stay. He came in to see me and said, 'How does it feel to have quinsies?' He was rather amused by the word, it was like something from Edward Lear to him, I think. I said: 'It's like having hat pins driven into your ears.' And then perhaps six months later I went into St Bart's to have my tonsils out. I was rather old for the operation, I was about twenty. The reason it had been delayed was that Verily thought that I had a wonderful career as a treble for ever, so she didn't want my tonsils interfered with. Anyway, I now had them ripped out and John Betjeman came to see me. All of the nurses were a-twitter that the Poet Laureate was coming to see me. And when he did arrive, he made up a poem about me, which began –

> Eddie lies upon Bart's bed,
> In to have his hat-pins out;
> Now that horrid quinsy's dead,
> Ed can sing and dance and shout.[25]

When Paul and Verily were in London, John often had breakfast with them. He would look down from his window at No. 43 Cloth Fair and Verily would raise her frying-pan in the window of No. 45 to signal he was to come across.[26] Sometimes he dined with the couple, too. Verily's son-in-law James Haldane O'Hare, a freelance television designer who lived in Ireland, met him at No. 41. O'Hare had come over to do some work for Granada Television. 'My fellow guests at dinner were John Betjeman and the [Dowager] Duchess of Devonshire [Elizabeth's mother]. It was the time of the three-day week imposed by Edward Heath. As I knew about the blackout, I had visited makers of church candles in Dublin. I opened up the candles for Verily, and the Duchess asked for a few candles to take home with her.'[27] O'Hare had heard quite a lot about John. In Ireland, the television designer was a friend of the Earl of Wicklow – the former Billy Clonmore – who had been at Oxford with John and was now a famous Dublin character, known as 'Mr Wick' and dispensing charity to the poor. From Wicklow, O'Hare had heard about John's wartime work in Dublin and his attempts to learn Gaelic. 'And in fact', O'Hare recalled, 'when I told John I had worked for Radio Television Éireann, he said straight away an Irish greeting, and I was quite thrown by his knowledge of Gaelic.'[28] O'Hare had also heard about John's Dublin posting from a colleague, Gerry O'Donovan.

He was a designer, like me; but his father, Seamus O'Donovan, was the ace of spies in Ireland in the war.[29] He was a top man, he was sent over to

Germany. And he told Gerry: 'John Betjeman was a *spy*.'[30] All the spies were on nodding acquaintance across the horseshoe bar of the Shelbourne Hotel.[31]

When Paul and Verily Paget visited Ireland, Lord and Lady Wicklow gave a party for them at Sandymount House, their fine town house near James Joyce's martello tower. O'Hare was invited, and later accompanied the Pagets on a tour of the architectural attractions of Dublin which John had listed for him as not to be missed.

The Pagets were staying at the Gresham [O'Hare remembered] and one of the nearest things we went to see was the Rotunda, where Candida was born. John had recommended the ceiling in the chapel, 'the finest rococo plasterwork outside Europe'; and it *was* – all these cherubs, but without the flashy gilding of Europe. Also on John's architectural 'shopping list' was Kingsbridge Station in Dublin (now Hewston Station) – 'a frontage like a palace'. I had never noticed it before. And Christ Church Cathedral, 'with restoration work by Street to stop the north side falling into the Liffey; and look at the stained-glass window by Brangwyn'.[32]

Verily also benefited from John's architectural knowledge. 'He used to take us on wonderful shuffles round the City,' she recalled. 'And one day I asked him: "Where did you learn all these amazing ins and outs?" He said: "There's not one word I have told you that I did not learn from either John or Paul" – because they'd been there forty years.'[33] The answer was calculated to please, and did; but it was not strictly true. John had known and loved the City for forty years before he met the Partners. By 1973, however, its charms for him were palling. 'The hellish noise of articulated lorries coming in from Europe in the small hours'[34] was one gripe. John also hated the New Brutalist buildings going up in the City, 'eggbox' architecture. In his poem 'Monody on the Death of Aldersgate Street Station', he wrote:

> Snow falls in the buffet of Aldersgate station,
>   Toiling and doomed from Moorgate Street puffs the train,
> For us of the steam and the gas-light, the lost generation,
>   The new white cliffs of the City are built in vain.[35]

Barry Humphries said: 'He used to be so hurt when the London he loved got changed by huge new developments . . .'[36] When Osbert Lancaster's stepson, the young journalist Max Hastings,[37] was about to go to America for a year, John gave him lunch, then a tour of the City views of St Paul's – 'none of which you will be able to see any more by the time you come back,' he told him.[38] 'Even at that age,' Hastings wrote to Candida in 1994, 'I was capable of perceiving the anxiety and melancholy so close to the surface.'[39] To add to John's misery, Paul Paget sold his five Cloth Fair houses for £90,000 to the Landmark Trust, a charity whose chairman, Sir John Smith, had married a sister of Verily's second cousin, the Duke of Grafton.[40] The Trust raised rents so that a woman John was fond of had to leave and the cloth shop closed down. The houses were turned into holiday homes with a high rental. By 1973 Parkinson's Disease was visibly undermining John's health. He often lost his balance. Penelope, who saw him at Christmas 1972, was concerned enough to write to Elizabeth Cavendish, suggesting that the two of them might take turns in looking after him. She was prepared to stay at Cloth Fair when necessary. She addressed directly the issue of John's relationship with Elizabeth.

> Naturally I was jealous when he first got fond of you, many years ago now. But over the years I have realised that from HIS point of view at any rate it has been a wonderful thing for him, as you are literary and I am not really, and you have provided the sort of companionship he needs and never really gets from me. I simply cannot get him to slow down now, can you? I mean I suggested, and Jock Murray thought it an excellent idea, that when he reached retiring age he should put a notice in the papers saying he could no longer afford a secretary and could therefore answer no more letters except from personal friends. Correspondence is KILLING him. And he should give up all, or nearly all, committee work so that he can have more time to relax and read. But WHO CAN MAKE HIM?? He has recently gone on to the board of governors of the King Edward's School in Oxford. WHY? Why give himself one more completely unnecessary chore at his age? Is there NO-ONE who can persuade him to cut down to what really interests him and to hell with the rest?[41]

The tribute to Elizabeth was handsome, and deserved; but clearly, too, there was an angry implied reproach: in effect, 'If you are meant to be looking after my husband, why is he being allowed to ruin his health by overwork?' Elizabeth diplomatically replied that she was touched by such a generous letter, and suggested Penelope get in touch with his doctor, John Allison, about his health.[42] Allison was fairly reassuring; but Penelope was still worried about making a proposed trip to India, in case John's condition (at that stage considered 'a prematurely early failing of his leg muscles')[43] should worsen. Elizabeth urged her to go and said she could cope.

In April 1973 John moved to No. 29 Radnor Walk, Chelsea, a few doors from Elizabeth's house in the same road.* To Penelope who, from whatever motive, had tried to dissuade him from moving, he wrote on 24 March 1973: 'I am getting very windy about the move to 29 Radnor Walk . . . as all you say about Cloth Fair is true. The views from the house are beautiful, the rooms are beautiful and so are the books . . .'[44] But the die was cast and on 27 April he sent her his first letter from Radnor Walk. He left a few relics in the City. Paul Paget wrote to him:

Following your move from Cloth Fair several of what we believe are your possessions seem to have been found in various temporary resting places. 1. Your CBE citation. 2. A Great Western Railway level-crossing sign. 3. A book of plates of Burges's Tower House.[45] 4. A scrapbook compiled by a Victorian architect. 5. A book on Danish houses (in Danish). 6. A book on art nouveau, in German. 7. A photograph of Cork Cathedral. 8. A number of appointments diaries . . . Possibly some are unwanted, and if you tell us we can throw them away with a clear conscience.[46]

* See Chapter 22, 'Radnor Walk'.

Spain, 1971: John surveys a less than picturesque scene

Mervyn Stockwood, John and Lady Elizabeth Cavendish in holiday mood

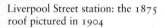

Liverpool Street station: the 1875 roof pictured in 1904

The plans for the station which John opposed in 1971

Opposite page

Brunel's Clifton Suspension Bridge over the Avon Gorge

Plans for the massive hotel which John helped to prevent rising beside the bridge

John on Southend pier with Simon Jenkins in 1976

With Valerie Jenkins (now Valerie Grove) in 1974

Dr Gregory Scott, who was one of his doctors in the late 1970s. John told him: 'I would be happy to die in your arms'; but in 1983 Scott committed suicide

The Poet Laureate at home

John with the Rev. Harry Williams in Jonathan Stedall's television series *Time with Betjeman*, 1981

With Osbert Lancaster in *Time with Betjeman*

At No. 29 Radnor Walk with Bevis Hillier in 1982. By now, the poet's face was 'frozen' by his Parkinson's Disease

Mary Wilson greets John at Scilly in 1981

Lady Elizabeth Cavendish

Opposite page

'Sir Les Patterson' (Barry Humphries) visits
John at Radnor Walk in Jonathan Stedall's
television series *Time with Betjeman*, 1981

John and Lady Elizabeth Cavendish at
Chatsworth – her family home – in the
same series

On 24 June 1983 John named
British Rail's main-line electric
locomotive No. 86229 after himself
in a ceremony at St Pancras station;
(*right*) Sir Peter Parker, chairman of
British Rail, and (*to his left*) Jim
O'Brien, general manager of the
London Midland region

John's grave, of Cornish slate, at
St Enodoc, Cornwall. Simon Verity
carved the extravagant lettering

20

'A HEAVY CROWN'

I do remember my dispute with [John Betjeman] over the Silver Jubilee poem, which was junk and senile junk at that . . . I consider that he was a rotten Poet Laureate, but it is such an absurd post anyway, that perhaps he was an appropriate occupant of it.

> Sir Nicholas Fairbairn QC, MP, letter to the author, 24 June 1992

After the success of *Collected Poems* in 1958, newspaper columnists tipped John as a future poet laureate. In fact, 'William Hickey' of the *Daily Express* jumped the gun by twelve years in February 1960 when Prince Andrew was born, by asking John to compose a poem to mark the event.

I had not chosen the easiest moment for Mr Betjeman ['Hickey' wrote]. He was taking a bath at the East Bergholt home of Mr Randolph Churchill, with whom he was staying. Mr Churchill shouted through the door of the bathroom and Mr Betjeman shouted back that it was very short notice, but he would do his best to oblige. 'Pass me a pencil,' he said.

Immediately after his bath, however, he had to leave to give a reading of Tennyson's poems to the Stour Valley Music Society in the village hall.

He did it admirably, I am told, and while reading he was also composing.[1]

The resulting poem was printed in the 'Hickey' column, under the heading 'THE POEM HE WROTE IN THE BATH':

> You might have thought the world absurd
> That could so advertise a birth
> With louder trumpets than that stable heard
> When our Creator came to earth
> But if you did, then you were wrong
> To let those brazen voices smother
> A deeper, universal song –
> Such as is sung by every mother.[2]

It was not the first time that a poet had, as it were, tried on the laurel for size. In 1736 the ill-fated Richard Savage contributed an ode to the *Gentleman's Magazine* as 'Volunteer Laureat [*sic*]'. And Cecil Day Lewis, who was likely to be a serious rival to John when the next laureate needed to be chosen, wrote a rather better poem on Prince Andrew's birth.

John's doggerel might have been a warning to those concerned with appointing a laureate. But in June 1960 his chances of gaining the laurel when the aged John Masefield should die were enhanced by his winning the Queen's Gold Medal for Poetry. It was Masefield who had suggested to King George V, in 1933, that the medal be instituted; and it was Masefield who recommended that John should receive it. The medal came as the culmination of a series of honours for John: the Duff Cooper Memorial Prize in 1958;[3] the William Foyle Poetry Prize in 1959;[4] and the CBE in the New Year's Honours list in 1960. Reporting the award of the Queen's Gold Medal, the Londoner's Diary of the *Evening Standard* suggested that 'it points what becomes a more and more accepted prediction: that Mr Betjeman will himself become the next Poet Laureate'.

Through his close friendship with Lady Elizabeth Cavendish, John was already on the fringe of 'court circles'. The *Standard* suggested that Princess Margaret's hand could be detected in the award of the gold medal.[5] Five months later, Geoffrey Moorhouse wrote in *The Guardian* that 'though John Betjeman's success has unfortunately something to do with the tag of being "Princess Margaret's favourite poet" – which he doubts – he had better get used to it. He may, after all, be the next poet laureate.'[6]

In 1962 John added further to his qualifications for a court place when he presented a masque to the Queen on the opening of the Festival of the City of London. Those who took part in the 'Entertainment' included Sir John Gielgud and the pop singer Tommy Steele, who had first become a teenage idol in the late 1950s with his hit song 'Never Felt More Like Singin' the Blues'.

'Atticus' of the *Sunday Times* wrote on 8 July ('The City Goes Gay'):

Last week I watched Sir John Gielgud, John Betjeman and Tommy Steele rehearsing the masque which Betjeman has written as the Festival's opening entertainment: it is to be performed before the Queen tomorrow evening at the Mansion House.

Betjeman's nostalgia for his youth was immediately apparent in the advertisements from the 1920s which were being flashed on a screen – Nestlé's chocolate, somebody's haircream, a poster for Noël Coward's 'Vortex'. 'And we'll throw in some blitz noises as well,' said Betjeman.

'Now, what was the name of that music-hall in Shoreditch High Street, Ran?'

Randolph Sutton, a veteran of vaudeville, put on a topper with a flourish, answered Betjeman's question, and broke into 'On Mother Kelly's Doorstep'.

Gielgud, waiting his turn, whistled the tune to himself. 'No, no, it's too much, that was my heyday,' he declaimed as he watched the screen. Then to me: 'It's the first time I've worked with Betjeman, you know – I haven't seen him since his Oxford days. What do I do? No Cockney accents, I'm afraid – I just read Samuel Pepys and that sort of thing. Tommy Steele does the accents.'

Betjeman was doing a shimmy to the music. 'I agreed to write this masque on one condition, my dear fellow – that they opened the Coal Exchange again. What a wonderful building! They're having an exhibition in it for the Festival, and after that, well, who knows?* Have you heard Tommy sing "What a Mouth"?'

William Charles interviewed John for the *Daily Express* on 9 July, the day the masque was to be presented to the Queen.

'London changes, but the people do not,' said the 56-year-old poet, after rehearsal yesterday. He sipped a cup of tea and added: 'I don't approve of many of the changes, you know.'

The Lady Mayoress (who changes every year) swooped down the staircase. 'It's a wonderful show, Mr Betjeman,' she said.

Betjeman smiled. Lady Hoare is *his* Lady Mayoress, after all, for he is one of the few thousand people who actually live in the City . . . 'I have lived there – I use sleeping-pills and ear-plugs against the noise – for 10 years,' he said . . .

Betjeman clapped a straw boater on his head, and we walked through the steel-and-glasss canyons around the Mansion House.

'Oh, vast unbeautiful blocks!' cried Betjeman. 'These buildings make you feel like an insect . . .'

That evening, as the Queen and her party arrived at the Mansion House, two actors dressed as the Guildhall giants Gog and Magog, one of them armed with a spiked ball on a chain, declaimed from the balcony these words by John:

GOG: When this great City where you see me stand
　　　Was only salty creeks and soggy land

* See Chapter 8, 'The Coal Exchange'.

>   I looked at Magog wading through the flood
>   And longed to push him backwards in the mud.
> MAGOG: Aeons ago I rose from river fog
>   Hunting my rival there, the giant Gog
>   For centuries since they've kept us in Guildhall
>   And here's my chance to slay him once for all.

The giants then fought a battle which ceased as the Queen reached the steps of the Mansion House.

>   GOG: Magog! Hold back, here comes our country's Queen
>   MAGOG: Hold back yourself, there must not be a scene
>   GOG: We giants here your Majesty to greet
>   MAGOG: Lay down our age-long weapons at your feet.[7]

The masque was presented in the Egyptian Hall of the Mansion House. It told the story of the City. 'London thou art the flower of cities all . . .' Gielgud spoke William Dunbar's line. Then Tommy Steele sprang out from the wings, singing the old music-hall song 'What a mouth, what a mouth, what a north and south – blimey, what a mouth he's got!' Peter Maxwell Davies (who was twenty-seven) and Richard Rodney Bennett (twenty-six) had composed settings for the Festival. Jacqueline du Pré, who was seventeen, gave her first public performance – the Boccherini cello concerto – on a 1672 Stradivarius given to her anonymously.

Queen magazine reported on the Festival. 'The Queen, who wore a tiara with her shimmering pale blue lace dress, walked to her place through a guard of honour of Pikemen and Musketeers of the Honourable Artillery Company in their scarlet uniforms and sat with the Lord Mayor and Lady Mayoress. After the performance the Queen enjoyed a buffet supper and met all those who had taken part in the entertainment.'[8] There was dancing in the street. 'For the first time in 150 years,' *Queen* reported, 'wine was sold in the streets from 5 pm to 11 pm . . . It was served by girls in Elizabethan dress, but Humphrey Lyttelton's band struck a 20th-century note.'[9]

John Masefield died on 12 May 1967. Two days later, Anthony Curtis[10] wrote in the *Sunday Telegraph*:

> Why perpetuate the archaic institution of Poet Laureate? Isn't the death of John Masefield the moment to terminate what has become a charming absurdity?
>   After all, even two days after his death no one is going to pretend that those four and six line verses that he used to contribute so punctiliously

on important Royal and State occasions represent a side of his work in which posterity is likely to be the least bit interested. Perhaps his own attitude to them may be gathered from the fact, which has just been revealed, that he always used to include a stamped addressed envelope with the manuscript [in sending it to *The Times*] in case it should prove to be unacceptable.

Curtis answered his own question by suggesting that the laureateship should be continued 'as tangible evidence of our faith in the potential of the language'. But that did not mean, he wrote, that the post should go to a great innovator. Gerard Manley Hopkins would have been unsuitable for the post: 'you are much better off with someone like his friend Robert Bridges, who did the job admirably'. The occasions on which a laureate might be expected to utter were changing. 'On the day when Britain either succeeds or fails to get into the Common Market the Laureate will be presented with a splendid challenge . . .' Curtis's short list of the poets best able to respond to such a challenge was: John Betjeman, C. Day Lewis, Edmund Blunden and Robert Graves. 'Of these four it is Betjeman and Day Lewis who seem to me to have the kind of occasional gift that would be required to enable this kind of poetry to be taken seriously again. The ability to produce it is one of our national assets and we ought to think twice before allowing it to dwindle to nothing.'

Masefield's death suggested a subject for one of the *New Statesman*'s 'Weekend Competitions'. Competitors were asked 'to write a respectful poem upon the death of the old Poet Laureate, in the style of John Masefield, or a comical poem upon the appointment of the new Poet Laureate, in the style of Robert Graves, C. Day Lewis, John Betjeman or any other candidate'. The results were published on 9 June. Only one competitor (myself, as it happens) was quoted as having chosen the Masefield option.[11] Prizes went to 'a Graves, a Larkin and two Betjemen'. Peter Veale contributed one of the two 'Betjeman' poems:

> . . .
> My praises of tennis girls, kindly viewed hitherto,
> Could get me, as Laureate, into a row.
> And let me remind you I caused quite a dither, too,
> Calling for bombs to be rained upon Slough.
> So spare me, I beg you, the pain of selection,
> For when the thing's offered it's hard to say 'No'.
> If naught else will move you, here's one last objection:
> My name doesn't sound very *English*, you know.[12]

By Christmas 1967 the new Laureate had still not been appointed.
On Christmas Eve the *Sunday Express* published an interview with
John by Graham Lord.

If Poets Laureate were chosen simply for their popularity [Lord wrote]
there is little doubt that John Betjeman would get the job as John
Masefield's successor.

Not only do his verses sell better than any other living British poet. His
appearances on television have also given him a fireside fan club, a vast
suburbia of Betjemaniacs, all enamoured of his mild eccentricity, his
quietly humorous niceness.

Apparently he also has sex appeal. Usually reliable sources inform me
that he is even cuddlier than Dudley Moore [sometimes known as 'Cuddly
Dudley'].

So it seems as if Betjeman the Pop Personality has almost engulfed
Betjeman the poet. Among his Christmas cards this year was one from a
female admirer addressed to *Sir* John Betjeman.

Before the interview, John had said he would not talk about the poet
laureateship – 'That wouldn't be right. I hate any form of competition
and treating the candidates like a lot of racehorses.'

But somehow we got round to it [Lord wrote]. He is a kindly man. With
a smile, he explained to his secretary: 'This chap has a sort of innocence.
You think you've got to help him in his work or he'll get the sack.'

So, for the sake of my job, we talked about the Poet Laureateship.

When Masefield died, Betjeman's wife Penelope told me that even if he
were offered the job he'd turn it down. Was that still true?

'I wouldn't refuse it,' he said. 'That would be very arrogant. But I
wouldn't like it. I'd get so many more of these letters and manuscripts.

'But anyway, I don't think I would be chosen. If it's to be an honour
then why choose only one poet? And if it's to be political verse, which was
superbly done by Dryden, or State verse – superbly done by Tennyson –
then it should be the sort of person who enjoys writing occasional verse.
A sort of A.P. Herbert.

'And if it's to be an honour for poetry then it's invidious that there
should be only one Poet Laureate.'

Should it be a post held in rotation?

'I think that's quite a good idea. But it all smacks of Arts Council and
I don't like it very much.'

Graham Lord's article was headed 'The man who'd rather not be
Poet Laureate'. Some of John's friends were beginning to suspect that

he didn't want to be Poet Laureate in much the same way as the tar baby didn't want to be thrown into the tar. But this time it was not to be. On 2 January 1968 it was announced that C. Day Lewis had been appointed.

It was from John, however, not from Day Lewis, that Prince Charles requested a poem on his investiture as Prince of Wales at Caernarvon Castle in 1969. As we have seen, the Prince and the poet met at a dinner-party given by Harry Williams. Prince Charles recalled:

> I think it was the first time I had met John Betjeman. I don't think I had met him at my grandmother's house at Royal Lodge in Windsor. It was a very convivial occasion. There were quite a lot of people there – among them, the two he mentions in the poem, [Robin] Hastings Bass [later Lord Huntingdon], who was the son of a trainer in Hampshire (he himself became a trainer and trained one or two horses for the Queen) and Eddie Woods, the son of the Dean of Windsor, Robin Woods, later the Bishop of Worcester. They were people I knew at Cambridge.
>
> I thought it was the greatest possible fun, and John Betjeman was extremely enjoyable. We had one of those marvellous evenings afterwards: he told all sorts of stories and I think he read some poems. It impressed me enormously, and I remember thinking what fun he was, how amusing – he made me laugh a great deal.[13]

As Prince Charles left the party, he said to John, 'I want a poem out of you on my Investiture in Wales.' He slightly raised his hand. 'And that', he added, 'is a command.' Remembering from his Oxford days how King Richard II had urged John Gower to write him a poem, and how Gower had proudly described the bestowing of the commission in his *Confessio Amantis* (completed 1390), John in 'A Ballad of the Investiture 1969' described how the charge had been laid on him. He cast the poem in the form of a 'rhyming letter', detailing the journey from Euston to Wales, then the rapt moments of the ceremony in which the Queen crowned her son. The poem ended:

> You knelt a boy, you rose a man.
> And thus your lonelier life began.

Asked in 1985 if those lines expressed what he had felt at the time, Prince Charles said, 'I don't think so, really, no. I mean, I think it's a bit of poetic licence. It was a nice way to put it – I can see what he was getting at, from the point of view of responsibility; and I suppose it does become lonelier, depending on how much responsibility one has. But when do you suddenly "transit" between a boy and a man? I don't know. It used to be marked by the transition from short trousers to long ones – a sort of assumption of the toga – but in my case even that was delayed, because at Gordonstoun we wore shorts.'[14]

In the same year as the Caernarvon ceremony, John was knighted. He received over a thousand letters of congratulation, from both friends and strangers. Angus Wilson wrote:

That your *Herald* review set my books on the right road would alone suffice – but seriously, it is the greatest pleasure to me as to thousands and thousands of others who have attended your adolescent dances, your beach cricket, and wept with you at the Café Royal and the Cadogan Hotel. Long years of rhododendrons and pony clubs to you.[15]

Nancy Mitford wrote from Versailles: 'If I had accepted your invit-ation – "Since Miss Pam won't marry me I think you had better"[16] – I should now be a lady. Alas too late.'[17] John told Lord Longford: 'Ever since I heard of it I have been wondering who suggested it and got it through what sort of committees . . . I haven't noticed any change in my status in Wantage or indeed in the City. I still can never find a taxi when I want one. But I suppose the magic will work when I'm dubbed.'[18] Penelope was cross that the dubbing at Buckingham Palace was on the same day as the Arab Horse Show at Windsor; but in the end she managed to attend both events.[19] It meant little to her to be the Hon. Lady Betjeman. John, too, did not take the honour too seriously, recalling Napoleon's words to an aide on instituting the Légion d'Honneur – 'It is by such baubles that men are led.'[20] But for him there was a Tennysonian romance about a knighthood; and the accolade was proof that the man with the funny foreign name had been accepted by – received into – the British Establishment.

On 22 May 1972 Cecil Day Lewis died at Lemmons, Hadley Wood, Hertfordshire, the home of Kingsley Amis. He had been staying there with his wife, the actress Jill Balcon, while she made a television play at Elstree Studios. (The last poem Lewis wrote was 'To All – Lemmons'.) John attended the memorial service: he was photogra-phed with the grieving Jill Balcon on his arm.[21] Reporting the death on the front page of *The Times*, Philip Howard, later literary editor of the newspaper, wrote: 'The Laureateship has always been a heavy crown. It carries, besides the burden of writing ceremonial verse to order, a fee of £70 a year, with £27 "in lieu of a butt of sack".'[22] Two days later, Geoffrey Handley-Taylor, author of books on the laureates Masefield and Day Lewis, wrote in to correct Howard: it was an old journalistic misconception that the Laureate was expected to write ceremonial verse. Even in Victoria's reign, he pointed out, Prince

Albert had confirmed that the Poet Laureate was not required to write official odes on great occasions. The principal duty of the Laureate now was to recommend to the sovereign each year the name of the poet who should receive the Queen's Gold Medal for poetry – as Masefield had recommended John in 1960.[23]

Howard's article also provoked a letter from (Sir) Edward Pickering, a former editor of the *Daily Express* who was head of the International Publishing Corporation.

Day Lewis wore the heavy crown with distinction – and with courage. Yet already voices can be heard questioning and criticizing the existence of the laureateship. Surely this is the moment when we should seek a greater recognition of the written and spoken word and not be demeaning them still further . . . The Arts Council lavishes millions on opera . . . Poetry languishes . . . Even Sir John Betjeman's fame rests rather more on his television appearances, as the Apostle of Victoriana, than on his deserved reputation as a poet.

Is this not the time for the Musician in Number Ten [Edward Heath] to demonstrate – both by an appointment and by the recognition that goes with it – that the words matter as much as the music?[24]

On 24 May *The Times* published an article headed 'W.H. Auden is favourite to become the new Poet Laureate'. The article was by the young reporter Timothy Devlin, a son of the judge Lord Devlin. 'Mr Auden', he wrote, 'is believed to be favoured by the official bodies who are consulted before the Prime Minister makes his choice . . .' However, as Devlin recorded, the Prime Minister's office was emphasizing that the post had to go to a British subject. Auden had become an American citizen in 1946, so he would have to become a British citizen again to qualify. Auden himself soon scotched any such plan. 'Mr Auden "cross" at Laureate rumours' ran a *Times* headline of 22 June. The article asked a question. Day Lewis had died six days before the Queen's uncle, the Duke of Windsor. What if he had died six days after him – would he have been called on to write a poem? The question was in the last degree rhetorical – the British royal family had little love for the late Duke and there was no possibility of the Queen's requesting a valediction. However, Auden was prepared to answer the question. 'When the Duke died, I thought about what I would write if I had been Poet Laureate. It would have been a difficult task; and my sympathy would have gone out to anyone asked to undertake it.' Auden called the suggestion that he might be made poet laureate 'a load of bosh'. It made him 'very cross indeed'. He added: 'I do not covet the post; I have no desire for it'. He did not intend to change back his citizenship. If anything more were needed to ensure that the Conservative Government would not forward his name to the Queen, it was Auden's mischievous afterthought that 'there should be a clear understanding that the Poet Laureate could write on controversial issues, as well as the traditional ones.' Rather than write on the Investiture of the Prince of Wales, he would prefer to compose a 'poem of thanks' that 'the prince's unnerving moment when his feet caught in the rigging of his parachute while he was making a jump did not end in disaster'. That, he said, would be 'much more fun to write'.

Other candidates being mentioned were John Betjeman, Roy Fuller (then Professor of Poetry at Oxford), Stephen Spender, Philip Larkin, Ted Hughes and William Plomer. Spender effectively ruled himself out by telling Devlin: 'If I had to write about a public event, I would want to write about the bombing of Haiphong,[25] which I am sure would not be very suitable.' Larkin was thought to have dished his chances by publishing a poem that began, 'They fuck you up, your mum and dad,' a sentiment unlikely to be endorsed by the Queen.

Some of the younger poets were backing Adrian Mitchell, the left-wing Liverpool poet. He told Devlin: 'If Mr Heath is wise enough to offer the post to me, I am crazy enough to accept it. But I would rather be Ambassador to Chile.' The Women's Lib movement was making a great stir in 1972. Germaine Greer's *The Female Eunuch* had been published in 1970. So the *Times* diarist's speculation on 29 June 1972 that 'It is quite possible that the next Laureate will be a poetess' was in the spirit of the age – though most feminists would deplore the word 'poetess'. The diarist understood that Sir John Hewitt, secretary for appointments to the Prime Minister, had 'netted several women in his list of contenders'. Among the names being canvassed were Kathleen Raine, Ruth Pitter and Elizabeth Jennings. Osbert Lancaster, in one of his *Daily Express* cartoons, showed two feminists with 'Women's Lib' badges campaigning for Mary Wilson to be appointed. (Harold Wilson, with his pipe and Gannex coat, is in the background.)

Some correspondents to *The Times* felt the post should be open to all English-writing poets everywhere. Mr P. D. Hazard of London wrote to suggest Soyinka (Nigeria), Braithwaite (West Indies), Heaney (Belfast) and Judith Wright, whom John had sought out on his Australian trip in 1961.* But Hazard added: 'Failing this kind of Blakean utopianism, I can assure you Sir John will much more than merely do.'[26]

In a controversy of this kind, *The Times* was still, in 1972, the paper whose views counted for most. On 22 June it weighed in with a lead

---

* See Chapter 7, 'Australia 1961'.

Osbert Lancaster's cartoon in the *Daily Express*, 2 June 1972

editorial headed 'WORTH MORE THAN A TUN OF SACK'. The leader suggested that the main value of having a poet laureate was that the periodic rows over the succession drew attention to poetry. 'Now that Mr W.H. Auden appears to have scratched himself from an event in which he was attracting most of the big money the field is as open as after Crowned Prince dropped out of the starters' list for the Derby. The list of possible entries is still long, but the form book is a doubtful guide . . .' If the selectors skipped down a generation they would find 'much promising material' – Larkin, Hughes, Causley. But, the leader-writer warned, 'There are risks, perhaps, in appointing too young a man – who knows what age may turn him into?'

The names now at short odds were Roy Fuller, Stephen Spender and John Betjeman, in that order. (Ladbroke's, who had John at 6–1, said that they were hoping 'only for nice, friendly bets'.) The *Times* leader-writer made his choice clear:

But of course it is Sir John Betjeman on whom the public money is being laid. He is one of the few poets since Kipling and Newbolt to become not only known by name but even to be sometimes quoted. He has done for girl athletes what Kipling did for private soldiers. And the extraordinary thing about the Betjeman story is that, though the scope of his popularity owes a great deal to television, he has never modified his style to win a wider audience. It is public taste that has changed. Verses which were first admired by a small group of his contemporaries are now spread around every Christmas from uncle to niece and nephew to aunt with the same abandon that earlier was accorded to Rupert Brooke or Elroy Flecker. It is a remarkable development, and the laureateship would be a fitting seal to it. There is also the not unimportant consideration that Sir John is more likely to produce verse worthy of a public occasion than is anyone else . . .[27]

On the day this editorial appeared, *The Times* also carried a report, by the biographer Richard Holmes, on the first of four days of informal poetry readings at the Institute of Contemporary Arts, London. The readings were a warm-up for the fifth London Poetry International which was to open at the South Bank later that week. Holmes reported:

Sir John Betjeman came to launch the sessions clutching a straw shopping bag from which he drew nine new poems by Philip Larkin. Hospitals, late night despondencies, accidents, invitations, aging: each a clear, grave anecdote. Such nonconformist sermons were very chastening at lunchtime, read with almost sinister good-humour. *Carpe diem* indeed, I thought, studying Betjeman's pale blue socks. There was a wild rumour that Betjeman had disappeared in a taxi with Peter Jay, Festival adviser, reading him Wesley's Hymns from the newly published *Faber Book of Religious Verse*.[28]

Two days later, the architectural historian Priscilla Metcalfe wrote to *The Times*: 'Twenty-five years ago there was published in New York a slim volume of poems and prose by the then Mr Betjeman under the odd title *Slick but Not Streamlined*, the whole selected and introduced by Mr Auden.' John Betjeman's 'equally engaging preface' to that book of 1947 had a 'prophetic last sentence': 'I try to create an atmosphere which will be remembered . . . when England is council houses and trunk roads and steel and glass factory blocks in the New Europe of after the war.' Miss Metcalfe concluded that Sir John Betjeman would write his own 'Locksley Hall Sixty Years After' without waiting as long as Tennyson did. 'That would be worth a most tolerable deal of sack.'[29]

At the beginning of October the Prime Minister wrote to tell John that he was recommending to the Queen that she should consider appointing him poet laureate. On 9 October, when John was on holiday in Trebetherick, his secretary in London was telephoned from

No. 10 Downing Street with the news that the appointment was confirmed: 'Summoned by Telephone Bell' as *The Guardian* later put it. The *Evening Standard* broke the story on its front page the next day – ' "Dumbfounded and humbled" Betjeman new Poet Laureate'. 'The Londoner', for whose column in the *Standard* John had once written, told how the office of poet laureate had started when James I granted a pension to Ben Jonson. Dryden, Wordsworth and Tennyson had held the post. The Laureate had traditionally received a butt of sack until 1790 when Henry James Pye said he would rather have the cash.[30]

On the same day, there was an untoward incident when John was interviewed on BBC radio about his new duties. The broadcast was interrupted for about thirty seconds by the voice of 'Lord Haw-Haw' – William Joyce, the traitor hanged for broadcasting German propaganda during the Second World War. BBC officials explained: 'The announcer in our continuity studio was rehearsing for a later programme, "Fifty Broadcasting Years". In switching on the tape he accidently switched it into the network.'[31]

The daily papers of 11 October carried the news of the appointment and editorial comment on it. An article by Ron Boyle in the *Daily Express* ('NEW TOP POET – It's John Betjeman') called him 'a cherubic imp'. On the telephone from Cornwall he told Boyle, 'The older I get, the slower I write.' Boyle noted that 'Canary wine is no longer available. But according to Grants of St James's one butt (or 600 bottles) of sack would cost the Queen . . . well over £700.' Osbert Lancaster drew a jubilant pocket cartoon to celebrate his old friend's success.

'I was surprised and humbled when I heard that I was to be appointed,' John told John Winder of *The Times*. 'Then I was very pleased. I love poetry and hope that my brother poets, many of them much better poets than I, will not be jealous.' He said he was pleased to be in the succession of Wordsworth, Tennyson and Bridges, 'but not quite so pleased to be the successor of Alfred Austin. I am sure he wrote some good poetry. I have been reading his work looking for it.' Philip Larkin told Winder he thought it 'an enormously appropriate appointment', and added: 'In the eyes of a great many people, from the royals down to the humblest television watchers, he has become identified with so much of the nation's cultural heritage.'

The Times had also sent Tim Devlin to interview John in Cornwall. 'I don't think I am very good,' he told him, 'and if I thought I was any good I wouldn't be any good.' Devlin reported:

Dressed in his characteristic rough coat and baggy trousers, with his feet in red slippers up before the fire, he remarked on the silence of the night. 'Listen to the waves,' he said. 'You can hear the high tide on the beach,

'I say, Daphne, isn't it *super* about the new laureate?!'
(Osbert Lancaster's cartoon in the *Daily Express*, 11 October 1972)

a few hundred yards away. This is where I spent the happiest days of my childhood.'

He added that he didn't watch much television, 'except for Alf Garnett, who is outrageous' – 'but I'm going to watch myself on television tonight. We are going to have a grand celebration with all my childhood friends at the home of Mrs David, the widow of the Bishop of Liverpool who was formerly Headmaster of Rugby. She has a colour television set.'

John told Devlin that he was interested in former laureates. 'Henry James Pye, in the late eighteenth century, who was lampooned in the Four-and-Twenty Blackbirds nursery rhyme,[32] was a very good poet. He wrote a very good poem called "Faringdon Hill" but he was laughed at.' Asked if becoming Laureate might sound the death knell of his talent, John said, 'I should think it would have . . . had I not been in Australia for three months. That has restored my confidence, because the Australians took me for what I was without dipping into my past.' Devlin commented: 'If there has been any failure, it is his portrayers who have failed him. We have always been blinded by his eccentricity and have portrayed him as a lovable uncle from a Trollope novel preserving the past, but not so much as the serious poet he has always striven to be.'

The *Daily Telegraph* also sent a journalist hotfoot to Cornwall – Keith Nurse, its arts reporter, who walked along Daymer Beach with John. 'Chuckles and frequent gales of laughter laced his attempts to explain his poetic outlook to the continuing stream of callers whose cars jammed the narrow lane down to the beach.' John told the *Telegraph*'s 'Peterborough' columnist: 'I just think how pleased my parents would be if they were still alive.' An editorial in the same issue of the *Telegraph* welcomed the appointment, beginning with face-tiousness and rising to an almost Biblical cadence.

The poet laureate's sounds a funny old job. And some might suppose that, in Sir JOHN BETJEMAN, a funny old buffer has been found to fill it.

Yet some of our very greatest poets have been Laureates . . . Would they have been ashamed of Sir JOHN? Would they have been in some way shocked by his bubbling love of life and fun and old buildings and common things? Why should they not have enjoyed these traits in him, as we do? Would they have thought his friendliness and lovable eccentricities unseemly? Surely not: the more fools if they did. Would they have despised his ready comprehensibility – they, who also wrote to be understood?

His fervent love for this country, for its landscape and people – did they not share it? Would they have thought his themes trivial? Some are, perhaps: though very moving poems have been written about trivial things. But love, death, faith, doubt, lust, pity, terror, pain, joy and sorrow – these are not little things. Nor can any poetry be trivial which, like Sir JOHN's, encompasses them all, and pierces the heart in doing so.

David Holloway, the *Telegraph*'s literary editor, was less welcoming. There could be no doubt, he wrote, that the Queen had made the most popular choice. 'But it must be said that if the office of Poet Laureate should be given to the best poet in the land, then Sir John Betjeman would not be the first choice.' Holloway thought that if a vote had been taken among published poets, the laurel would have gone to Roy Fuller, 'a better poet than Sir John, though less of a public figure'. However, Holloway fairly noted that John was one of the few poets of the day who had written 'royal' poems, citing 'Death of King George V' (1936). And he conceded that John was also appropriate in that, 'in a secular age [he] is a genuinely religious poet . . .'.

Interviewed by Dennis Barker of *The Guardian*, John said he would write only when moved and otherwise 'remain a silent thrush'. He added: 'Isn't that a beautiful remark? I just made it up.' Perhaps he was remembering Horatio Bottomley's gibe about Robert Bridges – 'the dumb Laureate'. John spoke truer than he knew. It was over a year before he wrote any 'official' poem; and whatever Prince Albert might have said in Victoria's reign, journalists persisted in suggesting that it was the Laureate's duty to write poems on 'royal' occasions.

John received from the Lord Chamberlain, Lord Maclean, the handsome warrant, headed by the royal arms, which attested that 'Sir John Betjeman, CBE, C.Litt is by The Queen's Command hereby appointed into the Place and Quality of Poet Laureate in Ordinary to Her Majesty.' The archaic wording reminded him that his kinsman, Gilbert Betjemann, had been Musician in Ordinary to the previous reigning Queen of England, Victoria. In replying to the Lord Chamberlain, John asked that the meagre emolument might be converted back into drink – half-bottles of champagne. His morning visitors, from 1972 onwards, were usually offered 'some of the royal bubbly'.

To the many friends and strangers who wrote to congratulate him on the appointment, John sent a foolscap sheet of paper printed with the words

THANKYOU
    OH
THANKYOU

– sometimes scribbling an extra message below. *The Times* reported on 28 November: 'There are now two secretaries working away on what they call "the congratters", and Sir John's diminutive house in Cloth Fair is still overflowing with them. Some 5,500 have been received so far and more come in daily. "He's been very good," says his regular secretary.' John's Oxford friend Pierce Synnott sent, from Ireland, a poem in Latin to congratulate him.[33]

In 1972, Kingsley Amis interviewed him in an *Omnibus* programme about being Laureate, drawing this response from John: 'I like rhythm and rhyme because I think it's far harder to write *without* rhythm and rhyme. Rhyme gives you ideas which would never have occurred to you. I think there's such a thing as a Muse . . . The Muse, oh what an inventive creature!'

In December a two-part television film called *Thank God It's Sunday* (directed by Jonathan Stedall) was broadcast on successive Sundays on BBC1.* The *Times* Diary noted: 'Sir John Betjeman, the poet laureate, must be the only television commentator who writes his scripts in blank verse . . .'[34]

In January 1973 the *Times* diarist reported that letters written by John were beginning to fetch high prices. 'Hand-written ones are becoming scarcer each year, because the poet laureate feels his writing

---

* See Chapter 23, 'Heaven and Hell on Television: The Seventies'.

is so illegible it would be an insult to the recipient not to have them typed.' John Wilson, an Oxfordshire dealer in historical documents, was offering £10 on average for a letter from John and said that an 'interesting' letter might be worth as much as £50. Duncan Andrews, a New York businessman, had been collecting John's letters and manuscripts for some years; his quest for more had helped inflate the market. 'I dictate about fifty letters a day,' John told *The Times*, 'but they are mainly declining to attend meetings. I was not a great letter-writer in my youth and I don't think my early letters will be easy to find. But I did write fan letters to authors, particularly to Anthony Hope. Once I got such a charming letter in reply.'[35]

On 11 September 1973 John went to London Zoo for a lunch given by the *Sunday Times* to celebrate Cyril Connolly's seventieth birthday. Among the guests was Cecil Beaton, who observed John 'with trousers too short walking like a toddler on the sands. He only lacked a bucket and spade.'[36] In his speech, Connolly described his early encounters with several friends present at the party. 'In London,' he said, 'I was lucky enough to work for a demon editor with fire in his belly, a commanding figure who wouldn't even let me smoke in his office, invariably referred to by his initials J.B.' In the next edition of the *Sunday Times*, 'Atticus' explained: 'This turned out to be Sir John Betjeman, who chortled his disbelief.'[37]

The first big test of John's skills as laureate was Princess Anne's wedding to Captain Mark Phillips on 14 November 1973. By the end of October he was already panicking. At a wake after W. H. Auden's memorial service in Oxford, he told Philip Larkin that he wanted 'to pack in the Laureateship'.[38] Candida records that he became so worried about it that in the end his doctor decided to take action.[39] 'He rang up [Sir] Rennie Maudslay, an old patient of his, who was Keeper of the Privy Purse, and asked him to ask the Queen to speak to JB. She confirmed to him that it was indeed not a *duty* to write something every time there was a Royal occasion. But somehow the *public* expected it of him . . .'[40]

On 12 November the headline above Philip Howard's article in *The Times* was 'Awesome machinery of a royal wedding is moving inexorably into top gear'. The couple had met as Olympic riders – their courtship might have been the perfect subject for a Betjeman poem if John had been able to allow himself even the mildest levity or satire in his Laureate poems. Instead, he 'recycled' the pavement/enslavement rhyme which he had first used in serenading Mary Shand in Bath. He wrote:

> Hundreds of birds in the air
> And millions of leaves on the pavement,

And Westminster bells ringing on
  To palace and people outside –
And all for the words 'I will'
  To love's most willing enslavement.
All of our people rejoice
  With venturous bridegroom and bride.

Trumpets blare at the entrance,
  Multitudes crane and sway.
Glow, white lily in London,
  You are high in our hearts today!

John admitted to Tim Devlin in *The Times* that this was 'one of the most laborious things he had ever written' and 'not the best poem he had ever penned'.[41] He told Devlin: 'I wanted it to be quite clear, very simple and not like a Christmas card.' The first and second lines had helped to carry the piece along. His explanation of the poem's genesis was a surprise to those who assumed that the word 'palace' was a reference to Buckingham Palace.

> I was in front of Westminster Abbey and looking at that awful mess that they are doing in the car park and envisaging how it could all be changed, how Parliament Square could be cut off from traffic. And when I talked about the palace, I meant Westminster Palace, as it could be restored to be, not Buckingham Palace. These were my thoughts, with the leaves falling from the trees, that inspired the opening.[42]

Being Poet Laureate had not affected his talent, John told Devlin. 'But what would have been a death knell to my talent would have been writing about Princess Anne if I had had to write anything horsey.'[43]

Michael Leapman, the *Times* diarist, began what became a long campaign of denigration of John's laureate work, with an item about the wedding poem.

> *The Incorporated Linguist* has asked its readers to translate this gem into a language of their choice. No prizes. To show the way it is done, they persuaded one T. Lindkvist to translate it into Swedish and then, ignoring the original, to translate the Swedish back into English. Some may think the result just as good as the original:

> Bedded with leaves is the ground,
> And bird-flights wheel high among buildings.
> Then shall the bell-metal peal

Over palace and people and land,
All for a simple 'I will'
To love which its bondage is gilding:
What can we do but exult
When a bride and bridegroom join hands?[44]

A week after the royal wedding, at a private ceremony in Buckingham Palace, the Duke of Edinburgh, as President of the Royal Society of Arts, presented John with the society's Albert Medal for services to poetry and the appreciation of architecture. On 1 June 1974, at the instigation of Robert Aickman, founder of the Inland Waterways Association, John declaimed a poem at the opening of the Upper Avon at Stratford, in the presence of Queen Elizabeth the Queen Mother. The poem, which referred to 'The meadows which the youthful Shakespeare knew', ended with an apostrophe which might have been written by a Georgian or Victorian laureate –

Your Majesty, our friend of many years,
Confirms a triumph now the moment nears:
The lock you have re-opened will set free
The heart of England to the open sea.

Also in June, John received an honorary doctorate of letters at Oxford – the return of the Prodigal Son. A photograph in *The Times* showed him receiving it beside Lord Hailsham, the Lord Chancellor, who was given a doctorate of civil law.[45] In October, John unveiled a memorial plaque to W. H. Auden in Poets' Corner at Westminster Abbey.

Two months later, Cyril Connolly died and John contributed an article about him to the *Sunday Times*.[46] A remark in the piece caused one of John's old dragons, Geoffrey Grigson – the dreaded 'Griggers' – to rear up with a letter of furious expostulation in the next week's *Sunday Times*.

I have no wish to quarrel over the passing of Cyril Connolly. *Requiescat in pace*. But a statement in John Betjeman's tribute to him seems to me so disgraceful as to demand a protest.

He explained that Connolly was cut off from the London literary life of the Thirties because temperamentally he was 'neither Left Wing nor homosexual'. No such double passport to that 'life' was ever required. As far as Connolly was concerned, some writers who are now taken to denigrate the Thirties were repelled by what they took to be Connolly's mixture of social and aesthetic attitudes. In matters of value they saw him as a late and provincial acolyte of much that they rejected.

However, the disgracefulness of Betjeman's remark resides in that collocation of Left Wing and homosexual, that repetition of a smear. It ill fits the man who earlier this week was laying a wreath on the Abbey stone of W.H. Auden.[47]

John left this letter unanswered.

In November 1974, the first fruits of his laureateship were published by John Murray in a new collection, *A Nip in the Air*. As the poet's seventieth birthday was less than two years ahead, the implication of the title was obvious. But John may also have had in mind a *Private Eye* cartoon by Candida's friend William Rushton: a kimonoed Japanese is floating above two businessmen, one of whom remarks to the other, 'Nasty Nip in the air, Lobethrust.'[48] (The joke was recycled for a state visit to Britain of Emperor Hirohito.) In sending the book to friends, John repeated the quip that the book was 'not about a Japanese aviator' or joked, 'I hope the Japanese ambassador won't be offended.' As usual, John had first thought of off-putting titles. In May Jock Murray had firmly steered him away from *Penultimate Poems* and *Last Words*. He had also vetoed Osbert Lancaster's suggestion, *A Few Early Laurels*.[49] The work of garnering poems for the volume had begun in December 1973 when Murray had written to Squadron-Leader David Checketts, private secretary to Prince Charles, to ask if the Prince would allow John's 'Ballad of the Investiture, 1969' to be included. The Prince had no objection.[50] In March John wrote to Alan Ross, editor of the *London Magazine*, to ask him to retrieve for him the poems he had published. Among them was 'Executive', beginning:

> I am a young executive. No cuffs than mine are cleaner;
> I have a Slimline brief-case and I use the firm's Cortina . . .

The make of car may have been suggested by an advertisement in the guide to Wantage Church, to which John wrote an introduction.

In June 1974, John wrote a poem to mark the seventieth birthday of Patrick Kinross, and it was decided to include it. When he sent a copy of the poem to Mary Lutyens (Mrs J. G. Links), who had known John and Kinross well in the 1920s, she replied with a nostalgic poem of her own, recalling those days in Yeoman's Row, London, and in particular John's response to the rejection of his marriage proposal to Pamela Mitford.[52]

> I envied the friendship of male towards male
> When John once appeared more than usually pale;

It was known that his fate would be settled that day.
Had his Pamela said yes or had she said nay?
That her answer'd been 'no' was as plain as his face
As his friends gathered round in a loyal embrace:
'Her ankles are thick and her hair a dyed fleece' –
In a trice John was toasting his lucky release.
And John has been weighted with honours and fat
(Though no less loveable for that).[53]

Up to and during August, there was much debate between Jock
Murray and John as to which poems should be included in the new
book and which omitted. They considered printing John's verse script
for the television film *A Passion for Churches*,* but decided against:
the words were intended as an accompaniment to the pictures on the

---

* See Chapter 21, '*A Passion for Churches*'.

screen, and would not work on their own. Then there was the poem
originally entitled 'The Mistress', which began:

> Isn't she lovely, the mistress,
> With her wide apart grey green eyes.
> And her drooping lips and when she smiles
> The glance of amused surprise . . .

The poem was inspired by an elegant woman John admired at the
Grosvenor Chapel in South Audley Street, where he and Elizabeth regularly worshipped after he moved to Radnor Walk. John did not know
her name.[54] She was in fact Joan Price, the beauty editor of *Harper's
Bazaar* (later *Harper's & Queen*).[55] John and Jock agreed that the poem
should go in, but under the more decorous title 'Lenten Thoughts of
a High Anglican'. When it was published in the *Daily Express* as a
'trailer', *Private Eye* lampooned it –

> Lovely lady in the pew,
> Goodness, what a scorcher – phew!
> What I wouldn't give to do
> Unmentionable things to you.
>
> If old God is still up there
> I'm sure he wouldn't really care.
> I'm sure he'd say, 'A little lech
> Never really harmed old Betj.'[56]

The main sticking-point, in choosing the poems to go into *A Nip in
the Air*, was over John's poem about the journey to Diss with Mary
Wilson.* Elizabeth Cavendish wanted it omitted. She argued that it
might lead to the taunting of John in the press; but was she, perhaps,
just a little bit jealous of his friendship with the Prime Minister's wife?
Jock Murray wrote to Tom Driberg on 2 August:

[John] came in here last night, felt guilt about family and has decided to
dedicate *A Nip* to his grandchildren though he wishes he could dedicate
it to you too.
    One urgent point: Elizabeth appears to be working on him to omit the
Mary Wilson poem. Her reasons may be many but she evidently mentioned to him the danger of the Press being able to make improper capital
out of it. I have told him that both you and I are strongly in favour of it

---

* See Chapter 15, 'Mary Wilson and a Journey to Diss'.

going in. If you really are in favour please support me on this. Meanwhile at her suggestion via John I have been forced to send a copy of it to Sparrow for his views – oh dear![57]

Murray posted the poem to Sparrow but sent a follow-up letter on 5 August: 'My spies have just reported that Mary Wilson knows that the poem is coming in the next slim volume and she is delighted – this means that John would be in a hole if he now removes it. What odd corners he does get himself into! I can only pray that the poem comes up to your astringent standard.'[58] Luckily, Sparrow approved. 'I think the poem is rather pleasant, and quite up to the standard of the Laureate's light verse,' he wrote to Murray on 7 August. '. . . I quite see Elizabeth's point about the possibility of pulling John's leg about the Mrs Wilson poem. I think I would have advised him to take the risk, and published all the same . . .'[59] Murray wrote to Driberg the next day, 'Your letter to JB about the Mary Wilson poem has done the trick. Congratulations. So the poem stays.'[60]

A poem potentially much more incendiary than the 'Diss' one was 'Shattered Image'. After a lot of worried discussion between Jock Murray and John, it was included in the new book. John Bayley devoted a paragraph of his *Listener* review to describing and praising it.

Two poems are much more carefully laid out [than 'Executive'] under the taxidermist's glass. 'He and She on the Costa Blanca' superlatively dissects the before and after of a retirement dream. 'Shattered Image' is much denser and more sombre: the soliloquy of a successful young man, a Catholic convert with an excellent advertising job, who is probably to be proceeded against for interfering with children. It is a nightmare picture in modern Victorian genre, and, as is appropriate to such pictures, it strikes an attitude at us rather than attempting to move us. Betjeman's own total absorption in, and enthusiasm for, every kind of aesthetic experience is like a zany but holy dowsing gift which is momentarily transferable to us: never more so than here. Once we begin to read the poem . . . we are completely helpless, spellbound to the end.[61]

When *A Nip in the Air* was published, John asked his then secretary, Magda Rogers, to say that 'Shattered Image' was a poem which he had written many years before and which she had found in a desk drawer.[62] But in fact the inspiration of the poem was an Old Bailey case of 1968 in which one of John's Wantage neighbours, the interior decorator Oliver Ford, was fined £700 for 'gross indecency' with guardsmen.[63] In June 1969 John had written to Mary Wilson: 'As to that queer poem, I am going to try to change the crime – I can't do it to the Armed Forces, the only other crime which comes in the act, because then it will be too obviously Oliver Ford. I think I shall hint more at the crime. The point is that it should be an unacceptable crime. There aren't many.'[64]

Letters of 1968 from Oliver Ford to John show how kind and sympathetic John was at that time of crisis, when it looked as if Ford might go to prison.[65] In altering the poem, John did two things to dissociate Rex, the central character, from Ford. First, he changed his profession from decorator to public relations officer. Second, he changed his offences from sex with guardsmen to sex with a minor, Sidney Alexander Green, whom Rex nicknames 'Aleco'. (*Aleko* was the title of a homosexual novel of 1934, by Kenneth Matthews, in the collection of Colonel Kolkhorst which John had discreetly helped to sell after the Colonel's death.)[66]

That John should have read 'Shattered Image' to Mary Wilson shows the trust he had in her judgement and the closeness of their relationship, which was not just a mutual-congratulation society or a pact for cosy teatime readings of Tennyson and Newbolt. On his poem about the painter Julius Olsson – of whose works they each owned an example – he consulted not only Mary,[67] but also Tom Driberg. Originally, the first two lines read –

> Over what Bridge-parties that luscious sea
> Has sparkled in its frame of bronzed gold . . .[68]

Driberg criticized the scansion of these lines. 'I knew there was something odd about it and you have found it you clever old thing,' John replied.[69] In *A Nip in the Air* the poem opened –

> Over what bridge-tours has that luscious sea
> Shone sparkling from its frame of bronzèd gold . . .[70]

Driberg's other reservation about the poem was characteristically expressed:

In the sestet . . . the long witholding of the !, though fascinating, no doubt, to women readers (recalling as it does the male's deliberate postponement of an erotic climax) is unjustifiable and has complicating side-effects. It should perhaps come after 'walls'.[71]

In the printed version, John omitted all exclamation marks. The deft ending of the poem was ostensibly about Olsson, but perhaps there was a hint of autobiography in it, too.

'It isn't art. It's only just a knack' –
    It fell from grace. Now, in a change of taste,
See Julius Olsson slowly strolling back.[72]

John's reputation, like Olsson's, was taking a turn for the better. His self-confidence was slower to return. He still had the persecution-complex about journalists that he had painfully exposed in his 1960s poem 'Tregardock' –

Only the shore and cliffs are clear,
    Gigantic slithering shelves of slate
In waiting awfulness appear
    Like journalism full of hate . . .[73]

In August 1974 he wrote to Mary Wilson: 'I have been having a terrible time in the newspapers – misrepresented, lied about, often with the best intentions, and made so nervous I hardly dare put pen to paper.'[74] In an interview with Graham Lord published in the *Sunday Express* three days earlier, he had been defensive about his poem on Princess Anne's wedding. ('It was an unhappy squib, but I can't think why people were so rude about it.') But gradually, reassured by such friends as Mary Wilson and Jock Murray, he steeled himself to a new assertiveness. By publication day, 18 November, he was even prepared to make a defiant case for the Princess Anne poem in a *Daily Express* profile by Peter Grosvenor headed 'Betjeman is back – with a nip for his critics'.

He's . . . feeling rather more vexed than hurt at the reception which greeted his first official poem – the one on Princess Anne's wedding.

Hundreds of birds in the air,
And millions of leaves on the pavement . . .

It was meant to be like an Impressionist painting, capturing the wedding day in a series of vivid impressions.
    'It was criticized by silly asses who don't understand poetry and expected some heroic verses on the Princess. You know the sort of thing . . .'
    He began to extemporize:-

Thou art the spirit of equestrian pride,
Thou ridest gracefully through the countryside . . .

Then he rolled his eyes heavenwards in horror. 'Anyone can write rubbishy rolling couplets like that. And that's what some of them wanted. Well, they didn't get it.'[75]

The reviews of *A Nip in the Air* were more consistently good than those of any other of John's books. 'Betjeman at his best' was the heading of Elizabeth Jennings's review in *The Scotsman*. 'There is not a bad poem in this large collection,' she wrote.[76] John Press, one of John's successors in the George Elliston chair at Cincinnati,[77] wrote in the *Times Literary Supplement* that the poet had lost 'neither his idiosyncratic view of the world nor his ability to convey it in verse'.[78] In *The Tablet*, John Heath-Stubbs opined that 'The present volume will not disappoint Sir John's admirers.' He thought 'Shattered Image' was 'a poem of remarkable psychological insight'.[79] Philip Toynbee, not always friendly toward John, wrote in *The Observer*, 'Betjeman has become savage,' adding: 'The muted elegiac tone of *Summoned by Bells* has sharpened into an overt horror at the facts of life and death: sudden cries of extreme pain have pierced the wry nostalgia.'[80] From Toynbee, that was praise. The *Birmingham Post* considered that 'Fruit' was 'perhaps the most beautiful and moving short poem he has written'.[81] The *Daily Telegraph Magazine* praised his ear for the inflexions of speech: 'He reproduces faultlessly the gentle lament of a retired couple miserable in Spain, a prison chaplain's oily platitudes, the hideous jargon of a young executive.'[82] In *The Listener*, John Bayley wrote: 'The eye for life is as sharp as ever, and the rhythms as crisp as a Worcester apple.'[83] Clive James suggested in the *New Statesman* that 'he can be called light-minded only by the thick-witted'.[84]

A number of the reviewers commented on John's increasing preoccupation with death. T.C. Worsley, who had been at school with him at Marlborough, complained in the *Financial Times* that for his generation the poems spoke less of nostalgia than of mortality.[85] Only a few of the reviews were openly hostile. Lyman Andrews, in the *Sunday Times*, felt that John had been 'constricted by being Laureate'.[86] The *Daily Mail* thought the volume 'not only slim but undeniably slight in content'.[87]

Sales were excellent. On 18 January 1975 *The Bookseller* reported Murray's apology that 'the large demand for John Betjeman's *A Nip in the Air* meant that some booksellers may not have had their orders supplied in the last few days before Christmas. A reprint is in hand and will be available by the first week in February.' By 26 January the book had risen to No. 8 in the *Sunday Times*'s bestseller list.

On 26 April 1976, under the heading 'Idle muse', the *Times* Diary attacked John with a new malevolence.

Francis Kinson, who writes for our Business News section on Saturdays, is upset by the Poet Laureate's failure to produce a poem for the Queen's fiftieth birthday – or indeed for any royal occasion since his appointment in 1972 except Princess Anne's wedding. He has therefore penned these *Lines to a Laureate*:

> O Betjeman, bard manifest
> Of poesy topmost flower,
> Pray hearken to our stern behest –
> Thou should'st be living at this hour.
> Too long, alas, the lyre hast slept,
> Grown rusty is the dithyramb,
> Thy dactyl lieth ivy crep't
> And lo, thou givest not a damn.

Another stanza demanded 'Did God, who moulded Blake, mould thee?' and the last stanza ran:

> Rest on thy laurels, laureate,
> Priest of the social shibboleth
> Conserve thy Muse inviolate,
> For yawns thou'd better'st save thy breath.

In May 1976 Prince Charles wrote to John from a 'creaking, tossing ship in the middle of the English Channel' in his capacity as chairman of the King George Jubilee Trust, which was to administer a charitable appeal to coincide with the Queen's Silver Jubilee in 1977. 'I am determined that it should be as much of a success as possible . . .' he wrote. 'It would be marvellous if you could find the time to construct one of your masterpieces of scansion for the Queen's Jubilee . . . I would be enormously grateful, personally, if you felt able to conjure up your muse! . . . I am sure you will agree that a Silver Jubilee is something to be remembered with suitable splendour.'[88] It was only seven years since Charles had been pleased by John's lines on his investiture as Prince of Wales. He did not realize the extent to which Parkinson's Disease had depleted his powers.

When James Lees-Milne dined at Radnor Walk on 8 June with John, Elizabeth and Frank Tait, 'JB recited in so far as he could remember it the ode on the Queen's Silver Jubilee which he has completed after much sweat and tears and submitted to the Sovereign. She is delighted with it, and so is the D. of Edinburgh, even over some complimentary and funny stanzas, not for publication, about HRH discreetly walking behind.'[89]

In July the *Times* Diary belatedly caught up with the news that John was to collaborate with Malcolm Williamson, Master of the Queen's

Music, to write a 'Jubilee hymn' to mark the Queen's Silver Jubilee. 'For Sir John,' it suggested, 'the enterprise will help appease his critics, who complain that he has not written sufficient royal verse since becoming Laureate, and that he takes his duties unseriously.'[90] The next day, the diarist gave his list of imaginary new books for holiday reading, including *When I am Prime Minister* by Margaret Thatcher – not, in retrospect, a very well-aimed sneer. Among the books was *My Royal Poems* by Sir John Betjeman. 'This slim volume – a single folded sheet – contains the celebratory work performed by Sir John since he became Poet Laureate (HMSO 10p.)'[91]

The Diary had another dig at John in August 1974, after he launched an appeal for the restoration of the tower of St Anne's, Soho, a church which had been largely destroyed by a bomb in 1941.

> Sir John, in a straw boater and a pale blue woollen tie, affably announced that he had managed to compose six couplets to commemorate the occasion.
>
> In fact his verses, properly counted, do not seem to add up to quite such a considerable achievement, but here they are in full:

> High in the air two barrels interlock
> To form four faces of this famous clock.
> Reduced to drawing-room size this clock would be
> A Paris ornament of 1803.
> Let's make it go again: let London know
> That life and heart and hope are in Soho.

> Members and supporters of the Soho Society, who intend to make a community centre of the derelict and allegedly cat-infested tower, were delighted.[92]

There was another snipe from the Diary in November, when the Ephemera Society ('they collect things the rest of us throw away') held an exhibition at the office of a papermaking company in Soho. Maurice Rickards, a writer and designer, had founded the society a year before and had persuaded John to become president. 'It's a bit of a spectator sport with him,' Rickards confided to Leapman, indicating 'Sir John's sole contribution to the show, a bookplate which says simply "John Betjeman".'[93]

John Nankivell remembers how he and his then girlfriend, Bess Cuthbert, helped to get John over the 'trauma' of writing the Silver Jubilee poem that Prince Charles had requested.

We had this cottage down in a valley near Penelope. We paid a rent of one of my drawings a year for it, from a dear friend of Bess's. We'd often go up to see Penelope and we'd plan to be at the cottage when John was staying with her, so that we could visit both of them.

In 1977 John had got into a really bad state, because he had been asked to write this poem and he had not got round to doing it at all. He just could not think of anything. He was in despair about it. In fact, there was a time when Prince Charles had written to him – earlier – and asked him to do something and John had literally sent him a postcard saying 'No.' We said, 'You can't send him something like that!' He said, 'Well, I did.'

He couldn't contemplate thinking about the Silver Jubilee poem. His mind went a complete blank. So we sat down one afternoon – he, Bess and I – and we began inventing doggerel verses with him. I can't remember how the thing turned out or whether we recognized any bits and pieces of it as being by Bess and me; but certainly we had a very, very funny afternoon, working out various lines. We'd had a little bit to drink. The humour flowed and he of course laughed as well. By the end we were all almost in tears about the things we were turning out. They weren't ribald, just amusing. And in the end John managed to produce something. It may have borne no relation to what we were talking about in Cusop; but I think that afternoon softened the trauma for him.

Every time something like this turned up he'd get really upset about it. He knew how ridiculed many of the previous laureates had been when they produced official verse. He'd hate the thought of it and he'd despair: he was going to make a mess of it; it would be rubbished by everyone; and he'd be regarded as the usual disastrous laureate who's a waste of space.[94]

John managed to send his 'Jubilee Hymn' to Prince Charles in the month the Prince requested it, though his letter enclosing the poem was inadvertently put on a 'B' pile in the Prince's private office so that he did not see it until several days after it had arrived at Buckingham Palace.[95] Only with the publication of Jonathan Dimbleby's biography of Prince Charles, in 1994, was Charles's reaction to the poem made public. 'When he finally read it, he was aghast, though he noted with uncharacteristic understatement that "this poem is not exactly what I was expecting".' Dimbleby added:

Doubtless conceived 'in humble duty', Betjeman's five stanzas were lacklustre to the point of pastiche, without that verve which had rightly earned him a reputation as a great contemporary poet. The Prince was so dismayed that he contemplated asking the Poet Laureate to try again, but since the Queen had already given her approval to a modified version of the same poem to be put to music by Malcolm Williamson . . . he decided reluctantly not to press the matter.[96]

On 6 February 1977, the Jubilee Hymn, set to Williamson's music, was performed for the first time at the Royal Albert Hall. It was received with loud, long applause from an audience of 5,500. However, on the next day *The Times* quoted Nicholas Fairbairn, Conservative MP for Kinross and West Perthshire, who described the hymn as 'absolutely pathetic . . . the most banal, ninth-rate piece of child's verse. It has none of the mystery of poetry about it.'[97] Fairbairn, who later became Solicitor-General for Scotland, was a flamboyant and eccentric figure. He wore grotesque tartan suits and listed his recreations in *Who's Who* as 'making love, ends meet and people laugh'. Proposing that John should be given a different kind of sack from that traditionally enjoyed by poets laureate he promised that he would write a better Jubilee hymn himself.[98]

Penny Symon reported in *The Times* of 7 February 1977 that John was 'very upset about criticism of his silver jubilee hymn'. He had told her: 'The words were meant for singing, not reading, and therefore have plentiful long vowels. "God Save the Queen" is not poetry, but it sings well. This was written to sing well.' Three days later Fritz Spiegl wrote to the paper to say that the Jubilee Hymn compared well with effusions by earlier poets, for example Eusden's address to George II, which contained the couplet 'Thy virtues shine particularly nice, Ungloomed with a confinity to vice' or Shadwell's to William III after the King had been wounded at the Battle of the Boyne – 'But Heav'n of you took such Peculiar Care That soon the Royal Breach it did repair'.[99] There was also some comfort for John in Nicholas Fairbairn's promised rival hymn, which was generally agreed to be even more feeble than John's. Several members of the public sent John letters of support.[100] On 21 February he replied to one, from Matthew W. Jones: 'I was enchanted to have your kind letter. As Prince Philip said in a letter to me, "Please don't forget that criticism is much easier than creation and the persecution of individuals has always been the pleasure of thick-headed bullies . . ." '[101]

In October 1977 James Lees-Milne went to see his doctor, John Allison, who was also John's physician.

He talked about John B., in his indiscreet fashion, because we are both such friends. I respect his confidence accordingly. Says J's health is much affected by his happiness and unhappiness. The fact that Paul came over from USA and was nice to his father has helped to make him better. Allison says J.B. suffers terrible guilt over Paul. Why on earth? That now he suffers badly from press persecution; references to 'our ageing laureate', and such-like wounding phrases, notably *The Times* in its boring Diary on the middle page. J.B. complained to me about this. If I saw such criticism I would at once write to Rees-Mogg[102] in protest. I would always champion J.B. in any and every instance.[103]

John was again in need of some championing in May 1980 when he was once more attacked in *The Times*. The Arts Council had paid him a fee of £2,000 to choose the winner of the £7,500 National Book Award for Children's Literature. John decided it should go to Colin Dann for his story *The Animals of Farthing Wood*, published by Heinemann. Brian Alderson, *The Times*'s respected children's book editor, commented: 'It is a result that has been met with anything from incredulity to ridicule among critics who reckon to know something about children's books.'[104] Allowing that Alderson was clearly piqued at not having been consulted himself, his report was damning. It could not be said that Sir John was 'experienced in the assessment of children's books', for all 'his benign aspect'. It was difficult to see how his status in relation to the subject matched that of his fellow judges – Kingsley Amis for fiction and Dame Veronica Wedgwood for biography. Alderson, who ridiculed the brief essay John had written in handing down his judgement, would have expected some account of the reasoning that led to the selection of the short list and 'a fairly rigorous explanation of why the winner deserved its £7,500'. In the case of *Farthing Wood*, this might have included some discussion of 'its derivative plot and characterization, together with some attempt to "place" it in a genre that includes such writers as Fortescue and Adams, Hoban and Grahame'. But all John had provided was 'a disarmingly avuncular set of comments which ramble around matters of book production as much as they do literary merit'.

Supremely absurd, to Alderson, was John's remark that *Farthing Wood* 'deserves the award because it looks like a book, even when the dust-wrapper is off'. Further, one could 'hardly catch £7,500-worth of enthusiasm' in John's '(true) remark that Mr Dann has no "ear for rhythm"'. Brian Alderson thought Dann's work 'embarrassingly amateurish'. Taxpayers' money had been wasted. Alderson liked John's own book for children, *Archie and the Strict Baptists*, which had recently caused some annoyance to Strict Baptists. He would defend it, he said, against Teachers Against Teddy Bears. But that one book did not qualify John as a judge of children's literature.[105] At least some populist vindication of John's choice came later, when *The Animals of Farthing Wood* was adapted into a hugely successful international television series.

Also in 1980, the Queen Mother, who was as old as the century (and was to outlast it), celebrated her eightieth birthday. *The Times* reported on 4 August that two thousand people had sung 'Happy Birthday' to her as she walked through Sandringham Park after attending morning service in the parish church the day before. Then she had returned to Clarence House for the birthday celebrations on 4 August. *The Times* published the poem John had written for the occasion.

> We are your people
> Millions of us greet you
> on this your birthday
> Mother of the Queen.
> Waves of good will will go
> Racing out to meet you
> You who in peace and war
> Our faithful friend have been.
> You who have known the sadness of bereavement
> The joyfulness of family jokes
> And times when trust is tried.
> Great was the day for our United Kingdoms
> And God bless the Duke of York
> Who chose you as his bride.

The lines 'Waves of good will will go Racing out to meet you' were a neat inversion of a line John had written in *Summoned by Bells*, about his father's bullying conduct on Cornish holidays in John's adolescence – 'Black waves of hate went racing round the room.'[106]

Even though in April 1981 he had a stroke, John still wanted to write a poem to celebrate the marriage of Prince Charles to Lady Diana Spencer on 29 July. *The Times* of 27 July reported that 'Sir John, aged 75, will not be able to attend the service. A friend said: "He is not very well. The poem is his personal gift." '

The poem read:

> 'Let's all in love and friendship hither come
> Whilst the shrill Treble calls to thundering Tom,
> And since bells are for modest recreation
> Let's rise and ring and fall to admiration.'
> Those lines are taken from a ringer's rhyme

Composed in Cornwall in the Georgian time
From the high parish church of St Endellion,
Loyal to the Monarch in the late Rebellion.
Loyal to King Charles the First and Charles the Second,
And through the Georges to our Prince of Wales,
A human, friendly line that never fails.
I'm glad that you are marrying at home
Below Sir Christopher's embracing dome;
Four square on that his golden cross and ball
Complete our own Cathedral of St Paul.
Blackbirds in City churchyards hail the dawn,
Charles and Diana, on your wedding morn.
Come college youths, release your twelve-voiced power
Concealed within the graceful belfry tower
Till loud as breakers plunging up the shore
The land is drowned in one melodious roar.
A dozen years ago I wrote these lines:
'You knelt a boy, you rose a man
And thus your lonelier life began.'
The scene is changed, the outlook cleared,
The loneliness has disappeared;
And all of those assembled there
Are joyful in the love you share.[108]

Perhaps because of the general awareness that John was ill, this poem attracted less harsh criticism than his earlier exercises in royalism. There were even some compliments. Prebendary Edwin Stark congratulated John for his 'delightful reference to the association of Prince Charles with the delectable duchy of Cornwall by mentioning St Endellion'.[109] Philip Howard, in reporting on the wedding, took up the theme of John's 'A human, friendly line that never fails':

In the familiar Reformation words with which millions of English men and women have wed for more than three centuries, the Prince of Wales was married to Lady Diana Spencer. It was a grand act in the theatre of kingship: one of the last great ceremonies of the British monarchy this century. It was a colossal media spectacular, watched and wondered over by hundreds of millions at the round world's imagined corners.

In a mysterious way it was a rite of passage also for the British nations, which still measure their calendrical progress by such royal landmarks: another step to the music of time by which the English monarchy has personified English history and made it human for more than a thousand years.[110]

But there were also some gently teasing remonstrances about John's poem. K.H. Oldaker of London N14 commented on the lines beginning 'Blackbirds . . .': 'I fear not. It is the moulting season. Patriotic blackbirds may endeavour to raise a twitter or two even if they do themselves a mischief in the attempt. But it has to be said – if you want blackbirds at the wedding, get married in the spring.'[111]

Mrs E. Maimie Sharp of Whittlesford, Cambridge, sprang to John's defence. 'Sir John Betjeman is the most distinguished poet of our time and is surely entitled to use poetic licence. In this year of royal rejoicing, many more blackbirds have, strangely enough, been twittering gaily on my lawns, especially during the dawn chorus, whether they are moulting or not.'[112] (Were Laureate Pye's four-and-twenty blackbirds fluttering somewhere in John's subconscious?) The Cambridge chemist Lord Todd OM, FRS wrote to *The Times* with a different grouch: 'Replying to Sir John Betjeman's Wedding Ode, Mr K. H. Oldaker . . . observes that blackbirds do not sing in July. Nor, to Scottish ears at least, does "morn" rhyme with "dawn" at any season.'[113] It was the very rhyme John had used, as a boy, in one of his earliest poems, the aborted:

> Through the humble cottage window
>   Streams the early dawn.
> O'er the tossing bay of Findow
>   In the mournful morn.[114]

Paul Johnson has written: 'Even the best of the twentieth-century Laureates, John Betjeman, seemed to lose all his talent once the laurel was nailed to his brow.' Why did John fail so miserably in the rôle in which almost everybody thought he would excel? It was partly that his health was failing – as Penelope said, 'he has gorn orf'.[115] His near-reverence for the Queen at the head of the Church of England inhibited his usual sense of humour. And the whole idea of 'writing poetry to order' (however much the Queen might assure him that this was not required of him) went against the grain. He had always jibbed against authority, and to have anybody, from the *Times* diarist upwards, suggesting what he should write was anathema to him. He could not be himself. Interviewing him in 1974, Graham Lord had reported:

'One knows poetry can't be written to order,' he says, pointing towards the heavens. 'One just waits for something to come through from The Management upstairs and The Management can be very capricious.'[116]

Beyond that, all that can be said in mitigation is that John was not as dreadful a laureate as Alfred Austin, who wrote:

> Spring is here! Winter is over!
> The cuckoo-flower gets mauver and mauver.[117]

The honour of the laurel belonged to the classical world. John Sparrow, the classicist, applied to John's tenure a famous Latin tag, Tacitus' words on the Roman emperor Galba: 'Omnium concensu, capax imperii, nisi imperasset' (In the opinion of all, he was worthy to rule – had he not ruled).[118]

21

A PASSION FOR CHURCHES

'Men hate beauty. They think it wicked.' Sir John Betjeman talks to the television camera, coldest of listeners, as to a very old friend who can be trusted not to show impatience at anything he might say. Were it to do so he would turn his back and walk off, in the equally sure knowledge that it would follow him: Betjeman's back is growing in persuasive moral fervour.

Michael Ratcliffe, reviewing *A Passion for Churches*
in *The Times*, 9 December 1974

After the success of *Metro-land*, Eddie Mirzoeff was encouraged by Robin Scott, the Controller of BBC2, to make another Betjeman film for television. Mirzoeff looked for a subject which would involve John to the same degree but would take him and the viewer into a different world. It seemed to him that John's relationship with the Church of England was like his relationship with suburbia – 'something he was passionate about, had written about and saw in a way that was unique to him'.[1] And, like the pleasures of suburbia, the life of the Church of England had not been touched on much before, on television. The idea appealed to John.

Mirzoeff suggested that, just as the Metropolitan Line had been the 'spine' of *Metro-land*, giving the film shape and coherence, a single diocese should be chosen as a focus for the Church of England film. The question was, which diocese? Ted Roberts thought Salisbury would be an ideal choice – 'The architecture is so stunning, everybody's idea of what a cathedral should look like; and it's set in the heart of Wessex.'[2] But John wanted Southwark, which for him had two great advantages: it was conveniently near his London home and the Bishop was his friend Mervyn Stockwood. In March 1973 John, Elizabeth Cavendish and Mirzoeff dined with Stockwood in Southwark.

It was positively the most unpleasant evening I can remember – *ever* [Mirzoeff recalls] – battling through on behalf of the BBC. I was not at all taken by his personality, and still less taken by the set-up he had there, of young Arab boys going round looking after him, in a number of different ways.

Betjeman obviously was a great chum of his, but could see, absolutely see, halfway through the evening, that it was a total disaster. And there was no question about it: the following morning, well, I was furious, because of the way Mervyn Stockwood had behaved, which I thought was very, very rude, actually. He was so arrogant and *de haut en bas*; he more or less ignored me. He was really *horrible*. And I wasn't his cup of tea, either, there was very little doubt about that. Also, he was being offhand about what help he was prepared to give us. John Betjeman was very sensitive, wrote all the right kind of letters to both parties; but it was clear that Southwark was not it. In any case, I didn't think an inner-city diocese was the sort of place we should be doing with John. It had all the wrong vibes to it. I mean, we weren't all about deprivation and lack of housing and general misery.[3]

John wrote Mirzoeff an apologetic letter after the Stockwood dinner. ('John McGlashan . . . has written an appreciative letter about Southwark. Its old Bishop woke up yesterday morning in a penitent mood and thought he'd gone a bit far. Feeble and I thought he had been fasting during Lent and lost his proportion . . . He only feared that he might have wounded you. I said I would try to put it right.')[4] But John was still urging that 'Southwark is the right place for a celebration.'[5]

Eddie Mirzoeff lost no time in letting him know how opposed he was to that idea. In a letter of 6 June 1973 John, who was down in Cornwall, conceded that 'our meeting with Mervyn was a bit of a flop'.[6] Attempting to deflect Mirzoeff's anger with humour, he wondered whether the effects of tourism on the Church might make a good subject. 'As I was walking up a lane to Pentire yesterday I saw one of those cocoons containing hundreds of caterpillars which had shrivelled up the leaves and twigs. It seemed to me like tourism . . .'[7] Four days later he sent another idea: how about comparing a town church with a country church, and men's communities with women's communities? For the country church he suggested Blewbury, Berkshire, where the Vicar was his cricket-loving friend Hugh Pickles, whom he had first known as a curate at Wantage. 'If this hasn't given you enough to think about,' John teasingly added, 'ask the Bishop of Southwark!'[8]

Then Ted Roberts, who had edited *Metro-land* and was to edit the new film too, suggested the diocese of Norwich. He was himself Norwich-born and bred, and his parents still lived there. 'I was afraid that everybody would think I just wanted to promote my home team, so to speak,' he recalls. 'But I think it was a good idea, because in East Anglia you have the most dense collection of medieval churches in Christendom. So there was a visual richness.'[9] And the diocese of Norfolk had one other great recommendation. In Norfolk lived Billa Harrod. Not only was she very close to John; she had written the Shell Guide to Norfolk for him, was much involved in helping to save redundant churches, and was a friend of the Bishop of Norwich, Maurice Wood. 'She loved having John to stay,' Mirzoeff says, 'and he usually felt very relaxed and at home in her house. So from that point of view it was a goer. And also it was clear, early on, that one would find characters who had the true essence of the old-fashioned Church of England in them. People like Canon Blackburne, the Chaplain of the Norfolk Broads, who clambered about on narrow boats. He was the uncle, curiously enough, of the man who signed the expenses of our BBC department at that time, Martin Blackburne. That was another good reason for us to film in Norfolk!'[10]

In January 1974 John, Mirzoeff and the latter's secretary, Jane Whitworth, stayed with the Harrods at the Old Rectory at Holt in Norfolk. (Sir Roy Harrod, the economist, was still *compos mentis*, though a few years later he had become confused.) They explored the diocese. It was a generally happy visit, though there was one untoward incident. 'We were stopped by the police on the old A11,' Mirzoeff recalls. 'Jane was driving and speeding – *unquestionably* speeding. John was sitting in the front passenger seat and I was in the seat behind. And there was this wonderful sight of John slowly descending in the seat, lower and lower, and finally disappearing completely, down into where you put your knees, in order to prevent himself being seen by the policeman. He had this vision of a headline saying POET LAUREATE CAUGHT SPEEDING.'[11]

On 24 January, after they had returned to London, John wrote Mirzoeff a letter covering four pages of foolscap, beginning: 'I am still reeling with delight at the soaring majesty of Norfolk and our tour there with Jane Whitworth . . .'[12] He then set down his ideas for the film.

I think the obvious is best and that the film should be our earthly pilgrimage expressed in the sacraments and psalms of the C of E to which most people belong even though they may have forgotten. It will stir memories. Phrases from the Book of Common Prayer, especially the General Thanksgiving, that Norwich invention – the psalms and hymns A[ncient] and M[odern] will wander through the script much of which should be spoken by someone with a Norfolk accent, and a *strong* Norfolk accent.[13]

He had been reading *Walsingham Way*, a book by his friend Colin Stephenson. It had convinced him that the Shrine of Our Lady of Walsingham could not be ignored in the film. 'The pilgrimage was of European fame before the Reformation and though I don't much like relic worship myself, things do get an extra quality when they have been revered for centuries by thousands. They are something like the monarchy.'[14] He even thought that some holy water from Walsingham could be sprinkled over the camera lens 'to surprise and bless our readers [*sic*]!'.[15] What he wanted at all costs to avoid was 'solemnity and conscious do-goodery and taking ourselves too seriously'.[16] The film must be 'natural and life-like and full of jokes like Chaucer and some of those carved bosses and bench-ends we saw'.[17] The film would be given shape by the progression of the Sacraments.

> We begin church with Baptism in the font at Trunch . . . Then we have Sunday School and all over Norfolk in glass and wood and stone are school scenes, the beating of bottoms as in the porch at Cley or in the Cathedral. Then we can have Confirmation and a Bishop's hand and the words and flaxen or reddish Norfolk hair on boy or girl or adult. Then we must have a village wedding, the coming out from the cottage and all the finery and ribbons on the hired car and illegal confetti and the relations in the pews . . . And now the keepers of the house tremble and the grinders cease and mourners go about the streets and that will bring us to a village funeral, the motor hearse and professional undertaker.[18]

John sent a copy of the letter to Billa Harrod, who replied: 'I *love* your idea for the film.' She added: 'Your visit made us feel *young* again, like when we used to come out to Uffington when we were first married.'[19] Just as with the *Metro-land* film, Mirzoeff thought most of John's ideas unworkable, though he was pleased by his enthusiastic involvement. But Mirzoeff did adopt the progression of Sacraments as the film's framework. A letter was even sent to Norgate Bros, under-takers, of Horstead, with a view to having a grave dug in the church-yard there;[20] but eventually Mirzoeff decided that the subject of death was too daunting for John, and abandoned the sequence.

One thing on which John and Mirzoeff did not agree was the title of the projected film. Mirzoeff wanted to call it *Failed in Divinity*. He thought it wonderfully ironic that John, so renowned as an expert on churches and religious observances, should have been ploughed in the elementary Oxford examination. He wanted to begin the film with John standing on the steps of the Examination Schools in Oxford, that 'Anglo-Jackson' building, and declaiming the lines about his débâcle, from *Summoned by Bells* –

> Failed in Divinity! Oh count the hours
> Spent on my knees in Cowley, Pusey House,
> St Barnabas', St Mary Mag's, St Paul's,
> Revering chasubles and copes and albs!
> Consider what I knew of 'High' and 'Low' . . .
> Failed in Divinity! O, towers and spires!
> Could no one help? Was nothing to be done?[21]

From the first, John showed resistance to the proposed title. 'Why he disliked it so much,' Mirzoeff says, 'I never . . . *divined*.'[22] In 1960, when *Summoned by Bells* was published, John had been happy enough to reveal his academic humiliation of the late Twenties. But in 1960 he was still describing himself, in *Who's Who*, as 'journalistic hack'. Now, fourteen years on, knighted and Poet Laureate, perhaps he was less inclined to be paraded in a dunce's cap. Whatever the reason, this was a battle John was determined to win, and, as Anthony Powell wrote, he had 'a whim of iron'.[23] Against that determination, even the strong-willed, resourceful and diplomatic Mirzoeff could not prevail. For a time John pressed for *Norfolk Pilgrimage* as an alternative title,[24] but Mirzoeff felt that did not adequately indicate what the film was about. Very late in the day the two men compromised with *A Passion for Churches*, though Mirzoeff still regrets the loss of *Failed in Divinity*. 'It would have been a beautifully ironic title – because by the end of the film you'd feel he had told you a vast amount.'[25]

In March 1974 John and Mirzoeff again stayed with Billa Harrod, this time bringing with them the BBC researcher Christine Whittaker, who had worked on *Metro-land*. They made great progress in choosing sites for filming; but the visit was marked by a weird incident.

We were absolutely convinced that that Old Rectory was haunted [Mirzoeff says]. It was the only occasion in all my work with the BBC that I have been visited by a spirit or ghost. The house is a rambling old place in deep M.R. James country. We were put into different parts of it. At four o'clock in the morning I suddenly woke with a start, a very sudden awakening. I don't usually do that. I felt there was something odd; but there was no actual manifestation. There was no sudden coldness – it was freezing anyway in that bedroom! Nevertheless, a very odd sensation. I picked up my watch eventually; put the light on, rather in trepidation – nothing there. I looked at the watch: dead on four o'clock. That was it. I went back to sleep and thought no more about it.

The following day, after we'd had our breakfast and said goodbye to Lady Harrod and Sir Roy, we were driving away and Christine Whittaker – who still works at the BBC [1997] – said, 'I'm never going back to that place again.' I said, 'Why not?' and she said, 'I woke up in the middle of the night suddenly and heard a voice calling my name.' I said, 'It must have been Sir Roy.' And she said, no, it definitely wasn't Sir Roy, she could tell the difference. It was absolutely strange and frightening. So I asked, 'What time was it?' – because we were in different corners of the house. And she said, 'Well, I managed to look at my watch and it was exactly four o'clock.' So clearly we both woke up for some reason at four o'clock, and that's as far as it went. But we were both convinced that something odd had happened, and we never stayed there again. It did not in any way stop Lady Harrod from being a great help all the way through the filming.[26]

Mirzoeff does not remember any talk with John about the 'haunting', but – if only not to seem a spoilsport – John must have acknowledged some frisson of the supernatural, because, when Billa Harrod heard about the experience, she wrote to Mirzoeff:

I was slightly horrified – but *very interested* – to hear that you, and Christine, and John B, had had disagreeable experiences in our spare room. Was it the yellow room facing the front of the house?. . . John certainly slept in the yellow front room but I slightly discount his experiences as he has slept in that room many times before without any complaints! He was tired, and worried about, and by, Penelope, who was sleeping next door in the blue room, on *his* bad night.[27]

Billa Harrod asked Mirzoeff and Christine Whittaker to give a full description of their experiences, 'because I do *not* want to put my friends into haunted rooms and I am much too frightened by the news of *your* discomfort to dare to sleep there myself to find out'.[28]

Otherwise, the March visit was a success. There was a meeting with the Bishop of Norwich. 'Maurice Wood was very Low Church and not, you'd have thought, Betjeman's cup of tea,' Mirzoeff says. 'But actually he was really lovely in the way he welcomed us to the diocese. The first time Christine and I turned up for research, it was an afternoon, and he swept across from a cloister with his gowns flowing – "My *dears*!" he said, "you must come to Evensong." And afterwards he had a conversation with me which I've always treasured. "I can tell", he said, "that you are rather High Church." Well, I'm not C of E at all!'[29] The Bishop was less enthusiastic when Mirzoeff sent him a sheet of his rough ideas for the film. 'I must be open with you,' the Bishop wrote on 19 March, 'and say that it looks very much like a "seven sacraments walk through Victorian Norfolk", which, delightful though this may be, is unlikely to be a factual picture of the Church of England.'[30] Mirzoeff hastened to reassure him: 'The film is a *personal* view by Sir John Betjeman of what he finds attractive and sympathetic in the institution of the Church of England.'[31] The Bishop gave his assent.

John wrote to Mirzoeff, after their return to London, 'It seems to me that there are two pilgrimages in *Norfolk Pilgrimage*, as I have named our film. One is Walsingham which cannot be left out. The other is the soul's journey in Norfolk and time from birth to death and we hope eternal light in life after death.'[32] The 'visual bonanzas', he added, would include carved wooden roofs such as that at Knapton and painted screens like that at Ranworth. And 'We mustn't forget the royal touch with Sandringham Church and the Lycett Green mansion of Kenhill – an untouched Edwardian interior.'[33] He had enjoyed driving round Norfolk and introducing Mirzoeff to the glories of East Anglian church architecture. 'I did not pretend to know anything about it,' Mirzoeff says. 'I remember sitting in one church and saying "cle-re-story". He said: "I call it 'clear-story'." '[34]

But the 'Norfolk Pilgrimage' also had a poignancy for John. He was revisiting the county where, in early childhood, he and his father had been friends, before they quarrelled. In his poem 'Norfolk' he had written –

> How did the Devil come? When first attack?
> These Norfolk lanes recall lost innocence . . .[35]

He particularly remembered his father when, with Mirzoeff, he 'did a recce' on the River Bure. They met a Mr Cook whose parents-in-law had known the Betjemanns. On 18 March 1974, John wrote to thank Cook for a sketch he had sent him, and treated him to an autobiographical flashback.

I was delighted to receive the charming ink sketch of the Anchor Inn, Coltishall. I so well remember mooring there overnight in my father's cruiser called the *Morning Calm*, and she nearly always was becalmed, that cruiser, for she never won a race! She was very beautiful and built at Doxham by the Press brothers. As for the Anchor Inn, I can remember happy visits there and sitting in the drawing room where there was a piano and some old-fashioned music which my mother sang and which made my friend Ronald Wright (later a monk at Ampleforth and now dead)[36] collapse with laughter. It seemed a wonderful unexplored land above the locks at Buxton and Lammas in those days and we used to go there in the dinghy. I shall treasure this ink drawing for it is just as I remember the place with that stepped Dutch gable-end. I return the photograph of Mrs Cook's

parents. I well remember them and the welcome there used to be once one
had come round the reach at Belaugh to what seemed like home . . .[37]

Filming began on 8 April, and the first scene was at Belaugh on the
Bure. Resigned, by now, to John's implacable hostility to the *Failed in
Divinity* title and the opening scene in Oxford, Mirzoeff asked him
how he first came to appreciate churches. John replied that he thought
it was the outline of Belaugh church tower against the sky, when his
father took him sailing and rowing on the Bure, that had given him 'a
passion for churches; so that every church I've been past since, I've
wanted to stop and look in'.[38] For the first scene in the film, Mirzoeff
asked John to repeat this explanation while rowing a dinghy on the
Bure. Disaster followed.

John *could* row [Mirzoeff recalled] – in the same way as he could play
golf – but not as well as when he was younger. And in one of the tapes he
was rowing, facing backwards, as one does, and he hit the bank. Instead
of going straight down the middle of the river, he edged towards the side;
and there was this extraordinary sight of him toppling, terribly terribly
slowly, in the boat, with his legs in the air. It was one of those awful
moments – both extremely funny and, obviously, very concerning, because
you don't want poor old Sir John to drown in the River Bure.

We rushed him into – it so happened – the near-by rectory. We knocked
at the door and said, 'We have a poet here, he's soaking wet. Could you
possibly take him in and dry his clothes?' And this intensely filthy, disreputable old rector with egg stains all down his front and clothes which
hadn't been dry-cleaned for twenty-five years, had us in. A charming man,
clearly a sort of throw-back to the nineteenth century. He wrapped up Sir
John in a dressing-gown and dried his trousers.

I had a falling-out afterwards with the cameraman, John McGlashan.
Because when we came to see the rushes, and we all waited to see this
moment, we found it wasn't there. We thought: Why not? What happened?
And we eventually found that John McGlashan had deliberately exposed
that bit of the film by running it back, to make sure it could not be used.
And what worried me was that McGlashan had not had the confidence in
me to think . . . you know, he was going to make sure that Sir John was not
made a laughing-stock. I thought he should have had the confidence in his
director to know that he wouldn't do that. I felt very upset about that.[39]

The row-boat episode had one happier sequel. Enough of the footage
of John rowing survived to use in the film. A still from it, published in
Radio Times,[40] inspired an oil painting by the Royal Academician
Ruskin Spear, which John liked so much that it was reproduced on the

sleeve of *Sir John Betjeman's Britain*, one of the records he made with Jim Parker.*

John emerged from the rectory dried out and unscathed. But it was an ominous start; and the incident showed up John's growing infirmity. Those of the crew who had worked with him on *Metro-land* two years earlier noticed the decline in his strength and his difficulty in walking. 'He needed to be wrapped up very well,' Mirzoeff remembers, 'and he came out with one of those Puffa jackets, which Billa or somebody had insisted he wore. I said, "No, it looks terrible, we can't have you walking around like that in the film." He said, "Well, I need something." And we were in Swaffham and we went in a gents' outfitters and he bought a terrible blue plastic mac. In the film, it trails behind him like a gown. He called it "my Swaffham". There were a lot of jokes of that kind.'[41] Ted Roberts, who stayed in London awaiting the film to edit, had a postcard from John. 'It was written in broad Norfolk. The combination of broad Norfolk and John's handwriting was damn' near impossible to decipher. It was signed "Jack Saxmundham".'[42]

After the boating upset at Belaugh, the filming went well. The weeks of research had suggested many vignettes of Church of England life. In the church at Trunch, with its magnificent carved wood font-cover, baby Cherry Ann Schamp was baptized. One of the film's reviewers wrote that Cherry Ann 'went scarlet and screamed the font down';[43] the Dean of Norwich complained, 'the baby looked positively in pain'.[44] At Ranworth, the art restorer Pauline Plummer was uncovering a medieval painting, 'a hundredth of an inch at a time', on the chancel screen. 'It's by no provincial hand,' John judged. 'It's rather a masterpiece.'[45] At Norwich Cathedral, Bishop Wood played host to the picture-hatted Mothers' Union –

> Bawdeswell greets Stratton Strawless,
> Potter Heigham is on terms with Little Snoring,
> North Creake sits beside Melton Constable,
> And for everyone there's the chance to meet the Bishop.[46]

The Bishop, in a red cassock and holding a crook, said: 'Here we've got Bishop Salmon's palace, about 1320 . . . As opposed to having your lunch in the cloisters, or, as today, sitting out here in the garden – we would have given you an enormous sit-down lunch. [To his wife] We weren't married in those days, darling!' Realizing that the last sentence was open to misconstruction he corrected himself: 'Bishops weren't allowed to marry [in the Middle Ages].'[47]

---

* See Chapter 25, '*Banana Blush*'.

At Weston Longville the Rector, the Rev. C. G. 'Jimmy' James, was shown typing copy for the parish magazine, with just that arch touch of sauciness that clergymen can allow themselves:

> We send belated birthday greetings to Mr Walter Pardon of Weston Longville who reached the splendid age of 89 years on February 17th. Little Johnny Atherton aged eight-and-a-half years broke his leg on February 17th – bad luck! – we hope you get well soon, Johnny. It is only a rumour but there is talk of a sponsored streak for church funds. By whom, we wonder?[48]

John chipped in: 'Not, I think, by members of the Parochial Church Council at Letheringsett, the PCC.'[49] Billa Harrod was a member of the Letheringsett PCC. So was Miss Cozens-Hardy, who had taken umbrage at John's poem about the Cozens-Hardy mausoleum.[50]

South Raynham had been chosen for the filming of that quintessential Church of England function, a garden fête. The fête was held at South Raynham Grove, the home of Mrs Eve ('Puffin') Le Strange and formerly the rectory. 'Let battle commence!' said the Rector, the Rev. Stephen Pritt. A local newspaper reported: 'Visitors were also "shot" as they paid their money at the entrance. Those on the lawn included Marquess and Marchioness Townshend,[51] Sir Roy and Lady Harrod and their son Dominick.'[52] After the filming, John told the Harrods a favourite story, of a fête organized by a Miss Helen Hunt. 'A white glove was found near the Lucky Dip. The Vicar got up on his dais and innocently announced: "Anyone who has lost a glove can go to Helen Hunt for it!" '[53]

At St Mary Bylaugh, John climbed up to the decks of a three-decker pulpit. At St Margaret, Felbrigg (the parish church of his old Oxford friend Wyndham Ketton-Cremer),[54] he chatted to a party of brass-rubbers led by Mrs Dawson of Apple Acre, Blofield, and was photographed with them for the *Eastern Daily Press*, beaming down,[55] though in fact he rather disapproved of the 'antiquarianism' of brass-rubbing, and memorial brasses were an art form that left him cold. (In the voice-over later superimposed, he says: 'I wonder who fall to their knees here today. Oh, the new cottage industry, brass-rubbing. Medieval effigies tell us nothing of the people they represent, they're so calm and bland and self-controlled.')[56]

The Sacrament of marriage was filmed at Lyng Church, where the bride's father, Canon Townshend, was priest.[57] The young bridegroom was Nigel McCulloch, who is now Bishop of Manchester.

> We bought Nigel and Celia McCulloch a BBC wedding present [Eddie Mirzoeff recalls]. I asked the secretary to buy it, and she got a coffee-maker.

And I said, 'John, this is from all of us and you've got to write a little poem to go with it.' He put it off and put it off; and finally we could put it off no longer. He was being given a special journey on a steam train, round the inner London railway that has Olympia on it. And, as Olympia is near where we then worked, at Kensington House, I telephoned John and said, 'I'm coming to Olympia and I want you to write something down.' And there he was with the bosses of British Rail. I rushed up – 'Hello, John! You've *got* to write something.' The British Rail bosses looked on in surprise. And he wrote:

> Nigel and Celia, may you be
> Fonder of coffee than of tea.

That was his moving epithelamium! He was there at the wedding, in the congregation. And we gave Nigel and Celia all the material that we shot – the parts that were not used in the film. By the way, we found out later that neither of them likes coffee, so the gift was a dead loss.[58]

The bells that pealed after the wedding were those not of Lyng Church, but of Wiverton, so that John could introduce Billy West, captain of the tower and sixty years a ringer. 'Ah, that's music in the ear,' West says. 'Once that gets hold of you – I suppose it's like smoking cigarettes – once that gets hold of you – that, that's a drug, you can't get rid of it. There's something about it, I don't know what it is, but you'd go anywhere for it. If there weren't somewhere where there were some bells, I'd go crazy, I know I should.'[59]

The next three sequences were of Ditchingham, Walsingham and Sandringham. At Ditchingham, John admired the work of the sisters of All Hallows Convent – wafer-making and bee-keeping. At Walsingham, he showed the old station now turned into an Orthodox church with golden minarets ('The Orient come to East Anglia') and then the shrine with its coachloads of pilgrims. Royal permission had been obtained for the filming in Sandringham Church.[60] John arrived at the church in a 1936 Bentley lent by Humphrey Boardman of Hoveton[61] – 'Sandringham is the Queen's country estate. The parish church is used both by the villagers and the royal family. It seems appropriate to arrive in style.'[62] Inside, he pointed out the altar of solid silver 'given by Mr Rodman Wanamaker, a very rich American admirer of our royalty', a statue of St George by Sir Alfred Gilbert of *Eros* fame; and a plaque where King Edward VII had sat: 'THIS SEAT was occupied by my beloved husband from the year of our marriage 1863 till 1910 when the LORD took him to HIMSELF – ALEXANDRA.'

Though both John and Mirzoeff were on the look-out for Church of England 'characters', the Rev. Ronald Cooling of Martham was almost too much of an Ealing Comedy caricature, and John serious doubts about including him. Before becoming a clergyman, Cooling had worked as a nautical instrument-maker and ship's-compass adjuster.[63] Now he was a model-railways fanatic. The film showed him in an upper room of the vicarage, engrossed in the task of oiling a model steam locomotive which he had begun making in 1971; he was now completing the chassis. In the voice-over, John intoned: 'In his room above, the Rector, Father Cooling, model engineer, oils his parish wheels; and indeed they run themselves most smoothly.'[64]

Ted Roberts and others who had worked with John on *Metro-land*, noticed that he had lost some of his élan. 'We felt that the spark that was there in *Metro-land* had started to wane,' Roberts says.[65] But there was one piece to camera in the Norfolk film as inspired as the *coup de théâtre* in *Metro-land* when, in Voysey's old house, John had played truant from the agreed script. He was keen to show the 'sculptured gold' work of his old friend Sir Ninian Comper in Wymondham Abbey and in Lound Church. At Lound, he paused while descanting on Comper's gilding, turned to look direct into the camera, and said:

> I knew Comper. He died a few years ago and he looked rather like that advertisement for Colonel Sanders' Kentucky Chicken. Little white pointed beard; and he spoke in a very lah-di-dah manner – 'my wark, doncha know, in that charch'. And his wark in this charch is really marvellous.[66]

'The Colonel Sanders comparison, the personal memory, the acting – John had put none of these into the rehearsal,' Mirzoeff says.[67] John went on to talk of the altar hangings in which pink predominated. 'It's called "Comper Pink", and he had it specially made in Spain. He used to buy scarlet silk and there have it bleached in the sun till it was just the shade he wanted.' Here John gave a sly look to camera. ' "Incomperable," as people used to say.'[68] Again, Mirzoeff remembers, the pun was a spontaneous embellishment of the script.[69]

But, with all the caricatures and jokes, John was intent on conveying to the viewer the spiritual essence of the Church of England. For him, this was most tellingly illustrated by the Vicar of Flordon, Bill Fair, saying Offices in an empty church. Father Fair was Irish. 'We have done tose tings which we ought not to have done,' he declared.[70] For John, he had the simplicity of the Celtic saints.

> It doesn't matter that there's no one there.
> It doesn't matter when they do not come.
> The villagers know the parson is praying for them in their church.[71]

...oment, Mirzoeff brought John into three redundant
...es to make jokey comments about the new uses to
... being put. At St Edmund Fishergate, now used as a
...re was a terrible pun about souls and soles. St Lawrence
...studio by young artists. ('Better that than let the building fall.) At St Mary Coslany, where the watercolourist John Sell
Cotman was baptized and Old Crome married, the present congregation were 'well upholstered' (overstuffed furniture). Then on to Smith's
Knoll lightship, the furthest point of the Norwich diocese, twenty-two
miles out to sea. Trinity House on Tower Hill, London, had given
Mirzoeff permission to film the Rev. Maurice Chant, Chaplain of the
Missions to Seamen in Great Yarmouth, coming aboard to meet the
men and listen to their problems.[73] On inland waters, Canon
Blackburne, Chaplain of the Norfolk Broads, was shown summoning
'the floating members of his flock' to an Easter service.

The film was building to its climax, the dawn of Easter Day on Ness
Point, Lowestoft, the easternmost tip of England. Easter Day fell on 14
April that year. Canon Douglas Caiger, who was to conduct the open-
air service, told Mirzoeff in advance, 'As far as I can gather, the sun is
due to rise about ten minutes to six.'[74] Osbert Lancaster later described
the scene at Ness Point, more Turner than Cotman – 'in the background the flaming sky of dawn and great breakers exploding on the
seawall with, down in the front, the interdenominational congregation
accompanied by a Salvation Army band out-trumpeting the clash and
bluster of a force nine gale'.[75] Then the film cut to the quietist faces of
old ladies in red cloaks and black witch hats –

> Peaceful their lives are, calm and unsurprising,
> The almshouse ladies here at Castle Rising;
> And suited to the little brick-built square
> The Jacobean hats and cloaks they wear.[76]

The film ended with the pealing bells of St Peter Mancroft (' "Is
risen today?" "Is risen today?" they plead') and scenes of people going
to church. John knew that fewer than half of his viewers would be
God-fearing. His audience would include atheists and agnostics;
Christians who had let their faith slip; people who loved the Church
of England as part of English life and its churches as tabernacles of
preserved history, without subscribing to its doctrines. His carefully
pitched last words made concessions to most of these groups.

> The faith of centuries is in the sound
> Of Easter bells, that ring all Norfolk round;

And though for church we may not seem to care,
It's deeply part of us. Thank God it's there.[77]

When filming *Metro-land*, John and the crew had spent only one
night away from home. With *A Passion for Churches*, they were on
location for weeks at a time. 'There was a lot of socializing in pubs at
lunchtime,' Mirzoeff says. 'John was absolutely lovely with the crew
around him, telling them stories – all the old stuff, stories of his youth,
of his days as a prep-school master, that sort of thing. All the jokes he
loved about film paraphernalia. (We had the same recordist as we had
on *Metro-land*, Simon Wilson.) But in the evening it was slightly
different, for various reasons. One of them was that Penelope came up
and stayed for several days.'[78]

Penelope's arrival on the scene was a complication that no one had
bargained for, and not everyone welcomed. She stayed with John both
at Holt and in Norwich. Like the Pipers, the Harrods had remained
loyal to her and did not approve of John's liaison with Elizabeth
Cavendish. Learning that John would be away from Elizabeth and
safely *chez* Harrod or in a Norwich hotel, Penelope gatecrashed the
party. Her presence unsettled John, stirring more feelings of guilt to
add to those he felt about his father.

For me [Mirzoeff recalls] the most memorable thing that happened, in
personal terms, was that after Penelope left the Maid's Head Hotel, the
big old hotel in Norwich, just John and I were left alone. All the others
had gone out – John McGlashan was always going to Indian restaurants.
And we had the most extraordinary talk, the only time I had a talk like
that with John. Extremely personal. It started with his talking about
Penelope. Then he talked about Paul – 'the Powlie', as he called him – and
his desperate sadness at what he felt was his failure to build bridges, to
keep him alongside. He'd gone, left for Canada or somewhere as a musician. There was no contact. And John was feeling guilt, terrible terrible
guilt.

So I said to him, 'Why don't you *write* to him? Why don't you write
and say what you feel? Why don't you say that you have this affection for
him which you have failed to communicate?' He said: 'I can't do it.' I
said: 'Come on, you can.' I went on and on about this, though it wasn't
my business at all. He said he would write, but I don't think he did. This
long talk brought us very close together. I never felt closer to him, as a
human being, than I did that night. One felt one broke through the jokes
and the performance to the real person – who was, on that occasion, a
very sad, unfulfilled, guilt-ridden person. It made you feel very warm
towards him.[79]

In their off-duty hours, Mirzoeff found that John was an extraordinarily knowledgeable guide to East Anglia. 'He knew his way round. He
not only knew all the churches; he knew where the bookshops were,
and we went into lots of them. There was a marvellous bookshop at
Reepham. They just left it open in the evening, nobody there. You
walked in, took what you wanted, and left money in a bag hanging on
the door. Amazing to think about now.'[80] Another bookshop John liked
was The Scientific Anglian, which he called 'The Scientific Anglican'.
There he found several books illustrated by the Scottish colourist Jessie
M. King,[81] a disciple of Charles Rennie Mackintosh. Some of these he
gave to members of the crew. Not all the recipients appreciated the
dainty *art nouveau*; the gifts were lost, or left behind in Norfolk.

John was in one of his very generous moods [Eddie Mirzoeff remembers].
Elizabeth Jane Howard[82] was sent out by the *Radio Times* to write an
article about the filming. She stayed several days. She was very grand – she
would only talk to John and she wouldn't talk to any of us. But she
insisted on taking him into various antique shops and saying, 'That's
absolutely wonderful, John, you must buy it.' So he would be carrying
round these paintings and things that she made him buy. The moment she
left, he gave them to us. I've still got a lovely painting that he gave me. We
all did rather well.[83]

As Kingsley Amis's then wife, Elizabeth Jane Howard already knew
John well. She may not have endeared herself to the crew, but with her
novelist's eye she was able most effectively to evoke John's pattern of
life in Norfolk in the *Radio Times* article, which was headed, ' "I like
a bit of High" '.

'I'm a dreadful old fraud.' This audible mutter was made after about fifteen
strangers had accosted him in the streets of Norwich: 'Sir John Betjeman?
I *so* much enjoyed your last programme / book of poems / reading / . . .'

'Thank you, that's very kind of you.' His responses to these interrupting
encounters had been invariably gentle and courteous. He never swanks,
never snubs anyone, and they are congratulating him upon numerous real
achievements. Of course he is not a fraud . . .

When I joined him, he had been working with the unit for at least two
weeks and seemed to be enjoying it: he'd got everybody to feel – in varying
degrees – amused, respectful and protective. To do this, he doesn't have to
put on an act – he simply goes on being himself, but, as it were, with a bit
of a vengeance. 'I am enjoying myself' is a reprise. Sometimes it is true.
He'd bought himself a cheap blue plastic mac at Swaffham Woolworth's
('my Swaffham') and a green felt hat at Holt ('my Holt'). These garments,

contriving almost at once to look as though their owner had never been without them, went everywhere, together with his airline bag.

He worked hard that day, patiently doing the same thing again and again, until all the technicians felt that they had got what they wanted. He must have been tired, but it was hard to tell how tired, since he will self-protectively give the appearance of being far older, more frail and uncertain than he really is.[84]

At the end of the afternoon's filming, she and John were to drive to King's Lynn. She thought that all he would want to do would be to get there in time to have a rest before dinner. Not at all. 'It was one of those windy, sunlit evenings of early summer. He did not wish to travel on main roads – there was a church at South Creake that he would like to show me.'[85] So they went off to South Creake – 'one of those lovely churches with a flock of carved wooden angels . . . poised in the roof'.[86] He told her, 'My old car slows down automatically when we come to a church.'[87]

They drove on slowly to King's Lynn. 'I do hate rushing about,' he said. 'The frightful way that people brush past you in the street. "*So* sorry"; they're not in the least.'[88] She noted that 'He does walk very slowly, sometimes shuffling – "doddering" would be the unkind word for it . . .'[89] In the bar 'he drank terrifyingly horrible wine out of tiny one-glass bottles and tried to pay for everybody's drinks. His generosity is continuous and complete – "Money is simply to buy off anxiety." '[90] The next day and a half he was not filming. They spent the time driving, walking, looking at churches and antique shops.

He enjoys bouts of wilful rapture. There was (I thought) a rather unprepossessing boy/girl who provoked an outburst. '*What* a lovely girl! I thought with those trousers and those freckles she was a boy, but she was a girl! Didn't you think she was perfectly lovely? I thought she was beautiful,' and so on. I think this is all part of the scheme to keep affectionate laughter going. He is extremely sensitive to other people, and it is his way of having a rest from them.[91]

On their way back to Norwich they decided that all modern architects should be rounded up and shot.

'Picture windows! Open planning! And those terrible thick, white rails round gardens! What *are* they for?'

Only any good for enclosing a hippopotamus, I suggested.

A screech of laughter. 'Quite right! Oh *dear*! That's *very* good!' He always gives you full marks for trying.[92]

John told Howard that he loved making films for television; but at the end of the article she observed, 'He has a proper aversion to being hectored, bullied and made to do things, and somewhere, very deeply hidden, one suspects a streak of that ruthlessness essential for the self-protection of any working artist'.[93] That John possessed such a faculty, Eddie Mirzoeff was to be made painfully aware in the editing of the film.

After the filming, he drove John back to London. 'John had been in the best of form, extremely alive and cheerful,' he recalled. 'But the closer to London, the more tense he got. By the time we reached the suburbs, he had got into a state of abject terror. It was all to do with having been away from Elizabeth, the likelihood of being late, and what was going to happen when we turned up in Radnor Walk – maybe having to confess that Penelope had been with him. It was extraordinary to see this transformation.'[94]

The editing went much less smoothly than the filming. 'For me,' Mirzoeff says, 'it was just another film; and Ted is a standard C of E chap. But for John, this was a subject terribly close to the core of his being. It mattered to him; it mattered enormously; and he therefore found it quite difficult. He was very, very uncertain about how it was going to be received, and whether we could show certain sequences, get away with them – sequences which seemed to us totally harmless.'[95]

John was specially worried about the Walsingham scenes. He felt distaste for the shrine, as both Romish and suburban; but he knew that some revered it and others would be repelled. 'I could feel that sequence looming up,' Mirzoeff says. 'He knew that very soon he would have to find words for that part of the film. He was getting more and more uncomfortable. He thought: images of the Virgin Mary, in a film about the Church of England – how would people take this? He knew it had been filmed with great beauty by John McGlashan, who cares tremendously for very High ritual and had composed the candles in exactly the right place and so on. It wasn't the sort of sequence of which you could say, "Oh, this is no good, we'll just lose it." It was wonderful; but how were we going to treat it?'[96] Everything depended on the words John would write to go with the pictures. In the end, he found a way round what seemed an insoluble problem, by a series of rhetorical questions –

The Shrine of Our Lady of Walsingham. 1930s red-brick Romanesque. But inside is the goal of all the pilgrims. And very peculiar it is.

I wonder if you'd call it superstitious. Here in this warm mysterious holy house, the figure of Our Lady and Her Child. Or do you think that forces are around – strong, frightening, loving and just out of reach, but waiting, waiting, somewhere to be asked?[97]

Then he emphasized the foreignness of Walsingham (never a compliment from John) and praised the Church of England for its tolerance in embracing it.

> I've seen processions like this in Sicily;
> You can see them in the streets of Malta, too.
> But it's an exotic flowering of the C of E,
> Here in a Norfolk garden.
> The Anglican church has got a bit of everything.
> It's very tolerant – and that is part of its strength.[98]

John made a similar point in talking with Ted Roberts. 'It's the quality of *doubt* that makes the Church of England – which the Roman Catholics don't have. They have certainties.'[99] At times John fell back into his old easy relationship with Roberts, in the Soho cutting-room, each improving on the other's verses. As a verse voice-over for the garden fête at South Raynham, Roberts originally wrote:

> God bless the Church of England,
> The rectory lawn that gave
> A trodden space for that bazaar
> That underpinned the nave.
> We must dip into our pockets
> For our hearts are full of dread,
> There's all the more to pay for now
> The roof's been stripped of lead.[100]

John said, 'Oh, that's awfully good,' but altered the last two lines to –

> At the thought of all the damage
> Since the roof was stripped of lead.[101]

At other times, John seemed to be suffering from acute writer's block. He reached a stage when he could not write anything. 'There were a lot of very short days,' Ted Roberts remembers. 'He'd say, "Well, I think we're doing quite well. I'm going home now, and I'll be back at eleven tomorrow." And you'd had half an hour, you know. Eddie was tearing his hair out.'[102] Mirzoeff tried to be sympathetic about John's anxieties. 'So many things were too close to the bone. He kept saying to me, "This is very very important to me. I can't treat this easily." '[103] But time was getting short, and one essential part of the commentary remained unwritten. Mirzoeff needed from John some words to link the brass of Sir Simon and Lady Margaret Felbrigg to the wedding of Nigel and Celia McCulloch. Surely this should not be a difficult transition – from medieval marriage to modern marriage.

> It was the last thing [Mirzoeff recalls]. We'd done the front of the film and we'd done the end of the film. We'd added this and we'd added that. Gradually, as with a jigsaw, we were filling in the last bits, and we'd got stuck with this hole. We were due to record the commentary the next day. There was no way we could put it off any longer. But John just couldn't do it. In the past, Ted and I had between us done a lot of drafts for him, saying 'roughly this?' and so on. And I was saying this to him now: 'Come on, John, it's not difficult; why can't you say this?' – when, suddenly, he snapped, like *that*. And I have never seen it before or, thank God, since; but it was terrifying, because he literally yelled, he lost his temper in a way that you can't imagine the lovable teddy-bear figure of the jolly Poet Laureate doing. He felt he was being pushed too far and he felt I was asking more than he could give.
>
> He said: 'I'm an old man and I can't do this sort of thing to order. I'm nearly seventy and I'm not being treated as I should be.' He went on and on. It was absolutely frightening to see this temper, and embarrassing. One just sat there and there was this anger which was obviously an accumulation of frustration, but it was serious anger. One couldn't go on. So when all this had come out, I finally said, 'Well, I'm going to go. I can't deal with this.'[104]

Mirzoeff went into another cutting-room, and for two or three days Ted Roberts acted as an intermediary. He would come in to Mirzoeff with a piece of paper, saying, 'What about this? This is what we've managed to get so far.' Mirzoeff would say, 'No no no!' Roberts remembers: 'When I went back to John, I'd try to defuse the situation. I'd say, "Let's relax for a moment. Now, I think what Eddie is hoping we might be able to do here is . . ." '[105] After a while Mirzoeff and John got back on speaking terms, though Mirzoeff called him 'Sir John' for some time afterwards.[103] Mirzoeff made another film with John, but feels that they never quite recovered their old relaxed relationship. 'Always at the back of our minds there was an awareness of that moment, that terrible row, which was caused by . . . just pressure, pressure of timetables. I couldn't see what he was finding so difficult.'[106] In the end, John overcame his block and made a fine, poetical link between the Felbrigg brass and the Lyng wedding.

Interior of church
and zoom out to
discover brass rubbing

> . . . Sir Simon and Lady Margaret Felbrigg. He, a
> Garter Knight, and she a cousin of the Queen.
>
> It must have been the day of days, The day they
> took their vows . . .

Cut to wedding
sequence – Lyng Church[107]

John was almost as worried by what was being left out of the film
as what was going in it. In particular, he was upset that the Mass – to
him the most holy of the Sacraments – was to be omitted. What would
his critics say of a portrait of the Church of England which left out
Holy Communion? Sending Billa Harrod a copy of his recorded
script, he wrote:

> It will not mean much to you without the visuals, and it reads like pretty
> good tripe . . .
>   Of course as always happens we took yards more film than we actually
> used. My great regret is that the Mass at South Creake is omitted.[108] Eddie
> said it was too confused and when I saw it I could see what he meant . . .
> The highlight is Puffin's Fête – you never know what film is going to do.
> I should have liked the highlight to be the Mass, but it looked very com-
> plicated on the screen.[109]

On 6 August 1974 John wrote to Mirzoeff asking to see the film
before a final version was assembled.

> I ask this because quite a lot of things were left out which we filmed, e.g.
> Confession, the Mother's Union procession, the South Creake Sung Mass
> and I want to get an impression of the overall effect of the film.
>   Why I ask this is because it is my religion which is being filmed and I
> will be held responsible for views expressed and because emphasis and
> omissions and deletions are so much easier appreciated when the thing is
> assembled.[110]

Meanwhile, Mirzoeff was faced with a new difficulty, potentially
more hazardous than the row with John.

> We'd made this film about the Church of England from our then depart-
> ment, I think it was called Documentary Features. What it absolutely was
> not was the Religious Department. It had come to the attention of the
> Head of Religious Broadcasting that a film had been made about the C
> of E which had not come under his aegis, so he hadn't got any say in it.

And for territorial reasons, largely, he said, 'This is wrong. It has to be vetted by me.'

My then head of department, who was the piratical Desmond Wilcox,[111] said, 'No way does this go through him!' So this was going to be a good battle. In the end, we compromised. We would show him the film as completed but he did not have rights over it. Nevertheless, if we showed it to him, he could actually create a lot of fuss if there were things in it that he didn't like.

John got into quite a state about it and so did I. He got into a state because, O dear God, the C of E is going to carry on, in the shape of the Head of Religious Broadcasting – he was the head of the whole of religion in the BBC.[112]

After all Mirzoeff had gone through in making the film, he was not going to let it be sabotaged at this late stage. How could the Head of Religious Broadcasting be neutralized? Mirzoeff hit on a masterly stratagem.

This was the same sort of period that John was seeing a lot of the Prime Minister's wife, Mary Wilson – they were going to Diss, and so on,* it was part of the East Anglia thing that was going on. So I said to John, 'Why don't we have a screening for the Head of Religious Broadcasting and let Mary Wilson see it too?' She wanted to see it; and we thought this would trump the Head of Religious Broadcasting's king or queen with an ace which he would never have expected. So John got on the phone to Mary Wilson and said, would she like to come to a screening, and that these were the circumstances; and she, good trouper that she was, said yes. And it was, I think, one of the best diplomatic cards we've ever played.

It was a delicious sight to see this gentleman walk into the viewing theatre in Lime Grove after we'd all had lunch in the Lime Grove Club with Mary Wilson. She and John were sitting together. And he walked in, thinking, 'I'm going to . . .' I said: 'This is Sir John Betjeman and this is Mrs Mary Wilson' – the Prime Minister's wife. And you could see his face fall. I mean, what's he going to do, poor man? He's not going to sit there making a fuss. He sat there with an unconvincing smile on his face, said, 'Really wonderful' – and we never heard a word from him again.[113]

The film was transmitted on BBC2 on 7 December 1974 at 10.05 p.m., clashing with *Match of the Day* on BBC1 at 10.10. The day before, Osbert Lancaster previewed it in the *Times Literary Supplement*. He applauded the choice of Norfolk, which had not only the noblest

---

* See Chapter 15, 'Mary Wilson and a Journey to Diss'.

churches in the land but also 'more notably idiosyncratic incumbents than any county in England'.[114]

> Vicars who preached in black gowns from rat-infested three-deckers, rectors whose chasubles outshone those of All Saints, Margaret Street, gourmandizing parsons, hunting squarsons, saints such as Fr Maude-Roxby of Norwich,[115] refugees from Trollope such as Bishop Herbert,[116] libidinous scallywags such as the ill-fated Rector of Stiffkey,[117] all have flourished there in my lifetime. How right is the poet to emphasize the variety and tolerance of the Establishment! Here the whole spectrum of Anglican worship and practice is sympathetically revealed, from the Ultramontane goings-on at Walsingham to the liturgical Disneyland of Series III.[118]

Under the Old Pals' Act, Lancaster wrote that 'In this medium, *A Passion for Churches* is, I think, Sir John's masterpiece to date.'[119] But most of the other critics, while praising the film, saw in it a falling-off from the near-perfection of *Metro-land*. Nevertheless, in *The Times*, Michael Ratcliffe noted that Mirzoeff was a producer who got the best out of John, 'knowing precisely when to let him go on and when to administer a judicious change of mood'.[120] Chris Dunkley observed in the *Financial Times*: 'It takes the mind of a poet, and an unusual poet at that, to see the middle classes as worthy of considerable notice and, having done so, to make this clear to the audience. Betjeman does this in the same way that poets have always revitalized the seemingly mundane: by enveloping it, and then extruding it in a form which is still recognizably familiar to the audience, but with a number of new surfaces facing the light in such a way that one's attention is drawn back sharply.'[121]

Dennis Potter, then the television critic of the *New Statesman*, tried his hand at a Betjeman parody by reviewing the film in verse. A formidable writer in prose, he was oddly pedestrian in poetry and took liberties with metre and rhyme which would have made John wince.

> Summoned by trailers I gladly switched on
> *A Passion for Churches* by dear Sir John
> In which the Poet Laureate told us
> Of his love for spires and towers enormous . . .
>
> The poet ambled along a cloistered track
> In a straw boater and a plastic mac
> Talking of vaporous clouds turned to stone
> And old ladies praying above creaking bone

Rectors with soft pink cheeks and model trains
Bishops granted purple smiles and addled brains . . .

Here in a quiet house beyond the green
The rector types out the parish magazine
We saw his finger typing birthday greeting
   Saw his smirk about the sponsored streaking
   Watched a wedding between Nigel and the bride
   A girl called Celia dry-mouthed at his side . . .

But Nigel and Celia and the rest
Are probably trying to do their best.
The collecting box may not be a heist
Carried out by an absent Jesus Christ
And though I doubt if it's true, all that,
I'll worship a guide in a soft felt hat . . .[122]

In the chorus of praise there was just one dissenting voice. The review in the local paper, the *Eastern Daily Press*, was headed 'A Surfeit of Churches'. It suggested that John and Mirzoeff had tried to stuff far too much into one film. 'The muse had hardly time to settle upon [John Betjeman] before he was bringing to our attention yet another piece of ecclesiastical architecture.'[123] In the critic's view, it had been 'a whistle-stop tour' and John had completely missed the point of Norwich and Norfolk. There was a comic sequel.

We had a repeat very soon [Mirzoeff remembers]. It was one of those programmes that was so successful, there was a demand for it. We put out just the same programme, of course. And the *Eastern Daily Press* review on *that* occasion said: 'They have taken to heart our strictures. Now, at last, it is exactly what it should have been.'
Not one syllable, not one shot, had been changed![124]

RADNOR WALK

John Betjeman has been associated with the City of London (Cloth Fair) and with deepest Cornwall for so long that it came as a surprise to find him living in Chelsea, a mere pebble's throw from that sewer of trendiness, the King's Road.

> Wilfred De'Ath, 'The lonely Laureate',
> *Illustrated London News*, March 1974

In 1970–71, while Penelope was away in India with John Nankivell and the three Elizabeths, John visited Rupert and Candida more often at their home in Chepstow Villas, Notting Hill. There were grandchildren now: Lucy, Imogen and Endellion (named after the saint of one of John's favourite Cornish churches) were born in the Sixties, David and John in the Seventies.[1] 'He enjoyed his grandchildren's company,' Candida writes, 'but only when they were quiet. (He hated noise, and yelling children were one of his worst nightmares.) He would open his mouth hugely and his eyes would twinkle when he saw them. He always brought stacks of presents.'[2] He also took the children on outings.[3]

In his sombre fiftieth-birthday letter of 1956, John had told Penelope that he left it to her whether and when to sell The Mead. By 1972 the logic of selling it had become irresistible. In February John wrote to a friend to say that Penelope had decided to sell the house. 'It is impossible to let so large a place or to keep the vandals out, or pay for the upkeep out of income.'[4] By April she had had two offers for The Mead, one of £42,000 from a developer, and another of the same amount from her nephew Christopher Chetwode, who worked for the estate agents Knight, Frank and Rutley and also wanted to develop it.[5] Altruistically, she sold it for less to a Tibetan family who, she thought, would not allow it to be despoiled. They took possession on 4 July 1972[6] but, as Candida sourly notes, soon sold it for a large profit.[7] The Betjemans' furniture was stored by the Barings; Penelope's books and papers by

John Sparrow at All Souls.[8] John wrote a poem, 'On leaving Wantage. July 1972', which was published in the parish magazine. It ended:

> From this wide vale, where all our married lives
> We two have lived, we now are whirled away
> Momently clinging to the things we knew –
> Friends, foot-paths, hedges, houses, animals –
> Till, borne along like twigs and bits of straw,
> We disappear below the sliding stream.[9]

In February 1973 John wrote to Penelope: 'I am quite all right, do not worry about me. E[lizabeth] has bought a house in her street and I have given notice for 43 [Cloth Fair]. I have severely cut down my work and have got a part-time secretary called Mrs Mountain.'[10] The house Elizabeth had bought for him was No. 29 Radnor Walk, Chelsea, just a few doors away from her own house at No. 19. His next-door neighbour at No. 31 (when in London) was Christopher Ewart-Biggs, British Ambassador to the Republic of Ireland. (In 1976 he was killed by the IRA, and John helped to comfort his widow, Jane.)[11]

John put it about that he had been driven from Cloth Fair by the noise of lorries delivering carcases to Smithfield Market at dawn; but it was clear to his friends that his main reason for moving was to be near Elizabeth. The move ratified the love affair which had now lasted for over twenty years. There was also a more practical reason for moving to Chelsea. In the two years since 1971, John's health had noticeably declined. The debilitating effects of Parkinson's Disease had begun to appear, in the shuffling gait which Lord Longford wrongly took to be part of an 'old man' act.[12] John now needed, if not twenty-four-hour care, a watchful eye kept on him. Whatever she may have been to him in the earlier years of their relationship, in the Seventies Elizabeth also became something of a nurse to him, almost a nanny.

Chelsea was once described in *Country Life* as 'London's Latin Quarter'.[13] In the eighteenth century, Ranelagh Gardens had given it a reputation for fashionable raffishness. This was maintained in the later Cremorne Gardens, painted by Whistler. In the late nineteenth century, Wilde and Frank Miles, Shannon and Ricketts[14] had brought to it their greenery-yallery decadence, and Lillie Langtry, a mistress of the Prince of Wales, lived next to the Cadogan Hotel. The ardent womanizer Augustus John became principal of the Chelsea Art School in 1903 and survived into the 1960s.[15] In the 1950s the district was the arena of the 'Chelsea Set', rich, stylish and hell-raising – the men in 'Chelsea boots', the women with bell-tent skirts. In the Swinging Sixties the King's Road was a rival to Carnaby Street as a promenade of the Beautiful People, a sort of human art gallery. At one end of the King's Road was the silver-clad Chelsea Drugstore; towards the other (in snob terms, the 'wrong' end) the Granny Takes a Trip shop, selling retro clothing and erotic prints after Beardsley; between the two, the trendy Arethusa Club and Mary Quant's shop with its 'pelmet' mini-skirts. Hippieism prevailed when John moved in, though by the end of the Seventies the King's Road had become the centre of the new, Establishment-hating Punk movement.

Like Old Church Street, where he had spent some of the less happy years of his childhood, Radnor Walk led off the King's Road. If a competition had been held to design a setting into which he would not fit, Chelsea in the Seventies could well have been the winner. His peculiar dislike of dogs has been noted.[16] In Radnor Walk he had to pick his way through deposits of dogs' mess, a sort of pedestrian slalom. The Thames stank: he mentioned it as 'awful' in a letter of 1974 to Patrick Cullinan.[17] The noise of the lorries at Cloth Fair was replaced by that of sports-car engines being gunned and motor-bikes revving up in the small hours as young bloods left the Arethusa Club with their 'birds'; and there was usually a hubbub at the Chelsea Potter pub on the corner of Radnor Walk. (The Chelsea Pottery, whose fine glazed earthenwares are today collected as 'antiques', was *in* the Walk, a few doors from Elizabeth's house.) If John wanted to do some shopping, he had to brave the Hieronymus Bosch pageant of the King's Road – a bald old-timer shuffling with his string bag past druggy young people with harlequin clothes and mad haircuts (dyed Mohicans in the Punk era). He was almost as out of context as Margaret and Denis Thatcher, who lived in Flood Street, parallel with Radnor Walk and next to the verdigris-domed emporium of Antiquarius antiques market.

There were old friends within reach: the Blakistons in Markham Square; Lord David Cecil and his historian son Hugh in Wellington Square; Osbert Lancaster and Anne Scott-James in Belgravia; Michael Astor in Swan Walk;[18] Cecil Beaton in Pelham Place; Margie Geddes in South Kensington – but he felt isolated, a faded chrysanthemum in an orchid house. Even the old friends were not all a comfort. He was very fond of Margie Geddes, whom he had known since the 1920s when he taught her brothers at Heddon Court. He saw a lot of her in the Radnor Walk years, and her letters to him were so affectionate as almost to qualify as love letters.[19] But John no longer got on with the Blakistons as well as he had done when they visited Uffington in the 1930s. Noel Blakiston was irritated that John always made the same jokes when he met them. At the beginning of the Second World War, when working at the Public Record Office in Chancery Lane, Blakiston had received the top secret order: 'Collect Magna Carta and proceed to Chipping

Sodbury' (where the document was to be stored, to protect it from air-raids). And his wife Giana (*née* Russell) had an entomologist relation who, when Giana was bitten by a flea, captured it in a matchbox and wrote a catalogue entry recording: 'Habitat: Miss Georgiana Russell'. 'Every time John comes to see us,' Noel Blakiston complained in 1976, 'we get, "Proceed to Chipping Sodbury HAW HAW HAW" and "Habitat: Miss Georgiana Russell HAW HAW HAW".'

The King's Road did not have the sort of old-fashioned, ceremonious restaurants that John liked, such as Rules, Wilton's, the Café Royal Grill Room and the Charing Cross Hotel. The nearest restaurants to his taste – Charco's and Au Père de Nico – were too near for a taxi ride, too far for a stroll. One evening he decided to try the Chelsea Kitchen, in a cramped King's Road cellar. Sitting on a wooden bench with an assortment of students from Italy, France and Greece, he politely asked them where they all came from. They told him. Then one of them asked, 'And where do *you* come from?' He later recalled: 'I left with an *au revoir* on my lips, and an *adieu* in my heart.'[20] Eventually he found an Italian restaurant to his liking near the non-King's Road end of Radnor Walk, within easy walking distance, the San Quintino. He was there for lunch most days, often with friends from outside Chelsea. As Eddie Mirzoeff had found, having lunch with him could be something of an ordeal. For a start, he knew he was the cynosure of all eyes: as the tattooed-all-over man at Speakers' Corner proclaimed, 'I'm not paranoiac! Everyone *is* looking at me!'[21] And after a while John would begin making comments on the other people in the restaurant, in a stentorian whisper. 'I say, do you think those men are *executives*? I expect they're discussing "profit margins" and "feasibility surveys". And that chap over there – is that gel his secretary, do you think? I wonder if they're going back to his flat after lunch.' You could see the man's ears reddening.[22]

The move to Radnor Walk was a turning-point in John's relations both with Elizabeth Cavendish and with Penelope. In the daytime he worked at No. 29 – the house ostensibly his – mainly dictating letters about poetry and threatened buildings, to a succession of secretaries. But he spent the nights at Elizabeth's house down the road, No. 19.[23] Up to this time the London gossip columnists had not been able to pin a 'relationship' on John and Elizabeth. Now they closed in like hounds on a fox breaking cover. The two separate houses in Radnor Walk could not quite be reckoned a 'love nest'; but on 21 August 1974 the *Daily Express* printed an insinuating story headed 'Old friend Lady Elizabeth comforts Betjeman', with a photograph of the couple together several years earlier. John knew that the paragraph would distress Penelope. As late as 1972 – just after The Mead was sold – she had still been able to talk, in a television interview, as if she and John were together.

The great thing about John [she said] is that he gets over rows very quickly, and my technique has usually been to pay no attention to him when he gets in a passion and that annoys him all the more. So on the whole it's probably better if I do have a bit of a row. I think we have less rows than we used to when we married. One of the worst rows was when I threw his teddy-bear Archie out of the window. He very nearly divorced me on that one, and Archie would have been the co-respondent . . .

You might call it a stormy marriage, but fundamentally John and I are terribly fond of each other and I shall be terribly sad if he dies first and he'll be very sad if I die first.[24]

After the gossip paragraph appeared, John wrote to her:

I did not like all that probing and prying in the *Express*, I felt very sorry for you, what business is it of theirs, fuck them. It is absolutely lovely here in London in August because the dog messes on the pavement dry up much quicker. I laugh a lot when I think about your labour camp[25] but what the *Sunday Express* ought to have said was that you are a very distinguished Indologist in your own right which is what you have always wanted to be and it has only recently been broken to me by John Allison, my doctor, and by Elizabeth that I had to be moved here last year because I was not fit to be left alone in the City with no-one else in the house. I am really much better now but will never be able to walk fast and far or keep up with the grandkiddiz. But you will be doing that as you are a much better person in all respects than yours truly.[26]

Penelope replied from *her* new house – on stationery which she had had printed, in red, 'No telephone thank God'. After The Mead was sold, she had had some thoughts of living in a convent. 'We all wondered whether the nuns would drive her mad first, or she them,' Mollie Baring said.[27] But instead Penelope had moved to a glorified cottage on the Welsh border, at Cusop, near Hay-on-Wye, Herefordshire. She called it 'New House', but John always referred to it as 'Little Redoubt' (or 'LR'), and to Hay-on-Wye as 'Kulu-on-Wye', after the part of India on which Penelope had written her book of 1972. 'You need not worry AT ALL,' Penelope wrote. 'I am blissfully happy up here in the L.R.'[28] This was half true. The house, with stabling for her pony Golliwog ('We call him "Chocolate" when we enter him for horse shows, so as not to break the race relations laws')[29] was in good riding country, on the edge of a beetling forest. She could ride to Hay-on-Wye, which had been turned into 'the largest second-hand bookshop in Europe' by Richard Booth, the self-styled 'King of Hay'.[30] (Among other buildings, an old cinema was filled with books.)

Penelope made a particular friend of one of Booth's assistants, Michael Cottrill ('Cotters'), a pleasant, learned and intelligent man who was twenty-five in 1973. Lady Mary Clive, Lord Longford's sister, was another congenial neighbour within easy reach, at Whitfield Court, a Georgian mansion at Allensmore, Herefordshire.[31] Richard Booth introduced Penelope to the celebrated transsexual April Ashley, who was sometimes invited to New House dinner parties. Penelope also got to know Jonathan and George Howells, two bachelor brothers in their sixties who lived on the eastern side of the Black Mountains in a white farmhouse.[32] She brought along, to meet them, her friend Bruce Chatwin, whom she was 'cushioning' after his separation from his wife Elizabeth. 'The story she told of them (and which captured my imagination)', Chatwin recalled in 1982, 'was that sometime before the War their mother, seeing them to show no signs of interest in the opposite sex, had sent them to the fair at Hay-on-Wye to meet some young ladies. They came back with crestfallen faces, never having seen girls in short skirts before. This put them off forever.'[33] They became the central characters of his novel *On the Black Hill*, published in 1982 and later filmed. Penelope, who had already been transmuted into fiction by Lord Berners and Evelyn Waugh, was the 'Philippa Townsend' of Chatwin's book.[34] Nicholas Shakespeare, Chatwin's biographer, suggests:

> He may have got the idea of twins from the Greenway family who lived a mile from Penelope Betjeman at Wernagavenny and whose telephone ensured that Bruce returned repeatedly. 'I always go over to Olive to use the telephone,' said John Betjeman.[35]

Penelope did eventually invest in a telephone; but it was one of the few mod cons at New House. She had the fanciful idea that it might still be possible for her to lure John away from Elizabeth and persuade

John's sketch of Penelope's dog, Ben

him to live with her at Cusop. She put a bed in a downstairs room so that he would not have to toil up the stairs. He came to stay, but was appalled by the Spartan accommodation, inadequately heated by the temperamental boiler which Penelope called 'The Crem'. He did his best to like her dog Ben, and made an impressionistic sketch of him in one of his thank-you letters.[36]

When April Ashley came to dinner, John asked her why she had decided to change sex. She replied, 'I thought, darling, "If you can't beat them, join them!"'[37] On future visits, John made sure that he spent most of his time with Penelope at Mary Clive's house. There was no danger of his decamping from Chelsea.

Penelope was delighted to find that John Nankivell was sharing a cottage, in a valley near Cusop, with his girlfriend Bess Cuthbert. She knew and liked Bess too. She had first met her through the Baring family, when Bess was going out with Nigel Baring (known as 'Ball' Baring from his exploits with young women).[38] Nankivell had got to know Bess in India when she broke with her 'rather grand' Scottish family to teach in a public school in Hyderabad, with maharajahs' sons among her pupils. 'I think we kissed for the first time at the Taj Mahal,' Nankivell recalled; 'and then we had a very happy relationship for about ten years.'[39] It was Nankivell who would drive John to Mary Clive's house and pick him up again 'from amid his cigarette butts'.[40] Nankivell usually had lunch with Lady Mary, her son George and John. 'Once, Sheridan and Lindy Dufferin were also there. At that time I did not know about the deep affection John had had for Sheridan's father.'[41] Nankivell also drove John and Penelope to tea with Major Gerald and Mrs de Winton at Maesllwch Castle, 'one of the three or four great castles of the Wye. Dry rot had virtually demolished it, except that an amazing tower was still there.'

> The de Wintons [Nankivell remembers] asked John to recite some poetry. He recited Tennyson. They were sitting with their backs to the window, with John between them and Penelope and myself watching. He recited the Tennyson and it was so moving; Mrs de Winton was in tears over it.[42]

A few months before the exposé about Elizabeth and himself appeared in the *Daily Express*, John had written Billa Harrod a letter to thank her for her hospitality to him and Eddie Mirzoeff when they were 'doing a recce' for the television film about Norfolk churches.* In it he tried to set down what he felt about his 'Two loves I have . . .' dilemma, while evidently bearing in mind that Billa was decidedly in Penelope's camp rather than Elizabeth's.

---

* See Chapter 21, 'A Passion for Churches'.

Your kindest action to me in our long and loving friendship was to speak to me so kindly and clearly of Penelope. I love her. *But I cannot live with her for long without quarrelling.* I sensed her anguish when we went to the cinema last night with Emily [Villiers-Stuart]. I cannot bear to hurt her. She kissed me on the cheek when she got out of the taxi last night and I went back to Radnor Walk.

You said being loved is a great burden. I have lived so long apart from Penelope, that Elizabeth now loves me more than anyone else in the world. I cannot hurt *her* either, any more than I can Penelope. I depend on Elizabeth for food and for my body and mind. She is v much part of me too.

Both P and E feel threatened. Fear steps in and with it hatred and anger. It is difficult. I *think* Penelope would be wounded if we separated, though she says that is what she wants to do. I don't want to, but may have to because she will precipitate it in rage at E and all Cavendishes. I can understand her rage and misery. She won't believe how much I love her. I think she needs to be given her rights and dignity. She is okay at Kulu-on-Wye and insecure in London with me in the enemy's camp. I must buy, if it ruins me, a camp for her in London where she can entertain her friends with me.

In all this awful storm of misery, the one thing I cling to is my love for Penelope *and* for Elizabeth who has given up marriage and a family life with her own children, out of love for me.

I think, but am not sure, that P is more defenceless than E and must therefore be propped up by a London base as well as Kulu-on-Wye. Radnor Walk would never do. It is too near the enemy, though P has tried to be friendly with E.

Ora pro nobis [pray for us] . . .[43]

Penelope gave her view of the situation in a letter of 1975 to Lord Kinross.

Alas I seldom come to London now tho' with an old person's ticket one can go half price in mid wk . . . but as E. doesn't want me to go to John's house in Chelsea, there is not much point in going up! It's so artifical just lunching with him at the RAC [Royal Automobile Club]. I *hate* that club whereas I liked the Athenaeum & the Garrick but he has resigned from those . . .

But for E, I could never have gone back to India so often. I am so grateful to her in so many ways & would love to be friends & share John – as Jock Murray says that some men need two wives! – but she refuses to see me & John gets terrible guilt whenever he goes to stay either in Kulu-on-Wye or at . . . Candida's & starts fussing about his train back to London almost before his arrival at Hereford or Chippenham. As he is in a very bad state of health it would be cruel to insist on his staying longer & put him in a worse state of dichotomy than ever, but last time he came (two wk-ends ago) he said he wanted so much to stay on but that E. did not like being left alone in London & obviously she hates his coming to us (C. or me). It's the old story of a middle-aged woman without children being unfulfilled (a psychological FACT) & clinging to her man in a completely possessive way. I am so lucky in having Paul & Candida & now FOUR enchanting grandchildren. P. is doing very well with his electronic music (teaching & composition) though he is obviously not destined to achieve FAME like his Papa . . . [44]

Penelope had offered John a divorce, even though she was a Roman Catholic.[45] Whether from religious scruples or from fear of adverse publicity, he declined the offer. And he never did buy her a London house or flat. Possibly he could not afford to; more probably, he preferred to keep his two loves a healthy distance apart. It was true that Penelope had tried to make friends with Elizabeth, and been politely repulsed. Magda Rogers, who was John's secretary from 1974 to 1977, remembers that Penelope had to make an appointment to see John.[46] 'Elizabeth was very definite about not seeing Penelope,' Jonathan Stedall recalls, 'and I can quite see why she did that. It was not out of animosity. She knew that Penelope was a very powerful personality and would kind of take over.'[47]

Stedall saw a lot of John, Elizabeth *and* Penelope in the 1970s. He sometimes stayed at No. 29 Radnor Walk. And in the early part of 1973 he was filming Penelope in India. When, in 1972, John had been told of the plan to make the film, he had laughed and said to Stedall, 'That will be a battle of wills!'[48]

He was right [Stedall said]. It is quite difficult being a producer. It *is* a battle of wills. You have to be sensitive to the people you're filming; but you also have to be the boss. The film about Penelope in India was for a series called *One Pair of Eyes*. The whole idea was to show someone's passionate enthusiasm for something. She really agreed to it because she was keen on the Indian temples. I kept telling her, 'It has got to be about *your* enthusiasm for the temples'; but when we were actually filming, she got frightfully annoyed – 'Don't film *me*! Film the temples!' It also made her cross that we wanted to stop and film all the time, while she wanted to get on with the travelling.[49]

When the film was screened in January 1974, John saw it at Elizabeth's house with Cecil Beaton, Elizabeth and her sister, Lady Anne Tree, the film director Barney Platts-Mills[50] and his wife Marion.[51] They were in constant fits of laughter, especially at the scene in which Penelope floated across the Ganges on an inflated buffalo skin; between her and the skin was an emaciated Indian lying flat on his stomach and feebly flapping his hands in the water to give the eccentric craft some momentum. (Penelope was not a lightweight.) 'We were all held spellbound by it,' John wrote to Penelope on 31 January. '. . . I think it is the best thing Jonathan has done . . .'[52]

Elizabeth liked Stedall: Magda parodied her attitude towards him as '*Dear* little Jonathan!'[53] When he stayed at No. 29, he was absorbed into the ménage at No. 19, too. He remembers Princess Margaret's visits.

She wasn't a very relaxing person to be with. She made it difficult, because part of the time she was very matey – one of us – and then she'd become the little Princess. Quite a few times I was at dinner at No. 19 and she'd turn up at about 11.00 when we were all about to go to bed, and she'd want scrambled egg. And there was this kind of etiquette that you don't go to bed until she leaves – and she had bugger all to do.

The Princess told me a lovely story. When John first moved to Radnor Walk, it was gradually becoming gentrified; but a very working-class family lived opposite No. 19. They had a lot of children, and John and Elizabeth got to know them. One evening Princess Margaret turned up at No. 19 and was ringing on the doorbell and this little girl with a grubby face came across the street and said, 'Aw, Feeble's gorn to a dance!'[54]

At dinner parties, Stedall met Elizabeth's circle of friends. 'They tended to be gay men,' he said.[55] Harry Williams often stayed at No. 29. Elizabeth's next-door neighbour at No. 21 was Frank Tait, an Australian child psychiatrist whose close friend was Billy Henderson, a painter and former ADC to Lord Linlithgow when Viceroy of India, who had stayed on as Comptroller to Lord Wavell. (Tait and Henderson also had a cottage in Tisbury, Wiltshire.) Two BBC men were often at No. 19: the German-born Peter Adam, who was in Berlin throughout the Second World War but rose to be director of the BBC television series *Arena* – employing, among others, Julian Jebb;[56] and (Sir) John Drummond, who had persuaded the Australian Broadcasting Corporation to put up money for John's 1972 films in Australia.

From [then] on [Drummond wrote in his memoirs] I saw him regularly, and grew also to know and to love his companion, Lady Elizabeth Cavendish, a woman of remarkable strength of character and beliefs . . . Every meeting was both entertaining and instructive. We went to see an exhibition called 'The Destruction of the Country House', which Roy Strong had organized at the V&A. There was a big gallery full of pho- tographs of demolished houses. John went round and, in highly audible tones, to the consternation of the other visitors, commented on the hideousness and architectural shortcomings of almost all those that had gone. The only good ones, he said, had caught fire or collapsed of their own accord. 'Why the mourning?' John asked. 'The best have all been saved.' But there would have been less mileage in 'The Saving of the Country House'.

John had a line of quiet asides that was memorable too. About a fierce woman producer with whom he had made a short film on the Isle of Man, he said, 'I would like her to chastise me – and I don't mean pretend.' Of a good-looking young male director, 'Brings out the Scoutmaster in us all.'[57]

John and Elizabeth had also been friends of James Mossman, the gay BBC journalist who committed suicide in 1971. Jonathan Stedall remembers that the playwright Peter Shaffer – a friend of Peter Adam (and formerly of Mossman) – was also a frequent guest at No. 19.[58] It was one of the cases that Elizabeth Cavendish heard as a magistrate that gave him the plot of his play *Equus*, first presented at the Old Vic Theatre in July 1973.[59] A boy had blinded six horses with a metal spike. When arraigned in court, he would only chant the jingles of contemporary television advertisements, such as 'A Double Diamond works wonders, works wonders, works wonders', to the tune of 'There's a hole in your bucket, Eliza, Eliza'. An Elizabeth Cavendish-like figure, a compassionate magistrate called Esther Salomon, appears in the play. She begs a psychiatrist to take on the boy's case: 'There's something very special about him.'[60] Frank Tait helped Shaffer with the 'child psychiatry' aspect of the play.

Cecil Beaton, who met the playwright at Tait and Henderson's country cottage in the year *Equus* was at the Old Vic, wrote in his diary:

> Shaffer struck me as being strangely stagey, though why someone who has been writing successfully produced plays for so long should not have been slightly tainted, and using stagey jargon, I do not know. But for so intellectual a writer, it surprised me to find echoes of John Gielgud in his personality and also in his physical appearance. The texture of his white, ivory-smooth skin, his general colourlessness and his large nose were very like John. So too his manner. But he is a far more truthful person. He doesn't indulge in persiflage. He would not make an effect by saying anything that he did not feel. He is not interested in effects, or getting a laugh. He is always on the search for new ideas, a person to be much admired and respected.[61]

Raymond Leppard – from 1972 principal conductor of the BBC Northern Symphony Orchestra – was one of the people who could always make John laugh, sometimes with risqué jokes. In 1974 he stayed with John and Elizabeth in Cornwall. 'He will fit in v well to

Trebetherick,' John wrote to Penelope in advance of the visit.[62] John and Elizabeth often saw Jeremy Fry, who was to have been best man to Antony Armstrong-Jones at his wedding to Princess Margaret in 1960, but had been hastily replaced by Roger Gilliat when a past homosexual 'indiscretion' came to light.[63] In 1975 Fry moved into the flat above James Lees-Milne's in William Beckford's old house in Lansdown Crescent, Bath. Lees-Milne described him in his diary that year:

> Jeremy still beguiling, handsome with dark hair curling down his neck, just the right length. Wears spectacles which somehow suit him. Elegant suit, long jacket, pale blue linen shirt with long, rounded points to collar . . . He always holds the stage; must be in the limelight. Simply his charm and endearing manners, for is he not shallow and vain? I must ask him one day. He is lovable. Like David Herbert [son of the fifteenth Lord Pembroke] he carries off every unconventional impulse with aplomb.[64]

A great friend of Fry's – the two went on many holidays together – was the play-and film-director Tony Richardson, predominantly gay, even though he had two daughters by Vanessa Redgrave during their five-year marriage. He, too, was in John and Elizabeth's circle. As early as 1969, Cecil Beaton recorded 'a quiet dinner at home with Eliz. Cavendish', attended by Frank Tait, Patrick Garland and himself.

> The conversation was by no means all bawdy . . . Talk was also of the remarkable 'village' and its 'inhabitants',[65] bought by Tony Richardson and the goings on, in which Eliz. stayed as a spectator this weekend, a great deal about juvenile delinquency (Eliz., a magistrate, had today sent a child to a reform school for stealing £2,000) [and] about the Budget . . .[66]

Richardson enlivened any dinner-party. Lindsay Anderson, in his introduction to Richardson's posthumously published memoirs, wrote: 'His way of speaking was, I suppose, his most remarkable characteristic; indeed it was (it still is) difficult to repeat Tony's remarks about anything without adopting that suppressed Northern accent, a certain flamboyance, a delivery more rhetorical than intimate . . .'[67] Through Rupert and Candida, John became a friend of Terence Stamp, the star of *Far from the Madding Crowd* (1966). A central figure of the Swinging Sixties, Stamp was the boyfriend of another, the model Jean Shrimpton. When Stamp wanted to move into a set of rooms in Albany, Piccadilly, John was asked for a testimonial. He wrote to Colonel A. L. Chetwynd-Talbot, the secretary of Albany: 'I can assure you that he is honourable, quiet, sober and a keen vegetarian. In addition to this he is honest, good company and entertaining as well as a most distinguished actor.'[68] Stamp's application was successful.

Also in John's and Elizabeth's circle was the novelist Robin Maugham, a nephew of Somerset Maugham and son of a lord chancellor, whose viscountcy he had inherited. ('Never forget that I am a peer of the realm,' was one of his crowing catchphrases.)[69] He had gained some réclame when his novel *The Servant* (1948) was filmed in 1965 with a screenplay by Harold Pinter and a subtly ambiguous performance by Dirk Bogarde. Maugham lived in Brighton with the prolific writer Hector Bolitho, who in 1938 had persuaded John to contribute an essay on Jacob Epstein to a book he edited, *Twelve Jews*. After the success of *The Servant*, some predicted that Maugham would overtake his uncle as a major novelist. It did not happen; though John gave his novel *Behind the Mirror* a glowing review in the *Daily Telegraph* in 1955[70] and in the 1970s agreed to write five sonnets for Maugham to work into the narrative of his novel *The Barrier*. This was a story of inter-race love in India. As the narrator was the white woman in the affair, Maugham was able to indulge in torrid descriptions of dark, sinewy male bodies – 'The skin of his thighs was so smooth that every part of their surface glittered like a mirror.'[71] (Had the book been published twenty years later, it might have been eligible for the *Literary Review*'s Bad Sex Award.) In the sonnets he supplied, John entered into the spirit of the thing –

> Is He not good, the God who such rapture gives?
>   Such overflowing ecstasy of joy.
> Youth, let me touch your warm enticing skin
> That I may know my lover breathes and lives.
>   My own, my darling sunkiss'd supple boy,
> If this is sinful, what is wrong with sin?[72]

That last line could be taken as a retort provoked by Pauline ethics; and John revived the theme in another sonnet:

> Adultery! The moon and stars permitted it.
>   Adultery! I'm numbered with the thieves.
> Adultery, and it was I committed it
>   I hear it in the whisper of the leaves . . .[73]

James Lees-Milne was the bisexual man whom John and Elizabeth saw most often. His incomparable diaries are a window into the couple's life and a mournful periodic bulletin on John's declining health. He was also a friend of Penelope, whom he had known since the early 1930s, before her marriage to John.[74]

Unlike some of John's friends – the Pipers and Harrods, for example – who were dismayed by John's abandoning Penelope and taking up with Lady Elizabeth, Lees-Milne was happier to meet a John discreetly escorted by Lady Elizabeth than a John resoundingly accompanied by Penelope. When Penelope was planning to leave Wantage in 1972 and came to inspect some derelict cottages near his home in Somerset, Lees-Milne confided to his diary: 'Truly I hope she does not come to live within a mile of us. I don't think I could bear it. I love her dearly, but she is impossible to be with for more than two hours. She bulldozes one, is utterly self-centred. She overwhelms and overbears.'

Like Cardinal Newman and Osbert Sitwell, Lees-Milne was an indifferent novelist and an inspired autobiographer. He excelled in the keeping of his diary. He had, in fuller measure than any of his contemporaries, the qualities that make a diarist: honesty; a facility for putting down what one observes and feels without too much straining through the muslins of the intellect; concern for other people; the kind of interest in oneself that Gore Vidal has called 'objective narcissism'; a memory for dialogue; an awareness of setting (in this Lees-Milne, with his experience as a National Trust adviser, was a professional); an eye for significant detail; a sense of humour with a condiment dash of malice; a willingness to make a fool of oneself; a skin too few. There was art, but predominant was the compulsion to tell.

For the last fifteen years of John's life, the diaries are a kind of Greek chorus.

11 March 1972

Penelope telephones to say they are leaving Wantage and she doesn't know where she is going to live. Says John will never tear himself away from London and will die there in harness; that he hates going away for weekends and so seldom goes to Wantage (I did not tell her that he is staying with us next weekend *and* with Elizabeth); and he would rather she took a small house right away, possibly in the Welsh Marches where he could retire for weeks on end. It is extraordinary how people deceive themselves. Poor Penelope, surely she must realise that John does not want to live with her at all. And surely she must know that on the contrary he goes off weekend after weekend at a time. I suppose it is pride which makes women cling to delusions of this sort, rather than face the ugly truth. Yet she is eminently sensible, and cherishes her independence.

18 March 1972

John Betj and Eliz: Cavendish to stay weekend. I met them in Kemble. John now shuffles rather than walks, such short shuffles that he scarcely raises his feet. It is a habit, he admits, but it is a sad one. We tease him about it. Feeble and I walked with the dogs round the valley below Winner Hill and Foxholes, where we saw hounds the other side of the valley. A still and beautiful afternoon; we could hear the voices of huntsmen clearly. She said 'That's David Somerset's voice, swearing at someone or something. I could never be mistaken . . .'

21 March 1972

I asked John if he ever saw Lionel Perry. He said,

> 'Literary Lionel sitting in his den
> Was visited by lots and lots of homosexual men.'

My love for JB is very deep. I am sure that hundreds of his friends believe they are the chief confidant and the one friend with whom he is most at ease. I don't kid myself to this extent. But I am sure I am one of his most intimate friends. With him confidences pour out, fun, folly, tears, wisdom, recitations, extracts from the *DNB* [*Dictionary of National Biography*], *Burke's Peerage*, shouts of laughter, jokes about his friends, fear of the after-life and God's retribution, total disbelief in the whole thing, genuine deep devotion to the Church, what a mixture; what torments he suffers, what enjoyment he extracts from life. I wish he were not so physically collapsed. He has a huge paunch, and the shuffling! He and Feeble no longer keep up pretence that they are not totally and permanently attached. She does not ever seem to get bored, or irritated by his ceaseless fantasizing.

Walking to church he said, 'I wonder what the bell-ringer will look like.' I said, 'Boy bell-ringers would be plain, spotty and wearing spectacles.' 'Yes,' he said, 'men don't make passes at boys wearing specs.' We were mistaken. Our bell-ringer was a very pretty little boy with a cream complexion. After matins the headmaster buttonholed John who was made to go to Rosehill for coffee. The boys came up with autograph books. J. is pursued wherever he goes. In the afternoon I took him to Westonbirt. In the library the girls were poring over their books. One with flaming red hair and wearing blue jeans was lolling lasciviously across a table. She sent him into ecstasies. These thrills and what he calls letchings are sheer fantasy.

22 April 1972

At [Lord] Abinger's request I asked John Betj. If he would give an address in Westminster Abbey in July to mark the 150th anniversary of Shelley's death. He said no, for he did not like Shelley. He agreed with Tennyson in declaring that Shelley was not worth Keats's little finger. Life like a dome of many-coloured glass staining the white radiance of eternity – makes no sense at all. All that rot about the skylark. Besides he was silly as a man, and wrong-headed. Leigh Hunt was a far better poet. So I have had to disappoint the Keats-Shelley Committee. JB said Anthony Blunt was a great Shelley fan. Would he not do? Or the Poet Laureate. [C. Day Lewis]? But the latter had already been asked and declined because of his bad health.

In February 1973 John visited Lees-Milne in Bath and stayed the night of the 2nd. That evening, Burnet Pavitt, the bachelor managing director of Roche, the chemicals firm, and a trustee of the Royal Opera House, Covent Garden, came to dinner in Lansdown Crescent. Lees-Milne noted:

> JB's humility is touching. To everyone who approaches him he speaks courteously; and when they leave him, he complains. After dinner last night he said to Burnet Pavitt, 'After you, please. You are so distinguished. I am only a fraud who has got away with it.' A trifle disingenuous?[75]

The next day John and Lees-Milne looked at Bath architecture and had lunch at the Hole in the Wall restaurant. John was everywhere recognized.[76] He told Lees-Milne of a recent encounter with their old Oxford friend John 'The Widow' Lloyd. After Lloyd had had an accident, John had taken him to his room at Brooks's and put him to bed. The Widow, in writing to thank him, said, 'This must be the first occasion of a Poet Laureate tucking a bachelor into bed since Tennyson did it to Arthur Hallam.'[77] On 6 May, when Elizabeth Cavendish rang him to ask if she and John might stay on the 19th, Lees-Milne wrote in his diary: 'How I love that dearest man, and dearest woman.'[78] Bath was a convenient staging-post for the couple on their way to Cornwall. With Lees-Milne, his wife Alvilde and their old housekeeper Miss Barrett they watched *Metro-land* on the television. Lees-Milne was shocked at how old John had become, though he thought he looked worse in the film made some months before.[79]

On 20 May the two couples had lunch at Cerney House, near Cirencester, with Quentin Craig. ('Never have I seen a Regency house more mauled within,' Lees-Milne wrote.)[80] Alvilde drove Elizabeth there, and Lees-Milne took John, who was in a confiding mood.

> He told me Penelope, although she had wanted to marry him, probably was never in love with him; that she is quite impossible to live with; that he does not know if his son is alive or dead, for his last letter was returned from the dead-letter office in New York. He is worried over lack of money. His secretary costs him £50 a week and he does not earn enough to cover

this item of expense. The demands made on him now he is Laureate bring no financial return, and much work. Showed us a letter he has just received from the Duke of Kent who offers his services in preventing London being totally transformed. John must go and see him. Another letter, from [Edward] Heath, asking him to translate a Portuguese poem into English to be put to music by Arthur Bliss and played to the Portuguese President on his visit to the Queen. And so it goes on . . . As we drove past Malmesbury John said, nodding to a signpost, 'In that village I had my first experience of sex with the son of the Vicar. It was in a punt on the river. I was quite spent. That night the brother came into my room, but I was too shocked by what I had done with the other, during the afternoon, and so lost a second opportunity.' He was then fifteen. We agreed that no subsequent escapades have eclipsed those early schoolday ones.[81]

John and Elizabeth again stayed a night with the Lees-Milnes on their way back from Cornwall on 16 June, bringing a canary as a present for Alvilde and for Lees-Milne a book of London statues photographed by the young Prince Richard of Gloucester.[82] John was amused to hear that (Sir) Julian Hall had put Lees-Milne into *The Senior Commoner*, a novel written at Eton forty years before.[83]

While we were eating [Lees-Milne wrote] John said, 'Oh, let's have a squint at it.' He always wants to look up a reference, read a passage of verse immediately. This is what I like. So I fetched the book, and read a letter tucked inside which Julian had written me in 1934 after the book had come out. 'Must be ninety per cent,' said John. 'Yes, I can tell from that letter that he's queer,' Feeble said. Then added, 'Tony Snowdon says he always knows that when people like you and me they're bound to be queer.'[84]

The next day, Lees-Milne noted:

John never misses Eucharist here, and Elizabeth accompanies him. A[lvilde] said when they had gone that E's love and solicitude for him were boundless. In church she would not let him kneel on the altar steps where the rails were not, but took that place herself so that he would have a rail to rest his arms against.[85]

In December, Lees-Milne was dining with Rosamond Lehmann at an Italian restaurant opposite Buckingham Palace mews, when someone tapped on the window. It was Osbert Lancaster, who was beckoned to join them. He had walked from the Beefsteak Club where he had sat next to Cyril Connolly. Alvilde, who dined that evening with John and Elizabeth, later told Lees-Milne that 'Cyril wanted to dine with them but Elizabeth sent him away because she only had three cutlets.'[86] Was Elizabeth being mean and inhospitable? Couldn't she have rustled up some other dish for Connolly, like the scrambled eggs that were there when Princess Margaret asked for them? Quite possibly her motive in turning Connolly away was to avoid taxing John, who would need to be on top form in conversation with the critic.

Besides James Lees-Milne, Cecil Beaton, another acute twentieth-century diarist, was a friend of John and Elizabeth, and kept John in his sights, both photographically and in his journals. He photographed the couple in his Pelham Place house with Cathleen Nesbitt, the actress whom Rupert Brooke had loved and almost married.[87] When John spoke at Noël Coward's memorial service in May 1973, Beaton noted that he was 'in second gear'.[88] In March 1974 John and Elizabeth witnessed a horrifying attack on Beaton by Robert Heber Percy, who lived up to his nickname, 'the Mad Boy'. All of them had been invited to Peter Quennell's sixty-ninth birthday party. Among the other guests was Lady Mary Dunn (née St Clair-Erskine), to whom John had once proposed marriage.[89] She was with her husband, Sir Philip Dunn, whom she had married in 1933, divorced in 1944, but remarried in 1969. Beaton liked to leave parties early. Knowing this, Evangeline Bruce, wife of the American ambassador, said she would telephone for a taxi. Both of them waited in the hall while other guests were leaving. The Dunns, old friends of Beaton, passed him, 'followed by the "Mad Boy" Heber Percy, who wore his asinine grin'. Suddenly Heber Percy gave Beaton a terrific blow on the chin. 'This sent me a few inches further away from him so that he aimed a most terrific, frenetic kick at my balls. The aim failed, or my overcoat softened the pain, but I found myself down the three front door steps on the pavement.'[90] Heber Percy then shot 'punches of ungoverned rage' at his face. 'I was being seriously beaten up.'

The Mad Boy was paying off a very old score. In a published diary, Beaton had stated that Lord Berners's family had been surprised and disappointed at being bypassed in his will in favour of Heber Percy, but that Berners's last days were not happy ones. Heber Percy had gone to a lawyer with a view to suing but had been told he had no case. 'So he had waited his chance to take the law into his own hands, break it and give me my comeuppance.'[91] The 'mugging' only ended when Sir Philip Dunn came back and pulled Heber Percy off Beaton. 'My nose was not broken, neither were my teeth. My face was very sore and some blood came from my ear. But I was safe. Eliz C. and John B. were terribly upset . . .'[92] Kenneth and Kathleen Tynan took him home in their car.[93] Beaton considered suing Heber Percy but 'decided against facing up to so much worry and bad publicity, and to forget the whole bloody business'.[94] Beaton's biographer, Hugo Vickers, records: 'Heber Percy laughed frequently as he recalled the incident in later years.'[95]

In the same month as the Beaton mugging, the *Illustrated London News* published an interview with John by Wilfred De'Ath, better known as a television producer than as a journalist. (He later won less welcome fame by serving jail terms for decamping from hotels without paying his bills.)[96] Some of the article was jokey ('He has been dubbed the Macaulay of *Mon Repos*, the Donne of *Dunromin* . . .'), but De'Ath also elicited from John more naked candour than any previous interviewer had done.

> After greeting me warmly [De'Ath wrote] he conducted me out of the ground floor study where his secretary was struggling with the day's pile of letters and into an exquisite little drawing room on the first floor where he immediately began to talk about death:
> 'I dread the prospect of extinction more than anything,' he told me. 'I can't bear the thought that life may just have been a cruel joke. I think I'd rather be alive in hell than extinct.'[97]

De'Ath asked him, didn't his Christian belief provide an adequate shield against his malaise of the soul?

> 'Well, sometimes it does and sometimes it doesn't, you know. I've had long moments of thinking Christianity isn't true, but on the whole I'm convinced that it is . . . In my youth I was attracted to the Quakers and I used to go to their meetings, but I think that was chiefly to avoid going to confession. I was much troubled by sex as a young man – I suppose most young men are. With me a sense of sin was always inextricably involved with sex and in my book masturbation was as bad as, if not worse than, murder . . . and I hated having to confess it.'[98]

James Lees-Milne was at Radnor Walk again in July, to ask John to autograph a book for the prize-giving of a school near the Lees-Milnes' home. 'I said to John, "Just add under your name *Poet Laureate*. This will give immense pleasure." He did so. Then leant back and murmured, "What a fraud I feel," and a look of intense anguish passed across his eyes.' But Lees-Milne thought John looked much better than when he had last seen him, with 'a good fresh colour'. Elizabeth said that John no longer drank spirits, and 'only wine – no port – after six'.[99] Much of the conversation that day was about Lees-Milne's former lover, the royal biographer James Pope-Hennessy, who had been murdered the day before. Young thugs had rammed a hairnet down his throat in an attempt to torture out of him the whereabouts of the large advance he had received for a biography of his friend Noël Coward.[100] (It had long since been spent.)

A month later, John stayed with Rupert and Candida. They had just moved to Blacklands, near Calne in Wiltshire beside the River Marden. The large Georgian house was in a bad state of repair: the top two floors had been gutted by fire. 'It had had a lot of money lavished on it and the grounds in the nineteenth century,' Candida writes, 'and none since.'[101] She sold David Hockney's portrait of her in the Ossie Clark dress, to pay for a tennis court; a plaque designated it 'The Hockney Court'. On 5 August 1974 John wrote to Mollie Baring: 'Darling Mollie, I am writing this on the terrace in the sun looking south to the downs at Wibz's new abode. Rupert is working the motor mower, the children rush about; only the downs and expensive-looking horses are still. It will make the most beautiful house and garden and has affinities with Ardington.'[102] The next day, he wrote Candida a verse thank-you letter from Radnor Walk.

Darling Wibz,
    Ta ever so for a glorious idle stay in the Wiltshire summer.

> Ta for the view from the brick-walled garden
> On to the downland over the Marden
> Ta for the monotone, evenly-flowing
> Of Rupert's football and Rupert's mowing.
> Ta to Lucy for bringing a chair
> That I might bask in the Wiltshire air
> Ta for Imo I never will find
> One so gentle, and loving and kind
> Ta to Delli whose eyes so round
> Go rolling about with never a sound
> And over it all the long day through
> Ta oh wonderful Wibz to you.

Love, MD [Mad Dadz][103]

Perhaps John had learned from the mistakes he had made with his own children; he seemed to relate to his granddaughters much better. He wrote them letters, sometimes in rebus form. After the first Blacklands Christmas he wrote to Candida: 'I can't forget Delli's rapturous, thrilling singing in the hall. The spreading meadow and limestone on one side, the hump of downland on the other . . . Your well-organized work greatly impressed the lazy, self-pitying, fat, bald, old reprobate who signs himself your old dad.'[104] In 1975 a son,

David, was born to Rupert and Candida. John went to Calne for the christening by Gerard Irvine.[105] Another son was born in 1978, who was named John after his grandfather.[106] David Lycett Green was born on 21 May. The next day was Tom Driberg's seventieth birthday. John wrote a poem to celebrate the event, including the couplet

> Testy at breakfast, difficult at tea
> But in the evening, oh how free, how free![107]

At the end of May 1975 John went to Canada to attend a seminar on High Victorianism. John Julius Norwich, who organized the event, had obtained him a fee of £2,000.[108] John, Elizabeth, Norwich, Hugh Casson and Asa Briggs flew first class to Toronto. John managed to lose his braces *en route*. When the party was greeted at the airport by Jack Jamieson of the Baptist McMaster University, John's trousers fell down; Jamieson lent him his belt.[109] The trip was a success. Lord Norwich told Candida: 'John was surrounded by scores of admiring teenagers the whole time we were there – he *never* stopped signing his books they brought him, always something different, "*Le maple leaf toujours*" and such like.'[110] After the seminar the British party travelled by train through the Rockies to Vancouver. John sat in the observation car, swigging rye whisky.[111] Back in England, he sent a verse thank-you to Carson Kilpatrick (senior) and his family with whom he had stayed in Toronto – head of the publishing house which issued the Canadian editions of his poems. Headed 'Rye-on-the-Rocks For Ever', it began:

> Carson and Anne Kilpatrick
> Are beautiful children to me:
> Carson is strong and his hair is long
> And his eyes are as blue as the sea.
>
> Anne has a peach complexion
> And beautiful curves and hips;
> When she looks in her brother's direction
> There's a secret smile on her lips . . .

And it ended:

> Oh, rye-on-the-rocks for ever!
> And I'm glad that I'm still alive
> While Carson and Anne Kilpatrick
> Are living on Vesta Drive.[112]

In November 1975 John stayed with Penelope again at the Little Redoubt. They visited Lady Chetwynd at her '1870-ish fantasy palace of tiles and iron and coloured marbles and steep gables' at Barmouth.[113] John wrote to Penelope on 1 December: 'I love you as much as I ever did and this visit was like old times. I saw a very good telly last night on hell. It was a film. It said hell is now and is separation from God. Quite true.'[114] This letter was a harbinger of the mental torment he suffered in the next year. On 17 March 1976 he wrote to Harry Jarvis, 'I have a very strong feeling that this earth is going to crack beneath me and I will sink into fire through mattresses of chicken-wire, telephone cables and sewage pipes which compose the ground under our feet in Radnor. On Monday the whole of it was bathed in an ominous violet pink light.'[115] It did not help that, on his morning constitutional, peering into the window of the King's Road boutique called Sex, he saw his name in the list of 'Hates' on a T-shirt which Bernard Rhodes, Malcolm McLaren and Vivienne Westwood[116] had designed for the shop. The shirt was intended to be a manifesto and a 'poem', as well as an article of clothing. John was fourth in the long list of Hates on the front of the shirt, after Television, Mick Jagger and the Liberal Party. The 'Loves' which appeared on the back included Christine Keeler, the Society for Cutting Up Men, Ronnie Biggs and Rubber.

On 11 April 1976 John went to Romania for just over a week with Elizabeth Cavendish, Jonathan Stedall and Stedall's cameraman, John McGlashan. They were making a 'recce' for Stedall's television film *The Long Search*, about the Orthodox Church in Romania. Stedall recalls:

I think what appealed to John in Romania – because we spent a lot of time in the country, in the villages – was that it was like medieval Europe. Each family had a pig and a cow and a cart. In one place, sheep were grazing in a churchyard. 'Much nicer than an ATCO [mowing machine],' John said. Everyone went to church on Sunday. The most important person in the village was the priest; then the doctor. John loved it. Because I was interested in the Church, and, although Romania was under Ceaucescu and was a very nasty place in some ways, we were looked after by the Church; and Ceaucescu's policy, unlike that of the Soviet Union, was to leave the Orthodox Church alone.

We went to monasteries quite a lot, and convents, and had the best wine and the best food. At one monastery we had quite a lot to drink. Then we had to stand at the end for grace, and Elizabeth got the giggles. She is a terrific one for getting the giggles. She told me that when she went to Holland with Princess Margaret they had to listen to a very poker-faced man delivering a speech about dams. And he told that story about the boy

putting his finger in the dyke; and both the Princess and Elizabeth ha~
control giggles.

We had a long coach journey back to Bucharest – we'd been right up in the north and we'd been travelling two or three hours. We were all tired, absolutely silent. And then John's voice suddenly piped up: 'I am enjoying the boredom.'

We went on another trip – again we'd had a long day. We were heading towards this town appropriately called Brasov, and we had an interpreter called Horia. It was late and it all looked pretty grim and John said, 'Horia, what's the chief industry of Brasov?'

Horia said, 'Cement.'

'Is the hotel we're going to stay in tonight made of cement?'

'Yes.'

'I was afraid so.'[117]

Patrick Kinross died on 4 June of cancer of the intestine. On 8 June, James Lees-Milne was at Radnor Walk again.

Since Patrick was to have dined with me this evening, Feeble and John Betj. had me to dine with them. JB very unhappy over P's death. Frank Tait there too. Very sympathetic man. Slightly sardonic smile, yet compassionate, funny, very. He walks in an engagingly joyous manner as though at any moment he might levitate.[118]

Kinross's funeral was on 11 June, at Paddington Green Church. John gave the address and was therefore unable to attend the funeral, the same day, of his old Admiralty boss, Richard Hughes, at St Martin-in-the-Fields. James Lees-Milne, at the service for Kinross, found it hard to control his emotion. He wrote in his diary: 'Paddy [Leigh Fermor] read one lesson with his difficult voice. John Betjeman's address from the pulpit most beautiful. His excellent, calm, quiet, professional delivery. He likewise very moved . . .'[119] But Lees-Milne also wrote: 'Oh dear. Dreadful to watch JB's painful ascent to and descent from the high pulpit. Osbert [Lancaster] there looking a million [years old].'[120]

Privately and publicly, John's seventieth birthday, on 28 August 1976, was celebrated in style. Rupert and Candida held a party for him at Blacklands.[121] Jonathan Stedall made a television film of *Summoned by Bells*, in which John retraced his early life. Even though Stedall was the producer, John did not enjoy it. On 14 June he wrote to Candida: 'Jonathan has been filming with me today in burning heat at Gerrards Cross. Some people like lumps of meat hot and red with over-indulgence were lunching at the horrible Greyhound Inn, Chalfont St Peter. And would not budge up so as to let us have seats

443

...from filming.'[122] And he told James Fox, who con-
...day article about him to the *Radio Times:*

...thing has been the most devastating experience. I had no idea
...f draining effect it has on one. Very upsetting. Was I very difficult
over th... filming, Magda?* Yes, I think so. It did upset me most surprisingly.
I felt as though I were undressing in public and showing my parts. I hadn't
thought about it very much. I just went about my way and then suddenly
found myself confronted with the things I'd seen as a child, which I hadn't
seen since, and it looked much smaller, then it grew big again. That was
what was so surprising. It was just as awful.

Swain's Lane [where the boys lay in wait for him] was every bit as alarm-
ing as it was when I went there as a child from Highgate Junior School. All
those roads to school were the same.[123]

'I had to go back to the very earliest places I can remember,' he
wrote to Penelope on 8 September, 'and see Ernie's grave in Highgate
Cemetery and a passport photograph of Bess and remember nursery
things. It was like being the bath water and running down with it as
part of the London drains. And then suddenly the BBC girded its loins
and started a sort of fiesta so that I find myself not myself but a public
figure and quite inhuman.'[124]

Stedall's film, which incorporated Edwardian archive footage,
would have been thought outstanding if the public had not already
seen Mirzoeff's *Metro-land*. Under the headline 'The Betjeman question left unresolved', Sylvia Clayton of the *Daily Telegraph* made the
inevitable comparison: 'Unlike the brilliantly successful *Metro-land*,
in which Sir John was a lively guide to the landscape, this film introduced his verses as a "voice over" and showed him in once familiar
haunts as a silent, saddened figure in a variety of hats, playing no more
active part than his battered Teddy bear, Archibald.'[125]

John Sparrow gave a talk about him on the radio, in which he said:

Looking back, I can only say that if anyone had told me fifty years ago at
Oxford that my undergraduate friend, that exuberant, irreverent,
mocking, light-hearted, mischievous elf, would be transformed into a
pillar of the Establishment . . . I would have laughed him to scorn . . . The
miracle is that John Betjeman has achieved all this *without* any transformation – and of course without any pretence and without any compromise
on his part . . .[126]

* Magda Rogers, his then secretary.

John wrote to Sparrow after the broadcast: 'I was entranced by what Penelope has called your loyal piece about me on the wireless. I listened to it, preening myself like an old queen and scarcely believing it was true. All the same you've said it and you would never tell an untruth and you have always been a friend.'[127]

The *Radio Times* of 28 August (which included the James Fox interview) gave its cover to a coloured drawing of John by Adrian George. John had wanted to be depicted with his teddy-bear, but – as George complained to Janet Street-Porter – Elizabeth Cavendish put her foot down about that, saying that it would make John look infantile.[128] So, instead, George drew him holding a copy of *Tiger Tim's Weekly* comic – hardly less infantile, some might feel. When Osbert Lancaster saw the drawing of John, he thought he looked, in his battered felt hat, like an elderly Sapphic headmistress, and redrew him with silvery curls, holding Radclyffe Hall's lesbian novel of 1928, *The Well of Loneliness*.[129]

Five days after John's seventieth birthday, James and Alvilde Lees-Milne drove to Hay-on-Wye to deliver a copy of Lees-Milne's new book, *William Beckford*, to Michael Cottrill at Richard Booth's bookshop.[130] Afterwards they called on Penelope at Cusop, without prewarning, bringing a picnic lunch with them.

> She was busily cooking in the kitchen [Lees-Milne wrote]. Received us as though we had been with her all the morning, went on cooking, talking, talking without cease, treating us with her extraordinary detached, candid manner. Is a round little tub with close-cropped grey hair, wearing a brown one-piece garment, trousers, the legs very tight, also the behind, which is enormous. From the behind a thick hair was dangling like a tail, of which she was totally unconscious. She is very worried about John. Thinks his health is impaired by what she calls his 'dichotomy', i.e., his divided allegiance to her and Feeble. She says F. is very possessive and John is afraid of her, which isn't true. Thinks John is killing himself with drink and drugs which his doctor plies him with. This is far more likely. It was distressing to see how old he has become, for in the film given on his seventieth birthday he walked like Charlie Chaplin, as though his legs did not belong to him. Very sad film, for he did not speak throughout. A background recitation in his voice taken from *Summoned by Bells*. At the very end he broke into that delicious smile, made a joke and came alive.[131]

HEAVEN AND HELL ON TELEVISION: THE SEVENTIES

Of all the things we have done together, I think *Belfast* is the best.

John Betjeman to Ken Savidge, 9 August 1977

The early 1970s were the apogee of John's television career, with the Australian films of 1972, *Metro-land* in 1973, and *A Passion for Churches* in 1974.* In 1976 he made the televised version of *Summoned by Bells* that he enjoyed so little. At the beginning of the decade he made his exuberant films with Margaret McCall, *Four with Betjeman*. He was in his element wandering down the staircase of the Eastern Grand Hotel, reflecting on Gilbert Scott's career and pointing out curly ironwork by Skidmore of Coventry. His programme about the gardener Gertrude Jekyll and the architect Edwin Lutyens – whom John familiarly called 'Ned', as one who had known him – displayed his dual ability to sketch in background ('The architecture of the simple life goes with vegetarians, fruitarians, H. G. Wells, Bernard Shaw, garden suburbs and bowls of pot-pourri and lavender sachets in the linen cupboards') and his skill in analysing the legacy of a historical episode. ('The great contribution England made to architecture in the last century and at the beginning of this was the small, well-built house made of local materials designed to fit in with the landscape and which looked as if it had always been there.')

He demonstrated the same twin talents in another of the McCall programmes, about the Ritz Hotel, London, the earliest steel-frame building in Britain. First, the atmospheric introduction: 'As soon as

---

* See Chapters 16, 'Back to Australia'; 18, '*Metro-land*'; and 21, '*A Passion for Churches*'.

you come in, you're impressed by its quiet stateliness and you begin to think, "Oh, have I got dirty nails? Am I properly dressed?" ' He mentions the building's date – 1906 – but does not reveal that it was the year of his own birth, too. Again, he is clear what, in the perspective of time, the building stood for: 'The last fling of a great age. And the Great War brought it to an end.'

In 1972 John made a two-part film with Jonathan Stedall, *Thank God It's Sunday*. Much of it was a send-up, by a churchgoing Christian, of the secularization of the Sabbath. One was awakened by:

> The newest feature of our Sunday streets
> On double time, if on the day of rest –
> The deafening dawn chorus of the drills.

His harshest words were saved for the Sunday newspapers, whose critics, over the last few years, had often belaboured him:

> Steady on just and unjust falls the rain
> Across the soaking acres of the grass,
> Over wet pavements and by dripping boughs
> We pilgrims plod to the last shrine of all,
> The best attended and the most revered –
> The sacred altar of the Sunday press.
> What's in; what's out; what's on.
> We ought to know, for if we don't
> We won't be thought informed. Willingly
> We make offerings at the shrine.

One of John's most successful programmes was *Vicar of This Parish* (1976), produced by Patrick Garland. The impression of one eccentric talking about another was established at once by John's oblique, discursive introduction.

The diaries of the Rev. Francis Kilvert were discovered by my friend William Plomer. He spoke it 'Ploomer' and people who didn't know used to call it 'Plummer'. He was chiefly a poet and he had a round head, round eyes and a round, drawling voice. He died in 1974. And he specialized in the unexpected. He lived in bungalows and council houses. And here is a typical example of William's humour which he told me once. There was a lady sitting on a bus with a child on her knee and whose child was sucking one of those lollies on a stick. And a lady in a mink coat came and sat down next to them and the child wiped its lolly on the mink coat of the lady next door. And the mother said: 'Don't do that, Mavis – you'll get 'airs all over it.'

That was William's delight in the unexpected, and he showed the same delight in the unexpected in the Victorian parson Francis Kilvert, whose diary he edited . . .

It was clear that to some extent John identified with Kilvert. His final words about him could have been said about himself.

Everyday life did not seem to him ordinary and humdrum. Even what he called the humble and uneventful seemed to him curious and wonderful, therefore enjoyable . . . He wanted to give it a lasting shape, to communicate it to others to entertain them. And this was the impulse of an artist.

In 1977 John made one last film with Eddie Mirzoeff, to mark the Queen's Silver Jubilee in that year.

Aubrey Singer was the boss man here [Mirzoeff recalled] – he may have been managing director by then. He was saying, 'I *demand* a helicopter series called *The Queen's Realm* which is going to come from Scotland and Wales and England; and you', he said, 'will do it.' We'd all done this helicoptering before. He said, 'You know how to do it.' But none of us wanted to set foot in a bloody machine again because we'd actually been filming for three years fairly continuously. Since then, one of our number had had an accident in a helicopter, and everyone said, 'Enough's enough. These are dangerous things.' We really didn't want to do any more.

So what we did was to print all the films we had actually made of which there were about fourteen; and we used other helicopter material that other people had shot. Somehow, we created a film out of that. Not one frame was specially shot. Everything was extant in the library.[1]

Mirzoeff, who was working on another film, gave all the helicopter footage to Ted Roberts and asked him to work out what could be done with it. Eventually the two men decided that it might be a good idea to do something based on the seasons, particularly as one of the helicopter films was *Around the Seasons*. The words would be an anthology of English poetry. Mirzoeff first approached Geoffrey Grigson, whom he regarded as an anthologist of genius. On the telephone, Grigson sounded enthusiastic; but when Mirzoeff sent him the scripts of the helicopter films (of which some were written by John) saying 'You'll get a sense of what we've done,' Grigson sent back a curt note, 'I'm afraid I can't take on this project.'[2] Mirzoeff thinks he was put off by the discovery that John was involved. So Mirzoeff went back to John and said, 'Look, if we do lots of the work, could you possibly try and tie it all together?' John agreed to help.

Mirzoeff formed a small team, including his wife, and they 'just read day and night, looking for seasonal stuff'. They would say to John, 'We've found these ten poems, John. What do you reckon?' John was good negatively, Mirzoeff remembers. 'He'd say "no" quite clearly. So quite a lot of stuff went out because he didn't like it. He was more hesitant in saying "Yes". There were many "maybe" s.'[3] John did come up with a few things the rest of the team would never have thought of, such as a Hilaire Belloc poem about electricity and a passage from Elizabeth Barrett Browning. Gradually the plan of the film took shape; and all the time Ted Roberts was giving thought to the music that should be played.

The main question was [Mirzoeff recalls] should we use John to read the poems, or actors? John was now getting on. Also, I thought it would be misleading to have him reading – people would think they were all poems by him. So in the end he read his own bits and voices read the other bits – Michael Hordern, Richard Pasco, Prunella Scales. And that did not go down well in Radnor Walk, let me tell you. Lady Elizabeth had done her best to stop John being taxed by the work; but when we got these actors, she felt he had been marginalized. They had not been very keen on his working in the first place, but once he actually did get involved they wanted to maximize the impact of it. It was silly, because the thing was hugely successful. Everyone loved it. And John got credited with the choice of the poems, too! I had the fun of taking the film along to the then editor of the *Times Literary Supplement*, John Gross, and saying, 'How many of these can you get?' As you'd expect, he was very good at guessing the poets – but there were quite a few he didn't get.[4]

By a piquant irony, Derek Jarman's film *Jubilee* had its première at about the same time as *The Queen's Realm* was transmitted. With its killings and sexual wantonness, it was almost a Satanic negative of John's and Mirzoeff's elegiac vision of the country, though there were curious points of contact between the two films, for example in their views of stately homes. Jarman recognized that these were 'the indispensable prop for the English way of life' – 'Any film or TV series that has one is half-way to success.'[5] Filming at Longleat, Jarman naturally focused on the erotic murals by the then Lord Weymouth (now Marquess of Bath), though he was persuaded to cut a scene 'that had Hitler painting those lurid murals – "We came to Dorset. It's the perfect place for retirement. Josef suggested it after we met in Berlin." '[6] This was the time of punk, of Sid Vicious and Johnny Rotten. Crowds showed the Queen great affection when she went on public 'walkabouts' in a Hardy Amies suit and tasselled hat. But for a new generation of disaffected and 'disadvantaged' young people, Jarman's subversive vision had more to say than lines of Elizabeth Barrett Browning recited with BBC vowels above aerial views of downland. John caught their mood and responded to it with fear in his poem 'Chelsea 1977'.[7]

In the late 1970s, John also made his last films with Ken Savidge, *Betjeman's Belfast* and *Betjeman's Dublin*. His old friend, after a time as a consultant in Pakistan and 'a rather unhappy period in the foreign relations department of the BBC', had asked to be a producer again. He was told, 'If you are determined to work at the coal face, it will have to be in Northern Ireland.'[8] So Savidge moved to Ulster.

> And, knowing John's delight in many of the buildings of Belfast, I thought it would be a good idea to do thirty minutes on them. But at first – not from him, but from Elizabeth – there was great resistance. 'Oh, he will be kidnapped, he will be assassinated!' We got over that and in any case he had connections there, for example with the Dufferins at Clandeboye. So we embarked on this. He was most hospitably received. The BBC really pushed the boat out.[9]

For the best part of a week, John stayed outside Belfast in 'a rather nice place near Bangor'. The filming went smoothly. John visited a Church of Ireland church on the Shankill Road, a Methodist church in the centre of the city, the Seamen's Mission – 'everything was done in inscriptions on flags on the floors' – and the gasworks. The City Hall was 'the gorgeous and culminating extravaganza' with which the televised tour ended. 'In this misty mountainous country,' John said, 'skyline is all-important . . . Every dull, clinical slab that goes up makes the bronze, marble and stained glass of the City Hall more precious.'[10] The film was shown on BBC1 on 12 November 1976. In 1977 John wrote to Savidge: 'Of all the things we have done together, I think *Belfast* is the best. Well proportioned, right timing and plenty of jokes.'[11]

In the same letter, he asked Savidge to arrange a party for the crew of the inevitable sequel about Dublin. 'I will pay. I think I owe this to the great and neglected race, the Anglo-Irish and to the Church of Ireland.' By that time, he was too infirm to go to Ireland; but with all his wartime experience of Dublin he was able to suggest the full itinerary and recorded a commentary. His voice was still steady. The film opened in the University Church, where his commentary began:

> I wonder where you think we are? Italy perhaps – Rome or Ravenna? Well, you are quite wrong because this magnificent basilica is right here in the centre of one of Europe's thriving capital cities, and, if you haven't

guessed by now, we are of course in Dublin – and that's the Irish flag flying over the country's most celebrated building: the Post Office in O'Connell Street.[12]

For a moment John was shown in Radnor Walk, continuing his introduction. Then the camera swung along the Liffey and out to Castletown, 'the largest Palladian house in Ireland', where William Conolly, first Speaker of the Irish House of Commons, had lived. In his original script, preserved by Ken Savidge, John wrote: 'Speaker Conolly liked a good show for his money. Instead of getting lots of picture frames, he got these pictures first and then arranged the plaster round them.' In the final commentary this was omitted and the film moved on to the fine monument Speaker Conolly's widow put up to him. 'It stands in an unlighted mausoleum in the old Protestant churchyard at Celbridge, and it's by Thomas Carter, a statuary of Hanover Square, London.' Of course the Rotunda, where Candida was born, had to be shown. John mentioned that it had replaced a rotunda where 'the Irish pianist and composer John Field, whom Chopin much admired, first played in public at the age of nine'. Then to St Mary's Chapel of Ease at the top of Granby Row – 'the Black Church, it's called, – why, nobody seems to know' – and on to the Four Courts, the Guinness Brewery, the Custom House and Dublin Castle, where, in the Strawberry Hill Gothic chapel, John was able to show off his knowledge of Francis Johnston. 'There's Jonathan Swift over the north-west entrance and you'll see he takes precedence over St Peter beneath him.'

After vistas of Georgian squares, with fanlights above their doors, John talked expansively about Kingsbridge station, Dublin, designed by Sancton Wood, and the Egyptian-style Broadstone station by John Skipton Mulvany, the runner-up in the Kingsbridge station competition. Then back for a longer look at Newman's University Church and on to Trinity Library to see the eighth-century Book of Kells. John thought Trinity Engineering School 'arguably the most exciting building in Dublin' – the old engineering school in the Venetian–Islamic style, which Ruskin admired so much that he gave its co-architect Benjamin Woodward the commission for the University Museum, Oxford. The tour ended with the Trinity Provost's House (1759). 'Elegant and perfectly proportioned, it does all that good architecture ought to do, it doesn't crush you, it lifts you up . . .' John's commentary was completed by early October 1978 and was screened at Christmas. The BBC showed what they thought of it by putting it out at 11.00 p.m., after *The Liver Birds*, *The Dick Emery Christmas Show* and *International Show Jumping*.

Though clearly in decline, John was still capable of animated contributions to chat shows. As with *Desert Island Discs* on radio, he was the only person invited to appear three times on Michael Parkinson's television shows[13] – once with the camp *Carry On* comedian Kenneth Williams and the actress Maggie Smith and once with the Lancashire singer Gracie Fields, whom he had first seen forty years before in the otherwise deserted theatre at Alexandra Palace.[14] Williams and Maggie Smith decided they would recite John's 'Death in Leamington' in his presence. Williams wrote in his diary:

> To TV studios for the 'Parkinson Show'. I was introduced to Sir John Betjeman and he was a great delight. One of the most lovable and kindly gentle people I've ever met. On the show itself, it all got very woolly and serious and Maggie went terribly *posh*. She was obviously intensely nervous. When I got on, I wasn't much better and I was foolishly babbling about train strikes being against the essence of socialism etc. so I will doubtless reap the whirlwind of indiscretion. I read the Betjeman poem with Maggie – holding the book between us – and it worked very well.[15]

Anyone watching the third Parkinson programme of 1977 would have thought John on top form. He recited his poem 'A Russell Flint' (about 'Freckly Jill') to the music of Jim Parker, played live. And he gave fluent answers to Parkinson's questions.

Parkinson: When exactly did you last write a poem or try to write a poem in recent weeks?

John: About three days ago I was trying to do one on Peterborough Cathedral, a beautiful building which has got in it a chapel called St Sprite and I imagine that's the Holy Spirit, and it's such a nice name for a chapel, I thought I'd try and do a thing about the Sprite in Peterborough Cathedral. I got the first words out and have now lorst them.

Parkinson: You've lost them? Mislaid them?

John: Mislaid them.

Parkinson: Can't you remember them?

John: No.

Parkinson: So what are you going to do?

John: Hope I'll find them again.

John told Parkinson, 'I started as a journalist, as you did – and it teaches one to write things simply and not like government department forms.'

Parkinson: Advertising slogans and phrases have always been a part of your poetry, haven't they? You've always stuck them in there. What's the fascination you have?

John: I think sitting in the Underground and seeing things like:

> Whatever her Party, the smart young thing,
> It's certain she'll vote for a Bravington ring.[16]

Parkinson: And Virol.

John: 'Anaemic girls need it'. And Iron Jelloids! Mazawattee tea! I think they're most beautiful names.

Candida was watching the programme. She later wrote: 'Although there was jollity in his air and the audience laughed at almost everything he said, I could detect a fear in his eyes. He told me afterwards it had been one of the most frightening experiences of his life. He was terrified that he was going to be asked difficult questions.'[17] He need not have worried. 'Is your poetry *relevant*, do you think?' Parkinson asked. '*No*, thank God.'

THE 'GREEN GIANT' AND OTHER CAMPAIGNS: PRESERVATION IN THE SEVENTIES

Unless something is done, [J. D.] Sedding's irreplaceable church and the works of art designed especially for it will be destroyed for ever and dispersed.

John Betjeman, *A Plea for Holy Trinity Church, Sloane Street*,
London 1974

As early as 1958, *The Times*, reviewing John's *Collected Poems*, said of him: 'He has established a personal regency over contemporary taste.'[1] By 1970 he had become something more practical – a sort of ombudsman for conservationists throughout the country. The *Times* Diary reported in October 1970: '[He] gets some 50 letters daily on threatened buildings, redundant churches, old market places, Victorian town halls, etc, and most generate three or four letters at least. "I was made to be a writer, and I'm being turned into a Post Office." '[2]

In December he signed, with his old *Daily Herald* colleagues Michael Foot and Marjorie Proops (by now the *Daily Mirror*'s 'agony aunt'), as well as Pevsner, Lord Silkin and Summerson, a letter on London motorways. Great harm would be done if the inner and intermediate motorway sections of the Greater London Development Plan were allowed to go ahead. The scheme would involve 'the wholesale destruction of 20,000 homes'. Instead, public transport should be improved.[3]

In March 1971 he was once more on the warpath against unsightly street lamps. With the scientist Ernst Chain, Osbert Lancaster, Pevsner and others, he described as 'deplorable' two thirty-five-foot lamp standards within inches of each wing of the seventeenth-century College of Arms.[4] In May he attacked new buildings put up by Barclay's Bank in 'what is left of the charming limestone market town in the heart of Peterborough': 'So deeply ingrained is the doctrine that "modern" is cheaper, that some large firms and local authorities really believe it is essential to build in concrete and steel and glass. Quite often it is just as cheap to use load-bearing walls, brick, stone and wood, and thus help to preserve the environment.'[5]

He was not only called upon to sign letters of protest; he was also in demand as a witness at public hearings. In March 1971 he told an inquiry at Bristol that the city 'would suffer at the hands of commercial enterprise' if the Grand Hotel Company were allowed to build a £1 million hotel on the slopes of the Avon Gorge.[6] He described Brunel's 1829 suspension bridge across the gorge as 'an effortless conquest of space' and pointed out that Brunel had been inspired by the setting. John was brought into the campaign by Penelope's cousin Lord Methuen, whose action group had secured the services of a fiery young barrister, Paul Chadd (later QC).[7] Chadd recalls:

In 1969 the Grand Spa Hotel (now the Avon Gorge Hotel) wanted a new car park and ballroom. Discussions with the Bristol city planners led the owners to realize that more profit could be made by putting a hotel on top of the car park – a building eight storeys high, 250 feet long and 200 feet from the bridge. For the owners, there were two snags: first, work on construction had to begin by 31 March 1971 to qualify the hotel for a Government grant of £1,000 per bedroom, then on offer for new hotels; second, opposition to such a large building was to be expected. (That was recognized in a letter to the planners from the architect dated 23 June 1970.) Neither the Grand Spa Hotel nor the architects nor the officers of the planning department nor counsel selected to serve the city breathed a word of this; it all went on behind closed doors. The public remained in happy ignorance of what was proposed for one of the prime monuments of nineteenth-century British engineering, in one of the finest settings alongside the gorge.

January 1971 saw three devastating days. On 8 January a routine check by a small amenity group revealed what was afoot. On the 13th the Royal Fine Art Commission in London said that it could see nothing wrong with this size of building on this site. And on 27 January, in the face of growing public protest, outline permission for the development was given by the Bristol planning committee.

The amenity societies formed an action group. A letter-writing campaign was organized. That was threatened before it began by a postal strike; but the action group provided a private postal service and 1,200 letters of protest soon landed on the desk of Peter Walker, the then Minister for the Environment. The only hope for the bridge and the gorge was for him to revoke the permission that had been granted. *The Observer*, *The Guardian* and *The Times* kept the battle before the public. Tony Aldous of *The Times* had been at Bristol University, and he wrote a report that one couldn't quite call impartial. He wrote: 'Should an eight-storey building . . . be permitted to spoil the dramatic scenery of the Avon Gorge?' The public got really worked up about it. In Bristol people would walk into a pub and ask, 'Any news yet?' 'No news yet.'

On 5 March the Minister announced that he was considering revocation and that he intended to hold an inquiry. He sent down an inspector who was a high-flyer, Stanley Midwinter. His report was wholly in our favour and against the developers. We thought we'd won. But even this did not halt the philistine councillors in Bristol. So angry was the leader of the Conservatives that they were preparing on 17 March 1971 to approve the scheme, even though the inquiry was going to be held. A week later, bulldozers appeared on the site. The hotel company was desperate for some work on the foundations to begin in order to qualify for the Government grant of £126,000 on the proposed 126-room hotel. The local authority did nothing to stop them. All they had to do was *start* work; and luckily, no great harm was done.[8]

The inquiry was held on 17 May. Paul Chadd had prepared his case with care. He had managed to get from the architects their elevations of the new hotel. He had then had professional photographs taken of the gorge and bridge and superimposed on them scale versions of the drawings to show how overpowering the hotel would be (see plate). 'In their drawings, the architects had put dainty trees in front of the car park – but you couldn't have planted trees there, it was solid rock.' The witnesses Chadd had lined up included the modernist architect Berthold Lubetkin, who, two years earlier, had moved with his wife Margaret to a house barely a hundred yards from the gorge. John's old *Architectural Review* colleague James Richards also attended. But Chadd considered John his star witness.

I gave lunch to him and Lady Elizabeth Cavendish before the hearing [he says]. My impression was that he was diffident; despondent, too. He said, '*They always win*,' and it made me quite sad. So it gave me great pleasure to ring him up later and say, 'We've won.' He was nervous, uncomfortable in the witness box; but he created the Betjeman atmosphere. Everybody liked him. Even the tough counsel on the other side was courteous to him. 'My wife enjoys your television programmes very much,' he said, in a rather patronizing and I suppose 'sexist' way. James Richards was analytical; but John gave the *flavour*. The combination was ideal. One of the things John said was that he was worried about the effect of the hotel windows at night. The bridge is the only thing illuminated there – it *would* have made a big difference.[9]

Although the Avon Gorge development was stopped, the Bristol hearing was not quite the end of the matter. On 29 May 1971 a news report appeared in *The Times* under the headline 'SIR JOHN BETJEMAN'S EVIDENCE "INACCURATE" '. William Huntley, for the developers, said that the project's opponents had made 'gross misrepresentations' about it and had circulated 'despicable posters which showed the hotel the wrong size'. Huntley added: 'A statement made by Sir John Betjeman that the hotel would urbanize the Gorge was grossly inaccurate. Sir John came here post-haste from Cornwall to give evidence, without seeing the plans.'

A year later, John was alarmed by reports that, when Piccadilly Circus was redeveloped, the Criterion Restaurant (the 'Cri' of his early poem 'The 'Varsity Students' Rag') would come down. This would be 'an irreparable loss of an exquisite Victorian restaurant and theatre of the [eighteen-]seventies. These were Thomas Verity's finest work, with, in the restaurant, most of the original decorations surviving under the usual formica'. He bitterly concluded: 'Would the Authorities please confirm that they are not hand in glove with the property developers, and that when a building is listed as being of architectural and historical interest this means that it is worth preserving and cannot be handed over to make way for mere speculative office development?'[10]

The letter inspired an article by *The Times*'s star reporter, Philip Howard, headed, 'MEMORIES LINGER LIKE CIGAR SMOKE'. He called the Criterion 'an oasis of Victorian elegance in the howling wasteland of griddles and cockney taverns and amusement arcades in Piccadilly Circus'. The theatre, he wrote, had the oldest auditorium still in its original state in London. 'On public tours . . . the exclusively royal lavatory behind the royal box is a favourite attraction. The large, functional black box opens on a miracle of Victorian closet-work, in which garlands of blue flowers decorate the china bowl.' It would be, Howard thought, 'a crime to sink such an extraordinary memory-haunted place in the concrete foundations of an office tower'.[11] In June, Westminster City Council asked the Piccadilly planners to think again about the Criterion. It was saved, and John wrote an article about it, on its centenary, in the '1874' issue of *The Connoisseur* published to celebrate the centenary of Churchill's birth (1974).[12]

The Duke of Grafton and others wrote to *The Times* in October 1972 to complain of a proposal to develop four hundred acres to the east of Bury St Edmunds for industry and two thousand houses. On 4 October, just a week before his appointment as Poet Laureate was made public, John's letter supporting the Duke appeared at the top of the *Times* letters page. He wrote of 'the proposed suicide of

Bury St Edmunds': 'It is almost unbelievable that such a thing can happen in an ancient and historic town of national importance . . . To build housing estates on this irreplaceable and untouched eastern side of the town is even worse than if the GLC suddenly decided to turn all London's open spaces and public parks into brick and concrete.'[13] There is a note almost of hysteria in this, perhaps indicating the tension John felt over the impending announcement of his appointment. The development he opposed did take place in the 1980s, in the area now called Moreton Hall, to the east of Bury.

In January 1973 he signed a letter with Lady Dartmouth, Simon Jenkins, Osbert Lancaster, Denys Sutton and myself suggesting a 'Wider Use for Somerset House' as a gallery for British art. The letter counted the National Gallery among those collections 'obliged to keep most of their best paintings in store'.[14] Sir Edward Playfair, who became chairman of the National Gallery that year, took a token revenge for his defeat over St Pancras. 'It is sad to see this myth propagated by such friendly, sensitive and well-informed people.' All the gallery's paintings, he insisted, were on show.[15]

In June 1973 John wrote, again with Simon Jenkins, on the City of London Corporation's threat to demolish the east end of Christ Church, Newgate, 'a major work by Wren and the last of his surviving churches which has not yet been restored after war damage'. The reason the Corporation gave for the demolition was a road scheme which was claimed as the western termination of Route 11 (London Wall): in fact, John and Jenkins wrote, it offered no direct link.[16] In November John protested at an application by Josiah Wedgwood & Sons to demolish Barlaston Hall, Staffordshire, a Grade I listed building designed by Robert Taylor and built between 1756 and 1758. 'This is another case', John wrote, 'where an owner has permitted a country house of major architectural importance to remain empty for 20 years. It is now in a state of almost utter disrepair.'[17] A *Times* article urged, 'Think again, Wedgwood.'[18] Wedgwood did think again: if they had not, a genuine eighteenth-century work would have been destroyed by a company best known today for the manufacture of eighteenth-century pastiches. Barlaston Hall was restored. Including it in his 2003 book *England's Thousand Best Houses*, Simon Jenkins wrote: 'The library bow window has roundels of Shakespeare and, now, of John Betjeman, hero of the conservation movement to which we owe the survival of this house.'

A threat to Southend pier, in February 1974, touched John more personally. It would cost £1.5 million to repair the pier over ten years, *The Times* reported; total demolition would cost £800,000, only partly offset by the income from scrap. It happened that the foremost authority on English piers, Cyril Bainbridge, was then night news editor of

The Times. On 16 February he contributed an article headed 'How far to the end of the longest pier in the world?' On 22 February John wrote, 'I am one of millions who have used Southend Pier as the nearest place to London for real sea-air, recreation and complete change of scene . . . In winter or summer the pier is a delight with its tram-way, once of toast-rack type, running for a mile and a third into a wide prospect of sea and sky. There is all the advantage at the end of the pier of being right out to sea and no feeling of sea-sickness.' He hoped the preservation of the pier would be considered 'not merely of local interest but . . . of national importance'. The pier was saved.*
Equally successful was John's campaign of 1974 to prevent further replacements of medieval statues on the west front of Wells Cathedral. John protested with Henry Moore and others at the 'depressingly bad standard' of the new carvings, and in August the Cathedral Advisory Committee of the Church of England halted the work.[19]

Also in August, John wrote with Casson, Pevsner, Basil Spence and Jack Simmons to try to save the Royal Agricultural Hall, Islington – the 'Aggie', built in 1862 'on the same heroic scale as the Crystal Palace and St Pancras station'. John Stuart Mill had addressed the Reform movement in it. 'It would be a great tragedy, tantamount to an historical amnesia, if the Royal Agricultural Hall were to be razed from the London townscape.'[20] However, Cedric Price wrote, 'Sir John Betjeman and his friends must be suffering from architectural amnesia to compare that third-rate building with the Crystal Palace. I look forward to their appeal for the saving of Earls Court. Thank goodness they were all too young to appeal on behalf of old Newgate Jail.'[21] The Hall's owner, Ronald Lawrence, had withdrawn a plan to renovate it, after what he described as 'prolonged controversy and indecision'. The 'Aggie' was saved, however, and is now the Business Design Centre, Islington.

John's most significant campaign of 1974 was in defence of Holy Trinity Church, Sloane Street, London – the church on which he had written a poem in the 1930s.[22] As Dr Gavin Stamp has written, this was an important case, as it exposed the vulnerability of historic churches under historic-building legislation: if they were in use, no protection was guaranteed, no matter how fine they were. John wrote: 'Holy Trinity is a celebration of the Arts and Crafts movement. It only lacks a bishop's throne to be the Cathedral of West London.'[23] It was full of stained glass and metalwork by such artists as Sir Edward Burne-Jones, F. W. Pomeroy and Hamo Thorneycroft.

* On John's visit to Southend pier with Simon Jenkins, see Chapter 26, 'Simon Jenkins and a Trip to Southend'.

I recall [Dr Stamp writes] that JB thought that emphasis on the financial problems with the church – estimates for repair rapidly escalated – was just a cynical ploy to redevelop the site. One Lord Cadogan had given the site of the first church, another had given more land and paid for [J. D.] Sedding's church. Now their successor was more interested in promoting a scheme to redevelop the church site altogether with Cadogan Estate land immediately adjacent. JB would point out that Lord Cadogan and the Rector were old friends, that both the Cadogan Estate and the Church Commissioners would benefit financially from building a block of flats with a worship centre on the site near Sloane Square, and that all those involved – churchwardens, the Church Commissioners' surveyors, Lord Cadogan – were Freemasons. I am sure he was right.[24]

Holy Trinity was badly damaged in 1941, and although re-roofed by 1951 it was never thoroughly restored. By 1969 the Rector, the Rev. A. B. Carter, was complaining about the cost of the building: 'My job is to preach Christianity – not beg for funds.'[25] In June 1971 plans were announced to demolish the church and redevelop the site.[26] John condemned these as 'the height of irresponsibility'. The Greater London Council and the Victorian Society also vehemently opposed the scheme.

It should be stressed [Dr Stamp writes] that JB's rôle was not only in generating publicity . . . for he wrote careful, forceful letters to all involved. I have a copy of one he sent to D. H. Piper, churchwarden and Mayor of Chelsea, 17 July 1974. 'I believe that the P.C.C. must now face the fact that redevelopment, however tempting, is out of the question under the present Pastoral Measure, and that in the future public opinion is likely to demand a strengthening rather than a relaxation of measures for the protection of buildings of architectural interest . . . To speak of an architectural masterpiece in terms of "obsolete plant" is counterproductive and can only result in loss of public sympathy when it is most needed.'[27]

It was about the time of that letter – mid-1974 – that John contacted Stamp. He knew him because Stamp had approached him in 1973, via Gerard Irvine, asking if he would write a short introduction to a book of architectural fantasies Stamp had drawn, *The Architect's Calendar*.[28] John admired Stamp's drawings, which might have been the work of an accomplished 'black-and-white' artist of *c*.1904. He now asked him to make drawings of Holy Trinity which he would offer to the parish to sell, to generate both income and publicity – knowing that the offer would be declined. *A Plea for Holy Trinity Sloane Street* was published in 1974 with an ironic foreword by John – 'After a long period of thought and prayer the Rector and congregation have decided that there is no way of retaining the present building as a centre of worship except by pulling it down and building a new church. Unless something is done, Sedding's irreplaceable church and the works of art especially designed for it will be destroyed for ever and dispersed.'[29] John and Stamp both made sure that the booklet generated a great deal of unwelcome publicity for the parish and Lord Cadogan.[30]

'That did the trick,' Stamp concludes; though he also credits John with strengthening the campaign by a second poem he wrote about Holy Trinity, published in the *Sunday Times* on 15 September 1974, above a photograph of the chancel screen and one of Pomeroy's bronze angels –

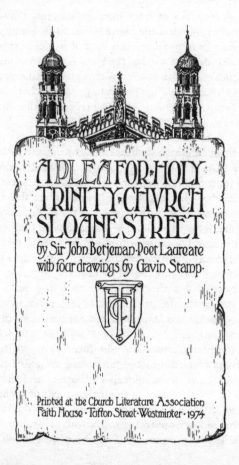

A PLEA FOR·HOLY TRINITY·CHVRCH SLOANE STREET
by Sir John Betjeman·Poet Laureate
with four drawings by Gavin Stamp·

Printed at the Church Literature Association
Faith House·Tufton Street·Westminster·1974

> Bishop, archdeacon, rector, wardens, mayor
>> Guardians of Chelsea's noblest house of prayer.
> You your church's vastiness deplore
>> 'Should we not sell and give it to the poor?'
> Recall, despite your practical suggestion,
>> Which the disciple was who asked that question.

This was written the year after John was publicly criticized for his poem about Princess Anne's wedding. The stab of satire proved how effective he could still be when he chose his own subject and his emotions were engaged.

Gavin Stamp feels that the Holy Trinity campaign had a number of valuable long-term consequences.

> There was no more talk of redevelopment after this although as Peyton Skipwith says in his guide to the church (2002), Holy Trinity remained generally closed and was 'as though in a state of parochial sulks' for the following two decades. The hand of the Victorian Society in fighting for the best nineteenth-century churches was strengthened; it eventually became possible for Historic Buildings grants to go to churches in use and the C of E tightened up its own mechanisms for protecting churches while public attention was focused on the ecclesiastical exemption . . .[31]

In 2002 Peyton Skipwith dedicated his fine guide to Holy Trinity: 'IN MEMORIAM J. D. Sedding, George 5th Earl Cadogan and Sir John Betjeman, architect, patron and preserver, respectively, of the Church of The Holy Trinity, Upper Chelsea'. The tribute to John was just. When he passed that church, towards the end of his life, he knew that, but for him, it might well not be standing; and that was some consolation for the scandalous demolition of St Agnes', Kennington, the George Gilbert Scott jr church he had vainly tried to save in the Fifties.

Yet another pier was threatened in January 1975, the West Pier at Brighton, an ethereal silvery structure then 108 years old.[32] Even people only in their thirties in 1975 could remember, in the 1940s, the Victorian slot-machine tableaux still in macabre use on the pier – 'The Miser's Dream' and 'The Execution of Mary Queen of Scots' in which a miniature axe swung down and the queen's composition head fell with a satisfying clunk on to the floor, and the ghost train and the helter-skelter and the decorous sepia glimpses of frothy petticoats above plump Victorian ankles in the flicker-cards of 'What the Butler Saw' machines. In March 1975, about three hundred people marched along Brighton promenade to protest at the plans, among them the actor John Mills, who punned, 'What have we got left in England except piers and royalty?'[33] John had written the campaigners a letter of support. The pier was reprieved – though it was later allowed to fall into ruin, a mess of mangled minarets.

In June, John and others wrote to *The Times* in concern for the White Horse of Uffington. 'In our opinion the White Horse is in great danger. The protective fence has recently been removed . . . The distinctive outlines are now being eroded.'[34] (Ironically, one of John's co-signatories was Geoffrey Grigson, who was to recall, soon after John's death in 1984, that in the 1930s John had stood on the backside of the White Horse and 'gravely cursed' him, after he had rejected 'The Arrest of Oscar Wilde at the Cadogan Hotel'.)[35]

In July 1975 John launched a national appeal to save old farm buildings at Coate, near Swindon, where Richard Jefferies was born and spent most of his life. The outbuildings were constructed by Jefferies's father, James, about 1840.[36] The appeal for £7,000 was a sequel to John's campaign of 1938 for the Jefferies–Williams Memorial. Once again, Henry Williamson gave his support, though this was by now a mixed blessing, as older people had not forgotten his fascist views. Nevertheless, enough money was raised to restore a stable, dairy and pigsties.

John was girding himself for a greater campaign, nearer his heart. In February 1975 he had written to me that there was much he wanted to talk about under three headings, one of which was 'Liverpool Street station and Hotel and Broad Street station', a topic which 'must be confidential for the moment'.[37] In August – the day after the Government announced that two bays of the Liverpool Street train sheds of 1872 were to be listed as Grade II – John and others wrote to *The Times* to oppose British Rail's plans to redevelop Liverpool Street and Broad Street and the Great Eastern Hotel.

British Rail were claiming that, because of the future operating requirements of the station, all the existing buildings at Liverpool Street must be demolished and replaced by a brand new station. Allegedly to pay for the new station, they were proposing 'a vast commercial development', consisting of 840,000 square feet of lettable office space, a shopping centre, and a new 300-bed hotel, at a total cost of £120 million. John and his allies counter-claimed that this total redevelopment was unnecessary; the station could be brought up to date by adapting the existing buildings. 'Liverpool Street's trainsheds, with their breathtaking fan-vaulting and aisle-and-transept form, can be described as a cast-iron citadel of the railway age . . .' John wrote. 'The Great Eastern Hotel . . . contains some of the most spectacular Victorian and Edwardian interiors in London.' He and his co-signatories suggested that the City of London, as the local planning authority, should mount an exhibition to put forward both cases to the public.[38]

On 11 August, P. R. Dashwood, managing director of the British Railways Property Board, irritably replied that the Liverpool Street Station Campaign (LISSCA) had *already* mounted an exhibition, in advance of the exhibition planned by British Railways Board. 'They gave us no prior notice of their intentions, less still did they invite us to exhibit our proposals alongside theirs.' He was annoyed that LISSCA were continuing to claim that 'It has been *proved* that . . . total redevelopment is unnecessary . . .' That, Dashwood wrote, was just not true. 'It would be rash for me to challenge Sir John Betjeman's well known lyrical description of Liverpool Street, but I suspect that the vast number of travellers who use this essentially functional building do not see it in the same way.' On the same page, his argument was reinforced by a letter from P. C. Hyde 'on behalf of the long-suffering East Anglian commuters', who complained of the overcrowding on trains from Liverpool Street. 'Sentiment is a fine emotion, but sentiment will not improve services from Liverpool Street . . . The Great Eastern Railway has far too long been the Cinderella of British Rail services.' And Alan Delgado asked: 'Have Dr Nuttgens, Sir John Betjeman and others ever trudged up (or down) the "elegant Florentine stairway" at Broad Street station carrying a bag in the rush hour? . . . Have they, I wonder, struggled with luggage up and down the staircases at Liverpool Street station to reach the platform they require?'[39] John replied that he agreed about the complications of finding the Underground stations and taxi ranks at Liverpool Street. 'But the righting of these wrongs need not involve the destruction of the present stately trainsheds. As we know from the brochure published by the developers, the City skyline will be submerged in an enormous bulk of offices stretching from Broad Street to Bishopsgate. Under these, as crushed and puzzled as they are at Euston, will be the passengers at Liverpool Street if this grandiose scheme is realized.'[40] A compromise was reached. Bernard Kaukas, who was chief architect of British Rail at the time, recalls:

> It was not true that the big commercial development was necessary to pay for the new station – something the preservationists constantly claimed. British Rail had no remit from the Government to use the money for that. It was true that the Government pressed on us the idea of commercial development. I think I did eventually get John to see that it wasn't British Rail architects who said, 'Let's pull down all this muck and put up something new.' We were servants of the Government. Early on, I realized that all that the preservationists really cared about was the western train shed;

they didn't worry much about the offices. And we *did* compromise – we very quickly decided that the western train shed should remain.[41]

In November 1976 John wrote with Lord David Cecil and Lady Birkenhead to appeal for £30,000 for the Keats Memorial in Rome.[42] In May 1977 – the year of the Queen's Silver Jubilee – he made a 'Jubilee appeal' with Trevor Huddleston (by now Bishop of Stepney) for three churches by Hawksmoor – St George in the East, Christ Church, Spitalfields and St Anne, Limehouse. Because St George's had been bombed, it had received 'war damage' money for restoration; but the other two churches needed 'financial resources quite beyond the capacity of the local Christian community'.[43] Christ Church, Spitalfields, finally received an adequate grant from National Lottery funds in 1996.

In June 1977 John sent a letter of support to the Grasmere Village Society, which aimed to save Wordsworth's village from 'the wrong sort of development'.[44] In the same month, he was 'sad to hear of the impending destruction of the Countess of Huntingdon chapel surviving in what is left of Worcester'. The building of 1804–15 was 'like the hold of a wooden ship'. He implored the City Fathers of Worcester to find a use for it before it was too late.[45] The building was saved and renovated and is now an arts venue in the centre of Worcester, known as Huntingdon Hall.

In September, the *Times* Diary, never friendly toward John when the left-wing Michael Leapman was diarist, made fun of his campaign to save St Mary-le-Strand.

Sir John Betjeman managed to perplex a church-full of conservationists yesterday after summoning them by bells to St Mary-le-Strand. The aging Poet Laureate, who was last in the news over that awful Silver Jubilee hymn of his, was at the church to launch a £400,000 appeal to clean and restore it.

He chose the occasion to expound what he called a rather hopeless dream, which had one anxious about him. Sir John, who is now 71, said he had a vain desire to arrive at the church via the Thames, which he thought should be unembanked and widened.

'In my dream you would arrive on an unembanked Thames with the water flowing under the arches of Somerset House,' he said. 'One would arrive by barge, disembark and walk up the steps into the great square of Somerset House and across it to St Mary-le-Strand. It would be the most marvellous architectural walk in London, probably in Europe.'[46]

John described the church's interior as 'a baroque paradise'. The 260-year-old building by James Gibbs needed cleaning and restoration, which would cost £400,000. 'Sir John's other plans . . . are expected to cost a little more,' the Diary suggested.[47] To raise funds for the campaign, John wrote a poem about the church. Rendered in neat calligraphy and printed, it was sold as a parchment-like broadsheet. The verse was vigorous; the signature underneath it painfully shaky.

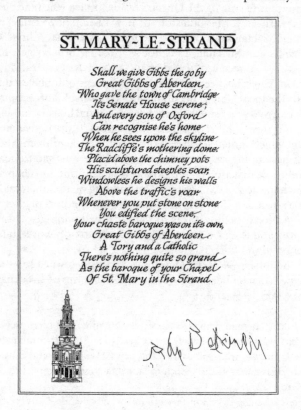

ST. MARY~LE~STRAND

Shall we give Gibbs the go by
Great Gibbs of Aberdeen,
Who gave the town of Cambridge
Its Senate House serene;
And every son of Oxford
Can recognise he's home
When he sees upon the skyline
The Radcliffe's mothering dome:
Placid above the chimney pots
His sculptured steeples soar,
Windowless he designs his walls
Above the traffic's roar
Whenever you put stone on stone
You edified the scene,
Your chaste baroque was on its own,
Great Gibbs of Aberdeen
A Tory and a Catholic
There's nothing quite so grand
As the baroque of your Chapel
Of St. Mary in the Strand.

In September 1977 John went on a pious pilgrimage to Stoke Poges churchyard, to appeal for £5,000 to restore the classical sarcophagus to Thomas Gray's memory which had been erected in 1779 by John Penn, grandson of the founder of Pennsylvania.[48] In February 1978 the National Trust acquired the Crown Liquor Saloon, Belfast (1885), one of the most ornate pubs in Britain. They were influenced by John's praise of the building: 'The Crown Liquor Saloon is a many-coloured tavern. Look at the detail with the same care you would if you were on an antiquarian church crawl.'[49] Stained-glass windows, shattered in an IRA bomb blast, had been replaced.

In June 1978 John, with the actor Marius Goring and other members of a trust for the restoration of Wilton's Music Hall, said they could not support a plan to restore the Victorian music hall in the East End of London. Goring thought the owner's plans were inadequate to turn the building into a working theatre.[50] Wilton's was saved. In September John, with Lady Antrim, Lady Longford and Julian Jebb protested at a proposed tower block which would 'dwarf and darken the courtyard' of the Pheasantry, Chelsea – a short walk from John's home in Radnor Walk.[51] In the same month, with Peter Pears, Robert Gittings, Jon Stallworthy, Norah Smallwood, Ian Parsons and others, John proposed a memorial to the war poet Wilfred Owen, who was killed in November 1918, a week before the Armistice. The memorial would be in the village church of Dunsden, near Reading, where Owen had been lay assistant to the Vicar from 1911 to 1913, and where his parents were buried.[52]

In March 1979 John launched the celebration of the 150th anniversary of London's bus service, travelling to the Guildhall in a horse-drawn bus plastered with Colman's Mustard advertisements and walking unsteadily in front of the bus in a parade.[53] In July he became president of a new National Piers Society.[54] In September he deplored the destruction of more Georgian houses in Bloomsbury.[55] He was visiting Southend Pier in July 1980. The pier was again threatened with closure, after a bad fire of 1976. John repeated his remark about being able to go to sea without being sea-sick.[56]

In a letter to The Times (16 January 1980), the Archbishop of Canterbury, Donald Coggan, with Henry Moore and Lord Alexander of Tunis, fired a salvo in what was to be John's last great conservation battle. They complained that the proposed tower of the European Ferries office block, opposite the Tate Gallery on the south bank of the Thames, would be nearly twice as high as Big Ben – 'so colossal that it is known as "The Green Giant", being clad in green glass, or by local campaigners as "The Incredible Hulk of the South Bank".' A front-page Times news report on 14 January had named John among the tower's opponents. Four days later, Lord Duncan-Sandys, president of the Civic Trust, was quoted as saying that the block would be 'the thin edge of the wedge', leading to 'a forest of giants'. (The tower was to be 500 feet high and 260 feet wide.) But in the same issue of the paper, the developers' architect, E. L. Howard, making the case for the building, said that the Archbishop and his co-signatories had complained of 'a lack of publicity' but, in reality, the developers had taken pains to ensure publicity. There had been two public exhibitions, 'one of them within 100 yards of the Archbishop's London residence'. The Archbishop and the other correspondents had described the building as clad in green glass. 'This is not so,' Howard wrote. 'It is clad in a light tinted glass giving an appearance of transparency . . .' And on 24 January proponents of the plan called a meeting to answer what they called 'misleading and ill-informed criticisms'. Sir Peter Shepheard, Professor of Architecture and Environmental Design at Pennsylvania University, described the tower as 'probably one of the most distinguished [buildings] since the Second World War'. On 7 June a *Times* news report appeared, headed 'Green giant objectors fear failure'. The protesters expected the 'giant' to win when Michael Heseltine, Secretary of State for the Environment, announced that he would make his decision within the next four weeks. Lady Wynne-Jones, chairman of the Friends of Chelsea, said, 'If the block goes ahead it will be disastrous for London. It will be death to the city; the greatest tragedy you can imagine. The identity of the city will be completely lost.' Lord Duncan-Sandys called the tower 'this vast green slab'. On 23 June, in a Lords debate, peers attacked the 'monstrous green giant project'. The next day, a shareholder of European Ferries, R. Arnold Rosen, attacked the 'green giant' at the company's annual general meeting and asked to see the files on the scheme. Rosen, a barrister, said, 'I deplore the policy of this company in wanting to build out of all proportion from what has been built already.' Some of the proposals, he said, were 'more worthy of Attila the Hun than a public company'. On 18 July 1980, Michael Heseltine rejected the 'green giant' scheme for the South Bank. He made the announcement 'to a visibly surprised audience at the Royal Institute of British Architects' annual conference in Newcastle-upon-Tyne'.[57]

John was to be involved in a few other campaigns. In 1980 Clevedon pier was threatened with destruction. He had known it since the days when he used to stay at Clevedon Court with his schoolfriend Sir Arthur Elton. The pier was a delicate structure, built out of railway metal. It had partially collapsed, and the local authority said it could not go on repairing it and that it was 'dangerous'. An inquiry was held and once again Paul Chadd represented the protesters. He asked John if he would be a witness. John was by now too ill to attend, but adopted a stratagem he had last used in 1935 when he was unable to attend the 'Evening of Bad Taste' party in London:[58] he sent a recorded message. This time it was a short tape-recording. Of Clevedon he said, 'I think it is a gem among the coastal towns'; of the pier, 'It is such a beautiful and elegant cast-iron structure. It recalls a painting by Turner or etching by Whistler or Sickert or even a Japanese print . . .'[59] And he read plangent lines of Tennyson about Clevedon. 'It wasn't so much what John said,' Chadd recalls. 'The essence of it was his *voice*, like the disembodied voice in a séance.'[60] Chadd thought John's plea had some effect. 'But what was probably more convincing than his romantic description of the pier was the economic argument we put forward: demolition was going to cost a hell of a lot!'[61] Clevedon pier has been completely restored.

In 1981 John raged at a proposal to demolish part of Alfred Waterhouse's Natural History Museum, and again appealed for funds to save St Mary-le-Strand. ('It looks like a grotto inside and its outside is familiar to all Londoners from the cover of the Strand Magazine.')[62] In November 1981 he attacked a proposal to build a new estate in the grounds of Witanhurst, below Highgate Village, a house he had known since early childhood.[63] (In 2002 it became the setting for *Fame Academy*, a series on BBC television; the rich neighbours complained about the noise the would-be pop stars caused.) And in August 1982 he wrote a letter – as erudite and eloquent as ever – when he heard that St Barnabas, Pimlico was to become redundant.[64] But the vanquishing of the 'green giant' was his last grand victory. It symbolized the way a preservationist David could defeat a Goliath of a developer. It had been a model campaign: the protest by a formidable group of people, rather than one person; the branding of the building as the 'green giant', a picturesque smear-phrase that fitted easily into newspaper headlines; the mention of 'opposite the Tate Gallery', as though the nation's art heritage were somehow imperilled; Duncan-Sandys's prophecy of a 'thin end of the wedge' (exactly the tactic John had used in the Letcombe Bassett fight);[65] the speeches in Parliament; the keeping up of a constant din of protest until the Government capitulated. John did not intervene directly with a letter, but he allowed his name to be brandished, and his influence was felt behind the scenes. He had been at Magdalen with Duncan-Sandys; as a Chelsea resident he was in touch with the Chelsea Society; the Archbishop was a friend and consulted him on architectural questions.

The Times said of Michael Heseltine's speech to the RIBA conference that it 'went beyond specific planning issues and amounted to an indictment of much that has happened to the physical face of Britain in the past 35 years'.[66] Heseltine had no doubt carefully chosen a gallery to play to, though he was not without credentials as a preservationist. In 1979 he had yielded to the plea of the newly formed Thirties Society (now the Twentieth-Century Society) – of which John was a patron – to list the Art Deco Firestone factory, but the developers demolished the building the night before the order was due to come into force.[67] Heseltine's speech to the architects at Newcastle could be read as a benediction on everything John had striven for in more than half a century of preservation campaigns.

Mr Heseltine said that the quality of a generation's architecture was perhaps the most conspicuous legacy it left behind. The buildings constructed now and those that were retained and conserved would remain long after the day-to-day political battles were forgotten.

'Who, a century from now, will care about the political issues which dominate this week's national newspaper headlines?' he asked. 'Very few of these will survive as a memorial of our generation.

'But if we take the wrong decision now on how to use sites properly in the centre of our capital, we shall not be so easily forgotten nor, dare I say, forgiven.'[68]

Illustration by Gavin Stamp for the 1974 booklet about Holy Trinity, Chelsea, which he compiled with John

BANANA BLUSH

I must write to tell you . . . how entranced I am with your brilliant and sympathetic music to my verses. They [*sic*] give the poems a new dimension and are as varied as a Gala Performance at the Palladium, or better still, the Empire or the Alhambra, Leicester Square.

Sir John Betjeman, letter to Jim Parker, 22 March 1974

It was John's affection for the Isle of Man that led, indirectly, to his making four records between 1974 and 1981, combining his poetry with the music of Jim Parker. Like his favourite college at Oxford, Pembroke, the island was slightly off-beat, an unobvious choice. Perhaps his first interest in it was inspired by Walter Scott's novel *Peveril of the Peak*, which, he told H.S. Goodhart-Rendel in 1949, 'started a romantic craze for the Isle of Man'.[1] He made references to the island in his poem 'The Exile', published in 1938,[2] and contributed an essay on it to the book *Portraits of Islands* (1951).[3] He admired its Victorian architecture, the houses Baillie Scott had built while living there, the narrow-gauge railways,[4] the silver and watercolours of Archibald Knox,[5] the poetry of the Manxman T.E. Brown and the novels of Hall Caine, whom he described to Simon Jenkins as 'the Shakespeare of the Isle of Man'.[6] He bought a supply of Manx postage stamps; when using them, he printed on the envelopes, with a rubber stamp: 'Note the charming Manx stamp.'[7] In the late 1970s he was patron of the Isle of Man Festival.[8] 'The island', he wrote, 'is all an old sensualist like me could desire.'[9]

In 1970 John was asked if he would give a reading of Kipling at the Royal Court Theatre, Chelsea. He was flattered to be invited, and liked the idea of appearing on stage, but was dubious about presenting a programme of Kipling. 'Imperialism' was then notably out of favour, and in any case he preferred Newbolt. He replied: 'I will do Kipling, if I can also do T.E. Brown.'[10] The Royal Court's response was 'Who?', but after John had spent an evening explaining his enthusiasm for the Manx poet, his suggestion was accepted. He said that he would read

.. Kipling works, but that somebody with a Manx accent, or who could 'do a Manx accent', must be found for the Brown poems. His old Oxford friend Douglas Cleverdon, now at the BBC, suggested that the man for the job was William Bealby-Wright, who had grown up on the Isle of Man, with a Manx mother.[11] Although Bealby-Wright's normal way of speaking was British upper-middle class, he could do a Manx accent very convincingly. The Royal Court programme was a success; later, John and Bealby-Wright made a long-playing record of Brown's poetry and prose, *Manxman*.

Through the show and the recording, John became a friend of Bealby-Wright and his wife Susan Baker, often visiting them and their young children at their house on Parliament Hill, Highgate, the land of his own earliest memories. Bealby-Wright remembers John's pointing up at 'a rather hideous block of flats opposite the Magdala pub' and saying, 'Look! Early Crittall [the manufacturers of metal window-frames]!'[12] John was fascinated to hear about Bealby-Wright's parents: his mother, the Manxwoman, was Jane Bacon, who had been a leading lady at the Old Vic in the 1920s; his father, George Bealby, who had committed suicide when William was a year old, was a Grand Guignol actor whose first wife had been Mabel Beardsley, the sister of Aubrey Beardsley, so William could almost claim to be a 'step-nephew' of the artist.[13] Susan Baker's father had also been an actor.[14]

The couple were both members of a group called the Barrow Poets, which read poetry and played music in pubs.[15] 'Eventually,' Susan Baker recalled, 'the performances in pubs got so packed out that even the landlord couldn't get to the Gents.'[16] A forceful character, in 1960 she took charge of the Barrow Poets. In 1963 they made their first appearance at the Aldeburgh Festival. Poetry 'took off' in the 1960s, bringing popularity to the Barrow Poets and the Liverpool Poets who included Roger McGough and Adrian Henri. The 'Barrows' read other people's poems (among them, some of John's) and their own, with musical accompaniment. Susan Baker played the violin; Bealby-Wright played an extraordinary one-man-band instrument called a cacofiddle. They sometimes gave as many as two hundred concerts a year. 'There is not a festival we haven't played in,' Susan Baker says.[17] They made commercially successful tours of America. No book was published of the Barrow Poets' poems. They operated like a musical pop group, with live performances and later with records. People came and went in the group, but by the end of the Sixties it had solidified into six members: Susan Baker and William Bealby-Wright, with Cicely Smith, Heather Black, Gerard Benson and the composer–oboist–pianist Jim Parker.

Born in 1934, Jim Parker had grown up in wartime Hartlepool. He had worked in an accountant's office for two years after leaving school

Susan Baker   Jim Parker   Cicely Smith   William Bealby-Wright   Heather Black Gerard Benson

at sixteen – 'but I really wanted to be a musician so I joined the army, the Dragoon Guards band, which doesn't exist any more'.[18] By now he was based in County Durham, whose rich local authority gave him a large grant to study at the Guildhall School of Music for four years. Next he joined the Birmingham Symphony Orchestra as an oboist. Then he freelanced in London for a while before meeting the Barrow Poets. He was invited to join the group. 'It became a full-time occupation for about eight years.'[19]

Apart from his skills as an oboist and pianist, Parker's great value to the Barrow Poets was that he could look at a poem and write incidental music in character with it. 'It was much more interesting than playing the oboe in an orchestra,' he says. 'When the poetry boom eased off, *we* eased off and eventually I moved across to writing music for records and television programmes. But it was quite big for a time. At one stage we actually did the Queen Elizabeth Hall for seven nights, with some afternoon shows as well. We made a lot of records for different companies. You could go along to companies in those days with an idea – you'd sell about twelve copies of the resulting record; then you'd wait for a few months and approach another company with another idea.'[20] In 1972 they made the record *Joker* for RCA and the records *Outpatient* and (for children) *Magic Egg* for Decca. Bealby-Wright, who had studied art at the Ruskin School in Oxford, designed record-sleeves in hippie style. A splinter-group of the Barrow Poets, known as Doggerel Bank (Baker, Bealby-Wright, Parker) recorded *Silver Faces* (1973) and *Mr Skillercorn Dances* (1975) for a company in Wardour Street, London, called Charisma. It was owned by an enterprising if slightly fly man, Tony Stratton-Smith, who had previously run reggae groups and edited *The Football Year Book*. The producer of the Doggerel Bank records was Hugh Murphy, described by Susan Baker as 'a boy with long hair and one earring, very working-class . . . an interesting person'.[21]

Baker and Bealby-Wright invited Murphy to stay; he said at dinner one day, 'I'd love to produce John Betjeman poems.'[22] Murphy admired John for reasons quite other than those which made the poet the darling of the Women's Institutes. 'To me – even though it was in the midst of the Sixties when I discovered it – Betjeman's time was roughly the same sort of time in history as mine. When he was young it was the Twenties, and the Twenties were incredibly exciting as well . . . There was a parallel.'[23] Murphy wanted the poems to have a musical accompaniment. Susan Baker told him: 'We know John Betjeman very well. I'll introduce you to him, but only if you promise to use Jim Parker as composer.'[24] When Murphy returned to England, he took the idea to Tony Stratton-Smith, who liked it. John had just become Poet Laureate. Here, perhaps, was a poetry-and-music record that would sell more than twelve copies. Before attempting to set any of John's poems to music, Parker bought a record of his reading them, on the Argo label, to find out how he delivered them. 'He had a very definite interpretation of each poem,' Parker says. 'He was an extremely good performer. He never spoke in tempo. Some people can adapt and do a *Sprechgesang* [spoken song] but I had the feeling that he would not be comfortable doing that. Somehow I had to work out a way to let him speak his poems just as he usually did, *not* in tempo.'[25]

Susan Baker telephoned John to invite him to dinner, broaching the idea of a musical record. John was doubtful about the plan – 'I always thought poetry was its own music,' he said – but he accepted the invitation. In the big music room at the Parliament Hill house, where the Barrow Poets had often rehearsed their performances, William Bealby-Wright spoke the words, while Jim Parker accompanied him on a portable harmonium. 'John was tickled pink by this miniature harmonium,' Parker recalls. 'It was the size of a small coffin; the legs came down. It was the sort of small instrument that seaside performers used to take on to the beach.'[26] John was delighted by the settings, though he vetoed one poem, about death. He had a try at reciting the poems with the musical accompaniment (he knew all his poems by heart). It was not a success. Bealby-Wright recalls:

His voice had a most natural rhythm which sometimes spread over the music in the right sort of way; but we had great trouble with one poem.

I thought it might be a good idea if I stood in front of him and mouthed it. And I thought, what I've got to do is mouth it as dramatically as possible so that he will follow it. And he was just mesmerized by this idiot face in front of him, with rolling eyes and gestures. The whole thing was a total fiasco . . .[27]

In spite of this set-back, John was so impressed with Parker's settings that he agreed to make a record.

During the next few weeks John, Jim Parker and Murphy worked out which poems should be chosen. It was Murphy who thought of the title *Banana Blush*, from John's early poem 'The Flight from Bootle', which begins:

> Lonely in the Regent Palace,
>   Sipping her 'Banana Blush',
> Lilian lost sight of Alice
>   In the honey-coloured rush.

'There were fifty minutes' worth of time on the record,' Parker remembers, '– poetry and music. Much more music than poetry. I got a system worked out: each poem would have a tune, that would be the "theme". It probably wouldn't happen at the same time as the poem. It would start; then the poem would take over; then a rest for John – music for two or three stanzas. I wasn't sure how John would take to this, but we agreed where it would stop. All he had to do was to read the poem, up to where it said "stop".'[28] As with his settings for the Barrow Poets, Parker looked at each poem carefully and gave it whatever music it seemed to suggest – 'Lagondas purring down the drive' music for 'Indoor Games near Newbury'; 'geysers, and waste pipes chuckling into runnels' music for 'Business Girls'; 'shimmering water' music for 'Youth and Age on Beaulieu River, Hants'. Many of the poems were of Twenties and Thirties subjects. Though Parker had never played in a palm-court trio, he had played in dance bands as well as military bands and knew how to mock up a *thé dansant* sound.

The recordings were made in a studio in Willesden.[29] John was usually driven there by Hugh Murphy. Each morning Murphy would pick him up in Radnor Walk and strap him into the passenger seat of his Volkswagen Beetle. 'And I'd take different routes each day . . . And he'd point out things, all the time. I was passing Kensal Rise. He'd tell me who was buried there. He'd be looking up, he'd see the tops of buildings and remember what they used to be. I had a running commentary by John Betjeman. I didn't really appreciate it at the time.'[30] Murphy added:

> All the musicians were sitting there with their headphones on when we got there. 'Hello!' – and he brought out his little packet of pastilles because he knows when he's talking his voice goes, and he was putting a pastille in his mouth – 'Hello, how are you?' And I got him comfortable and put mikes in front of him and said, 'Is it okay?' And Betjeman had *not the first sense of rhythm*. He couldn't count a bar. He just sat there while they went through it. And at the end he said, 'Oh, that was lovely. That was absolutely *lovely*.' He thought every take was great. I don't think he was intimidated by the fact that he had to do it to music, because he wasn't aware that there was a problem – that there were eight bars and then you had to come in. He thought he could just talk anywhere and it would be all right. So it was quite difficult. That's why I had to be with him all of the time to tell him exactly where to come in or direct the engineer to drop in at the right time, and I'd say, 'Leave a gap here.'[31]

Instrumentally, Parker used 'a sort of Thirties dance band. We tried to get the atmosphere of the Thirties – a kind of innocence.' He did what he often did on records, which was to subdivide the material into various sessions, using a big band on one and a small band on another. 'It all balanced up: we'd get in one session on the pieces which were most crucial to having a lot of musicians and then try to economize on the others. The biggest we had was about fourteen players – four saxes, four brass, three rhythm with a few other people: Susan played the violin, I and my younger brother Tom played the piano, someone played the banjo. In "Business Girls" we used a steel guitar – I don't know why, except that it sounded nice, which is a good enough reason. That again was Hugh Murphy's idea. He said, "You should use a steel guitar." I said, "What's that?" I worked out it was what we used to call a Hawaiian guitar, electric. There used to be a group called Felix Mendelssohn and his Hawaiian Serenaders donkeys years ago, they used to play "Come back to wherever it was . . . Aloha, Aloha", all that. It's used today in American country music. If you see Dolly Parton there's often a chap with a thing on a table that looks like a zither. This is the steel guitar. It has a pedal on it, they can sustain it and do swoops. Rod King played it on *Banana Blush*.'[32] Susan Baker played the mandoline for John's reading of 'Longfellow's Visit to Venice'. Parker noticed that 'John's American accent was not spot on – he said "Tintoretto" when he should have said "Tinnoreddo" – but somehow that was right, it would have seemed too "clever" to have a perfect imitation. He was better on the north-country accent for "A Shropshire Lad", though I remember he told me that when he went to Hull to see Philip Larkin, John went up to a bar and ordered a drink in his northern accent, to amuse Larkin, and the barmaid said, in a huffy voice, "We don't speak laike that in Hull." '[33]

A strong musical rhythm runs through most of the settings. 'The idea was', Parker says, 'that this was essentially a pop label. Tony Stratton-Smith wanted to sell records, he didn't want an esoteric setting, the sort that Schoenberg did. And I agreed with him. The poems are very immediate, very accessible, and I felt the music ought to be the same. So that is why quite a lot of them have a rhythm going through them, although it wasn't actually a modern rhythm most of the time, it tended to be a fairly old-fashioned and traditional rhythm; but then they weren't modern poems, they were very traditional and well-structured.'[34]

John read his words in a glass box in the studio. 'I brought him in, he knew where to stop,' Parker says. 'On that first record there is a slight problem in hearing the words sometimes – we dealt with that in later records. If you raised the level of the voice, you also raised the saxophones. They call it "spill" in the record industry. You say, "Can we have a bit more trumpet?" They turn the trumpet up and you get the saxes as well, because they're spilling on to each other's mikes. Obviously John's glass box wasn't totally soundproof. He was wearing headphones: the music came to him through one of them, his own voice through the other.'[35]

Parker adopted an old music-hall device for getting round the problem of John's not speaking in strict tempo. 'I used what are called "till ready" bars, because otherwise I would have had to write the music to fit exactly the time he was going to take, out of tempo, to get to a certain point. Sometimes one can do that; but if there's a rhythm going, one can't. So I had this sort of "till ready" system. "Till ready" was a thing used in music-hall – you know, you'd get this *RROOM*-boom-boom-boom, *RROOM*-boom-boom-boom, and eventually, after several goes and a few jokes they'd come in. "Till ready" is exactly what it is: you play till they're ready to start the song. It was the same idea, really, except that I was waiting for John to finish rather than waiting for him to come in. If John was falling behind we'd play the repeat bar a few times.'[36] There was one exception. Listening to 'Business Girls' on the Argo label, Parker had realized that John read that poem more or less in time. So 'Business Girls' was recorded live; music and words together, with no 'till ready' bars. 'Where he goes a bit over the end of the music, it doesn't really matter; and if he finishes a bit too soon, that doesn't matter either, because it works.'[37]

A BBC radio programme, listening in on one of the recording sessions, captured some of the frustrations:

> *John Betjeman*: 'Love so pure . . . Love so strong . . .' Oh! my brain's going.
> *Jim Parker*: Don't worry; we'd better try that again, I think.
> *John Betjeman*: I forgot it all.
> *Jim Parker*: Yes, yes. It went all right, then it sort of disintegrated. We'll do another take.[38]

Hugh Murphy paid tribute to Parker's skill and tact in working with John. 'It's Jim's sensitivity to the whole thing and his understanding that poetry is poetry and music is music and that the king, with John Betjeman, is the words. All [Jim] is doing is highlighting, like an artist would put a dab of white on an eye to bring an eye alive.'[39] Bealby-Wright thought that the secret of Parker's rapport with John was that 'Jim had learned the hard way, as we all had – with a pub audience that was quite free to answer back or leave or suggest that we do so, not a captive poetry-loving audience – to give an impression, in the opening bars, that "This is going to be all right, it's not going to hurt." '[40] There was no pretension that what was being done was 'important' – in contrast with the two groups of poetry-readers that had prevailed in the Sixties – 'Allen Ginsberg's group, who arrived like prophets from the Old Testament and bellowed' and the other school 'epitomized by Margaret Rutherford with a gold microphone in a pulpit'.[41]

Hugh Murphy designed the sleeve of the record, in Art Deco 'Banana Blush' colours – pink, lemon yellow and ice blue. On the front was a sepia photograph of John by John Garrett in the poet's 'Aren't I a card!' attitude. On the back were pictures of the recording sessions at Willesden, including one of John looking old and bewildered, his head clamped between giant headphones like the beef in a hamburger. Jim Parker asked him to inscribe one record sleeve. He drew himself with a beard and dedicated the record to Parker's daughter Claire, who was then three years old.[42]

Tony Stratton-Smith's confidence in the enterprise was justified. The record was generally well reviewed and sold well too. On 22 March 1974 John wrote to Parker:

Dear Jim,
    I must write to tell you, albeit on a typewriter for the sake of legibility, how entranced I am with your brilliant and sympathetic music to my verses. They [*sic*] give the poems a new dimension and are as varied as a Gala Performance at the Palladium, or better still, the Empire or the Alhambra, Leicester Square. I am thrilled with their effectiveness, and

many people have written to me saying how much they enjoy the record. Are you rich? I am certain you should get a large and fair percentage of the proceeds if the record sells to the waiting millions who have so far been deprived of its lyrical assistance. George McBeth [sic], while I was writing this letter, rang me up to congratulate you on the music.

Yours ever,

John B.[43]

At the same time, John was mildly worried that his becoming a pop artist might give offence at the Palace. To forestall any criticism he wrote to Major Sir Rennie Maudslay, Keeper of the Privy Purse and Treasurer to the Queen:

> I committed a lapse of taste last month and I will not be surprised if I am dismissed from my honourable office. A respectable and literary pop group called the Barrow Poets wanted me to recite some of my verse to music. This I did and was pleased with what little of the result I heard. However, the publicity of the pop world is so appalling that I was not prepared for it. They called the pop record 'Betjeman's Banana Blush'. They've had a T-shirt made for me to wear which I've refused to do. It had on it, in white letters, this frightful title. Well, I have made my confession, reverend father. It is up to you to give me my penance, counsel and absolution, if you can.[44]

The courtier replied: 'I can echo the admonition from *Hamlet*, "O shame, where is thy blush?" But as this is your first offence I am prepared to offer you a more gentle reproach from *Henry V* – "Put off your maiden blushes."'[45] John played down the record's merits in an interview with Graham Lord of the *Sunday Express*. 'The cover is the most appalling yellow and pink,' he told him, 'and it has a photo of me completely bald and sitting on a chair giggling. As for one of the pictures on the back, one friend saw it and wrote to me, "Dear Dracula".'[46] Another of the pictures on the back, which showed John holding a drink and kissing Susan Baker, attracted the notice of the Queen. 'Who is that woman?' she asked.[47]

Jim Parker did not make much money out of the record; but its success did bring him money in the long run. Unlike the Barrow Poets and Doggerel Bank records, it made his name. In 1979 the *Sprechgesang* record 'Captain Beaky', with lyrics written by Jeremy Lloyd and spoken by the actor Keith Michell, achieved Parker's ambition of breaking into the pop charts – 'I actually had to go along to *Top of the Pops* [on BBC television] to supervise Michell's performance.'[48] A second 'Captain Beaky' record appeared in 1980. Parker was much in demand for writing television theme music, such as that for the Michael Dobbs serials *House of Cards* and *To Be the King*.

The Parker settings for *Banana Blush* became popular in live performances too. The Nash Ensemble gave one at the Royal Festival Hall in June 1974. John attended and made a short speech: 'Thank you very much for coming. And thank you for finding your way through all this concrete'.[49] He wrote to Jim Parker on 6 June: 'I loved the music. I loved the acting and the audience. I even grew quite fond of the Festival Hall and this all because of Nash Ensemble and you. Many thanks.'[50]

In spite of some arguments over money, Jim Parker agreed to co-operate with Tony Stratton-Smith in making a second Betjeman record. John was enthusiastic. Parker thought that this time some sort of theme should link the poems chosen: perhaps they could be poems about women? John agreed. The title was to be *Late Flowering Love*, a squeamish adaptation of one of the poems' titles, 'Late Flowering Lust'. Parker thought up the title. 'Having suggested it, I thought, "Oh God, that's a terrible title" and I rang up and said, "Look, forget that title, it's awful," but by that time they'd got very keen on it and they wouldn't change it.'[51] Another meeting was held with John, to choose the poems. The selection included 'Station Syren', 'Sun and Fun' and 'Invasion Exercise on the Poultry Farm'. Parker did not want to make a second record with a Thirties band sound. He decided to use a consort of viols, combining it with a Fifties style of band, because a lot of the poems were post-war and would benefit from the 'big band' sound. The consort of viols, by contrast, would be ideal for the Arts and Crafts ambience of 'Narcissus'. 'Viols have a sound flatter than normal strings, which have a very warm sound; the viols make a much reedier noise.'[52] For the poem 'Late Flowering Lust', the consort of viols was combined with bass, guitar, vibraphone and timpani. The record was made on a tight budget. Parker had to work out how many musicians he could afford, at a sessions fee of £17 a musician – slightly more for the leader and for those who doubled on more than one instrument. 'I saved on the piano by doing it myself,' he says. 'Anything I could do myself, I tended to do, just so that I could save money and buy another musician who'd play something else.'[53]

On one of the two larger band sessions the famous jazz trumpeter Kenny Baker was the lead trumpeter. He performed a brilliant *ad lib* solo on 'Station Syren'. Parker played the piano with 'Sun and Fun', partly to economize and partly because a piano was what the night-club proprietress, the poem's subject, might have played. He recorded a play-out for the end of that poem which was also to be the end of the record, a coda for saxophone and rhythm section. 'Nearly all popular records at that time ended with a "fade", and ours did too.'[54]

When the recording was finished and edited, Parker played to John, who commented, 'By Jove!'[55]

Like *Banana Blush*, *Late Flowering Love* was recorded at the Willesden studios. John took Parker to Willesden Church, not to see the graves of Charles Reade and his mistress Laura Seymour, of whom he had written in his poem 'In Willesden Churchyard', but 'to interrogate the incumbent', as he put it, about the miraculous appearance, hundreds of years before, of a Black Madonna. 'So we met the Vicar,' Parker recalls, 'and we went to the very spot where this Madonna was supposed to have appeared. And it certainly sticks in my memory because it was absolutely pouring with rain. But it didn't make the slightest difference to John. He just ploughed on through the graveyard. I ended up with a terrible cold, but he seemed fine.'[56] George Melly was recording a jazz album in another studio at Willesden on the same day and was surprised to bump into John; even more surprised to hear he was recording a music album too. 'He seemed in a good humour about it,' Melly thought, '– tickled and pleased.'[57]

Two years later, in 1977, Tony Stratton-Smith thought of another reason to make a Betjeman record. John was the Poet Laureate and 1977 was the year of the Queen's Silver Jubilee. As the 'special selling point' of the record, he wanted John to write a poem for the jubilee and asked Parker to get Malcolm Williamson, the Master of the Queen's Music, to set it to music to issue on a jubilee record. 'That did not come about,' Parker says. 'We ended up with a record that had very little royal about it except the cover and John's poem on the Death of George V. It was more a celebration of Betjeman than the Queen.'[58] The record sleeve, based on the painting by Ruskin Spear of John rowing a dinghy in a boater, credited 'The New Philharmonia'. 'What that meant', Parker remembers, 'was as many members of the orchestra as I could afford – about twenty.'[59] One of the poems John read on the record was 'Hunter Trials', with a martial Parker accompaniment. 'It was not a terribly suitable poem for John to recite,' Parker thinks. 'In general, nobody ever read Betjeman better than Betjeman: attempting to do so, is like trying to play Richard III after watching the film of Olivier in the part. But here, he was an elderly man reading a young "Thelwell" girl's part. He *almost* got away with it. When I've performed it live, it has usually been with Eleanor Bron, who does it terribly well – "Miss Blewitt says Monica threw it" and all that. I think Prunella Scales would also be very good. John does it in a rather droll way which has its own charm; but when Eleanor Bron does it, she does it in time – *de diddly diddly dee* – and that's really more effective.'[60]

The record was issued as *Sir John Betjeman's Britain*. As a concession to the jubilee idea, the second side was about London. One of the poems John read was 'South London Sketch, 1944', which contains the lines

> Where the waters of the Wandle do
> Lugubriously flow.

As a break from recording, John and Parker went off to have a look at the River Wandle. 'It's just down in Wandsworth – dark brown, treacly, absolutely filthy,' Parker says. The two men stood on a small bridge and looked down. 'It really *is* "lugubrious", isn't it?' John said.[61]

As before, it was often Hugh Murphy who drove John to and from Willesden. When they returned to Radnor Walk, John would usually offer him a malt whisky. 'And he enjoyed just sitting there and watching me drink it,' Murphy said.[62] John was rather smitten by the young producer. '[He] has long, gold hair and one earring,' he told *The Observer*, 'but he's a wonderful fella.'[63] And Murphy said of John: 'I got the chance of meeting somebody who brought his time with him . . . It wasn't quite a falling in love; but in a way it was *like* falling in love, because it's a big experience.'[64] One day, John came to Murphy's office in Knightsbridge. 'We had a lovely girl there called Judy London, who was thin and very good-looking – long red hair and freckles. And he fell in love with her like you wouldn't believe. I took him home and he said, "Who was that beautiful girl? Those freckles!" She reminded him of a girl whom he wrote about.'[65] That girl, of course, was 'Freckly Jill'.[66]

As a change from Murphy, Jock Murray drove John to one of the recording sessions. Murray realized to his surprise that John – usually so fretful and nervous before any performance – was actually looking forward to the session.[67] Parker noticed how well John got on with the recording crew. 'He knew his own worth, of course, but he understood other people's value too – knew he'd be lost without them, in fact. He'd listen attentively if anybody had a point to make, whoever it was. Anyone could chip in, he didn't mind. One of the engineers told him that he'd got something wrong in his poem 'Harrow-on-the-Hill': Kenton is not to the west of Harrow, it's to the east. Without a murmur, John at once altered the line in question to, "There's a storm cloud to the eastward over Kenton", on the recording.'[68]

In 1981 Parker found an excuse to make another record with John, which was to be the last. The film-maker Charles Wallace had made a television programme and a short cinema film based on the earlier records, using the tracks he liked best. He wanted to make another Betjeman film, so he egged Parker on to persuade John to record some new arrangements. Wallace suggested the poems he would like to be recorded, among them 'Death in Leamington', 'Slough', 'Exeter' and

'The 'Varsity Students' Rag'. John agreed and the record
ally issued as *Sir John Betjeman's 'Varsity Rag*. (The inside
bore a drawing of John by Julia Whatley, perhaps the best
ever made of him.)

Cartoon of John by Julia Whatley

'John was very happy to do the record,' Parker recalls, 'because he
was doing very little at that time. It gave him something to get on
with.'[69] But Parkinson's Disease and a stroke had enfeebled him. 'He
was frail and I have to say he does sound a lot frailer. He was visibly
tired. With *'Varsity Rag* we recorded the voice first. That meant John
didn't have to come into the studio at set times any more. He came in
totally at his leisure, with nobody waiting around, so he didn't have to
rush to finish, he was just on his own. We took as many takes as we
needed, and the poems were recorded in bits. I wrote the music round
what he recorded. With the poem "'Varsity Rag" he did, for once,
actually say it in time.'[70]

Jim Parker continued to visit John at Radnor Walk. He admired the
way Lady Elizabeth Cavendish looked after him. One evening Parker
was having a drink with John and Jonathan Stedall, the television film-
maker. The telephone rang and Stedall answered it. Cupping his hand
over the receiver he whispered to John: 'Elizabeth is coming round and
she's bringing Little Friend.'

'Oh *no*!' John said. Turning to Jim Parker he asked, 'Will you stay
as well? Princess Margaret is coming to supper.' Parker did stay and
helped keep the Princess entertained in John's small dining-room.[71]

Three years later, Parker played some of John's favourite music at the poet's memorial service in Westminster Abbey, including Ketèlbey's 'In a Monastery Garden'. 'John was not very musical,' he says,

> but he liked music and words that went well together, as in hymns and music-hall songs. He loved Edgar Bateman's 'The Houses In-Between' –
>
> > Wiv a ladder and some glasses,
> > You could see to 'Ackney Marshes;
> > Wiv some tackle and a pulley
> > I'd enjoy the view more fully –
> > *If it wasn't for the 'ouses in-between.*
>
> One time, I played him a record of a music-hall song – I can't remember which. When it finished, John asked 'Who wrote that?' I told him. 'He was a *genius*', he said.[72]

To John, the best example of words going well with music was the Savoy Operas of Gilbert and Sullivan, which he had enjoyed ever since taking part in *The Pirates of Penzance* at the Dragon School. He had paid special tribute to Gilbert at his home, Grims Dyke, in the *Metro-land* film.* 'On occasions,' Jim Parker recalls, 'John would introduce me and say, "He's Sullivan and I'm Gilbert" – typically, he didn't put himself first. I think he always fancied a rather Gilbert and Sullivan relationship, and that is what we had. I wrote him the odd card signing it "Sullivan" and he wrote the odd card signed "Gilbert".'[73]

The records came out during years when John's reputation, as Laureate, was at low ebb. The presentation of some of his best earlier poems, in such an appetizing form, helped revive his popularity. A lot of people who might not have read the poems listened to the records. Parker modestly disclaims any responsibility for rehabilitating John. 'But the records did turn up on an awful lot of desert islands.'[74]

---

* See Chapter 18, '*Metro-land*'.

SIMON JENKINS AND A TRIP TO SOUTHEND

Thank God for you.

Sir John Betjeman, letter to Simon Jenkins, Easter Monday 1971

I should have written long before this to thank you for our Southend trip. From the first glance at that overgrown cemetery in Tower Hamlets to the last sunset rays over the spreading estuary.

Sir John Betjeman, letter to Simon Jenkins, 9 November 1976

Every ten years since 1841 (except for the war year 1941) a census has been held in Great Britain. In recent decades, the census has usually provoked a public row. The British do not take kindly to being asked personal questions or to being categorized and put on file. In 1951 an old lady burned her census form in a frying pan outside the House of Commons. She said she would have burned her ration book too, but it had come on to rain. In the same year John's friend Rose Macaulay wrote to Father Hamilton Johnson: 'They tell us [the census] is all absolutely private, so that burglars can put "Occupation: burglary", without the least apprehension. I wonder if they do.'[1] The 1971 census caused a controversy bigger than any before or since. There were three reasons for this. The number of questions had been greatly increased; one of the questions, on parents' origins, was taken by some to be racist; and for the first time computers were to be used to record the results. This last innovation gave rise to fears of a 'data-bank society' in which confidentiality would be threatened and details might even be sold. There were dark mutterings about *Nineteen Eighty-Four* and Big Brother. The leader of the Liberal Party, the suave opportunist Jeremy Thorpe, saw a chance to make political capital out of these fears. He stirred the anti-census feeling into a frenzy.[2] Bernard Levin, writing about the 'juicy and enjoyable' uproar in *The Times* of 15 April, dwelt with some pleasure on 'the imminent prospect of Mr Jeremy Thorpe being led away with gyves upon his wrist'.[3]

The dispute over the census also prompted an article by the *Evening Standard* columnist Simon Jenkins, who took a line different from all the other columnists. At twenty-seven, Jenkins – a future editor of both the *Standard* and *The Times* – was the blue-eyed boy of the *Standard*'s then editor, Charles Wintour. He had made a name as a writer on London architecture; it was in this year that his book *A City at Risk* was published. On 20 April Jenkins wrote in the *Standard*:

> The great census rumpus has at least served one useful purpose. It has brought under the spotlight one of London's most long-standing scandals – the use of Somerset House.
>
> Last week, while the Registrar-General, Michael Reed, did battle in his room with the Press, pressure groups and assorted MPs, I sloped off to wander round the block of offices in his command.
>
> The home of the Inland Revenue, the Registry of Births, Marriages and Deaths and the Probate Registry, Somerset House is no mere civil service building. It is one of the most magnificent palaces in London, on one of the best sites and dominating the finest view. It is quite absurd that it should be used for offices which are totally inaccessible to the public.

Jenkins suggested that Somerset House should be opened up, as soon as possible, to house one of the great national art collections, preferably the 'disgracefully neglected' British art collection at the Tate Gallery. 'Where better to show off the works of Hogarth and Stubbs, Gainsborough and Constable, and above all the still unexhibited masterpieces of Turner, than the river front of Somerset House?' Of the Registrar-General's office, with its plaster swags, ornate friezes and painted cameos, Jenkins wrote: 'What on earth is all this doing hidden behind forbidding doormen and special permits and used for storing mere statistics?'

One telling point that Jenkins neglected to make was that Somerset House had, after all, been the original home of the Royal Academy. But John Betjeman made it in a letter he wrote to the *Standard* in Jenkins's support.

> Simon Jenkins . . . rightly deplores the present misuse of Somerset House in the Strand.
>
> What could be one of the finest eighteenth-century squares, not just in the United Kingdom but in Europe, is at present a private car park for tax collectors and registrars in the very heart of London.

The public is excluded from the galleries and chambers, specially designed for the Royal Academy and the houses which contained the learned societies either side of it.

There is a great shortage of public gallery space in London. Somerset House should be allowed to revert to its original purpose. One can understand the reluctance of the present occupiers to leave so gracious an eighteenth-century retreat but their work of registration and collecting taxes could be equally well done in a modern slab.[4]

Here was a sweet revenge on bureaucracy, taxmen, senior civil servants and the 'slave state', with a deft sideswipe at New Brutalist architects. It was a perfect moment to strike. Tax-collectors are never loved; and now the Registrar-General was in public disfavour too. In May the matter was aired in the House of Commons. Julian Amery, Minister for Housing and Construction, was asked whether he would move the Registrar-General and his staff to other premises, in order to allow Somerset House to be used as a national gallery for art. The Minister replied that though he sympathized with the suggestion, he 'must have regard to the practical difficulties'. But in two years, under further pressure from a caucus led by John and Jenkins, the registry had been ejected and the rooms hung with Turner paintings. Later, much more of the building was turned into galleries; though the Sir Arthur Gilbert collection of 'micro-mosaics' and silver, presided over by a waxwork effigy of the property mogul Sir Arthur, in yellow tennis shorts, might not have been quite what John had in mind for the space.[5]

When John's letter arrived at the *Standard*, Simon Jenkins telephoned to thank him. John asked him to lunch. The two men already knew each other; in 1969 John had had lunch with Jenkins and Jenkins's friend Anne Riches, daughter of the Bishop of Lincoln.[6] The men were on Christian-name terms by December of that year, when John, signing himself as 'ex-journalist', wrote to Jenkins to praise articles he had written on the Strand and on the future of London. Earlier in 1971 John had attended the launch party for Jenkins's book *A City at Risk*.

It was my first book [Jenkins said] – just a collection of pieces from the *Standard*, the sort of thing you should never produce. We had a party in some garret somewhere, some tiny little place up a long flight of stairs. The people there were all sort of London conservation lobby. I think Betjeman had been through quite a rough time. He'd produced some poems that hadn't worked, he'd been a bit under the weather. But he really wanted to come to this party, and he came. Wheezing up the steps. And he came into

the room and a silence fell, that he should have come. And he looked round
the room, taking in every person in turn, quite astutely; and then, realizing that people were waiting for some great word from the most dignified
guest, he simply stood up very straight and said: 'Ahh: *friends*.'[7]

Less than a year after Jenkins's article on Somerset House appeared,
John and Jenkins had lunch together in Covent Garden. They met at
Boulestin, the grand old subterranean restaurant founded by X. Marcel
Boulestin in the 1920s. John had known Boulestin, who, he remembered, had issued a gramophone record on 'How to Make the Perfect
Omelette'. John and Jenkins had cocktails in the pretty bar (soon to be
ruined). Murals by Marie Laurençin had already been removed for fear
of theft, but sub-cubist paintings by Jean Laboureur remained between
the curly trellises of lighting fixtures. Lunch was in the cavernous main
salon with its soup-brown walls and massive chandelier. The restaurant
was patronized by old grandees who had known it since it opened –
Lord Hailsham, Lord Eccles, Cyril Connolly, Anthony Powell – but also
by younger celebrities who had discovered its buried treasures, among
them the thriller writer Len Deighton and the artist Alan Aldridge, who
had illustrated *The Beatles' Songbook*. Jenkins reminded John that
Boulestin was threatened with demolition by Greater London Council
planners. 'John Betjeman, who has become the butt of everyone's
favourite tale of architectural destruction, was quite punch-drunk on
the subject of the Covent Garden redevelopment,' Jenkins wrote a few
days later. 'He merely said, "Oh dear, oh dear," pulled his ancient
brown trilby down over his head and stalked out into the sun.'[8]

What began as a brief stroll back to the car had by teatime extended
into 'an Odyssey of London sights and characters', as Jenkins recorded
in an article of 27 April, 'A walk through Betjeman's London'.

> His knowledge is encyclopaedic. A woman once approached him and said,
> 'Mr Betjeman, I saw something perfectly horrible the other day. I know
> you'll love it.'
>
> Yet his judgments are always exhaustively researched and scrupulously
> fair. And as far as the 19th century is concerned, he could write a com-
> plete vade-mecum to the London offices of Victorian architects.

The two men walked past the *Country Life* offices where Jenkins
had worked when he first went into journalism. 'As we walked past,'
Jenkins recalled in 1990, 'he started reminiscing about Christopher
Hudson, the old editor of *Country Life*, and how Lutyens had
designed everything in there; and he knew everything that was going
on behind the façade of the building, and of course was deploring the

fact that it had been taken over by George Newnes, and then taken over by IPC – and all sorts of horrors were happening.' Going in an easterly direction, they passed an undistinguished warehouse on the corner of Wellington Street. 'Could it, oh could it, be early Maufe?' John asked. Jenkins noted how, like so many of John's sentences, that one scanned perfectly. Later on they looked up the building, and it *was* by Sir Edward Maufe.[9]

Down towards the Strand, the Lyceum caught John's eye. The manager was a grey-haired man in an old blazer, who treated a visit from Sir John Betjeman as he might one by the Queen Mother. 'Oh yes, Mister Betjeman, as you wish. Do go wherever you please. We used to have Henry Irving here, you know.' The tour, which took in Australia House, the Waldorf Hotel, the Theatre Royal in Drury Lane and the Bridge House restaurant near London Bridge (Regency banisters under a thick coating of dirt; and an extraordinary ballroom), ended where it had begun, in the streets round Covent Garden. There they bumped into Osbert Lancaster, stumping along to Fleet Street to sketch the topical antics of Maudie Littlehampton.

'There are a number of dreadful things I must tell you about,' Lancaster said.

'Oh yes,' John said, 'do.'

Jenkins left them gossiping away. He sent John a copy of the *Standard* article he wrote about the tour. John replied from Trebetherick on 3 May: 'Fight on! Fight on!' His message continued: 'Delighted, dear Simon, with your piece. You know what's happening? The world is feeling Seifert[10] swindled it. Did he? Not consciously, possibly; but in fact yes. Old Osbert I should think will be delighted too . . .'

Another architectural jaunt Jenkins made with John began at Baker Street station, whose buffet had inspired John's poem 'The Metropolitan Railway'. 'This is one of the most beautiful buildings in London,' John said. Jenkins thought, 'This really is going too far.' As usual, John knew who the architect was.

He said, 'This was the true heir of Norman Shaw' [Jenkins recalled in 1990]. If you look at it, you can see what he means: huge arched windows on the ground floor, and so on. We went round the whole of the building and he pointed out all these – when was it, 1910 I suppose, 1915, that building? – all the architectural features and how important they were. But we then went round the back and there's a building called Sarah Siddons House next to it, which is an 1880s, I suppose, or 1890s block of flats, with a wonderful stained-glass window in the stairwell at the back, by someone like Burne-Jones, of Sarah Siddons. I remember thinking, how did John Betjeman *know* this?[11]

At the back of Baker Street station, John showed Jenkins the offices of the Metropolitan Railway Company in white faïence tiling, with the emblems of the railwayman's art embossed and rampant on the façade. 'It's a marvellous building from behind,' Jenkins said in 1990. 'And again, I suddenly realized, one thing Betjeman did was to show you a building of which you or I would have thought "How boring" all our lives, and absolutely brought it to life.'[12]

Jenkins remembers his friendship with John as a series of these architectural tours. Most of them began with lunch in the main dining-room of the Charing Cross Hotel, later named the Betjeman Room. 'The food was unspeakable,' Jenkins recalled, 'but he introduced me to Sancerre, a Loire wine, now very fashionable. I'd never had it before, but they had it at the Charing Cross Hotel, in the old British Railways wine cellar. And he used to say, "It doesn't matter how disgusting the roast beef is; we can have the Sancerre."'

After one such lunch, they took a taxi to Southwark. Jenkins remembers the trip mainly for an episode which showed John's insecurity.

He always had a real horror of Irish drunks [Jenkins recalled in 1990]. We were walking through Borough Market and I remember he wanted to go to Southwark Cathedral, and there were three Irish drunks on a bench in the little Close of the Cathedral. And he simply wouldn't go past them. I said, 'John, they're really harmless old boys,' but he said, 'Oh, no, I won't go' – it was as if there were a bull in the Close. And I noticed whenever I was walking with him anywhere, he had an absolute horror of drunks. He thought they'd attack him. I often wondered whether he'd had that experience. But of course he was a very sensitive chap.

Once we went to St Paul's Cathedral and he wanted to show me one of the monuments in the crypt. We walked to the Cathedral, to the steps down to the crypt. It must have been about 5.45 and the crypt was closing at 6.00. And the verger on duty said, 'I'm sorry, gentlemen, it's closed.'

And I said, 'Look, it's closing at 6.00. It's now 5.45.'

'Well, no people are admitted after 5.45.'

'We're just going to see one thing down there. Our money's as good as anyone else's. Please can we go down?'

'No, it's an absolute rule.'

And Betjeman simply flew off the handle. He went completely mad. He shouted: 'Listen, I was a night watchman on this Cathedral in the war. I'm a Friend of this Cathedral. I'm a friend of the Dean. How dare you not let me into the crypt? It's outrageous. *Do you know who I am?*'

And the hapless verger, who was a really unpleasant character, suddenly realized who he was and said, 'Oh, Sir John, I'm most awfully sorry, I do beg your pardon; please, please come down.'[13]

Although the verger had capitulated, John now refused to go in. He would not lay off the man, but harangued him for some minutes more: 'NO! NO! NO! I won't have this. It's an outrage. This place has gone to the dogs, it's absolutely outrageous. I am going to report this to the Dean.' Jenkins was embarrassed. 'He just went on and on,' he recalled.[14]

In 1973 John said to Jenkins, 'We must do Middlesex.'[15] They decided to explore the churches within two miles of Terminal One at Heathrow Airport. The area had been left surprisingly undeveloped. The airport's swift expansion after the Second World War had imposed a freeze on the land around it, partly with an eye to future acquisition, partly because it was assumed that nobody would want to live in houses so near a runway. Farms, manors, churches, fields, lanes all stayed as they were, locked in the past. Trunk roads and motorways cut separate paths, leaving old byways undisturbed.[16]

'We got in a car and we simply tottered round all these little churches,' Jenkins said. 'Within two miles of Terminal One is a circle of these great old Middlesex churches, all of which you could visit if your plane was delayed a couple of hours. And John Betjeman knew them all.'[17] The car stopped at the southern edge of the perimeter road at Heathrow, and the two men got out. John stood surrounded by a seemingly endless wasteland of aircraft hangars, restricted areas, sparking-plug factories and deserted petrol stations. 'Ah,' he said with deep satisfaction, 'rural Middlesex, rural Middlesex – one of the very best counties.' The fuel crisis of 1973 had made that corner of the Home Counties more tolerable than usual. Traffic was much reduced, and it was possible to imagine what the old village of Heathrow must have been like before the coming of the airport.

John gave Jenkins an idea of the treats in store for him. 'Up to the north of the BOAC hanger', he said, 'lies the old estate of Cranford House, once home of the Berkeleys. Then round past the motorway link to medieval Harlington and on to Harmondsworth with its delightful village green. Then Longford on the old Bath Road. And down towards the reservoirs before Staines we will see the spire of Stanwell Church across the moor. And then there's Bedfont, and Hounslow, and Feltham, and . . .'

Back in the car, they left the M4 at the Feltham and Air Cargo Exit at Heathrow. 'At this point,' Jenkins wrote, 'you are just twenty yards from one of the loveliest medieval churches in Middlesex (which has many), and barely a mile from the main BOAC Jumbo hangar.' The church was St Dunstan's, Cranford – all that remains, apart from the park and some stables, of the Cranford House estate. Its Tudor tower juts up from yews and elms, with the motorway roaring past at roof height. 'Betjeman shuts his ears to it and wanders in through the old wicket gate, up the path and into the church. There, in the chancel, stands a splendid renaissance alabaster monument to one Sir Robert Aston. "And look here," he says, pointing to a tombstone. "John Finall Cook 1771–1856, who left as his epitaph that he was 'the worst-used Irish constable in England, which office he held for more than half a century'. How sad." ' The showpiece of Harmondsworth was its great tithe barn, known since the Domesday Book but largely undiscovered.

'It's really a cathedral,' says Betjeman, approaching it across the muddy farmyard in which it still serves its original purpose. 'The biggest and noblest medieval barn in the whole of England. Built, I'd say, at the end of the 14th century.' He rubs its vast walls as a tailor might feel fine silk. 'Pudding stone, they used to call it in this part of Middlesex. Isn't it beautiful.'

Getting inside entailed crawling under locked doors and up through the bales of hay inside. Betjeman burrowed up through the hay like a mole to admire the magnificent nave and roof supported on vast oak columns with huge wooden vaults.

He carried that hay round with him on his suit for the rest of the day with great pride. He would gaze at it and murmur, reverently, 'Harmondsworth hay.'[18]

These were the last days of John's agility. 'He was already *supposed* to be crippled,' Jenkins observed in 1990.

The two men battled on beneath the main take-off flight-path to Longford. 'I do believe that's the Duke of Northumberland's river we've just crossed,' John said. 'And what an excellently laid hawthorn hedge.' To the right lay the village of Colnbrook, a coaching stage in the great days of the Bath Road. Now it was almost deserted. John and Jenkins took part and counterpart in a duet of disgust at the way its lovely inns and coach-houses had been left to rot by Buckinghamshire Council.[19]

South of Heathrow, Jenkins noted, it took real imagination to squeeze romance out of the environment. Landing beacons festooned the cabbage fields as far as the eye could see. Hideous fencing surrounded endless restricted areas. Everywhere there were things that ran on petrol. But at Bedfont was another church, St Mary's, 'sandwiched in a hellish maelstrom between the A30 and the A315'.

Betjeman approaches the church nervously [Jenkins wrote]. 'It's the only church in Middlesex that I've never been inside because nobody ever seems to have a key,' he wails. 'Once upon a time the yews in the churchyard were part of a great hedge and cut into fantastic topiary peacocks. The cockneys would come down from London for the day to see them:

"Darn ta Bedfont!" Now they've gone, and the cockneys don't come any more. And I bet it's locked.' Locked it is, and the topiary peacocks are a sorry sight. Such incidents upset Betjeman more than is reasonable, as if the art to which he offers his devotion is purposely humiliating him.[20]

By the end of their tour, John and Jenkins had encircled Heathrow. John shouted, above the roar of a jet, 'Look, there's Hounslow West on the Piccadilly Line, where the air hostesses alight.' He added: 'No, we won't take the motorway back, but the Great West Road, past the Gillette Building by Banister Fletcher and all those traffic lights we used to race in our motor-cars to pass before they turned red . . .'[21]

In the early days of John's friendship with Jenkins, the two walked long distances together. 'Later on,' Jenkins said, 'he always insisted on driving. But then you'd end up getting out of the car to look at something, and you'd walk and walk and walk and forget where you'd left the car.'[22] When Jenkins and his friend the journalist Valerie Jenkins (later Grove) took John on a tour of north-west London in 1974, they noticed that he was 'very unsteady'. Valerie Grove took them to her old school, Kingswood Grammar School; Jenkins showed them over his *alma mater*, Mill Hill School, 'which of course Betjeman knew the architecture of, completely'; and they also visited Harrow, of which John felt himself 'spiritually an Old Boy'.[23]

John was '*extremely* unsteady', Jenkins remembered, by 1976, the year of a memorable jaunt the two made to Southend. On 22 July, Jenkins wrote to John:

> Could I possibly try something out on you? As you may know, the Architectural Heritage Fund was set up at the end of the dreaded European Architectural Heritage Year. The idea is an estimable one of giving money to put old buildings back into shape and then re-let them on some sort of economic basis – making the Fund eventually self-supporting.
>
> Someone had the bright idea (I think Raine Dartmouth, that was) of asking local amenity societies to raise money towards the initial Fund with coffee mornings and other such events. This yielded only a drop in the ocean, but much worthy activity nonetheless. By far the most successful society has been Southend who have raised twice as much as the next largest, Stamford! I am writing on behalf of various people to see whether there would be any chance of your 'receiving' a cheque from the Southend society on behalf of the Fund – since you are also, I see, patron of that society. They would give you a great reception and would leave the choice of time and date entirely to you.
>
> An additional reason for my writing, however, is that I would love to make one of our erstwhile expeditions out of it.[24]

John was enthusiastic about the plan. Jenkins wrote an account of the trip, not for publication in the *Evening Standard*, but to preserve his memories of the day. He had arrived in Chelsea in a taxi to take John to Fenchurch Street station.

Collecting John Betjeman [he wrote] is like launching a ship: a slow ponderous progress across the street towards the car door with me wondering at every step whether the thing would sink. On this occasion I was late. He was on the phone to my office attempting to discover where I was and getting nowhere. His conversation with goodness knows whom was made further complicated by my arriving in the middle of it. (I discovered later that pandemonium was breaking out at the office over where I might be if I wasn't with JB – not helped by his having vanished from the line suddenly.) Despite the weather he fervently refused to take more than a flimsy plastic mac and his flat cap. Gone are the days of the black overcoat and pork-pie hat. A day out at Southend called for more proletarian garb.

The taxi driver thought us mad. We took him via the sole remaining bit of Doulton's in Lambeth, then back and forth over the various bridges to look at the 'curly bits'. But he knew Southend well. He often took his boys fishing there and JB warmed to him no end when he remarked that 'I could do with a quid for every jar I've drunk in a Southend pub.'[25]

Jenkins found that John was 'totally obsessed' with a visit he had made as a boy to the church in the forecourt of Fenchurch Street station. By now, the church was only a crypt beneath a modern development. 'But there – you can still see the trees in the old churchyard,' John said, pointing to 'a thoroughly squalid patch of open space beneath an office block'. Jenkins thought: how wonderful to be able to invest any pattern of the City streets with their pre-war glory.

But Fenchurch Street was not much changed; and the ticket clerk gave satisfaction by asking, 'Single, day return, or will you be staying the night?' This prompted one of John's musings-aloud. 'Staying the night! Could it be at the Royal Hotel? Done in I'm sure. Or perhaps the Palace – Oh what a night that might once have been!' Jenkins noticed how John adopted his characteristic pose of 'standing, feet firmly on the ground, hand on some rail or baluster and eyes peering skyward in search of joy'. The interior of the station had recently been tactfully repainted – 'cared-for without excessive restoration', Jenkins noted. The stair rails had been left. 'Look at those rails!' John cried. 'Made when rails were rails. And the finials! Pure London, Tilbury and Southend Gothic revival!'[26]

Jenkins was delighted to find that their train had no corridors. He knew of old that John hated 'the offchance of human encounter over which he has no control'. In any case, as John observed, there were unlikely to be many travelling first class on the 11.32 from Fenchurch Street to Southend. 'They'll all be safely tucked up in their offices. Offices by Seifert, but then back to Southend by the London, Tilbury and Southend line.'

Fenchurch Street runs eastwards out of the City on a viaduct. 'It's a dramatic sudden exit,' Jenkins wrote, 'almost reminiscent of New York as one crosses the bridge into Manhattan. The old viaduct ruined many a good view of the City – and many a fine house round the Minories – but now at least it provides a few views itself.' The Tower of London, Tower Bridge, then St Katharine's glanced by as the train picked up speed. Then the backs of the houses in Leman Street, some with sash windows, mansard roofs and chimney stacks with original brickwork. John kept up a running commentary: 'They can't get rid of the churches. There's no finer view of St George's. Watch for it. You get a quick glimpse on the right. St Paul's Shadwell. Soon there'll be St Anne's Limehouse, possibly Hawksmoor's greatest. Oh the things one can see from the Fenchurch Street Line!'

On through unknown suburbs. Out beyond elm parks towards Upminster, where, Jenkins wrote, 'weird Underground trains moved like worms uncovered on the lawn'. Would they see the Upminster windmill? John wanted him to see it more than anything, but only suburban semis appeared on the horizon. They passed a gaunt Georgian house surrounded by scrub. Jenkins thought it 'extraordinarily spooky'. John said: 'Look, Bleak House. A borstal, probably, a detention centre. Nameless things go on there at night.' On the left, virtually the only good view of Stepney Cemetery was to be had – a dash of wildness and mystery in the heart of the East End. 'What a place! Look at it! It's like Highgate Woods. There are gravestones in there . . . How sinister. Can you imagine what unmentionable things must go on in there at night? Murders and crimes – every night, I should think. *Unmentionable* things. I should think you could well set a thriller there. Stepney Cemetery. Imagine it.'

Suddenly a curve of neat grass viaduct veered away towards dockland. 'There it goes, look. The Poplar Loop of the Broad Street Line. What a railway. It's going to Blackwall station. I used to take a ticket to Blackwall station just to stand there by the Thames. It's a terminus. Derelict now, I should think.' Not only was the line disused, the rails had been taken up. Jenkins thought it would make 'a splendid overhead ramble – without hurting or displacing a soul'.

Stepney East railway station, the words 'GENERAL WAITING ROOM' still in frosted glass on the window. 'No, there'll be no first-class waiting-room here,' John said. 'Not many first-class travellers from Stepney East. Do you know, I once saw a graffito here which said "Cockney Power".' Upton Park, citadel of cockney soccer. 'Ah yes, do you know the brother of the manager of the football team here was our curate at Wantage?' (Like the good journalist he is, Jenkins later tried to confirm this fact with Ron Greenwood, but drew a blank.) 'Basildon. Horrible. Do they really have a railway station at Basildon? Probably just garages. Sprung fully formed from some drawing board or other. We'll come to the middle soon – it's probably called the art centre. Yes, here it is, with those mosaics on the wall. Best seen in a steady drizzle . . . Look, some gypsies; this whole area is like Charles Dickens, Peggoty. We'll be in Chalkwell soon, Classy Chalkwell. In half an hour you could hear the soft flip of playing cards, bridge parties, with the car outside and much talk of how much her husband earns. Leigh-on-Sea: it's the Hampstead of Essex; Chalkwell is the Finchley. And here's Southend, oh this is exciting, so many good things, and all on the Fenchurch Street Line. It must be the nearest country to London, Hadleigh Castle, the soft light on the sudden hillocks – that's Essex, real Essex. Look at the station, a real station. And there's a big Jewish hotel on the left.'[27]

There was a steady, relentless drizzle, but John liked that: 'It keeps Southend just for us, no people around.' He got off the train with his cloth cap pulled down on his head and the plastic mac round his shoulders. In an old airline bag he was carrying an embossed volume of the Southend poet Robert Buchanan.[28] In 1990 Jenkins recalled an unfortunate incident just after their arrival.

Betjeman had a very delicate flashpoint – I knew that from our encounter with the verger at St Paul's. When we got off the train at Southend, the station was totally deserted except for a mother and child waiting on the platform. We got off the train, and Betjeman was, frankly, acting. 'Ah! Wonderful place, Southend!' you see. Well, that station was ghastly. He went up to this woman and said, 'Isn't it marvellous, living in Southend, my dear? You are so lucky, living in Southend.' Anyway, she thought this man was completely crackers, and turned away and covered up her child. Betjeman was furious. He expected her to say, 'Oh, Sir John, how grateful I am . . .' but clearly she had no idea who he was. And that got him into a really bad mood.[29]

The two men turned towards the new high-street precinct, but the sight of modernity in the distance led their steps back towards the sea. They passed Brightwell's Stores. John was sure that Brightwell must have been a staunch churchman and a man of good works, simply because of the old-fashioned character of the store. It was in that street,

Jenkins remembered, that Charlie Chaplin, young from London, asked 'What on earth is that big blue thing at the bottom end of the street?' It was his first sight of the sea. 'Deserted pavements and plodding old people,' John commented. 'What do they say to each other in retirement? "Well, my dear, what shall we do today? The pier? No, we did that yesterday. The promenade? No, you decide. *You* decide. I decided yesterday." They probably end up at the Palace Hotel bingo.'

> The hotels are now all flats or decaying [Jenkins wrote]. There's only one good restaurant and our search for a bar ended in a maelstrom of Musak and flocked wallpaper – 'give us something sort of Georgian – you know, Regency'. Two elderly queens came in adorned with hairpieces. The smell of a fryup. 'The only good business in Southend is fishing tackle. It's better than Brighton, especially when it's grey. Oh dear, and all at the end of the Fenchurch Street Line.' Restaurant – a whisky sour and scallops. 'No dear, we don't have cockles, not here, you get them round the corner'.
>
> 'I say, there are some French people at the table behind us. It *must* be a good place.' He tastes the whisky sour. 'You know, I think this must be the best restaurant in all England – don't you think?'[30]

After lunch, they strolled down Royal Terrace. 'You could get a house there for £10,000,' John said, 'but it would need a lot spent on it. £10,000 – it's worth ten times that. Look at the view, always changing. Let's find Buchanan's grave – here it must be, what a marvellous spot. Palace Hotel, like Broderick's in Scarborough, only better. And St Erkenwald's, like a great ship there.' His slow walk speeded up occasionally, then slowed again. 'Who lives in Southend? Discriminating people. I would live here – and travel up to Fenchurch Street. And look at this bookshop – a complete set of Hall Caine, the Shakespeare of the Isle of Man. £7.50. Done. It was a boom town in the Twenties and it will be so again. Look at the Palace Hotel – bar for residents only. Imagine it in its great days. "Now, dear, you wanted to come to the seaside and here it is – now enjoy it."'

It was time for the official part of the day. Because of John's infirmity Jenkins had ordered cars to take them from one part of Southend to another. He had also arranged, because he knew John liked to be made a fuss of, a reception by civic dignitaries and a good showing by the local press. 'But what he really wanted to do was to see the pier. Unfortunately, the pier had just burned down, there had been this terrible fire. And the dignitaries said, "We're awfully sorry, Sir John, but the pier train is out of action, because of the fire." It was pouring with rain, it was a really ghastly day. He said: "We'll walk." And dammit, he did. No stick – he just strode out the length of that wretched pier.

I was slightly miffed, because I had actually got all these cars to take him a hundred yards here and a hundred yards there. It was all a bit of a show on his part.' At a ceremony in the Westcliff Hotel, John read out long extracts from Robert Buchanan – 'an appalling poet', in Jenkins's view. The Buchanan volume was presented to the local conservation society and John duly received the cheque from the society for the Architectural Heritage Fund.[31]

They returned to Fenchurch Street in the evening, both exhausted – John from showing off all day and walking too far, Jenkins from watching over his capricious companion. On 9 November 1976 John wrote to Jenkins from Chelsea:

Dear Simon,

I should have written long before this to thank you for our Southend trip. From the first glance at that overgrown cemetery in Tower Hamlets to the last sunset rays over the spreading estuary. I should have said much more at that little ceremony in the Westcliff Hotel. I should have said that the Pier is really the making of Southend's landscape. By its immense length the Pier draws the sea towards the visitors, even when the tide is right out. It also unites sky and sea. It *is* Southend. It will kill the town to destroy it and make the town to put it back into repair with a nice, spidery, flimsy folly to gather shore and sky together. Robert Buchanan would have liked this, so might have Swinburne whom he so harshly attacked. You do a great local public work by keeping the Standard a local paper . . .

Yours ever with great gratitude,

John B.[32]

Southend pier, in spite of two severe fires, survives. And one of the two miniature locomotives that carries visitors to the end of the pier and back is named *The Sir John Betjeman*.[33]

'...AS I LOSE HOLD'

The street is bathed in winter sunset pink,
The air is redolent of kitchen sink,
Between the dog-mess heaps I pick my way
To watch the dying embers of the day
Glow over Chelsea, crimson load on load
All Brangwynesque across the long King's Road.
Deep in myself I feel a sense of doom,
Fearful of death I trudge towards the tomb.
The earth beneath my feet is hardly soil
But outstretched chicken-netting coil on coil
Covering cables, sewage pipes and wires
While underneath burn hell's eternal fires.
Snap! Crackle! Pop! the kiddiz know the sound
And Satan stokes his furnace underground.

John Betjeman, 'Chelsea 1977', *Uncollected Poems*, London 1982

In 1977 John made a new friend – the bookseller Reg Read, who served him as librarian, companion and court jester. Infiltrating and absorbed into the ménage at No. 29 Radnor Walk, and to some extent into that at No. 19, Read had an intimate view of John's day-to-day life for eight years, until the poet's death. Long before he met John, he had heard a lot about him from 'Dusty' Miller, who worked at Frank Hollings's bookshop underneath John's flat in Cloth Fair. (Miller, who was sorting John's papers and handled the sale of much of the Betjeman archive to the University of Victoria, British Columbia, died in August 1977.)[1] One night in the Fifties Read was in a Smithfield pub when he overheard one of the meat porters talking to another. 'That geezer Betjeman! He's always coming home and has lost his key. Do you know what he did last night? He came across to the market and said, would we get a ladder and get him in? Which we did; and before we knew where we were it was four o'clock in the morning. Because he insisted on pouring out the old guzzler, didn't 'e?'[2] Read told a bookseller friend of his about that incident.

He said, 'Have you ever met him?'

I said, 'No.'

He said, 'Oh, I'll fix it. I'm president of the Piers Preservation Society. I'm due to see John Betjeman about the society. Why don't you come along?'

I went, but I was late. The arrangement was that I would be at Radnor Walk around ten o'clock. As it was, I had a call to go and buy some books, and that held me up. By the time I got down to Radnor Walk my friend had already gone in. I didn't know the number of the house – I had no need to know it, as we'd arranged we'd meet outside the house and go in together. So I knocked at various doors and I eventually found John Betjeman lived at No. 29.

We took to each other absolutely. He plied me with bubbly; later on, I continually got blamed by Lady Elizabeth for his drinking too much. We had a wow of a morning. I commented about his books – how the sets had been broken up. Volume I was on the top shelf, Volume III on the bottom shelf and so on. Chaos! He said, 'What are you doing tomorrow?' I said, 'Why?' He said, 'Well, you're criticizing my books; you might as well come and put them in order.' So I became his librarian. If he felt very grand, he'd say, 'librarian and literary companion'.[3]

The next day, Read began putting the books in order; but before he could make much headway John had a new idea. 'He said: "I think they should be *catalogued*." (I think it was: anything to keep our friendship going.) He said: "You can go upstairs into the parlour. There's a typewriter up there." We had great fun. Because of the amount of materials tucked away, he didn't always remember where things were; so he'd get great pleasure when I took a book downstairs, perhaps an 1890s poet – "Oooh, isn't it lovely!" '[4] Not all Read's discoveries pleased John.

I had a desk in the study with John, and in the bookcase above my desk there was a fair quantity of books by Evelyn Waugh. Many were presentation copies, signed by Waugh to John or Penelope, or both of them. And in my excitement at finding these I said, 'Oh, *look*!' He was furious, because he considered – rightly or wrongly – that Evelyn Waugh had been responsible for the breakdown of his marriage. 'He was cruel,' he was this, he was that – John went berserk. Then he said, 'Let's have some more bubbly,' and the matter was dropped. I was surprised those books stayed where they were; because one day I happened to say, 'What a lovely collection of Nikolaus Pevsner you've got.' My *God*!

'*Don't mention his name!*' John maintained that Pevsner never went to the buildings. He said that he used to gather up any university undergraduates and put them on bicycles and send them off to gather information. 'Well,' John said, 'they don't know anything. They probably don't even go to the places; they can tell him anything they like.' Of course, this was nonsense; but he just couldn't stand Pevsner. He made me put all the Pevsners into boxes and take them down to the cellar. 'Put them in the darkest corner you can find,' he said.[5]

Read had a profound knowledge of books. Born in Kingston-upon-Thames in 1930, he was educated 'mainly in air-raid shelters' but also attended classes in Pitman's shorthand. His mother wanted him to become a journalist; instead, he became secretary to Stephen Dykes Bower, surveyor of the fabric at Westminster Abbey.[6] His interest in architecture, history and books was stimulated. While working for Dykes Bower, Read saw an advertisement: an assistant was wanted by Percy Muir of Elkin Mathews, a firm of London booksellers specializing in modern first editions. Because of the war, the firm had moved to Takeley in Essex. Read was given the job. 'It was a wonderful opportunity for me to learn everything,' he says. 'I came back from the interview and my mum asked, "What kind of books do they sell?" I said, "It looks as if it is all Bibles." It wasn't: it was *bibliographies*.'[7] He stayed for eighteen years, sometimes buying large collections, such as those of the wood-engravers Eric Gill (through his brother, Evan Gill), Joan Hassall and Reynolds Stone. He also helped to prepare the IPEX* exhibition at Olympia (1963). Next he joined Nigel Traylen, who was running Beeleigh Abbey Books, the antiquarian-books section of Foyle's Bookshop in Charing Cross Road, London. Christina Foyle often sent him round to Francis Bacon's Kensington studio to buy his sketchbooks. Eventually Read acquired bookshops of his own in Highgate, Islington and Charing Cross Road.

He was bisexual: left his wife to live with another man, a fellow bookseller with a shop in Cecil Court. He felt about his wife much as John felt about Penelope: 'I loved her, and we get on; but I can't live with her. Twenty-four hours and I'm nearly up the wall!'[8] John quizzed Read about his sex-life and played along with the camper side of his nature. Read remembers: 'I went to a Chelsea café one morning with John and his then secretary, Elizabeth Moore. It was the time of Wimbledon and there was quite a lot of the Wimbledon set in there. We went to this restaurant about 11.00 in the morning and it was filling up with people having coffee. And John, in a voice which could be heard across the room, said "Look at that waiter's bum! It's like two apples. Reg! Invite him over – then maybe I might be able to brush against him with my hand." '[9] Another time, it had

---

* IPEX: International Printing Machinery and Allied Trades Exhibition.

been arranged that John would speak the next Sunday at a Baptist
church near Radnor Walk.

> As he and I passed the church, on a morning walk [Read recalls] he said,
> 'Stop! Reg, stop! I'm going to ask you something. Have I told you the
> subject of my talk in this church next Sunday?' I said, 'No, I don't think
> so.' 'Well,' he said (looking round to make sure there were other people
> listening), 'I shall climb up into the pulpit. I shall look over the congre-
> gation. And I shall say: "The subject of my talk this evening is *The
> Importance of Exposing One's Private Parts in Public as Often as
> Possible*." '[10]

John enjoyed Read's racy anecdotes about the book world. While
with Foyle's, he told John, he had discovered a batch of letters by
T. E. Lawrence together with Royal Air Force documents which not only
threw doubt on the Deraa incident as recounted in *The Seven Pillars of
Wisdom* but showed that on his final RAF enlistment Lawrence bore no
scars but when he left there were 'scars on buttocks'. These papers were
talked about at the Antiquarian Booksellers' Association Fair, where
they were sold, as 'Read's bum papers'.[11]

John had a taste for the scatological. 'He loved smutty stories,' Read
says. 'And naughty postcards.'[12] John gave him a drawing he dashed off
after some po-faced designer had stated on television: 'With any design
feature, I am primarily interested in whether it serves its purpose. That
is: does it work? *Does it come off?*'[13]

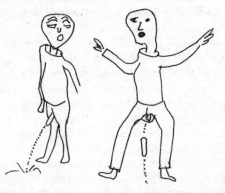

Jonathan Stedall also remembers John's Rabelaisian streak. 'He got
very irritated if journalists who rang up asked him to spell his name.
He would shout into the telephone: "B for bugger; E for entrails; T for
turd; J for jockstrap" and so on.'[14]

Read did not get on particularly well with Lady Elizabeth Cavendish, and relations were not improved by an unfortunate incident.

I was invited to see John at No. 19, when he wasn't feeling well [Read remembers]. I got the okay from him to examine just about everything. So I was down in the basement sorting things out; up in the loft, sorting things out. And, this day, he had the idea that I should go up and look at the papers above the wardrobe in his bedroom at No. 19. So I did that thing.

There wasn't anything very exciting there. So, as one does, one moved from one room to another. And there in the adjoining room was a big cupboard full of clothes. Above it was a mass of boxes. Standing on a chair I got to reach these boxes. They were full of bundles of letters. And I had just started to undo the first bundle when I realized these were love letters from Elizabeth to John and from John to Elizabeth. Something said to me I mustn't look at these things, but before I could put them back and get myself off the chair, up comes a *tank engine* – Lady Elizabeth, of course. And there was I standing on the chair with these letters in my hand. She hauled me down. 'How *dare* you! These are *private*' – and she grabbed the letters. I mean, her reaction was quite understandable; but I had acted in all innocence. Lady Elizabeth already thought me a 'bad influence'; now she must have thought me some kind of spy.

I said to John, 'I think I've upset Elizabeth. I was looking through your papers and I happened on some love letters.' He almost laughed; and I even wondered if he had intended me to find them.[15]

By contrast, Read made great friends with Penelope on her rare visits to Radnor Walk. He was invited to stay at Cusop. 'Much of the conversation was about how unreasonable John was regarding the temperature of the house. But it *was* cold!'

One of the things we had to suffer at No. 29 [he recalled] was that at least once a month Penelope would phone up wanting money. She was quite clear about it. She didn't keep it vague. She'd say she needed the money, otherwise the telephone would be cut off – that's when she *got* a telephone. John used to reach the point where he guessed that this demand was coming soon. He'd say, 'I bet that's Penelope,' and I'd answer the telephone and have to make up some excuse. She'd say to John: 'Unless you give me some money I'll be cut off, you won't be able to make any contact with me; I won't know how you are.'

Eventually he would send her some money. My guess is he kept her pretty short. About every fortnight he would ask Elizabeth Moore, 'How is my money situation?' She'd say, 'You're all right.' She would tell him how much he had in his current account. Of course it was never enough. 'Oh, I won't be able to manage!'[16]

John still managed to entertain his friends in style. In 1977 he gave lunch at Au Fin Bec in Draycott Avenue to Gerard Irvine, his sister Rosemary Irvine (headmistress of a girls' school near Winchester) and Duncan Fallowell, the editor of a 'punk' magazine, *Deluxe*. Twenty-nine in 1977, Fallowell had first met John as a schoolboy at St Paul's School. He had gone on to Magdalen College, Oxford, and the two had kept up a correspondence.[17] The guests were asked to come to Radnor Walk first. Fallowell arrived before the others and recorded his conversation with John, which he published in *20th Century Characters* (1994). Like John's banter with Penelope and the Sharleys in 1963, Fallowell's recording gives a fly-on-the-wall impression of John at ease in friendly company, conjuring exactly what it was like to be with him before his face became frozen and his speech impaired by his illness. Fallowell wrote:

The following conversation took place at Sir John's house in Chelsea in the middle of a sunny day: blue sky, daffodils, and daisies. There are two background activities: (1) The rapid progress through bottles of champagne. These were by Dagonet and the speed is faster than usual because they were half bottles. (2) The attempts to take some snaps with an over-sophisticated polaroid camera.

'You've done your hair up in a new colour!' was the first thing he said with his toothy, crooked grin . . .

'No, I went to the tropics.'

'That's very brave of you. In the summer I like to go north, to the Faroe Islands, mist-laden Atlantic wonders. It stays cool up there. They roof their churches with sods. Would you like to have a little bubbly? Mr. Glover, where are you? [Mr Glover was the odd-job man.] Oh, there you are, let's have another glass. And let's have another bottle.'

DUNCAN: I'm a bit late actually. The King's Road is blocked off.
SIR JOHN: It's not the punks is it?
DUNCAN: No, steamrollers. They're making a new road.
SIR JOHN: *Mechanical* punks . . . Can't offer you a cigarette. Haven't got any.
DUNCAN: I've got some Camels.
SIR JOHN: I love the smell of it.
DUNCAN: Have you an ashtray?
SIR JOHN: Use that Chelsea Arts bowl. They kindly presented it to me, the Chelsea Potters, a lovely firm.

DUNCAN: Why did you move from the City? I loved Cloth Fair.

SIR JOHN: Driven out by the noise. I really liked the City better. But you know that great Barbican thing glaring down at one. Horrible great thing. It's only in the morning that you need this champagne to drink, you know.

DUNCAN: What do you have in the afternoon?

SIR JOHN: Sometimes I have a rest.

DUNCAN: I've brought some gadgets. This one is American. It's supposed to take polaroid pictures. Somebody told me how to use it but I've forgotten.

SIR JOHN: Do you want to take a picture?

DUNCAN: I thought I might. The picture shoots out of the bottom here and you watch it developing under your eyes.

SIR JOHN: Oh, let's have a go! Am I against the light do you think?

DUNCAN: Er, possibly . . .

SIR JOHN: Is this the first you've taken?

DUNCAN: I took some in a pub. You are supposed to hold it very still. They were a complete mess . . .[18]

Fallowell had recently been to India, and asked John if he had received his postcards.

SIR JOHN: Yes, I did! Lovely. Those wonderful Raj churches which should have been in Surrey or Edinburgh.

DUNCAN: I sent one of St Paul's Cathedral in Calcutta.

SIR JOHN: That's obviously wonderful.

DUNCAN: It's the Regency version of Canterbury Cathedral.

SIR JOHN: Is it well attended, St Paul's Calcutta?

DUNCAN: Mm, well, the out-patients department is. They have a crack saviour service in jeeps.

SIR JOHN: High?

DUNCAN: No, they can't really afford the candles. But they're eccentric. I heard a sermon there about Thackeray. He was born in Calcutta.

SIR JOHN: I've never been there but my wife has.

DUNCAN: I saw her in Hay-on-Wye, incidentally.

SIR JOHN: I used to go and stay there but she has no water or electricity or heating and all the windows are open with the wind whistling through the place – well, I'm rather frightened to go now in case it kills me. But I like Hay very much.[19]

Fallowell talked about the reception of his work.

DUNCAN: I received a poisonous letter from a writer called Michael Moorcock.

SIR JOHN: Who is he?

DUNCAN: He writes fantasies for children and hippies, churns it out. Pretty feeble stuff, and I said so. He said that if I said so again he'd break both my legs with an iron bar.

SIR JOHN: Where did you run him down?

DUNCAN: In print.

SIR JOHN: Oh, they never forgive print. They think it's going to be there forever. I always believe anything that's said against me. And if anything is said in my favour I think they're only trying to be nice. To this day I think that. And I can only remember things said against me.[20]

Gerard Irvine and Rosemary Irvine arrived. ('He is in a soutane, is very jolly and flushed and eighteenth-century looking. His sister is more contained, wears intelligent shoes, and has a dry sense of humour.')[21] Rosemary drove them all to Au Fin Bec. 'There was a moment of frisson while crossing the King's Road, followed by some disorientation in a cul de sac. There were several ribald remarks about a certain block of flats used for prostitution . . . We eventually found ourselves at the destination and hit the dry martinis.'[22] They had Oeufs Benedict which 'broke and dribbled to perfection', veal, spinach, red wine and fruit. 'Our talk grew bawdy.'[23]

Fallowell's chapter gives the flavour of John's life in the late 1970s. There is the light badinage; there is the heavy drinking. He is still interested, inquiring. But we also hear what he really thinks of Penelope's house. And, beyond the jokes and the conversational patball, there are hints of inner misery. Reg Read often found him in tears. 'Many an afternoon he would sit in the large chair and he'd weep. The tears would be flowing down his face: the thought that Jesus was going to cast him into hell because of what he'd done to Penelope.'[24] When Harry Williams was staying, he was able to comfort John, telling him that the marriage to Penelope had been a mistake and that he was destined to be with Elizabeth.[25] John's physical condition worsened; and he became more and more disaffected with Chelsea. All his hatred of Chelsea boiled over in his poem 'Chelsea 1977' (printed at the head of this chapter). John made no fewer than six drafts of the poem; he later made a present of them to Read. The penultimate version which – unlike all the earlier drafts – was typewritten, ended with ten lines which were deleted from the poem when it was finally published. They expressed John's longing to escape from Chelsea and cross the river to the diocese of Southwark, ruled by his friend Mervyn Stockwood.

The diocese of London was a waste
From which I vainly strove to leave in haste.
I could not lift my limbs, my feet were clogged;
London was over-peopled, over-dogged.
If only I could move a little faster
But move I could not here where fear was master.
The Diocese of Southwark was a friend:
Across the Thames my misery might end,
Where suddenly the spreading brickwork yields
To public open space called Myatt's Fields.[26]

At the bottom of the draft, after a gap and some geometric doodles, John has typed in – in fainter ink – the couplet which replaced those ten lines in the published version. It was one of those flashes of inspiration which he credited to 'The Management' –

Snap, crackle, pop the kiddiz know the sound
And Satan stokes his furnace underground.[27]

'Snap! Crackle! Pop!' (in the published poem John put in the exclamation marks) was the advertising slogan used to promote Kellogg's breakfast cereal Rice Krispies, which make a popping sound when milk is poured on them. By this stroke John converted the ten rather laborious and self-pitying lines into a bolt of black humour.

A friend John used to visit in Soho wrote a parody of the poem, entitled 'Soho 1977' –

I saw Wifebeater's House* in sunset glow
And shuffled past St Barnabas (too low);
Upon my arm, the daughter of a duke
Took care to steer me round lagoons of puke.
I finally sat down in Soho Square
Upon a newly vandalized park chair,
And splinters of the wood stuck in my arse,
While from St Patrick's came the strains of Mass.

* In 1977 the present author was living in Goldbeaters House, Manette Street, Soho, where JB visited him. JB called the building 'Wifebeater's House'. The building was owned by Miss Christina Foyle of Foyle's Bookshop; and in the lobby was a foundation stone engraved 'LAID BY THE POET LAUREATE' (John Masefield). 'Every nice girl's ambition,' JB commented.

Deep in myself I felt my tummy rumble
And for my Rennies I began to fumble;
O for De Quincey's drug (or Collis Browne);*

---

* Dr Collis Browne's Chlorodyne was a stomach-settling liquid which had recently been banned by the Government because of its opium content.

The street was bathed in winter sunset pink

The air was redolent of kitchen sink

Between the dog mess heaps I picked my way

To watch the *dying* embers of *the* baleful day

Glow over Chelsea, *London* crimson *grown* load on load

All Brangwynesque *across* the long King's Road

Deep in my self I felt a sense of doom

Deep in myself *the soul* was but a tomb

beneath my feet was hardly soil

But outstretched chicken coil *on* coil

And underneath cobbles pipes and wires

And wonder them all round Hell's eternal fires

escape! escape!

London The Diocese of London was a waste

I looked across

The Diocese of Southwark

If only I could move a little more a little further

But more I could not for my fear was weather

The Diocese of Southwark

His Greek Street house was near; it's now pulled down.
And very soon they'll pull me down as well
To where the Devil waits for me in hell.
I know what hell will be: exhaust-pipe fumes,
And kiddiz running wild through all the rooms;
And Pevsner's *Penguin Guide to the Inferno*

And buildings by Goldfinger – 'Hello, Ernö!'*
And 'Goodbye, Feeble!' for Penelope,
Who's still my legal wife, must soon join me.
With forks they'll rip the jodhpurs off her hips;
Together we will fry like fish and chips;
And, when we're cooked, the fiends will wrap us up
In greasy copies of the *Times Lit. Supp.*
I'd rather writhe in everlasting pain
Than be wrapped up in Grigson and John Wain.[28]

One source of misery, at least, was removed in 1977. The only thing that had detracted from John's enjoyment of his seventieth-birthday celebrations in 1976 was that no greeting arrived from his son. 'Not a bleep from Paul, who is still hung up in his subconscious . . .', John had written to Penelope.[29] But in the summer of 1977 the long alienation of father and son ended when Paul brought to England a beautiful girlfriend, Linda Shelton. John was greatly taken with her. He wrote to Candida's mother-in-law, Lady Grimthorpe, 'Our son Paul appeared this summer with a smashingly pretty and humorous girl from Missouri. They lightened life and warmed the cockles of my heart. They stayed at Blacklands.'[30] (In May 1979 Penelope and John received a telegraph: 'Linda and I are getting married on Saturday May 19th at the Advent Lutheran Church on 93rd Street and Broadway, New York. Please be there in spirit although we do not expect you there in body. Paul and Linda.'[31] The young Betjemans were to have three children, Thomas, Timothy and Lily.)

James Lees-Milne still saw a lot of John and Elizabeth. He had been concerned when the couple stayed with him just before Christmas 1976, *en route* for Cornwall. He wrote of John:

He has aged alarmingly. Can hardly move. Passed the shuffling stage. Has to be guided along. With difficulty was able to enter our front door and collapse on an upright chair. There he sat till dinner, and ambled to the kitchen. Getting him upstairs and down the following morning a slow and laborious process. Talked after dinner about religion, and discussed how few practising Christians today really believed implicitly, whereas those of our grandparents' generation did believe without question, not all of course, but the majority. John said he *hoped*. Hope was greater than charity. All we could do was to hope.[32]

---

* Ernö Goldfinger (1902–87). Hungarian-born British modernist architect.

The diarist enjoyed a jollier dinner 'with John and Feeble' in August 1977.

> F. has lost weight through a diet. She eats little and drinks nothing at all. John looking better, but very shuffly. Is suffering from Parkinson's, which he discusses merrily. Takes an infinity of pills. A lovely joyous evening. John quoting from a newly discovered [sic] queer vicar, the Revd _____ Bradford,[33] who wrote sentimental poems to boys in the 1920s. Very funny about his two new loves, one a girl secretary, two an announcer on TV, a young man whom Feeble and I both find repulsive. He is the sort of youth, John said, whom he would have fallen for at school and been turned down by. When the said announcer appeared on the screen John addressed him in heart-rending terms of endearment and howls of laughter.[34]

Later in 1977, Jock Murray gave John lunch at the Charing Cross Hotel. 'John was putting on his "helpless" act,' Murray recalled. 'He said, "Oh, Jock, my fork is wobbling so much, I can't get the food to my mouth." I said, "Maybe not, John; but I notice you don't seem to be having so much trouble with the *wine glass*." '[35] In November 1977 John stayed with Penelope again at Cusop and she consented to worship with him at Hereford Cathedral. The Roman Catholic Church had relaxed its rule forbidding its members to attend Anglican services. 'I have never felt so happy and fulfilled,' John wrote to Penelope; '. . . the happiness still steals over me like radiant heat.'[36] Penelope had not yet acquired a telephone. John wanted to work out a system by which she would make regular calls to him at stated times. 'I very much like talking to you on the telephone. It is like those daily letters Woad and Mrs Woad [Penelope's parents] wrote to each other.'[37]

On 16 March 1978, James Lees-Milne attended a meeting of the Royal Society of Literature at which John took the chair and Roland Gant, literary editor at Heinemann, spoke on John Masefield. 'Very dreary lecture and dreary delivery,' Lees-Milne wrote. 'We dined afterwards with dear Sheila Birkenhead. Silly old John had invited Gant and Mrs Gant to join the party. I drove to Wilton Street with Sheila who a little ruefully said how much more fun we would have had without these people whom none of us knew. In fact Gant turned from being dull to a very boring, pleased-with-himself oaf. Elizabeth Cav. didn't like him one bit.'[38] (In Gant's defence, it should be said that he was a friend and publisher of Anthony Powell, who liked him a lot.)[39]

The ordeal of chairing the meeting may have contributed to the heart attack that John suffered a few days later. Candida was driving

home from London to Wiltshire when she heard on the car radio that
her father had been rushed into the Royal Brompton Hospital.

My own heart came up into my mouth [she wrote] and I continued round
the roundabout in the rain and sped at over a hundred miles an hour back
to London. I kept him alive in my mind. I could do nothing but say the
Lord's Prayer constantly. As I drove up the Fulham Road I saw thirty or
forty press men outside the Royal Brompton Hospital. It was raining even
harder. I still kept JB alive in my head. I did not ask them any questions.
I parked the car and walked into the hospital with my head down and eyes
on the ground. I didn't ask the porter if my father was dead. I still kept
him alive. I asked what ward he was in and went up to the fourth floor
saying the Lord's Prayer all the way up in the lift. He was alive. I sat by his
bed and held his hand. He had the softest hands I had ever felt on a man,
and when I looked back, I realised it was because he had never done a
stroke of manual work in his life.[40]

Slowly he regained his strength. In May he was well enough to travel
to Cornwall with Elizabeth, staying with the Lees-Milnes on the way.
James Lees-Milne scuttled home from Roy Harrod's memorial service
in Oxford Cathedral, in time to welcome them. Also of the house
party were Lees-Milne's nephew Richard Robinson and a friend of
his, James Bettley.

They are going on a tour of Victorian country houses in July [Lees-Milne
wrote] and wanted to pick our brains. John delighted by this, and by
them of course, and very sweet to them. He is more crippled than ever;
has difficulty in getting from the drawing-room to the kitchen, and has
to be cajoled, and pulled by Elizabeth who is encouraging, and patient.
He has to take dozens of different pills which he forgets. She reminds
him; she in fact puts him to bed, and gets him up in the morning. He told
me that without her he would die. Yet on Sunday morning he insisted
on coming to church, not the early service, but Matins at 11.15 and
Communion after. I feared great difficulties, but once out of the car he
walked bravely from the gate. On his feet, and on the flat, and rested after
a good night, he is better. Is stricken with Parkinson's, kept very under
control by the drugs. As we approached the church door we were overtaken by a bevy of girl guides from their camp at Bath Lodge. 'Oh dear,
they will be disturbing!' he said. 'It would of course be worse if they were
boy scouts.'[41]

Back in Radnor Walk in July, John had regained enough vim to write
an irascible letter to Williams Brothers, a Fulham building firm, asking

'for how many more days the noisy machine you installed for a building on the King's Road corner of this residential street is to continue?. . . It does start very early in the morning and work becomes impossible.'[42] The builders sent an apology and the noise ceased ten days later.[43]

By 25 September John could write to Penelope: 'I am very much better if I do very little each day . . . Next time you come, you must come and see Chelsea Hospital [the Royal Hospital, built 1682–90 by Sir Christopher Wren]. I can manage the walk . . .'[44] By October he travelled again to Cornwall with Elizabeth. On the way they once more spent a night with the Lees-Milnes, who had moved to a house at Badminton.

> I would say he is rather more decrepit than before [Lees-Milne wrote on 10 October]. Mind active as ever, and quoting reams of poetry which always puts me at a disadvantage. Has re-read *The Deserted Village*, which was the first poem he knew, for his father read it aloud to him. He now realises that all his own poetry stemmed from it.[45] After we had been sitting in the drawing-room A[lvilde] said come and look at the sunset. John said he would like to be driven round the park. So I drove him, and we came out at Little Badminton and I took him to look at the outside of the church. The lights were shining through the windows and we heard singing. This determined him to join Evensong. It turned out to be Little Badminton's Harvest Festival. The tiny church was packed. We sat at the back beside the font. I was not properly dressed, wearing a pullover. All the rich farmers and their wives dressed to kill; and Master and Mary [the Duke and Duchess of Beaufort] in the front row . . .[46]

On 28 November the Lees-Milnes dined with John and Elizabeth at No. 19 Radnor Walk, which was 'more topsy-turvy than usual, the builders in process of installing a heating system'.[47] Lees-Milne found the heat 'asphyxiating', but John said he could never, himself, be too warm. Some of the talk was about the Jeremy Thorpe case: the Liberal leader had been charged, with others, with conspiracy to murder Norman Scott, his former lover. (All the defendants were later acquitted.) 'John said that in no circumstances was he ever shocked by sex cases. A[lvilde] said, not even when children are seduced? Never, John answered.'[48]

During 1978 he wrote a foreword to *Temples of Power*, a limited-edition book about power stations by Gavin Stamp, illustrated with lithographs by Glynn Boyd Harte.[49] The foreword began: 'Electricity is the daintiest handmaid of Science.'[50] The book was reviewed in the *Times Literary Supplement* in *ersatz* Betjeman stanzas.[51] John attended the launch party at the National Liberal Club, ceremonially cutting a cake in the shape of Battersea Power Station (a building once described as 'an upended billiard table') – pink icing with marzipan chimneys.[52]

In July 1979 Lees-Milne invited John and Elizabeth to dine at his club, Brooks's, with himself, Alvilde and the young historian Michael Bloch, for whom the diarist had conceived a platonic passion.

> I think A[lvilde] liked M[ichael] [Lees-Milne wrote], though she finds him looking, as she says, unhealthy. After dinner, M. and John had a long talk about Uranian [homosexual] verse, and liked one another. I worry about John, who is worse. Find walking a great effort. E. leads him by the arm, making encouraging noises as one would to a recalcitrant horse. He has both sleeves of his shirt, without links, hanging over his hands. This, and his staggering gait, make him seem drunk after dinner. I felt sad. A. and I drove away, having put John in his car, and leaving Michael on the pavement.[53]

A month later, the Lees-Milnes lunched with Penelope at Cusop. James noted that she 'talked of John as if he were still hers. Deplored his addiction to drugs: he takes every medicine which is going, and they conflict with one another'.[54]

In 1979 John stayed at Churchill, Letterkenny, Co. Donegal, to have his portrait painted by Derek Hill. The bachelor artist lived in a classical Regency house set in woodland; Reynolds Stone had made a wood-engraving of it to head Hill's stationery. While painting, Hill kept John entertained with gramophone records of Douglas Byng and with reminiscences of Marlborough: he had been a pupil after John and shared his dislike of A.R. Gidney.[55] Hill used oil paints with almost the technique of a watercolourist, thinning the pigments with turpentine, rather than relying on impasto, glazes and scumbling in the manner of the Old Masters. But he achieved a remarkable likeness of John: the lustrous brown eyes below quizzical eyebrows; the slightly bulbous nose; the lopsided mouth, expressive of both hesitancy and humour. Painter and sitter visited Lionel Perry, who lived near-by, no longer the 'Golden Boy' of Oxford days, but a paunchy old roué. Perry recited some of John's 'indecent' poems, of which he (like John Edward Bowle, Oswell Blakeston and Cecil 'Granny' Gould of the National Gallery, London) had a cherished collection. One, about a masturbatory encounter between two schoolboys behind a cricket pavilion, ended:

> Oh Neville, dear, how could you squirt
> That filthy stuff all down my shirt?[56]

Hill also took John to meet the American Henry McIlhenny at Glenveagh Castle, with its famous landscape gardens.[57]

The Betjemans were together again for Penelope's seventieth birth-day on St Valentine's Day, 1980 ('*the* day in my life,' John assured her);[58] but two days later John and Elizabeth were guests of the Queen Mother at Royal Lodge, Windsor Great Park[59] – 'surely a change in the tradition of royalty never to countenance domestic irregularities' Lees-Milne noted.[60] He added:

> John was given a bedroom next to the Queen Mother's and not next to E's. Nevertheless she went to say goodnight to him and tuck him up. She told the policeman on duty, who apparently sits all night on a chair outside the QM's bedroom, to see if John needed anything during the night, which this kind man did.[61]

Sir Roy Strong, then director of the Victoria & Albert Museum, and his wife, the theatre designer Julia Trevelyan Oman, were also at Royal Lodge that weekend. Strong heard of an incident involving a group of the Queen Mother's guests – among them Elizabeth Cavendish and Sir Frederick Ashton, founder choreographer to the Royal Ballet.

> The story came to me direct from Fred Ashton [Strong writes]. He recalled how the bathroom door at Royal Lodge was suddenly flung open and Lady Eliz said 'And here is Sir Frederick's bathroom.' Fred was sat on the loo com-pletely pole-axed and said, 'Thank goodness I had a dressing-gown on.' The moment was dissolved to mirth by Liz Cav. screaming with laughter.
> We went four times to Royal Lodge for Qu. Eliz's 'Arts' weekend – I didn't write them all up in my diary. Latterly, it was Ted Hughes. J.B. got dropped when he became too difficult to cope with – he drank so heavily that it was [Sir] Martin Gilliat's[62] task to carry him upstairs somehow, undress him & put him to bed.[63]

The state of John's health ruled out some of the treats he and Elizabeth had been looking forward to. On 2 July 1980 he wrote to Penelope: 'I have come to the conclusion that I cannot accept an invitation I had to visit Gothland in the Baltic. A beautiful island of flowers and rocks and Hanseatic Romanesque. It would mean foreigners, different food and no protection unless Jonathan [Stedall] came, which he can't at the moment.'[64] But that year John and Elizabeth did visit the Scillies again. Arriving by helicopter, they were greeted by Mary Wilson with a bouquet of flowers, and stayed in a house owned by Prince Charles.[65] Also, John was still up for trips to the English seaside, though not always with his partner's blessing. Reg Read remembers something of a showdown with Elizabeth Cavendish in 1980.

One morning John came into his office at No. 29 – into his den – and said, 'Oh, Reg, what are we going to do? The Lung of London is going to be demolished! Southend pier.' So he sits himself down and I said, 'Explain.' He says, 'Oh, look!' and he showed me a cutting to the effect that Southend Council had agreed to a development which would mean that the whole of the pier would come down. So out came the bottles.

We got to about 11.00 and he said he was going to write to Southend Corporation and the Victorian Society and so on. He was very fond of the Lung of London. And suddenly I thought, 'I know: we'll get this on television.' I said, 'We'll go to Fenchurch Street – now you know you like Fenchurch Street – and we'll go to Southend-on-Sea. I'll arrange for a wheelchair to be available. And you know the television people, you know the press people.' 'Oh, wonderful, wonderful!' Within half an hour we had fixed it all up. John phoned various people. Elizabeth Moore said, 'Don't tell Elizabeth; there's no need for her to know until it happens.' Oh, it was fatal. As soon as Elizabeth Cavendish walked in, John spilt the beans. It was fatal to tell him 'Don't tell Elizabeth,' because he told her everything. She was furious – 'Certainly not . . . Quite unnecessary . . . Out of the question.' So nothing more was said or done, but indirectly we heard Lady Elizabeth's views, via Mrs Alford, the cleaning lady, whom John used to regale with champagne. Elizabeth was saying to Mrs Alford, 'Reg is very irresponsible. A very bad influence on Sir John.'

Rene Alford told us that Lady Elizabeth was dead against the trip – 'Supposing something happens' – this, that and the other.

The day of the trip was fast approaching so I thought I'd try and reason with Lady Elizabeth. I went down to No. 19 and said, 'Why don't you come with us, make a day of it?' She hit the ceiling. 'Certainly not!' She more or less said, over her dead body. Anyway, came the day of departure. It was like The Thirty-Nine Steps, everyone going round whispering.

We were trying to get him out of her house without her knowing. The trouble was that John used to come up from No. 19 looking as if he had just got out of bed – he probably had. But because he was going to Southend and was going to be filmed, we had to make sure he was smartened up a little. So arrangements were made that he should groom himself a bit without making it too obvious to Lady Elizabeth. In due course he walked up with his second-best suit on and his tie not quite tied in a neat knot, and what remained of his hair brushed: it was reasonable. And I was waiting by the door of No. 29 to get a cab, and Lady Elizabeth realized that we were going. You could tell from where we were at No. 29 that she was yelling. So I went down to her house and said, 'Sorry, Lady Elizabeth, but I did ask you to come with us. Why don't you? There's still time.' 'No!' She was so angry she could hardly speak. The cab came along and we all piled in, and there was Lady Elizabeth in the middle of the road, making frenzied gestures.[66]

At Fenchurch Street station, John spotted a journalist he knew and, to Read's dismay, asked him to travel down to Southend in their compartment. 'So for the whole of the journey this reporter was firing questions at John; and John was getting so worked up, that he arrived at Southend not in the best of moods. But we had a marvellous time at Southend. A police constable attached himself to us, pushing the wheelchair. The visit was well covered on telly and in the newspapers; and we saved the pier.'[67]

On 21 July 1980 Lees-Milne went to tea with Michael Bloch at the Oxford and Cambridge Club and found that he had also asked the writer Lady Caroline Blackwood, daughter of John's Oxford friend Basil Dufferin. 'Chain-smoking, churchyard cough, beautiful blue staring eyes, raddled complexion,' the diarist noted. 'A difficult girl. No come-back, no return of the ball.'[68] He went on to drinks with John and Elizabeth. When Elizabeth left the two men to attend a meeting, Lees-Milne talked about his encounter with Caroline Blackwood. John told him of his unrequited love for Dufferin.[69] In return, Lees-Milne described his passionate embraces, at Eton, with Tom Mitford[70] – 'lips to lips, body pressed to body, each feeling the opposite fibre of the other'.[71]

J's eyes stood out with excitement. And then? he asked. And then, I said, when Tom left Eton it was all over. He never again had any truck with me, and turned exclusively to women. J's eyes filled with tears.[72]

The eyes of a character obviously based on John fill with tears in a novel by Anthony Burgess published that same year.[73] The book was *Earthly Powers*, which has perhaps the most arresting first sentence in modern literature – 'It was the afternoon of my eighty-first birthday, and I was in bed with my catamite when Ali announced that the archbishop had come to see me.'[74] Burgess, an inveterate umbrage-taker, was envious of John's knighthood. In the novel – which kind friends soon drew to John's attention – he portrayed, with maximum malice, a Poet Laureate, Dawson Wignall. (Did Burgess, who knew so much, know that Dawson was the maiden name of John's mother?)[75] Wignall is contemptuously described: 'a round, duckdownheaded, hamsterteethed children's book illustration of a benign humanoid who held the office John Dryden had once held'.[76] Vulnerable himself, Burgess was adept at detecting other people's vulnerabilities. Over thirty years earlier, in *Scott-King's Modern Europe*, Evelyn Waugh had satirized John's fantasies about schoolgirl prefects.[77] Burgess went further, making explicit the charges of perversion and fetishism and garnishing the attack with a parody of John's verse – clever, funny and lethal. The narrator, a novelist, is about to meet the Laureate:

> Near the original Quiller-Couch edition stood, not wellthumbed, not favourite, the revised *Oxford Book of English Verse*, bloody Val Wrigley as editor. I took this down and lay on the couch with it, looking for the inevitable selection from Dawson Wignall. I did not much care for what I found – insular, ingrown, formally traditional, products of a stunted mind. Wignall's themes derived from Anglican church services, the Christmas parties of his childhood, his public school pubescence, suburban shopping streets; they occasionally exhibited perverse velleities of a fetishistic order, though his droolings over girls' bicycles and gym tunics and black woollen stockings were chilled by whimsical ingenuities of diction. For this sort of thing, then, he had been honoured by the monarch:
>
> > Thus kneeling at the altar rail
> > We ate the Word's white papery wafer.
> > Here, so I thought, desire must fail,
> > My chastity be never safer.
> > But then I saw your tongue protrude
> > To catch the wisp of angel's food.
> > Dear God! I reeled beneath the shock:
> > My Eton suit, your party frock,
> > Christmas, the dark, and postman's knock!

I returned the book to the shelf and took down *Who's Who* . . . There he was: Wignall, Percival Dawson – not yet OM but tinkling with other awards. His list of literary achievements was exiguous enough, spare output being the mark of a gentleman writer, but the autobiographical epic called *Lying in Grass* was probably the dehydrated equivalent of ten of my watery novels . . .[78]

John, whose earthly powers were failing, was at the stage of life at which one assesses what one has achieved and what one has failed to achieve. When he asked, 'Mirror, mirror, on the wall . . .?' there leered back at him the effigy which Burgess had created to stick pins in. He brooded over it. Not only was it mortifying in itself, a public humiliation; it was upsetting, too, to be made aware that there was anyone who despised and disliked him enough to mount such an attack. The rave reviews for Burgess's book did nothing to salve the wounds.

As John's *Angst* intensified, Reg Read and Elizabeth Moore encouraged people he liked to visit him. 'He was sometimes embarrassed,' Read says, 'because he lost control of his body, pooped his pants. So it had to be friends who knew him well.'[79] Barry Humphries was always welcome. So were Margie Geddes, Kingsley Amis, Mary Wilson, Alan Ross, editor of the *London Magazine*, the broadcaster Robert Robinson, who had compèred television quiz shows in which John had taken part, and Richard Boston, editor of the magazines *Vole* and *Quarto*.

Boston was the tenant, next-door neighbour and friend of Osbert Lancaster (whose biography he later wrote) in a thatched cottage at Aldworth, Berkshire – the 'A' of John's television *ABC of Churches*. He remembers visiting John in Radnor Walk in the 1970s and sharing with him one of the orgies of mirth that the poet still occasionally enjoyed. The name of John's old boss on *The Architectural Review*, Hubert de Cronin Hastings, cropped up in the conversation.

John was not very communicative [Boston writes] until (at an agreeably early stage in the mid-morning) champagne arrived. Things livened up quickly. The webbed feet of the Hastings family were mentioned. I asked whether this was a matter of pride or concern for de Cronin Hastings, and whether John had information about Hastings's own feet. The subject-matter and the champagne combined/combusted into laughter from both of us that was uncontrollable. We tried to move on to other topics but after a few words one or the other of us would remember the webbed feet and crack up. John soon became tired and it was clear that his attention-span was brief so we agreed to continue the conversation another day – which, regrettably, I think we never did.[80]

The 1970s had brought Barry Humphries sobriety and fame. In 1976 – 'the happiest year I have known', he said – he had his first great

London success with *Housewife-Superstar*. Dame Edna's one-woman show was introduced by another of Humphries's characters, the gross, drunken, priapic 'Australian cultural attaché', Sir Les Patterson: 'I'd like you all to give her a warm hand on her opening and give her the clap she so richly deserves.'[81] John was at the Apollo Theatre to witness the triumph he had predicted for Humphries fourteen years earlier.[82] In 1979 he attended his wedding to the surrealist artist Diane Millstead at Marylebone Register Office, along with Sir John Rothenstein, John Wells, Nicholas Garland and Joan Bakewell. (Diane had a bouquet of 'gladdies'.)[83]

As John lapsed into illness and Humphries increasingly went on tours abroad, the two men saw less of each other. When Humphries did visit John, he thought he was 'very much in the grip of alcohol. There was a lot of booze: champagne in pewter tankards in the morning; drinks before lunch; drinks at lunch; drinks after lunch; drinks in the evening. It all built up – and he was mixing it with anti-depressant pills. Most people didn't notice because of the fun of it all. It looked like merriment, generosity, enjoyment, celebration – but the truth was, he was pissed.'[84]

For John, the most welcome visitor of all was Osbert Lancaster. 'I have a strong memory of Osbert and John at Radnor Walk, with Osbert sitting on the sofa,' Jonathan Stedall says. 'There is that thing about somebody you know really well, that you can sit in silence together. I had the feeling of a real closeness there – more than, I would say, with Jock Murray.'[85] In August 1980 John said to Read, 'Oh Reg, we must go to Covent Garden for lunch. Shall we ask Osbert?'

So a telephone call was put through to Osbert. He turned up. We got down to Covent Garden. There was a huge queue. I took one look and said, 'I'll see what I can do.' So I did a great act of 'I've got the Poet Laureate with me' – did a queue-jump. The waiter made it a condition that I must get him John Betjeman's signature. We got down to eating. Osbert decided to leave – which had happened before. So poor old John was landed with the bill. We made our way to the front of the house to go, and the waiter comes charging up about his autograph.

The waiter says: 'I hope you don't mind me saying so: you might be the Poet Laureate but I think the poem you wrote for the Queen Mother's eightieth birthday was bloody awful!'

John went the colour of your shirt [white] with rage. I said, 'Come on, John'; but he turned to the waiter and said, 'Have you ever tried to write poetry?' He said, 'You don't realize how difficult it is to write poetry to order.'

I grabbed him by the arm. I said, 'Come along, come along. I'll get a cab.' He was *shaking*, in the lobby. I got him out into the road and I said,

'Now, John, I'll go and get a cab down at the court – Bow Street. You stand there. Don't move.' I left him clutching a bollard. And I hadn't been gone more than thirty seconds before, 'Reg! Reg!' I thought, 'Oh God, are we going through that manure process again? Has he messed himself?' So I went back. I said, 'Oh for goodness sake, John! How can I get a taxi unless you . . . what is the matter?'

'Just look over there,' he said.

I followed his gaze to a row of neatly stacked black high-powered motor-cycles, glistening in the sun.

'We don't need a taxi,' he said. 'We'll go home on one of them. *Just think of all that power between your legs*!' He was laughing, the whole situation was defused.[86]

Reg Read had to steer John through another crisis in September 1980, over the publication of *Church Poems*, a selection illustrated by John Piper. There had been a temporary falling-out between John and Piper. When, in 1976, I approached Piper for an interview about John, he agreed to talk, but added, 'He and I are not really on speakers at the moment.' The discord between the two old friends had arisen because Piper's son Edward was now the designer of the Shell Guides. John Betjeman hated his designs, and said so; John and Myfanwy Piper took offence and their son's side.[87] John said to Reg Read, 'Do you know, Reg, Mr Piper does not like me. He's never really liked me at all.' Read said, 'Come on, John, you've known each other for years; you've worked together; he's one of your best friends.' John said, 'No, he doesn't like me. He's jealous. Because my name appears first, before his. It's I who get mentioned, not Mr Piper.'[88] Read thought John was acting like some petulant medieval king, excluding people from his court.

The Betjeman–Piper friendship was far too deep for the bad feeling to last. As so often, Jock Murray's gentle, wise and humorous diplomacy came into play. He jollied the two men out of their antagonism. The two Johns' collaborating on *Church Poems* set the seal on reconciliation.

'There was great excitement at No. 29 in September 1980,' Reg Read recalled.

Jock Murray was coming round with these special copies for John to sign. John signed them, and off they went by courier, to Buckingham Palace, Clarence House and so on. A little later, Jock turned up with ordinary copies. John said, 'How lovely! Oh, Jock, you've done me proud!' When Jock left, John said to me, 'I'll give you a copy.' So he signed a copy. I was looking through it and he said, 'Read some of my poems to me.' So I just read at random. I came to the end of one poem, and John said, 'Go on, finish it.' I said, 'There isn't any more.' He said, 'Oh, yes, there is! There are several more lines. Where's the end of the poem?' We read other poems and there were other changes. I think Murray's had cut the poems to avoid adding another four pages – to save money.

Well, John went absolutely spare. The result was that I grabbed the phone. I said, 'Don't let's waste time; let's get through to Jock.' I did the talking. I said Sir John was very upset, and what were they going to do about it? I said, 'Sir John insists that the special copies should be got back. And he insists that the book be reprinted.' John was in such a state.

Well, they rushed round the palaces and elsewhere getting back the copies. They didn't get them all. They didn't get mine! John said, 'Tell Jock I'll pay to get it reprinted.' I said, 'Not on your life! It's their mistake,' I said. 'I can see why they did it, to save an extra fold of paper.* They hoped you wouldn't notice.' Two weeks later we heard that the poems would be reprinted, 'but there will be a delay'.

John later asked Jock, 'Any idea why the poems were cut?' 'Yes,' Jock said. 'The proofs blew out of the window.' Really, I thought that was on the level of 'The dog ate my homework'![89]

The corrected edition was published in March 1981. Peter Gammond and John Heald record, in their *Bibliographical Companion to Betjeman* (1997), that a number of the faulty copies 'survived the withdrawal and are now collectors' items'.[90]

There was more trouble over another book of the 1980s in which John had a hand. In the late 1970s he had met at a country-house party Lady Fergusson of Kilkerran, the sister of his old Oxford friend Michael Dugdale. She told him that Dugdale, who had died in 1971, had written a number of poems, which she thought deserved publication. John said, 'Send them to me; and if I like them, I will pay to have them privately published.'[91] When the poems were sent to him, he did like them, and suggested to Frances Fergusson that they should be published under the striking title *An Omelette of Vultures' Eggs* (the heading of one of the poems). John arranged that the printing should be done by Francis Cleverdon, the son of another Oxford friend, Douglas Cleverdon.

Weeks went by [Reg Read recalls]. John made a telephone call to Francis Cleverdon. So lo and behold one lunchtime Francis Cleverdon turned up at

---

* This is not very likely. The saving would have been negligible.

Radnor Walk. He almost didn't seem to know what we were talking about. The typescript disappeared from John's desk, Francis Cleverdon took it away. Weeks and weeks went by. Frances Fergusson kept phoning up, asking 'When's the book coming out?' We had to ask Francis Cleverdon how things were going on and it seemed to me that he didn't know himself – he was doing it through a friend of a friend, something like that. Then he turned up with the books all finished. John said, 'This is no good. I promised Frances Fergusson I would write a foreword; we'll have to rearrange it.' It was all taken away. More weeks went by and the foreword didn't get written. Lady Fergusson was getting very impatient.

One day John said, 'Pull up a chair. I'll give you the gist of what we're going to say – and you write it.' I went upstairs and I typed an introduction to the poems. I read it over to him. Roars of laughter. 'You must sign it,' I said. 'It's *yours*.' Later it caused big trouble. Apparently there was a mistake in the foreword. Of course Lady Fergusson spotted it and insisted the copies be withdrawn. I think eventually we compromised with an *erratum* slip. And of course John didn't want to know about that, although it was *his* mistake that I'd repeated.

The books were sold at £40 each, but there were some copies over and above the numbered limited edition. Lady Elizabeth had those. John was not supposed to sign those – he was only supposed to sign the limited edition. But he did sign them.[92]

The *Vultures' Eggs* episode is memorable to Reg Read for another reason.

Francis Cleverdon, who was young and good-looking, turned up with the final copies. John said, 'Now Reg will take you to a very nice pub he knows, for lunch' – lots of nudges and winks at me. So I took Francis Cleverdon to a pub I knew, the Harlequin, next to Sadler's Wells Theatre. It was not notable as a gay bar, but it was theatrical. We arrived late: it was okay for drinks, but too late for lunch. That evening I went back into the pub. The landlord said, 'You're barred.' 'Why?' I asked. 'Quite clearly you brought that under-age boy here with illicit purposes in mind.' I was completely taken aback. So I went across to the King's Head. I told the landlady, Blanche, 'I'm barred from the Harlequin,' and explained what had been said. She said, 'You come back in half an hour and I'll see what I can do about this.' When I came back, she had made several badges inscribed, 'BARRED FROM THE HARLEQUIN'. We all went over to the Harlequin wearing them.

The next day I had lunch with John and Lady Elizabeth. He said, 'I was hoping you would fall in love with Francis. We were looking forward to hearing about that, weren't we, Feeble?'[93]

In March 1981, John was still well and tranquil enough to reply in his most exuberant strain to Alice Hardy, a woman who had had something of a fling with him in his Admiralty days in 1944,[94] and who had written to him every year since then.

> Darling PE* [he wrote],
>
> I loved your annual letter. As you know, you are the original of 'In a Bath Tea Shop', the shortest poem I wrote.[95] I'm so glad to hear of old friends and so sad for Eileen Molony.[96] I think of her sitting with me in the little branch line to Iron Acton, she will remember it if she is well enough. I loved her deeply and she was a very good producer, the slave of the lady who was head of her department.[97] That was the most creative time of my life, everything was thrilling and the Avon flowed through Clifton Gorge and under that mighty mosquito of a bridge.[98]
>
> I wouldn't half mind that book of Teddy Wolfe's.[99] I would buy it on the strength of your recommendation. I'll ask my accountant if I can afford the two hundred pounds . . .[100]

In April John went to stay with Elizabeth at Moor View, near Chatsworth. On Easter Sunday he lingered in bed. Elizabeth told him to hurry up or they would be late for church; but she soon found that he could not speak or move his right arm.[101] He had suffered a stroke and was admitted to the Royal Hallamshire Hospital in Sheffield. He stayed there over a month and was attended by the neurologist Dr Cyril Davies-Jones, to Candida's eye 'extraordinarily good-looking'.[102] Penelope and Elizabeth played Box and Cox in visiting hours. 'I hope your hozzie smells nice,' Sandy Stone (alias Barry Humphries) wrote from Melbourne on 29 May.[103] That same day, James Lees-Milne wrote in his diary, after he and Alvilde had visited John in the hospital on their way to Chatsworth:

> [He] has a room to himself which, such is his distinction, they will not allow him to pay for. Room a sort of glass eyrie at top of tall modern block. Like being in a glass box, for the walls are seemingly of white glass. I would find it depressing looking out at view of ugly modern blocks and chimneys and distant grey hills. John sitting in chair, much thinner in face, with slight twist to his mouth which disturbs customary picture of him. Alert but not cheerful and longs to get away, after six weeks. Feeble there, of course, motors in every day and now takes him for drives.[104]

John was out of hospital by the time of his seventy-fifth birthday, 28 August 1981. To mark that anniversary, the Celandine Press published

---

* Programme Engineer. See note 94 to this chapter.

A Garland for the Laureate: verses by over twenty poets in an edition of 350 copies. On the title-page was a woodcut by Miriam Macgregor of a garland of wild flowers. Among the poets represented were Dannie Abse, Kingsley Amis, Patricia Beer, Alan Brownjohn, Charles Causley, Patric Dickinson, Roy Fuller, Ted Hughes, Elizabeth Jennings, Philip Larkin, A. L. Rowse, Sacheverell Sitwell, Stephen Spender, R. S. Thomas, Anthony Thwaite and Laurence Whistler. Even the old enemy John Wain contributed. The book was not ready for August, but was presented to John as a surprise in November. Many of the poets, including Larkin and Thomas, came to Radnor Walk for the ceremony, bringing bottles of champagne and smoked salmon sandwiches.[105] On 4 December, John wrote to John Pringle of the Celandine Press, whose idea the book had been, 'The wild flowers in the Garland are inno-cently beautiful and make me think of the Christian names of the nurses who attended me at the Royal Hallamshire.'[106]

Lees-Milne saw John again in March 1982, ten months to the day after his diary entry about the hospital visit. At Radnor Walk for dinner, he was shocked by his condition.

When I arrived, he was sitting in his usual chair under the window, his belly swollen and prominent. Not his usual self, but quieter than usual. No guffaws of laughter, and when amused he gave a funny little half-snigger, half-grunt as though it were painful for him to laugh outright. But I tried to cheer him. He began by reciting a new poem he was writing: 'Sir Christopher Wren / Was dining with some men / He said "If anyone calls / Say I'm building St Paul's." '* 'No, you have not got it right, love,' said Elizabeth. Moving him to table for dinner was a great effort. She walked backwards, holding his outstretched hands. He groaned, as though with pain, and moved to the table in a kind of dancing movement like an old bear. It was rather piteous. Talked of Gavin Stamp. I said how nice he was and clever. J. said he was a very good writer and had a column in *Private Eye* on architecture, under assumed name.[107] J. said he (John) was only interested in young men. Wanted to go to bed with them. This did make him laugh outright. I said, 'We must get used to the fact that this is impossible now.'[108]

Lees-Milne again dined with John and Elizabeth on 15 June.

Noticeable declension since my last visit. J. barely spoke. Must have had another little stroke by the slipped look of his face on right-hand side. Enormous blown-up stomach. Movement from his chair to dinner table

* Garbled version of well-known lines by E. Clerihew Bentley.

most painful. Was told not to help. Nice friendly old Anglican monk [Harry Williams] staying. While Elizabeth supported J.'s shoulders the monk gently kicked J's feet. Thus they dragged him, bent sideways like a telephone pole half blown over, to the table. I sat beside him. Tried to tease him into amusement. Barely succeeded. Yet yesterday, he was televised sitting in his chair.[109] I said, 'I suppose you were talking about yourself as usual?' He laughed in the old way. He said, 'No, I was catty.' Strange reaction . . . Left feeling very sad. Cannot believe he will survive the year.[110]

On 19 August 1982, John was visited in Radnor Walk by Paul Wigmore. The photographer and writer had become a friend of Penelope through attending one of her lectures on Hindu temples and stayed with her at Cusop. He asked her if she could persuade John to meet him. 'I can hear her voice again, the unmistakable voice of command recognized by Himalayan mules and coolies. "Yes of course," she said. "But you MUSTN'T STAY MORE THAN TEN MINUTES. D'you understand?"'[111] As Wigmore came into the small front room at No. 29, John turned his head stiffly towards him, hardly able to smile because of his strokes and Parkinson's Disease. But Wigmore soon realized that his mind was as agile – and poetical – as ever.

We talked and talked and drank champagne. Liz Moore had to go out for ten minutes and asked me to look after him. This I did, including answering the phone and knocking my glass of Moët on to the floor and soaking the carpet.

'Help yourself to more,' he said. 'Oh, this is fun!' . . .

The phone rang again after his secretary returned. One of the papers. What was his reaction to hearing that Naseby Field was to have a road built through it? He thought for a moment. 'Tell them it's like cutting a man in half,' he said. Then, after a pause, 'Alive!'[112]

There were still flashes of the old wit. A friend told him how the Roman Catholic monk Bede Griffiths, who had been at Magdalen, Oxford, with John, had gone out to India with a view to 'reconciling' the Roman Catholic and Hindu faiths. 'I suppose,' said John, 'he's trying to combine Mumbo and Jumbo in roughly equal proportions.'[113] I had lunch with him in a Chelsea Restaurant. John ordered the salmon-like fish called smelt. Delivering it to our table, the waiter asked him, 'Are you smelt, sir?' John: 'Only by the discerning.'

In October 1982 John Murray published a selection of poems by John which (with two exceptions) had never appeared in book form before. I had found them among his papers at the University of Victoria, British Columbia; and he had given the choice his approval. The verses, dedicated to Elizabeth, appeared under the title *Uncollected Poems*. Kingsley Amis said, 'Perhaps they should have stayed that way,'[114] and John suggested the alternative title *Barrel Scrapings*.[115] Most of the reviews were of the kind that Jock Murray diplomatically described as 'unhelpful', though the selection contained poems as good as '1940', 'Interior Decorator' and 'The Retired Postal Clerk'; and in 2001 the verses were subsumed into a new edition of the *Collected Poems*.

John confounded James Lees-Milne's prediction that he would not survive 1982. 'By 1983,' Candida writes, 'he often looked sad and haunted behind his long, clear gaze. He would spend each morning at number 29, sitting at his Swedish-made pine table opposite his gentle secretary, Elizabeth Moore, whom he always called "Dorinda" and who lived on the other side of the street.'[116] Candida felt that, in a way, the letters that still poured in 'anchored' her father, gave a structure to his day. But 'his dictated replies got shorter and shorter. Sometimes Elizabeth Moore would write them herself and say that JB was not feeling well and could not do this or that.'[117]

One thing John did consent to do was to attend a lunch in his honour at Fishmongers' Hall on 7 April 1983, under Pietro Annigoni's exquisite portrait of the Queen. It was his second-to-last public appearance. John Mallet, who was keeper of the Ceramics Department at the Victoria & Albert Museum, presided over the event, and recorded it in his diary.

> Lunch for the Poet Laureate at the Fishmongers' today. This arose from the initiative of John Gough,[118] who heard how Sir John Betjeman had earlier had to miss lunch in the Hall with Mervyn Stockwood, former Bishop of Southwark. As the Prime Warden wasn't available I was asked to act as host and sit at the head of the table next to Sir John. On the other side of him sat his nice secretary, who helped him from time to time when his hands failed him. He has Parkinson's disease and arrived in a wheel chair. Nevertheless, though considerably aged since I met him a few years back following [an] oyster-smack race in the mouth of the Thames, his memory still seemed good, though his concentration came and went a little. He ate and drank well enough, getting through two platefuls of oysters in the time it took me to eat one. If I am asked what we talked about I find it hard to say. I did not think it felt right to ask personal questions (such as had Miss Purey-Cust got in touch with him after the programme on television in which he claimed her as his first and most passionate love). John Gough and I talked with him a bit about Holy Trinity, Sloane Street, whose nice vicar plus wife was there. Also present was a . . . ginger-haired wine-merchant who claimed to have collected every scrap that Betjeman had ever written. I felt a bit sorry for the old

man when this keen little fellow tried to discuss poetry with him. Perhaps it was some sense of inadequacy in paying for his lunch with sparkling chat that made Betjeman turn anxiously to me after one of his periods of silence, and say: 'I hope you don't mind if I'm not *discussing* things.' I did my best to reassure him by saying with what I hope was warmth of feeling: 'Not at all. It's so nice for us having you here.'

After lunch we wheeled him through the Hall looking at things, though I have an idea his eyesight is pretty bad and he couldn't see much. But he seemed to enjoy it for a time and when he looked like tiring I hustled his wheel chair down into the lift and John Gough drove him home. I hope the old boy enjoyed himself; I think he did. Several times he threw back his head and opened his mouth in a loud, boyish clap of laughter.[119]

TIME WITH BETJEMAN

The current television series, 'Time with Betjeman', allows us to study his face. Like most old faces, it has collapsed somewhat, but is still watchful, the eyes moving from speaker to speaker, faintly apprehensive.

When he himself says something, there is a hint of the old nostril-lifting irony, the corners of the mouth turning down crookedly; then suddenly comes the uproarious back-of-the-pit horse-laugh wide open, all teeth and creases. And above it the extraordinarily powerful skull, like a Roman bust, or a phrenologist's model waiting to be marked into thirty-three sections and labelled with Superior Sentiments and Reflective Faculties. Impossible to characterize such features: the top half is authoritative, perhaps a famous headmaster, but lower down is the schoolboy: furtive, volatile, ready to burst out laughing, never entirely at ease.

> Philip Larkin, review of Patrick Taylor-Martin's *John Betjeman: His Life and Work, The Observer*, 10 April 1983

In 1981 and 1982 – the last period when John was articulate – Jonathan Stedall made a series of seven television programmes with and about him, entitled *Time with Betjeman*.[1] It was akin to the retrospective exhibition of a painter; instead of paintings, extracts from his earlier television films were shown. Though they ranged from one of John's earliest surviving televised broadcasts – at Exeter College, Oxford, in 1954 – to 1982 in Radnor Walk and Cornwall, they were not in chronological sequence, nor grouped under themes. Stedall made each episode a gallimaufry, a kind of lucky dip. At one moment one was watching the youngish, vital John mounting a diatribe against modern office blocks; at the next, the John of 1982 was slumped in an armchair, talking with old friends or haltingly answering Stedall's questions about his life and beliefs. For the viewer, the effect was 'Through all the changing scenes of life'; for John himself, it must have seemed more like the cliché about near-drowning – 'The whole of my life flashed before me.' To somebody already familiar with his television work – a Betjemaven, so to speak – the main interest of the series was to see the poet in the Eighties, his state of body and mind. Never, before or since, has there been so intimate a delving into a writer's life so near its end.

Stedall presented, as well as produced, the programmes, where necessary trundling John about in a wheelchair. Episode one began with
part of Julian Jebb's 1968 film *Marble Arch to Edgware*. A shot of a
sign reading 'URBAN CLEARWAY'. John stepping on to a bus –
'Well, now we're really off. We're going through that part of the
Edgware Road which everybody thinks *is* the Edgware Road, just face-
less shops and flats . . .' Stedall chips in:

> Some of John Betjeman's most effective films have been attempts to draw
> attention to what he calls 'the vandalism of planners'. This film was full
> of such moments and is only one of many gems from the Betjeman archive
> that we're dipping into in this series.

Back to John in 1968. Sign: 'VEHICLE PARK'.

> Pretty awful, isn't it? I mean, a lot of people think that the whole of the
> Edgware Road is like this. Thank goodness it isn't quite as squalid as this is.
> Modern, clean lines, I suppose – that bridge over there, with more modern,
> clean lines cutting across it. Where I'm standing was the Metropolitan
> Theatre of Variety. D'you remember, everybody famous used to come here:
> Dan Leno, Max Miller, Marie Lloyd. And look! I mean, it almost makes you
> like planning, doesn't it, for the lack of it there is here. Look! They've put a
> car park on the site. They needn't have taken it down at all.

Here an old photograph of the music-hall is shown, the *art nouveau*
lettering of 'Metropolitan' on its marquee almost exactly like that
above Hector Guimard's Paris Métro entrances.

Cut to John sitting with John Osborne and Stedall in Radnor Walk
and listening to a long-playing record of *Max at the Met*: 'Now '*ere's*
a funny thing. I went 'ome last night – now *there's* a funny thing . . .'
John tells Osborne this was T. S. Eliot's favourite record.

> *Osborne*: [Max Miller] was banned by stuffy organizations like the BBC.
>   They're all very innocent jokes really.
> *Stedall*: When did you first go to the music-hall, John?
> *John*: I went to the Chelsea Palace when I was, I suppose, fourteen.
> *Stedall*: Who took you? Your father?
> *John*: No, I went on my own. I thought it was rather marvellous to go to
>   somewhere that wasn't a cinema.
> *Stedall*: Would you say you were influenced by the music-hall?
> *John*: I'd say I cribbed it. I was always waiting for the band to start up and
>   those red curtains in front of the brass rail parted and there was
>   paradise.

Stedall asks if he ever thought of becoming an actor. 'No,' John replies. 'Only as a schoolmaster. Being a schoolmaster is being a variety artiste. You have to hold an audience.'

The next part of episode one is a flashback to a Michael Parkinson show of 1977, with John's reciting 'A Russell Flint' to the music of Jim Parker. Stedall reveals that the inspiration of the poem was John's secretary, 'Freckly Jill'. In answer to Parkinson's question 'Which, of all the jobs you did, Sir John, on the way to being a poet, did you enjoy most?' John had replied, 'Undoubtedly, being a schoolmaster.' In the 1982 programme, Stedall comments: 'John Betjeman did not have the same enthusiasm for being a school*boy*.' Some of the Marlborough scenes from the 1976 *Summoned by Bells* film follow, ending with John's sitting with boys in the chapel. This scene gives Stedall a link to John and Osborne in Radnor Walk, discussing the New English Bible, which both deprecate.

> *Osborne*: Nobody knows what 'through a glass darkly' means, do they? – but they *know* what it means. They can't explain it. Because it's poetry. You take away the poetry, you take away the meaning.

Stedall asks John Betjeman if he knows what people in the Church think about the New English Bible. 'I don't know any who're in favour of "withitry". It's like the town centre at Croydon: an awful square nothing.'

Stedall explains that, unlike many writers, John likes to work in the film cutting-room, sometimes labouring for hours to find the right words for the pictures in front of him. He wheels him, in his wheelchair, up to Document in Soho, where Stedall has arranged for Eddie Mirzoeff and the film editor Ted Roberts to watch a screening of *Metro-land* with John and himself. Stedall tests John, to see if he still remembers the film-makers' jargon that used to amuse him. John is stumped by the phrase 'creeping sync'.

> *Roberts*: Creeping sync is when a shot starts and the sound matches the lip movements at first and gradually as the shot progresses it gets further and further apart and more and more ludicrous. And it's very difficult to cure. There's no known cure.
>
> *John*: Oh dear, how lovely.
>
> *Stedall*: Do you know what 'hair in the gate' is?
>
> *John*: It's something you can't cure until you put in a new bit of film. Is that it?
>
> *Roberts*: Yes, you can have the job.

The four men watch John miss the golf ball at Moor Park.

    Mirzoeff: There was no intention to miss it.
    Stedall: Did you do another take with John hitting the ball properly?
    Mirzoeff: We were going to; but I think it was John McGlashan who said,
       'You can use that. That's funnier than any driving off could be.'
    John: And it was.

Episode one ends with a memorable exchange.

    Stedall: John, do you ever at all regret the amount of time you've spent
       making programmes when you could have been writing poems instead?
    John: I like to think they *are* poems.

*   *   *

Stedall begins episode two with a seaside scene from the film he made with John in 1972, *Thank God It's Sunday*. In it, John comments on the people shown. Of two rugged-looking workers he says, '[They] may well be admirals.' He mocks the oarsmanship of a middle-aged lady in a dinghy. And then – still in the 1972 film – John, as Stedall puts it, starts playing a game he is fond of: delivering, on screen, an imaginary letter of complaint about the film – in a suitably pompous voice. This one begins:

Wheelhouse Grange,
Albatross Lane,
Havant

To the Chairman of the Governors,
BBC, London

Sir,
    I was disgusted to find the BBC had had the effrontery to turn its cameras on the private marine activities of our English coast, and, what is more, on a Sunday morning, when they should all have been in church.
    My aunt, who is not an expert oarswoman, was shown on the screen without her permission. My own picnic party, with my niece and daughter, was also filmed without permission, as was a party of my staff who were on holiday at Burnham-on-Crouch. How would you like to have the private moments of your family life shown to millions and commented on facetiously by a man with an unpronounceable name? Is nothing sacred?

The four viewers of 1982 giggle about this; but then Stedall produces a letter he actually received, about four years after the 1972 film was screened.

Dear Mr Stedall,

I have for a long time felt I must write to you regarding your excellent programme *Thank God It's Sunday*, shown on television quite some time ago. I happened to be the lady in the dinghy about whom you remarked . . . 'my aunt, who's not a very expert oarswoman . . .' I would like to explain. My husband and I were returning to Ichenor. The dinghy was driven by an outboard motor and at the time we were being photographed the engine had been switched off as the water was too shallow; also it was too shallow to be able to row, so I had to dig the oar into the gravel to heave us along to the shore. Hence the obvious opinion of me not being a good oarswoman.

Quite honestly I was delighted to be shown on television, as was also my husband Donald. Many of our friends saw the programme. By the way, the two men walking across . . . who you thought might be admirals, were scrubbers and painters of boats.

John greeted this with his most eldritch laugh.

Stedall: But that kind of letter that you made up, John, we did get letters awfully like that.
John: Good. Yes. I love them. I think they always ought to be critical and about details and can't possibly be answered back. And they ought to leave one . . . [he gropes for the word – possibly 'chastened'?] ashamed and bewildered.

The 1982 film then tracks back to 1955, for a Shell programme John made for ITV about Chastleton House, Oxfordshire, which had been the home of the Jones family since it was built in 1603. The house had been a royalist strongold in the Civil Wars. John hid in the secret cupboard in which the original owner, Arthur Jones, had hidden from Cromwell's men. A second *coup de théâtre* was to remove from an embossed box the Bible which King Charles I used on the scaffold –

'What I am holding now, Charles I held as he stepped out to the block in Whitehall. These pages were the last the royal martyr saw.'

Back to Radnor Walk in 1982, and John's secretary Liz Moore is reading out a letter from a would-be poet asking for advice. She says John receives an average of twenty letters a day.

Stedall: If the poem is not good, what do you say?
John: 'It doesn't scan.'

John's daughter Candida calls in, blonde and elegant. Stedall asks her what John was like as a father.

Candida: Made us laugh a lot. Still does. He tried to put us on to old churches – 'Not *another* old church!' . . . From about eight to four-teen I resented that terrifically because it involved making every journey far longer . . . Do you remember we had a revolution in Exeter Cathedral?

John: Oh yes, that was marvellous.

Candida: We just walked . . . Powlie and I walked out and refused to look.

The scene shifts to Smithfield, with Stedall pushing John along in a wheelchair. John talks about the market's architect, Sir Horace Jones: 'He was the City Architect. He was a dear old thing. He was so fat that they had to carve a half-circle out of the council table in the RIBA [the Royal Institute of British Architects] in order to fit him in.' John mimics the growly cockney voice in which he thinks Sir Horace would have spoken.

Back to Radnor Walk, and Barry Humphries is visiting – not in drag. Stedall asks what John had thought of Australia on his first encounter with the country.

When I got there it was nothing like what I thought it was going to be like. A most beautiful place. The light is what you notice. It's like being inside a diamond . . . And the flowers! It's as if you went to Cheltenham and it was buried in bougainvillaea.

Humphries warns him that Sir Les Patterson, the 'shadow Australian cultural attaché', may call in. He does: 'This, Sir Benjamin, is very much in the nature of a pilgrimage for me.' Admiring the books lining the walls, he assures John, 'They're deductible.' He adds:

My wife Gwen – that's Lady Patterson, but Gwen to you – and I are very great fans. I think the first poem of yours I admired, if I may say so, sir, was 'I must go down to the sea again'. And 'Quinqueremes of Nivea'.

Stedall cuts to part of John's 1972 film in Australia, in which he is praising Henry Eli White's State Theatre, Sydney, the Art Deco palace of 1929. Back to Barry Humphries (as himself).

Humphries: Because you admired it, I think that's the only reason they didn't pull it down.

John: You don't mean it? Well, thank God.

Humphries: So you can always think of that, if you're feeling gloomy.

John: And what about that marvellous theatre by Burley Griffin?

Humphries: The Capitol, in Melbourne. What they did with that was, you only admired the ceiling. So they destroyed the whole theatre and left the ceiling. And honestly, in the guide books it says: 'And don't miss Burley Griffin's ceiling.'

There is talk of Conder and Phil May and of a painting which Humphries commissioned from Arthur Boyd as a present for John in 1965, which Boyd dashed off on a cigar-box lid. John shows off his tarantulas preserved in resin. Irene Alford, the cleaning lady, comes in to Hoover. The insects give her the creeps.

'You can dust the spider,' Stedall teases her.

'No, thank you.'

*   *   *

Episode three opens at Crowcombe, in the Quantock Hills, Somerset, in 1960. It is a black-and-white film, and John is careful to describe the colours of brick and stone. From the church, with its toppled spire-top in the graveyard like some eccentric's monument, John moves to Crowcombe Court, home of the Trollope-Bellew family 'since the Conquest'. On to 1967 and a conversation about hymns with Robin Ray. And back to 1982 again, with John and Stedall joining John and Myfanwy Piper in Harefield Church, Middlesex – a church the artist had first visited with John in the late 1930s. John is on form in this setting.

Stedall: Do vicars have good taste, in general?

John: The holier the man, the worse the taste.

And again:

Piper: Why do you suppose we all like churches so much?

John: Because they're there, whatever happens.

It was also a chance for Myfanwy to acknowledge herself the inspiration of 'Myfanwy at Oxford' and to reveal that John had given her a copy of the poem 'all beautifully illustrated with things cut out from the *Girl's Own Paper* and *Little Folks*'.

In the same episode John descants on the Crofton beam engine at
the summit of the Kennet and Avon Canal, a Cornish engine of 1880:
'Listen to the strong, satisfied noises it makes.' Kingsley Amis interviews him (1972) about being Laureate. There are extracts from the
Tennyson film of 1968. Forward to 1982 and Stedall reads a letter from
Penelope in the Himalayas – an irresistible excuse to show again the
film of her crossing the river on the inflated buffalo skin. John is
handed a Latin translation of his poem 'The Exile' and struggles to
read it. And the poets who contributed to *A Garland for the Laureate*
make their surprise arrival with Jock Murray. Lady Elizabeth
Cavendish is twice shown on screen greeting the distinguished guests,
sometimes with a kiss, at the front door.

*   *   *

Episode four begins with the sarcastic lines from *Thank God It's
Sunday* about the 'shrine' of the Sunday newspapers and the 'dawn
chorus' of the pneumatic drills. Switch to a studio in Maybury
Gardens, Willesden, where John is making a record with Jim Parker
and his musicians.

Stedall: John, do you consider yourself musical?
John: No. I can't sing in tune, and therefore I was always told by my
    parents that I wasn't musical.
Stedall: But you like music?
John: Oh yes, I can hear it in my inner ear and I suppose I know when a
    thing is out of tune . . .

John fluffs a line in reciting, with the music, 'Indoor Games near
Newbury'. He stops for a break.

Stedall: Was there a real Wendy, John?
John: Yes. I suppose you could say it was Peggy Purey-Cust. A largish gold-
    haired creature. No sex in it at all, just love; and I see myself entirely as
    a passive creature in it all.
Stedall: Did you fall in love a lot as a little boy?
John: Yes. I wonder if she's still alive and if so where she lives and whether
    she's as beautiful as I thought she was. Purey-Cust was the name of the
    Dean of York.[2] Must have been a relation.

During the break, John shows that his 'whim of iron' has not atrophied.

John: If I could have a throat pastille – if I may coin a French word.
Stedall: There's some water here, John.

John: It is not as good as . . . oh, I daresay I'll be all right. Some soft Zubes
    or something would be quite good.
Parker: We'll send out for some.

In the awkward silence that follows, John once again plays the game
of visiting on himself some criticism, mimicking a dialogue between
two imaginary carpers:

I don't think he was so good on the day at Maybury Gardens.
Oh, what makes you think that?
Well, he didn't seem to concentrate. It might have been stage fright.
I rather doubt that.

Next, old film of John in Cornwall is interspersed with his being
pushed by Stedall through Cornish landscape and chatting to an old
friend, Cesca Sharpe, who remembers him when she was four and he
was a grandee of an Oxford undergraduate. 'I chiefly remember your
sticking on my nose little labels with jagged edges,' she says. Quizzed
about his father, John says he thinks he was very interested in churches
but didn't like to say so as it wasn't 'manly'. It was golf that had
brought Ernest Betjemann down to Cornwall. John had played golf
and tennis, with little success.

Stedall: Did you ever sail, John?
John: Yes.
Stedall: Did you enjoy that?
John: No.
Stedall: Why?
John: I was sick.

The programme then switches to Pusey House in Oxford, where
John gazes soulfully at the golden Comper decoration. Then to
Radnor Walk for a discussion about religion, with Harry Williams
and Stedall.

Stedall: Do you go to church, John?
John: Yes. I used to think it was boring when I was at school – but much
    nicer than the other boys! Now I can't do without it: I think it fulfils
    something.
Harry Williams: When I first knew you, years and years ago, the sort of
    churches you preferred were definitely Anglo-Catholic; but I think that
    now you are much more drawn to what I would call ordinary Church
    of England, that is to say, a sort of church which is averagely Anglican

and what you used to call 'middle stump'. I think you feel at home. Am
I right in that?
John: Absolutely.

Stedall then shows an extract from *A Passion for Churches*, including John's inspired lines of verse commentary

> What would you be, you wide East Anglian sky,
> Without church towers to recognize you by?

In Radnor Walk again, Stedall reminds John that in a radio broadcast
on Tennyson about ten years ago, he had said: 'He held a very vague
faith such as mine.' Would John stand by that? Williams interrupted:

I detect beneath the surface of your poetry . . . a view of life not as bloody
but as terrifying, as full of horror.

John agrees with this. 'I'm frightened a lot of the time. Who isn't?'

Stedall: *Love* of life, too. I suppose the two can coexist?
Williams: That's the doubt and the faith. It's expressed in his poetry. I
    mean, the way he loves life – that's the faith. And when he feels the
    terror and horror – that's the doubt.
Stedall: What do you fear most, John?
John: Pain . . . I remember hearing somebody say, 'Of course as a Christian
    I'm bound to believe in eternal life; but I prefer the idea of extinction.'
    That was a very good man, said that. And I thought it was really the
    most awful thing you could say. And now I find it's true.

Stedall asks if John reads the Bible much. He replies, not much,
though he likes the Psalms and well-known passages like 'Let us now
praise famous men . . .' Williams says that one of the things he has 'not
so much learnt as caught' from John is that 'in order to say something
real and profound you have to be simple'. There is no pretension about
John's poetry.

Williams: Pretension is what you don't like, isn't it?
John: It can be very funny.
Williams: You can laugh at religious pretension.
John: Yes: nothing I like more than the niceties of 'High' and 'Low'
    church . . .
Stedall: Harry became a monk. Would that ever appeal to you, that life?

John: No, too ascetic. I wouldn't like having to do without anything. I
   need to be indulged all the time.
Stedall: Do you think he would make a good monk, Harry?
Williams: I think he would, probably because it's not half so ascetic as outsiders imagine it to be. [Looking at Williams, one could believe that.]

Stedall asks if John had ever thought of becoming a clergyman. 'Only
as a means of making myself felt, not really out of charity at all. Out
of love for my fellow human beings? No, I don't think so.'
   Williams suggests that when John laughs at other people it is a sign
that he likes them.

Stedall: Do you laugh at Harry?
John: All the time.

Williams claims that the whole of theology is funny 'because it is man
talking about God – it's like trying to play Beethoven's ninth symphony on a tin whistle'.

*   *   *

At the start of episode five, John is discovered sitting with Osbert
Lancaster. There is a brief flashback to the 1954 film (*Conversation
Piece*) in Nevill Coghill's Oxford rooms, in which John, at forty-eight,
springs to his feet and performs spoof Shakespeare – a yokel and a
lord – in front of Coghill, Lord David Cecil and A. L. Rowse. Then
back to Osbert Lancaster, who recalls how he met John in the OUDS
before John was expelled for 'going too far'.

Stedall: What was John like?
Lancaster: . . . Never quite reverent enough about various Oxford institutions. Very enjoyable.
John: I read Welsh.
Lancaster: You read Welsh. That was your final triumph. When you had to
   take a Pass degree, at the last moment it was discovered you could take
   an optional language, Welsh. It cost them God knows what because they
   had to bring down a Welsh-speaking tutor from Aberystwyth every
   tutorial. It was a good tease, that was.

Stedall asks if John can still speak any Welsh. John recites the verb
'to be'.
   We see John revisit Sezincote in the 1976 adaptation of *Summoned
by Bells*; then in Wadham College, remembering Maurice Bowra.

Lancaster: [Bowra] completely freed one from the fear of going too far.
Stedall: Did you both like Oxford?
Lancaster: Oh, I enjoyed every minute.
John: So did I.

Osbert recalls how John managed to charm Lady Chetwode, though 'she was a terrible fiend in her way'.

John: She *looked* very fierce and *was* very kind.
Stedall: What about the Field-Marshal?
John: He was less adaptable.

Next, John and Lancaster are shown attending a meeting of the GLC's historic buildings committee in the winter of 1981. Both have been advisory members for the last fourteen years. The subject under discussion is a proposed extension to the Tate Gallery. Predictably, Lancaster thinks the extension 'should not take place at all': instead, he would like to see paintings loaned to provincial galleries, as they are lent in France. 'It may', he adds, 'be more trouble for people writing theses; but pictures aren't painted for people writing theses. They're painted for the general public.' John: 'I absolutely agree with Osbert about that.'

After an extract from John's (and Stewart Farrer's) 1965 television play, *Pity about the Abbey*, Ashley Barker, the GLC's Surveyor of Historic Buildings, joins John and Stedall. His rôle is to suggest the influence that John has had on the appreciation of architecture – once described by the poet as 'a public art gallery that is always open'. Stedall refers to John's book of fifty years earlier, *Ghastly Good Taste*.

John: I was quite wrong in those days. I thought that everything that was tasteful was wrong, and that everything should be natural. I thought everything was getting better and that the simpler things were, the better they were. I was not in favour of elaboration in architecture.
Barker: Still, John was making us look. As a student I saw what I was told to see. There are two things: there's seeing, and then there's admitting to yourself that the evidence of your eyes is right . . . John made one unafraid to believe one's own eyes.

Stedall asks John if he would have liked to be an architect. No, he would not have enjoyed the maths involved. Returning Barker's compliments, John congratulates him on the restoration of Covent Garden.

Barker: We've come through to another age now, because whereas accepted
wisdom would have said, 'But you can't hope to keep very much,' in conversations now people say automatically, 'Ah, that wouldn't happen
now, would it? They'd never be allowed to pull that down now' . . . Our
committee used to be called 'The Hysterical Buildings Committee'.
They never tired of the joke.

Ashley Barker thought John could take a lot of the credit for this
change in attitude.

Stedall: John, what would you say that modern buildings celebrate?
John: Nothing, on the whole. The idea that they could be easy to *dust*. I
remember somebody saying he didn't like the Natural History Museum
because it was 'such a dust trap'.

Then Stedall incorporated in the episode scenes from Margaret
McCall's *Four with Betjeman* films of 1970 – the one on St Pancras
station; the one on Miss Jekyll and Lutyens; and the one on the Ritz,
ending with the canal ride past 'Street's brick church in Paddington'.

*   *   *

In episode six, John is shown driving, with enjoyment, an electric
Harrod's van – an extract from the film *That Well-Known Store in
Knightsbridge* (1971). 'They're bound to invent something as good as
this after the noise and fumes of internal combustion.' In Radnor
Walk again, Liz Moore reads him a letter ('Dear Grandpapa') from his
grandson David. Then off to Murray's offices at No. 50 Albemarle
Street, where John, Stedall, Jock Murray and John Sparrow are dis-
cussing corrections to the proofs of John's *Uncollected Poems* (1982).

Stedall: John, do you mind this process going on?
John: No, I rather like it.

Cut to an old film – early 1960s – of *John Betjeman Goes by Train*. The
journey is from Kings Lynn to Hunstanton (pronounced 'Hunston' by
some Norfolk locals). John gets out at Snettisham (pronounced
'Snetsham') to sit on the platform; behind him, 'SNETTISHAM' and
'GER' (Great Eastern Railway) spelt out in a flowerbed. Back to
Albemarle Street.

Stedall: Jock, do you think that John's involvement with radio and television has been important in making him much more widely known and
appreciated?

Murray: Very important . . . John can correct me if I'm not right, but I
should have thought that it has stimulated him to create things that he
would never have created.

John agrees.

The conversation turns to poetry. John says he enjoys Newbolt
because 'he's easy to understand'. He does not like Donne's poems –
'things that Kingers [Kingsley Amis] calls "brain-twisters" '. He likes
the Manx poet T. E. Brown: cue for an extract from his 1970 film *Look
Stranger: Isle of Man*, on top of Snae Fell. Back at Murray's, John
recites Tennyson. When he declaims poetry, his age falls off him; as
with a chronic stammerer who is able to sing, there is complete fluency.
Asked about Hardy, he says, 'I think he's almost my favourite modern
poet' – and one recalls that John was in his twenties when Hardy died.
Asked what it is he likes about Hardy, he answers: 'You can always tell
he's written it. Couldn't be by anyone else. And it gives the impression,
his poetry, of being taken out of a local newspaper and treasured.'
Which living poets does he admire? John nominates 'old Philip'
(Larkin) and mischievously quotes, again without a stumble, the
whole poem beginning, 'They fuck you up, your mum and dad . . .'
Sparrow is asked what are the outstanding qualities of John's poetry.
He dodges the question, but the four men identify what they consider
John's main subjects – among them, churches, architecture, death and
the fear of the unknown.

John: Fear . . . I'm very timid and by nature a masochist.
Stedall: But a lot of your poems are very funny . . .
John: Death frightens me. Desperately frightens me.

Sparrow reads John's poem 'A Child Ill' aloud. Stedall asks John if it
was about Paul. In his reply, John comes close to acknowledging that
he has mismanaged his relationship with his son: 'It wasn't that Paul
was ill. I thought he *might* be ill. One is always afraid of losing people.
I made the mistake, probably, of thinking my son belonged to me,
which he doesn't.' Again John is questioned about contemporary
poets.

Stedall: Auden you knew. And you like his verse?
John: I liked him even more than his verse.

There follows what for many is the *pièce de résistance* of all seven
episodes. Stedall had driven John back to Uffington while Penelope
was trekking in India. Now the film is played over to Penelope in

a studio, with John beside her; and she contradicts almost everything he says on screen. Showing John Garrards Farm, in pouring rain, Stedall says: 'Your two children were born here before the war, weren't they?'

> *John*: Yes.
> *Penelope*: Neither of them. One in London, one in Dublin. [She might have added that Candida was born *during* the war.]

On screen, John tells Stedall, 'the house was run for horses'.

> *Stedall*: Did you ever ride?
> *John*: No.
> *Penelope*: He did. I took him out, yes. This is *all* wrong!
> *Stedall*: Was he any good?
> *Penelope*: No. I'll tell you. Robert Heber Percy bought a very old grey cob to take Lord Berners out riding on, Gerald Berners. It was a fleabitten grey. And I borrowed it for John. I took him out on the downs one day, and it was so lame in every leg . . . it could hardly hobble along. We went up on the downs, beyond White Horse Hill. We got into a huge field full of little bullocks, sort of yearling bullocks. And you know how inquisitive they are. They all rushed round us and started chasing John, who set spurs to this old grey who galloped off up the hill and John shouting, 'You've brought me here to kill me! You've brought me here to kill me!' And I laughed so much I nearly fell orf.

On screen are seen the telegraph posts on White Horse Hill that John had protested about when they went up.

> *John*: They put up these dreadful poles and wires which really drove us out, they were so ugly. They looked like a monkey up a stick. You couldn't see White Horse Hill . . . Opposite there was this dear old boy, a gardener, called Townsend, and he said: 'I think it loivens up the place a bit.' Gosh, I was so angry.
> *Stedall*: That was why you moved, was it?
> *Penelope*: No! We moved because the farmer wanted the house for his second son.

Asked if she had enjoyed John's spell in Dublin, she said: 'I loved it. Except it was a bore going to diplomatic cocktail parties. Once I had Candida, I bosom-fed her for eleven months in order to avoid cocktail parties.' Had she liked Farnborough? 'I loved it – marvellous riding country. I think John didn't like it because we were treated rather as

lords of the manor, had to do things in the village all the time.' And
Wantage?

> *John*: I liked it because it looked rather like a railway station, without a
> platform.
> *Stedall*: I remember when I first met you there, Penelope, you gave me a
> slide show of Indian temples and I wasn't allowed to speak.
> *Penelope*: Lies! I've never *heard* such lies!

Stedall asked Penelope about King Alfred's Kitchen. She: 'If I were
prime minister I would make a law that poets must not go into business. John started the blasted place . . .'

*   *   *

Episode seven, and first we are plunged into a *Monitor* programme of
1960, produced by Peter Newington. The subject is national exhibitions; and in the extract we see and hear how John – in a short burst
of patter – can combine satire, pathos and nostalgia.

> I've always been fascinated by exhibitions and the architecture of exhib-
> itions and here we are on the National Festival of Britain site of 1951 and
> can you remember how tremendously modern it seemed, and contempo-
> rary? And there's something very sad now, looking at it, how quickly
> 'Contemporary' rusts and decays – how the concrete cracks and the pools
> which were meant to swim with goldfish are muddied over and have got a
> little oil on the surface; and how those masts over there, dashed off with
> a pencil with such *joie de vivre* in 1949, now, in 1960, seem rather point-
> less and sad, but also infinitely romantic.

Great novelists rarely make their heroes wholly heroic or their villains exclusively evil; they understand the complexity and ambivalence of human nature. Similarly John, in this fragment of
commentary, is having a go at Hugh Casson (the 1951 Festival's director of architecture) and at the gimcrack techniques of modern building; but beyond this mockery he offers something more generous and
more profound, a 'Vanity of Human Wishes' moral. He remembers
and understands the Festival afflatus of only nine years earlier, the
need that was felt for brightness and celebration both to counter post-
war austerity and as a signal that Britain had recovered from the war.
The Festival was funny, but it was also 'infinitely romantic' – in both
respects like, say, the Eglinton Tournament of 1839.[3]

In episode seven, the *Monitor* extract is followed by the delicious Butlin's sequence of the 1969 *Bird's-Eye View*. Cornish and Dragon School extracts from the *Summoned by Bells* film complete a kind of sampling-flask of John at his televisual best. Cut to Cornwall, where John is in his wheelchair with Stedall in attendance. And here comes the most famous exchange of the entire series.

Stedall: Do you have any regrets, John?
John: Yes. I haven't had enough sex.

Amused by his own repartee, John takes a while to regain his composure, but is soon giving honest answers to Stedall's other questions.

Stedall: John, would you like to have had brothers and sisters?
John: Yes. I think so. I used to think not. Then I used to think it's more interesting. But I don't like the idea of sharing.
Stedall: That's what brothers and sisters are meant to teach you to do.

There is more talk about death.

Stedall: Do you remember that thing that your friend Harry Williams said, that death is like letting go?
John: Yes. That's a very good description of it. Letting go.
Stedall: Have you minded getting old, John?
John: Yes. Because I don't feel so well. Growing old is the most disillusioning thing we have to go through. It isn't easier to be alive now we're old. Now *I'm* old.
Stedall: Can you explain, John? Why is it disillusioning?
John: I think it's because . . . I'm very worried about this *Guinness* thing [a 'Guinness' label on his windcheater].
Stedall: I've cut mine off.
John: I wish I'd cut mine off. I don't like advertising.
Stedall: Are you changing the subject?
John: No. Well, I suppose I am, yes.

Colour drains from the screen as we return to John's black-and-white 1964 film about Cornwall – his rapture about saints, his rage against 'caras'. Back to Cornwall in 1982 and John soliloquizes.

> I think poetry is life and you can't do without it. It's a sense of exhilaration in us all. It makes life worth living – especially here. It is for me the perfect place to be. *And* London. I love the City too. In fact everything is made by contrasts.

Stedall: You're a Londoner, really, aren't you?

John: Yes. Cockney. Cockney with a rather classy accent which I've cultivated.

Stedall asks him about his having been a journalist.

John: It's to do with observation. And using my eyes and feelings have always been part of my life – a most important part.

Stedall: It was a very good training.

John: Oh, *very* good. You can't do anything unnecessary in journalism.

John talks about the *Daily Express* 'house complaints' column he wrote in the Thirties when 'I was very much on my uppers', and tells the story of the man with the next-door neighbour who had 'an enormous frig that makes a terrible noise all night long'. John adds: 'He asked what he should do about it. I didn't know.'

Stedall ends his series where he first met John, in his cottage in Cornwall. Trebetherick is in sunshine and the two men sit in the garden. As a corollary to his remarks about Kilvert, John says: 'I think everything is a pattern. It's assembling patterns and arranging things in order. It's all anything is, is arranging – rearranging – the order.'

The noise of a delivery van is heard.

John: Mother's Pride.

This prompts Stedall to comment on how John loves jargon and television commercials.

John: Yes. The vulgarer they are, the more I admire them . . .

Stedall: You don't like the news?

John: No, I'm not in the least interested in the news. I don't think it's of any importance at all.

Stedall: Have you ever been interested in the news and current affairs?

John: No, never. As an undergraduate, I became very 'Left' in order to annoy my father and mother . . .

Stedall: Was your father very right-wing?

John: No. I think he was a very nice man and I'm only beginning to see that now he's dead. A very nice man and a very funny man and good-humoured. I'm peevish. But he wasn't [though] he used to get into bad tempers.

Aware that Stedall's film was probably his last chance to say things 'on the record', John used the opportunity to make his peace with his father, in effect apologizing for his misjudgement of him and explicit hatred of him. There is the sense of a resolution.

> *Stedall*: John, do you think your father really resented your becoming a poet, as opposed to going into the family business?
> *John*: No. I think he was secretly rather pleased. Yes, he *was* pleased.
> *Stedall*: Was there a bit of a poet in him?

In answer to this last question, John quoted the lines Ernest had given him to start him off on a poem about Frank Bramley's painting in the Tate Gallery, 'Hopeless Dawn', repeating:

> He was a nice man. I'm beginning to see that now – too late. But I expect in Eternity he knows I'm fond of him – which I certainly *wasn't* at one time. Fear . . . 'Perfect love casteth out fear.' I had great fear of him. He was a large man, deaf . . . my mother was very kind, could always be got round.

The van is heard on its return journey.

> *John*: That's nice, that's Mother's Pride come back. There it is, they've had a loaf. You can find nowhere that's quite silent . . . People are afraid of silence, but nothing is silent. All the time there's something bubbling up.
> *Stedall*: John, is there anything that you feel quite unshakable about in your convictions, whatever anyone else says?
> *John*: No. No, I don't think there is anything. I don't think I'd ever lay down the law . . . I *hope* 'The Management' is benign and in charge of us. I do very much hope that.
> *Stedall*: Hope rather than belief?
> *John*: Yes, certainly hope. Hope's my chief virtue.

He gazes at the lawn, trees and flowers at the end of the garden. 'Lovely here,' he murmurs.

> *Stedall*: Finished?
> *John*: Yes.

Some people thought it was a mistake to make a series of films of John in his enfeebled state. In 1994 the novelist, biographer, columnist and critic A. N. Wilson wrote, perhaps characteristically:

> During the sad period of Sir John Betjeman's decrepitude, a man in a cap called Jonathan Stedall had the idea of pushing him around in a wheelchair and asking him a lot of damn-fool questions.

You could not be sure, even in these circumstances, whether Sir John was not playing to the gallery (interrupting the barrage of questions to listen to a passing Mother's Pride van for example). But in the years that have passed one imagined Stedall (a BBC producer) repenting of having put Sir John through all this.

Not a bit of it. We turned on the telly on Sunday night (*Time Enough! or Not Enough Time!* BBC2) to find Stedall squatting beside the wheel-chair while Betjeman, in the last stages of Parkinson's disease, wandered in his speech. I have often wondered in geriatric wards, or when visiting old friends in the final stage, that those who devote themselves to caring for the old seem positively to enjoy the aspects of the work which most of us would find most distressing. Dark thoughts about such matters are precisely the kind out of which Betjeman made poetry . . .[4]

Stedall himself has said that he regrets not filming John a year or two earlier.[5] But, while acknowledging that in 1982 John not only had difficulty with his speech but could not always hold on to a line of thought, he feels that there was one advantage to leaving the filming so late. Through infirmity, John's defences were down. 'He was almost totally unselfconscious in front of the camera. The performer in him was largely laid aside . . . He became more transparent, more truly what he was in essence.'[6]

HIS LAST BOW

Does it all have to end?

> Sir John Betjeman to James O'Brien, general manager, London
> Midland Region, British Rail, after the naming of the *Sir John
> Betjeman* locomotive, St Pancras station, 24 June 1983

On a summer evening in 1953, Elizabeth Cavendish's future neighbour, Frank Tait, was exploring Oxford. The young Australian doctor, son of a Geelong schoolmaster, had graduated in medicine at Melbourne University in 1947 and had come to England in 1950 to study psychiatry. As part of his training he took a six months' course in neurology at Stoke Mandeville Hospital. Every Thursday, he went into Oxford for an out-patients' clinic with Dr Ritchie Russell, a celebrated neurologist.

> After clinic was over [Tait recalled], I was walking round Oxford, spitting with resentment and envy at the people who were there at the University, and not at Melbourne University, the hideous desert of a campus where I had been. I was walking through what I now know was Lincoln College and saw a notice saying 'TONIGHT AT 8 O'CLOCK: "THE STATE OF THE ENGLISH NOVEL" – LORD DAVID CECIL'. So I went back at 8 o'clock and pretended to be an undergraduate, and was absolutely enchanted by this extraordinary man, whose voice was going all over the place, his hands moving round. It was a delicious talk.[1]

Two days later, on the Saturday, Tait went to lunch with John and Myfanwy Piper at Fawley Bottom Farmhouse, near Henley-on-Thames. He had been introduced to them in 1951 by his friend John Cranko, the young choreographer of the Sadler's Wells Theatre Ballet. Over drinks, Tait told the Pipers how much he had enjoyed David Cecil's lecture. 'Guess who's coming to lunch!' Myfanwy said.[2] Soon afterwards, Cecil arrived with John Betjeman. Both were wearing striped blazers and straw hats: it was regatta time at Henley. Tait had not met John before, and had had little chance to talk with

Cecil after the lecture. At lunch he found both men 'scintillating'. He was amazed by their range of historical reference. 'I mean, I'd had a reasonable education at a good school – but I'd never seen anything in my life that was more than a hundred years old. My idea of a good building was the Geelong post office, built in about 1850. I had seen a great deal of Nature, but not so much of what Man had achieved.'[3]

John asked Tait what he did.

'I'm training to be a psychiatrist.'

'Oh, it must be so lovely having a psychoanalysis and being able to lie on a couch for an hour and *talk filth*.'[4]

The next time Tait stayed with the Pipers, sleeping in what they called 'the book room', he found a copy of John's *First and Last Loves* (the prose anthology which Myfanwy had edited in 1952) on one of the shelves, and was as taken by his writing as he was by John himself. The two men met again at Leicester House, Henley-on-Thames, the large house to which Osbert and Karen Lancaster had moved in 1953. John and Tait became friends. John visited the younger man in the latter's basement flat in Eccleston Square (known as 'the coal hole') and stayed with him in the cottage Tait shared with his close friend, Billy Henderson, in Tisbury, Wiltshire. On one of their trips to the country, Tait drove John past the Victoria & Albert Museum. John gestured in the direction of the ornate, turn-of-the-century building. 'The great thing about architecture', he said, 'is that it can't answer back.'[5]

Also in the Tisbury ménage was William Giles, who had been Henderson's manservant since the 1930s. Born in Staffordshire in 1910, he had left school at fourteen to become a coal miner, but illness had forced him to leave the mines and he had come to London in service. 'John was fascinated by William's experiences,' Tait said. 'William told him how he had had to run along with a metal rod and poke it between the wheels of the wagons coming out of the mine, as a brake. He used to go to work at five o'clock in the morning and come out at three o'clock – he didn't see daylight for the whole of that time. I can remember John's intense questioning, and his understanding of that particular sort of horror.'[6]

In 1963 Tait moved from 'the coal hole' to No. 21 Radnor Walk, Chelsea – next door to Elizabeth Cavendish at No. 19. He was now a psychiatrist with the Inner London Education Authority (ILEA), working with 'maladjusted children' – mainly children with emotional problems, not children who were intellectually retarded. Elizabeth Cavendish, as a justice of the peace, was also interested in child welfare, so Tait was a particularly congenial neighbour. Even before John moved to No. 29 Radnor Walk in 1973, he and Lady Elizabeth were seeing a lot of Frank Tait and Billy Henderson.

A year after Tait moved to Chelsea, he held a small dinner-party there to introduce John to one of his best friends, Jill Parker – a thirty-nine-year-old doctor who was married to Peter Parker, later chairman of British Rail. She was the daughter of Sir Ernest Rowe-Dutton, a Treasury official who had served in the Berlin and Paris embassies before the war and had retired in 1951 as a director of the International Monetary Fund and of the International Bank in Washington.[7] In 1943, when she went up to Oxford to read medicine, Jill had dark hair and 'a long equine face like a Chardin'.[8] She was a *femme fatale*: her string of boyfriends included John Godley (later Lord Kilbracken) and Kenneth Tynan, to whom she was briefly engaged. Jill broke off the engagement when her father persuaded her that Tynan would not permit his wife to have a career as a doctor. Tynan and Jill never spoke again, but he dedicated his first book to her.[9]

At Oxford Jill also encountered the dashingly handsome Peter Parker, who played Hamlet, as Tynan snidely put it, 'as if he badly wanted to be king'. Parker and Jill met again in New York in 1950, when he was at Cornell University studying industrial relations and she was on an obstetrics fellowship at a Brooklyn hospital. They were married in 1951; Parker had just been defeated in the General Election as Labour candidate for Bedford. In 1952 Jill became the first medical officer at Unilever House. Fired in 1957 for taking two maternity leaves, she joined a National Health Service practice in Palace Gardens Terrace, London, with a patient list of four thousand in a catchment of Kensington and Notting Hill Gate. It was run from the white-stuccoed early-Victorian house in which Max Beerbohm had been born.[10]

Jill Parker made an immediate hit with John at Frank Tait's dinner-party in 1964. She was vivacious, winningly direct and – what appealed to him most – chronically susceptible to humour. Elizabeth Cavendish was not present, Jill remembered.

> It was just *hilariously* funny. We laughed fit to bust all the time. Frank Tait will say absolutely anything, he's frightfully 'rude'. So John felt uninhib-ited and made these very rude jokes – marvellous descriptions of how his father had tried to teach him the facts of life, and how he must be most frightfully careful not to meet any buggers – and so on. I can't possibly remember all our conversation, but I was reminded of a description of people coming out from having had dinner with Sydney Smith, and having to hold on to the railings so as not to fall over with laughter.[11]

Not long afterwards, John met Peter Parker at a dinner-party held by Elizabeth Cavendish in Radnor Walk. 'It was an entirely relaxed

.....nter,' Sir Peter Parker recalled. 'John knew Jill, so there was no problem – in fact, it was almost seamless, not knowing John and knowing John.'[12] Parker was already an admirer of John's poetry. In his poorer days, before he became a highly paid manager, he had made pocket-money by reading poems on BBC radio at £1 a session. One of the poems he had been asked to read was John's 'Indoor Games near Newbury'. He had fluffed the line 'Spingle-spangled stars are peeping' – blurting out 'bingle-bangled'.[13]

John and Parker had much in common. Both were insiders who felt, in some way, outsiders. Both had shone in Oxford dramatics. They had extravagant charm: Parker wrote of Lord Mountbatten, under whom he had served in the war, that he had 'a practised charm – and why not practise?'[14] Both Parker and John wanted to please others and hated to say no. Neither found it easy to decide whether he was on the left wing or the right. As a child in Shanghai (where his father was an engineer), Parker had seen capitalism at its most rampingly corrupt. War service abroad, latterly as an intelligence officer, had given him 'a first inkling of management'. After the war he worked for the Labour Party. He loved the poetry of William Blake, whose 'antimaterialism' delighted him.[15] On the other hand, he was full of American business-school precepts and in his later career seldom took over a company without 'rationalizing' it by sacking many of the staff. (At British Rail he began as overlord of 214,000 people and reduced that number by 38,000.) He picked up directorships of private companies as a squirrel gathers beechmast: his engaging phrase for this practice, 'going plural', passed into City jargon. He was an easy target for Conservatives who wanted to suggest that socialists are hypocrites. When he was convicted of drunken driving in 1977, the *Daily Telegraph* commented that his disqualification would cause him little inconvenience as he had a chauffeur-driven gold Rolls-Royce and a gold rail pass.[16] John was no businessman, but he recognized that some of the contradictions in Parker's character were parallelled in his own. The two men willingly succumbed to each other's charm.

John became a friend of the Parker family. He visited them at their country home, a medieval farmhouse at Minster Lovell, Oxfordshire, and wrote a quatrain (now lost) about the romantic garden Jill was creating there.[17] In London, he took Jill and her children on expeditions. He would turn up on the doorstep of their house in Brunswick Gardens, Kensington, holding his bag and sometimes his teddy-bear. Jill remembers one jaunt she and her son Oliver, then twelve, made with him.

John said: 'How would you and Olly like to come to Somerset House?' – it was when they had the Thames exhibition. So Olly and John and I went in a taxi. John had on his Betjeman-type hat. It was sort of lunch-hour. We marched into Somerset House, and it was one of the days when he leaned very far backwards all the time – more alarming than leaning forwards, really. And he got into the oval hall, and there were quite a few people. They all saw John coming and stood there, looking at him. He stood in the middle. He said: 'We'll go up by the stairs, we'll not take the lift.' So we went incredibly slowly up the stairs, with John leaning so far back that Olly and I, behind him, had our hands raised ready to stop him falling. He seemed to know every banister on the way. He would stop and say: 'From this angle you can see that angle of the door – marvellous!' We finally got to the top, and by this time he had a crowd round him, who were waiting for him to pronounce about the pictures exhibition. He looked round, and there's a little painted ceiling with clouds – I don't think actual cherubs, but clouds and gilt and stuff. He looked round and lifted his chin: he was obviously going to declaim, and I think he knew that everybody was listening. And he said, in a great big voice: 'THANK GOD FOR THE REGISTRAR-GENERAL!'[18] which was the last thing anybody expected him to say. They expected him to say something artistic.[19]

In 1978, John's private doctor, Dr John Allison,[20] had a heart-attack at a dinner-party John was himself attending; he died three days later. John had already become a National Health patient of Jill's, and now, after some hesitation, he decided to put his faith entirely in her practice. 'I think Lady Elizabeth didn't really want me to be his GP,' Jill said. 'She wanted him to have one of the royal doctors. And when I became his doctor, she thought that I wasn't being sufficiently professional. He would insist on starting with a glass of claret. I would try to ask him what was the matter, but she would come upstairs and find us in fits of laughter over something. *Both* in fits, you see. But I mean it was the only way to talk to him about whatever medically needed to be done.'[21] Jill diagnosed Parkinson's Disease but thought John was fortunate in that, although he had the typical difficulty in walking which British doctors call a 'festinant gait' and the French *la marche aux petits pas*, he suffered only a little of the tremor associated with out-and-out Parkinson's. She prescribed L-dopa drugs for him. Jill's mother, Lady Rowe-Dutton, who had had the same illness, had been greatly helped by Dr Kevin Zilkha of the National Hospital for Nervous Diseases – 'the Hospital for Nervous Wrecks', as John called it. So Jill sent John to him. 'As with any doctor he ever went to, Kevin fell for him, and John was very well looked after. He never really got . . . I mean, Parkinson's can be soul-destroying. It held up his walk, but not more than that, I would say. It was certainly not the cause of his death.'[22]

Some of the patients at the Palace Gardens Terrace practice were private; most were National Health. Sir Hugh Fraser, the Conservative Member of Parliament, was a private patient; his socialist wife Lady Antonia and her children were NHS. John thought it almost *sans-culotte* to be a National Health patient. It did not occur to him that he should make an appointment.

He just rang up one day [Jill recalled] and said, 'I've got to see you now. It's an *emergency*. It's really terrible – and I'm coming in a taxi. And he put the phone down. My surgery was full of people. He came in and sat in the surgery waiting-room. The place was electric. Everybody was watching him: you know he often looked as if he was just about to say something, when he wasn't. He sat there, I think he had Archie with him. And of course everybody in the surgery recognized him and was frightfully impressed and amazed. And I cheated slightly, because I wasn't going to keep him waiting through *too* many patients. And anyway, if it was an emergency . . . And then he came in and sat down. He said: 'I don't know what to do. I've been too wicked – over Penelope and Elizabeth. Do you think I'll go to hell?' This was the emergency! I took it as a great compliment that it was a thing he should discuss with me. I'm sure it never crossed his mind that this was not a medical problem, nothing to do with me. It just sort of seized him. That was the important thing at that moment. And, you know, you wanted to . . . you didn't quite want to laugh, you wanted in a way to jerk him out of it and say, 'Oh, come on, John, don't be so ridiculous, you've been doing this for thirty years perfectly happily.' But at that moment it was real. So I said: 'I shouldn't think so. I don't think you'll go to hell. You just feel guilty because you're a guilty sort of person.'[23]

John called Palace Gardens Terrace 'the little toy surgery', because he was often seen, not by Jill, but by one or other of the practice's two young partners, Dr Christopher Calman and Dr Gregory Scott (see plate). 'They both had curly hair and they did look very young,' Jill said. 'John would say: "I want to come and see you." I would say, "Well, I can't be there on Tuesday" – or whatever it was. And he'd say, "Never mind, the little boys will be there, and I *love* the little boys!" Of course they weren't really little boys, and I didn't tell them what he said because I thought they'd be hurt.'[24]

When Christopher Calman visited John in Radnor Walk, he found him suffering from acute anxiety. John had developed a phobia about crossing the cracks between the paving-stones on the pavement of Radnor Walk. Calman took him outside, where he 'carried out some basic behaviour therapy', making him go back and forth across the cracks.[25] Possibly the phobia was related to the superstition,

John trying on Mervyn Stockwood's episcopal headgear. He commented, in paraphrase of John Greenleaf Whittier's lines: 'Of all sad words of tongue and pen, The saddest are these: "It *mitre* been"'

In 1963, at the height of the campaign to save the London suburb of Bedford Park, John's friends Tom Greeves and Peter Clarke designed a Christmas card, 'The Battle of Bedford Park'. The opponents facing each other include (*left*) John, in boater, with Nikolaus Pevsner, in mortar-board; (*right*) Sir John Summerson

John was best man at the wedding of Verily Anderson and Paul Paget at St Bartholomew the Great, London, on 10 August 1971. *Left to right*: Paul Paget; Verily Anderson; John; Eddie Anderson; Alexandra Anderson; Janie Hampton (her husband, Charles Hampton, behind her); and Marian O'Hare. Joyce Grenfell, 'a rather mature bridesmaid', took the photograph

John on the grand staircase of the City Hall, Belfast, during the filming of *Betjeman's Belfast* by Ken Savidge in 1978

Lord Snowdon photographed John between blue and gold trains to accompany a profile of the poet by Susan Barnes (Crosland) in the *Sunday Times* colour magazine of 30 January 1972

John in a recording session with the musician and composer Jim Parker, in Jonathan Stedall's television series *Time with Betjeman*, 1981

With John Sparrow in *Time with Betjeman*

On the cliffs at Trebetherick in Jonathan Stedall's television film
Summoned by Bells, 1976

In front of Blisland Church, Cornwall, in *Time with Betjeman*

At a luncheon at Euston House, after a British Rail locomotive was given his name on 24 June 1983: Jim O'Brien, general manager of the London Midland region, presents John with a model of the demolished Euston Arch, while Gillian, Lady Parker and Rupert Lycett Green look on perpetuated by generations of nursemaids and nannies, that bears will leap out on children if they tread on a crack.

The Times of 10 March 1976, which carried a picture of John celebrating, with Henry Moore and Lady Birk, the designation of part of Somerset House as a Turner gallery, also recorded that Dr Christopher Calman, aged thirty, had been suspended from the medical register for three months for 'serious professional misconduct' after admitting having sexual intercourse with an eighteen-year-old girl patient. The girl's mother told the court that after the incident she had visited the doctor at his surgery. 'I smacked him hard, as hard as I could,' she said. When Calman returned to the surgery, Lady Antonia Fraser insisted that her daughters be removed from his care and transferred to Dr Gregory Scott. 'She knew there would be no hanky-spanky with *him*,' said Scott's lover, the novelist John Stevenson.[26] Jill Parker was incensed by Lady Antonia's decision, and wrote her a letter of protest; but Lady Antonia, who to the glee of *Private Eye* was holidaying in Haiti with the playwright Harold Pinter (her future husband), did not relent.[27]

Gregory Scott, who was twenty-eight in 1976, made no secret of his homosexuality. He and Stevenson, who first met at the ordination of a mutual friend, moved in the High Church circles of Mervyn Stockwood, the turbulent Bishop of Southwark, and the Rt Rev. J. R. Satterthwaite, Bishop of Fulham and Gibraltar, who lived in the same street as the Parkers and was a patient of the practice. A few doors along from the house Scott and Stevenson shared in Fielding Street, Stockwell, lived Dr Peter Southwell, who had been Scott's boyfriend in their student days at Guy's Hospital. (He disappeared in Kenya in 1988, soon after Julie Ward was murdered there.)[28] Greg Scott had fair, shoulder-length hair and the face of a decadent schoolboy, and wore floral shirts and flared trousers. He was well-read in British writers of the 1890s and the inter-war years; when he and Stevenson met Alec Waugh in Tangier, Scott showed such an intimate knowledge of 1930s writers that Waugh said it was hard to believe he had not been alive in that decade.[29] Scott wrote a biography of Leigh Hunt; corresponded with Michael Holroyd about his life of Lytton Strachey;[30] and formed a complete collection of early Penguin books.[31] 'You should have been the doctor,' he told Stevenson, 'I the writer.' Because of Beerbohm's association with the Palace Gardens Terrace house, Scott covered the walls of his consulting-room there with reproductions of 'Max' cartoons. At home, he had the original of Max's caricature of the Victorian dramatist Sydney Grundy.[32]

In April 1977, not long after Calman had treated John for his pavement-cracks phobia, Jill Parker took Scott to Radnor Walk to meet the poet for the first time. Scott wrote up the red-letter day in his diary.

As a result of being told [about the paving-stones episode] I was aware . . . that he suffered from considerable feelings of anxiety or Angst as he refers to it. Oddly, an article about him in a reference book written in 1963 refers to his fear of death, something that assails him more than ever. John [Stevenson] sees this attitude, the High Anglican afraid to meet his maker, as typical of Betjeman's generation, a feeling perhaps shared by W.H. Auden and Tom Driberg. The source of the fear is supposedly that the FAITH is not strong enough and that hell may await the sinner who has committed the unforgivable sin of thinking that there is no God.[33]

As Jill Parker drove Scott down to Chelsea, she explained 'Betjeman's domestic set-up'.

Betjeman lives at 29 Radnor Walk [Scott wrote] and his 'close friend', Lady Elizabeth Cavendish, lives a few doors along. In fact, Betjeman uses his own house really as a sort of study and actually sleeps, eats etc. at Lady Elizabeth's. The lady in question is fiftyish, grey hair, matronly in an authoritative way and it comes as no surprise that she is a JP. She is a sister of the Duke of Devonshire and therefore indirectly related to Diana Mosley, Evelyn Waugh's great friend . . . Lady E. or 'Feeble' as Betjeman calls her, obviously fulfils the role of nurse, companion, sister, mother etc. to her ward, who is unfortunately in need of these varied attentions . . .

The door of the house was opened by a young man, reminding me of Philip [the boyfriend of a Cambridge don]. He ushered us in, holding a book open in one hand, and announced in languid tones that he and John had just been reading some uproarious poems. As we entered the hall, I noticed that the side of his face was . . . disfigured by a scar running from temple to chin . . . It later transpired that this man is John Byrne, one of the people who run Bertram Rota [the London booksellers]. He had been going through all Betjeman's books and had found a poem by Evelyn Waugh (with a drawing of the Crystal Palace on it) and also many letters from Waugh to Betjeman . . . I would have very much liked to ask Betjeman what had happened to Evelyn Gardner, Waugh's first wife, who according to Powell is still very much alive. This was obviously not the moment to raise such a personal enquiry, however. At the top of the stairs, Betjeman awaited us, leaning against the door frame. He and Jill embraced, and I was introduced. Jill told him firmly that he could call me by my Christian name. Very slowly Betjeman shuffled a couple of steps into the room behind him. There he stood by the arch dividing the two halves of the room and didn't move for nearly half an hour, except to turn towards the front of the house when we all sat down. In the back half of this double drawing room was a table on which was a large model of a church (? St Mary's in Penzance) made entirely of shells. Somebody suggested that a light was needed, so Betjeman fiddled with a switch, muttering that if he lit up the church, we would be able to see it better. A dim bulb lit up inside the model, emphasizing its rather kitsch appearance.[34]

John Byrne again mentioned the poems he and John had been reading, and John passed Scott the book, commenting that the best poems were marked in pencil.

'Can we talk freely in front of him?' he asked Jill, as if I was too innocent-looking for words. I asked him if he was implying that I was shockable, as that was certainly far from the case. Looking at the book I could see why he had made this enquiry. The poems were by one of the Uranian poets, a Rev. Davidson who had been a Cambridgeshire cleric.[*35] When I showed recognition of this school of poetry, Betjeman was obviously pleased and was amused when I later pointed out that they were also known as 'the bathing shed school of poetry'. Glancing through the book, I quickly realised that the poems were fine examples of the pederastic school of poetry at its most overripe stage. The poems were all about moonstruck friendships where pubescent boys expressed undying love for each other. Suddenly, on prompting from Betjeman and John Byrne, I found myself reading one of them. After each verse, Betjeman encouraged me – 'Go on! Go on!' The poem was luckily not too provocative and in fact each verse finished with a twee refrain about eating Banbury buns on the beach! Even so I became nervous as I went on and read the last verse rather poorly. We all, except Betjeman, then sat down and were given some wonderful burgundy. This represented only a small part of Betjeman's official salary as Laureate – twelve butts of sack. This hereditary payment has evidently been amplified over the years, and when we went along the road to Feeble's house, the hall was virtually impassable with cases of vintage claret and burgundy from floor to ceiling. I couldn't resist turning to Betjeman in the hall and saying 'Well, if you ever decide you've had enough, what a way to go!'

While we sat sipping burgundy, Betjeman encouraged John Byrne to read more of John Davidson's Uranian poems. In fact several more were read to the point where it became a little embarrassing, particularly since it so firmly underlined Betjeman's pederastic interests. Jill laughed heartily as yet another poem was recited, but commented afterwards on Byrne's tactlessness.[36]

Eventually Byrne left, and Jill and Scott were able to address John's medical problems.

* John Byrne has told the author that the poet read was not in fact Davidson, but the Rev. Dr E. E. Bradford.

By this time [Scott continues] Betjeman was seated beside me . . . Jill says
that his cardio-vascular system is OK and that his apparent infirmity is all
due to his Parkinson's Disease. He has seen a neurologist [Kevin Zilkha]
about this and is on L-Dopa but it doesn't seem to help much. The three
features of Parkinson's Disease are rigidity, tremor and bradymysesia.
He doesn't seem at all disabled by the first two of these – perhaps they are
controlled by the L-Dopa – but the third symptom disables him almost
totally. Obviously prone to depression and anxiety, he can hardly bear his
present immobility. He bemoaned the fact that he will probably never be
able to get on a bus again and asked plaintively 'Am I going downhill? Do
you think this is it? Am I going to die?' This may sound self-pitying, but
in fact such comments were interspersed with witty utterances and his old
sparkle and charm still pervade his whole behaviour. He also bemoaned
the fact that his creative powers have totally disappeared.

'I haven't written a poem for years. Will I ever write one again?' Jill strenu-
ously contradicted him, but he is obviously in such a restricted state men-
tally and physically that lack of creative impetus is hardly surprising.[37]

John told Scott that he was delightful and that he would be happy
to die in his arms. He asked if he had seen many people die.

I rather evaded answering this question in detail. (In fact, I haven't seen
many people at the moment of death, and usually they were unconscious.)
He then went on to describe his difficulties at night. Early morning waking
is a huge problem, and he obviously gets desperate, lying in bed, worrying whether he is going to die. Even something as simple as walking to the
toilet is a huge ordeal for him, as it takes so long, and next week I am to
order a commode for him.

I suggested that what he experienced at night must certainly be worse
than anything he could experience after death, and that, therefore, death
itself should be seen only as a release and not as something to fill him with
terror. He was quite taken with this idea.

I reminded him of Timothy d'Arch Smith's book *Love in Earnest*, about
the Uranian poets.[38] Betjeman actually went to visit Davidson at his parish,
suggesting the extent of his interest in the subject . . . I also mentioned
[Rupert] Croft-Cooke's *Feasting with Panthers*,[39] for which Betjeman
expressed great enthusiasm. We agreed how interesting the 90s were, and
looking up at the mantelpiece with his slightly skew-eyed twinkle, he
exclaimed 'Oh, I do like a little decadence, you know.'[40]

While Jill Parker and the 'toy surgery' boys were ministering to
John's body, Peter Parker was doing wonders for his ego. In 1976 Parker
was appointed chairman of British Rail. (He was knighted in 1978.)

The railway system still bore scars from the 'axe' of Dr Richard Beeching, who in the 1960s had cut a large number of 'uneconomic' branch lines. Parker, with his business-school philosophy, was prepared to pay guarded tribute to Beeching: he had done 'a magnificent job with the wrong terms of reference'. He could understand the 'dramatic reasoning' behind Beeching's actions – to 'clear the past from our sight and concentrate on finding a future'. He saw his own task as quite different. 'I had to get the act together. Above all we needed to draw inspiration from the entrepreneurial past, from our great days, and this could help us to correct an imperfect present . . .'[41] In John Betjeman – already well known to the public as a nostalgic railway-lover – he saw the ideal instrument for such a policy. He was fond of John, and genuinely wanted to do him honour; but he also hoped, as he recalled in 1990, that John would help to 'energize' his plans for British Rail. (Was there also some hope of gagging John's public criticism of British Rail's developments and demolitions if British Rail honoured him, stopping his gob with sweets?)

You see, when I came into the railway [Parker said in 1990], they had given up steam. They had given up any relationship with steam. Beeching, whatever his qualities were, was certainly not in that sense imaginative. He never saw the importance of holding the sympathy of the customer, putting it at its crudest; and steam is a remarkable thing because it warms people up. I caught on to that idea when I measured the number of books out on steam trains. About 400 were published each year, there was an immense passion behind this – a head of steam, if you like. These books did not just appeal to the sort of person of whom the professional railman says, rather warily, 'He's an enthusiast.' I suddenly saw that there was this huge area of interest, and it had been absolutely cut off. British Rail staff had been discouraged from collaborating with it. And of course I, approaching it from my little spoke of commitment, came to exactly where John was. I could see that this was a perfectly viable, romantic commitment and our people should stick with it. I mean, I put on the 150th anniversary of the Liverpool–Manchester line, and I had people flying in from Texas.

In the logic of sheer marketing, you came to the same conclusion. You found that the little boys' clubs were bigger than they had ever been – they were still taking down train numbers. There was this area of imagination in the whole thing, the past. And then again, I'd been educated reasonably well, but nobody had ever told me about Brunel. Fancy going through all that, including Oxford, and not picking up something about him! There was an area of our history to be reclaimed, of enormous energy and courage, people doing extraordinary things, crossing Chatmoss and so on.

I kept using the standards of these people, these great names, to goose up interest in railway affairs; and John knew that I had soon got committed to that, because I encouraged the steam clubs. So there was never a sense that I needed to be jogged: we were both going in the same direction. In fact, Betjeman was the ideal person to energize the programme.[42]

Although John's primary interest in the railways was the architecture of the great stations, he also instinctively preferred steam trains to electric and diesel ones – the old locomotives that charged across the landscape trailing clouds of glory. He was the first member of the preservation society that kept the Talyllyn Railway, Wales, in action from 1951, and opened its museum at Tywyn, Gwynedd, in 1965. 'At every level I found that John was interested,' Peter Parker said. He thought that John benefited from the collaboration with British Rail, too.

He was anything but an outsider in one sense; in another sense, he was never quite with us where an organization or a bunch of men had a major external purpose. I mean, his relationships were a kind of distinguished club of relationships, but not a working or an organizational relationship; and I think it must have been an amazing thing for him to see people arranged in that kind of a pattern of purpose. There was something there which would relate him to the way the world was going. I mean, the world is run by terrifying organizations. I felt, from the very first time we talked railways, that he was on the outside looking at something which he could learn about, almost like Kipling could learn bridges to do a story; but his way into it was the arrangement of people doing what he felt they loved to do. That was what he was always harping on – 'Aren't you lucky to be in this thing!' He didn't see it in battle terms, the thuggery of Treasury wars or civil servants or unions; instead, he saw all these people in modern times associated with something which seemed by its sheer narrative demand each day to sort of harmonize something.[43]

In July 1977 Peter Parker joined Jill late at a dinner-party and found John there too. It was coffee-time and guests were moving to another part of the room, but John waved to him and asked if he would join him at the table because his legs were beginning to bother him. 'I walk like a crab.'[44] He again told Parker how lucky he was to work with railway people, the best sorts in the world.

'You know, I carry a book by a railwayman around with me most days,' John added. He pulled from his pocket a small book: Parker noticed that the soft black cover had become 'curved to the pear-drop shape of the Betjeman hip'.[45] The book was *Joy to Know*, a collection of 'prayers and thoughts' by Walter Sinkinson, a retired signalman. John had been sent the book in 1975 by his friend Trevor Huddleston, Bishop of Stepney. Sinkinson had spent twenty-seven years working on the railway in the small Yorkshire town of Mirfield. He knew Huddleston through the Community of the Resurrection there, of which Huddleston, like Harry Williams, was a senior member. Technically, few of the poems were much higher than parish-magazine standard; some were indistinguishable from George Elliston's Cincinnati verses. What attracted John was the serene certainty of Sinkinson's faith; he also enjoyed the touches of railway lore that enlivened the imagery.

The next day, Parker found out who Sinkinson was and wrote to him to say how much John Betjeman enjoyed his work. By coincidence, his letter crossed with one from Sinkinson to him. The old man wrote in a copperplate script, telling Parker that he had heard him on the wireless being interviewed about the railways and that he had mentioned William Blake: would Sir Peter be at all interested in poems and prayers which he had tried to write in the Blakean spirit? 'Some were enclosed,' Parker remembered. 'They were truly Blakean, full of Mental Fight . . .'[46]

Parker asked one of his lieutenants, Bernard Kaukas, to keep in touch with Sinkinson. Kaukas visited Sinkinson and his wife Mary in their Mirfield council house. He wrote to John of the railwayman's 'simple, unaffected goodness' and added, 'I now find myself liking the man so much that I am in danger of possibly overpraising him and his work.'[47] Through Kaukas, another book of Sinkinson's poems was published, *Branch Line Charm*, with a preface by Peter Parker. John wrote Sinkinson several letters, sometimes addressing him as 'Dear Laureate of the Lines'. When his copy of *Joy to Know* wore out, he asked for another: 'It is the perfect answer to the powerlessness and the tedium of hate.' John also corresponded with Kaukas as to whether it might be possible to publish an 'epic' that Sinkinson had written about the railways – though in fact the epic remains unpublished in the National Railway Museum, with six huge volumes of tinted drawings in which Sinkinson illustrated the complexity of railway signalling regulations.

In 1977, Peter Parker appointed Bernard Kaukas to be director of environment for British Rail. It was a newly created post. Like 'ecology', 'environment' was 'in': the Ministry of Works had become the Department of the Environment in 1970. A warm-hearted and genial, if sometimes peppery, man, Kaukas had previously been chief architect of British Rail and development director for the BR Property Board. One of the first things Parker asked him to do, as director of environment, was to think of some way of honouring

John Betjeman. 'We must move quickly: he's not at all well,' Parker said.[48]

Kaukas had already known John for some years before they began corresponding about Walter Sinkinson. During his time as chief architect (1968–74) he had been irritated by an article in which John had written of 'the passé architectural department at British Rail'. Kaukas had written John a letter, of which the burden was: 'If you think that the architect's department of a nationalized industry is able to make decisions to destroy this or pull down that, you know *nothing* about our business. We're servants, professional tradesmen. And though we may say, "Oh God, have we really got to do this?" we think "Well, yes, it's part of our business." We are put in this odd dichotomous situation of saying: "Well if we had our own way, of course – if the Government would give us some money and the Board would say okay – of *course* we'd restore the buildings; but, as it is, we have to get on with our real life." '[49]

Kaukas had first met John in 1969, when the British Rail Board was considering what to do with the glass roof of Paddington station after a man had fallen through the glass and been killed. Kaukas recalled:

The Health and Safety at Work people, who had a different name in those days, said that if we were going to carry on with this ridge-and-valley glass roof, we had to provide walkways all the way over that great expanse – which would have looked ridiculous from the outside. So we said, what happens if we provide plastic sheets? – no one's going to fall through a plastic sheet, they're going to bounce off. And they said, yes, that would be all right. So we spoke to the Royal Fine Art Commission and told them what we wanted to do; and I can remember the day when we produced a half-inch scale model of the great train shed with the actual shapes of the plastic glazing and so on, and we took it on to the concourse. We had Sir Basil Spence, Sir Colin Anderson, Sir John Betjeman, Sir Hugh Casson and one other knight – we had five knights – and they were all looking at the roof and discussing it, and John Betjeman put his arm round my shoulder and said, 'Don't let anybody touch Wyatt's scrollwork.' You remember at the end there's this wonderful scrollwork. He wasn't making trouble; he was looking about with a properly observant eye.[50]

The Royal Fine Art Commission agreed to the plastic sheeting. It turned out a disaster. Kaukas had been assured by the civil engineers that the plastic would be treated on the underside with a coating that would resist stains. 'It was completely untrue,' he says. 'After some years, the diesel fumes put a brown coating all over the underside of the plastic. If you went to an adjacent shed where there was still glass, it was quite clear, the light was still coming through; but it was not coming through the plastic. The only answer of course is the expensive answer of electrification.'[51]

In 1976 William McAlpine (now Sir William) invited Kaukas on a trip to 'circumnavigate' London in a private train on 6 May. Accepting, Kaukas suggested that McAlpine might care to invite John Betjeman too. McAlpine, who had never met John, was keen to meet him – and John accepted the invitation. Bill McAlpine was the great-grandson of Robert McAlpine ('Concrete Bob') who, beginning as a coal miner, had become the biggest speculative builder in Scotland by 1869 and later built the Lanarkshire and Ayrshire Railway and the West Highland Extension. (His constructing Glenfinnan Viaduct in massed concrete gave him his nickname.) Bill McAlpine, who had joined the family business, was forming a railway museum on his estate at Farley Hill, near Henley-on-Thames. It included a working railway with a signal-box, a tunnel and a wooden station removed plank by plank from Somersham, Cambridgeshire. (An Italian lady, visiting the McAlpines' mansion, said, 'It's a lovely house. What a pity it's so near the railway line.')[52]

The 'McAlpine Special' left Kensington Olympia at 10.50 a.m. on 6 May 1976. Behind a modern diesel engine rolled four classic carriages from the collection: Great Eastern Railway Saloon No. 1 (1920), Caledonian Railway Saloon No. 4 (1897), Great Western Railway Brake First Saloon No. 9004 (1930) and London & North Eastern Railway Restaurant Buffet Car 24287 (1939). When John had arrived, Bill McAlpine and his wife Jill had taken him into the Twenties saloon, with its mahogany panelling and leather button-back seats. McAlpine recalls:

> John Betjeman said: 'This is marvellous. Look at that light there!' It was a cut-glass and brass thing. I said, 'Well, I'm terribly sorry, but my fellow got that in York last week.' It was the only thing in the vehicle that wasn't original. But it was a bit of a compliment to my fellow for choosing something that looked right, even to John Betjeman.[53]

The saloon had been built at Stratford Works by the Great Eastern Railway in 1920 for use by the general manager, Sir Henry Thornton, on official journeys and inspections. It was the last saloon built by the GER and was unique for that railway in having an open balcony at one end with ornamental railings and steps down to the lineside. Presumably this North American feature was ordered by Thornton, who was an American.

Bill McAlpine chatted with John for a while. John was amused to hear that he wanted his body, after his death, to be thrown into the

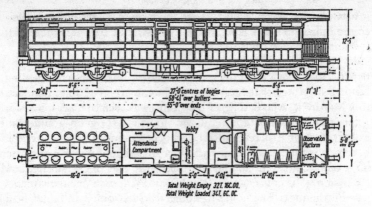

Total Weight Empty 32T. 16C.0Q.
Total Weight Loaded 34T. 6C. 0C.

boiler of the Flying Scotsman. As the antique saloons moved southward through West Kensington and the western edge of Chelsea, with
a view down the Kings Road to the left, McAlpine left John in the
observation car with Bernard Kaukas and strolled off to talk to his
other guests.

> Sir John had brought with him a large-scale Bacon's Atlas of London, *circa*
> 1927 [Kaukas recalled]. We sat together in what I can only describe as a
> blissful session. I identified exactly where we were passing, looking for
> churches and any other interesting buildings we could see, while he dis-
> coursed happily on the great Victorian architects who had been responsible.
> We finished our tour at West Kensington where a BBC crew were waiting to
> whisk him away. I took care to ensure that he took with him all the papers
> he brought on to the train, and finally handed him the atlas. 'That's not
> mine,' he said. 'It's yours.' Slightly puzzled, I pressed it on him. Only when
> he twice repeated with a smile 'It's yours' did I realize that he was making a
> present of it to me.[54]

John's natural attitude to British Rail architects was antagonism:
there was nothing they could put up that would placate him for what
they were pulling down. But after the McAlpine Special jaunt, he
regarded Bernard Kaukas as a friend. 'There were one or two instances',
Kaukas wrote, 'when he received very ratty letters from (among others)
the Victorian Society complaining about what we were not doing, or
what they thought we intended to do, to railway buildings. He would
send me the correspondence and tell them that he had done so: "I have
sent your letter to my friend Bernard Kaukas who, I know, will deal with
the matter," or words to that effect. As I was invariably cast as the villain
of the piece I was rather amused.'[55]

When Peter Parker asked Kaukas to think of a way of ho[...]
John, Kaukas replied that as John was Poet Laureate, the hon[...]
to be something lasting: 'anything else would be trivial.' Per[...]
building could be named after the poet. Kaukas's first suggestion was
the Abercorn Bar at Liverpool Street station. This was rejected on
commercial grounds – since people were used to saying, 'Let's meet at
the Abercorn Bar.' Eventually it was decided to rename the restaurant
at the Charing Cross Hotel after John. This grand, high-Victorian
room was at the time named the Simon de Montfort Room, after the
thirteenth-century baron who once owned the land around Charing
Cross and who forced Henry III to grant the first English parliament.
John had described it as 'the best proportioned Victorian hotel dining-
room in London'. The hotel, built in 1864, was designed by Edward
Middleton Barry, son of the architect of the Houses of Parliament. It
had been one of John's haunts when he was young, a place where a
group of his friends would meet. At that time there had been a comfortable bar with leather-bound books, 'and there', John told Parker,
'one used to have a drink and look out on to all the people going down
to their trains, poor things'.[56]

The renamed Betjeman Restaurant was opened on 24 January 1978.
The evening was divided into three episodes: a saloon trip to four
London termini; a reception and the naming of the restaurant at the
hotel; and a dinner afterwards for John and a few friends. The general
manager, Southern Region, allowed his own saloon to be used for the
evening visit to four termini:[57] the Thames was to be crossed six times
on four of the City's bridges. The saloon left Victoria at 6.12 p.m. and
travelled by way of Blackfriars and Cannon Street to Charing Cross –
a journey of just over forty-five minutes. 'Light refreshments' were
served to John, Elizabeth Cavendish and twelve other guests.

Jill Parker was in the train party, but her husband had a bad leg and
did not join them for the ride, though he was at Charing Cross station,
with gold-braided officials, to greet them. 'I remember waiting anxiously for this train of John's to come in,' he said, 'because it was the
equivalent of bull-fighting, in railway terms, to run it across London
at this hour of the night, without disrupting traffic. It was a period of
commuter militarism – I mean, if anything had gone *wrong*, can you
imagine . . .?'[58] The train arrived on time and Parker hobbled on to
thank the staff. He said to one of the railwaymen: 'Does Sir John
know everything, or is it an amateurish knowledge?' The man was
'quite awed'. He said: 'Oh no, he knows everything. He's really
serious.'

'*What* does he know?'

'He knew my father had built some warehouses along the line.'[59]

Jill was also impressed by John's knowledge. 'As we were going through south London somewhere, and turning, he suddenly said: "Oh, we must be about half-way round the Catford loop, are we?"'[60]

John's slow walk from the train to the hotel was 'like a royal progress'.[61] For the first time in anyone's memory, the entrance to the hotel from the concourse had been opened, so he was able to walk up the staircase, rather unsteadily. He found time to tell Bernard Kaukas how much he wished to see the painted hardboard panelling removed from the decorative wrought-iron balustrading.[62] Under the chandeliers of the restaurant about forty guests assembled to hear Peter Parker give an address. The purpose of the celebration, he said, was to name the room after 'Sir John Betjeman, Railwayman Extraordinary – and one of our greatest and toughest customers'. Betjeman's genius, he said, was 'an infinite capacity for taking trains'. He spoke of John's toughness too: 'Sir John has been at his most relentless in reminding railways of the treasures that we have in trust from our history.'[63] The vexing question of the moment was Liverpool Street station. Parker knew that John was fiercely opposed to BR's plans for developing the station: as a token of propitiation, he handed him an album of photographs of carved brickwork cherubs in the Liverpool Street tympana which were 'among the wonderful things to preserve there'. The cherubs are all performing railway tasks, such as pulling signal levers and laying sleepers. Kaukas, an accomplished amateur book-binder, had himself bound the sheets of photographs into the album, with a poem he had written about the figures, 'Great Eastern Cherubim'.[64]

When Peter Parker had finished his tribute, John stood up to reply. 'But he didn't really make a speech,' Parker remembered. 'He just said: "Ooohh! Ooooooohhh! Oo!" Just an extraordinarily happy crowing noise, it was absolutely amazing. I mean, maybe two or three lines came out of it, but the place was in an uproar; it was just this lovely cooing noise. And then he pointed to bits of the room: "Those arches!" And he said how lucky everybody was to be in the railways and what a good idea all this was. And then he collapsed in great sighs of laughter and the party melted away.'[65]

During the reception, Parker noticed Bernard Kaukas with Walter Sinkinson and his wife in a corner at the back. The Sinkinsons had been invited down to meet John, although John had not been told they were coming. 'But, inexplicably, there was no surprise at all,' Parker wrote. 'Bernard brought Walter through the crowd, and before he could introduce him, in the midst of all that chatter and excitement, John stared a moment and said quietly, "You must be Walter Sinkinson."'[66]

It was a gala day for the old railwayman, and he later wrote about it in his parish magazine. On the morning of 24 January, he and Mary had travelled by Pullman to King's Cross, thence to Stepney, where Bishop Huddleston had invited them to stay overnight, after the reception. (Huddleston was away at a bishops' conference, but the Sinkinsons were welcomed by his housekeeper and her husband, old friends.) At 6.45, slightly nervous, they pushed their way through the revolving doors of the Charing Cross Hotel.

After first calling at our respective cloakrooms [Sinkinson wrote] we were ushered into *the* room. A few guests were already there. We were given champagne. Very soon we were feeling relaxed, being introduced to members of British Rail . . .

Then someone said 'Sir John's over there. Near the door.' I looked. Yes, JB was standing in the middle of a group, one of whom had a microphone and a cassette.

Waiters were kept busy replenishing glasses, offering delicacies. In walked Mr Parker. Soon he came up and greeted us. 'You must be Mr and Mrs Sinkinson. Come. Meet John.'

This was the moment. Mr Parker introduced us to the great man . . .

The man with the cassette held the microphone invitingly, to record what the Laureate was saying about a little blue book (minus wrapper) he had taken from his pocket: 'Bishop Huddleston sent it to me. Prayers, meditations, poems . . . I always carry the book with me. When I feel depressed, I find a quiet spot and read it. It gives me comfort.'

Sir John seemed determined to give *Joy to Know* a moment of glory.[67]

Sinkinson recorded that after John's speech and the applause that followed, Peter Parker took John by the arm, saying, 'And now you have some unveiling to do.'

The two friends went through the doorway leading to a corridor, at the end of which was the renamed restaurant. A huge basket of flowers was just inside, hiding the interior from our gaze. Above the entrance was the inscription 'The Betjeman Restaurant' with a pink silhouette of JB's profile, wearing a boater, tilted slightly backward. We must have hesitated. Turning, Mr Parker motioned us to follow. 'Come. Please! This is what it's all about.' We all made our way along the corridor, stopped opposite a curtain on the wall on our left. On each side of the curtain were framed illustrated poems by JB. Thirteen in all. 'Pull the cord, John,' said Mr Parker. John obeyed. A white plaque was revealed . . .

The Chairman then, again, took his friend's arm. Together they passed the multi-floral basket; they disappeared into that part of the Charing Cross Hotel which now proudly bears the Betjeman name.

We examined the exhibits on the wall. One, an original manuscript donated by the publishers, John Murray. There was a photograph of a laughing Sir John waving from a Metropolitan train third-class door-window.[68]

At the small dinner-party after the reception, John sat between Jill Parker and Bernard Kaukas's wife, Pamela. In a thank-you letter to Kaukas, John wrote of 'the divine Mrs Kaukas'.[69] At the time she was working at Conservative Central Office, but John soon found out that she had formerly worked on the *Catholic Herald* which had offices near Smithfield Market – not far from his old flat in Cloth Fair. Perhaps prompted by Pamela's Midland accent (she was brought up in the Potteries) John asked whether she had seen *Coronation Street* recently, the long-running television serial about midland folk.[70] 'Oh yes!' Pamela said, and asked 'Is Ernie Bishop really dead?' as he had been shot in a recent episode.[71] After a little more small-talk, some of it with Jill Parker, John asked Pamela whether she ever thought about dying, did that worry her? 'I had told him I was a Catholic, so the question wasn't so strange to me. I said I thought the worst part would be leaving people. I can't remember anything else he said at the dinner, but I noticed, as you *do*, his napkin sliding off his knees, and I didn't know whether to pick it up or not, being the lady. You know, I hate to be forceful, but I did, very gently.'[72]

There were two desserts: a chocolate boater, and zabaglione in frosted glasses, each glass decorated with 'JB' in blue icing. The waiters wore white gloves.

The next day, John wrote Peter Parker a rapturous thank-you letter:

Dear Peter,
    While it is still fresh in my memory I must recall for you, and for all of us who were there, what is one of the happiest evenings of my life. After the rush and Reg's brilliant driving round to Platform 8 at Victoria to the brightly lit haven where the ladies of the party were sitting, we did that Venetian tour through the South of London. I wish you had been on it. When we turned the lights out we glided over tracks where human foot had scarcely trod particularly between Cannon Street and Blackfriars. Sometimes the moon was on our left and sometimes on our right. We did not mind as we were gliding through heaven with lights sparkling in the tidal Thames and various inhuman chunks of Colonel Seifert glittering in the dark. Jill brought us all together and seemed to be the gondolier, though the driver, at each change, seemed to know the route as if he had walked it. What is the capital of England? When I think of it in terms of good architecture, I think it is Liverpool but last night London became a capital again particularly when we stepped into the station entrance of

Edward Middleton Barry's masterpiece, the Charing Cross Hotel. There is a very fine account of him in the *DNB* [*Dictionary of National Biography*] and I am so glad we had that reception in the really superb anteroom with its triple arches, before walking down the corridor to that noble domed dining room.

So strong is Barry's architecture, so precise and clear-cut his mouldings that hardly any colour is needed. Your speech, dear Peter, filled me with modesty and delight. I could feel throughout the room the affection in which you and Jill are held.

It was wonderful to find the catering and engineering and architectural sides of the railways, all like a moving tulip bed in Barry's uplifting setting. I think the Ritz is the best Edwardian hotel interior in London. I am sure Barry's Charing Cross Hotel is the best Victorian classical interior though the Great Eastern comes near to it. What a good thing it is that the hotel architectural side has not gone too 'with it' and most of the architecture, even the GW, is still there waiting behind plyboard. It is a wonderful hotel though, the Charing Cross, and Mr Jack knows it and so do Mr Whittingham and the staff. When I am feeling particularly anonymous, I shall visit that exhibition in order to restore my ego.

I feel uplifted, fulfilled, contented but not, I hope, complacent about last evening for which I cannot thank you and British Railways [*sic*] enough. Mr Bernard Kaukas has given me a beautiful album of those brick tympana in Liverpool Street of cherubs in the nude shovelling coal, wielding axes, surveying and signalling . . . With it is a poem showing his deep love for railways. Love always wins. The railways are delivered from Beeching who was too much like a machine for anything so human as railways. Thank you, oh thank you.

Yours ever,

John B.[73]

John did revisit the Betjeman Restaurant, on a 'test run' with Jill Parker. On the way up the staircase, he was pleased to note that British Transport Hotels had taken his hint and that the plywood had been removed from the wrought-iron staircase.

The staff knew that we were coming [Jill Parker recalled], so we were ushered to a good table. But I think John was a little bit shattered by the food that day. Unbelievably tough meat! But he kept looking round, he didn't really care about the food. He just thought it was wonderful to come there and have it called his room. He kept getting up and saying, 'Look at these mouldings, aren't they marvellous!. . . It was a case of slogging through the meal and having a good time, just him being so pleased. He did do this thing constantly – at first you thought 'He means it' but then you found he did it *all* the time – 'I don't know when I've had a better time! Oh, I do think this is the happiest day of my life.'[74]

In March 1978 Peter Parker went into the Middlesex Hospital for an operation on his leg; and John, overcoming his fear of hospitals and his hatred of 'hospital smell', visited him. He brought with him a copy of his children's book *Archie and the Strict Baptists*, which Murray had recently published with illustrations by Phillida Gili, some of them loosely based on John's originals. On the flyleaf John wrote:

For Peter's convalescence. Middlesex 1978
A Dog Lover's Poem
Big and barking and smelly is my landlady's dog
It has tits all over it and turds the size of a log
I know I must try to like it for it's ever so fond of me
And must never attempt to strike it if it thinks I'm the trunk of a tree.[75]

This rhyme (which soon found its way into a newspaper gossip column) was the final recrudescence of John's lifelong canophobia, which first surfaced mildly in his 'Ode to a Puppy' (1920), then more viciously in his Oxford playlet *The Artsenkrafts* and his poems 'Senex' and 'Chelsea 1977'.

Word got around the hospital that John was visiting Parker.

There were a lot of nurses, little Filipino nurses, lots of foreigners [Parker said]. John was sitting there and the buzz got round. They kept popping their heads in to look. There was one huge Australian nurse, who was quite capable of picking me up. She came round and I could see John looking at her – she was his kind of sporty girl. She accompanied him when he left me, the lift was very close by. John was by this time *very* charming. Suddenly he said, 'Oh, are you from Sydney?' He said he had been to a modern art exhibition in Sydney. They were all listening in awe. The lift was just coming, I could hear him round the corner. He said, one thing had puzzled him: there was a big wellington boot just near the entrance of the exhibition. 'A big wellington boot. Full of custard.' He said: 'I looked it up in the catalogue, and it was called "Pus in Boots".'[76] And then the lift closed.[77]

John's own health was declining. Increasingly, he was attended by Dr Gregory Scott, in whose arms he had said he would be happy to die. Two surviving letters from John to Scott, though not fully dated, suggest growing familiarity and growing dependence. The first letter, dated '21 Nov', was almost certainly written in 1979, the year in which *Studies in Seduction*, by Scott's friend John Stevenson, was published.

Dear Doctor Scott,

I am so glad to have a letter from you and with good news. I am so sad to be typing a reply. My hand is still too unsteady to write clearly. I am very pleased to have a numbered signed copy of John Stevenson's Studies in Seduction, to which I shall be yielding next week. I can see that it is compulsive dialogue. The man on the cover of the Best Seller is very like the Ayatollah. Life is real, life is earnest, Two things stand alone, Silence in another's trouble, sorrow in your own.

Ella Wheeler Betjeman[78]

The second letter is undated. Its greater familiarity and the more precarious state of John's health suggest that it was the later of the two.

Dear Greg,

I must write to thank you for saving my life. The great Kevin Zilkha said you had done it with that injection and can you pass on my thanks to Jill. I hope the other little boy is well again in the toy surgery. Once again thank you very much for your kindness and competence.

Yours ever,

John B.[79]

In the spring of 1983, John and Scott were participants in a black comedy of errors. When John had become Jill's patient, she had told him that he must not expect visits, although the partners would try to visit him from time to time. On an April evening in 1983, Gregory Scott was calling on several patients in South Kensington, the southern border of the practice, and decided he would just be able to get over to Chelsea and see John as well. One of the first patients he called on was a Miss Alexandrov who was dying of motor-neurone disease. When he arrived, he found that her sister, a former tennis champion, was visiting her. 'I'm afraid your sister is getting worse,' he said. 'It's remorseless: it's up to the neck now. She's paralysed and as you can see she can hardly speak, can hardly do anything. The end must be quite close.'

Leaving Miss Alexandrov and her sister, Scott made seven more visits that evening. The last visit was to John at Elizabeth Cavendish's house. At each house he visited, Scott made a note of the telephone number. Then he drove home to Stockwell. He was on call for the night. At about 3.00 a.m. the telephone rang. It was Miss Alexandrov's sister, ringing to say that the old lady had just died. 'Thank you for letting me know,' said Scott, with expressions of sympathy. 'I'll fill out all the necessary forms in the morning.'

'Oh, we can't wait till the morning!' said the sister. 'I want the body out of the house tonight.' Scott said he was not at all sure that was possible, but that he would see what he could do. He then telephoned the undertaker, who was not too surprised to be woken in the middle of the night. They had a short discussion.

'You mean, she wants us to go round there immediately? Why immediately?'

'I don't know, but she wants it immediately.' There was an embarrassed pause.

'Well, of course, it can be done; but it *is* the middle of the night, and there will have to be an extra charge for that.'

Scott said: 'Just tell me what it's going to involve and what it's going to cost, and she'll have to make the decision herself.' The undertaker gave him the information. Now Scott had to ring back Miss Alexandrov's sister. He referred to his list of telephone numbers. Unfortunately, several of them had the prefix 352 – a code covering both Kensington and Chelsea. He dialled the number. After several rings, a cultured female voice answered. There was no need for Scott to identify himself: he was simply continuing the conversation of ten minutes before. So he said: 'I've got on to the undertaker, and he says it is perfectly possible, but it will cost an extra hundred pounds.'

There was a long pause at the other end of the line. It was 3.15 in the morning. Lady Elizabeth Cavendish may have thought – recognizing Scott's voice – that the worst had happened and that she was being informed in a somewhat curious way, though why it should involve extra money must have been a mystery. 'Then they had a rather strange conversation,' said John Stevenson, who heard the whole story from Scott. 'Lady Elizabeth took it very well. She said, "I quite understand . . ." And then Greg had to get back to the motor-neurone lady's sister. Of all the numbers he had taken down that day, the only one which could possibly have caused such confusion was Betjeman's. He was the only other patient who was in anything like a critical condition.'[80] John Stevenson could not resist applying to the incident a parody of William Johnson Cory's lines:

> They told me, Heraclitus, they told me you were dead;
> They woke me up at half-past three, and got me out of bed.

Gregory Scott committed suicide three months later, in July 1983. He went to a Surrey valley and took alcohol and 100 Tuinal tablets. His father, a well-known Liverpool psychiatrist, had taken his own life in 1961, and Gregory had shown suicidal tendencies at least since 1972, when he had drawn at the end of his diary a man lying on the ground with a bottle of gin and a packet of barbiturates. In retrospect, his remark to John Betjeman in 1977 about the stocks of wine in Radnor Walk – '. . . if you ever decide you've had enough, what a way to go!' – also seems ominous. Jill Parker decided not to tell John of Scott's death. He was by then very ill: 'It would have been terribly depressing for him.'[81]

John made his last public appearance in June 1983, two weeks before Scott's death. In July 1980, James O'Brien, deputy general manager of the London Midland Region, had written to Peter Parker asking if he would invite John Betjeman to allow his name to be used on a locomotive, with a naming ceremony at St Pancras station if John were well enough. John would thus become British Rail's third 'living loco': the first two were Harold Macmillan, the former Prime Minister, and Lord Olivier, the actor. Parker at once agreed, but in fact the naming ceremony did not take place until 24 June 1983.

> I was quite worried that we weren't going to have the ceremony in time [Parker said], because he was nosediving quite fast. But the day came, and he was absolutely super. He was in a wheelchair by then. We wheeled him through the totally restored ticket office, which he had been wonderful in championing. There had been all sorts of ideas there, and, much nerved by him, we had battled through. I remember him looking up and seeing all this wonderful colouring, superbly picked out.[82]

Accompanying John, as the wheelchair was manoeuvred alongside the train, were Elizabeth Cavendish and both of his children – Paul was over from America with his wife. There was also a buzzing throng of railway enthusiasts with notebooks and cameras; after the ceremony they were going to ride on the *Sir John Betjeman* to Bedford and back, at £10 a ticket.

Peter Parker made one of his polished speeches. He spoke of John's campaigns to save the railway buildings heritage; of the famous lost battle over the Euston Arch that ironically became the rallying-point to fight on; of 'the frays (I put the word no higher)' which had developed since then, and the courtesy and understanding British Rail had received from Sir John, which were very much appreciated. The power of John's arguments, he added, had been responsible for the Board's decision, seven years before, to create an Environment department with a special remit to examine carefully its building heritage policy. 'I think it may fairly be said that disasters no longer occur, and that, as this great building exemplifies – the Return of the Pink Pancras! – much money and effort is now being expended in conserving our buildings.' (The Peter Sellers film *Return of the Pink Panther* had been released in 1974.) Parker ended: 'I can think of no person who better deserves to have his name running through the countryside, towns, villages and cities which he has described so amusingly, so evocatively and so touchingly.'[83]

With some help, John pulled a cord to draw aside the curtain covering the gleaming 'SIR JOHN BETJEMAN' plaque on the locomotive. The crowd cheered. He tried to speak to them, but failed.

> When we got to the train [Parker recalled] at first he said he wasn't going to say anything; but when people began applauding he said he wanted to say something, and a thin little ribbon of a mike was pushed in front of him. But no one could hear a word. He did speak, and of course he did not realize that his whisper wasn't catching anything. So we had, I'd say, sixty seconds when he was speaking and none of us could hear. It was a very still moment. He was looking round as if he were wondering what was happening.[84]

The *Sir John Betjeman* electric locomotive 86229 left for Bedford, pulling carriages with railway enthusiasts at every window. John was not on board. He was going off to a private luncheon in 'the Mess' at Euston House, headquarters of the London Midland Region. As James O'Brien (by now general manager) wheeled him from the dais, John said: 'Does it all have to end?'[85]

'He then behaved with complete merriment,' Peter Parker remembers. 'We went back to lunch. The photographs taken at lunch show what tremendous form he was in. Elizabeth [Cavendish] was feeding him, but there was no embarrassment around the table of any sort. A spellbound situation.'[86]

The other guests at the luncheon – who again included Walter and Mary Sinkinson – had dressed crab or lobster mayonnaise and a collation of cold meats, but O'Brien had arranged for John to have a plate of oysters, his favourite dish. After lunch, O'Brien presented him with a model of the Euston Propylaeum. The exquisite irony of this was not lost on John, who in his letter of thanks to O'Brien wrote: 'I look at the model of the Euston Arch every day. I am glad to think that it will survive us all.'[87]

Jill Parker remembers John at the luncheon going into his usual act – 'Oh my goodness! Oh dear! I don't know *when* I've had such a good time!' But she thought 'He really did love it, although it made him very tired. I think that was the sort of occasion that Elizabeth [Cavendish] would slightly frown on, because it made him so tired – but in fact it was *worth* being tired, it didn't matter if he was tired, I always thought.'[88] Three days after the ceremony, John wrote to Peter Parker: 'I can't express my thanks enough to you and to the Board of British Railways [*sic*] for its so generous treatment of me on Friday. It was a memorable day indeed and after it all things an anticlimax.'[89]

'... WHOSE DEATH HAS ECLIPSED THE GAIETY OF NATIONS'

Lord, let me know mine end, and the number of my days: that I may be certified how long I have to live.

Psalm 39

John Betjeman was staying with us once at Biddesden when he had a terrifying dream, that he was handed a card with wide black edges, and on it his name was engraved, and a date. He knew this was the date of his death.

Diana Mosley, *A Life of Contrasts*, London, 1977

All through your life you were mindful of Death,
And you met him at last on the way to Polzeath.

Stanley J. Sharpless, 'Sir John Betjeman', in *How to Become Absurdly Well-Informed about the Famous and Infamous*, ed. E. O. Parrott, London 1987

Two weeks after John was honoured in the locomotive-naming ceremony, James Lees-Milne did 'what I would never do for anyone else' – drove to London to dine with John and Elizabeth, returning to Badminton the same evening. He arrived at Radnor Walk at eight o'clock.

After all I need not have come. Feeble sweetly welcoming and cooked delicious roast chicken breast, and provided strawberries and cream. John slumped in his arm chair by the window, watching Coronation Street when I arrived, at an angle to the screen, two feet from it. Made signs of recognition. Spoke little. Mouth down at both sides. Difficult to elicit interest or response, yet I think fairly pleased to see me. Did not move to the table.

Feeble put a board across arms of chair and gave him his helping, tied a bib, gave him a spoon. He toyed with his helping. Just like a baby. His trousers totally loose, not tied to body by belt or braces. I talked to Feeble during dinner. J heard what we said and did not join in beyond a grunt or two. Then his nurse came. 'Do you want to go to bed, darling?' Feeble said at 8.45. 'Yes, I think so.' The nurse piloted him upstairs. I did not see him again. Talked to Feeble and left at 9.30. She said he was lucky, for he had no pain, and was not lonely. Mind clear. Was read to by a young actor every afternoon. Is wheeled to his house every morning where his secretary opens letters and answers them for him.[1]

Other old friends continued to visit John. Kingsley Amis, in his memoirs, contrasted him before and after he entered what Mary Wilson, in a poem, called 'the speechless years'.[2]

I cherish a portrayal of John as seen by my old friend Susan Allison,[3] for many years his part-time secretary and, more lately, mine too. She describes how his statutory mid-morning half-bottle of champagne could be brought forward to eleven a.m. with the aid of an elaborate display of casualness on his part or deferred by her dangling the completion of another horrible couple of letters. He would dictate all of these straight into Susie's typewritten text, sending her a devious look when he came to a hard word, breaking off every so often to leaf through Who's Who or Debrett and read aloud 'the hobbies and habits of one or another usually eccentric, always indigent Irish peer, embellishing his reading with some scandalous titbit from memory or mischief.' . . .

At the end, John was finally incapacitated by Parkinson's Disease, and that incomparably expressive face became set into a mute unchanging mask. I went and read poems to him, some of them by his much-admired Newbolt, not 'Drake's Drum' but later pieces like 'The Nightjar'. His stare remained as blank as before but I know the words reached him.[4]

Robert Robinson also came to see John in the last years.

It took me long enough to make up my mind to visit Betjeman after he had the stroke [he wrote]. 'Just go on up and read to him,' said Elizabeth Cavendish when I arrived at Radnor Walk. She was doing the dishes, someone had made his bed, and he was sitting in a chair in a corner of the bedroom. 'Must be dreadful to lose your speech when it's the thing that makes you who you are,' said Elizabeth in a matter of fact way which she must have used to other visitors, to let them off having to say something themselves. I'd brought *The Everyman Book of Light Verse* of which I was editor, and told him it had just come out.

He sat, the expression on his face pleasant but fixed, quite unchanging. I read a few poems out of the book, some of his own, wondering whether he would like the familiar echoes or resent some chump barging in and making free with the stuff. I offered a sort of commentary, making it sound like a conversation, as one does, but wondering whether things he'd said to Josée and me over the years was anything he could put up with hearing again. I told him his own jokes in the Do you remember mode: as when he'd overheard a lady buttonholding T. S. Eliot and asking him, 'Do you pronounce your name Leon M. Leon or Layon M. Lyon?', and someone else who always pronounced the word 'poetry' as 'poytry'. And when I read him a verse or two of 'How to Get On in Society', a smile appeared, but oh, from a long way away.[5]

In September 1983 John had another heart attack. Lees-Milne again visited him and Elizabeth at Radnor Walk on 13 October.

JB sitting in his old armchair between window and fireplace looking different again since that bad heart attack. Totally bald, egg-shaped and dead white. A silent Buddha. Did not speak at all except to ask me, 'How's the Dame?' Eliz. says he rarely speaks now. Likes to be read to. No explanation for the heart attack.[6] Might have another tomorrow, or in two years' time.[7]

Elizabeth wrote to Patrick Garland: 'John was doing so well against all the odds, but for some reason he has become very withdrawn and I find it agonizing seeing him look so sad and tormented and being unable to help him at all.'[8] He could speak a little, even compose lines of verse. Gerard Irvine, who called in often to give him communion, thinks that the last verse John ever composed was this couplet, suddenly uttered after a long silence:

> Of all the things within this house that are by me possessed
> I love, oh yes, I love by far, my *ironing* board the best.[9]

There were still visits to Cornwall and Derbyshire with Elizabeth. After John had attended the Hallamshire Hospital in December 1983, Dr Cyril Davies-Jones wrote to Jill Parker: 'I told Elizabeth Cavendish that there is no indication to treat him vigorously in any way because I do not think he would be improved, and I cannot see him going on for all that much longer.'[10]

James Lees-Milne saw John for the last time on 1 February 1984.

In evening went to see John Betj. at Radnor Walk. Worse than ever. Very tragic. Sitting in his chair like a sack, his head lolling to one side. Feeble went up, kissed him and said she would set him straight. Promptly the head fell to the other side. Did not recognize me. I left feeling very sad.[11]

In December 1983, Penelope had taken her and John's eldest grandchild, Lucy, on a three-month 'educational tour' of India.[12] Penelope had to return in mid-February to act as a lecturer on two Linblad cruises. She was paid $100 a day for a month.[13] 'This means', she wrote to Jessie Sharley in April, 'I will be able to take our second granddaughter Imogen to India either this autumn or early in 1985.[14] She is the intellectual member of the family and if her A levels are good enough ... Marlborough College may put her forward for the Oxbridge Entrance Exam ...'[15] She added:

I went to see John when I returned to London at the end of March and he smiled and said Yes several times when I asked him questions but otherwise he never speaks at all now and just sits in a chair with Archie and has a trained nurse in attendance who is going up to Derbyshire with him for three weeks at Easter. It is terribly sad as he used to be so active, but at least he does not suffer any pain except when he has strokes and I pray daily when his time comes God will take him in his sleep and that he won't have any more painful strokes.[16]

In May, John went to Cornwall with Elizabeth and his nurses, Carole and Vicky. 'Please relax . . . and don't drink any WHISKY,' Penelope wrote to him.[17] Candida came down to Trebetherick and read him Evelyn Waugh's *The Ordeal of Gilbert Pinfold*. 'He was utterly happy in Trebetherick,' she later wrote. 'I could see it in his eyes.'[18] John's close friends were keeping a kind of metaphorical vigil: they knew the end could not be far off. On 18 May, his and Elizabeth's friend (Sir) John Drummond had a disconcerting experience.

Among the exhibitions in 1984 [he recalled in his memoirs] was one devoted to the wardrobe and memorabilia of Dame Edna Everage. I went to the official opening, performed by the Dame herself in full fig. I knew Barry Humphries only slightly, but we shared a deep affection for John Betjeman. Noticing me in the crowd, he asked a gallery attendant to bring me round to see him. Sitting back with his stockinged legs on the table, drinking a cup of tea between engagements, he asked me if I had news of John, who was in hospital and likely to die at any moment. He said he had talked to Kingsley Amis, who had been going to the hospital to read to John, and wondered if I had been in touch with Elizabeth Cavendish. All this was a normal part of our shared concern for a much loved friend. But, though he can apparently do the voice when wearing male clothes, he cannot stop using the voice when got up as Edna, and I found it quite intolerable to be talking about the imminent death of one of my most cherished friends with this shrieking virago. I have always had more than a soft spot for Dame Edna, since she bears a dangerous resemblance to my mother's sister, but in these circumstances she was too much and I excused myself apologetically. John Betjeman died the next day.[19]

John was due to return to London by ambulance on 19 May. Candida is sure that he heard of this arrangement and that he decided he wanted to die at Treen.[20] Elizabeth read to him on the evening of the 18th and Carole watched over him that night. He died peacefully at 8.30 a.m. Elizabeth later wrote to Billa Harrod:

> I truly think those last months he was more serene and at peace than I have ever known him . . . He died on the most beautiful sunny morning with the sun streaming into the room and the French windows open and the lovely smell of the garden everywhere. Carole was holding one of his hands and me the other and Vicky was just gently stroking his head and he had old Archie and Jumbo in each arm and Stanley the cat asleep on his tummy. He was completely conscious right up to that last moment. We none of us moved for nearly an hour afterwards and the sense of total peace was something I shall never forget.[21]

Elizabeth telephoned Candida, who rang her mother in Herefordshire. Candida went into the garden at Blacklands and picked all the parrot tulips she had planted the autumn before, put them in the back of her car and drove down to Cornwall.[22] That day John's death was a main item on the television news programmes. In the pubs, people talked about him, though it was Cup Final day.[23] On 20 May most of the Sunday newspapers ran long and affectionate obituaries. *The Observer*'s headline was: 'Betjeman the people's poet dies'. On another page, Kingsley Amis, under the heading 'Frightfully good, old Betjeman', added an appreciation of his friend: 'In our century he has few equals and no superiors.' The *Sunday Times* published an essay by John Piper. The *Sunday Express* called John 'the man who took verse into the best-seller lists'.

On one point, two of the Sunday news reports seemed at variance. The *Sunday Times* claimed that 'Buckingham Palace sent a private message of sympathy to Lady Betjeman . . . who had been "amicably separated" from Sir John . . . Sir John's long-standing friend Lady

Elizabeth Cavendish was at the family home yesterday, but declined to speak.' The *Sunday Express*, for its part, reported that 'The Queen sent a private message of sympathy to Sir John's home close to the Camel estuary in Trebetherick, Cornwall.' Both reports may have been true. It was proper that the Queen should send condolences to her Laureate's widow; it would also have been natural for her to write to Elizabeth Cavendish, whom she had known since they were children together. On the Monday, Philip Larkin wrote the obituary in the *Daily Telegraph*: 'Truly he has created, as Wordsworth said all great and original writers must, the taste by which he was relished.' *The Times*, too, judged John 'a true original'. Even the *New York Times* gave space to the news on its front page.

The funeral took place in St Enodoc Church in Cornwall on 22 May. It was a day of driving rain. The *Guardian* reporter, John Ezard, wrote of 'a horizontal monsoon and an umbrella-splintering wind'.[24] The sand was so wet that the two gravediggers were worried that their work would collapse. Mourners were drenched as they struggled on foot towards the church's witch-hat spire. Penelope, Paul, Candida and Elizabeth were there, with Jock Murray, Billa Harrod and James Lees-Milne. The cortège parked on the St Enodoc golf course, which was closed for the day as a mark of respect.

> The undertaker and six pall-bearers [John Ezard wrote] drove through the dunes until the track ran out three hundred yards away. Then they got out and bore the coffin very slowly and precisely through the rain up the winding slope to the lych gate, with still more valleys of dunes stretching in the background to the long rollers of the sea.
>
> They carried the coffin not on their shoulders but in old-country fashion, on struts waist high, so that they could use the coffin rests in the middle of the lych gate when they reached it. As they walked the spectacle composed itself into the lines of a nineteenth-century coastal village painting by John Singer Sargent.[25]

James Lees-Milne had spent the night before at Lanhydrock[26] with 'the dear Trinicks' – Michael Trinick of the National Trust and his wife Elizabeth. He hired a taxi to Trebetherick and arrived there at about 11.30 a.m., meaning to call on Elizabeth Cavendish and leave his suitcase in the cottage, but Elizabeth and a party of her friends were already in the street. 'I offered to give them a lift. But E said, You can't drive. Can only walk. So I dismissed taxi, got out and carried my blue suitcase. Mercifully had put on galoshes in the car.'[27] He had to shut his umbrella, which threatened to blow inside out. The church interior was 'dark as pitch, save for a few oil lamps and candles'. Jock Murray recalled that 'The lady verger fortunately had a torch and she shone it in the aisle, rather like a cinema usherette, so that people could read their hymnals.'[28] Lees-Milne was put into a two-seater pew next to Murray, 'who whispered throughout'. In front of them were Billa Harrod and Penelope. 'The battery of wind and rain somewhat distracted concentration on the service and checked emotion,' Lees-Milne wrote. 'Nevertheless a moving occasion.'[29] The lessons, one of which was read by Paul, were from Isaiah, Ecclesiasticus and the Apocrypha, 'with its tribute to the modest youthfulness of writers of poetry'.[30] The Rev. Anthony Gent said: 'Sir John was a man of humility, humour, simplicity of manner, and had an insight into the things which really matter in life.'[31] The congregation of more than a hundred sang John's favourite hymns – 'The Church's One Foundation' and 'Dear Lord and Father of Mankind'. Lees-Milne wrote of the coffin-bearers: 'They, poor things, dripped throughout service on to the floor, and I felt them shivering.'[32] He stood in the porch with others while the simple coffin was carried out into the torrential rain. It was buried beside the lych gate. Barely twenty yards away, fresh flowers had been placed on the grave of John's mother.[33]

The service was a delicate operation. Jock Murray was reminded of the 1950 film *The Happiest Days of Your Life* (produced by John's wartime friend Sidney Gilliat), in which, by a clerical accident, a girls' school moves in with the boys at a boys' school, and when the girls' parents visit, desperate attempts are made to prevent their seeing any boys.[34] Penelope and Elizabeth did not speak to each other. After the ceremony, there were two distinct wakes. Lees-Milne, who had telephoned Elizabeth, not Penelope, to ask if he would be welcome at the service, walked back across the field, with Lady Anne Tree, to the cottage, where a fire was burning.

> Given toasted sandwiches and a glass of whisky. The others went to a neighbouring house for luncheon with Penelope whom I did not see to talk to. And Billa. Silent embrace in the rain. Poignancy of sitting on John's little deathbed with Archie, teddy bear, and Jumbo propped against pillow. Anyway I have paid my respects to the best man who ever lived and the most loveable.[35]

Lees-Milne was, of course, a partisan mourner, one of John's oldest surviving friends. But John Ezard noticed how a group of what, in cliché terms, would have been called 'hard-bitten journalists', who had been allowed to stand under the lych gate with their notebooks and cameras, were affected by the rainswept ceremony. 'The scale of the place was so intimate and Betjemanesque that as they peered out they made an ashamed discovery. It is possible, even when rainwater is streaming down people's faces, to tell that they are also crying.'[36]

In a note in the *Sunday Express* on the day John's death was reported, Graham Lord had recalled John's telling him that he wanted just his name and dates on his tombstone. 'A well-designed stone, well-proportioned. Made out of local stone. Simple. Like a good title page.'[37] It was not to be. The lettering on the gravestone was of Gothic floridity – 'like something out of *Gormenghast*', Jock Murray thought.[38] The inscription was carved by Simon Verity, best known today for the figures he has carved in the Church of St John the Divine, New York. A few days before the funeral, an old Cornishwoman famed for her garrulousness had been buried in a near-by plot. 'Not much chance of John Betjeman's resting in peace,' a local commented.[39]

On 26 May, *The Spectator* honoured its former columnist with no fewer than three articles, all by *Private Eye* writers. Gavin Stamp wrote that it was 'that marvellous book' *First and Last Loves* that had first stimulated his interest in architecture when he was still at school. Richard Ingrams recalled John's melancholia and religious temperament. Auberon Waugh, incensed by what he considered a patronizing leader about John's death in the *Daily Telegraph*, wrote:

> In France less important writers than Betjeman are given state funerals. Streets, squares, whole new towns are named after them. I would suggest that his light may well go on burning with a fiercer brightness as the years go by. I would certainly imagine that his poetry will be being read with pleasure and profit long after the dimmest provincial university has finally cleared its shelves of Eliot, Pound and Auden. His place may yet prove to be among the truly great – and we will be shown the greater fools for not having seen it.

It was inevitable that poets would write threnodies for John. One poem (of which a couplet stands at the head of this chapter) was by Stanley J. Sharpless, a regular winner of the *New Statesman*'s literary competitions. Charles Thomson – to whom John wrote in 1982, 'I don't know what a poet is but I know you are one'[40] – wrote two commemorative poems, of which one asked plaintive questions modelled on the 'And is it true?' of John's poem on Christmas.[41]

> So will his poetry not last?
> So did his heart outweigh his head?
> So did he seek an unreal past?
> John Betjeman is dead.[42]

Thomson answered these and the other questions in his poem:

> His poems will survive.
> He entertained with what he said
> And brought the simple things alive.
> And though today the mourners cry,
> The work he gave, the life he led
> And all who hold him dear deny
>   John Betjeman is dead.[43]

Perhaps the best of the *in memoriam* offerings was by the extraordinary polymath Roy Dean, diplomat, arms-control expert, twice winner of the *Times* National Crossword Championship and holder of the world record for the fastest verified solution.[44] His 'Homage to Betjeman' was based on John's 'Hymn'.[45] Like that early poem, it can be sung to the tune of 'The Church's One Foundation'. The five stanzas included these three:

> The comedy of manners
> Was his essential strain;
> Pretentious snobs and planners
> Were mocked in tones urbane.
> He did not seek to lecture,
> But taught us to admire
> Victorian architecture
> In arch and roof and spire . . .
>
> He sang the muscled maiden,
> The fragrant Surrey pines,
> The cliffs with blossom laden,
> Suburban railway lines.
> And while a handsome station
> Was lauded in his verse,
> He showed that restoration
> Could lead to something worse.
>
> A morbid dread of dying
> Disturbed his later years,
> Though friends were always trying
> To dissipate his fears.
> May all his troubles cease now
> Where waves assault the rock,
> And may he rest in peace now
> In far St Enodoc.[46]

The memorial service held at Westminster Abbey on 24 June confirmed four lines in Roy Dean's opening stanza –

> His lyrical achievement
> We all could understand,
> And pangs of keen bereavement
> Were felt throughout the land.[47]

In the congregation were most of John's surviving friends, and many people who had never known him but had applied for tickets to pay their respects. Three formidable diarists were present and recorded the occasion: Anthony Powell, James Lees-Milne and Peter Parker (not to be confused with the former chairman of British Rail), who was writing the biography of John's old friend Joe Ackerley, the novelist and literary editor. All three were given seats at good vantage points. Powell wrote:

V[iolet] and I to London for the John Betjeman Memorial Service at Westminster Abbey. We had booked seats. I arrived about an hour before the (11.30) start, and was first occupant of the Choir Stalls. I was taken up aisle with great pomp by a verger, between already full rows in the nave of the Abbey. I felt that the resentment at this was almost audible (V said later, unprompted, she too had same sensation) . . . Philip Larkin and Monica Jones appeared in the row behind us, later joined by Kingsley Amis. The block opposite included Peter Quennell (a faint smile on his skull-like features), a couple (said to be the architect/journalist Gavin Stamp & wife) who rather exhibitionistically brought small baby with them; Richard Ingrams (face agonizingly racked) with wife; Peter Fleetwood-Hesketh (an old friend of V's, Eton contemporary and colleague of mine in War Office, architectural buddy of Betjeman's); Grey Gowrie;[48] no doubt others one knew.[49]

Lees-Milne recorded:

John Betjeman's memorial service. Extremely impressive. We were given the best possible seats, 2 stalls in the choir. Alas, A [lvilde] unable to attend owing to sprained wrist. I sat next to Michael Tree. I think he wept, I certainly did at times. Emma Tennant[50] next to A's vacant seat. Noticed four fine chandeliers hanging like pear drops in the crossing.[51]

Peter Parker, who attended the service with a friend, wrote:

We filed in through the West Door, watched by crowds behind the barricades, and were guided to our seats in the South Lantern, a block behind the family and with a splendid view of the pulpit and lectern. As we entered, Jim Parker's band were playing Elgar, 'Favourite School Songs' and 'A Selection of Hymn Tunes', and this set the tone of the entire proceedings: celebratory, idiosyncratic and really rather moving.[52]

Not all the congregation thought Jim Parker's style of music appropriate – as the Rev. John Richards, priest and author, later hinted in a long poem about the service, 'Summoned by Love':

> With syncopation some feared pandemonium,
> Dignity-clutching they tried to look solemn –
> Walked as if mourning, while brass and euphonium
> Bounced mighty oompahs off archway and column.[53]

Parker observed the arrivals.

We bobbed up and down as, unseen from where we sat, assorted royalty filed in to the strains of 'Nimrod'. The family, led by Candida Lycett Green in a beautiful grey outfit with pillbox hat and veil, trotted round the back to take their seats. Lady Betjeman was also in grey, her bosom resting down by her belt, her face like a disgruntled pekinese. Strings of children. Last of all, in shuffled an old man in a grubby raincoat, his thin hair brushed forward Caesar-style, held in place by a hairnet.[54]

The three diarists gave their impressions of the service – as it were, three artists painting the same scene. Powell contrasted the extravagant honour being done to John with his own memory of the scruffy joker of the 1920s.

Service a tremendous affair, the Archbishop of Canterbury [Robert Runcie] in charge; Prince of Wales reading the Lesson (which he did well), perfectly right for the Poet Laureate. The address by a cleric named Harry Williams, who emphasized how much Betjeman loathed the smoothness of business executives.[55] (Williams himself gave an unrivalled example of ecclesiastical smoothness, and for ingratiating himself in other ways Betjeman too unequalled.) After a polite reference to Penelope Betjeman as wife, he spoke of 'thirty years' help and support from another', tho' Elizabeth Cavendish was not mentioned by name. Finally, in obeisance to the Prince of Wales, adding how much Betjeman would have agreed with 'certain recent remarks about architecture'. One could not help indulging in rather banal reflections about the seedy unkempt (but never in the least unambitious) Betjeman of early days, snobbish objections to him at Oxford, Chetwodes' opposition to the

ned at the last by all this boasted pomp and show. It was
ie feat.[56]

s Lees-Milne, too, reflected 'how amazed JB would have been
ha ne known forty, fifty years ago when I first knew him, of this
national hero's apotheosis, which is what it was'.[57]

Before service opened we listened to John's favourite tunes, from *In a Monastery Garden* to Elgar and school songs he loved. Immediately long procession of twenty-five to thirty clergymen I would guess – dear old Gerard Irvine prancing among them – followed by Archbishop of Canterbury in white mitre. Feeble to whom I blew a kiss in a stall five away from mine was lunching with him afterwards. Billa [Harrod] very shocked. 'Most unbecoming in the Archbishop entertaining not the widow but the concubine.' The Prince of Wales read first lesson beautifully, strong, good voice, slowly, pausing in right places. Jock Murray read the second. Equally well until the very last sentence when he was deeply moved, and could barely get the words out in a whisper. Somehow it seemed apposite and was rather touching. I congratulated him when we left. He said, 'By Jove, I barely made it,' and was clearly upset. So I wrote and told him how effective it was . . . Harry Williams's address was excellent and he paid oblique tribute to Feeble's thirty years' friendship and nursing. The Abbey packed with close friends and unknown friends and admirers. Special prayers written for John. Much emphasis upon the love he inspired . . . I walked out with Tony Powell and found Anne Rosse at the west end. She motored me to our restaurant, Como Lario [*sic* for Comolario].[58]

Peter Parker wrote:

The choir burst into some Croft as a vast procession of robed clerics stumped up the nave, croziers and candles held aloft. Red, gold and green; but one old gent in a blue robe trimmed with ancient rabbit, which looked as though it had been run up by the housemaster's wife . . . for a school production of Shakespeare. Runcie cloaked and mitred. Then silence for the Bidding: 'We meet to thank God for Sir John Betjeman, a national figure whose death has eclipsed the gaiety of nations . . .', and we were off, the Dean of Westminster reading the eye-pricking speech with great dignity.[59]

The Dean, Edward Carpenter, spoke of the way John had 'cast an aura of romance and nostalgia over ordinary and familiar things' and of 'his firm commitment to Christian Faith held within a reverent agnosticism'.[60] Then 'Immortal, Invisible' was sung. Parker described the

Prince of Wales as 'very much the Head of School, a handsome figure suddenly rather vulnerable in front of so vast a congregation'. He added: 'Sir Osbert Lancaster, immobile in a wheelchair, brought out [an] ear-trumpet, which he directed towards the lectern.'[61]
Alan Bennett, also present, wrote in his diary:

> Prince Charles at Betjeman's memorial service. Never read the Bible as if it means something. Or at any rate don't *try* and mean it. Nor prayers. The liturgy is best treated and read as if it's someone announcing the departure of trains.[62]

Peter Parker's account of the service continued:

The choir, unseen, sang out Stanford's setting of Psalm 150 – absolutely glorious. Then Jock Murray, somewhere out of sight in the nave, read the second lesson, his voice faltering. This was followed by another hymn from the choir as the Rev. Harry Williams, friend of Betjeman and 'out gay', was escorted to the pulpit by [a woman] in green robes. I had thought this figure was a curly-headed young man specially chosen for Rev. H.W., until I saw court shoes poking out from beneath the green hem. The address seemed to say all the right things, without being particularly distinguished.

Then we all stood for 'When I survey the wondrous crawss' . . . which Robin Ray,[63] in an ancient television programme, had suggested was rather bloodthirsty.

'Well, that's all to do with theology,' Betjeman had retorted.

> ' "His dying crimson like a robe,
>   Spreads o'er his body on the Tree;
> Then I am dead to all the globe,
>   And all the globe is dead to me."

'I don't see that there's anything . . . That seems to me very grand poetry.'

Then prayers, including a marvellous thanksgiving for Betjeman's 'earthly pilgrimage', especially 'for his delight in trains and railways and the Underground'. John Oaksey read 'Trebetherick'[64] and Prunella Scales[65] read 'South London Sketch, 1844', and we all sang 'Praise to the Holiest in the height'. Runcie gave the Blessing, and the bells, unheard over the organ within, rang out. Jim Parker's ensemble played a selection from *Banana Blush* as we filed out into the nave and shuffled towards the door alongside [Philip] Larkin – tall, with deaf-aid – and [Kingsley] Amis – blown up like a bullfrog. The Duchess of Devonshire (the happy recipient of £21.2 million from a sale of Old Master drawings last Tuesday) and

Lady Mosley representing the Mitfords. The latter a very good advertisement for fascism: bird-bright, immaculate in black-edged tweed, a black
Alice-band thrust into grey hair worn utility-short, briskly stepping forth,
glancing round with extraordinarily blue eyes. Only the deaf-aid suggested
decay. 'Isn't that Percy Sugden from *Coronation Street*?' I said to Philip,
and it was. He was standing in the doorway with Alf Roberts and Rita
Fairclough, whose hair and face are bright orange. No Brian Tilsley.
Unseen. Lady Elizabeth Cavendish and a Mrs Jackson, formerly Miss Joan
Hunter Dunn. Michael Gough,[66] very distinguished in grey suit, shirt and
bow-tie; Jonathan Stedall with a child aloft; a roseate Stephen Spender;
Lord Snowdon, subdued and alone (his former wife [Princess Margaret],
representing HMQM [Queen Elizabeth the Queen Mother], resplendent
in black, with a hat trimmed with crow's feathers, had sat in the Quire);
Lord Longford, very tall and unkempt in an extraordinarily ill-fitting
morning suit, shoelaces trailing dangerously, like the lugubrious butler in
a West End farce; Terence Stamp; the David Dimblebys;[67] and so on and
so forth.

   We congregated outside with some of the heralds, who had formed a
distinguished but effete group in immaculate suits (my own was £10 from
West Hampstead Oxfam). Lady Mosley at the wheel of a Mercedes saw
her chance and nearly mowed us down . . .[68]

It was natural that Diana Mosley should attend. She was one of
John's oldest friends. He had known her before she married Bryan
Guinness and had remained her friend after she married Sir Oswald
Mosley (with Adolf Hitler a guest at the wedding breakfast) and after
she was imprisoned in the Second World War as a potential danger to
the realm. But there was a macabre aptness to her materializing at the
service. It was as if she were there to witness the enforcement of a
Faustian bargain. For under her roof, over fifty years before, John had
dreamed – or so he thought – the exact date of his death.[69]
A memorial service was also held at Magdalen College, Oxford,
and a Requiem Mass at Pusey House, where John had worshipped as
an undergraduate. Penelope wrote to Father Ursell, the principal of
Pusey House:

I will come with a friend (who is driving me to Oxford as I have no car &
it is too far for my bike or pony cart) to the Requiem Mass . . . I would
much rather just join the general congregation & not go in a front pew. I
do hope you don't mind but the whole thing is very traumatic & I feel
BOGUS. As I am sure you know JB settled with Elizabeth Cavendish for
the last ten or twelve years & altho' I saw him occasionally & we were on
good terms, E. did not like us meeting & she looked after him thro'out the

Parkinson period. Of course I told J.B. I would divorce him if he wanted to marry E, but he IMPLORED me not to.

I have got to be in a front pew in W[estminster] A[bbey] as I am John's official widow but I can't face it at Pusey House as well.

Officially, as you know, I can't receive Holy Communion in an Anglican church. I have once done so with J.B. but as this is an official requiem there would be so much talk from both camps if I did, that I honestly think it will be more tactful if I just make a spiritual communion. I very much want to hear Gerard [Irvine]'s address. I would love to meet you afterwards.[70]

On 27 October 1984 *The Times* reported, under the headline 'Betjeman leaves £1,000 to colleges', that the poet had left an estate valued at £200,775 net: a modest sum, considering that his poems had sold in their millions. The Marquess of Anglesey and Lady Elizabeth Cavendish were to be his literary executors. John left £500 each to the fabric funds of Magdalen and Keble Colleges, Oxford – each of which had made him an honorary fellow.[71] Gerard Irvine was left John's Tuke painting of callipygous bathers.[72]

Twelve years later, on 11 November 1996, John's family and friends came to Westminster Abbey again for the dedication of a monument to his memory in Poets' Corner. It was an eighteenth-century stone cartouche which had been found in the triforium, still in its original crate.[73] As John was not armigerous, the Abbey's Surveyor, Dr Donald Buttress, originally designed an Underground train to go in the cartouche above the inscription – in allusion to the poet's enthusiasm for Metro-land.

Buttress remembers:

I treated the train front in a heraldic way – boldly coloured in red, black and white. The 'joke' amused *some* of the [Abbey's architecture advisory] panel – not *all*, since art historians tend to take themselves rather

seriously – but it was not liked by someone . . . who perhaps thought the Abbey too serious a place for frivolity. At very short notice therefore I redid the upper shield having a low-relief 'Gothick' bell-frame and bell which I thought would allude to *Summoned by Bells*.[74]

The 'swash' lettering on the tablet was designed by John's friend David Peace.[75]

John Betjeman's extended family had grown: there were great-grandchildren now.[76] His friends were depleted: Osbert Lancaster, among others, had died since 1984. Patrick Leigh Fermor, another classic writer of the 'Murray stable', gave the address. In this taber-nacle of English antiquity, and to a congregation whose freshest memory of John was as a sad old man in a wheelchair, Leigh Fermor was able to conjure an image of the poet as he had first known him, in 1931, when John had given a lecture to his school, King's, Canterbury.

He was twenty-five and nothing about this slim, dinner-jacketed figure, with his dark, rather floppy hair, his chalky pallor and his vivid and mobile mouth, in the least resembled any of our previous lecturers. His large dark eyes looked rather forlorn . . . His discourse was light, spontaneous, urgent and convincing, and it began with a eulogy of the spare and uncluttered lines of the Parthenon and this led on, astonishing as it may sound today, to a eulogy of the spare, uncluttered lines of the modern architecture of Le Corbusier and the Bauhaus School . . . and the merits of ferro-concrete and the simplicity of tubular steel furniture were rapturously extolled. Conversely, not an aspidistra, not an antimacassar was spared, and the slide of a half-timbered Victorian villa was dismissed with a pitying wave – 'and that's a tribute to Anne Hathaway, I suppose'. Wonderful jokes welled up in improvised asides and when, as if by mistake, the simple joke of a slide of Mickey Mouse playing a ukelele dropped on to the screen for a split second, it brought the house down. We reeled away in a state of gaseous exhilaration and the result would have been the same, whatever his theme.[77]

This resurrection of the springtime Betjeman – in some ways the antithesis of his later public persona – was as telling as the celebrated coda of Lytton Strachey's *Queen Victoria*, in which the mind of the dying Queen flits back constantly to images of the young Prince Albert.[78] Mary Wilson unveiled the monument. Leigh Fermor revealed how the antique stone had been discovered a few years before.

It was blank then [he said] but it is inscribed now with his name, and raised forever on the flank of a pillar, like a hatchment. He would have

liked the uprush of the clustered piers overhead and the interlock of the
cloisters over there . . . Not many steps away sails the great vaulting of
Henry VII's chapel; John always gloried in the thought that fan tracery
was England's one original contribution to architecture; it only exists in
the British Isles, like grouse. He would rejoice in his surroundings, and we
all of us rejoice with him, for he has bestowed great gifts on us . . .[79]

EPILOGUE

What were his life's keepings?

Geoffrey Grigson, 'John Betjeman', *Recollections*, London 1984

I think one of the strengths of Mr Betjeman's poetry is that he has refused to relinquish emotions and situations that other poets have let slip into the film and the novel and other mass-media: it can lead to sentimentality, but on the other hand it can lead to works such as Hardy's *Satires of Circumstance*. And since I have mentioned Hardy, I should like to end by quoting a sentence he copied into his diary from Leslie Stephen: 'The ultimate aim of a poet should be to touch our hearts by showing his own, and not to exhibit his learning, or his fine taste . . .' I think this even more relevant now than it was then, and one reason why I regard Mr Betjeman's poetry as important is that it bears it out so well.

Philip Larkin, Q, 11, Hilary 1955; reprinted in *Further Requirements*, London 2001

Somebody with a taste for the epigrammatic might suggest: 'John Betjeman's life was lived wholly within the twentieth century; but all his interests lay outside it.' (Love affairs excepted, of course.) He was famous for liking and preserving Victorian architecture. He wrote in a style that Tennyson would not have found outlandish. He was a man of religion in an age of irreligion.

It is a tenable debating case; but the arguments against it are stronger. Betjeman was a Bright Young Thing in the 1920s. He wrote with a post-Freudian freedom about sex, from 'Get on the bed there and start' in 'Clash Went the Billiard Balls' to 'Late Flowering Lust' and the sympathetic treatment of homosexuality in 'Monody on the Death of a Platonist Bank Clerk', published before homosexuality between consenting adults in private was made legal in Britain. He was a pioneer of the new medium of television. And, despite all his huffing and puffing about the 'infernal combustion engine', he helped, with the Shell Guides, to encourage people to explore Britain's heritage by motor-car.

In the long run, more cars meant dangerous pollution; but Betjeman has been claimed as an ecological trail-blazer. Michael Foot wrote in 1970: 'How many of the anti-pollutionists or community-preservers of the 1970s may look for their inspiration to early Betjeman? . . . He anticipated and, maybe, excited the modern outcry against the desecration of England in general and London in particular . . .'[1] Betjeman's hymn for ecologists, 'We spray the fields and scatter The poison on the ground', was published in 1966, the same year as Rebecca West's *The Birds Fall Down* and three years after Rachel Carson's *Silent Spring*.

He was able to conjure and capture the *Zeitgeist* of every decade he lived through (except the Eighties, when he was too ill); as examples, the Twenties children's party in 'Indoor Games near Newbury' and the caustic send-up of a young Sixties blade in 'Executive'. Betjeman may have felt culturally *dépaysé* from the late Fifties onwards, but his *Summoned by Bells* (1960) has plausibly been hailed as the first clarion of the Swinging Sixties, heralding the 'Let it all hang out' philosophy of the decade.[2] A much less benign view of that book is taken by Andrew Sanders, Professor of English Studies at Durham University. In *The Short Oxford History of English Literature* (2000 edition) he writes:

> Although Betjeman claimed in his gushy, blank-verse autobiography *Summoned by Bells* to have presented a volume of his schoolboy poems to 'the American master, Mr Eliot', his later verse never revealed much of a response to Eliot's metrical, intellectual and lexical novelty.[3]

That is rather like demanding: Why did Ronald Firbank never take up kick-boxing?

Sanders is rebuking Betjeman for not being 'modern'. In the sense in which professors of English Studies use the word (experimental; mimicking the 'fragmentation' of twentieth-century society), Betjeman was not modern; yet in another sense of the word he was more modern than Eliot himself. His friend Richard Ingrams wrote in 1984: 'He was never, as some opponents held, an obsolete fuddy-duddy . . . More so than many of today's poets he wrote about the modern world.'[4] Though Betjeman is eternally associated with 'nostalgia', we learn far more about the world he lived in, from his poetry, than we learn about the world Eliot lived in, from Eliot's. If only in that respect, Betjeman is the more modern of the two.

In 1971, in attempting – as Auden had done before him – the difficult task of introducing Betjeman's poetry to American readers, Philip Larkin wrote: 'The quickest way to start a punch-up between two British literary critics is to ask them what they think of the poems of

Sir John Betjeman.'[5] The 'critical response' to him had always been
polarized: Betjephiles versus Betjephobes. In 1937 Auden and
MacNeice, in their *Letters from Iceland*, called him

the most
Remarkable man of his time . . .[6]

In the same year, Isaiah Berlin described his contributions to Graham
Greene's magazine *Night and Day* as 'embarrassing rubbish'.[7] The
detractors became more vocal after the great success of *Collected
Poems* in 1958 – not least, perhaps, because those who were rival poets
were jealous.

In October 1958 the critic A. Alvarez – himself a modernist poet[8] –
returned to England from America, where he had been lecturer in creative writing at Princeton. He found the English literary scene
becalmed, partly, he thought, because some of the more combative
critics were in America: Kingsley Amis at Princeton, John Wain at the
MacDowell Colony, Philip Toynbee on tour and Kenneth Tynan in
New York.

> The fog remained undisturbed [Alvarez wrote]. But not for long. On 1
> December the calm was disastrously shattered. With the young men off
> the field, the Old Guard moved back in force. The occasion was the pub-
> lication of *The Collected Poems of John Betjeman* [*sic*], with a preface,
> for no apparent reason, by Lord Birkenhead. Now, Mr Betjeman is a
> skilful, harmless, minor writer of light verse, who is most successful when
> hymning *les petits plaisirs des riches*; he writes little panegyrics on bully-
> ing tennis girls, the nostalgia of boarding schools and the hidden charms
> of Victorian architectural monstrosities. His subjects, in short, are the
> rather delicious trials and tribulations of being upper middle class. He
> also writes bad, religiose poems about death.[9]

At the time Alvarez wrote his article, 33,400 copies of Betjeman's
Collected Poems had been sold in two and a half months. 'This',
Alvarez wrote, 'is almost certainly a good many more than the
Collected Poems of T. S. Eliot sold in as many years.' He added:

> In terms of literature, the fact that Mr Betjeman's book has become a best-
> seller – and the first poetry best-seller since heaven only knows when –
> means quite simply, I think, that the revolution called 'modern poetry', on
> which all our critical standards are founded, never took place for a huge
> proportion of the English poetry-reading public. They are still living in
> some hazy pre-Prufrock Never-Never Land. All the creative efforts of

Eliot, Yeats and Auden, and the painful fight to establish critical standards and a fresh tradition by men like Richards, Leavis and Empson, have apparently done no good at all.[10]

Alvarez did not include Betjeman in his 1962 anthology *New Poetry*; but Betjeman found room for Alvarez in his poem 'Shattered Image', weaving him into a piece of melded snobbery and campery no doubt calculated to annoy the left-wing heterosexual. In the poem, the accused paedophile muses:

> And this new flat is such a good address –
> One seven Alvarez Cloister, Double-you-one,
> (No need to put in Upper Berkeley Street):
> Under-floor heating, pale green wall-to-wall,
> Victoriana in the sitting-room.
> Mother insisted on the powder-blue.[11]

Alvarez's attack showed the main gripes and grievances of the Betjephobes. In their view, Betjeman was 'light' (frivolous) and snobbish, and was writing from and for the upper-middle class. Above all, he was considered a poetic reactionary, a foe of modernism. As a friend of Eliot, the last thing he wanted was to be pushed into the ring of a literary prize-fight with such a heavyweight. But, like it or not, his poetry is the antithesis of Eliot's. His poems are of great clarity. Eliot had written that 'Poets in our civilization, as it exists at present, must be *difficult*.'[12] His critics accused him of being obscure. By a piquant irony, one such adversary was Betjeman's *bête noire* C. S. Lewis (who resembled him in ways neither of them would have found it easy to acknowledge).[13] In his poem 'A Confession', Lewis wrote:

> I am so coarse, the things the poets see
> Are obstinately invisible to me.
> For twenty years I've stared my level best
> To see if evening – any evening – would suggest
> A patient etherized upon a table;
> In vain. I simply wasn't able.[14]

The critics who took Alvarez's line about Betjeman tended to be left-wing disciples of Eliot. Reviewing Betjeman's *Collected Poems* in 1959, the poet Thom Gunn – then still in his twenties – wrote of his poem about the 'mountainous' sports girl Pam: 'The target is obvious, and so is the manner of shooting. It is not difficult to imagine Hermione

Gingold[15] delivering these lines, dressed as a man. And they would probably be all the better with a faint tune in the background.'[16] Gunn did concede that among Betjeman's more serious verse, 'astonishingly, there is . . . a small number of exceptionally good poems, if one has the patience to search them out . . . That Mr Betjeman often misuses his talent does not obscure the fact that it is considerable.'[17]

John Wain entered Betjeman's private demonology in 1960 by his review of *Summoned by Bells* under the headline 'A Substitute for Poetry', in which he wrote that the verse-form Betjeman chose needed 'no more skill than is shown by the men who write the jingles on Christmas cards'.[18] Four months later, Philip Toynbee, describing *Summoned by Bells* as 'an almost unmitigated disaster', added:

> This failure does have the unfortunate tendency of making us look back with more severity on the earlier work – if only in the sense that it tempts us to withdraw the benefit of the doubt which we had sometimes awarded him.

Alvarez and Gunn, Wain and Toynbee all thought that Betjeman was upholding a tradition that needed to be smashed. The same point was made, more subversively, by Joe Orton and Kenneth Halliwell, in 1962. In that year, the future playwright and his latently homicidal lover were sent to prison for defacing library books.[19] The vandalism was innovative and surreal. Orton had pasted a monkey's head in the middle of a rose on the cover of the *Collins Guide to Roses*, and a female nude over a book of etiquette by Lady Lewisham. But the *pièce de résistance* was the facelift Orton gave the jacket of Derek Stanford's *John Betjeman*, which had been published in 1961. The mannered photograph of the poet wearing a boater and smoking through a long cigarette-holder was replaced by 'a pot-bellied old man tattooed from head to toe and clothed only in a skimpy swimsuit'.[20] Orton and Halliwell were targeting the Establishment they held in contempt. One way of doing that was to get at Betjeman, who was later described as its 'mascot'.[21] The same kind of thinking inspired the 'T[hem]-Speak' T-shirt sold in the Sex boutique in Chelsea, with Betjeman listed as a top 'Hate'.[22]

As far as the universities were concerned, the Betjephobe critics were preaching to the converted. In 1969 the future poet James Armstrong[23] applied for a university place to read English. Twenty years later, Charles Thomson – a poet admired by Betjeman[24] – described what happened.

> There is one area where Sir John Betjeman's work is received less than enthusiastically. Philippa Davies [founder of the Betjeman Society]

comments: 'One of our aims is to get him recognized by British universities, where he is not yet studied.' Folkestone singer and poet James Armstrong . . . discovered this neglect to his cost during an interview for university admission. When asked about his favourite poets he mentioned a particular liking for John Betjeman and 'waxed lyrical about his satire, irony and presentation of modern English life'.

To the board's response that Betjeman could surely be considered as only a minor English poet, James replied intrepidly that he thought 'in years to come Betjeman would stand out as one of the major English poets of the century'. This produced a result he had not anticipated: 'I could see them looking at me in a curious way as if I'd just got off a spaceship . . . and I realised I wasn't going to get a place at King's College, Cambridge.'[25]

Almost ten years later, when Murray published a selection by John Guest entitled *The Best of Betjeman*, it was reviewed in the *New Statesman* by the poet and critic Ian Hamilton. He began by admitting that in the late Fifties hostility towards Betjeman was almost a 'knee-jerk reaction' by young writers such as himself.

Needless to say, it wasn't *just* his popularity that stuck in the throats of the more steely critics of the day. He was despised for this, of course, but what really riled the hatchet men (or so they said) was that he'd somehow done the dirty on Poetry by dishing out a sugared substitute for the real thing. The real thing at that time was meant to be difficult, 'committed', and prosodically experimental. Betjeman's stuff was simple, idly snobbish and trippingly traditional in metre. It was also lots of other things: insular, ingratiating, churchy, smug and so on. He was thought by many to be the arch-enemy of What Needed to be Done in poetry. I seem to remember vaguely accepting that this was the case, without having read much Betjeman beyond the odd anthology piece. After all, the indictment sounded pretty well conclusive: popular, rhymes and scans, goes on about tennis clubs and subalterns . . . a clear case, it seemed, of What Needed to be Done In.[26]

If anybody – including the then still living Betjeman – imagined that this paragraph was to be the prelude to a breast-beating *mea culpa*, he was disappointed. Hamilton was repelled by Betjeman's inverting phrases for the sake of the rhyme, and in his review impudently rewrote two Betjeman stanzas, wreaking havoc with their metre and rhyme in order to invert the inversions.[27]

Betjeman's fame as a television 'eccentric' was harmful to his reputation as a poet. Alan Bennett and John Wells did lifelike comic impressions of him. (Bennett's 'Betjeman' gazed moonily after a departing

London bus and murmured: 'I wonder where it's orf to. Newington Butts? Whipp's Crorss?') Alan Pryce-Jones quipped: 'It was John's fate to be sent down in his youth, and sent up in his old age.'[28] In 1982 the writer and librarian Alan Bell contributed to *The Times* a profile of Betjeman which (to Bell's irritation) a sub-editor headed: 'By Appointment: Teddy Bear to the Nation'.[29] The label stuck. The 'cuddly' image still further exasperated the modernists. After the poet's death in May 1984 the critics, who had had few enough inhibitions about putting the boot in while he was alive, felt free to say whatever they wanted. The publication, late that year, of my book *John Betjeman: A Life in Pictures*, provoked a snarling poem by Gavin Ewart, a poet admired by Larkin.[30] Published in the *London Review of Books* in December, it contained these lines, with Ewart's gloss in the right-hand margin:

When I see yet another work of hagiography
concerning Sir John Betjeman,
it makes me want to vomit!
Show me, I want to say, please, the 'geography'   *an old*
of the house!   *euphemism for*
But Betjeman wasn't nasty, in fact very far from it. *lavatory, toilet*
                                                      etc.

It's probably the Murrays who are such penny-turners
(Byron's one was a Philistine).
John's an important asset,
One of the few real genuine poetic earners,   *more copies*
man not mouse,   *sold than any*
in many a crowd-pulling, wide, populist facet . . .   *poet since*
                                                      Tennyson

I'd rather they honoured Grigson or Bunting
or anyone less televised.
Someone anti-life, grim, retiring!   *Roy Fuller*
Less of the stately homes, horses, hunting, landowners, *perhaps?*
the young drunk rich ones so self-admiring . . .[31]

Though the late poet's alleged snobbery and his preoccupation with middle-class mores are reprobated here, the poem is less a squib against Betjeman than against the cult of Betjeman. The green-eyed monster probably lurks behind this piece of satire: one feels that when Ewart suggests that Grigson or Bunting should be honoured, he is really demanding: 'What about *me*?' A cult of Grigson was never a hot probability.

'Griggers', too, had it in for Betjeman – though he was fair-minded enough to recommend him for radio work in the 1940s.[32] The two men had never been on easy terms after Grigson turned down a Betjeman poem for the magazine *New Verse*.[33] Betjeman had to apologise for giving an unsavoury character in a short story the name 'Grogson';[34] played elaborate practical jokes on Grigson;[35] and, in Barry Humphries's view, 'never forgave' him.[36] Grigson gave as good as he got. Betjeman was still alive when he dismissed him as 'the lowbrow's middle-brow' in *The Private Art: A Poetry Notebook* (1982).[37] Grigson wielded his famous 'billhook' with greater ferocity a few months after Betjeman's death, in *Recollections* (1984).

How many have asked what [Betjeman] really stood for; if he was indeed quite real, and if he was not, on second thoughts, some kind of changeling found under a castor oil plant in the suburbs?

Often the insults have been more insulting, and even bitter and scornful. What were his life's keepings? Wasn't it odd to make verse – skilfully to be sure – into a parody of verse, using forms and metres, even rhythms, adapted from hymn books both to mock those who enjoy them and think them to be the eternal essence of poetry, and to make them enjoy being mocked? 'Culture' without difficulties, 'culture' easily come by, without problems . . .

Indignation asks . . . what have we expected the 'modern' poet to be? Serious.[38]

Grigson ended his essay:

Do I believe, as I have been told, that after some . . . pinprick Betjeman climbed from his house at Uffington and cursed me from the backside of the White Horse? Why not? John Betjeman showed himself a kindly and forgiving man; but I detested and still detest his verses, or most of them.[39]

In May 1985, a year after Betjeman's death, Anthony Thwaite assembled a group of poets to give their views on him in a BBC Radio 3 discussion. Thwaite himself had never been enthusiastic about Betjeman's poetry;[40] and in the programme the dice were a little loaded against the dead poet. Donald Davie admitted that 'He is infernally difficult to get any sort of critical callipers on.'[41] But the Northern Irish poet Tom Paulin was unambiguously hostile.

He represents that anti-intellectual antiquarian strand that there is in English culture. For me, he goes with a children's book I once read about a character called Molesworth, who tends to find things like old ear-trumpets in Hull. It's the kind of whimsy which, after a while, becomes terrible and

frightening and surreal and bizarre, because of its enormous, trivializing
stupidity.

I don't think the work develops. I frankly find him a very absurd figure.
I can remember having a conversation with a French friend of mine and I
explained to him that the Poet Laureate of England slept every night with
his teddy bear – he just fell on the floor laughing with total incredulity. I
think that when one looks at Betjeman from a European perspective he
does seem to be an utterly ridiculous figure. Because he's so much on the
surface, there's no complexity there: really he would interest somebody
with a sociological approach to literature, and I think one could construct
an interesting argument based on that. But in purely literary terms I don't
think there's any interest at all, though one might like to compare him
with Marvell. There's something similar there, though I think Marvell is a
marvellous, great poet – that fascination with long, hot afternoons and
big girls is there in Marvell. It's there in Lewis Carroll. Perhaps it's the
tradition they belong to, phantasmagoric Anglicanism.[42]

On the same programme, however, Kingsley Amis defended his old
friend from the charge of 'cosiness'.

I remember distinctly the first poem that sank in, which was 'Croydon' in
his first collection. I had naturally taken him to be what so many people
already thought him to be and so many people still think of him as – a
light, entertaining, extremely funny versifier. But then, you see, I paid
especial attention to 'Croydon', because I grew up near there.

> In a house like that
> > Your Uncle Dick was born;
> Satchel on back he walked to Whitgift
> > Every weekday morn.

Notice the 'morn' there: I thought, 'This is sly fun going on.' It's like an
affectionate little postcard – a suburban scene. But then we see that it isn't
just that and it ends with saying

> the steps are dusty that still lead up to
> Your Uncle Dick's front door.

> Pear and apple in Croydon gardens
> > Bud and blossom and fall,
> But your Uncle Dick has left his Croydon
> > Once for all.

And I remember thinking, 'My God, I hadn't bargained for that.' It's a
very characteristic Betjeman thing, of course: it's that horrible dig in the

ribs. Very often the message is, it seems, in the midst of life we're in death. It's not always that way but in the midst of ordinary, boring, amusing, vaguely entertaining life there's something unexpected done with incredible speed and incredible concentration.[43]

Both during Betjeman's life and after it, his greatest cheerleader was Kingsley Amis's best friend, Philip Larkin. While the Betjephobes reviled Betjeman for not being 'modern', Larkin made that very quality the keystone of his defence of him. Reviewing the *Collected Poems* in the magazine *Listen* in 1959, he wrote:

> The chief significance of Betjeman as a poet is that he is a writer of talent and intelligence for whom the modern poetic revolution has simply not taken place.[44] For him there has been no symbolism, no objective correlative, no T. S. Eliot or Ezra Pound, no rediscovery of myth or language as gesture, no *Seven Types* or *Some Versions*, no works of criticism with titles like *Communication as Discipline* or *Implicit and Explicit Image-Obliquity in Sir Lewis Morris*. He has been carried through by properties and techniques common to all but his immediate predecessors: a belief that poetry is an emotional business, rather than an intellectual and moral one, a belief in metre and rhyme as a means of enhancing emotion, a belief that a poem's meaning should be communicated directly and not by symbol.[45]

In 1983, in his review of Patrick Taylor-Martin's study of Betjeman, Larkin made the case for the humorous poems which had earned the poet a reputation as 'just a funny man'.

> The trouble with the Plain Man's evaluation of Betjeman, putting one's money on the 'serious' poems and trying to forget the rest ('bad poems by his own standards, and not even very good light verse'), is that it misses the primitive, farcical, even Dionysian element in his work that expresses an essential side of his personality that may even power the rest. Mr Taylor-Martin's struggle with Captain Webb ('the nonconformist industrial setting is fondly described') ignores the sheer thumping silliness ('The *gas* was on in the Institute, The *flare* was up in the *gym*') that is the whole intoxicating point.[46]

This was an amplification of a comment Larkin had made in a conversation with Neil Powell: 'I think it's significant that a lot of Betjeman's poems are funny – quite often there are things that you can only say as jokes. He is rather like the fool that speaks the truth through jokes, though that's a horribly literary way of putting it.'[47]

In 1961 the novelist Jocelyn Brooke,[48] in a biographical and critical study of Betjeman, had also suggested that his humorous verse should, as it were, be taken seriously. He took issue with Lord Birkenhead's assertion, in his introduction to the *Collected Poems*, that 'John Betjeman is not a "funny" poet . . .' If a writer of verse made one laugh almost continuously, how, Brooke asked, was he to avoid being regarded as a funny poet?

> The trouble is that, since the Romantic Revival, we have tended to draw an arbitrary and largely artificial distinction between 'serious' and 'light' verse. It is arguable, indeed, that this dichotomy had its origins at an even earlier date, and Aldous Huxley considers that 'the secret of being lyric-ally funny, of writing comic verses that are also beautiful', died with the Elizabethans (*Texts and Pretexts*) . . . It might perhaps be said of John Betjeman that he has rediscovered this long-lost faculty for being 'lyrically funny', though with him the blend of fun and lyricism has little in common with its Elizabethan counterpart.[49]

Brooke thought that the same rare quality could be claimed for Edward Lear, some of whose comic verse was 'hauntingly beautiful'; and Betjeman greatly admired Lear.[50] Brooke also suggested that, in his blending of nostalgia and humour, Betjeman might be compared with Firbank, 'whose nostalgic passion for the "*fin de siècle*" was bal-anced by his capacity for poking fun at it'.[51]

As James Armstrong discovered, academe had set its face against Betjeman; but in the 1980s both a future Oxford don and an Oxford professor broke the ostracism and acknowledged Betjeman's genius. When the poet Craig Raine reviewed Patrick Taylor-Martin's book in 1983, he was poetry editor at Faber & Faber, Eliot's publishers. Subsequently a fellow in English at New College, Oxford, he has written a book entitled *In Defence of T. S. Eliot*[52] and, though he defends him on the charge of having been an anti-Semite rather than a bad poet, he *is* an admirer of Eliot's poetry. So his praise for Betjeman in 1983 showed that a regard for Eliot and an enthusiasm for Betjeman need not be mutually exclusive, as Philip Larkin had implied they were in *All What Jazz*, in which he asserted that poetry had been ruined by Eliot, art by Picasso and jazz by Charlie Parker.[53] Raine wrote in 1983:

> It is useless to approach [Betjeman's poetry] in the Arnoldian spirit of high seriousness. Betjeman is not interested in the noble application of ideas to life. He is interested in the thing itself – life – and he succeeds marvellously, without recourse to the Grand Style . . .

You can scarcely understand Betjeman's poetry ~~~~~
that he writes 'badly' in order to write well. It is a b~~~~~
which has disorientated his critics. In essence, Betjem~~~~~
dated, antique style – Timeless Classical by Golden Tr~~~~~
it with ephemeral detail, knowing that nothing ages~~~~~
eternal and that nothing lasts like dross. By and large, ~~~~~ ~~~nes
break every modernist rule. They might have been writte~~~~~ ~ne spirit of
contradiction, with Ezra Pound's 'A Few Don'ts By an Imagiste' propped
open at his elbow. It is futile, however, to set up a conflict between Betjeman
and modernism, as Alvarez and Wain do, and as Betjeman's greatest
admirer, Larkin, seems to do. It is possible to admire Eliot and Betjeman –
but only if you can see that Pound's eminently sound rules have been
broken by an exceptional poet.[54]

The Oxford professor who championed Betjeman was John Bayley.
His review of the first volume of this biography, published in 1988,
contained perhaps the most sympathetic appreciation ever of the emotional appeal of Betjeman's poetry.

Betjeman was probably the most sociable and conversable poet of this
century, but his poetry is best discovered on one's own, and read in private.
I remember doing that, as an undergraduate, and the world revealed was
as magical as that of Auden had been at school. It was not Betjeman's
fashionably social and ecclesiastical world. Like Auden's minefields and
pitheads and scars where kestrels hover, through which one tiptoed in a
state of heightened and excited awareness, it was a plangent but impersonal world of suburban joy and beauty, Odeons flashing fire, electric
trains swinging low down the line through resin-scented fir-trees; Uncle
Dick dying; sardine games in furry cupboards; the six o'clock news and a
lime-juice and gin. It was pure romance, the light that never was on sea or
land, the something ever more about to be, the familiar made wondrous
and strange.

And sex, and love, as in all romance. They were immanent in the scent
of the woods, the packet of Weights squashed in the grey sand of Surrey,
the Edwardian plantations of Upper Lambourn making the swelling
downland, far surrounding, seem their own. Most moving of all, the end
of 'Love in a Valley' (from *Continual Dew*, 1937):

> Portable Lieutenant! They carry you to China
>   And me to lonely shopping in a brilliant arcade;
> Firm hand, fond hand, switch the giddy engine!
>   So for us a last time is bright light made.

It made me shed ecstatic tears. The complex mastery in it is in fact very
great: the history and locality; the contemporary mechanics and outmoded

all rushed along with seeming effortlessness by the brilliant transformation of Meredith's metre, in which exultation is not replaced by loneliness and sadness, but mingled in with it. A total newness and lack of
self-consciousness finds paradoxical expression in Victorian music, thus
confounding the modernist pundits who maintained that new verse needs
totally new form.[55]

It was Betjeman's bad luck to coincide with the rule of modernism.
In the years of this cultural totalitarianism it was as bleak a fate to be
a poet of rhyme and metre as it was to be a representational painter in
the almost coeval heyday of abstract expressionism. There had been,
perhaps, a need for a 'clearing of the decks' after the sentimentality
into which Victorian poetry (with a few exceptions) and Victorian
painting (with fewer) had fallen; but this ruthless scouring seemed to
last interminably, leaving the decks as bare and bleached as cuttlefish
bone. Why should a poet or painter, if he felt more at home in a past
style, take up a disruptive, experimental, new one? The idea that one
should work in the style which one found most congenial was
eloquently expounded by Betjeman in a letter of 1939 to Ninian
Comper – an architect despised by modernists for designing twentieth-
century buildings in a neo-Gothic style.

> I know, for myself, that you solved for me an architectural puzzle I could
> never understand. I would see an aeroplane or underground train and
> think 'lovely architecture' and I would see Greenwich Hospital and think
> the same thing. How can I like them both? Why is the new Regent Street
> bad?[56] It wasn't until I saw your work and knew at once that this was great
> architecture that I solved the puzzle. I saw then that it was not the ques-
> tion of the age we live in, but of the creative gift in an architect and the
> sincerity of the man. I saw as I sat in St Cyprian's [Marylebone], propor-
> tion, attention to detail, colour, texture and chiefly the purpose – the
> tabernacle as the centre of it all. This is as much of the present age as the
> aeroplane. It is not aping a past age, that is bad; or what pretends to be
> modern and is not; that is worse.[57]

Mutatis mutandis, these words can be applied to Betjeman's poetry.
Because, by chance, we happen to be born in a particular time, we are
not necessarily obliged to write or paint in the prevailing style, when
there are other, well-tried styles to choose from. Horace had made
that point in the first century BC, in the *Ars Poetica*.[58] Shakespeare
made it again in Sonnet 76, in which he implicitly answered those who
wondered why he did not adopt the exciting shock tactics of the

Metaphysical poets.[59] When Thomas Hardy gave up writing novels after the furore over *Jude the Obscure* in 1895 and concentrated on poetry (an almost exact reversal of the career of Sir Walter Scott after he declined to be Laureate in 1813), he did not have to accommodate himself to 'modernism'; but the poets of Betjeman's generation were all but dragooned into doing so. For some of them, no coercion was needed: to them, modernism was a glorious liberation, a breaking of pointless, archaic restraints. To others, it seemed an irksome imposture, passing off a *fricassée* of arbitrarily chopped-up prose,[60] inconsequential gobbets, foreign quotations and impenetrable symbolism as poetry.

On what Larkin called Eliot's 'fatal phrase'[61] about the desirability of poetry's being difficult, Betjeman commented: 'It's easy to be difficult.'[62] And on the notion of modernism as an unshackling of poetry from wearisome conventions: 'There is a difference between liberty and taking liberties.'[63] But he was not a pathological or doctrinaire anti-modernist.[64] He was much more tolerant towards the modernists than they were towards him. Rather as he accepted that some Christians were temperamentally more drawn to 'Low' worship than to 'High', he understood the appeal of the looser genres to some of his friends. What he objected to in modernism was what he principally disliked about Roman Catholicism: its authoritarian stance, its insistence that all should follow its diktats or be pariahs.

By writing in traditional forms he cast himself – metaphorically and, as Laureate, literally – as a royalist when the puritans were coming to power. Up to the seventeenth century, writers relied on rich patrons and the Church for a living. For a time patrons were still important, but from the seventeenth century journalism offered an income. In the twentieth century, poets began writing for a new readership, university English departments and what Larkin called 'the whole light industry of exegesis'.[65] To be easily understood no longer commanded respect. But Betjeman and Larkin held that a good poem needed no interpreter: the whole point of a poem was that, by its concentration, emotional power, originality of expression or other qualities – its creator's *ichor* – it should convey its meaning with more immediacy, more strikingly, than the same thought or image couched in prose. 'Poetry is the shorthand of the heart,' Betjeman wrote to an Australian woman fan. 'I've just thought that up: rather good, don't you think?'[66]

In her book *Romanticism and its Discontents* (2000), Professor Anita Brookner listed the characteristics of the Romantic. Two of them – nostalgia and terror – we readily recognize in Betjeman; but the one that fits him best is the last on her list, 'the conviction of a secret destiny or calling'.[67] In *Summoned by Bells*, Betjeman wrote:

> I knew as soon as I could read and write
> That I must be a poet . . .[68]

This was confirmed by Brenda Thompson, who was at kindergarten with him before the First World War. She remembered that when she and another small girl were comparing the lengths of their hair in the playground, Betjeman suddenly exclaimed with great emphasis: 'I'm going to have long hair when I grow up and be a poet.'[69]

Betjeman may be credited with one romantic trait not listed by Professor Brookner. At the end of *Young Betjeman* I suggested that 'His was the desolation of the Romantic whose vision of the world is eroded by the world's reality.'[70] Ann Wolff (*née* Hope), who in 1929 was four years old and daughter of the headmaster of a prep school where Betjeman taught, went much further: 'All the time I knew him he gave the impression of someone who has early looked closely at life and profoundly despaired, and from then on he was filling in time until his death.'[71] *Could* that be true of the vivacious jester Betjeman, the lovable, genial Betjeman, everybody's favourite uncle, national teddy-bear? Ann Wolff may have had a specially jaundiced view of him, as he allegedly 'victimized' her;[72] but the anguish in several poems and the undertow of melancholy in others need explaining.

His fear of death and hell – expressed in a number of his poems,[73] and witnessed at its most extreme by Reg Read[74] – originated in his indoctrination by his 'hateful' Calvinist nurse, Maud.[75] His guilt-feelings intensified as he broke with Penelope and lived with Lady Elizabeth Cavendish. (His was a classic instance of 'the love of two women'. It was not a case of 'How happy could I be with either, Were t'other dear charmer away!'[76] Rather, he found in each woman qualities which he missed when with the other – for examples, Penelope's scholar's brain and Elizabeth's ministering attentiveness.) Betjeman had faith, but – as was acknowledged by the Dean of Westminster at his memorial service[77] – the faith was assailed by doubts. We see them at the end of his poem 'Good-bye' ('With Judgement or nothingness waiting me, lonely and chill') or the end of 'Aldershot Crematorium' ('"*I am the Resurrection and the Life*": Strong, deep and painful, doubt inserts the knife'); in the repeated question 'And is it true?' in 'Christmas' and in the last lines of the poem about his father, 'On a Portrait of a Deaf Man' –

> You, God, who treat him thus and thus,
>   Say, 'Save his soul and pray.'

> You ask me to believe You and
> I only see decay.

In poems like these, Betjeman seems to be challenging God to give him answers, rather as Gerard Manley Hopkins – as a priest, a much more committed Christian – does in 'The Loss of the Eurydice' ('it concerned thee, O Lord: Three hundred souls, O alas! on board')[78] and in 'Carrion Comfort' –

But ah, but O thou terrible, why would'st thou rude on me
Thy wring-world right foot rock? Lay a lionlimb against me? scan
With darksome devouring eyes my bruisèd bones? and fan,
O in turns of tempest, me heaped there, me frantic to avoid thee and flee?[79]

Hopkins finds answers to his questions ('Why? That my chaff might fly; my grain lie, sheer and clear') but Betjeman is left floundering. In the television series *Time with Betjeman*, he recited favourite lines from Tennyson's 'Crossing the Bar' –

> Twilight and evening bell
>   And after that the dark!
> And may there be no sadness of farewell,
>   When I embark;
>
> For tho' from out our bourne of Time and Place
>   The flood may bear me far,
> I hope to see my Pilot face to face
>   When I have crost the bar.

After reciting those lines, Betjeman defiantly emphasized: ' "I *hope* to see my Pilot" – not "I *shall* see my Pilot",' and added, 'Tennyson said: "There lives more faith in honest doubt, Believe me, than in half the creeds."'

Craig Raine thinks that Betjeman's early poem 'Exeter', about the doctor's intellectual wife, 'describes a loss of faith, *tout court*'.[80] That is debatable, as is James Lees-Milne's belief that Betjeman cared more about church architecture than the Sacraments.[81] In 1974 Betjeman told Wilfred De'Ath: 'I've had long moments of thinking Christianity isn't true, but on the whole I'm convinced that it is.'[82] He had enlarged on this in a handwritten essay of unknown date (but before 1961) preserved at the University of Victoria, British Columbia.

Perhaps a religious history should come first. It is interwoven into my life more than anything else. I have rarely fully believed & equally rarely fully disbelieved. But when I look at my friends, those who have remained deepest and & most lastingly in my affections have been those who are religious. Bill Bouman, the son of a Dutch journalist, with whom I played until I was eight – for he went with his family to Holland in 1914 or 1915 – I found again, parents, sisters and all only last year living above a station arcade at Kingsbury in the Edgware district. He was unmarried & parish church activities played a large part in his life. Ronnie Wright, my next oldest friend through Dragon School & in the holidays at public school stage when he was at Ampleforth & I at Marlborough, is now a Roman Benedictine monk. Cracky William Clonmore my friend of Oxford days & early London life, having been an Anglican deacon, is now an R.C. layman. Colonel Kolkhorst, though professedly agnostic, is obsessed with death & charity & most of his friends are either priests or R.C.'s. Maurice Bowra, a man full of religion though no churchgoer; the late Brother [*illegible* – Adrian Bishop?], his friend & mine, who became an English Benedictine lay brother. Alan Pryce-Jones (in & out the church of Rome; ~~in & out the duchesses, that's the way the Caption goes~~) which he now is trapped in, with duchesses to take him home, Pop goes the Captain).[83] Edward Longford who takes off his hat to every [Church of Ireland] church; the niceties of 'high' 'low' & 'broad' have long been a bond with my closest friends. Indeed people not interested in church have never interested me so much as those who are. Sometimes it was simply looking at churches that brought me friends – John Piper for instance, who with Goldilegz his wife was received into the C. of E. before the war. Osbert Lancaster is another churchy friend & his wife Karen was received into the C. of E. from Rome. My nearest & dearest have always been my friends & I think religion has been our chief bond.

I wonder what I mean by religion? It ought to be, of course, that personal devotion to Christ which I envy in others & try, on retreats, to emulate. But I believe my religion is largely one of fear. Endlessness used to terrify me ~~& still does~~ even more than it does now. That early dream of rising in a lift to a wooden hut floating on a grey sea which stretched on for ever, & seeing outlined against it a tall figure with horns which I knew to be the devil: the sound of the bells of St Anne's Church on winter nights with the sense of Highgate cemetery beyond. And with that fear of endlessness, goes the terror of punishment & the deep sense of guilt connected with sex. 'Honour thy father & mother that thy days may be long in the land which the Lord thy God giveth thee.' I am so frightened even now of dishonouring my parents that I ~~cannot~~ do not like to put the blame on them for the fear & guilt by which I am obsessed. They are both dead & cannot answer back & I want to see them again & hear what they have to say to me. By their standard, I have done well for myself. But by my own & by what may be theirs now? No.[84]

An atheist or agnostic could cite that passage as an example of the pernicious effects of religion. Betjeman, who – with all his intermittent doubts – can fairly be described as a religious poet,[85] might have disagreed with that estimate; but the religious terror instilled into him at an early age never left him. From early childhood, too, he suffered feelings of insecurity: because of his foreign name and the real danger of attacks on German (or presumed German) families during the Great War;[86] and because of his family's social position, with a father 'in trade'.[87] The word 'safe' recurs again and again in his poetry, as in two phrases on consecutive pages of *Summoned by Bells* – 'Archibald, my safe old bear' and 'Safe, in a world of trains and buttered toast'.[88] It may have been partly because he was an only child and wanted a surrogate sibling that he made such a voodoo fetish of Archie; but the bear may also have served the purpose of Linus's 'security blanket' in the American strip-cartoon 'Peanuts', something soft and familiar to cling on to in a daunting, bewildering world. The element of infantilism in Betjeman has to be reckoned with. He freely – gleefully – admitted that he was a case of arrested development – 'arrested, I should say, about the age of thirteen'.[89] That he remained, in some degree, a child himself – a state of mind urged by Christ – not only helps to explain his amazing ability, in his poems, to put himself inside a child's skin (L. P. Hartley's novels are the only contemporary writings of comparable child-empathy);[90] it may also account for his disturbing and sometimes reprehensible behaviour towards his own children. In his soul-baring letter of 1949 to Penelope, he admitted that he had been jealous of the children ('Between them they have taken you away from me . . .').[91]

John Bayley sees Betjeman's infantilism as yet another Romantic trait. His review of *Young Betjeman* was headed 'Heartless Genius', and in it he wrote:

Betjeman, as private genius and poet, was completely heartless, real leprechaun. Before his admirers rush in to denounce such a judgment and give a thousand instances of his kindness and warmth, both in his life and in his poetry, let me explain. He had no heart like a small child who has not yet learnt the use of one, or how to cultivate it. Like Poe and Shelley in their best poems he had about this an absolute lack of self-consciousness. It is the Romantic's truest gift; and with it he can wholly overcome the difference between his own awareness and an external existence. The old lady in 'Death in Leamington' is not seen or imagined or felt or pitied – she is *there*; she is absolute in terms of her setting.[92]

(Fifteen years later, in a book on Iris Murdoch, A. N. Wilson was to say much the same of Bayley himself, in curiously similar words, though without the sympathetic gloss: 'Inside this uncomplaining little leprechaun there was a screaming, hate-filled child.'[93] He also wrote of him, what is probably not true of Bayley, but was possibly true of Betjeman: 'Like a spoilt child, [he] reacts petulantly to the presence of other, real children invading his space or claiming the attention of his Protectress or Playmate.')[94]

It may have been Betjeman's sense of insecurity, again, that caused him to give people disobliging nicknames – a way of feeling superior to them. No doubt it also made him overreact to what he considered slights, and to bear undying grudges. He was socially aspiring too, and has been called a snob; but his snobbery was of the Disraelian sort which thought it romantic that the same family had lived on the same patch of land for hundreds of years, in magnificent buildings. It was romantic to stay at Pakenham Hall (now Tullynally) where the great Duke of Wellington had wooed his wife Kitty Pakenham; in the Gothic splendour of Billy Clonmore's Shelton Abbey; or, in later years, at Chatsworth, as almost part of the family. One of Disraeli's heroes, dying, 'babbled of strawberry leaves'; and Betjeman died in the arms of a duke's daughter.

English society, at the time he was writing, was still deeply class-conscious; it would have been remiss of him, as a writer of (among other forms) *vers de société*, to ignore that fact. He had, though, great rapport also with Smithfield meat porters, railwaymen and London taxi-drivers. He was never the Evelyn Waugh type of snob, rude to waiters. Betjeman certainly married for love; but, if a kind heart could come with a coronet – if one could also have a rich peer as a father-in-law – it didn't hurt. It was Lord Chetwode who bought the Betjemans the finest house in which they ever lived, at Farnborough.[95]

Betjeman felt guilt at not living up to his own father's expectation that he would enter the family firm as 'the fourth generation'. Evelyn Waugh, who knew how to touch people's sore points, was malevolently funny about this in his diary when *Summoned by Bells* was published –

Betjeman's biography. John demonstrates how much more difficult it is to write blank verse than jingles and raises the question: *why* did he not go into his father's workshop? It would be far more honourable and useful to make expensive ashtrays than to appear on television and just as lucrative.[96]

Betjeman's whole life could plausibly be interpreted as a Hamlet-like appeasement of his father's ghost – one long refutation of Ernest Betjemann's prophecy that his son would turn out a ne'er-do-well, 'Bone-lazy like my eldest brother Jack';[97] one long yearning for the benediction, 'This is my beloved son, in whom I am well pleased.'[98] With Betjeman, art came before ambition; but still he craved the glittering prizes, emblems of success. This tendency showed up early, when he was at the Dragon School. The boys were asked to draw a strip-cartoon, illustrating 'how you would rescue and revive a drowning person'. Betjeman won the competition and his drawing was printed in the school magazine. In the last frame of the cartoon, the three brave rescuers are shown. On the left lapel of each is pinned a medal as large as a dinner plate.[99] This 'going for a gong' trait continued in adult life. Betjeman made light of his accolade; but it was something he had set his heart on. What might Ernest Betjemann have felt if he had been able to witness the memorial service of Sir John Betjeman, with the Prince of Wales reading 'Let us now praise famous men'?

In 'An Eighteenth-Century Calvinistic Hymn', an early work, Betjeman wrote:

> I am not too sure of my Worth,
>   Indeed it is tall as a Palm;
> But what fruits can it ever bring forth
>   When Leprosy sits at the helm?[100]

He was unsure of his own worth, and prone to self-abasement. (His partiality for dominatrix figures may have been linked to that aspect of his psyche.) Because he went to such pains to put his weaknesses on show, it was easy for his critics to harp on them and to miss his good qualities. He was in general kind, sympathetic, sensitive to other people's distress; though he liked to pretend that self-interest motivated that side of his character, often advising: 'Cast thy bread upon the waters, and it shall return unto thee – *buttered*.'[101] You felt you could tell him things you would not tell anyone else: he was non-judgemental because he understood. When Brenda Thompson confessed to him, at their first school, that she had cribbed a piece of verse that she had presented as her own, she was sure that 'With John the stark truth was right, and safe, he would not "split" because he would understand . . .'[102] He showed kindness in finding schools for Joan Hunter Dunn (Jackson)'s sons when their father died and in reassuring Anne Baring that she had done nothing monstrous when she was threatened with expulsion for painting King Alfred's statue; kindness, and courage too, in taking on, as temporary secretaries, unfrocked priests; and in comforting Oliver Ford when the interior decorator was up on a charge.[103]

As anyone who reads his poems would guess, he was a wit. He also liked people who made *him* laugh, such as Barry Humphries and Reg

Read. Even when his health was at vanishing-point, he could still produce memorable one-liners on television shows – as when he assured Michael Parkinson that his poetry was not 'relevant'.[104] But some critics were prepared to make larger claims for him. In his essay in *Listen* (Spring 1959), Philip Larkin wrote that Betjeman was 'one of the rare figures on whom the aesthetic appetites of an age pivot and swing round to face an entirely new direction'.[105] Twenty years later, introducing the selection of Betjeman's poems for Americans, he quoted that earlier opinion and wondered if it had proved justified. He thought it had.[106] More than thirty years further on, we can ask again: was Betjeman the 'pivotal' influence on poetry that Larkin suggested? Larkin acknowledged himself a disciple of his – worrying that he might come to seem 'a sort of cut-price Betjeman'[107] – though some of Larkin's own disciples have done their best to exculpate him for what they took to be an embarrassing association.[108] And spoors of Betjeman can be detected in poets of a more recent generation – Craig Raine, James Fenton, even Seamus Heaney.[109] But *pivotal*?

Betjeman himself was under no illusions about his standing in English literature. For him it was not enough that his poems received some cordial reviews or that they sold – as Alvarez crossly observed – better than Eliot's. He was conscious of being an outsider, of swimming against the current, of being never accepted into a poetic élite which was as untabulated but as actual as the British Constitution. Journalists might call him 'the most popular poet since Kipling' or even 'since Tennyson'; but when there was a book or exhibition about 'Poets of the Thirties', he was not included with Auden, Day Lewis, Spender and MacNeice.

Betjeman revolutionized British taste in favour of Victorian architecture;[110] if he had done only that, he would be numbered among the great tastemakers, with Horace Walpole and William Beckford, Ruskin, Whistler and Wilde. And he demonstrated the miraculous potential of television. But in terms of poetry he did not, in Larkin's words, cause 'aesthetic attitudes' to 'swing around'. The most he achieved in poetic tastemaking was to show young poets that they did not necessarily have to write in a modernist style. Poets as good as Fenton, John Fuller, Heaney and Raine adopt metre and rhyme as the mood takes them.

In his preface to the American edition of Betjeman's poems, in 1971, Larkin asked: 'Can it be that, as Eliot dominated the first half of the twentieth century, the second half will derive from Betjeman?'[111] It did not happen. Most of the poetry now published still owes far more to Eliot. No questions on Betjeman are asked in university English Literature examinations. There is not a single mention of him in the

1,383 pages of *The New Princeton Encyclopedia of Poetry and Poetics* (1993)[112] or in the 626 pages of *A Companion to Twentieth-Century Poetry* (2001).[113] It is as if he has been excommunicated from English literature.

In 1958 Betjeman wrote about the 'Ern Malley' hoax perpetrated in Australia: two poets, by cobbling together random lines and words, persuaded the editor of a modernist journal to publish them in the belief that they were the work of a talented new poet. 'This hoax', Betjeman wrote, 'put an end to intellectual pretentiousness in Australian poetry'.[114] In 2003 the Australian-born Peter Carey based his novel *My Life as a Fake* on the Ern Malley affair. The London *Sunday Times*, reviewing it, smugly observed that 'The Ern Malley hoax began as a satire on modernism. Carey has skilfully and satirically turned it around in order to vindicate the creative imagination.'[115] No, modernism has not been toppled.

Yet there has been a shift in perspective. The biographer Jad Adams, reviewing the second volume of this biography in *The Guardian*, described Betjeman in his opening sentence as 'one of the greatest twentieth-century poets'.[116] Adams admits that he expected a torrent of hostile letters from *Guardian* readers, but none arrived.[117] A sign that both modernism and Betjeman are being reappraised was an article on poetic reputations contributed to *The Guardian* in 2003 by James Fenton. He wrote:

> When we look at the art of our contemporaries, and we try to distinguish good from bad, we should also be aware that the criteria we are using will modify over time. Some things now worshipped will fall entirely from grace. Others will, in due course, gain a proper appreciation. Some things will fall into undeserved neglect before returning again to favour.[118]

Those words might almost be a line-by-line translation of what Horace wrote in the *Ars Poetica* nineteen centuries earlier.[119] Fenton added:

> Thinking back to the poetry my friends and I read at about the age of twenty [that is, in about 1969], and what we thought of it, I am reminded that T. S. Eliot, both as a poet and as a literary critic, was considered fundamental. Ezra Pound, on the other hand, was always controversial. His advocates were passionate and that put his detractors on their mettle.
>
> There was Modernism: were you for it or against it? If you were for it, how wholeheartedly were you for it? I remember people saying about W. H. Auden that he had, as it were, had his encounter with Modernism, absorbed what he wanted, and then moved on in his own sweet way. And

this wasn't considered good enough. It was as if he hadn't quite taken Modernism seriously.

Somewhere in the background, in our view of twentieth-century poetry, there were figures who, while they could not be ignored entirely, did not fit into the scheme of things. Thomas Hardy was one of them. A. E. Housman and John Betjeman were on the same list for different reasons. A friend once said to me that you would have to consider the possibility that our whole concept of the Modernist tradition was beside the point, and that the real tradition was to be traced through people like Housman. This was an unspeakably sophisticated thing to say – it seemed to me – wildly improbable, but also wickedly seductive.[120]

'Modernist tradition' seems an oxymoron, like 'odourless stinkbomb' or 'animated sphinx'. The point of 'modernism' was to disrupt and overturn tradition – 'the shock of the new' and all that. Perhaps we have reached the stage at which 'modernism' is beginning to seem *passé*: rather like the man in the fairy tale who was unable to shudder (even when they put his grandmother under a steam hammer), we have lost the power to be shocked. Rebellion that becomes orthodoxy is no longer rebellion. As for the 'unspeakably sophisticated' notion of a 'real tradition' to set against modernism, I suggested in *Young Betjeman* (1988) that 'There was a tradition of social realism in English poetry which had only recently gone underground and which surfaced again in [Betjeman].'[121] It was like a river which flows for a while underground, then bursts forth in a bubbling spring. Professor John Carey 'reckoned' this idea enough to quote it in his book *The Intellectuals and the Masses* (1992),[122] but I find that something like it had already been broached by Larkin, if not in so many words.[123]

Although Fenton was clearly reluctant to countenance the 'rival tradition' theory, in his article of 2003 he showed himself open to something almost as unthinkable to the modernists: second thoughts about Eliot.

As time passed, Auden's reputation grew, and many of the objections to him faded away and lost their force or even their meaning. Eliot became problematic, and not just over the issue of anti-Semitism. Some American readers today think *Four Quartets* represented a decline of his gifts – the opposite of what we used to believe.[124]

If anything could be more startling than Fenton's being critical of Eliot, it was a wholehearted defence of Betjeman in December 2003 by the avant-garde poet Michael Horovitz, in reply to yet another attack by the late, waspish Ian Hamilton. Horovitz was reviewing a new selection, *The Best Loved Poems of John Betjeman*.

In *Against Oblivion: Lives of the Twentieth-Century Poets*, Ian Hamilton pretended to a community of opinion regarding John Betjeman, when he wrote:

> Betjeman had the equipment for manufacturing slick, sociological, light verse, but whenever he attempts to engage our sympathies beyond the point of mere smiling acquiescence, he finds it impossible to adapt – or should one say escape? – an ingrained showmanship, a look-at-me predictability.

No one who has read Betjeman's many sombre poems such as 'The Cottage Hospital', 'Death in Leamington' or 'Devonshire Street W.1' ('No hope. And the iron knob of this palisade / So cold to the touch, is luckier now than he. / "Oh merciless, hurrying Londoners! Why was I made / For the long and painful deathbed coming to me?"...') could have ascribed 'look-at-me predictability' to their author. How I wish that pompously censorious critics would make it clear that they are speaking only for themselves.

This new *Best Loved* collection brings together around seventy poems, of which the vast majority categorically refute Hamilton's superficial dismissal ... Even 'A Subaltern's Love-song' with which Hamilton himself chose to represent Betjeman, and which is given pride of place at the front of *Best Loved*, actually veers subtly away from bourgeois certainties and leaves the reader – like the speaker of the poem – contemplating the unpredictability of potential fates that lurk beneath the confident surface of Home Counties sports club rituals ...[125]

In the article about his friendship with Betjeman that he contributed to the Prince of Wales's magazine *Perspectives in Architecture* in 1994, Barry Humphries suggested that the poet's fate might be similar to the one Betjeman had claimed for the painter Julius Olsson RA –

> 'It isn't art. It's only just a knack' –
>   It fell from grace. Now, in a change of taste,
> See Julius Olsson slowly strolling back.[126]

Ten years on, there were these signs that Humphries's prediction was coming true. In February 2004 Betjeman even received a grudgingly half-respectful mention in the latest volume of The Oxford English Literary History, *The Last of England?* by Randall Stevenson, although Stevenson is an out-and-out modernist or, as he would say, post-modernist ('colloquial language within exact, conventional poetic forms . . . elegantly asserted rhymes and rhythms . . . some of the grander styles of the Victorians, wryly counterpointed against a disdainful vision of contemporary life . . .').[127]

As the balance-scales of reputation are adjusted – Eliot down a bit, Betjeman up – it is natural to wonder: what will be Betjeman's eventual place in English literature? There is Jad Adams's assessment: 'one of the greatest twentieth-century poets'. Craig Raine thinks Betjeman 'succeeds marvellously' in presenting 'life', but all the same Raine's essay is in the nature of an affectionate put-down: 'he writes "badly" in order to write well'. And then there is the Grigsonian view that the poems are piffling and detestable.

A biographer has to be on his guard against making exorbitant claims for his subject. Setting aside, for a moment, the rôle Larkin assigns Betjeman – of valiant heresiarch against modernism – I believe Betjeman's poetry will last and will still be read with enjoyment in hundreds of years' time. He is a pre-eminent poet of places – in Harold Acton's words, 'the genius of the *genius loci*'.[128] His skill in conveying places' character is hardly surpassed in English literature. Wordsworth has it in *The Prelude*; but often poets ostensibly dealing with places – Gray in his *Elegy* or T. S. Eliot in *Four Quartets* – are more interested in telling us their thoughts in or about Stoke Poges or Little Gidding than in evoking those places themselves, as Betjeman would do. If England stays much the same, it will be delightedly recognized in Betjeman's poems; if ruined, it will survive in them.

Some of his admirers think his reputation will rest on his 'serious' poems, such as 'Death in Leamington'. In accord with Larkin, I think it is more likely to rest on his humour – the humour which even sidles into 'Death in Leamington' ('Oh! Chintzy, chintzy cheeriness, Half dead and half alive!'). Poets greater than Betjeman have written on love and death; but in (say) satire of the English middle classes in the Fifties, he is incomparable; those poems have a historical, as well as literary, value. And, just as humour invades the 'serious' poems, so the humorous ones are not all exclusively funny. There is a parallel with his friend Nancy Mitford, whose biographer writes:

> The theatre director Peter Brook, who in 1950 staged a play that Nancy had translated from the French, wrote to me that what he remembers most about her was that she was '*light*, light in the way that the French use the word'. To the English, of course, lightness has implications of frivolity and foolery. In the French, however, lightness is not merely what you do when you can't manage heaviness. It has, as Peter Brook so perceptively wrote, an 'absolute value', a worth and a weight of its own.[129]

The lightness of Betjeman's poetry is the Unbearable Lightness of Being.

There is often deep emotion in Betjeman's humour. We might be inclined to smile at Jennifer in 'Beside the Seaside', 'last year's queen' of the children playing organized games on a Cornish beach, who is mortified at being ousted as the favourite of Mr Pedder (short for 'pederast'?), the organizer; but Betjeman so completely feels the misery of her humiliation, that we feel it too. Compassion is one of the most piercing qualities of his poetry – the compassion he felt, even as a child, when he experienced a 'wave of pity',

> seeing children carrying down
> Sheaves of drooping dandelions to the courts of Kentish Town.[130]

Again, in 'Devonshire Street, W.1', after the death-sentence pronounced by the doctor, there is a hint of satire in the last stanza. Betjeman, though, knows that a reader with anything like his own understanding of human ways will not smile superciliously, but recognize the lines' poignancy and their truth: this is just the way a wife *might* deal with such a cataclysm, trying to deflect her husband's mind from the horror with a familiar murmured mantra about bus numbers so that – in Eliot's clever, arid phrase – he will be 'Distracted from distraction by distraction'.[131]

> She puts her fingers in his as, loving and silly,
>   At long-past Kensington dances she used to do
> 'It's cheaper to take the tube to Piccadilly
>   And then we can catch a nineteen or a twenty-two.'

The husband in Devonshire Street is doomed; but the Kensington flashback is light – as flashbacks are. In Betjeman's poem '1940', in which he imagines Penelope killed in an air-raid, he brings her before us with a comical, cartoonist's touch – 'the nut-shaped head' – but ends with the diapason blast:

> Oh bountiful Gods of the air! Oh Science and Progress!
> You great big wonderful world! Oh what have you done?[132]

John Betjeman was happy to be compared to William Cowper, George Crabbe and Winthrop Mackworth Praed, all of whom he admired; but his range was greater than theirs, and they did not have the twentieth century to grapple with. He was, at the least, the very model of a major minor poet; and of course he was more besides – architectural historian, conservationist and television star, an authenticated National Treasure, archetype of the species. If he had not written a line of verse he would deserve a place in the national pantheon. Like Dr Johnson and Oscar Wilde, he imprinted and impressed his personality on his age. As a result, the word 'Betjemanesque' – apparently first used by John Edward Bowle in his Marlborough diary in 1924[133] – entered the language. It joined bowdlerize, boycott, banting, Bradshaw, Belisha beacon, Biro, Benedictine, Bewick's swan, buddleia and Byronic in the *Oxford English Dictionary*. In 1961 Cummings could draw Betjeman alongside President Kennedy as one of the six men best known to Britons. That fame was temporal. Betjemania is over; but the Betjemanesque survives, and will survive.

APPENDIX 1

A Walk with Mr Betjeman
by Tom Driberg, (*New Statesman*, 6 January 1961)

Mr John Betjeman has described himself, with characteristically bilingual modesty, as 'the Ella Wheeler Wilcox *de nos jours*'. It might be juster to find in him – at least in his tastes and aspirations – something of Hopkins (since he, too, loves 'the weeds and the wilderness' and 'all things counter, original, spare, strange'), and to liken his personality, with the manic–depressive alternations of mood common in his verse, to that of Edward Lear. Mr Betjeman, like Mr Lear (who wept 'by the side of the ocean', as well as 'on top of the hill'), weeps almost all the time – by the ocean-side from which rises the hideous bulk of a nuclear power-station, on the hilltop threatened by an eruption of huts and wireless masts. Mr Lear, it will be remembered, liked to purchase 'chocolate shrimps from the mill'. Betjeman's chocolate shrimps are the treasured vestiges of pre-industrial or early-industrial architecture now vanishing as fast as the unspoiled coast and country which he loves equally.

Such agonies and delights are present to John with almost unbearable intensity in the City – the City of London – in which he has a working maisonette hard by the Norman church of St Bartholomew the Great and the hospital which he visits regularly. It is a rare pleasure – one which fell to me recently – to spend some hours exploring the City on foot with Mr Betjeman.

It would indeed be difficult, with traffic as it is, to undertake such an expedition otherwise than on foot – though, when I arrived in Cloth Fair at the appointed time, empty-handed and not wearing trouser-clips, he gave me a glance of slight disapproval and said: 'I've booked a table at the Mermaid . . . As you haven't brought a bicycle, we shall have to walk.' I did not mind: it was a crisp day of pale winter sunshine. We set out across the open square of West Smithfield, several persons who may have been bummarees saluting Mr Betjeman with the respectful familiarity now transferred from the squirearchy to the television 'personality'. He waved lingeringly towards the hospital on our left: 'You know the Hogarth staircase there.'

Then he pulled me across the road, dodging a van whose driver looked more alarmed than angry, turned towards the main hospital and its southward extensions and said: 'If you stand *here*' – he described an arc from left to right – 'you can see the deterioration of architecture since the early nineteenth century superbly done . . . It's really a complete perspective of English architecture in stone for so long as there were load-bearing walls – E.E., Perp (look, over to the left, there), then there's that seventeenth-century brick, Middlesex style, mannered Wren style, then Regency, then good early Victorian, then fussy late Victorian, then hopelessly fussy Edwardian.'

We walked downhill past St Sepulchres, Holborn Viaduct; the drinking-fountain here was the first erected (1859) by the Metropolitan Drinking Fountain Association. St Sepulchre's was near the gateway to the City as you approached it from the west; its stately fifteenth-century tower is hidden by the tall new cube of Remington House. If I had noticed it before, I had never realised why Old Bailey – the street – widens out towards its northern end where a green wooden hut now stands. This extra space was for the crowds who came to watch the public executions. So were the pubs opposite – the Magpie and Stump and the rest.

Betjeman: 'You remember the *Ingoldsby Legends*? They hired rooms at the inn and then drank too much while waiting for the hanging, and slept through it.' What is usually called the Old Bailey – the Central Criminal Court – is 'a very dull job by E.W. Mountford, a winner of competitions who used to get people into his office who could draw in the styles of the assessors.' It replaced Dance's Newgate jail – 'a masterpiece, though a grim masterpiece, with rusticated stone and iron chains let into the walls; based on Piranesi . . .'

We went on south and down. The City sky was a riot of new cubes. Mr Betjeman gave a gesture of distaste towards one of them: 'Look at that —— thing there! A straight piece of copybook contemporary, disregarding the lines of Ludgate Hill . . .' But he was full of praise for a Midland Bank branch by T.W. Collcutt (architect of the Imperial Institute, a famous defunct restaurant, the Holborn, and the Palace Theatre – the first theatre to be constructed with cantilevered circles and, therefore, no pillars to block the view): 'See – granite base, terra cotta above, and then brick . . . Look at that moulding' – he stroked it – 'how delicate . . .'

In Black Friars Lane he stopped again, and made me look round. It was almost the only point in the City, he said, from which any of

Wren's steeples could still be seen as he meant them to be seen, rising above buildings three or four storeys high: from here we could see St Martin's, Ludgate, and St Bride's. And here was another treasure, intact: Apothecaries' Hall, its seventeenth-century buildings set about a secluded courtyard, like a college or almshouse quadrangle. 'It's very nice, isn't it? I can't think why it's still up. I suppose it's because it's Early.' Then, through a void soon to be filled by the new offices of *The Times*, we had the last sight we shall have from there of the dome of St Paul's, radiant in the late-afternoon sun, and were soon at the busy Blackfriars road-junction.

Here are two curiosities for amateurs of Victoriana: a pub, the Black Friar, whose exterior and interior décor is 'the most perfect *art nouveau* in London', with marble and mosaic panels and elaborate bronze reliefs of monks quaffing (signed Henry Poole RA) and such texts as 'Industry is all'; and, on the dreary front of Blackfriars station, a quaint matching of the holiday resorts to which Victorian travellers could set forth hence – Herne Bay and Lausanne, Margate and Leipsic [*sic*], Beckenham and Baden-Baden, Walmer and Wiesbaden, Westgate-on-Sea and St Petersburg. (Mr Betjeman once went in and asked for a ticket to St Petersburg: the clerk referred him to Victoria (Continental) without a flicker of surprise.) Oh, and just round the corner, towards the bridge, looking sadly tatty, is the Blackfriars District Railway station: most of the thousands who pass it daily probably haven't noticed that it's in the Moorish style.

A restorative break at the Mermaid (including Cornish mead) fortified us for the walk along Upper Thames Street. Betjeman: 'This is the only part of the City that's concerned physically with merchandise, not just with stockbroking. You can see the Thames actually being used . . . You remember Uncle Tom?' – an allusion to *The Waste Land*. 'Look at "Carron warehouse" over there: the same words in three styles of lettering, of different periods – the oldest by far the best.'

There were still sunlit glimpses of St Paul's (to our left) and the river (to our right). Once we saw St Paul's through trees growing wild in a square plot, a regular Hopkins wilderness of weeds and rusty tins, with two broken-down benches. This was a churchyard once – St Peter's, Paul's Wharf: the church was not rebuilt after the fire of 1666. 'How squalid!' I said.

Betjeman: 'Oh, I'd rather it like this . . . rather than municipal-tidy.'

Near-by we saw a strange new concrete structure. 'Well,' he said, parodying a brisk business voice, 'we're hoping to make a speedway from Upper Thames Street to St Nicholas Cole Abbey . . .' Then another glimpse of the gleaming river drew us down a lane, Trig Lane: 'York stone, these pavements.' Opposite, the Bankside power-station

belching. Betjeman: 'I've often wondered why they bothered to declare
the City a smokeless zone when that bloody thing pours out smoke all
the time.'

An iron bollard (once a gun); bent railings; chalk graffiti; the high
tide chuffing and slapping against the granite steps – 'and a Vicat Cole
sky* behind Sir Howard Robertson's Shell tower,' he intoned rhythmic-
ally, as if improvising a poem . . . 'Look at Southwark Bridge,' he cried.
'By Sir Ernest George. The least-known bridge in Britain – and the
least-used. You can park your car on it. I always use it when I bicycle
to the south.'

Some gulls flapped towards us, screaming. 'And the Tower Bridge
. . . Look, I think you can just see it. They've taken the ironwork off
the top, so that the whole point of the design is gone.' Back to Upper
Thames Street: it was a weekday, but the scene was empty but for one
thin man, rather knock-kneed – 'That man looks like a drawing by
Lowry, doesn't he?' Then Wren's churchless tower of St Mary
Somerset, plain and grey, a red GPO telephone-box nestling at its base:
'sensitively placed, the kiosk, isn't it?' Then the little high-gabled
square called Queenhithe: 'you see, that's interesting – there was an
attempt to make London look like Bruges' . . . The graceful, baroque
three-storied turret-steeple of St James's Garlickhithe . . . Vintners'
Hall . . . 'But for sheer brickwork, and how to deal with blank spaces,
you can't beat these flanks of Cannon Street station' – whose terminal
cupolas looked almost Venetian in the sunset glow.

We hurried on, past the incense-fragrance of St Magnus the Martyr,
overshadowed by the monstrous proximity of Adelaide House, and
past the fish-fragrance of Billingsgate; for further east, in Lower
Thames Street, is a building which Mr Betjeman is anxious to save from
demolition – the Coal Exchange, built in the 1840s by J.B. Bunning,
and historically notable as well as striking of aspect, since it has the
world's first large prefabricated cast-iron dome and cast-iron internal
galleries with mouldings in the form of cables.

Demolition is threatened in connection with a road-widening
scheme; Mr Betjeman showed how the road could be widened *and* the
Coal Exchange saved – but this might involve some slight interference
with the dull Custom House opposite, 'and the civil servants are so
entrenched there'. Perhaps, too, the City Corporation, which owns the
rest of the Coal Exchange block, would like to clear the whole site and
let Mr Cotton or someone build a skyscraper on it.

* George Vicat Cole (1833–93), English landscape painter specializing in harvesting
and river scenes.

Soon the short day was done. We had a cup of tea in a Lyons, where a large, stout business-man came up to Mr Betjeman and said, in words that were a compendium of what is always said in these vapid approaches: 'Pardon me, I trust you're very well, sir. I spoke to you some years ago – you wouldn't remember.'

This encounter enhanced the melancholy of the evening. Out into one of the winding lanes that still survive, bright with clustering small shops: 'That's what the City should be.' But then, overhead, a colder brightness – 100, 200 office-windows, identical rectangles of fluorescence, in a vertical cube that soared without aspiring or inspiring, utterly devoid of feature or character, not even copybook contemporary: '. . . and that's what they're doing to the City – trying to make it like Piccadilly or New York'. But then we came out into the grandeur of Leadenhall Market. 'There!' said Mr Betjeman, like one who breathes Alpine air after a foetid tunnel; and he stood with arms open, like a priest as he says 'Dominus vobiscum.'

The crowds were hurrying homeward. It was too late to go and walk through the Barbican area . . . Time to see only one more church, St Mary-at-Hill – 'often ignored', said Mr Betjeman, 'because of its plain outside: the interior is one of the – oh, the most magnificent in the City'. And so it seemed; and we admired Wren's 'Byzantine quincunx' dome and the carved woodwork and the huge staircase sweeping up to the pulpit. The present incumbent's predecessor was the late Prebendary Carlile, of the Church Army. 'In those days,' he told us, 'there was royalty galore coming here.'

The verger explained the scriptural significance of the unicorn in the royal arms: 'The horn is the horn of David, the tail . . .' But the notice-board outside seemed to epitomize the City: it was designed to advertise, in large lettering, the Christian Evidence Society; but the words were almost obscured by public notices of ward elections and of a meeting for the granting of billiard licences.

Appendix 2

THE LAST OF PENELOPE

In 1985, Penelope Betjeman put her house at Cusop on the market and prepared to move into a convent at Llandrindod Wells.[1] She wanted to free money for Paul and to be able to go to India whenever she liked.[2] She began giving her possessions to her children and organized her papers in box files.[3]

In 1986 Christina Noble, who ran Indian tours, asked Penelope if she would take her place as leader of a Himalayan trek in April; she herself was having to drop out because of family problems.[4] Penelope agreed to do it. Before leaving she said goodbye to Jessie Sharley and Ottilie Squires, both of whom strongly sensed that she was saying a final farewell.[5] On 1 April she took the train from Hereford to London on her way to Heathrow airport.[6] On the train she met a friend, Thomas Dunne. As it drew into Paddington, she said:

> I think I might never come back from this trip. The funny thing is, if I die on the mountains, I know that everyone will say what a wonderful death I have had. They'll say, what a wonderful way to go, it is just as she would have liked! But I don't want to die now at all, I've so much to do.[7]

Penelope left London on 5 April with the West Himalayan Tour party.[8] She and the fourteen tour members stayed first in Simla, where she had fallen in love with Sir John Marshall in 1931.[9] The party included Ronnie and Judith Watson, a couple in their late sixties from Berkshire; a doctor and two Queen Alexandra nurses retired from the Royal Navy. Christina Noble had assigned Paddy Singh, an Indian ex-soldier, to act as Penelope's support and help organize the porters and ponies.[10]

On 11 April, Penelope was up exceptionally early and was ready packed when Ronnie Watson emerged from his room opposite hers.

'You're up terribly early,' he said.

'I know,' she replied. 'I feel as though I might be on my way to heaven.'[11]

Penelope's granddaughter, Imogen Lycett Green, has written about that day in her book *Grandmother's Footsteps* (1994). By her account, a long mountain walk the party had planned was hindered by landslides and fallen trees; but Penelope was determined to get to the hamlet of Mutisher, where there was a temple with beautiful bronze door knockers.[12]

> . . . Penelope reached Mutisher on her pony where . . . two tour members (one of whom was a nurse) and a couple of the porters were waiting . . . [she] got down off her pony and climbed three high steps up towards the temple. She sat down on the third and she rested her head against the stone wall. She shut her eyes for a moment.
>
> The nurse turned round: 'Come on, Penelope, we've got to make Khanang [rest house] – let's get going.'
>
> Penelope didn't move. The nurse walked up the steps to her. She shook her, she shouted at her, but there was no movement.
>
> The nurse tried artificial respiration, the temple priest began to wail. Prem, one of the porters, turned on his tail and leapt up the mountain to where Paddy and the other members were waiting on the hillside.
>
> 'Come quick, come quick, Lady Penelope, oh, Lady Penelope,' he wailed.[13]

In Imogen's account, the doctor was quickly on the scene. Penelope was dead.

It is an affecting story but, in the view of Judith Watson – who, unlike Imogen, was on the tour with Penelope – it is not entirely accurate. 'Imogen's account is over-dramatized,' she writes. 'At Penelope's death there was no nurse; there were no steps; there was no temple!'[14] Judith has written her own description of the tour, *A Walk in the West Himalayas* (1996). In her version, Penelope has left Mutisher village, in the hot sun, when after a few minutes she says to Edith Schmidt, a German pharmacist on the tour, 'Let's sit down for a bit.' After a rest, Penelope sets off riding again. She is then thought to have fainted. It is Edith Schmidt (not one of the two ex-Navy nurses) who tries to resuscitate her – in vain.[15] Villagers carry her on their shoulders up the mountain to Khanang.

It was decided to cremate her on a funeral pyre in the Hindu fashion.[16] Bruce Chatwin, who had just completed the first draft of *The Songlines* beside a lake near the Nepalese border, read the news of her death in *The Times of India*, dropped everything and got to the funeral.[17] On 24 April he wrote to Patrick Leigh Fermor:

> Yesterday morning, her friend Kranti Singh and I carried her ashes in a small brass pot to a rock in the middle of the River Beas which was carved

all over, in Tibetan, with the Buddhist mantra, O the flower of the lotus. He tipped some into a whirlpool and I then threw the pot with the remainder into the white water. The flowers – wild tulips, clematis, and a sprig of English oak-leaves (from the Botanical Gardens in Manali) vanished at once into the foam.[18]

When Imogen Lycett Green went to India in 1992 (on the journey recorded in *Grandmother's Footsteps*), she made a detour to Khanang to place an engraved stone there in Penelope's memory. The stone had been commissioned by Candida, who had composed, with Billa Harrod and Bruce Chatwin, the words to be cut on it –

In memory of Penelope Valentine Hester Betjeman, writer and traveller, born 14th February 1910, wife of John Betjeman Poet Laureate, and daughter of Field Marshal Lord Chetwode, Commander-in-Chief of the Indian Army 1930–35 and of Lady Chetwode. On 11th April 1986 she died in these hills she had loved so long.[19]

Cricketing boys used the monument as a wicket: 'I think Penelope would have been pleased about that,' Christina Noble says.[20] It was damaged and had to be replaced. A second memorial to Penelope was set up in another stretch of wild country she had loved, the Ridgeway in Berkshire.

ACKNOWLEDGEMENTS

As with the previous two volumes, my first and greatest debts of gratitude are to John Betjeman, for authorizing this book and recording some recollections for it, and to Penelope Betjeman, for giving all possible help until her death in 1986; and I make grateful acknowledgement to their Estates.

The late Jock Murray and his son, my contemporary and friend John R. Murray, commissioned this biography and oversaw the publication of the earlier volumes at the old Albemarle Street, London offices known to Lord Byron. I thank them and their fellow directors for their help and their patience. Following the takeover of John Murray by Hodder Headline in 2002, I have been given equal encouragement from Roland Philipps, managing director, with the third and final volume.

Four other people have ensured a happy continuity. Grant McIntyre, though no longer a director of John Murray, has edited this volume with the same judiciousness, tact and meticulous care that he brought to the last one. Once again, Peter James has been a matchless copy-editor. Again, too, Caroline Westmore has seen to it that the operation has run as smoothly as such a complex and sometimes difficult enterprise can run. I am delighted that Douglas Matthews, who indexed the earlier volumes so well, has undertaken the index of this one too. I feel immense gratitude to all four.

My late parents, Jack and Mary Hillier, read some of the chapters and gave wise counsel. Alan Bell, formerly Librarian of the London Library, also offered welcome advice.

Yet again, my sister Mary Thompson has been of incalculable help. Her rôle is acknowledged in a not too perplexing cipher in the dedication of this volume. My brother-in-law Nigel Thompson, my niece Amy Vincent and her husband Richard, and my nephew Oliver Thompson have also contributed, both in practical ways and by their sympathetic interest in my work.

Duncan Andrews of New York early made available to me his treasured collection of Betjemaniana.

The Royal Literary Fund made me a grant which, while it was specifically not to aid me in finishing the book, made life easier while I did so. I am most grateful to its Trustees and its Secretary, Eileen Gunn.

I have had exemplary help from the staff of the Bodleian Library, the British Library, the BBC Written Archives at Caversham, near Reading, the Huntington Library, San Marino, California, the London Library, Trinity House, London and above all from the McPherson Library of the University of Victoria, British Columbia, Canada – where most of Betjeman's papers are lodged. Individual acknowledgements to some of the librarians and archivists of these and other institutions appear below.

HRH The Prince of Wales kindly talked to me, at Kensington Palace in 1985, about his friendship with John Betjeman.

Many others who knew the poet have been good enough to grant me interviews. I am specially obliged to those whose relationship to him was so significant that whole chapters have been built around them and named after them: the Andersons and Pagets;

Barry Humphries (who took time off from a gruelling American tour to make a long transatlantic telephone call to me); Sir Simon Jenkins, an old friend and colleague; John Nankivell; and Lady Wilson of Rievaulx. Just as great, in many cases, are the contributions of the Baring family to the 'Wantage' chapter; of the late Tom Greeves to 'The Battle of Bedford Park'; Bernard Kaukas to 'The Euston Arch'; Edward Mirzoeff to '*Metroland*' and other chapters about Betjeman's television career; Jim Parker to *Banana Blush*; Sir Peter and Gillian, Lady Parker to 'His Last Bow'; Reg Read to '. . . As I Lose Hold'; and Jonathan Stedall to *Time with Betjeman*.

The late James Lees-Milne typed out for me all the passages in his diaries relating to Betjeman, and in a later session gave me extra information about the other people mentioned in those extracts. Sometimes the passages differ slightly from the versions subsequently published by John Murray. I am deeply grateful to the diarist for going to such trouble on my behalf; grateful, also, to his literary executor Michael Bloch both for his friendship and for his acceptance that Lees-Milne intended me to make use of his diaries in this biography.

I have tried to remember everyone who helped me, and beg forgiveness if I have left anyone out of the list of names that follows: Brother James Abson; the late Sir Harold Acton; Jad Adams; Nick Adams; Philippa Allen; the late Mario Amaya; the late Sir Kingsley Amis; Mark Amory; Edward Anderson; James Armstrong; Clive Aslet; Susan Baker; the late Desmond Baring; the late Mollie Baring; Nigel Baring; Professor John Bayley; William Bealby-Wright; Guilford Bell; William Bell; the late Nicolas Bentley; June Berliner; Robert Berliner; Diana Berry; Georgia Berry; Andrew Best; Jerry Bick; Lady Rachel Billington; the late Georgiana Blakiston; the late Noel Blakiston; John Boorman; Richard Boston; Richard Bourchier; Lord and Lady Briggs; Jenny Brumhead, Assistant Community Library Manager, Worcester Library; Dr Donald Buttress, Surveyor Emeritus of the Fabric of Westminster Abbey; Professor John Carey; Humphrey Carpenter; the late Sir Hugh Casson; Manuel Catral; the late Lord David Cecil; Paul Chadd QC; Anna-Mei Chadwick; the late Cyril Connolly; the late Dame Catherine Cookson; the late Lady Diana Cooper; John Toop Cooper; Anthony Curtis; Anne Dalgety; Jake Davies; Philippa Davies, founder of the Betjeman Society; the late Sir Henry d'Avigdor-Goldsmid; Roy Dean; Frank Delaney; the late Earl of Drogheda; Professor Katherine Duncan-Jones; the late Lady Mary Dunn; Brian Edwards; the late Lady Elton; Julia Elton; the late Sir Nicholas Fairbairn QC MP; Duncan Fallowell; Professor James Fenton; Dr Christine Ferdinand, Fellow Librarian of Magdalen College, Oxford; Adam Fergusson; the late Lady Fergusson of Kilkerran; the late Peter Fleetwood-Hesketh; Louise Fletcher; the Rt Hon. Michael Foot; the late Christina Foyle; Luke Franklin; Mario Galang; Peter Gammond, ex-Chairman of the Betjeman Society; Patrick Garland; Simon Garwood; the late Sir Arthur Gilbert; Sir Martin Gilbert; Antony Giles; Ellie Giles; Jonathan Gili; Phillida Gili; Anton Gill; Mark Girouard; Mark Glazebrook; Chandra Gopal; the Duke of Grafton; the late Col. Andrew Graham; the late Ian Grant; Ti Green; the late Vivien Greene; Eleanor Greeves; the late Joyce Grenfell; John Gross; Valerie Grove; the Rev. William Gulliford; the late John Hadfield; Martin Haldane; Petronella Haldane; Janie Hampton; the late P. J. R. Harding; the late Robert Harling; David Harrison; Dominick Harrod; Lady Harrod; the late Sibyl Harton; Sir Max Hastings; Lady Selina Hastings; John Heald, Chairman of the Betjeman Society; the Rt Hon. Lord Healey; the Rt Hon. Sir Edward Heath; the late Dr Winifred Hector; Brenda Herbert; Cicely Herbert; the late David Herbert; the late Derek Hill; Anthony Hobson; Sue Hodson; Stella Hollister; Alexander Hollweg; the late Diana Holman-Hunt; Michael Holroyd; Sir Alistair Horne; Aaron Howard; Anthony Howard; Philip Howard; the late Archbishop Trevor Huddleston; the late Sir Ian Hunter; the Rev. Prebendary Gerard Irvine; Rosemary Irvine; the late Walter Ison; Joan Jackson (the former Joan Hunter Dunn); the late Edward James; the Rev. Canon Eric James; the Richard Jefferies Society; Sir Simon Jenkins; Stephen Jessel; Dr D. P. Johnson, Librarian-in-Charge, Oxford Union Society; Girish Karnad; Dr Saras Karnad; the late Pamela Kaukas; John Keay; Diana

Kendrick; Francis King; the late Lord Kinross; Professor James Kirkup; Hester Knight; Hiromichi Kurumada; Marie-Jaqueline Lancaster; Mollie Lawrence; the late Sir Osbert Lancaster; Patrick Lawrence; Anthony Lejeune; Raymond Leppard; Jeremy Lewis; Roger Lewis; John Linnell; the late Elizabeth, Countess of Longford; the late Earl of Longford; Christopher Loyd; Dorothy Luft; Sir William McAlpine; Margaret McCall; Celia McCulloch; Bishop Nigel McCulloch; the late K. B. McFarlane; John Mallet; Philip Mansergh; Yvonne Mansergh; Ved Mehta; the Rt Rev. Hugh Montefiore; Amanda Morgan; His Honour Judge Hugh Marsden Morgan; the late Rev. Marcus Morris; Patt Morrison; the late Malcolm Muggeridge; the Rt Hon. Lord Justice Mummery and Lady Mummery; the late Dame Iris Murdoch; Ann Norman-Butler; Belinda Norman-Butler; Lord Norwich; James O'Brien; James Haldane O'Hare; Felicity O'Mahony; Father Barry Orford; Professor Nicholas Orme; Rona Orme; Verity Orme; Christine Outhwaite; the Rev. Tony Outhwaite, former Master of the Hospital of St Cross, Winchester; Verily Anderson Paget; George D. Painter; Thomas Pakenham; Valerie Pakenham; Peter Parker; Michael Parkinson; Philip Parks; the late David Peace; Jenny Pearson; the late Edmund Penning-Rowsell; the late Lionel Perry; Dr William Peterson; Chris Pelter; Miriam Phillips; Michael Pick; the late John Piper; the late Myfanwy Piper; Tony Platt, Keeper of the Lapidarium, Westminster Abbey; the late Sir Edward Playfair; the late Roy Plomley; the late Anthony Powell; Tristram Powell; the late Lady Violet Powell; Alan Powers; Professor John Press; Dr Judith Priestman; the late Marjorie Proops; the late Alan Pryce-Jones; David Pryce-Jones; Craig Raine; Dr Marilyn Ravicz; the late Dr Robert Ravicz; Len Rawle; Anne Reed; James Reeve; the late Sir James Richards; the Rev. John Richards; Jenny Richardson; Nicholas Richardson; Hilary Rittner; the Hon. Lady Roberts of the Royal Library, Windsor Castle; Magda Rogers; the late Dr A. L. Rowse; Joan Ryan; Eunice Salmond; John Saumarez Smith; Kenneth Savidge; the Rev. Canon Michael Saward; Lynn Sayer; Martin Sayer; the Rev. John Schaufelberger; the late Dr Gregory Scott; Professor Colin Seymour-Ure; the late Bart Sharley; the late Jessie Sharley; Veronica Sharley; the Rt Rev. Lord Sheppard of Liverpool; Ned Sherrin; Leslie Sherwood; the late Robin Skelton; Peyton Skipwith; Anthony Smith, President of Magdalen College, Oxford; Sir John Smith; the late Alison Smithson; Peter Smithson; Neil Somerville; the late John Sparrow; the late Sir Stephen Spender; Kirsty Squires; the late Ottilie Squires; Dr Richard Squires; Dr Gavin Stamp; John Stevenson; the late Bishop Mervyn Stockwood; the late Reynolds Stone; Dr Graham Storey; the Hon. James Stourton; Janet Street-Porter; Sir Roy Strong; the late Sir John Summerson; A. G. Swift; Dr Frank Tait; Natasha Talyarkhan; Rishad Talyarkhan; the late A. J. P. Taylor; Jean Sharley Taylor; Patrick Taylor-Martin; Erreg Thami; Charles Thomson; Dr Edmund Thomson; the late George Malcolm Thomson; Brenda Thompson; Laura Thompson; Brother Philip Thresher; the editorial staff of the *Times Literary Supplement*; the late Elizabeth Tollinton; Roger Trayburn, of Swindon Libraries; Ion Trewin; Terry Tuey; Katie Vaughan, Searchroom Assistant, Bury St Edmunds Record Office, Suffolk; Hugo Vickers; the officers of the Victorian Society; the editorial staff of the *Wantage Herald*; Graham Warhurst; Sarah Waters; the late Auberon Waugh; the late Ben Weinreb; Vivienne Westwood; Paul Wigmore; Edward Wild; Tessa Wild; the Rev. Harry Williams; Ann Wolff; the late Joan Woods (Joan Maude); the late Judith Wright; the late Lord Wyatt of Weeford; Carolyn Wylie; Deane Wylie; Billie Yarbrough; Raymond Yarbrough; the Rt Hon. Lord Young of Graffham; Rory Young.

NOTES

Abbreviations

BBCWA   BBC Written Archives Centre, Caversham Park, Reading
CLG   Candida Lycett Green
interview   This denotes a tape-recorded interview with the author, conducted at the stated date
JB   John Betjeman
JBLP   Bevis Hillier, *John Betjeman: A Life in Pictures*, London 1984
JBNFNL   Bevis Hillier, *John Betjeman: New Fame, New Love*, London 2002
JBP   John Betjeman's papers
PB   Penelope Betjeman
Victoria   The McPherson Library of the University of Victoria, British Columbia, Canada
YB   Bevis Hillier, *Young Betjeman*, London 1988

Chapter 1: Wantage

1 On the Barings and Ardington House, near Wantage, see *JBNFNL*, pp. 455–57.
2 See *ibid.*, p. 455.
3 PB, interview, 1978.
4 JB, conversation, 1977.
5 *Wantage Herald*, 20 April 1960.
6 *Ex inf.* Christopher Loyd, interview, 1989.
7 *Ibid.*
8 Mollie Baring, interview, 1976.
9 *Ibid.*
10 Mollie Baring, interview, 1989.
11 *Ibid.*
12 JB, *Letters*, ed. CLG, ii, 136n.
13 JB to Sister Brigitta, 4 February 1958. JB, *Letters*, ed. CLG, ii, 136.
14 JB, *Letters*, ed. CLG, ii, 136n.
15 Mollie Baring, interview, 1989.
16 *Ibid.*
17 JB to Mollie Baring, 25 July 1960. Kindly shown to the author by Mrs Baring.
18 *Ibid.*
19 *Ibid.*
20 *Ibid.*
21 Mollie Baring, interview, 1989. The late Mrs Baring's account is confirmed by a story in the *Wantage Herald* of 27 September 1950, headed 'Statue daubed again'.
22 On Glenton, see *JBNFNL*, pp. 511–14, 516–18.
23 William Glenton, *Tony's Room: The Secret Love Story of Princess Margaret*, New York 1965, p. 75.

24 *The Noël Coward Diaries*, ed. Graham Payn and Sheridan Morley, London 1992, p. 438.

25 On 4 October 1964 Coward wrote in his diary: 'A lovely evening with the Dowager Duchess of Devonshire and John Betjeman.' On 3 December 1967: 'While in London I recorded some poems, me on one side and John Betjeman on the other.' *Ibid.*, pp. 576 and 656 respectively.

26 Cole Lesley, in *The Life of Noël Coward*, London 1977, pp. 1–2, records that at Coward's memorial service at St Martin-in-the-Fields on 24 May 1973 JB described St Alban's Teddington (where Coward was christened) as 'a fine, soaring Gothic Revival building . . . It looks like a bit of Westminster Abbey that has been left behind further upstream.' And on p. 481: 'Sir John Betjeman . . . composed and wrote the address:

> We are all here today to thank the Lord for the life of Noël Coward.
> Noël with two dots over the 'e'
> And the firm decided downward stroke of the 'd' . . .

Philip Hoare in *Noël Coward: A Biography*, London 1995, p. 519, writes of the memorial service: 'John Betjeman . . . spoke of St Martin's as a "beautiful great eighteenth-century theatre of a church . . . it is precise, elegant and well-ordered. Like Noël." '

27 *Ex inf.* Dr Richard Squires, interview, 1976.

28 JB, *Letters*, ed. CLG, ii, 157.

29 Dr Richard Squires, interview, 1976.

30 Hinge and Bracket: drag artistes. George Logan and Patrick Fyffe (1942–2002) played, respectively, Dr Evadne Hinge and Dame Hilda Bracket – musical ladies far older than themselves. See Fyffe's obituary, *The Times*, 14 May 2002.

31 JB, *Letters*, ed. CLG, ii, 157.

32 The Rev. John Schaufelberger, interview, 1976. In JB's poem 'Harrow-on-the-Hill' (*Collected Poems*, 2003 edn., p. 148) there is a similar parallel between sea and transport.

33 The Rev. John Schaufelberger, interview, 1976.

34 Three of the Betjemans' more 'upper-class' friends in the Wantage area made this point in interviews with the author. Sibyl Harton also expressed surprise at the friendship (interview, 1976).

35 Veronica Sharley, interview, 1989.

36 After leaving Wantage, JB wrote to Jessie and Bart Sharley (4 October 1973): 'I did enjoy myself at dear old 6 Portway in that house where I have so oft indulged myself by looking at my own image in programmes.' (Shown to the author by the late Mrs Sharley.)

37 Veronica Sharley, interview, 1989.

38 Jessie Sharley, interview, 1989.

39 *Ibid.*

40 Veronica Sharley, interview, 1989.

41 JB to Veronica Sharley, 20 October 1964. Shown to the author by Ms Sharley.

42 JB to Veronica Sharley, 17 July 1965. Shown to the author by Ms Sharley.

43 JB to Veronica Sharley, 9 August 1974. Shown to the author by Ms Sharley.

44 Veronica Sharley interview, 1989.

45 Jessie Sharley, interview, 1989.

46 *Ibid.*

47 Veronica Sharley, interview, 1989.

48 (Ricardo) Hercules Fuque Bellville (b. 1939), son of the test pilot Rupert Bellville who married Jeannette, daughter of General S. O. Fuqua, the United States military attaché in Spain. See Burke's *Landed Gentry* under 'Bellville of Tedstone Court, Herefordshire'.

49 Veronica Sharley, interview, 1989.

50 JB, *Letters*, ed. CLG, ii, 157.

51 The Hon. Peter Jay (b. 1937), who married a daughter of the Rt. Hon. James Callaghan and was later British Ambassador to Washington and Economics Correspondent of the BBC.

52 Quoted, Patrick Marnham, *The Private Eye Story*, London 1982, p. 19.

53 The present author contributed a short story to that issue of *Mesopotamia* and Nicholas Orme, now Emeritus Professor of History at Exeter University, drew cartoons for it alongside Rushton's.

54 Marnham, *op. cit.*, p. 19.

55 *Ibid.*, p. 50.

56 *Loc. cit.*

57 The last paragraph of Marnham, *op. cit.*, p. 230, is:

> [*Private Eye*'s] twentieth year, 1981, ended with the first-ever glossy cover and the news that after years of boardroom butchery Jocelyn 'Piranha Teeth' Stevens had at last been fired by Express Newspapers. It had taken 522 issues, two thousand libel writs and millions of pounds, but if 'Piranha Teeth' had finally learnt that firing Candida Betjeman from *Queen* magazine was just not on, it had been worth every moment.

58 JB, *Letters*, ed. CLG, ii, 157.

59 It rhymed 'taut as a drum' with 'bum'. *JBP*.

60 See JB, *Letters*, ed. CLG, ii, 416 and n. JB's first 'Nooks and Corners' column appeared in *Private Eye* on 21 May 1971.

61 JB, *Letters*, ed. CLG, ii, 157.

62 *Ibid.*, 158.

63 A photograph of JB reciting 'Congo' at Knighton Bushes is reproduced in *JBLP*, p. 128.

64 See *YB*, p. 239.

65 PB, interview, 1980.

66 *Ibid.*

67 *Ibid.*

68 *Ibid.*

69 PB to JB, n.d. *JBP*.

70 On the Baccarat scandal, see Sir Philip Magnus(-Allcroft), *King Edward the Seventh*, London 1964, pp. 222–29.

71 Jonathan Aitken, *The Young Meteors*, London 1967, p. 30.

72 *Loc. cit.* For a photograph of Rupert Lycett Green wearing a 1960s Blades suit, see Rodney Bennett-England, *Dress Optional: The Revolution in Menswear*, London 1967.

73 Aitken, *op. cit.*, p. 30.

74 PB to Rupert Lycett Green, 4 April 1963. *JBP*.

75 *The Times*, 27 May 1963. For a more detailed account of the wedding, see *Wantage Herald*, 30 May 1963.

76 Christopher Sykes wrote to JB on 26 May 1963: 'I saw a picture of your dial in the piper attending the wedding of your daughter, like, dressed doubtless in garments formerly owned by a deceased author from over the seas. I have known the Lycett Greens all my life on account of Yorkshire like and think your daughter has married into a very nice group of humans.' (JB, *Letters*, ed. CLG, ii, 208.)

77 Stella Hollister, interview, 1989.

78 On Angela Wakeford, see *JBNFNL*, pp. 597 and 704 n. 29.

79 Jessie Sharley, interview, 1989.

80 The Rev. John Schaufelberger, interview, 1976.

81 JB, *Letters*, ed. CLG, ii, 208.

82 CLG, *Over the Hills and Far Away*, London 2003 edn., p. 77.

83 *Ibid.*, p. 78.

84 PB is quoted, *ibid.*, pp. 78–79.

85 On the origins of the phrase 'Swinging London', see B. Hillier, *The Style of the Century*, London 1990 edn., pp. 162–63.

86 *The Ossie Clark Diaries*, ed. and introduced by Lady Henrietta Rous, London 1998, p. 109 n. 34. CLG herself writes, in *Over the Hills and Far Away*, *op. cit.* pp. 55–56: 'Rupert and I were often referred to as "The Tailor and Cutter" (the name of the rag trade magazine) because I seldom spoke and, through no fault of my own, my mouth, when in repose, turns downwards, causing people in the street to say to me, "Cheer up, love, it'll never happen." '

87 Tape, September 1963, kindly copied for the author by Ms Veronica Sharley.

88 *Ibid.*

89 JB to John Sutro, 26 November 1963. JB, *Letters*, ed. CLG, ii, 265.

90 *Ibid.*, 265n.

91 Tape, September 1963, kindly copied for the author by Ms Veronica Sharley.

92 *Ibid.*

93 Ann Fleming to Evelyn Waugh, 15 November 1964. *The Letters of Ann Fleming*, ed. Mark Amory, London 1985, p. 361.

94 Veronica Sharley, interview, 1989.

95 *Ibid.*

96 On Sir Henry d'Avigdor-Goldsmid, see *JBLP*, p. 78. The d'Avigdor-Goldsmids' house, Somerhill, was in Kent.

97 Mollie Baring, interview, 1989.

98 JB, *Letters*, ed. CLG, ii, 253.

99 *Loc. cit.*

100 JB wrote to Evelyn Waugh 1958? (JB, *Letters*, ed. CLG, ii, 162): 'I stayed last Saturday with John Osborne, a man I like very much and who (rightly) thinks you are the finest living writer in England.' CLG writes (*ibid.*, 163n.): 'JB had recently become a friend of the playwright John Osborne and had been to stay at his mill house in Sussex . . .' The mill house was The Old Water Mill, Hellingley, near Hailsham, Sussex. (John Osborne, *Almost a Gentleman: An Autobiography*, London 1991, vol. ii: *1955–1966*, pp. 221–2.)

101 Osborne, *op. cit.*, p. 243.

102 *Ibid.*, p. 254.

103 John Osborne, *Inadmissible Evidence*, London 1965, p. 108.

104 JB to John Osborne, 10 September 1964. JB, *Letters*, ed. CLG, ii, 281.

105 Tristram Powell, conversation with the author, 1988.

106 John Osborne, *Inadmissible Evidence*, London 1965, p. 19.

107 'He thought he would be found out to be the fraud he believed he was,' JB, *Letters*, ed. CLG, ii, 157. See also JB's notes for a prize-day speech to the boys of Giggleswick School, including 'A FRAUD WHO HAS GOT AWAY WITH IT'. *JBLP*, p. 152.

108 John Osborne, *Inadmissible Evidence*, London 1965, p. 30.

109 *Ibid.*, p. 41.

110 The Rev. John Schaufelberger, interview, 1976.

111 JB, *Letters*, ed. CLG, ii, 236n.

112 Dr Richard Squires, interview, 1976.

113 Quoted, PB, interview, 1976.

114 Quoted by JB in a letter to PB, 5 March 1963. *JBP*.

115 JB to PB, 5 March 1963. *JBP*.

116 JB to Harry Jarvis, 16 November 1963. JB, *Letters*, ed. CLG, ii, 263. On Tom Parr see *The Unexpurgated Beaton Diaries*, introduced by Hugo Vickers, London 2003 edn., pp. 279, 403; and *Beaton in the Sixties: More Unexpurgated Diaries*, introduced by Hugo Vickers, London 2003, pp. 108, 134–35, 319, 324, 332.

117 The Kitchen was sold in June 1961. JB, *Letters*, ed. CLG, ii, 203.

118 JB to PB, 19 June 1961. *JBP*.

119 Mollie Baring, interview, 1989.

120 JB to PB, 9 June 1964. JB, *Letters*, ed. CLG, ii, 276.

121 *Ibid.*, 276–77.

122 *Ibid.*, 277.

123 JB said this to the author, 1972.

124 Dr Richard Squires, interview, 1976.

125 See *JBNFNL*, p. 465.

126 Dr Richard Squires, interview, 1976.

127 *Ibid.*

128 *Ibid.*

129 JB, *Letters*, ed. CLG, ii, 252.

130 *Ibid.*, 252–53.

131 *Ibid.*, 253.

Chapter 2: 'Vic Soc.' and 'The Dok'

1 James Lees-Milne, interview, 1993.
2 On Linley Sambourne, see B. Hillier, *Cartoons and Caricatures*, London 1970, pp. 48–49 and 52. Lord Snowdon made a film about No. 18 Stafford Terrace, with JB as presenter. An extract from it was shown in Edward Mirzoeff's television programme *John Betjeman: The Last Laugh* (BBC2, 29 December 2001).
3 *Victorian Society archives.*
4 *Ibid.* JB was a member of the Georgian Group. See *JBNFNL*, p. 408.
5 *Victorian Society archives.*
6 *Ibid.*
7 *Ibid.*
8 *Ibid.*
9 Tom Greeves, interview, 1990. 'It was a summer evening,' Greeves recalled of that occasion. 'My friends from the Architecture School said, "I expect he'd like to see a bit of Cambridge afterwards." We gave him some refreshment, and we said, "We won't show him any of the usual sights of Cambridge. We'll show him the sort of things that probably he's never seen before" – the industrial Victorian area of Cambridge which included the gasworks and all those houses round the railway sidings. And he was very polite and said he'd enjoyed it.'
10 Peter Clarke, 'Non-Stopography', *Punch*, 13 October 1954.
11 *Victorian Society archives.*
12 *Ibid.*
13 *Ibid.*
14 *Ibid.*
15 *Ibid.*
16 *Ibid.*
17 Tom Greeves's scrapbook. Shown to the author by the late Tom Greeves.
18 JB had tried to persuade P. Morton Shand to join the Victorian Society, but Shand had replied (21 October 1958, JB, *Letters*, ed. CLG, ii, 148n.): 'Not even you yourself lived in, or *knew*, the Victorian Age. I did, and the horror of it abides with me to this day . . .' JB wrote back to him (28 October 1958, JB, *Letters*, ed. CLG, ii, 148):

> The Victorian Society is necessary of course but it is very hard to get it working on an effective footing, if I may use a rather nice term which all we adminstration boys like to employ. I am surprised and delighted to find that far the best members of the Victorian Society are young men with a burning passion for saving Norman Shaw and those sort of people.

> And Graham Lord, interviewing him for the *Sunday Express* (11 December 1966), wrote: 'Then he will tell you, with a defensive grin, that nearly all the people on his side are under forty. "You won't find the Victorian Society composed of a lot of greybeards . . ."'

19 Ian Grant, interview, 1994.
20 *Ibid.*
21 *Victorian Society archives.*
22 *Ibid.*
23 Ian Grant, interview, 1994.
24 *Ibid.*
25 *Ibid.*
26 *Ibid.*
27 *Ibid.*
28 *Ibid.*
29 *Ibid.*
30 *Victorian Society archives.* 'The Committee . . . instructed the Secretary to write to British Railways asking for information and likewise to the London County Council.'
31 On JB's earlier association with Fleetwood-Hesketh, see *YB*, pp. 362–65.
32 Peter Fleetwood-Hesketh, interview, 1977.

33 Frances Partridge wrote in her diary on 18 July 1965 (*Other People: Diaries 1963–1966*, London 2001 edn., pp. 145–47):

> Doddington Hall, Lincolnshire . . . I took to [Steven Runciman] very much . . . Other guests – who should they be but 'delightful Peter Hesketh', whom Julia marked down years and years ago as a possible husband, now matched with an elderly-looking wife. I wonder what Julia would think of 'delightful Peter' now. He's an architectural expert and for many long hours yesterday – six days – we all racketed around looking at houses all over the flat plate of the Lincolnshire countryside. I enjoyed visiting Grimsthorpe, built by Vanbrugh and inhabited by the Ancasters . . . Lady Ancaster showed us round . . . Then 'delightful Peter' insisted on taking us to look at one of his old homes now an open prison, gloomy, derelict and charmless, and kept up a running commentary of 'There used to be a wood here. My father planted this avenue. There used to be five gates on this road.' Steven Runciman looked round and muttered to me, 'I'm not impressed.' The general conversation in the car was all about properties, inheritances and ancestry. The extraordinary smugness of tone – 'Who was *she*?' 'Oh yes, that belonged to old Lord Liverpool.' 'Oh, was he the one with the wooden leg?' 'Yes, did you know him?' 'Why, very WELL INDEED!' 'Oh, really?' The snobbishness, the slow self-confident drawl in which all these exchanges were made – and they were pursued to incredible lengths – gradually sickened me . . . Boasting, not communication, is the petrol firing these engines of talk. Ideas, where are they?

In 1952 Julia Strachey had in fact married Lawrence Gowing, a painter of the Euston Road group, eighteen years her junior.

34 On 22 October 1970, JB wrote to Rupert and Candida Lycett Green (JB, *Letters*, ed. CLG, ii, 406): 'I liked the curious admixture of booksellers and Fortune Euston and Pe'ter Fle-'it! wood Hésketh. I cannot write down his curious enunciation.'

35 The tape-recording was played to the author by the late Tom Greeves.

36 See *Country Life*, vol. 139, 17 March 1966, pp. 600–04.

37 *Victorian Society archives*.

38 Mario Amaya, 'The Roman World of Alma-Tadema', *Apollo*, December 1962, pp. 771–78.

39 Ian Grant, interview, 1994. There appears to be some confusion here. Nikolaus Pevsner, in *London: The Cities of London and Westminster*, London 1973 edn., p. 220, states that the National Provincial Bank, Bishopsgate, was by John Gibson; in the same book (p. 257n.) he states that the Westminster Bank of 1861 in Lombard Street was by C. O. Parnell – 'Italian in a debased palazzo style' – and that it was replaced by the National Westminster Bank (1963–69) by Mewès & Davis, seven storeys high. It is likely that Grant was referring to the Bishopsgate bank by Gibson.

40 *Victorian Society archives*.

41 *Ibid*.

42 Ian Grant, interview, 1994.

43 *Victorian Society archives*.

44 *Ibid*.

45 *Ibid*. Between 1963 and the present, Fitzjohn's Avenue has been all but ruined by demolitions and rebuilding in styles at variance with the original architecture.

46 Quoted, Ian Grant, interview, 1994.

47 Canon Eric James, typewritten essay sent to the author, 1990.

48 *Victorian Society archives*.

49 Ian Grant, interview, 1994.

50 Dr Timothy Mowl, *Stylistic Cold Wars: Betjeman versus Pevsner*, London 2000.

51 *Ibid*., pp. 29–30.

52 Quoted, *ibid*., p. 83.

53 *Loc. cit*.

54 See *ibid*., p. 84.

55 On JB's friendship with P. Morton Shand, see *YB*, pp. 328–30 and 392–96.

56 Mowl, *op. cit*., p. 95.

57 *Loc. cit.*

58 See *ibid.*, p. 126.

59 Mowl writes (*ibid.*, p. 121); 'John Newman has discovered three instances of Pevsner humour in the forty-six volumes of *The Buildings of England*.' (Mowl suggests a fourth.) By contrast, JB's Shell Guides were full of such asides as (in *Cornwall*) 'If you try to like wasps they will like you.'

60 *Das Englische in der Englischen Kunst* (1931). See Mowl, *op. cit.*, p. 76. In 1955 Pevsner developed the same subject in his Reith Lectures. See Mowl, *op. cit.*, pp. 138–45.

61 Quoted, *ibid.*, p. 157.

62 In other words, somebody who liked the Victorian age for such camp curios as waxed fruit under glass domes, as collected by early enthusiasts for Victoriana, including Robert Byron and Harold Acton.

63 JB to John Summerson, 14 June 1966. JB, *Letters*, ed. CLG, ii, 319.

64 Quoted, Mowl, *op. cit.*, p. 100.

65 The article, 'The Seeing Eye', appeared in *The Architectural Review* in 1939.

66 Quoted, Mowl, *op. cit.*, p. 107.

67 *Ibid.*, p. 106.

68 See Chapter 11, 'The Battle of Bedford Park'.

69 Derwent May, *Critical Times: The History of the Times Literary Supplement*, London 2001, p. 287.

70 *Ibid.*, p. 288.

71 Quoted, *ibid.*, p. 351.

72 Quoted, *ibid.*, p. 286.

73 Mowl, *op. cit.*, p. 113.

74 *Time and Tide*, 12 January 1952, p. 40.

75 JB to James Lees-Milne, 26 March 1952. JB, *Letters*, ed. CLG, ii, 23.

76 JB to P. Morton Shand, 31 October 1952, JB, *Letters*, ed. CLG, ii, 31.

77 JB, *First and Last Loves*, London 1952, p. 5.

78 Mowl, *op. cit.*, p. 126.

79 Quoted, *ibid.*, p. 127.

80 A. L. Rowse, letter to the author, 26 January 1986, quoting Alan Rome and concurring.

81 Father Anthony Symondson SJ, 'John Betjeman and the Cult of JN Comper', *Thirties Society Journal*, No. 7, 1991.

82 JBP.

83 Mowl gives a précis of the review, *op. cit.*, pp. 127–28. He comments, 'John was usually completely at sea on matters Anglo-Saxon, but here his Saxon scholarship was deadly in its accuracy. Either he had spent days researching the review or had taken the informed advice of a local Durham historian.' Alternatively, it is possible that JB consulted such learned friends as John Bryson, Stuart Piggott and Sir Thomas Kendrick.

84 Mowl, *op. cit.*, p. 128.

85 On Clifton-Taylor at Oxford, see *YB*, p. 178.

86 JB to Alec Clifton-Taylor, September 1953. JB, *Letters*, ed. CLG, ii, 43.

87 Quoted, Mowl, *op. cit.*, p. 145.

88 Peter Clarke, 'A Period Piece', *Punch*, 2 November 1955. Clarke originally entitled the poem 'Poet and Pedant', but that was toned down in the title given to the published piece.

89 Shown to the author by the late Ian Grant. The remaining stanzas run:

3
Zu jeder church in London
   Ich schoss in froher Eil
Und hab' schon 'was gefunden
   In echt Rundbogen-style.
'So beefy und hamfisted'.
   Ich hatt' ein damgoodlook
But soon es war gelisted
   In meinem Penguinbook.

4

Ich ging einmal nach Ealing –
  Ach! wie ein schönes dorf –
To list a Georgian ceiling
  Restored by Edward Maufe.
Und dann sofort nach Morden
  Im audo I did scorch
To note a church by Porden,
  Mit 'veryrumourved porch'.

5

To go out on the bendl'
  Ach! das ist wundershön!
Mit Herrn Goodhart-Rendel
  Und Johanu Sommersohn.
Gross Scott! But we are noisy
  Und have such lustigkeit,
We can't distinguish Voysey
  From Temple Moore or Tite.

6

I fly across the Atlantik
  Und talk both day and night
On Baukunst und der Antik
  Und style of Franklloydwright,
Till Hitchcock cries 'Quit stoogin'!
  If ain't no doggone good
To call Augustus Pugin
  'A chip off Sancton Wood.'

7

Once on perambulation
  I walk twelve miles or more
To note an elevation
  In style of Norman Shaw.
The rooms were full of dampness,
  The cellars full of mice.
I note 'Perhaps by Champneys,
  Not specially nice'.

8

All else shall be resisted
  Till ev'ry stone und brick
Is fianlly gelisted
  By Herr Professor N—k.
Mit broadcast, book and lektur
  Rolls in der £.S.D.
Der Britisch Architektur –
  Ach! dats der game for me.

90 See Mowl, *op. cit.*, p. 146.
91 JB to Lady Juliet Smith, 5 December 1963. JB, *Letters*, ed. CLG, ii, 303.
92 JB to John Piper, April 1966. JB, *Letters*, ed. CLG, ii, 303.
93 *Victorian Society archives*.
94 *Ibid.*
95 *Ibid.*
96 Quoted, Tom Greeves, interview, 1990.
97 Ian Grant, interview, 1994.

said, "It's entirely your fault." But it *wasn't.*' Ian Grant, interview, 1994.

Society archives. In 1963 Richard (later Lord) Beeching (1913–90), then chair- the British Railways Board, issued his notorious report suggesting major cuts in 'unprofitable lines'. Between 1965 and 1970 the 'Beeching axe' reduced passenger lines by one-fifth and the number of stations by one-third.

100 *Tom Greeves scrapbook.*
101 Tom Greeves, interview, 1990.
102 *Tom Greeves scrapbook.*
103 Patrick Leigh Fermor, 'In Honour of John Betjeman', *Cornhill Magazine*, Summer 1954, pp. 379–80.
104 Alan Bennett, 'Place-Names of China', *The Faber Book of Parodies*, ed. Simon Brett, London 1984, pp. 58–59.
105 *Tom Greeves scrapbook.*
106 *Ibid.*
107 *Ibid.*
108 *Ibid.*
109 See *YB*, pp. 378–79.
110 'Britain's national austerity favoured cheap solutions to architectural problems, and cheap solutions tended to be logical Modernist ones.' Mowl, *op. cit.*, p. 114. JB's view had been expressed in *The Architectural Review* in September 1939, the month war broke out:

> Instead of despairing of what we have always been told is ugly and meretricious, [John Piper] has accepted it at its face value and brought it to life. He has made us look a second time, without any sense of satire, moral indignation or aesthetic horror. He has done the job of an artist.

111 Mowl, *op. cit.*, p. 166.
112 JB, 'Death in Leamington', *Collected Poems*, 2003 edn., p. 2.
113 JB, *Letters*, ed. CLG, ii, 470n.

Chapter 3: The Daily Telegraph

1 Roger Chetwode, Penelope's brother, committed suicide on 14 August 1940. Osbert Lancaster commented (interview, 1978): 'When war came, those field-marshals' sons found it impossible to live up to their fathers' records; they felt inadequate. Lord Gort's son [the Hon. C. S. Vereker] also took his own life.' As recorded in *YB* (p. 404), the late Lord Longford thought that 'John's kindness and sympathy after Roger Chetwode committed suicide . . . (when John called on the Field-Marshal and wisely insisted he continue to go to work to take his mind off the tragedy)' finally ended the animosity which had existed between John and his father-in-law.

Anthony Powell wrote in his journal, 6 July 1988 (*Journals 1987–1989*, London 1996, p. 119):

> Roger Chetwode (who seemed a reasonably nice Lower Boy, was a contemporary of mine at school) apparently played a malign part in anti-Betjeman behaviour after the marriage [of JB and Penelope]. An interesting aspect of this is that Roger Chetwode, if hearty, was also by no means a fool, even tho' lacking in Betjeman's poetic 'cultural' gifts, an extrovert, jolly in manner, a terrific social snob and climber, go-getter in busi- ness (he made a fortune on Wall Street in his early twenties), he was at the same time, like Betjeman in many of these characteristics, also deeply melancholic. Indeed, for no apparent reason, he committed suicide at the beginning of the war. No doubt Betjeman's poetry and his religiosity kept him from suicide, as similar characteristics might have done for Roger Chetwode *mutatis mutandis*.

2 JB to Nicolas Bentley, [? December] 1931, JB, *Letters*, ed. CLG, i, 86.
3 Sir Osbert Lancaster, interview, 1978.
4 Powell, *op. cit.*, pp. 61–62.

5 Duff Hart-Davis, *The House the Berrys Built*, London 1990, p. 20.
6 *Loc. cit.* Kenneth Rose, who reviewed books alongside JB during Ziman's tenure, writes of
'Z' (letter to the author, 23 November 1996): 'He was a ghastly fellow. He would say to the
most distinguished reviewers, "I hope you will not begin your review, 'This book . . .'"'
7 *Daily Telegraph*, 1 June 1983.
8 *Daily Telegraph*, 28 March 1952.
9 *Daily Telegraph*, 18 January 1952.
10 Thom Gunn, 'Elvis Presley', *The Sense of Movement*, London 1957, p. 31.
11 *Daily Telegraph*, 5 February 1954.
12 *Daily Telegraph*, 13 February 1954.
13 *Daily Telegraph*, 20 March 1953.
14 *Daily Telegraph*, 14 March 1952.

> Barbara Pym is a splendid humorous writer. She writes about that world which is much
> bigger than people suppose, of professional men – clergymen, doctors' widows, the
> higher but not the top grades of the Civil Service, naval officers and their wives,
> gentlewomen who are not yet quite distressed. There are those who will find 'Excellent
> Women' tame, with its fussing over church bazaars, 'high' and 'low' churchmanship,
> a boiled egg for lunch and a cup of tea before going to bed, but to me it is a perfect
> book . . . Conscious charm by a professional ladies' man, quarrelsomeness from an old
> school friend, rows about where to put the lilies in the chancel at Easter, are subjects
> which suit her acid powers of description. 'Excellent Women' is England, and, thank
> goodness, it is full of them.

15 *A Very Private Eye: The Diaries, Letters and Notebooks of Barbara Pym*, ed. Hazel Holt
and Hilary Pym, London 1984, entry of 4 March 1938, p. 65.
16 Letter to 'Jock' (Robert Liddell), 23 May 1938. *Ibid.*, p. 81.
17 Quoted Hazel Holt, *A Lot to Ask: A Life of Barbara Pym*, London 1990, p. 160.
18 *Loc. cit.*
19 *Daily Telegraph*, 31 August 1956.
20 *Daily Telegraph*, 29 March 1956.
21 Dame Catherine Cookson, letter to the author, 15 November 1996.
22 *Daily Telegraph*, 16 November 1951.
23 *Daily Telegraph*, 7 November 1958.
24 *Daily Telegraph*, 4 March 1955.
25 *Daily Telegraph*, 20 June 1958.
26 *Ibid.*
27 *Daily Telegraph*, 19 July 1957.
28 *Daily Telegraph*, 27 February 1953.
29 *Daily Telegraph*, 10 April 1953.
30 *Daily Telegraph*, 27 February 1953.
31 *Daily Telegraph*, 1 August 1952.
32 *Daily Telegraph*, 31 October 1952.
33 *Daily Telegraph*, 14 November 1958.
34 In this he took much the same view as Evelyn Waugh. When Waugh was interviewed by
Julian Jebb for the *Paris Review* in 1962, the following interchange took place:

> *Jebb*: Does this [an interest in drama, speech and events] mean that you continually
> refine and experiment?
> *Waugh*: Experiment? God forbid! Look at the results of experiment in the case of a
> writer like Joyce. He started off writing very well, then you watch him going mad
> with vanity. He ends up a lunatic. (*A Dedicated Fan: Julian Jebb 1934–1984*,
> ed. Tristram and Georgia Powell, London 1993, p. 65.)

35 *Daily Telegraph*, 22 May 1953.
36 *Summoned by Bells*, London 1960, p. 43.
37 *Daily Telegraph*, 8 May 1953.
38 *Daily Telegraph*, 7 November 1952.

39　*Daily Telegraph*, 8 July 1955.

40　*Daily Telegraph*, 5 July 1957.

41　*Daily Telegraph*, 3 June 1960.

42　*Daily Telegraph*, 9 November 1956.

43　*Daily Telegraph*, 22 February 1952.

44　*Daily Telegraph*, 28 May 1954.

45　*Daily Telegraph*, 16 April 1953.

46　*Daily Telegraph*, 30 June 1951.

47　*Daily Telegraph*, 28 December 1951.

48　*Daily Telegraph*, 9 February 1951. Through his friendship with W. H. Auden, JB was a friendly acquaintance of Christopher Isherwood.

49　*Daily Telegraph*, 16 February 1951.

50　*Daily Telegraph*, 18 January 1952.

51　*Daily Telegraph*, 22 November 1957.

52　*Daily Telegraph*, 9 January 1959.

53　*Daily Telegraph*, 28 September 1956.

54　*Daily Telegraph*, 10 August 1951.

55　*Daily Telegraph*, 7 March 1952.

56　Edmund Wilson, diary entry for 12 January 1954. *The Fifties: From Notebooks and Diaries of the Period*, ed. Leon Edel, New York 1986, p. 116.

57　*Daily Telegraph*, 23 December 1955.

58　*Daily Telegraph*, 14 November 1952.

59　JB to Alan Pryce-Jones, 25 February 1951. JB, *Letters*, ed. CLG, i, 532.

60　*Ibid.*, i, 532n.

61　*Daily Telegraph*, 2 March 1951.

62　*Daily Telegraph*, 6 November 1953.

63　*Daily Telegraph*, 17 November 1954.

64　JB, *Letters*, ed. CLG, ii, 45n.

65　JB to Patrick Kinross, 9 October 1953. JB, *Letters*, ed. CLG, ii, p. 45.

66　*Daily Telegraph*, 10 June 1955.

67　*Daily Telegraph*, 3 February 1956.

68　*Daily Telegraph*, 13 September 1958.

69　*Daily Telegraph*, 11 May 1951.

70　*Daily Telegraph*, 16 July 1951.

71　See Evelyn Waugh to Nancy Mitford, 23 March [1951]. *The Letters of Nancy Mitford & Evelyn Waugh*, ed. Charlotte Mosley, London 1996, p. 215.

72　*Collected Poems*, 2003 edn., p. 273.

73　*Summoned by Bells*, London 1960, p. 66.

74　*Daily Telegraph*, 10 November 1952.

75　*Daily Telegraph*, 22 January 1954.

76　*Collected Poems*, 2003 edn., p. 160.

77　*Daily Telegraph*, 10 June 1951.

78　*Collected Poems*, 2003 edn., p. 288.

79　*Daily Telegraph*, 1 May 1959.

80　*Collected Poems*, 2003 edn., p. 289.

81　*Daily Telegraph*, 11 June 1954.

82　*Daily Telegraph*, 27 May 1955.

83　*Daily Telegraph*, 2 March 1956.

84　*Daily Telegraph*, 28 February 1958.

85　*Daily Telegraph*, 5 August 1955.

86　*Daily Telegraph*, 21 November 1960.

87　*Daily Telegraph*, 15 May 1957.

88　*Daily Telegraph*, 31 October 1958.

89　*Loc. cit.*

90　*Daily Telegraph*, 23 October 1959.

91　*Daily Telegraph*, 7 June 1957.

92 James Kirkup, *A Poet Could Not But Be Gay*, London 1991, p. 27.

93 Walter Ison, letter to the author, 21 March 1997.

94 Christopher Woodward, obituary of Leonora Ison, *The Independent*, 16 December 1996.

95 Quoted, Walter Ison, letter to the author, 21 March 1997.

96 Leonora Ison was born at Wendover on 4 July 1904, the third child of Edward John Payne and his wife Emma Helena Leonora (*née* Pertz). Her father was a fellow of University College, Oxford, Recorder of Wycombe, a historian, musicologist and expert on the violin and the viola da gamba. Leonora's mother had two eminent grandfathers: James John Garth Wilkinson (1812–99), a homeopathic physician who translated Emanuel Swedenborg's works and was a friend of Henry James; and the German historian Georg Heinrich Pertz (1795–1816), editor of the *Monumenta Germaniae Historica* and court librarian first in Hanover and later in Berlin. (*Ex inf.* Walter Ison, typewritten essay on his late wife sent to the author with his letter of 21 March 1997.)

97 On JB's dealings with Robert Harling, see *JBNFNL*, pp. 126–31, 133–34 and 138.

98 Walter Ison, letter to the author, 21 March 1997.

99 JB to Leonora Ison, 28 March 1961. Shown to the author by the late Walter Ison.

100 JB to Leonora Ison, 10 October 1961. Shown to the author by the late Walter Ison.

101 JB to Leonora Ison, 22 February 1962. Shown to the author by the late Walter Ison.

102 JB to Leonora Ison, 19 September 1962. Shown to the author by the late Walter Ison.

103 See *JBNFNL*, pp. 517–18, on which Leonora Ison's drawings of the Rotherhithe buildings are reproduced.

104 JB to Leonora Ison, 10 February 1964. Shown to the author by the late Walter Ison.

105 Walter Ison explained (letter to the author, 21 March 1997): ' "Old Cartographer". This appellation came about during a rather bibulous dinner at the House of Lords attended by JB and his guest, my wife. I think it was given by [Ivor] Bulmer-Thomas for the Friends of Friendless Churches. On parting JB sent me a greeting, but said "Cartographer" instead of the intended "Topographer", referring to my work on The Survey of London.' JB mentioned 'the Old Cartographer' or 'the OC' in nearly all his letters to Leonora Ison.

106 JB to Leonora Ison, 27 July 1964. Shown to the author by the late Walter Ison.

107 Another example of JB's thoughtfulness towards Leonora Ison: 'I enclose my article for our next assault. It seems cruel to ask you to go to Peterborough in this weather, and we have already illustrated the west front of the cathedral so that is out . . .' (JB to Leonora Ison, 13 January 1964. Shown to the author by the late Walter Ison).

108 JB to Leonora Ison, 27 July 1964. Shown to the author by the late Walter Ison.

109 Walter Ison, letter to the author, 8 March 1997.

110 Frank Delaney, *Betjeman Country*, London 1983, p. 12.

111 In the early 1980s, the present author was one of the late John Anstey's features editors.

112 JB to Mary Wilson, 27 June 1969. JB, *Letters*, ed. CLG, ii, 383.

113 JB to Patrick Leigh Fermor, 18 October 1969. JB, *Letters*, ed. CLG, ii, 392.

Chapter 4: Summoned by Bells

1 C. R. N. (Dick) Routh, an Eton master who compiled a small dictionary of national biography.

2 (Sir) Rupert Hart-Davis (1907–99), publisher. He was a friend of JB. On 16 November 1958 he wrote to George Lyttelton (see note 3) that he had just attended Rose Macaulay's memorial service. 'Betjeman, unusually neat in a tail-coat, read the lesson very well . . . Outside afterwards Betjeman rather spoiled his effect by wearing a battered brown round pork pie hat, which combined with the tail-coat to give an effect of the Crazy Gang.' (*The Lyttelton Hart-Davis Letters 1955–1962: A Selection*, ed. Roger Hudson, London 2001, p. 166.)

3 The Hon. George Lyttelton (1883–1962), second son of the fifth Lord Lyttelton (who later became the eighth Viscount Cobham). Eton housemaster. Like Rupert Hart-Davis (see note 2), he was a friend of JB. On 12 February 1959 he wrote to Hart-Davis: 'After good-nighting you [at the Literary Society], Roger [? Fulford], Betjeman and I drifted into a neighbouring pub where hoi polloi were in force. We were the only men wearing hats

and they came in for a good deal of derision – J.B.'s rightly, for it was almost non-existent in depth, and sat on the noble brow like the crest of a waxwing . . .' (*ibid.*, p. 177).

4 Stephen Spender wrote:

> Who live under the shadow of a war,
> What can I do that matters? . . .
>
> (Spender, *Collected Poems*, London 1955, p. 37.)

5 'You know, I think it's only when we're young that an autobiography is interesting That's why I ended mine at this point [just after Oxford] because it still has in it things we share in common – struggles at home, struggles at school and then struggles to get a job.' JB, BBC television film *Summoned by Bells*, produced by Jonathan Stedall, 1976.

6 Cecil Roberts (1892–1976), author and journalist.

The late Dr A. L. Rowse wrote of Roberts (letter to the author, 17 July 1990), 'It was well known that as a young man he had been the Duke of Kent's lover; he boasted of it.'

Roberts first met JB in 1929 when the poet was twenty-three (Roberts, *The Bright Twenties*, London 1970, p. 400), beginning 'a lifelong friendship'. The two met from time to time, often at the Garrick Club. In another volume of his memoirs (*The Pleasant Years*, London 1974, p. 115), Roberts describes an encounter with JB in August 1952:

The day after my return [from a trip to Leicestershire] John Betjeman came to lunch, from his home at Wantage. His eyes were shining when he walked in. He told me he had had an encounter with his Muse while motoring over the Chilterns. He had composed a poem! Standing there by the hearth, he recited it. And since one poem deserves another, I wrote one, about his hat which, on leaving, he forgot. I hesitated about posting the hat to him. It was an old brown felt one, shapeless, greasy, with the band missing and two holes in the crown. It seemed hardly worth the postage, but I sent it, knowing one has an affection for old things. My friend Norman Birkett [Lord Birkett of Ulverston] learned my poem, 'The Old Brown Hat', by heart and recited it in the Judges' Robing Room at the Law Courts to a fellow Lord of Appeal who liked poetry.

Roberts's poem, 'The Old Brown Hat (John Betjeman's)', is printed in his *Selected Poems 1910–1960*, London 1960, p. 137 and begins:

> From Wantage way, half-Horace and half-Puck,
> You came when Spring renewed the meads, and stood,
> One foot upon my fender, fresh in luck
> From an encounter in a Chiltern wood . . .

and ends:

> Later, when you had gone, and wondering at
> The spell that words have put on us long years,
> I suddenly saw your old brown, battered hat,
> Forgotten – and, somehow, came near to tears.

7 Cecil Roberts, *The Pleasant Years*, London 1974, p. 236.
8 Quoted, *loc. cit.*
9 *John Murray archives.*
10 John G. Murray, conversation with the author, 1963.
11 *John Murray archives.*
12 *Ibid.*
13 *Ibid.*
14 See *YB*, p. 118.
15 *John Murray archives.*
16 *Ibid.*
17 *Ibid.*

18 *Ibid.*
19 *Ibid.*
20 *Ibid.*
21 *Ibid.*
22 *Ibid.*
23 *Ibid.*
24 *Ibid.*
25 *Ibid.*
26 *Ibid.*
27 *Ibid.*
28 *Ibid.*
29 Sir Osbert Lancaster, interview, 1978.
30 *John Murray archives.*
31 *Ibid.*
32 JB to CLG, November 1959. JB, *Letters*, ed. CLG, ii, 156.
33 JB to PB, 10 February 1960. JB, *Letters*, ed. CLG, ii, 156.
34 *John Murray archives.*
35 *Ibid.*
36 *Ibid.*
37 John Murray, publishers, owned the *Cornhill Magazine*, founded in 1860 and once edited by W. M. Thackeray. It folded in 1975.
38 *John Murray archives.* The poem, 'Edward James', had appeared in *Punch* on 29 October 1958.
39 *John Murray archives.*
40 *Ibid.*
41 *Ibid.*
42 *Ibid.* Derek Stanford's *John Betjeman* was published by Neville Spearman, London, in 1961.
43 *John Murray archives.*
44 *Ibid.*
45 *Ibid.*
46 *Ibid.*
47 *Ibid.*
48 *Ibid.*
49 *Ibid.*
50 *Ibid.*
51 *Ibid.*
52 *Ibid.*
53 *Ibid.*
54 *Ibid.*
55 *Ibid.*
56 *Ibid.* George Malcolm Thomson (1899–1996), journalist and author; sometime editor of the *Daily Express*.
57 *Ibid.* The Rev. Marcus Morris (1915–89), who had founded the boys' comic *Eagle* in 1950, was managing director of the National Magazine Company, the British subsidiary of Hearst in New York, which owned *Harper's Bazaar* (later amalgamated with *The Queen*), *Good Housekeeping* and other magazines. See Sally Morris and Jan Hallwood, *Living with Eagles: Marcus Morris, Priest and Publisher*, Cambridge 1998.
58 Douglas Cleverdon (1903–87) had been a friend of JB's at Oxford. He was features producer of the BBC, London, 1943–69. On him, see *JBNFNL*, p. 524. His wife, Nest, also a friend of JB, died in 2004.
59 *John Murray archives.*
60 *Ibid.*
61 *Ibid.*
62 *Ibid.*
63 *Ibid.*

64 *Ibid.*

65 JB supplied the somewhat imprecise explanation: 'Blob work is an expression for a kind of child's painting fashionable in the early part of the [twentieth] century.' Mrs White also wanted to know what 'Oxford marmalade' was. JB wrote: 'Cooper's Oxford marmalade manufactured near the railway station is to be found on the breakfast tables of all dons and the more discerning undergraduates. The words "Oxford marmalade" are sufficient to suggest the other dishes which make an Oxford breakfast.' *John Murray archives.*

66 *John Murray archives.*

67 *Ibid.*

68 *Ibid.*

69 *Ibid.*

70 *Ibid.*

71 On the Addison Road house see B. Hillier, *Pottery and Porcelain 1700–1914*, London 1968, pp. 255–56 and colour plate XII. On Halsey Ricardo, see Michael Holroyd, *Lytton Strachey*, vol. i, *The Unknown Years*, London 1967, p. 28.

73 *John Murray archives.*

74 *Ibid.*

75 *Ibid.*

76 *Ibid.*

77 *Ibid.*

78 *Ibid.*

79 *Ibid.*

80 *Ibid.*

81 Philip Larkin, 'The Blending of Betjeman', *The Spectator*, 2 December 1960.

82 *John Murray archives.*

83 *Ibid.*

84 For a reproduction of the cartoon, see *JBLP*, p. 121.

85 *John Murray archives.*

86 *Ibid.*

87 *Ibid.*

88 Cutting in *ibid.*

89 *Ibid.*

90 *Ibid.*

91 *Ibid.*

92 *Ibid.*

93 *Ibid.*

94 George Seferis (real name Georgios Seferiadis) (1900–71), Greek poet, essayist and diplomat. He was Greek Ambassador in London, 1957–62. In 1963 he won the Nobel Prize for Literature.

95 *John Murray archives.*

96 Philip Harding had been at Marlborough and Oxford with JB (see *YB*, pp. 101, 108, 111, 113, 129, 132, 168, 191 and 360). He remained a friend and usually stayed with the Betjemans at Christmas when the couple were still together. JB was mildly satirical about him in a letter of 4 June 1965 to Deirdre Connolly: 'Philip Harding, Cyril will recall, is the brother of the late Archie Harding. "Everything he touches turns to ashes," as his sister-in-law once said to me, and now he edits those extraordinary supplements thrown away with *The Times*' (JB, *Letters*, ed. CLG, ii, 293).

But Harding was *not* a bore, as the present author, who was appointed to his first job by him, and whose first boss he was, can testify.

97 Sandy Baird: presumably Seymour Alexander McDonald Baird, BA at Magdalen College, Oxford, 1925.

98 Alexander Gray Macindoe matriculated at Magdalen College, Oxford, in 1925, as did JB.

99 Denzil Templer Branch matriculated at Magdalen College, Oxford, in 1925, as did JB.

100 On Kolkhorst's nickname, as remembered by JB, see *YB*, p. 142.

101 Michael Dugdale, diary entry for 28 November 1960. Shown to the author by Dugdale's sister, Frances, Lady Fergusson of Kilkerran.

102 *John Murray archives*.
103 *The Observer*, 27 November 1960.
104 *Punch*, 28 December 1960, p. 951.
105 *Sunday Times*, 27 November 1960.
106 *Sunday Express*, 27 November 1960.
107 *Newsweek*, 5 December 1960.
108 *Daily Express*, 29 November 1960.
109 *John Murray archives*.
110 *Ibid.*
111 *The Bookman*, November 1960.
112 JB to William Plomer, 3 December 1960. JB, *Letters*, ed. CLG, ii, 194.
113 *John Murray archives*.
114 *The Spectator*, 2 December 1960.
115 *John Murray archives*.
116 Dr F. R. Leavis (1895–1978), Fellow of Downing College, Cambridge, editor of *Scrutiny*, 1932–53 and author of books establishing a narrow, dogmatic canon of 'approved' works of English literature. A hammer of writers whom he considered unserious.
117 Rupert Hart-Davis to George Lyttelton, 12 January 1961. *The Lyttelton Hart-Davis Letters 1955–1962: A Selection*, ed. Roger Hudson, London 2001, p. 292.
118 Martyn Skinner papers, Bodleian Library, Oxford.
119 *Collected Poems*, 2003 edn., p. 263.
120 On 30 March 1960, Edward James wrote to JB:

> My dear John,
> How are you? How is Penelope? Bless you both! I trust you are flourishing as you deserve to be. Would your boy be large enough to fit into one of the suits I had made for me before the War – and never wore, because I had grown out of it before the tailor (Radford Jones) delivered it? So it is still as good as new. Or would he be too big for it? I cannot quite calculate what age he would be. I used to be still very slender in 1939; but I am not tall. Is he a giant now?
> You may be surprised to hear from me after so many years. You may also have been hurt, perhaps, not to hear from me fully – after the poem which appeared in *Punch*. It amused me and touched me deeply. Also it was all true, even the more improbable details . . . (*Victoria*.)

121 See note 42 to the present chapter.
122 *The Observer*, 14 March 1961.
123 *Sunday Times*, 27 November 1960.

Chapter 5: Back to Cloth Fair

1 JB, *Letters*, ed. CLG, ii, 153.
2 JB, conversation with the author, 1972.
3 Osbert Lancaster, conversation with the author, 1978.
4 JB, *Letters*, ed. CLG, ii, 374.
5 *Ibid.*, 153.
6 *Loc. cit.*
7 Harry Jarvis, CLG interview, 1994. JB, *Letters*, ed. CLG, ii, 154.
8 JB, *Letters*, ed. CLG, ii, 153.
9 *Ibid.*, 154.
10 JB to Harry Jarvis, 19 August 1960. JB, *Letters*, ed. CLG, ii, 154.
11 JB, *Letters*, ed. CLG, ii, 59.
12 JB to Jack Beddington, 2 January 1954. JB, *Letters*, ed. CLG, ii, 154.
13 According to CLG: JB, *Letters*, ed. CLG, ii, 59.
14 *Collected Poems*, 2003 edn., p. 282.
15 JB, *Letters*, ed. CLG, ii, 84n.

16 JB to PB, 19 August 1955. JB, *Letters*, ed. CLG, ii, 84.

17 *Collected Poems*, 2003 edn., p. 234. CLG confirms the poem is 'about E[lizabeth] C[avendish]': JB, *Letters*, ed. CLG, ii, 84n.

18 JB to the Rev. Harry Williams, 25 March 1960. JB, *Letters*, ed. CLG, ii, 184–85.

19 Harry Jarvis, CLG interview, 1994. JB, *Letters*, ed. CLG, ii, 154.

20 *Collected Poems*, 2003 edn., p. 365.

21 Kenneth Allsop (1920–73), television presenter and author.

22 *Daily Mail*, 9 December 1960.

23 *Ibid*. Ella Wheeler Wilcox (1855–1919) was the trite American versifier who wrote:

> Laugh, and the world laughs with you;
> Weep, and you weep alone . . .

24 JB drew a picture of the millipede in a letter to Candida, 19 February 1958. JB, *Letters*, ed. CLG, ii, 157.

25 *Everywoman*, December 1960.

26 *Ibid*.

27 *Ibid*.

28 Sir Gerald Kelly, PRA (1879–1972). The artist, who had once shared a house with Monet (conversation with Sir Gerald Kelly, 1960), painted portraits of W. Somerset Maugham and T.S. Eliot. (The latter is illustrated in *JBNFNL*, plate 16.) Reproductions of his paintings of a Burmese girl were bestsellers in the 1950s. His sister married Aleister Crowley, the black magician.

29 The magazine used these words of JB, broken up, under a series of photographs of him. (See *JBNFNL*, Plate 68.)

30 *Everywoman*, December 1960.

31 JB, *Letters*, ed. CLG, ii, 155.

32 *Ibid.*, 255.

33 John G. Murray, speech at P.E.N., 1984.

34 JB, *Letters*, ed. CLG, ii, 115n.

35 Part of JB's letter to Ian Fleming is quoted by Andrew Lycett, *Ian Fleming*, London 1995, pp. 432–33.

36 Ian Fleming to JB, 10 December 1963. JB, *Letters*, ed. CLG, ii, 254. Fleming went on to say that JB's world would 'outlive by centuries the rather grimy vulgarities of my friend James Bond'.

Chapter 6: The Euston Arch

1 Quoted *Manchester Guardian*, 12 March 1955; and see *JBNFNL*, p. 500.

2 Other examples: William Langland was believed to have foretold the Reformation with a line in *Piers Plowman*, 'then shall the abbot of Abingdon get a knock of the king . . .'. In the essay in which Karl Marx suggested that 'History always repeats itself, the first time as tragedy, the second time as farce,' he referred to the way the French revolutionaries of the 1790s had mimicked the moralistic bloodletting of the ancient Romans; but in the 1590s Shakespeare had already predicted that emulation, in *Julius Caesar*:

> Brutus: . . . How many ages hence
>   Shall this our lofty scene be acted over,
>   In states unborn, and accents yet unknown!

In his Moral Essay 'On the Use of Riches', Pope forecast the destruction of the Duke of Chandos's great house, Canons –

> Another age shall see the golden ear
> Embrown the slope and nod on the parterre,
> Deep harvests bury all his pride has planned
> And laughing Ceres reassume the land.

In 'Locksley Hall', Tennyson clairvoyantly predicted commercial airlines, bombing and aeroplane dog-fights –

> For I dipt into the future, far as human eye could see,
> Saw the Vision of the world, and all the wonder that would be;
>
> Saw the heavens fill with commerce, argosies of magic sails,
> Pilots of the purple twilight, dropping down with costly bales;
>
> Heard the heavens fill with shouting, and there rained a ghastly dew
> From the nations' airy navies grappling in the central blue . . .

(Tennyson was again anticipated by Shakespeare's *Julius Caesar* (II, 2) –

> Calphurnia: . . . Fierce fiery warriors fought upon the clouds
>   In ranks and squadrons and right form of war . . .

Even the choice of words – Shakespeare's 'squadrons', Tennyson's 'Pilots' – is seer-like.)

In 1867 Thomas Hardy wrote a poem entitled '1967', mentioning summer and love – a hundred years before the Summer of Love. And Kipling in his poem 'Romance' satirized the way Victorians looked back on bows and arrows and sailing ships as romantic; he guessed that one day people would feel the same way about the steam trains of his own age –

> Confound Romance! and, all unseen,
> Romance brought up the Nine Fifteen.

JB was the living fulfilment of that prophecy. A further example of *his* prescience: speaking of Lindsey House, Chelsea, formerly the house of Count Zinzendorf, the eighteenth-century leader of the Moravians, he said to Bryan Guinness: 'There I believe you are going to live,' and he lived there for two years (JB, *Letters*, ed. CLG, i, 107).

3 *The Architectural Review*, vol. 74, September 1933, opposite p. 105.
4 *One Foot in the Past* (BBC2 television), June 1993.
5 The Transport Act of 1947 largely nationalized the railways of Britain, under a Labour government. The Act replaced the railway companies by a British Transport Commission (BTC), an Executive and a number of regions. The BTC – reporting to the Minister of Transport – controlled the Railway Executive (RE) and other divisions of transport, including roads and inland waterways. Under the Executive, six new regions were established: Eastern, London Midland, North Eastern, Scotland, Southern and Western – with their headquarters, respectively, at London (Liverpool Street), London (Euston), York, Glasgow, London (Waterloo) and London (Paddington). By mid-1948 the title 'British Railways' was being used on locomotives and station notices.
   Under a Conservative government, the Transport Act of 1953 abolished the RE and gave greater authority to the regions. Between 1953 and 1962 the BTC managed the British Railways divisions. By the Transport Act of 1962 the BTC was dissolved and separate boards were set up for each of the main services formerly run by the Board, including British Railways. In a 'streamlining' of the early 1960s, the name 'British Railways' was changed to 'British Rail'.
6 Bernard Kaukas, interview, 1990.
7 Quoted *ibid*.
8 *Ex inf.* Bernard Kaukas, interview, 1990.
9 JB, *Letters*, ed. CLG, ii, 181n.
10 Quoted by Lord Eccles, conversation with the author, 1969.
11 See *JBNFNL*, pp. 567, 569.
12 Lord Wyatt, interview, 1995.
13 JB, *Letters*, ed. CLG, ii, 180–81.

14 *The Times*, 23 April 1960.

15 On the Betjemans' attendance at the royal wedding, see Chapter 1, 'Wantage', of the present volume.

16 In *Birmingham Buildings*, Newton Abbot 1971, JB's friend Bryan Little (see *JBNFNL*, p. 273) illustrates Philip Hardwick's Curzon Street terminus at Birmingham (finished 1838), which survived as a goods depot.

17 Sir Frank Markham MP, letter to *The Times*, 28 June 1960.

18 *The Times*, 6 July 1960.

19 On the dispute over the rose garden, see B. Hillier, 'The Boase Garden', *The Betjemanian*, vol. 9, 1997–98, pp. 10–38.

20 *The Times*, 22 July 1960.

21 *Loc. cit.*

22 *Daily Express*, 19 April 1960.

23 *The Times*, 22 April 1961.

24 Edward, Lord Bridges (1892–1969), son of the Poet Laureate Robert Bridges, was chairman of the Royal Fine Art Commission, 1957–58, and of the British Council, 1959–67. JB greatly disliked him and Bridges is the 'senior civil servant' of the Betjeman poem 'Mortality' (*Collected Poems*, 2003 edn., p. 288). One of JB's main objections to Bridges was that he had – in JB's view – 'stuffed the RFAC with *practising* architects who were the bugbear of his predecessor David [Lord] Crawford', converting it from a Royal Fine Art Commission into a 'Royal Fine Architecture Commission' offering 'jobs for the boys'. (JB to James Lees-Milne, 3 April 1963. JB, *Letters*, ed. CLG, ii, 244–45.) JB thought that laymen should preponderate on the RFAC; practising architects might tend to allow old buildings to be demolished to make room for their new ones.

25 *The Times*, 27 September 1961.

26 This clip of film was shown in Dr Dan Cruikshank's contribution to *One Foot in the Past* (BBC2 television), June 1993.

27 *The Times*, 17 October 1961.

28 *Ibid.*

29 J.M. Richards, *Memoirs of an Unjust Fella*, London 1980, p. 216.

30 *The Times*, 17 October 1961.

31 *Loc. cit.*

32 Richards, *op. cit.*, p. 216.

33 *Loc. cit.*

34 Sir Hamilton Kerr, first Bt. (1903–74). Conservative MP for Oldham, 1931–45; for Cambridge, 1950–66. Parliamentary private secretary to Harold Macmillan in the Fifties, when Macmillan was Foreign Secretary and Chancellor of the Exchequer.

35 Peter Fleetwood-Hesketh, interview, 1977.

36 Sir Hugh Casson, in *One Foot in the Past* (BBC2 television), June 1993.

37 José Manser, *Hugh Casson: A Biography*, London 2000, p. 208.

38 Alistair Horne, *Macmillan 1957–1986* (vol. ii of the official biography), London 1989, p. 252. In a footnote, Horne refers to Macmillan's diary for 24 October 1961.

39 *The Times*, 4 November 1961.

40 Bernard Kaukas, interview, 1990.

41 *The Times*, 7 November 1961.

42 'Mr Valori, who is getting £12,000 for the job – too small a sum to include the dismantling and numbering of the immense blocks of sandstone – says that £50,000 could still save the arch.' Astragal, *The Architects' Journal*, 11 October 1961, p. 585. (As that issue went to press, scaffolding was going up but demolition had not yet begun. By that stage the Victorian Society had raised only £800.)

43 *The Times*, 7 March 1962.

44 Anecdote relayed to the author by Sir Simon Jenkins.

45 Bernard Kaukas, interview, 1990.

46 Bernard Levin, *The Pendulum Years: Britain in the Sixties*, London 1970, p. 44.

47 JB and John Gay, *London's Historic Railway Stations*, London 1972, pp. 125–26.

48 Quoted by Sir John Summerson, interview, 1977.

49 Alison and Peter Smithson, who had met at Durham University and married in 1949, later designed the Economist building, London (1959–64), the British embassy, Brasilia (1964–65), Robin Hood Gardens, London (1966–70) and the Garden Building of St Hilda's College, Oxford (1967–70), but their main contribution to architecture was as theorists and propagandists.

50 Alison and Peter Smithson, *The Euston Arch and the Growth of the London, Midland and Scottish Railway*, London 1968, p. 7.

51 *The Times*, 14 October 1968.

52 Oliver Marriott, *The Property Boom*, London 1967, p. 158.

53 *Ibid.*, p. 161.

54 *Ibid.*, p. 164.

55 See *ibid.*, p. 165, for a summary of Hillman's article of July 1964.

56 Marriott, *op. cit.*, p. 166.

57 Bernard Kaukas, interview, 1990.

Chapter 7: Australia 1961

1 The deputation to Harold Macmillan, of which JB was a member, presented its case on 24 October, five days before JB flew to Singapore and Australia.

2 JB to PB, 21 October 1961. *JBP*.

3 JB to PB, 27 October 1961. *JBP*.

4 JB to PB, 25 October 1961. *JBP*.

5 JB to PB, n.d. *JBP*. The injunction was accompanied by a drawing of PB being shot at by brigands.

6 JB, 'Aspects of Australia', *Vogue* (London), February 1963, p. 101.

7 Nevil Shute (real name Nevil Shute Norway) (1899–1960), English-born Australian novelist. JB had known him in his (JB's) childhood, when Shute stayed at Rock, Cornwall, near the Betjemanns' holiday home at Trebetherick. Shute emigrated to Australia after the Second World War. His novels include *A Town Like Alice* (1950) and *On the Beach* (1957).

8 JB, 'Aspects of Australia', *Vogue* (London), February 1963, p. 101.

9 *The New Oxford Book of Australian Verse*, chosen by Les A. Murray, Oxford 1986, p. 50.

10 'Dreams', *The Oxford Book of Australian Literature*, ed. Leonie Kramer and Adrian Mitchell, Melbourne 1985, p. 727.

11 Douglas Stewart, 'Two Englishmen', *Collected Poems 1936–1967*, Sydney 1967, p. 13.

12 *The New Oxford Book of Australian Verse*, chosen by Les A. Murray, Oxford 1986, p. 189.

13 Douglas Stewart, 'A Country Song', *ibid.*, p. 50. 'Brumby (also brumbee, brumble): Australian word (origin unknown) for a wild or unbroken horse' (*OED*).

14 Judith Wright, 'The Blind Man', *A Human Pattern: Selected Poems*, London 1992 edn., p. 39.

15 JB to PB, 31 October 1961. *JBP*.

16 *Ibid.*

17 *Ibid.*

18 *Ibid.*

19 JB to PB, 1 November 1961. *JBP*.

20 *Ibid.*

21 *Ibid.*

22 JB to PB, 4 November 1961. *JBP*.

23 *Ibid.*

24 JB to PB, 7 November 1961. *JBP*.

25 JB to PB, 11 November 1961. *JBP*.

26 Rodney Hall (ed.), *The Collins Book of Australian Poetry*, Sydney and London, 1981, pp. 4–5.

27 JB, 'Aspects of Australia', *Vogue* (London), February 1963, p. 100.

28 *Loc. cit.*

29 JB to PB, 17 November 1961. *JBP*.

30 JB, 'Aspects of Australia', *Vogue* (London), February 1963, p. 100.

31 Judith Wright (McKinney), letter to the author, 28 January 1995. Wright died in 2000. See her obituary in *The Times*, 27 June 2000.

32 Judith Wright (McKinney), letter to the author, 28 January 1995.

33 JB, 'Aspects of Australia', *Vogue* (London), February 1963, p. 100.

34 CLG, *Letters*, ii, 205.

35 JB to PB, 18 November 1961. *JBP*.

36 David Marr (ed.), *Patrick White Letters*, London 1994, p. 197.

37 *Ibid.*, p. 645.

38 Patrick White to Frederick Glover, 20 November 1961. Marr, *op. cit.*, p. 201.

39 JB, *Daily Herald*, 21 September 1948. Quoted Marr, *op. cit.*, p. 74n.

40 I am grateful to Dr Edmund Thomson for this information. Cynthia Nolan (*née* Reed) committed suicide in 1974. See the obituary of Sir Sidney Nolan (1917–92), *The Times*, 28 November 1992.

41 JB, 'Cheltenham', *Old Lights for New Chancels* (1940). Patrick White had not enjoyed his years at Cheltenham; in 1969 after seeing the Lindsay Anderson film *If . . .*, he wrote to Frederick Glover, 'The buildings of my old school . . . added to the horror of the story . . .' (Marr, *op. cit.*, p. 348).

42 Patrick White to Ben Huebsch (1876–1964, publisher), 11 September 1956. Marr, *op. cit.*, p. 107.

43 Patrick White to Owen and David Moore, 7 June 1957. Marr, *op. cit.*, p. 119.

44 Patrick White to Frederick Glover, 28 November 1971. Marr, *op. cit.*, p. 389.

45 Patrick White to Pepe Mamblas (1893–1985, Spanish diplomatist and nobleman), 20 May 1973. Marr, *op. cit.*, p. 412.

46 Patrick White to Jean Scott Rogers, 16 March 1931. Marr, *op. cit.*, p. 5.

47 JB to PB, 23–24 November 1961. (The letter was written over two days.) *JBP*.

48 *Ibid.*

49 *Ibid.*

50 JB to CLG, 26 November 1961. JB, *Letters*, ed. CLG, ii, 224.

51 *Ibid.*

52 JB to PB, 29 November 1961. *JBP*.

53 On the relationship between Arthur Cameron Corbett, son of Lord Rowallan, and April Ashley, see Duncan Fallowell and April Ashley, *April Ashley's Odyssey*, London 1982, pp. 115–18, 120–21, 122, 123–29, 131, 132, 137, 138–39, 146–50, 153, 154, 206–11, 215–26, 219, 220–21. Corbett and Ashley went through a marriage ceremony in Gibraltar; but the marriage was later ruled void by an English court on the ground that Ashley was not a woman.

54 In his letter to PB of 29 November 1961, JB referred to Fiona Corbett as 'Wibz's friend'. *JBP*.

55 JB, 'Aspects of Australia', *Vogue* (London), February 1963, p. 100.

56 JB, 'Men and Buildings: Clear Light, Colour and Space', *Daily Telegraph*, 18 December 1961.

57 JB to PB, 29 November 1961. *JBP*.

58 I am grateful to Mr Philip Parks for the information about his late parents' attendance at JB's lecture.

59 Recalled by Mr Philip Parks.

60 In the early 1890s the Australian architect Edward E. Raht designed a new building for the Equitable Life Assurance Society of the United States, on the north-west corner of Collins and Elizabeth Streets in Melbourne. It was in an 'Americanized Renaissance' style. In 1923 the building was sold to the Colonial Mutual Life Assurance Sociaty. Between 1959 and 1960 it was demolished by Whelan the Wrecker. The 'New Brutalist' building erected on its site in 1960 – making use of some of the original granite – is the one JB disliked on his 1961 visit.

61 *Ibid.*

62 On the Rev. George Bridle, Vicar of Wantage, see *JBNFNL*, pp. 8–9, 91, 238.

63 JB to PB, 2 December 1961. *JBP*.

64 *Ibid.* The cutting – presumably a newspaper report of a JB lecture, mentioning the Duchess of Westminster, has not survived with the letter. *JBP*.

65 JB, 'Men and Buildings: Clear Light, Colour and Space', *Daily Telegraph*, 1 December 1961.
66 JB to PB, 4 December 1961. *JBP*.
67 *Ibid*.
68 JB to PB, 2 December 1961. *JBP*.
69 JB, 'Men and Buildings: Clear Light, Colour and Space', *Daily Telegraph*, 18 December 1961.
70 *Ibid*.
71 *Ibid*.
72 *Ibid*.
73 *Ibid*.
74 *Ibid*.
75 *Ibid*.
76 *Ibid*.
77 *Ibid*.
78 See *YB*, p. 121.
79 It may have been JB's familiarity with the decorations of the London Coal Exchange (much on his mind at this date) that suggested this simile.
80 JB, 'Aspects of Australia', *Vogue* (London) February 1963, p. 101.
81 Quoted, JB, *Letters*, ed. CLG, ii, 304–05.
82 JB, 'Beneath the Wattle Tree', *Daily Express*, 27 January 1964.
83 Neville Cardus, *Daily Express*, 27 January 1964.
84 JB, 'Beneath the Wattle Tree', *Daily Express*, 27 January 1964.
85 JB, 'John Betjeman's Kangaroo Island: Old-Fashioned Betjemanesque Pleasures', *Daily Telegraph Magazine*, 5 January 1968.

Chapter 8: The Coal Exchange

1 *Victorian Society archives*.
2 Henry-Russell Hitchcock wrote extensively about the Coal Exchange in his *Early Victorian Architecture in Britain*, London and New Haven 1952, i, 295, 298, 316, 317, 320–41, 343, 359, 402; (illustrations) ii, section X, 14–24.
3 *Loc. cit*.
4 JB to Judith Scott, 17 March 1956. JB, *Letters*, ed. CLG, ii, 58.
5 Marshall Sisson (1897–1978), architect, author and treasurer of the Royal Academy, 1965–70.
6 Quoted, JB, *Letters*, ed. CLG, ii, 99.
7 *Victorian Society archives*.
8 *The Times*, 17 September 1958.
9 *The Times*, 15 October 1958.
10 *Loc. cit*.
11 *Victorian Society archives*.
12 *The Times*, 23 October 1958.
13 *The Times*, 25 October 1958.
14 *Loc. cit*.
15 *The Times*, 29 October 1958.
16 *Loc. cit*. On the successful campaign by JB and others to save Albert Bridge – which links Chelsea and Battersea, London – see *JBNFNL*, pp. 566–67.
17 *The Times*, 29 October 1958.
18 *The Times*, 30 October 1958. Lord Young (Mrs Thatcher's Secretary of State for Trade and Industry) has assured the author that he was not the David Young who wrote this letter.
19 *Victorian Society archives*.
20 *Ibid*.
21 *Ibid*.
22 *Ibid*.
23 *Ibid*.
24 *Ibid*.
25 *Ibid*.

26 *Ibid.*
27 *Ibid.*
28 *Ibid.*
29 *Ibid.*
30 *Ibid.*
31 *Ibid.*
32 *Ibid.*
33 *Ibid.*
34 *The Times*, 9 February 1961.
35 *Loc. cit.*
36 *Loc. cit.*
37 *The Times*, 10 February 1961.
38 Joke retailed to the author by Mr John Toop Cooper of *The Times* in 1964. However, it must be acknowledged that this quip has been credited to other speakers and about other persons. For example, Ned Sherrin, editor of *The Oxford Dictionary of Humorous Quotations* (Oxford 1995, p. 295) attributed it to Maurice Bowra 'on being told he should not marry anyone as plain as his fiancée', giving as his authority Hugh Lloyd-Jones in *Maurice Bowra: A Celebration* (1974). Against this, Francis Wheen writes (*Tom Driberg: His Life and Indiscretions*, London 1990, p. 248): 'On seeing a photograph of Ena [Driberg] in the *Daily Herald*, Winston Churchill allegedly roared: "Oh well, buggers can't be choosers!"'
39 *The Times*, 10 February 1961.
40 *Loc. cit.*
41 *Loc. cit.*
42 *Loc. cit.*
43 *Loc. cit.*
44 *Loc. cit.*
45 *Loc. cit.*
46 *Loc. cit.*
47 *Loc. cit.*
48 *Loc. cit.*
49 *Loc. cit.*
50 *Loc. cit.*
51 *Loc. cit.*
52 *Loc. cit.*
53 *Loc. cit.*
54 JB to Woodrow Wyatt, 18 February 1961. Shown to the author by Lord Wyatt.
55 *Ibid.*
56 *Victorian Society archives.*
57 *Ibid.*
58 *Ibid.*
59 *Ibid.*
60 *Ibid.*
61 *Ibid.*
62 *Ibid.*
63 *Ibid.*
64 *Ibid.*
65 *Ibid.*
66 *Ibid.*
67 *Ibid.*
68 Peter Fleetwood-Hesketh, interview, 1977.
69 *Victorian Society archives.*
70 *Ibid.*
71 *Ibid.*
72 *Ibid.*
73 *Ibid.*
74 *Guardian*, 22 February 1962.

75 *City Press*, 3 March 1962.
76 *The Times*, 7 March 1962.
77 *The Times*, 8 March 1962.
78 *Loc. cit.*
79 *Loc. cit.*
80 *Loc. cit.*
81 Hugh (later Lord) Molson (1903–91), Conservative MP and Minister of Works, 1957–59. He was also known as 'Preters', having pompously stated that he was 'preternaturally interested' in politics. See *The Diaries of Evelyn Waugh*, ed. Michael Davie, London 1976, pp. 72n. and 187n.
82 *The Times*, 8 March 1962.
83 *Loc. cit.*
84 *Loc. cit.*
85 *The Times*, 9 March 1962.
86 *Loc. cit.*
87 *Loc. cit.*
88 *Loc. cit.*
89 *Loc. cit.*
90 *Victorian Society archives.*
91 *Ibid.*
92 *Ibid.*
93 *Ibid.*
94 *Ibid.*
95 *Ibid.*
96 *Ibid.*
97 *The Times*, 3 August 1962.
98 *Loc. cit.* The Victorian Society's annual report (*Victorian Society archives*) claimed that 'the Ministry had, in fact, planned to list the building in 1958 but, when informed then by the City that it was likely to be demolished, decided that "there was no useful purpose to be served" by completing the legal formalities of listing: "in the circumstances the building will not be added to the list at the moment, but, of course, if it should still be standing when we have a general revision of the list for the city, we shall add it then"!'
99 *Victorian Society archives.*
100 *Ibid.*
101 *Sunday Times*, 12 August 1962. Ernestine Carter and JB had known each other when they both worked in the wartime Ministry of Information. See *JBNFNL*, p. 180.
102 *The Times*, 21 September 1962.
103 *Victorian Society archives.*
104 *Ibid.*
105 *Ibid.*
106 *Ibid.*
107 *Ibid.*
108 *The Times*, 19 October 1962.
109 *Victorian Society archives.*
110 *Ibid.*
111 *Ibid.*
112 Peter Fleetwood-Hesketh, interview, 1977.
113 *Victorian Society archives.*
114 *Ibid.*
115 *Ibid.*
116 *Ibid.*
117 *Steel and Coal*, 19 October 1962.
118 *Victorian Society archives.*
119 *Ibid.*
120 *The Times*, 17 October 1963.
121 Cutting in *Victorian Society archives.*

122 Cutting in *Victorian Society archives*.

123 On Philip Harding, see *YB*, pp. 101, 108, 111, 113, 129, 132, 168, 191, 360; *JBNFNL*, pp. 74, 144, 149; and JB to Deirdre Connolly, 4 June 1965, JB, *Letters*, ed. CLG, ii, 293.

124 The author worked for Philip Harding on *The Times* in the early 1960s and became familiar with this apophthegm.

Chapter 9: A Natural Showman: Television in the Sixties

1 Kenneth Savidge (b. 1927) joined the BBC West Region in Bristol in 1951.

2 Kenneth Savidge, interview, 2000.

3 *Ibid*.

4 Quoted, *ibid*.

5 Quoted, *ibid*.

6 JB, *Letters*, ed. CLG, ii, 258.

7 Kenneth Savidge, interview, 2000.

8 On Ewart Garland, see JB, *Letters*, ed. CLG, ii, 357n.

9 Kenneth Savidge, interview, 2000.

10 *Ibid*.

11 See Evelyn Waugh, *A Little Learning*, London 1964, pp. 227–28 and 229. Also *The Letters of Evelyn Waugh*, ed. Mark Amory, London 1980, pp. 616 and 623–24; and Selina Hastings, *Evelyn Waugh: A Biography*, London 1994, pp. 135, 144, 172–73, 173n., 613 and 615.

12 Kenneth Savidge, interview, 2000.

13 *Ex inf.* Brother Young's nephew, the late John Young of *The Times*, London.

14 Kenneth Savidge, interview, 2000.

15 That is, the art historian Kenneth Clark (Lord Clark) (1903–83). *Private Eye* gave him the nickname 'Lord Clark of Civilization' in reference to his television series *Civilization*.

16 (Sir) Patrick Moore (b. 1923), astronomer.

17 Kenneth Savidge, interview, 2000.

18 *Ibid*.

19 JB, *Letters*, ed. CLG, ii, 257.

20 That is, Senior Service cigarettes.

21 JB, *Letters*, ed. CLG, ii, 257.

22 Kenneth Savidge, interview, 2000.

23 *Ibid*.

24 *Ibid*.

25 *Ibid*.

26 *Ibid*. Knowing JB's fondness for the technical jargon of television, two of the crew which had worked with him composed for his seventieth birthday in 1976 this poem, a pastiche of JB's poem 'Dorset' –

> ODE TO THE LAUREATE ON THE OCCASION OF HIS 70th BIRTHDAY
> by P. West and K. Savidge
>
> Light's abode, Celestial Scanner,
> See the bench ends gleaming bright
> As with bashers, pups and 2ks
> Jack adjusts the Molish* light.
> 'Check your focus – tilt down Teddy –
> Can the Artiste see his cue?'
> While Eric Benn, Ken Savidge, Geraldine Manning, Ray Burgess, Bill Jones,
>   Alan Hitchcock and Ted Bragg prepare themselves to tape Take Two.

* A reference to Mole Richardson (Electrics) Ltd, now defunct.

Note: The names in the last line of this stanza are put in not out of malice, nor for their euphony, but simply for old times' sake.

27 Quoted, *ibid*.

28 *Ibid.*
29 *Ibid.*
30 From the original script of 1964 preserved by Kenneth Savidge.
31 JB to Maria Aitken, 17 May 1962. JB, *Letters*, ed. CLG, ii, 231.
32 *Come to an End* was reshown as a tailpiece to the revival of JB's 1962 films in 1997.
33 Jonathan Stedall, interview, 2003.
34 *Ibid.*
35 Quoted, JB, *Letters*, ed. CLG, ii, 327.
36 (Dame) (Muriel) Diana Reader Harris (1912–96), headmistress, Sherborne School for Girls, 1950–75.
37 Maria Aitken to JB, n.d. JB, *Letters*, ed. CLG, ii, 231n.
38 Jonathan Stedall, interview, 2003.
39 *Ibid.*
40 *Ibid.*
41 Maria Aitken to Lady Aitken, June 1962. JB, *Letters*, ed. CLG, ii, 231n.
42 JB, *Sherborne*, 1962.
43 *Ibid.*
44 *Daily Express*, 1 September 1994.
45 JB, *Marlborough*, 1962. See also 'Film exposes "lost" Betjeman poem', *The Independent*, 1 September 1994.
46 JB, *Devizes*, 1962.
47 JB, *Crewkerne*, 1962.
48 JB, *Northlew and Swindon*, 1962.
49 *Ibid.*
50 JB, *Devizes*, 1962.
51 *Ibid.*
52 Sir Thomas Lawrence (1769–1830), English portrait painter. He was appointed limner to George III in 1792 and in 1820 became president of the Royal Academy.

   JB was only half right. Though Lawrence's father was indeed landlord of the Black Bear at Devizes from 1772, Lawrence was in fact born in Bristol in 1769.
53 JB, *Devizes*, 1962.
54 JB, *Sidmouth*, 1962.
55 JB, *Bath*, 1962.

   Ten years later, JB helped Adam Fergusson – a nephew of his Oxford friend Michael Dugdale – wage a tremendous and largely successful campaign to save Bath. On 9 May 1972, when Fergusson was in the middle of 'a wonderful knockabout correspondence conducted through *The Times* . . . on the subject of Bath', JB wrote to him:

   > Dear Mr Fergusson,
   >   What a smashingly good reply to those silly planners and architects – which is which by the way? Or are they both? – what a good article on Bath. Keep it up. Attack these arrogant charlatans . . .
   >   I like to think you are Michael Arthur Stratford Dugdale's nephew. If so, Hurrah! He is pleased in Heaven, for there he undoubtedly deserves to be. He had your clarity of mind and witty, pithy way of saying things & the same passion for architecture and contempt for humbug.
   >   Many many thanks for your writings.
   >   Don't bother to reply. Writing replies is a nuisance . . .
   >   (Letter shown to the author by Mr Fergusson).

   James Lees-Milne (interview, 1990) recalled that JB particularly disliked the work, in the Bath area, of the modern architect Howard Stutchbury. 'He hated the houses he had built across the river [Avon]. He thought they looked like rabbit-hutches, so he called them "stutches".'

   In 1972 JB wrote verses to introduce Fergusson's book *The Sack of Bath* (London 1973). Most of the verses are reprinted as 'The Newest Bath Guide' in *Collected Poems,* 2003 edn., pp. 303-4; but, with JB's permission, Fergusson excised ten lines, of which he has kindly sent the author a copy:-

It doesn't matter just once in a while
To desert the old-fashioned Palladian style
For Greek or for Gothic; although I must own
I like to see both in our good local stone.
Please keep down the height and consider the sky
And the look of the trees and the buildings near-by.
But rulings like these didn't suit very well
The monster who gave us the Empire Hotel

And Bath University surely did right
In placing its factories well out of sight.

Adam Fergusson thinks that the 1973 book, with John's other verses, did help to save Bath from further 'erosion', by causing the outcry and protest movement that led to the implementation of 'conservation areas'.

56 Hugh Hebert, 'Laureate's Lost Land', *The Guardian*, 30 August 1994.

57 Alan Bennett's *Talking Heads* was published as a book by BBC Books, London, in 1988.

58 The programme went out on 1 January 1963. *BBCWA*.

59 *BBCWA*.

60 John Boorman, letter to the author, 7 February 2004.

61 Alan Bennett, *Writing Home*, London 1998 edn., p. 565.

62 Larkin's letters to Patrick Garland concerning the film were sold at Sotheby's 11 July 1996, lot 303. This letter was quoted in the catalogue. Patrick Garland writes (letter to the author, 4 September 2004): 'The attraction of the Larkin film, although they did admire each other, was as much Hull as Larkin himself. "The Venice of the North" as John called it, although I felt sympathy for that jazz-musician friend of George Melly, Mick Mulligan, who, walking round Hull in the pouring rain after a gig, said: "I still prefer fucking Venice."'

63 Quoted, *loc. cit.*

64 Quoted, *loc. cit.*

65 Quoted, *loc. cit.*

66 On Edward, Lord Bridges, see p. 648, n. 24.

67 JB to Lord Esher, 17 May 1966. JB, *Letters*, ed. CLG, ii, 317.

68 Lord Esher to JB, 20 May 1966. Quoted, JB, *Letters*, ed. CLG, ii, p. 318n.

69 'Mr Betjeman – Delightful as a Man with a View', *The Times*, 28 April 1966.

70 JB to CLG, 11 November 1966. JB, *Letters*, ed. CLG, ii, 325.

71 JB to Duncan Fallowell, 29 November 1966. JB, *Letters*, ed. CLG, ii, 325–26. The Pre-Raphaelite artist William Holman Hunt (1827–1910) painted *The Scapegoat* in 1854–55 and it was hung in the Royal Academy in 1856.

72 JB to David Higham Associates, December 1966. Quoted in a letter of Higham Associates to Margot Robbins of the BBC, 14 December 1966. *BBCWA*.

73 *Ibid.*

74 David Higham Associates to Margot Robbins, 14 December 1966. *BBCWA*.

75 Internal BBC memo, December 1966. *BBCWA*.

76 Anthony Burgess, *You've Had Your Time*, London 1990, p. 105. It is only fair to note that Burgess had reason to be prejudiced against *Call My Bluff*. He made the social error of actually knowing what one of the rare words meant (*loc. cit.*).

77 For example, at Riverside Studios on 20 March, 4 April, 16 May, 23 May, 22 August and 2 September 1965. *BBCWA*.

78 Robert Robinson, *Skip All That: Memoirs*, London 1996, p. 158.

79 Burgess, *op. cit.*, p. 104.

80 *Ibid.*, pp. 104–05. The publisher Anthony Blond (b. 1928) makes amusing reference to JB in his memoirs, *Jew Made in England* (London 2004). At p. 142:

'Fuck Collins, bravo Anthony Blond!'
    Certainly not the sort of epistle one would expect from the future Poet Laureate. It did not rhyme or scan, but John Betjeman wrote it all right, about my proposal to publish a new edition of *Ghastly Good Taste*.'

Blond did publish the new edition, in 1970. He observes (*ibid.*, p. 143): '. . . it must have been too much of a period piece for the mass of Betjeman's fans who, according to our sales reps, wanted to see his face on the jacket of the book, as they had on television. I have always been a bit of a purist – a fatal refinement in a publisher.

One of Blond's anecdotes concerns the award of a poetry prize for children; he, John and Roger McGough were the judges (*loc. cit.*).

81 JB to (Sir) David Attenborough, 2 January 1967. *BBCWA*.

82 On Terence de Vere White (1912–94), see his obituary in *The Times*, 18 June 1994; also, *JBNFNL*, pp. 238, 386.

83 Sir Winston Churchill had died in 1965 and been given a state funeral.

84 JB to Terence de Vere White, 1 November 1967. JB, *Letters*, ed. CLG, ii, 118.

85 Stephen Hearst to JB, February 1968. Quoted by Hearst in internal BBC memo to Miss S. Hewitt, 5 February 1968. *BBCWA*.

86 JB to Stephen Hearst, February 1967. Quoted, *ibid.*

87 Edward Mirzoeff, interview, 1992.

88 *Ibid.*

89 Edward Roberts, interview, 1992.

90 Edward Mirzoeff, interview, 1992.

91 *Daily Telegraph*, 7 April 1969.

92 Edward Mirzoeff, interview, 1992.

93 *Ibid.*

94 Sir Edward Pickering, *Tennyson Research Bulletin*, November 1990. Quoted, JB, *Letters*, ed. CLG, ii, 356.

95 JB to Sir Edward Pickering, 26 September 1968. JB, *Letters*, ed. CLG, ii, 355–56.

96 *A Dedicated Fan: Julian Jebb 1934–84*, ed. Tristram and Georgia Powell, London 1993, p. 106.

97 *Ibid.*, p. 110.

Chapter 10: Barry Humphries

1 Quoted, Barry Humphries, *More Please*, London 1992, p. 330.

2 Barry Humphries, 'The Dame and the Laureate', *Perspectives in Architecture* (magazine), vol. i, issue 2, May 1994, p. 16. The author is grateful to the Hon. Lady Roberts of The Royal Library, Windsor Castle, for a photocopy of this article.

3 Peter Coleman, *The Real Barry Humphries Story*, London 1990, p. 47.

4 Interview with Barry Humphries recorded by 3BM Television for the Channel 4 programme *The Real Betjeman* (2000). Kindly supplied to the author by Marion Milne of 3BM.

5 Barry Humphries, *More Please*, London 1992, p. 203.

6 See *YB*, p. 11.

7 Barry Humphries, 'The Dame and the Laureate', *Perspectives in Architecture* (magazine), vol. i, issue 2, May 1994, p. 16.

8 *Loc. cit.*; also Barry Humphries, *More Please*, London 1992, p. 205.

9 Barry Humphries, 'The Dame and the Laureate', *Perspectives in Architecture* (magazine), vol. i, issue 2, May 1994, p. 16.

10 *Loc. cit.*

11 Barry Humphries, *More Please*, London 1992, p. 17.

12 *Ibid.*, p. 143.

13 *Ibid.*, p. 118.

14 *Ibid.*, pp. 178–79.

15 *Ibid.*, p. 131.

16 *Ibid.*, p. 143.

17 *Ibid.*, p. 157.

18 *Ibid.*, p. 182; and Coleman, *op. cit.*, pp. 50 and 52–53.

19 Barry Humphries, *More Please*, London 1992, p. 185.

20 *Ibid.*, p. 189.

21 *Ibid.*, p. 188.

22 *Ibid.*, p. 189.

23 *Ibid.*, p. 192; and Coleman, *op. cit.*, p. 58.

24 Barry Humphries, *More Please*, London 1992, p. 192.

25 *Ibid.*, p. 194; also Coleman, *op. cit.*, p. 58.

26 Barry Humphries, *More Please*, London 1992, p. 203.

27 Quoted, YB, p. 22.

28 Kenneth Slessor (1901–71), Australian poet. For examples of his verse see *The Faber Book of Modern Australian Verse*, ed. Vincent Buckley, London 1991, pp. 7–16; and *The Collins Book of Australian Poetry*, chosen by Rodney Hall, London 1981, pp. 122–30.
    JB met Slessor on his visit to Australia in 1961. See JB, *Letters*, ed. CLG, ii, 242 and 424.

29 Quoted, Coleman, *op. cit.*, p. 160.

30 Clive James, *Falling Towards England*, London 1985, pp. 159–64. In the book James calls Humphries 'Bruce Jennings'. He writes of him (p. 160): '[Jennings] was known to take luncheon at Rules in the company of his admirer, John Betjeman.' Also (*loc. cit.*): 'Jennings left you in no doubt of his brilliance, though in some fear that his monologues might never end.'

31 Barry Humphries, telephone conversation with the author, 2003.

32 Barry Humphries, *More Please*, London 1992, p. 206.

33 On Conder, see *loc. cit.*

34 *Ibid.*, p. 194.

35 *Ibid.*, pp. 194–95.

36 Barry Humphries, telephone conversation with the author, 2003.

37 *Collected Poems*, 2003 edn., p. 48.

38 *Ibid.*, p. 351.

39 JB also referred to Ardath cigarettes, in a prose sketch in the *London Mercury* (August 1933). See YB, p. 351.

40 John Lahr, *Dame Edna Everage and the Rise of Western Civilization*, London 1991, p. 93.

41 *Collected Poems*, 2003 edn., p. 163.

42 Coleman, *op. cit.*, p. 12.

43 *Collected Poems*, 2003 edn., pp. 74–75.

44 Lahr, *op. cit.*, p. 125.

45 *Barry Humphries' Treasury of Australian Kitsch*, Melbourne 1980.

46 Barry Humphries, *More Please*, London 1992, p. 126.

47 The Theatre Royal 'Victim Map' for this show is illustrated by Lahr, *op. cit.*, p. 100.

48 Nicholas Garland, quoted *op. cit.*, p. 171.

49 Barry Humphries, *More Please*, London 1992, p. 126.

50 *Loc. cit.*

51 *Ibid.*, p. 99.

52 Coleman, *op. cit.*, p. 52.

53 Barry Humphries, *More Please*, London 1992, p. 198.

54 Coleman, *op. cit.*, p. 63.

55 Barry Humphries, *More Please*, London 1992, p. 198; also, telephone conversation with the author, 2003.

56 Barry Humphries, *More Please*, London 1992, p. 200.

57 *Ibid.*, p. 205; also, Barry Humphries, *My Life as Me*, London 1992, p. 205.

58 Quoted, Barry Humphries, *More Please*, London 1992, p. 330.

59 *Ibid.*, p. 210.

60 *Ibid.*, p. 213.

61 *Ibid.*, p. 216.

62 *Ibid.*, p. 217.

63 *Ibid.*, p. 216.

64 Dame Edna Everage [i.e. Barry Humphries], *My Gorgeous Life: An Adventure*, London 1989, p. 214.

65 Lahr, *op. cit.*, p. 170.

66 *Loc. cit.*

67 Everage, *op. cit.*, p. 215.
68 Coleman, *op. cit.*, p. 72.
69 Barry Humphries, *More Please*, London 1992, p. 218.
70 *Loc. cit.*
71 *Ibid.*, p. 220.
72 *Ibid.*, pp. 237–38.
73 Lahr, *op. cit.*, p. 171.
74 Barry Humphries, *More Please*, London 1992, p. 228.
75 'Chunder': vomit. See *ibid.*, p. 219; and Lahr, *op. cit.*, p. 172.
76 Coleman, *op. cit.*, p. 87.
77 See note 75 of this chapter.
78 Barry Humphries, *More Please*, London 1992, p. 229.
79 Coleman, *op. cit.*, p. 90.
80 Dame Laura Knight (*née* Johnson) (1877–1970), English painter and designer. Often took circuses as her subject and was markedly more interested in painting women than men.
81 Robert Anning Bell (1863–1933), British artist. Barry Humphries recalled (telephone conversation with the author, 2003): 'Anning Bell did the murals at the Horniman Museum, which was John's favourite museum, because no one ever went there. He proved it by leaving a sandwich on top of a glass case. Months later, it had not been moved.'
82 One of Tuke's best-known paintings, *August Blue*, is mentioned in JB's poem 'Monody on the Death of a Platonist Bank Clerk', *Collected Poems*, 2003 edn., p. 275. On Tuke, see *YB*, pp. 125 and 427 n. 15; *JBNFNL*, p. 458; and Chapter 11, 'The Battle of Bedford Park', in the present volume.
83 Barry Humphries, *My Life as Me*, London 2002, pp. 293–94.
84 Barry Humphries, telephone conversation with the author, 2003.
85 *Ibid.*
86 Phil May (1864–1903) was born in England but from 1885 to 1888 he drew for the *Sydney Bulletin*.
87 Barry Humphries, telephone conversation with the author, 2003.
88 Barry Humphries, *More Please*, London 1992, pp. 246–48.
89 Quoted, Coleman, *op. cit.*, pp. 72–73.
90 Interview with Barry Humphries recorded by 3BM Television for the Channel 4 programme *The Real Betjeman* (2000), kindly supplied to the author by Marion Milne of 3BM.
    In an obituary article on JB (*Sunday Times*, 20 May 1984), John Piper wrote that JB had 'quoted [Barry Humphries] incessantly'.
91 The finely printed and illustrated books of the Vale Press were issued between 1896 and 1904 (Colin Franklin, *The Private Presses*, London 1991 edn., p. 81). The press was run by the artist Charles Ricketts (1866–1931), who lived with his lover Charles Shannon (1863–1937) in The Vale, Chelsea. The press published forty-eight works, including as one work a complete Shakespeare in thirty-three volumes (*ibid.*, p. 82). Llewellyn Hacon was involved with the press. It is said that William Morris on his deathbed wept at the sight of some Vale Press books. See also Maureen Watry, *The Vale Press*, London 2001.
92 Barry Humphries, telephone conversation with the author, 2003.
93 Quoted, Lahr, *op. cit.*, p. 221.
94 Quoted, *ibid.*, p. 222.
95 JB, conversation with the author, 1982; and Barry Humphries, telephone conversation with the author, 2003.
96 Barry Humphries, *More Please*, London 1992, p. 289.
97 *Ibid.*, p. 290.

Chapter 11: The Battle of Bedford Park

1 Tom Greeves, interview, 1991.
2 Tom Greeves, *Bedford Park*, London 1983; and material about the suburb in the late Tom Greeves's scrapbook.

3 Tom Greeves, interview, 1991.

4 Material about Bedford Park in the late Tom Greeves's scrapbook.

5 On William De Morgan, see B. Hillier, *Pottery and Porcelain 1700–1914*, London 1968, pp. 26, 240, 242–58 and 331.

6 W.B. Yeats, *Autobiographies*, London 1989, p. 113.

7 *Loc-cit.*

8 On Conrad Noel, the 'Red Vicar' of Thaxted, see *YB*, p. 223, and JB, introduction to *Ghastly Good Taste*, London 1970 edn., p. xxiv.

9 G.K. Chesterton, *The Man Who Was Thursday*, London 1944 edn., p. 5.

10 G.K. Chesterton, *Autobiography*, London 1936, p. 139.

11 *Daily Telegraph*, 11 August 1960.

12 JB, letter to Peter Clarke, 15 November 1952. Copy shown to the author by the late Tom Greeves.

13 Tom Greeves, interview, 1991.

14 *Ibid.*

15 JB's poem appeared in the *London Magazine*, October 1965.

16 Tom Greeves, interview, 1991.

17 *Ibid.*

18 Tom Greeves, letter to Frank Adams, 12 February 1963. Copy shown to the author by the late Tom Greeves.

19 Undated cutting in the late Tom Greeves's scrapbook.

20 Tom Greeves, interview, 1991.

21 *Ibid.*

22 Sir Albert Richardson died in 1964.

23 Tom Greeves, interview, 1991.

24 Arnold Walker, letter to JB, 12 May 1963. Copy shown to the author by the late Tom Greeves.

25 On Charles Clore and Jack Cotton, famous property developers of the 1960s, see Oliver Marriott, *The Property Boom*, London 1967. Many pages of the book are devoted to both men.

26 Copy shown to the author by the late Tom Greeves.

27 Tom Greeves, interview, 1991.

28 Quoted, *ibid.*

29 See Chapter 6, 'The Euston Arch'.

30 Copy shown to the author by the late Tom Greeves.

31 The card is reproduced in the colour plate section.

32 Quoted, Tom Greeves, interview, 1991.

33 Quoted, *ibid.*

34 Ian Fletcher (ed.), *Romantic Mythologies*, London 1976.

35 Tom Greeves, interview, 1991.

36 *Ibid.*

37 Theobald von Bethmann Hollweg (1856–1921), German Imperial Chancellor before and during the First World War.

38 Ben Pimlott in *Harold Wilson*, London 1992, p. 347, writes that in 1964 Wilson's political secretary Marcia Williams (later Lady Falkender) had 'a brief, doomed affair with John Allen'. Stephen Dorril and Robin Ramsay in *Smear!*, London 1991, pp. 75–76, write that 'Allen had proposed marriage to Marcia in 1965 but withdrew it.' He stayed in the 'kitchen cabinet' until 1970. Wilson said to Allen (p. 76): 'Do you realise I've spent more time on your private life than I have on the Vietnam war?' On this subject see also *Sunday Times*, 19 July 1981.

39 Schmutzler's book was translated into English by JB's Oxford friend Edouard Roditi (on whom, see *JBLP*, p. 61).

40 Robert Schmutzler, *Art Nouveau*, London 1964, p. 4.

41 Andrew Best, letter to the author, 25 July 1991.

42 Text of JB's speech in the late Tom Greeves's scrapbook.

43 JB, *First and Last Loves*, London 1952, p. 140.

44 Mark Glazebrook's former wife, Elizabeth, telephone conversation with the author, 1991.

45 Mark Glazebrook, interview, 1991.

46 *Ibid.*

47 Dr (later Sir) Roy Strong was director of the National Portrait Gallery from 1967 to 1975.

48 Hugh de P. Glazebrook (1855–1937), portrait painter.

49 Mark Glazebrook, interview, 1991.

50 *Ibid.*

51 *Ibid.*

52 William Rimington Glazebrook (1864–1954), president of the Liverpool Cotton Association 1916; Sheriff of Denbighshire, 1940.

53 Reginald Field Glazebrook (1899–1986), a director of the Liverpool and London and Globe Insurance Company.

54 Mark Glazebrook, interview, 1991.

55 JB called Tuke 'the Boucher of the Boy Scouts'. See *YB*, pp. 125 and 427 n. 15.

56 Mark Glazebrook, interview, 1991.

57 Alexander Hollweg, telephone conversation with the author, 1991.

58 Tom Greeves, interview, 1991.

59 Quoted, *ibid.*

60 *Ibid.*

61 Quoted, *ibid.*

62 The nursery rhyme begins: 'Hark, hark! The dogs do bark; the beggars have come to town . . .'

63 Tom Greeves, interview, 1991.

64 Samuel Sanders Teulon (1812–73), English Gothic revival architect of Huguenot ancestry. Among his designs were Totworth Court, Gloucestershire (1849–52), Shadwell Park, Norfolk (1856–61), St Mary's, Ealing (1861–74) and St Stephen's, Rosslyn Hill, Hampstead, London (1868–71).

65 Tom Greeves, interview, 1991.

66 *Ibid.*

67 *Ibid.*

68 JB to Tom Greeves, 22 February 1983. Shown to the author by the late Tom Greeves.

Chapter 12: High and Low

1 Lord Birkenhead to John G. Murray, 10 January 1966. *John Murray archives.*

2 JB to CLG, 31 January 1960. JB, *Letters*, ed. CLG, ii, 182.

3 The poem 'Archibald', omitted from *High and Low*, was published in *Uncollected Poems*, London 1982. It was presumably written in 1956, as it contains the line (in the sixth stanza), '"You're half a century nearer Hell"'. (This is what JB's teddy-bear Archibald seems to be saying to him in the year JB was fifty.)

4 John G. Murray to Lord Birkenhead, 23 March 1966. *John Murray archives.*

5 *London Magazine*, June 1965.

6 Lord Birkenhead to John G. Murray, 23 March 1966. *John Murray archives.*

7 *Ibid.*

8 John G. Murray to Lord Birkenhead, 29 March 1966. *John Murray archives.*

9 Quoted by John G. Murray, letter to Lord Birkenhead, 22 March 1966. *John Murray archives.*

10 *John Murray archives.*

11 The poem 'When father went out on his basic' was finally published in *The Betjemanian*, vol. 7, December 1995, pp. 8–9. It begins:

> When father went out on his basic
> With Muriel, Shirley and me,
> We drove up to somebody's mansion
> And asked them to give us some tea.

> 'Get out of that there. We're the workers
> The mansion is ours, so to speak
> As Dad turns a handle at Sidcup
> For twenty-five guineas a week.'

> 'I'm paid by the buffet at Didcot
> For insulting the passengers there.
> The way they keeps rattlin' the door knob
> Disturbs me in doin' my hair' . . .

12 Lord Birkenhead to John G. Murray, 1 April 1966. *John Murray archives.*

13 The meaning is indeed mysterious to later generations. One would expect 'basic' to be an abbreviation of 'basic training', the 'square-bashing' that new recruits to the services had to undergo, learning to march and to perform arms drill – but the use of the word in this poem does not give that sense.

14 Lord Birkenhead to John G. Murray, 13 April 1966. *John Murray archives.*

15 See John G. Murray, letter to Lord Birkenhead, 27 April 1966. *John Murray archives.*

16 *John Murray archives.*

17 Quoted in an aggrieved letter from John G. Murray to Lord Birkenhead, 22 June 1966. *John Murray archives.*

18 For Byron's 'Epistle to Mr Murray' (1817) see John R. Murray, *Variations on Number Fifty*, London 1964, p. 5.

19 As recorded in a letter from John G. Murray to JB, 3 June 1966. *John Murray archives.*

20 See John G. Murray to Lord Birkenhead, 15 June 1966. *John Murray archives.*

21 See John G. Murray to JB, 27 June 1966. *John Murray archives.*

22 It is not known what JB's late, provocative title for the book was.

23 John G. Murray to JB, 16 September 1966. *John Murray archives.*

24 John G. Murray, memorandum to staff, 2 July 1966. *John Murray archives.*

25 Lord Birkenhead to John G. Murray, 10 June 1966. *John Murray archives.*

26 *Ibid.*

27 John G. Murray to Lord Birkenhead, 15 June 1966. *John Murray archives.*

28 See JB, *Letters*, ed. CLG, ii, 323–24 and 324n.

29 John G. Murray to JB, 15 August 1966. *John Murray archives.*

30 John G. Murray to JB, 12 October 1966. *John Murray archives.* JB acceded to the BBC's request. The *Radio Times* for 1 November 1966 announced that at 8.30 p.m. in *The World of Books* programme on the Home Service, 'John Betjeman presents poems from his collection High and Low, published yesterday.'

31 Penelope Chetwode, *Kulu*, London 1972.

32 *The Scotsman*, 12 November 1966.

33 *Ibid.*

34 *Ibid.*

35 (Dame) Judi Dench (b. 1934), British actress.

36 *The Scotsman*, 12 November 1966.

37 Craig Wylie of Houghton Mifflin, telegram to John G. Murray, responding to Murray's letter of 31 August 1966. *John Murray archives.*

38 John G. Murray to Craig Wylie, 23 September 1966. *John Murray archives.*

39 Craig Wylie to John G. Murray, note sent with suggested American 'blurb' for *High and Low*, n.d. *John Murray archives.*

40 JB, *Letters*, ed. CLG, ii, 310.

41 On 2 October 1966 Jane Boulanger of John Murray sent Houghton Mifflin – who had requested the information because of copyright law – the following list of poems going into *High and Low* but not previously published:

'Old Friends'	'Monody on the Death of a Platonist Bank Clerk'
'The Small Towns of Ireland'	'Good-bye'
'Ireland's Own'	'Five O'Clock Shadow'

'An Edwardian Sunday . . .'	'Perp. Revival i' the North'
'Uffington'	'Agricultural Caress'
'Anglo Catholic Congresses'	'Meditation on the A30'
'The Commander'	'Reproof Deserved'
'The Hon. Sec.'	'Caprice'
'A Lament for Moira McCavendish'	

However, this list should be accepted with caution. It was presumably based on what JB told Murray; and, though his memory for church architects was remarkable, his memory for other minutiae could be more erratic.

42 *Vogue*, November 1957.
43 The Betjeman–Skinner correspondence is in the Bodleian Library, Oxford. For examples of JB's letters to Skinner, see JB, *Letters*, ed. CLG, ii, 142, 183, 283 and 301.
44 *John Murray archives.*
45 *Sunday Times*, 6 November 1966.
46 *The Tablet*, 24 December 1966.
47 *The Observer*, 6 November 1966.
48 Auden made this comment in his introduction to the selection of JB's poems he made for American readers in 1947, *Slick But Not Streamlined*, Garden City, New York, pp. 9–10.
49 *New Statesman*, 23 December 1966.
50 *Country Life*, 19 January 1967.
51 *Punch*, 9 November 1966.
52 Anthony Powell, *Journals 1987–1989*, London 1996, p. 62.
53 *John Murray archives.*
54 *Evening News*, 8 December 1966.
55 *The Observer*, 18 December 1966.
56 Philip Larkin to John G. Murray, 25 October 1966. *John Murray archives.*
57 *Sunday Express*, 11 December 1966.
58 *Ibid.*
59 *Ibid.*
60 *Ibid.*
61 The letter is quoted by John G. Murray in a letter to Mrs Deane of David Higham Associates, 14 March 1978. *John Murray archives.*

Jock Murray decided that two of JB's slim volumes, after they were absorbed into *Collected Poems*, were worth reprinting. They were reprinted; and one of the two was *High and Low*. Hence Murray's letter to JB asking for permission to reprint and JB's humorous acceptance of the suggestion. As is usual with reprints, a reduced royalty was offered. However, after *High and Low* was reprinted, Murray's received an angry telephone call from Higham saying that Higham had the rights for *High and Low* – looked after the copyright on behalf of JB, an arrangement that applied to that book only. Jock Murray wrote to Higham to say he was very sorry; he had not remembered that such an arrangement existed. And then Mrs Deane of Higham wrote back to say, 'Don't worry; it's all right.' (*Ex inf.* John R. Murray, telephone conversation, 2004.)

Chapter 13: John Nankivell

1 Shown to the author by John Nankivell.
2 John Nankivell, letter to the author, 22 May 2001.
3 On the *Nanskevall* family of St Wenn, Cornwall, see Davies Gilbert, *The Parochial History of Cornwall*, London 1839, iv, 139.
4 John Nankivell, interview, 2003.
5 JB's essay on Ilfracombe appeared in *First and Last Loves*, London 1952, pp. 225–28. ('Ilfracombe is the end of everything . . . It is an epitome of seaside history . . .')
6 John Nankivell, letter to the author, 22 May 2001.

7 Samuel Sanders Teulon (1812–73), English Gothic-revival architect of Huguenot ances-
  try. Among his designs were Totworth Court, Gloucestershire (1849–52), Shadwell Park,
  Norfolk (1856–61), St Mary's, Ealing (1861–74) and St Stephen's, Rosslyn Hill,
  Hampstead, London (1868–71).

8 William White (1825–1900), English Gothic revival architect. In 1847 established a prac-
  tice in Cornwall. He designed (among other buildings) the Old Rectory, Columb Major,
  Cornwall (1849–50), All Saints, Notting Hill, London (from 1852), St Saviour's, Aberdeen
  Park, London (1865) – where JB's parents were married in 1902 – and Humewood, Co.
  Wicklow (1873–77).

9 William Burges (1827–81), English architect. Among his most famous buildings are
  Cardiff Castle (from 1866), Castell Coch, Glamorganshire, Wales (1872–91) and his own
  Tower House, Melbury Road, Kensington, London (1875–81). The Tower House was
  bequeathed to JB in 1962. (See *JBNFNL*, p. 559.)

10 John Nankivell, letter to the author, 22 May 2001.

11 On the 'indefatigable' Henry Hems of Exeter, see Nikolaus Pevsner, *North Devon*,
  Harmondsworth 1952, p. 117.

12 John Nankivell, interview, 2003.

13 *Ibid.*

14 *Ibid.*

15 *Kennet Review*, vol. 4, no. 2, March 1962, pp. 34–36.

16 John Nankivell, interview, 2003.

17 *Ibid.*

18 *Ibid.*

19 *Ibid.*

20 Lewis Hosegood's publications include *Portraits and Places* [verse], Dulwich Village 1960.

21 Quoted, John Nankivell, interview, 2003.

22 *Ibid.*

23 *Ibid.*

24 Frank Lake (1914–82) and his brother Brian, both of whom wrote on 'clinical theology'.

25 R.D. Laing (1927–89), British psychiatrist noted for his 'alternative' approach to the treatment of schizophrenia. Among his published works are *The Self and Others* (1951) and
  The Divided Self (1960).

26 John Nankivell, interview, 2003.

27 On Margaret O'Brien, see *JBNFNL*, p. 451.

28 Quoted, John Nankivell, interview, 2003.

29 *Ibid.*

30 John Nankivell, letter to the author, 22 May 2001.

31 *Ibid.*

32 On Lord Methuen, see *JBNFNL*, p. 85.

33 John Nankivell later commented (interview, 2003): 'He may have been psychic – but it
  didn't stop him falling into the canal that day.'

34 On Froxfield, Hampshire, see Arthur Mee, *Hampshire with the Isle of Wight* (The King's
  England), London 1939, pp. 168–69.

35 John Nankivell, letter to the author, 22 May 2001.

36 The Rev. Hugh Pickles became Vicar of Blewbury in 1963.

37 John Nankivell, letter to the author, 22 May 2001.

38 John Nankivell, interview, 2003.

39 On Cranmore Tower (1862), see Maxwell Fraser, *Companion into Somerset*, London
  1947, p. 43.

40 As examples: on 31 August 1967 JB wrote to Nankivell: 'Stick to the 2nd cheque as I would
  like to stick to that oil of the Sparrow unless you want more of it. I have grown v fond of
  it . . .' Nankivell recalls (note to the author, 15 July 2003): 'I had painted in oils a tiny
  picture of the pretty Sparrow pub in Letcombe Regis which John B loved and bought as
  a present for a godson.' Also, JB wrote to Nankivell on 27 September (?) 1967: 'I am
  delighted with the Uffington & Woolstone pictures – particularly the pencil sketch of the
  cottage by the church with a bit of the old school on the right . . .' Nankivell explains

(note to the author, 16 July 2003): 'It was a commission by him for a wedding or godchild present . . .' Both letters from JB shown to the author by Mr Nankivell.

41 John Nankivell recalled (interview, 2003):

Miriam Fletcher, my friend in Wantage, had a young Guernsey potter, Graham Newing, staying with her. He had decided he didn't want to live in Guernsey any more, so he upped and brought his family back to England. He didn't have a job at the time so he stayed with Miriam in Wantage for a few weeks.

I had read 'William Hickey' in the *Daily Express*, who said that the young Lord Weymouth – Lord Bath's eldest son – was starting an art group at Longleat and that he was wanting to gather together individual artists, including a potter. So I very bravely phoned up his lordship from a callbox one day, expecting to speak to a refined young gentleman who lived in a dark green penthouse apartment in a very sophisticated James Bond style on the top floor of Longleat; and I said, 'I know a potter', and was amazed when Weymouth said, 'Bring him down.' So I took Graham down and we were taken into these great painted rooms with modern paintings in the old part of the house with a Baroque room all covered with his lordship's paintings and his lordship with bare feet and a very correct butler and his wife. And Graham was invited to join the group – he still lives at Westbury and has a very successful pottery. Lord Weymouth said to me, 'Would you like to come too?' 'Oh, no,' I said. I had a very nice life in Wantage, thank you very much. I lived in Challow Park; I had all these new friends, including John Betjeman.

Anyway, Graham got on well there; and eventually Miriam and her husband Joe, who was a very good woodworker, decided to go there too. His lordship was acquiring all these craftspeople. He would acquire a photographer, an engraver, a silversmith, a jeweller and so on in the hope that one day this little community which was painting his walls – once they'd finished his murals – would be doing their own things. They'd be doing pottery, glass, sculpture and so on. They'd be a little art colony. I did get involved in some of the painting and in creating stained glass. A BBC producer called John King made a documentary, one of a series on 'communes' – very Sixties. And I remember his saying, 'Of course, this is the best time for people like you. Now you're in the full flush of enthusiasm. In a few years' time you'll all be falling to pieces.'

One bonus I got from the adventure was the picture frames. When Weymouth was a young man he had painted in every style imaginable. They weren't the 'rude' paintings of later years. These were his young-life works – mock Picassos, mock Van Goghs, mock everything. All these pictures of his had been poorly framed in mottled and textured white frames. He had them all cut out of their frames and we, as his painters, had to stick them on the walls of his house in oil borders. So he had a whole load of these empty frames which he very kindly lent me when I had the exhibition in Exeter.

42 John Nankivell, interview, 2003.

43 JB wrote to John Nankivell on 11 January 1968: 'I am so glad to have your letters and to know all went well with Michael Croucher. I thought it would. He works slowly but something will happen in the end.' (Letter shown to the author by Mr Nankivell.)

44 On 25 February 1970 JB wrote to John Nankivell:

Yesterday I had lunch with some young publishers called Mitchell, Beazley . . . I am connected with the firm. I mentioned your name as someone who might be willing to illustrate the first of a new series of books we had thought of. In fact I told them you were *the* man for the job, and they will pay you as some impersonal combine is at the back of them. I thought it would be a good idea to produce a series of books on towns illustrated by an artist and for pedestrians, and to sell fairly cheaply. The pictures and format are of course the most important thing. I thought of a map of the town in the fly leaf, and marked on it numerically the places from which the artist's views were taken. The point of the views would be that what you illustrate is what appeals to your eye, regardless of date, the text would be short and mention the architects of the buildings and other relevant bits of history. One wants to have the place looked at from the pedestrian's point of view, alleys, turns in a road, details that appeal. One would like of course to do Ilfracombe, which you have so memorably illustrated, but I don't think enough people go to Ilfracombe to justify that subject as the first in the series. There are, on the other hand, places which everybody goes to and nobody has looked at, such as Swansea and Cardiff and Chatham and Middlesbrough, but there are also towns which are good for tourist trade, and the books about which are either the Town Clerk's brochure or Pevsner, neither of which opens the eyes. I thought it would be a good idea to do one of the towns that the Ministry of Housing and Local Government is putting into repair, or making it into a conservation area, or whatever it is called, an obvious one of these is Chichester. The other towns they are going to do are York, Chester and I've forgotten the fourth. You will be hearing from one of the young publishers, probably by this post. I go to Chicago until the 5th, but if you are free to come up to London after that do fix a date, if you want me to be there, but you may like to negotiate it on your own . . . (Letter shown to the author by John Nankivell.)

On 16 March 1970, JB wrote to James Mitchell of Mitchell Beazley, sending a carbon copy to Nankivell:

Dear James (or whoever opens this letter and has power to 'implement' it)

I have had an idea about the [*illegible*]. John Nankivell has written to tell me he had an enjoyable and useful meeting with Nick Russell and will be coming up in April.

Get a copy of Tallis's London recently republished from the original of 1840 for the London Topographical Society by a firm called Natalie and Maurice at 8gns [guineas]. It is an oblong book bound in a swell way and with hundreds of plates. I propose that we should make a new Tallis of Chichester, York, etc. When you see the Tallis reproduction you will know what I mean. We could get an architectural draughtsman to draw the façades of each historical street in the centre of the town, chain stores, garages and all and we could get the companies whose names appeared in the drawings to pay for them if they wanted to, like they did in Tallis's time.

John Nankivell himself may like to do these drawings but any architectural draughtsman of humour (Robin Wyatt at Seely and Paget, for instance) could draw in that flat, linear style the main streets. John's drawings could emphasize the good things and go down the side streets which are not Tallisised. Chichester is an admirable example to start with.

Thus the book is an oblong in thin boards or cardboard with a map over the fly leaves indicating where John has drawn and let us say 8 or 10 pages of his drawings intermingled with factual and sometime furious and sometimes delighted text and across the double spread formed by the middle of the 32 pages the Tallis of the main streets. It may not be necessary to stick exactly to this format but it is a way of being neither Shell nor Pevsner and more informative than either and, I think, prettier.

I don't think it in the least matters if a lot of the book is out of date as far as shops are concerned and threatened buildings in a year or two after publication. It will add to its value as a memorial of what once was an attractive town.

I am in Cornwall till next Tuesday but Jackie Davis [his secretary] can get hold of me if you tell her you want to talk about this on the telephone. (Copy shown to the author by John Nankivell.)

45 JB, letter to John Nankivell, 25 February 1970. Shown to the author by Mr Nankivell.
46 Elizabeth Simson, artist. On her, see Nicholas Shakespeare, *Bruce Chatwin*, London 1999, p. 242.
47 Bess Cuthbert, school teacher, who became John Nankivell's girlfriend. See *loc. cit.*; also, Chapter 20 of the present volume, 'A Heavy Crown'.
48 In a letter of this year to Stuart Piggott, JB described Nankivell as 'a young male pencil artist of real talent'. JB, *Letters*, ed. CLG. ii, 371.
49 JB to the Rev. Wilfrid Harry Jarvis, 15 September 1970. JB, *Letters*, ed. CLG, ii, 404.
50 Stuart Piggott's diary, 6 August 1968. Quoted, Shakespeare, *op. cit.*, p. 196.
51 The research fellow was Ruth Tringham, 'a red-haired Marxist . . . the first westerner to excavate in Moldavia'. (Shakespeare, *op. cit.*, p. 198). She added: 'In as much as either

could have loved another person, they loved each other. My impression is that Stuart was in love with him' (*ibid.*, p. 213). Piggott's marriage had ended in divorce 'because of, you know, not having children', Sibyl Harton said (interview, 1976). However, Nicholas Shakespeare is sceptical of Tringham's opinion and considers (*ibid.*, p. 213) that Piggott's diaries suggest that 'he felt sorry for Bruce rather than attracted to him'.

52 Quoted, *ibid.*, p. 242.
53 John Nankivell, interview, 2003.
54 Shakespeare, *op. cit.*, p. 242.
55 *Ibid.*, p. 244.
56 *Ibid.*, p. 247.
57 Bruce Chatwin to Michael Cottrill, July 1986. Quoted, *ibid.*, p. 378.
58 John Nankivell recalls that Lady Elizabeth Cavendish dropped John at the gallery in Duke Street, St James's, then immediately drove off – because she knew that Penelope was going to be present at the private view.
59 The phrase was introduced by Reyner Banham as the title of his book *The New Brutalism: Ethic or Aesthetic?*, London 1966.

Chapter 14: Pylons on the March: Preservation in the Sixties

1 On the history of the campaign to save the Great Barn at Avebury, I have been given great help by Mr Brian Edwards. Most of the correspondence and other papers relating to the controversy over the barn are now lodged at Lackham Agricultural College; but Mr Edwards made copies of some key documents which he has sent me.
2 Stuart Piggott, interview, 1989.
3 Brian Edwards, telephone conversation, 2003.
4 Copy of letter sent to the author by Brian Edwards.
   On 19 December 1959 JB wrote to Lord Moyne: 'I have this day written to Lord John Hope M[inistry] of W[orks] & to John Smith of Coutts . . . of Nat. Trust enclosing the correspondence & saying I will hold up signing the letter to *The Times* until negotiations have failed . . .' (Wiltshire Rural Life Society, Lackham College, Wiltshire). In his reply, dated 'January 1960', Lord John Hope wrote:

   I think you know that the National Trust consider themselves bound by the general policy, which was agreed at the time when the tripartite arrangements were made between them, the late Mr Keiller and ourselves for the preservation of Avebury, that as and when buildings reach the end of their useful life they shall be handed over to us for demolition.
      On the other hand, I am certainly not anxious to see this barn demolished (or to have the job of demolishing it) and I would be just as well pleased to see it preserved. The trouble is that I am advised that it is not a building of such value architecturally or archaeologically that I could make any money available for its preservation . . . (Wiltshire Rural Life Society, Lackham College, Wiltshire).

6 (Henry) Robin Romilly Fedden (1908–77), National Trust officer and author, mainly of travel books. For an appreciation of him at the time of his death, see James Lees-Milne, diary entry for 21 March 1977. *Through Wood and Dale: Diaries 1975–1978*, London 2001 edn., pp. 155–56.
7 *Ex inf.* Brian Edwards. The correspondence is at the Wiltshire Rural Life Society, Lackham College, Wiltshire.
8 Brian Edwards, telephone conversation with the author, 2003.
9 Brian Edwards, 'Avebury and Other Not-So-Ancient Places: The Making of the English Heritage Landscape', in *Seeing History: Public History in Britain Now*, London, 2000, pp. 65–79.
10 Lyrics by Ray Davies of the Kinks.
11 Brian Edwards, telephone conversation with the author, 2003.
12 *Ibid.*

13 I am grateful to Mr Norton for writing to me about his correspondence and encounter with JB.

14 I am grateful to Mr Norton for a copy of this letter.

15 I am again indebted to Mr Norton for a copy of this letter.

16 Thanks are again due to Mr Norton for a copy of this letter.

17 The poem is printed in David Bland, *Ouseley and His Angels: The Life of St Michael's College, Tenbury and Its Founder*, Windsor, Berkshire 2000, pp. 209–10. I am grateful to Brother James Abson for kindly drawing the book to my attention.

18 Bland, *op. cit.*, p. 219.

19 Quoted, *loc. cit.*

20 JB, conversation with the author, 1971.

21 Bland, *op. cit.*, p. 224.

22 *Ibid.*, p. 234.

23 *Ibid.*, p. 261.

24 Quoted, *loc. cit.*

25 *Ibid.*, p. 291.

26 *The Times*, 27 April 1962.

27 *The Times*, 22 June 1962.

28 *The Times*, 26 September 1962. On Charles Clore and Jack Cotton, see Oliver Marriott, *The Property Boom*, London 1967.

29 *The Times*, 30 October 1962.

30 *The Times*, 18 June 1963.

31 *The Times*, 21 June 1963.

32 *The Times*, 3 December 1963.

33 *The Times*, 4 November 1963.

34 *The Times*, 30 October 1965.

35 *Ibid.*

36 *The Times*, 23 February 1966.

37 *The Times*, 4 March 1966.

38 *The Times*, 5 March 1966.

39 JB to Sir Giles Gilbert Scott, 27 January 1944. JB, *Letters*, ed. CLG, i, 337–38.

40 Sir Giles Gilbert Scott to JB, 2 February 1944. JB, *Letters*, ed. CLG, i, 338n.

41 *The Times*, 8 September 1966.

42 *The Times*, 10 September 1966.

43 *The Times*, 12 September 1966.

44 Sir Edward Playfair, letter to the author, 3 January 1996.

45 I am grateful to Dr John Maples for this information.

46 *The Times*, 11 March 1967.

47 *The Times*, 18 April 1967.

48 *The Times*, 4 August 1967. Professor Hancock's letter had been published in the issue of 26 July 1967.

49 *The Times*, 17 July 1968.

50 *The Times*, 17 July 1969.

51 *Ibid.*

52 Lady Pamela Berry to JB, 22 February 1970. JB, *Letters*, ed. CLG, ii, 375.

53 Quoted, *loc. cit.*

Chapter 15: Mary Wilson and a Journey to Diss

1 Charles Garrett Ponsonby Moore, eleventh Earl of Drogheda (1910–89). A protégé of Brendan Bracken, whose house in Lord North Street (later the home of Jonathan Aitken, MP) he occupied. (JB refers to the street in his letter to Mary Wilson, 26 February 1974. JB, *Letters*, ed. CLG, ii, 476.) Lord Drogheda was chairman of the Royal Opera House, Covent Garden, 1958–74, and of the Financial Times Ltd, 1971–75 (managing director, 1945–70).

2 Lady Wilson, interview, 1982. In his memories, *Double Harness* (London 1978, p. 263), Drogheda gave a slightly different account of the occasion; though as he misremembered its date (assigning it to the première of Visconti's *Trovatore* in 1964), his version may not be reliable.

> Visconti himself was to give us three other productions in coming years, a handsome serviceable *Trovatore* in 1964/5, to the première of which I invited Mrs Harold Wilson, who had been recently installed in 10 Downing Street and of whom I had read in a newspaper profile that opera was among her enthusiasms. As company for her I thought that it would be a good idea to invite John Betjeman, and I said to him, 'Please come and exercise your charm on the wife of the Prime Minister. Covent Garden's grant may depend on you'. He duly complied. During the music he was more hypnotized by the harpist in the orchestra than by the action on the stage: but during the intervals Mrs Wilson was captivated by him, with the result that regularly thereafter he was invited for tea at No. 10. She most certainly enjoyed the evening. I remember her comparing it with some of her official functions where she said that she felt like a tethered goat. She was obviously not in a position to determine our grant, but at least her enjoyment at Covent Garden could not have hurt our cause.

3 JB, *Letters*, ed. CLG, ii, 339n.
4 JB to Mary Wilson, 12 November 1967. JB, *Letters*, ed. CLG, ii, 339.
5 *Ibid.*, ii, 340.
6 Conventionally abbreviated into some such phrase, what Wilson actually said in a broadcast of 19 November 1967 was: 'From now the pound abroad is worth 14 per cent or so less in terms of other currencies. It does not mean, of course, that the pound here in Britain, in your pocket or purse or in your bank has been devalued.' *The Oxford Dictionary of 20th Century Quotations*, ed. Elizabeth Knowles, Oxford 1998, pp. 330–31.
7 Mary Wilson to JB, 27 November 1967. JB, *Letters*, ed. CLG, ii, 340.
8 There is some doubt as to the precise date on which the Garrick dinner took place. JB's letter, 'Oh dear. Never again the Garrick' (JB, *Letters*, ed. CLG, ii, 343), is dated 3 December 1967. However, Mary Wilson's letter of thanks for the dinner (*Ibid.*, 343n.) – 'Thank you for last night' – is dated 5 December. JB is more likely to have got the date wrong than Mary Wilson, so the dinner was probably on the evening of 4 December.
9 On 9 March 1964, three years before he met Mary Wilson, JB wrote to Leonora Ison, the woman who illustrated his 'Men and Buildings' articles in the *Daily Telegraph* (on her, see Chapter 3):

> I would like to do a piece about Diss, in Norfolk, for my next article. If only you could cross the mouth of the Thames in a rowing boat to Ipswich, you could get there quite quickly, without having to go round by Liverpool Street. If you do go to Diss, avoid the King's Head, which is one of the worst hotels I've stayed in. It is a charming town built round a mere. It has a good service of trains to London and no main road and it has neither grown nor shrunk and is a happy community with the inevitable East Anglian blends of nonconformity in charming chapels down side-streets, a market place and handsome flint church, too vigorously restored inside. The prettiest home of descent [*sic* for dissent] is the Unitarian chapel on Park Field, exactly suited to your pencil and with a view of the mere beyond it. Another good view is the Shambles in the market place (a Georgian colonnade threatened with destruction) and the knapped flint porch of the church beyond. There are steep little streets like Market Hill with its sudden view of the Greek revival Corn Exchange and there is good late Georgian in Mount Street, notably Admiral Taylor's house, Mount Pleasant. John Oliver, the antique dealer, or Dr Hyde would, I am sure, show you round if you go. They are as anxious to save Diss as you, the old Cartographer [Leonora's husband, Walter Ison] and
>
> Yours,
>
> John Betjeman

(Shown to the author by Walter Ison.)

It may have been just coincidence that in March 1964 JB decided to write about Diss, part of which was under threat. A cynic, however might note that in February 1963 Harold Wilson had become leader of the Labour Party after the death of JB's old friend Hugh Gaitskell in January. Journalists began to take an interest in Wilson's wife Mary, as a potential future First Lady, and her birthplace, Diss, was mentioned. Wilson's chances of becoming prime minister went up in October 1963 when the feeble Lord Home succeeded Harold Macmillan in that post. Did JB choose to write about Diss with a view to interesting Mary Wilson in him?

10 JB, *Letters*, ed. CLG, ii, 313.
11 See his letter to Mary Wilson of 6 April 1969. JB, *Letters*, ed. CLG, ii, 363.
12 Mary Wilson to JB, 4 January 1968. JB, *Letters*, ed. CLG, ii, 345.
13 JB to Mary Wilson, 5 January 1968. Shown to the author by Lady Wilson of Rievaulx.
14 Lady Wilson, interview, 1982.
15 *Ibid.*
16 *The Poetical Works of Henry Wadsworth Longfellow*, London 1893, p. 481.
17 John McCrae, 'In Flanders Fields', 1915. The *Oxford Dictionary of War Quotations*, ed. Justin Wintle, London 1989, p. 307.
18 Lady Wilson, interview, 1982.
19 JB, *Letters*, ed. CLG, ii, 313.
20 Lady Wilson, interview, 1982.
21 JB, *Letters*, ed. CLG, ii, 314.
22 *Ibid.*, 313.
23 *Ibid.*, 314.
24 *Ibid.*, 313.
25 Mary Wilson's poems about the Isles of Scilly have been collected in *A Journey to Scilly*, St Mary's Isles of Scilly, n.d.
26 JB to Mary Wilson, 16 August 1969. Shown to the author by Lady Wilson.
27 JB to Mary Wilson, 11 January 1968. Shown to the author by Lady Wilson.
28 JB to Mary Wilson, 26 October 1969. Shown to the author by Lady Wilson.
29 JB to Mary Wilson, 10 December 1969. Shown to the author by Lady Wilson.
30 Lady Wilson, interview, 2003.
31 Mary Wilson, 'Mamzelle', *New Poems*, London 1979, p. 64.
32 JB to Mary Wilson, May 1971. Shown to the author by Lady Wilson.
33 JB to Mary Wilson, September 1971. Shown to the author by Lady Wilson.
34 *Collected Poems*, 2001 edn., p. 341.
35 Lady Wilson, interview, 1982.
36 *Ibid.*
37 This is the version of the poem which appeared in *A Nip in the Air* (London 1974) and *Collected Poems* (1985 edn., pp. 414–15). For the original draft and a note on JB's emendations see JB, *Letters*, ed. CLG, ii, 349–50.
38 Nye used poetic licence: the Latin for Hell is 'Dis'.
39 *The Times*, 12 December 1974.
40 Lady Wilson, interview, 1982.
41 Mary Wilson, 'Reply to the Laureate'. It was published in her *New Poems*, London 1979, p. 53. JB gave her permission to print his 'Mind's Journey' beside it.
42 *Sunday Times*, 14 March 1976.
43 *The Times*, 21 March 1976.
44 Robert Lusty, *Bound to Be Read*, London 1975, p. 135.
45 The present author first encountered Joan at dinner at the Garrick Club with Mr John R. Murray.
46 Lusty, *op. cit.*, pp. 135–36.
47 JB to Mary Wilson, summer 1970. Shown to the author by Lady Wilson.
48 Lady Wilson, interview, 2003.
49 Fison's was and is a well-known fertilizer. There was no Sir Monty Fison, but there was in 1975 a Sir (Frank Guy) Clavering Fison who lived at Crepping Hall, Suffolk.
50 Joe Haines (b. 1928), chief press secretary to the Prime Minister.

51 Andrew Delahunty in *The Oxford Dictionary of Nicknames*, Oxford 2003, p. 97, lists:

> *Lady Forkbender* Marcia Williams, Lady Falkender (b. 1932). Prime Minister Harold Wilson's private and political secretary 1956–73. Given a life peerage in Wilson's resignation honours list in 1974, she was dubbed Lady Forkbender in the satirical magazine *Private Eye*. As well as playing on her name, this alluded to Uri Geller (b. 1946), the Israeli psychic performer who came to fame in the 1970s with his demonstrations of bending cutlery, stopping watches, and other feats.

52 *Private Eye*, 30 May 1975.
53 Quoted, Lady Wilson, interview, 2003.
54 Lady Wilson, interview, 2003.
55 JB to Mary Wilson, 2 February 1970. Shown to the author by Lady Wilson.
56 JB to Mary Wilson, summer 1974. Shown to the author by Lady Wilson.
57 JB to Mary Wilson, n.d. but about May 1970. Shown to the author by Lady Wilson.
58 JB to Mary Wilson, 17 October 1974. Shown to the author by Lady Wilson.
59 JB to Mary Wilson, 18 March 1976. Shown to the author by Lady Wilson.
60 JB to Mary Wilson, 20 March 1970. Shown to the author by Lady Wilson.

Chapter 16: Back to Australia

1 Shown to the author by PB. On 26 October JB had written to (Sir) John Drummond, who set up the films (JB, *Letters*, ed. CLG, ii, 421n.):

> I like the idea of doing an Australian film or films . . . They could be a revelation over here and I daresay in Australia too, of the superlatively good eighteenth- and nineteenth-century architecture and planning and layout of suburbs to be found in that country. I'd also like some marsupials ambling about, and horned lizards walking up garden fences . . . Subjects I should like to do are: 1) the architecture of Horbury Hunt, e.g. Newcastle and Grafton and Armadale Cathedrals; 2) the City of Brisbane and along with it some Drysdale-looking country town; 3) Sydney's Georgian and later architecture; 4) Ballarat, a town I have never visited but which I am told has splendid relics of its golden days. The possibilities are so immense, I don't really know where to start. The Botanic Gardens at Melbourne are worth a film to themselves, along with the Mint and the Governor's house. The railways of Australia, the steamers to Manley, unvisited places like Zeehan in Tasmania, with its empty Opera House and cyclamen-scented ruined streets. The marvellous paintings of Australia done by Tom Roberts, Conder, Streeton and the Boyds. Drysdale desert scenes. It is too beautiful for words. The Australians take it for granted and we don't know about it.

The visit to Chicago did not, in fact, take place.
2 *Ibid.*
3 *Times Literary Supplement*, 23 June 1972.
4 Shown to the author by PB.
5 See *YB*, p. 19.
6 Shown to the author by PB.
7 *Ibid.*
8 JB to the author, 14 September 1971.
9 On Dr Frank Tait, see the beginning of Chapter 29. 'His Last Bow'.
10 *Betjeman in Australia* (BBC and ABC television), 1972.
11 Margaret McCall, interview, 1991.
12 *Ibid.*
13 Ian S. MacNiven, *Lawrence Durrell: A Biography*, London 1998, pp. 558, 590, 611.
14 Margaret McCall, interview, 1991.
15 *Ibid.*
16 *Ibid.*

17 *A Dedicated Fan: Julian Jebb 1934–1984*, ed. Tristram and Georgia Powell, London 1993, p. 14.

18 On that film, *Marble Arch to Edgware* (one of a BBC series called *Contrasts*, screened in 1968), see Chapter 9, 'A Natural Showman: Television in the Sixties'.

19 On the film *Tennyson: A Beginning and an End*, which JB made with Julian Jebb in 1968–69, see *ibid*.

20 Margaret McCall, interview, 1991.

21 *Ibid*.

22 *Ibid*.

23 *Ibid*.

24 *Ibid*.

25 *Ibid*.

26 *Betjeman in Australia* (BBC and ABC television), 1972.

27 Margaret McCall, interview, 1991.

28 *Betjeman in Australia* (BBC and ABC television), 1972.

29 *Ibid*. JB wrote to CLG from Brisbane on 14 October 1971 (JB, *Letters*, ed. CLG, ii, 422): 'Saw a spider four inches long in a private house "toilet" (a v[ery] dainty toilet) and filmed it.'

30 Margaret McCall, interview, 1991.

31 *Betjeman in Australia* (BBC and ABC television), 1972.

32 *Ibid*. Presumably this was the 'lovely rubber centipede' to which JB referred in his letter of 29 September 1971 to CLG (JB, *Letters*, ed. CLG, ii, 420).

33 *Betjeman in Australia* (BBC and ABC television), 1972.

34 *Ibid*.

35 Margaret McCall, interview, 1991.

36 *Betjeman in Australia* (BBC and ABC television), 1972.

37 *Ibid*.

38 *Ibid*.

39 JB, *Letters*, ed. CLG, ii, 420–21.

40 Margaret McCall, interview, 1991.

41 *Betjeman in Australia* (BBC and ABC television), 1972.

42 *Ibid*.

43 PB, interview, 1976.

44 See *YB*, p. 189.

45 *Betjeman in Australia* (BBC and ABC television), 1972.

46 *Ibid*.

47 *Ibid*.

48 *Ibid*.

49 *Ibid*.

50 Louis Raemakers (1869–1956), Dutch cartoonist who gained international fame during the First World War with his anti-German cartoons. After 1916 he worked for some years in England. He was also a cartoonist in the Second World War.

51 *Betjeman in Australia* (BBC and ABC television), 1972. Sir Frank Brangwyn RA (1867–1956), English painter and graphic artist. His designs for the House of Lords were rejected as too flamboyant for their setting; in 1933 they were acquired by the Guildhall, Swansea, where they remain. A painter of Imperial splendours.

52 *Ibid*.

53 Julian Jebb, conversation, 1970.

54 *Betjeman in Australia* (BBC and ABC television), 1972.

55 Margaret McCall, interview, 1991.

56 JB, *Letters*, ed. CLG, ii, 421–22.

57 *Ibid*., 422.

58 See Tristram Powell's Introduction to *A Dedicated Fan: Julian Jebb 1934–1984*, London 1993, p. 13.

59 Margaret McCall, interview, 1991.

60 *Betjeman in Australia* (BBC and ABC television), 1972.

61 *Ibid.*

62 *Ibid.*

63 JB, *Letters*, ed. CLG, ii, 424.

64 *Ibid.*, 423.

65 On Reggie Ross-Williamson, see *JBNFNL*, Chapter 13, 'Ireland'.

66 JB, *Letters*, ed. CLG, ii, 423.

67 *Loc. cit.*

68 *Betjeman in Australia* (BBC and ABC television), 1972.

69 *Ibid.*

70 CLG writes (JB, *Letters*, ed. CLG, ii, 378): 'This second trip to Australia was not as successful as his first, partly because Julian Jebb was unhappy in love which caused a lot of tension . . .' Jebb committed suicide in 1984.

71 Margaret McCall, interview, 1991.

72 Humphries and Beresford were discussing plans for the film *Barry McKenzie Holds His Own* (Australia, 1974).

73 Barry Humphries, telephone conversation with the author, 2001.

74 Margaret McCall, interview, 1991.

75 *Ibid.*

76 Port Arthur was named after Governor Sir George Arthur, later of Upper Canada. One of James Lees-Milne's aunts had married an Arthur. On 12 December 1971 JB wrote to James and Alvilde Lees-Milne (JB, *Letters*, ed. CLG, ii, 425–26): 'Of course in Tazzie, Governor Arthur is made out to be the wickedest man who ever lived. He certainly did authorize the abo [rigine] hunt so that there are no aborigines left in Tasmania . . . Arthur brought *order* to Tazzie but was recalled to Upper Canada. Is there a life of him? It would be worth writing. I think he may be much maligned . . .'

77 *Betjeman in Australia* (BBC and ABC television), 1972.

78 *Ibid.*

79 *Ibid.*

80 *Ibid.*

81 *Ibid.*

82 *Ibid.*

83 *Ibid.*

84 *Ibid.*

85 This is the version of the poem published in *A Nip in the Air*, London 1974, p. 41. CLG (JB, *Letters*, ed. CLG, ii, 426–27) gives an earlier version, sent to Edith and Oliver Garratt, who owned a house opposite Treen in Trebetherick, Cornwall) on 31 December 1971, indicating that JB made a number of changes before it appeared in *A Nip in the Air*.

86 Frances Partridge, diary entry for 7 December 1972. *Life Regained: Diaries 1970–1972* (vol. 6), London 1999 edn., p. 236.

87 Frances Partridge, diary entry for 15 December 1972. *Ibid.*, p. 237.

88 Frances Partridge, diary entry for 25 December 1972. *Ibid*, p. 242.

89 *Ibid.*, p. 243.

90 *Loc. cit.*

91 Shown to the author by PB.

92 James Lees-Milne wrote in his diary on 28 June 1972 (*A Mingled Measure: Diaries 1953–1972*, London 1994, pp. 254–55):

At 4.30 [Alvilde] and I left, and motored to London for John Betj's film première on Australia, and dinner after. While having drinks at the bar of the cinema Tony Snowdon arrived, ran up to us and talked about Bath. Full of vitality and cheer. Then Princess Margaret arrived, followed by the Prince of Wales. I was taken aback not having expected such. Elizabeth Cavendish presented us one by one. Then Princess Margaret came up to Tony and, small though he is, she almost tiptoed to kiss his ear, and whisper. Tony said, 'You know Jim?' 'Yes,' she said, and moved away. After the film we went to Rules restaurant in Maiden Lane where John had hired an upstairs room, with a single table. We were a party of ten, including Princess Margaret, Prince Charles and Tony. I sat next to Mary Duchess of D. and a nice youngish man, whom only afterwards I learnt was Patrick Garland. Opposite him sat the girl he is living with, a film star, placed next to the P. of W., on Elizabeth's right. Then Tony, then A. on John Betj's left, John, Princess M., John Drummond who had produced the film, the Duchess, me, Garland. I hardly spoke a word to the royals, but watched them closely. Prince Charles is very charming, and very polite, shook hands with us all and smiled. P.M. is far from charming, is cross, exacting, too sophisticated, and sharp. She is physically attractive in a bun-like way, with trussed-up bosom, and hair like two cottage loaves, one balancing on the other. She wore a beautiful sapphire and diamond brooch. She smoked continuously from a long holder, and did not talk to John once. [On another occasion, Princess Margaret told the Hon. James Stourton that she greatly disliked JB, but had to put up with him for Elizabeth's sake; this remark was witnessed by the art dealer Christopher Gibbs. *Ex inf.* Mr Stourton, conversation, 2003.] Prince Charles at 11 asked Elizabeth if he might leave, for he had to motor to Portsmouth. He said he was tired, and looked worn out. E. patted his hand and said, 'Of course, love, Sir,' and beckoned to John. We all rose. He shook hands with us, Princess M. kissed him and Tony called out, 'Good-night, Charles.' 'Good-night, Tony.' E., who had taken her shoes off under the table, walked barefoot downstairs and into the street to see the P. off. She said to the driver, 'Mind you drive carefully.' P.M. while she was out of the room picked up E.'s shoes and put them on her plate. This annoyed Tony who said, 'It is unlucky, and I don't like it.' So P.M. took them off, put them on her chair, and walked to the window. A. said to me, 'You must go and talk to her,' but I knew she didn't want me to. She said she wanted to leave. Indeed it was time. Finally she induced Tony to take her, after E. had said that I would drive her in my Morris. Thank God I didn't have to. In following her, Tony made us all promise to come back to Kensington Palace. Which we debated. I did not want to go because I thought P.M. would not be pleased. The Duchess said to me as we left, 'Well!' – nothing further.

However we went to the palace since the Duchess accompanied us, and we knew she would not stay long. Tony met us in the courtyard and explained to me the architecture; what was Wren's work, what his. Their apartments were very well done by Tony in mock William Kent style. P.M. more gracious to me in her own house and took me into the dining-room. But I did not find conversation very easy or agreeable.

93 John Drummond, *Tainted by Experience: A Life in the Arts*, London 2000, pp. 196–97.

Chapter 17: The Church of England Ramblers

1 H.A. Williams, *Some Day I'll Find You*, London 1982, p. 230.
2 Sir Edward Heath, interview, 1990.
3 See *JBNFNL*, p. 281.
4 Princess Margaret fell in love with Group-Captain Peter Townsend, an equerry to the King, but in 1955 was forced to renounce him because he was divorced.
5 Bishop Mervyn Stockwood, interview, 1990.
6 *The Times*, 2 February 2001.
7 Joyce Grenfell, *The Time of My Life*, London 1989, p. 68 (her journal entry for 20 March 1944).
8 *The Times*, 2 February 2001.
9 Bishop Mervyn Stockwood, interview, 1990.
10 *Ibid.*
11 Bishop Hugh Montefiore writes of Harry Williams in his (Williams's) days as chaplain of Westcott House (1948–51), in *Oh God, What Next?* (London, 1995, p. 69): '[He] was not yet the radical don who set the theological world by the ears with *The True Wilderness*: he was at that time the ex-curate of All Saints, Margaret Street, the high-church member of staff who had spent hours in the Confessional in London, and whose views were (if you can credit it) very conservative and orthodox.'

12 H.A. Williams, *The True Wilderness*, London 1965.

13 PB, interview, 1977.

14 H.A. Williams, *Some Day I'll Find You*, London 1982, pp. 163–75 and *passim*.

15 Quoted, *ibid.*, p. 209.

16 *Loc. cit.*

17 Simon Stuart wrote (letter to the author, 16 March 2001): 'I was sent to see Harry [Williams] when he was at Westcott by Fr. Denis Marsh – a Franciscan C of E friar. I was in a muddle at the time about (homo) sex and religion. Harry told me to read Augustine's *Confessions* and I went so far as to carry a copy in my pack to Finnish Lapland in July '57, but never opened it. Then Harry was made Dean of Trinity and I suppose the association developed therefrom.'

18 *Ex inf.* Bishop Mervyn Stockwood, interview, 1990.

19 Hugh Montefiore, *Oh God, What Next?*, London 1995, pp. 144–45.

20 Ned Sherrin, letter to the author, 16 March 2001.

21 Bishop Mervyn Stockwood, interview, 1990.

22 *Ibid.*

23 *Ibid.*

24 *Ibid.*

25 In his autobiography, *Father Figure* (London 1972, p. 165), Beverley Nichols confessed that he had tried to kill his father.

26 Bishop Mervyn Stockwood, interview, 1990.

27 *Ibid.* The master was of course A.R. Gidney.

28 *Ibid.*

29 Mervyn Stockwood, *Chanctonbury Ring: An Autobiography*, London 1982, p. 39.

30 On JB's *Spectator* article about Billy Graham, see *JBNFNL*, p. 531.

31 Stockwood, *op. cit.*, pp. 99–100.

32 *Loc. cit.*

33 *Ibid.*, p. 103.

34 Bishop Mervyn Stockwood, interview, 1990.

35 On Munir Elhawa, see Michael De-la-Noy, *Mervyn Stockwood: A Lonely Life*, London 1996, pp. 186–87, 196 and 198.

36 Caryl Brahms, critic and novelist, writer of film, television and radio scripts. In *Too Dirty for the Windmill: A Memoir of Caryl Brahms*, written with Ned Sherrin (London 1986, p. 62), she recorded: 'Ned and I always looked forward to Mervyn's mid-Lent parties. So many different sorts of people, and we were among those always asked to stay on to luncheon, after the drinks. John Betjeman would be there with Elizabeth Cavendish, Norman Hartnell, Hywel Bennett and his wife, Cathy McGowan ... Jennie Lee, David Owen.' JB wrote a preface for Caryl Brahms's book *Gilbert and Sullivan: Lost Chords and Discords*, London 1975. Ned Sherrin recalls (letter to the author, 14 March 2001): 'I rather think we gave him lunch when Caryl asked him to write the piece. It may have been on that occasion that I gave him a lift back to Radnor Walk and as we bowled along Royal Avenue I called it "the soft under-belly of Chelsea", which made him laugh a lot.'

On Caryl Brahms, see also Ned Sherrin, *A Small Thing – Like an Earthquake: Memoirs*, London 1983, pp. 21–22, 33, 41, 45, 52–53, 62, 74, 76, 80, 93, 99, 100, 116, 119, 120, 123–24, 150, 159, 163, 164–84, 202–04.

37 Ned Sherrin, letter to the author, 14 March 2001.

38 Dr Michael Ramsey (1904–88), was Archbishop of Canterbury from 1961 to 1974.

On 4 November 2002, Canon Michael Saward, sometime Canon Treasurer of St Paul's Cathedral, wrote to the author:

In October 1967 I took up the post of the Church of England's Radio and Television Officer with special responsibility for Michael Ramsey's (the Archbishop of Canterbury's) broadcasts.

One of my first tasks, a week later, was to be present at a televised discussion at Lambeth Palace between the Archbishop and John Betjeman. As the new boy, I had not been involved in the planning so I simply stood and watched, with growing embarrassment, as these two elderly men, both in their sixties, sat together on a settee in Ramsey's study and giggled and simpered like two adolescent schoolgirls. It was quite distressingly camp and I watched the looks of distaste and unbelief on the faces of the TV camera crew who were clearly as sickened as I was at such a fatuous performance. Betjeman's only redeeming feature was to take us all afterwards (minus Ramsey) to a brassy Victorian pub in Tottenham Court Road where he noisily dispensed alcohol to all and sundry.

I had no difficulty in seeing why it was that C. S. Lewis had so disliked him when Betjeman was one of his Oxford students in the 1920s . . . I enjoyed Betjeman's verse but thought him a good example of what A. N. Wilson calls 'High Church pansyism'.

39 Shown to the author by Bishop Stockwood.
40 Robert George Miles became Vicar of St Nicholas with Christ Church, Deptford, in 1961; Hugh Everingham Wallace, Vicar of Christ Church, North Brixton, in 1955.
41 Shown to the author by Bishop Stockwood.
42 Lord Sheppard of Liverpool, letter to the author, 9 March 2001.
43 Ned Sherrin, letter to the author, 14 March 2001.
44 H.A. Williams, *Some Day I'll Find You*, London 1982, pp. 225–26.
45 *Ibid.*, p. 226.
46 De-la-Noy, *op. cit.*, p. 187.
47 H.A. Williams, *Some Day I'll Find You*, London 1982, p. 227.
48 *Ibid.*, p. 229.
49 *Loc. cit.*
50 JB, *Letters*, ed. CLG, ii, 324.
51 *Ibid.*, 323.
52 *Ibid.*, 324.
53 A reference to JB's television programme *A Man with a View*. See Chapter 9, 'A "Natural Showman": Television in the 1960s'.
54 Simon Stuart's book, *Say: An Experiment in Learning*, was published in London in 1969. JB gave him extensive advice on the writing of it, in letters of 1 September 1966 and 24 November 1966 (shown to the author by Mr Stuart). Stuart later wrote *New Phoenix Wings: Reparation in Literature*, London 1979.
55 JB, *Letters*, ed. CLG, ii, 324.
56 In 1966 Stuart wrote JB a letter, complimenting him on his poems, with particular mention of a poem with implications of homosexuality, 'Monody on the Death of a Platonist Bank Clerk'. JB replied (24 November 1966): 'That was about the kindest thing you could have done to have written about my verse. I've no confidence in my verses and a letter from someone I admire as I do you, gives me some. Ta ever so. Ah yes that bank clerk! And have you studied Narcissus [JB's poem 'Narcissus']? Have a look at Maurice Bowra's Memoirs (wildly funny & v good) & see what John Sparrow looked like . . .' copy sent to the author by Mr Stuart.
57 Simon Stuart, letter to the author, 14 March 2001.
58 *Ibid.*
59 *Ibid.*
60 H.A. Williams, *Some Day I'll Find You*, London 1982, p. 230.
61 Dr Graham Storey, telephone conversation with the author, 1997.
62 Mervyn Stockwood, *Chanctonbury Ring*, London 1982, p. 96.
63 Bishop Mervyn Stockwood, interview, 1990.
64 Ned Sherrin, letter to the author, 14 March 2001. In his autobiography, *A Small Thing – Like an Earthquake*, London 1983, p. 146, Sherrin describes a visit of Zsa Zsa Gabor to London to appear in the film *Up the Front*.

. . . I gave a small dinner party for her. The guests included Mervyn Stockwood, Bishop of Southwark, who always loves life, friends and rubbing shoulders with showbiz. Some years before, at Hywel Bennett's wedding to Cathy McGowan, I had sat him next to Roger Moore, producing a Sunday newspaper photograph captioned, 'What the

Bishop said to the Saint.' This time the legend was equally predictable – 'What the
Bishop said to the Actress.' I sometimes wondered if Mervyn minded these gross
exploitations, but I was reassured later on going through his press cuttings book to find
that both photographs were duly pasted in.

65 Bishop Mervyn Stockwood, interview, 1990.
66 JB, *Letters*, ed. CLG, ii, 332.
67 *Ibid.*, 347.
68 Ex inf. Simon Stuart, letter to the author, 14 March 2001.
69 H.A. Williams, *Some Day I'll Find You*, London 1982, p. 273.
70 *Ibid.*, p. 270.
71 *Loc. cit.*
72 *Loc. cit.*
73 *Ibid.*, p. 272.
74 *Ibid.*, p. 273.
75 *Ibid.*, p. 272.
76 *Ibid.*, p. 273.
77 *Loc. cit.* Williams notes of JB, 'he is no longer like that'.
78 *Loc. cit.*
79 *Ibid.*, p. 274.
80 *Loc. cit.*
81 JB to Lord Wemyss, 16 April 1968. JB, *Letters*, ed. CLG, ii, 350.
82 JB, *Letters*, ed. CLG, ii, 351n.
83 H.A. Williams, *Some Day I'll Find You*, London 1982, pp. 288–89.
84 *Ibid.*, p. 289.
85 *Ibid.*, pp. 289–90.
86 John Byrne. On him, see Chapter 29, 'His Last Bow'.
87 H.A. Williams, *Some Day I'll Find You*, London 1982, pp. 290–91.
88 Jonathan Dimbleby, *The Prince of Wales*, London 1995 edn., p. 127.
89 *Loc. cit.*
90 *Ibid.*, p. 137.
91 HRH The Prince of Wales, interview, 1985.
92 H.A. Williams, *Some Day I'll Find You*, London 1982, p. 296.
93 JB to Mary Wilson, 14 January 1969. JB, *Letters*, ed. CLG, ii, 358.
94 *Collected Poems*, 1985 edn., p. 409.
95 *Ibid.*, p. 410.
96 *Loc. cit.*
97 Dimbleby, *op. cit.*, p. 163.
98 Quoted, Osbert Lancaster, interview, 1977.
99 'Father Miles' was almost certainly Robert George Miles, deacon 1936, priest 1937. From
    1961 Vicar of St Nicholas with Christ Church, Deptford, Diocese of Southwark.
100 Shown to the author by Bishop Stockwood.
101 *The Channings*: novel of 1861–62 by Mrs Henry Wood.
102 Shown to the author by Mr Stuart.
103 JB to Mary Wilson, September 1971. JB, *Letters*, ed. CLG, ii, 420.
104 Simon Stuart, letter to the author, 14 March 2001.
105 *Ibid.*
106 Evelyn Waugh, 'Gaudí', *The Architectural Review*, June 1930, pp. 309–11.
107 Simon Stuart, letter to the author, 14 March 2001.
108 In his poem 'Beside the Seaside' (*Collected Poems*, 1985 edn., p. 157) JB wrote:

> Green Shutters, shut your shutters! Windyridge,
> Let winds unnoticed whistle round your hill! . . .

109 Simon Stuart, letter to the author, 14 September 2001.
110 *Ex inf.* Bishop Hugh Montefiore, letter to the author, 28 February 2001.

111 *Ibid.*
112 *The Ulick O'Connor Diaries 1970–1981: A Cavalier Irishman*, London 2001, p. 17.
113 Bishop Hugh Montefiore, letter to the author, 28 February 2001.
114 *Collected Poems*, 1985 edn., pp. 381–82.
115 Bishop Mervyn Stockwood, interview, 1990.
116 *Ibid.*
117 Bishop Mervyn Stockwood, interview, 1990.
118 *Ibid.*
119 Francis Wheen, *Tom Driberg: His Life and Indiscretions*, London 1990, p. 373.
120 The poem was shown to the present author by Bishop Stockwood. It begins, 'My Lord of Bristol, fearing that He might get muddled with his Hat . . .' and ends, 'I think it might be rather better To don his purple-pink biretta.'
121 Shown to the author by Bishop Stockwood and quoted with his kind permission.
122 Shown to the author by Bishop Stockwood.

Chapter 18: Metro-land

1 See YB, Chapter 8, '*The Secret Glory*'.
2 See *ibid.*, p. 321.
3 *Loc. cit.*
4 JB, conversation with the author, 1972. On JB and Machen, see also Anthony Lejeune, 'Memoirs of Machen' in *Arthur Machen: A Miscellany*, ed. Father Brocard Sewell, Llandeilo 1960, p. 33.
5 *Evening Standard*, 26 March 1934.
6 Edward Mirzoeff, interview, 1990. Except where otherwise indicated, Mr Mirzoeff has supplied all the information in this chapter.
    J. M. Richards's book was published in 1946. Mirzoeff's statement should, however, be qualified by reference to the earlier pro-suburbia passages by Arthur Machen, mentioned at the beginning of this chapter. Richards's book was reissued in 1973, to feed the new interest in suburbia that JB's film had created.
7 *Daily Herald*, 19 June 1945.
8 JB to Robin Scott, 9 May 1971. I am grateful to Edward Mirzoeff for kindly showing me a copy of this letter.
9 'Electric trains are lighted after tea' is a phrase in 'Harrow-on-the-Hill'. 'Middlesex' begins:

> Gaily into Ruislip Gardens
> Runs the red electric train . . .

And JB gave the title 'The Metropolitan Railway' to his poem about the Baker Street station buffet –

> Early Electric! With what radiant hope
>   Men formed this many-branched electrolier,
> Twisted the flex around the iron rope
>   And let the dazzling vacuum globes hang clear,
> And then with hearts the rich contrivance fill'd
> Of copper, beaten by the Bromsgrove Guild.

10 'The restaurant has been gutted, the doors are closed. Stuck to one of them, a note, written on brown paper: "Ann – hope you get this message, sorry about wrong directions. The Allsop Arms is on Gloucester Place remember. Hope to see you there later on. Bye for now and love Brian. X." The stained-glass frieze, with its doltish medieval figures, still lines the lintel; in the restoration, the decorative panels and the mock medieval crest inside will vanish.' Frank Delaney, *Betjeman Country*, London 1983, p. 207.

11 See B. Hillier, 'The St John's Wood Clique', *Apollo*, June 1964, pp. 410–15.

12 Walpamur: brand of distemper paint. Edward Mirzoeff remembers: 'It took a *very* long time for us all to manage to come up with a three-syllable common domestic Neasden-ish name.'

13 Delaney, *op. cit.*, p. 214.

14 In the copy of his poems which I asked him to sign when I first met him in 1971, JB wrote: 'from John Betjeman, an Old Harrovian in all but fact'. Frank Delaney (*op. cit.*, p. 215) remembered how 'Handing out assorted collected school boaters in party humour he always chose the Harrow ribbon: around the piano he led with the Harrow School Song.' JB's nickname for the Old Harrovian Sir John Summerson, 'Coolmore', was Summerson's *nom de plume* as a journalist; but John also (Summerson said) 'linked it with my way of writing and linked it also with one of his highly eccentric public school fantasies. He held that Harrovians wrote the best prose, instancing Winston Churchill, Wyndham Ketton-Cremer and perhaps rather surprisingly Sir Bernard Docker, with a few others, including me. He called it "cool Harrovian prose".' At a dinner to celebrate his honorary doctor-ate at Oxford, John began his speech, 'I like things that are overshadowed – like Harrow.'

15 On JB's friendship with Voysey, see *YB*, pp. 261–63 and 272.

16 Len Rawle, meeting of the Betjeman Society, 11 July 1992.

17 Peter Schaffer to JB, 27 February 1973. *JBP*.

18 Edward Mirzoeff writes (letter to the author, 21 July 2000): 'The point of this line was to half-remind the audience of Cliveden and Christine Keeler and the swimming pool . . .'

19 As early as 1957 he praised the Art Deco Carew Tower in Cincinnati; and in 1971 he wrote to me, after looking through a copy of the catalogue of the Art Deco exhibition which David Ryan and I organized in Minneapolis in that year, '. . . I am now totally converted to *moderne* and Wallis, Gilbert and Partners' (the well-known architects of the Hoover factory and other extravagantly Deco buildings).

20 On Margaret ('Margie') Geddes, *née* Addis, see *YB*, pp. 288–89; also *JBLP*, p. 75.

21 On Jill Parker, see Chapter 29 of the present volume, 'His Last Bow'.

22 On Queenie Avril, see *YB*, p. 12.

23 *Evening Standard*, 27 February 1973.

Chapter 19: With the Andersons, the Pagets and Joyce Grenfell

1 See obituary of Lord Mottistone, *The Times*, 5 December 1996.

2 Dr Winifred Hector, interview, 1998.

3 On Kenric Rice and the Bruces, see *YB*, p. 242.

4 Verily Anderson Paget, interview, 1999.

5 Verily Anderson, *The Last of the Eccentrics*, London 1972, pp. 186–87.

6 Elizabeth Bowen's review is quoted on the jacket of later editions of *Spam Tomorrow*.

7 JB to Laurie Lister (who directed Joyce Grenfell's revues), 4 May 1947. JB, *Letters*, ed. CLG, i, 411. The lady JB invented for Joyce Grenfell was called Sylvia Paddington, a pseu-donym he sometimes adopted in the *New Statesman*.

8 Verily Anderson Paget, interview, 1999.

9 *Ibid.*

10 See Verily Anderson, *The Last of the Eccentrics*, London 1972, pp. 167–98, 206–8, 212–13 and *passim*.

11 Verily Anderson Paget, interview, 1999.

12 *Ibid.*

13 *Ibid.*

14 Joyce Grenfell to Virginia Graham, 7 June 1971, *Joyce and Ginnie: The Letters of Joyce Grenfell and Virginia Graham*, ed. Janie Hampton, London 1998 edn., pp. 411–12.

15 Verily Anderson Paget, interview, 1999.

16 *Ibid.*

17 *Ibid.*

18 Janie Hampton, *Joyce Grenfell*, London 2003 edn., p. 221.

19 Verily Anderson Paget, interview, 1999.

20 On the architecture of Templewood, see Clive Aslet, 'An Interview with the Late Paul Paget 1901–1985', *Thirties Society Journal*, no. 6, 1987.

21 JB to Paul Paget, 4 August 1969, JB, *Letters*, ed. CLG, ii, 389.

22 Edward Anderson, interview, 1999.

23 *Ibid.*

24 *Ibid.*

25 *Ibid.*

26 Verily Anderson Paget, interview, 1999.

27 James Haldane O'Hare, interview, 1999.

28 *Ibid.*

29 On Seamus O'Donovan's espionage activities, see Enno Stephan, *Spies in Ireland* (first published in German as *Geheimauftrag Irland*, Hamburg 1961), London 1963 edn., pp. 23–25, 27–38, 48–50 and *passim*.

30 On the strong probability that JB had some 'intelligence agent' duties when press attaché to Sir John Maffey in Dublin during the Second World War, see *JBNFNL*, pp. 229–37.

31 James Haldane O'Hare, interview, 1999.

32 *Ibid.*

33 Verily Anderson Paget, interview, 1999.

34 JB, 'The City', *Observer Magazine*, 24 July 1977.

35 *Collected Poems*, 2001 edn., p. 217.

36 Barry Humphries, CLG interview, 1994, JB, *Letters*, ed. CLG, ii, 373.

37 (Sir) Max Hastings (b. 1945), journalist and author. Son of Anne Scott-James by the journalist and author Macdonald Hastings. Successively editor of the *Daily Telegraph* and the *Evening Standard*. Knighted 2002.

38 (Sir) Max Hastings, letter to the author, 4 September 1999.

39 (Sir) Max Hastings, letter to CLG, 1994. JB, *Letters*, ed. CLG, ii, 373.

40 On JB's encounter with Sir John Smith in the Scottish islands in May 1959, see *JBNFNL*, p. 599.

41 JB, *Letters*, ed. CLG, ii, 439–40.

42 *Ibid.*, 440.

43 *Loc. cit.*

44 *Ibid.*, 462.

45 Presumably *The House of William Burges ARA*, ed. by R.P. Pullen, London 1886.

46 Paul Paget to JB, May 1974. JB, *Letters*, ed. CLG, ii, 441.

Chapter 20: 'A Heavy Crown'

1 *Daily Express*, 17 February 1960.

2 *Ibid.*

3 See *JBNFNL*, pp. 609–11.

4 Miss Christina Foyle, conversation with the author, 1978. Miss Foyle was not amused to be told by JB, at the prize-giving ceremony, that her bookshop was hopelessly old-fashioned and much in need of modernizing.

5 *Evening Standard*, 24 June 1960.

6 *The Guardian*, 22 November 1960.

7 I am grateful to the late Sir Ian Hunter, the organizer of the Festival, for showing me this script.

8 *Queen*, August 1960.

9 *Ibid.*

10 Anthony Curtis was literary editor of the *Sunday Telegraph*, 1960–70. On his career, see his autobiography, *Lit Ed*, London 1998.

11 *New Statesman*, 9 June 1967.

12 *Ibid.*

13 HRH The Prince of Wales, interview, 1985.

14 *Ibid.*

15 Angus Wilson to JB, quoted JB, *Letters*, ed. CLG, ii, 369.

16 On JB's unsuccessful proposal to Pamela Mitford, see *YB*, pp. 299–303, 383 and 389. on his light-hearted proposal to Nancy Mitford, see *JBNFNL*, p. 317.

17 Nancy Mitford to JB, 14 June 1969. JB, *Letters*, ed. CLG, ii, p. 369.

18 JB to Lord Longford, 25 June 1969. JB, *Letters*, ed. CLG, ii, pp. 369–70.

19 JB, *Letters*, ed. CLG, ii, 370.

20 JB, conversation with the author, 1971.

21 The photograph is reproduced in *JBLP*, p. 146.

22 *The Times*, 23 May 1972.

23 *The Times*, 25 May 1972.

24 *Ibid.*

25 Haiphong, the principal port of North Vietnam, was bombed by the United States in 1972.

26 *The Times*, 24 June 1972.

27 *The Times*, 26 June 1972.

28 *Ibid.*

29 *The Times*, 28 June 1972.

30 Henry James Pye (1745–1813) had owned Faringdon House, later owned by JB's friend Lord Berners.

31 *The Times*, 11 October 1972.

32 Iona and Peter Opie record in *The Oxford Dictionary of Nursery Rhymes*, Oxford 1997 edn.:

> When Henry James Pye was appointed Poet Laureate in 1790 his first ode, a very poor one, was in honour of the king's birthday and was full of allusions to the 'vocal groves and the feathered choir'. George Stevens immediately punned, 'And when the PYE was opened the birds began to sing. Was not that a dainty dish to set before the king?' [This was a pun on an old English rhyme.]
>
> Byron referred sarcastically to Pye in 'The Vision of Judgment', stanza xcii: 'The monarch, mute till then, exclaim'd "What! what! Pye come again? No more – no more of that!" '

33 On JB's friendship with Pierce Synnott, see *YB*, 170, 180, 197–203, 290 and 316. JB wrote to thank him for the Latin poem on 30 November 1972. JB, *Letters*, ed. CLG, ii, 456–57.

34 *The Times*, 14 December 1972.

35 *The Times*, 18 January 1973.

36 *The Unexpurgated Beaton Diaries*, introduced by Hugo Vickers, London 2002 edn., p. 376.

37 *Sunday Times*, 16 September 1973.

38 JB, *Letters*, ed. CLG, ii, 442.

39 *Loc. cit.*

40 *Loc. cit.*

41 *The Times*, 12 November 1973.

42 *Ibid.*

43 *Ibid.*

44 *The Times*, 15 November 1973.

45 *The Times*, 24 June 1974.

46 *Sunday Times*, 1 December 1974.

47 *Sunday Times*, 8 December 1974.

48 The cartoon is illustrated in Humphrey Carpenter, *That Was Satire That Was*, London 2000, p. 197.

49 As John G. Murray mentioned in a letter to JB of 23 May 1974. *John Murray archives*.

50 Squadron-Leader David Checketts to John G. Murray, 4 December 1973. *John Murray archives*.

51 As JB told John G. Murray in a letter of 29 March 1973. *John Murray archives*.

52 See note 16 to the present chapter.

53 Mary Lutyens to John G. Murray, 9 January 1974. *John Murray archives*.

54 JB, *Letters*, ed. CLG, ii, 443. JB wrote in the *Sunday Express*, 13 May 1973 (quoted, *loc. cit.*):

> She was the most beautiful creature; she had a slightly sad expression, and I didn't even know her name – but it was probably all the better for that . . . I like there to be a mystery between me and my beloved, and I don't think there was anything wrong with looking at her in church. I don't think there's anything wrong with loving the beauty of the human figure whether it's in the church or in the street. I'm not in sympathy with people who think that anything to do with physical good looks is not being profound or deep, or who think it's wicked to think about what people look like when they go to church: as if you couldn't really love someone unless she was a State Registered Nurse.'

55 A photograph of Joan Price appeared on the 'Contributors' page of *Harper's Bazaar*, March 1969.

56 *Private Eye*, 25 May 1973. Quoted, JB, *Letters*, ed. CLG, ii, 443.

57 *John Murray archives*.

58 *Ibid.*

59 *Ibid.*

60 *Ibid.*

61 *The Listener*, 5 December 1974.

62 Magda Rogers, conversation with the author, 1974.

63 See 'Guardsmen case man fined £700', *The Times*, 7 May 1968.

64 JB to Mary Wilson, 27 June 1969. Shown to the author by Lady Wilson of Rievaulx.

65 *Victoria*.

66 JB, *Letters*, ed. CLG, ii, 414.

67 See Chapter 15, 'Mary Wilson and a Journey to Diss'.

68 *John Murray archives*.

69 *Ibid.*

70 *Collected Poems*, 2001 edn., p. 298.

71 Tom Driberg to JB, n.d. *John Murray archives*.

72 *Collected Poems*, 2001 edn., p. 298.

73 *Ibid.*, p. 239.

74 JB to Mary Wilson, 21 August 1974. Shown to the author by Lady Wilson of Rievaulx.

75 *Daily Express*, 18 August 1974.

76 *The Scotsman*, 4 January 1975.

77 On Professor John Press, see *JBNFNL*, p. 703 n.62. In 1974 Professor Press wrote the British Council pamphlet *John Betjeman* ('Writers and Their Work', no. 237).

78 *Times Literary Supplement*, 10 January 1975.

79 *The Tablet*, 21/28 December 1974.

80 *The Observer*, 24 November 1974.

81 *Birmingham Post*, 30 November 1974.

82 *Daily Telegraph Magazine*, 22 November 1974.

83 *The Listener*, 5 December 1974.

84 *New Statesman*, 22 November 1974.

85 *Financial Times*, 28 November 1974.

86 *Sunday Times*, 24 November 1974.

87 *Daily Mail*, 21 November 1974.

88 HRH The Prince of Wales to JB, 13 May 1976. Quoted by Jonathan Dimbleby, *The Prince of Wales*, London 1995 edn., p. 282.

89 James Lees-Milne, diary entry for 8 June 1976. *Through Wood and Dale: Diaries 1975–1978*, London 2001 edn., p. 97.

90 *The Times*, 6 July 1976.

91 *The Times*, 7 July 1976.

92 *The Times*, 2 August 1976.

93 *The Times*, 3 November 1976.

94 John Nankivell, interview, 2003.

95 Dimbleby, *op. cit.*, p. 282.

96 *Ibid.*, p. 283.

97 *The Times*, 7 February 1977.

98 *Loc. cit.*

99 *The Times*, 10 February 1977.

100 JB, *Letters*, ed. CLG, ii, 512.

101 Quoted, *loc. cit.*

102 William (later Lord) Rees-Mogg was Editor of *The Times*.

103 James Lees-Milne, diary entry for 11 October 1977. *Through Wood and Dale: Diaries 1975–1978*, London 2001 edn., p. 205.

104 *The Times*, 7 May 1980.

105 *Loc. cit.*

106 *Summoned by Bells*, London 1960, p. 84.

107 *The Times*, 5 February 1981.

108 *John Murray archives.*

109 *The Times*, 10 August 1981. JB appropriated Prebendary Stark's expression 'delectable duchy' as an ironic heading to a poem about Cornwall in which he abominated its 'cara' (caravan) sites and litter. (*Collected Poems*, 2003 edn., pp. 306–07).

110 *The Times*, 30 July 1981.

111 *The Times*, 31 July 1981.

112 *The Times*, 5 August 1981.

113 *The Times*, 4 August 1981.

114 *Summoned by Bells*, London 1960, p. 20. (The poem was aborted because, on searching through a gazeteer, JB found there was no such place as 'Findow'.)

115 PB, conversation with the author, 1981.

116 *Sunday Express*, 18 August 1974.

117 I am grateful to Mr John Toop Cooper for this quotation.

118 John Sparrow, conversation with the author, 1982.

Chapter 21: A Passion for Churches

1 Edward Mirzoeff, interview, 1997.

2 Edward Roberts, interview, 1997.

3 Edward Mirzoeff, interview, 1997.

4 JB to Edward Mirzoeff, 2 April 1973. BBC files, kindly made available by Mr Mirzoeff.

5 *Ibid.*

6 JB to Edward Mirzoeff, 6 June 1973. BBC files, kindly made available by Mr Mirzoeff.

7 *Ibid.*

8 JB to Edward Mirzoeff, 10 June 1973. BBC files, kindly made available by Mr Mirzoeff.

9 Edward Roberts, interview, 1997.

10 Edward Mirzoeff, interview, 1997.

11 *Ibid.*

12 JB to Edward Mirzoeff, 24 January 1974. BBC files, kindly made available by Mr Mirzoeff.

13 *Ibid.*

14 *Ibid.*

15 *Ibid.*

16 *Ibid.*

17 *Ibid.*

18 *Ibid.*

19 Lady Harrod to JB, 29 January 1974. Copy in BBC files, kindly made available by Mr Edward Mirzoeff.

20 Letter from Christine Smith (BBC assistant) to Norgate Bros, 27 February 1974. BBC files, kindly made available by Mr Edward Mirzoeff.

21 *Summoned by Bells*, London 1960, pp. 108–09.

22 Edward Mirzoeff, interview, 1997.

23 Anthony Powell, *Daily Telegraph*, 23 July 1988.

24 See JB letter to Edward Mirzoeff, 5 March 1974, quoted later in the present chapter and referenced in note 32.

25 Edward Mirzoeff, interview, 1997.

26 *Ibid.*

27 Lady Harrod to Edward Mirzoeff, 22 April 1974. BBC files, kindly made available by Mr Mirzoeff.

28 *Ibid.*

29 Edward Mirzoeff, interview, 1997.

30 The Rt. Rev. Maurice Wood, Bishop of Norwich, to Edward Mirzoeff, 19 March 1974. BBC files, kindly made available by Mr Mirzoeff.

31 Edward Mirzoeff to the Bishop of Norwich, 20 March 1974. Copy in BBC files, kindly made available by Mr Mirzoeff.

32 JB to Edward Mirzoeff, 5 March 1974. BBC files, kindly made available by Mr Mirzoeff.

33 *Ibid.*

34 Edward Mirzoeff, interview, 1997. 'Clear-story' is the generally accepted pronunciation of clerestory.

35 JB, *Collected Poems*, 2001 edn., p. 168.

36 On Father Ronald Wright, see *YB*, 41–42, 47–49, 116 and 139.

37 JB to Mr Cook, 18 March 1974. Copy in BBC files, kindly made available by Mr Edward Mirzoeff.

38 Recording script of *A Passion for Churches*, kindly made available by Mr Edward Mirzoeff.

39 Edward Mirzoeff, interview, 1997.

40 *Radio Times*, 5 December 1974.

41 Edward Mirzoeff, interview, 1997.

42 Edward Roberts, interview, 1997.

43 Michael Ratcliffe, *The Times*, 9 December 1974.

44 The Very Rev. Alan Webster to Edward Mirzoeff, 9 December 1974. BBC files, kindly made available by Mr Edward Mirzoeff. Webster had been Dean of Norwich since 1970.

45 *A Passion for Churches*, 1974

46 *Ibid.*

47 *Ibid.*

48 *Ibid.* Reviewing this part of the film in *The Times* (9 December 1974), Michael Ratcliffe noted of the parish magazine: 'the front page headline really did read "Hello Sailors, and Welcome".'

49 *A Passion for Churches*, 1974.

50 Shown the poem, Miss Cozens-Hardy took exception to the lines (*Collected Poems*, 2003 edn., p. 228) in which JB suggested that villagers did not like to pass near Lord Cozens-Hardy's 'curious mausoleum' for fear of seeing his ghost. For this reason, when the poem was printed in *The Saturday Book* of 1956, JB altered the name to 'Lord Barton-Bendish'; but 'Cozens-Hardy' was later restored in the *Collected Poems*. For the autograph of the poem, and the illustration of the mausoleum, by John Piper, which accompanied its publication in *The Saturday Book*, see *JBLP*, p. 132. See also David Watkin, 'Letheringsett Hall, Norfolk: The Home of the Lady Cozens-Hardy', *Country Life*, 5 January 1967, pp. 18ff.

51 The seventh Marquess Townshend (b. 1916) was a director of Anglia Television. He and his wife lived at Raynham Hall.

52 Dominick Roy Harrod (b. 1940), journalist, broadcaster and economist.

53 *Ex inf.* Sir Roy Harrod, conversation, 1976.

54 See R.W. Ketton-Cremer, *Felbrigg: The Story of a House*, London 1962; a pedigree at the end traces the author's ancestry from the fifteenth century.

55 *Eastern Daily Press*, 9 April 1974.

56 *A Passion for Churches*, 1974.

57 Canon Horace Lyle Hume Townshend, Rector of Lyng, Norfolk.

58 Edward Mirzoeff, interview, 1997.

59 *A Passion for Churches*, 1974.

60 In March 1974 arrangements were made with Jane Astell, Assistant, Royal Liaison, Villiers House, London. BBC files, kindly made available by Mr Edward Mirzoeff.

61 Correspondence with Mr Humphrey Boardman. BBC files, kindly made available by Mr Edward Mirzoeff.

62 This information comes from an undated cutting from the *Yarmouth Mercury* in the BBC files, kindly made available by Mr Edward Mirzoeff.

63 *A Passion for Churches*, 1974.

64 *Ibid.*

65 Edward Mirzoeff, interview, 1997.

66 *A Passion for Churches*, 1974.

67 Edward Mirzoeff, interview, 1997.

68 *A Passion for Churches*, 1974.

69 Edward Mirzoeff, interview, 1997.

70 *A Passion for Churches*, 1974.

71 *Ibid.*

72 *Ibid.*

73 Christine Smith of the BBC made the arrangements with Mr George Thompson, External Relations Officer, Trinity House, Tower Hill, London EC4. BBC files, kindly made available by Mr Edward Mirzoeff.

74 Canon Douglas Caiger to Edward Mirzoeff, 20 March 1974. BBC files, kindly made available by Mr Edward Mirzoeff.

75 Osbert Lancaster, 'The Laureate in vision', *Times Literary Supplement*, 6 December 1974.

76 *A Passion for Churches*, 1974.

77 *Ibid.*

78 Edward Mirzoeff, interview, 1997.

79 *Ibid.*

80 *Ibid.*

81 Jessie Marion King (Mrs E.A. Taylor) (1876–1949). Painter and illustrator. Studied at the Glasgow School of Art. A fine *art nouveau* illustrator. Much of her work was on parchment, delicately outlined and tinted. On her, see Simon Houfe, *The Dictionary of Nineteenth-Century British Book Illustrators*, Woodbridge, Suffolk 1996, pp. 198–99.

82 Elizabeth Jane Howard (b. 1923), novelist. In 1965 she married (Sir) Kingsley Amis; the marriage was dissolved in 1983.

83 Edward Mirzoeff, interview, 1997.

84 Elizabeth Jane Howard, 'I like a bit of High', *Radio Times*, 7–13 December 1974.

85 *Ibid.*

86 *Ibid.*

87 *Ibid.*

88 *Ibid.* JB had made much the same complaint in *The Spectator* in 1957. See *JBNFNL*, p. 547.

89 Elizabeth Jane Howard, 'I like a bit of High', *Radio Times*, 7–13 December 1974.

90 *Ibid.*

91 *Ibid.*

92 *Ibid.*

93 *Ibid.*

94 Edward Mirzoeff, interview, 1997.

95 *Ibid.*

96 *Ibid.*

97 *A Passion for Churches*, 1974.

98 *Ibid.*

99 Edward Roberts, interview, 1997.

100 *Ibid.*

101 *Ibid.*; and *A Passion for Churches*, 1974.

102 Edward Roberts, interview, 1997.

103 Edward Mirzoeff, interview, 1997.

104 *Ibid.*
105 Edward Roberts, interview, 1997.
106 Edward Mirzoeff, interview, 1997.
107 *A Passion for Churches*, 1974.
108 Edward Mirzoeff wrote on 18 October 1974 to break the news to the Rev. L.H.M. Smith of South Creake that the Mass sequence was not going to be used. Smith replied on 21 October, 'We are all bitterly disappointed.' BBC files, kindly made available by Mr Mirzoeff.
109 JB to Lady Harrod, 19 August 1974. Copy in BBC files, kindly made available by Mr Edward Mirzoeff.
110 JB to Edward Mirzoeff, 6 August 1974. BBC files, kindly made available by Mr Mirzoeff.
111 Desmond Wilcox (1931–2000), television producer and journalist. He was Head of General Features, BBC, 1972–80. He married Esther Rantzen in 1977.
112 Edward Mirzoeff, interview, 1997.
113 *Ibid.*
114 Osbert Lancaster, 'The Laureate in vision', *Times Literary Supplement*, 6 December 1974.
115 Herbert Suffield Maude Maude-Roxby, deacon 1906, priest 1907. Church of St Mark, Lakenham, 1906–11. Vicar of St John the Baptist, Timberhill (with All Saints from 1929), City and Diocese of Norwich from 1918. Chaplain of St Augustine's Lodge, Norwich, from 1930. He appears in *Crockford's Clerical Directory* for 1938 but not that for 1939.
116 Rt. Rev. Percy Mark Herbert (1885–1968), Bishop of Norwich, 1942–59.
117 Rev. Harold Davidson (1876–1937), Rector of Stiffkey. He appeared before the Norwich Consistory Court charged with immoral practices, and was unfrocked. Later he appeared in a lion cage in a menagerie and was mauled to death. Malcolm Muggeridge, who gives a summary of the scandal in *The Thirties, 1930–1940, in Great Britain*, London 1940, pp. 165–67, compares him with the early Christians who were thrown to the lions.
118 Osbert Lancaster, 'The Laureate in vision', *Times Literary Supplement*, 6 December 1974.
119 *Ibid.*
120 Michael Ratcliffe, *The Times*, 9 December 1974.
121 Chris Dunkley, 'A passion for Betjeman', *Financial Times*, 11 December 1974.
122 Dennis Potter, 'Good Sir John', *New Statesman*, 13 December 1974.
123 *Eastern Daily Press*, 9 December 1974.
124 Edward Mirzoeff, interview, 1997.

Chapter 22: Radnor Walk

1 Lucy was born in 1964, Imogen in 1966, Endellion in 1969, David in 1975 and John in 1978.
2 JB, *Letters*, ed. CLG, ii, 371–72.
3 *Loc. cit.*
4 JB to the Rev. Wilfrid Harry Jarvis, 8 February 1972. JB, *Letters*, ed. CLG, ii, 427.
5 PB, interview, 1980.
6 JB to John Edward Bowle, 4 July 1972. JB, *Letters*, ed. CLG, ii, 432.
7 *Ibid.*, 433.
8 *Loc. cit.*
9 Photocopy from the Wantage parish magazine of 1972, supplied in 1976 by the Rev. John Schaufelberger. In later printings (e.g. *Collected Poems*, 1985 edn., p. 368), the last line was changed to 'We sink below the sliding stream of time'.
10 JB to PB, February 1973. Quoted, JB, *Letters*, ed. CLG, ii, 440. On 5 March 1973 JB wrote to Mary Wilson, 'The new Jackie [i.e. successor to his secretary Jackie] is called Mrs Mountain from Hindhead and is, I should think, Conservative. She seems kind and calm like a ward sister.' Letter shown to the author by Lady Wilson of Rievaulx.
11 On the assassination of Christopher Ewart-Biggs, see *The Times*, 22 July 1976.

12 After the late Lord Longford had attended the unveiling, by JB, of a memorial tablet to W.H. Auden in Westminster Abbey in 1974, he suggested to the present author that JB was putting on an 'old man' act. (On the unveiling of the tablet, see *The Times*, 3 October 1974.)

13 According to Martin Summers, art dealer, in the BBC2 documentary programme *Chelsea Tales* screened on 17 September 2003.

14 Frank Miles, artist and friend of Oscar Wilde. Richard Ellmann writes in *Oscar Wilde*, London 1987, p. 57: '[Wilde's] friends in Magdalen [College, Oxford] were not homosexual but the artist Frank Miles probably hovered on the edges, as might be inferred from the great interest taken in him by Lord Ronald Gower with whom he went off to Paris.' Miles's father, Canon Miles, forced his son to give up his friendship with Wilde. On Charles Ricketts and Charles Hazelwood Shannon, see p. 659, n. 91.

15 See Michael Holroyd, *Augustus John: A Biography*, London (i) 1974, (ii) 1975.

16 See *YB*, pp. 66 and 202.

17 JB to Patrick Cullinan, 13 August 1973. JB, *Letters*, ed. CLG, ii, 465.

18 The Hon. Michael Langhorne Astor (1916–80), son of the second Viscount Astor and brother of the Hon. David Astor, who was editor of *The Observer*, 1948–75. Was MP for the Eastern Division of Surrey, 1945–51. Farmed 1,000 acres of Oxfordshire.

   CLG records (JB, *Letters*, ii, 516) that JB and Lady Elizabeth Cavendish stayed with Michael Astor on the Island of Jura.

19 *JBP*.

20 JB, conversation with the author, 1972.

21 Quoted Heathcote Williams, *The Speakers*, London 1964, p. 39.

22 This passage describes the author's own experience of lunching with JB at San Quintino.

23 As noted by Jonathan Stedall and Reg Read. (On the latter, see Chapter 27, '. . . As I Lose Hold'.)

24 *The Listener*, 17 August 1972.

25 JB was referring to a joke about PB's helpers at Cusop, made by Graham Lord in the *Sunday Express*, 18 August 1974.

26 Quoted, JB, *Letters*, ed. CLG, ii, 441.

27 Mollie Baring, interview, 1978.

28 Quoted, JB, *Letters*, ed. CLG, ii, 441.

29 PB said that to the author when introducing him to pony-riding at Cusop in 1976.

30 JB knew Richard Booth's aunt, Viva King, widow of William King of the Victoria & Albert Museum, who was a *salonnière* in South Kensington.

31 James Lees-Milne, who visited Whitfield Court with his wife Alvilde, described it as 'a delightful, "dim" later Georgian house, unpretentious with nice rounded window bays extending from ground floor to roof-line . . . A family house set in unspoiled, remote country. Full of family portraits, a large cosy library, whole house crammed with books, old morocco and modern.' In the same diary entry he described Lady Mary Clive as 'delightful, intelligent, well-read and unpretentious like all Pakenhams'. James Lees-Milne, *Deep Romantic Chasm: Diaries 1979–1981*, ed. Michael Bloch, London 2003 edn., p. 108.

32 I am indebted for this information and that which follows about Bruce Chatwin and the Howells brothers to Nicholas Shakespeare, *Bruce Chatwin*, London 1999, Chapter XXVIII, 'Border Country'.

33 Bruce Chatwin to Graham C. Greene, 8 June 1982. Quoted, *ibid.*, p. 378.

34 'She was a short and very courageous woman with large wrinkles at the edge of her slaty eyes, and silver hair cut in a fringe. She spent several months of each year riding alone round India on a bicycle.' Bruce Chatwin, *On the Black Hill*, London 1998 edn., pp. 229–31. Chatwin made the brothers in his novel twins – which the Howells brothers were not Nicholas Shakespeare, *op. cit.*, p. 377, states that PB was the original of Chatwin's 'Philippa'. That is certainly true; but the bicycle-riding-in-India aspect of Philippa probably owes more to Dervla Murphy, who wrote *Full Tilt: Ireland to India with a Bicycle*, London 1965. PB preferred horses to bicycles.

35 Shakespeare, *op. cit.*, p. 382.

36 JB to PB, 28 June 1976. JB, *Letters*, ed. CLG, ii, 502.
37 PB, interview, 1980.
38 According to both John Nankivell and Dr Richard Squires – interviews respectively 2003, 1976.
39 John Nankivell, interview, 2003.
40 *Ibid.*
41 *Ibid.*
42 *Ibid.*
43 JB to Lady Harrod, 13 February 1974. JB, *Letters*, ed. CLG, ii, 473.
44 PB to Lord Kinross, 11 December 1975. Huntington Library, San Marino, California.
45 PB, interview, 1976.
46 Magda Rogers, interview, 1982.
47 Jonathan Stedall, interview, 2003.
48 Quoted, *ibid.*
49 *Ibid.*
50 Barney Platts-Mills made the film *Bronco Bullfrog* in 1970.
51 JB told PB of the audience her film had had in a letter of 31 January 1974. JB, *Letters*, ed. CLG, ii, 472.
52 *Ibid.*
53 Magda Rogers, interview, 1982.
54 Jonathan Stedall, interview, 2003.
55 *Ibid.*
56 Peter Adam, *Not Drowning But Waving: An Autobiography*, London 1995, p. 335. In the same book, Adam records (p. 275) that 'Jim Mossman . . . lunched with the Queen Mother at Diana Cooper's, who was devoted to him, or with Elizabeth Cavendish and John Betjeman.'
57 John Drummond, *Tainted by Experience: A Life in the Arts*, London 2000, p. 196.
58 Jonathan Stedall, interview, 2003.
59 *Ibid.*
60 Peter Shaffer, *Equus*, London 1973, p. 20.
61 Cecil Beaton diary, 1973. *The Unexpurgated Beaton Diaries*, introduced by Hugo Vickers, London 2003 edn., pp. 390–91.
62 JB to PB, 24 April 1974. JB, *Letters*, ed. CLG, ii, 470.
63 John Osborne wrote (*Looking Back*, London 1999 edn., pp. 466–67):

> We [he and Jocelyn Richards] had struck up some sort of acquaintance with Roger and Penelope Gilliatt at Tynan-like gatherings in their flat in Lowndes Square. He was a rather stern, saturnine neurologist, who had become an overnight celebrity on account of the reluctant part he played in the melodrama that had been created when it was sniffed out by a creepy hack that Tony Armstrong-Jones's best man at his wedding to Princess Margaret, Jeremy Fry, had once been involved in a youthful homosexual scandal. The subsequent clamour of outraged morality was deafening, threatening to become an issue of constitutional proportions.
>
> Fry was dumped overnight and replaced with desperate haste by Roger, whose respectability was ironclad.

See also Theo Aronson, *Princess Margaret: A Biography*, London 1997, pp. 178–79:

> No sooner had it been announced that Jeremy Fry would be the best man than rumours began circulating about his conviction for a homosexual offence eight years before. By 6 April [1960], one month before the wedding, he was obliged to announce that he was suffering from an attack of jaundice and would therefore be unable to act as best man. The fact that he had just returned from a skiing holiday, looking fit and tanned, did nothing to dispel public scepticism.

Aronson further records that, with Fry out of the running, it was hoped that another of Armstrong-Jones's friends, Jeremy Thorpe, might fill the vacancy; but discreet inquiries by the Special Branch uncovered the same 'homosexual tendencies' that had made Fry 'unsuitable'. Eventually, Roger Gilliatt was chosen – 'if not exactly an intimate friend of the prospective bridegroom . . . at least an undeniably heterosexual one'.

64 James Lees-Milne, diary entry for 20 September 1974. *Ancient as the Hills: Diaries 1973–1974*, London 2000 edn., pp. 193–94.

65 Richardson had bought Le Nid du Duc near La Garde-Freinet in France. See Tony Richardson, *Long Distance Runner: A Memoir*, London 1993, p. 202.

66 Cecil Beaton diary, 1969. *Beaton in the Sixties: More Unexpurgated Diaries*, introduced by Hugo Vickers, London 2003, pp. 333–34.

67 Lindsay Anderson, introduction to Tony Richardson, *Long Distance Runner: A Memoir*, London 1993, p. xiv.

68 JB to Col. A.L. Chetwynd-Talbot, 13 June 1972. JB, *Letters*, ed. CLG, ii, 432.

A profile of Terence Stamp in the *Sunday Times* of 21 March 2004 recorded that 'His lionization was complete when Candida Lycett Green, John Betjeman's daughter, composed a swoony poem, "Miss Knightsbridge," in which each verse ended with the words "I'm *frightfully* keen on Terence Stamp".'

69 Quoted, Bryan Connon, *Somerset Maugham and the Maugham Dynasty*, London 1997, p. 268. This book also records an occasion when JB and Robin Maugham were fellow guests at Beverley Nichols's house (pp. 213–14); and describes how JB persuaded Maugham not to write a novel suggesting that Joseph of Arimathaea had made plans to fake the death and resurrection to confirm Christ's claim to be the true Messiah. JB told Maugham that the Church would be 'outraged at the portrayal of Christ as a political pawn' (p. 341).

70 Robin Maugham wrote to JB in 1955: 'I must write to let you know how much your review of *Behind the Mirror* meant to me. It came out at a moment when I felt really depressed and it just made all the difference – to me and needless to say to the book. I am awfully glad you liked it. And I shall now go ahead and write another one.' Quoted, JB, *Letters*, ed. CLG, ii, 59.

71 Robin Maugham, *The Barrier*, London 1976, p. 87.

72 *Ibid.*, pp. 112–13 and 195.

73 *Ibid.*, pp. 98 and 193.

74 See *JBLP*, p. 92; also James Lees-Milne, diary entry for 18 June 1984. *Holy Dread: Diaries 1982–1984*, ed. Michael Bloch, London 2001 edn., pp. 193–94.

75 James Lees-Milne, diary entry for 3 February 1973. *Ancient as the Hills: Diaries 1973–1974*, London 2000 edn., p. 13.

76 *Ibid.*, p. 12.

77 Quoted, *ibid.*, p. 13.

78 James Lees-Milne, diary entry for 6 May 1973. *Ibid.*, p. 38.

79 James Lees-Milne, diary entry for 20 May 1973. *Ibid.*, p. 42.

80 *Loc. cit.*

81 *Loc. cit.*

82 James Lees-Milne, diary entry for 16 June 1973. *Ibid.*, p. 49.

83 (Sir) Julian Hall (1907–74), eleventh Baronet.

84 James Lees-Milne, diary entry for 16 June 1973. *Ancient as the Hills: Diaries 1973–1974*, London 2000 edn., p. 50.

85 James Lees-Milne, diary entry for 17 June 1973. *Loc. cit.*

86 James Lees-Milne, diary entry for 11 December 1973. *Ibid.*, p. 110.

87 See plate in the present volume for Beaton's photograph of JB and Elizabeth Cavendish with Cathleen Nesbitt and Beaton's secretary Eileen Hose. On Cathleen Nesbitt, see *ibid.*, pp. 7, 112–17, 131–33, 203 and 251.

88 *Ibid.*, p. 351.

89 See *YB*, pp. 284–86, 305 and 359.

90 See Beaton, *op. cit.*, p. 416.

91 *Ibid.*, p. 417.

92 *Ibid.*, p. 418.

93 *Loc. cit.*

94 *Loc. cit.*

95 Beaton, *op. cit.*, p. 418 n.1.
96 On De'Ath's incarcerations (the first was in 1993) see Anthony Howard's column, *The Times*, 7 October 2003.
97 Wilfred De'Ath, 'The lonely Laureate', *Illustrated London News*, March 1974, p. 45.
98 *Loc. cit.*
99 James Lees-Milne, diary entry for 9 July 1974. *Ancient as the Hills: Diaries 1973–1974*, London 2000 edn., p. 173.
100 See *The Times*, 9 July 1974; and *loc. cit.*
101 JB, *Letters*, ed. CLG, ii, 483.
102 JB to Mollie Baring, 5 August 1974. Shown to the author by the late Mrs Baring.
103 JB to CLG, 6 August 1974. JB, *Letters*, ed. CLG, ii, 483.
104 JB to CLG, 30 December 1973. JB, *Letters*, ed. CLG, ii, 444.
105 See JB to PB, 1 December 1973. JB, *Letters*, ed. CLG, ii, 493.
106 *Ibid.*, p. 541n.
107 JB to Tom Driberg (who was created Lord Bradwell in 1975), 22 May 1975. JB, *Letters*, ed. CLG, ii, 492.
108 JB, *Letters*, ed. CLG, ii, 448.
109 *Loc. cit.*
110 Quoted, *loc. cit.*
111 *Loc. cit.*
112 *Loc. cit.*
113 JB to PB, 1 December 1975. JB; *Letters*, ed. CLG, ii, 493.
114 *Loc. cit.*
115 JB to the Rev. Wilfrid Harry Jarvis, 17 March 1976. JB, *Letters*, ed. CLG, ii, 495.
116 Bernard Rhodes was later manager of The Clash, Malcolm McLaren of the Sex Pistols. Vivienne Westwood (b. 1941) is a leading fashion designer.
117 Jonathan Stedall, interview, 2003
118 James Lees-Milne, diary entry for 11 June 1976. *Through Wood and Dale: Diaries 1975–1978*, London 2001 edn., p. 97.
119 James Lees-Milne, diary entry for 11 June 1976. *Ibid.*, p. 98.
120 *Ibid.*, p. 99. Sir Osbert Lancaster died in 1986.
121 A photograph of JB with Osbert Lancaster at his seventieth birthday-party at Blacklands is reproduced in JB, *Letters*, ed. CLG, ii, Plate 19a.
122 JB to CLG, 14 June 1976. JB, *Letters*, ed. CLG, ii, 501.
123 Quoted, James Fox, 'Poet in pursuit of his past', *Radio Times*, 28 August 1976.
124 JB to PB, 8 September 1976. JB, *Letters*, ed. CLG, ii, 505.
125 Sylvia Clayton, 'The Betjeman question left unresolved', *Daily Telegraph*, 30 August 1976.
126 Transcript of John Sparrow's talk. *JBP.*
127 JB to John Sparrow, 8 September 1976. JB, *Letters*, ed. CLG, ii, 506.
128 *Ex inf.* Janet Street-Porter, conversation with the author, 1976.
129 Both the *Radio Times* cover and Lancaster's parody of it are reproduced in colour in *JBLP*, p. 148.
130 James Lees-Milne, diary entry for 3 September 1976. *Through Wood and Dale: Diaries 1975–1978*, London 2001 edn., pp. 117–18.
131 *Ibid.*, p. 118.

Chapter 23: Heaven and Hell on Television: The Seventies

1 Edward Mirzoeff, interview, 1997.
2 Quoted, *ibid.*
3 *Ibid.*
4 *Ibid.*
5 Derek Jarman, *Dancing Ledge*, London 1984, p. 273.
6 *Ibid.*, p. 176.

7 On this poem, see Chapter 27, "'. . . As I Lose Hold'".
8 Kenneth Savidge, interview, 2000.
9 *Ibid.*
10 Quoted, *Radio Times*, 12 November 1976.
11 JB to Kenneth Savidge, 9 August 1977. JB, *Letters*, ed. CLG, ii, 515.
12 Script preserved by Kenneth Savidge and shown by him to the author.
13 Michael Parkinson, telephone conversation with the author, 2000.
14 See *JBNFNL*, p. 555.
15 Entry for 17 February 1973. *The Kenneth Williams Diaries*, ed. Russell Davies, London 1993, p. 444.
16 JB introduced a Bravington ring into one of his poems, 'Station Syren' (*Collected Poems*, 2003 edn., pp. 195–96) –

> . . . So maybe the Air Vice-Marshal
> Will buy her a Bravington ring.

17 JB, *Letters*, ed. CLG, ii, 514.

Chapter 24: The 'Green Giant' and Other Campaigns: Preservation in the Seventies

1 *The Times*, 4 December 1958.
2 *The Times*, 24 October 1970.
3 *The Times*, 5 December 1970.
4 *The Times*, 26 March 1971.
5 *The Times*, 7 May 1971.
6 *The Times*, 21 May 1971.
7 I am greatly indebted to Mr Chadd (interview, 2003) for his recollections of the Bristol inquiry and for copies of relevant documents and photographs.
8 Paul Chadd QC, interview, 2003.
9 *Ibid.*
10 *The Times*, 1 May 1972.
11 *The Times*, 2 May 1972.
12 *The Connoisseur*, January 1974.
13 *The Times*, 2 October 1972.
14 *The Times*, 5 January 1973.
15 *The Times*, 8 January 1973.
16 *The Times*, 30 June 1973.
17 *The Times*, 19 November 1973.
18 *The Times*, 18 November 1973.
19 *The Times*, 1 August 1974.
20 *The Times*, 15 August 1974.
21 *The Times*, 19 August 1974.
22 *Collected Poems*, 2003 edn., p. 47. On the history of the campaign to save Holy Trinity, Sloane Street, I am most grateful to Dr Gavin Stamp (who was much involved in the campaign) for his recollections and much other material besides.
23 JB, *A Plea for Holy Trinity Church Sloane Street*, London 1974.
24 Dr Gavin Stamp, essay on Holy Trinity, Sloane Street, sent to the author in 2003.
25 *Ibid.*
26 *Ibid.*
27 *Ibid.*
28 *Ibid.*
29 JB, *A Plea for Holy Trinity Church Sloane Street*, London 1974.
30 Dr Gavin Stamp, essay on Holy Trinity, Sloane Street, sent to the author in 2003.
31 *Ibid.*
32 *The Times*, 16 January 1975.

33 *The Times*, 18 March 1975.
34 *The Times*, 6 June 1975.
35 Geoffrey Grigson, *Recollections Mainly of Artists and Writers*, London 1984, pp. 7 and 169.
36 *The Times*, 19 July 1975.
37 JB, letter to the author, 23 February 1975.
38 *The Times*, 9 August 1975.
39 *The Times*, 13 August 1975.
40 *The Times*, 18 August 1975.
41 Bernard Kaukas, interview, 1990.
42 *The Times*, 30 November 1976.
43 *The Times*, 3 May 1977.
44 *The Times*, 13 June 1977.
45 *The Times*, 20 June 1977.
46 *The Times*, 15 September 1977; see also *Sunday Times*, 4 September 1977.
47 *Ibid.*
48 *The Times*, 15 September 1977.
49 *The Times*, 1 February 1978.
50 *The Times*, 26 June 1978; see also *Sunday Times*, 25 September 1977.
51 *The Times*, 26 September 1978. On the Pheasantry, see also B. Hillier, 'The Pheasantry', *Harper's Bazaar*, June 1969.
52 *The Times*, 22 September 1978.
53 A photograph of this event is reproduced in *JBLP*, p. 144.
54 *The Times*, 12 July 1979.
55 *The Times*, 28 September 1979.
56 *The Times*, 31 July 1980.
57 *The Times*, 19 July 1980.
58 See *JBNFNL*, pp. 46–50.
59 Transcript of the tape JB sent to Clevedon, preserved by Paul Chadd QC.
60 Paul Chadd QC, interview, 2003.
61 *Ibid.*
62 *The Times*, 27 January 1981.
63 *The Times*, 28 November 1981.
64 *The Times*, 3 August 1982.
65 See *JBNFNL*, pp. 390 and 420–21.
66 *The Times*, 19 July 1980.
67 At the time, the present author was chairman of the Thirties Society. The Firestone factory was for the society what the Euston Arch was for the Victorian Society: the martyr that every preservation group needs to draw to public notice the need for action.
68 *The Times*, 19 July 1980.

Chapter 25: Banana Blush

1 JB to H.S. Goodhart-Rendel, 13 July 1949. JB, *Letters*, ed. CLG, i, 478. On JB and the Isle of Man, see Claire Clennell, *Dreamers of Dreams: An Island Musical Odyssey – Mananan International Festival of Music and the Arts: The First 25 Years*, Erin Arts Centre, Isle of Man, 2000, pp. 9, 19, 20, 23, 26, 33, 36, 39, 55, 67 and 68.

Mrs Eunice Salmond, an Isle of Man journalist, recalls (letter to the author, 9 November 2000):

I heard John Betjeman was staying at the Fort Anne Hotel, a building made famous as the home of Sir William Hillary who founded the Royal National Lifeboat Institution from his observations of ships in distress on the rocks below his home overlooking Douglas Bay. Betjeman was staying with his constant companion Lady Elizabeth Cavendish . . . As a local journalist I rang to seek an interview with the great man. He told me he was much too busy with visits to many places and to the Museum. My heart sank but then, almost as an afterthought, he told me he was going to see Glencrutchery House which had rooms designed by the Victorian architect Baillie Scott. Would I like to go with him? Would I!

We drove up the driveway to this house, last resided in by one of the Island's Deemsters (High Court Judge). I cannot remember anyone being with us but as we entered the empty drawing room, I exclaimed: 'Oh! *My Fair Lady*!' 'Why did you say that?' he demanded. I explained that I had not long before seen the film in which Audrey Hepburn ran in despair to the house of Professor Higgins's mother. The drawing-room there had the same inglenook fireplace and possibly similar tiles and brass canopy. 'Clever girl!' replied Betjeman. 'I loaned my book on Baillie Scott to Cecil Beaton when he was designing the sets for *My Fair Lady*.' That visit took place in the early 1960s.

I was to see Betjeman at other times – I have one memory of him trudging round the corner of the Villiers Hotel, a Victorian paradise as well as a landmark, his squashed panama on the back of his head, laden with paper bags containing Manx rock.

My memories of him echo with his love of the Isle of Man. He would sometimes stay in B and B places, like Peel for instance. There was nothing grand about him . . .

The most precious memories come from an October evening in 1972. I don't know how it came about, but Betjeman expressed a wish to see a collection of Archibald Knox paintings owned by a friend of mine. It was arranged for teatime on All Hallowe'en . . .

I went out to greet the rather doddering Poet Laureate and to help him alight from his car. In the near distance some Cubs were singing the Celtic song 'Ginny the witch, *Hop tu Naa*' (All Hallows' Eve). 'What is that?' he asked as we stood on the pavement. 'Sing it to me,' he demanded. I did my best with the flattest of tones – the song begins, 'Jenny the Witch flew over the house, To fetch a stick to lather the mouse.' I told the Cubs I wanted them to come inside and sing for the Poet Laureate. 'Never met one of those, Ma'am,' said the tiniest Cub. That over, Sir John stayed for a long time studying the watercolours. In his typical fashion and tone, he murmured, 'We are as near heaven tonight, in this house, as any of us will ever be.'

2 The poem appeared in his collection *Sir John Piers*, Mullingar 1938. *Collected Poems*, 1985 edn., p. 81.

3 *Portraits of Islands*, ed. Eileen Molony, London 1951. It will be remembered that Eileen Molony was the BBC Talks producer at Bristol to whom, in 1945, JB sent a letter beginning, 'Ah, my darling dark yellow-stockinged Amazon . . .' See *JBNFNL*, p. 291.

4 Graham Warhurst (letter to the author, 13 November 2000) writes: 'My own involvement was to arrange a special train to take people, and Sir John Betjeman as guest of honour, from Port Erin to Castletown where one of the concerts of the Erin Arts Festival was held . . . From memory this was in 1975 and 1976. The local railway was, and still is, operated using its original Victorian and Edwardian locomotives and rolling stock. This, of course, appealed to Sir John, especially as I had arranged for the Directors' first class saloon (of 1905) to be in the train with a seat reserved for him.'

5 See note 1 of the present chapter; also, Mrs Dorothy Luft writes (letter to the author, 2 November 2000): 'It is known that in October 1961 Sir John bought twenty-three watercolours by Archibald Knox from the Manx Museum, to which they had been donated under Knox's will.'

6 Sir Simon Jenkins, conversation with the author, 1976.

7 Mrs Eunice Salmond, letter to the author, 9 November 2000.

8 Clennell, *op. cit.*, p. 68.

9 JB to H.S. Goodhart-Rendel, 13 July 1949. JB, *Letters*, ed. CLG, i, 479.

10 William Bealby-Wright, interview, 1990.

11 *Ibid*.

12 *Ibid*.

13 *Ibid*.

14 Susan Baker, interview, 1990.

15 The Barrow Poets started in 1951 as a group of friends, mainly at London University and the Slade School of Art, who wanted to sell poems as broadsheets during the Festival of Britain. The actor Patrick Wymark and his wife Olwen were involved; she tried to obtain a licence from the London County Council to sell broadsheets, but failed. The group were called the Barrow Poets because Patrick Wymark had acquired a street-market barrow, from which it was intended to sell the poems. As the LCC did not give permission, the barrow was left at Wymark's parents' house in Grimsby, but the name stuck. In 1952 Susan Baker, then a student at the Royal College of Music, began playing the violin with the Barrow Poets. The group became linked with Poetry and Plays in Pubs, an organization founded by Sybil Thorndike and others before the war. Posters were put up in pubs to advertise that 'The Barrow Poets will be here tomorrow', and the performers received £2 each a night. (*Ex inf*. Susan Baker, interview, 1990.)

16 Susan Baker, interview, 1990.

17 *Ibid*.

18 Jim Parker, interview, 1990.

19 *Ibid*.

20 *Ibid*.

21 Susan Baker, interview, 1990.

22 *Ibid*.

23 Hugh Murphy, on the radio programme *Softly Croons the Radiogram*, produced by Rob Ketteridge, BBC 1991.

24 Susan Baker, interview, 1990.

25 Jim Parker, interview, 1990.

26 *Ibid*.

27 William Bealby-Wright, interview, 1990.

28 Jim Parker, interview, 1990.

29 Morgan Studios, Maybury Gardens, Willesden.

30 Hugh Murphy, on the radio programme *Softly Croons the Radiogram*, BBC 1991.

31 *Ibid*.

32 Jim Parker, interview, 1990.

33 *Ibid*.

34 *Ibid*.

35 *Ibid*.

36 *Ibid*.

37 *Ibid*.

38 This extract was played on the radio programme *Softly Croons the Radiogram*, BBC 1991.

39 Hugh Murphy, *ibid*.

40 William Bealby-Wright, *ibid*.

41 *Ibid*.

42 Jim Parker, interview, 1990.

43 JB to Jim Parker, 22 March 1974. Shown to the author by Mr Parker.

44 JB to Major Sir Rennie Maudslay, 1974. The letter was read out on the radio programme *Softly Croons the Radiogram*, BBC 1991, though the letter's precise date was not given.

45 Major Sir Rennie Maudslay to JB, 1974. *Ibid*.

46 Graham Lord, 'The day Sir John was called Dracula by a friend', *Sunday Express*, 18 August 1974.

47 *Ex inf*. Susan Baker, on the radio programme *Softly Croons the Radiogram*, BBC 1991.

48 Jim Parker, interview, 1990.

49 Quoted by Jim Parker, interview, 1990.

50 JB to Jim Parker, 6 June 1974. Shown to the author by Mr Parker.

51 Jim Parker, interview, 1990.

52 *Ibid*.

53 *Ibid*.

54 *Ibid*.

55 *Ibid*.

56 Jim Parker, on the radio programme *Softly Croons the Radiogram*, BBC 1991.

57 George Melly, *ibid*.
58 Jim Parker, *ibid*.
59 Jim Parker, interview, 1990.
60 *Ibid*.
61 *Ibid*. JB's description of the River Wandle in his 1944 poem was confir
   later, by J. Hillier in his book *Old Surrey Water-Mills*, London 1951:

> A pilgrimage up the Wandle these days is a harrowing experience. In places it is still sufficiently a 'country' river, with grassy banks and tall old trees, for one to be shocked by the unhappy state of most reaches, the way it is harnessed to mercenary and usually noisome enterprises, and smothered under streets and houses as though it were a drain. In fact, had it been encased in concrete conduit along its entire length we should have been spared these poignant reminders, breaking out like spasmodic poetry in the prosaic topography of Mitcham and Merton and Wimbledon . . .

62 Hugh Murphy, on the radio programme *Softly Croons the Radiogram*, BBC 1991.
63 *The Observer*, 17 March 1974.
64 Hugh Murphy, on the radio programme *Softly Croons the Radiogram*, BBC 1991.
65 *Ibid*.
66 Hugh Murphy got hold of the wrong end of the stick. He thought that the girl about whom John had written had been a model of the watercolourist Sir William Russell Flint; but in giving his poem about 'Freckly Jill' at the Garrick Club the title 'A Russell Flint', JB was merely indicating the sort of beauty she was.
67 John G. Murray, interview, 1990.
68 Jim Parker, interview, 1990.
69 *Ibid*.
70 *Ibid*.
71 *Ibid*.
72 *Ibid*.
73 *Ibid*.
74 *Ibid*. Parker was, of course, referring to the popular radio programme *Desert Island Discs*, in which celebrities were and are asked to choose the records with which they would wish to be stranded on a desert island. Devised in 1941 by Roy Plomley, and for many years presented by him, it is now the longest-running series on BBC radio.
   Plomley wrote in his book *Desert Island Discs*, London 1977 edn., pp. 58–59:

> Another celebrated railway buff [besides the Rev. W. Awdry, author of *Thomas the Tank Engine*] is Sir John Betjeman who, on the occasion of the first of his two appearances in the series, recorded on a sunny afternoon in 1954, chose a collection of railway noises as one of his discs as well as songs by Randolph Sutton and John McCormack, and the bells of Thaxted Church in Essex. He and I had already done a lot of broadcasting together in *We Beg to Differ*, in which he was a reserve member of the gentlemen's team. One day, a member of the ladies' team was talking about the drab clothes habitually worn by men, and she was obviously getting at John Betjeman, who was wearing a dark suit and a sober tie. After enduring the jokes patiently for a while, he rose to his feet and said, 'Things are not always what they seem,' and threw open his jacket to show that it was lined in crimson. It was hardly good radio, but it was beautifully timed and brought a whoop of delight from the studio audience. It also revealed a facet of a delightful but complex nature.
>
> After our *Desert Island Discs* recording, we came out of Broadcasting House at about a quarter past five. 'It'd be nice to have a drink,' I said, 'but it's a quarter of an hour before opening time.'
>
> 'Let's walk up to Marylebone Station,' said John. 'By the time we get there the buffet will be open.'
>
> 'All right,' I said. 'Er – but why Marylebone Station? Are you catching a train?'
>
> 'No,' he replied, 'but the station is a beautiful example of Victorian railway architecture, and it's the only buffet in London where one can hear birdsong.'

They seemed two excellent reasons, so we set off in the sunshine up Portland Place, feeling relaxed and cheerful, having finished our day's work. Another of the discs he had chosen was a catchy May Day song, sung by Cornish villagers, and after a while we both began to sing it. Then, because we felt like it, we began to dance as well.

We sang and danced our way along the pavement, which was almost deserted. Then, bearing down on us, we saw the dignified figure of a very senior BBC official indeed, wearing, as all very senior BBC officials should, an Anthony Eden hat and a double-breasted blue Crombie overcoat, and carrying a briefcase and a rolled umbrella. We saw his eyebrows shoot up as he observed the two broadcasters come dancing towards him.

But the future Poet Laureate wasn't in the least abashed. 'Ah, my dear fellow,' he called. 'Come and dance with us.'

And, bless his heart, he did. We all three sang and danced together, belatedly celebrating May Day in far-off Padstow, and then John and I continued on our way to Marylebone Station . . .

(On the May Day song and the 'obby 'oss festival in Padstow, Cornwall, see *YB*, pp. 88–89.)

After Plomley's book appeared in 1977, JB made a third appearance on *Desert Island Discs*.

Chapter 26: Simon Jenkins and a trip to Southend

1 Rose Macaulay, *Letters to a Friend 1950–52*, ed. Constance Babington-Smith, London 1961, p. 63.
2 See *The Times*, 14 April 1971.
3 *The Times*, 16 April 1971.
4 *Evening Standard*, 22 April 1971.
5 The Sir Arthur Gilbert collection, housed on the river side of Somerset House, was opened by Queen Elizabeth the Queen Mother in May 2000. One of the exhibits was a waxwork of Gilbert in yellow tennis shorts.
6 (Sir) Simon Jenkins, interview, 1990.
7 *Ibid.*
8 *Evening Standard*, 27 April 1971.
9 Sir Edward Maufe (1883–1974), architect. His works include Guildford Cathedral, buildings for Oxford and Cambridge colleges and St Thomas's, Hanwell. In 1974 (the year of Maufe's death), JB wrote to the architect, praising the Hanwell church. See JB, *Letters*, ed. CLG, ii, 477.
10 Robin (also known as Richard) Seifert (1910–2001), architect. Hon. Lt.-Col. Designed, among other buildings, Centre Point, St Giles's Circus, London; and the Royal Garden Hotel, Kensington. JB detested most of his work.
11 (Sir) Simon Jenkins, interview, 1990.
12 *Ibid.*
13 *Ibid.*
14 *Ibid.*
15 *Ibid.*
16 *Ex inf.* (Sir) Simon Jenkins, interview, 1990; and Simon Jenkins, 'Betjeman's flight of fancy', *The Times*, 16 October 1993.
17 Simon Jenkins, 'Betjeman's flight of fancy', *The Times*, 16 October 1993.
18 *Ibid.*
19 *Ibid.*
20 *Ibid.*
21 *Ibid.*
22 (Sir) Simon Jenkins, interview, 1990.
23 *Ibid.*

24 Simon Jenkins to JB, 22 July 1976. Copy shown to the author by (Sir) Simon Jenkins.

25 Unpublished account of the Southend trip, 1976, shown to the author by (Sir) Simon Jenkins.

26 *Ibid.*

27 *Ibid.*

28 Robert Buchanan (1841–1901), poet, novelist and popular dramatist. Among his works are *Poems including London Poems*, 1866, and *Collected Poetical Works*, 1880. See *DNB*.

29 (Sir) Simon Jenkins, interview, 1990.

30 Unpublished account of the Southend trip, 1976, shown to the author by (Sir) Simon Jenkins.

31 *Ibid.*

32 JB to Sir Simon Jenkins, 9 November 1976. Shown to the author by (Sir) Simon Jenkins.

33 I am grateful to my cousin, Mr Antony Giles of Leigh-on-Sea, Essex, for taking me for a ride on the *Sir John Betjeman* at Southend. On 13 November 2003, the Southend Tourist Office confirmed to me that the train was still running.

Chapter 27: '. . . As I Lose Hold'

1 See JB's letter of 12 September 1977 to Keith Miller, about the death of his father 'Dusty' Miller. JB, *Letters*, ed. CLG, ii, 528–29.

2 Quoted, Reg Read, interview, 2003.

3 *Ibid.*

4 *Ibid.*

5 *Ibid.*

6 In 1973 JB unsuccessfully tried to obtain a knighthood for Dykes Bower. See JB's letter to (Sir) Edward Heath, 26 January 1973. JB, *Letters*, ed. CLG, ii, 458.

7 Reg Read, interview, 2003.

8 *Ibid.*

9 *Ibid.*

10 *Ibid.*

11 *Ibid.*

12 *Ibid.*

13 *Ibid.*

14 Jonathan Stedall, interview, 2003.

15 Reg Read, interview, 2003.

16 *Ibid.*

17 On Duncan Fallowell (b. 1948), see JB, *Letters*, ed. CLG, ii, 588.

18 Duncan Fallowell, *20th Century Characters*, London 1994, pp. 256–57.

19 *Ibid.*, p. 258.

20 *Ibid.*, pp. 262–63.

21 *Ibid.*, p. 264.

22 *Ibid.*, pp. 266–67.

23 *Ibid.*, p. 267.

24 Reg Read, interview, 2003.

25 PB, interview, 1978.

26 Copy of JB's typescript kindly supplied by Mr Reg Read.

27 JB, 'Chelsea 1977', *Collected Poems*, 2003 edn., p. 392.

28 I am grateful to Mr Alan Bell for having preserved a copy of this poem.

29 JB to PB, 8 September 1976. JB, *Letters*, ed. CLG, ii, 506.

30 JB to Angela, Lady Grimthorpe, 7 November 1977. JB, *Letters*, ed. CLG, ii, 529.

31 JB, *Letters*, ed. CLG, ii, 516.

32 James Lees-Milne, diary entry for 23 December 1976. *Through Wood and Dale: Diaries 1975–1978*, London 2001 edn., p. 138.

33 On the 'Uranian' poet Dr E. E. Bradford, and JB's visit to him, see *YB*, pp. 176–77 and *JBNFNL*, pp. 14, 62–63, 65, 190–91 and 259.

34 James Lees-Milne, diary entry for 11 August 1977. *Through Wood and Dale: Diaries 1975–1978*, London 2001 edn., p. 179.

35 John G. Murray, interview, 1989.

36 JB to PB, 3 December 1977. JB, *Letters*, ed. CLG, ii, 530.

37 *Loc. cit.*

38 James Lees-Milne, diary entry for 19 March 1978. *Through Wood and Dale: Diaries 1975–1978*, London 2001 edn., p. 240.

39 Anthony Powell describes Roland Gant of Heinemann (1919–91) as 'my friend and publisher' in *To Keep the Ball Rolling: The Memoirs of Anthony Powell*, vol. iii, *Faces in My Time*, London 1980, p. 44. In his speech at a Heinemann lunch at Claridge's, 8 April 1986, Powell said: 'With every book I write I feel it would never have appeared without Roland ...' (*Journals 1982–1986*, London 1995, p. 227). On 17 January 1988 Powell wrote in his diary, after lunch with Roland Gant and his wife Nadia, 'nice to see Roland again' (*Journals 1987–1989*, London 1996, p. 76).

40 JB, *Letters*, ed. CLG, ii, 517–18. CLG also writes (*ibid.*, p. 550): 'After that first heart attack in 1978, Gerard Irvine had rushed over from St Matthew's in Great Peter Street to the Royal Brompton Hospital and given JB the last rites.'

41 James Lees-Milne, diary entry for 22 May 1978. *Through Wood and Dale: Diaries 1975–1978*, London 2001 edn., p. 257.

Richard Robinson and James Bettley were both twenty-year-old Oxford undergraduates in 1978. Robinson remembers little of the evening, 'except all of us getting very overexcited about prep school and chanting "Jute-Hemp-Sisal", those being key ingredients of early geography lessons it would seem for us all.' (Letter to the author, 29 June 1990). James Bettley, who later joined the staff of the Royal Institute of British Architects, kept a diary. In his entry for 20 May 1978 (of which he has kindly supplied the present author with a copy), he made the understandable mistake of assuming that the woman with JB (in fact Lady Elizabeth Cavendish) was his wife:

> Dressed and left Moor Wood at about 7.15 and drove to Badminton – dinner with R[ichard]'s uncle Jim Lees-Milne. Betjeman and wife there when we arrived – B dressed in perfect manner in smart suit, collar of shirt in a dreadful mess, badly tied rust-coloured tie, right cuff without link. Crashed heavily into a delicate chair after the introductions. Seemed uncertain of us to begin with, but soon warmed up and seemed almost excited by the whole affair. Conversation before dinner general, Sir John drinking whisky and taking a great liking to potato crisps. Two comments: 'I like a good peer – an Irish peer – run to seed' and 'Live for pleasure' – great admiration for the Bishop of Southwark because of his worldliness (last to leave a ball at Bath, at 4 a.m.). Rumours of orgies vigorously denied. At dinner we talked first of geography and 'Jute Hemp and Sisal', that great trio. J.B. kept on exclaiming 'Jute! What *is* it?' Then of links with the past – J.B. and JL-M both knew Bosie, Lord Alfred Douglas, and had letters from him. Excellent food – J.B. dribbling soup slightly down his chin ... Lady B. old, slightly unconventional: large tummy, corduroy trousers, standing with hands in pockets, back to the fire. Talkative in a quieter way than Sir John – who despite a certain vagueness was always quick in conversation and laughed a very great deal – more so, he said, than for a long time.

Among the things Bettley wanted to talk about was the fact that his mother, *née* Jean McIntyre, had been JB's secretary at the Ministry of Information during the war. 'He wrote her a poem but, alas, it was blitzed and she is now dead, Bettley wrote (letter to the author, 4 July 1991).

42 JB to Williams Brothers, Builders, 14 July 1978. JB, *Letters*, ed. CLG, ii, 538.

43 *Ibid.*, 538n.

44 JB to PB, 25 September 1978. JB, *Letters*, ed. CLG, ii, 541.

45 JB told PB much the same: *loc. cit.*

46 James Lees-Milne, diary entry for 10 October 1978. *Through Wood and Dale: Diaries 1975–1978*, London 2001 edn., p. 286.

47 James Lees-Milne, diary entry for 28 November 1978. *Ibid.*, p. 297.

48 *Loc. cit.*

49 Glynn Boyd Harte (1948–2003), artist. He had already collaborated with JB. His obituary in *The Times* (19 December 2003) began:

> It can hardly have been coincidence that Glynn Boyd Harte's first significant work of illustration was a collaboration with John Betjeman on *Metro-land*. For in many ways, Boyd Harte was a Betjeman among painters. He shared many of the same nostalgias for Victoriana and the oddities of English life, and adopted many of the same slightly fogeyish attitudes.
>
> For this reason, no doubt, he was never taken entirely seriously as an artist; as with Betjeman among poets, there was often a faint hint of patronization in critical views of him, along with a suggestion that he had – perhaps wilfully, perhaps perforce – proclaimed himself a minor, reactionary artist, a big fish in a small pond . . .

In their *Bibliographical Companion to Betjeman*, Canterbury 1997, Peter Gammond and John Heald list the earlier collaboration under 1977 as follows:

> [Souvenir of] METRO-LAND. *Original Lithographs by* Glynn Boyd Harte illustrating Verses taken from the BBC Television Film METRO-LAND (1973) produced by Edward Mirzoeff . . . Warren Editions (Jonathan & Phillida Gili), London, 15 November 1977. Limited edition of 220 boxed copies, signed by John Betjeman & Glynn Boyd Harte + 25 Sets of the 16 lithographs.

50 Gavin Stamp and Glynn Boyd Harte, *Temples of Power*, London 1979, p. 2.

51 The present author reviewed the book in the *Times Literary Supplement* on 25 December 1981.

52 JB, *Letters*, ed. CLG, ii, 539n.; and conversation with Dr Gavin Stamp, 2003.

53 James Lees-Milne, diary entry for 25 July 1979. *Deep Romantic Chasm: Diaries 1979–1981*, ed. Michael Bloch, London 2003 edn., p. 41.

54 James Lees-Milne, diary entry for 20 August 1979. *Ibid.*, p. 45.

55 Derek Hill, interview, 1979.

56 Quoted, Lionel Perry, interview, 1979.

57 Derek Hill, interview, 1979.

58 JB to PB, 14 May 1980. JB, *Letters*, ed. CLG, ii, 562.

59 James Lees-Milne, diary entry for 19 February 1980. *Deep Romantic Chasm: Diaries 1970–1981*, ed. Michael Bloch, London 2003 edn., p. 76.

60 *Loc. cit.*

61 *Loc. cit.*

62 Sir Martin Gilliat (1913–93), private secretary to Queen Elizabeth the Queen Mother, 1956–93.

63 Sir Roy Strong, letter to the author, 7 December 2003.

64 JB to PB, 2 July 1980. JB, *Letters*, ed. CLG, ii, 563.

65 Lady Wilson, interview, 2003.

66 Reg Read, interview, 2003.

67 *Ibid.*

68 James Lees-Milne, diary entry for 21 July 1980. *Deep Romantic Chasm: Diaries 1979–1981*, ed. Michael Bloch, London 2003 edn., p. 101.

69 On this conversation, see *loc. cit.*; also *JBNFNL*, p. 328.

70 Tom Mitford (1909–45), son of the second Lord Redesdale. Like JB's friend Basil Dufferin, he was killed in action in Burma.

71 James Lees-Milne, diary entry for 21 July 1980. *Deep Romantic Chasm: Diaries 1979–1981*, ed. Michael Bloch, London 2003 edn., p. 101.

72 *Loc. cit.*

73 Anthony Burgess wrote, in *Earthly Powers*, London 1981 edn., p. 36:

> Wignall nodded and nodded, putting crumbs of the cake to his mouth, smiling down some long vista of the years at perhaps some fateful childhood party in Hampstead or

an as yet uncorrupted Golders Green. I settled myself again and brought out, thinking to give pleasure to their author, the lines I had read that afternoon:

> But then I saw your tongue protrude
> To catch the wisp of angel's food.
> Ah God! I quailed beneath the shock:
> Your something something party frock.

'Shut it,' he cried. *Shock* was right. 'Shut it, shut it. It's nothing to you except a chunk of—' His eyes now were the ones to fill. 'All over, it's all over. Sorry,' he sniffed to his hostess, who wrinkled painfully though not in bewilderment: she had entertained plenty of authors in her time. And then to me: 'Sorry. It's just that – Growing old isn't easy,' he said loudly to the children, who had been crumbling cake in what I took to be embarrassment . . . 'Everything's spat upon now. Everything.'

74 *Ibid.*, p. 7.
75 See *YB*, p. 8.
76 Burgess, *op. cit.*, p. 27.
77 See *JBNFNL*, p. 301.
78 Burgess, *op. cit.*, pp. 23–24.
79 Reg Read, interview, 2003.
80 Richard Boston, letter to the author, 2004.
81 Quoted, John Lahr, *Dame Edna Everage and the Rise of Western Civilization: Backstage with Barry Humphries*, London 1991, p. 112.
82 See Chapter 10, 'Barry Humphries', in the present volume.
83 Peter Coleman, *The Real Barry Humphries Story*, London 1990, p. 158.
84 Barry Humphries, telephone conversation with the author, 2003.
85 Jonathan Stedall, interview, 2003.
86 Reg Read, interview, 2003.
87 PB, interview, 1978.
88 Reg Read, interview, 2003. As early as 1971 JB wrote to Mary Wilson: 'The literary world is malicious and personal. I suffer under [Geoffrey] Grigson and his like and even under people who pretend to be friends (e.g. John Piper and his wife) who feel, one knows, that one is "trivial" and not "important". One of the agonies of publishing is that you get such attacks.' (JB to Mary Wilson, 25 June 1971. JB, *Letters*, ed. CLG, ii, 416.)
89 Reg Read, interview, 2003.
90 Peter Gammond with John Heald, *A Bibliographical Companion to Betjeman*, Canterbury 1997, section 81B2a.
91 *Ex inf.* Reg Read, interview, 2003.
92 *Ibid.*
93 *Ibid.*
94 'Alice Hardy first met JB in 1943 [*sic*, for 1944] when she was married to her first husband Mr Jennings and JB was working for the Admiralty in Bath. He was making a broadcast under the auspices of Geoffrey Grigson in the Bristol BBC studios: "I came into the Listening Room in order to put him on the air, being the Programme Engineer, now called Studio Manageress, and John said, 'Who's that girl?' And Griggers from a great height said, 'That's your PE.' At that time everybody in the BBC and probably elsewhere too was bristling with initials, and, coming upon this latest one, John burst into a great chortle of enchantment, so infectious that I joined in too, and that's how our friendship started up, and how henceforth I was called PE."
    'JB fell in love with her. They were both away from their families and missing them. "It was all lovely and gorgeous and funny," remembers Alice Hardy. "We used to go into Bath tea shops together. When John wrote 'In a Bath Tea Shop' I said to him, 'You may be a "thumping crook", but I'm *not* "an ordinary little woman".' He admitted it was not a physical description of us but of a couple we had been watching." JB wrote to

Alice, 17 July 1944, "I've had rather a pang in this heart, sitting here at Fortt's having tea, at seeing a girl who is obviously you with rather skinny shoulders and J. M. Barrie hair sitting by a gallant RAF boy. He's nuts about her, I can see from his eyes. She's got her back to me. I hope it's not you. Because he's not like Jennings . . . My dear thing, just go over that day again – the bicycle, the iron stairs, the sweet on the carpet, the constant change of dress, the quiet of Clifton treetops and the U[nion] J[ack] flag beyond them, shopping . . . the drunk lunch with Beadle and Co. – then the sleep in that little cell of a bedroom, tea, love – my ruined raped Wendy – the rocks, Teddi Wolfe, the wonderful walk back. Oh heaven! What a height we reached . . . I'm in a hell of a tangle. I love you: I love you: keep your few eyelashes free from blast.'" (JB, *Letters*, ed. CLG, ii, 569.)

95 This might seem to contradict Tom Driberg's description of JB's couplet 'I sometimes think that I should like To be the saddle of a bike' as 'the shortest erotic poem in our language' (*YB*, p. 258); but when Jonathan Gili asked John Piper if he would illustrate that couplet for a private press publication, Piper declined on the grounds that the original poem was far longer and *very* erotic. (*Ex inf.* Jonathan Gili, telephone conversation with the author, 2002).

96 On Eileen Molony see note 3 to Chapter 25 above.

97 Eileen Molony's boss at the BBC was Mary Semeris, head of Schools Talks. (JB, *Letters*, ed. CLG, ii, 570.)

98 On JB's successful action to save the Avon Gorge and the Clifton suspension bridge from being overshadowed by a big hotel, see Chapter 24, 'The "Green Giant" and Other Campaigns: Preservation in the 1970s'.

99 'Edward Wolfe RA was a great friend of Alice Hardy [then Alice Jennings] and JB and they were always going to his studio by the river for drinks made of Metatone, a sort of wartime tonic which tasted quite like Vermouth, and gin stored in milk bottles made illegally by university students. Wolfe, always broke, had made a limited edition of prints illustrating the *Song of Solomon*.' (JB, *Letters*, ed. CLG, ii, 570.) On Wolfe see also *JBNFNL*, pp. 280–81.

100 JB to Alice Hardy, 2 March 1981. JB, *Letters*, ed. CLG, ii, 569.

101 *Ibid.*, 552.

102 *Loc. cit.*

103 Quoted, *ibid.*, 553.

104 James Lees-Milne, diary entry for 29 May 1981. *Deep Romantic Chasm: Diaries 1979–1981*, ed. Michael Bloch, 2003 edn., p. 149.

105 JB, *Letters*, ed. CLG, ii, 573n.

106 *Loc. cit.*

107 Dr Gavin Stamp wrote (and still writes) a column in *Private Eye* about architecture under the *nom de plume* 'Piloti'.

108 James Lees-Milne, diary entry for 29 March 1982. *Holy Dread: Diaries 1982–1984*, ed. Michael Bloch, London 2003 edn., pp. 17–18.

109 As part of Jonathan Stedall's television series *Time with Betjeman*.

110 James Lees-Milne, diary entry for 15 June 1982. *Holy Dread: Diaries 1982–1984*, ed. Michael Bloch, London 2003 edn., pp. 29–30.

111 Paul Wigmore, unpublished autobiography. Kindly shown to the author by Mr Wigmore.

112 *Ibid.*

113 JB, conversation with the author, 1982.

114 (Sir) Kingsley Amis, conversation with the author, 1982.

115 JB, conversation with the author, 1982.

116 JB, *Letters*, ed. CLG, ii, 556. There was a good reason for giving Elizabeth East a nickname: it would have been confusing to have had two Elizabeths in Radnor Walk.

117 *Loc. cit.*

118 John Gough, whose career was in insurance, was elected to the court of the Fishmongers' Company (*ex inf.* John Mallet).

119 John Mallet, unpublished diary entry for 7 April 1983. Photocopy kindly supplied by Mr Mallet.

Chapter 28: Time with Betjeman

Except where otherwise stated, all the quotations in this chapter are from the BBC series *Time with Betjeman*, produced and presented by Jonathan Stedall and first screened in 1983.

1 Jonathan Stedall (interview, 2003), explained the genesis of the *Time with Betjeman* series:

> The last thing I did with John was *Time with Betjeman*. That really grew. I was working in the documentary department at the BBC and I'd done a series with Malcolm Muggeridge called *Muggeridge Ancient and Modern* – and that was a sort of television autobiography. Muggeridge had made a number of films about his younger days – one with Kevin Billington in India and one in America; and the idea was to do an entire television autobiography, filling in the gaps – which is what we did. So I was dipping into the archives, but also talking to Malcolm and driving him around. I'd done that and it was my initiative that we should do a similar kind of thing with John, which is what we did; but the difference was that, while the Muggeridge series involved only Malcolm and his wife Kitty, with Alec Vidler coming in briefly, with John we brought in many people – John and Myfanwy Piper, Osbert Lancaster, Barry Humphries and of course Penelope, and others.

2 Arthur Perceval Purey-Cust (1828–1916), Dean of York, 1880–1916.

3 In 1839 the Eglinton Tournament was staged by Archibald Montgomerie, thirteenth Earl of Eglinton – a sort of pageant with jousts in medieval fancy-dress. It is seen now as part of the Victorian Gothic Revival.
   See Ian Anstruther, *The Knight and the Umbrella: An Account of the Eglinton Tournament 1839*, London 1963.

4 A. N. Wilson, 'Mother's Pride Passing By', *Sunday Telegraph*, 15 May 1994.

5 Quoted, JB, *Letters*, ed. CLG, ii, 554.

6 Quoted, *ibid.*, 555.

Chapter 29: His Last Bow

1 Dr Frank Tait, interview, 1990.
   Alan Bennett in a television lecture on JB, told how the poet saw another David Cecil talk advertised, on 'Reading'. Attending it, he was disappointed to find that it was on the art of reading, not on the town of Reading, as he had imagined.

2 Quoted, Dr Frank Tait, interview, 1990.

3 *Ibid.*

4 Quoted, *ibid.*

5 Quoted, *ibid.*

6 *Ibid.*

7 Gillian, Lady Parker, interview, 1990.

8 Peter Parker, *For Starters: The Business of Life*, London 1989, p. 59.

9 The book was *He That Plays the King*, London 1950.

10 Lady Parker, interview, 1990.

11 *Ibid.*

12 Sir Peter Parker, interview, 1990.

13 *Ibid*

14 Sir Peter Parker, *op. cit.*, p. 27.

15 *Ibid.*, p. 39.

16 *Ex. inf.* John Stevenson, interview, 1990.

17 Lady Parker, interview, 1990.

18 The Registrar-General had his office at Somerset House.

19 Lady Parker, interview, 1990.

20 On Dr John Allison (1926–78), see *The Letters of Kingsley Amis*, ed. Zachary Leader, London 2000, p. 807n. Kingsley Amis wrote to Elizabeth Jane Howard on 17 September 1976, after dining with Allison and his wife Susan: 'v. gd fun with John [Allison] getting rather pissed in his most amiable vein, full of stories about Arab billionaires'. After Allison's death in 1978, his wife did secretarial work both for Amis and for JB. (See Chapter 30, '. . . Whose Death Has Eclipsed the Gaiety of Nations'.)

21 Lady Parker, interview, 1990.

22 *Ibid.*

23 *Ibid.*

24 *Ibid.* In fact, Calman and Scott knew of JB's nickname for them, and were not offended.

25 Dr Calman's visit to JB was described by Dr Gregory Scott in his unpublished diaries. Shown to the author by Mr John Stevenson.

26 John Stevenson, interview, 1990.

27 *Ex. inf.* Dr Gregory Scott's unpublished diaries. Shown to the author by Mr John Stevenson.

28 On Dr Peter Southwell see *The Times*, 18 January 1989, and *Sunday Times*, 17 September 1989 and 29 October 1989.

29 *Ex. inf.* John Stevenson, interview, 1990.

30 Michael Holroyd, conversation with the author, 1990.

31 On Scott's collection of Penguin books, see B. Hillier, *The New Antiques*, London 1977, pp. 54–57.

32 John Stevenson said (interview, 1990): 'I remember Greg was very nervous, his hands were trembling at the thought of buying this "Max" original. It was the cheapest thing at a West End exhibition of Beerbohm's work, in the 1970s. All the Wilde sketches and things like that were £2,000, £3,000; but this was only £300 because nobody at the exhibition, apart from me, apparently, knew who Sydney Grundy was. He was the Alan Ayckbourn of the 1890s – wrote dozens and dozens of successful situation comedies.'

33 Dr Gregory Scott, unpublished diary. Shown to the author by Mr John Stevenson.

34 *Ibid.*

35 See T. S. Eliot, Hugh McDiarmid and Maurice Lindsay on John Davidson's life and works in *John Davidson: A Selection of His Poems*, London 1961. Eliot claimed to have been influenced by Davidson.

36 Dr Gregory Scott, unpublished diary. Shown to the author by Mr John Stevenson.

37 *Ibid.*

38 Timothy d'Arch Smith, *Love in Earnest: Some Notes on the Lives and Writings of English 'Uranian' Poets from 1889 to 1930*, London 1970.

39 Rupert Croft-Cooke, *Feasting with Panthers: A New Consideration of Some Late Victorian Writers*, London 1967. JB was a friend of Croft-Cooke. See JB, *Letters*, ed. CLG, ii, 45 and 232.

40 Dr Gregory Scott, unpublished diaries. Shown to the author by Mr John Stevenson.

41 Sir Peter Parker, *op. cit.*, p. 265.

42 Sir Peter Parker, interview, 1990.

43 *Ibid.*

44 Sir Peter Parker, *op. cit.*, p. 265.

45 *Loc. cit.*

46 Sir Peter Parker, interview, 1990.

47 Bernard Kaukas to JB, 16 August 1977. Copy shown to the author by Mr Kaukas.

48 Quoted, Bernard Kaukas, interview, 1990.

49 *Ibid.*

50 *Ibid.*

51 *Ibid.*

52 Quoted by Sir William McAlpine, interview, 1990.

53 *Ibid.*

54 Bernard Kaukas, interview, 1990.

55 *Ibid.*

56 Sir Peter Parker, interview, 1990.

57 Bernard Kaukas (interview, 1990) said: 'For the saloon trip, the blessing of the general manager, Southern Region, had to be obtained. Even as chairman of British Rail, Peter Parker couldn't just click his fingers and summon this, that and the other. The railways used to be like the Holy Roman Empire – in exactly the same way, those princes knew the limits of their autonomy and the Emperor knew how far he could go; and if the princes wanted to hold something back from the Emperor, they jolly well could do. In the railways, the general managers were the princes.'

58 Sir Peter Parker, interview, 1990.

59 Quoted, *ibid*.

60 Lady Parker, interview, 1990.

61 Sir Peter Parker, interview, 1990.

62 Bernard Kaukas, interview, 1990.

63 Quoted, JB, *Letters*, ed. CLG, ii, 514.

64 Two of the stanzas ran:

> Arrested is each little arm
> In frozen motion to the task;
> Imperious gesture, visage stern,
> Belie the plump cherubic forms
> Whose concentration tells us that
> True effort needs no caveat.
>
> And hidden midst the foliage
> Or curvilinear cusps and scrolls,
> Like elementals, engineers
> And Superintendents-of-the-Line
> Peer balefully as though aware
> That dividends are lurking there.

65 Sir Peter Parker, interview, 1990.

66 Sir Peter Parker, *For Starters*, London 1989, p. 266.

67 Walter Sinkinson, Mirfield parish magazine, 1978.

68 *Ibid*.

69 JB to Bernard Kaukas, 26 January 1978. Shown to the author by Mr Kaukas.

70 JB loved the soap opera *Coronation Street*. In a *New Statesman* advertisement for the programme, he was quoted as saying he was in 'paradise' when he watched it; and he made a visit to the cast – a photograph taken on that occasion appears in *JBLP*, p. 154.

71 Pamela Kaukas, interview, 1990.

72 *Ibid*.

73 JB to Sir Peter Parker, 25 January 1978. Shown to the author by Sir Peter Parker.

74 Lady Parker, interview, 1990.

75 Shown to the author by Sir Peter Parker.

76 This was a Barry Humphries joke. See Peter Coleman, *The Real Barry Humphries*, London 1990, p. 28.

77 Sir Peter Parker, interview, 1990.

78 JB to Dr Gregory Scott, 21 November [1977]. Shown to the author by Mr John Stevenson.

79 JB to Dr Gregory Scott, n.d. Shown to the author by Mr John Stevenson.

80 John Stevenson, interview, 1990.

81 Lady Parker, interview, 1990.

82 Sir Peter Parker, interview, 1990.

83 The author was present on this occasion and took a note of Parker's words.

84 Sir Peter Parker, interview, 1990.

85 James O'Brien, letter to the author, 19 September 1990.

86 Sir Peter Parker, interview, 1990.

87 JB to James O'Brien, 27 June 1978. Shown to the author by Mr O'Brien.

88 Lady Parker, interview, 1990.

89 JB to Sir Peter Parker, 27 June 1983. JB, *Letters*, ed. CLG, ii, 578.

Chapter 30: '. . . Whose Death Has Eclipsed the Gaiety of Nations'

1 James Lees-Milne, diary entry for 6 July 1983.
2 In 1984, after JB's death, Mary Wilson visited an exhibition devoted to him and his works at the National Theatre, London. It included a recording of JB's voice. As a result she wrote this poem, entitled 'At the Exhibition':

> Ah, but the voice, after the long silence!
> It was the voice which drew the startled tears.
> Unheralded, already half-forgotten,
> It struck like sudden music on our ears
> And brought us back, with gentle modulations,
> To days long gone – before the speechless years.

(Sent to the author by Lady Wilson of Rievaulx.)

3 Susan Allison was the widow of JB's and Kingsley Amis's former doctor, Dr John Allison (1926–78). See *The Letters of Kingsley Amis*, ed. Zachary Leader, London 2000, p. 807n. See also note 20 to Chapter 29, 'His Last Bow', in the present volume.
4 Kingsley Amis, *Memoirs*, London 1991, p. 266.
5 Robert Robinson, *Skip All That*, London 1996, p. 199.
6 CLG writes that the heart attack was 'due to a coronary thrombosis'. JB, *Letters*, ed. CLG, ii, 556.
7 James Lees-Milne, diary entry for 13 October 1983.
8 Quoted, JB, *Letters*, ed. CLG, ii, 556–57.
9 Quoted, *ibid.*, 557.
10 Quoted, *loc. cit.*
11 James Lees-Milne, diary entry for 1 February 1984. James Lees-Milne, *Holy Dread: Diaries 1982–1984*, London 2003 edn., pp. 145–46.
12 PB to Jessie Sharley, 8 April 1984. Shown to the author by the late Mrs Sharley.
13 PB added in her letter to Jessie Sharley (*ibid.*): 'The Linblad cruises were quite extraordinary, seventy Americans on the outward cruise from Bombay round Sri Lanka and up to Madras where the first passengers disembarked and the second lot of sixty-four got on board and we returned to Bombay. They were all incredibly rich and go on five or six trips a year and this one cost $6,000 each for just a fortnight *excluding* their return fare to America, and as most of them came from California that added an extra $1,000! They certainly were in a different income group from us and also spent colossal sums on antique shops buying mostly rubbish.'
14 PB did take Imogen on a tour of India, as the latter recalled. (Imogen Lycett Green, *Grandmother's Footsteps*, London 1994.)
15 PB to Jessie Sharley, 8 April 1984. Shown to the author by the late Mrs Sharley.
16 *Ibid.*
17 Quoted, JB, *Letters*, ed. CLG, ii, 581.
18 *Loc. cit.*
19 John Drummond, *Tainted by Experience: A Life in the Arts*, London 2000, pp. 313–14.
20 JB, *Letters*, ed. CLG, ii, 181.
21 Quoted, *loc. cit.*
22 *Loc. cit.*
23 See the letter from John Ezard to CLG, quoted JB, *Letters*, ed. CLG, ii, 583.
24 *The Guardian*, 23 May 1984.
25 *Ibid.*
26 The grandest house in Cornwall, built in the early seventeenth century for the first Lord Robartes (cr. 1625), a Truro tin and wool merchant.
27 James Lees-Milne, diary entry for 22 May 1984.
28 John G. Murray, interview, 1990.
29 James Lees-Milne, diary entry for 22 May 1984.
30 *Daily Telegraph*, 23 May 1984.

31 *Ibid.*

32 James Lees-Milne, diary entry for 22 May 1984.

33 *Ibid.*

34 John G. Murray, interview, 1984.

35 James Lees-Milne, diary entry for 22 May 1984.

36 *The Guardian*, 23 May 1984.

37 Graham Lord recalled JB's words in the *Sunday Express*, 20 May 1984.

38 John G. Murray, conversation with the author, 1990.

39 Quoted by PB, conversation with the author, 1984.

40 JB to Charles Thomson, 17 May 1982. JB, *Letters*, ed. CLG, ii, 575.

41 JB, 'Christmas', *Collected Poems*, 2003 edn., p. 154.

42 Charles Thomson, 'In Memoriam Sir John Betjeman 1906–1984', *The Betjemanian*, vol.
    1, December 1989, p. 33.

43 *Ibid.*

44 Born in 1927, Roy Dean entered the Diplomatic Service. As director of the Foreign and
    Commonwealth Office's Arms Control and Disarmament Research Unit from 1976 to
    1983, he played an important rôle in support of the East–West arms-control negotiations
    which eventually led to the end of the Cold War.
        He has twice won the *Times* National Crossword Championship. (The first time, in
    1970, Tom Driberg was a contestant, and finished 198th.) Since that year Dean has held
    the world record for the fastest verified solution. On retirement in 1987 he started a new
    career as a writer.

45 JB, 'Hymn', *Collected Poems*, 2003 edn., pp. 3–4.

46 Roy Dean, 'Homage to Betjeman', *Mainly in Fun*, London 2002 edn., p. 64. A framed copy
    of the poem now hangs in St Enodoc Church, Cornwall.

47 *Ibid.*

48 Alexander Patric Greysteil Ruthven, second Earl of Gowrie (b. 1939), later Minister for the
    Arts and chairman of the Arts Council of Great Britain.

49 Anthony Powell, diary entry for 29 June 1984. *Journals 1982–1986*, London 1995, p. 114.

50 Lady Emma Tennant, niece of Lady Elizabeth Cavendish. Not to be confused with the
    writer Emma Tennant, daughter of the second Baron Glenconner.

51 James Lees-Milne, diary entry for 29 June 1984.

52 Peter Parker, journal for 29 June 1984. Kindly transcribed for the author by Mr Parker.

53 The Rev. John Richards, 'Summoned by Love', 1984. Mr Richards kindly gave permission
    for this stanza from a longer poem to be quoted.

54 Peter Parker, journal entry for 29 June 1984. Kindly transcribed for the author by Mr
    Parker.

55 Most of the Rev. Harry Williams's address was printed in *The Listener*, 5 July 1984, p. 16.

56 Anthony Powell, entry for 29 June 1984. *Journals 1982–1986*, London 1995, p. 114.

57 James Lees-Milne, journal for 29 June 1984.

58 *Ibid.*

59 Peter Parker, journal for 29 June 1984. Kindly transcribed for the author by Mr Parker.

60 The Dean's bidding speech was printed in the Abbey service sheet. *John Murray archives.*

61 Peter Parker, journal for 29 June 1984. Kindly transcribed for the author by Mr Parker.

62 Alan Bennett, diary entry for 30 June [*sic* for 29 June] 1984. *Writing Home*, London 1998
    edn., p. 185.

63 Robin Ray (1934–98), son of the comedian Ted Ray. Musicologist, actor, broadcaster and
    writer. He interviewed JB about his favourite hymns in an *Omnibus* television programme.

64 John Geoffrey Tristram Lawrence, second Baron Oaksey (b. 1929), racing correspondent
    to the *Daily Telegraph* and the *Sunday Telegraph*. In 1959 he married Victoria 'Tory'
    Dennistoun, who had become JB's secretary in 1958. (See *JBNFNL*, p. 511.) The marriage
    was dissolved in 1987 and Lord Oaksey married again in 1988.

65 Prunella Scales (Mrs Timothy West), actress.

66 Michael Gough (b. 1917), character actor. Appeared in the film *Richard III* (1956) and in
    Hammer horror films. A friend of (Sir) Alec Guinness, in biographies and autobiogra-
    phies of whom there are several mentions of him.

67 David Dimbleby (b. 1938), broadcaster; m. 1967 Josceline Rose Gaskell (m. diss. 2000). Josceline Dimbleby (b. 1943) is a cookery and travel writer.

68 Peter Parker, journal for 29 June 1984. Kindly transcribed for the author by Mr Parker.

69 See quotation from the late Lady Mosley in the epigraph to this chapter.

70 PB to Father Ursell, 17 June 1984. Pusey House archives. The author is much indebted to Father Barry Orford of Pusey House for kindly drawing this letter to his attention and providing a photocopy of it.

71 *The Times*, 27 October 1984.

72 Shown to the author by the Rev. Prebendary Gerard Irvine on a visit to his home, 1995.

73 Tony Platt, Keeper of the Lapidarium at Westminster Abbey, has recalled (interview, 2004):

> The Lapidarium is a collection of stones and other artefacts which have either fallen off or been knocked off the Abbey over the centuries – a sort of three-dimensional archive. I became involved in the Betjeman memorial because the cartouche which now forms the memorial was originally in my collection. It was thought originally to have been an unused cartouche; but when we came to clean it – because we were going to use it as one of the exhibits in a 1995 exhibition that we had in St Margaret's Church, to mark the completion of the restoration work – we found that there were in fact traces of a painted inscription on it; but unfortunately not enough for us to work out – not decipherable. That being so, we cleaned the rest of it off and it went into the exhibition. It is probably early eighteenth century.
>
> When the question of putting up a memorial to Sir John came up, Donald Buttress, Surveyor of the Abbey, thought that this cartouche would make a particularly appropriate memorial for him; and it developed from there. The cartouche didn't have a supporter, so Donald designed a supporter which is a little stack of books. I don't think anybody would realise it, but a mistake was made. One of the books is *The Book of Common Prayer*, so it has 'BCP' carved on it. The other one was intended to be the Authorized Version of the Bible but unfortunately, when it was carved, they put 'KJV' – King James Version – on it, and it was pointed out, after it had been carved, that there is no such thing as a 'King James Version' – it is the *Authorized* Version. So while the lettering 'BCP' was gilded, the 'KJV' wasn't – you can hardly see the initials, but you can just feel them if you run your fingers over the stone.

74 Dr Donald Buttress, letter to the author, 5 April 2004. I am greatly obliged to Dr Buttress for kindly providing copies of his original drawings for the Betjeman memorial.

75 The late David Peace wrote about the commission in 'A Club Member's Work in Westminster Abbey', *Arts Club Journal*, Autumn 1997, pp. 16–17; and in 'John Betjeman 1906–1984: The Memorial', *The Betjemanian*, vol. 9, 1997–98, pp. 52–54. David Platt (interview, 2004) described how Peace obtained the commission.

> I had a bit of a hand in putting David Peace and Donald Buttress together. At evensong one day I was on duty in my other capacity as an honorary steward in the Abbey, and I knew that Donald was going to be attending and occupying his own stall as Surveyor. I had met David Peace on two or three occasions – but socially rather than professionally. And he turned up for the service. It just happened that earlier in the day I'd been talking to Donald about the lettering for the memorial and he wasn't very happy about it. He said he'd show me the lettering he had drafted, later. He turned up with the sketches for the lettering in his pocket. So we were talking about it just before the service and he said, 'This doesn't seem quite right. What do you think?' And I said, 'Well, I'm not an expert on lettering, but I know a man who is – and he's sitting in the stall next to you, because I've just put him there.' They did know each other anyway; but Donald took the pieces of paper out of his pocket in the fifteen minutes or so before the service. They discussed the design. David Peace took the drawings away with him and within twenty-four hours had produced that lovely scrollwork.

Dr Buttress recalls (letter to the author, 5 April 2004) that Peace travelled to York to supervise the letter-cutting at Dick Reid's workshop.

76 At the unveiling and dedication service on 11 November 1996, flowers were placed at the foot of the memorial by JB's great-grandchildren, Jasmine and Archie Ward.

77 (Sir) Patrick Leigh Fermor's address on 11 November 1996. *John Murray archives.*

78 Strachey wrote (*Queen Victoria*, London 1921, pp. 309–10):

> She herself, as she lay blind and silent, seemed to those who watched her to be divested of all thinking – to have glided already, unawares, into oblivion. Yet, perhaps, in the secret chambers of consciousness, she had her thoughts, too. Perhaps her fading mind called up once more the shadows of the past to float before it, and retraced, for the last time, the vanished visions of that long history – passing back and back, through the cloud of years, to older and ever older memories – to the spring woods at Osborne, so full of primroses for Lord Beaconsfield – to Lord Palmerston's queer clothes and high demeanour, and Albert's face under the green lamp, and Albert's first stag at Balmoral, and Albert in his blue and silver uniform, and the Baron coming in through a doorway, and Lord M. dreaming at Windsor with the rooks cawing in the elm-trees, and the Archbishop of Canterbury on his knees in the dawn, and the old King's turkey-cock ejaculations, and Uncle Leopold's soft voice at Claremont, and Lehzen with the globes, and her mother's feathers sweeping down towards her, and a great old repeater-watch of her father's in its tortoise-shell case, and a yellow rug, and some friendly flounces of sprigged muslin, and the trees and the grass at Kensington.

79 (Sir) Patrick Leigh Fermor's address on 11 November 1996. *John Murray archives.*

Epilogue

1 Michael Foot, 'The poet who got there first', *Evening Standard*, 14 April 1970.

2 Professor John Sutherland includes *Summoned by Bells* in the 1960s section of his book about bestsellers, *Reading the Decades*, London 2003, pp. 53–54.

3 Andrew Sanders, *The Short Oxford History of English Literature* (2nd edn.), Oxford 2000, p. 607.

4 *The Spectator*, 26 May 1984. On JB as a chronicler of the contemporary world, see also the present author's Introduction to JB, *Uncollected Poems*, London 1982.

5 Philip Larkin, 'It could only happen in England', *Cornhill Magazine*, Autumn 1971, p. 21.

6 W. H. Auden and Louis MacNeice, 'Auden and MacNeice: Their Last Will and Testament', *Letters from Iceland*, London 1937. A more extended quotation from the poem, including these lines, appears as the epigraph to *JBNFNL*.

7 Isaiah Berlin to [the American jurist] Felix Frankfurter, 23 August 1937. *Flourishing: Letters 1928–1946*, ed. Henry Hardy, London 2004, p. 251.

8 As examples, see the poems 'Summertime' and 'Apparition' in A. Alvarez, *Autumn to Autumn and Selected Poems, 1953–76*, London 1978, pp. 16 and 28 respectively.

9 A. Alvarez, 'London Letter', *Partisan Review*, 1959, p. 286.

10 *Loc. cit.*

11 *Collected Poems*, 2003 edn., p. 326.

12 Quoted by Philip Larkin, 'The Blending of Betjeman', *Required Writing*, London 1983 edn., p. 129.

13 For examples, their allegiance to and writings about the Church of England; their living with women not their wives; their detestation of developers (Lewis wrote of 'contraceptive tarmac'); their lack of susceptibility to modernist poetry.

14 C. S. Lewis, 'A Confession', *Poems*, London 1964, ed. Walter Hooper, p. 3.

15 Hermione Gingold (1897–1987), deep-voiced actress of stage and screen, mainly in comedy rôles.

16 Thom Gunn, 'Poets English and American', *Yale Review*, Summer 1959, p. 618.

The English-born Gunn had studied at Stanford University in California under the poet and critic Yvor Winters. When Gunn died in 2004, the poet Clive Wilmer wrote, in an obituary in *The Independent* (29 April 2004): '[Winters] thought Modernism a false turning; he none the less encouraged Gunn to learn from Modernist virtues . . .' In the same article, Wilmer noted:

> The American side of him experimented with what he called 'openness', the looser forms of avant-garde America. His achievements in this manner are substantial, but he was more obviously at home in the standard metres and rhyme, which he used in a strictly traditional manner.

17 Thom Gunn, 'Poets English and American', *Yale Review*, Summer 1959, p. 618.

18 John Wain, 'A Substitute for Poetry', *The Observer*, 27 November 1960.

19 I am indebted for the account of what Orton and Halliwell did in 1962, and what happened to them, to John Lahr, *Prick Up Your Ears*, London 1978, Chapter 3.

20 *Ibid.*, p. 94.

21 By Anthony Thwaite, 'The teddy bear and the critics', *The Listener*, 23 May 1985, p. 20.

22 See Chapter 22, 'Radnor Walk', in the present volume.

23 James Armstrong's books of poems, privately printed, include *Spiders on Toast* (with Geraldine Aldridge, Finchley 1999); *Only a Game* (Dover 2000); and *Every School Should Have a Clown* (Dover 2003).

24 See letter from JB to Charles Thomson, 17 May 1982. JB, *Letters*, ed. CLG, ii, 575. In January 1999 Thomson founded, with Billy Childish, the Stuckist art movement.

25 Charles Thomson, 'The Betjeman Society', *Kent Life*, August 1989, p. 46.

26 Ian Hamilton, 'Tripping Up', *New Statesman*, 22 and 29 December 1978, p. 881.

27 *Loc. cit.*

28 Alan Pryce-Jones, conversation with the author, 1985.

29 Alan Bell, The *Times* Profile, 'By Appointment: Teddy Bear to the Nation', *The Times*, 20 September 1982.

30 See Philip Larkin, 'Horn of Plenty: Gavin Ewart', *Further Requirements*, ed. Anthony Thwaite, London 2002 edn., pp. 320–25.

31 *London Review of Books*, 21 December 1984.

32 See *JBNFNL*, pp. 384–85.

33 See *YB*, p. 358.

34 See *JBNFNL*, p. 385.

35 In the Thirties, when JB and Grigson were being televised at Alexandra Palace, JB persuaded Grigson – like himself, in full make-up – to go, during a break, to look at an 'uninteresting' Victorian church. Grigson recalled (*Recollections*, London 1984, p. 164) that they were followed by a policeman, who evidently thought them a pair of flagrant 'pansies'. On another occasion Grigson was obliged to share a bed with Betjeman at the Royal Clarence Hotel, Exeter, with Archie the teddy-bear tucked up between them (*loc. cit.*).

36 See Barry Humphries, *My Life as Me: A Memoir*, London 2002, p. 296.

37 Geoffrey Grigson, *The Private Art: A Poetry Notebook*, London 1982, p. 55.

38 Geoffrey Grigson, *Recollections*, London 1984, p. 164.

39 *Ibid.*, p. 169.

40 See what Thwaite wrote in *Isis* in 1954 when *A Few Late Chrysanthemums* was published – *JBNFNL*, p. 495.

41 'The teddy bear and the critics', *The Listener*, 23 May 1985, p. 20.

42 *Loc. cit.*

43 *Loc. cit.*

44 Larkin was presumably echoing what A. Alvarez had written about JB in 1959, as quoted above, in this chapter.

45 Philip Larkin, 'Betjeman En Bloc', *Further Requirements*, ed. Anthony Thwaite, London 2002 edn, p. 207.

46 Philip Larkin, 'Brief for Betjeman', *Ibid.*, p. 336.

47 Philip Larkin, 'A Conversation with Neil Powell', *Ibid.*, p. 29.

48 On Brooke, see Anthony Powell's introduction to Jocelyn Brooke, *The Orchid Trilogy*, London 1981.

49 Jocelyn Brooke, *John Betjeman*, London 1961, p. 11.

50 See *Summoned by Bells*, London 1960, p. 58; also, *JBNFNL*, pp. 249, 437 and 548.

51 Brooke, *op. cit.*, p. 11.

52 Craig Raine, *In Defence of T. S. Eliot*, London 2000.

53 Philip Larkin, *All What Jazz*, London 1970, pp. 10–13.

54 Craig Raine, *Haydn and the Valve Trumpet*, London 1999, p. 314.

55 John Bayley, 'Heartless Genius', *London Magazine*, August/September 1988, p. 119.

56 On JB's objections to the new Regent Street, see *YB*, pp. 362, 453 n. 64; and his poem '1930 Commercial Style', *Collected Poems*, 2003 edn., pp. 363–64.

57 JB to Ninian Comper, 12 October 1939. JB, *Letters*, ed. CLG, i, 242.

58 See *Horace for English Readers*, trans. E. C. Wickham, Oxford 1903, p. 354.

59 Sonnet 76 begins:

> Why is my verse so barren of new pride,
> So far from variation or quick change?
> Why, with the time, do I not glance aside
> To new-found methods and to compounds strange?
> Why write I still all one, ever the same,
> And keep invention in a noted weed,
> That every word doth almost tell my name,
> Showing their birth and where they did proceed?...

60 For example, in the sequence *Positives* (1966), written to accompany photographs by his brother Ander, Thom Gunn wrote:

> In a family there is
> a sense of many doing
> many things, all different,
> absorbed in different rooms.

How, one might ask, are those lines any improvement on the unexceptionable, if unprofound, prose sentence, 'In a family there is a sense of many doing many things, all different, absorbed in different rooms'?

To advance the same argument from the opposite direction, consider Vladimir Nabokov's poem 'On Translating "Eugene Onegin"' (1955).

> What is translation? On a platter
> A poet's pale and glaring head,
> A parrot's screech, a monkey's chatter,
> And profanation of the dead . . .
>
> (*Poems and Problems*, London 1972, p. 175)

Of this one can ask: could anybody, in prose, convey so vividly and effectively the idea that a translation of a great poet can never match up to the original?

61 Philip Larkin, 'The Blending of Betjeman', *Required Writing*, London 1983 edn. p. 129.

62 Quoted, Alan Pryce-Jones, interview, 1976.

63 *Ibid.*

64 For example (as quoted in *JBNFNL*, p. 254) he wrote in the *Daily Herald* on 18 October 1944: 'There is little doubt that the greatest established poet writing in Britain today is T. S. Eliot.'

65 Philip Larkin, 'The Blending of Betjeman', *Required Writing*, London 1983 edn., p. 129.

66 JB to Anne Reed, 23 September 1976. Copy kindly provided by Mrs Reed.

67 Anita Brookner, *Romanticism and its Discontents*, London 2000.

68 JB, *Summoned by Bells*, London 1960, p. 16.

69 *YB*, p. 22.

70 *Ibid.*, p. 405.

71 *Ibid.*, pp. 224–25.

72 *Ibid.*, p. 224.

73 Poems which express JB's fear of hell include 'An Eighteenth-Century Calvinistic Hymn' (*Collected Poems*, 2003 edn., p. 8); 'N.W.5 & N.6' (*ibid.*, pp. 231–32); and 'Chelsea 1977', (*ibid.*, p. 392).

74 See Chapter 27, '". . . As I Lose Hold"', of the present volume.

75 See *Summoned by Bells*, London 1960, pp. 6–7.

76 The lines, from John Gay's *The Beggar's Opera* (xiii, air xxxv), became well known through their use by Dennis Price in the 1949 film *Kind Hearts and Coronets*.

77 The Dean ascribed to JB 'a reverent agnosticism' (printed order of service. *John Murray archives*).

78 *The Poems of Gerard Manley Hopkins*, ed. W. H. Gardner and N. H. Mackenzie, London 1967, p. 72.

79 *Ibid.*, p. 99.

80 Raine, *op. cit.*, p. 31.

81 James Lees-Milne, interview, 1987.

82 Wilfred De'Ath, 'The lonely Laureate', *Illustrated London News*, March 1974, p. 45.

83 JB's nicknames for Alan Pryce-Jones were 'Boggins' and 'Captain Bog'.

84 *JB P.*

85 My friend Professor Nicholas Orme of Exeter University, a committed Church of England Christian, has sent me some views on JB as a religious poet which he has kindly permitted me to cannibalize in the note which follows. (He may be contributing an article on the subject to the *Church Times* before this volume appears.)

Betjeman ranks as one of the three great exponents of Christianity in the twentieth century, the others being G. K. Chesterton and C. S. Lewis. Both Lewis and Betjeman write about religion in an accessible way; but Lewis expects you to be or become a Christian while Betjeman reaches out to a readership beyond the Christian market. He appeals to those who have a yearning for Christianity but do not want to become too involved – what Grace Davie has called (in her book of this title) *Believing without Belonging*. (Betjeman's own position was perhaps closer to 'belonging without believing'.) These are people who like visiting parish churches when there is nothing going on in them, like them as landmarks, enjoy the sound of *distant* bells. They turn up once or twice a year, at Harvest or Christmas, to 'buy into' something traditionally British – Betjeman satirizes the type in his 'Diary of a Church Mouse':

> it's strange to me
> How very full the church can be
> With people I don't see at all
> Except at Harvest Festival.

Betjeman serves these people by avoiding Lewis's theology and dogmatics and by candidly voicing his doubts.

In spite of his reservations, he can fairly be called a religious poet. He deals with religious context and atmosphere, especially those of churches and chapels. In this respect he is unusual. Most religious poets have trafficked in personal experiences and glimpses of the divine, not in surroundings. George Herbert wrote a long poem on 'The Church', which deploys church furnishings to make religious and moral points; but this is nearer to allegory than Betjeman's substantive interest in church furnishings. Yet Betjeman's interest is not merely antiquarian, because these things to him are numinous – they are creations of religious culture, are touched by religious usage; and their beauty can lead people into religion. (He wrote – in prose – of the interior of Blisland Church, Cornwall: 'It brings you to your knees.')

He writes of people whose lives find stability through religion, like the Felixstowe nun. He may simply be projecting – in the manner of Chaucer or Browning – the feelings and beliefs of people with whom he does not necessarily agree; but he at least respects and sympathizes with the religion of his characters. He is a poet of guilt and mental suffering. He is very strongly aware of his own guilt – about his parents ('Remorse') and about Penelope ('Pershore Station. . .') and of other people's guilt

('Original Sin on the Sussex Downs'). He is also aware of the slights and injuries to him and the suffering they have caused in his life. His interest in these matters is religious to the extent that he sees sin as an absolute; and while he does not dissect the theology of it, his attitude is traditional Christian orthodoxy: mankind is fallen and sin is the lasting result.

Betjeman does not tell us much about God: in this he differs from the great religious poets like Donne, Herbert, Vaughan and Hopkins. How he would like to think of God is adumbrated in 'A Lincolnshire Church': someone who *is*, creator and saviour, in the sense of making us safe. It is a very Old Testament God: there is much in the Psalms (for which he expressed special fondness) that presents God in that way, 'a very present help in trouble'. But more dominant in Betjeman's mind is the terror of God –

'World without end.' What fearsome words to pray . . .

Some might say that, in terms of religion, he is shallow. They would say he does not explore 'God's nature' or 'God's relationship with us'. Betjeman is more interested in the clutter of religion – pews, screens, stained-glass windows. That is the religion of many people, and this partly explains why he has been so much read. Most people who go to church do so because it is a different sort of place from home, often ancient and beautiful; to be with people like themselves; and to take part in a familiar repetitive experience that somehow reassures them. They are not Christians in order to argue, analyse or proclaim religion. Betjeman was a typical majority Christian of his time – as also in seeing the Church in terms of his own past life, rather than that of the future. For those who wished to argue and analyse, there was always 'St C. S. Lewis's Church'.

86 See *YB*, pp. 2–3.

87 See *ibid.*, p. 41.

88 JB, *Summoned by Bells*, London 1960, respectively pp. 4 and 5. I am grateful to Mr Jonathan Stedall for pointing out the recurrence of 'safe' in JB's poems (interview, 2003). The other recurrent word is 'lonely'.

89 JB, conversation with the author, 1971.

90 JB gave particularly warm praise to Hartley's novel *Eustace and Hilda* in a *Daily Herald* book review of 1947. See *JBNFNL*, pp. 250–51.

91 JB to PB, 2 June 1949. JB, *Letters*, ed. CLG, i, 460.

92 John Bayley, 'Heartless Genius', *London Magazine*, August–September 1988, p. 119.

93 A. N. Wilson, *Iris Murdoch as I Knew Her*, London 2003, p. 260.

94 *Ibid.*, p. 15.

95 See *JBNFNL*, pp. 285–86.

96 Evelyn Waugh, *Diaries*, ed. Michael Davie, London 1976, p. 777.

97 JB, *Summoned by Bells*, London 1960, p. 84.

98 Matthew, iii, 17.

99 The cartoon is reproduced in *JBLP*, p. 24.

100 *Collected Poems*, 2003 edn., p. 8.

101 JB in conversation with the author at various times, 1971 to 1984.

102 Quoted, *YB*, p. 22.

103 On Oliver Ford, see Chapter 20, 'A Heavy Crown', in the present volume.

104 See Chapter 23, 'Heaven and Hell on Television: The Seventies', in the present volume.

105 *Listen*, vol. iii, no. 2 (Spring 1959), p. 14.

106 Philip Larkin, 'It could only happen in England', *Required Writing*, London 1983 edn., p. 216.

107 John Haffenden, *Viewpoints: Poets in Conversation*, London 1981, p. 119.

In *Critical Quarterly*, Winter 1986, appeared an article by the academic Bill Ruddick, '"Some ruin-bibber – randy for antique": Philip Larkin's response to the poetry of John Betjeman'. Ruddick presented examples of what he considered was JB's direct influence on Larkin. 'Certain Betjeman poems', he wrote, 'continued to resonate in Larkin's mind . . .'

The appearance of the 'little shuttered corner shops' of Betjeman's brilliant Pre-Raphaelite burlesque 'The Licorice Fields at Pontefract' as the 'shut shops' of Larkin's moving poem 'MCMIV' is a good instance, though it would need extensive quotation to suggest the extent to which Betjeman's skill at the miniaturization or vignette-presentation of landscape is assimilated into Larkin's poem.

Ruddick thinks Larkin was most influenced by JB's 'mastery of the precise', and by 'the discovery of spiritual significance in moments that at first seemed ordinary'. He finds most echoes of JB in the title poem of *The Whitsun Weddings*, describing a Betjemanesque train journey from Hull to London. Larkin's 'A hothouse flashed uniquely' recalls JB's 'an Odeon flashes fire' in 'The Metropolitan Railway'. Larkin's train nears London –

> We slowed again,
> And as the tightened brakes took hold, there swelled
> A sense of falling, like an arrow-shower
> Sent out of sight, somewhere becoming rain.

Ruddick convincingly suggests that these lines owe something to JB's 'Sunday Morning, King's Cambridge', in which the poet marvels at the Perpendicular roof –

> And with what rich precision the stonework soars and springs
> To fountain out a spreading vault – a shower that never falls.

108 As examples: James Booth in *Philip Larkin, Writer*, London 1992, p. 69, writes: 'Even more misleading, because so vigorously promoted by Larkin himself in his later years, is the parallel with the older poet Betjeman'; and (p. 76) he derides 'the absurdity of Larkin's respectful admiration for Betjeman's minor talent, quoting with approval Christopher Ricks's disparaging comments on Betjeman.

And Professor J.R. Watson, in *Philip Larkin: The Man and His Work*, ed. Dale Salwak, London 1989, p. 91, writes:

> In Dylan Thomas's work, wrote Philip, 'the voice and the style are indissoluble', and earlier in the same essay he observed that 'a poet always thinks of his poems as being read in his own voice.' . . . It is that voice which makes Philip Larkin's poems different from those of his contemporaries, even from those of John Betjeman which he so loved and admired. Bill Ruddick has recently drawn attention to the echoes of Betjeman in Larkin's poetry, but Betjeman's voice was very different: it never lost that self-indulgent nursery and prep-school quality which was then mixed with old-fashioned Oxford-isms – 'orf' and 'crors' instead of 'off' and 'cross' When Larkin picked up echoes and resonances from Betjeman, he transformed the echo into a different sound.

109 Of the poets writing in English in the generation of JB's children, most were modernists, but there was a gradual relaxation of the iron rule that had prevailed. One might take as representative figures the poet and Oxford don John Fuller, born in 1937, the same year as JB's son; the Irishman Seamus Heaney, born two years later; Craig Raine, born in 1944, two years after JB's daughter; and James Fenton, born in 1949, who succeeded Heaney as Professor of Poetry at Oxford.

In a 'Verse Letter to John Fuller' (*The Memory of a War: Poems 1968–1982*, Edinburgh 1982, p. 53), Fenton listed, among those who would not enjoy Fuller's verse,

> Dull imagists, the strictly free,
> Po-faced admirers of H.D.*

* Hilda Doolittle (1886–1961), American Imagist poet, who wrote under her initials. She was briefly engaged to Ezra Pound, and was married to Richard Aldington from 1913 to 1937.

In the Fifties that would have been heresy. The main influences on Heaney included Hopkins, Hardy, Yeats and Auden, of whom he has written ('W. H. Auden, 1907–73', in 'Ten Glosses', *Electric Light*, London 2001, p. 55):

> He was a barker of stanzas, a star turn, a source of instruction,
> And the definite growth rings of genius rang in his voice.

But in Heaney's poetry, too, it is possible to detect the odd tipping of the cap to JB. When, in recalling barefoot runs of 1957 on college lawns, Heaney writes ('Nights of '57', *ibid.*, p. 55) –

> The older I get, the quicker and the closer
> I hear those labouring breaths and feel the coolth,

we think of JB's lines on his mother's death ('Remorse', *Collected Poems*, 2003 edn., p. 182) –

> But my neglect and unkindness – to lose the sight of them
> I would listen even again to that labouring breath.

Heaney's 'purring cars', in 'Funeral Rites', remind us of JB's 'rich the makes of motor purring' in 'Indoor Games near Newbury'. And when Heaney, wishing he were back with his friends in Rosguill in 1960, writes ('The Gaeltacht', *Electric Light*, London 2001, p. 44) –

> And Paddy Joe and Chips Rafferty and Dicky
> Were there talking Irish, for I believe
> In that case Aoibheann Marren and Margaret Conway
> And M. and M. and Deirdre Morton and Niamh
>
> Would be there as well

it is tempting (while not forgetting 'Widdecombe Fair') to draw a parallel with JB's roll-call of his childhood friends in Cornwall in 'Trebetherick' –

> We waited for the wreckage to come swirling into reach,
> Ralph, Vasey, Alastair, Biddy, John and I.

When Craig Raine writes a poem on the Betjemanesque subject 'Houses in North Oxford' (*Collected Poems, 1978–1999*, London 2000, p. 19), he does so in modernist style. But 'Baize Doors' (p. 210) is his 'Death in Leamington'. In it, the lines –

> a *Reynolds News* between her floor
> and the opened skull

are Betjeman out of Donne; and the dying fall of the end also recalls JB's early poem –

> A pair of bellows prayed in the hearth.
> The kitchen fire fell to its death.

Like Raine, James Fenton has written a poem on North Oxford – 'South Parks Road' (*The Memory of a War: Poems 1968–1982*, Edinburgh 1982 p. 77). It is not in rhyme, but parts of it are unmistakably School of Betjeman – for example,

> Birdlime on windscreens and a drain spluttering
> Froth under the laburnums,

110 Although JB did more than anybody else to change British taste in favour of Victorian architecture and Victoriana, he was not the first to espouse the cause. Albert Capper, in *A Rambler's Recollections and Reflections*, London 1915, describes the Piccadilly flat of a young guardsman – an ambassador's son – home on sick-leave from the Front in the First World War:

> When you are shown into his dining-room you walk straight into 1840 and you feel almost as though you were bowing low before the young Queen at Buckingham Palace, and that poor Lady Blessington and D'Orsay were chatting together on the sofa beside you, a very correct early Victorian sofa, but very uncomfortable . . . In the decoration of this Victorian dining-room he is as plucky as he would be in the trenches – he shrinks from no mid-century horror: false fruit in glasses; false fruit by itself. I absent-mindedly took up a pear to bite it – ugh! Appalling decorations in the direction of vases, and huge, perfectly hideous jugs with early Victorian ships and early Victorian sentimentalities indelibly inscribed upon them . . .

Astonishingly, Lytton Strachey, seen as the great iconoclast against the Victorian age, wrote to Vanessa Bell on 1 March 1919:

> By-the-bye, what is your view of the Albert Memorial as a work of art? It's not easy to consider it impartially – one's earliest memories are so intertwined with it – surely we must have met on those steps in long clothes? – but surely there's a coherence and conception about it not altogether negligible? – Compared, for instance, to the memorial to Victoria opposite Buckingham Palace, it certainly stands out. At any rate, it's not a thing one can easily forget. (Quoted, Michael Holroyd, *Lytton Strachey: The Years of Achievement, 1910–1932*, London 1968, p. 370n.)

111 Philip Larkin, 'It could only happen in England', *Required Writing*, London 1983 edn., p. 218.

112 Edited by Alex Preminger and T. V. F. Brogan.

113 Edited by Neil Roberts.

114 See Chapter 7, 'Australia 1961', in the present volume.

115 *Sunday Times*, 7 September 2003.

116 Jad Adams, 'Notional Treasure', *The Guardian*, 2 November 2002.

117 Jad Adams, conversation with the author, 2003.

118 James Fenton, 'Chapter and verse on reputation', *The Guardian*, 23 July 2003.

119 See note 58 to this chapter.

120 James Fenton, 'Chapter and verse on reputation', *The Guardian*, 23 July 2003.

121 *YB*, p. 340.

122 John Carey, *The Intellectuals and the Masses: Pride and Prejudice among the Literary Intelligentsia, 1880–1939*, London 1992, p. 66.

123 Philip Larkin, 'The Blending of Betjeman', *Required Writing*, London 1983 edn., p. 129.

124 James Fenton, 'Chapter and verse on reputation', *The Guardian*, 23 July 2003.

125 Michael Horovitz, 'Laughter laced with pain', *The Spectator*, 6 December 2003.

126 Barry Humphries, 'The Dame and the Laureate', *Perspectives in Architecture*, vol. i, issue 2, May 1994, p. 16. The author is grateful to the Hon. Lady Roberts of The Royal Library, Windsor, for a photocopy of this article.

127 Randall Stevenson, *The Last of England?* (vol. 12, 1960–2000, in *The Oxford English Literary History*), Oxford 2004, pp. 171–72.
    Stevenson's book received some lacerating reviews (see, for example, that by Professor John Carey in the *Sunday Times*, 22 February 2004). Betjeman's best work falls outside the period Stevenson is covering, but still he writes about him. He would like to bundle him in with the poets of 'The Movement' – among others, Elizabeth Jennings, John Holloway, Thom Gunn, Philip Larkin, D. J. Enright, Kingsley Amis, John Wain, Donald Davie and Robert Conquest – as a kind of prototype, elder-statesman Movement poet. Stevenson has very little time for most Movement work. To him it is not 'challenging' (the euphemism modernists have devised for Eliot's off-putting 'difficult' – as though what we all seek when we read a poem is a gruelling tussle with meaning). Disgracefully,

in Stevenson's view, the Movement poets went, in Davie's phrase, 'much further than halfway to meet [their] readers'. Stevenson writes: 'Whether or not they were committed to *real* honesty, Movement poets were determined to *sound* straightforward and down-to-earth.' Worse still, they gave others 'an excuse for writing straightforwardly'. Though he gives Betjeman some lukewarm praise, he concludes that 'much of [his] work was humorous and unchallenging', (p. 172).

128 Sir Harold Acton, letter to the author, 1977; and see *YB*, p. 165.
129 Laura Thompson, *Love in a Cold Climate: Nancy Mitford*, London 2003, p. xii.
130 JB, 'Parliament Hill Fields', *Collected Poems*, 2003 edn., p. 101.
131 T. S. Eliot, 'Burnt Norton, III', 'Four Quartets', *The Complete Poems and Plays of T. S. Eliot*, London 1969 edn., p. 174.
132 JB, '1940', *Collected Poems*, 2003 edn., p. 395.
133 See *YB*, p. 101.

Appendix 2: The Last of Penelope

1 Imogen Lycett Green, *Grandmother's Footsteps: A Journey in Search of Penelope Betjeman*, London 1994, p. 351.
2 *Loc. cit.*
3 *Ibid.*, p. 353.
4 Judith Watson, *A Walk in the West Himalayas*, privately printed, Edinburgh 1996, p. 1.
5 Jessie Sharley and Ottilie Squires, interviews, respectively 1989 and 1990.
6 Lycett Green, *op. cit.*, p. 354.
7 Quoted, *loc. cit.*
8 *Loc. cit.*
9 See *YB*, p. 375.
10 Lycett Green, *op. cit.*, p. 356.
11 *Ibid.*, p. 357.
12 *Ibid.*, p. 358.
13 *Ibid.*, pp. 358–59.
14 Judith Watson, letter to the author, 9 March 2004.
15 Watson, *op. cit.*, p. 18.
16 Lycett Green, *op. cit.*, p. 360.
17 Nicholas Shakespeare, *Bruce Chatwin*, London 1999, pp. 459–60.
18 Quoted, *ibid.*, p. 460.
19 Lycett Green, *op. cit.*, p. xiii.
20 Christina Noble, telephone conversation with the author, 2004.

SELECT BIBLIOGRAPHY

All the books consulted, quoted from or drawn upon during the writing of this biographical trilogy are given references in the notes at the end of each volume. The purpose of this limited bibliography is to offer others interested in John Betjeman's life a core selection of works which will enable them better to appreciate and understand him.

Books by Betjeman with autobiographical content

Collected Poems, John Murray, London 2003 edn.
First and Last Loves, John Murray, London 1952
Ghastly Good Taste, Anthony Blond, London 1970 edn.
An Oxford University Chest, John Miles, London 1938
Summoned by Bells, John Murray, London 1960

Betjeman's letters

John Betjeman Letters, ed. Candida Lycett Green, vol. i: *1926 to 1951*, Methuen, London 1994
John Betjeman Letters, ed. Candida Lycett Green, vol. ii: *1951 to 1984*, Methuen, London 1995

Books with contributions by Betjeman of autobiographical interest

T. S. Eliot, ed. Tambimuttu and Richard March, Frank & Cass, London 1965 edn.
The Future of the Past: Attitudes to Conservation 1174–1974, ed. Jane Fawcett, Thames & Hudson, London 1976
Hugh Gaitskell 1906–63, ed. W. T. Rodgers, Thames & Hudson, London 1964
Little Innocents, ed. Alan Pryce-Jones, Cobden-Sanderson, London 1932
My Oxford, ed. Ann Thwaite, Robson, London 1977
(with David Vaisey) *Victorian and Edwardian Oxford from Old Photographs*, Batsford, London 1971

Bibliographies

A Bibliographical Companion to BETJEMAN, compiled by Peter Gammond with John Heald, The Betjeman Society, Canterbury 1997.
 The bibliography on which Dr William Peterson of the University of Maryland has been working for many years, is eagerly awaited

Books about John Betjeman

Jocelyn Brooke, *Ronald Firbank and John Betjeman*, Longmans, Green & Co., London 1962
Frank Delaney, *Betjeman Country*, Hodder & Stoughton, London 1983
Bevis Hillier, *John Betjeman: A Life in Pictures*, John Murray/Herbert Press, London 1984
John Press, *John Betjeman*, British Council, London 1974
Lance Sieveking, *John Betjeman and Dorset* (pamphlet), Dorset Natural History and Archaeological Society, Dorchester 1963
Derek Stanford, *John Betjeman: A Study*, Neville Spearman, London 1961
Patrick Taylor-Martin, *John Betjeman: His Life and Work*, Allen Lane, London 1983

Books with references to John Betjeman

The Letters of Kingsley Amis, ed. Zachary Leader, HarperCollins, London 2000

Kingsley Amis, *Memoirs*, Hutchinson, London 1991

Beaton in the Sixties: More Unexpurgated Diaries, ed. Hugo Vickers, Weidenfeld & Nicolson, London 2003

The Unexpurgated Beaton Diaries, ed. Hugo Vickers, Phoenix, London 2003 edn.

Alan Bennett, *Writing Home*, Faber, London 1998 edn.

Anthony Blond, *Jew Made in England*, Timewell Press, London 2004

Wilfred Blunt, *Married to a Single Life*, Michael Russell, Salisbury 1983

Wilfred Blunt, *Slow on the Feather: Further Autobiography 1935–1959*, Michael Russell, Salisbury 1986

C. M. Bowra, *Memories 1898–1939*, Weidenfeld & Nicolson, London 1966

Anita Brookner, *Romanticism and its Discontents*, Viking, London 2000

The Diaries of Sir Robert Bruce Lockhart, ed. Kenneth Young, Macmillan, London 1973

Anthony Burgess, *Earthly Powers*, Hutchinson, London 1980

John Carey, *The Intellectuals and the Masses: Pride and Prejudice among the Literary Intelligentsia 1880–1939*, Faber, London 1992

Humphrey Carpenter, *W. H. Auden: A Biography*, Allen & Unwin, London 1981

Miranda Carter, *Anthony Blunt: His Lives*, Macmillan, London 2001

Helen Cathcart, *Princess Margaret*, W. H. Allen, London 1974

Bruce Chatwin, *On the Black Hill*, Vintage, London 1998 edn.

Kenneth Clark, *Another Part of the Wood*, John Murray, London 1974

The Ossie Clark Diaries, ed. Lady Henrietta Rous, Bloomsbury, London 1998

Peter Coleman, *The Real Barry Humphries*, Robson, London 1990

John Cooney, *Charles McQuaid: Ruler of Catholic Ireland*, The O'Brien Press, Dublin 1999

Lord Drogheda, *Double Harness*, Weidenfeld & Nicolson, London 1978

John Drummond, *Tainted by Experience: A Life in the Arts*, Faber, London 2000

Dame Edna Everage (Barry Humphries), *My Gorgeous Life: An Adventure*, Macmillan, London 1989

Duncan Fallowell, *20th Century Characters*, Vintage, London 1994

Robert Fisk, *In Time of War: Ireland, Ulster and the Price of Neutrality 1939–1945*, Deutsch, London 1983

Peter and Leni Gillman, *'Collar the Lot': How Britain Interned and Expelled its Wartime Refugees*, Quartet, London 1980

William Glenton, *Tony's Room: The Secret Love Story of Princess Margaret*, Bernard Geis Associates/Pocket Books, New York 1965

Richard Percival Graves, *Richard Hughes: A Biography*, London 1994

Geoffrey Grigson, *Recollections Mainly of Artists and Writers*, Hogarth Press, London 1984

Selina Hastings, *Evelyn Waugh: A Biography*, Sinclair-Stevenson, London 1994

Mark Haworth-Booth, *E. McKnight Kauffer: A Designer and his Public*, Gordon Fraser Gallery, London 1979

Christopher Hollis, *The Seven Ages: Their Exits and their Entrances*, Heinemann, London 1974

Michael Holroyd, *Lytton Strachey: The Years of Achievement 1910–1932*, London 1968

Alistair Horne, *Macmillan 1957–1986* (vol. ii of the official biography), Macmillan, London 1988

Barry Humphries, *More Please*, Viking, London 1992

Barry Humphries, *My Life as Me*, Michael Joseph, London 2002

Richard Ingrams and John Piper, *Piper's Places: John Piper in England and Wales*. Chatto & Windus, London 1983

A Dedicated Fan: Julian Jebb 1934–84, ed. Tristram and Georgia Powell, Peralta Press, London 1993

John Lahr, *Dame Edna Everage and the Rise of Western Civilization*, Bloomsbury, London 1991

John Lahr, *Prick Up your Ears*, Allen Lane, London 1978

Osbert Lancaster, *All Done from Memory*, John Murray, London 1967

Osbert Lancaster, *With an Eye to the Future*, John Murray 1967

Philip Larkin, *Further Requirements*, ed. Anthony Thwaite, Faber, London 2002 edn.

Philip Larkin, *Required Writing*, Faber, London 1983

James Lees-Milne, *Ancient as the Hills: Diaries 1973–1974*, John Murray, London 2000 edn.

James Lees-Milne, *Through Wood and Dale: Diaries 1975–1978*, John Murray, London 1999 edn.

James Lees-Milne, *Deep Romantic Chasm: Diaries 1979–1981*, ed. Michael Bloch, John Murray, London 2003 edn.

James Lees-Milne, *Holy Dread: Diaries 1982–1984*, ed. Michael Bloch, John Murray, London 2003 edn.

Bernard Levin, *The Pendulum Years: Britain in the Sixties*, Cape, London 1970

C. S. Lewis, *Collected Letters: Books, Broadcasts and the War*, ed. Walter Hooper, HarperCollins, London 2004

Robert Lusty, *Bound to Be Read*, Cape, London 1975

Louis MacNeice, *The Strings Are False*, ed. E. R. Dodds, Faber, London 1965

J. P. W. Mallalieu, *On Larkhill*, Alison & Busby, London 1983

Patrick Marnham, *The Private Eye Story*, Deutsch, London 1982

Oliver Marriott, *The Property Boom*, Hamish Hamilton, London 1967

Penelope Middleboe, *Edith Olivier from her Journals 1924–48*, Weidenfeld & Nicolson, London 1989

Caroline Moorehead, *Sidney Bernstein: A Biography*, Cape, London 1984

Timothy Mowl, *Stylistic Cold Wars: Betjeman versus Pevsner*, John Murray, London 2000

Harold Nicolson, *Diaries and Letters 1939–1945*, ed. Nigel Nicolson, Collins, London 1967

David O'Donoghue, *Hitler's Irish Voices: The Story of German Radio's Irish Service*, Beyond the Pale, Belfast 1998

John Osborne, *Almost a Gentleman: An Autobiography*, vol. ii: *1955–1966*, Faber, London 1991 edn.

John Osborne, *Inadmissible Evidence*, Faber, London 1965

Peter Parker, *Ackerley: A Life of J. R. Ackerley*, Constable, London 1989

(Sir) Peter Parker, *For Starters: The Business of Life*, Cape, London 1989

Anthony Powell, *To Keep the Ball Rolling: Infants of the Spring*, Heinemann, London 1976

Anthony Powell, *To Keep the Ball Rolling Messengers of Day*, Heinemann, London 1978

Anthony Powell, *To Keep the Ball Rolling: Faces in My Time*, Heinemann, London 1980

Anthony Powell, *To Keep the Ball Rolling: The Strangers All Are Gone* Heinemann, London 1982

Anthony Powell, *Journals 1982–1986*, Heinemann, London 1995

Anthony Powell, *Journals 1987–1989*, Heinemann, London 1996

Anthony Powell, *Journals 1990–1992*, Heinemann, London 1997

Craig Raine, *Haydn and the Valve Trumpet*, Picador, London 2000 edn.

Stephen Regan (ed.), *Philip Larkin: Contemporary Critical Essays*, Palgrave Macmillan, Basingstoke, Hampshire 1997

J. M. Richards, *Memoirs of an Unjust Fella*, Weidenfeld & Nicolson, London 1980

Cecil Roberts, *The Bright Twenties*, Hodder & Stoughton, London 1970

Cecil Roberts, *The Pleasant Years*, Hodder & Stoughton, London 1974

Robert Robinson, *Skip All That*, Century, London 1996

J. D. Scott and Richard Hughes, *The Administration of War Production* (History of the Second World War, United Kingdom Civil Series), Longmans, Green & Co., London 1955

Nicholas Shakespeare, *Bruce Chatwin*, The Harvill Press/Cape, London 1999

Lance Sieveking, *The Eye of the Beholder*, Hulton Press, London 1957

Randall Stevenson, *The Last of England?* (vol. xii, 1960–2000. *The Oxford English Literary History*), Oxford University Press, Oxford 2004

John Sutherland, *Reading the Decades*, BBC, London 2002

Laura Thompson, *Life in a Cold Climate*, Review, London 2003

The Diaries of Evelyn Waugh, ed. Michael Davie, Weidenfeld & Nicolson, London 1976

The Letters of Evelyn Waugh, ed. Mark Amory, Weidenfeld & Nicolson, London 1980

Evelyn Waugh, *A Little Learning*, Chapman & Hall, London 1964

Trevor West, *Horace Plunkett, Co-Operation and Politics: An Irish Biography*, Colin Smythe/
    Catholic University of America Press, Washington DC, 1986
Terry Whalen, *Philip Larkin and English Poetry*, Palgrave Macmillan, Basingstoke, Hampshire
    1986
Harry Williams, *Some Day I'll Find You*, Mitchell Beazley, London 1982
Mary Wilson, *New Poems*, Hutchinson, London 1979
Derek Wood, *Attack Warning Red: The Royal Observer Corps and the Defence of Britain 1925
    to 1975*, Macdonald & Jane's, London 1976
Derek Wood with Derek Dempster, *The Narrow Margin: The Battle of Britain and the Rise of
    Air Power*, Arrow, London 1969 edn.
The Journals of Woodrow Wyatt, ed. Sarah Curtis, Macmillan, London 1999 edn.

INDEX

ABC of Churches (TV programme), 183–6
Abse, Dannie, 525
Ackerley, Joe Randolph, 584
Ackroyd, Peter, 79
Acton Gazette, 224
Acton, Sir Harold, 616
Adam, Peter, 430–1
Adams, Frank, 224
Adams, Jad, 613, 616
Adams, Mary, 191
Adams, Maurice, 233–4
Adelaide, Australia, 158, 161
Adelphi, London, 264
Adrian, Edgar Douglas, 1st Baron, 308
Agutter, Jenny, 305
Aickman, Robert, 381
Aitken, Jonathan: *The Young Meteors*, 14
Aitken, Maria, 188–9
Albemarle, Walter Keppel, 9th Earl of, 177
Albert Bridge, London, 168
Albert, Prince Consort, 371
Alderson, Brian, 393
Aldous, Tony, 456
Aldwych Theatre, London, 129
Alexander, Shane William Desmond, 2nd Earl, 467
Alexandra, Princess, 311
Alexandrov, Miss, 571–2
Alford, Irene, 516, 535
Allen, John Scofield and Philippa, 228
Allen, Walter, 105
Allison, Dr John, 361, 392–3, 425, 553
Allison, Susan, 576
Allsop, Kenneth, 120–1, 123
Allsopp, Bruce: *Decoration and Furniture*, 42
Alma-Tadema, Sir Lawrence, 37
Alvarez, A., 595–6, 603, 612
Amaya, Mario, 37
Amersham, Buckinghamshire, 330, 345
Amery, Julian, 487
Amis, (Sir) Kingsley: success in 1950s, 54; on *Call My Bluff*, 193; selects *High and Low* as book of year, 246; Cecil Day Lewis dies at home of, 370; as judge in National Book Award for Children's Literature, 393; visits JB, 519;

contributes to *A Garland for the Laureate*, 525; disparages JB's *Uncollected Poems*, 527; interviews JB on being Laureate, 526; on poetry, 542; on JB in old age, 576; obituary tribute to JB, 579; at JB's memorial service, 587; at Princeton, 594; defends JB's poetic reputation, 600; *Lucky Jim*, 55
Ancient Monuments Society, 135
Anderson, Sir Colin, 562
Anderson, Captain Donald, 354
Anderson, Eddie, 358–9
Anderson, Janie (Mrs Charles Hampton), 357
Anderson, Lindsay, 432
Anderson, Rachel, 357
Anderson, Verily *see* Paget, Verily
Andorra, 324
Andrew, Prince (Duke of York), 363–4
Andrews, Duncan, 379
Andrews, Lyman, 388
Anglesey, Henry Paget, 7th Marquess of, 242, 589
Anne, Princess Royal: wedding to Mark Phillips, 379, 387, 389, 462
Annigoni, Pietro, 527
Anstey, John, 78
Antrim, Elizabeth, Countess of, 467
Antrim, Randal MacDonnell, 13th Earl of, 271
Architectural Heritage Fund, 493, 498
Architectural Review, The, 39–41, 126, 137, 166, 331, 346
Armstrong, James, 596–7, 602
Around the Seasons (TV film), 448
Ashley, April, 157, 426–7
Ashton, Sir Frederick, 515
Astor, Michael, 98, 423
Attenborough, (Sir) David, 195, 292
Attlee, Clement, 1st Earl, 121, 129
Auden, W.H.: preface to *The Faber Book of Modern American Verse*, 65; tipped as Poet Laureate, 371–3; memorial service, 379; JB's liking for, 542; fear of death, 556; promotes JB's poetry in USA, 593–4; John Bayley on, 603; reputation, 612–14
Austin, Alfred, 397

Australia: JB visits (1961), 146–62, 204; JB
   on architecture in, 159–60; JB revisits
   (1971) to make TV films, 289–91,
   294–305, 534
Avebury, Wiltshire: Great Barn, 259–61
Avon Gorge, 455–7

Baccarat Scandal (1891), 13
Bacon, Jane, 472
Baillie Scott, M.H., 51, 471
Baily, Michael, 144
Bain, Joe, 323
Bainbridge, Cyril, 458
Baird, Alexander, 103
Baker, Kenny, 480
Baker, Susan (Mrs William Bealby-Wright),
   472, 474, 476, 479
Bakewell, Joan, 520
Balcon, Jill (Mrs Cecil Day Lewis), 370
Balliol College, Oxford, 37
Bangkok, 293–4
Baring, Anne, 2–4, 22, 611
Baring, Desmond, 1–2
Baring, Mollie: friendship with JB, 1–3;
   and vandalism of school statue, 3–4;
   on JB's relations with Elizabeth
   Cavendish, 21; and Penelope's attitude
   to Elizabeth Cavendish, 25; JB writes
   to from Palermo, 315; on Penelope's
   proposed move to convent, 425; letter
   from JB at Lycett Greens, 440
Baring, Nigel, 1, 427
Baring, Peter, 1
Barker, Ashley, 174, 540–1
Barker, Dennis, 377
Barlaston Hall, Staffordshire, 458
Barnes, George, 151, 242
Baron, Alexander: The Human Kind, 62
Barr, Andrew, 203
Barrington-Ward, Robin, 137
Barrow Poets, 472–5, 479
Barry, Sir Charles, 298
Barry, Edward Middleton, 565, 569
Barry Humphries Scandals, The (BBC TV
   series), 217
Bateman, Edgar: 'The Houses In-Between',
   484
Bath: JB visits, 436
Bath, Alexander George Thynn, 7th
   Marquess of (earlier Lord Weymouth),
   256, 449
Batsford, Brian, 174
Bayley, John, 385, 388, 603, 609–10
Bealby, George, 472
Bealby-Wright, William, 472–4
Beardsley, Aubrey, 208–9

Beardsley, Mabel, 472
Beaton, (Sir) Cecil, 379, 423, 429, 431–2,
   438–9
Beddington, Jack, 118
Bedford Park: campaign to preserve, 38,
   41, 182, 221–35, 259; Greeveses in, 219;
   housing design, 220–1; Festivals, 232–3
Bedford Park Society, 38, 225–8, 232, 235
Beeching, Richard (later Baron), 559
Beer, Patricia, 525
Beerbohm, Sir Max, 551, 555
Behrens, Derick, 219
Belfast: JB's film on, 450; Crown Liquor
   Saloon, 466
Bell, Alan, 598
Bell, Guilford, 291
Bell, Robert Anning, 216
Belloc, Hilaire, 355, 449
Bellville, Hercules, 9
Bence-Jones, Mark: Paradise Escaped, 58
Bendigo, Australia, 296
Benét, Stephen Vincent, 65
Bennett, Alan: parodies of JB's verse, 49;
   Talking Heads series, 192; at JB's
   memorial service, 587; imitates JB, 597
Bennett, Hywel, 317
Bennett, Jill, 279
Bennett, (Sir) Richard Rodney, 366
Benson, Gerard, 472
Bentall's (store), Kingston-on-Thames, 100
Bentley, Eric Clerihew, 53, 73
Bentley, Nicolas, 53
Beresford, Bruce, 302
Berkeley, Sir Lennox and Freda, Lady, 216
Berlin, Sir Isaiah, 100, 594
Berners, Gerald Hugh Tyrwhitt Wilson, 9th
   Baron: doves, 15; home, 119; limericks,
   349; and Heber Percy, 438; riding, 543
Berry, Michael (later Baron Hartwell), 52
Berry, Lady Pamela (née Smith; later Lady
   Hartwell), 52, 274
Berry, Patricia, 52
Best, Andrew, 228–9
Bethlehem, 194
Betjemann, Bess (Mabel Bessie; née
   Dawson; JB's mother): in JB's
   autobiographical poem, 81–2, 85
Betjemann, Ernest Edward (JB's father): in
   JB's autobiographical poem, 81;
   accent, 298; JB visits grave, 444; JB
   describes in Time with Betjeman, 537,
   546–7; JB's relations with, 610–11
Betjeman, (Sir) John: moves to Wantage, 1;
   lacks TV set, 6–7; contributes to
   Private Eye, 10; at Candida's wedding,
   14; conversation recorded at Sharleys,

16–20; on reading poetry aloud, 18–19; marriage relations, 21, 26, 230–1, 241, 258, 405, 428, 506, 606; relations with Elizabeth Cavendish, 21–3, 118–20, 411, 425, 427–8, 437, 606; and Osborne's *Inadmissible Evidence*, 22–3; concern over son Paul, 24, 393, 411; and founding of Victorian Society, 27–32, 34–5, 51; memory, 33–4; declining attendance at Victorian Society, 34–5, 38–9, 48; awarded CBE, 35, 365; parodied, 49–50, 367–8; reviews for *Daily Telegraph*, 52–75; schoolmastering, 62, 124; homosexual feelings, 66, 315; papers bought by University of Victoria, 74, 499, 526; articles on architecture for *Daily Telegraph*, 75–7; leaves *Daily Telegraph*, 78; popularity as poet, 109–10, 121; on becoming a poet, 110–11; employs ex-clergymen as secretaries, 117, 147; returns to Cloth Fair from Rotherhithe, 117, 120; trip to Bavaria and Venice (1955), 119; interviewed, 120–3, 240–1, 246–7, 365, 368, 375, 378, 387, 439, 452–3; social life and circle, 124, 431–3, 436–8, 550–2; and Euston Arch campaign, 129–30, 138, 141–2, 145; visit to Australia (1961), 146–62; suffers from Parkinson's Disease, 162, 296, 345, 361, 389, 422, 483, 511–12, 527, 553, 558, 576; and campaign to save Coal Exchange, 163–4, 167, 172–3, 178, 182; tipped as future Poet Laureate, 171–3, 363–74; television programmes and appearances, 182–95, 292, 297–9, 330–47, 405–7, 443–4, 446–50, 529–48; speaks at Sherborne School for Girls, 188–9; in Holy Land, 194, 240–1; takes helicopter rides for TV programmes, 197–9; enjoys Barry Humphries's performance at Establishment, 214; sensitivity to criticism of poems, 236, 349–50; poetry reviewed, 243–7; preservation and protest campaigns, 259–74, 454–70; friendship with Mary Wilson, 275–80, 285–8; knighthood, 276, 370; revisits Australia (1971) to make TV films, 289–91, 294–305; dancing, 297; drinking, 302, 439, 500, 520; holidays abroad with Church of England Ramblers, 314–17, 323–5; golfing, 340; writes commentary for TV films, 348–51; as best man at Pagets' wedding, 357; moves to Radnor

Walk, Chelsea, 361, 422–4; literary honours and prizes, 364, 381; presents masque for Queen, 364–6; autograph letters sold at high prices, 378–9; poem on Princess Anne-Mark Phillips wedding, 379–80, 387, 462; Oxford awards honorary doctorate, 381; reputation rises, 387–8; criticised in *The Times*, 388–90, 393; composes ode on Queen's Silver Jubilee, 389–91; poem for Charles-Diana marriage, 394–6; poem on Queen Mother's 80th birthday, 394; suffers strokes, 394, 483, 524; health decline, 396, 406, 443, 516, 519–20, 525–6, 570, 576–8; performance as Laureate, 396; rowing-boat mishap, 405–6; dress, 406, 412–13, 517; Elizabeth Jane Howard writes on, 412–14; and grandchildren, 421, 440; visits Penelope at Cusop, 427, 442, 511; and difficulty of maintaining two loves, 428–9; sees Penelope's Indian TV film, 429–30; religious faith, 439, 510, 537–8, 607–9; relations with children, 440, 609; visit to Canada, 441; visits Romania, 442–3; gives address at Kinross's funeral, 443; seventieth birthday, 443; in TV film of *Summoned by Bells*, 443–4, 446; advocates Somerset House as art gallery, 458, 486–7; records poems with Jim Parker music, 474–84; escorts Simon Jenkins on tours of London and Middlesex, 488–93; Charing Cross Hotel restaurant named for, 490, 565–9; horror of drunks, 490; rebukes St Paul's verger, 490–1; fondness for smutty stories, 502; entertaining, 504–6; chairs Royal Society of Literature meeting, 511; heart attacks, 511–12; portrait by Derek Hill, 514; Queen Mother entertains, 515; mocked in Burgess's *Earthly Powers*, 518–19; contributes foreword to Dugdale's *Omelette of Vultures' Eggs*, 522–3; entertained at Fishmongers' Hall, 527; makes up letters of complaint to BBC, 532–3; riding, 543; on growing old, 545; Jill Parker becomes doctor, 553; phobia over pavement cracks, 554–6; fear of death, 556, 606–7; and British Rail's developments, 559–64; and Paddington station glazing, 562; dislike of dogs, 570; railway locomotive named for, 573–4; death and funeral, 579–82; tributes to, 582–3; memorial

Betjeman, (Sir) John (*cont.*)
services, 584–9; estate and will, 589;
Poets' Corner monument, 589–90;
poetic reputation, 592–606, 612–18;
infantilism, 609–10; teddy bear
(Archie), 609; personal qualities,
610–12; relations with father, 610–11;
social aspirations, 610–11; effect on
public taste, 612; achievements, 618;
Driberg's article on (text), 618–23;
WORKS: 'Agricultural Caress', 242;
'Aldershot Crematorium', 606;
'Archibald', 237; *Archie and the
Strict Baptists*, 393, 570; 'The Arrest
of Oscar Wilde at the Cadogan
Hotel', 463; *The Artsenkrafts*, 570;
'Autumn 1964', 21; 'Back from
Australia', 304; 'A Ballad of the
Investiture 1969', 369, 382; *Banana
Blush* (record), 155, 475–6, 479–81;
'A Bay in Anglesey', 242; 'Beneath
the Wattle Tree' (article), 161;
'Beside the Seaside', 18, 617; *The
Best Loved Poems of John Betjeman*,
615; 'Business Girls', 475–7;
'Caprice', 243; 'Chelsea 1977', 450,
499, 506–7, 570; 'A Child Ill', 542;
'Christmas', 606; *Church Poems*,
521–2; 'Clash Went the Billiard
Balls', 592; 'The Cockney Amorist',
118–19, 242; *Collected Poems*
(1958), 80, 90, 236, 363, 454, 594,
601; *Collected Poems* (1970), 248;
'The Commander', 242; *Continual
Dew*, 90, 96, 603; 'Cornish Cliffs',
239; 'The Costa Blanca', 326; 'The
Cottage Hospital', 615; 'Croydon',
600; 'Death of King George V', 377;
'Death in Leamington', 452, 483,
609, 615–16; 'Delectable Duchy',
271; 'Devonshire Street, W1', 17,
615, 617; 'Diary of a Church
Mouse', 17; 'Edward James', 115;
'An Eighteenth-Century Calvinistic
Hymn', 611; 'Epic' (unpublished),
80; 'Essex', 62; 'Executive', 382,
385, 593; 'Exeter', 483, 607; 'The
Exile', 471; *A Few Late
Chrysanthemums*, 62, 71, 239, 331;
First and Last Loves, 42, 229, 250,
550, 582; 'The Flight from Bootle',
475; 'Fruit', 388; *Ghastly Good
Taste*, 40, 195, 211, 540; 'Goodbye',
242, 606; 'Guilt', 120; 'Harrow-on-
the-Hill', 482; 'Harvest Hymn',
243; 'He and She on the Costa

Blanca', 385; *High and Low*, 71–2,
239–40, 242–8; 'The Hon. Sec.',
242; 'How to Get On in Society',
577; 'Hunter Trials', 481; 'Huxley
Hall', 70; 'Hymn', 583; 'In a Bath
Tea Shop', 524; 'In the Public
Gardens', 119; 'In Westminster
Abbey', 211; 'In Willesden
Churchyard', 242, 481; 'Indoor
Games near Newbury', 475, 536,
552, 593; 'Inexpensive Progress',
239, 243; 'Interior Decorator', 527;
'Invasion Exercise on the Poultry
Farm', 72, 480; 'John Betjeman's
Kangaroo Island' (article), 162;
'Jubilee Hymn', 391–2; 'Lake
District', 276; 'A Lament for Moira
McCavendish', 242; 'The Last
Laugh', 281; *Late Flowering Love*
(record), 480–1; 'Late Flowering
Lust', 480, 592; 'Lenten Thoughts
of a High Anglican', 384; 'The
Licorice Fields at Pontefract', 72;
'Lines written to Martyn Skinner',
114, 242; 'Longfellow's Visit to
Venice', 476; 'Love in a Valley', 603;
'Matlock Bath', 243; 'Meditation
on the A30', 238; 'The
Metropolitan Railway', 334;
'Middlesex', 210; 'A Mind's Journey
to Diss', 281–2, 384–5; 'Monody on
the Death of Aldersgate Street
Station', 360; 'Monody on the
Death of a Platonist Bank Clerk',
69–70, 592; 'Mortality', 71, 238,
242; *Mount Zion*, 53, 112;
'Myfanwy at Oxford', 535;
'Narcissus', 223, 235, 237; *1940*,
527, 617; *A Nip in the Air*, 71, 282,
304, 382–8; 'Norfolk', 404; 'Ode to
a Puppy', 570; 'The Olympic Girl',
72; 'On leaving Wantage', 422; 'On
a Portrait of a Dead Man', 606; *Pity
about the Abbey* (play, with Stewart
Farrer), 192–3, 266, 540; *A Plea for
Holy Trinity Church, Sloane Street*,
460–1; *The Pocket Guide to English
Churches*, 272; *Poems in the Porch*,
183–4; 'Reproof Deserved *or* After
the Lecture', 72; 'The Retired Postal
Clerk', 527; 'A Russell Flint', 242,
452, 531; 'Senex', 570; 'Shattered
Image', 385–6, 388, 595; *Sir John
Betjeman's Britain* (record), 481;
Slick but Not Streamlined, 374;
'Slough', 483; 'South London

Sketch, 1844', 482, 587; 'Station Syren', 480; 'A Subaltern's Love-song', 615; *Summoned by Bells*, 60, 70, 79–116, 121–2, 401–2, 593, 596, 606, 609–10; 'Sun and Fun', 480; 'Trebetherick', 587; 'Tregardock', 242, 387; *Uncollected Poems* (1982), 526–7; 'Upper Lambourne', 17; 'The 'Varsity Student's Rag', 36, 457–483; 'Wantage Bells', 18; 'Youth and Age on Beaulieu River, Hants', 475

Betjeman, Linda (*née* Shelton; Paul's wife), 510

Betjeman, Paul (JB-Penelope's son): Veronica Sharley's infatuation with, 9; embraces Mormonism, 24; JB feels guilt over, 24, 393, 411; in USA, 24–5; seeks job with David Hicks, 146; relations with JB, 290, 542; musical life in USA, 429; marriage, children and reconciliation with JB, 510; accompanies JB to train-naming ceremony, 573; attends JB's funeral, 580–1.

Betjeman, Penelope, Lady (*née* Chetwode; JB's wife): moves to Wantage, 1; class confidence, 2; friendship with Sharleys, 6; gives lectures, 7–8; and Candida's marriage settlement, 14; at Candida's wedding, 15; broadcasts, 16, 20; conversation recorded at Sharleys, 16–20; on trip to Spain, 16, 146–7, 150; attitude to Elizabeth Cavendish, 21, 25, 361, 428; marriage relations, 21, 26, 230–1, 241, 258, 405, 428, 506, 606; and Paul's conversion to Mormonism, 24; travels, 25; writes on India, 25; converts to Catholicism, 56, 312; letters from JB on Australian trip, 149–52, 154, 157–9; Nankivell meets, 254; spends year in India, 256–8, 289, 421; final trip to India, 258; reports attempted rape in Turkey, 258; and JB's reaction to Bowra's death, 290; and JB's Australia films, 305; criticises Harry Williams, 308; concern over JB's health, 361, 445; opposes JB's move to Radnor Walk, 362; and JB as prospective Poet Laureate, 368; on JB's knighthood, 370; on JB's health decline, 396; visits JB in Norfolk during filming, 411, 414; sells The Mead, 421; and JB's move to Radnor Walk, 424; moves to Cusop, Herefordshire, 425–7; depicted in

Chatwin's *On the Black Hill*, 426; JB visits at Cusop, 427, 442, 511; makes TV film in India, 429–30, 536; friendship with James Lees-Milne, 434; Lees-Milnes visit, 445, 514; on Sparrow's radio talk on JB, 445; money demands on JB, 503; seventieth birthday, 515; visits JB in hospital, 524; friendship with Wigmore, 526; in *Time with Betjeman* film, 542–4; takes granddaughter Lucy to India, 578; and JB's death and funeral, 579–81; at JB's memorial service, 585, 588; in JB's *1940*, 617; death and funeral in India, 624–6; *Two Middle-Aged Ladies in Andalusia*, 16

Betjeman Society, 596

Betjeman's Belfast (TV film), 450

Betjeman's Dublin (TV film), 450

Biarritz, 323–4

Bird, John, 213

Bird's-Eye View (TV series), 196–9, 331, 545

Birk, Alma, Baroness, 555

Birkenhead, Frederick Smith, 2nd Earl of, 236–40, 602

Birkenhead, Sheila, Countess of, 465, 511

Birmingham Post, 106

Bishop, Adrian, 99, 289

Black, Heather, 472

Blackburne, Canon Hugh Charles (*later* Suffragan Bishop of Thetford), 400, 410

Blackburne, Martin, 400

Blacklands (house), near Calne, Wiltshire, 440, 443

Blackwood, Lady Caroline, 517

Blades (tailors), 135

Blakeston, Oswell, 514

Blakiston, Noel and Georgiana, 423–4

Bloch, Michael, 514, 517

Bloom, Ursula: *The Abiding City*, 59

Bloomfield, Rev. Harry, 6

Bluebell Line (Sussex), 332–3

Blunden, Edmund, 367; *Poems of Many Years*, 61

Blunt, Anthony, 124

Boardman, Humphrey, 408

Bonas, Ben, 103, 124

Bond, Norman, 224

Bonham Carter, Lady Violet, 260

Boorman, John, 192

Booth, Richard, 425–6, 445

Boothroyd, Basil, 244, 246

Borrow, George: *The Bible in Spain*, 16

Bosanquet, Theodora, 14

Boshier, Derek, 15
Boston, Richard, 519
Bottomley, Horatio, 377
Boulanger, Jane, 91, 96, 98
Boulestin, X. Marcel, 488
Bouman, Bill, 237, 608
Bowen, Elizabeth, 55, 355
Bowes & Bowes (Cambridge bookshop), 100
Bowle, John Edward, 124, 514, 618
Bown, Jane, 310
Bowra, Sir Maurice: praises JB's poetry, 242; protests against M4 route, 264; death, 289; JB reminisces about, 539–40; religious views, 608
Boyd, Arthur, 535
Boyle, Ron, 375
Boyne, Colin, 136
Bradford, Rev. E.E., 349, 511
Bradshaw, Maitland, 26
Bragg, Melvyn, Baron, 195
Brahms, Denzil, 103
Brandon-Jones, John, 39
Bridges, Edward, Baron, 134, 193, 242
Bridges, Robert, 367, 377
Briggs, Asa, Baron, 441
Briggs, R.H.C., 30
Brighton: West Pier, 462
Brigitta, Sister (St Mary's headmistress), 2–4
Brisbane, Australia, 153, 161, 291, 299
Bristol: development plans, 455–7
British Broadcasting Corporation (BBC): broadcasts extracts from Summoned by Bells, 94, 100; JB claims expenses from, 188, 194–5; and Barry Humphries broadcasts, 217–18
British Council: sends JB to Australia, 146–7, 161
British Railways: and Euston Arch, 128–9, 131
British Transport Commission, 127–30, 133–4
Britten, Benjamin (later Baron), 261, 355
Broad Street station, London, 463
Broadbent, John, 111
Broadley, Philip, 291–3
Bron, Eleanor, 213, 481
Brook, Peter, 616
Brooke, Jocelyn, 602; The Passing of a Hero, 60
Brooke, Rupert, 438
Brookner, Anita: Romanticism and its Discontents, 605
Brothers, William, 512

Brown, T.E., 471, 542
Browning, Elizabeth Barrett, 449–50
Brownjohn, Alan, 525
Bruce, Evangeline, 438
Bruce, Lenny, 213
Bruce, Rev. Rosslyn, 354–6
Brunel, Isambard Kingdom, 455, 559
Bryson, John, 87, 103
Buchanan, Colin, 267
Buchanan, Robert, 496–8
Buechner, Frederick: A Long Day's Dying, 63
Bunning, J.B., 622
Burges, William, 36
Burgess, Anthony, 195; Earthly Powers, 517–19
Buttress, Donald, 589
Byng, Douglas, 514
Byrne, John, 556–7

Cadogan Estate, 460
Cadogan, John, 5th Earl, 462
Caiger, Canon Douglas, 410
Caine, Hall, 471
Call My Bluff (TV programme), 195
Calman, Dr Christopher, 554–5
Camden Park, New South Wales, 295
Campbell, Patrick, 195; Patrick Campbell's Omnibus, 72
Canada: JB visits, 441
Canberra, Australia, 156, 160, 162
'Caps and Mitres' (group), 326–7
Cardus, Neville, 162
Carey, John, 243, 614
Carey, Kenneth, 316
Carey, Peter: My Life as a Fake, 613
Carpenter, Edward, Dean of Westminster, 586, 606
Carr, Jonathan T., 220–1, 223
Carter, Rev. A.B., 460
Carter, Ernestine, 179
Carter, Thomas, 451
Cartland, (Dame) Barbara, 312
Carus-Wilson (of St Bartholomew's hospital), 9
Casson, Sir Hugh: at founding of Victorian Society, 29; protests at Euston Arch demolition, 138–9; and preservation of St Edmundsbury Theatre Royal, 261; in Canada with JB, 441; protests at demolition of Royal Agricultural Hall, 459; JB criticises, 544; and Paddington station glazing, 562
Casson, Margaret MacDonald, Lady, 29
Causley, Charles, 74, 373, 525

Cavendish, Lady Elizabeth: JB's relations with, 21–3, 118–20, 411, 425, 427–8, 606; Penelope's attitude to, 21, 25, 361, 428; advises JB on *Summoned by Bells*, 87, 94, 97; in Derbyshire with JB, 90, 94; nickname ('Feeble'; 'Phoeble'), 118; and Princess Margaret's wedding, 131; meets Kenneth Savidge, 184, 437; sees Barry Humphries off to Australia, 212; visits Bedford Park Festival, 233; and publication of JB's poems, 236–7; in JB's poems, 242, 245–6; visits Scilly Isles with JB, 287; accompanies JB on BBC trip to Australia, 292–4, 301, 304; visits Lord David Cecil, 305; friendship with Stockwood, 307–8, 310, 313–14, 316, 323–5; opposes Harry Williams' move to Mirfield, 320–2; disapproves of Simon Stuart's fiancée, 325; and JB's Parkinson's Disease, 361; in court circle, 364; requests omission of JB's Diss poem from collection, 384–5; visits Stockwood with Mirzoeff, 398; and JB's move to Radnor Walk, 422–4; as magistrate, 431–2, 550; visits Romania with JB, 442; prevents picture of JB with teddy bear, 445; and Silver Jubilee film, 449; and Bristol Gorge protest campaign, 456; cares for JB, 483, 526, 575–6; poor relations with Reg Read, 500, 503; loses weight, 511; in Cornwall with JB, 512–13; Queen Mother entertains, 515; opposes JB's trip to Southend, 516–17; and JB's stroke at Moor View, 524; friendship with Frank Tait, 550; entertains in Radnor Walk, 551; and Jill Parker's becoming JB's doctor, 553; on British Rail trip with JB, 565; Gregory Scott mistakenly informs of JB's death, 572; accompanies JB to train-naming ceremony, 573–4; and JB in old age, 576–8; at JB's death, 579–80; at JB's memorial service, 585–6, 588; as JB's literary executor, 589

Cecil, Lord David, 195, 305, 423, 465, 549–50
Cecil, Henry, 125
Cecil, Hugh, 423
Celandine Press, 524–5
Chadd, Paul, 455–6, 468
Chain, (Sir) Ernst, 454
Chamberlin, P., 174
Chance, Donovan, 83, 86
Chant, Rev. Maurice, 410
Chaplin, Charlie, 497

Charing Cross Hotel, London, 490, 565–9
Charles, Prince of Wales: at private view of JB's Australia film, 305; at Cambridge University, 322; investiture as Prince of Wales, 322–3, 369; JB writes 'Ballad of the Investiture' for, 369, 382; requests JB poem for Queen's Silver Jubilee, 389, 391; marriage, 394–5; reads lesson at JB's memorial service, 585–7, 611
Charles, William, 365
Charteris, Hugo, 125
Charters Towers, Australia, 294–5
Chastleton House, Oxfordshire, 533
Chatsworth House, Derbyshire, 129, 610
Chatwin, Bruce, 257–8, 625–6; *On the Black Hill*, 426
Chatwin, Elizabeth, 257–8
Chavasse, Christopher Maude, Bishop of Rochester, 306
Checketts, Squadron-Leader David, 382
Chelsea, 422–4
Chesterton, Frances (*née* Blogg), 221
Chesterton, G.K., 185, 221
Chettoe, C.S., 174
Chetwode, Alice Hester Camilla, Lady ('Star'), 442, 540
Chetwode, Christopher (Penelope's nephew), 421
Chetwode, Field Marshal Philip, Baron, 43, 192, 610
Chetwode, Roger (Penelope's brother), 52
Chetwynd-Talbot, Colonel A.L., 432
Chetwynd-Talbot, Rev. Arthur, 5
Chisholm, John, 77
Chorleywood, 341–4
Christ Church, Newgate, 458
Christ Church, Spitalfields, 465
Church of England: JB-Mirzoeff TV film on, 398–407, 417–18; JB's devotion to, 398
'Church of England Ramblers Association', 314–18, 323–6
Churchill, Sir Winston: on Driberg, 170
City Press, 181
Civic Amenities Act (1968), 47, 233
Clark, Sir Kenneth (*later* Baron): advises on aims of Victorian Society, 28, 31, 37, 235; Associated TV programme with JB, 101; encourages JB to visit Australia, 147; television appearances, 186; supports preservation order on Robert Street (Adelphi), 264
Clark, Ossie, 15–16
Clark, Robert, 144–5

Clarke, Peter: and founding of Victorian Society, 29–30; imitations, 36; lampoons JB and Pevsner, 43, 45; parodies of JB, 48–50; death, 50; visits Behrens, 219, 221; and Bedford Park, 221–2, 224, 227

Clarkson, Tom: *The Pavement and the Sky*, 63

Clayton, Sylvia, 444

Cleese, John, 307

Clevedon pier, 468

Cleverdon, Douglas, 94, 100, 472

Cleverdon, Francis, 522–3

Clifton-Taylor, Alec, 43

Clive, George, 427

Clive, Lady Mary, 11–12, 426–7

Clonmore, William Forward-Howard, Baron *see* Wicklow, 8th Earl of

Cloth Fair, City of London: fire, 77; JB returns to, 117, 120; JB moves from, 422

Clowes, Mark, 95

Clowes, William & Sons (printers), 95–6

Coal Exchange, London, 47, 163–82, 206, 259, 622

Cobbold, David, Baron, 309

Cocteau, Jean, 5

Coggan, Donald, Archbishop of Canterbury, 467

Coghill, Nevill, 539

Cole, George Vicat, 622

Coleman, Peter, 210–11, 215

Coleridge, Samuel Taylor, 185

Collcutt, T.W., 620

Collins, William (publisher), 95

Colville, Lady Cynthia, 3–4

Come to an End (TV programme), 188

Comper, Sir Ninian, 42–3, 409, 604

Compton-Burnett, Dame Ivy, 54, 66; *Darkness and Day*, 57

Conder, Charles, 205, 209, 216

Conesford, Henry Strauss, Baron, 176

Connell, Amyas, 346

Connoisseur, The (magazine), 457

Connolly, Cyril: reviews JB's *High and Low*, 243; seventieth birthday, 379; death, 381; Elizabeth Cavendish and, 437–8; *Enemies of Promise*, 79

Conolly, William, 451

Contrast: Marble Arch to Edgware – A Lament by John Betjeman (TV programme), 196, 530

Conversation Piece (film), 539

Cook, Peter, 212–15

Cookson, Dame Catherine, 57

Cooling, Rev. Ronald, 408–9

Cooper, Lady Diana, 216, 352

Cooper, Duff (1st Viscount Norwich), 125

Cooper, Elizabeth, 338

Cooper, William, 54–5

Coote, Colin, 53–4

Corbett, Fiona, 157

Corcoran, Christopher, 256

Corfield, Frederick, 179

Cornhill Magazine, 92, 94

Cornwall: in JB's *Summoned by Bells*, 85–6, 91; in *Time with Betjeman* film, 546–7; JB visits with Elizabeth, 577–8; *see also* Trebetherick

Coronation (1953), 55

Cotman, John Sell, 410

Cottrill, Michael, 426, 445

Council for the Care of Churches, 165

Country Life: denounces Compton-Burnett's novels, 66

Coward, Noël, 5, 102, 438

Cowderoy, Cyril, (Catholic) Archbishop of Southwark, 312–13

Cowper, William, 617; 'The Poplar Field', 274

Cozens-Hardy, Miss, 407

Crabbe, George, 617

Crabtree, Eric, 312

Crane, Walter, 221–2, 229

Cranko, John, 549

Criterion Restaurant, London, 457

Croft-Cooke, Rupert, 68; *Feasting with Panthers*, 558

Crofton Beam Engine, 255

Croucher, Michael, 256

Cubitt, W. and L., 127

Cullinan, Patrick, 423

Cummings (cartoonist), 113–14, 618

Curtis, Anthony, 366–7

Curtis, Frederick, 128

Cusop, near Hay-on-Wye, 425–7, 445, 511, 624

Custom House, London, 169–74

Cuthbert, Elizabeth, 257, 390–1, 427

Cuthbertson, Peggy, 13

Daily Express: and serialisation of *Summoned by Bells*, 94; reviews *Summoned by Bells*, 107; JB writes for, 161, 223, 225, 546; on JB's liaison with Elizabeth Cavendish, 424–5, 427

Daily Herald, 52–3, 260, 262, 331, 335

Daily Telegraph: JB reviews for, 52–75; JB writes on architecture for, 75–7, 159; praises JB's *Summoned by Bells*, 101; and campaign to save Euston Arch, 129, 135, 141

Dale, Anthony, 227
Daley, Victor, 148
Dance, Monica, 38
Dann, Colin: *The Animals of Farthing Wood*, 393–4
Dartmouth, Raine, Countess of, 458, 493
Darwin, Erasmus, 147
Dashwood, P.R., 464
David Higham Associates (JB's agents), 194
Davidson, Rev. John, 557–8
Davie, Donald, 599
Davies, (Sir) Peter Maxwell, 366
Davies, Philippa, 596
Davies-Jones, Dr Cyril, 524, 577
d'Avigdor-Goldsmith family, 2
Dawson, Canon, 267
Day Lewis, Cecil, 364, 367, 369–71, 612
Day-Lewis, Sean, 198, 350
Dean, Roy, 583–4
De'Ath, Wilfred, 439, 607
Debenham, Sir Ernest, 97
Debenham, Sir Gilbert, 97
Debenham, Virginia, 96, 98
Decoration (magazine), 75
Deedes, William (*later* Baron), 172
de Ferranti, Sir Vincent, 175
Delaney, Frank: *Betjeman Country*, 78, 334, 337
Delgado, Alan, 464
De L'Isle and Dudley, William Philip Sidney, 1st Viscount, VC, and Jacqueline, Viscountess, 156
de Maré, Eric, 95, 168, 270
De Morgan, William, 37, 97, 221, 223, 234
Dench, Dame Judi, 241
Dennistoun, Tory *see* Oaksey, Victoria, Lady
Desert Island Discs (radio programme), 452
de Sousa, Tony, 16
'Destruction of the Country House, The' (exhibition), 430–1
Devizes, Wiltshire, 190–1
Devlin, Timothy, 371–2, 376, 380
Devonshire, Deborah, Duchess of, 587
Devonshire, Evelyn, Dowager Duchess of, 3, 305, 320, 359
de Winton, Major and Mrs Gerald, 427
Diana, Princess of Wales (*née* Spencer), 394–5
Dickens, Monica: *The Winds of Heaven*, 58
Dickinson, Patric, 525
Dieppe, 292
Dimbleby, David, 10, 588

Dimbleby, Jonathan, 322, 391
Diss, Norfolk, 275, 281–4, 384
Dobbs, Michael, 480
Dobson, Austin, 61
Dobson, Rosemary, 148
Document Films, 348, 350–1
Dods, R.S., 160
Doggerel Bank (poets' group), 473, 479
Donne, John, 542
Dragon School, Oxford, 90
Driberg, Tom (*later* Baron Bradwell): reads and corrects typescript of *Summoned by Bells*, 81–3, 92–3, 98; at launch party for *Summoned by Bells*, 103; friendship with JB, 124; in campaign to save Coal Exchange, 170–2, 174, 176, 179; reads JB's poems in *High and Low*, 239–40, 246; on preserving Houses of Parliament, 267; at Stockwood's parties, 312; with 'Caps and Mitres' group, 326–7; and Diss poem in JB's *A Nip in the Air*, 384; JB consults over poem, 386; seventieth birthday, 441; fear of death, 556; *The Best of Both Worlds*, 79; *Ruling Passions*, 79; 'A Walk with Mr Betjeman' (text), 617–23
Drogheda, Garrett Moore, 11th Earl of, 275
Drummond, Sir John, 305, 430, 578
Dublin: JB's film on, 450–1
Duff Cooper Memorial Prize, 365
Dufferin, Sheridan Hamilton-Temple-Blackwood, 5th Marquess, and Serena Belinda, Marchioness of, 427, 517
Dugdale, John, 103
Dugdale, Michael, 103–4; *An Omelette of Vultures' Eggs*, 522–3
Duncan-Sandys, Duncan Sandys, Baron, 467–9
Dunkley, Chris, 419
Dunn, Lady Mary (*née* St Clair-Erskine), 438
Dunn, Sir Philip, 438
Dunne, Thomas, 624
du Pré, Jacqueline, 366
Durrell, Lawrence, 292
Dykes Bower, Stephen, 501

Eccles, J.F., 265
Eden, Anthony (*later* 1st Earl of Avon), 165
Edensor, Derbyshire, 3
Edward VII, King (*earlier* Prince of Wales), 13
Edwards, Brian, 260–1
Edwards, Marcus, 228

Elek, Paul, 95
Eliot, T.S., 530, 593–5, 602, 612–14,
    616–17; *Four Quartets*, 614, 616
Elizabeth II, Queen: JB presents masque
    for, 364–6; Silver Jubilee, 389–91,
    448–9; sends tribute on JB's death,
    579–80
Elizabeth the Queen Mother, 394, 515
Elkington, George, 261, 263
Ellis, Royston, 74
Elton, Sir Arthur, 199, 468
Emery, Winifred, 339
Enterprise Neptune, 270–1
Ephemera Society, 390
Epstein, Sir Jacob, 433
Esher, Lionel Gordon Baliol Brett, 4th
    Viscount, 193
Esher, Oliver Sylvain Baliol Brett, 3rd
    Viscount: in Victorian Society, 29–33,
    36, 141; death, 39; and threat to Coal
    Exchange, 166–7, 169, 173, 180
Establishment Club, London, 213–14
Euston Arch, 35, 47, 126–45, 163, 174, 259
Euston Centre, 144–5
Euston, Hugh Denis Charles FitzRoy, Earl
    of *see* Grafton, 11th Duke of
Euston station, 127–8, 131, 140, 142
Evans, (Dame) Joan, 259–60
Everage, Edna *see* Humphries, Barry
Everywoman (magazine), 122–3
Ewart, Gavin, 598
Ewart-Biggs, Christopher and Jane (*later*
    Baroness), 422
Exeter College, Oxford, 87
Ezard, John, 580–1

*Faber Book of Modern American Verse,
    The*, 65
Fair, Rev. William, 409
Fairclough, Leonard, Ltd (contractors),
    135–6
Fallowell, Duncan, 194, 504–6
Farrer, Stewart: *Pity about the Abbey* (play,
    with JB), 192, 266
Faulkner, William: *Requiem for a Nun*, 55
Fawcett, Jane, 47, 268
Fawkes, Wally ('Trog'), 273
Fedden, Robin, 260
Felbrigg, Sir Simon and Lady Margaret,
    415–17
Fenchurch Street station, London, 494–5,
    516, 517
Fenton, James, 612–14
Ferguson, Jocelyn, 240
Fergusson of Kilkerran, Louise Frances
    Balfour, Lady (*née* Dugdale), 522–3

Fermor, Patrick Leigh: parodies of JB's
    verse, 49; and JB's leaving *Daily
    Telegraph*, 78; reads lesson at Kinross's
    funeral, 443; gives address at
    dedication of JB monument, 590; told
    of Penelope's death, 625
Ferriday, Peter, 169
Festival of Britain (1951), 55, 69, 544
Festival of the City of London (1962),
    364
Field, Barron: *First Fruits of Australian
    Poetry*, 147
Field, John, 451
Fielding, John, 144
Fields, Gracie, 452
Firestone Factory, London, 469
Fisher, Geoffrey, Archbishop of
    Canterbury, 311–12
Fishmongers' Hall, London, 527–8
Fiske (of City of London's architect's
    department), 180
Fitzjohn's Avenue, Hampstead, 235
Fleetwood-Hesketh, Peter: as secretary of
    Victorian Society, 35–7, 179; writes for
    Daily Telegraph, 77; and Euston Arch
    campaign, 138–9; and Coal Exchange,
    169, 175, 179–80, 182; meets William
    Norton with JB, 262; at JB's memorial
    service, 584
Fleming, Ann, 21, 125, 289
Fleming, Ian, 125
Fleming, Peter: *The Sixth Column*, 71
Fletcher, Sir Banister, 493
Fletcher, Ian, 228
Fletcher, Miriam, 252–3
Foot, Michael, 454, 595
Foot, Paul, 10
Ford, Oliver, 385–6, 611
Foreign Office (building), Whitehall, 47
Fortune, John, 213
Foster, William, 240–1
Four with Betjeman (TV series), 291–2,
    446, 541
Fox, James, 444–5
Foyle, Christina, 501, 507n
Foyles Poetry Prize (1955), 126
Fraser, Lady Antonia, 554–5
Fraser, Sir Hugh, 554
Freeman, Jennifer: *Built Environment*,
    181
Frost, Sir David, 213, 307
Frost, Ernest: *A Short Lease*, 60
Fry, Jeremy, 432
Fry, Maxwell, 264–6
Fuller, John, 612
Fuller, Roy, 372, 525

Gaitskell, Hugh, 87, 133, 192
Gammond, Peter and John Heald: *Bibliographical Companion to Betjeman*, 522
Gant, Roland, 511
Garland for the Laureate, A, 525
Garland, Nicholas, 215, 520
Garland, Patrick, 185, 192, 305, 447, 577
Garland, Rodney: *The Heart in Exile*, 67; *The Troubled Midnight*, 67
Garrett, John, 488
Garrick Club, 125, 195, 276, 284
Gascoigne, Bamber, 214
Gaunt, William, 33, 35
Gay, John: *London's Historic Railway Stations*, 142
Geddes, Margaret ('Margie'; *née* Addis), 349, 423, 519
Gent, Rev. Anthony, 581
George, Adrian, 445
George, Ernest, 622
Georgian Group: and Euston Arch, 128, 140; and Coal Exchange, 170–1
Gibbs, James, 465
Gibbs, Lewis: *Gowns and Satyr's Legs*, 72
Gidney, A.R., 39, 211, 514
Gielgud, (Sir) John, 66, 364, 366, 431
Gilbert, Sir Alfred, 408
Gilbert, Sir Arthur, 487
Gilbert, Sir William Schwenck, 338–9, 484
Giles, William, 550
Gilfoyle, William, 298
Gili, Phillida, 570
Gill, Rev. Colin, 326
Gillard, Frank, 183
Gilliat, Roger, 432
Gilliat, Sidney, 581
Gilliatt, Sir Martin, 515
Girouard, Mark, 32, 35, 169–70, 174, 258
Gittings, Robert, 467
Glanville, George, 340–1
Glazebrook, Elizabeth, 228–30
Glazebrook, Mark, 228–32
Glazebrook, Rimington, 231
Gleichen, Count, 2
Gloag, John, 134
Gloucester, Henry, Duke of, 46
Gloucester, Prince Richard of, 437
Glover, Frederick, 155
Glyn, Sir Stephen, 138
Godwin, E.W., 220, 224
Goldbeaters House, Soho, 507n
Goldfinger, Ernö, 510
Golding, (Sir) William, 54
Gollancz, Sir Victor, 66
Goodhart-Rendel, H.S., 29, 31n, 65, 158, 471

Gordon, Adam Lindsay: *Bush Ballads and Galloping Rhymes*, 148
Goring, Marius, 466–7
Gosling, Nigel, 29
Gosse, Noel, 97
Gough, John, 527–8
Gough, Michael, 588
Gould, Cecil ('Granny'), 514
Gowrie, Alexander Patric Greysteil Ruthven, 2nd Earl of, 584
Grafton, Hugh Denis Charles FitzRoy, 11th Duke of (*earlier* Earl of Euston), 261, 323, 457–8
Graham, Andrew, 124–5
Graham, Billy, 311
Graham, E.R.B., 36
Graham, Virginia, 357
Grant, Ian: as secretary of Victorian Society, 32–4; resigns secretaryship, 35; on preservation of Victorian buildings, 37; on Pevsner, 39, 47; and threat to Coal Exchange, 169
Grasmere Village Society, 465
Graves, Robert, 291–2, 367
Gray, Diana, 188
Gray, Thomas, 466, 616
Greater London Development Plan, 454
Green, G.F.: *In the Making*, 61, 70
'Green Giant' building, South Bank, London, 467–8
Green, Henry (i.e. Henry Yorke), 80; *Pack My Bag*, 79
Greene, Graham, 55
Greenhalgh, Dr George, 251
Greenhalgh, Mary, 251–2, 256
Greer, Germaine, 206
Greeves, Eleanor, 219, 221, 225, 233
Greeves, Thomas, 29–30, 36, 47, 48; and Bedford Park, 219–23, 225–9, 232–5
Grenfell, Joyce, 307, 355–7
Grenfell, Julian, Baron, 309, 311
Griffiths, Bede, 526
Grigson, Geoffrey, 109, 244, 381, 448, 463, 510, 598–9, 616
Grims Dyke, Harrow Weald, 338–9, 341, 484
Grimthorpe, Angela, Lady (Candida's mother-in-law), 510
Grindlay, J.O., 176
Grogan, Arthur, 232–3, 235
Gross, John, 195, 243, 449
Grosvenor, Peter, 387
Grounds, Roy, 178
Grove, Valerie, 493
Guardian, The (newspaper): on Coal Exchange, 176

Guest, John, 284; (ed.) *The Best of Betjeman*, 597
Guggenheim, Solomon, 315
Guildhall Art Gallery, London, 168, 170
Guinness, Desmond, 13
Gunn, Thom, 55, 74, 595–6
Gunnis, Robert, 156
Gurney, Rachel (*later* Bruce), 356

Hailsham, Quintin Hogg, Baron, 270, 312
Haley, Sir William ('Oliver Edwards'), 137–8, 141
Hall, Sir Julian: *The Senior Commoner*, 437
Hall, (Sir) Peter, 261
Halliwell, Kenneth, 596
Hamilton, Ian, 597, 615
Hampstead Garden Suburb, 233, 265
Hancock, Sir Keith, 271
Handley-Taylor, Geoffrey, 370
Harding, Philip, 103, 182
Hardwick, Philip, 126–7, 132, 138, 142
Hardy, Alice, 524
Hardy, Thomas, 542, 605, 614
Harling, Robert, 75
Harper's Bazaar (magazine), 93–4
Harpur, Charles: *Thoughts*, 147
Harris, Dame Diana Reader, 189
Harris, Richard, 36
Harrod, Dominick, 407
Harrod, (Sir) Roy, 87, 400, 402, 407, 411, 512
Harrod, Wilhelmine, Lady (*née* Cresswell; 'Billa'): JB stays with in Norfolk, 400–2, 406–7, 427; disapproves of Elizabeth Cavendish, 411, 586; JB sends copy of Churches script to, 417; at JB's funeral, 580–1; at JB's memorial service, 586; composes epitaph for Penelope, 626
Harrow, 337–9
Hart, Derek, 120
Hart-Davis, Duff: *The House the Berrys Built*, 53
Harte, Glynn Boyd, 258, 513
Hartley, L.P., 609; *My Fellow Devils*, 54
Hartnell, Sir Norman, 312
Harvey, Brian, 77
Hassall, Christopher, 263–4
Hastings, Hubert de Cronin, 346, 519
Hastings, (Sir) Max, 360–1
Hastings Bass, William Edward Robin Hood (*later* Earl of Huntingdon), 322, 369
Hawthorne, (Sir) Nigel, 191

Hay-on-Wye, 425, 445
Hazard, P.D., 372
Heaney, Seamus, 372, 612
Hearst, Stephen, 196
Heath, Sir Edward, 306, 359, 371–2
Heath-Stubbs, John, 388
Heathrow, 491–3
Heber Percy, Robert, 15, 438–9, 543
Hector, Winifred, 354
Heddon Court (school), Cockfosters, 88, 243
Henderson, Billy, 430–1, 550
Henri, Adrian, 472
Henriques, Sir Basil, 66
Herbert, David, 432
Hereford Cathedral: iron choir screen, 267–8
Heseltine, Michael, 468, 469
Hewitt, Sir John, 372
'Hickey, William' (newspaper columnist), 363
Hicks, David, 146
Higgins, Molly, 96
High and Over (house), Amersham, 346
Higham Associates *see* David Higham Associates
Hill, Derek, 514
Hillier, Bevis: JB befriends, 258; suggests using Somerset House as art gallery, 458; *John Betjeman: A Life in Pictures*, 598; *Young Betjeman*, 606, 609, 614
Hillman, Judy, 145
Hilton Hotel, London, 139
Hitchcock, Henry-Russell: on Coal Exchange, 165, 174; *Architecture: Nineteenth and Twentieth Centuries*, 64–5
Hoare, Lady, 365
Hoare, Samuel, 356–7
Hobart, Tasmania, 158, 161, 301–2
Hocking, Cliff, 212, 218
Hockney, David, 15, 231–2, 324, 440
Hodgson, J.J., 131
Hodgson, Ralph, 74
Hoff, Reyner, 299
Holder, Eric, 215
Holford, Sir William, 46, 266
Hollings, Frank (bookshop), 205, 499
Hollis, Christopher, 121
Hollister, Stella, 14
Hollom, Vincent, 327
Holloway, David, 54, 377
Hollweg, Alexander, 228, 232
Holmes, Richard, 374
Holy Land: JB visits to make TV film, 194, 240–1

Holy Trinity Church, Sloane Street, London, 459–62, 470, 527
homosexuality: JB reviews books on, 66–9; JB's feelings of, 66, 315; and literary autobiographies, 80; in Australia, 155
Hood, Canon A.F. (Freddy), 117
Hood, Thomas, 334
Hope, John Humphrey, 88
Hopkins, Gerard Manley, 367, 607
Horace: *Ars Poetica*, 604, 613
Hordern, Michael, 449
Hornby, Nicolette, 12, 15, 289
Hornby, (Sir) Simon, 12
Horne, (Sir) Alistair, 139
Horovitz, Michael, 614–15
Hosegood, Lewis, 252
Hospital of St Cross, Winchester, 185
Housman, A.E., 614
Howard, E.L., 467
Howard, Elizabeth Jane, 195, 412–14
Howard, Mrs F. (*née* Dawson; JB's aunt), 97
Howard, Philip, 370, 379, 395, 457
Howells, Jonathan and George, 426
Howerd, Frankie, 312
Huddleston, Trevor, Bishop of Stepney, 465, 561, 567
Hudson, Christopher, 488
Hughes, Richard, 12, 443
Hughes, Ted, 372–3, 515, 525
Humphries, Barry: friendship and affinity with JB, 204–12, 215–17, 519; background and career, 206–8, 211; London stage parts, 207, 215; marriage breakdowns, 207, 218; poetry, 210–11; hate-figures, 211; performs in Melbourne, 212; plays Establishment Club, 213–14; depression, 218; and JB's second visit to Australia (1971), 291, 297, 301–2, 535; makes TV film on Dieppe, 292; at private view of *Metro-land*, 352; on JB's dislike of changes to London, 360; success as performer, 519–20; marriage to Diane Millstead, 520; writes to JB in hospital, 524; visits JB in Radnor Walk for *Time with Betjeman*, 534–5; as Sir Les Patterson, 534–5; as Dame Edna Everage, 578–9; and JB's not forgiving Grigson, 599; makes JB laugh, 611; on JB's reputation as poet, 615; *My Gorgeous Life*, 213
Humphries, Emily (Barry's daughter), 216
Humphries, Tessa (Barry's daughter), 215–16

Hunt, Horbury, 160
Hunt, Leigh, 436
Huntley, William, 457
Hussey, Christopher, 29, 31–3, 170
Huxley, Aldous, 602
Hyde, P.C., 464

Ilfracombe, 249–50, 256
Ince Blundell Pantheon, near Liverpool, 259
India: Penelope in, 256–8, 289, 578, 624–6
Ingle, L.D.C., 89, 96
Ingrams, Mary (*née* Morgan), 10
Ingrams, Richard: friendship with Candida, 10; on JB's dislike of Pevsner, 40; cuts Barry Mackenzie strip in *Private Eye*, 215; obituary tribute to JB, 582; at JB's memorial service, 584; on JB's modern world, 593
Irvine, Rev. Prebendary Gerard, 146, 205, 326–8, 460, 504, 506, 577, 589
Irvine, Rosemary, 504, 506
Isherwood, Christopher, 63–4; *Lions and Shadows*, 79
Ison, Leonora, 75–8
Ison, Walter, 75

Jackson, Joan Hunter (*née* Dunn), 588, 611
Jackson, Peter, 280
James, Rev. C.G. ('Jimmy'), 407
James, Clive, 208, 388
James, Edward, 115
James, Canon Eric, 38, 92
James, Henry, 274
Jamieson, Jack, 441
Jarman, Derek, 449
Jarvis, Rev. Wilfrid Harry, 5, 117–18, 120, 442
Jay, Peter, 10, 374
Jebb, Gladwyn (*later* 1st Baron Gladwyn), 125
Jebb, Julian: filming with JB, 195–6, 199–200, 203, 530; diary published, 203; in Australia filming with JB, 294, 299–304; homosexuality, 300; JB turns against, 301–2; exhaustion after Australia trip, 304–5; works for Peter Adam, 430; protests at 'Green Giant' building, 467
Jefferies, Richard, 463
Jekyll, Gertrude, 446
Jellicoe, George, 2nd Earl, 176–7
Jenkins, Elizabeth, 54–5
Jenkins, (Sir) Simon: as JB's protégé, 258; reviews *Metro-land*, 352; campaigns for Somerset House as art gallery, 458,

Jenkins, (Sir) Simon (*cont.*)
486–8; JB recommends Hall Caine to, 471; tours London and Middlesex with JB, 488–93; visits Southend with JB, 493–8; *A City at Risk*, 486–7
Jenkins, Valerie *see* Grove, Valerie
Jenks, Mrs (secretary of Victorian Society), 33
Jenner, Father Jack, 229
Jennings, Elizabeth, 372, 388, 525
Jerusalem, 194
John XXIII, Pope, 311–12
John, Augustus, 209
Johnson, Father Hamilton, 485
Johnson, Paul, 396
Jones, Sir Horace, 534
Jones, Matthew W., 392
Jones, Monica, 584
Jonson, Ben, 281
Jordan, Robert Furneaux, 95, 176
Joseph, Sir Keith (*later* Baron), 130, 133, 171–5, 182
Jourdain, Margaret, 66
Journey to Bethlehem (TV film), 194
Joyce, William ('Lord Haw-Haw'), 375
Just a Show (Barry Humphries revue), 217

Kauffer, E. McKnight, 96
Kaukas, Bernard, 128, 140, 141, 145, 464, 561–6, 568–9
Kaukas, Pamela, 568
Keeler, Christine, 17
Keiller, Alexander, 259, 261
Keir, Sir David Lindsay, 37
Kelling, E. Bassett, 158
Kelly, Sir Gerald, 124
Kendall, Henry, 147
Kennet, Edward Hilton Young, 1st Baron, and Kathleen (*née* Bruce), 355
Kennet, Wayland Young, 2nd Baron, 47
Kenny, Sean, 213
Kerouac, Jack, 54
Kerr, Sir Hamilton, 139
Kerr, Peter, 298
Keswick, Margaret, 14
Ketton-Cremer, Wyndham, 407
Keynes, John Maynard, Baron, 268
Kilbracken, John Godley, 3rd Baron, 551
Kilmartin, Terence, 104
Kilpatrick, Carson and Anne, 441
Kilvert, Rev. Francis, 447–8, 546
King Alfred's Kitchen, Wantage, 25, 544
King George Jubilee Trust, 389
King, Jessie M., 412
King, Rod, 476
Kinglake, A.W., 148

King's Cross station, London, 268
King's Road, Chelsea, 422–4
Kinks, the (pop group), 260
Kinross, Patrick Balfour, 3rd Baron, 68, 154, 216, 382, 428; death, 443
Kinson, Francis, 388
Kipling, Rudyard, 471–2
Kirkup, James: *The Descent into the Cave and Other Poems*, 74–5; *A Poet Could Not But Be Gay*, 74
Kirkup, 'Barone' Seymour, 75
Knight, Dame Laura, 215
Knowles, Sir Francis, 259
Knox, Archibald, 471
Kolkhorst, 'Colonel' George, 83, 103, 608
Kunzer, Joan (*née* Larkworthy), 271

Laboureur, Jean, 488
Lacey, Charmian, 34
Lahr, John, 214
Laming, Barbara, 283
Lancaster, Colonel C.G., 172
Lancaster, Karen, 21, 608
Lancaster, (Sir) Osbert: meets Stockwood circle, 3; wife's death, 21; on Paul Betjeman, 24; at founding of Victorian Society, 29–30; Lord Chetwode compliments, 43; proposed illustrations for *Summoned by Bells*, 90–1; drawing of JB, 99, 445; on JB's employing ex-priests, 117; and Prudential building, 118; wealth, 118; friendship with JB, 124, 520; illustrates Andrew Graham novels, 125; meets Barry Humphries, 216; declines to write preface to JB's poems, 237–8; cartoon on Poet Laureateship for woman, 372–3; celebrates JB's appointment as Poet Laureate, 375–6; suggests title for JB's book of poems, 382; describes Ness Point, 410; reviews *A Passion for Churches*, 418–19; home in Belgravia, 423; and James Lees-Milne, 437; at Patrick Kinross's funeral, 443; protests at proposed developments, 454; suggests Somerset House as art gallery, 458; meets JB on tour of London, 489; and Richard Boston, 519; in TV film *Time with Betjeman*, 539–40; at JB's memorial service, 587; death, 590; religious faith, 608
Landmark Trust, 361
Larkin, Philip: reviews JB's *Summoned by Bells*, 99, 107, 110; TV programme on, 192; reads JB's *High and Low*, 246;

tipped as Poet Laureate, 372–4, 614; welcomes JB's appointment to Laureateship, 375; and JB's wish to give up Laureateship, 379; JB visits in Hull, 477; contributes to *A Garland for the Laureate*, 525; JB praises, 542; writes obituary of JB, 580; at JB's memorial service, 584, 587; introduces JB's poetry to American readers, 593; admires Gavin Ewart, 598; champions JB as poet, 601–3, 612, 616; on Eliot's desiring poetry to be difficult, 605

Lascaris, Manoly, 155

Laski, Marghanita, 56

Laurençin, Marie, 488

Lawrence, Ronald, 459

Lawrence, T.E., 502

Lawrence, Sir Thomas, 191

Leapman, Michael, 380, 390, 465

Lear, Edward, 602

Lear's Bookshop, Cardiff, 100

Leavis, F.R., 110

Le Carré, John: *The Spy Who Came In from the Cold*, 23

Lees-Milne, Alvilde, 305, 436–7, 445, 513–14

Lees-Milne, James: on Anne Rosse, 27; and founding of Victorian Society, 29; JB complains to of Pevsner, 42; and Great Barn at Avebury, 260; replies to Sir Edward Playfair, 269–70; at dinner for JB's Australia film, 305; JB reads Queen's Silver Jubilee ode to, 389; on JB's failing health, 392–3, 510, 525, 527; on Jeremy Fry, 432; friendship with JB and Elizabeth, 433–9, 443, 510–11, 514; diaries, 434–5; on Lord Kinross's death, 443; JB stays with after heart attack, 512–13; on JB's staying with Queen Mother, 515; meets Caroline Blackwood, 517; on JB in hospital, 524; visits JB and Elizabeth in Radnor Walk, 575; sees JB for last time, 577; attends JB's funeral, 580–1; at JB's memorial service, 584–6; on JB's religious feelings, 607; *William Beckford*, 445

Lehmann, Rosamond, 29, 437; *The Echoing Grove*, 59

Leigh, Vivien, 157

Leighton, Frederic, Baron, 37

Leighton House, London, 37

Leighton, Margaret, 5

Leppard, Raymond, 308, 431

Lerwick, Shetland Islands, 318–19

Le Strange, Eve ('Puffin'), 407

Levin, Bernard, 141–2, 195, 485

Levy, Joe, 144–5

Lewis, C.S., 39, 87, 211, 595

Lewisham town hall, 261–3

Liddell, Robert, 56

Lindsay, Vachel: 'Congo', 11

Littlewood, Joan, 212, 215

Liverpool: Albert Docks, 48

Liverpool Street station and hotel, London, 463–5, 566

Lloyd, Father (of Isle of Purbeck), 184

Lloyd, Jeremy, 479

Lloyd, John ('Widow'), 436

Logue, Christopher, 15; *Songs*, 71–2

London: motorway box, 273; development changes, 360–1

London in the Country (TV film), 344

London County Council (LCC): and Euston Arch, 127–9, 133, 145

London, Judy, 482

London Magazine, 230–2, 237, 382

London Poetry International, fifth (1972), 374

London on Sunday (TV film), 344

Longford, Elizabeth, Countess of, 467

Longford, Francis Aungier Pakenham, 7th Earl of, 312, 370, 422, 588

Look Stranger: Isle of Man (TV film), 542

Lord, Graham, 246–7, 368, 387, 396, 479, 582

Lost Betjemans, The (TV film), 189, 191

Lovecraft, H.P., 64

Loyd, Christopher, 2, 255

Luard, Nicholas, 214

Lubetkin, Berthold and Margaret, 456

Lutyens, Sir Edwin, 77, 446, 488

Lutyens, Mary (Mrs J.G. Links), 382

Lycett Green, Candida Rose (*née* Betjeman; JB's daughter): dislikes move to Wantage, 1; at Barings' in Ardington House, 2; at St Mary's school, 3; on Schaufelberger and Bloomfield, 6; friendships and romances, 9–11, 13; sacked by Jocelyn Stevens, 10, 12; as debutante, 11–12; engagement and marriage to Rupert, 12–14; cancer, 13; hippie period, 13; honeymoon trip round world, 15; London social life, 15–17; welcomes Elizabeth Cavendish into family, 22; on changes to The Meads, 26; and writing of *Summoned by Bells*, 91; on JB's employing clergymen as secretaries, 117; and JB's relations with Elizabeth Cavendish, 120; JB praises in interview, 123;

Lycett Green, Candida Rose (*cont.*)
on JB's social success in Australia, 154; letters from JB in Australia, 157, 296, 299–300; and JB's pub-visiting while filming, 186; letter from JB in Jerusalem, 194; Nankivell meets, 254; accompanies JB to Oving protest meeting, 274; and JB's friendship with Mary Wilson, 276, 278–9; and JB's anxiety about Laureateship, 379; children, 421; JB visits in Notting Hill, 421; JB stays with in Wiltshire, 440; moves to Blacklands, near Calne, 440; celebrates JB's seventieth birthday, 443; watches JB on Parkinson TV show, 463; learns of JB's heart attack, 511–12; on JB in old age, 527; appears in *Time with Betjeman*, 534; accompanies JB to train-naming ceremony, 573; and JB's death and funeral, 579–80; at JB's memorial service, 585; *Over the Hills and Far Away*, 13

Lycett Green, David (JB's grandson), 441, 541

Lycett Green, Sir Edward, 13

Lycett Green, Endellion (JB's granddaughter), 421, 440

Lycett Green, Imogen (Mrs Augustus Christie; JB's granddaughter), 421; *Grandmother's Footsteps*, 625–6

Lycett Green, John (JB's grandson), 441

Lycett Green, Lucy (JB's granddaughter), 290–1, 297, 421, 578

Lycett Green, Rupert: engagement and marriage to Candida, 12–14; founds Blades, 13–14; children, 421; JB stays with, 440; at JB's seventieth birthday, 443

Lynam, Joc, 21

Lynam Thomas, Peggy, 21

Lyons, Eric, 142

Lyttelton, George, 113

Lyttelton, Humphrey, 366

McAlpine, Jill, Lady, 563

McAlpine, Robert, 563

McAlpine, Sir William, 563–4

MacArthur, John, 295–6

Macaulay, Dame Rose, 485; *The Towers of Trebizond*, 56

McCall, Margaret, 234, 291–5, 297, 299–302, 304, 446, 541

McCarthy, Mary: *Cast a Cold Eye*, 64; *Memories of a Catholic Girlhood*, 64

McCubbins, Frederick: *Lost in the Bush* (painting), 304

McCullers, Carson: *The Ballad of the Sad Café*, 59

McCulloch, Celia (*née* Townshend), 407–8, 416, 420

McCulloch, Nigel, Bishop of Manchester, 407–8, 416, 420

McGlashan, John, 344, 405, 411, 414, 442, 532

MacGonagall, Teresa, 20

McGough, Roger, 472

McGowan, Cathy, 317

Macgregor, Miriam, 525

Machen, Arthur, 345; *The Secret Glory*, 330

McIlhenny, Henry, 514

Macindoe, Alec, 103

Mackenzie, (Sir) Compton: *Sinister Street*, 108

MacKenzie, Rachel, 92

McKinney, J.P., 153–4

McKinney, Meredith, 153

Mackintosh, Charles Rennie, 42

Maclean, Charles Hector Fitzroy Maclean, Baron, 378

Maclean, Donald, 66–7

Macmillan, Harold (*later* 1st Earl of Stockton): and Euston Arch controversy, 133–6, 138–41; John Bird parodies, 213; Heath complains of Stockwood's elevation to, 306

MacNeice, Louis, 124, 594, 612

Mädchen in Uniform (film), 327

Magdalen College, Oxford, 133

Malcolm, Mary, 335

Mallalieu, J.P.W., 60

Mallet, John, 527

'Malley, Ern' (hoax poet), 613

Man, Isle of, 471–2, 542

Man with a View, A (TV programme), 193

Marble Arch to Edgware (TV film) *see* Contrast

Marchant, Geneviève Gérard, 280

Margaret, Princess: marriage to Antony Armstrong-Jones, 5, 131, 432; JB's poem on wedding, 93; friendship with JB and Elizabeth, 105–6, 430, 438, 483; sees JB's Australia films, 305; and award of Queen's Gold Medal for Poetry to JB, 364; in Holland with Elizabeth Cavendish, 442–3; at JB's memorial service, 588

Markham, Sir Frank, 132–3

Marlborough College Register, 89

Marlborough school: in JB's *Summoned by Bells*, 70, 83–6, 89–90, 95–6, 531; old boys' reunion, 124; JB films at, 189–90

Marples, Ernest, 135, 139, 141
Marriott, Oliver: *The Property Boom*, 144–5
Marshall, Arthur, 195
Marshall, Sir John, 624
Marshall, Michael, Bishop of Woolwich, 326
Martin, Kingsley, 94
Martin, Sir Leslie, 267
Martin, Ruth, 103
Marvell, Andrew, 600; 'To His Coy Mistress', 3
Marx House (Marx Memorial Library), Clerkenwell Green, 272
Masefield, John, 364, 366–8, 507n, 511
Matthews, Kenneth: *Aleko*, 368
Maud (JB's nursemaid), 606
Maudslay, Major Sir Rennie, 379, 479
Maufe, Sir Edward, 489
Maugham, Robin, 433
May, E.J., 230, 235
Mead, The *see* Wantage
Mears & Stainbank, 96
Meath, Gerard, 243
Melbourne, Australia: JB visits, 156, 160–1, 205–6; seeks to acquire Coal Exchange, 178–9; JB films in, 297–8, 302
Melly, George, 481
Menzies, Jill, 242
Mereworth Castle, 196
Mermaid Theatre, London, 169
Mesopotamia (*Mespot*; magazine), 10
Messel, Oliver, 29
Metcalfe, Priscilla, 374
Methuen, Paul, 4th Baron, 255, 260, 455
Metro-land (TV film), 162, 330–48, 350–3, 398, 444, 446
Metropolitan Line (London Underground railway), 330–3, 336, 398
Michell, Keith, 479
Michelmore, Cliff, 120
Midwinter, Stanley, 456
Miles, Bernard, Baron, 169, 261
Miles, Father, 323
Miller, 'Dusty', 205, 499
Miller, Jonathan, 213
Miller, Max, 530
Milligan, Spike, 215
Mills, D.G., 177
Mills, (Sir) John, 462
Millstead, Diane: marriage to Barry Humphries, 520
Mirfield, Yorkshire: Community of the Resurrection, 318, 320, 322

Mirzoeff, Edward: makes *Bird's-Eye View*, 197–8; makes *Metro-land* film with JB, 330–3, 335–52, 398, 531; makes *A Passion for Churches* film with JB, 398–412, 419–20, 427; visits Stockwood with JB, 398–9; ghostly experience at Harrods', 402–3; and JB's demands over editing, 414–18; makes Queen's Silver Jubilee film, 448–9; and *Time with Betjeman*, 531–2
Mitchell, Adrian, 372
Mitchell Beazley (publishers), 256
Mitford, Nancy, 370, 616; *The Blessing*, 69
Mitford, Pamela, 370, 382–3
Mitford, Thomas, 517
Mittelholzer, Edgar: *The Weather in Middenshot*, 66
Mlinaric, David, 16
modernism, 604–5, 613–15
Mole, William: *Trample an Empire*, 62
Molony, Eileen, 524
Molson, Hugh, Baron, 176
Monitor (TV programme), 544–5
Montagu, Edward Douglas-Scott-Montagu, 3rd Baron, 66
Montefiore, Elisabeth, 325
Montefiore, Hugh, Bishop of Birmingham, 309, 312, 325
Moor Park Golf Club, 339–40
Moor View, near Chatsworth, 524
Moorcock, Michael, 505
Moorcroft, Roy, 128
Moore, Dudley, 213
Moore, Elizabeth, 501, 503, 516, 519, 526–7, 533, 541
Moore, Henry, 459, 467, 555
Moore, John, 272
Moore, Patrick, 186
Moore, Roger, 317
Moorehead, Alan, 300
Moorhouse, Geoffrey, 364
Morris, Marcus, 94
Morris, William, 30, 39, 165, 222–3, 323
Mortimer, Penelope: *A Villa in Summer*, 62
Mortimer, Raymond, 104–5, 116
Mortlock, Canon, 33
Mosley, Diana, Lady, 588
Mosley, Sir Oswald, 588
Mossman, James, 431
Motion, Andrew, 192
Mott, Nevill, 308
Mottistone, Henry John Alexander Seely, 2nd Baron, 117, 174–6, 354, 358
Mounsey, Deborah Jane: marriage to Simon Stuart, 325

Mountain, Mrs (JB's secretary), 422

Mountbatten, Louis, 1st Earl, 552

Mountford, E.W., 620

Mowl, Timothy: on JB-Pevsner feud, 39–43, 51

Moyne, Bryan Guinness, 2nd Baron, 259–60, 588

Mozley, Charles, 101

Muggeridge, Malcolm, 244–6

Muir, Percy, 501

Munir (El Fhatah), 312, 327

Murdoch, Iris, 54–5, 57

Murphy, Hugh, 474–6, 478, 482

Murray, John ('Jock'; publisher): JB writes guides for, 41; and publication of JB's Summoned by Bells, 79, 82, 87, 89–103; and JB's work for other publishers, 95; on reviews of Summoned by Bells, 106–7, 109, 113; on JB's entertaining at The Garrick, 125; publishes JB's High and Low (poetry), 236–40, 242–3, 246–8; and JB's decline in old age, 361; publishes JB's A Nip in the Air, 382–5, 387–8; drives JB to recording session, 482; entertains JB, 511; publishes (and cuts) JB's Church Poems, 521–2; reconciles JB and John Piper, 521; publishes selection of JB's previously unpublished poems (1982), 526–7; in Time with Betjeman film, 541–2; attends JB's funeral, 580–1; on JB's gravestone, 582; reads lesson at JB's memorial service, 586–7

Nairn, Ian, 176

Nankivell, John: meets JB, 249–50, 254; background, 250–3; JB befriends, 254–6, 258; accompanies Penelope to India, 257–8, 421; and JB's Silver Jubilee ode, 390–1; lives close to Penelope in Herefordshire, 427

Nash, Frances, 284

Nash, Ogden, 125, 284

Nashdom Abbey, Buckinghamshire, 99

National Book Award for Children's Literature, 393

National Film Archive (NFA), 333

National Provincial Bank, Bishopsgate, 37

National Trust, 259–61, 270–1

Natural History Museum, London, 469

Neasden, 335–6

Neave, Airey and Diana, 2

Negus, Arthur, 196

Nesbitt, Cathleen, 438

Neven-Spence, Sir Basil, 319

New Statesman (journal), 49; 'Weekend Competition', 367

New York Times, 105, 112

New Yorker (magazine): publishes extracts from Summoned by Bells, 91–3, 95, 99–100

Newbolt, Sir Henry, 471, 542, 576

Newington, Peter, 544

Newman, John, 47

Newman, John Henry, Cardinal, 434

Nice Night's Entertainment, A (Barry Humphries show), 212

Nicholas Brothers (Canadian company), 136

Nichols, Beverley, 310–13; Twenty-Five, 79

Night and Day (magazine), 594

Noble, Christina, 624, 626

Norfolk: diocese chosen for TV film on Church, 399–400, 403–5

Norman-Butler, Belinda, 29

North, Alexander, 160, 303

Northern Ireland, 279

Norton, William, 261–3

Norwich, John Julius Cooper, 2nd Viscount, 352, 441

Norwood, Sir Cyril, 87

Novak, Captain (helicopter pilot), 197–8

Nuns on the Run (film), 229

Nurse, Keith, 377

Nuttgens, Joseph Edward, 464

Nye, Robert, 282

Oaksey, John Lawrence, 2nd Baron, 117, 587

Oaksey, Victoria, Lady (née Dennistoun; 'Tory'), 117

O'Brien, Flann, 59

O'Brien, James, 573–4

O'Brien, Margaret, 253

Observer, The (newspaper), 104

O'Connor, Ulick, 325

O'Donovan, Gerry, 359–60

O'Donovan, Seamus, 359

O'Hara, Archbishop Gerald Patrick, 312

O'Hare, James Haldane, 359–60

Old Chiswick Protection Society, 224

Oldaker, K.H., 396

Oldaker, Max, 207

Olssen, Julius, 209, 280, 386–7, 615

Oman, Julia Trevelyan (Lady Strong), 515

One Pair of Eyes (TV series), 429

One Thousand Years at Milton – from Milton Abbey (TV programme), 188

Orchard, The (house), Chorleywood, 341–3, 346

Orton, Joe, 596

Osborne, Charles, 207

Osborne, John: friendship with JB, 22; sends postcard to JB, 34; amused by Barry Humphries, 214; meets Mary Wilson with JB, 279; in TV film with JB, 530–1; *Damn You, England*, 22; *Inadmissible Evidence*, 22–3

Owen, Wilfred, 467

Paddington station, 562

Paget, Paul, 117, 309, 354, 356–62

Paget, Verily (*formerly* Anderson; *née* Bruce), 354–60; *Spam Tomorrow*, 355

Pakenham Hall (now Tullynally), 610

Pakenham, Thomas, 32, 36, 47

Palmer, Sir Mark, 13

Parker, Claire, 488

Parker, Gillian (Jill), Lady: diagnoses JB's sleepiness, 351; background, 551; JB meets, 551–2; as JB's doctor, 553, 558; friendship with JB, 555–8, 560; protests to Lady Antonia Fraser, 555; and British Rail's honouring JB, 565–6, 568–9, 574; and Gregory Scott's suicide, 572; and JB's health decline, 577

Parker, Jim, 406, 471–84, 531, 536, 585, 587

Parker, Oliver, 552–3

Parker, Sir Peter, 551–2, 558–62, 565–8, 570, 573–4

Parker, Peter (biographer), 584–6

Parkinson, Michael, 452–3, 531, 612

Parks, Charles and Dorothy, 158

Parks, Philip, 158

Parr, Tom, 25

Parry, Dennis: *Sea of Glass*, 72

Parsons, Ian, 467

Partridge, Frances, 36, 304–5

Pasco, Richard, 449

Passion for Churches, A (TV series): JB compares Comper to Colonel Sanders in, 43; verse scripts, 383; suggested, 398–401; title, 401–2; making of, 402–11, 446; editing, 414–16; broadcast and reviewed, 418–20; passage shown in *Time with Betjeman*, 538

Paterson, A.B. ('Banjo'), 148

Patterson, Sir Les *see* Humphries, Barry

Paulin, Tom, 599

Peace, David, 590

Pearce, Maresco, 209

Pears, Sir Peter, 467

Pearson, Frank Loughborough, 299

Pearson, John Loughborough, 299

Penguin Book of Australian Verse, 147

Penn, John, 466

Penning-Rowsell, Edmund, 95, 101

Perry, Lionel, 318, 514

Perspectives in Architecture (magazine), 615

Perth, Australia, 158

Peters, Fritz: *Finistère*, 66–9

Pevsner, Sir Nikolaus: absent from founding meeting of Victorian Society, 27–8, 31; Peter Clarke parodies and lampoons, 29–30, 43–5; cited in support of National Provincial Bank building, 37; as chairman of Victorian Society, 39, 46, 48; JB's hostility to, 39–43, 46–7, 49, 51, 358, 500–1; character and qualities, 46–7; death, 46–7; achievements, 51; deprecates demolition of Euston Arch, 130–1, 138; and Hampstead Garden Suburb, 165; defends Coal Exchange, 170, 174–5; in Bedford Park campaign, 227–8, 235; joins JB in protests about developments and demolitions, 266, 454, 459; *Buildings of England* series, 41, 46

Pheasantry, Chelsea, 467

Philip, Prince, Duke of Edinburgh, 381, 389

Phillips, Captain Mark, 379

Phipps, Simon, Bishop of Lincoln, 307–8, 314–15

Pickering, Sir Edward, 199, 371

Pickles, Rev. Hugh, 255

Piggott, Stuart, 257, 259

Pinches, John (medallists), 142–3

Pinter, Harold, 555

Piper, D.H., 460

Piper, Edward, 521

Piper, John: subscribes to *Private Eye*, 10; at founding of Victorian Society, 29; and JB's feud with Pevsner, 46; and writing of *Summoned by Bells*, 80; as prospective illustrator for *Summoned by Bells*, 90–1; friendship with JB, 124; illustrates JB's *Poems in the Porch*, 183n; protests at M4 route, 264; falls out with JB, 521; illustrates JB's *Church Poems*, 521; Frank Tait visits, 549–50; religious beliefs, 608

Piper, Myfanwy, 80, 521, 535, 549–50, 608

Pitman, Robert, 105, 111

Platts-Mills, Barney and Marion, 429

Playfair, Sir Edward, 268–70, 458

Plomer, William, 109, 314, 372, 447–8

Plumb, J.H., 75

Plummer, Pauline, 406

Poet Laureate: JB as prospective, 363–8, 371–4; rôle questioned, 366–7; duties, 370–1; JB appointed, 374–8
'Pomp and Circumstance' (TV film), 297
Poole, Dorset, 193
Poole, Henry, 621
Pope-Hennessy, James, 29, 439
Pope-Hennessy, Sir John, 29
Port Sunlight, 233
Potter, Beatrix: *The Tale of Mrs Tittlemouse*, 342
Potter, Dennis, 419
Pound, Ezra, 603, 613
Powell, Anthony, 53, 246, 402, 511, 584–6
Powell, Georgia, 203
Powell, Noel, 601
Powell, Tristram, 23, 203, 292
Powys, John Cowper, 54–5
Praed, Winthrop Mackworth, 617
Preece, Ruby, 339
Presley, Elvis, 55
Price, Cedric, 459
Price, Joan, 384
Pride of Place (TV programme), 196
Priestley, J.B., 137; *Festival at Fairbridge*, 69
Pringle, John, 525
Pritchett, (Sir) Victor S., 112, 195
Pritt, Rev. Stephen, 407
Private Eye (magazine): and *Mespot*, 10; lampoons JB and Negus, 196; Barry Humphries contributes to, 215; 'Mrs Wilson's Diary' column in, 276, 284; on Neasden, 335; lampoons JB poem, 384; Gavin Stamp writes in, 525
Profumo, John, 17
Proops, Marjorie, 454
Pryce-Jones, Alan, 41, 66, 112–13, 598, 608
Pryce-Jones, David, 107
Pugin, Augustus Welby Northmore, 51
Punch (magazine), 92, 94, 104, 244
Purey-Cust, Peggy, 536
Pusey House, Oxford, 588
Pye, Henry James, 375–6
Pym, Barbara, 54–6

Queen's Gold Medal for Poetry, 364, 371
Queen's Realm, The (TV film), 448–9
Quennell, (Sir) Peter, 113, 438, 584

Radio Times (magazine), 444–5
Radnor Walk, Chelsea, 361–2, 422–4
Raine, Craig, 602, 607, 612, 616
Ramsey, Michael, Archbishop of Canterbury, 313
Ratcliffe, Michael, 419

Raven, Charles, 307
Rawle, Len, 332, 343–5
Ray, Robin, 535, 587
Raynes, Father Raymond, 4
Read, Reg, 499–502, 506, 516–17, 519–23, 606, 612
Redgrave, Vanessa, 432
Reed, Michael, 486
Reedman, Robert, 26
Rees-Mogg, William, Baron, 29, 393
Regent's Park Terraces, London, 129
Reid, Alastair, 73
Reindorp, George, Bishop of Guildford then of Salisbury, 309
Reynolds, Bayley, 169
Rhondda, Margaret Haig Thomas, Viscountess, 243
Ricardo, Halsey, 97
Rice, Kenric, 354
Richards, (Sir) J.M., 29, 32, 39, 41, 137–8, 166, 268, 272, 456; *Castles on the Ground*, 331
Richards, Rev. John, 585
Richardson, Sir Albert, 174, 226
Richardson, Philip and Susan, 317
Richardson, Tony, 432
Riches, Anne, 487
Rickards, Maurice, 390
Ritz Hotel, London, 446–7
Robbins, Margot, 194
Robbins, Michael, 333
Robert Street, London, 264
Roberts, Cecil, 80, 99
Roberts, Edward (Ted): edits *Bird's-Eye View*, 198; works on *Metro-land*, 331–3, 348–51; edits film for Stedall, 344; writes verse, 348–9; and TV film of English Church, 398–9, 406, 409, 414–16; and Queen's Silver Jubilee film, 448–9; on TV technical terms, 531
Robertson, Fyfe, 120
Robertson Sir Howard, 622
Robinson, John (*later* Bishop of Woolwich), 309, 312, 317
Robinson, Richard, 512
Robinson, Robert, 519, 576
Rogers, Magda, 385, 429–30, 444
Rolt, L.T.C.: *The Thames from Mouth to Source*, 41
Romania: JB visits, 442–3
Rome, Alan, 42
Rooke, T.M., 221
Room in Chelsea Square, A (anonymous novel), 68
Ross, Alan, 230, 382, 519
Ross-Williamson, Eileen, 300

Rosse, Anne, Countess of (*née* Messel): co-founds Victorian Society, 27–30, 32–3, 37, 46, 51, 586; manner, 36

Rosse, Laurence Michael Harvey Parsons, 6th Earl of: and founding of Victorian Society, 27, 29, 31–2; and Great Barn at Avebury, 260

Rossmore, William Warner Westenra, 7th Baron, 309, 325

Rothenstein, Sir John, 520

Rous, Lady Henrietta, 16

Rouse, Hannah, 298

Rouse Hill House, New South Wales, 298

Routh, Richard, 114

Rowallan, Arthur Corbett, 3rd Baron, 157

Rowallan, Thomas Godfrey Polson Corbett, 2nd Baron, and Gwen, Lady, 157

Rowe-Dutton, Lady, 553

Rowland, Sir William, 177

Rowse, A.L., 42, 265, 315, 525, 539

Royal Agricultural Hall, Islington, 459

Royal Automobile Club, London, 8

Royal Court Theatre, Chelsea, 471

Royal Fine Art Commission: and Euston Arch controversy, 133–4, 141; and Coal Exchange, 173; and JB's play *Pity about the Abbey*, 193; and Avon Gorge plans, 455; and Paddington station glazing, 562

Royal Lodge, Windsor Great Park, 515

Royal Society of Literature, 511

Runcie, Robert, Archbishop of Canterbury, 585–7

Rushton, William, 10–11, 284, 335, 382

Russell, Bertrand: *Satan in the Suburbs*, 59

Russell, Leonard, 75, 89, 100–1

Russell, Dr Ritchie, 549

Rylands, George ('Dadie'), 261

St Agnes' church, Kennington, 462

St Anne (church), Limehouse, 465

St Anne's, Soho, 390

St Edmundsbury Theatre Royal, 261

St George in the East (church), London, 465

St John's Wood, London, 331, 335

St Mary-le-Strand, London, 465–6, 469

St Mary's, Bryanston Square, 270

St Mary's school, Wantage, 2–5

St Michael's College, Tenbury, Worcestershire, 263–4

St Pancras station, London, 47–8, 267–70

St Paul's cathedral, London: precincts, 266, 271, 360–1

Sale, George, 26

Salinger, J.D., 54; *The Catcher in the Rye*, 65

Sambourne, Linley, 27, 31

Samuel, Godfrey, 193

Sanders, Andrew, 593

Sang, Frederick, 164

Sansom, William, 63; *A Touch of the Sun*, 54; *A Bed of Roses*, 70

Satterthwaite, J.R., Bishop of Fulham and Gibraltar, 555

Savage, Gordon, Bishop of Buckingham, 117

Savage, N.J., 271

Savage, Richard, 364

Savidge, Kenneth, 183–8, 450–1

Say, David, Bishop of Rochester, 306

Scales, Prunella, 449, 481, 587

Schamp, Cherry Ann, 406

Schaufelberger, Rev. John, 5–6, 15, 24

Schmidt, Edith, 625

Schmutzler, Robert, 228–9

Scholfield, R.J., 216

Scilly Isles, 287–8, 516

Scott, Sir George Gilbert, 267, 462

Scott, Sir Gilbert, 267–8, 446

Scott, Sir Giles Gilbert, 268

Scott, Dr Gregory: friendship with JB, 554–8, 570–2; suicide, 572–3

Scott, Norman, 513

Scott, Father Richard, SJ, 158

Scott, Robin, 331, 398

Scott, Sir Walter, 605

Scott-James, Anne (*later* Lady Lancaster), 21, 423

Sedding, J.D., 460–2

Seferis, George, 102

Segsbury school, Wantage, 251

Shaffer, Peter, 345

Shakespeare, Nicholas, 426

Shakespeare, William: Sonnet 76, 604

Shand, Mary, 379

Shand, P. Morton, 39–40, 42

Sharley, Bart, 6–9, 15–16, 18

Sharley, Diana, 6, 9, 16, 18

Sharley, Jessie, 6–9, 15–16, 18, 578, 624

Sharley, Veronica (Ron), 6–8, 16, 19–21

Sharp, E. Mamie, 396

Sharpe, Cesca, 537

Sharpless, Stanley J., 582

Shaw, Christine, 224

Shaw, Norman, 38, 41, 219–20, 222–4, 229, 338–9

Shearing, Joseph: *The Abode of Love*, 335

Shell Guides, 41, 46

Shelton Abbey, 610

Shepheard, Sir Peter, 468

Sheppard, David, Baron, Bishop of Woolwich then of Liverpool, 309, 312–13, 323, 325

Sheratt, Frank, 187–8

Sherborne School for Girls, 188–9

Sherrin, Ned, 309, 312–13, 317

Shetland Islands, 318–20

Shot Tower, London, 168, 177

Shrimpton, Jean, 213

Shute, Nevil (i.e. Nevil Shute Norway), 147

Sicily, 314–15

Sidmouth, Devon, 191

Silkin, Lewis, 1st Baron, 454

Simmons, Jack, 459

Simms, Eric, 336

Simpson, Archibald, 298

Simson, Elizabeth, 257–8

Singapore, 149–50

Singer, Aubrey, 448

Singh, Paddy, 624–5

Sinkinson, Mary, 561, 566–7, 574

Sinkinson, Walter, 560–2, 566–7, 574; Branch Line Charm, 561; Joy to Know, 560–1, 567

Sitwell, Sir Sacheverell, 525

Skelton, John, 281

Skelton, Robin, 73–4

Skidmore and Sons, of Coventry, 267

Skinner, Martyn, 114, 242

Skipwith, Peyton, 462

Slater, G.H., 136

Slessor, Kenneth, 208

Smallwood, Norah, 467

Smirke, Sir Robert, 167

Smith, Cicely, 472

Smith, Edwin, 95

Smith, Sir John, 361

Smith, Lady Juliet: Northamptonshire (Shell Guide), 46

Smith, Maggie, 452

Smith, Timothy d'Arch: Love in Earnest, 558

Smithson, Alison and Peter, 143

Smyth-Piggott, Rev. John Hugh, 335

Snow, Julian, 130

Snowdon, Antony Armstrong-Jones, 1st Earl of: marriage to Princess Margaret, 5, 131, 432; in Rotherhithe, 77; at dinner for showing of JB's Australia films, 305; TV film on growing old, 318; organises Prince of Wales investiture, 322; on homosexuals, 437; at JB's memorial service, 588

Society for the Protection of Ancient Buildings (SPAB): and Victorian Society, 30–2, 35; and Euston Arch, 128, 140; and Coal Exchange, 165, 168; and Bedford Park, 222

Somerset House, London, 458, 486–8, 555

South Wales Motorway (M4), 264

Southend: pier, 458–9, 467, 497–8, 516; JB visits with Simon Jenkins, 493–8; JB visits with Reg Read, 516–17

Southwell, Dr Peter, 555

Soyinka, Wole, 372

Spain, 317–18, 323–6

Sparrow, John: reads and comments on JB's typescript of Summoned by Bells, 81–2, 85–6, 92–3, 114; at Bowra's funeral, 289; epitaph on Bowra, 289–90; reads JB's poems for A Nip in the Air, 385; on JB as Laureate, 397; stores JB's books and papers, 422; radio talk on JB, 444–5; in Time with Betjeman film, 541–2

Spear, Ruskin, 405, 481

Spectator (magazine): JB writes in, 311; obituary tributes to JB, 582

Spence, Sir Basil, 251, 459, 562

Spencer, Bernard, 74

Spender, (Sir) Stephen: reads draft of Summoned by Bells, 90, 94; reviews Summoned by Bells, 108; tipped as Poet Laureate, 372–3; contributes to A Garland for the Laureate, 525; at JB's memorial service, 588; reputation, 612; World Within World, 79

Spiegl, Fritz, 392

Spurrier (town planning officer), 225

Squires, Dick, 24, 26, 257

Squires, Ottilie, 624

Stallworthy, Jon, 467

Stamp, Gavin, 258, 459–62, 470, 525, 582, 584

Stamp, Terence, 432–3, 588

Stanford, Derek, 92, 115; John Betjeman, 596

Stark, Rev. Edwin, 395

Stedall, Jonathan: first works with JB, 188–9; makes film on St Michael's College, 264; JB reports on Church of England Ramblers to, 317; JB stays with, 333; JB double-books film-making with, 344; makes Thank God It's Sunday, 378, 447; films in India with Penelope, 429; Elizabeth Cavendish's liking for, 430; on Peter Shaffer's visiting Elizabeth, 431; in Romania, 442; makes film of Summoned by Bells, 443–4; visits JB, 483; on JB's bawdy streak, 502; and

JB's proposed trip to Gothland, 516; makes *Time with Betjeman* TV series, 529–48; on Osbert Lancaster at Radnor Walk, 529; at JB's memorial service, 588

Stevens, Rodway, 178, 180

Stevenson, John, 555–6; *Studies in Seduction*, 570–1

Stevenson, Randall: *The Last of England?*, 615

Stewart, Douglas, 148–9, 152, 154

Stock Conversion (company), 145

Stockdale, Alderman Sir Edmund, 177

Stockwood, Mervyn, Bishop of Southwark: circle and friendships, 38, 306–13, 323, 326, 555; holidays abroad, 316, 325; forms 'Caps and Mitres' group, 326–7; writes humorous verse, 327–9; Mirzoeff visits with JB, 398–9; JB misses Fishmongers' Hall lunch with, 527

Stoke Poges, 466

Stone, Reynolds, 76, 514

Storey, Graham, 309, 314, 316

Strachey, Julia, 36

Stratton-Smith, Tony, 474, 477–8, 481

Street, G.E., 184

Street-Porter, Janet, 445

Stride, Desmond, 264

Strong, Sir Roy, 430, 515

Stross, Sir Barnett, 179

Stuart, Simon, 240, 308, 314–15, 318, 323–5

Sugden, Peter, 588

Sullivan, Sir Arthur, 484

Summerson, Sir John: JB appeals to in St Pancras station campaign, 40; praises Leonora Ison, 75; in Euston Arch controversy, 131–2, 134, 136–8, 143; hears JB's annual speech to SPAB, 165; opposes Bedford Park conservation, 227–8, 235; campaigns for St Mary's Bryanston Square, 270; protests about London motorways, 454

Summoned by Bells (TV programme), 443, 446, 539

Sumner, John, 206

Sunday Times: and serialisation of *Summoned by Bells*, 94, 97, 100–1, 104; and controversy over Coal Exchange, 179; prints JB's and Mary Wilson's poems, 283

Sutherland, Graham, 292

Sutro, John, 17, 18n

Sutton, Denys, 458

Sutton, Ian, 46

Sutton, Randolph, 209, 365

Swan, Michael: *The Paradise Garden*, 72

Sydney, Australia, 151, 153–6, 161, 299–301

Tait, Frank, 291, 389, 430, 443, 549–51

Take It or Leave It (TV programme), 195

Talyllyn Railway, Wales, 560

Tasmania, 153, 157–8, 301–4

Taylor, Elizabeth: *The Sleeping Beauty*, 55

Taylor, Harry, 224–6, 228, 235

Taylor-Martin, Patrick, 601–2

Teheran, 293

Tennant, Emma, 584

Tennyson: A Beginning and an End (TV film), 199–203

Tennyson, Alfred, 1st Baron, 199–201, 538, 542; 'Crossing the Bar', 607

Tennyson, Sir Charles, 200, 202–3

Tennyson, Emily, Lady, 200

Tewkesbury: Church Street, 272

Thank God It's Sunday (TV film), 378, 447; 532–3, 536

That Well-Known Store in Knightsbridge (TV film), 541

Thatcher, (Sir) Denis, 423

Thatcher, Margaret, Baroness, 129, 423

Thirties Society (*now* Twentieth-Century Society), 469

Thomas, Brian, 358

Thomas, Dylan, 73; *A Prospect by the Sea*, 73

Thomas, Father, 184

Thomas, R.S., 525

Thompson, Brenda, 606, 611

Thompson, Rev. J.M., 87

Thompson, Lovell, 96, 102

Thomson, Charles, 582–3, 596

Thomson, George Malcolm, 94

Thornton, Sir Henry, 563

Thorpe, Jeremy, 485–6, 513

Thwaite, Anthony, 525, 599

Time with Betjeman (TV series), 529–48, 607

Time and Tide (magazine), 42–3, 74, 242

Times, The (newspaper): on Tower House, 36; reviews *Summoned by Bells*, 108–9; and demolition of Euston Arch, 127, 129–30, 134–8, 141, 143–4; and threat to Coal Exchange, 166–9, 171, 173, 180; on JB's television qualities, 193; and JB's preservation campaigns, 260–1, 265–6, 271, 455–9, 463, 465; on award of Laureateship, 371–5; attacks JB for failure to write poems for royal occasions, 388–90; criticises JB for

Times, The (newspaper) (*cont.*)
  choice of children's book award, 393;
  publishes JB's royal poem, 394; reviews
  JB's *Collected Poems* (1958), 454
Times Literary Supplement: JB writes in,
  41, 43; reviews *Summoned by Bells*, 110
Timms, Rev. R.N., 146
Todd, Alexander Robertus Todd, Baron,
  396
Tomkinson, Cyril, 307
Tong, Rosalind (Barry Humphries' second
  wife), 207, 212, 216, 218
Tonight (TV programme), 120
Toronto, 441
Tower House, Melbury Road, London, 36
Town and Country Planning Act (1967),
  47
Townshend, George, 7th Marquess, and
  Ann, Marchioness, 407
Toynbee, Philip, 388, 594, 596
Tranby Croft, near Doncaster, 13
Traylen, Nigel, 501
Trebetherick, Cornwall, 19, 21, 578–80
Tree, Lady Anne (*née* Cavendish), 119,
  305, 429, 581
Tree, Michael, 90–1, 94, 101–2, 119, 196,
  305, 584
Trinick, Michael and Elizabeth, 580
Trog (cartoonist) *see* Fawkes, Wally
Tuke, Henry Scott, 209, 231–2
Turnbull, Sir Richard and Lady, 36
Tynan, Kathleen, 438
Tynan, Kenneth, 213, 438, 551, 594

Uffington White Horse, 463, 543
University of Victoria, British Columbia,
  74, 499, 526
Ursell, Father, 588

Valori (demolition contractors), 136
Valori, Frank, 140–1, 178, 179–81
Van Oss, Oliver, 125
Vansittart, Peter: *A Little Madness*, 60
Veale, Peter, 367
Verity, Simon, 582
Verity, Thomas, 457
Vicar of This Parish (TV film), 447
Vickers, Hugo, 439
Vicky (JB's nurse), 578–9
Victorian Society: founded, 27–33, 51, 165;
  early secretaries, 33–5, 47; meetings,
  33–4; offices, 35–6; activities, 37–9;
  efficacy, 47; and Euston Arch, 127,
  135–6, 138, 140; and Coal Exchange
  campaign, 165, 169–71, 174–5, 178,
  180–2; and Bedford Park campaign,

  228; and Lewisham town hall, 261–2;
  campaigns for Holy Trinity Church,
  Sloane Street, 460, 462
Victorian Society Annual, 47
Villiers-Stuart, Emily, 428
Voysey, C.F.A., 40, 341–3, 409

Wain, John, 54, 104–5, 107, 510, 525, 594,
  596, 603
Wakeford, Angela, 15
Walker, Arnold, 226, 228
Walker, Peter, 455
Wallace, Charles, 482
Walsham, Biddy (*later* Crookshank), 85–7,
  97
Walsingham, 401, 404, 408, 414–15, 419
Wanamaker, Rodman, 408
Wantage: JB moves to (The Mead), 1, 544;
  JB rents out and divides The Mead,
  25–6; Penelope sells property in, 26;
  Penelope rents out The Mead during
  trip to India, 256; The Mead sold, 421
Ward, Stephen, 17–18
Warwick Society, 270
Waterhouse, Alfred, 469
Watkin, David, 258
Watkin, Sir Edward, 336
Watson, Judith, 624; *A Walk in the West
  Himalayas*, 625
Watson, Ronnie, 624
Waugh, Alec, 555
Waugh, Auberon, 582
Waugh, Evelyn: letter from Ann Fleming
  on Osbert Lancaster, 21; published
  works, 54; Catholicism, 55; attempts
  to convert JB, 56, 125; praises Nancy
  Mitford's *The Blessing*, 69; writes on
  Gaudí, 324; JB's hostility to, 500;
  snobbery, 610; *Decline and Fall*, 330;
  Scott-King's Modern Europe, 518; *The
  Ordeal of Gilbert Pinfold*, 58, 578
Waverley, Ava, Viscountess, 286
Wedgwood, Josiah & Sons, 458
Wedgwood, Dame Veronica, 393
Weinreb, Ben, 142
Wellington, Gerald Wellesley, 7th Duke of,
  156
Wells Cathedral, 459
Wells, John, 10, 265, 284, 520, 597
Wembley, 336–7
Wemyss, Francis David Charteris, 12th Earl
  of, 320
West, Billy, 408
Westbrook, Eric, 178
Westminster, Loelia, Duchess of, 156–8
Wheeler, John, 39, 211

Wheeler, Sir Mortimer, 165, 170–1, 173, 260

Whistler, James McNeill, 221

Whistler, Laurence, 525

White, E.B., 91

White, Henry Eli, 301, 534

White, Katharine, 91, 93, 95

White, Patrick, 155

White, Terence de Vere, 196

Whitehall: proposed development, 267

Whittaker, Christine, 340–1, 402–3

Whitworth, Jane, 400

Wicklow, William Forward-Howard, 8th Earl of (*earlier* Baron Clonmore), 359–60, 608, 610

Wickman, Lena, 284

Wigmore, Paul, 526

Wilby, Joseph, 266

Wilcox, Desmond, 418

Wilde, Oscar, 208, 221, 330

Wildeblood, Peter, 66

Wilkins, William, 261

Wilkinson, James, 75

William Morris Society, 30

Williams, Rev. Harry A.: and Paul's conversion to Mormonism, 24; JB confesses love for Elizabeth Cavendish to, 119; in Church of England Ramblers, 240, 308, 313–14, 323–4; moves to Mirfield (Community of the Resurrection), 318, 320–2, 561; and Prince of Wales, 322, 369; and Simon Stuart, 325; stays with Elizabeth in Chelsea, 430; visits JB, 506; stays with JB in Radnor Walk, 526, 537; discussion with JB in *Time with Betjeman*, 537–9; on death, 545; gives address at JB's memorial service, 585–7; *Some Day I'll Find You*, 308; *True Resurrection*, 314; *The True Wilderness*, 314

Williams, Kenneth, 452

Williams, Norman and Margery, 151, 153, 155

Williams, Tennessee, 66

Williamson, Henry, 463

Williamson, Malcolm, 389, 392, 481

Willson Rev. Martin, 183–4

Wilson, A.N., 547, 609

Wilson, (Sir) Angus, 195, 370

Wilson, Arthur, 13

Wilson, Dennis Main, 217

Wilson, Edmund, 65–6

Wilson, Harold (*later* Baron), 276, 279, 307

Wilson, John, 379

Wilson, Mary, Lady: and JB's writing for *Daily Telegraph Magazine*, 78; friendship with JB, 275–80, 285–8, 519; visits Diss with JB, 281–3, 384–5; poems published, 284; letter from JB in Australia, 300; letter from JB on Prince Charles's revue song, 322; letter from JB on trip to France and Spain, 324; as prospective Poet Laureate, 372–3; and JB's poem 'Shattered Image', 385–6; JB complains to of bad press coverage, 387; invited to see *A Passion for Churches* film, 418; on JB in old age, 476; JB meets in Scilly Isles, 516; unveils Poets' Corner monument to JB, 590

Wilson, Simon, 333–4, 411

Wilton's Music Hall, London, 467

Wiltshire Folk Life Society, 261

Winder, John, 375

Windsor, Edward, Duke of, 371

Wing, Buckinghamshire: proposed airport, 274

Wintour, Charles, 486

Witanhurst (house), Highgate, 469

Wolfe, Edward, 524

Wolfenden Report (1957), 66

Wolff, Ann (*née* Hope), 606

Wolfit, (Sir) Donald, 261

Wood, Maurice, Bishop of Norwich, 400, 403, 406

Woods, Edward, 322

Woods, Robin, Bishop of Worcester, 369

Woodyer, Henry, 263–4

Worcester: Huntingdon Hall, 465

Wordsworth, William: *The Prelude*, 616

Worsley, T.C., 388

Wright, Brenda (Barry Humphries' first wife), 206

Wright, Judith, 148–9, 153–4, 372

Wright, Ronald, 404, 608

Wyatt, Benjamin, 129

Wyatt, Woodrow (*later* Baron): campaigns for Euston Arch, 129–31, 133, 141, 170; and threat to Coal Exchange, 173

Wylie, Craig, 242

Wynne-Jones, Rusheen, Lady, 468

Yeats, William Butler, 221, 229, 235

Yorke, Henry *see* Green, Henry

Young, B.A., 92

Young, David, 168

Young, Dick, 185

Zennor, Cornwall, 265

Zilkha, Dr Kevin, 553, 558, 571

COPYRIGHT ACKNOWLEDGEMENTS

Acknowledgement is gratefully made to the following for permission to reproduce. Details of text material quoted can be found in the Notes. It has not proved possible to trace all copyright holders, but anyone inadvertently overlooked should contact John Murray Publishers. A. Alvarez. *The Architectural Review*. *Built Environment*. James Bettley. Bloomsbury: John Lahr, *Dame Edna Everage and the Rise of Western Civilization*; Cape: Robert Lusty, *Bound to be Read*. Century: Robert Robinson, *Skip All That*. Chatto & Windus: Geoffrey Grigson, *Recollections: Mainly of Writers and Artists*; Lytton Strachey, *Queen Victoria*. *City Press*. The Estate of Peter Clarke and Tom Greeves. *The Collins Book of Australian Poetry*. Constable: Caryl Brahms and Ned Sherrin, *Too Dirty for the Windmill: A Memoir of Caryl Brahms*. *Country Life*. *Daily Express*. *Daily Mail*. *Daily Telegraph*. Roy Dean. *Evening Standard*. *Everywoman*. Faber: John Drummond, *Tainted by Experience: A Life in the Arts*; John Osborne, *Almost a Gentleman: An Autobiography* and *Inadmissible Evidence*; Craig Raine, *Haydn and the Valve Trumpet*. James Fenton. The late Lady Fergusson of Kilkerran. Bernard Geis Associates and Pocket Books Inc.: William Glenton, *Tony's Room: The Secret Love Story of Princess Margaret*. *Guardian*. *Harper's & Queen*. HarperCollins: Frances Partridge, *Diaries*. Heinemann: Anthony Powell, *To Keep the Ball Rolling (Memoirs)* and *Journals*. Hodder & Stoughton: Cecil Roberts, *The Pleasant Years*; Mervyn Stockwood, *Chanctonbury Ring*. Elizabeth Jane Howard. Hutchinson: Kingsley Amis, *Memoirs*; Anthony Burgess, *Earthly Powers*. *Illustrated London News*. Michael Joseph: Barry Humphries, *My Life as Me*. The late Julian Jebb, and Tristram and Georgia Powell. Sir Simon Jenkins. Bernard Kaukas. William Kimber: Roy Plomley, *Desert Island Discs*. Little, Brown: Jonathan Dimbleby, *The Prince of Wales: A Biography*. *London Magazine*. *London Review of Books*. Macmillan: Dame Edna Everage (ie. Barry Humphries), *My Gorgeous Life*; *Philip Larkin: The Man and his Work*, ed. Dale Salwak; Imogen Lycett Green, *Grandmother's Footsteps: A Journey in Search of Penelope Betjeman*. John Mallet. Mitchell Beazley: H. A. Williams, *Some Day I'll Find You*. Mowbray: Michael de-la-Noy, *Mervyn Stockwood: A Lonely Life*. *The New Oxford Book of Australian Verse*. *New Statesman*. *New York Times*. *Newsweek*. *Observer*. Tom Paulin. *Perspectives in Architecture*. *Private Eye*. Punch Ltd. *Radio Times*. Random House Group: Marcel Proust, *In Search of Lost Time*. Robson Books: Peter Coleman, *The Real Barry Humphries*. St Mary le Strand Church. *The Scotsman*. The late Dr Gregory Scott and John Stevenson. Secker & Warburg: Jonathan Aitken, *The Young Meteors*. *The Spectator*. Sir Roy Strong. *Sunday Express*. *Sunday Times*. Charles Thomson. *The Times*. *Times Literary Supplement*. Timewell Press: Anthony Blond, *Jew Made in England*. Viking: Barry Humphries, *More Please*. Vintage Books: Duncan Fallowell, *20th Century Characters*. *Vogue*. Weidenfeld & Nicolson: Lord Drogheda, *Double Harness: Memoirs*; J. M. Richards, *Memoirs of an Unjust Fella*; *The Unexpurgated Beaton: The Cecil Beaton Diaries as They Were Written*, introd. Hugo Vickers; *Beaton in the Sixties: More Unexpurgated Diaries*, introd. Hugo Vickers. Lady Wilson of Rievaulx. 'Village Green Preservation Society' by Ray Davies © 1968 Davray Music Ltd and Carlin Music Corp – London NW1 8BD – All rights reserved. Used by permission.